ARCTIC OCEAN
BARENTS SEA
KARA SEA
LAPTEV SEA
Taymyr Peninsula
Siberia
RUSSIA
SEA OF OKHOTSK
Kamchatka
BERING SEA
FINLAND
SWEDEN
POLAND
GERMANY
UKRAINE
ROMANIA
Black Sea
GREECE
TURKEY
CYPRUS
SYRIA
IRAQ
IRAN
KAZAKHSTAN
UZBEKISTAN
TURKMENISTAN
AFGHANISTAN
PAKISTAN
MONGOLIA
CHINA
TIBET
NEPAL
INDIA
JAPAN
(NORTH) KOREA
(SOUTH)
Sea of Japan
PACIFIC OCEAN
TAIWAN
PHILIPPINES
Philippine Sea
VIETNAM
THAILAND
CAMBODIA
MALAYSIA
SRI LANKA
MALDIVES
Bay of Bengal
Arabian Sea
SAUDI ARABIA
YEMEN
OMAN
EGYPT
LIBYA
TUNISIA
CHAD
NIGER
NIGERIA
SUDAN
ETHIOPIA
SOMALIA
KENYA
UGANDA
TANZANIA
ZAIRE
CONGO
GABON
ANGOLA
ZAMBIA
MALAWI
ZIMBABWE
MOZAMBIQUE
BOTSWANA
NAMIBIA
SOUTH AFRICA
MADAGASCAR
MAURITIUS
SEYCHELLES
INDONESIA
PAPUA NEW GUINEA
SOLOMON ISLANDS
Banda Sea
Arafura Sea
Timor Sea
CORAL SEA
AUSTRALIA
WESTERN AUSTRALIA
NORTHERN TERRITORY
QUEENSLAND
SOUTH AUSTRALIA
NEW SOUTH WALES
VICTORIA
TASMANIA
TASMAN SEA
INDIAN OCEAN
FEDERATED STATES OF MICRONESIA
NORTHERN MARIANAS
PALAU
Caroline Islands

MANAGEMENT

THIRD EDITION

MANAGEMENT

Principles and Practices

David H. Holt

James Madison University

Prentice Hall, Englewood Cliffs, New Jersey 07632

Library of Congress Cataloging-in-Publication Data

Holt, David H.
Management : principles and practices / David H. Holt. — 3rd ed.
p. cm.
Includes bibliographical references and index.
ISBN 0-13-553934-X
1. Management. 2. Industrial management. I. Title.
HD31.H6225 1993
658.4—dc20 92-26438
CIP

Dedicated to
my wife, Judith K. Holt,
whose life I have forever altered
with this task.

Acquisitions editor: Alison Reeves
Development editors: Thom Moore / Stephen Deitmer
Production editor: Eleanor Perz
Copy editor: Carole Freddo
Cover and interior design: Suzanne Behnke
Photo research: Teri Stratford
Prepress buyer: Trudy Pisciotti
Manufacturing buyer: Patrice Fraccio

Printed in the United States of America
10 9 8 7 6 5 4 3 2 1

ISBN 0-13-553934-X

Prentice-Hall International (UK) Limited, *London*
Prentice-Hall of Australia Pty. Limited, *Sydney*
Prentice-Hall Canada Inc., *Toronto*
Prentice-Hall Hispanoamericana, S.A., *Mexico*
Prentice-Hall of India Private Limited, *New Delhi*
Prentice-Hall of Japan, Inc., *Tokyo*
Prentice-Hall of Southeast Asia Pte. Ltd., *Singapore*
Editora Prentice-Hall do Brasil, Ltda., *Rio de Janeiro*

Brief Contents

Contents

PART ONE ■ INTRODUCTION

Chapter 7 Strategic Management 194

Chapter 8 Tactical and Operational Planning 226

PART THREE ■ ORGANIZING

Chapter 9 Organizing: Bringing Together People and Resources 262

PART FOUR ■ LEADING AND LEADERSHIP

Chapter 15 Managing Change and Conflict 472

Chapter 16 Toward More Effective Communication 508

PART FIVE ■ CONTROLLING: MANAGING FOR RESULTS

Chapter 17 The Controlling Function 546

Chapter 18 Production and Operations Management Control 588

Chapter 19 Management and Information Systems 626

PART SIX ■ MANAGEMENT CHALLENGES

Chapter 20 Entrepreneurship 658

Chapter 21 Career Management 694

Preface

When work began on the first edition of this text in 1982, I felt a sense of responsibility to emphasize the role of *quality management*. That sense of responsibility became apparent after spending several years in Japan and Europe and watching the rapid changes being made by foreign managers intent on competing with American enterprises. At the time, the quality message was not thoroughly accepted, and it took several years before Americans began to deeply appreciate the challenges. Nevertheless, we created a textbook that buzzed with quality and productivity issues. For the second edition, we decided to emphasize *global competition* also, and readers were ready for that. Quality and productivity continued to be themes woven into the fabric of our presentations.

In this edition, the messages of *globalization, total quality management*, and a *commitment to productivity* remain strong. They are supplemented by many other important themes, not least of all the requirement that managers strive toward *ethical behavior*, and that we all embrace a sense of *social commitment* to humanity and to our world environment. In the preface to the second edition, I suggested that changes in European and Pacific Rim nations would significantly alter global competition and that managers prepare themselves for the twenty-first century. That suggestion prompted several cynical replies, yet since then, enormous changes have occurred in the former Soviet Union, Eastern Europe, the Middle East, and Asia. The cynics aside, "fundamentals of management" can no longer be bounded by culture or gauged by political definitions of nation-states. Sometime after the beginning of the twenty-first century, "principles" courses may be relegated to history and replaced, I predict, not by existing courses such as organizational behavior or international management, but by a yet-to-be-defined discipline that encompasses management on our planet. Perhaps that suggestion will draw some response, and response is welcome because I learn from those concerned enough to challenge issues.

Meanwhile, before that new discipline evolves, and before we come to terms with how to live with global humanity and strife, managers must pick up the gauntlet of competition. By the year 2000, America will have a strong foundation of managers who experienced revolutionary changes in Western technology, and they will have been part of the transition era away from a low-tech industrial economy to a high-tech information society. They will have tremendous opportunities for exciting careers, and many will venture overseas.

As a result of global changes, managers will rapidly adjust to a *global mentality*. Recognizing that changes in Europe will realign our major trading partners in 1992, changes in China will create new opportunities and competitors in the Pacific Rim, and changes in the former Soviet Union may lead to an era of economic cooperation with Eastern Bloc countries, we are beyond the age of insular nations vying for a few select markets.

I am drafting this preface only 12 hours before leaving for the airport, and during the coming months, my schedule will take me to the People's Republic of China, Thailand, Hong Kong, Japan, and the former Soviet Union. A few years ago, this would have been unthinkable, but today it may provide a glimpse of yet further changes leading toward that "predicted" new discipline in planetary management. I will be touring with students in Asia, working as a consultant for Procter & Gamble in China, training Chinese managers in Hong Kong, working on curriculum design in Bangkok, and introducing free-market economics and the concepts of entrepreneurship to factory managers in a Russian industrial city. Having spent several years in Europe and Japan, I am already sensitive to America's tremendous national resource of innovative managers, and I am convinced that innovation will remain the strength of our nation in the next century. We have an extraordinary technological basis and educated professionals capable of meeting any challenge. However, it will require academic vigilance to maintain that advantage. We cannot be impertinent as a nation about our past successes.

I was concerned in writing this edition, as I was with the last, that we had only scratched the surface of a trend in global business management. As a result, our team of editors and colleagues who helped prepare much of the supplemental materials responded to the challenge of providing students with the best, real-world information on global management issues. I have prepared special features in each chapter to illustrate *Global Trends.* Interesting scenarios, cases, videos, and supplemental exercises highlight companies throughout Europe, Asia, and neighboring countries in North America. Commentary on U.S. firms operating overseas has been integrated into discussions throughout the text, and international trends toward strategic global alliances are presented whenever the opportunity presents itself. An international chapter is presented early in the text, and we emphasize changes that have most recently occurred. However, the text will never be complete or even satisfactory to me because it is impossible to articulate all that is needed in less than encyclopedic space.

I have also tried in this edition to retain students' interests in their immediate objectives. The most pressing objective, of course, is to graduate and find meaningful work. A new chapter on *career management* is presented to focus on this concern. Although it is positioned at the end of the text, the material can stand alone and be addressed at any time, in almost any course. As educators, we certainly have a mandate to help students in their career planning, and although we might lecture on such weighty topics as global strategic alliances, most students are still wrestling with course schedules and decisions about planning their majors. Consequently, most examples throughout the text are written with students in mind. I have tried to understand where their heads are during the early preparation stage of their careers, and the specific chapter on careers acts to focus those concerns on better career management.

With that said, we have a tremendous challenge to open students' minds to a huge number of topics. Students are certainly headed toward different careers than most of us were pursuing when we were their age, and they will have to be much more adaptable than we were in a rapidly changing world. They will manage in a global economy, reconcile multicultural issues within their organizations as the work force becomes more diversified, redefine business ethics in a socially acceptable framework of their own making, and embrace the ever-present mandates of commercial competition that underpin a free world and market economy. Along the way, they must adapt to an age of information technology. The role of information technology has been featured early in planning and organizing chapters, but a special chapter on information systems management focuses on the topic. Throughout the text, we have stressed the importance of *multicultural* management, and we have introduced students to changes in how *team management* is prevailing to change organizational processes.

Several important topics—*group technology*, *self-managed work groups*, and *group processes*—are emphasized in Chapter 11, where we focused our efforts to present topics previously treated lightly. Major changes in management are also taking place, and it was essential to address the concept of *transformational leadership* in Chapter 14. Unlike the "transactions" approach to leading that addresses role responsibilities for effective administration, the transformational approach underscores major shifts in organizational endeavors. It often comprises a complete redefinition of where the organization is headed, and those leaders who fit this role are profiled throughout the text.

The concepts of *entrepreneurship* and innovation are threaded into nearly every chapter through examples of new ventures, creative enterprises, and innovative managers. The chapter on entrepreneurship (Chapter 20) has been substantially rewritten, reinforcing fundamental concepts, yet raising the level of discussion beyond the scope of small business to encompass the meaning of new-venture creation in a market economy. The role of the small-business owner, however, is equally important, representing more than half of all commercial enterprises in the United States. Consequently, entrepreneurs and small-business owners are given balanced coverage with those entrepreneurial managers in major public and private organizations.

We have also made an attempt to address *women in management* and the status of *minorities.* These are often difficult topics to present, and they are more difficult to illustrate because we have not yet created a culture where women and minority employees have sufficient opportunities for careers in leadership roles. If there is one regret we have in writing this text, it is the fact that we were frustrated by the lack of useful information about women and minority managers and their real-world experiences. It is clear that competent leaders in many fine companies are addressing these issues, but they need to come forward—to go public—with their efforts and values, driving forward to help change the system as well as to provide the inspiration needed to improve our managerial environments. We are, however, making changes to improve opportunities and redress problems that have plagued many organizations for generations.

It is my hope that the third edition addresses these changes. It represents several years of hard work and careful thought, and I have tried to incorporate the constructive suggestions of reviewers. Prentice Hall assembled an editorial team to challenge me to write accurately and effectively. Although we intended to "revise" and not to "rewrite," this edition is substantially new. The book content is entirely my doing, and while I owe a great deal to reviewers and close colleagues who opened my mind to better ideas and changes in content, the text is my endeavor. I say this with a sense of pride, but also to alert readers that I have total responsibility for errors and omissions.

My colleagues, reviewers from throughout the world, and the Prentice Hall staff deserve greater accolades that I can offer for providing insights, examples, recommendations, and a vast assortment of ancillary materials. Collectively, they have helped to provide an instructional package with enriched opportunities for students to study management. Our objective has not been to outgun the competition or to find ways to improve sales, but to provide students with the best educational package possible. Often heated disagreements took place among those working on text materials, and all of us, being strong-willed participants, battled to defend our positions. However, an interesting pattern of decisions emerged. *We made decisions based on our perception of how the materials would benefit students.* Quality work to benefit students was our foundation for agreement, and we accept the challenge of making continuous improvement in the quest for that ultimate achievement.

FEATURES OF THE REVISED TEXT

The third edition is similar in format and writing style to the previous edition, and we retained features that were proven beneficial. We have added features such as boxed examples in global management and ethics to enrich student learning. Video cases have been written specifically for each chapter, and cases have been selected to reinforce student learning. Our obligation in writing this text has been to convey to students knowledge of management, and we recognize that instructors must have the best tools available to support their students. Most instructional materials, test banks, supplemental information, and exercises have therefore been fashioned to enrich the teaching experience. We hope that we have addressed both student and instructor needs through our efforts.

Chapter Outline. At the front of each chapter is an outline of major topics and their secondary subjects to guide readers.

Chapter Objectives. Each chapter begins with selected focal objectives for learning, each one coordinated with the chapter summary. These are aligned with the chapter outline so that students can see there is indeed a correlation between what they are supposed to learn and what is covered.

Chapter Framing Stories. Each chapter begins with a real-world example to introduce the student to the chapter's topic. We return to this example at the end of the chapter to reinforce the chapter coverage. Opening examples are *positive* illustrations of good management practices in well-known organizations or good examples of effective management practiced by well-known individuals.

Checkpoints. At the end of each major section within the chapters, we have posed "checkpoint" questions. There are between 20 and 30 questions in each chapter. They are positioned to prompt student review at strategic points and so reinforce learning. Checkpoints replace the traditional review questions often listed at the end of chapters that are rarely read by students. Checkpoints also provide an instant review process so that students can digest smaller increments of information and engage in a form of self-testing.

Margin Definitions. A glossary of terms and definitions are positioned in page margins nearest to the topics being discussed. The vocabulary of management is emphasized with margin materials, and brief definitions provide additional learning reinforcement. The instructor's edition includes guidelines, symbols for a systematic way to integrate exercises and ancillary materials for class lectures, and carefully prepared annotations to assist instructors with their presentations.

Artwork. There are approximately 100 full-color photographs in the text. These were carefully selected to enhance student learning and to attract their attention to important concepts. In addition, the text has more than 150 drawings, diagrams, or exhibits. All of the line drawings have been redrawn for clarity.

A Synopsis for Learning. At the end of each chapter, the opening objectives are restated and discussed. The synopsis concludes each chapter by reconfirming the objectives and focusing students' attention on mainstream issues.

Management Applications. At least one contemporary illustration of how management principles are applied is highlighted in each chapter. This material is set off in an "applications box" to supplement chapter discussions, thereby enhancing a student's understanding of management concepts. Many of these focus on smaller, entrepreneurial companies.

Global Trends. Real-life examples have been selected from American and foreign companies engaged in global business operations. These are positive examples of companies and their managers designed to help students understand the nature of international management.

Ethics in Management. A new feature, this boxed material emphasizes ethical practices by managers and socially responsive organizations to enrich students' understanding of ethical problems and their solutions in management.

Examples. Every effort was made to reinforce concepts with illustrative examples woven into presentations. These examples are taken from industry, service firms, major manufacturers, entrepreneurial ventures, and not-for-profit enterprises and include well-known companies and managers. In most instances, they are contemporary examples that rely on the most recent information available, just prior to final printing. In a rapidly changing world, we recognize that some examples will become obsolete by events; mergers and acquisitions, for instance, change organizations more quickly than we can revise textbooks. Nevertheless, the examples are specific to existing companies, and although events change the world in which we live, this too can be an important lesson for students.

End-of-Chapter Cases. Each chapter has a section called *Skill Analysis,* which consists of two short cases. Every case is real, although a few are disguised to protect individual identities. The range of cases is extensive with selections from industry, service firms, government, public agencies, and social organizations. One of the cases has a corresponding video in the ABC News/Prentice Hall Video Library; these videos are available to show in class either to start or extend classroom discussion of the case.

Skill Practice Exercises. An experiential exercise for each chapter has been prepared for classroom use or more extensive out-of-class assignment. Recommendations for their use are included in the instructor's materials together with supplemental readings, discussion points, and ancillaries.

Integrative Cases. The text is divided into six parts, each part consisting of complementary chapters. At the end of each part, an integrative case pulls together material from that part's chapters. The part cases are longer than end-of-chapter cases, broadening an instructor's options for classroom discussions or out-of-class assignments. Each case is drawn from real-world incidents and has recent citations for student research.

SUPPLEMENTS

While the ancillary materials are extensive, our main objective was to make them useful for both instructors and students. We recognize that few instructors will use a majority of these materials, but because class sizes and teaching methodologies vary widely, we have tried to provide a broad range of optional supplements. Following is a list of the supplements; a more complete description appears in the *Annotated Instructor's Edition.*

Annotated Instructor's Edition (AIE). Dennis Patzig of James Madison University again shared his teaching expertise with us in preparing the *AIE.* The margin annotations provide a wealth of additional examples, anecdotes, and teaching tips for virtually every topic in the text.

Instructor's Resource Manual (IRM) with Transparency Masters. This was prepared by Dr. Mary Coulter of Southwest Missouri State University, who has had considerable experience in developing a variety of teaching materials and pedagogical features for Prentice Hall. The IRM contains lecture outlines and teaching notes for all in-text cases and exercises, chapter outlines keying in all supplements, and transparency masters for all text figures.

Applications Pack. Karen Wiggenton and Mark Usry brought their international, entrepreneurial, and teaching experience to bear in preparing this compendium of handout-formatted applications. There is an extra case and an extra exercise, with teaching notes, for each chapter as well as teaching notes for using *Management Live!* with the text. These same cases and exercises (without the teaching notes) are included in the *Study Guide.*

PH Color Transparency Masters for Management—Series C. This set of 150 color transparencies contains art from the text as well as other sources. The "Coordinated Resource Annotation" in the *AIE* and chapter outlines in the *IRM* and *Lecture File Folders* cross-reference them with chapter material. Each color transparency is accompanied by an interleaf with an extended explanatory annotation.

Test Item File. James Pettijohn of Southwest Missouri State University carefully prepared this test bank of over 2000 items. Each question is page-referenced, coded as to level of difficulty, and labeled as factual or applied. With the third edition we have implemented a new program called ATLAS (Academic Testing and Learning Analysis System) to check each question for accuracy and overall quality. The *Test Item File* is also available in a computerized format called the *PH Test Manager* and through our *PH Telephone Test Preparation Service.*

Lecture File Folders. A handy manilla file folder for each chapter has preprinted on it the chapter outline with all relevant supplementary items keyed into it.

Prentice Hall/New York Times Contemporary View Program. This complimentary newspaper-formatted supplement contains articles that correspond directly with chapters and topics in *Management,* Third Edition. Updated twice a year to ensure timeliness, it offers students a view of all kinds of textbook concepts in practice.

Desktop Order: Hypercard Simulations for Management (Site License). For Apple Mac users, this "simulation" on desktop order is also an actual tool students (and managers) can use to plan and organize their work.

Micromanaging Site License. Ten Lotus-based exercises organized along the management functions help students see that knowing how to use a computer can make them more efficient managers.

The ABC News/Prentice Hall Video Library for Management, Third Edition. This video library contains all the videos that correspond with the in-text video cases. There are 21 videos in all, ranging on average from 5 to 15 minutes. See the *Annotated Instructor's Edition* for a complete list of all videos in the library and a full description of the program.

Management/Management Live! Package, Third Edition. Written by Robert Marx, University of Massachusetts at Amherst; Todd D. Jick, Harvard University; and Peter J. Frost, University of British Columbia, *Management Live! The Video Workbook* is an experiential workbook with topic overviews followed by a series of exercises for students to do before, during, and after class and accompanying readings. At least one of the in-class exercises in each chapter has a video component; the videos are available free upon adoption of *Management Live!* (one per department only) either by itself or shrinkwrapped at a substantial discount, to *Manage-*

ment, Third Edition. *Management Live!* has its own *Instructor's Manual* with thorough teaching notes for all the exercises. For teaching notes specifically relating *Management Live!* to *Management,* Third Edition, see the *Applications Pack.*

Management/Acumen Edition, Third Edition. *Acumen: Educational Version* is a personalized self-assessment program that gives students feedback on 12 characteristics relevant to their managerial acumen. Each assessment disk allows three assessments. Used by many worldwide corporations, such as UPS, this software program is available at only a minimal price when shrinkwrapped to *Management,* Third Edition.

Student Guide. In addition to offering review and test practice, the study guide contains an extra case and an extra exercise per chapter. (These same exercises and cases are available on handout masters in the *Applications Pack.*)

Modern Business Decisions. Developed by Richard Cotter, Emeritus University of Nevada, and David Fritzsche, University of Washington, this is a team-oriented computer simulation. The components include a *Player's Manual, Instructor's Manual, Program Disk* for the professor, and a *Decision Disk* for the student.

Managing an Organization: A Workbook Simulation. By Gary Oddou of San Jose State University, this is a noncomputerized workbook simulation organized along the management functions.

Management Applications: Exercises, Cases, and Readings. This is a supplemental book of brief case incidents and exercises along with a mix of classics and recent articles (both academic and practitioner-oriented).

Readings in Management. By Phillip DuBose of James Madison University, this is an extensive collection of readings organized along the management functions.

ACKNOWLEDGMENTS

Few people read the acknowledgments in any book, but I hope that those involved with this text will take a moment to do so. This edition is significant because it was not expected to be written. At least, it was not supposed to be finished by me. In the summer of 1991, when we were set to launch the revision, I was diagnosed with cancer and given a matter of months to live. This was particularly difficult to deal with because my wife and I are still a long way from peaking in our careers and we have three sons in their late teens. My wife and I took off quickly for Europe for an extended holiday that stretched from the north of Scotland to the French Riviera. We traveled the Alps, dined well, sampled the best wines of Germany and France, gambled in Monte Carlo, partied in Italy, swam in the Med, and romped in the summer snow that prevails in Switzerland.

Meanwhile, I'm sure that Alison Reeves and the Prentice Hall staff were on the verge of panic. They get nervous when I leave the country for a few days—even when well. Imagine the trauma when I disappeared for many weeks with a death sentence hanging over my head. Needless to say, I survived, and we have completed the textbook without compromising our professional principles. During the past year, however, I underwent major surgery, radiation treatments, months of chemotherapy, and have endured side effects nearly as bad as the disease itself. The reason I am bringing this up in the acknowledgments is that without the extraordinary support of the people involved in this project, I am convinced that I would not have survived. Had Prentice Hall not supported my efforts to make the revision, I may simply have given up hope.

The book itself became the ultimate focus for living, and without it, I would not have had the motivation to continue. The process of writing kept my mind sharp and my senses pointed toward a single goal, and I learned more about values, goal-directed behavior, and priorities during the past year than in all previous years of my life. Consequently, I have many people to thank, and my brief comments here will never be sufficient to reveal the profound gratitude that I feel for each person's effort, each gesture of support, and every contribution no matter how insignificant they may have appeared to be.

My doctors initially gave me time to try to do the book, then they gave me the strength to endure. They include Keith Vest, Greg Montgomery, Brian Robinson, Robert Kyler, John Glick, the surgical team of Harrisonburg Surgical Associates, the University of Virginia surgical consultants, and the Rockingham Memorial Hospital Cancer Center. Nurses gave me the care and emotional support to work while in the hospital, to recover quickly, and to overcome many extremely difficult problems. They include the staff nurses at Rockingham Memorial Hospital in surgery, surgical recovery, ward nurses on the surgical wing, ward nurses and specialists on the cancer wing, and the nurses and staff in the cancer center. The support staff and specialists were extraordinary, and I thank them all for their personal care and their keen interest in seeing me succeed.

I am particularly grateful to those talented colleagues who have an "equity interest in" our instructional package. Dennis Patzig, Karen Wiggenton, and Mark Ursy of James Madison University created the Annotated Instructor's Edition and the Applications Pack. They also gave me valuable insights and personal support in research.

Considerable information and immense support were provided by friends and international scholars. My special thanks to the following colleagues from the Chinese University of Hong Kong: K. C. Mun, M. K. Nyaw, Bob Terpstra, Julie Yu, Japhet Law, and Bob Westwood. I sincerely appreciate help provided by David Forsyth from the University of the South Pacific, Fiji; Irene Chew of the National University of Singapore; Cemal Talug, Ankara University, Turkey; Gerard Tocquer, CERAM, Sophia Antipolis, France; Erkan Benli, Undersecretary, Ministry of Agriculture, Turkey; Masami Hirata, Bunka Women's University, Tokyo, Japan; Daniel Morales Ramos, ITESM, Monterrey, Mexico; Sotos D. Boukis, Deree College, Athens, Greece; John Habert, International Student Exchange, France; and the Commerce Faculty attached to the U.S.-China Business Council, Beijing.

Thanks to my German friend Holger Gossman of Rolls Royce; Bob Glucksman and Hugh Parker, principals, Witgang Far East Ltd., Bangkok; Car Villacorta, president, Orient Integrated Development, Manila; Ross Silver, International Consulting, London; Mikchail Matorin, general director, Ural Mountain Industrial Management, Russia; K. S. Ma, director, Junwell Ltd., Hong Kong and Guangzhou, PRC; Mansfield Mok, Hoare Govett Asia, Ltd., Hong Kong; I. Ng, Namura Securities, Tokyo; Sin Moon-tong, Hong Kong Government; George Tam, Securities and Futures Exchange, Hong Kong; Barin Ganguli, Asian Development Bank, Manila; Nurhan Ulger, senior partner, ALCA, Turkey; W. K. Lo, managing director of Computer Products Asia-Pacific Ltd., Tai Wai and Shenzhen, PRC; John Zinkin, CEO, Gilman Ltd., London and Hong Kong; and Paul Nix, director, Procter & Gamble, Guangzhou Ltd., PRC.

Corporate executives in the U.S. who provided personal assistance and advice include: Charles H. Sweet, director of international strategy, Checchi Corporation; Charles O. Conrad, president, PolyChem Associates, Inc.; James B. Strang, president, Spokes Etc.; John D. Hunt and Wayne Hall, co-directors, Foress Systems; Rita Scales-Modi, Head to Toe; Jimmy Calano, CEO, CareerTrack; Donald D. Boroian, chairman, FranCorp; Sam Black, director of quality, Caterpillar Inc.; Richard E. Turner, president, Falconer Glass Industries, Inc.; Paul Bush, CEO, Bush Industries, Inc.; Stew Leonard, chairman, Stew Leonard's, Inc.; James F. Gibney, vice president sales, Marriott Corporation; John Robertson, president, Robertson Marketing Group; Jackie Hayter, Pinehurst Hotel and Country Club; Richard E. Marriott, Marriott Corporation;

Warren Avis, Avis Corporation; Robert Kaiser, ExImBank; Alan Larson, U.S. State Department; John Holt, associate, Price Waterhouse; and Richard Gardner, senior partner, Dominion Computer Systems.

Those colleagues who especially supported me during the critical period of illness include: Carolyn Dexter, Pennsylvania State University; George Westacott, SUNY Binghamton; John Yanouzas, University of Connecticut; Janice Beyer, University of Texas at Austin; and Heidi Vernon-Wortzel, Northeastern University. The entire College of Business faculty at James Madison University, with few exceptions, supported my research, helped my family, provided personal support and friendship, and organized meals for my family to relieve the pressure of events while I was in treatment. These people have a special place in my life, and each in their own way helped make the book a reality.

Others that contributed to my understanding and presentation of management concepts include: Jeffrey Lenn, George Washington University; Harry G. Harris, California State University—Fresno; Bruce D. Phillips, SBA Office of Advocacy; Raymond Smilor, University of Texas at Austin; Donald L. Sexton, Ohio State University; Ignace Ng, University of Victoria; Carol Ann Meares, U.S. Department of Commerce Productivity Center; Rick Lundquist, State University of New York, Fredonia; and Tom Chisholm, West Georgia College.

Prentice Hall editors and their staff have provided exceptional support, and considering the circumstances, they stuck by me through many problems, failed deadlines, and anxious moments to honor a commitment that they could easily have avoided. Alison Reeves, assistant vice president and executive editor, spearheaded this revision and provided insight, leadership, and energy to bring our "instructional text" team together. Eleanor Perz, Thom Moore, and Marilyn Miller played key roles in getting this edition out the door. Other Prentice Hall people whose dedication meant so much are Frances Russello, Joyce Turner, Trudy Pisciotti, Patrice Fraccio, Kris Ann Cappelluti, Esther Schwartz, Diane Pierano, Sue Behnke, and Stephen Deitmer.

I had exceptional research support from my graduate assistant and Chinese exchange student, Tanya Au, who never faltered in her responsibilities, and in spite of working here, in a culture foreign to her own, she proved to be exceptionally capable. I was assisted at James Madison University by Marsha Shenk and Bernidine A. Click, secretaries in the Center for Entrepreneurship and the Department of Management, respectively. Marsha and Bernie are far more than secretaries, however. Together with Karen Wiggenton, they organized support networks during my illness and took care of details too numerous to list. I owe them a debt of friendship and gratitude that I will never be able to repay. I am also extremely grateful to Robert E. Holmes, Dean of the College of Business, and Daniel Gallagher, Chair of Management, for protecting my professional interests and arranging my work to fit unpleasant circumstances. My thanks to each of these individuals for their understanding and inspiration.

My wife, Judith, has endured my frustration, sacrificed her energy to care for me, suffered because of my often unpleasant behavior and pain, yet motivated me at the worst of times and reprimanded me when I needed scolding. Earlier versions of the text were written for my sons. I wanted to create a legacy of success through hard work, and because I am a poor role model in so many ways, I had hoped to write this one from a position of strength to reinforce an image they could emulate. That opportunity may have passed like so many others, but part of the book's success (and it is a success just by being completed) is due to the inspiration I absorbed by having three sons.

Kevin, the oldest, was entering college as an honor student in music when I finished the second edition, and now he is a junior majoring in international business. He achieved what I could not by earning a 4.0 in his course work, and although he still has more to complete, he has held out to me a relentless challenge to excel. Bryan has just graduated from high school and remains unfocused and fun-loving. As a result, he has a richer, more varied life than most. He will be the entrepreneur, the one who leads the parade and sets a cadence apart from others. Sean, the youngest, is about to return from a year in France as a high school exchange student, where he finished third in his class. He accomplished this in an environment where only French was written and spoken, lived with French "parents," and sat the French exams. Who said Americans can't compete with foreign students!

I have learned more this year about living than I knew existed, and my family has become more dear to me than any endeavor. My contributions, whatever they are, are only dim shadows of great things so many individuals are doing. So although this has been an unusual experience for me, I am unpretentiously honest when I say that I am grateful for having the opportunity to be part of something worthwhile.

DAVID H. HOLT
Professor of Management
James Madison University

MANAGEMENT

1

Management Perspectives

OUTLINE

Focus of This Text

Defining Management

Organizations
Organizational Purpose
Formal and Informal Organizations
The Essence of Organizations

The Process of Management
Planning
Organizing
Leading
Controlling
Emerging Concepts in Management

The Role of the Manager
Interpersonal Roles
Informational Roles
Decisional Roles
How Managers Spend Their Time

The Management Hierarchy
Division of Responsibility
Management Classifications
Functional and General Managers
Managerial Skills

Entrepreneurs

Global Dimensions of Management

Productivity—A Challenge for Innovative Managers
Recent U.S. Productivity
Management Productivity and Innovation
Changes Affecting Management

OBJECTIVES

- Define management, and discuss future perspectives for management careers.
- Explain what constitutes an organization, and discuss the differences between formal and informal organizations.
- Explain the process of management, and discuss the concepts of planning, organizing, leading, and controlling.
- Name the different sets of managerial roles, and give examples of each.
- Name the three basic levels of managers in the management hierarchy and briefly describe each.
- Describe entrepreneurship as an important dimension of our free enterprise system.
- Discuss how global competition is changing our views about managing organizations.
- Explain the connection between quality and productivity.

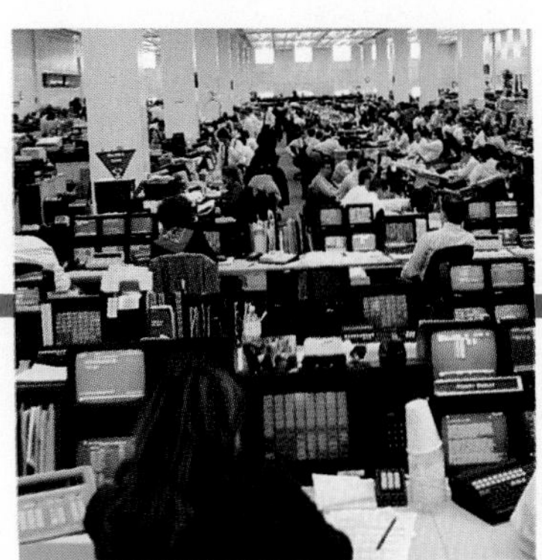

MANAGERS at Shearson Lehman Hutton want both to have the most efficient organization in the brokerage industry and to make effective decisions for client investments. Those objectives seem obvious, yet until a few years ago, they were not considered important; the company was concerned primarily with how many transactions a broker could conclude. With more than 16 million U.S. investors, selling stocks and bonds is a competitive business. Every brokerage firm strives to attract disgruntled customers from other firms and works equally hard to retain current clients. At Shearson, the emphasis is now on quality services through effective management rather than on quantity of sales.

Shearson's parent, American Express, instigated the new focus by urging Shearson's managers to become obsessed with quality service. To attain quality service, Shearson's managers had to commit themselves to building an organization with skilled personnel. American Express sent in teams of experts to help construct the organizational systems and to train managers. Their mandate was to create a critical mass of skilled managers who were innovative and dedicated to quality. Before American Express intervened, Shearson's customer transactions were late 80 percent of the time and the amount received was wrong 20 percent of the time. Now, after six years of effort, Shearson is one of the best-managed brokerage firms in the country. Transactions are processed twice as fast as they were six years earlier with nearly 99 percent accuracy. The company also retains more clients than before and enjoys a larger share of the securities market.

American Express made a similar commitment to quality in its other subsidiaries. At IDS Financial Services, its financial planning subsidiary, account planners are trained in management processes. Account managers integrate research and investment services to meet customer requirements, rather than to generate sales, and all company personnel are admonished to make customer satisfaction their first priority. "Now even the worst of our 6,500 planners is better than our average planner used to be," says Chairman Harvey Golub.[1] One indicator of the firm's success is that in four years the percentage of clients who leave has dropped by more than half.

As we shall see in this text, management acumen is an intangible, yet very important, asset; it is a form of intellectual capital. In service organizations such as American Express and its subsidiaries, intellectual capital is a competitive weapon. Clients buy services from a company because of that company's collective knowledge and skill in using its knowledge. This applies to banks, brokerage firms, software consultants, advertising agencies, telecommunication companies, and entertainment media, among others. As we shall see, customers also buy products from manufacturers who demonstrate they have the intellectual capital to manage effectively and to provide reliable, high-quality, safe products. As you read this chapter, think of management knowledge as intellectual capital; it may be America's most valuable asset.

American managers today face the enormous challenge of safeguarding their companies against global competition. Not long ago, the United States held nearly two-thirds of the world market in the ten leading industries ranging from automobiles to microelectronics. Today the United States can claim leadership in only three of those major industries—aerospace, paper and pulp products, and computers and office equipment. We also enjoy a substantial edge in many smaller industries, including medical instrumentation, biogenetic engineering, and agricultural chemicals, but our basic industries, such as automobiles and steel, are clearly under siege by aggressive foreign competitors. Services—most importantly, banking, telecommunications, and merchandising—are also besieged by global competition. In terms of trade, productivity, and gains in domestic standard of living, the United States was outperformed during the decade of the 1980s by France, Italy, West Germany, the United Kingdom, and Japan, though in absolute terms, this country is still the dominant economic power in the world.[2]

Critics never tire of reminding us that the United States has lost its competitive edge, and although there is an uneasy truth to their assertions, American industry is rebounding. Managers of our Fortune 500 companies are repositioning their corporations to compete as global enterprises, and many are joining forces with foreign companies to create new foreign ventures. Xerox and Fuji, for example, created a joint venture, Fuji Xerox, to engage in reprographic research and sales of document-processing office equipment throughout Asia. Procter & Gamble's joint venture with the Guangzhou Soap Company in the People's Republic of China manufactures and sells Zest soap and Head and Shoulders shampoo in Asian markets. Similar strategic alliances exist for products marketed in the United States. Daewoo, a South Korean corporation, and General Motors coproduce the Pontiac Lemans. Group Bull (France) is allied with Honeywell (U.S.) and NEC (Japan) to produce and market microelectronics and microprocessors in Europe and the United States. American companies became involved in nearly 4,800 similar ventures in 1990, and this pace of globalization is expected to continue.[3]

Although the United States suffers from lagging productivity, high levels of consumer and international debt, and cumbersome business organizations, American managers look to the twenty-first century as a new age of economic opportunity. Global markets offer extraordinary challenges beyond the perennial need to compete with Japan. It will be necessary in this new era to build new alliances in Western Europe, open new enterprises in Eastern Europe, take American industry to the developing nations of Africa and South America, and become involved in the economic restructuring of the Commonwealth of Independent States. At the same time, U.S. managers must help solve the pressing domestic problems of marginal gains in productivity, an inadequate education system, and organizational inefficiencies that result in high costs and low quality in both products and services.

To accomplish these enormous tasks, we require a new generation of managers who are well educated in both domestic and international affairs, committed to quality performance, and prepared to make the investments in technology and human resources that are essential for American business to compete globally. Most important, America must enrich its most valuable asset—intellectual capital. As noted earlier, management acumen is a form of intellectual capital. The cumulative effect of expertise, knowledge, and leadership skills may provide the distinctive competitive edge required in the coming century.

The purpose of this text is to provide students with the fundamental concepts of management as a foundation on which to build intellectual capital. Our principal theme is that American managers must embrace the challenge of becoming global citizens who can successfully lead their companies into the next century. Consequently, the theme of the globalization of American enterprise will be reinforced as we present the principles and practices of management.

FOCUS OF THIS TEXT

This text is about ways to manage organizations effectively. It follows a "functional" or "process" format that emphasizes *planning, organizing, leading,* and *controlling*—the fundamental responsibilities of managers in all organizations. We will focus on the concepts of quality and productivity. We will explore management roles, not simply in manufacturing, but also in service industries, government, and entrepreneurial enterprises, both in the United States and in the world.

The text also addresses the extraordinary transformation that is taking place as we leave the era of electromechanical industrialization and enter the age of information technology.[4] This technological revolution is stimulating many cultural changes that have far-reaching implications for managing human resources. Innovation is the key to this transformation, for it is innovation that enhances quality and productivity.

To begin our study, we must develop a background of management concepts. Therefore, we open this chapter with a practical definition of management, then address the general features of business organizations. These provide the foundation for our description of managerial roles in relation to organizational responsibilities. Later in the chapter, we will describe changes taking place in industrialized societies that have important implications for managers.

DEFINING MANAGEMENT

Management can be defined as "the art of getting things done through people." This definition was expressed in 1918 by Mary Parker Follett, a notable management scholar who studied how work was accomplished in organizations. Although the definition is simple, it captures the essence of management.[5] An expanded definition based on our "functional" approach is that management is the process of planning, organizing, leading, and controlling that encompasses human, material, financial, and information resources in an organizational environment.

management
The art of getting things done through people.

This expanded definition emphasizes that management is best viewed as a *process* that is employed to accomplish organizational objectives. During Operation Desert Storm, for example, the chairman of the Joint Chiefs of Staff, General Colin Powell, spent thousands of hours in planning meetings, strategy sessions, and organizational deliberations with hundreds of military and government personnel. The objective of operations against Iraq in 1990 (prior to the outbreak of war) was to get Iraq to withdraw its invasion forces from Kuwait. Powell explained how field operations progressed logically through an "evolving process" of interrelated decisions that began with economic sanctions and ended with military action backed by the United Nations. Operations required extraordinary leadership and control, both of which were vested in Powell's field commander, General Norman Schwarzkopf, who was celebrated for his coordination of diversified coalition forces. When war came, Schwarzkopf was able to achieve military objectives by "getting the best from thousands of men and women who were part of a peculiar organization."[6]

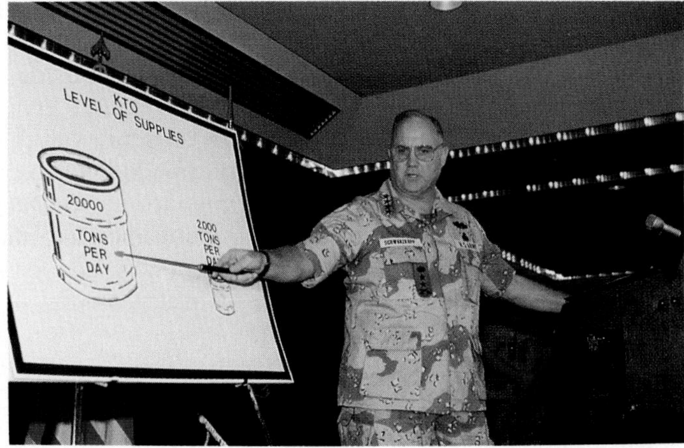

Style refers to how managers choose to work within the management process. During Operation Desert Storm, it was clear that the management styles of Generals Colin Powell and Norman Schwarzkopf were different but complementary.

As we shall see later, there are styles of management that differ over time and between individuals and organizations. *Style* refers to how managers choose to work within the management process. General Powell, for example, is a polished executive, dressed always in a crisp uniform and working through teams of advisers and colleagues to make decisions. In public, he is the image of the controlled leader, respected for his quiet but strong demeanor. In contrast, General Schwarzkopf prefers battlefield attire and has a flair for making individual command decisions. In public, he often makes vehement statements, yet he is respected as a leader who can rally support from his troops. Each man has unusual talents that are well suited to his organizational environment.

CHECKPOINT

- Define management and what it means to manage others in an organization.
- Discuss the process of management and what it means to "be a manager."

ORGANIZATIONS

organization
The structure of relationships that exists when two or more people mutually cooperate to pursue common objectives.

Organizations exist when two or more people mutually cooperate to pursue common objectives. An organization, therefore, is more than a gathering of individuals; shoppers in a busy supermarket do not constitute an organization, nor do crowds of people at a ball game. An organization consists of people working together to achieve common objectives, and while we often pursue interests independently as shoppers or sporting fans, we are also members of a great many organizations. We work jointly with others in our families, we are part of a collective student body in school, and we are members of teams, clubs, and religious groups. Some of us are involved in many organizations. Others have fewer formal organization ties, but even informal associations with friends are types of organizations. In both formal and informal organizations, membership is characterized by *mutual cooperation* in the pursuit of *common objectives*. When a group of friends get together for a party, common objectives surface. These may be simple, such as having fun or relieving stress, but the party does not "simply happen." Its organizers assign tasks, such as buying food and arranging for entertainment, and the party is successful when these tasks are well organized and effectively accomplished.

Organizations allow us to overcome our individual limitations. Through combinations of human effort and resources, we achieve far more than we could acting independently. For example, one bricklayer working alone to build a wall has to mix mortar, carry bricks to the wall, and then lay the bricks. He does his work task by task, often with a lot of wasted motion—climbing up and down ladders and so on. Three persons, each separately assigned to mix mortar, carry bricks, and build the wall, can outperform three individual bricklayers doing all three tasks themselves. Similarly, ten students preparing for a party can coordinate their activities to accomplish more with less total effort than the same students could acting independently. This is called *synergism*. Synergy means that the results of combined efforts are greater than the sum of individual efforts. Industrial nations have prospered through the synergism of well-managed organizations that have developed specialized and well-coordinated systems of work.

Organizational Purpose

Organizations have many purposes. For example, manufacturers create products, banks provide financial services, schools offer educational opportunities, and fire departments furnish protection. In business schools, we have typically approached the study of organizations from an industrial perspective, focusing on manufacturing enterprises. Manufacturing remains the preeminent economic sector. It still employs more people than the service sector, but there are now more white-collar service jobs than blue-collar jobs, and there is a growing number of service organizations in Western economies. Typical service organizations are hospitals, recreation enterprises, airlines, and postal delivery. Many new services have emerged from information technology, including software consulting, financial planning, biogenetic research, and computer systems support.

Although every organization has its particular objectives, all organizations have one common purpose: to provide value for stakeholders. **Stakeholders** are those individuals and groups that have interests in, or are affected by, an organization's performance. Thus investors (stockholders in a corporation) depend on a firm for dividends; employees depend on it for their livelihoods; taxpayers rely on it to contribute to the public welfare; consumers depend on its products and services; and community businesses look to it for their own continued growth and prosperity. Just as governments exist to provide valuable social benefits, so do manufacturers exist to provide valuable products to consumers and service organizations to provide valuable services to clients. When an organization fails to provide value, its reason for existence ends. Thus we arrive at a more useful definition of organizations: They are formal associations that combine human activities, resources, capital, and information for the purpose of providing something of social value.[7]

stakeholders
Those individuals and groups that have interests in, or are affected by, an organization's performance.

Formal and Informal Organizations

Formal organizations consist of two or more people involved in a mutual effort with formal authority to achieve common objectives. **Informal organizations** do not have deliberate structures of authority and their members need not work together to achieve common objectives. Just before the breakup of the Soviet Union into the Commonwealth of Independent States, for example, Westinghouse created a formal international alliance group with Soviet and European experts in air traffic control to renovate Soviet air traffic control systems. The group spent nearly a year setting up its authority system and defining what was to be accomplished. This international alliance is working as a formal organization to bring Soviet technology and policies into line with established international standards. Informally, several group members regularly get together over coffee to discuss the practicalities of air traffic

formal organization
Two or more people involved in a mutual effort with formal authority for creating tangible benefits.

informal organization
Two or more people involved in a mutual effort without deliberate structures of authority or the necessity of common objectives.

control. Westinghouse and its alliance are formal organizations with structured authority and clear objectives, but the coffee-room gatherings are not organized or required to achieve anything in particular.[8]

Management education focuses on formal organizations because "formality" presumes human effort is deliberately focused on common objectives. Informal organizations permeate our lives, but they arise spontaneously and are often temporary. We will explore them more thoroughly in Part Three. It is important here to note that management is concerned with formal organizations—those that are deliberately structured with common objectives, clarity of purpose, and two or more individuals working together. Our party example is not one of a formal organization if it represents a group of friends getting together on a Saturday night. However, if the party is a scheduled fraternity affair or a civic program, then someone is likely to have responsibility for management. The "manager" will plan the event, gather resources, direct activities, and control behavior. Managers at Chrysler, IBM, Citicorp, and CNN have similar responsibilities for planning, organizing resources, directing activities, and controlling results.

The Essence of Organizations

Formal organizations are generally concerned with a transformation process in which managers are responsible for creating tangible benefits. Managers achieve results by transforming resources into added value for stakeholders through a synergistic process. The concept of resources has been refined slightly from the general economic list of "labor, capital, land, and entrepreneurship" to "people, capital, materials, technology, and information."[9] We include under the category of "people" the entrepreneurial efforts of innovative persons and the leadership capabilities of managers.

Peter F. Drucker, one of this century's most prolific management writers, epitomized organizational and managerial activity when he noted that we have become a society of organizations, designed to be immortal, that are run by professional managers. In Drucker's view, the wealth-producing forces of the economy today are intangible and nonmaterial resources. These include the intellectual and organizational skills of creative leaders with entrepreneurial verve who not only transform resources but also make work interesting and meaningful to those involved in it.[10]

Drucker emphasizes that it is the combination of personal skills and innovation that drives our economy forward, with management catalyzing the transformation. Perhaps this is the essence of a free enterprise society. Bearing these points in mind, we will now look more closely at the *process of management* within formal organizations.

CHECKPOINT

- Why is membership in an organization characterized by mutual cooperation in the pursuit of common objectives?
- Explain what is meant by "synergism," and how specialization can produce group results that are greater than the sum of individual efforts.
- How do organizations influence our lives, and what responsibilities do managers have for enriching and protecting stakeholder interests?

THE PROCESS OF MANAGEMENT

The activities that make up the managerial process are commonly called the *four functions of management*. Although these are interrelated activities that separately have little meaning, we can better understand management by studying each activity in isolation. Figure 1-1 shows the model of this process.

Planning

Managers develop organizational objectives by planning. This activity is said to precede all other managerial functions, but of course it cannot take place in a vacuum. Plans evolve within organizations, usually while people are working and resources are being used and controlled. **Planning** is the process of defining an organization's objectives and determining how to achieve them. Objectives are benchmarks for measuring future performance. As managers, we plan today based on our assumptions about what will happen in the future. We seek direction for current and future actions and solutions to current problems in order to prevent future problems. In other words, managers plan so that organizations can move forward with the best probability of success.

planning
One of the four major functions of management. It is the process of defining organizational objectives and then articulating strategies, tactics, and operations necessary to achieve those objectives.

George Steiner, a leading scholar in the field of strategic planning, defines planning as deciding "what is to be done, when it is to be done, how it is to be done, and who is to do it."[11] Larger, more complex organizations face more daunting planning tasks than their smaller counterparts. Managers in large firms frequently tackle heady issues. Major power companies, for example, are currently preparing for the decade of the 2030s because it takes that long to plan, fund, and build a new power plant. Imagine trying to determine the electricity needs of a large city decades from now. What power sources will be used in the year 2030? What sort of computer technology will be employed to control electric generation?

Smaller entrepreneurial firms seldom face issues as intangible and far-reaching, but their need for planning is equally critical. Clothing store managers who fail to plan for new fashion changes might easily find themselves with outdated inventory. A supermarket manager who makes a 1 percent error in costs may earn no profits because 1 percent is often the total net profit in retail groceries.

So many factors affect organizational performance that is rarely adequate for managers to make decisions solely on inspiration. The planning function implies a formal, structured approach to help them *do the right things* while keeping clear objectives in mind. Intuition plays an important role, particularly for experienced managers, but effective planning is not a spontaneous exercise. It is the active process of establishing where one wants to be at a specific point in the future. Important elements of planning and decision making are addressed in Part Two.

FIGURE 1-1 The Functional View of Management

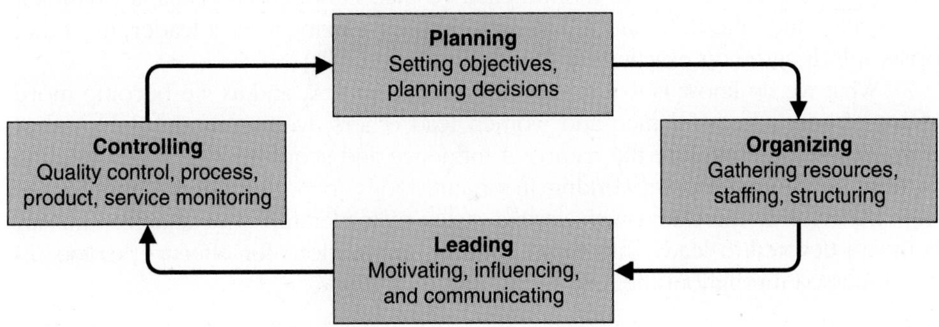

Organizing

Managers must organize human and material resources to carry out their plans. Resources must be gathered and allocated, and the work of an enterprise must be coordinated. Gathering resources includes *staffing,* or the organization of human resources. It also includes purchasing materials, securing financing, and providing facilities. Once a firm understands its needs and sets about gathering resources, an allocation process evolves. Human resources are grouped in logical divisions of labor, schedules of operations are defined, and lines of communication are forged to ensure coordination of tasks.

organizing
The function of gathering resources, allocating resources, and structuring tasks within an organization.

These **organizing** activities occur within the context of a specifically designed structure. The job of organizing requires a deliberate *configuration* for the firm that defines how authority is structured, how communication flows, and how tasks are accomplished. This configuration differs from organization to organization and depends largely on the nature of each firm's work. For example, a manufacturing company will choose a structure based on production methods and technology, a university will choose a form of departmentalization that allows groups of professionals to work somewhat independently, and a hospital may require careful delineation of services within a structure that enhances working relationships among its medical activities.

We expand these concepts in Part Three, which is devoted to organizing, but there is an added dimension of organizing addressed in Part Four that is concerned with leadership. This dimension is the *philosophy* of organization, which influences how we combine human resources with rapid changes in modern technology. In Part Four, we discuss, for example, how American firms are moving toward participative systems. Participation means involving subordinates in decisions that traditionally have been handled by individual managers.

"Getting organized" obviously means much more than defining structures, assigning jobs, and bringing together essential resources. A firm cannot function in anarchy. "Getting organized" implies the creation of a harmonious work environment, and harmony is largely the result of effective leadership.

Leading

Leadership implies a system of inequalities in which superiors influence subordinates—in other words, managers in authority direct human behavior to achieve organizational objectives. Several descriptive terms have been used interchangeably to describe the **leadership** function. These include "motivating," "actuating," and "directing." They all have in common the assumption that managers *influence* behavior. Exactly *how* they do this is subject to interpretation. Historians and philosophers have tried for centuries to understand how great men and women achieve extraordinary success. Some people's success has been attributed to charisma or to a dominant personality. Others seem to have been "born to lead," to have inherited the traits necessary to achieve monumental results. Although charisma, a dominant personality, and inherited traits are all capable of producing a great leader, most theorists still disagree on exactly how leaders are made.

leadership
The management function of influencing others to strive toward performance that achieves organizational objects; also called *directing*.

What we do know is that leadership can be studied, and as we become more aware of how successful men and women lead others, we can model the process ourselves. We can explore the nature of influence and acquire some understanding of what influences people working in organizations to perform well. We can see how behavior is correlated with certain styles of leadership. The chapters in Part Four are devoted to leadership topics, but the implications for effective leadership are discussed throughout the text.

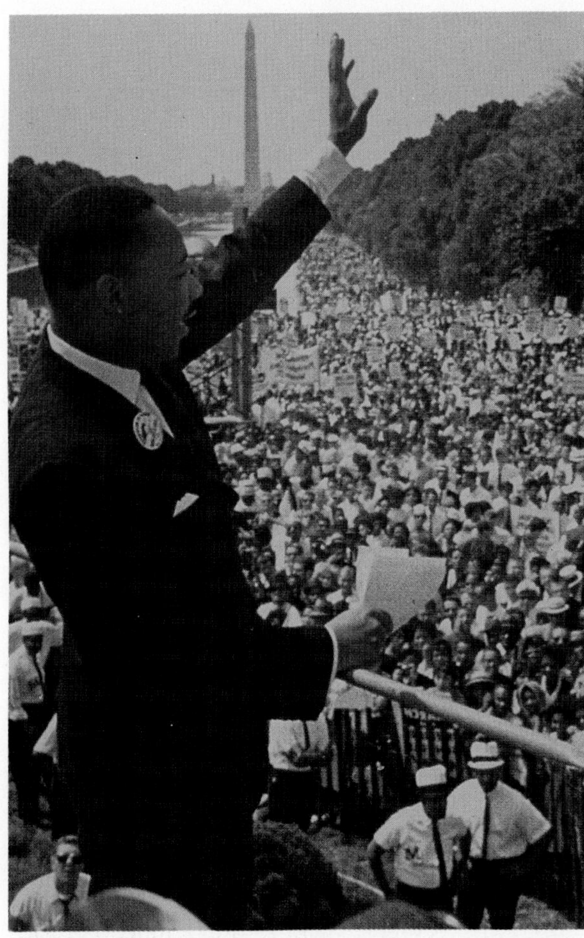

Dr. Martin Luther King, Jr., is widely regarded as one of the most charismatic leaders of all time. In recognition of his efforts to secure basic civil rights for all citizens, King was awarded the Nobel Peace Prize in 1964.

Controlling

Managers have the daily responsibility to "keep things on track." This function of steering performance toward desired results is called **controlling**. The task is rather complex. Managers must evaluate performance, recognize problems, anticipate crises before they occur, avert catastrophes, and simultaneously make hundreds of little decisions that can be the difference between ultimate success or failure.

controlling
The management function of monitoring performance and adapting work variables to improve results.

Controlling is the complementary activity of planning. Managers *plan* to determine what to do and *control* to ensure it is done correctly. The three mainstream topics of managerial control are *coordinating, monitoring,* and *adjusting performance*. In order to accomplish these activities, managers must have *standards* of performance. Consequently, the control process begins with definitions of performance standards, and with these established, managers can coordinate work, measure and monitor work progress, and make adjustments when necessary to keep performance directed toward attaining those standards.

This process should be familiar to students, who work toward course standards (grades), receive regular monitoring (exams), and usually change their study habits (adjust performance) to stay on track toward their grade objectives. Every organization has similar control processes and various means of achieving desired results. IBM has rigid quality control standards on computer manufacturing, Frito-Lay carefully controls its field distribution system to ensure nearly perfect on-time delivery of fresh snack foods, and CBS carefully monitors its program performance through television ratings and consumer surveys.

The nature of control and the assortment of control mechanisms have changed with advances in information technology. Cost accounting and auditing—both primarily control activities—-have been redefined by computer applications and information science. Production, purchasing, financing, and most other corporate functions utilize information technology for enhanced control systems. These topics are developed more thoroughly in Part Five; and, collectively, the control topics address productivity, a central theme of this text.

Emerging Concepts in Management

In the final chapters of this text, students are challenged to think beyond the function of management in large organizations. Entrepreneurship is introduced as a pervasive force in a free enterprise economy. Entrepreneurship is concerned not only with small businesses but also with creating and nurturing new, high-growth ventures. Every Fortune 500 company began as a small enterprise, and nearly every giant corporation was formed by a farsighted entrepreneur who took unusual risks to succeed. We will study celebrity entrepreneurs such as Steven Jobs of Apple Computer and Mitch Kapor of Lotus Development Corporation and present the success stories of lesser-known, but equally interesting, entrepreneurs such as Tom Monaghan of Domino's Pizza and Debbi Fields of Mrs. Fields Cookies.

We conclude the text with a concise presentation on careers. This final chapter will outline how organizational careers evolve, pitfalls of career development, and particular challenges facing young managers in the future. One of those challenges, for example, is managing a dual-career marriage in which two young adults must reconcile separate careers while attending to their joint family interests. Another aspect of career development is the increasing trend of sending managers overseas to work for multinational companies. With the rapid advance toward a globalized economy, expatriate assignments have important implications for career advancement.

Our remarks about the functions of management and the flow of topics within the text are meant to provide fundamental definitions of organization and management. We will return to the capstone topics such as entrepreneurship and career development after fully addressing the principles of management in the following chapters. Now that we have these summary points in mind, we will focus on the persona of a manager and his or her organizational skills.

CHECKPOINT

- Define each function of management: planning, organizing, leading, and controlling.
- Explain how the functions of management are interrelated to constitute the "process of management."
- Describe an example of this process and the activities related to each function of management.

THE ROLE OF THE MANAGER

A widely quoted study by management researcher Henry Mintzberg shows that managers have three general "sets of behavior." Each set has several associated roles, as Figure 1-2 illustrates. Mintzberg's conclusions followed from an intensive study of selected organizations in which he identified patterns of behavior stemming from two conditions: first, managers have *formal authority* over others; and second, managers

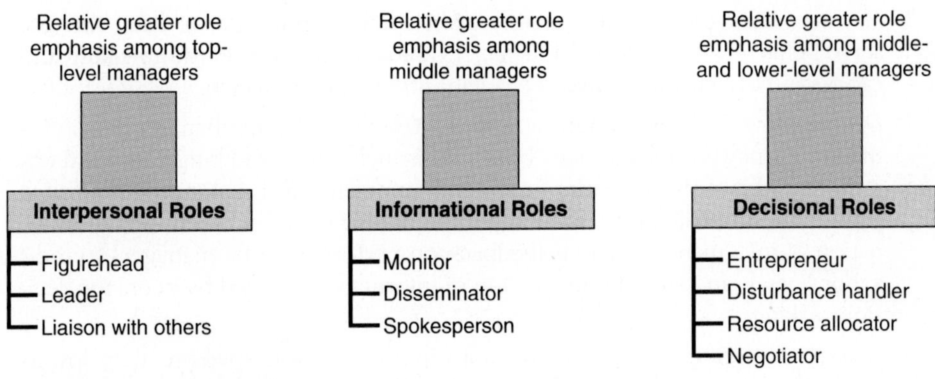

FIGURE 1-2 Managerial Roles

Source: Adapted from Henry Mintzberg, "The Manager's Job: Folklore and Fact," *Harvard Business Review*, July-August 1975.

enjoy *differentiated status* according to rank. These two factors are instrumental in determining interpersonal relations with superiors, peers, and subordinates. Also, the roles that evolved from these interpersonal relations were found to be similar in all organizations studied.[12]

Interpersonal Roles

The first set of behavior concerns interpersonal roles, and Mintzberg identifies three managerial roles within this set:

1. *Organizational Figurehead.* Executive managers perform a number of ceremonial duties such as representing the firm at public affairs and overseeing official company functions. Lower-level managers also have ceremonial duties, but usually of lesser importance, such as attending employees' weddings, greeting visitors, and acting as hosts for customers.
2. *Leader.* This role encompasses a range of duties suggested earlier, including motivating subordinates, guiding work-related behavior, and encouraging activities that help achieve organizational objectives. Managers at all organizational levels have leadership duties, although they vary in intensity according to the specific tasks and activities.
3. *Liaison.* All managers find themselves acting as liaisons between groups and individuals that are part of, or come into contact with, an organization. The liaison role is important for establishing relationships with suppliers, coordinating activities among work groups, and encouraging the harmony needed to ensure effective performance. Top-level executives are more concerned with external liaisons than lower-level managers, and these include relationships with government agencies, competitors, consumers, and public special interest groups. Lower-level managers are primarily concerned with internal liaisons to coordinate activities among interrelated work groups.

Informational Roles

Informational roles, as the term implies, involve communication among individuals and groups, but managers must also be adept at gathering and using information to help make effective decisions. Moreover, they should be able communicators who can transmit information and articulate decisions. Mintzberg sees managers as performing three informational roles:

1. *Monitor.* Managers monitor activity, solicit information, gather data, and observe behavior. Well-informed managers are prepared for decision making and can redirect behavior to improve organizational performance.
2. *Disseminator.* Here communications are reversed. Rather than receive information, managers transmit it to others. This includes articulating plans and objectives laid out by superiors to their subordinates and making performance reports on subordinates to their superiors. It also includes downward dissemination of information, such as feedback on performance by managers to their subordinates, and lateral transmission of information needed by peers for decision making.
3. *Spokesperson.* Top executives are more important spokespersons than lower-level managers. A firm's policy on competition, its philosophy of investment, and its commitment to safety are common topics in executive speeches. Managers at all levels, however, are spokespersons. For example, when department heads meet to discuss operating budgets, they must be prepared to present information in support of their budget requests.

Decisional Roles

Mintzberg identifies four decisional roles that reflect managers' choice-making responsibilities:

1. *Entrepreneur.* In recent years, entrepreneurs have been identified with commitment to innovation, specifically to starting new companies based on innovative products or services. Managers do not necessarily start their own firms, but those in complex organizations act as entrepreneurs by seeking innovative ways to use resources and technologies.
2. *Disturbance Handler.* This may be the best-understood role of managers because they have always had the primary responsibility for resolving problems. It may also be their most stressful role, for managers seem to be constantly faced with disturbances that threaten the harmony and effectiveness of their organizations.
3. *Resource Allocator.* This third managerial role links the planning and organizing functions. Managers must plan to meet their objectives and distribute resources accordingly. There will never be sufficient time, money, material, or manpower to accomplish all that is expected, so resource allocation often means carefully proportioning *scarce* resources.
4. *Negotiator.* The allocation process affects the manager's role as a negotiator. When scarce resources must be shared among many operating units, managers with superior negotiating skills will have an advantage over their less-skilled counterparts. Negotiating extends to many activities both inside and outside the firm. For example, purchasing managers negotiate material prices and terms, personnel managers negotiate wages and conditions of employment, marketing managers negotiate sales, and labor relations managers negotiate union contracts. Negotiation, of course, does not connote "conflict," but it does imply personal bargaining between individuals who may have different expectations.

How Managers Spend Their Time

Managers are often required to alternate among roles. In fact, the pace of change can sometimes be hectic. Mintzberg's research reveals how much time managers at different organizational levels spend in each of their roles. For example, chief executive officers (CEOs) spend about 59 percent of their time in scheduled meetings, 10 percent in unscheduled meetings, 22 percent at their desks, and about 6 percent on the telephone. The remaining 3 percent is spent on all other activities. By adding these percentages, you can see that CEOs devote 75 percent of their time to communicating.

Middle-level managers also spend a great deal of time in scheduled and unscheduled meetings, on the telephone, and on desk work. In contrast, first-line managers (the lowest level of management) are more involved with short, unscheduled meetings to address operational issues. Also, first-line managers spend more time than other managers in direct communication with nonmanagement workers about daily tasks.

Mintzberg's work represents a milestone in our understanding of how managers perceive their roles; current research is even more revealing. In 1988, Fred Luthans reported on his intensive four-year study of managers, which, unlike Mintzberg's, included individuals at all organizational levels.[13] Mintzberg's general role models were supported, but Luthans found greater emphasis among managers on *human interaction* and on *communicating*. He also observes that formal planning, decision making, and controlling are crucial management activities, but that they are seldom the result of intuition. In addition, he identifies "real managers" as those who, embracing the challenge of organizational initiative, are innovative and productive. These characteristics distinguish *real managers* from *successful managers*. Successful managers survive, and may even be promoted, because of uncontroversial behavior, administrative efficiency, or a combination of good socializing and politicking. In contrast, real managers forge ahead, driving their organizations to higher productivity, creating quality products and services, and setting the pace for innovative endeavor. Figure 1-3 illustrates these differences in role behavior. In the next section, we explore managerial roles at various levels in the organizational hierarchy.

FIGURE 1-3 The Activities of Real Managers

Source: Fred Luthans, "Successful vs. Effective Real Managers," *The Academy of Management Executive,* Vol. II, No. 2 (1988), pp. 127–132. Reprinted with permission.

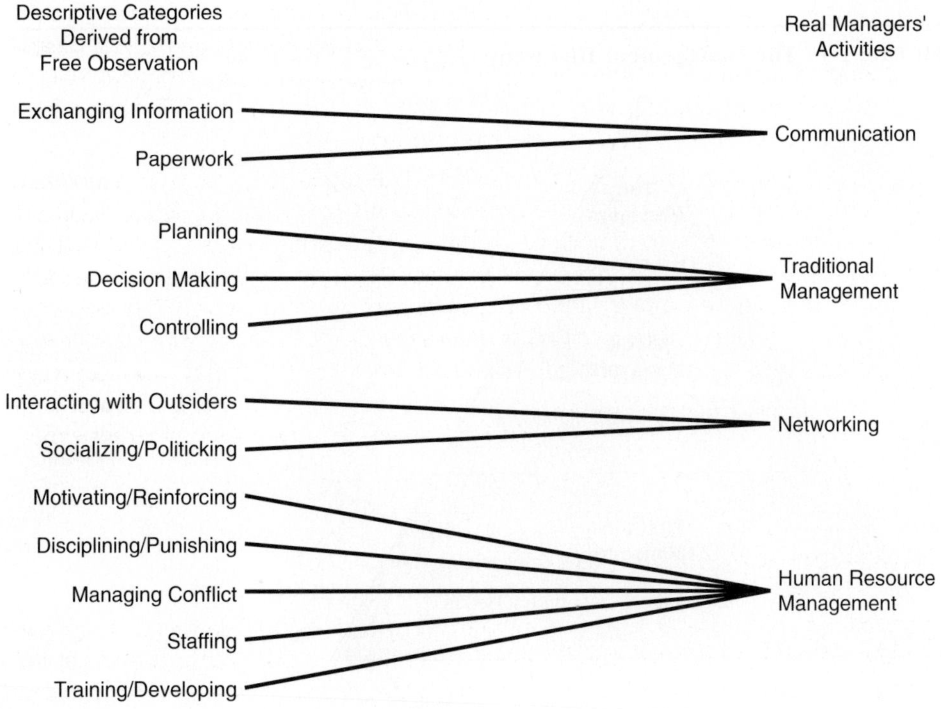

CHECKPOINT

- Describe responsibilities a manager might have in relation to each of the three interpersonal roles of figurehead, leader, and liaison.
- Informational roles imply communication. Discuss the roles of monitor, disseminator, and spokesperson.
- What do managers do in their decisional roles of disturbance handler, resource allocator, and negotiator?
- Explain how managers at different levels in an organization spend their time planning, organizing, leading, and controlling.

THE MANAGEMENT HIERARCHY

As organizations grow, a *hierarchy of management* evolves with fewer managers at higher levels and many more at lower levels. This management pyramid is shown in Figure 1-4. As you can see, executives are at the pinnacle, whereas first-line managers, such as shop supervisors, are near the bottom, close to operational workers. Between these two extremes are middle managers. They occupy a variety of specialized positions such as running departments, managing divisions, and overseeing plants. Principles of management apply equally to managers at every stratum, but the relative emphasis of activities changes at each level.

Many considerations influence the structure of a management hierarchy. Larger organizations simply cannot be managed by a few people, and as companies grow, increasing authority is delegated to an expanding cadre of lower-level managers. The complexity of operations, the type of technology employed, the geographic diversification of the firm, and the range of products or services managed also influence the hierarchy. Other factors include the number of individuals one person can manage and how work groups are structured. These points are discussed in the chapters on organization (Chapters 9–12).

FIGURE 1-4 The Management Hierarchy

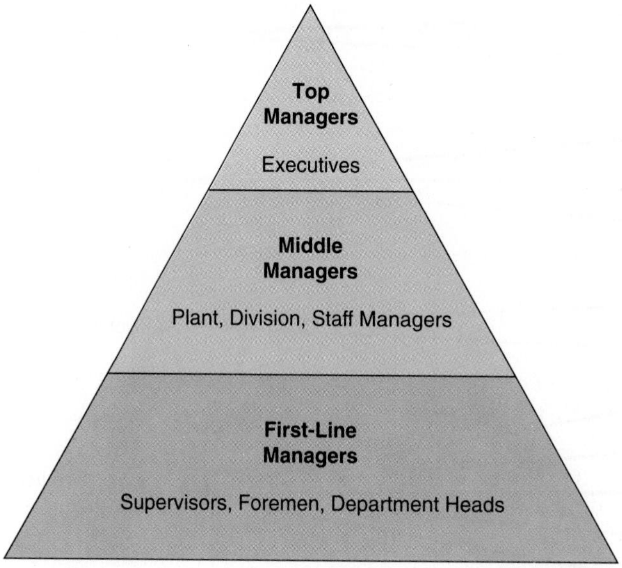

Division of Responsibility

While some organizations have few layers of management, others have many layers. Hierarchies evolve as a form of vertical division of labor. Executives concern themselves with far-reaching issues and grand, long-term plans. They cannot become involved in everyday operations and also concentrate on decisions with major consequences. Operational responsibilities are therefore delegated to lower-level managers. The extent of this vertical layering depends on the nature of the organization. Universities typically have between four and six levels. Manufacturers often have between seven and ten layers. Service organizations, such as hospitals, may have as few as three or as many as twelve levels.

During the era of rapid industrial growth that followed World War II, U.S. firms added levels of management and created more complex, "taller" organizations, but currently the trend is toward "downsizing." Many large companies, including IBM, Ford Motor Company, and Chrysler Corporation, have reduced their number of management levels. Service organizations are becoming "flatter," with fewer strata and more people reporting to each manager. In effect, firms are becoming "leaner and meaner," which means more responsibility for fewer managers.[14] These changes reflect changing expectations for participative leadership and changes in information technology, which together have reduced the need for middle managers in coordination roles.

Management Classifications

There are three clear categories of management in the hierarchy: *top management, middle management,* and *first-line management*. Even in the federal government's eighteen management levels, individual positions can be classified as belonging to one of these three categories. Let's look more closely at each.[15]

Top management. The chief executive officer is by definition one person heading an organization. In rare instances, two or more people share the leadership of a firm. For example, both Hewlett-Packard and Intel Corporation, two of America's leading high-tech Silicon Valley firms, have co-chairmen with joint authority. Most firms, however, vest CEO authority in one person. Top management also includes a few highly selected executives who share the huge work load of the CEO—the corporate treasurer, the chief financial officer (CFO), and a few other specialists. In large diversified firms, top management includes executive vice presidents and division presidents who are responsible for strategic decisions.

Top managers are distinguished from other managers by the scope and nature of their responsibilities. They make decisions that can ruin an organization or lead it to take prodigious strides in profitability and growth. They determine long-range objectives, dictate the cadence of change, and establish a philosophy of leadership. Not least of all, they set the standards for ethical behavior and guide their organizations toward socially responsive endeavors. These characteristics can be seen by studying prominent corporate leaders. For example, John Scully, CEO of Apple Computer corporation, brought to that company new growth objectives, new strategies for marketing, and a new style of leadership that differed significantly from that of Apple's celebrity founder Steven Jobs. Lee Iacocca, CEO of Chrysler, became one of America's most notable industrial leaders by reversing the auto company's downslide. Both Iacocca and Scully are well known because they assumed top management roles under highly publicized adverse circumstances and succeeded, but other, lesser-known CEOs have equally difficult responsibilities. For example, John Akers, chairman of IBM, is involved in a massive restructuring of the corporation while under heavy competitive pressure by other major computer manufacturers.[16]

Middle management. Multiple levels of individuals are sandwiched between executive managers and first-line managers. Unlike top managers, whose positions can be fairly well described, middle managers occupy a wide variety of positions in many strata that are hard to define. Plant managers, accounting managers, public relations officers, department heads, regional sales managers, and managers in charge of specialty areas, such as data processing or market research, are all middle managers.

Most middle managers supervise subunits of an organization; they direct the activities of other managers. Middle managers typically do not manage nonmanagement employees except those workers in specialty units such as data processing or accounting. In primary work environments—for example, manufacturing or sales—middle managers almost always have several lower-level managers reporting to them. In manufacturing, lower-level managers may be shop supervisors. In sales, they may be sales managers. Middle managers' responsibilities are largely dictated by the philosophy of organization prevailing in their firms.[17] For example, middle managers in a company with a flattened structure (few levels) will participate in many top-level decisions, but will also be close to actual operations. To use Mintzberg's model, they will have significant responsibility in "interactive roles," but these will embrace the "real managers'" activities of communicating and human resource management described in Luthans's model.

Taller organizations—those with more layers of management—tend to insulate each layer through more rigid reporting systems and job titles. In these companies, upper-echelon middle managers have decision-making responsibilities closely associated with top management. In contrast, lower-echelon middle managers focus more on operations (actual tasks and processes) and coordinate work with first-line managers.

First-line management. Supervisors are generally called "first-line managers" because they constitute the first level above operational, nonmanagement personnel. They include floor supervisors, head tellers in banks, military sergeants, and charge nurses in hospitals. The majority of managers in nearly all organizations are supervisors who spend most of their time with employees. Their duties consist of technical control of operations, direct communication with employees, and resolution of immediate problems associated with specific tasks.

Unlike many higher-placed managers, first-line managers tend to rise from employee ranks. Their roles differ from those of other managers in three substantial ways. First, they are expected to possess greater technical skills for hands-on work. Second, they are charged with the greatest responsibility for managing employee problems, resolving schedules, and controlling behavior. Third, they initiate most operational reports. This means first-line managers shoulder the burden of transmitting most of the information generated in an organization.[18]

First-line managers are highly visible. Their superiors expect them to support higher-level objectives, report on employees' performance, and implement decisions made at higher levels. Employees expect them to provide direction and training, represent the work group, and make equitable decisions on schedules, raises, and grievances. Their peers expect them to coordinate interrelated activities and to harmonize interdepartmental relationships.[19]

It is no wonder that first-line managers feel they are constantly on the firing line. They are forced to make tough decisions, and many don't believe they have been given sufficient training to be held accountable for those decisions.

One of the ironies of management education is that first-line managers, who do most of the hands-on "managing," are the least trained in management techniques. Most first-line managers have never read a textbook on management, and only those in our largest corporations have access to formal in-house training programs. Some authors argue strongly that one of the advantages of Japanese companies is that most of their supervisors are college-educated and well trained to man-

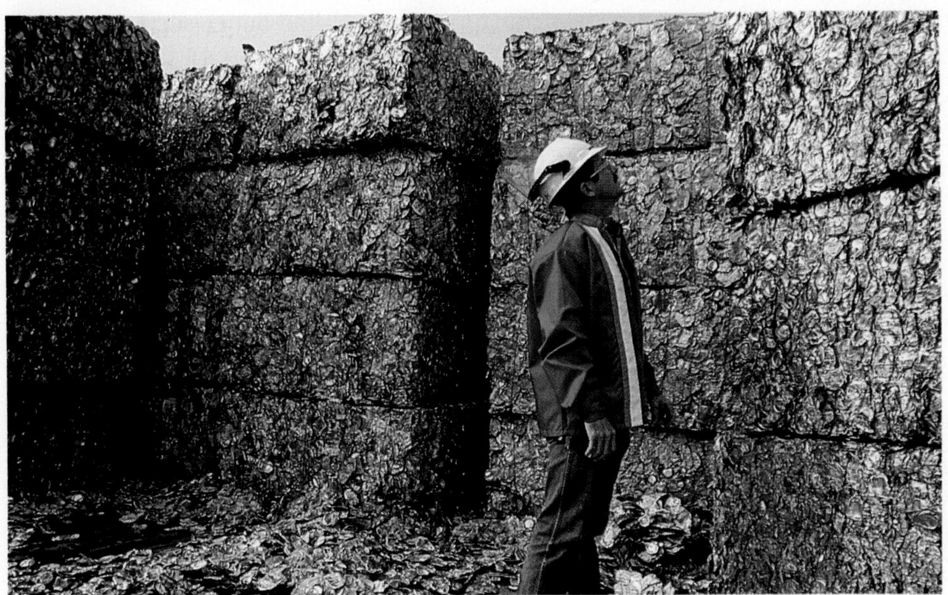

Although they shoulder an enormous amount of responsibility, first-line managers often have little training in formal management techniques. This supervisor at Alcoa's Knoxville, Tennessee, beverage-can sheet factory surveys bundles of aluminum cans fresh off the boxcar. Alcoa pays over $230 million per year for cans that, as recycled aluminum, supply fully one-seventh of the company's primary aluminum needs. Recycling saves the company 90 percent of the labor and capital costs and 95 percent of the energy costs required to produce new aluminum.

age human resources.[20] Management skills at the first-line level may become even more important if, as Peter Drucker notes, changes in information technology shift more responsibility for coordinating activities away from middle managers toward first-line managers. Drucker points out that many firms are eliminating entire levels of middle management, particularly where information systems can provide effective linkage between top-level executives and operations. John Akers eliminated nearly 6,000 middle-management positions at IBM between 1988 and 1990, then announced a general staff reduction of nearly 47,000 for 1992.[21] Lee Iacocca cut two complete levels of middle management from Chrysler during the 1980s. In each instance, first-line managers were given expanded leadership roles and were held more accountable for decisions previously made by a cadre of middle managers.[22]

Functional and General Managers

The hierarchy of management described by top, middle, and first-line management is a *vertical* division of labor. Management is also divided *horizontally* along functional lines of authority. **Functional management** reflects a kind of specialization in which authority is vested in managers according to their fields of expertise. Department heads are delegated narrow slices of authority over particular areas. For example, accountants are usually grouped within a single department and given broad-based authority for accounting, but restricted from involvement in production or sales. Accounting may be further subdivided into departmental sections such as payroll, payables, cost accounting, and auditing. Subunits within a large personnel department may include labor relations, recruitment, benefits administration, compensation management, and affirmative action.

functional management
A definition of management authority based on expertise and specialization.

Functional managers are not all experts in professions such as accounting or personnel. Actually, most of them are in line positions. **Line managers** are concerned with primary organizational activities such as marketing and production. De-

line manager
A person who has direct control over primary operations of an organization such as production.

partments are, in turn, defined according to functional line duties such as production control, receiving, sales, shipping, and customer service. Functional management positions developed out of the rapid expansion of individual firms during the 1940s and 1950s. For example, the growth of our factory system required specialized production managers. A commensurate increase in competition led to sales and marketing positions. The complexity of commerce also nourished financial management positions. Horizontal specialization spread rapidly to include managers adept at materials management, purchasing, logistics, market research, advertising, and many other areas.

general manager
A person who oversees collective operations and supervises multifunctional subordinate activities.

Generalists, or **general managers,** usually oversee collective operations that include several functional managers. Plant managers are generalists, responsible for the totality of their plant operations. Division managers have similar roles in corporations. Top managers, by definition, are also generalists. These executives and upper-middle-level managers may have moved up to their positions from lower-level functional positions in "line" areas such as production or marketing. A number of higher-level generalists in manufacturing are engineers by training, and it is not unusual to find executive positions filled by financial specialists. Historically, a few top general managers "came up from the ranks" or carved out careers from nonmanagement jobs, but this is extremely rare today.

Managerial Skills

Managers in different occupations obviously need different skills. Those who specialize in functional areas tend to focus their energy on the technical aspects of their jobs, but they also lead others. In contrast, those in general management positions have to manage a variety of people in many different situations, and this calls for integrative leadership skills. Research by Robert L. Katz, a specialist in organizational theory, has shown that all managers have similar skills in three important areas: *technical, human,* and *conceptual.*[23] He also notes that managers at different levels in an organization tend to emphasize one type of skill more than others, a finding that is reinforced by Fred Luthans.[24] Figure 1-5 shows the relative intensity of different skills at the three management levels.

Conceptual skills. Managers spend much of their time communicating with others, making decisions, and solving problems. People with the ability to look at organizational problems from a broad conceptual base usually make decisions more consistent with organizational objectives. Top managers must go one step further to envision the long-term needs of the firm and make decisions that serve the entire organization. Conceptual skills are far more crucial for executives than for lower-level managers. For example, American executives who can envision an expanding global economy in which we will one day be actively trading in China will make decisions today that will prepare their organizations for those future opportunities. First-line managers in the same companies do not have to deal with such broad conceptual issues, but are concerned with meeting weekly production quotas.

Human skills. All managers must acquire human skills, for all managers must lead, motivate, and influence others to achieve organizational objectives. Today a disproportionate number of middle managers find themselves in coordinating roles where human skills are emphasized: fine-tuning interpersonal relations, developing harmonious relationships among work groups, and motivating others. First-line managers also play a significant role in motivating others, and if the trend toward reducing the number of middle managers continues, first-line managers will become more accountable for activities that require human skills.

Skills Needed by Managers | **Relative Importance by Management Level**

Conceptual

Ability to solve long-term problems and view the total organization as as interactive system

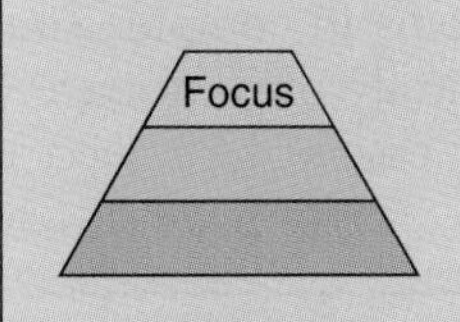

Human Relations

Ability to work effectively, lead, and ensure harmonious interpersonal relations

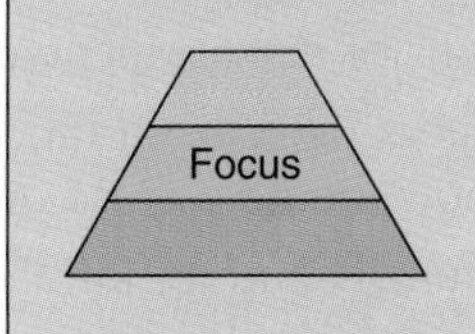

Technical

Ability to use tools, apply specialized knowledge, and manage processes and techniques

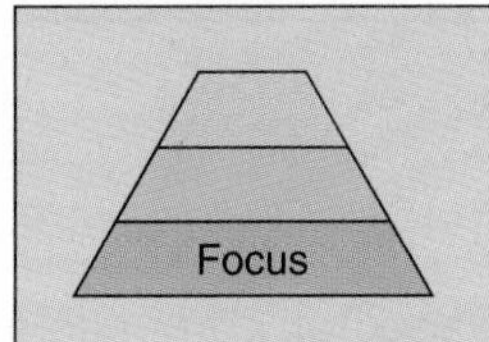

FIGURE 1-5 Managerial Skills

Source: Adapted from Robert L. Katz, "Skills of an Effective Administrator," *Harvard Business Review,* September-October 1974.

Technical skills. First-line managers, as well as many middle managers, are intensively involved in technical operations. They are expected to apply their education, job experience, and expertise to make things happen. Although lower-level managers cannot ignore conceptual and human skills, they focus on daily decisions involving technical operations and specific tasks assigned to their work groups. First-line managers are also typically evaluated on how well they accomplish those tasks, so technical expertise is important to their career success.

A perspective on skills. All three types of skills vary tremendously among individual managers and organizational positions. There are no hard-and-fast rules for establishing which skill is most important at any given time, yet clearly managers

The man with the tie on is Alabama Gas CEO Mike Warren, who's obviously not afraid to get his hands—or his clothes—a little dirty. Managers at every level ideally possess an appropriate mix of technical, human, and conceptual skills. Determining which skills are most important in a certain situation or at a certain time requires intelligence and flexibility.

cannot advance up the hierarchy without conceptual abilities and strong human relations skills. Similarly, top managers need not be technically expert if they can lead others well and solve problems in complex situations. In the next section, we discuss entrepreneurs who typically own, manage, and operate their own ventures. A broad range of skills is often essential for successful entrepreneurship.

CHECKPOINT

- Explain the classifications of management and give an example of each.
- How do general managers differ from functional managers? Give an example of each and state how their roles are distinguished.
- Describe conceptual, human, and technical skills and how they differ in importance for executives and first-line managers.

ENTREPRENEURS

Our discussion so far has focused on corporate management, but new ventures and small businesses also offer substantial opportunities for managers. During the last decade, small businesses created more than 6 million new jobs for Americans, while the largest corporations—those in the Fortune 500—cut employment by more than a million jobs. There are about 16 million small firms in the United States, accounting for roughly 97 percent of all nonfarm businesses; these companies typically have fewer than 1,000 employees and do less than $10 million in sales.[25]

entrepreneur
An individual who assumes the risk of starting a new business, creating a new commercial product or service, and consequently seeking profitable rewards within a free enterprise system.

Firms that are small but growing, innovative, or high-risk ventures are generally called *entrepreneurial.* **Entrepreneur** is a French word used during the sixteenth and seventeenth centuries to describe persons who contracted their services. It originally applied to actors, building contractors, mercenaries, and others who bore the risk of their own enterprise rather than work within established organizations.[26] While the literal meaning of "a go-between" or "one who undertakes service for a fee" has been lost, the connotation of free enterprise has prevailed. There are numerous modern examples of entrepreneurs who launched highly successful firms from independent and often humble beginnings. In fact, many of our largest companies began in ramshackle garages, not least among them Hewlett-Packard, McDonald's, Macy's, and the Ford Motor Company. Andrew Carnegie and J. P. Morgan laid the foundations of our steel industry, Edwin H. Land founded and managed Polaroid Corporation, and John D. Rockefeller fashioned an oil empire that nurtured hundreds of other companies.

Many entrepreneurs have been forgotten even though their companies have become part of the American heritage. Rowland H. Macy, for example, failed four times at the dry-goods business during the mid-1850s, an example of the high risk—and persistence—associated with entrepreneurship. It was his fifth attempt in 1858 in New York City that ultimately led to Macy's department store. More recently, four entrepreneurs named Andreas Bechtolsheim, Vinod Khosla, Bill Joy, and Scott McNealy started a company with little capital and a rented apartment. The company, Sun Microsystems, is now a $1.3 billion leader in computer technology.[27]

Managers of entrepreneurial organizations must become generalists, able to assume a broad range of duties as well as to make executive decisions. Entrepreneurs also typically risk their personal wealth and reputations to pursue a new venture. But not every entrepreneur is to be found in a "small" business. Entrepreneurs also exist in established corporations. Research and development efforts in many firms confirm this observation. A celebrated example occurred in Boca Raton, Florida, where a small team of corporate adventurers created the IBM Personal Computer. We explore entrepreneurship in Chapter 20.

CHECKPOINT

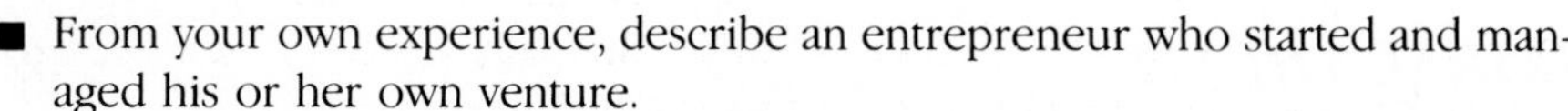

- From your own experience, describe an entrepreneur who started and managed his or her own venture.

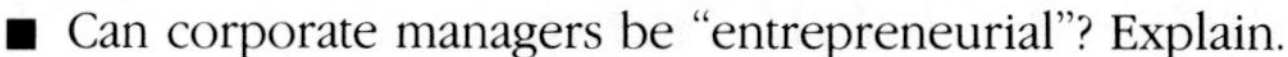

- Can corporate managers be "entrepreneurial"? Explain.

GLOBAL DIMENSIONS OF MANAGEMENT

Nearly 40 percent of all U.S. corporate profits are derived from overseas investments, and American firms account for about 17 percent of gross world output in noncommunist countries. Many of our largest companies earn more than 50 percent of their gross revenues from foreign operations.[28] In turn, American managers today must cope with the increasing influence of foreign firms operating in the United States; this competition is stiff in electronics, automobiles, computers, petroleum, and food products, among others.

Managing in a global environment requires a comprehensive perspective that includes knowledge of trade, finance, and the political economics of selling to and buying from foreign companies. International managers must operate overseas facilities, coordinate foreign subsidiaries of domestic corporations, and compete with a multitude of companies in diversified cultures.

Increasing globalization of business is an undeniable fact of corporate life, and with so many important changes occurring throughout the world, managing in the international arena can no longer be studied as an interesting addendum to a principles course. The importance of the international management theme has been emphasized for business school education in the 1990s by the AACSB (American Assembly of Collegiate Schools of Business). Consequently, we will introduce students to international management early in this text, in Chapter 3. Although the entire text remains focused on "principles" of management, the international theme will be evident throughout the chapters and in many of the accompanying cases.

CHECKPOINT

- Based on an overview of the chapter, what challenges do you envision for managing in a global economy?
- What attributes might a manager need to be effective in a firm that operates internationally?

PRODUCTIVITY—A CHALLENGE FOR INNOVATIVE MANAGERS

The concepts of management we have introduced suggest diverse career directions for young managers entering the world of commerce. The familiar corporate world of domestic competition is, of course, the fundamental model explored in this and most other management texts, but it is not the only model. The world of entrepreneurs, for example, has been receiving much scholarly attention lately. Within the scope of entrepreneurial activity are new-venture creations, high-risk business operations, and small-business management. We have also noted the increase in global competition, which is compelling managers to study international relations. Every arena of business poses its own managerial challenges. Yet the ultimate challenge is for managers to create a nation of highly productive organizations, large and small,

GLOBAL TRENDS
Texas Instruments—A Global Team

As the first U.S. semiconductor company to go international, Texas Instruments now operates in more than thirty countries on five continents. It has nineteen overseas plants and research ventures with twenty-eight European and three Japanese companies. In 1991, TI became the world's leading non-Asian producer of microchips.

TI created the first commercial silicon transistor in 1954, and when the company manufactured transistors for the first commercial transistor radio later that year, it demonstrated to the world the practicality of these components in commercial products. In 1958, TI invented the integrated circuit, which revolutionized the electronics industry by reducing the size, weight, and cost of electronic equipment, making possible a wide range of new commercial, industrial, and military products. The company introduced the first integrated circuit computer in 1961, and in 1967, it unveiled the world's first hand-held calculator. In 1978, TI developed the first single-chip speech synthesizer; in 1984, the first multiport video RAM; and in 1987, the first single-chip artificial intelligence microprocessor.

These milestones in innovation instigated tremendous challenges in management and organization, stimulating the company to create an information network within the firm that links more than 50,000 computer terminals through a worldwide communications system. Simultaneous communication among thousands of managers and engineers in numerous locations redefined organizational relationships toward teamwork and away from bureaucratic strata. Today TI is not viewed merely as another American firm doing business abroad but as a transnational corporation. Its Italian plant near Rome, for example, includes a $700 million investment by the Italian government as part of a $1.2 billion package. Semiconductor products developed and manufactured there are sold throughout Europe as Italian products, yet the technology used in Rome was developed through TI's Japanese venture with Fujitsu. European sales of the Italian-made products are coordinated through TI's facilities near London.

Sources: "Milestones in Innovation," a report by Texas Instruments, Dallas, Tex., 1988; Jonathan B. Levine, "Texas Instruments: Digging in Against the Japanese," *Business Week,* June 3, 1991; and "Chairman's Letter to Shareholders," Texas Instruments *Annual Report,* 1991, p. 2.

profit and nonprofit, that will ensure a competitive economy, jobs, growth, and a high quality of life.

productivity
The relationship of combined inputs such as labor, materials, capital, and managerial verve to outputs such as products or services. It is the summation of quality performance that results in more efficient utilization of organizational resources.

Productivity is the measurement of *net quantity output* related to the *total resources used.* Any product, service, or performance result can be evaluated in tangible terms using such techniques as market prices, units of parts produced, and number of people served. These results are then compared to the effort and resources needed to create them. For example, to grow a bushel of corn requires land, tools, seed, water, fertilizer, and hours of labor to plant, weed, and harvest. If a farmer can produce more corn using fewer resources per bushel of corn harvested, his productivity increases. Productivity measurements have historically focused on "labor-hours" as the primary input. Using this measurement as an illustration, a manufacturer who produced 100 units in a previous period using 10 labor-hours and produces 110 units in the current period with the same 10 labor-hours experiences a 10 percent increase in productivity. Labor-hours continues to be the standard for

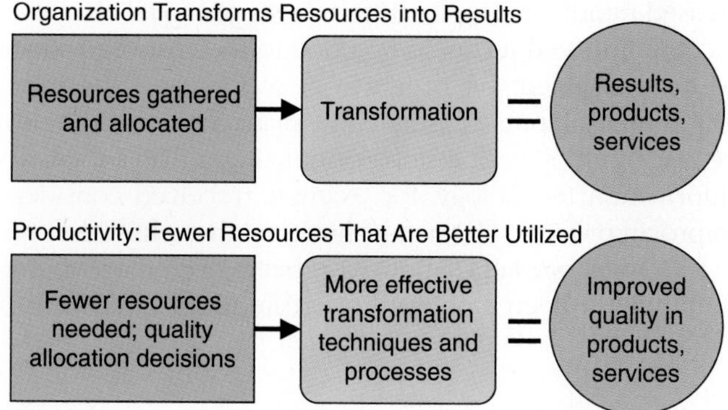

FIGURE 1-6 Organizational Model and Productivity

statistical comparisons, but it is a poor indicator of performance. Other resources must be included in the equation—capital, materials, energy, and information.

Figure 1-6 illustrates two dimensions of organized activity. First, most organizations exist to "transform" collective forms of resources into new products or services, as shown in the top part of the figure. Second, productivity is a relationship between resource inputs and the results of the transformation process, as shown in the lower part. Increases in productivity are achieved in at least three general ways. Resources can be reduced (while results are held constant); processes can be improved (increasing quality and quantity); and results can be improved by raising quality (using similar resources and processes).

Our definition of productivity emphasizes the output part of the equation—"net good quality output." The crucial word here is **quality.** If we measured pure output without considering how many units were rejects, productivity would be based entirely on how rapidly we are able to manufacture the greatest number of products. That would be like judging the performance of a hospital on how fast patients can be treated without considering whether they are made well in the process. Similarly, in producing material goods, the number of good products must be evaluated, with defective work subtracted from results. A defective product, obviously, uses the same resources as a good product, but it does so without adding value to the process. Productivity, therefore, depends on how quality can be improved; in effect, it means using fewer resources to create a quality product or service at lower cost. This result is achieved largely through innovative combinations of resources, new technologies, creative leadership, and effective control systems that encourage employees to do quality work.

quality
The concept of doing things better, not just more efficiently.

Recent U.S. Productivity

Between 1948 and 1967, private business productivity in the United States grew at an average annual rate of 3.1 percent. That was the best record among industrialized nations during the postwar period. Our productivity rate dropped to 2.3 percent between 1967 and 1973, however, and then it fell even more, to about 0.8 percent between 1973 and 1980. During the 1980s, it improved to an annual 3.5 percent rate, but as noted earlier in the chapter, our performance still lags behind that of our foreign competitors. Japan, for example, posted annual average productivity gains during the sample period of nearly 7 percent.[29]

Initial reactions to U.S. productivity "losses" centered on labor. Critics claimed that American workers were lazy, that they had lost the traditional work ethic, and that labor unions had strangled our industries. Actually, labor became a lower percentage cost of manufacturing during this time. Energy costs nearly doubled, however, and material costs increased rapidly during the 1980s. Costs of capital also rose as interest rates climbed, and sophisticated technology added to the cost of production. Resource relationships have changed, yet productivity continues to be measured with labor-hours as the primary input. Consequently, management still tends to focus on squeezing more out of employees instead of utilizing a firm's total resources more effectively. Information technology, for example, received considerable fanfare as a means of improving white-collar productivity, yet there has been no appreciable improvement. White-collar workers simply have been given more to do, and more people and machinery have been employed to create more information, whether needed or not.[30]

Managing Productivity and Innovation

effectiveness
The result of making decisions that lead to doing the right things, which helps to fulfill the mission of an enterprise.

efficiency
The result of making decisions that lead to doing things right, which helps to achieve objectives with fewer resources and at lower costs.

innovation
Finding new ways to use or combine resources to create new products, services, processes, or technologies.

Managerial effectiveness is related to the *total* productivity of a firm's resources, not just labor or materials or energy or any other partial factor of performance. And while **effectiveness** (doing the right things) is critical, prosperity also requires **efficiency** (doing things right). Managers must efficiently use resources for the greatest results. Consequently, quality workmanship, quality materials, quality systems, and quality decision making add to the total productivity of a firm. When national productivity increases, it means that collectively we have generated better results while using our resources more effectively.

Every manager must therefore focus on improving his or her environment so that productivity increases. Higher productivity often requires **innovation**. Innovation means creating new technology, developing new systems, and combining resources *creatively* to enhance total performance. The backbone of every organization is the collective performance of its managers and their work groups. The ultimate challenge of management is to achieve organizational objectives through the most effective use of resources. The only way to achieve these objectives is by a commitment to quality in every organized activity.

These principles are not specific to manufacturing; service organizations have similar responsibilities to customers and similar resources—human and material—to manage. The role of entrepreneurial activity in creating new processes and providing new technologies also cannot be underestimated. Innovation is at the heart of entrepreneurship, and it is needed equally by established firms and new ventures. In a global economy, where competition is increasingly across geographic boundaries, the role of innovation is accentuated. Throughout the text, we discuss innovation and productivity as important issues for future managers.

Changes Affecting Management

In summary, these are the factors that are beginning to affect managers now and are most likely to affect them in the year 2000 and beyond.[31]

1. *Frequent Changes.* A global economy signals pervasive involvement in world affairs, world trade, and the tensions associated with international competition. Managers must adapt to peoples and cultures unlike their own. Affluence among people of industrialized nations has induced new perceptions of work and leisure, while people in emerging nations must struggle with economic and political hardships.
2. *Technology Innovation.* Rapid and conspicuous changes will occur in technology, including robotics, telecommunications, biogenetics, and similar fields. Overseeing these changes will require greater sophistication by leaders better educated in technical disciplines than the present generation of managers.

MANAGEMENT APPLICATION

Innovation: Taking Chances at Johnson & Johnson

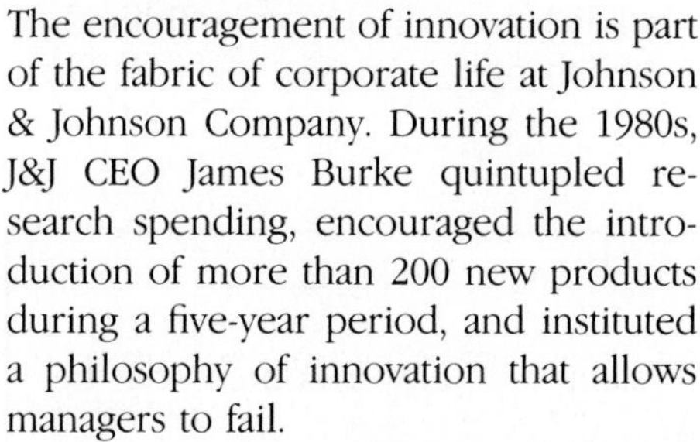

The encouragement of innovation is part of the fabric of corporate life at Johnson & Johnson Company. During the 1980s, J&J CEO James Burke quintupled research spending, encouraged the introduction of more than 200 new products during a five-year period, and instituted a philosophy of innovation that allows managers to fail.

His first stay at J&J lasted only one year. In 1953, he left, feeling stifled and bored. Before his departure, Burke suggested that J&J create a new-products division. In less than three weeks, he was back to head this division. Burke set to work developing new ideas, until he was summoned to the office of the chairman, General Robert Wood Johnson. It seems that one of Burke's first new-product innovations, a children's chest rub, had failed dismally.

General Johnson asked Burke, "Are you the one who just cost us all that money?" Burke nodded. The General said, "Well, I just want to congratulate you. If you are making mistakes, that means you are making decisions and taking risks. And we won't grow unless you take risks."

J&J's new CEO since 1989, Ralph S. Larsen, is out to make his own corporate legends. His goal: to retain the decentralization and entrepreneurial spirit that have created J&J's 166 separately chartered companies while working toward more integration of these companies. Larsen likens himself to a symphony conductor who must simultaneously guide and inspire his musicians. He must guide J&J managers to eliminate redundancies, share more services, and streamline relationships with larger clients while at the same time allowing these managers the creative freedom they are used to. Larsen knows that he's taking a chance, but then, taking chances is what J&J has built its success on.

Sources: Kenneth Labich, "The Innovators," *Fortune,* June 6, 1988, pp. 50–64; Laura L. Nash, "Johnson & Johnson's Credo," in *Corporate Ethics: A Prime Business Asset* (New York: Business Roundtable, 1988), pp. 77–104; and Joseph Weber, "A Big Company That Works: J&J's Ralph Larsen Gives His Units a Lot of Latitude—and They Produce," *Business Week,* May 4, 1992, pp. 124–132.

3. *Shifts in Resource Allocations.* Sharply defined changes are occurring in energy development, natural resources, capital markets, and labor relations. Developing nations are wealthy in natural resources; industrialized nations are relatively shallow in those resources. Labor has become less important as a factor of production than the combination of resources and capital for transforming goods and services.
4. *Growth in Services.* Industrial management, and most management theory, evolved during the growth period that followed World War II. This focus on management is being replaced by one on services, such as recreation, health care, and telecommunications. Intellectual resources, such as expertise in information technology and robotic engineering, are becoming more important than physical resources, such as minerals and steel production capacity.
5. *Changing Expectations.* Employees are becoming more accustomed to participative decision making; they expect different relations than they have now with managers. Similarly, younger managers expect different relationships with older managers.

6. *Social Influences.* Special interest groups, and society in general, expect managers to behave ethically. Environmental concerns, equality legislation, and constitutional issues are redefining how we view corporate social responsibility.

This list is hardly exhaustive, but it makes it clear that managers of the future—those currently being trained in colleges and universities—will face extraordinary challenges. Management is barely beyond the embryonic stage of development; there has been less than a century of theory building compared to several hundred centuries for many sciences. It follows that greater changes in management are likely to occur as research in the field expands.

CHECKPOINT

- Define productivity and formulate an example of how resources can be used effectively to improve productivity.
- Quality performance enhances productivity. Explain this statement and show how poor quality wastes resources.
- Poor productivity in America has been blamed on a "lost work ethic." Analyze this statement and explore how innovation affects productivity.

AT THE BEGINNING OF THIS CHAPTER, we discussed the changes Shearson Lehman Hutton was making to provide high-quality customer service rather than merely high sales volume. These were important changes because they forced managers to redefine their roles to generate customer confidence that their company could provide fast and accurate service. Previously, the company had emphasized convincing investors that they could make more money with Shearson than with a competitor. Other Wall Street firms followed similar strategies, and many still do, but Shearson managers have become obsessed with creating an organization committed to quality service.

Managerial roles changed drastically in the process. Instead of spending most of their time on sales accounts, Shearson managers now spend a majority of their time improving internal operating systems. This involves marketing, of course, but it also involves better planning, enhanced control systems for customer accounts and internal transactions, and more effective leadership to improve both employee and customer relationships. As quality has improved at Shearson, productivity and long-term profitability have also improved. Managers are committed to getting things done that reinforce the long-term success of their organization.[32] ■

A SYNOPSIS FOR LEARNING

1. Define management, and discuss future perspectives for management careers.

   Management is the process of getting things done through others. Managers' major responsibilities are defining what is to be done, organizing resources, guiding others toward accomplishing their tasks, and controlling performance. Planning, organizing, leading, and controlling form the outline of this text. Future managers will find exceptional opportunities in global affairs, and they will find equally rewarding challenges in small, high-growth ventures.

2. Explain what constitutes an organization, and discuss the differences between formal and informal organizations.

   Organizations exist when two or more people mutually cooperate to pursue common objectives. Thus people combine their talents and resources to achieve more collectively than they could working independently. Formal organizations have deliberately defined objectives that take into account their stakeholders' interests; they also have specific purposes. Informal organizations arise spontaneously and may have no formal purpose or objective, yet their members have mutual interests and work together to satisfy them.

3. Explain the process of management, and discuss the concepts of planning, organizing, leading, and controlling.

   The process of management includes four *functions* of management that are interrelated activities. Managers *plan* in order to provide objectives. *Organizing* is concerned with gathering resources necessary to carry out plans. *Leading* is the "influence" process through which managers in authority direct human behavior to achieve objectives. *Controlling* is the management function of steering performance toward desired results.

4. Name the different sets of managerial roles, and give examples of each.

   Interpersonal roles include figurehead, leader, and liaison. *Informational roles* include monitor, disseminator, and spokesperson. *Decisional roles* include entrepreneur, disturbance handler, resource allocator, and negotiator.

5. Name the three basic levels of managers in the management hierarchy and briefly describe each.

   Strategic managers are top operating executives and decision-making boards who guide the company in fulfilling long-term objectives. They are concerned with the broad-based mission and major objectives to be accomplished, as well as with providing a philosophy of leadership to organizational members. Tactical managers are those just under executive ranks and in several lower strata, including divisions and departments. They can be specialists, such as auditors, or operational managers, such as sales directors, but they deal with near-term objectives such as quarterly or annual sales and budgets. First-line managers are those who interact directly on a daily basis with operational, nonmanagement employees. They hold positions as supervisors, foremen, and office managers, and they are concerned with immediate performance results, daily scheduling, and personal leadership and guidance of the work force.

6. Describe entrepreneurship as an important dimension of our free enterprise system.

   Large and complex organizations began in humble surroundings as entrepreneurial ventures. Every major company can trace its roots to innovative individuals. Entrepreneurship is the act of starting new ventures by combining resources in unusual ways to create new commercial endeavors.

7. Discuss how global competition is changing our views about managing organizations.

   American managers must cope with increased competition at home from foreign companies that have been able to establish strong markets by offering high-quality products at reasonable prices. One of the important challenges for future American managers is to regain our competitive posture in the world economy.

8. Explain the connection between quality and productivity.

   Productivity is achieved by reducing the total resources used to provide reliable products or services. Workmanship, effective purchasing, proper sales forecasting, careful performance control, good inventory management, and innovative methods in production or services add to a company's quality profile, and as these improve, so does productivity.

SKILL ANALYSIS

CASE 1 Characteristics of Top Managers in U.S. Firms

The editors of *Fortune* magazine recently surveyed the nation's top corporate recruiters to determine "America's Most Wanted Managers." The results suggest a number of attributes that recruiters agree are essential for becoming the chief executive officer of a major corporation. In subsequent articles, *Fortune* profiled several of America's most successful CEOs. Attributes found through the survey are summarized below, followed by four selected CEO profiles.[33]

- *Action-oriented.* One of the key characteristics desired in a chief executive was the ability to "act," to get things done. Most recruiters agreed that too many managers are competent planners who cannot follow through to implement plans.
- *Visionary.* Managers must have the ability to envision where the organization should be headed in the long run and understand how it might get there.
- *Intuitive.* Recruiters used various terms to describe the ability of top managers to think on their feet, make quick judgments, and bring a constructive view of the future into decision making.
- *Self-confident.* Having a "healthy ego" permits strong leadership, ambition, and acceptance of necessary changes.
- *Capable of Managing Change.* Managers in top-echelon positions must be able to motivate others to accept necessary changes, implement drastic changes smoothly, and translate innovation into success.
- *Technically Competent.* Recruiters placed strong emphasis on advanced degrees, profit-and-loss experience, steady progress in operating ranks, experience in international business, and excellent communication skills. The inclusion of experience in international business is another indication of the increasing global orientation of most major U.S. corporations.
- *A Pattern of Accomplishment.* This characteristic emphasizes "results" over promotion through the ranks. Although many top executives did move systematically up through the management hierarchy, others switched jobs and companies, leaving behind a succession of accomplishments that built their careers and set the stage for a top-leadership position.

- *Commitment.* Recruiters generally agreed that the one common denominator of all top-ranked executives is their commitment. The commitment may be to the firm, to the task at hand, or to plans that require difficult decisions. Top executives have been willing to pay a heavier price than others to choose the right thing to do and then ensure it gets done.
- *Other Observations.* Recruiters noted that almost all executives on their most wanted list were happy and secure in their present positions. These individuals are sensitive to others, versatile, exceptionally capable of dealing with numbers, energetic, and have almost unbelievable energy. They were also described as ethical, imaginative, and able to generate loyalty and admiration from subordinates.

Sam Walton, who passed away on April 5, 1992, was no less than a legend. Founder and CEO of Wal-Mart, he was called America's most successful merchant. He was also one of the wealthiest men in the world, yet he did not launch the Wal-Mart empire until he was forty-four years old. Before opening his first store, Walton had successfully managed several retail stores, been an avid merchandising purchasing agent, and served with distinction as a U.S. Army officer. As a youngster, he was a state champion high school quarterback, Eagle Scout, and student council president. Walton made Wal-Mart into the largest U.S. retail organization, with 2,000 store locations and $40 billion in annual sales. For years, he was an active manager who visited every store at least once each year, handled all key management promotions personally, and oversaw corporate purchasing.

Jane Evans, president and CEO of Crystal Brands, once dreamed of being a field agent in the foreign service. She is fluent in French, German, Italian, and Spanish, and her global outlook serves her well in her worldwide endeavors to market Monet, Izod Lacoste, and Ship 'N Shore women's apparel. Her rise to the top began as a shoe buyer for Jarman; she was the most astute international buyer the company had had. She progressed to become the first woman in senior management and president of Butterick Fashion Marketing, a division of American Can. This led to the position of senior vice president at General Mills. At Crystal Brands, Evans is described as innovative and fearless, able to manage change and to instigate visionary breakthroughs.

John F. "Jack" Welch, chairman of General Electric, has transformed his giant corporation from a stagnating appliance company into a global enterprise with diversified interests in aerospace, electronics technology, and, incidentally, appliances, operating on four continents. GE makes more than 2,000 products, ranging from 65-cent light bulbs to billion-dollar power plants. The company produces locomotives, jet engines, robotics, heavy appliances, and telecommunications equipment, and has services ranging from consumer credit to entertainment, including NBC. Since Welch became CEO, dozens of product divisions have been sold, including the entire line of GE small appliances, and dozens of product lines have been enhanced or added, including jet propulsion engineering and space communications technology. Jack Welch is described as a charismatic leader who believes in giving people responsibility for self-management. He has hired dozens of consultants to help redefine the GE culture as one of "personal empowerment" where employees are expected to participate in decisions and managers are expected to counsel and support employees, not boss them. Every GE employee is encouraged to be creative, to put forward new initiatives, and to be entrepreneurial. Company incentives, such as bonuses and recognition programs, reinforce this concept. Welch demands superior performance, and he backs a philosophy of hard work and high productivity. He has also instituted one of the most extensive corporate training programs in the world to help employees enhance their skills and their careers.

Case Questions

1. Compare Mintzberg's "executive roles" with the characteristics described as common among America's most wanted managers.
2. Discuss how these executive characteristics can enrich a manager's ability to improve corporate performance in a global economy.
3. Explore the concept of productivity and how top executives might view their role of encouraging it in a competitive environment.

VIDEO CASE The Personal Computer Revolution—Bone or Bane?

The computer revolution began when Steven Jobs and Stephen Wozniak launched Apple Computer in 1976, and it skyrocketed in 1981 when IBM introduced its PC. Since then, millions of personal computers have been sold and thousands of innovations have transformed the computing industry. However, statistics show that 85 percent of offices equipped with PCs use them primarily for word processing, and 60 percent of all managers use PCs for simple spreadsheet applications. Few PCs are used for more complex computing tasks, and only 12 percent are configured for educational purposes. Consequently, leaders in the industry are asking themselves whether the technological revolution they envisioned is really taking place, and if the PC is the instrument of productivity it was meant to be.

Steven Jobs, CEO of Next Computer, the company he founded after leaving Apple; once described the personal computer as the "bicycle of the twentieth century," giving man capabilities unheard of before its introduction. Jobs also believes that the expensive stand-alone system is unnecessary today. His Next computer is expensive, complicated, and designed for the "high-end" technology required in office systems, engineering design, graphics, and specialized telecommunications made possible through data-base networks. But he believes that smaller machines efficiently designed for dedicated word processing and simpler data management tasks will suffice for most offices.

William Gates III, the thirty-something billionaire founder and mastermind of Microsoft Corporation, believes the future of PCs rests on the usefulness of software. Today's software allows people to access stock markets, shop by computer, handle their bank accounts, investments, and taxes on a PC, and do more than 10,000 customized applications ranging from interactive games to complicated engineering designs. People are only beginning to recognize the power of personal computers as they learn to use the software that's available.

James Cannavino, president of IBM's Entry Systems Division which makes the IBM PC, envisions more powerful systems and software. He believes that with global "cloning" of popular systems, they will soon be as common (and perhaps as inexpensive) as typewriters were a few years ago. This viewpoint is echoed by Andrew Grove, CEO of Intel, the company that manufactures chips and microelectronic components for many U.S. computer systems. Grove points out, however, that PCs are creating a special problem in society, a distinction between the "haves" and "have-nots" in terms of computer literacy. PCs and courses on computing are becoming common in elementary and secondary schools with the money and trained teachers capable of supporting computer education—which means primarily white, upper-middle-class schools. Inner-city schools with large minority populations lack the resources or personnel to train students.

Even more significant is the fact that most computer education is at the mere "literacy level," described by John Sculley, Apple's CEO, as training students in writing skills using block letters and one-syllable words. The few students who are really learning computing skills are enthusiasts who form a technical elite. Meanwhile, in business organizations and most universities, the pervasive use of PCs as word processors or glorified calculators has resulted in a generation of secretaries and clerks who are skilled at these applications working for computer-illiterate bosses. Sculley notes that it isn't unusual to find a secretary capable of managing budgets on a PC or of creating interesting graphic desktop presentations, while the boss fumbles around with a memo or uses E-mail to track an appointment.

Perhaps the most controversial viewpoint is held by Michael Dell, founder of Dell Computers, who at the age of twenty introduced the first PC that sold for under $1,000 and who has since challenged industry leaders with nearly $1 billion in global sales. Dell sees the PC as like the telephone a hundred years ago—an instrument bound to become so common and so important to every home and business for data management and communication that the next generation will be swept into using the technology. Today's educators, he contends, are in danger of being run over by the revolution because they are teaching the buggy whip methods of computing without realizing that soon the horse will be gone and expertise with buggy whips will be useless.

The potential of PCs, Dell and others contend, is showing up right now in how organizational work is being redefined. Fundamental access to information and the ability to create global telecommunications through multimedia applications is starting to transform the work environment. Under the leadership of enthusiasts and the computer elite, the technology is on the brink of explosive growth, and under the leadership of office staff, the use of PCs to enhance work flow and data management is beginning to alter human relationships.

Case Questions

1. Explain how personal computers—and, indeed, computer literacy—is affecting education and the way we work.
2. Personal computers are only one small dimension of the general revolution in information systems. Futurists predict major changes in factory automation, office management, and human productivity based on exponential growth in technology. Discuss how recent changes in technology have affected our organizations and patterns of work-related behavior.
3. Discuss the social implications of PCs if, as predicted, they become as common as telephones. Also, in your own view, how has computer technology affected human relationships, and what problems might occur in this area in the future?

Sources: Brenton R. Schlender, "The Future of the PC," *Fortune,* August 26, 1991, pp. 40–48; "Jobs and Gates Together," *Fortune,* August 26, 1991, pp. 50, 54; and Mark Taber, "Can OfficeVision Take Off with Notes?" *Datamation,* February 15, 1992, pp. 65, 68.

SKILL PRACTICE EXERCISE IN SELF-PERCEPTION

Introduction

The admonition to "know thyself" has existed for a long time, and yet most findings reveal that the majority of people are very poor self-evaluators.

People of high status may hate to see change for fear that it will undermine their position. Conversely, successful people may feel so secure that they view further change and development not as a threat, but rather as a challenge. Moreover, unsuccessful people may be goaded to new effort by their failures. Thus there are many pros and cons to the question of whether an adult can or should change.

Those who a few years ago would confidently reel off characteristics of the successful leader in community affairs or business now acknowledge that many different kinds of people can function effectively as leaders. Attention has shifted from the qualities of leadership to the roles and functions of leaders and to the variety of contributions different individuals can make to a group.

How we perceive ourselves is crucial to how we perceive and deal with others. Our self-image is a major force in our behavior patterns.

Self-Perception Rating Scale

Instructions: Each paragraph below gives a description of personal characteristics that might or might not be true of you. For each statement try to determine the degree to which the statement is typical of you. Try to be as objective as you can. Rate each statement according to the following scale:

7 The statement is very much characteristic of me
6 The statement is somewhat characteristic of me
5 The statement is slightly characteristic of me
4 The statement is neither characteristic nor uncharacteristic of me
3 The statement is slightly uncharacteristic of me
2 The statement is somewhat uncharacteristic of me
1 The statement is very much uncharacteristic of me

______ 1. I resent suggestions, hold to my present ways, and tend to resist pressures to change.

______ 2. I am orderly, and tend to systematize things and people.

______ 3. I am disorganized, and live in a state of "clutter."

______ 4. I do each day's work well but resist and resent evaluation. I am inclined to get involved in busywork and avoid tasks that call for a lot of future planning and preparation.

______ 5. I tend to do a lot of dreaming, and have been sometimes referred to as an "idea" person but accused of having lost a sense of proportion or perspective.

______ 6. I spend much of my time and energy in criticizing political parties, school, work, other people, and so on.

______ 7. I am a "worrier." Often I worry about things that have not happened or about things that are already over.

______ 8. I am sarcastic, sometimes toward others in my presence and sometimes toward others who are not present.

______ 9. I am likely to "nag" if things aren't going well.

______ 10. I am a procrastinator, putting off decisions until I have sought out and questioned others; often it is then too late to take the best action.

______ 11. I am what people could call "decisive." I am efficient, size things up quickly, and act so as to get results right away.

______ 12. I avoid becoming entangled in other people's emotional problems and usually find some excuse to get away from people who are about to "unload" on me.

______ 13. I consider myself an honest person. I am often quite frank even if the truth is painful to others.

______ 14. I am quite sensitive and often take things said very personally. I am likely to "fly off the handle" with little provocation.

______ 15. I find it very difficult to "step down in responsibility" to make room for others. Once I have gained a position with status, I find it difficult to give it up.

When you have finished completing the scale, transfer your rating for each paragraph to a separate piece of paper and turn it in anonymously to your professor.

Complete Your Feedback Chart

This chart will be easier to complete if you draw a horizontal line across it at the neutral value (4). Then plot your individual values. Your professor will give you the group average values; plot this on your chart to provide a comparison. The chart is for your own information and will not be given to the instructor.

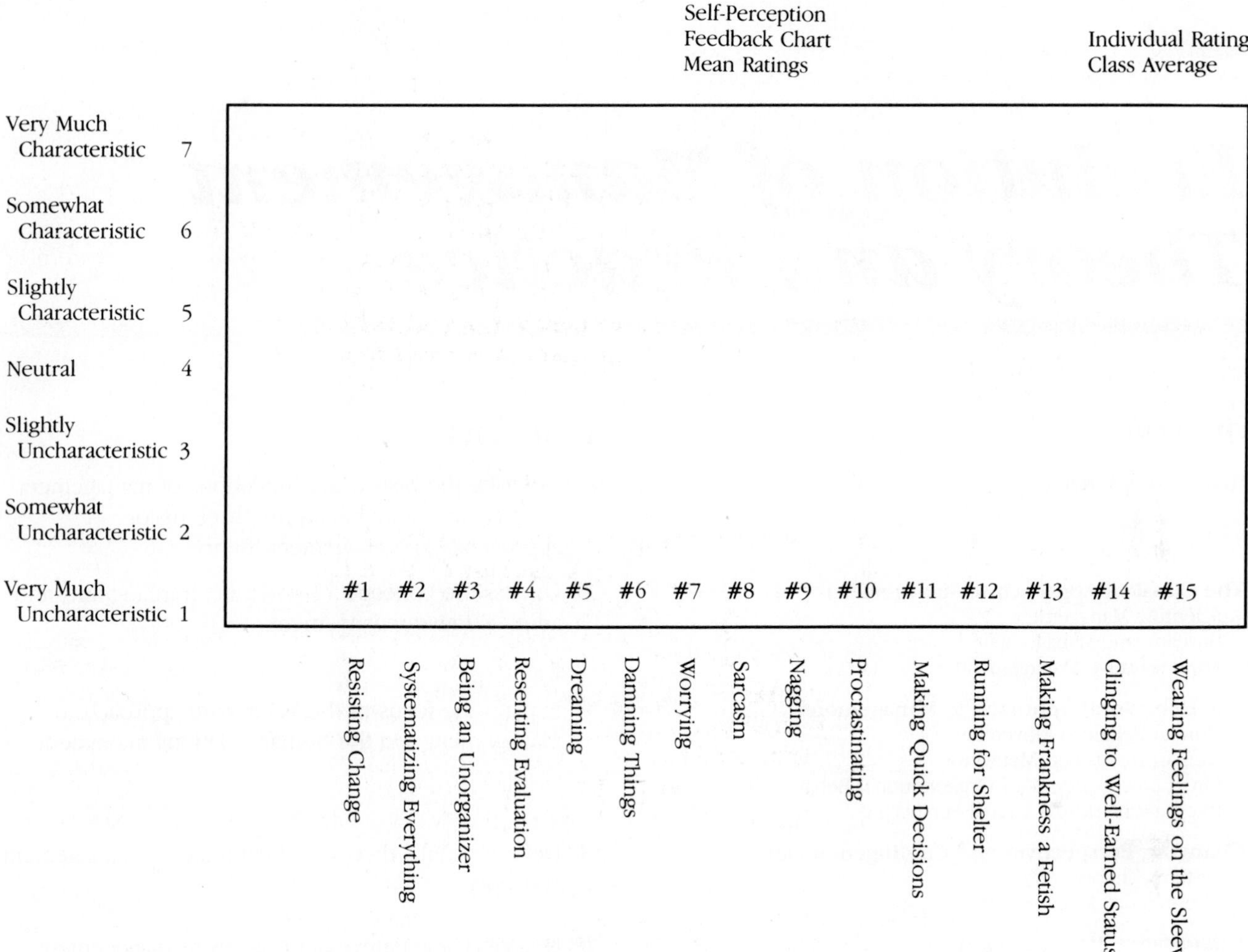

Source: Copyright 1981, Richard E. Dutton. Reprinted by permission.

2

Evolution of Management Theory and Practice

OUTLINE

Historic Legacies

The Classical Approach to Management
- Scientific Management
- Bureaucratic Management
- Administrative Management

The Behavioral Approach to Management
- Human Relations Movement
- Human Needs and Motivation
- Integrative Concepts of Organizational Behavior
- Integration and the Global Perspective

Changing Perspectives and Contingency Views
- Systems Theory
- Contingency Management

Quantitative Management
- Operations Management
- Information Systems for Management

OBJECTIVES

- Describe the historical foundations of management practice, and understand the three major approaches to management theory.
- Discuss the concepts of scientific, bureaucratic, and administrative management.
- Explain the focus of the behavioral approach to management and the human relations movement.
- Define systems theory and contingency management concepts.
- Describe quantitative approaches to management and the role of information systems.

GENERAL MOTORS CORPORATION, perhaps the world's largest bureaucracy, experienced in April 1992 what many business watchers call a coup: GM's Executive Committee, chaired by Procter & Gamble CEO John G. Smale, took control of the troubled automaker, effectively putting GM Chairman Robert C. Stempel on notice that the board wants the pace of change at GM to be accelerated. This places even more pressure on GM, whose management and work force have undergone major changes at an already relatively fast pace since the early 1980s.[1]

Prior to stepping down as GM's chairman in 1990, Stempel's predecessor, Roger B. Smith, reorganized top management. As CEO, he created two vice chairman positions: one to coordinate domestic subsidiaries such as Electronic Data Systems, Delco Electronics, and Hughes Aircraft; and the other to coordinate global operations. Today, income from global operations alone represents a third of GM's total profits. In addition, Smith launched several programs during the 1980s aimed at "active listening" by managers and "new-culture decision making" emphasizing teamwork.[2]

Most of GM's 750,000 employees praised the changes as long overdue, but there were many skeptics who saw plant closings, reorganization, and new technology as job killers. After Smith stepped down, Stempel set about to make these changes pervasive and accepted throughout GM's global corporation. He proposed a "Framework for Greatness" that focuses on quality products, customer satisfaction, and employee involvement. By 1991, Stempel had extended this concept to first-line managers in thirty divisions by *empowering* labor-management teams at shop-floor levels to make many of their own decisions. At the Saturn subsidiary, consensus decisions are common, and they work. This sentiment was echoed by an experienced machinist, once a UAW shop steward and foe of management. He said, "I thought it was all a bunch of crap at first. . . . 'How's your dog, John? Is the family okay?' . . . You know, sugar-coated stuff. But then I realized that most managers were sincere. They enjoyed being pleasant, and they were concerned. We started to come together on our work, and the team evolved. We honestly work damn well together."[3]

However, such changes in the boardroom and on the shop floor, accompanied by massive worker layoffs, have so far not been enough to help GM's slow productivity growth, sinking market share, and steep losses in the early 1990s. GM Director John Smale and the rest of the GM Executive Committee know that no amount of sugar will help the bitter medicine of their coup go down any easier at GM. Nevertheless, they believe they have stopped a disease that could have turned terminal.

As we race toward the twenty-first century, consider how the theories and concepts introduced in this chapter will affect how you will one day manage.

Management is as old as human society, but until the modern era, little was done to establish a body of knowledge about how to manage. Several thousand years of actual management practice preceded management theory. The industrial revolution compelled us to address management for the first time as an independent subject. Then, as complex organizations emerged in the early 1900s, scholars began to turn their attention to management theory. Following World War II, the industrialized nations embraced management research, and business leaders became interested in graduates skilled in management concepts. This focus led to the growth of business schools and management as a field of study.

Recently, a tremendous interest in management techniques has generated a proliferation of research and many publications, including educational texts. Popular books on management dominated nonfiction best-seller lists during the past decade, and business magazines such as *Fortune* and *Business Week* are sold worldwide. This deluge of new information prompted management writer Harold Koontz to suggest that we have created a "management theory jungle" of conflicting approaches and concepts.[4] Figure 2-1 outlines the major approaches to management theory, most of their chief proponents, and the theories arising from these approaches.

The concepts and theories presented in this text will not clear a path through the jungle. There is no wizardry we can conjure up to define one foolproof way of managing because there are too many differences among organizations to suggest one best way to manage. An appreciation of the history of management, however, may help students clarify their expectations for management roles. Therefore, we begin this chapter with a brief review of contributions made to management by leaders prior to the industrial revolution. Changes in management practice took place slowly during the first hundred years of the industrial revolution, and it was not until well into the twentieth century that new systems of management emerged. These early changes and the evolution of management in thought and action are the main thrust of this chapter.

FIGURE 2-1 Management Theories

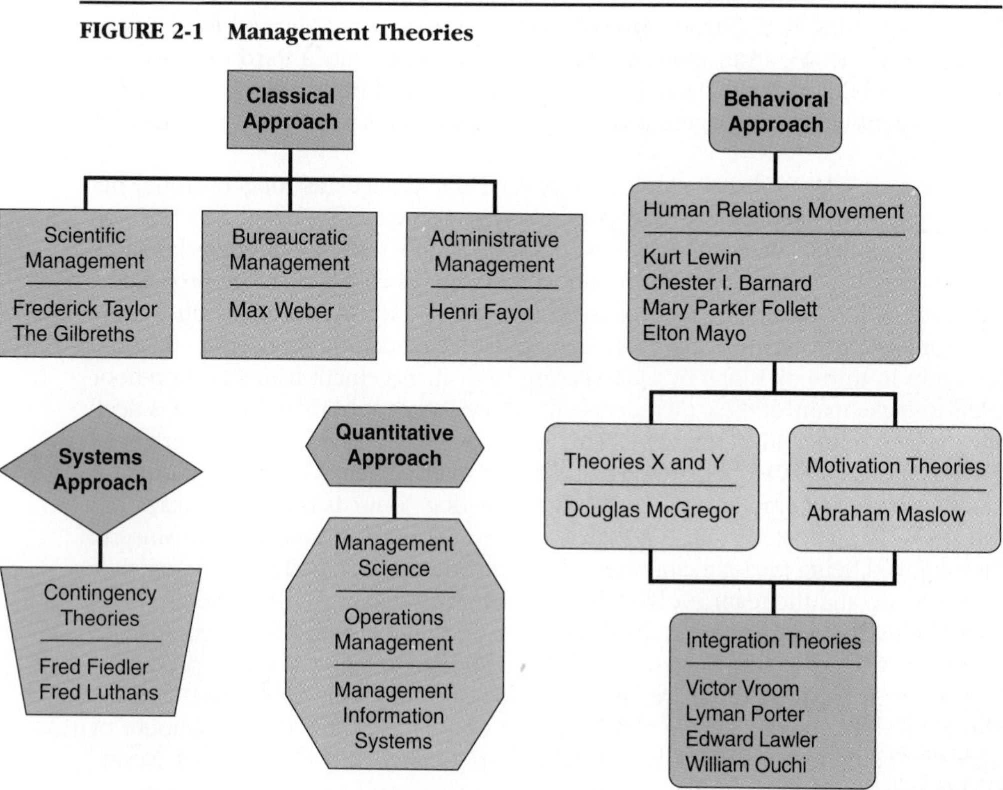

HISTORIC LEGACIES

Heroic leaders who conquered and ruled vast empires capture our imagination. We are astounded by the accomplishments of Alexander the Great. The Athenian statesman and general Pericles established a golden age in Athens founded on successful trade and commerce. And the Roman Caesars, some famous and some infamous, forged an immense empire still reflected in today's political boundaries. What often escapes our attention is that great leaders need tremendous managerial skills. Alexander did not simply march halfway across the known world with sword and shield in hand. Pericles did not create a wealthy state by luck alone. The Romans did not control a complex empire for hundreds of years without exceptional management systems. But the remnants of these civilizations give us little of a concrete nature to draw upon for management theory.

Roman accomplishments endured longer than those of most early civilizations. For nearly 500 years, Rome ruled a dozen countries with matchless administrative competency. Contemporary organizations often reflect Roman authority structures. Western military hierarchies, for example, reflect the carefully structured layers of command, ranging from infantry squads to field commanders, of the Roman legions. Our public administration systems reflect the authority once vested in Roman officials, the Roman senate, and a network of government and provincial agencies that managed public works, tax collection, and transportation. The legacy of Roman management is strong.

The organizations of antiquity are only shadows of the enormous corporations we now manage. Management techniques of past eras would be insufficient today. We could not rely on the wisdom of Solomon or the zeal of Caesar to control our destinies. Yet these leaders and many other great individuals have given us a foundation of management.

The first great modern social experiment in managing others came when *Robert Owen* (1771–1858), an owner of fabric mills in New Lanark, Scotland, sought to motivate workers by modifying their oppressive factory environment. Owen created incentive pay systems, provided safe working conditions, helped workers acquire housing, and instituted one of the first performance evaluation systems. His fabric mills were extremely profitable, and Owen became known for his humane treatment of employees. Many of the values he endorsed are similar to the tenets of conciliatory management popular today. Unfortunately, Owen's great social experiment ended with his death.[5] Many of his ideas were only recently rediscovered.

CHECKPOINT

- Identify the contributions to management made by early cultures, especially the Romans.
- Describe how the inspired leader Robert Owen tried to improve management.

THE CLASSICAL APPROACH TO MANAGEMENT

Unprecedented growth during the industrial revolution prompted three types of management theory. The first, called *scientific management,* focuses on production efficiency. The second, called *bureaucratic theory,* is concerned with structuring organizations. The third, labeled *administrative management theory,* seeks to establish universal principles of management. Collectively, these are known as the *classical approach to management.*

Scientific Management

At the beginning of this century, the industrial process was little more than a collection of traditional skills. There was a "factory" system both in Europe and in North America that exploited human labor and sought only the greatest output. Assembly-line techniques had not yet been developed, and workers were treated rather like the machines they operated. Jobs were almost randomly assigned, and employees worked very long hours. Techniques of work had advanced little since *Adam Smith* inspired the concept of **specialization** in his famous 1776 economic treatise *The Wealth of Nations*.[6] Smith explained how production of straight pins could be increased by assigning different workers to do different tasks. One person would specialize in drawing out wire, another would straighten it, another would cut it into pin lengths, a fourth would grind points, and others would attach pin heads, package, and stack the product. By having individuals specialize instead of each making pins one at a time, a company could produce thousands rather than dozens of pins a day. Specialization resulted in the *division of labor,* whereby tasks were broken down into narrowly defined jobs. These were repetitious, but highly efficient.

specialization
Defining tasks that relate to expertise and then horizontally separating jobs for formal activities.

Frederick Winslow Taylor (1856–1915) revolutionized industrial processes by making a systematic study of work and scientifically developing methods of production. Taylor is called the "father of scientific management" because he created a mental revolution about how to get things done in organizations. At the time, his ideas were considered so extraordinary that Congress held hearings with Taylor testifying in 1912, and initiated a nationwide investigation into scientific work methods. Congress criticized Taylor for dehumanizing and exploiting workers because his ideas focused on engineering jobs to rigid performance standards. Much of modern-day industrial engineering is based on Taylor's concept that, given certain production capabilities, there is "one best way" to accomplish a task.[7]

Taylor believed that both companies and employees would benefit from more systematic work methods, higher productivity, and efficient management processes. In his view, management was a science that could be extended to every job. He proposed, therefore, a system of **scientific management** based on the four principles shown in Exhibit 2-1.

scientific management
A major approach to management advocated by Frederick W. Taylor that focuses on standardized work methods and rational selection of employees coupled with training and job development.

piece rate
An approach to compensation whereby employees are paid for each unit of work completed.

Scientific management became a method of maximizing efficiency by studying individual jobs and establishing optimal standards of performance. Workers were then hired to fill those jobs based on their skills. Taylor also felt that money motivated employees to work harder, and he developed the concept of **piece-rate** work whereby a person is paid for each piece of work completed or each operation assigned. For example, seamstresses assigned to sew pockets on shirts would receive, say, 10 cents a pocket. The more pockets they sewed, the more they would get paid. This system is still used today in many firms.[8]

Among Taylor's contributions were instituting job analysis, time-and-motion studies, standardization of processes, efficiency techniques, and productivity measurements to systematically track labor costs. He also championed worker rest periods and introduced the idea of training for both managers and employees. His methods of "engineering jobs" have been strongly criticized, but perhaps history has been too harsh. True, he did stand over workers with a stopwatch to determine the most efficient ways to work, but he also developed safer work methods. His pioneering studies abolished traditional haphazard job assignments and unrelenting hours of work. These were sensational changes when Taylor implemented them more than eighty years ago.

Frank Gilbreth (1868–1924) and *Lillian Gilbreth* (1878–1972) formed an unusual husband-and-wife team who made significant contributions to scientific management. Frank's motion studies led to more productive ways to accomplish tasks; Lillian was a psychologist who became known for her research on fatigue and the effects of work on employees. An extraordinary woman, she complemented her life as

EXHIBIT 2-1 Taylor's Four Principles of Scientific Management

Taylor's Principle	Related Management Activity
1. Develop a science for each job with standardized work implements and efficient methods for all to follow.	Complete time-and-motion study to determine the best way to do each task.
2. Scientifically select workers with skills and abilities that match each job, and train them in the most efficient ways to accomplish tasks.	Use job descriptions to select employees, set up formal training systems, and establish optimal work standards to follow.
3. Ensure cooperation through incentives and provide the work environment that reinforces optimal work results in a scientific manner.	Develop incentive pay, such as a piece-rate system, to reward productivity, and encourage safe conditions by using proper implements.
4. Divide responsibility for managing and for working, while supporting individuals in work groups for what they do best. Some people are more capable of managing, whereas others are better at performing tasks laid out for them.	Promote leaders who guide, not do, the work; create a sense of responsibility for group results by planning tasks and helping workers to achieve those results.

a mother of twelve children with professional accomplishments in industrial psychology.[9]

Frank Gilbreth used motion pictures to study the structure of tasks. His most famous research was a motion study of bricklayers. He identified eighteen individual motions a worker used, motions that presumably had been part of bricklaying since ancient times. By changing the task structure, he was able to reduce the eighteen motions to five, which resulted in a more than 200 percent increase in productivity. This led him to a career of motion studies on tasks throughout industry. Today **motion study,** the study of the physical actions required to complete a task in the most efficient manner possible, has become part of our management language. Industrial engineers have combined Frank Gilbreth's methods with Taylor's to redesign jobs.

motion study
The study of physical actions required to perform a task in the most efficient way possible.

While her husband was doing his motion studies, Lillian Gilbreth was concerned with individuals and their performance at work under stressful conditions. She published her first paper in 1912—a doctoral thesis with her name disguised—and thereafter devoted herself to improving employee working conditions. Building on Taylor's ideas of rest periods, she advocated standard work days, scheduled breaks, and normal lunch periods. Her work also influenced Congress to establish child labor laws and develop regulations for protecting workers from harsh and unsafe conditions.

Henry Gantt (1861–1919), a consulting industrial engineer, focused on "control" systems for shop-floor production scheduling. His Gantt Charts are com-

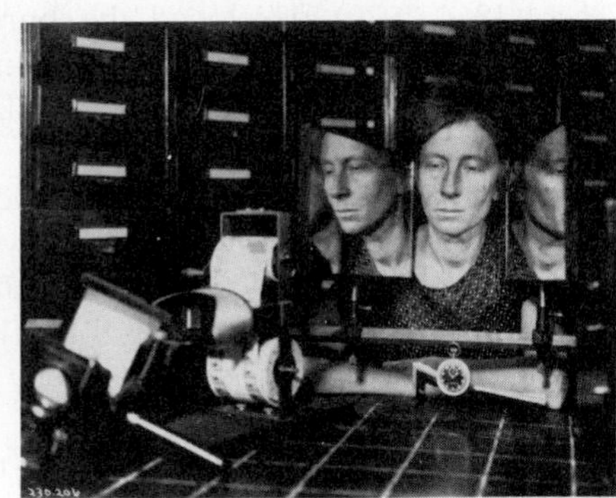

Lillian and Frank Gilbreth invented a wide variety of procedures and instruments that benefited industry and people. However, the couple is perhaps best known for having devised instruments that helped measure the most efficient ways to accomplish certain tasks.

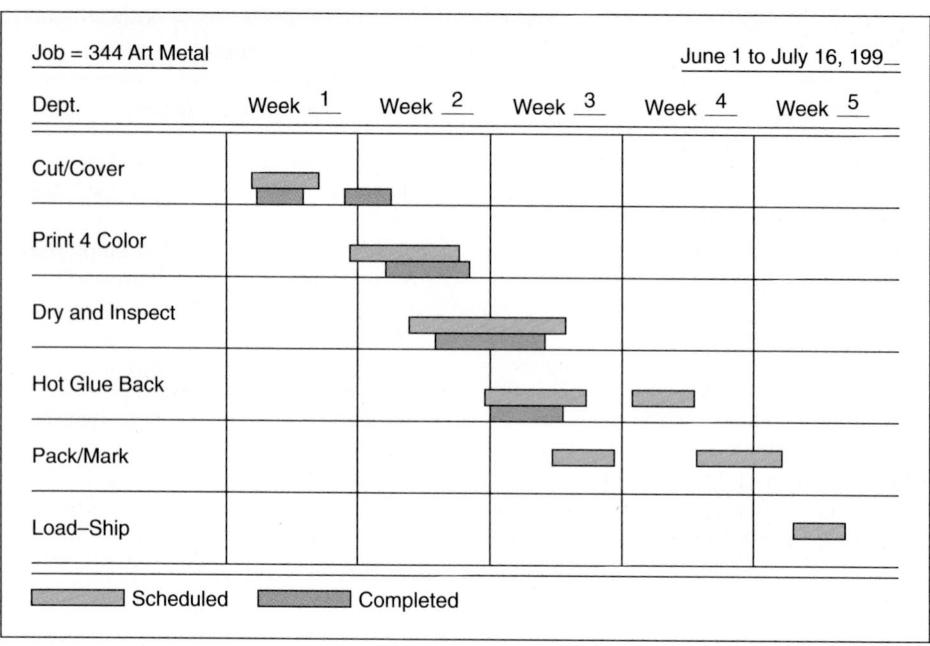

FIGURE 2-2 Gantt Chart for Book Bindery

Gantt Chart
A graphic illustration (usually a bar graph or diagram) that indicates time allocations for sequential operations and traces progress, routing, scheduling, and tasks in time intervals.

gainsharing
A method of bonus compensation based on a formula that shares profits or productivity gains among investors and employees.

mon today and have been adapted for computerized scheduling applications. The **Gantt Chart** illustrated in Figure 2-2 is a graphic means of coordinating the flow of work. It is a progress report in visual form that identifies stages of work and operational deadlines. Gantt also established quota systems and bonus systems for workers and managers who met or exceeded their quota standards.

Gantt's control system and bonuses supplementing basic wage rates are similar to the **gainsharing** concept currently acclaimed as the newest method of motivating employee performance. Gainsharing uses control techniques to monitor performance, compare results with established work standards, and pay employees bonuses in addition to base wages when results exceed standards.

Bureaucratic Management

bureaucracy
A model of organization based on defined positions, formal authority, and a regulated environment that includes well-documented rules, policies, and procedures.

The term *bureaucracy* evokes images of the federal government, a large, inefficient organization, and lots of red tape. Indeed, the word **bureaucracy** has become synonymous with bloated organizations. Most bureaucracies also have rather inflexible rules and a preponderance of regulations. Still, a large part of the industrialized world is modeled on bureaucracy, and basic principles of bureaucratic management dominate the way we think.

Max Weber (1864–1920) developed the bureaucratic model as a rational method of structuring complex organizations. He sought to define an ideal system where positions were well defined, the division of labor was clear, objectives were explicit, and a clear chain of authority existed.[10]

Managing organizations that consist of thousands of individuals in hundreds of locations would be impossible without a rational system, and although we tend to avoid the label, bureaucracy has provided the organizational mechanisms needed to build large companies like GM, Exxon, and IBM. The connotations of inflexibility, coldness, and dehumanization were not intended by Weber when he introduced his bureaucratic model.

If we view rational organization in Weber's terms, there is nothing wrong with the concept of bureaucracy. Most of us prefer to have clear objectives, well-structured authority, and formal guidelines. Weber also believed that employment decisions should be based on merit so that more productive and skillful people would rise to the top. The superiority of bureaucratic organization rests on defining positions and then filling them with qualified individuals. Weber was perhaps the first to address the problems of establishing a productive organization, and his ideas have inspired research in contemporary organizational theory.

The bureaucratic system has been criticized as inhumane because it first specifies jobs and then slots human beings into them. Bureaucracies have also been attacked for their propensity to "formalize," and thus "complicate," everything through rules and regulations. Recently, they have been charged with throttling creativity, and our current emphasis on innovation fosters a cultural bias against bureaucratic systems.[11]

Still, large organizations rely on formal systems of management in rational structures, and even very small firms, such as neighborhood stores, tend to define authority within a chain of command and to establish rules that all employees are expected to follow. Large, complex organizations—whether government agencies or private enterprises—simply could not function without bureaucratic guidelines. Even companies aspiring to participative management require employees to accept authority and adhere to standards of behavior.

Administrative Management

Perhaps the most influential classical theory is administrative management. Administrative management emphasizes management principles from a **functional perspective.** The significant contribution of administrative management has been the definition of the general duties, or functions, of managers within a framework of clearly articulated guidelines, or principles.

functional perspective
An approach that explains managers' responsibilities and activities according to general principles of management for planning, organizing, leading, and controlling.

Henri Fayol (1841–1925), a French engineer who became managing director of one of France's largest coal mining businesses, was the first to propose a comprehensive list of administrative management principles. His fourteen principles are summarized in Exhibit 2-2. Today we generally recognize four functions of management distilled from Fayol's original list: planning, organizing, leading, and controlling. Fayol believed that his principles had universal application and published them in a book, *General and Industrial Management,* in 1916. Although he was a contemporary of Frederick Taylor, Fayol's book was not widely distributed until 1949. The functional view of management is, therefore, a relatively recent perspective in American literature.[12]

EXHIBIT 2-2 Fayol's 14 Principles of Management

1. *Division of Work.* Specialization belongs to the natural order of things. The object of division of work is to produce more and better output with the same effort. This is accomplished by reducing the number of objects to which attention and effort must be directed.
2. *Authority and Responsibility.* Authority is the right to give orders and responsibility is its essential counterpart. Wherever authority is exerted, responsibility arises.
3. *Discipline.* Discipline implies obedience and respect for the agreements between the firm and its employees. Establishing agreements binding a firm and its employees should be one of the chief preoccupations of industrial heads. Disciplinary formalities emanate from these agreements, and may involve sanctions judiciously applied.
4. *Unity of Command.* An employee should receive orders from one superior only.
5. *Unity of Direction.* Each group of activities having one objective should be unified under one plan and one head.
6. *Subordination of Individual Interest to General Interest.* The interest of one employee or group of employees should not prevail over that of the company or broader organization.

(*continued*)

EXHIBIT 2-2 (continued)

7. *Remuneration of Personnel.* To maintain their loyalty and support, workers must be given a fair wage for services rendered.
8. *Centralization.* Like division of work, centralization belongs to the natural order of things. However, the appropriate degree of centralization varies from one organization to another. The problem is to find the measure that will give the best overall yield.
9. *Scalar Chain.* The scalar chain is the chain of superiors ranging from the ultimate authority to the lowest ranks. It is an error to depart needlessly from the line of authority, but it is an even greater one to adhere to it to the detriment of the business.
10. *Order.* A place for everything and everything in its place.
11. *Equity.* Equity is a combination of kindliness and justice.
12. *Stability of Tenure of Personnel.* High turnover breeds inefficiency. A mediocre manager who stays is infinitely preferable to an outstanding manager who comes and goes.
13. *Initiative.* Initiative involves thinking out a plan and ensuring its success. This gives zeal and energy to an organization.
14. *Esprit de Corps.* Union is strength, and it comes from harmony among the personnel.

Source: Abridged from Henri Fayol, *General and Industrial Management* (London: Sir Isaac Pitman & Sons, 1949), pp. 20–41.

For years, Fayol's ideas were overshadowed by Taylor's scientific management concepts because industrialists were preoccupied with production issues in a rapidly expanding economy. The leadership function surfaced in management research during the late 1950s, and Fayol's concern with organizing emerged as an important consideration in the 1960s. Not until the 1980s did his planning function become a conscious management theme, and the controlling function became popular only recently as managers began to realize the importance of meeting global competition through high-quality products and services. If most of Fayol's principles seem self-evident today, that is because his functional approach now dominates the study of management. In retrospect, his contributions represent an important transformation in management thought.

CHECKPOINT

- Identify and discuss Frederick Taylor's contributions to management theory, and state how his contemporaries provided the foundation for scientific management.
- Describe bureaucratic management, and contrast the advantages and disadvantages of a bureaucratic organization.
- Four primary principles of management have been derived from the writings of Henri Fayol. What are they? Choose several principles from Fayol's original list, and describe them in terms of current management practices.

THE BEHAVIORAL APPROACH TO MANAGEMENT

behavioral approach
An approach that explains how managers influence others to achieve organizational objectives through human relations and motivation.

Although Henri Fayol's principles embrace human behavior and leadership, he was not among the mainstream theorists who formulated the **behavioral approach** to management. The behavioral approach—sometimes called the *behavioral science approach*—emerged from research by behavioral scientists, including sociologists, psychologists, and anthropologists, who sought ways to improve organization effectiveness by modifying individual and group behavior.

Three distinct eras are associated with behavioral concepts. The first was the 1920s, when research inspired what we now call the *human relations movement*. The second was the post–World War II period, when theorists focused on *human needs and motivation*. The third era is occurring now, as we search for *integrative concepts* that satisfy the dual necessities of meeting employee needs and improving productivity.

Human Relations Movement

The human relations movement focused on individuals working in group environments. Managers and employees were studied in terms of group dynamics. Early contributors to the movement concluded that by improving workers' satisfaction with their jobs, companies could improve their performance. Thus managers were encouraged to be more cooperative with workers, to upgrade the social environment at work, and to reinforce individual employees' self-images.

Several pioneers in human relations made contributions that are still influencing the way we manage today. Prominent among them is *Hugo Münsterberg* (1863–1916), a German psychologist and philosopher often regarded as the founder of applied psychology. Münsterberg spent many years as a visiting professor at Harvard University. In 1913, he published *Psychology and Industrial Efficiency,* a textbook in which he advanced breakthrough ideas in industrial psychology and provided a critical linkage between scientific management and human endeavor.[13]

Kurt Lewin (1890–1947) examined the effects of different types of leadership and wrote extensively about group behavior. His work emphasized the importance of teamwork and, consequently, the importance of managers capable of working with and leading work groups.

Like Henri Fayol, *Chester I. Barnard* (1886–1961) was a practitioner. He was president of New Jersey Bell Telephone, and at the height of his career, he published a book, *The Functions of the Executive* (1938), in which he advocated employee training, group processes, and conciliatory management relations that would enhance cooperation between employees and supervisors.[14] The concepts of Lewin and Barnard are amplified in Part Four, where we discuss motivation, leadership, and organizational change.

Mary Parker Follett (1868–1933) was another of the founders of the human relations movement. She felt that managers were responsible for motivating employees to pursue organizational goals enthusiastically, not simply to obey orders. She rejected the notion that managers should be groomed to give orders, believing instead that they should be trained to work with employees toward the attainment of common objectives. Follett laid the groundwork for studies in group dynamics, conflict management, and political processes in organizations. Later theorists built on her work to contribute to advancements in industrial psychology and sociology.[15]

George Elton Mayo (1880–1949) pioneered experimental research on human behavior in work settings. Mayo and a Harvard University research team conducted a series of experiments at the Western Electric Company's Hawthorne plant in Illinois.[16] The experiments began in 1924 and spanned several years. The first experiment focused on changing the physical lighting in the company's relay assembly test room. Mayo hypothesized that he could find one best method of illumination that would result in optimal productivity. What his team found, however, was that *every* change in illumination resulted in higher productivity. Another experiment was conducted with the plant's bank wiring room employees. Several types of piece-rate incentive pay systems were implemented, with Mayo's researchers hypothesizing that they would discover one best pay system for motivating employees. Instead, they found that workers were equally motivated under a variety of pay systems.

Mayo realized that the Hawthorne employees had not reacted to illumination or incentive pay but to attention and recognition. Subsequent experiments by Mayo

These six young women took part in Elton Mayo's assembly room experiments at Western Electric's Hawthorne plant. The Hawthorne studies were important because they clearly showed that the most motivated employees are those whose managers possess strong interpersonal skills.

confirmed that employees are made to feel good about themselves and the value of their jobs by the intervention of researchers. He concluded that improved human relations, social contacts, and behavioral rewards (such as recognition) were important for motivating employees.

Hawthorne Studies
Social and psychological experiments conducted at Western Electric Company during the 1920s that revealed how human relations affected productivity.

The **Hawthorne Studies** are an enduring contribution to management thought, and the implications of Mayo's work are far-reaching. Ever since these famous studies, organizations have been viewed as social systems with both formal and informal patterns of authority and communications. Mayo was joined in his research by two Harvard colleagues, Fritz J. Roethlisberger and William J. Dickson. Together, they were among the first to suggest that managers need interpersonal skills for counseling employees, diagnosing personal and group needs, and balancing technical needs for productivity with human needs for job satisfaction.[17]

These conclusions may seem perfectly reasonable today, but in the context of the industrial society of Mayo's time, they were exceptional. Mayo did his research before the era of collective bargaining and safety regulations, when the standard workday exceeded ten hours and children worked alongside adults. Factories were dim and cavernous; managers were expected to behave like "straw bosses"; and employees were considered little more than productive units much like machines. (In fact, machines, being more expensive, were usually better treated.) When Mayo and his colleagues published their research findings, many people thought their conclusions were irrational.

Human Needs and Motivation

motivation
The concept of behavioral change as a result of an influence that alters an individual's performance.

The second era of behavioral research emphasized **motivation.** This research focused on employees' personal needs and how those needs influenced performance. Contributions to motivation theory by several important scholars immediately after World War II inspired greater efforts to understand individual behavior in work environments. This focus led to a field of study called *organizational behavior*. We will introduce only two noteworthy motivation theorists here. However, because organizational behavior is so important to management, we will take up this discussion again in the chapters in Part Four.

Douglas McGregor (1906–1964) brought a fresh perspective to management by challenging leaders to think of employees as responsible, capable, creative indi-

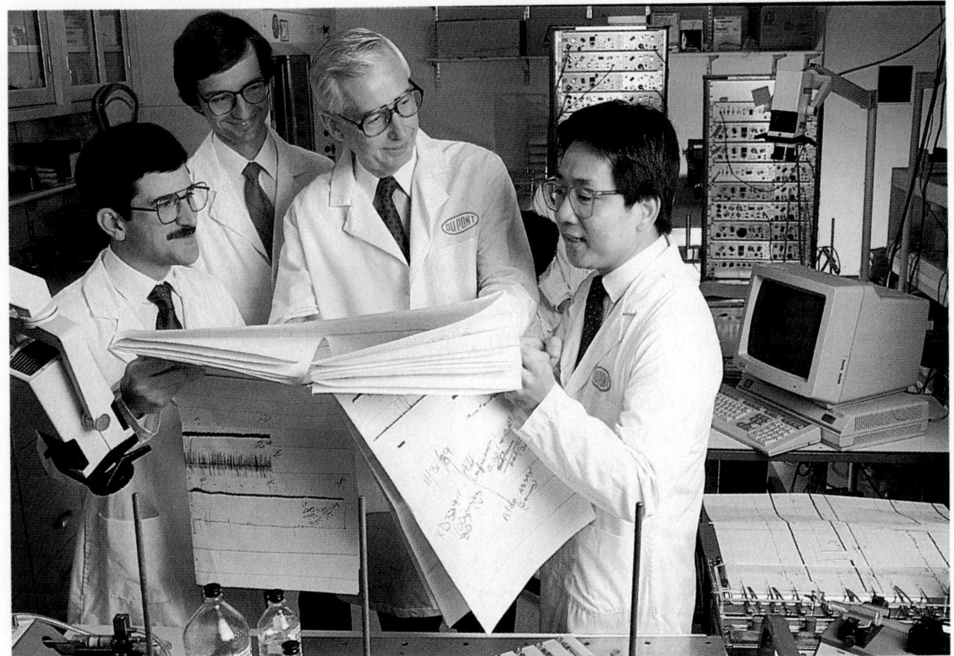

Theory Y managers view their employees in optimistic terms. Du Pont CEO Edgar Woolard (center) believes that "employees have been underestimated. You have to start with the premise that people at all levels want to contribute and make the business a success."

Source: Brian Dumaine, "Creating a New Company Culture," *Fortune,* January 15, 1990.

viduals. McGregor felt that throughout most of human history leaders had treated the people under them as irresponsible and lazy. He called this approach to management **Theory X.** Theory X assumptions commit managers to a pessimistic view of human nature, and Theory X managers tend to be autocratic, control-oriented, and distrustful. McGregor identified a second perspective, **Theory Y,** that reverses these assumptions. Theory Y managers view employees in optimistic terms as individuals who want to be challenged by their work, who prefer self-control, and who are capable of responsible, independent judgment.[18] McGregor's assumptions about Theory X and Theory Y management are outlined in Exhibit 2-3. We will revisit and expand upon these ideas in Chapter 14.

Theory X
A set of assumptions that employees are lazy, unambitious, and must be coerced to work; hence, a managerial approach based on fear tactics.

Theory Y
A set of assumptions that employees are generally responsible, want to do meaningful work, and are capable of self-direction; hence, a managerial approach based on conciliatory behavior.

Abraham Maslow (1908–1970), a contemporary of McGregor, based his theory of human behavior on the idea that individuals work to satisfy unfulfilled needs.[19] He suggested a hierarchy of needs through which everyone progresses. Thus a person may initially work to earn money for food and shelter, but once these fundamental needs are met, the employee will require more complicated rewards, such as respect, recognition, and self-fulfillment. Maslow's *hierarchy of needs* is an important cornerstone for motivation theory, and it is developed thoroughly in Chapter 13.

EXHIBIT 2-3 McGregor's Assumptions on Theory X and Theory Y

Theory X	Most human beings dislike work and avoid it whenever possible; they must be forced, threatened, and directly controlled in order to achieve organizational goals. Most people are lazy, prefer to be directed, shun responsibility, have little ambition, and want security. The average human being avoids leading and wants to be led.
Theory Y	Work is natural, and most people prefer the physical and mental effort of working. Commitment to objectives is also a natural state for most individuals, particularly when rewards are associated with achievement. Human beings can exercise self-control, prefer self-direction, and have the capacity for innovation and creativity. Under most reasonable circumstances, the majority of people will accept responsibility, and many individuals seek leadership rather than the security of being led.

Source: Adapted from Douglas McGregor, *The Human Side of Enterprise* (New York: McGraw-Hill, 1960), pp. 33–34 and 47–48.

GLOBAL TRENDS

The Monolith of Japanese Management Has a Few Cracks

A first glance at Japanese management practices suggests a monolith of incredible successes and ideal results. Western managers have been both impressed and mystified by the achievements of their Japanese colleagues and have often bemoaned the West's inability to reach the standard set by the East. Upon closer examination, however, the Japanese management monolith reveals a few cracks and crevices.

The Japanese are known for endorsing lifetime employment, group processes, and a strong commitment by all employees and managers to their organizations and their jobs. However, it turns out that lifetime employment exists only in the largest corporations and only so long as the employee continues to be loyal and fully accepted by the organization. Furthermore, Japanese managers understand "group processes" as "harmonious behavior," which can preclude the kind of risk-taking behavior that is often essential for innovation. Finally, Japanese commitment can mean an almost feudal dedication to the company, and this type of dedication can stifle creativity and innovation.

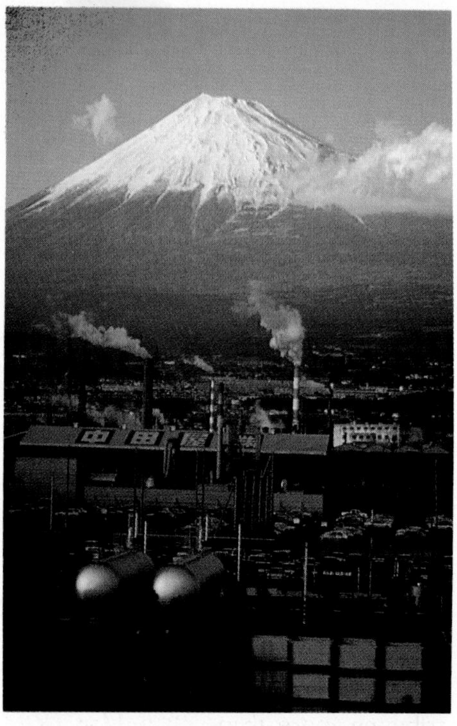

Consequently, while American companies are searching for ways to adapt many of the useful Japanese management practices, Japanese companies are searching for ways to encourage their

Integrative Concepts of Organizational Behavior

integrationist
A theorist who integrates concepts of several schools of management thought to suggest improved management practices.

Scholars have yet to reconcile the imperatives of the various concepts and perspectives on human nature with the practicalities of managing a complicated organization. Early human relations research was value-laden and more philosophical than practical. Classical theories, though practical, generally ignored the human side of enterprise. Behavioral scientists who followed McGregor and Maslow expanded their concepts and have attempted to integrate human behavior concepts with the practical necessities of managing organizations. These **integrationists,** among them *Victor Vroom, Lyman Porter,* and *Edward Lawler,* have taken McGregor's ideas, applied Maslow's need concepts, and studied how managers can use scientific techniques to achieve results. They have proposed methods of instituting systematic change in organizations, resolving conflict, achieving objectives through motivated employees, and improving group dynamics for greater productivity. The central theme of integration is that understanding human behavior is the key to effective

employees to be more innovative and risk-taking like Americans. Lacking American ingenuity, Japanese companies have come to the United States, bought or borrowed the best American technology, and applied their manufacturing skills to produce quality finished goods at lower prices and sell them back to the United States. For the past few years, however, Japanese companies have been sending their young managers and students to the United States to learn how to be more creative engineers and managers. Large companies have invested millions of dollars in research facilities in the United States, including a major facility at Princeton funded by NEC, and they have hired many of America's most creative scientists. Kobe Steel and Fujitsu have research centers in Silicon Valley, and sixteen of Japan's largest corporations have endowed chairs at MIT, contributing more than $30 million to establish educational liaisons for their students and scientists.

Japanese companies have also encouraged American companies to bring their research to Japan. Many leading U.S. companies have done so, including IBM, Du Pont, W. R. Grace, Dow Corning, Texas Instruments, Kodak, Pfizer, Digital Equipment, and Motorola. This has resulted in a transfer of innovative technology and a growing exchange of management practices between Japanese and American companies. From an economic standpoint, U.S. corporations have sold more than $2.5 billion in technology to Japan each year since 1988, while buying from Japanese companies only about $500 million annually. Americans working in Japan have learned Japanese management techniques first-hand, including methods of quality control and process engineering. Japanese working with Americans have learned how to "loosen up" and "buck the system," oft-cited requirements for bringing innovation into an organization. This mutual integration of ideas is changing management practices on both sides of the Pacific.

Sources: Susan Moffat, "Picking Japan's Research Brains," *Fortune,* March 25, 1991, pp. 84–96. See also Dori Jones Young, Stephen Hutcheon, and Joyce Quek, "Is Asia Breeding a Whole Pack of Tigers?" *Business Week: Innovation 1990, a Special Edition,* July 1990, pp. 152–155.

management, but that plausible management practices must be based on scientifically sound concepts.[20]

More recently, integrative approaches have focused on national trends in productivity and how organizations can improve their performance. This has led to substantial research on issues such as team building, organizational development, group processes, and interrelationships of technology and human endeavor. These topics are addressed in Chapter 10 on organizing, Chapter 11 on job and group processes, ,and Chapter 14 on leadership.

Integration and the Global Perspective

Given the global structure of many organizations and the intensity of international competition, it has also become important to understand global management concepts. Hence, some integrationists seek to combine the best of Western management techniques with those practiced overseas. Most notably, many Japanese management concepts have been integrated into American practice. McGregor's use of "X" and "Y" identifiers for management styles has been expanded to include *Theory Z,* which has become a convenient label for Japanese management techniques as practiced in the United States.

Theory Z
A reference to Japanese management practices of consensus decision making, quality circles, and employee participation to enhance productivity.

William Ouchi introduced **Theory Z** in 1981 to describe American adaptations of Japanese organizational behavior.[21] His theory is based on a comparison of management in Japanese organizations—called Type J firms—with management in American firms—called Type A enterprises. Exhibit 2-4 compares these two types of organizations. Ouchi recognized that cultural differences between the two nations prevent American managers from adopting Japanese techniques without modification. For example, Americans are highly mobile and often seek opportunities and career advancement by changing employers. Japanese workers, in contrast, tend to

EXHIBIT 2-4 Contrasts Between American and Japanese Organizations

American—Type A	*Mobile Employees.* Employees seek opportunities, advancement, and career changes by moving between employers and organizations. *Personal Decision Making.* Americans tend to rely on individual judgment and prefer to make decisions unilaterally, either as managers or as individuals controlling their own destiny. *Individual Responsibility.* Americans prefer taking personal initiatives and shouldering responsibilities as individuals rather than in groups. *Rapid Advancement.* Employees gain economically and socially from rapid advancement, with a premium on success as measured by promotions. *Specialization in Careers.* American organizations are founded on specialization of skills and labor; employees make career choices and follow specialized career paths. *Explicit Control Mechanisms.* Western nations emphasize explicit standards and controls for work and evaluation; employees expect explicit control mechanisms and guidelines. *Focused Concern for Employees.* American firms tend to view employees in their roles at work, paying less attention to the "complete" profile of the individual: family, social issues, personal health, and general well-being.
Japanese—Type J	*Lifetime Employment.* Japanese workers tend to make a lifetime commitment to their organizations and, in turn, organizations assume responsibility for lifetime employees. *Collective Decision Making.* Employees and managers seek consensus on decisions and endorse collective decision-making processes. *Group Responsibilities.* Japanese prefer group processes and accept group responsibilities through conciliatory communications: group rewards are not uncommon. *Slow and Systematic Advancement.* Employees rise slowly through established ranks; when opportunities arise for promotion, the loyalty and harmonious behavior of applicants are considered. *General Career Perspective.* Japanese organizations do not emphasize specialization but prefer flexibility and internal training so they can reassign personnel and develop skills among those who are members of the organization. Careers are linked to organizations, not professions. *Implicit Control System.* Japanese organizations emphasize quality control and process control methods, often with trained engineers in operational positions, but standards and work criteria are replaced by major objectives; control is left implicitly to shop-floor decisions. *Holistic Concern for Employees.* Japanese organizations take account of employees beyond the work environment and often aid in providing housing, day-care services, and mental and physical health counseling, among other things; employees are considered to be integral members of the total organization.

Source: William Ouchi, *Theory Z,* © 1981, Addison-Wesley Publishing Co., Inc., Reading, Massachusetts. Adapted from page 58. Reprinted by permission of the publisher.

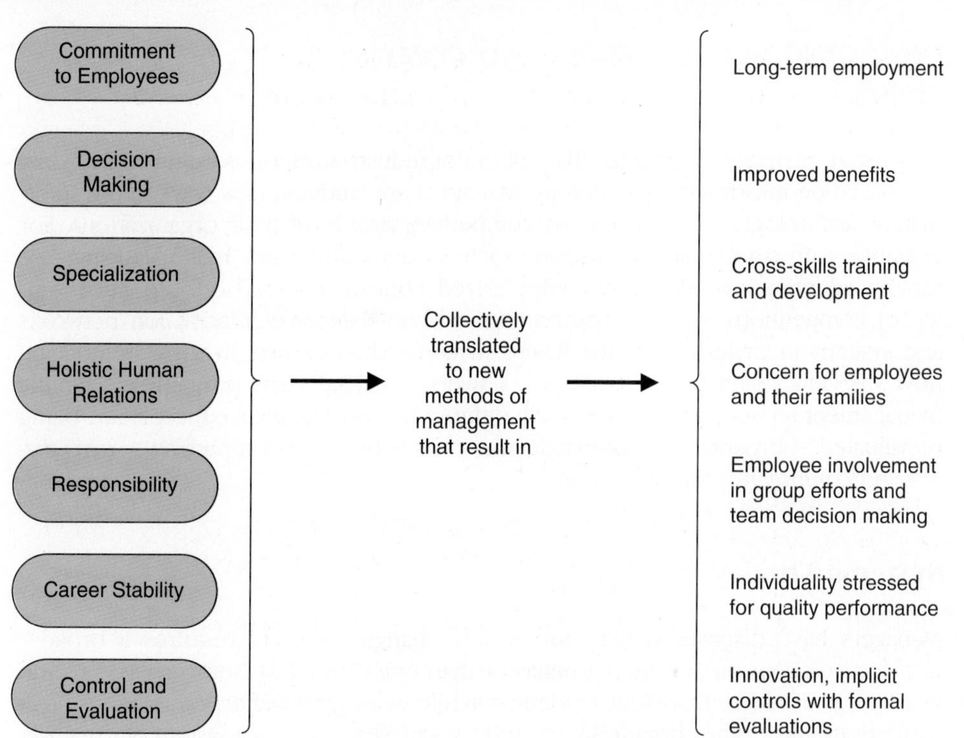

FIGURE 2-3 Type Z Organizations: The American Adaptation

regard a lifetime commitment to their organization as the ideal. Still, Ouchi discovered similarities between practices in America's leading firms and those in Japan. For example, at Hewlett-Packard and IBM, long-term employment has been the norm, even though it falls short of a lifetime commitment. Typical Type A firms rely on individual management decision making and Type J firms rely on collective decision making, but a number of excellent U.S. companies endorse a "collaborative" decision-making process closely approximating Type J behavior.

Perhaps the most important element in Theory Z is its combination of human relations concepts and scientific management techniques. The Type Z company endorses collective responsibility, a pervasive concern for employees, and a commitment to participative decision making. These organizations recognize individual and group needs, but simultaneously develop exceptional quality control techniques and scientific work methods. This style of management incorporates classical principles, behavioral tenets, and human relations concepts to emphasize quality and productivity. Figure 2-3 illustrates the characteristics of a Type Z company.

Theory Z has inspired scholars to study Type J (Japanese-type) and Type A (American-type) organizations and how Type Z organizations might evolve in the future. Western managers are currently fascinated by the idea of achieving "productivity through people" by adopting plausible aspects of Japanese management techniques. Best-selling books on management have underscored these themes, and many scholars have concluded that Theory Z has evolved beyond the "fad" stage and has become integrated into our corporate culture.[22]

CHECKPOINT

- What were the conclusions drawn by researchers during the Hawthorne Studies? Be prepared to critique these findings.
- Contrast McGregor's assumptions about workers in *Theory X* and *Theory Y*.
- After comparing American and Japanese management practices, discuss whether they are interchangeable. Could an American firm adopt Japanese techniques? Could a Japanese firm adopt American techniques?

CHANGING PERSPECTIVES AND CONTINGENCY VIEWS

Most astute managers recognize that the era of industrialization is being replaced by one based on information technology. Managers are studying new ways to use information technologies to improve the competitive profile of their organizations. For example, our smokestack industries, such as auto and steel manufacturing, are rapidly adopting robotics and computerized control systems to keep pace with global competition. Service organizations rely on extensive information networks and systems in order to survive. These dynamic changes are, in turn, influencing how we view management concepts. Universal management principles, scientific management techniques, and narrowly defined human relations concepts are being reevaluated. A broader view of management has evolved, encompassing *systems theory* and *contingency management*.

Systems Theory

Managers have discovered that our rapidly changing society requires a broader perspective about organizational behavior than one limited to work groups or individual organizations. Decisions made in a single work group affect other groups, organizations affect other organizations, and society as a whole is a system of organizations. This wider perspective alters how managers view their responsibilities and make decisions. They now need to adopt a *systems approach*.

system
A collective association of interrelated and interdependent parts; organizations are systems of divisions, departments, and specialized activities.

A **system** is a collective association of interrelated and interdependent parts. Even if it seems obvious that organizations are systems, managers have too often defined their roles within singular "parts" without viewing the "whole" of their enterprise. Just as the human body is a system with organs, muscles, bones, a nervous system, and a consciousness that links all the parts together, an organization is a system with many interdependent parts that are linked by the social dynamics of human beings working together. Machines and technology are part of our systems, but systems are defined by relationships among human beings.[23]

The systems approach provides a frame of reference for managers who must make decisions in a constantly changing environment. Decisions should be approached with consideration for the total organization and how it fits into a society of other organizations. Figure 2-4 illustrates this concept. Managers not only influence their own systems but also affect other managers and their systems. In a hospi-

FIGURE 2-4 A General Systems View

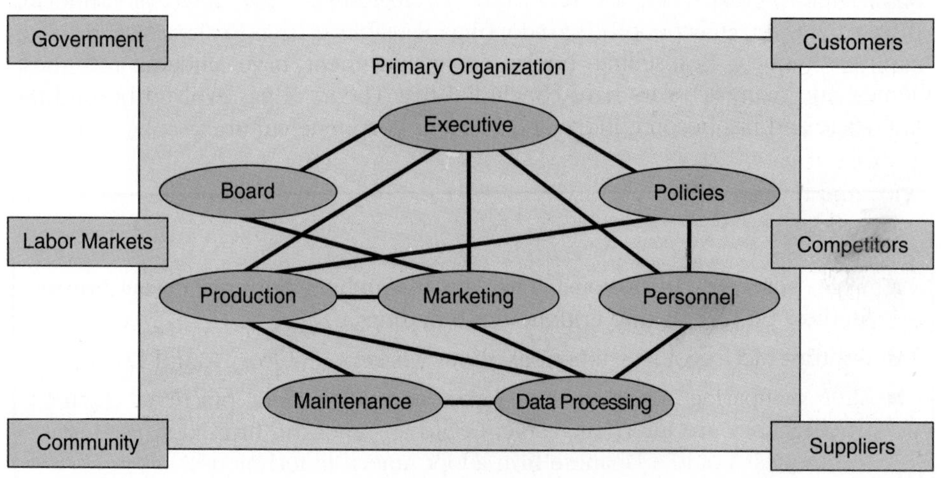

tal, for example, decisions in support areas such as X-ray departments and laboratory services affect the scheduling of patient care by ward nurses. For a company like Hasbro Toys, plastic toy manufacturing is dependent on the timely delivery of raw materials, production capacity, labor scheduling, and many other subsystems working together.

Equally important to systems within a company are external systems that can affect that organization's decisions. They include, but are not limited to, other organizations, community social systems, special interest groups, and government agencies. For example, government policies on Medicare will affect hospital billing, a truck driver's strike will disrupt delivery of plastic resins to Hasbro, and a power failure will devastate a computer service firm. Consider the extraordinary success enjoyed in Operation Desert Storm when nearly twenty countries brought together hundreds of systems ranging from space satellite intelligence to foxhole food service (and, of course, weapons and personnel) to ensure a coordinated campaign to free Kuwait. The Gulf War provided a vivid picture of decisions being coordinated among diverse political, economic, and cultural systems to achieve Desert Storm objectives.

Systems theory has many important implications for management. Research shows that effective communication is crucial for managing any enterprise, and with the growth in multinational organizations, network systems for communication are vital. With the emergence of systems concepts and the development of information systems technology, we have entered an era filled with new fields, such as *computer-integrated manufacturing* and *management information systems*. These are among the changes that influence the way managers make decisions and control organizational processes. We address these issues, together with systems theory, at length in Chapters 17 and 18.

Systems theory has also led to research about the general principles of management. Contrary to Taylor's belief, there is no "one best way" of doing anything because human behavior changes with circumstances, and circumstances change with the dynamics of internal and external systems. Therefore, instead of searching for absolute theories with universal applications, scholars have begun to explore *contingency management* as a method of understanding systems dynamics.

Contingency Management

The problem with the universal principles of management promulgated by early theorists is that few principles really are universal. **Contingency management** has emerged to address this dilemma. Advocates of contingency management argue that managers should adapt their leadership behavior to accommodate different situations or, alternately, should be assigned to situations that suit their leadership styles. Rather than suggest "one best way" to manage, contingency management implies that there are many effective ways to behave as managers, each depending on the circumstances of the work environment.

contingency management
An approach to management that suggests leadership behavior should be adapted to accommodate different situations, or, alternatively, leaders should be assigned to situations that best fit their leadership styles.

Substantial support for contingency management comes from research showing that management methods used in one circumstance seldom work the same way in other circumstances. Parents find this out quickly when they realize that spanking one child may get good results, but spanking another can result in emotional disturbance. Some employees are best motivated by economic rewards, whereas others have a greater need for challenging work. Still others care mostly about protecting their egos. If employee performance is contingent on circumstances, effective management requires that supervisors be capable of rapidly analyzing changes and adapting their own behavior accordingly.

The initial research that led to a contingency view of management focused on *situational analysis*. Attempts were made to find common principles of management that applied generally to similar situations. Fred E. Fiedler was among the early pro-

MANAGEMENT APPLICATION
United Parcel Service

Founded in 1907, United Parcel Service (UPS) was the first commercial messenger service in Seattle, Washington. The firm grew rapidly because of its low-priced, efficient organization. UPS founder James E. Casey put a premium on customer service and pioneered new work methods.

During the 1920s, Casey hired Frank B. Gilbreth and a team of scientific management consultants to improve UPS work methods. Using time-and-motion studies, the team helped create loading, package-handling, and delivery procedures for a UPS network that extended along the West Coast. Casey also stressed the concept of company "culture" seventy years before it became a common phrase in management. He wrote a monograph at the end of World War I called "Determined Men" and distributed it among his employees as a guide to UPS performance. His philosophy for efficiency and service is still circulated today.

UPS still uses many of the careful methods it developed in its early years. Drivers are timed for deliveries, strict quotas are maintained for processing parcels, and schedules are rigorously monitored. A package sorter is expected to handle 1,124 items per hour and make no more than one mistake in every 2,500 parcels. Supervisors, through tight quality control, correct those few errors. *Quality* is the key word at UPS. Operating with more than 104,000 ground vehicles and 364 aircraft, UPS delivers nearly 11 million parcels and documents *every day* to 122 countries and territories in Western Europe, the Pacific Rim, and North America. With net earnings of about $900 million on $11 billion revenue, UPS is the most profitable U.S. transportation business.

The success of UPS is based on its exquisite system of human resources. The company has 220,000 employees who are committed to high-quality customer service. Internal promotions provide employees with excellent career opportunities, and they enjoy wages and benefits well above those of UPS's competitors. Managers have a liberal stock bonus plan based on profit sharing that gives them partial ownership in the company. Looking forward to the next century, UPS has a cadre of 2,000 engineers who are expanding a system of five mainframe computers and nearly 20,000 personal computers to electronically control parcels in transit. The company is also training employees for multinational operations in 41 countries. One of the most innovative projects will link UPS directly into a U.S. Customs computer system to ensure that what is shipped actually passes through customs. Although labor costs are high and the company has spent heavily on automation, productivity gains by UPS keep customer prices the lowest in the industry.

Source: Behind the Shield (Greenwich, Conn.: United Parcel Service of America, 1988), pp. 1–16; "UPS Initiates Expedited Document Delivery Service to 163 Countries and Territories," *News from United Parcel Service,* April 24, 1989; and Kenneth Labich, "Big Changes at Big Brown," *Fortune,* January 18, 1988, pp. 56–58.

ponents of contingency management. He stated that managers must identify specific responses to specific problems in specific circumstances, and that a given problem and its response would be unique in each situation.[24] Fred Luthans, a noted researcher in organizational theory, has extended Fiedler's work to identify four contingencies that must be addressed by managers:[25]

1. An organization's structure of management authority must match the demands of its environment.
2. An organization's structure of management authority must coincide with its system of technology.
3. Individual subsystems, such as departments and work groups, must match their particular environments, and management authority must coincide with the technical requirements of those subsystems.
4. The leadership behavior of managers in the organization, and in its subsystems, must be appropriate to situational demands.

This contingency viewpoint is important in the study of management because it alerts us to approach concepts and practices with some latitude. Just as important, because circumstances differ between work groups and can change abruptly, managers and their work groups are being *empowered* today with more decision-making authority so that they can respond to contingencies in an appropriate fashion.

CHECKPOINT

- Describe a system of organizations and how a manager's decision in one organization might affect other organizations.
- What are the fundamental considerations of contingency management?

QUANTITATIVE MANAGEMENT

The move toward an information society has fostered extraordinary changes in **quantitative management** techniques. These are the techniques used in numerical analysis of organizational problems, statistical studies, and mathematical model building to improve management decisions. One area of quantitative management is called **management science,** not to be confused with Taylor's "scientific management." Management science uses mathematical models for quantified decision making. Its methods involve rather sophisticated techniques, extensive use of statistics, and complex decision-making models. For example, a company will use consumer survey information to model probabilities of demand for its products or services, and on that basis will determine how much to produce. This will, in turn, trigger decisions about hiring employees, opening sales offices, contracting with suppliers for materials, and so on.

quantitative management
An approach to management based on decision theory, use of statistical techniques for problem solving, and application of mathematical models to organizational processes.

management science
An approach to management that relies on models and mathematical analysis to improve decision making; alternatively called *the quantitative school* or *operations research.*

The historic origins of management science are found in World War II, when the Allies developed hunt-and-kill tactics for enemy submarines. Using statistical models, military experts were able to locate German submarines with some degree of probability. They were also able to improve logistics between the United States and Europe, plan strategic troop movements, and deploy new weapons systems effectively. Today NASA administrators rely on these techniques for bringing together an awesome array of organizations and resources to accomplish space expeditions. Large firms embarking on major projects, such as the design of a new weapons system, use management science methods to plan for and coordinate the myriad details of such immense undertakings.

Most applications of management science are reserved for complex situations requiring highly specialized knowledge. Practicing managers benefit more from mathematical techniques developed in an area we call *operations management*. Computer technology has also led to the unparalleled growth of *computer-assisted information systems*, which have vastly improved the quality of work and the productivity of organizations.

Operations Management

operations management The application of quantitative techniques in production and operations control using analytical models to improve organization activities.

Operations management is concerned essentially with using quantitative methods for production and operations control.[26] These methods are not necessarily mathematically complex; most of them use simple statistics and are easily understood. In this area of applied management, some of the more useful techniques are inventory control models, material-handling procedures, purchasing systems, production scheduling systems, and cost-control processes. The obvious applications of operations management are in production environments, but less obvious applications have substantially improved service operations. For example, banks have used the new techniques for customer service systems, transaction processing, and electronic banking.

There are literally hundreds of applications for operations management techniques. Productivity has improved as a result of these applications because managers are better informed about operational effectiveness—they can simulate operations, monitor results, and reduce errors more effectively. In short, operations management methods enable managers to make better decisions.

Information Systems for Management

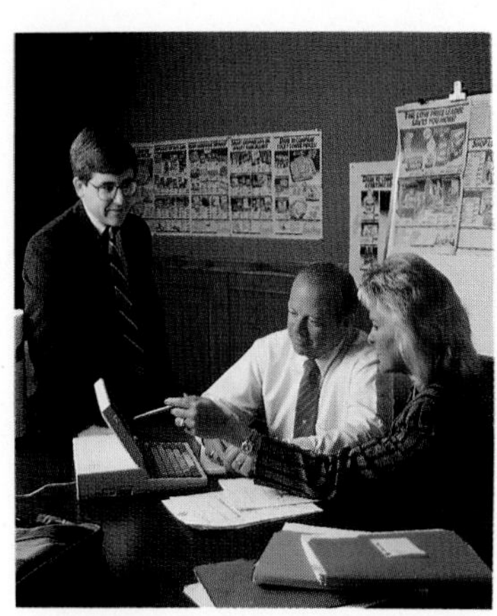

Computer-assisted information systems—everything from basic bar code scanners to a state-of-the-art checkout system called Visions to computer-initiated stock ordering by satellite—have helped Procter & Gamble get closer to its retailer customers. Here a Lucky Stores manager (center) learns a new computerized ordering system from P&G sales representatives.

Information was described in Chapter 1 as a *resource,* and that resource is managed through various types of *systems*. A telephone is, of course, part of an information system, but today we think in terms of *computer-assisted information systems*. During the past decade, we have progressed from general labels, such as "management information systems" (MIS), to specific labels, such as "computer-mediated communication systems" (CMCS) and "decision support systems" (DSS). The acronym MIS is still relevant, but now it refers to a specific type of integrated network that provides managers with information culled from large data bases. CMCS are very technical telecommunication systems, and DSS are usually stand-alone computer systems with software designed to help managers make decisions.[27] These are only three examples from among many, and a full chapter in Part Five is devoted to information systems.

From a management perspective, the rapid integration of information systems has fostered many changes in our organizations. All information systems include hardware, software, data, processes, and human beings. The nonhuman elements of these systems have changed dramatically with advances in microelectronics, network technology, and software innovations. Consequently, human beings must change to keep pace with the systems they use. This may mean little more than becoming computer-literate, and thus capable of using systems in daily operations. But it may also mean adapting to new relationships mandated by systems technology. For example, the CEO of Procter & Gamble, headquartered in Cincinnati, can correspond through his computer, "downloading" data or "uploading" reports instantaneously, twenty-four hours a day, with managers in Japan, Hong Kong, France, and Germany. Mail is electronic ("E-mail"), and even memoranda at Procter & Gamble are commonly conveyed through on-line electronic message centers. These innovations have redefined how P&G managers treat information and how they relate to one another.[28] We return to this theme in later chapters on organizing and controlling resources, and we address the implications of information technology for human relations and communication in Part Four. As a conclusion to this section, it is appropriate to note that the ultimate aim of information systems is to provide sufficient and accurate information to organizational users, and to do so in a timely fashion.

CHECKPOINT

- Explain how management science influences decision making and helps managers to be more effective.
- Describe operations management, and give an example of an application.
- Why is information considered a resource?

AT THE BEGINNING OF THE CHAPTER, we gave an overview of recent changes at General Motors Corporation. In the executive suite, a management coup by the GM Executive Committee in 1992 sought to greatly accelerate the pace of change at the giant automaker. However, massive changes have been in the making at GM since the early 1980s. Rather than "telling" employees what to do, GM managers are now encouraged to jointly determine responsibilities with their subordinates. Executives have also begun to meet informally, to listen to one another, and to emphasize teamwork. Unfortunately, the company has half a century of bureaucratic rationality to overcome, and its managers have been nurtured on what is ironically called "John Wayne individualism"—compete and win, win, win.

GM is beginning to recover from two decades of shaky performance that have resulted in plant closings, layoffs, and dozens of fadlike changes that were labeled "15-cent solutions to million-dollar problems." Today reorganization is being implemented through leadership training for more than 2,500 senior GM managers, and the company is pleased with its progress toward team building and worker participation. Buick engineers and plant workers made team decisions on designs for 1992 models, and new bonus systems rewarding innovative ideas were implemented in 1990. Now, CEO Robert C. Stempel and Director John G. Smale hope to proceed quickly with plans to change GM from a static bureaucracy to a flexible and innovative organization. ■

A SYNOPSIS FOR LEARNING

1. Describe the historical foundations of management practice, and understand the three major approaches to management theory.

   Though management owes much to ancient cultures, management theory only came of age with the industrial revolution. Scientific management evolved during the unprecedented economic growth of the nineteenth century. The accepted view today recognizes three approaches to management: classical, human relations, and quantitative. Systems theory and contingency management are also important approaches to management theory.

2. Discuss the concepts of scientific, bureaucratic, and administrative management.

   Scientific management holds that there is "one best way" to accomplish any task, which can be determined through scientific research. This "optimal" method can be used to define jobs, refine processes, and organize systems of work. Administrative management holds that there are certain principles of management that have universal application. Max Weber used the term *rational bureaucracy* to describe an ideal system in which positions are well defined, the division of labor is clear, objectives are explicit, and a clear chain of authority exists. Standardized systems provide a consistent approach to decision making. Perhaps the most influential approach to modern management, administrative management proposed fourteen important management functions that pertain to every manager in an organization. From these original fourteen functions, modern theory has distilled four: planning, organizing, leading, and controlling.

3. Explain the focus of the behavioral approach and the human relations movement.

   Behavioral studies have focused on leadership roles for managers, who must motivate employees to accomplish work in the most productive ways. Theorists within the human relations movement have studied situational variables—the complex interactions of individuals within work environments—and the nature of work itself.

4. Define systems theory and contingency management concepts.

   Systems theory requires managers to define their role within the entire system, which is made up of individual but interrelated parts that must be coordinated. *Contingency management* stresses that managers should adjust their leadership behavior to meet different situations or be assigned to positions more appropriate to their leadership styles..

5. Describe quantitative approaches to management and the role of information systems.

   Quantitative approaches are based on the concepts of management science, a theoretical field on the cutting edge of high-powered mathematical modeling that provides managers with information for making decisions. A specific management area called *operations management* is an applied discipline of systems control and decision making encompassing operational activities such as inventory control, scheduling, forecasting, budgeting, and materials management. Most of the models used are grounded in statistics and rely on computer technology. The rapid increase in microelectronic and computer innovations has resulted in a comparable growth in *information systems*. Information is a resource that managers require for daily decisions; with advanced systems, information is changing the way managers interact and how their organizations function.

CASE 1 Adapting Theory Z: Can It Be Done?

SKILL ANALYSIS

The following discussion illuminates attitudes toward Theory Z in some American firms. The conversation was among five executive managers and a consultant following a Theory Z seminar in Washington. Discussants included: Don, executive vice president for a telecommunications firm; Ross, president of a commercial printing firm; Cal, vice president of manufacturing for a company that makes mufflers and auto exhaust pipes; Alicia, executive operations officer for a large bank; Joan, president of a public relations firm; and Bob, the lead consultant at the seminar.

"What I don't understand about the Japanese," Ross said, "is how they get employees to cooperate in groups. I mean, we have quality circle groups who are supposed to get together and solve problems, but all they do is complain about pay or working conditions. My supervisors are pulling their hair out."

Don answered, "Ross, I know what you mean. We had that sort of thing for the first year or two . . ."

"Year or two! Good grief!" Cal exclaimed. "What the hell did you do about production control while this was going on for two years?"

"Well, there were lots of problems," Don said. "We found that it took time to get people thinking together rather than thinking in terms of 'We and Them' . . . you know, 'employees versus managers.' The biggest problem I had was with managers. My supervisors felt their authority had been stripped away when we told them they would work together with employees on problems."

"That was our problem at the bank," Alicia noted. "We had several really good lower-level managers who just couldn't reconcile giving orders one minute and then working as group members with subordinates the next. I haven't been very good at it myself. I've had to force myself to go with group decisions while quietly steering them away from trouble."

"Well, frankly," Cal said, "I think most of my employees lack the mental ability to handle a lot of our decisions. Hell, they aren't educated in statistics or quality control. Most wouldn't know what to do with profit figures, and certain accounting reports would blow their minds."

Joan turned to the consultant. "Bob," she asked, "you say you've been to Japan several times. How do they get employees to handle those sorts of issues? Are they trained in business schools or what?"

"Believe it or not, Japan has few formal business schools," Bob noted. "An employee is trained for needed skills on the shop floor. Quality circles are training vehicles as much as decision-making groups. But the crucial point is that few employees specialize. They are well educated in fundamentals, and then they enter firms where their abilities are honed in training programs."

"And what about their managers?" Joan asked.

"Managers tend to come from engineering backgrounds or other disciplines in the social sciences," Bob said. "College graduates start on the shop floor and move up slowly through the ranks. Promotions are based as much on personal characteristics, such as being able to get along with others, loyalty to the company, and history of harmonious work relations, as on technical skills and performance."

Cal was obviously uncomfortable with the direction of the discussion. "Can you see that happening here? I can't. Managers want fast promotions, too fast. Relying on personal characteristics would go over like a lead balloon with fast-track performers. Besides, we all want results and reward those who really get with it. You aren't suggesting we eliminate personal incentives, are you?"

"No," Joan interrupted, "I think what I hear is that we in America have been historically 'individualistic.' It's a cultural thing. We're not going to push a button and change people into 'group thinkers' all at once. What troubles me is whether we should. Don, you say you've been at this for a couple of years, what's the bottom line . . . what sort of results have you had?"

"You want hard data?" Don asked. "Well, our absenteeism dropped in half. Turnover has become a trickle. Safety has improved. And our customer service has increased remarkably."

"But has your productivity gone up?" Cal challenged. "That's the test. Have you made cost savings?"

"Yes and no," Don replied. "Yes, our productivity has gone up, but not in the traditional way of thinking. Our labor costs and man-hour efficiency rates haven't changed much. We actually pay more now as a percentage of total costs. But we have made dramatic savings in waste. Our scrap is way down and cost of material is lower. *Quality* went up . . . that's the key."

Case Questions

1. Using information from the chapter, identify as many differences as you can between Type A and Type J organizations.
2. Discuss the barriers to adopting group decision-making methods in American firms. Evaluate "individualistic" versus "collaborative" behavior.
3. Why do executives in the case have misgivings about adopting Type J techniques? Explain in terms of supervisors, values, and managers.
4. Find at least one article that contrasts American and Japanese management techniques. Summarize the key points for discussion.

VIDEO CASE Taking on the Boys Club: Can Management Theories Help?

Sexual harassment and *sex discrimination.* Ever since the nationally televised Thomas-Hill hearings in the fall of 1991, organizations and their employees have been more conscious of the hazards associated with sexual harassment, of which sex discrimination is just one. Clearly, the hearings made a strong impact on viewers. Sexual harassment and discrimination are not new problems, but they suddenly became more public and open to discussion. In fact, because of the furor raised by the allegations made by Anita Hill against Clarence Thomas after he was nominated to the U.S. Supreme Court, many executive education programs now include sexual harassment awareness in their training agenda. What do we know about the problems of sexual harassment and discrimination in the workplace? Where does it take place, what impact does it have on people, and what can be done about it? Classical and modern management theories can help us better understand the issues of sexual harassment and discrimination.

Sexual harassment can happen anywhere and at any time. It is a problem for men and women alike. It is just as likely to occur among assembly-line workers as among surgeons, attorneys, and business executives, although women in high professional positions often face sex discrimination as well as sexual harassment. As one reporter explains, "How can those biases follow women all the way up the corporate ladder? According to one historian, no matter how much women achieve, they are generally not valued as highly as men in the workplace." In fact, a massive multiyear study just completed for the U.S. Department of Education found that women earned better grades than men in high school and college. Yet despite their academic superiority, after they enter the work world, most women receive lower pay than men. In addition, professional women often hit what has been called the "glass ceiling"—that invisible barrier that prevents many qualified women from reaching the top of their professions. The glass ceiling represents a subtle, but pervasive, form of sex discrimination within organizations. And when a woman breaks through the glass ceiling, she may discover more sexual harassment and discrimination.

Dr. Frances Conley, the third woman in America to become a neurosurgeon, quit her position as brain surgeon on the faculty of prestigious Stanford University Medical School after enduring the sexual advances of her male colleagues for twenty-five years. Why did she put up with this treatment for so long? Conley replies, "Well, because I wanted to become a neurosurgeon. . . . I think you have to realize that at the time I entered the field, women were just very, very excited about getting an invitation and we didn't care about what the rules of the club were. We just had to get into the club." Now some women are willing to risk their careers to expose sexual harassment and discrimination. In fact, Conley's exposure of her humiliating treatment by male colleagues prompted Stanford to set up a task force to study the problem of sexual harassment of female doctors and students. After that disclosure, Dr. Conley announced she would return to her faculty position at Stanford.

Dr. Conley's actions, reported nationwide, heightened sensitivities about the obstacles faced by professional women everywhere. She was one of the lucky ones who took on "the club" and won her battle. But becoming a member of "the club" shouldn't have to involve a fight. Managers everywhere, in all types of organizations, need to be aware that the rules of admission into "the club" shouldn't include having to endure sex discrimination.

Case Questions

1. Would sexual harassment and sex discrimination be problems in a truly bureaucratic organization? Why or why not?
2. How do you think Frederick Taylor would have responded to the problems of sexual harassment and sex discrimination?
3. How could the integrative theories advanced by the behavioral approach to management be used to address the problems of sexual harassment and sex discrimination?
4. What solutions can systems and contingency theories of management provide to the problems of sexual harassment and sex discrimination?

Sources: Ronni Sandroff, "Sexual Harassment: The Inside Story," *Working Woman,* June 1992, p. 47ff; Joann S. Lublin, "Sexual Harassment Moves Atop Agenda in Many Executive Education Programs," *Wall Street Journal,* December 2, 1991, p. B1ff; and Alan Deutschman, "Dealing with Sexual Harassment," *Fortune,* November 4, 1991, p. 145ff.

CREATING A PSYCHOLOGICAL CONTRACT

SKILL PRACTICE

Introduction

The practices found within any organization are heavily influenced by the emergence and conditions of the "psychological contract." A psychological contract is implicitly formed between individuals and the organizations to which they belong. It deals with both the expectations of the *organization* and those of the *individuals* within it. While this "contract" is not *formally* agreed upon, it is a reality that has many implications for productivity and individual satisfaction.

The goal in this exercise is for the instructor to learn from the group members *their* expectations for the course: what *they* hope to learn, and where they see usefulness for this learning. Also, the instructor tries to learn what members feel they can *contribute* to the achievement of their expectations.

Instructions

A. Participants Get Organized

1. Class is divided into small groups of four or five persons each.
2. Each group elects a representative who will be interviewed.
3. The instructor will use the Question Guide for Instructors as the basis for his/her interview.
4. Representatives need to poll their groups on these five questions so they can accurately reflect the views of their group. You may wish to make some written notes on these views. (Step A = about 25 minutes)

B. Instructor Interviews Representatives

1. Representatives (one from each group) meet with the instructor. This can be done in the front of the room or in an adjacent room.
2. The instructor interviews each of the representatives. (Step B = about 15 minutes)

C. Participants' Interview of Instructor

1. Small groups re-form and select a different representative.
2. The groups should use the Participants' Interview Question Guide for the basis of their questions. You may delete/add items your group believes are irrelevant/relevant to your concerns. Representatives need to make sure they understand their group's key concerns.
3. Representatives interview the instructor (Note B-1 above.) (Step C = 15 minutes at least)

D. Comparison of Interview Results

There will always be distinct differences in the expectations of the participants and those of the instructor. The task then becomes how to narrow those differences through explaining why the (specific) goals of instructor and participants are *important*. Can the most important ones be viewed as *overlapping*? (Usually they *can*.)

This approach is very much like the management-by-objectives (MBO) approach and is very helpful in creating the understanding needed for a visible psychological contract.

Participants' Interview of Instructor: A Suggested Question Guide

You will have the opportunity to ask the instructor any questions you feel are relevant to effective learning during this course. (*Note:* It is important that you ask questions that are of real concern to you at this point. Only in this way can potentially important problems or conflicts be identified and managed.) You probably have many ideas of your own, and the questions asked by the instructor during the first interview should suggest others to you.

Some areas you may want to discuss are the following:

1. The instructor's theory of learning (i.e., how people learn)
2. The instructor's feelings on the question of evaluation
3. The instructor's role in the class
4. Any stereotypes the instructor may hold about you
5. Anything else you think is important

Be sure to ask specific questions. Think about the assumptions that may underlie your questions—for example, why you feel this is an important question. Test these assumptions by asking the instructor's opinion.

Instructor's Interview of Participants: A Question Guide

Few instructors ask group members to articulate their expectations for a class. During the ensuing interview, the instructor will try to gain an understanding of your views in the following general areas:

1. What are your goals for this course? To increase self-awareness? To learn theories? To get a grade? To apply learning in your job?
2. In what ways do you feel the instructor can best help you achieve your goals? Lecture, give examinations, lead seminar discussions? Let you work on your own? How do you feel about active, experiential learning?
3. What, if anything, have you heard about this textbook and/or this course from others?
4. What is the "best" thing that could happen in this course? What is the worst thing?
5. What are the participants' resources for this course (prior work experience, other courses in psychology, etc.)?

Source: D. Kolb, I. Rubin, and J. McIntyre, *Organizational Behavior,* 5th ed. (Englewood Cliffs, N.J.: Prentice Hall, 1991), pp. 9–23.

3

Global Management: Meeting the Competitive Challenge

OUTLINE

The Changing Global Environment
- From Red Square to Tiananmen Square
- Eastern Europe
- Reunification of Germany
- Europe After 1992
- The Pacific Rim
- Latin America
- Globalization of the U.S. Economy

Management Perspective
- International Business
- International Management
- Multinational Corporations
- Rationale of International Operations

Types of International Ventures

International Relations
- Host-Country Relations
- Parity: Head-to-Head Relations
- Home-Country Relations

Managing in the International Arena
- Culture
- Political Systems
- Skills and Technology
- Religious, Ethnic, and Gender Considerations
- Economic Systems
- Legal Systems

Looking to the Future

OBJECTIVES

- Describe some of the challenges to U.S. managers for doing business overseas and for accommodating foreign interests in the United States.
- Describe different approaches to managing multinational corporations.
- Describe how companies engage in export activities and expand overseas.
- Explain the implications of international business for host countries and explore the implications of trade competition between major powers.
- Describe the major considerations facing managers who must adapt to the international arena.

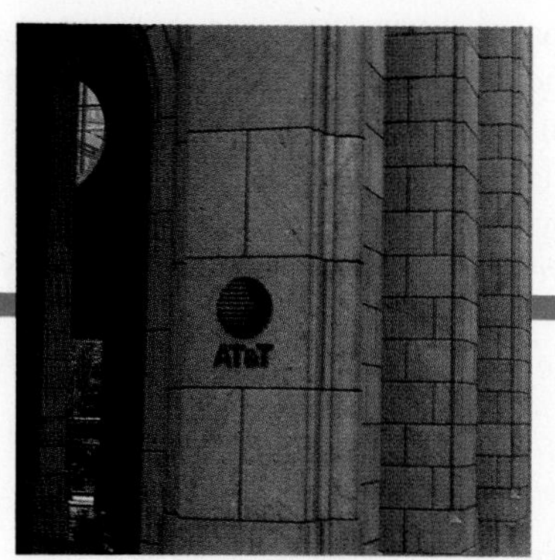

AMERICAN TELEPHONE AND TELEGRAPH is one of many global companies that use joint ventures to open global markets. A joint venture is a contract between two or more companies to invest in and pursue a business enterprise. In AT&T's view, joint venturing is a way to rapidly penetrate international markets. For example, AT&T has joint ventures with Italtel, Italy's major telecommunications company, with N. V. Philips, one of the Netherlands' largest companies and a major world manufacturer of electronics, and with Compania Telefonica Nacional de España, AT&T's counterpart in Spain. All three joint ventures combine AT&T's chip-making technology and expertise in computers with the marketing strength and manufacturing capabilities of its partners. The partners have common objectives for growth in Western Europe and early entry into new Eastern European markets.[1] AT&T also has alliances through its international division with companies in China, Hong Kong, Indonesia, Thailand, India, Mexico, and South Korea, yet AT&T is a relative newcomer to the international scene.

In 1925, the company sold its international holdings to International Telephone and Telegraph Corporation (ITT), and until recently remained almost totally isolated from world markets other than to service long-distance calls. AT&T had only 50 people employed overseas in 1983, yet by early 1991, the company employed 21,000 people in 40 foreign countries. AT&T earned 15 percent of its total 1990 revenue (about $5 billion) from foreign sales of equipment and services. The company expects to have 25 percent of its revenue from international sales by 1995, and that figure should exceed 50 percent by the year 2000.

Managers involved in global ventures such as those recently fostered by AT&T often find themselves engaged in a complicated web of trade that can be both exciting and confusing. For many Americans, their first experience with European and Japanese markets is shocking: they find that nearly 90 percent of all registered companies in the European Community and in Japan are engaged in international commerce. Today about half of all U.S. companies are engaged in international business, and like AT&T, many of these companies, and their managers, are newcomers to the international scene. Some, like ITT and Ford, have been international companies for half a century, but others, including IBM, GE, and Procter & Gamble, only became solidly involved in global business during the late 1970s.[2]

As American firms reach out to the world, companies from other nations come to America. International competition is an inescapable fact of managerial life, and the internationalization of our economy has meant integration of new techniques as well as the development of a worldview that accommodates the marketing of products and services in other cultures.

THE CHANGING GLOBAL ENVIRONMENT

The winds of change swept through Europe, Asia, and the Soviet Union as the world entered the 1990s. The Berlin Wall came down, East and West Germany reunified, Poland put its first "Solidarity" government into office, Czechoslovakia and Hungary turned out Communist Party leaders, and Rumanian dictator Nicolae Ceausescu was deposed and executed. Shortly before these events took place, the People's Republic of China capped ten years of "open door policy" by repressing democratic idealists with tanks in Beijing. All these events paled, however, in comparison to the seismic changes in the Soviet Union. The failed Soviet *coup d'etat* in August 1991 shook the foundations of Communism, and in its aftermath, the political and economic maps of the U.S.S.R. were redrawn.

From Red Square to Tiananmen Square

The Soviet Union no longer exists. Prior to the failed coup, it consisted of fifteen states, but now there is the eleven-member Commonwealth of Independent States, Georgia, a republic in the south, and the three independent Baltic countries of Estonia, Latvia, and Lithuania.[3] The new political boundaries are similar to those that existed prior to World War II, but economic boundaries have yet to be defined. The Commonwealth and new independent states have only begun to develop legal and economic infrastructures necessary for trade with the rest of the world. Many of these changes began when Mikhail Gorbachev unleashed his reform policy of *perestroika* ("restructuring") to reposition the U.S.S.R. for global business. Gorbachev's influence was also felt in China when, after a summit visit to Beijing, nearly 400,000

Fourteen years of negotiation preceded the opening of the first McDonald's in Moscow. But raising the golden arches in Russia was much more than a symbolic act: McDonald's means business. The Moscow McDonald's on Pushkin Square is four blocks from the Kremlin, boasts 700 indoor and 200 outdoor seats, employs 800 Russian citizens, and generates annual revenues of $80 million. McDonald's plans to open several more franchises in the Commonwealth republics in the near future.

people demonstrated for democratic reforms. Confronted with these demands, Chinese officials used troops to disperse demonstrators in Tiananmen Square, killing or injuring many people in the process.

Changes within the new Commonwealth reflect an impoverished economy where people face continual shortages of consumer goods and industrial stagnation. Economic reforms proposed before the attempted coup in 1991 began to open the economy to foreign investment. Several large companies such as PepsiCo and McDonald's entered into joint ventures with Soviet partners, and more than 600 major trade agreements were concluded between Western and Soviet firms under perestroika. Since the 1991 restructuring, independent republics and the new Commonwealth have been trying to create monetary and legal reforms to encourage open trade and global investments.[4]

In June 1989, when the Tiananmen Square disaster occurred, the People's Republic of China's supreme leader Deng Xiao-ping was in his tenth year of "four modernizations," an economic reform program aimed at opening China to Western trade. The ferocity of the repression that crushed the prodemocracy demonstrators set back China's international relations. Many nations boycotted China's products and withdrew plans for expansion in the PRC. Nevertheless, during the crisis year of 1989, China's exports to the United States were $17.5 billion, and imports of U.S. goods and services were nearly $20 billion. In 1990, there was an estimated increase of 6 percent in both exports and imports, a healthy growth rate even though lower than the annual average 9 percent increase during the 1980s.[5]

Eastern Europe

Recent events in Eastern bloc countries have made free-world markets accessible to an additional 140 million people.[6] Although effective buying power in Eastern Europe is expected to exceed $300 billion annually before the turn of the century, markets will not materialize overnight. In fact, most of Eastern Europe's industry and commercial infrastructure will have to be rebuilt before economic growth can occur. The most promising changes are likely to be in former East Germany, where "western" interests can underwrite development. Hungary is also promising because it has been a cooperative member of international trade organizations for several years and is relatively stable. Poland may emerge as a trading economy, although the country suffers from a defunct industrial base and soaring inflation.

Czechoslovakia has trade links with the West, but its economy is viewed as "mildly developing," with little to offer for export in exchange for Western goods and technology. The four remaining countries of Yugoslavia, Bulgaria, Albania, and Rumania are in political and economic disarray. Eventually, though, the trend in Eastern Europe is expected to be away from turmoil and toward positive change in global trade and international cooperation.[7]

Reunification of Germany

The fall of the Berlin Wall in 1989 may prove to have repercussions equally important to other changes in Eastern Europe and the former Soviet Union. After the wall came down, Germany reunified with an expanded population of 75 million people. Open borders also began to attract immigrants from nearby impoverished or besieged nations, and more than 300,000 people have resettled in the unified Germany. Prior to the demise of the wall, West Germany already had a strong economy and was positioned as the dominant economic force in central Europe. After unification, its economic influence alarmed leaders of other Western European nations who recalled how Germany had, twice this century, been able to economically and militarily challenge for world leadership.[8]

German unification also has placed the country in a leadership role for implementing changes in Eastern Europe and the Commonwealth of Independent States. Prior to unification, about 30 percent of West Germany's natural gas and 20 percent of its oil came from the Soviet Union, making it the single largest free-world trade partner with the Soviet Union. German technology found its way into the former Soviet Union, and the German deutschmark was the preferred currency of foreign exchange. After unification, trade between Germany and the Soviet Union increased dramatically, and then with the formation of the Commonwealth in 1991, it was Germany that took the lead in economic development, pledging $33 billion to help underwrite market reforms and trade alliances. Also, the Bonn government introduced new trade policies with the independent Baltic states, spearheaded negotiations for the peaceful withdrawal of Soviet troops from Eastern Europe, and began implementing widespread privatization programs in its eastern sector. Many of these policy initiatives and programs are being rapidly adopted in the Commonwealth, thrusting Germany even further into the role as Europe's foremost power.[9]

Europe After 1992

The twelve nations that make up the European Community (EC) have agreed with the seven nations that constitute the European Free Trade Association (EFTA) to link their countries into one vast, continental common market at the start of 1993. This extraordinary agreement, which unifies nearly 400 million people, has been called the "single market initiative for a post-1992 Europe."[10] These nineteen nations have become a confederation of "open border" nations where trade restrictions will be minimized during the next several years. This chapter's Global Trends feature describes the member nations and their trade associations.

The agreement will take years to implement fully, but even in its embryonic state, the European initiative is changing world trade relations. The new federation has created a cooperative market among the nineteen member nations that provides preferential trade without customs duties, discriminatory taxes, or trade quotas. People, goods, and services will flow freely among these member nations. Common Market studies indicate that the federation could experience an annual 7 percent increase in GNP and create 5 million new jobs before the end of the decade.[11] Nations outside the alliance will face stiffer trade barriers with Europe.

There is no comparable federation in North America or the Far East, but the United States and Japan set the cadence for economic activity in their regions. Japan and other Pacific Rim nations constitute a geographic region that is also a competitive market, and the United States is aligned with Canada through the U.S.–Canada Free Trade Agreement and is negotiating with Mexico to conclude a similar agreement. Although the North American and Asian regions have no legal premise similar to the EC/EFTA alliance, a tripartite trade environment will almost certainly emerge among Europe, Japan, and the United States. Harvard's Kenichi Ohmae has called this environment a *triad of power* that could dominate international trade in the near future. Global trade *within* these regions is expected to increase even as trade *between* regions becomes more complicated.[12]

Recognizing that they can no longer compete effectively with European companies for European customers, American corporations have established many joint ventures with European organizations. They have also located new facilities in Europe and positioned themselves to compete as European companies. Johnson & Johnson, for example, acquired Janssen Pharmaceutica in Belgium, thus becoming one of the ten largest pharmaceutical distributors in Europe. H. J. Heinz, the largest American producer of tomato-related processed foods, bought Copais Canning, the leading tomato processor in Greece, to establish a position within the European alliance. Also, in a unique move, the ultimate status retailer on New York's Fifth Avenue, Tiffany, opened a major store in Berlin's Grand Hotel.[13]

The Pacific Rim

The Pacific Rim comprises about twenty countries ranging from the oil-rich tiny kingdom of Brunei to superpower Japan. Together, the PacRim nations represent approximately 300 million people in market-driven economies (excluding China with 1.2 billion people). Many of these countries—Taiwan, South Korea, Indonesia, Malaysia, and Thailand—are eager to attract Western trade and investment. Some, like Singapore and Hong Kong, have international trade alliances and strong economies. Others, including the Philippines and Vietnam, are at awkward turning points and could either develop rapidly or stagnate, depending on political changes. The two countries of Australia and New Zealand are Western cultures with fully developed economies and strong trade alliances with Europe, North America, and other Pacific Rim nations.

Six of the smaller PacRim nations—Taiwan, South Korea, Malaysia, Singapore, Hong Kong, and Thailand—account for nearly three-quarters of all microelectronic consumer products imported into the United States. These include VCRs, microwaves, radios, CD players, televisions, telephones, small appliances, and microcomputer "clones." Many products with Japanese or European brand names (e.g., Sony, Panasonic, Philips, National, NEC) are manufactured in these countries. These tiny nations (Hong Kong is actually still a British colony) enjoy rapid growth and have high-tech industries with exceptional banking systems, skilled workers, excellent university systems, and thriving stock markets. Combined, their exports to the United States are equivalent to those of the Japanese.[14]

Japan and the United States continue to negotiate over sensitive "open" trade issues. The Japanese consistently export more than they import, and Americans want either trade restrictions on Japanese goods or increased exports to Japan in order to reduce the U.S. trade deficit. Yet many American firms do have operations in Japan, representing products that range from office software to space technology, and, in many areas, Japan depends heavily on U.S. imports. For example, Lotus, Microsoft, Genentech, and Mead Imaging have established markets in Japan, and the Japanese rely heavily on U.S. medical equipment, agricultural chemicals, instrumentation, pharmaceuticals, processed meat, and poultry.[15]

Latin America

Although news articles on Latin American countries tend to focus on drug raids and dictators, there is rapid economic growth in many Central and South American nations. United States exports to the 20 countries that comprise the so-called Latin-American Economic Sector nearly tripled to $60 billion between 1986 and 1991. European and Japanese investments in Latin American countries account for an additional $40 billion annually. For example, French-owned France Telecom has a 20 percent stake in Mexico's Telefonos de Mexico, which is also listed on the New York Stock Exchange and touted as one of fastest growing utility stocks available.[16] GM and Ford import from their Mexican affiliates four models of cars, GE has joint ventures in five Latin countries, and virtually all European and American petroleum companies have major investments in South America.

Most investments are in private industry, such as Caterpillar's joint venture in Brazil or Exxon's exploration consortium in Venezuela. However, as Latin countries expand, major public-sector funds are going into projects that help build infrastructure—roads, communication systems, banking, housing, industrial centers, and port facilities.[17]

As the leading Latin economy with the highest level of economic growth, Mexico has gained attention not only as a North American trade partner with Canada and the United States, but also as a "Pan-Pacific" nation with industrial ties to Japan, Hong Kong, Taiwan, and Singapore. Mexican President Carlos Salinas de Gortari has ag-

GLOBAL TRENDS

Redefining European Economic Boundaries

Western European nations have been making steady progress toward a single, unified economic community since the late 1950s, when seven continental countries reached their first cooperative agreement to control and share coal-based energy production. The so-called Common Market, originally six nations, was the outgrowth of this coal cooperative. Officially, it was known as the European Economic Community (EEC), an alliance achieved through the 1957 Treaty of Rome. The EEC expanded during the 1970s and early 1980s to twelve member nations, and it became known simply as the European Community (EC). From its headquarters in Brussels, the EC systematically reduced travel restrictions and trade quotas until members agreed to the "Single Market Initiative" that would eliminate all tariffs, quotas, and trade barriers among the EC nations after 1992.

While the EC was moving rapidly toward economic unification, seven other European nations were on a separate but parallel course of cooperation. The European Free Trade Association (EFTA) was formed in 1960 to provide a forum where member-nation delegates could resolve trade disputes and foster a cooperative environment for reciprocal export-import activity, customs duties, and currency exchange. Although the EFTA has attracted less public attention than the EC, it, too, has contributed to the infrastructure of banking, trade, transportation, multicultural enterprises, and European law that resulted in the current economic unification.

In 1991, a unification pact was signed whereby EC and EFTA members would create a single European economic community beginning in 1993. The pact produced more than 1,400 pages of laws and regulations on European activities, affecting 400 million people in nineteen nations. But 1993 is only a milestone date, one stage in the thirty-year effort to join forces among nations that, with few exceptions, have battled one another for centuries over economic and political issues.

The primary strategic objective under the pact is to create a unified Europe free of trade tariffs, custom duties, import licenses, quotas, and discriminatory taxes. The second objective is to eliminate barriers against people working in, or offering services to, any member nation beginning in 1993. This objective requires reciprocal recognition of professional qualifications, such as those for physicians, accountants, attorneys, and architects. The pact also calls for a "common agricultural policy" whereby all nations will liberalize trade of agricultural products. However, because farming methods, restrictions against agricultural chemicals, and standards for food processing differ substantially among European nations, this objective may take years to realize. The members have also agreed on a comprehensive environmental policy, but this, too, may take years to implement. The environmental objective will initially focus on clean air initiatives and transport emissions. Member nations have put in place a Council of Ministers and

gressively pursued foreign trade alliances in Asia, and he is pushing for passage of the North American Free Trade Agreement with the United States. Under the Salinas government, nearly three-quarters of Mexico's state-owned companies have been privatized, inflation has dropped from 160 percent to less than 20 percent, tariffs on imports have been drastically cut, and foreign ownership of companies inside Mex-

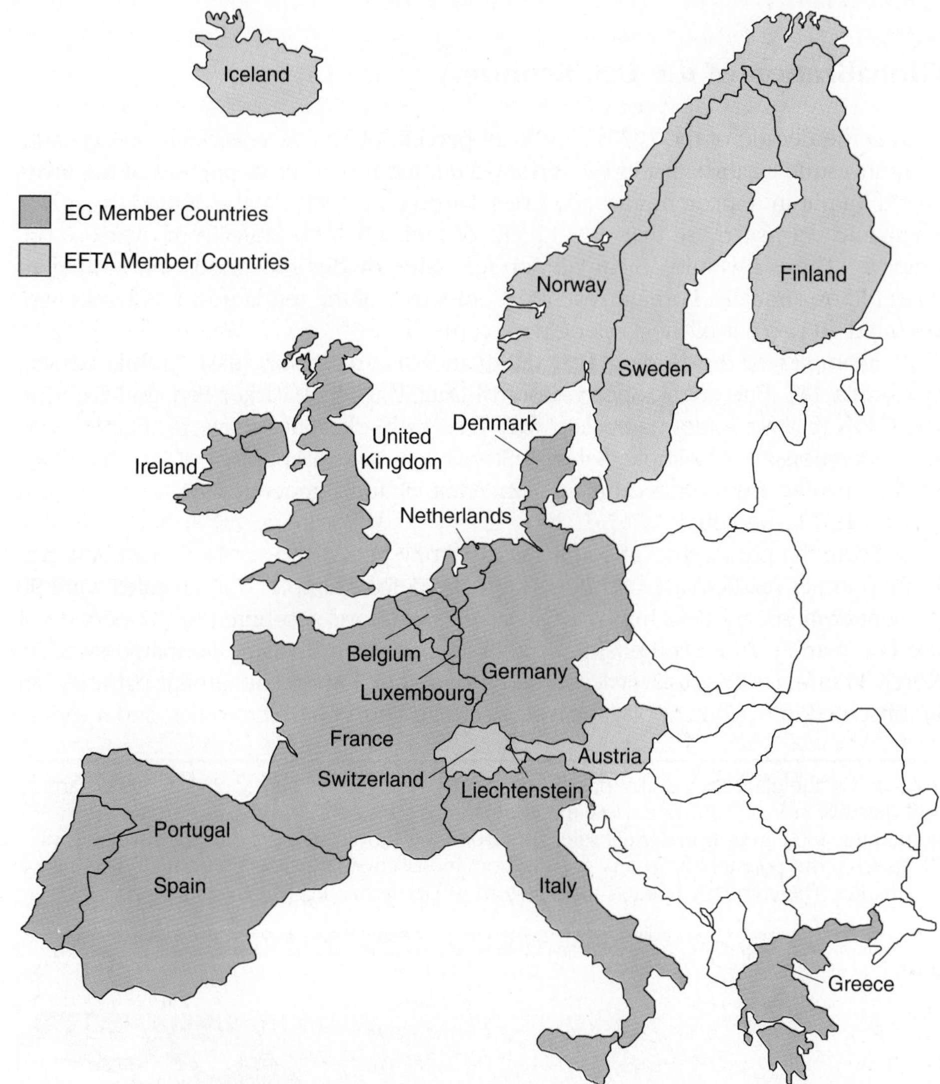

a European Court of Justice to administer pact initiatives, resolve disputes, and provide the legislative mechanism for a unified Europe. Finally, the pact provides a foundation on which to create a common European currency and a body of financial policies necessary to regulate trade and foreign currency exchange.

Sources: Stanley A. Budd, *The EEC: A Guide to the Maze,* 2nd ed. (London: Kogan Page, 1987), pp. 21–29; "EC Political Union: Dutch Courage," *The Economist,* September 28, 1991, p. 59; and Mark M. Nelson and Martin du Bois, "Pact Expands Europe's Common Market," *Wall Street Journal,* October 23, 1991, p. A10.

ico, once impossible, is now encouraged. These changes have resulted in major new investments and a growth rate of 4 percent.[18]

Companies that would not consider investments in Mexico only a few years ago now are concentrating their expansion efforts there. Zenith has moved its Taiwan operations to Mexico, providing quick access to North American markets and lower operating costs. Nissan has planned a $1 billion automotive plant in central Mexico. Corning Glass has a $300 million venture being built. In 1991, Lotus Development Corporation, Microsoft, and Compaq opened subsidiaries in Mexico City. And franchises, including McDonald's, Pizza Hut, and Baskin-Robbins, have facilities opening in every sizable city in Mexico.[19]

Globalization of the U.S. Economy

During the decade of the 1970s, nearly 25 percent of all U.S. corporate profits came from investments abroad, and U.S. firms accounted for about 10 percent of the gross world output in noncommunist countries. During the 1980s, many of the largest U.S. companies earned more than 50 percent of their gross revenue from overseas operations. These revenues included foreign sales of durable goods amounting to $460 billion annually. Foreign revenue from seven of the ten largest U.S. banks represented 40 percent of their operating income.[20]

Examples of the leading U.S. multinationals are Exxon, IBM, Mobil, Texaco, Coca-Cola, ITT, Burroughs, Sperry, Control Data, U.S. Steel, Parker Pen, and Caterpillar. Firms that we seldom associate with foreign markets also have profitable overseas operations. For example, Safeway Stores generates 38 percent of its annual operating profits from sales abroad, American Brands generates 41 percent, and McDonald's 17 percent.[21]

From the perspective of countries exporting goods and services to us, America is the premier marketplace of the world. In 1970, for example, U.S. car sales were 90 percent domestic models, but by 1990, Japanese imports accounted for 32 percent of the U.S. market, and a composite of other imports from Britain, Germany, Sweden, Korea, France, and Yugoslavia accounted for another 14 percent. Similar patterns can be observed in machine tools, apparel, footwear, consumer electronics, and a variety

---

Toys 'R' Us, the giant toy retailer based in Paramus, New Jersey, went global in 1985, starting with just five stores in Europe. Now the company has seventy-six stores in Europe generating $800 million in annual sales. But booming European sales did not distract Toys 'R' Us from the potential in Japan—a $6 billion annual toy market, second only to the U.S. toy market. The company opened its first store in December 1991 in Ibaraki, Japan.

Source: Robert Neff, "Guess Who's Selling Barbies in Japan Now?" *Business Week*, December 9, 1991, pp. 72, 74, 76. See also Patrick Oster and Igor Reichlin, "Toys 'R' Us: Making Europe Its Playpen," *Business Week*, January 20, 1992, p. 89.

of microcomputer "clones" and data processing equipment.[22] A disproportionate number of imports are coming from PacRim countries, which leads to notable trade imbalances. At the same time, however, there is growing interaction between European and North American companies—a point made at the beginning of this chapter with examples of AT&T joint ventures.

Another significant trend is the growing number of domestic operations that are foreign-owned. Many foreign corporations have U.S. operations, including Sony, Siemens, Toyota, Nissan, Honda, Philips, Volkswagen, and Volvo. Other foreign-owned companies are Royal Dutch Shell Oil, British Petroleum (BP Oil), A&P Stores, and Seagram Corporation. Many U.S. companies are substantially owned by foreign investors, including Mack Trucks, American Motors, W. R. Grace & Company, Ramada Inns, and Columbia Pictures.

Managers in all nations, regardless of what kind of organization they work for or what they do, face a world that is changing rapidly. These changes are forcing managers to educate themselves for a global economy and to learn how to manage their businesses in the heat of international competition. In the previous chapter, we examined how theories evolved to provide us with fundamental principles of management. In the remainder of this chapter, we introduce the concepts of international business and management, and examine how management practices are influenced by globalization.

CHECKPOINT

- Summarize the recent changes in Eastern Europe, Asia, and the Soviet Union, and discuss how these are likely to affect trade with Western nations.
- Describe the concept of *triad of power* and the growing importance of the new European Community federation.
- Discuss some of the challenges to U.S. managers both for doing business overseas and for adapting to foreign interests in the United States.

MANAGEMENT PERSPECTIVE

Several confusing terms are used by managers when alluding to global business. A good starting point for our discussion is to clarify these terms and provide a perspective for international management.

International Business

Major nations have been engaged in international business for centuries, but only a few firms in any nation have been engaged in international management for more than several decades. **International business** is a comprehensive concept that involves trade, finance, and the political economics of selling to, or buying from, companies in other nations. In contrast, **international management** is the ownership and management of assets in other countries.[23] Although international business has been going on since ancient times, very few firms have had to systematically concern themselves with planning, organizing, directing, and controlling global operations.

international business
Global transactions of a commercial nature that involve companies operating outside their home country.

international management
Managing overseas offices, branches, or subsidiaries of a multinational organization.

A glance through history gives an interesting perspective on how industrial nations evolved. The early city-states of Greece grew partly out of trading associations. Venice became wealthy by encouraging its merchants to travel the world to trade with a global citizenry. Britain colonized North America, India, and much of Africa through its trade associations. France, Spain, the Netherlands, and many other imperial powers thrived on mercantilism.

It is often forgotten that the American colonies were once trading arms of European nations. The governors assigned to the colonies by European monarchs were both political leaders and managers of their colony's business enterprises. A lingering connection to Europe influenced post-Revolutionary American attitudes toward international trade. By the end of the nineteenth century, the United States was second only to Great Britain in volume of transoceanic commerce.

International Management

Trading and actually managing in the international arena are quite different. A company that merely sells products to a foreign buyer is not concerned with international management. However, the enormous success of overseas sales has typically come from companies that have developed diversified international interests. Coca-Cola does not simply ship sodas to thousands of buyers around the world; it establishes businesses in hundreds of carefully chosen foreign locations with factories, distributors, bottlers, and managers. American managers who run overseas facilities must learn to plan, organize, direct, and control operations in substantially different cultural environments. They must also manage within unusual, sometimes volatile, political and economic situations.

Many managers of U.S. firms operating overseas are American citizens, but others are citizens of host countries. Both situations present problems. For example, a Nigerian manager running a Nigerian branch operation for an American-owned firm such as IBM must not only sell an American product in a very different culture, but also integrate the American company's policies with local management practices.

Multinational Corporations

multinational corporation (MNC)
A corporation that operates on a global scale with branches, outlets, distribution centers, facilities, or sales in foreign countries.

Multinational corporations (MNCs) conduct international trade and have overseas investments requiring international management expertise. The MNC label is convenient for distinguishing companies that own overseas assets from those that simply engage in foreign trade. MNCs must be concerned with foreign laws, politics, and economics as well as with managing host-country employees. Understanding international management begins with comprehending the rationale of multinational corporations. There are two philosophical approaches to managing MNCs, and each sets in motion a different corporate rhythm.[24]

geocentric multinational
A company that has diversified global operations but is controlled through decisions made by a centralized cadre of executives at the home office.

Geocentric corporations. **A geocentric multinational** has diversified global operations but is controlled by a centralized executive cadre at headquarters in the home country. Geocentric executives make strategic decisions that affect worldwide operations; they delegate little authority to overseas managers. For example, a senior executive in charge of international sales for aerospace lubricants may be among a hundred or more highly specialized personnel constituting the hub of strategic management. The aerospace lubricant sales executive can be responsible for several hundred worldwide sales programs from New York to Brisbane, Australia. A matter concerning sales in London will be weighed in relation to sales made in Saudi Arabia, Japan, and many other nations. Resource allocations for production, distribution, finance, and human resources, among other things, will be similarly evaluated for their global consequences. Figure 3-1 illustrates a geocentric organization.

Until 1991, IBM was the most notable example of an MNC organized geocentrically with an international division to promote its major products through a centralized executive team. IBM required that all foreign operations be completely owned and controlled by the parent company.[25] Each overseas facility manager reported di-

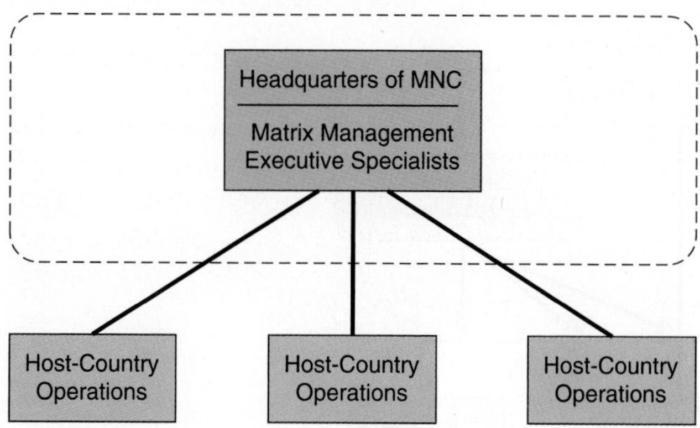

FIGURE 3-1 Geocentric Multinational Organization

rectly to the executive team at IBM's domestic headquarters, a team that included functional specialists in marketing, engineering, distribution, international law, finance, and many other areas. Field managers located overseas were often foreign nationals trained by IBM. However, the company did assign a significant number of American managers to senior overseas posts. The most noticeable characteristic of managing a geocentric organization is that all major decisions, as well as many operational ones, are made by headquarters executives. For IBM, that meant that executive teams were responsible for decisions on a global basis. Imagine making decisions one moment on operations in Japan and the next on marketing strategies in Spain, then discussing trade possibilities with one of the Baltic republics while team members are worried about inflationary effects on sales in Brazil! In 1991, IBM began to reorganize its foreign offices to allow greater local control of its operations. It remains to be seen whether this reorganization will end IBM's essentially geocentric management organization. In any case, geocentric MNCs have their special complexities and dangers, to which we will now briefly turn our attention.

Geocentric MNCs require exceptional information systems to monitor and control international operations. They also require management techniques that can assimilate opinions and coordinate decisions among many executives in a rather extensive management network. Moreover, each executive team must have an elaborate network of staff experienced in host-country operations.

A danger in managing a multinational company geocentrically is that a philosophy of ethnocentrism can strangle international cooperation. **Ethnocentrism** is the fundamental belief in the superiority of one nation (race, creed, or culture) over others. From a business viewpoint, ethnocentric behavior means that a company's managers impose their own standards and ethics on foreign operations while also drawing sharp lines between headquarters executives and their foreign subordinates.[26] Historical precedents include the practices of British trading companies in India under the Raj and American commercial domination of the Hawaiian Islands earlier this century.

ethnocentrism
The fundamental belief in the superiority of one notion (race, creed, or culture) over another.

Enlightened managers view such behavior as archaic, yet there are often understandable reasons why individuals promote **ethnocentric management.** National pride, for example, tempts us to endorse our management methods as superior to others, and managers are reluctant to consider new ideas. Also, many multinationals operate subsidiaries in *less-developed countries* (*LDCs*) that are just now on the brink of industrial growth. These LDCs include most emerging nations of Africa, South America, Southeast Asia, and the Middle East. What are considered to be rudimentary management concepts at home often seem futuristic advances in LDCs. It is extremely difficult in these circumstances to refrain from imposing industrialized management practices on host-country operations.

ethnocentric management
An approach to managing a global company whereby the home-office executives impose standards, ethics, and values on those who manage overseas operations.

polycentric multinational
A company with diversified global operations in which authority is decentralized, giving overseas managers broad-based authority for making decisions.

Polycentric corporations. If **polycentric multinational** is decentralized, with overseas managers given broad-based authority for making decisions. Most

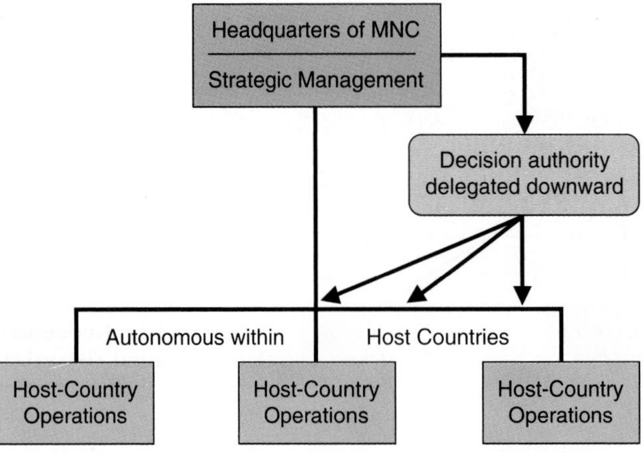

FIGURE 3-2 Polycentric Multinational Organization

polycentric organizations have semiautonomous operations within each host country. For example, Chrysler Corporation operates in the United Kingdom as Chrysler U.K., and Motorola, Inc., operates in Japan as Nippon Motorola. Like managers in a network of associated companies, managers in a polycentric organization make local decisions with little regard for the global consequences for other companies within the network. Figure 3-2 shows the polycentric structure, which is similar to that of many domestic corporations.

Corning Glass Works has been a pioneer in global diversification. The company entered its first joint venture in 1924 to produce glass in Europe. Today Corning is involved in forty major joint ventures with sixty-four different foreign companies. Many of these are as well known as the parent company, and include Dow Corning, Ciba-Geigy Corning, and Siecor. Corning Glass Works also has ten product divisions with operations in more than eighty countries. Virtually all of Corning's joint ventures are highly autonomous businesses, and foreign operations under the corporate umbrella have vested substantial control in host-country managers.[27]

A polycentric approach is plausible as long as the spirit of delegation is conspicuous and reinforced. However, an artificial attempt to create a polycentric multinational firm, one that on the surface is decentralized but is in fact rigorously controlled by the home office, can turn out to be disastrous. Host-country managers might ridicule home executives, avoid making decisions, or provide little support for a comprehensive corporate strategy. On the other hand, too little control at the suprastructure level is just as dangerous, for lack of strategic management can result in subsidiaries that are nothing more than a collection of loosely associated companies without a unified purpose.

Several interesting findings have emerged from research comparing the performance of geocentric and polycentric multinationals. Geocentric firms are more profitable, but have constrained growth because of decision-making burdens on the executive staff. Polycentric firms are less profitable, but they tend to expand more rapidly and gain a higher percentage of their income from overseas operations. Geocentric managers react more quickly to strategic problems on a global basis, but polycentric managers react more expediently to host-country problems and operational decisions.[28]

Neither the geocentric nor the polycentric philosophy for managing MNCs can be judged as categorically good or bad. Companies operating extensively in growth markets and in sensitive political environments are better advised to adopt polycentric methods if operational decisions require rapid localized decisions. Companies with interdependent operations would probably find geocentric management more effective. In fact, a company often has no choice because host countries may demand local control as a condition of doing business, or sensitive cultural idiosyncrasies may require a polycentric approach. For example, Japanese manufacturers in the United States are cautious about placing Japanese managers directly in charge of

American workers because of the potential for cultural clashes between employees and supervisors. Instead, American managers are trained in Japanese methods appropriate for the domestic environment. Honda Motors follows this model, and virtually all Honda employees and managers enjoy autonomy within their U.S. subsidiaries.[29] Perhaps the critical element in determining a philosophy of MNC management is the collective prerogative of senior management. If the top-management cadre wants to control in a geocentric manner, decentralized decision making—even if formally defined—simply will not occur.

Rationale of International Operations

In international business, often a "love-hate" relationship evolves between host and home-nation constituents. This is particularly apparent in LDCs because the technological superiority of industrialized nations such as Japan or the United States over nations in Africa or South America can easily breed envy and resentment on the part of the host nation. Such a mix can create a volatile business environment; at the least, there will be management problems. The relationship may be even more sensitive with nations positioned between these extremes, known as newly industrialized countries (NICs). Examples of NICs are Singapore and South Korea. NICs and LDCs provide opportunities for new markets and for overseas production facilities, but relationships with them are often tense because of unstable local politics.[30] Why, then, engage in business with them?

The answer lies in economic reality. Nearly every country has some strength on which to build a trade relationship. The theory of **comparative advantage** suggests that a nation with superior industrial technology can trade excess production at a profit while gaining goods and services it lacks from a trading partner.[31] The United States sells sophisticated weapons to Middle Eastern countries rich in natural oil reserves, and they, in turn, sell oil to the United States. If a perfect exchange is made, there is a balance of trade, with neither deficits nor surpluses. If, however, one country sells more than it buys, the purchasing country will run a trade deficit.

comparative advantage The economic strength one nation has relative to others based on natural resources, industrial technology, or cost-effective production. This strength permits favorable trade in gaining needed goods and services.

Thousands of companies operate in more than a hundred countries, each one bringing profitable goods and services to market because of an advantage it enjoys relative to its export market. Trading nations agree to use a common currency, often the U.S. dollar, to translate values of goods and services. Transactions are recorded and compared, and trade balances are calculated for all countries. Running accounts let nations know whether they have a trade deficit or surplus. Multiply a round-robin example such as the one in Figure 3-3 by several hundred thousand transactions daily, and you have some idea of the scope of international trade.

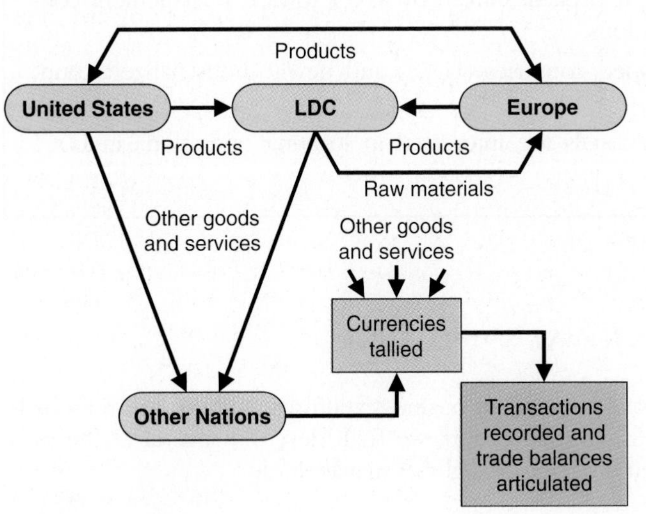

FIGURE 3-3 Conceptual Trading Process

Theoretically, each country benefits from these transactions. A nation's rationale for international trade is seldom merely to seek profit from an enviable comparative advantage, but rather to enhance its quality of life by importing goods and services that it lacks. A large number of the poorest African nations are rich in natural resources needed by the United States. Thus we import their staples, such as coffee, tea, and sugar. Similarly, we import many raw materials necessary for technological growth, such as petroleum, and numerous consumer products, such as radios, TVs, and automobiles. In return, we export goods and services in which we have a comparative advantage; a few of these are machinery, semiconductors, military hardware, telecommunications equipment, entertainment services, and medical technology. If we export precisely the same value of goods and services that we import, trade is in balance (assuming no complications such as foreign aid payments, loan defaults, or costly foreign wars). The United States currently has a trade deficit because of complications well beyond the scope of this text.

Trade and international business involvement occur for two reasons other than the economic and social benefits derived from comparative advantage: the expansion of financial resources and the realization of lower labor costs.

Financial resources. Multinational corporations realize that they can expand their financial resources through global associations. For example, a trading partner like Saudi Arabia has large capital resources created by an exponential growth in oil sales. By putting these capital resources to work through multinational investments, it can generate additional income and attract new technology to support its own industrial development. Thus a firm such as Caterpillar may be enticed to locate facilities in Saudi Arabia in exchange for financing and protected markets.

Lower labor costs. Another reason for going international is to realize lower labor costs. Labor rates vary considerably around the world. U.S. companies that manufacture computers, furniture, toys, and other products locate manufacturing facilities in low-wage areas such as Taiwan or Mexico to reduce total product costs. Paying low wages provides a comparative advantage for firms when reimporting these products for sale in home markets. Meanwhile, workers in overseas locations appreciate earning relatively high wages at American-owned plants, although their pay might seem exploitative by our standards.

CHECKPOINT

- Define and contrast international business and international management.
- Explain the different approaches taken by MNCs toward management control of foreign operations.
- Describe less-developed countries (LDCs) and newly industrialized countries (NICs).
- Explain why multinationals are interested in locating operations in LDCs and NICs.

TYPES OF INTERNATIONAL VENTURES

There are as many types of international business ventures as there are reasons to enter international business. In this section, we shall describe several of the most common ventures and their strategies for global management.

Exporting. The most fundamental type of international involvement is exportation. **Exporting** is a strategy of selling domestic products in foreign markets, usually through brokers or overseas distribution centers. By maintaining its manufacturing facilities at home, an exporting company makes few organizational changes other than to establish a channel for marketing overseas. This is the least risky method of becoming an international firm. For example, if foreign markets are tentative or politics shaky, an exporting company can sell its products through foreign brokers contracted as intermediary agents. By using agents, an exporter avoids foreign investment, but has little influence over how its products are marketed. Most small companies sell overseas this way, and several large corporations rely on brokerage contracts where the market does not justify investment in foreign facilities. Prior to reorganization in 1986, Du Pont generated nearly half its $1.3 billion foreign income in polymer products from agency contracts in more than a hundred different countries. By 1990, Du Pont had consolidated most of its operations for polymer sales in foreign markets under an international division, but the company still had agency contracts in many developing countries of Central America and Africa.[32]

exporting
A strategy of selling domestic goods or services overseas, usually through international brokers or distribution centers.

Where there is a substantial market, an exporting company may choose to eliminate middlemen by establishing foreign distribution centers, thereby taking control of its marketing and product distribution systems. This results in organizational change and additional management responsibilities for staffing foreign facilities. Staffing can be accomplished in two ways. Either a company hires local managers and employees to operate its distribution center, giving them substantial authority to develop markets and make operational decisions, or it transfers personnel from its domestic operations overseas. If it selects the first option, the firm will usually have to train foreign personnel, which can be problematical if the product being marketed uses sophisticated technology. If it chooses the second option, the company must train its own managers for international responsibilities, including how to operate in a culture where consumers and employees have different values, languages, and customs. For instance, ludicrous ad slogans can result when managers are ignorant of the foreign language. When 3M introduced Scotch tape in Japan with the ad slogan "It sticks like crazy," the Japanese interpretation was "It sticks foolishly." In Taiwan, the ad "Come Alive With Pepsi" was translated into Chinese as "Pepsi brings back your ancestors."[33]

Licensing. A common type of international business in this high-tech age involves licensing. **Licensing** is the process of contracting with other companies, granting to them proprietary rights to use technology, patents, copyrights, trademarks, or specific products or services. Licensing is a simple way to expand business overseas because the foreign licensee assumes the risk and investment of doing business. The domestic licensor may do little more than grant the right to use a trade name in exchange for royalties.[34] The Walt Disney Company, Inc., for example, licenses the right to manufacture Mickey Mouse electric toothbrushes to Hasbro Toys (with manufacturing in Europe and the Far East) in return for a royalty on sales.

licensing
In international business, the process of contracting with foreign companies, granting them the rights to use proprietary technology, patents, copyrights, or trademarks or to market products and services.

Licensing arrangements have typically focused on marketing successful products overseas through licensed agents and, with sufficient sales, on licensing overseas manufacturing. Today licensing extends to thousands of products and services, including fashion designs, watches, kitchen appliances, sporting goods, computer software, public relations, advertising media, and retailing. In some instances, this is a simple matter of contracting with retailers to distribute a product line such as Estée Lauder perfume or Liz Claiborne clothes.

franchising
A special form of licensing based on a contract that grants to a franchisee the right to offer, sell, or distribute goods or services through a business system created by the franchisor.

Franchising. **Franchising** is a special form of licensing in which a franchisor contracts to provide a complete business enterprise to a franchisee in return for certain fees and royalties. International franchises are similar to American franchises in which the franchisee is granted the right to offer, sell, or distribute goods or services

MANAGEMENT APPLICATION

American Brands Are Popular for Licensing

Owning rights to an American brand product is the fast track to success for many foreign businesses. U.S. corporations have more than 30,000 license agreements with foreign companies or agents to sell their products overseas. This is a relatively safe way to "go global" without having to invest or to become directly involved in foreign trade. Coca-Cola Company has used licensing since the 1920s; Compaq Computers launched its Asian operations through licensing in Japan and Hong Kong; and even a small company like Whampler-Longacre, a Virginia food processor, can sell nearly 5 million pounds of frozen chicken franks abroad each year without expanding its home base.

For the foreign entrepreneur, licensing means rapid access to products with global brand recognition. Alan Yeo, for example, owns a distribution company in Singapore that barely survived selling local Chinese foods. Then he acquired the license to sell Chun King foods (imported Chinese foods from the United States). Within two years, Yeo had contracts with major retailers in five countries for Chun King frozen and processed foods. This success led to licenses with several other major U.S. companies, including Pepsi, which he bottles in Singapore and Malaysia. Yeo now represents two dozen brand food lines, has sales in thirty-six countries, and grosses $200 million annually.

Sources: Courtesy of Charles Whampler, chairman, Whampler-Longacre Company, Harrisonburg, Virginia, November 1991. See also Louis Kraar, "Dedicated to Their Work," *Fortune,* Special Issues, Fall 1990, pp. 81–82.

under a *business system* created by the franchisor.[35] Franchise agreements vary widely, but in most instances, the franchisor provides facilities, equipment, materials, services, patent or trademark rights, management systems, and standardized operating procedures. Taken together, these constitute the business system, such as McDonald's, Precision Tune, or 7-Eleven.

A company franchising overseas has two advantages: it is able to enter foreign markets rapidly with a complete business concept; and it can quickly penetrate these foreign markets by using franchisees who have established business networks and successful reputations in their countries. Franchising allows a company to go international with less financial risk and lower costs than it would incur if it developed its own foreign subsidiaries.

Foreign franchises are highly visible examples of global expansion by Western interests. McDonald's giant restaurant in Gorky Street captured headlines for two years before its grand opening in 1990 as a celebrated Soviet free enterprise venture. It was by no means the first Western investment in the Soviet Union (now the Commonwealth of Independent States), and it was a Canadian organization that took McDonald's into Moscow, yet it seemed to represent a turning point in East-West relations. Visitors to Beijing (and the infamous Tiananmen Square) are often stunned to see the Kentucky Fried Chicken sign above one of the busiest franchises in China. Tourists in Tokyo, Hong Kong, and Singapore can shop at 7-Eleven markets, rent Hertz cars, and, of course, eat at McDonald's.[36]

Joint venturing. Foreign expansion can be accomplished through a **joint venture** that brings together companies from different nations to form a commercial alliance. Each company in a joint venture has a partial ownership position in the new enterprise. In contrast to licensing and franchising, which do not require investments by all parties, joint ventures are newly constituted enterprises in which the affiliates all make equity investments and consequently have ownership responsibilities.

joint venture
A contractual alliance between two or more independent companies, often including foreign government interests, to jointly invest in and pursue a new commercial enterprise.

Joint ventures are created to coalesce the unique strengths of each investing company. For example, GM joint-ventured with Toyota in 1983 to expand its small-car line in the United States. Toyota had the technology and expertise in small-car production to produce a high-quality product, and GM had the marketing and distribution strength to rapidly penetrate the American automotive market. The new enterprise, located in California, is called New United Motor Manufacturing, Inc. (NUMMI).[37] Each partner contributed $100 million in cash and assets to start NUMMI, and the original management team comprised an equal number of Japanese and American executives. Today NUMMI's line managers are all U.S. nationals, while Toyota personnel act as coordinators. Four senior Japanese serve as vice presidents among the eleven top positions. NUMMI produces the Geo Prizm for GM dealers and the Corolla sedan for Toyota dealers; both are manufactured using Toyota production technology, imported Japanese engines and transmissions, and domestically purchased U.S. parts.

Major joint ventures such as NUMMI are also called *strategic alliances* because today's diversified multinational companies are rapidly becoming involved in complicated international alliances positioned in major world markets. Xerox has joined with Rank (U.K.) to create Rank-Xerox, an information systems company in Britain that has manufacturing and distribution centers on three continents. Honeywell (U.S.) is joint-ventured with France's Bull and Japan's NEC for computer-integrated manufacturing systems. The combined Honeywell-Bull company also has backing from the French government in the form of equity grants for research and development.[38] Recall our discussion of McDonald's in Moscow. It, too, is a joint venture between the parent franchisor, a Canadian investor group, and the city of Moscow.

In each of these joint ventures, individual companies brought unique strengths to the affiliation, such as proprietary technology, expert marketing, experienced manufacturing, or access to capital investments. Sometimes a joint venture opens markets that would have otherwise have remained closed by trade barriers or import quotas. Fanuc (Japan) joined with General Electric to manufacture industrial robots in the United States, thus circumventing the import limitations imposed on Fanuc by the U.S. government.[39] Some companies enter into joint ventures to secure raw materials, others to take advantage of exceptionally low manufacturing wages. For example, the labor rate for a factory worker in mainland China is equivalent to less than $50 a month. For Western manufacturers, locating facilities in China can mean production costs that are only a fraction of those in comparable domestic facilities. Similar cost advantages, either in labor or materials, can be found in South Korea, Malaysia, Taiwan, Indonesia, and Mexico. American, Japanese, and European

This worker controls assembly-line operations at a gas range manufacturing plant in San Luis Potosi, Mexico. The plant, which turns out 800,000 units per year for sale in Mexico, the United States, and Canada, is a joint venture between General Electric and MABA, Mexico's largest appliance manufacturer.

Source: Nancy J. Perry, "What's Powering Mexico's Success," *Fortune*, February 10, 1992, pp. 109, 110, 114, 115.

companies have located ventures in these countries to manufacture a wide variety of products, including toys, running shoes, men's and women's clothing, radios, TVs, steam irons, toasters, industrial tools, and hundreds of different computer parts.[40]

Joint ventures are the preferred organizational vehicle for doing business in countries where politics are unstable or currencies are unconvertible. The Commonwealth of Independent States and the People's Republic of China have strict guidelines for joint venture management. Political turmoil in these countries has made it difficult to track data, yet as we entered the 1990s, indications were that more than 15,000 joint ventures with Western interests existed in China and approximately 600 joint ventures were operating in the former Soviet Union (and its autonomous republics).[41]

Wholly owned foreign operations. Unlike joint ventures that limit ownership and operational control, a wholly owned foreign operation is entirely owned and controlled by the parent company. This is the ultimate form of international involvement and has the highest degree of risk, as shown in Figure 3-4. A wholly owned foreign operation can be created in one of two ways: a company can set up an *overseas branch*, or it can acquire an existing overseas company as a *foreign subsidiary*.[42]

overseas branch
An extension of domestic operations located overseas that is wholly owned and managed by the parent company.

An **overseas branch** is part of the parent corporation and simply an extension of domestic operations. A branch of a Boston-owned company located in London is essentially the same as a branch located in New York City. Branch assets and liabilities are part of the domestic corporation. Profits or losses are part of the parent's financials, and taxes are paid in the parent's country on total company profits. Branch operations start from scratch and must be staffed, financed, organized, and managed like most new ventures. Unless the parent has a established reputation (e.g., Citicorp or IBM), a branch will have to fight for a competitive position alongside local companies.

foreign subsidiary
A company organized under a foreign legal code with separate liability and accountability, although wholly owned by a parent corporation.

A **foreign subsidiary** is a company organized under a foreign nation's legal code with separate legal and financial accountability. Specifically, the subsidiary has independent assets and liabilities, and it is taxed by the host nation. This form of wholly owned foreign operation can be an advantage if the foreign tax rate is lower than the domestic rate. Another advantage is that since the subsidiary is a separate legal entity, liability usually extends only to its operations, not to the parent. This can be important if the subsidiary is in a politically sensitive environment. A subsidiary can be created by the parent—in effect, starting from scratch in the overseas location—or it can be created by acquiring an existing foreign company. Acquiring an existing overseas company allows the parent to penetrate trade barriers immediately and avoid start-up complications by having a functional organization in place.

Entrepreneurs are particularly active in acquiring subsidiaries and operating overseas branches. Many small companies—some as small as one-person trading companies—are candidates for acquisition. Dickson Poon, for example, was the sole proprietor of a small watch retailing store in 1980, but through a combination of acquisitions and branch expansion, he owned ninety-six retail outlets in seventeen

FIGURE 3-4 Progressive Stages of International Involvement

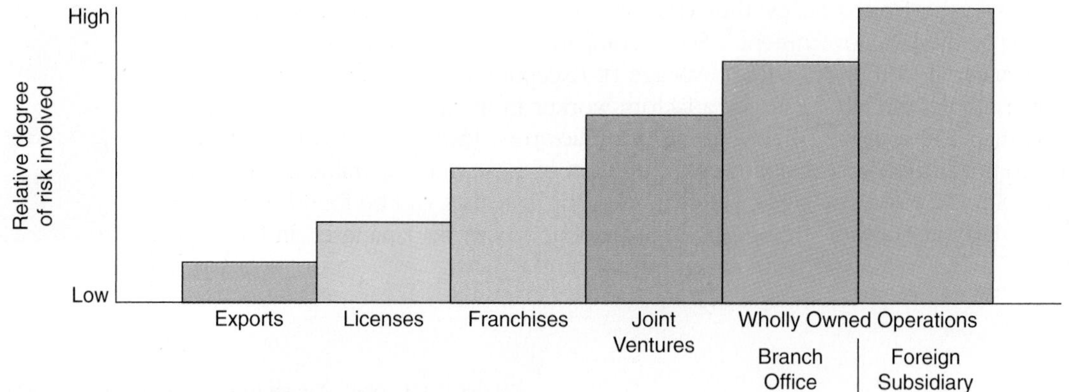

countries by 1990. Now called the Dickson Group, the company has exclusive fashion and jewelry shops representing such brands as Rolex, Chopard, La Montre Hermès, Polo/Ralph Lauren, Guy Laroche of Paris, Carrera, and Charles Jourdan. Dickson Poon built his company one location at a time, initially reinvesting meager earnings, then leveraging his group assets for loans. In 1986, he registered his company as a public stock corporation in Hong Kong, where he has subsidiaries. Today the Dickson Group has branches in West Germany, France, Switzerland, and the United Kingdom, and the company owns subsidiaries in Hong Kong, Taiwan, and Singapore.[43]

Transnational services. Though services are less tangible than products, most can be taken overseas through the same methods that work for product-based companies. Defining international services is something of a problem. For lack of a better term, they are called **transnational services,** indicating a borderless business concept.[44] This is the case for commercial banks, insurance companies, and accounting services that have similar professional responsibilities domestically and overseas. These service businesses do not export in the sense of shipping tangible products abroad, but they do generate earnings that register as foreign exchange through their branches or affiliated subsidiaries.

transnational services Professional and commercial services that are offered through contracts or provided to foreign customers through overseas branches and subsidiaries.

With due regard for legal considerations (such as host-country banking regulations), services can go international through methods similar to those used by manufacturers and merchandisers. One essential difference is that whereas manufacturers and merchandisers can often hire local employees easily, service enterprises usually rely on employees who have professional skills and are knowledgeable about local conditions. Also, service marketing requires customized client assistance because clients have unique requirements influenced by the culture, social values, economics, and political and legal systems in each country. Consequently, an American bank cannot take its domestic roster of services to Brazil or Thailand and expect the same success it has enjoyed at home. Few Brazilians need auto loans or mortgages, and few Thais use checking accounts. Life insurance policies are rare in socialist countries, and health-care services in many nations are provided by the government.

Consequently, overseas services must be tailor-made for specific foreign markets. Although executives may be from the home country, operational staff must be hired locally, for they must be able to deal directly with local clients as equals, not as foreign visitors. There are many opportunities for well-managed transnational services, particularly among emerging nations where managerial, technical, and educational expertise is lacking. Engineering companies such as Bechtel Corporation contract for dam building in Nigeria and power plant construction in Pakistan. Accounting firms such as Ernst & Young have scores of offices in countries from Finland to Kenya. Universities contract for overseas programs, student and faculty exchanges, and economic development consulting. Recently, new alliances of services have emerged, such as the Euromedicine Park in southern France. With support from twenty European and North American countries, the park maintains medical research facilities and offers medical consulting on a global basis.[45]

CHECKPOINT

- Describe different approaches to exporting products made domestically.
- Define and contrast licensing and international franchising.
- Explain how joint ventures are created and why they benefit the companies involved.
- Describe wholly owned foreign companies, using transnational services as examples.

INTERNATIONAL RELATIONS

International business involves two or more countries that often widely differ in cultural and social values. Home-country firms move into an international arena for many good reasons, and host countries enjoy numerous benefits from these relations. However, the relationship is not without tension.

Host-Country Relations

When a company enters a less-developed country, the host often benefits from the new jobs created. This is particularly true if LDC citizens are unskilled and have few opportunities to obtain wage-earning positions. Host countries also benefit economically from local spending by multinationals. Whenever companies build facilities, bring in equipment, and develop distribution systems, a tremendous amount of secondary economic activity begins. Each new venture expands the local tax base, creating revenue that pays for public services such as roads, water supply systems, and utilities. Also, an MNC usually transfers some highly skilled employees to LDC locations, and these people require housing, medical services, educational facilities, recreation, and shopping. Therefore, new ventures often create ripples of broad-based support activities.

Disadvantages to host countries, particularly LDCs, arise from the disruptive nature of new ventures.[46] The most emotional issue is the multinational corporation's influence in host-country politics, either directly through aggressive manipulation or indirectly through the sheer weight of its economic activity. Unethical activities such as bribery or direct meddling in host-country politics can be very disruptive. Ethics and social responsiveness are discussed in Chapter 4.

Even aggressive manipulation, however, is often less important than disruptions caused by the importation of values and behavior from high-tech cultures. American, British, French, German, and Japanese firms operating in remote parts of the world bring with them elements of their advanced industrial societies. Host-country peoples often cannot assimilate the knowledge or customs of these advanced societies without disrupting their traditional way of life.

Another problem is that some of the advanced techniques offered by MNCs are impossible to implement in many countries. It is difficult to train local employees to use a simple diesel engine when they have yet to understand a wrench. Introducing computers to a society that has not developed widespread consumer electricity presents almost insurmountable difficulties. When an MNC enters a host country with sophisticated technology, the benefits of employment, income, and a higher-quality lifestyle are often realized by only a small number of local citizens. From the host country's viewpoint, the scale in Figure 3-5 may never be in balance.

Parity: Head-to-Head Relations

parity
The condition of being equal in power, value, wealth, and status.

Even more sensitive than MNC–host-country relations is the rivalry that occurs when two nations with industrial parity compete for each other's markets. **Parity** is the condition of being equal in power, value, wealth, and status. Industrial parity between different nations exists when these nations enjoy comparable trade balances and trade relations that allow reciprocity for exports and imports. Historically, most of the world's wars have been rooted in economic competition. Britain and France waged war for much of the eighteenth century over economic dominance of European and colonial markets. The world wars of the twentieth century also had an economic basis.[47] Industrial parity can moderate international tensions, however, if sensible leaders seek mutually beneficial alliances.

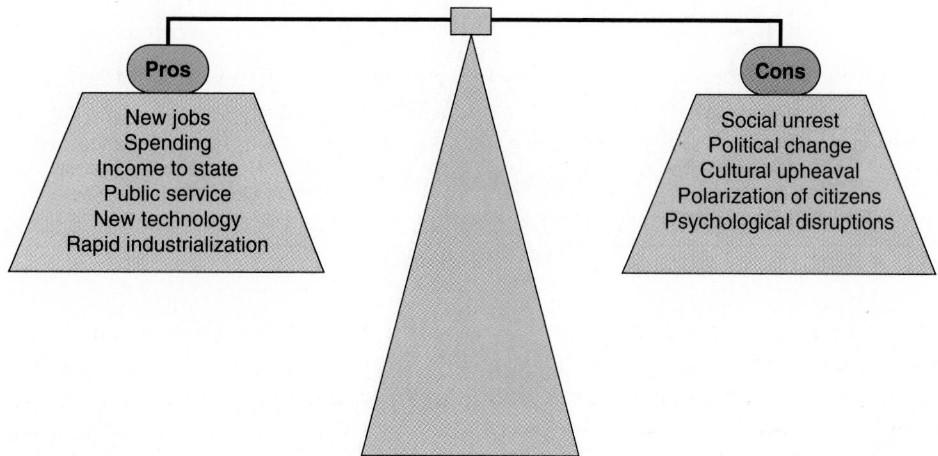

FIGURE 3-5 Host-Country Perspective of Advantages and Disadvantages of MNC Involvement

Tension arises when equilibrium is severely disrupted or when a nation aggressively competes for dominance. If unresolved, this tension can lead to collision-course competition. In 1980s, trade imbalances generated tension between Canada and the United States. Canada had become more expansionary, nearly doubling its export activity since 1970, and the United States was actively courting affluent Canadian markets while increasing its investment base in Canada's industrial sectors. The consequent tension initially prompted retaliation and political maneuvering by both sides. Then in 1988, cooler heads prevailed, and the two nations signed a cooperative trade agreement. The U.S.-Canada Free Trade Agreement seeks to realign imports and exports, stabilize currency exchange, and reduce artificial trade barriers between the two countries.[48]

The hazards of collision-course competition between industrial powers are most apparent today in U.S.-Japanese trade relations. Some experts suggest that tension between the two nations is increasing to the point where an economic showdown is inevitable. Others argue that despite strained relations, a cooperative level of competition is feasible. The size of the problem can be gauged by Japan's phenomenal success in world markets. By 1990, Japan was running a trade surplus with virtually every major industrial nation. Its 1991 surplus with the United States approached $80 billion. Japan dominates the Pacific Rim, and it is also the single largest foreign investor in the United States. Nearly one out of every twenty American workers is employed by a Japanese-owned firm.[49] With ownership of five of the ten largest world banks, dominance in electronics, and near-parity with the United States in automobiles and industrial machine tools, Japan is the second most powerful economic power.

Home-Country Relations

The extreme sensitivity of collision-course international competition illustrates the kind of difficulties multinationals face in their home countries. An obvious criticism of MNCs is that they export jobs along with their products and services. When MNCs are attracted to foreign shores by lower labor costs, the result is reduced employment opportunities at home. The same logic applies to capital investments. When MNCs build overseas and divert investment capital to remote facilities, domestic development lags. From a home-country perspective, the scale in Figure 3-6 will be unfavorably weighted. Proponents of this view argue for protective legislation coupled with higher tariffs to strengthen the domestic economy.

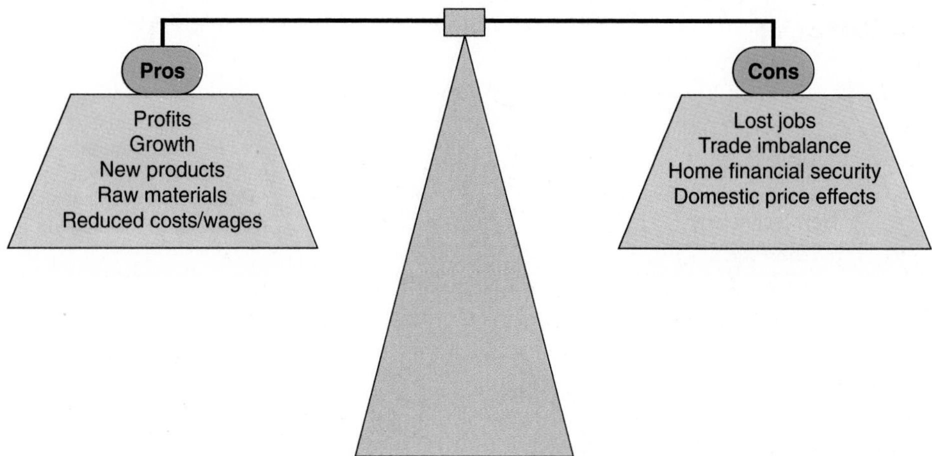

FIGURE 3-6 Home-Country Perspective of Advantages and Disadvantages of Multinational Business

There is another view of MNCs that directly contradicts this argument. Those who favor multinational corporations emphasize that the MNCs reimport lower-priced consumer goods that provide American consumers with an enriched quality of life. They also point to data showing high tax receipts from sales abroad and import duties. Finally, they suggest that the increased trade MNCs make possible helps eliminate trade imbalances.[50]

It is hard to reconcile the differences between these two extreme arguments. True, MNCs expand overseas to take advantage of low labor rates, inexpensive manufacturing facilities, and ready access to raw materials. They sell many products made overseas to foreign markets, but they simultaneously reimport a large percentage of them to sell in home markets.

CHECKPOINT

- Describe the advantages and disadvantages of international business for a host country.
- Discuss the concept of competitive parity and collision-course trade.
- Explain the advantages and disadvantages of international competition for the home country.

MANAGING IN THE INTERNATIONAL ARENA

It is not a quantum leap from domestic to global management. Richard N. Farmer, a long-time scholar of international management, strongly believes that good managers are quite capable of managing anywhere in the world, using skills very similar to those they use domestically. He acknowledges the need to adjust to different cultures, but insists that the functional requirements of managing an effective organization are similar across nations.[51]

Farmer's view is not universally shared. In a landmark study of four major nations—France, Great Britain, the Soviet Union, and the United States—David Granick noted substantial differences in management techniques. Other researchers suggest that management characteristics classified as "scientific" tend to be universal, whereas the "art" of managing human resources requires interpretation.[52] Major issues that influence the art of management overseas are discussed in this section.

Culture

Culture is the collective values, beliefs, and attitudes shared by members of a society that influence their behavior. It includes the national religious profile, language(s), ethnic heritage, stage of industrial development, and economic system. Because countries evolve from different roots and emerge as independent nations under their own social systems, cultural differences between nations and peoples can be pronounced. (We will discuss another kind of culture, organizational culture, in Chapter 10.) For example, Granick demonstrated that the management structure in French corporations is a three-tiered system with rigid downward communication and stratified authority based on class status. Class is largely determined by the schools from which managers graduate and their family ties. The result is an autocratic corporate environment that does not favor participative leadership methods. British firms retain some of the "old school ties" that assure graduates from top universities opportunities for rapid advancement, but the British have developed a strong collective bargaining system that forces companies to consider a much broader base in their decision making.

culture
A shared set of values and beliefs that determine patterns of behavior common to groups of people; organizational culture refers to patterns of behavior based on shared values and beliefs within a particular firm.

Management incentives also differ substantially from country to country. French executives receive extraordinary bonuses when productivity increases, but lower-level managers are largely ignored. In Britain, there are few bonuses at any level, yet most managers enjoy many nonwage benefits, such as cars and subsidies, that have no relation to changes in productivity. It is impossible to generalize about productivity bonuses in the United States because individual practices vary widely and are influenced by differences in industry and region.[53]

Culture is the primary force shaping these differences, and cultural differences are likely to provide the greatest difficulties to managers attempting to adjust to foreign environments. Managing in a less-developed country is far different from managing in one of the developed nations, yet managing in France also requires different skills and expectations than managing in Britain or the United States. Techniques of production, marketing, and financial management may be demonstrably similar in most industrial nations, but cultural factors determine how they are applied.

Political Systems

Differences in political systems also influence management behavior. Various forms of Marxism exist, or until recently did exist, in Eastern Europe, Asia, Africa, and Latin American nations. The European democracies of Britain, France, and Germany are closer to socialism than to American federalism. Several Middle East countries are governed by absolute monarchs who are also religious leaders. And for many nations, such as Iraq, the most familiar state of politics is an unstable dictatorship.

Managing in any of these systems requires making adjustments. In some systems, corporate forms of organization are illegal without a board appointed through political channels. In others, certain kinds of business are government owned, and free enterprise is circumscribed by socialistic ownership of resources. In still others, the government is a partner of the MNC, either because of direct government intervention, historical accident, or the country's efforts to support its own industries.

In France, the socialist government of François Mitterand has endorsed a policy of nationalization that is bringing more foreign-owned firms under government control. From Mitterand's viewpoint, France is actively "supporting" economic development by putting government resources behind its industries, but critics view this policy as one of interference. Following World War II, Great Britain nationalized its steel, rail, airline, and telecommunications industries. The government's basic motive was to create jobs for millions of workers. Today Britain is trying to encourage private ownership, yet the government continues to subsidize public transportation, steel, airlines, oil, and communications.[54]

In contrast, there is very little government ownership of industry in the United States. Although state and local governments own more than 25 percent of America's electric power industry, government does not directly invest in commercial enterprises. Still, foreign scholars view the United States as a heavily regulated economy, burdened with restrictive legislation and controlled through litigation, perhaps more so than most other industrialized nations.[55]

In Japan, corporations are financed largely by banks through debt instruments; Japanese exporters also benefit from huge government subsidies encouraging international expansion. Therefore, a Japanese automobile manufacturer will be capitalized differently than its American counterpart. Politically, Japanese companies have close relationships with government agencies, even though these fall short of the French socialist model. For example, Japanese executives are expected to follow government-mandated trade policies, and often confer with officials at the Ministry of International Trade and Industry (MITI) before making major decisions. MITI officials also regularly hold advisory positions in private firms, and company executives are similarly retained by MITI as advisers.[56]

Skills and Technology

Foreign operations often require a skilled labor force, but this is not always possible to find in less developed countries. Even when local managers are well educated by their own standards, their skills can be seriously lacking by our standards. When visiting Ghana several years ago, the author spoke with managers who ran a series of "cottage-style" sugar refineries. It was like glancing back to the late 1700s to see families of workers gathering sugarcane, cooking the roots, and squeezing sugar extract through what resembled large wringer washing machines. Village managers spoke of having been factory managers of a large modern sugar mill. We went to see the sugar mill, and found it rusting on the outskirts of a large clearing. The machinery was ruined, implements were scattered about, and several trucks were overgrown with weeds. When the plant was new, everyone saw it as the way to expand the sugar industry, but managers and employees did not understand the machinery and had no appreciation of maintenance. When the machinery began to wear from use, employees ignored the situation until rust and worn parts led to a complete shutdown of the mill. Then the local Ghanese returned to their cottages to mill sugar as they had done for centuries.

This is not a rare example. Many emerging countries have no common industrial knowledge or basis for education. Mathematics is often taught only to the extent needed for farming or herding. Language skills frequently do not exceed the level provided in missionary schools. Technology is known only to the extent of using simple equipment. Most emerging nations have one or two major cities, such as Lagos, Nigeria, or Lima, Peru, where the level of education is high compared to that in the rest of the country. Outside those population centers, country life continues in traditional ways, often without even simple forms of electricity or plumbing.

Hence multinational corporations operating in these countries must often transfer in skilled laborers as well as managers. In many instances, use of technology is limited by available systems and energy sources. For example, where electricity is unavailable for power looms, the appropriate technology for fabric manufacturing may be hand-powered looms.

Religious, Ethnic, and Gender Considerations

Religious and ethnic backgrounds and prevailing attitudes toward gender superiority present more complications for MNC managers. In India, for example, members of some ethnic groups, such as the Sikhs, consider themselves descended from a "warrior race" and avoid all industrial and commercial jobs. Others will not stoop to menial work but will only manage. Racial differences create problems worldwide. Some of those differences are pronounced, such as the severity of biases in South Africa; others can be quite subtle. For example, people of mixed racial descent in many South American countries are considered second-class citizens incapable of becoming well educated or holding managerial positions. In numerous societies, sexual inequality is commonplace, and an American female executive may be greeted with hostility. In Japan, a nation we regard as highly modern, women are rarely promoted to responsible positions. Women working in Japanese factories seldom achieve more than operating jobs, and they usually return to traditional roles as mothers and housekeepers once they bear children.[57]

Economic Systems

Politics and economics are intertwined in most countries. Whether a country has a Marxist or a capitalist system will dictate that country's economic priorities. Not all free enterprise systems are alike, however; there are major differences in currency, banking systems, trade associations, and the policies of supraorganizations such as the European Community (EC). And as we indicated earlier, even dominant systems are subject to change and, occasionally, major upheaval.

Domestic and multinational organizations have a difficult time keeping pace with so many changes. Managers find themselves constantly responding to such problems as international money exchange, price differentials, inflation, different methods of employee compensation, unstable consumer demand, and political decisions that affect economic activity. One implication for the near future is that organizations will resort to greater decentralization of authority. Local managers who are closest to operations and who can respond rapidly to changing circumstances will be given greater responsibility for decisions.[58]

Legal Systems

Laws and legal systems vary tremendously among nations. Managers ignorant of taxation policies in host countries, or unfamiliar with banking, lending, hiring practices, and safety requirements, can quickly get into trouble. The most sensitive issues concern legal interpretations of business dealings, such as paying money to conclude contracts. In 1977, the United States passed the Foreign Corrupt Practices Act, which made it illegal for American managers to offer bribes, gifts, or special favors in return for contract considerations abroad. In a country like Nigeria, where payoffs are a normal part of conducting business transactions, managers must choose between breaking American laws and refraining from doing business.[59]

CHECKPOINT

- Discuss how cultural differences influence management practices in different countries.
- Describe how government intervention in business affects management in different countries.
- Explain how managers in overseas locations are influenced by differences in local skills and technology.
- Discuss how international managers are influenced by host-country social and economic systems.

LOOKING TO THE FUTURE

A global perspective has become essential for a majority of organizations, yet global management grows more and more complex as emerging nations industrialize, political systems change, and multinationals proliferate. The first part of this chapter described the extraordinary changes occurring in Asia, Europe, and the Commonwealth of Independent States. From these often chaotic changes, newly defined political and economic systems are taking shape. In the aftermath of whirlwind changes in the former Soviet Union and Eastern Europe, nations are eager to establish infrastructures of government and industry that will allow them to participate in global commerce. The twelve-member EC has set in motion changes through the "single market initiative" that will substantially affect each member country long after 1993. In the Pacific, newly industrialized countries (NICs) have aggressively nurtured investment and trade on a global scale. Less-developed countries (LDCs), mainly those in Africa and South and Central America, seek economic development through strategic alliances with industrialized countries.

The fundamental principles of managing successful organizations differ little among established industrial nations. Nevertheless, even among the world's leading economies, there are many differences that require careful adaptation. When doing business in NICs, LDCs, and the economies evolving out of Marxism in the former Soviet Union and Eastern Europe, managers must make exceptional accommodations to reconcile differences in culture, education, technology, and legal, economic, and political systems. Consequently, the *art of management* is crucial to leadership of global enterprises and will be the preeminent challenge for future managers.

AT THE BEGINNING OF THE CHAPTER, we described how AT&T has begun to gain a foothold in global markets through joint ventures. Three of AT&T's ventures are with major companies in Spain, Italy, and the Netherlands, and the new companies created by these ventures market throughout Europe. Managing the joint ventures presents many problems since each must deal with unique European cultures. This is particularly interesting for companies in telecommunications, where a vast number of software programs, voice and visual media, and people who serve customers must accommodate more than two dozen languages through interconnected systems. The ventures also operate within twelve different political systems, and marketing and finance managers wrestle with as many as thirty different currencies. For AT&T, this is only the beginning. They expect to quadruple their efforts in the international arena before the end of the century.[60] ■

A SYNOPSIS FOR LEARNING

1. Describe some of the challenges to U.S. managers for doing business overseas and for accommodating foreign interests in the United States.

One major challenge is the "triad power" developing in the post-1992 European Community, Japan and the Pacific Rim, and North America. Giant new cooperative trading blocks are developing in each triad area. The United States,

Canada, and Mexico are drawing closer together through trade alliances, the EC and EFTA nations are solidifying into a huge trading region, and Japan is the center point for increased economic activity that includes the PRC, Taiwan, South Korea, Hong Kong, and Singapore, among others. Another major challenge is the emergence of Eastern Europe as global trading nations anxious to develop trade with the West. Yet another is the redefinition of economic activity in the former Soviet Union. In each instance, managers of all nations will soon find themselves dealing with substantially different cultures, languages, laws, currencies, peoples with unfamiliar social values, and uncertain political environments. At the same time, many foreign companies will be trying to establish markets in the United States and other Western nations. This means substantial changes in domestic competition and the flow of international investments.

2. Describe different approaches to managing multinational corporations.

Multinational corporations (MNCs) are managed in two different ways. In the first approach, called *geocentric,* authority is centralized in the home-country headquarters' executive staff, who control nearly all strategic and operational decisions. In the second approach, called *polycentric,* authority is widely delegated to managers in foreign positions. Although home-country executives remain responsible for the corporate portfolio, operational decisions—and often strategies for overseas subsidiaries—are left to host-country managers.

3. Describe how companies engage in export activities and expand overseas.

The easiest way to export is through contracts with agents who act as brokers, selling and distributing products made in other countries. As a company becomes more involved with trade, it may establish foreign distribution centers, staffing them with either host-country personnel or company employees transferred overseas. A third method is to license products or technology to existing overseas companies, who then manufacture, sell, and distribute the products, returning a royalty to the parent company. Companies can expand through joint ventures, which are commercial enterprises created through investments by two or more affiliated companies. A rapidly growing sector of international commerce is *transnational services,* which pursue research and professional services, or manage projects requiring home-country expertise.

4. Explain the implications of international business for host countries and explore the implications of trade competition between major powers.

Host countries benefit from international business through expanded employment opportunities, the introduction of new technology from the home country, and spending by multinationals to support personnel, facilities, and production. However, host-country societies—particularly those that are underdeveloped—can be disrupted, even overwhelmed, by the values and high-tech cultures MNCs bring with them. When major countries have comparable economic power and parity in technology or industrial development, there is a danger of economic conflict as they compete for the same markets. Europe 1992, the Pacific Rim, and the United States form a triad of power, each capable of comparable trade, technology, and economic sanctions.

5. Describe the major considerations facing managers who must adapt to the international arena.

Culture is a system of values, beliefs, and customs held by different peoples, and often sharp cultural differences prevail between regions and even within countries. Culture influences how people behave and work. Political and legal systems also vary widely, ranging from closed autocratic systems to free enterprise open-trade systems. Economic systems tend to mirror prevailing political and legal mandates, so managers must be keenly aware of host-country priorities and complications. In many regions of the world, people have not developed the skills or technologies to cope with modern industries, and managers often find that they must adapt their expectations accordingly. Religious and ethnic backgrounds also determine how work is accomplished, and in many societies, women's roles and opportunities seem to be unduly suppressed by Western standards. Managers in foreign posts often find themselves unable to cope with the ethical dilemmas that emanate from these circumstances.

SKILL ANALYSIS

CASE 1 Going International Is as Close as Mexico

Mexico and the United States have been trading partners for more than a hundred years. The United States is Mexico's number-one market for exports, and Mexico ranks third for United States exports behind Japan and Canada. During the past several years, exports to Mexico and U.S. investments with Mexican companies have accelerated. There are several important reasons for this increased activity. First, Mexico joined the General Agreement on Trade and Tariffs (GATT) in 1986, then signed a trade "understanding" with the United States to improve cross-border transactions in 1988. Under President Carlos Salinas de Gortari, Mexico has proposed a North American Free Trade Agreement, which, in 1992, was under consideration by Congress. Second, the Salinas government has brought inflation under control, cut trade tariffs from 100 percent to less than 20 percent (with many to be eliminated by 1995), and amended Mexican laws to allow foreign ownership of domestic companies. Third, Mexico has instituted several programs to encourage direct foreign investment. These include the *maquiladora* program, provisions for *sheltered* investments, and the *foreign joint venture* initiative.

The term *maquiladora* is derived from an old Spanish word, *maquila,* which referred to grain millers who would grind a farmer's grain into flour for a percentage of the milled flour. The concept was to share in productivity, and today, maquiladora is used to identify a domestic Mexican firm that transforms materials from a company of another nation into finished goods, which are sent back to the foreign firm for sale. With few exceptions, the finished products made in the Mexican maquiladora cannot be sold in Mexico.

An American company that contracts for maquiladora manufacturing benefits from unusually low labor costs and factory overhead, while Mexico benefits from having a new plant that employs workers and adds wealth to its economy. The American firm spends money, thereby improving Mexico's balance of trade payments, yet takes no income out of Mexican markets. The American company also benefits by having low-cost manufacturing without going halfway around the world to another low-cost location. Mexico is geographically convenient for shipping products to the United States—a fact not lost on other nations—and consequently, many Japanese firms, such as Nissan, are expanding into Mexico to manufacture products destined for North American markets.

The first maquiladora was started in 1966 in Juarez, Mexico, to make wood moldings. Today, there are more than 1,500 maquiladoras employing 400,000 people while supporting more than a million indirect supply and service jobs. The number of maquiladoras is growing by nearly 25 percent annually. Foreign companies with maquiladora contracts pay no import duties on materials used for manufacturing, and they enjoy complete exemption from export duties as long as the finished products are sent back out of the country. Under the *sheltered company* program, maquiladoras could be partially owned by foreign interests, and after July 1989, any foreign company could have a 100-percent ownership in a Mexican firm. Prior to this law, a Mexican company had to retain at least 51 percent ownership, which restricted foreign investments in maquiladoras and discouraged other forms of direct foreign investment. Under the sheltered company program, foreign companies can own real property in Mexico, which has enhanced development of franchising, housing, and commercial building.

Although the maquiladora program has been the most influential factor in Mexico's rapid economic growth, it has also been a catalyst for many of the legal changes in trade relationships and for growth in *joint ventures.* The joint venture initiative emerged from the maquiladora concept as a preferred way to attract investors from Europe, Asia, and North America. Through a joint venture, a company like Caterpillar can invest as a partner with the Mexican government and with private contractors to produce machinery that does not have to be exported. The joint venture, however, can be granted tax relief and given government-backed incentives, such as interest-free development bonds, to bring into Mexico much-needed new technology. Similarly, a joint venture between Price Waterhouse and several Mexican affiliates in Mexico City and Monterrey gave Mexico access to international consulting and management resources.

For manufacturers, relatively low labor and overhead costs are the primary considerations for establishing operations in Mexico. For example, a top-grade machine operator in a maquiladora earns on average $3.25 an hour. This is 50 percent higher than operator pay elsewhere in Mexico, yet far below the $25-an-hour rate a comparable worker would earn in the United States. Mexico also has a standard 48-hour workweek, whereas the standard workweek in the United States is 40 hours. There are only 7 paid annual holidays in Mexico, versus 12 or more in the United States and as many as 18 in Europe. Rising labor rates, reduced workweeks, and longer vacations in Japan, Germany, France, and Canada have attracted investments by companies from those nations. In fact, Mexico is attracting investments from Korea and Taiwan where labor rates average 38 percent higher than in Mexico, and are rising.

Mexican workers do not feel exploited, however, because they enjoy high wages, good benefits, improved public facilities, and enhanced technological training through maquiladoras and joint ventures. Communities with foreign investments also benefit from the economic activity, improved housing, and increased taxes. However, there has been some resistance to foreign interests, particularly to maquiladoras, by Mexican firms who see themselves being outbid for the best workers and skilled technicians. They also suggest that domestic investments are attracted to maquiladoras, thereby taking capital away from local firms. In the United States, labor unions are complaining that jobs are being exported to Mexico, further adding to domestic unemployment problems. United States firms affiliated with maquiladoras have relocated away from cities such as Buffalo and St. Louis to cities in the Southwest along Mexico's 2,000-mile border, thus weakening the economies of northeastern and midwestern cities.

Case Questions

1. Discuss advantages and disadvantages of the maquiladora program for the host country. Expand on the case using text criteria.
2. Describe advantages and disadvantages of relocating operations to a maquiladora for the home country. Expand on the case using text criteria.
3. What cultural, political, and social problems might a U.S. firm encounter in a maquiladora, a joint venture, or a wholly owned subsidiary under the sheltered operations initiative?

Sources: Don Hellriegel, "Maquiladoras: A Managerial Perspective," invited address to Managing in a Global Economy III, Eastern Academy of Management, June 11, 1989, Hong Kong; "We Have to Get Together," *Newsweek,* February 3, 1992, p. 41; and Nancy J. Perry, "What's Powering Mexico's Success," *Fortune,* February 10, 1992, pp. 109–115.

VIDEO CASE Made in America, but Sold Where?

Cracking the competitive Japanese market and other global markets has proved to be a tough task for many American companies. Often the lack of success in selling U.S. products globally, and particularly in Japan, is blamed on U.S. companies' failure to learn the language and culture of the countries in which they want to do business. A country's culture is a reflection of the values, beliefs, and attitudes of its citizens. An understanding of that culture is of paramount importance in marketing products and influencing consumer buying behavior. One American management school is addressing this issue by giving its students an opportunity to create marketing plans for companies hoping to crack the Japanese or other international markets.

The Thunderbird School of Management in Phoenix, Arizona, has long been acclaimed for its international management study program. Now a few selected graduate students at Thunderbird are getting the chance to work on real international marketing strategies for corporations. Corporate sponsors of the program pay $10,000 for a research grant to the school. In return, the companies get a team of six graduate students who work for four months researching a new market, presenting a product, and advising the company on how to launch it.

Hershey's Corporation used Thunderbird students to assist in developing an appropriate marketing strategy for selling its products in Japan. The challenge for the student team was to introduce a new boxed chocolate in the highly competitive Japanese market. A knowledge of the Japanese culture and language guided team members in developing their proposals. To understand the "chocoholic" tendencies of the Japanese, one team member conducted on-the-spot research. The result was the team's proposal for a new color for the box. Appreciation of how important order and arrangement are to the Japanese led the team to add a divider to the box to frame and protect each chocolate. Also, a trademark conflict forced the students to devise a new name for Hershey's product (Tribute). How did Hershey Corporation respond to the students' proposals? The company's export manager stated, "I thought they dealt with things as they are. They came up with relevant solutions [because they] recognized the problems."

Kellogg's and IBM have also participated in the Thunderbird program. In preparing an appropriate strategy for the Russian market, the challenge confronting Team Kellogg was to avoid offending the Russians by being too simplistic in introducing the product and explaining how to use it. The solution was to use the cereal box to educate and to sell. The box clearly conveyed the message that Kellogg's Corn Flakes is a cereal to be consumed with milk or milk substitutes in a bowl and with a spoon. Team IBM was faced with the issue of building interest among Bulgarian consumers in IBM PC2s. The team's solution: a mobile computer showroom.

Are the companies actually using the students' suggestions? Although not yet ready to commit to the student teams' global marketing recommendations, these companies have hired some of the people who participated in the program.

Case Questions

1. Why is it important for companies to understand the culture and language of a country in which they are hoping to sell their products?
2. What benefits do the students receive from this special program at Thunderbird School of Management? What benefits do the participating companies receive?
3. Critique the recommendations developed by Team Hershey for marketing a new boxed chocolate. Would you do anything different? If so, what?
4. Pick a product that you use every day. How would you market it in another country?

Sources: Drew Winter, "Selling Japan: Many Say It's Not That Tough," *Ward's Automotive World,* February 1992, Vol. 28, No. 2, p. 29; Jim Impoco, "Selling Toys to Tokyo's Tots," *U.S. News & World Report,* December 23, 1991, Vol. 111, No. 26, p. 54; and Candy Gourlay, "Wooing the Japanese Partner," *Marketing,* January 16, 1992, p. 16ff.

A ROLE EXERCISE IN A LESS-DEVELOPED COUNTRY ENTERPRISE

SKILL PRACTICE

Students may form into teams or work individually as instructed in class to research and present viewpoints concerning a new business school to be started in a small Middle East nation. The scenario of the nation follows:

Recently, this nation, which borders oil-rich Saudi Arabia, has suddenly become extremely wealthy because of massive oil strikes of its own. For this reason, as well as its lack of importance as a military power, the nation has become a prime area of multinational development. So far it has remained aloof from the wars and religious conflicts endemic to the Middle East; its citizens are predominantly Sunni Muslim, and the nation has encouraged trade with Europe and the United States.

The nation's leaders have recognized the importance of using revenues from oil exports to develop an industrial base for future growth. They have sent many young students to Western universities for training. Others have gone to work for multinationals and learned the most common techniques for production and marketing. However, very few host-country natives have actually held management positions. Most are nomadic by heritage and preserve a culture of rugged tribal individualism.

Two years ago, the nation endowed an expansion program for its major university. In addition to engineering studies, medicine, and agriculture, the university announced a new business school. Currently, business courses are taught by American and British professors on temporary contracts. As the curriculum expands, more professors will be needed, new textbooks will have to be selected, and programs will have to be well defined. There have been controversies as students complained about being taught topical subjects, such as management by objectives and participative leadership techniques, that they feel are unacceptable in their culture.

Most important, local leaders and most of the nation's emerging managers are uncomfortable with principles and concepts taught in management courses that disrupt their cultural norms. These include such matters as group decision making, assembly-line techniques that they feel enslave workers in unpleasant surroundings, and many of the motivational techniques, which they view as manipulative.

Assignment

Choose one of two role profiles if working in teams. One team should take the position of host-country citizens. Individuals on the team should represent (a) a business student in the new program, (b) a business professor asked to teach management using this text, (c) a manager returning to school for management training, and (d) a political leader concerned with economic growth of the nation.

The host-country team should prepare arguments that present the advantages and disadvantages of the proposed business school, together with critiques of a principles of management course, using this text and your course outline as an example. Discuss how business training will change the host nation, both pro and con, and how to improve the program to best match cultural priorities.

A second team composed of consultants from Europe or North America should prepare a similar brief and discuss issues to encourage a formal program based on Western techniques, practices, and educational priorities.

Remaining students should write a critique of the role presentations and evaluate the discussions for finer points concerning the institution of a formal business school curriculum. Examine the broader issues facing LDCs and the advantages and disadvantages of service contracts with Western technicians and professors brought to this nation to help form an industrial base.

4

Social Responsibility and Ethics in Management

OUTLINE

Social Accountability
- Business Ethics

Management Perspective
- The Ethical Context of Management
- Responding to Society's Expectations
- Whistleblowers
- Planned Responsiveness
- The Continuum of Response

Managerial Relationships
- Customers
- Employees
- Stockholder and Owner Interests
- Suppliers
- Competitors

Government Regulation
- The Case for Government Regulation
- The Case Against Government Regulation
- Reconciling the Issues

The Responsive Manager—A Changing Role
- Broadened Awareness
- Integrative Ability
- Effective Communications
- Political Sensitivity
- Intellectual Ability
- Ethics and the Growth of Responsible Management

OBJECTIVES

- Identify cultural and social changes influencing management decisions.
- Define and discuss ethical behavior in management.
- Discuss relationships between managers and their constituents.
- Explain the role of government regulation in business operations and discuss the cases for and against government regulation.
- Examine how managers can become more responsive to social issues.

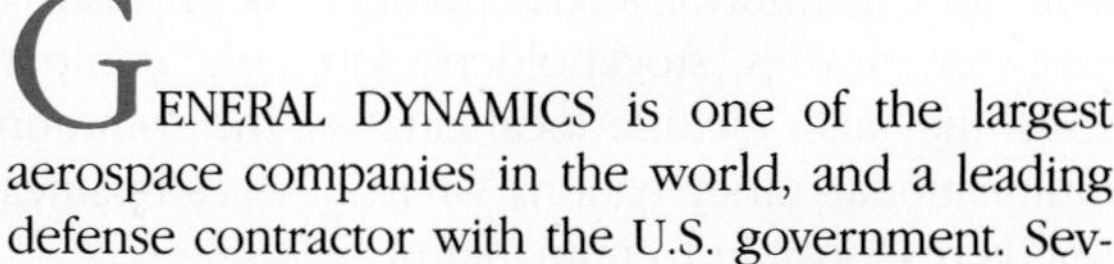

GENERAL DYNAMICS is one of the largest aerospace companies in the world, and a leading defense contractor with the U.S. government. Several years ago, the company also had the unpleasant experience of being the major target of Pentagon investigations into cost overruns and unethical business practices. After extensive congressional inquiries, it was determined that General Dynamics had front-loaded Pentagon contracts with high-priced materials, allowed expense accounts to far exceed acceptable guidelines, and charged the government for engineering mistakes the company should not have made. Moreover, the scandal was not confined to a few unethical managers. More than one hundred executives were asked to account to Congress for suspect costs and materials.

The scandal also aroused a sense of responsibility in General Dynamics executives. To their credit, these executives instituted an "ethics program" that is now considered a model for industry. The heart of the program is a twenty-page code of ethics that carefully describes to employees the company's expectations for business conduct. This is supported by monthly newsletters, a hotline that anyone can use to report misconduct, and a comprehensive training program. All new employees attend orientation workshops, and managers must participate in annual ethics programs. The company regularly holds seminars that focus on specific issues such as sexual harassment, improper use of expense accounts, rights of workers, and problems with AIDS in the workplace. More intense training occurs through a corporate ethics steering committee that provides employee counseling on such diverse topics as how to deal with attempted bribery when working overseas and how to write accurate cost estimates.[1]

As you read this chapter, consider how our expectations for ethical conduct can differ depending on time and location. What General Dynamics did recently may not have seemed serious twenty years ago. And United States companies that want to do business in Latin America must be prepared to deal with practices considered unethical at home, such as bribery.

Few organizations have survived for long without adapting to changing social conditions. Managers must therefore be responsive to social changes and make decisions that are acceptable both to their stakeholders and to the general society. An underlying concept of this text is that managers work in complex environments comprising other organizations and must be flexible and innovative to survive. But while managers struggle to survive in a competitive world, society holds them responsible for how they conduct themselves.

SOCIAL ACCOUNTABILITY

social responsibility
Refers to an organization's obligation to conduct business in such a way as to safeguard the welfare of society while pursuing its own interests.

This chapter focuses on managerial conduct and organizational responsibilities to society. **Social responsibility** is an organization's obligation to conduct business in such a way as to safeguard the welfare of society while pursuing its own interests. In a broader sense, social responsibility implies that managers are accountable to everyone who may be directly or indirectly affected by their actions. Ideally, it means that managers must protect the world's cultural, social, and ecological environments. This accountability is tempered by the immediate needs of society and pressure from an organization's stakeholders. As previously noted, stakeholders include the firm's employees, stockholders, suppliers, competitors, and customers. On a wide scale, they also include local citizens, the community, the nation, and, if the firm is multinational, other nations where it does business. On a grand scale, an organization is responsible to humankind.

Organizations do not operate in isolation from other organizations or from the complicated environment of political, social, cultural, and technological influences. Managers within organizations may feel more or less insulated from these external realities, but most of them recognize that they are ultimately accountable to others. Prior to World War II, however, managers obsessed with free enterprise generally ignored the social consequences of their activities. The nineteenth-century social Darwinist philosophy, stating that only the fit survive and the strongest survive best, prevailed in the United States. The implication was clear that for-profit organizations must earn maximum profits, concentrate narrowly on business activities, and resort to whatever means are necessary—with few restrictions—to accomplish their ends. At the turn of the century, this attitude was epitomized by the so-called robber barons who built empires in railroads, shipping, and oil exploration. Between World War I and World War II, social forces began to change the way Americans viewed industrial management. Miners revolted in the West Virginia coal fields, blue-collar workers formed powerful industrial unions to pressure management to make factory changes, and government passed strong legislation on work rules, employment, child labor practices, and social welfare. After World War II, rapid changes occurred in technology, economic activity, and social systems, and managers began to redefine their responsibilities beyond the paralyzing dimensions of social Darwinism.[2]

With these changes, a *systems* perspective emerged in organizations during the 1950s. Managers became accountable for their decisions to many other groups and organizations, including government agencies, political interest groups, suppliers, competitors, and organized labor unions. Not surprisingly, many managers resisted this "public" accountability, particularly in the area of human rights. Resistance, incidentally, was not confined to managers in private business organizations. Public school officials, elected state and local officials, and entire agencies of the federal government, including the FBI, also opposed such accountability. The result was more than a decade of constructive turmoil during the 1960s and early 1970s. This was a period of intense human rights legislation, when employees and consumers were consciously included as stakeholders in organizations. Today managers find themselves in complex relationships within their organizations and with external constituents, as shown in Figure 4-1.

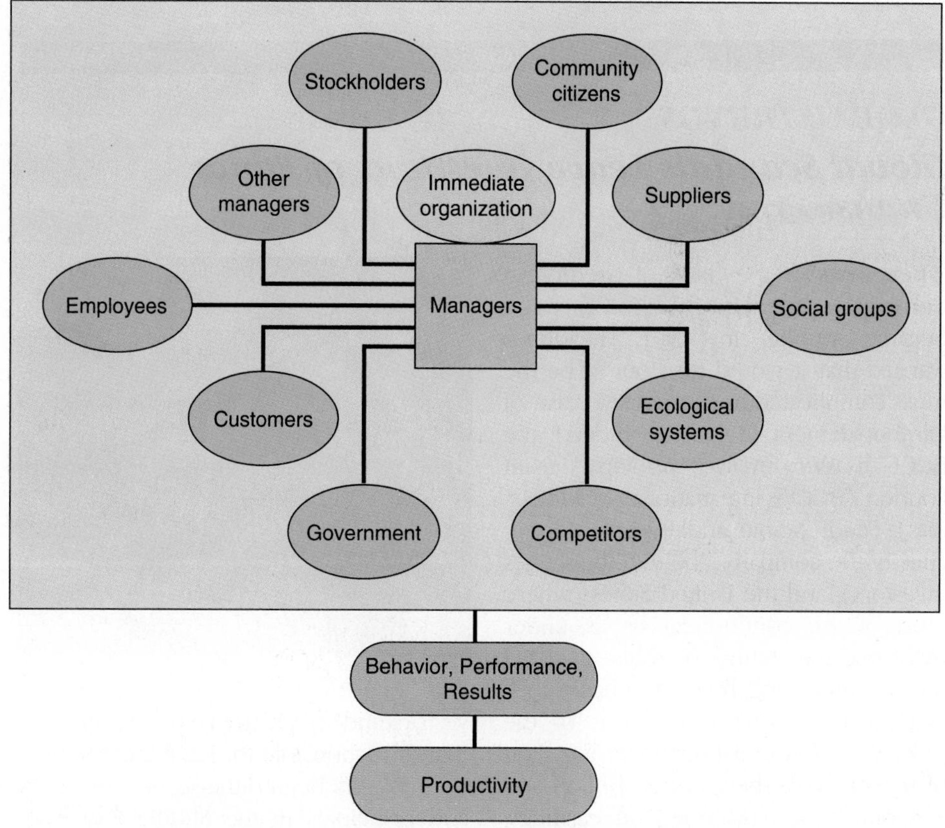

FIGURE 4-1 Expanding Systems of Relationships for Managers

As we near the twenty-first century, events throughout the world are ushering in another era of turmoil that everyone hopes will be a period of constructive change. Our global society has become smaller. Peoples in diverse cultures are trying to find ways to work and live together. Unfortunately, some are colliding violently. Recall from Chapter 3 how relationships in Eastern Europe, the Commonwealth of Independent States (the old Soviet Union, excluding Georgia and certain Baltic states) and Asia have engendered new multinational "strategic alliances." These organizations knit the globe together, and those people who manage them must be able to adapt to changes that include an emphasis on global human rights and a worldwide concern for the environment.[3]

Business Ethics

Ethics and social responsibility issues focus on leadership and often on how managers conduct themselves in a competitive environment. *Ethics* are concerned with standards of acceptable conduct stemming from morals. *Morals* are concerned with "rightness"and "wrongness" as defined by individuals, groups, or peoples. Consequently, ethical behavior by managers is often dictated by external circumstances and society's collective beliefs, attitudes, and values.

business ethics
The concept of moral right and wrong as applied to business enterprises, executive policies, and behavior.

Business ethics concerns moral right and wrong as applied to business enterprises, executive policies, and behavior. Because our major business institutions largely determine who will carry out the work of production, how that work will be organized, what resources that work will consume, and how profits will be distributed, we have become extremely sensitive to the *ethics* of accomplishing those tasks.[4] This sensitivity has led to pressure on government to regulate corporate behavior, and to a contrary pressure against intervention.

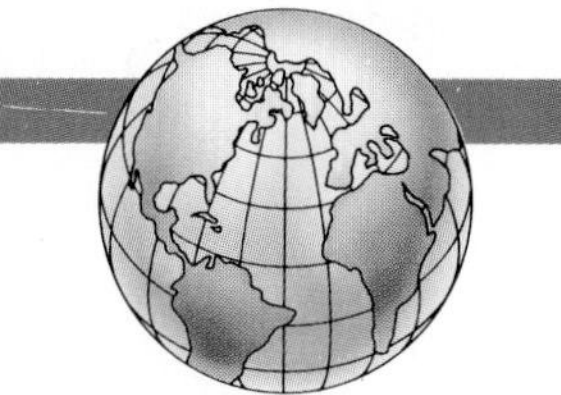

GLOBAL TRENDS

Global Scandals Leave Questions of Ethics Unanswered

When news of the Bank of Credit and Commerce International (BCCI) fraud became public in 1991, headlines warned that it would turn out to be the most complicated and expensive case of bamboozlement in history. Indeed, the BCCI disaster involves principals from London (BCCI's international headquarters), Saudi Arabia and Pakistan (domiciles of the company's behind-the-scenes investors), and the United States (where most of the commercial banks under BCCI became victims or tools of illegal money laundering, fraud, and bank stock manipulation). The dimensions of the scandal were astonishing: Over a period of several years, between $4 billion and $10 billion was siphoned off earnings, stockholders' equity, and depositors' interest.

Congressional hearings made it clear that BCCI's operations were grounded in extensive money laundering, influence peddling by BCCI attorneys and lobbyists, questionable methods of tax avoidance by the principals, and widespread bribes, payoffs, and unusually large "consulting fees" or legal retainers paid to individuals for unidentifiable services. In Great Britain, government authorities opened investigations that led to the discovery of far-reaching illegal activities around the globe. In the United States, the unethical behavior could lead to criminal indictments of the principals, consultants, attorneys, and lobbyists. In fact, most BCCI lawsuits will be settled in the United States, which has the majority of defrauded banks and investors and where the taxpayers are ultimately responsible for bank fraud losses.

BCCI's behind-the-scenes investors and principals in the Middle East may not only escape punishment, but will probably also enjoy the notoriety. At issue is a fundamental difference in business ethics between the West and other parts of the world. Saudi business is often conducted through "connections"—which in Western terms translates into influence peddling, payoffs for lobbying, and outright bribes. In Pakistan, laundering money and manipulating assets are considered "smart business." Also, beating Uncle Sam through tax dodges is laudable gamesmanship for some Middle Eastern investors.

Sources: Stephen J. Hedges, "Inside the BCCI Megascandal," *U.S. News & World Report,* August 12, 1991, pp. 27, 30–32; Susan Dentzer and Leslie Mandel-Viney, "How to Avoid Another BCCI," *U.S. News & World Report,* August 12, 1991, p. 33; and Marcus W. Brauchli and Peter Truell, "Family Shipping Firm Is One Reason BCCI Lost So Much Money," *Wall Street Journal,* August 15, 1991, pp. A1, A8.

Business ethics change as society changes, and the direction of societal change is not always predictable. Americans, for example, once tolerated slavery, and the United States is the only nation that has actually used nuclear weapons against another nation. Not every American alive at the time supported slavery or the decision to drop atomic bombs on Japan. Nevertheless, slavery endured for nearly a century

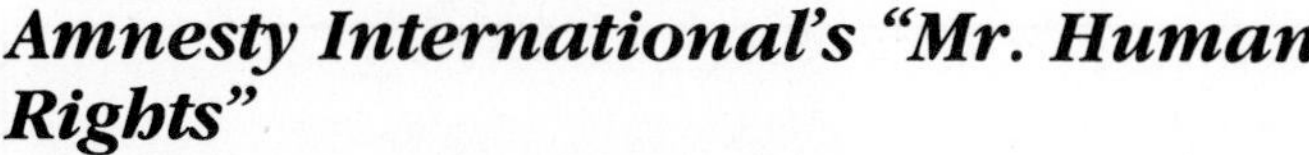

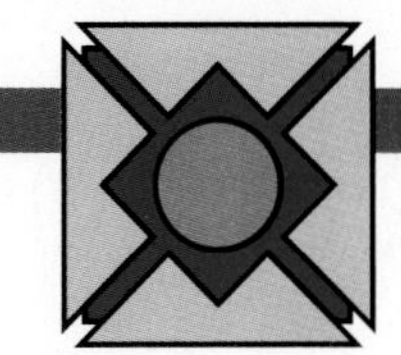

ETHICS IN MANAGEMENT

Amnesty International's "Mr. Human Rights"

Jack Healey, head of Amnesty International USA, is called Mr. Human Rights for activities that have taken him from boardrooms in Washington to tribal torture cells in Swaziland. An ex-priest who left his pastoral duties in rural Maryland to "take an active role in solving social problems," Healey is described today as a 50ish nondescript fellow in slightly rumpled clothes who is an organizational genius and the nemesis of third world thugs. He is credited with creating AI-USA, a human rights organization that has a celebrity list of patrons and active supporters ranging from ex-presidents to rock stars.

Bruce Springsteen, Sting, and Peter Gabriel headlined Healey's 1988 human rights *Now!* tour, which played in fifteen nations on five continents and was subsequently broadcast to more than fifty-eight nations. Sting, Sinéad O'Connor, and Jackson Browne starred in the 1990 concert, which was staged in Santiago, Chile, in a stadium only recently used by former dictator Augusto Pinochet to maim and murder thousands of people. Amnesty International and its subsidiaries, Human Rights Watch and Lawyers Committee for Human Rights, helped focus world attention on dictators like Pinochet, and received the Nobel Peace Prize in 1977 for their efforts.

Healey believes that human rights transcend domestic differences in ethics or culture, and he has set out to "vent some passion for social justice." Although helping to bring down dictators captures headlines, Healey is proud of simpler victories. He organized America's first charity walkathon in 1969 and raised $75,000 for his Freedom from Hunger Foundation. Since then, he has organized more than 600 walkathons and continues to support programs ranging from housing for the homeless in American cities to hunger relief for torture victims in Lesotho.

Under Healey, AI-USA has chartered more than 800 campus chapters and attracted more than 4,000 corporate patrons who support local and international charities concerned with human rights. Together, students, corporate managers, and Amnesty's staff bring tremendous pressure to bear on the world's political leaders.

Source: Michael Satchell, "Nemesis of Third World Thugs," *U.S. News & World Report,* August 26–September 2, 1991, pp. 60–64.

after the American Revolution, and there was only a muffled debate on the ethics of nuclear deployment by a few concerned scientists until well after World War II ended. Ethics are defined within a time period and within a framework of standards, expectations, and attitudes of people in a specific environment. Thus it is seldom certain how managers (or leaders of any organization, public or private) will be expected to act in the future with regard to ethical issues. Current examples of unresolved ethical disputes are abortion, employment rights of individuals with AIDS, and standards for toxic waste disposal.[5]

Managers must make decisions that take into account both society's prevailing ethics and the interests of their organization's stakeholders. Balancing the two accountabilities is often difficult, and there are few, if any, prescriptive answers to the dilemmas managers face. Perhaps that is why effective managers who make consistent ethical decisions are valued as socially responsible individuals. Throughout the remainder of the book, we shall introduce some of these individuals, their organizations, and their ethical dilemmas. These are set apart from the text as features called "Ethics in Management."

CHECKPOINT

- Explain how nineteenth-century attitudes toward business and social Darwinism influenced management behavior before World War II.
- Describe current notions of accountability in terms of social responsibility to stakeholders.
- Explain the meaning of business ethics and how standards of conduct can change as society's ethics change.

MANAGEMENT PERSPECTIVE

Periodic surveys show that too many American managers make unethical decisions and that too few organizations encourage socially responsible behavior by their employees. In one recent study, slightly more than 40 percent of 1,500 experienced managers said that they had violated ethical principles to meet organizational objectives.[6] In another study, a review of Fortune 500 companies revealed that over a ten-year period nearly two-thirds of these companies had managers involved in illegal activities.[7] These statistics, reinforced by headlines about the savings and loan scandals and insider trading on Wall Street, can easily create the impression that American business is generally unethical. In defense of business, it must be said that a majority of companies have a written *code of ethics* delineating standards for business conduct by their employees, and that more than 77 percent of all U.S. corporations with a net worth exceeding $100 million attach well-defined disciplinary provisions to their codes of ethics. Occasionally, managers in some of these companies make headlines by their unethical behavior, and their organizations suffer, but the vast majority of managers quietly go about their business without incident or intention to do wrong.[8]

The Ethical Context of Management

When managers are guilty of illegal activities, they are, by definition, unethical. But many problems arise from disputed values and attitudes rather than from illegal activities. For example, working women reported in a recent nationwide study that unethical behavior in their organizations included lying to managers and employees, permitting sexual harassment to take place, cheating on company expense accounts, nepotism, employee theft, discrimination based on sex or color, and lying to or misleading customers to close sales.[9] Several of these behaviors, such as discrimination and sexual harassment, are illegal acts that every company must act responsibly to prevent. Others, such as cheating on expense accounts and misleading customers, are unethical acts that every company should police as a matter of good business practice.

The Ethics Resource Center in Washington, D.C., studied 2,000 major U.S. corporations to find the most pressing ethical problems facing managers for the 1990s.[10] They found the following, listed in order of importance: (1) drug and alcohol abuse; (2) employee theft; (3) conflicts of interest; (4) quality control abuses; (5) discrimination in hiring, promotion, and job assignments; (6) misuse of proprietary information; (7) abuse of expense accounts; (8) plant closings and layoffs; (9) misuse of company assets; and (10) environmental pollution. Some of these problems, such as (1) and (8), are beyond managers' control; others, such as (5) and (10), occur because of poor management or weak company policies. Nevertheless, managers must try to eliminate unethical practices whenever possible and minimize their effects when they cannot be eliminated.

The current emphasis on business ethics does not mean that managers have only recently discovered morality or that their organizations have only recently become socially responsive. To the contrary, most of our leading companies have been concerned with ethical behavior for many years. Xerox Corporation had equal employment practices for hiring minorities a decade before affirmative action legislation was passed in 1972. Westinghouse Corporation instituted policies of equality in compensation and employee promotion to eliminate sex biases during the 1950s, nearly twenty years before the Fair Labor Standards Amendment of 1974. Du Pont introduced rigorous standards for hazardous waste disposal during the 1940s, long before the Environmental Quality Protection Act of 1970. Other companies, such as the Hewlett-Packard Corporation, established programs to enhance the work environment as far back as the 1930s. Consortia of companies and professional associations, including the American Institute of Certified Public Accountants, the Public Relations Society of America, the National Association of Manufacturers, and the Business Roundtable, have developed "codes of ethics" to guide members' behavior.[11]

Most professional associations deal with standards of ethical behavior as an extension of other issues. For example, the American Institute of Certified Public Accountants has established a code of conduct for members but focuses primarily on accounting rules and practices for CPAs. This is not the case with the Business Roundtable, which was founded in 1972 specifically to study business ethics and to refine corporate expectations for business conduct.[12] The Roundtable is made up of more than a hundred top executives from the nation's most respected companies, including American Express, Boeing, Champion International, Chemical Bank, John Deere, General Mills, General Motors, GTE, Hewlett-Packard, Johnson & Johnson, IBM, McDonnell Douglas, Norton, and Xerox. The spirit guiding the Roundtable can be traced to the period just after World War II, when major firms began asking how they were to conduct business in the new complex global environment.

In 1945, Boeing's CEO William Allen articulated a code of ethics that ranged from employee relations to contracting with foreign governments. Allen's approach was one of encouragement rather than regulation, and Boeing managers and employees not only accepted the code of ethics, but actually nurtured it. Under Allen, Boeing established a reputation for "squeaky-clean" behavior that endured for nearly three decades. Allen is reported to have had one standard for his own conduct: He wanted to do the right thing, not merely comply with the law or respond to pressure.[13]

Responding to Society's Expectations

Having a corporate code of ethics and having employees behave ethically do not necessarily make a company "socially responsible." Consider, for example, Nelson Mandela's viewpoint on American behavior toward South Africa. While touring the United States in the summer of 1990, he urged the continuation of sanctions against South Africa, but commented that although many U.S. companies comply with the boycott, thereby taking the correct ethical posture, they are doing little to actively improve the situation in South Africa. In Mandela's view, while "compliance" may protect a company (or a government) from the accusation of unethical behavior, that company (or government) should not be too quick to pride itself on having made a sufficient response to a serious social problem.[14] Merely having a record of no unethical behavior, therefore, does not make a company or its managers socially responsible.

MANAGEMENT APPLICATION

Hewlett-Packard's Commitment to Employees

Hewlett-Packard emerged from a garage during the 1930s to become one of the most admired corporations in America. Among the earliest high-tech entrepreneurs, William R. Hewlett and David Packard were in Silicon Valley forty years before it was known by that name. Commitment is the singular value on which HP was built, and while the firm has had a few minor layoffs and setbacks, it has always maintained a strong commitment to its "internal stakeholders," HP employees, as the following description shows:

> As products of the great depression, Bill and Dave decided that HP would not be a hire-and-fire organization. They felt job security was of the uppermost importance and built a company based on a loyal and dedicated work force. . . . An emphasis was placed on preserving the work force and finding the right niche for each person. The first employee was hired in 1939. . . . To protect employees, Bill and Dave established catastrophic medical insurance (in the late 1940s), which was virtually unknown at that time by other employers. An employee Stock Purchase Plan was established (in 1959) to allow a broad base of employee ownership. . . . HP established flex-time working hours during the 1960s, protected employees by cross-training them, retarded expansion when it appeared to put undue burdens on employees, and in 1986, celebrated 40 years of employee participation in management decisions.

Source: "Hewlett-Packard Company: Managing Ethics and Values," *Corporate Ethics: A Prime Business Asset* (New York: Business Roundtable, 1988), pp. 66–76.

Theoretically, the concept of social responsibility in business involves fulfilling the firm's social obligations, but scholars have not clearly defined what those social obligations are. From management's view, it makes sense to avoid criticism by "responding" to society's expectations because this will stave off controversy and preserve the firm's good image. But the specifics of responding are less clear. Should a company merely donate money to charities such as the United Way, or should it put its resources to work to help create shelters for the homeless? Should it be content merely to boycott South Africa because of that country's apartheid policies, or should it try to improve the situation, as Mandela suggested? One person's values will dictate one set of actions, whereas another person's values will dictate another—perhaps contradictory—set of actions. Trying to gauge society's collective values on many ethical issues is a monumental task.

corporate responsiveness Public perception of how a company reacts to protect the public interest or how it resolves questionable practices, not what the company does in absolute terms.

To escape this philosophical conundrum, managers are revising the meaning of *corporate ethics*. Instead of viewing corporate responsibility in absolute terms, many executives now view it in relative terms as **corporate responsiveness.** The rationale is that ethical behavior is judged by how well a firm is *perceived* to respond to an issue rather than by what it does in absolute terms. The "absolute facts" of a situation may mean little to the public. For example, in the public's perception, the absolute fact that the Ford Pinto had a flaw that caused its gas tanks to explode was not the issue; the reluctance of Ford to recall the flawed models was. Asbestos illness at John Manville chemical plants was a serious problem, but it was not the critical issue in lawsuits. Instead, litigation focused on whether managers knew about the asbestos situation and tried to rectify it. Some knew, none responded, and the firm went bankrupt.[15]

Whistleblowers

News of design flaws in the Ford Pinto was "leaked" to consumer safety advocates through "anonymous" tips from inside Ford Motor Company. Dangerous hazardous waste disposal practices at the Love Canal near Buffalo, allegedly by Hooker Chemical Company, were "revealed" to the press by a company engineer. Faulty O-ring seals that contributed to the space shuttle *Challenger* disaster in 1986 were described by Morton Thiokol engineers Allan McDonald and Roger Boisjoly before a presidential commission. In each instance, individuals who "blew the whistle" did so cautiously and in fear of losing their jobs. **Whistleblowers** are employees who go against their employers to publicly reveal unethical behavior. They do so as an act of conscience, frustrated by their company's lack of response (or outright cover-up) that allows an unethical practice to continue.[16]

whistleblowers
Employees who in an act of conscience go against their employers to publicly reveal unethical behavior.

Whistleblowers have little protection, and they risk a great deal by their actions. Even if they do not lose their jobs, they may well be passed over for promotion, personally harassed, assigned to unpleasant tasks, ridiculed by co-workers, and blackballed in their profession. Allan McDonald and Roger Boisjoly, for example, won the public's gratitude, but not their employer's. Both men were assigned to low-level jobs and labored long in obscurity before being reinstated. Many whistleblowers are dismissed, although recent court decisions have awarded fired whistleblowers damages and reinstated them in their jobs. This is hardly a satisfactory solution, however. Whistleblowers find little comfort in winning a lawsuit when their employers, peers, and, in some instances, families condemn their acts.[17]

Once again, the critical issue is not the "absolute facts" of an incident but the *perceived* response, or lack of one, by a company. This often leads to the implicit assumption that if things are so bad in one area that an employee feels compelled by conscience to risk his or her career to blow the whistle, the company is probably covering up many other unethical practices. That assumption may be substantiated by investigation, or it may turn out that the problem that prompted the whistleblowing was an isolated incident. Either way, the company will have to endure the repercussions of a public denunciation. Corporate responsiveness, therefore, is good business, and managers find that a *planned response* is the best and most profitable course of action.

Planned Responsiveness

Responsiveness implies two types of actions. In the first, managers recognize *potential* social problems and *proactively* do something about them before they become crises. In the second, managers are so jarred by events that they are *pushed* into reacting to those events. The second type of response involves dealing with problems that already exist.

An example of **proactive response** is self-initiated actions by a company to withdraw a defective product from the market. An example of **reactive response** is the same firm being forced to withdraw the defective product from the market. A forced response might be caused by something as simple as a local news story alleging that a product is defective. It can result in huge class-action lawsuits if the company does not respond in a way the public perceives to be appropriate. For example,

proactive response
A self-initiated action by a company to resolve, or protect against, unethical behavior.

reactive response
A forced action by a company to resolve problems or unethical behavior that is brought about by external pressure groups or government intervention.

the Gerber Products Company immediately recalled half a million jars of baby food following a news story in 1984 that reported glass fragments in their baby food. A full investigation was conducted by the Food and Drug Administration and by Gerber research teams, and the consumer complaints were found to be unwarranted: No glass fragments were found in Gerber's baby food. A second news story two years later again claimed that a customer had found glass slivers in Gerber's baby food. This time Gerber refused to recall their products and stated publicly that the allegations were false rumors. Once again, the FDA investigated thoroughly and exonerated the Gerber Products Company. Glass *was* found in the complainant's baby food, but the FDA concluded that it was the result of her dropping a grocery bag and cracking the baby food jar. The decision by Gerber executives not to recall their baby food jars, even though appropriate, was questioned by the public. Gerber's products were boycotted in some stores, and its baby food sales dropped off sharply for more than a year.[18] Society will evaluate the firm that "reacts," passing favorable judgment on managers who seem to respond expeditiously and honestly, while condemning those who do not.

The Continuum of Response

There are few hard-and-fast rules to guide managers toward an appropriate response, but there is a *continuum of social responsibility* with four types of responses serving as benchmarks. When a problem occurs, such as the rumors about Gerber's baby food, managers may deny any wrongdoing and resist taking any corrective action. They may also resort to a legal defense, using factual information to rationalize behavior that has merely met the "letter of the law." Or they may respond in earnest to resolve the problem, as Gerber executives did during the first recall of baby food. Finally, they may try to prevent the problem from occurring in the first place. For example, the FDA found that the Gerber Products Company had exceptional production technology that would prevent glass fragments from getting into baby food. These four responses are points on a continuum illustrated in Figure 4-2.[19]

- *Obstruction* is a categorical rejection of wrongdoing. Managers resist investigation and obstruct change, even to the point of fighting compliance laws in court.
- *Defense* is rationalization through meeting legal requirements—complying with the letter of the law to minimize cost and interference while using the law as a shield.

FIGURE 4-2 A Continuum of Managerial Response

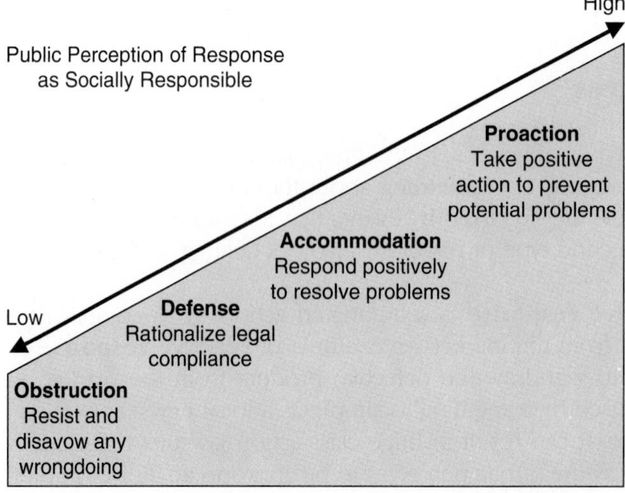

- *Accommodation* is the acceptance of social responsibility by taking positive ethical actions to rectify questionable activities and by initiating candid and open communications.
- *Proaction* is the planned effort to identify potential problems and to take positive and ethical steps to prevent questionable activities from ever occurring.

Clearly, it is less risky for a firm to take a *proactive* approach and create programs that will help avoid problems than to adopt a *reactive* approach, which invites public scrutiny. Reactive behavior implies "crisis management" and correlates to *obstructive* or *defensive* behavior on the continuum. Managers who choose *accommodation* are "reacting" to a problem after the fact, but theirs is a plausible and responsible response because they are candidly trying to resolve issues ethically. Since managers cannot anticipate every problem, accommodation may be the most they can do in a given situation. *Proaction* implies a conscious effort to avoid crises. Managers who consciously adopt proactive behavior establish effective relationships between their organization and its stakeholders. Managerial relationships are studied next to illustrate this point.

CHECKPOINT

- Define business ethics and explain why there has been increasing pressure on government to regulate corporate behavior.
- Explain why business leaders emphasize the need for professional "codes of conduct."
- What is meant by "social responsiveness"?
- Identify the primary types of responses on the "continuum of social responsibility."

MANAGERIAL RELATIONSHIPS

Managers must recognize that their organization exists within systems; for instance, it is one of the network of companies in an industry or one organization in the local community. Each part of a system, however, has a boundary separating it from other parts. For example, an organization has a purpose, a membership, and perhaps physical facilities that separate it from other organizations. College students and local citizens who are not part of campus life separate themselves with perceptual boundaries so that a "town and gown" system of two diverse groups evolves. In organizational terms, there are hundreds of internal and external systems of groups that must develop working relationships. These relationships are influenced by managers through *boundary-spanning roles*.

A manager who has a **boundary-spanning role** is responsible for linking the organization with its external constituencies.[20] This can be a *formal* responsibility prescribed for, say, a public affairs officer, who is expected to keep up with any changes that may influence a company's operations and to communicate information about the company to external constituencies. Purchasing managers are boundary spanners as they conduct business with suppliers; so are senior executives of corporations when they provide vital communications linkage with stockholders, lenders, competitors, government agencies, and customers.

boundary-spanning role A managerial responsibility created by proximity to external constituents to link those constituents' interests to the company's interests through effective communications.

A boundary-spanning role can also be *informal*. This role is implicit in the nature of the manager's job. Marketing managers are expected to span the boundaries between the company and its customers, to improve the company's image by being involved with the community, and to help the company be responsive to social is-

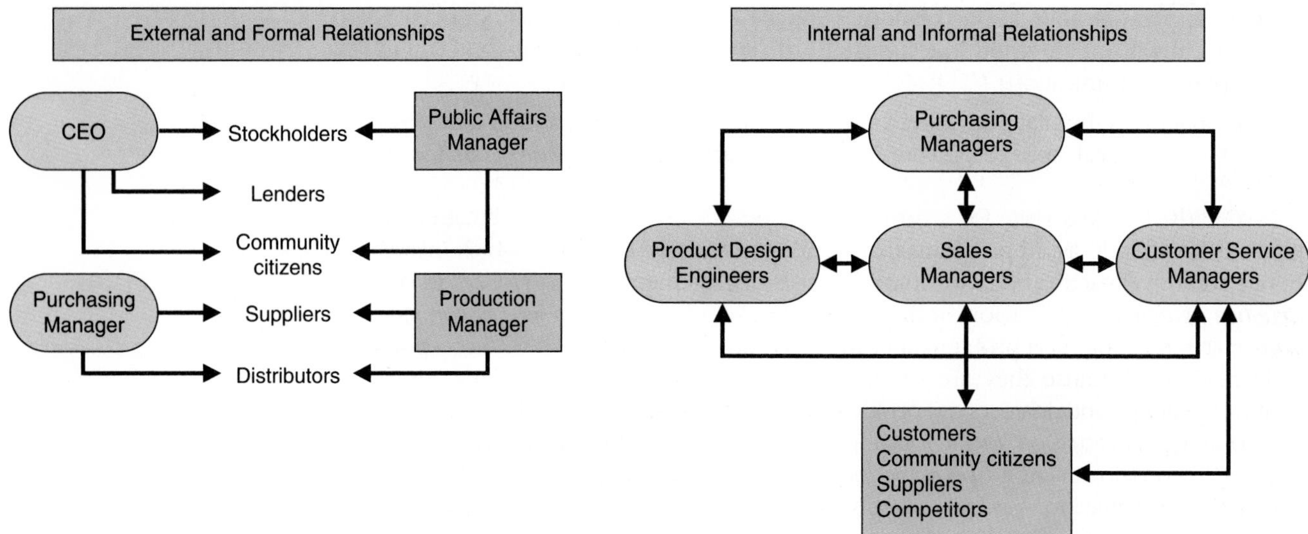

FIGURE 4-3 Boundary-Spanning Relationships

sues. Examples of informal boundary-spanning activities are joining a Rotary Club, doing volunteer work for the March of Dimes, and working with environmental groups to improve product packaging. Senior executives become involved in many external organizations to develop informal linkage with investors, lenders, potential customers, journalists, and legislators. William G. McGowan, for example, explained his role as the founder and chairman of MCI Communications Corporation as a "communicator" to the world beyond corporate walls. To make MCI succeed, he explained, he spent more than half of his time nurturing networks of associates and convincing potential customers that MCI could compete in a monopolized telecommunications industry.[21]

Boundary-spanning activities can also be internal to the organization and, here again, either formal or informal. Managers may be assigned formal spanning responsibilities to coordinate operations between departments such as production and marketing. Effective managers use informal boundary spanning to develop cooperative relationships between their departments. Some of these roles and responsibilities are shown in Figure 4-3.

Boundary-spanning activities are important because they bring together the components of an organization and help position the organization within its industry and community. Because *social responsiveness* depends on managers who are sensitive to their stakeholders, building good relationships with stakeholders is one of the manager's basic responsibilities. Primary stakeholders that all companies must consider are their customers, employees, investors, suppliers, and competitors.

Customers

All organizations have customers. Private-sector, for-profit firms sell products or services to customers. The federal government serves American citizens collectively. Schools have a customer base in students, parents, and the wider network of social organizations, such as future employers, who rely on well-educated youth for the next generation of employees. Some not-for-profit organizations may serve constituents that include the Red Cross, the Boy Scouts, and various charities. Figure 4-4 shows several of these relationships.

The term *customers* may sound inappropriate in some instances—one does not usually think of the Red Cross as serving customers—yet managers in all organizations must provide value to their clientele. Politicians who fail to serve the needs

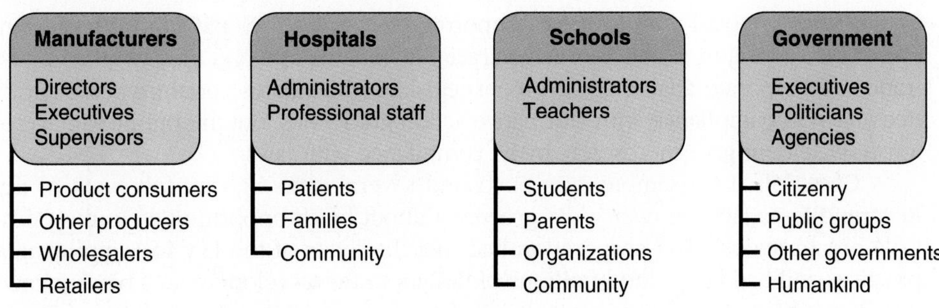

FIGURE 4-4 Customer, Client, and Constituent Relations

of their constituents will be voted out of office. Universities that fail to provide quality education will cause their students to switch to other schools. Even deserving organizations such as the Boy Scouts will lose public support and funding if their programs become shoddy or their leadership weak.

Social responsibility in customer relations means creating an exchange of value between buyers and sellers. That exchange may come through prices paid for products and services, votes, donations, or community support for programs. Social responsibility to customers has several broader meanings as well. It means providing safe and reliable products, being honest in advertising (or political campaigning), and embracing lawful and ethical behavior within the community. As we shall see later, social responsibility also includes the obligation of organizations to resolve social issues such as equal employment. Although these meanings go beyond a narrow interpretation of customer relations, the image a firm projects to its corporate citizenry influences customers and their decisions to do business with the firm.

Employees

Perhaps one of the most rapidly changing areas of management is attitudes toward employees. Until fairly recently, employees were viewed as elements in the economic development of the firm. More specifically, labor was treated as a factor of production. This viewpoint resulted in generations of adversarial relations between managers and their employees. Employees, for their part, saw managers as exclusively representing owners' interests. Today enlightened managers avoid this archaic relationship and encourage organizational members to take an active interest in their firm's fate.

Indeed, opinion leaders voice a growing belief that employees have property rights in their organizations stemming from their investments of time and labor. Peter Drucker believes these rights to be as valid as those of financial investors.[22] In Japan, the concept of an organization is not based on property rights or financial investments but on the collective membership of human resources. Therefore, the Japanese tend to view employees and managers as partners in a social entity. Consequently, community citizens, government agencies, and religious groups all feel they have a vested interest in how well many companies do.[23]

This philosophical change in organizational relations has instigated a number of efforts to involve employees in decision making. As we shall see later—specifically in Chapter 11 when we discuss group behavior and in Chapter 15 when we discuss leadership—various forms of participation and team management processes have evolved. Most derive from the idea that all individuals in an organization are responsible for their organization's conduct and are accountable for results.

A human resource viewpoint. A prevalent view of social responsibility concerns how organizations respond to society's expectations for human resource management in relation to employees. From this perspective, managers are held accountable for equal employment opportunities, equity in pay and promotion, elimination of unjust situations such as racial discrimination, and the lawful administration of corporate affairs. Government legislation mandates certain types of practices, such as compliance with affirmative action guidelines, but the public's image of a firm is seldom governed solely by its compliance with laws.

Coca-Cola, for example, was boycotted several years ago by followers of the Reverend Jesse Jackson over a disagreement about black opportunities in the Coca-Cola organization.[24] The corporation had met the letter of the law for employment practices and had committed millions of dollars to the development of black-owned distributorships. But Jackson's view was that the company was not doing enough. Embarrassed by the bad publicity, whether justified or not, Coca-Cola's leaders responded by focusing even greater attention on minority hiring, promotion, and support for black entrepreneurial ventures.

A dilemma of interpretation. There are many examples of managers being held socially accountable beyond legal guidelines for behavior within their organizations. For instance, sexual harassment is clearly undesirable behavior. When news stories break about sexual harassment within a company, community groups and customers are likely to react negatively, perhaps censuring the organization by taking their business elsewhere. Managers generally find it hard to know what to do about sexual harassment because there are so few guidelines for defining this sort of behavior. What is interpreted as harassment by one person may be an amusing experience for another. Yet the firm accused of allowing sexual harassment will find little advantage in pleading the difficulty of defining such behavior.[25]

In dealing with sexual harassment and other sometimes vague but equally sensitive issues, managers will be judged by their response rather than by their compliance with the law. As discussed earlier, an *obstructive* or *defensive* response in these situations will result in public condemnation with little concern for factual evidence in favor of the company. Managers must at least *accommodate* investigations into sexual harassment and, when possible, *proactively* establish policies for employee behavior that will minimize the likelihood of its occurring.

Employee relations. An organization's responsibility toward its employees is usually interpreted according to legal requirements for employment, job retention, and handling labor grievances. Managers rely on legislation for guidelines, but as noted earlier, many organizations spearheaded human relations programs years before required to do so by law. Xerox Corporation, for example, has followed a policy of affirmative action that transcends law. The Management Application titled "Success Is Color-Blind" introduces Barry Rand, one of the four executives sharing the presidency of Xerox Corporation.

Most managers think of equal employment opportunity and affirmative action legislation in regard to employee relations, and these in turn prompt discussions on discrimination. Discrimination in business is defined as the purposeful blocking of a candidate's employment or promotion opportunities on the basis of color, religion, ethnic background, or sex.[26] The courts have interpreted discriminatory practices to include inequalities in pay, work schedules, training, reassignment, and termination, but the central issue is whether minorities have had equal opportunities to be employed and to advance. This issue concerns all minorities, but the focus of attention in the United States has been on opportunities for blacks.

Bureau of Labor Statistics data show that since 1970, employment opportunities for blacks have consistently improved. In 1970, for example, only 1.3 percent of black Americans held managerial or professional positions; by early 1991, that percentage had increased to 15.7 percent, although much of the increase was attributed to the electoral success of black candidates in public office.[27] A 1985 survey of the Fortune 1000 companies revealed that only 1 percent of 1,362 top managers were

MANAGEMENT APPLICATION

Success Is Color-Blind—Barry Rand of Xerox

Addision Barry Rand is head of Xerox Corporation's U.S. marketing group, the core division for sales and service of Xerox Corporation. Rand is black, but his color has not been a factor in his success at Xerox. He started with the company in 1968 as a salesman and rose to his current position as head of a 33,000-employee division.

At Xerox, black people are spotlighted a little more than whites. Mistakes are amplified, but so are successes, and according to Rand, successful managers cannot afford to dwell on racism. "If I did, I'd go crazy," Rand said. "The issue is not black or white but good business. The U.S. is in a global trade war and we're trying to fight without all our troops. It's not a social issue or a moral issue. It's a business priority." Rand argues that a greater effort is needed to hire blacks and other minorities in major corporations, although he feels that in most instances American companies outpace affirmative action mandates by hiring, training, and promoting blacks. When Rand joined Xerox, the company already had minority hiring policies, educational support programs for minorities, and a "color-blind" promotion system that emphasized results.

According to Rand and other black executives, affirmative action was a bad idea in the first place, "a kind of racial spoils system." Blacks, he says, would rather simply have a level playing field, and many who advanced by merit resent the notion that fellow workers regard them simply as filling a quota to comply with affirmative action. Rand, who has an impressive reputation for inspiring his staff, explains success as the result of teamwork and the willingness to accept a variety of opinions and integrate them into management strategy. "The higher you get in an organization, the more important it is to have people tell you when you are right or wrong," he says. He emphasizes that a manager cannot create a successful team while worrying about a person's color or other personal characteristics. Xerox has developed a culture, in Rand's view, that rewards team results, and the company will support affirmative action—indeed, continue to set a pace ahead of legal mandates—to bring the best team players together.

Source: Courtesy of Xerox Corporation.

black; in 1988, the survey showed an increase to about 9 percent.[28] Clearly there has been a significant increase in black executives. Opportunities for African-Americans, as well as Hispanic-Americans and women, are expected to increase even more rapidly through the 1990s.[29] However, the statistics still show that all minority groups are substantially underrepresented in all professions and managerial positions. American corporations will undoubtedly be held more and more accountable to redress these social inequities. To do this they will have to go beyond the letter of the

Taylor Corporation, a printing business in North Mankato, Minnesota, with 5,000 employees, found it extremely difficult to recruit and retain married women, who make up nearly half of its work force. Therefore, several years ago, it launched a company-sponsored child-care facility and instituted a policy of flexible working hours to accommodate mothers' schedules. The child-care program has more than 150 children and costs Taylor $1,000 per child. Flexible work hours create some inconveniences for scheduling production, but the company reports that problems in recruiting, promoting, and retaining workers have been substantially eliminated.

law (complying with equal employment opportunity and affirmative action guidelines) to implement social programs that help resolve problems for minority groups. Examples of such actions are support for public school programs to help all disadvantaged youth, job training for existing employees to provide them with higher-level skills, and scholarship funding for professional degree programs.

Equal employment and affirmative action issues—though sensitive—are minor concerns of management compared with numerous daily issues involving employees. These issues include pay, benefits, work schedules, training, job assignments, relationships with other workers, relationships between employees and supervisors, safe working conditions, disciplinary policies, and resolution of personal problems such as drug and alcohol addiction. Employees are keenly aware of how managers address these issues, and they evaluate organizations from an internal perspective that transcends the law. Their perceptions are crucial because the productivity and internal effectiveness of a firm's operations rest largely on employee support. Figure 4-5 shows the causal relationships between employee perceptions and support for organizational programs. For example, employees will compare their benefits to those received by employees of other firms, and if their retirement benefits are less, insurance coverage is lacking, or compensation systems are inadequate, an adversarial relationship will emerge between employees and managers.

Beyond these objective issues, employees expect certain types of behavior from management. For example, they expect managers to discipline them fairly and to schedule work equitably. Effective managers, therefore, must consider employee

FIGURE 4-5 Employee Perceptions and Support

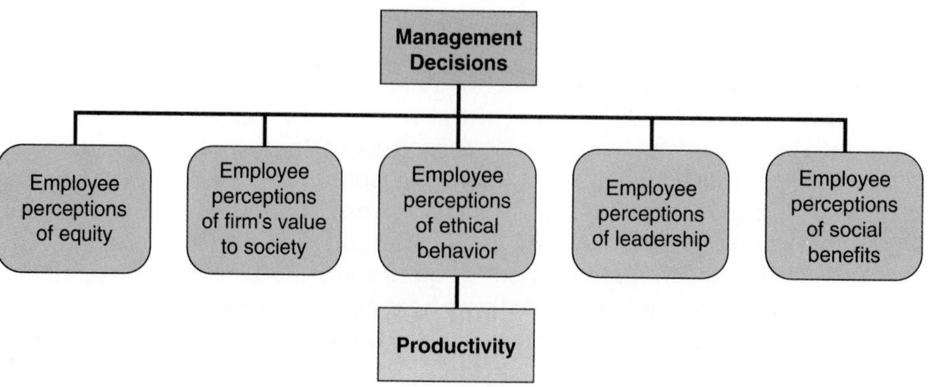

relations in terms of social accountability as well as in terms of legal mandates. A *proactive* response is most appropriate here; it encourages the development of programs, compensation systems, benefits, and employment policies that prevent problems from arising and improve employee satisfaction. Also valuable is an *accommodation* response in which managers seek to resolve employee problems without being defensive or obstructive.

Stockholder and Owner Interests

People who invest money in organizations form a unique special interest group. The prevailing model in free enterprise societies has been for corporate managers to make stockholder interests their first priority. This is based on the belief that those who take the financial risks of investing in a business should reap the highest profits possible from business operations. Focusing on profits, however, may lead to tunnel vision—a narrow perspective that puts short-run results ahead of long-term innovation. Senior managers develop a preoccupation with short-term results because they are often judged by investors and securities traders on their ability to maintain corporate financial strength in the short term.

The danger of short-run thinking is that long-term growth may be sacrificed to near-term profits. For example, a company's profits may be artificially boosted in the short run by taking large equipment depreciation expenses, but if the company continues to use aged equipment, its technology may become outdated. Innovative competitors might then easily capture markets with higher-quality, lower-cost products manufactured with state-of-the-art technology. Other common short-term profit tactics are to hold costs down by cutting personnel, minimizing benefits, or reducing training budgets. Cost reductions achieved this way will help boost profits in the immediate future, but in time, good employees will leave the firm, productivity will suffer, and the firm will face costly long-term reorganization.

Not all firms succumb to the short-run obsession. Most try to satisfy short-run profit objectives while striving to position their companies for long-term success. This is particularly important for unincorporated businesses that lack stockholders; an owner's personal investment is just as important to protect as outside capital. Partnerships and family businesses often rely on profits as their sole source of personal income. When short-run circumstances disrupt revenues, partnerships disintegrate, family members quarrel, and individual livelihoods are lost. Gearing up for long-term success is not easy when the cupboard is bare, and in these desperate situations, social issues are far down on an owner's priority list.

Suppliers

Suppliers, vendors, and contractors form a broad external network of stakeholder relationships vital to management. Organizations rely heavily on raw materials, service, parts, machinery, distribution, and supplies from many individuals and other organizations. Poor relationships with suppliers can result in poor-quality supplies, untimely deliveries, and high prices. Conversely, good relationships can avert these problems. Unfortunately, good relationships are difficult to maintain.

The spectrum of potential relationships runs from dominant supplier to dominant purchaser. Supplier-purchaser behavior can also be viewed as a spectrum running from close and friendly to cold and adversarial. The better the relationships between purchasers and suppliers, the more effective individual firms will be over time.

Bigger firms that place large orders can easily dominate smaller suppliers. When the purchasing firm has tremendous economic power, it can often dictate prices and terms to suppliers. The influence flows decidedly in one direction. For example, Wal-Mart, the world's largest retail merchandiser, has more than 12,000 individual suppliers. Because Wal-Mart's success rests on being able to offer consistently low customer prices, its purchasing managers must negotiate diligently with each supplier for the best price and terms.[30] Wal-Mart and other large buyers have a tremendous advantage, but not a mandate to bully smaller suppliers. If suppliers feel large client firms are flaunting their power, they may become uncooperative. Adversarial relationships can result in disrupted delivery schedules, unpleasant publicity, and contract disputes. These are costly to both parties.

Another concern is that suppliers know a great deal about their client companies' operations. If suppliers are bled by powerful purchasers, they may become promiscuous with information that finds its way to competitors. Motorola, for instance, provides microcomputer chips to forty different manufacturers of microcomputers, and has access to a great deal of information about computer specifications, production schedules, and sales projections of each buyer. If Compaq or IBM do not maintain good relationships with Motorola, proprietary information about their operations could perhaps "leak" out to several dozen competitors.

On the other side of the coin, it is possible for large and powerful suppliers to impose on their smaller clients by delivering goods at their own convenience, pricing at premium rates, and passing on unwanted products of poor quality. Customers in these instances are "price takers" who may not have alternative suppliers.

Competitors

Organizations compete with one another in recognized ways for customers and sales, but this level of competition is only a small part of the overall picture. Each organization must secure materials, workers, capital, and other resources essential to business, ranging from preferred distribution systems to legal rights to technological innovations. In relation to ethical behavior, competition must be viewed from two distinct perspectives: first, how companies compete for customers; and second, how they compete for resources.

Customer considerations. At the customer level, managers often gain unwanted news coverage from predatory pricing practices and manipulative promotions. The likelihood of callous behavior, perhaps outright consumer fraud, increases dramatically when competition intensifies. Prior to the 1960s, when pressure from consumer groups forced government to begin a program of legislative intervention, the public was often victimized by deceptive practices. Exhibit 4-1 summarizes key legislation designed to protect consumers. The results of these important acts include more truthful advertising, informative packaging, safety instructions, and legal remedies for consumers who have fallen prey to unscrupulous managers. Laws, however, are only tools that conscientious managers will use appropriately to make good decisions.[31]

Consumers are the primary beneficiaries of protective legislation, but companies within an industry also benefit. Penalties for making untruthful claims about a product have made unsavory practices costly. It is safer and usually more cost effective to simply improve the product's quality, thereby providing consumers with greater value for their money.

Resource considerations. There is relatively little regulation at the second level of competition: resources. The struggle for resources can be cutthroat; at the minimum, it is an arena of intense free enterprise. Significant research in this field has been conducted at the Harvard Business School and published by Michael Porter in his exceptional work *Competitive Strategy*.[32] Porter explains that organizations must not only have access to sufficient raw materials, but must also generate cost-effective relationships with resource vendors. He extends the concept of strong ven-

EXHIBIT 4-1 Selected Legislation Related to Consumers

Food, Drug, and Cosmetic Act Amendments of 1962	Require pretesting of drugs and related substances for safety and stated effectiveness and prescribe that all drugs be labeled with generic names.
Federal Cigarette Labeling and Advertising Act of 1965	Requires labels on cigarette packages warning consumers of hazards of smoking.
Fair Packaging and Labeling Act of 1966	Known as the *truth-in-packaging act,* mandates labeling for identification and use of household products, including sensitive ingredients and combinations.
Consumer Credit Protection Act of 1968	Known as the *truth-in-lending act,* requires full disclosure of all terms and conditions of finance charges for installment purchases and consumer loans.
Child Protection and Toy Safety Act of 1969	Expands requirements for child protection to include products related to electrical, mechanical, and thermal hazards.
Consumer Product Safety Act of 1972	Major legislation that established the Consumer Product Safety Commission, with authority for creating and policing consumer product safety standards and for controlling risk-related products, including legal remedies for injuries.

dor relationships to financial sources (bankers, money market brokers, and stockholders); subcontractors of equipment, tooling, and parts; and labor markets (employment bureaus, universities, and unions).

Organizations compete for raw materials on a daily basis. Purchasing managers vie for price advantages, quality materials, advantageous shipping schedules, and preferential treatment by suppliers. When purchasing is effective, a firm's cash flow is improved and its costs are minimized. If, for example, a company spending 40 percent of its money on material is able to acquire the same materials for 10 percent less, the difference represents "up-front" cash. This gain can be directly passed on to consumers through lower prices, resulting in a significant market advantage for the company. In many highly competitive industries, profits are rather small, so a slight savings in materials can have a huge impact on profit margins.

Competition for materials can sometimes result in unpleasant or illegal behavior. Bribery is not unusual, particularly if raw materials are located overseas, where "buying" supply contracts is a way of life. Special favors and gifts to suppliers are not uncommon, and other unethical tactics range from kickbacks to providing "escort services" for buyers. The importance of securing ample materials at favorable prices cannot be overemphasized, but clearly the potential for managerial misconduct is substantial.

Technology considerations. Competition for materials and supplies is mirrored by fierce competition for new technology and advantageous use of innovations. Patents, copyrights, and trademarks help protect organizations to some extent, but there is still a tremendous amount of corporate piracy. This activity is particularly evident in high-tech, high-growth industries such as computers and microcomputer software. Few guidelines exist for these growth industries. Even in those instances where the law is clear, piracy of innovations such as valuable software programs cannot be adequately policed.[33] Patents and other means of legal protection provide a form of legal retribution, but they cannot prevent the theft of technology to begin with. Thus they are of little help to a firm that has spent years perfecting a new product only to see it compromised, copied, or stolen by competitors.

Personnel considerations. Pirating of personnel is also a common business problem. Competition becomes conflict when organizations surreptitiously entice key managers, inventors, engineers, or other important personnel away from one another. The loss of a key molecular geneticist, software developer, or computer systems designer can destroy an emerging firm. Key individuals who change jobs take with them valuable knowledge of their previous organizations. Gaining an insider's view of a competitor's operations and familiarity with a competitor's proprietary technology gives the acquiring firm a tremendous advantage. It is not surprising that well-placed managers in high-tech firms enjoy huge under-the-table bonuses along with their extraordinary salaries and benefits. In an age when knowledge is a premium resource, corporate espionage has given new meaning to the task of personnel recruitment.[34]

CHECKPOINT

- What is a "boundary-spanning role" for managers?
- Identify and discuss the various constituents who influence managers and their decisions.
- How have employee-management relations changed in recent years? Argue from the viewpoint of property rights and employee expectations.
- Describe various aspects of competition and how managers must concern themselves with ethical relationships between competitors.

GOVERNMENT REGULATION

Competition is ultimately regulated by federal and local governments, and although laws sharply distinguish between legal and illegal conduct, many managerial decisions fall into a gray area where legality becomes a matter of interpretation. Courts are therefore called upon to rule on cases, and when these decisions become a matter of record, they add to the body of regulation. In most instances, court decisions simply clarify legislation, but clarification often means more restrictive interpretations of regulations that further limit managerial freedom to make decisions.

It is natural to think of business regulation as a federal province because the U.S. Congress has enacted nearly fifty major statutes in this area since the mid-1960s. State and local governments, however, also exert tremendous influence over businesses. For example, local authorities administer license laws, constrain business operating hours, regulate advertising, impose taxes, and police environmental protection laws. State governments regulate legal forms of business, hazardous waste disposal, insurance, and employment practices. Agencies at all levels of government exercise power over business. For example, the Internal Revenue Service exerts control through its interpretation of tax laws. At the executive level, presidential orders—called Executive Orders—carry the weight of law even though not enacted by Congress. It is not surprising that Americans have mixed emotions about legislative intervention. Those managers who spend time and money filling out forms and wrestling with regulations may feel harnessed to a system of lawful oppression. Yet managers who benefit from government intervention praise it for forcing improvements on society. Let us examine both viewpoints.[35]

The Case for Government Regulation

The federal government has a constitutional mandate to protect individuals through effective legal systems, to provide protection of property rights, to create services that benefit a majority of citizens, and to ensure the national security. It follows that services such as fire and police protection, court systems for adjudicating disputes, and military agencies are mandated government responsibilities. When government becomes involved in regulating how employees are hired, disciplined, fired, or retired, the mandate is far less clear. Supporters of government regulation point to an impressive body of evidence that business managers have exploited workers, mismanaged human resources, and made poor decisions about equal opportunities, thereby compelling our society to rely on government intervention to correct these abuses. The underpinning of this argument is that when business fails to manage itself effectively in areas that affect the general welfare, the only recourse is government coercion.[36]

Many business organizations benefit directly from regulations such as protective trade tariffs, antitrust legislation, fair pricing statutes, securities and investment regulations, truth-in-advertising laws, and a host of guidelines relating to safety, radiation control, credit reporting, bank reporting, and hazardous materials controls. Businesses are also aided by regulatory agencies such as the Food and Drug Administration, the Federal Communications Commission, the Interstate Commerce Commission, and the Securities and Exchange Commission. Not all managers agree that regulation by these agencies is beneficial, but supporters are able to cite advantages gained by firms and industries through regulatory controls.[37]

The arguments for government intervention often stereotype managers as categorically against regulation. They depict the typical business manager as a cold, unfeeling capitalist bureaucrat who pollutes rivers, dumps radioactive materials in school yards, and exploits employees to make a profit. Such stereotyping is unfortunate because the vast majority of managers are humane, responsible, and concerned citizens. Many also support government intervention, believing that regulation will not harm well-managed firms.[38]

The Case Against Government Regulation

Most arguments against regulation center on cost and profit issues. Social obligations, particularly those imposed by law, cost money. When reasonable, these costs are not a problem. But the burden of meeting government-imposed reporting standards, documenting behavior, and otherwise informing government agencies of business operations can be tremendous.

Economists have estimated that the direct costs of federal reporting exceed $100 billion annually, and even that estimate has been refuted as too low. A prestigious study by the Brookings Institution estimated that program costs associated with just one agency, the Environmental Protection Agency (EPA), are more than $50 billion per year, with annual increases approaching $10 billion projected for the early 1990s.[39] For all this cost, the study found no measurable improvement in environmental factors in any of the major EPA program areas.

Critics of regulation cite these extraordinary costs and the massive diversion of resources to unproductive ends as evidence against the social benefit of government regulation.[40] The effects on business are such that stockholders, consumers, and employees all come off losers. Stockholders lose in terms of reduced profits; hence, firms with stiff regulatory obligations tend to be less attractive to investors. Consumers lose by having to pay higher prices for goods and services. Finally, employees, particularly managers, suffer by having to redirect efforts away from productive operations toward compliance activities.

With all the information we have about the health dangers of smoking, it seems amazing to us today that an ad like this could have ever been used. The ad appeared in 1950. By 1970, the Public Health Smoking Act banned cigarette advertising on radio and TV. The FTC had already enacted the "Cigarette Rule" in 1965, which first required the now familiar "Surgeon General's" warning labels on cigarette packages.

The Brookings Institution study suggested several other, more subtle, problems with regulations. New enterprises, for example, must comply with many more regulations and meet more rigorous guidelines than established firms. The reason is that older firms simply could not continue doing business if they had to make sudden comprehensive changes to meet the levels of compliance required by newer legislation, so the legislation specifically exempted them. In contrast, new high-growth enterprises are hobbled by mountains of regulations administered by government agencies.

Opponents of government intervention maintain that in a free enterprise system government involvement must be minimized. Nobel Prize laureate Milton Friedman, the most outspoken critic of government regulation, argues that businesses exist to maximize economic benefits for customers, stockholders, and employees. He believes that a strong market system provides the best overall distribution of goods and services, and that government should confine its role to public issues and services for the good of society as a whole.[41]

Reconciling the Issues

Although there is no clear resolution in sight to the debate between those "for" and "against" government regulation, there is broad agreement about where we stand today. Recall that Adam Smith argued that a nation's wealth is measured in the total goods and services created by a robust free enterprise system. He emphasized business activities that increased this wealth. Thus the classic position, as argued in modern times by Milton Friedman, is that managers should focus their attention squarely on wealth creation. Progress—if that is the proper term for wealth creation—has always incurred social costs, including unemployment, pollution, poverty, discrimination, unsafe products, and unhealthy work environments. Because the traditional management perspective provided no clear solutions to these problems, government ultimately had to step in. Now we have a situation where public policy, regulation, and social pressure all require managers to consider their actions in light of how they will avoid or help to rectify social problems.[42]

At the macrolevel, business must provide society with goods and services within the parameters of a healthy economic system of competition. The macroperspective also includes solving the problem of providing the public with goods and

Recently released from a quarter-century of imprisonment, Nelson Mandela of the African National Congress has fought all his life against *apartheid*, the doctrine of keeping black and white cultures separate in South Africa. Apartheid is an enduring ethical issue for countries and businesses around the world, and the 1980s saw many American and European business leaders pull their companies and investments out of South Africa to protest the doctrine. Their message was received by South African business leaders, who in March 1992 strongly supported an important referendum that proposed to decrease the political power of the white minority and increase the power of the black majority.

services such as defense systems and utilities without shackling private enterprise. At the microlevel, individual firms and managers must find ways to incorporate public policy and social expectations into their daily business operations. Consequently, a socially responsible company will support public programs such as environmentally safe waste recycling efforts, and engender in its daily operations ethical behavior such as assuring equal opportunity and pursuing affirmative action. Although most managers agree their organizations should be socially responsible, few concede that government regulation is necessary or effective in achieving this end.

Business and environmental researchers at Harvard found that as we entered the 1990s, most business managers, government leaders, and environmental special interest groups were trying to do the right thing.[43] Their objectives with regard to many social issues were similar, and as world environmental, social, and humanistic problems escalate, there is a growing convergence of opinion on the need to find resolutions. Unfortunately, many efforts have proved disappointing because each group (business, government, and private interests) has worked independently, often in direct conflict with other groups' activities. In other words, everyone seems to agree on the objectives, but few agree about how to achieve them.[44]

CHECKPOINT

- Present the case for government regulation in terms of direct intervention into business affairs.
- Explore the arguments against government regulation that intervenes in business activities.
- How would you reconcile the differences between those who argue for and those who argue against government intervention?

THE RESPONSIVE MANAGER—A CHANGING ROLE

The rapidly changing role of business in society has altered managerial decision-making roles within companies and redefined a firm's relationships to other companies and societies on a global scale. Today government and business leaders in Europe and North America are confronted with problems such as how to help the former Soviet republics feed their people and to avoid economic collapse. They are sought after by East Europeans to help resolve that region's immense industrial pollution problem and to help create an infrastructure of commerce out of the ruins of state-run economies. They are pressuring South Africa to honor a code of human rights and debating international legislation on environmental waste standards, nuclear power, and conservation. Meanwhile, these leaders are confronted at home with the necessity to improve employment opportunities, clean up industrial and nuclear waste, redesign products to be safer, and ensure adequate health care for their own people.

These global and domestic concerns challenge managers to redefine their own roles even as they educate the next generation of managers to deal with still more complex relationships and problems. There are several specific skills that will help managers grow into these new roles. What follows is a brief discussion of these skills.[45]

Broadened Awareness

Managers need to broaden their awareness of internal and external forces that influence their organization. They now have to deal with a wide array of legislation, employee expectations, and external constituents, and must expect to be held accountable for their decisions. Traditional financial objectives are no less important than ever, but should be seen as only part of a much larger array of objectives.

This broadened awareness does not apply solely to executives. Managers at all levels must fine-tune their decisions to ensure organizational success. Social responsibility is a pervasive concern of people in positions of accountability. Few managers today, no matter how technically competent they may be, can get away with ignoring the broader system of constituents. Broadened awareness can be achieved through management education and development programs, but perhaps it is most successfully attained by those who teach themselves to consider the viewpoints of others when making decisions.

Integrative Ability

The collective process of organizational endeavor must be integrated. Some managers will have greater responsibility than others for integrating the behavior of subordinates in subunit operations, but it is essential at every level to coordinate functions. In more complex organizations, this process can be extremely difficult because many environmental and economic considerations must be integrated into managers' decisions. The stakeholders of an organization have expectations of performance that also must be considered. An associated skill for integrating behavior is empathy—the quality of being sensitive to others and aware of the ripple effect of one's decisions.

Effective Communications

In a world of intricate relationships, effective communication is critical to success. There are several important dimensions to this skill. Essentially, managers must be able to articulate expectations as well as listen effectively to discern the expectations of constituents. They must also be able to persuade others to behave in desired ways. Employees must be convinced to work toward clear goals, and stockholders must be encouraged to support management in strategies for long-term success. The public must be persuaded that the company is honest, ethical, and valuable to society.

Political Sensitivity

Even the best technical training does not prepare managers for survival in a complex organization. A firm's political environment is often unique, and managers must learn how to work in harness—to adapt to circumstances, form coalitions, direct group activities, participate according to leadership expectations, and respond to superiors' expectations. In effect, survival may require a great deal of personal accommodation. It might also require a change in careers for those who cannot reconcile personal and corporate ethics.

The implication is not that managers must bow to the whims of others or compromise their ethics, but that they must be sensitive to political reality and make appropriate and ethical decisions without abdicating responsibility. Organizations change partly because of changes in management behavior. Therefore, individual managers who find existing organizational behavior unacceptable cannot just ignore ethically difficult situations. Instead, they have the responsibility to implement changes that help the organization and enrich society.

Intellectual Ability

The multifaceted role of managers today calls for intellectual skills far greater than those needed in the past. Our global economy requires managers not only to be technically competent but also to be capable of adapting to different cultures and international business practices. Because the explosive changes of our information age are so overwhelming, some people focus too narrowly on analytical skills; they sharpen their abilities in quantitative techniques at the expense of their social skills. Quantitative skills are indeed important, but it is easy to become absorbed in them and neglect the human and emotional side of management. Quantitative skills should be supplemented by a liberal education so that managers can better relate to the external world and to their constituents.

Ethics and the Growth of Responsible Management

From an organizational viewpoint, developing an ethical culture may be the ultimate goal to ensure a progressive, socially responsible company. From the viewpoint of an individual manager, developing a sense of ethics to support consistent, responsible decisions is vital. A strong sense of ethics is arguably the preeminent factor in determining how managers will use their broadened awareness, integrative ability, communicative skills, political awareness, and intellect. Recall that ethics is concerned with morality as defined by the prevailing values of society. For managers within a particular organization, this means that social values must be understood, accepted, and communicated through a code of ethics that guides decisions and behavior.

Leading companies are instilling their employees with a strong ethical sensibility through ethics training programs and management development efforts.[46] General Electric, for example, has a code of conduct that anchors a program of ethics education. The GE program includes formal management development seminars, presentations by experts, and case studies to give managers and employees practical exposure to ethical dilemmas. IBM has annual ethics review seminars for employees throughout the company, and it holds indoctrination training for all new employees. Citicorp has developed The Citicorp Ethics Game, a board game accompanied by a sixty-page booklet of decisions and situations that constitute a comprehensive course for employees.[47] Nearly half of all Fortune 500 companies have some means of formal education in ethics. This is a proactive response to the general problem of irresponsible or naive decisions that violate public values and expectations for business conduct.

CHECKPOINT

- What is meant by "broadened awareness" and "integrative skills"?
- Describe "communicative skill" and "political sensitivity" as tools for improving managerial decisions.
- Considering how complex world affairs have become, what intellectual abilities are likely to be important to future managers?
- Explain how training and development programs are helping to promote an ethics culture for organizations.

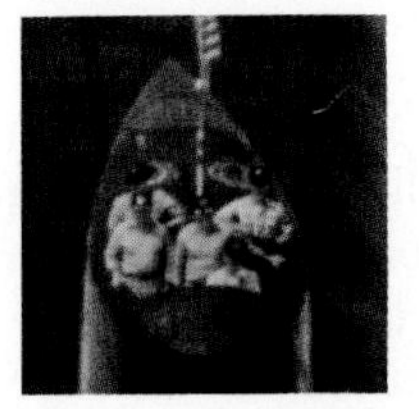

AT THE BEGINNING OF THE CHAPTER, General Dynamics was profiled as an example of a good company with a strong ethics program. The company, like many others, was induced to adopt this program by the questionable behavior of some of its managers. Many other companies, among them Hewlett-Packard, IBM, and General Electric, have long-standing codes of conduct and comprehensive training programs. Because some companies need goading, private interest groups bring pressure for greater government regulation, and because many managers still choose to operate their businesses in questionable ways, government regulation forces compliance. While there are few clear conclusions about how far the government should go in regulating business, it is indisputable that American managers are becoming more keenly aware of their social responsibilities.

Managers are challenged, however, by a global environment that is constantly changing and becoming more complicated. A corporate code of ethics is only a starting point for understanding how to make effective decisions when dealing with multiple cultures and peoples on several continents. Ethics are relative to each culture, and they can change dramatically over time at home as well as overseas. Constant attention to changing values among a company's stakeholders is thus mandated for effective management. ■

A SYNOPSIS FOR LEARNING

1. Identify cultural and social changes that influence management decisions.

Changes in technology, human rights, social systems, social demographics, competition, global enterprise, and scientific innovations affect not only the way managers behave but also how organizations are structured and how managers are accountable to society for their decisions.

2. Define and discuss ethical behavior in management.

Business ethics are concerned with moral right and wrong as applied to business enterprise and managerial behavior. *Ethics* are related to how managers accomplish their tasks, and this is largely determined by society's expectations for responsible behavior.

3. Discuss relationships between managers and their constituents.

Viewed from a systems perspective, managers have far-reaching responsibilities to many constituents. Constituents, called *stakeholders,* include employees, consumers, investors, suppliers, competitors, local citizens, and society at large. Managers have the responsibility to provide safe and reliable products to consumers and at the same time maintain profits for investors.

4. Explain the role of government regulation in business operations and discuss the cases for and against government regulation.

Government regulation is meant to protect society and to improve the quality of life for all citizens. Local authorities control licenses, regulate advertising, impose taxes, and police the environment. State agencies regulate employment practices and provide for public welfare. Federal agencies enforce safety rules, monitor product reliability, impose regulations for commercial drugs, and scrutinize interstate commerce. Arguments for and against regulation are framed in terms of government intervention in commercial enterprises. Those opposed to government intervention maintain that free enterprise and unrestrained trade produce the best products and services for consumers at the best prices. Those in favor of government intervention emphasize the need to protect consumers, suppliers, and competitors from exploitative practices, unfair pricing, discriminatory hiring practices, unsafe products, and unhealthy work environments.

5. Examine how managers can become more responsive to social issues.

   Individually, managers must accept a changing role in society. They must broaden their awareness of domestic and global social issues, and integrate new values into their organizations. By improving their communicative skills and becoming more politically sensitive to expectations by public constituents, managers can improve their organization's ability to respond effectively to social problems. Intellectual sensitivity to social issues helps managers make better individual decisions. These issues are emphasized in the ethics training and management development programs of many of our best companies.

SKILL ANALYSIS

CASE 1 Social Responsibility of Business: The *Exxon Valdez* Fiasco

Few sights are more beautiful than the Alaskan coastline. Towering snow-capped peaks rise from virgin forests and glaciers that form glistening cathedrals of ice around the gulf of Alaska. Nestled in an inlet near the top of the gulf lies the port of Valdez, a small fishing town that sits at the entrance to Prince William Sound. Founded during the Alaskan gold rush, it is the southern terminus of the Richardson highway and the Trans-Alaskan pipeline.

In the early hours of March 24, 1989, disaster struck Valdez. The tanker *Exxon Valdez* struck a reef in the sound and dumped eleven million gallons of oil into the sea.[48]

This was not the first catastrophe to strike Valdez. Exactly 25 years earlier, on March 24, 1964, a tidal wave resulting from the great Alaskan earthquake had leveled the port and destroyed most of the fishing boats there. However, Alaskans saw this first disaster quite differently. The tidal wave was an "act of God"; the oil spill was man-made and therefore preventable. At the very least, most Alaskans saw it as controllable. Unfortunately, those responsible were caught unprepared. The tanker's owner, Exxon, failed to control the damage immediately after the accident. This caused many Alaskans and many more people throughout the United States to question the company's willingness and ability to respond effectively to problems it had a hand in creating.

Exxon was unable to initiate cleanup efforts for well over two days. By then, the oil had spread into a slick that rapidly became uncontainable. Just as containment and cleanup efforts got under way, calm weather gave way to high winds that spread the slick from its initial 4 square miles to over 900 square miles. Aside from defiling over 400 miles of coastline, the slick created a deadly threat to the abundant marine and bird life in Prince William Sound.

Perhaps most disturbing to many Americans was the widely held notion that the disaster should never have happened in the first place. Among the first issues raised was that the *Exxon Valdez* was a single- rather than a double-hulled ship. (The double hull would have greatly reduced the likelihood of a leak, given the na-

ture of the accident.) Others pointed out that the accident might never have occurred had the company adhered to its own policies on alcoholism among its employees. The tanker's captain, Joseph Hazelwood, had a history of alcoholism and was determined by the Coast Guard to be drunk when the ship ran aground. Six years earlier he had undergone treatment for alcoholism under a company rehabilitation program. Exxon's policy called for immediate dismissal of any person who continued to drink after going through a rehabilitation program. The captain had been convicted on driving-while-intoxicated charges three times since completing the rehabilitation program.

Even after the tanker ran aground, a quick cleanup might have been possible had the necessary equipment and manpower been available. Alyeska, the consortium of oil companies that runs the Alaskan pipeline, had earlier reported, per contractual agreement, that it had a contingency plan that would provide resources sufficient to clean up a major spill within five hours of its occurrence. However, lulled by twelve years of shipping oil through Valdez without a major spill, Alyeska had let its equipment run down and no longer maintained full-time crews for handling spills.

The first crews and equipment to reach the spill did not do so until ten hours after it occurred. Booms intended to contain the oil and mechanical skimmers to scoop it up were barely enough to handle a spill one-hundredth the size of that at Valdez. Finally, the barge designed to receive the skimmed oil was under maintenance and inoperable until the following day.

Particularly infuriating to many residents and politicians were Exxon's early communiqués assuring that the disaster was under control and that beach cleanups and booming operations were well under way. Within a few days, however, company officials admitted that the cleanup had not yet begun. Exxon's chief executive officer, Lawrence Rawl, later blamed the delays on the intransigence of the Alaskan Coast Guard and a state environmental agency over the use of chemical dispersants, but many felt that the finger pointed squarely at Exxon.

Although huge numbers of birds, fish, and marine animals died as a result of the initial spill, the full implications of the disaster were not realized until later. Much of the oil coagulated and sank to the bottom of the sea, where it continues to slowly release toxic hydrocarbons. It is anticipated that these toxins will contaminate microorganisms, the small fish that eat them, and larger fish and animals all the way up the food chain. Some experts predicted that the fishing industry in Prince William Sound will be all but destroyed in years to come. However, CEO Rawl discounted these predictions about the spill's long-term impact on the environment, labelling those making them "prophets of doom." He claimed that the company would be able to completely negate any damage to the environment.

Environmental experts doubted Rawl's claims, and contended that nothing Exxon could do would ever return the environment to its former pristine state. To its credit, Exxon did mount a huge effort to make up for its earlier failures, albeit only under escalating public outrage, worsening public image, and the threat that Congress would refuse to award Alyeska the right to drill for oil in the Arctic National Wildlife Preserve. Exxon initially deployed a task force of 3,500 men and women to clean up the area and committed over $95 million to the effort. By 1991, the company had spent $3 billion on cleanup programs. Scientists have predicted that the total cost of the disaster—including lost revenues as well as the money spent on the cleanup effort—could eventually exceed $15 billion.

Recognizing Exxon's huge expenditures and efforts to solve the oil spill problem, a federal court fined the company only $150 million on criminal charges, ordered it to pay $100 million in restitution to the state of Alaska, and settled civil litigation charges brought against Exxon jointly by the federal government and Alaska for $900 million. However, Exxon still faces nearly 200 separate lawsuits by environmental groups, Native Alaskan authorities, and litigants from various wildlife, fishing, and tourist industries in Alaska.

Case Questions

1. Were the actions taken by Exxon immediately after the accident responsible or irresponsible? Explain your answer.
2. What steps can firms like Exxon take to prevent disasters comparable to those at Valdez?
3. What ethical questions were raised by the *Exxon Valdez* oil spill?

VIDEO CASE White-Collar Crime Doesn't Pay

The decade of the 1980s will long be remembered for the number of its publicized white-collar crimes and the people who committed them: Ivan Boesky, Michael Milkin, Dennis Levine, Charles Keating—names tied tightly to securities laws violations and the savings and loan scandal.

Numerous other illegal and unethical corporate activities were exposed during the 1980s. Consider the $400 hammers and $600 ashtrays billed by defense contractors to the Department of Defense (DOD). The DOD suggested to contractors that they appoint in-house watchdogs to control these kinds of abuses. In response, a spokesperson from the Corporate Ombudsman Association stated, "What the Defense Department obviously had in mind was someone who would, on a confidential basis, be able to receive telephone calls and reports from people working in the work environment about such things as fraud or mismanagement or cost overruns that they thought were unjustified." That is, the DOD wanted contractors to encourage "whistleblowing." Offering whistleblowers a confidential way to report illegal or unethical activities was seen as a step toward in-house policing.

New sentencing guidelines for federal judges dealing with white-collar criminals went into effect on November 1, 1991. The indent was to encourage companies to monitor the legality and ethicality of their own activities by providing punishment for white-collar crimes. The new guidelines have doubled the average fines for companies found guilty of such crimes as fraud. Thus a company responsible for a fraud of $1 million would face a minimum fine of $1 million. At the same time, the new guidelines stipulate that companies with compliance programs or ethics policies will be treated more leniently. Said the chairman of the committee that developed the new sentencing guidelines, "Crime committed within organizations can never be detected by law enforcement. We need to depend on the organization to self-police itself, to turn itself in."

According to one expert in the field of ethics, ensuring compliance with the law through self-policing is not enough, for focusing only on compliance means dealing with abuses and problems after the fact. Michael Josephson, president of the Josephson Institute of Ethics, believes that to avert ethical problems companies need to "acknowledge that being honest is an absolute, being fair is an absolute, being respectful is an absolute, and you don't just ask, 'What can I get away with under today's regulations?'" Corporate managers often find it difficult to make these kinds of commitments and resolutions. However, some companies are trying to be more ethical in their business dealings and are encouraging all their employees to act ethically in their business activities. For example, Pacific Bell Corporation has had an Office of Business Conduct and Standards since 1988. The ombudsman for Pacific Bell says about this department, "I believe that it gives employees and vendors a place to go where they can get their concerns and allegations aired."

Now that employee whistleblowing is legally encouraged, top managers cannot escape responsibility for misconduct in business dealings. In fact, the new sentencing guidelines state that if managers are judged to be "willfully ignorant," the corporation will be severely sanctioned. Will these new guidelines noticeably reduce illegal and unethical behavior in corporate America? Only the next few years will tell.

Case Questions

1. What are the good points about the new sentencing guidelines? What are the bad points? What changes, if any, would you make in the guidelines?
2. The chairman of the committee that developed these new sentencing guidelines stated that "We need to depend on the organization to self-police itself, to turn itself in." Do you think self-policing will work? Why or why not? What would you do to encourage self-policing in organizations?
3. You have been asked by your manager to design a way to protect whistleblowers within your organization. What suggestions would you make?
4. Find some examples in the media of companies that are being proactive in their ethical approaches. Describe what these companies are doing.

Sources: Nicholas M. DeFeis, "Implications of the New Sentencing Guidelines," *Bankers Magazine,* January–February 1992, Vol. 175, No. 1, p. 40ff; Mark Stevens, "Crime and Punishment," *Small Business Reports,* October 1991, Vol. 16, No. 10, p. 65ff; and "Make It Hurt," *The Economist,* May 4, 1991, Vol. 319, No. 7705, p. 71ff.

SKILL PRACTICE

WORK VALUES

Introduction

What do people want to get out of their work? What values do they want to fulfill through work?

In this exercise, you have an opportunity to think about your own priorities for what you want from work. You also have a chance to look at data on the priorities of others and compare your reasons for continuing to work with the answers given by a survey of business students by Nicholas Beutell and O. C. Brenner (1986).

Instructions

1. The instructor forms groups of five to nine persons. Each group should be composed *entirely* of *men or women.*

2. Each group meets separately in locations designated by the instructor. Group meetings should last *15 minutes* at most.
3. Each group performs the following tasks:
   a. *Without discussion* with others, rank-order the nine items in the survey under column A (Myself).
   b. Then decide *as a group* how you believe *most* people of the gender opposite that of the group would rank these items. Place those ranks under column B or C.
4. Appoint a spokesperson to present the group's conclusions to the entire class.
5. Each spokesperson has *5 minutes* to present his or her group's conclusions. *Male* representatives will speak *first*.
6. When all speakers have finished, the instructor will present the answers found in Beutell and Brenner's study.

The instructor will conduct a discussion of the issues raised by the exercise. The central issue seems to be the assumption that men and women want something different from work. (Minimum of 20 minutes)

What Do We Value in Work?

Instructions: Please *rank-order* the nine items in terms of how important they would be to you in a job. Indicate the most important reason by putting the number "1" by that item in column A (Myself). Put a "2" by the second most important, and so on, until you have put a "9" by the least important. (No ties, please.) When you have finished ranking the items for yourself, rank them in column B as you *believe* most male business students would rank them. (Think in terms of the average person rather than of individuals holding particular jobs.) Finally, rank-order the items as you *believe* most female business students would rank them in column C.

How important is it to you to have a job which . . .

	A Myself	B Men	C Women
1. Is respected by other people	______	______	______
2. Encourages continued development of knowledge and skills	______	______	______
3. Provides job security	______	______	______
4. Provides a feeling of accomplishment	______	______	______
5. Provides the opportunity to earn a high income	______	______	______
6. Is intellectually stimulating	______	______	______
7. Rewards good performance with recognition	______	______	______
8. Provides comfortable working conditions	______	______	______
9. Permits advancement to high administrative responsibility	______	______	______
My Sex:	______ Male		
	______ Female		

Source: R. J. Lewicki et al., *Experiences in Management and Organizational Behavior,* 3rd ed. (New York: Wiley, 1988), pp. 23–27. Reprinted by permission.

PART ONE INTEGRATIVE CASE

The Worst Industrial Accident in History

On December 3, 1984, a deadly gas leak at Union Carbide Corporation's plant near Bhopal, India, killed over 2,000 people and injured more than 200,000 others. It is the worst industrial accident ever recorded, and legal issues stemming from it may continue into the next century. More than $35 billion in lawsuits were filed against Union Carbide on behalf of victims. Stockholders filed another $1 billion in suits alleging management malfeasance. As a result, the company's stock fell, and investors have not been abundant in recent years.

The gas that leaked is methyl isocyanate, a highly toxic chemical used to make pesticides. It is several hundred times more lethal than cyanide, and so volatile that contact with another substance can create an explosion. This is essentially what happened at the Indian plant. The night before, a storage tank started boiling from moisture or some other substance that had gotten inside it. The night managers ignored instrument readings that signaled an unstable situation in the tank because, they explained later, the instruments were never correct, most being corroded. Even the safety cooling system designed to counteract a "boil" had been inoperative for more than a year. Several hours after the initial problem began, the emergency valves on the storage tank exploded, and toxic gas spewed into the air through a pipestack. Emergency procedures broke down when equipment failed and neutralizing agents could not be used to subdue the gas.

The gas moved as a cloud toward nearby villages and through crowded shantytowns. Victims choked to death as the gas filled their lungs. Thousands who escaped death were blinded by the caustic property of the gas. Thousands more were seriously burned by the chemical.

When the accident made headline news around the world, the thrust of the coverage was that a giant American company, Union Carbide, had been involved in the deaths of thousands of innocent persons in Bhopal, India. Warren M. Anderson, chairman of Union Carbide Corporation, never denied the company's responsibility. Indeed, within months, Anderson was on record with the full facts of the accident, offering over $200 million in compensation to victims. He was jailed (but quickly released) in India on criminal negligence charges, but he was never accused of being complacent or trying to cover up the issues.

The Union Carbide India, Ltd., plant was, in fact, a subsidiary of the American mother company, Union Carbide Corporation. But only a bare majority interest of 50.9 percent was held by the American company, and Union Carbide India, Ltd., had just one American executive on its board of directors. Moreover, although executives at the firm's U.S. headquarters controlled strategic planning, set major policies, and created technical directives for all divisions, the Indian plant operated almost autonomously. In fact, its key directors were from India and Hong Kong, and Indian managers handled all daily activities at all plant levels. Top Union Carbide executives in the United States controlled long-term budgets and capital assets, but U.S. managers acted as consultants, visiting the subsidiary locations and helping to correct problems, rather than as operating managers. Early in 1984, three top U.S. engineers had inspected the facilities and made a list of crucial things to correct, including corrosion on pipes and nonfunctioning emergency equipment. They also recommended safety precaution training for operators. Later, follow-up reports from the Indian managers indicated that the recommended corrective actions had been taken. Actually, however, they had not been completed.

Another factor that may have contributed to the accident was that the subsidiary had been losing money and local managers had initiated cost-cutting measures, including layoffs of operational personnel and reduction of maintenance costs. These actions resulted in stressful relationships between workers and managers, causing even more employees to leave. By the time of the accident, most experienced workers had departed and had been replaced largely by illiterate workers who knew little about the danger of the chemicals they came into contact with. Yet, despite these problems, Indian laborers continued to be eager to work for Union Carbide. In fact, the company represented a small economic miracle for many families in this remote region, providing jobs, medical benefits, improved housing, and social programs. Before the plant was built in 1969, the villages in this region were destitute. This was one reason that the government of India had urged Union Carbide to set up and operate the plant in Bhopal.

The Indian government also recognized that the rest of the country would derive tremendous social and economic benefits from the Bhopal subsidiary. And it did. For example, the pesticide made by the plant helped India cut grain losses by 10 percent. This figure represented an annual savings of 15 million tons of grain, sufficient to feed nearly 70 million people for a year. Because of the more plentiful harvests, starvation rates dropped. Perhaps as many as 20,000 Indians survived each year because of Union Carbide's pesticide program.

Before the accident, Union Carbide—the corporation as well as the subsidiary—had such an excellent reputation for safety that it was considered a model of social responsibility. The company complied with all Indian laws, and the mother company had instituted more rigorous safety standards than required by Indian law. Actually, India's environmental protection and safety laws were nearly nonexistent. Union Carbide had tough operating safety standards for handling materials and maintaining equipment, and had good inspection and control systems. In Bhopal, however, these systems broke down, and the result was an unparalleled disaster.

Case Questions

1. From a systems perspective, identify the various constituents, or "stakeholders," of Union Carbide Corporation. Explain the corporate responsibility to reconcile stockholder interests with the interests of the victims of the Bhopal accident.
2. Identify the various managerial groups involved and give your estimate of how each should have been held accountable for the Bhopal accident.
3. Critics argued that Union Carbide should never have built a plant that dangerous if it had only a few trained Indian managers and a work force of illiterate individuals to operate it. Take the viewpoint of American top management and argue for or against this view. Take the viewpoint of the Indian government and argue for or against this view.
4. Identify and discuss the social benefits and costs of the Bhopal plant to employees and local citizens of India. Then assume this plant was located in the United States and discuss the same potential benefits and costs.
5. Describe the differences between the U.S. and Indian cultural environments. Contrast how management principles would apply in each environment.

Source: Manuel G. Velasquez, *Business Ethics: Concepts and Cases* (Englewood Cliffs, N.J.: Prentice Hall, 1992), pp. 2–8. See also Subatra N. Chakravarty, "The Ghost Returns," *Forbes*, December 10, 1990, p. 108.

5

Decision Making

OUTLINE

The Nature of Decision Making
- Programmed and Nonprogrammed Decisions
- Adaptability in Decision Making
- The Role of Creativity

The Decision-Making Environment
- Certainty
- Risk
- Uncertainty

Techniques in Group Decision Making
- Brainstorming
- Nominal Groups
- Delphi Technique

The Role of Management Science

Rational Decisions and Problem Solving
- Diagnose the Problem
- Analyze the Environment
- Articulate the Problem or Opportunity
- Develop Alternatives
- Evaluate Alternatives
- Make a Choice
- Implement the Decision
- Evaluate and Adapt Decision Results

Toward More Effective Decision Making
- Use Information Effectively
- Enhance Systems for Decision Making
- Empower Those Who Must Implement Decisions
- Communicate Effectively
- Delegate Pragmatically
- Build on Strength

OBJECTIVES

- Describe how decision making is important to organizational success.
- Explain the concepts of certainty, risk, and uncertainty in decision making.
- Describe decision-making processes in brainstorming and nominal groups and discuss the Delphi technique for creative problem solving.
- Explain the role of management science techniques for decision making.
- Define and discuss a rational decision-making process.
- Explore guidelines for making effective decisions as managers.

WALT DISNEY introduced *storyboarding* as an organizational form of decision making hundreds of years after Leonardo da Vinci devised it to construct large murals. In creating the first storyboard, Leonardo made hundreds of small drawings—each representing part of a proposed mural—then affixed them to a wall so that he could study them. Disney appropriated Leonardo's visual technique, constructing a huge cork-covered wall and inviting teams of artists to pin their drawings to it, study a story plot, and develop a sequence of animation. He found that the storyboard encouraged a wealth of new ideas for stories, movies, and graphic innovations.

General Electric has built replicas of Disney's cork-lined wall to encourage creative thinking among its managers. Teams with a specific problem to solve gather at a meeting and each person jots down ideas on small cards that are pinned to the wall. The cards are arranged under various headings, such as "New Designs" or "New Manufacturing Methods." Team members then debate these ideas, discarding most, rearranging some, formulating new ones. GE first implemented the storyboard technique at its thirty-year-old dishwasher facility in Louisville, Kentucky, during the 1970s. In terms of ideas, it was a great success. Managers and engineers came up with a futuristic automated manufacturing plant with major product innovations. Not all team members enjoyed this type of decision making, however; some became disgruntled and others engaged in heated arguments with their colleagues.

Consider the advantages and disadvantages of group decision making. Would you advise GE to continue storyboarding? If so, what advice would you offer about how to improve the process?

Few human activities are more universal than decision making. We make hundreds of decisions each day and an extraordinary number in our lifetimes. Many decisions are simple, such as choosing clothes to wear or selecting food from a menu. Others are complex, such as choosing a major in college or purchasing a house. Managers face the same range of decisions, but unlike personal decisions, those made in organizations often affect thousands of other people. Consider the frenzy of corporate takeovers of the late 1980s that were fueled by junk bonds and megalomaniacal managers in banks, security firms, and companies targeted for leveraged buyouts. Purchase prices for companies were bid up on the strength of overvalued assets and secured by loans that created a fragile paper empire. The empire crumbled, several of the megalomaniacs went to prison, tens of thousands of investors lost money, and thousands of people lost their jobs. Add to this scenario the collapse of more than 700 savings and loan institutions that were, in part, drawn into competition for funds by junk bond raiders, and, in part, overextended by unscrupulous or naive managers. In the final analysis, the S&L debacle may cost taxpayers $500 billion, and it is expected to affect several hundred thousand homeowners, depositors, and employees.[1] The question being asked over and over again by congressional investigators and the public is this: How did so many people in so many organizations make so many bad decisions?

Many "bad" decisions began life as seemingly "good" decisions. For example, decisions such as revising tax laws, altering education requirements, imposing environmental laws, or passing antiabortion legislation may begin with the good intentions of public leaders. However, because decisions on such issues have far-reaching implications, they can help, or harm, millions of people and are therefore highly controversial. Consider a specific example of a little-known provision of the 1988 Congressional Trade Act. It requires the Commerce Department to make public thousands of scientific innovations from federal laboratories that have been developed through publicly funded research. Consumers will benefit from new medicines, household products, and computer enhancements, but executives of companies affected by this decision have mixed emotions about it. Those in larger firms, such as General Electric, Merck, and IBM, with the financial and marketing strength to commercialize scientific innovations, favor the provision. Hundreds of executives in smaller firms without financial or marketing strength are afraid they will be driven out of business.[2]

Obviously there is a tremendous difference between deciding what to eat for lunch and whether to pass a major trade bill, yet all decisions have similarities in terms of a conscious selection of actions based on some logical evaluation of circumstances. Because circumstances change, and because human beings are not only fallible but also emotional, different decisions are likely to be made under a variety of conditions. This is why it is important to understand the nature of decision making and how managers adapt to organizational situations to make effective decisions.

THE NATURE OF DECISION MAKING

Decision making is the process of defining problems, generating alternative solutions, choosing one alternative, and implementing it. The terms *decision making* and *problem solving* are used interchangeably in the context of management because managers constantly make decisions to resolve problems. For example, if a bank teller's cash drawer is short at the end of the day, the bank has a problem to resolve. The teller may be making mistakes, or something may be wrong with the bank's cash control methods. If the bank manager investigates and discovers that the teller has been making mistakes, a decision has to be made on how to correct the problem. The teller may be fired, given more training, or reassigned to work not requiring the same skills. Among those three alternatives, the bank manager may choose to train the employee further in cash control methods. If so, after the decision is implemented, the manager would closely monitor the employee's work to determine whether training had resolved the problem. If it had not, the manager would have to consider another alternative.

The definition of decision making should be expanded to include identifying opportunities, developing alternative action plans to take advantage of those opportunities, choosing one action plan, and implementing it. In discussing strategic planning in Chapter 7, we will stress opportunities for strategic decisions. Nevertheless, the *process* for solving problems or taking advantage of opportunities is the same. In making any decision, managers have the moral burden to help accomplish organizational goals without endangering others or misusing resources.[3] In the bank teller example, for instance, cash shortages may have occurred because of an inefficient method of handling customer transactions. If so, the manager has the opportunity not only to improve internal cash control but also to give customers improved service. He or she may select between computerizing teller transactions and adding more highly trained tellers. The choice, however, must take into account the bank's goals in the customer service area, the costs of implementing a new system, and how tellers' job responsibilities will change. Effective managers try to make logical decisions that take into consideration all relevant circumstances, people, and resources.

The nature of the decision, or the problem, will often dictate how we approach its resolution. The more complex or uncertain the issue, the more likely we will employ a *rational decision-making* technique, described in detail later in the chapter. Less complex problems or those with which we have had a great deal of experience may be resolved intuitively. In management, we also distinguish between decisions that are *programmed* and those that are *nonprogrammed*.[4] Figure 5-1 illustrates these two categories of decisions.

Programmed and Nonprogrammed Decisions

Programmed decisions are those that are made in predictable circumstances and have predictable results. Results are predictable because similar decisions have often been made before under similar, and recurring, circumstances. The high-tech age has enriched our language with new terms for old problems. *Programmed* is a term borrowed from computer jargon meaning "structured" and "having definite parameters." In making programmed decisions, therefore, managers have clear parameters and criteria, based on previous experience with similar problems. Problems are often structured and alternatives are well defined.

programmed decisions Decisions that have been made so often under similar circumstances that past experience provides clear guidelines for managers.

Many managerial decisions are structured through policy directives, rules, and procedures. For example, if it is company policy to discipline an employee who is

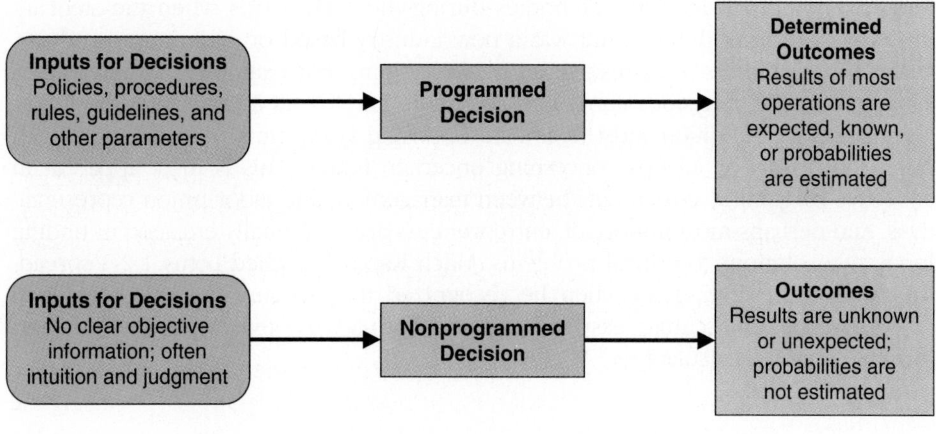

FIGURE 5-1 Programmed and Nonprogrammed Decisions

repeatedly absent, then a manager will simply follow procedures for documenting absenteeism and decide what disciplinary measures to take. Thus company policy may require a supervisor to write an official reprimand to warn an employee that he or she may be suspended from work without pay or fired if further unauthorized absences occur. The written reprimand goes into the employee's personal folder, and if absenteeism continues, the supervisor initiates the decision to suspend or fire the person.

Students must make programmed decisions throughout college. The decision to succeed at their studies entails attaining a certain grade average to pass, a certain cumulative grade point average to graduate, and credits from certain courses to satisfy particular degree requirements. Administrators make decisions about retaining students and awarding degrees according to programmed criteria.

Most programmed decisions are *routine* because managers understand the circumstances and the probable results of their decisions. Experienced managers will have made the same decisions many times before. Consequently, inexperienced managers will be able to find clear guidelines to help them make their decisions. Organizations adopt analogous processes to guide managers through complex decisions about production, marketing, financing, and a host of other situations. For example, a complex purchasing decision becomes routine after a manager buys materials several dozen times; decisions about pricing, how much to order, and choosing the best suppliers follow routine purchasing procedures. Programmed decisions reduce anxiety while improving quality in decision making. Organizations achieve greater stability in their operations and a more predictable pattern of behavior through them. Yet when managers have less discretion about their decisions, individual initiative suffers.

nonprogrammed decisions Decisions derived from unstructured analysis or generated from individual evaluation of nonroutine situations; decisions that lack clear analytical parameters or substantial precedent.

Nonprogrammed decisions are those that are made in unique circumstances and often have unpredictable results. Managers may either find themselves facing a problem that is ill-defined or in a situation that has never occurred before.[5] For example, Steven Jobs and Stephen Wozniak introduced the first Apple microcomputer in 1978 without knowing who would buy it or how it would be used. Tom Monaghan's Domino's Pizza franchises number nearly 3,000 today, yet when he founded the company, a "nonrestaurant" with total home deliveries had never been tried before.[6]

Executives almost always face nonprogrammed problems. Their task is to deal with changes that are often unforeseeable. Henry Mintzberg researched how executives make decisions and concluded they have four decision-making roles that require significant individual judgment.[7] You may recall that in Chapter 1 we examined these key management roles: disturbance handler, entrepreneur, negotiator, and resource allocator. Because each of these roles lacks structure, people in these roles are responsible for many unusual decisions. For example, resource allocators must find new, more efficient ways to use the firm's resources. Thus Henry Kaiser substituted aluminum for steel in car bodies during the early 1950s when the steel industry was in turmoil; the result was a new industry based on aluminum products. Disturbance handlers must resolve unusual problems. For example, first-line supervisors must make decisions about how to handle employees incapacitated by drugs. Negotiators by definition must assimilate opposing viewpoints or collaborate with other individuals or groups concerning uncertain issues. This is most apparent in collective bargaining agreements between management and labor union representatives. And perhaps most important, entrepreneurs are continually engaged in finding innovative solutions to critical problems. Mitch Kapor launched Lotus 1-2-3 spreadsheets for microcomputers when he recognized that accountants and bank loan officers wanted an accurate, easy-to-use, and easy-to-learn software program for performing complex calculations.[8]

Adaptability in Decision Making

In many cases, decisions are neither programmed nor nonprogrammed but fall into a gray area between the two extremes. Thus managers may have some information about a problem and some feeling for how a similar problem was handled before, yet still lack clear guidelines for making a decision. They are expected, therefore, to exercise discretion and to adapt to the situation. **Adaptability** is the ability to adjust to new or changed circumstances. Sales representatives quickly learn this, perhaps because they must constantly adapt to a variety of customers and changes in competition. Numerous factors intercede to alter decisions and to temper management behavior. Internal factors include the availability of money, materials, and personnel, as well as the nature of the work force, time requirements, and managers' personalities. External factors include economic conditions, customer expectations, competition, and social pressures.

adaptability
The ability to adjust to new or changed circumstances; a reaction to internal and external conditions requiring managers to adapt decisions.

Adaptability may be most important in emergency situations when managers have no time to seek information or to evaluate the problem thoroughly. In Bhopal, India, for example, a massive poison gas leak at a Union Carbide plant killed or injured several thousand people, yet several thousand more survived by the quick thinking of a plant supervisor who took the initiative to shut down the plant, evacuate employees, and help local villagers.[9] (A case on the Bhopal incident appears at the end of Part One.)

Adaptability in decision making is also essential to keep work activities on course, and this is a critical dimension of personal leadership. Managers often develop a strong intuitive sense about how to resolve problems quickly and efficiently without too much analysis. Quick-thinking managers are said to have a "Gordian knot" approach to decision making.[10] The Gordian knot, as you may recall, was a fabled knot tied around a sacred tree in Phrygia in Asia Minor during the time of Alexander the Great. It was said that whoever loosed the Gordian knot would rule the East. Many great men of the time studied the knot and tried to untie it. They all failed. Alexander, sword in hand, simply slashed the knot and went on to conquer most of Asia Minor. "Cutting the Gordian knot" has come to mean solving an intricate problem by bold and decisive action rather than by laboriously studying it and applying conventional wisdom.

Modern managers can become as entrapped by conventional wisdom as the great men of Alexander's day. They may bring reams of computer printouts and statistical data to bear on their problems when time and circumstances do not allow a detailed, rational analysis. For example, an overheating machine engine may require an expert mechanic for repair, but the immediate solution to the problem is to shut the engine down before further damage is done. However, there is a place for rational analysis of problems, and as we shall see later in the chapter, most complicated problems require careful consideration.

The Role of Creativity

Creativity is the ability to bring something new into existence. In business decision making, it is useful to think of creativity as a process of developing a new course of action for organizational work. Rather than just adapting to "keep on course," a manager creates a "new course" of action.[11]

creativity
The ability to bring something new into existence.

Consider how Richard and Maurice McDonald created the now-famous McDonald's chain and pioneered the American fast-food phenomenon.[12] They dreamed up the concept of "fast food" as a solution to several problems the McDonalds encountered in their drive-in restaurant. (See the Management Application for a brief relation of this story.) The main problem in 1948 was controlling the behavior

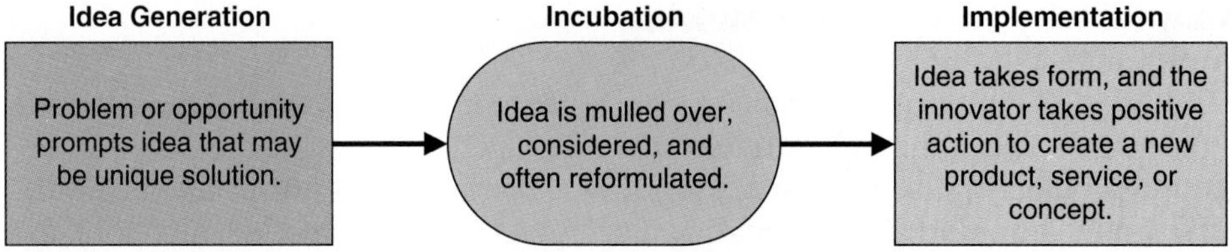

Idea Generation

Problem or opportunity prompts idea that may be unique solution.

Incubation

Idea is mulled over, considered, and often reformulated.

Implementation

Idea takes form, and the innovator takes positive action to create a new product, service, or concept.

FIGURE 5-2 Three Stages of Creativity

of McDonald's two dozen carhops. Carhops in those days were usually young women who waited on customers at their car windows. This was the conventional way that McDonald's, A&W Rootbeer, and most other drive-in restaurants conducted business. Unfortunately, keeping carhops was difficult, paying them was expensive, and the young women attracted male admirers who hung around the parking lot. The carhops also spent a great deal of time with male employees, not necessarily doing productive work. The McDonald brothers decided that the solution to their problems was the kind of restaurant where most customers would buy food from a simple menu at a counter and then leave. This would eliminate most of the cooks, busboys, waiters, and carhops. After instituting the changes, the brothers found it easy to open other restaurants under owner-managers because of the simplicity and low cost of their enterprise.

Creative decisions usually follow the three-stage process shown in Figure 5-2: idea generation, incubation, and implementation. In the three stages of this general model, a person (1) is alerted to a problem that requires a creative solution and generates ideas about novel solutions, (2) lets the ideas incubate for a period of time, and (3) then focuses on one choice to implement.[13]

Idea-generation stage. The idea-generation stage begins with a heightened awareness of a problem that has no obvious solution or with an individual's curiosity about doing something unusual. This stage is a *seeding process* in which people with fertile minds are open to new ideas. Alexander Graham Bell, for example, began a quest for a harmonic hearing aid after spending years teaching the deaf and hearing-impaired. His experiments led to the invention of a magnetic rod that could be "plunked" to produce various sound waves. This discovery was in the realm of physics; it did not automatically lead to the creation of a new product or process. In fact, Bell spent years studying his discovery and its possible applications for hearing aids before he invented the telephone. This initial period of discovery and research was Bell's "germination" period when new ideas were seeded in his mind based on the physics of sound transmission.[14]

Incubation stage. This is a period of "mulling it over" to allow an idea to formulate more clearly. The person "sleeps on" the problem to allow the subconscious to sort out possible solutions. This second stage can also be a period of fantasizing when the mind is allowed to wander beyond "rational" and known solutions. It is impossible to pinpoint exactly what goes on during the incubation stage, but during this time, an initial discovery or curious idea is transformed into something new and useful. Bell started this stage focusing his energy on hearing aids, but eventually the idea of a telephone as a communication tool took shape in his mind. Bell got this idea, the story goes, by calling his lab assistant Thomas Watson on a "harmonic telegraph wire."

Implementation stage. Once the person has an illumination (i.e., incubation has led to a clear new idea), he or she intensifies efforts to implement the idea. Thus Bell pursued the idea of a community with interconnected harmonic telegraphs, and the McDonald brothers hired Ray Kroc to market franchise outlets to replicate their concept of fast-food outlets.

MANAGEMENT APPLICATION

There Really Was a "Big Mac"

Richard and Maurice McDonald left their home in New Hampshire in 1920 and went to California to seek their fortunes. The brothers tried to break into Hollywood movies, operated a hot dog stand in Los Angeles, and ran a small movie theater during the rollicking twenties and depressed thirties. In 1940, Richard and Maurice (known as "Mac") settled in San Bernardino, then a rough but growing railroad town, and opened a new drive-in restaurant. The first McDonald's became a busy teenage hangout complete with short-skirted carhops and a hearty menu ranging from hamburgers to steak dinners. Between 1940 and 1948, the brothers managed this business much like other successful restaurants, but they were overwhelmed by employee problems. To solve them, they conceived the idea of a restaurant with a few standard take-away menu items served from a counter. The idea was to fill an order in 20 seconds rather than 20 minutes and eliminate carhops, waiters, and busboys. Take-away also eliminated dishwashing and the huge overhead expense of a curb-service parking lot.

The menu in 1948 was built around a tasty hamburger cooked to standard portions with standard condiments. Maurice introduced the "Big Mac" at 15 cents and a bag of fries at 10 cents. The simplicity of the business allowed the brothers to sell franchise rights for new locations, and the fast-food franchise business was born. In 1955, the brothers hired Ray Kroc to extend the McDonald's franchise chain beyond California. At the time, Kroc was a milkshake machine salesman, but he was a brilliant promoter who took most of his commissions in company stock. By 1961, the franchise chain had grown to 2,000 units and Ray Kroc, chief architect of that growth, was a major stockholder. The McDonald brothers, having been in the business for more than 20 years, were financially secure and ready to retire. They took a modest after-tax $1 million each from Kroc for the business.

Before he died in 1984, Ray Kroc had built a franchise empire of nearly 10,000 units on three continents. "Mac" McDonald retired to the countryside and died in 1971. Richard McDonald returned to New Hampshire, where he still enjoys having an occasional Big Mac and fries, although he is sometimes dismayed that few people realize there really was a Big Mac who spent a lifetime pursuing a dream and planting golden arches across America.

Source: Ellen Graham, "McDonald's Pickle: He Began Fast Food but Gets No Credit," *Wall Street Journal,* August 15, 1991, pp. A1, A5.

Creativity is seldom as simple as this outline of the three-stage process suggests. In fact, it usually takes tremendous time and resources before an idea emerges as a new product or new service. Thomas Edison, for example, spent a decade working on his idea for an electric light bulb, and he produced more than a thousand bulbs that didn't work before succeeding.[15] Managers are seldom involved in break-

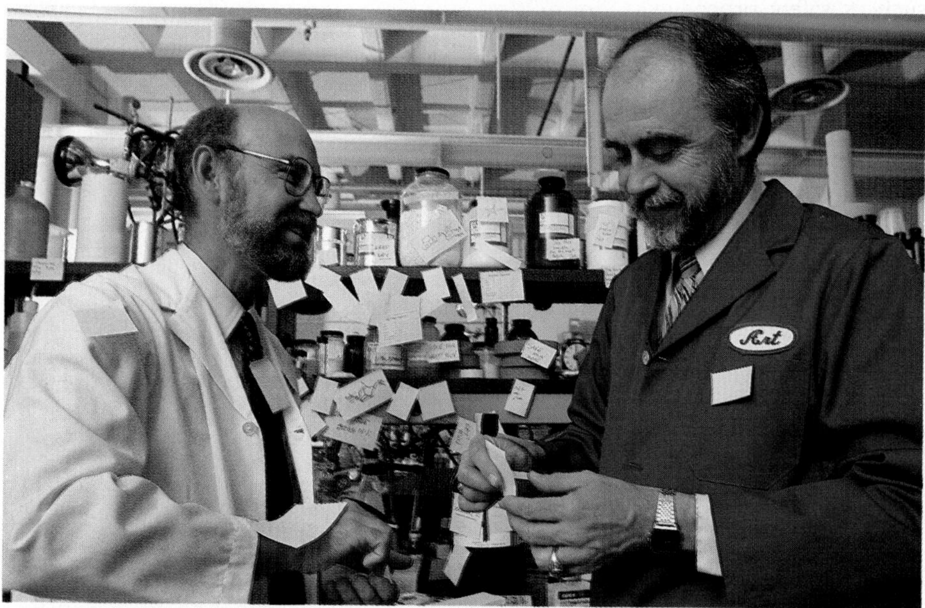

Art Fry, the inventor of Post-it Notes, is an excellent example of an *intrapreneur*. As a research engineer at 3M Corporation, Fry created a yellow pad with a gentle adhesive to paste notes and page markers inside his church choir's hymn books. When he tried to introduce the pad to his 3M superiors through official channels, he was ridiculed. Fry went ahead and developed his idea on his own time and distributed his pads to the company's executive secretaries. After several months, every office secretary was putting in purchase orders to replenish them, but no one knew where to buy the notes. Fry continued to "slip a few" pads to the secretaries, and it wasn't long before 3M management found out, backed his invention, and launched a new product line.

Source: Gifford Pinchot III, *Intrapreneuring* (New York: Harper & Row, 1985), pp. 7–9.

through inventions, but they often do make innovative decisions, and the creative process is the same, even though the problem may be something simple like how to improve an office filing system. Innovative solutions to office filing systems have inspired new file index systems, filing desks, computer storage disks, and, most recently, the networking systems that link several office computer stations into centralized storage and data retrieval bases.

entrepreneurship
The process of creating a new venture as an independent business endeavor, usually one positioned to grow and be profitable for the founders.

When new businesses are established through creative endeavor, we call the process **entrepreneurship,** a concept introduced in Chapter 1 and discussed more thoroughly in Chapter 20. The decision-making behavior of entrepreneurs has caught the interest of corporate executives who want to encourage greater risk taking and more innovation among their managers. There is good reason for this. During the 1980s, there was a steady decline in newly developed products by major corporations, and the number of patents registered by large U.S. companies decreased each year. During the same time, small enterprises (with fewer than 1,000 employees) registered 62 percent of all domestic patents and accounted for 65 percent of all new products brought to market.[16] Recognizing that they had to instill a sense of "venturing" in their managers, corporate executives started to emulate entrepreneurial behavior by backing innovative employees with company resources. This is called **intrapreneurship,** which is defined as the process of constructive change through innovation within an established organization.[17] (See Chapter 20.)

intrapreneurship
A term applied to corporate entrepreneurship (literally "intracorporate entrepreneurship"), suggesting innovation and new-venture creation from within established organizational boundaries.

Encouraging creative decisions necessarily means loosening the corporate harness. In an atmosphere that encourages creativity, there is less emphasis on programmed decisions—except, of course, to reinforce essential policies and rules, such as safety procedures. The mastery of nonprogrammed decision making—of reaching out beyond the frontiers of existing behavior—has become a valued managerial skill. Top-performing and innovative companies instill in their managers the habit of creative decision making. To ensure creativity, they also hire innovative people capable of challenging the status quo. It is no surprise to industrial analysts that firms such as Hewlett-Packard, IBM, 3M, General Electric, and Eastman Kodak are not only among the most admired but also among the most innovative corporations in America.[18] Internal decision making in each of these and other well-run firms has been substantially redefined. Employees are encouraged to participate in shop-floor decisions such as quality control; channels have been set up for evaluating new ideas; and managers seek to reward creative thinking, not subdue it. As a result, innovators such as Art Fry are encouraged, not ridiculed.[19]

CHECKPOINT

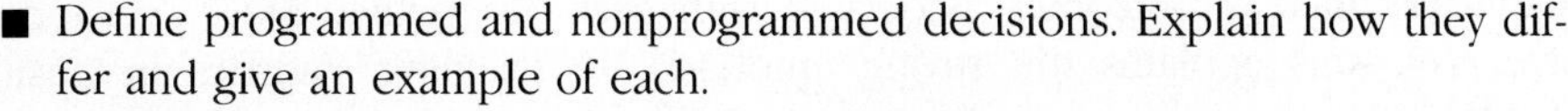

- Define programmed and nonprogrammed decisions. Explain how they differ and give an example of each.

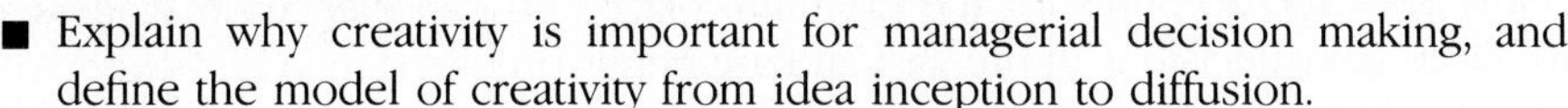

- Explain why creativity is important for managerial decision making, and define the model of creativity from idea inception to diffusion.

THE DECISION-MAKING ENVIRONMENT

To be good decision makers, managers do not have to be entrepreneurial or creative, but they must be able to adapt to circumstances and solve problems. Routine decisions are not difficult to make because similar decisions have been made in the past. These situations are seldom stressful, and managers have some sense of what the results of their decisions will be. In contrast, complicated situations or unique problems can be stressful, and managers can foresee little about the effects of their decisions. In these cases, they must approach decision making with caution, perhaps using lengthy analysis and seeking expert help. Essentially, it is the decision-making environment that dictates how managers approach these tasks.

Environmental factors influence some decisions more than others. When conditions are certain, decisions reflect "choice making" with few complications. Under conditions of risk or uncertainty, however, managers must grapple with complex issues. Figure 5-3 illustrates the three basic conditions for decision making, which we will briefly describe in turn.

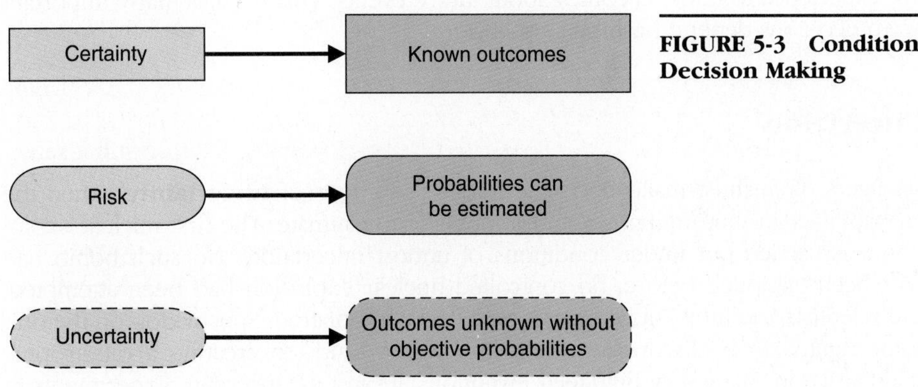

FIGURE 5-3 Conditions for Decision Making

Certainty

certainty
The condition of knowing the outcomes under each set of alternatives.

Conditions are **certain** when managers know outcomes under each set of alternatives. Therefore, one alternative will have a well-defined result, while another choice will have a different and equally well-defined result. Decision making under these conditions seldom requires a lengthy process of investigation; a manager just selects an alternative and takes action. To take a concrete example, a manager faced with choosing among several different pieces of machinery on the basis of purchase price will know what decision to make as soon as the prices of the machines are known: buy the least expensive item.

Risk

risk
The condition of not being certain about the outcome of a decision while also having enough information to sense probabilities.

When outcomes are not clear but managers have enough information to assess results, a condition of risk exists. **Risk** assumes that a manager can calculate statistically the probabilities of outcomes associated with each alternative. Most decisions involve risk. This explains the strong emphasis on teaching statistics in business schools. Risk also accounts for the premium placed on experienced managers who have faced risky decisions in the past and are better prepared than less experienced managers to judge probabilities of success or failure. Information and decision sciences play vital roles in decision making under risk conditions. The greater the amount of accurate and timely information managers have on a subject, the greater the likelihood that they can establish probabilities with reasonable reliability.

In organizational environments, the ability to estimate probabilities is important for making decisions about a wide array of investments, planning new products, entering new markets, estimating consumer behavior, and so on. In forecasting sales, for example, managers try to estimate how many customers are likely to buy products at a given price over a given period of time. Clearly, the best sales forecast can have errors because customers may say they will buy and then change their minds. This can happen for a variety of reasons, such as unexpected changes in competitors' prices, higher interest rates that frighten customers from buying on credit, and natural phenomena. During the summer drought of 1991, for example, fruit and vegetable prices went up because farmers lost crops, and beef prices soared because there was not enough water to support cattle. This disrupted food supplies and altered consumer buying patterns at grocery stores. By making use of statistical studies, however, food managers were able to adjust grocery inventories, thereby reducing the risk of having unsalable products in stock.

Experienced managers add an intuitive dimension to decision making by modifying estimates according to personal or subjective probabilities. An experienced marketing manager may have a feeling about how competitors will react to price reductions and modify the sales forecast accordingly. Managers use their past subjective experience to infer outcomes about future events. This is particularly important when decisions depend on human behavior.

Uncertainty

uncertainty
The condition of not knowing, and of having insufficient information to assign probabilities, in a decision situation.

Managers often must make decisions under conditions of **uncertainty,** when the probabilities are both unknown and impossible to estimate. The first nuclear explosion was carried out under conditions of utmost uncertainty. No such bomb had ever been exploded before; no controlled nuclear explosion had been attempted; and scientists had little knowledge of the effects of radiation. Speculation on the outcome ranged from discovering the bomb was a "dud" to creating a catastrophic chain reaction. Many new high-tech inventions are just as uncertain. Experiments in biotechnology, social research, and space exploration are so complicated, and we have such scanty information about their possible effects, that statistical probabilities are often little more than guesses.

Managers do not have to rely entirely on guesswork under conditions of uncertainty. By using *rational decision-making techniques* (described later in the chapter), they can tackle uncertain problems systematically. There are also several quantitative techniques that utilize information systems to help managers make *inferential* decisions, or "informed judgments"? We review these techniques momentarily. Under conditions of uncertainty, *behavioral methods* are favored by many managers. These use accumulated information gathered by experts in brainstorming sessions and several distinct models for tapping the greatest human information resource—the brain. Because these techniques rely on group processes, we address behavioral methods in the following section as group decision making.

CHECKPOINT

- Discuss how a decision is made under conditions of certainty, risk, and uncertainty. What differentiates each set of conditions?
- How would you describe "high-risk" and "low-risk" decisions?
- As a first-line supervisor, what type of decision would you most often have to make? Explain your answer. What if you were a top executive?

With the help of IBM funding, the University of Arizona developed a new way for people to sit down together and offer their new ideas to one another: the "electronic meeting." Participants gather around a table and use individual computer terminals to trade and "discuss" new ideas about specific issues. Because there is no talking and the entries are anonymous, some managers believe that this type of meeting could prove to be an excellent venue for informal as well as formal brainstorming sessions.

TECHNIQUES IN GROUP DECISION MAKING

Conditions of uncertainty or high risk often call for creative or novel decisions. In these situations, managers are just as challenged by the need to identify the right problem as they are by the need to develop a viable solution. After the 1991 abortive coup in the Soviet Union, business leaders and Western politicians found themselves guessing about its ramifications. Some sent up alarms about the lack of control over Soviet nuclear weapons and cautioned that the world could be on the brink of a nuclear holocaust. Others applauded the Soviet leaders and pronounced the advent of "peace in our time . . . finally." Still others felt the attempted coup would result in chaos, leading to riots and civil wars as ideological battle lines are drawn between democratic and communist forces. Since business leaders and politicians could not agree on the identity of the problems arising from the Soviet situation, they could not agree on how to develop viable solutions.[20] Equally perplexing situations exist closer to home. For example, escalating health-care costs have vexed Americans for decades, and managers everywhere question how to motivate their employees.

Powerful techniques have been developed for gaining insight into these types of problems. They are called techniques in *behavioral problem solving* and in *group decision making* because they rely on collective effects of human interaction among individuals who, through group efforts, draw inferential solutions to complex problems. Several of the most useful techniques are described here.[21]

Brainstorming

Getting people involved in the decision-making *process* is the key to all group approaches to problem solving, and brainstorming is perhaps the most interactive of all approaches. **Brainstorming** is a process of encouraging individuals in a group to be completely open, candid, creative, and spontaneous in their responses to a given problem. Human beings have been brainstorming throughout history, of course, but the concept of *organized brainstorming* implies the concentration of

brainstorming
Associated with group decision making and creativity, it is a technique for generating many diverse ideas in an atmosphere free from criticism and explicit boundaries.

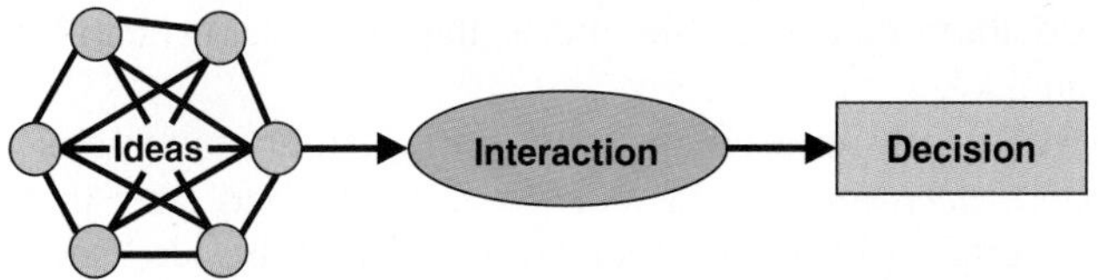

FIGURE 5-4 Brainstorming Relationships

group brainpower on a specific issue. This modern refinement brings together selected individuals with unique credentials to solve particularly complex problems. "Think tanks" such as the Rand Corporation frequently use this technique.

Brainstorming requires freedom of expression by individuals within groups, with as little structure as possible to allow the greatest degree of human interaction. Figure 5-4 illustrates the process, and several guidelines have been developed for effective brainstorming.[22]

- *Criticism* must be minimized because it is extremely difficult to be critical and creative simultaneously. The most effective brainstorming occurs when ideas are encouraged without constraint or intimidation. Even outlandish and apparently foolish ideas are often valuable because they can spark useful creative ideas by others. Criticism can occur after the brainstorming is done, when ideas with little merit can be discarded.
- *Limitations* should not exist on the number and variety of ideas developed during brainstorming sessions. A long list of seemingly worthless ideas frequently evolves into one creative, perhaps extraordinary, alternative. Getting to that point is seldom achieved in a flash of brilliance but rather through an evolutionary process.
- *Synergism* should be encouraged through collaborative contributions and a healthy competition to build on participants' ideas. An initial idea coupled with another, and another, and another leads to a collective result that is the principal advantage of brainstorming.

Research has shown that brainstorming is most effective in groups of five to seven individuals. Larger groups tend to bog down because of personal difficulties among group members. Longer periods of intensive group brainstorming are more productive than many short meetings. A collaborative solution takes time to form because it is an evolutionary process of wading through many, often worthless, ideas. When sufficient time is allowed, results can be impressive, but when brainstorming is hurried, participants can become combative rather than cooperative.[23]

Nominal Groups

nominal group
A panel established to develop ideas independently for resolving a particular problem that then, through an exchange of ideas, refines those ideas until a group consensus emerges.

A refinement of brainstorming is the **nominal group.** This technique follows many of the fundamental guidelines for brainstorming but allows individuals to develop their ideas independently. Panel members initially establish their common purpose, then set about developing ideas in isolation from one another. The group reconvenes from time to time to exchange ideas and share contributions. Members then return to independent investigation.[24]

Nominal groups (often called NGs) have been found more effective than unstructured brainstorming groups, producing more original ideas with more usable recommendations. Nominal groups avoid much of the potential for criticism and interpersonal conflict that is present in brainstorming groups. Also, more well-developed ideas come from nominal groups because members can work toward fully articulated solutions on their own. Collaboration is achieved when panel members collectively consider individual alternatives.[25]

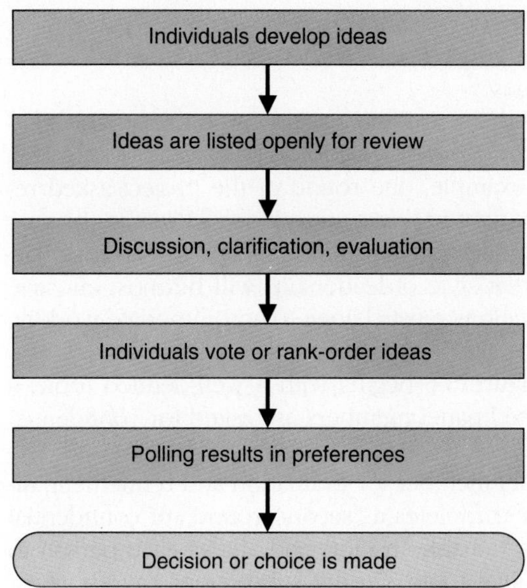

FIGURE 5-5 Nominal Group Technique

The recognized benefits of nominal groups have led to a formal method of decision making in organizations called the **nominal group technique (NGT).** This technique retains the advantages of group decision making while minimizing the potential conflict arising from individual biases. The NGT process shown in Figure 5-5 has the following four steps:[26]

nominal group technique (NGT)
A group decision-making process in which members independently identify solutions to a problem or alternative opportunities. Then, after options are fully articulated and discussed, members vote confidentially for preferences.

- *Step 1:* Panel members working independently develop and list ideas on a specific issue. Their ideas are privately conceived and written down without conversation or interaction with other group members.
- *Step 2:* Each panel member is individually queried on one idea in a "round robin" process. One person not involved in panel deliberations transcribes respondents' answers on a blackboard, or flip charts can be used to post answers conspicuously.
- *Step 3:* When all responses have been transcribed, panel members discuss, clarify, and elaborate points. Evaluation that highlights the advantages and disadvantages of each idea is encouraged.
- *Step 4:* Individual panel members silently and privately vote on ideas either by assigning a rank order or by using a predetermined rating scale for each idea. Votes are collected and tallied beside each posted idea, and decisions are based on pooled results.

A modification of the NGT procedure repeats steps 1 through 3, allowing panel members to flesh out new ideas or amplify recommendations prior to a vote. If a large number of alternatives result in no clear consensus for one idea, the process may be repeated, each time resulting in fewer ideas and more refinements.

Delphi Technique

Delphi technique
Used in forecasting, problem solving, and creative processes, the Delphi technique surveys experts through several rounds of investigation to develop a profile of information, ideas, or solutions.

The **Delphi technique** is a survey method of polling panel members on a well-defined problem. Unlike brainstorming and nominal group techniques, the Delphi technique does not bring individuals together in face-to-face meetings. Anonymity is maintained to encourage candid responses without the sociopsychological pressures of group interaction. Members are not only anonymous to one another but to coordinators as well. Polled responses are collected from individuals with guarantees against personal criticism or identification of respondents. Anonymity is particularly important when the Delphi technique is used within an organization to poll colleagues or co-workers on sensitive issues.

The Rand Corporation established the Delphi Project for military strategists during the 1950s.[27] It was initially used for developing futuristic scenarios of social, political, and military conditions. For example, one round of the project asked respondents, "What are the ten most important problems facing our society in the year 2020?" In organizational environments, questions are less dramatic but often as far-reaching. These may include asking what style of leadership will be most effective for the next generation or how organizations must change to accommodate working mothers.

The Delphi process shown in Figure 5-6 begins with a well-defined topic, a specific point for response. Then selected panel members are asked for confidential written responses in a "first-round" poll. All responses are transcribed into one document, which is then given to each panel member for evaluation and refinement. After seeing all responses, each member completes a "second round" of confidential response. This provides members with valuable insights and allows each person to refine his or her response to the original topic. During subsequent rounds of inquiry, members can substantiate their positions. The process is repeated until they achieve a consensus on the most important issues.

The Delphi technique is a compelling method of exploring complex issues without unwieldy analysis. It has the advantage of accumulating subjective information from experts without sacrificing personal beliefs and values. Delphi is plausible in situations of uncertainty or very high risk because a consensus decision galvanizes action in a democratic process.

A major disadvantage of the Delphi technique is that group members may achieve consensus by compromising. The optimal solution may languish when the weight of panel opinion swings toward a compromise. Mediocre compromises can be a critical problem if the panel of experts is not carefully selected or if members lack appropriate expertise or have strong personal biases. The Delphi technique has an advantage over nominal groups and brainstorming in that it permits large numbers of individuals to be queried without regard for location or sociopsychological characteristics. As noted earlier, the ideal in NGT and group brainstorming methods is between five and seven members. Delphi can solicit responses from many individuals on a global scale.

FIGURE 5-6 Delphi Method for Decision Making

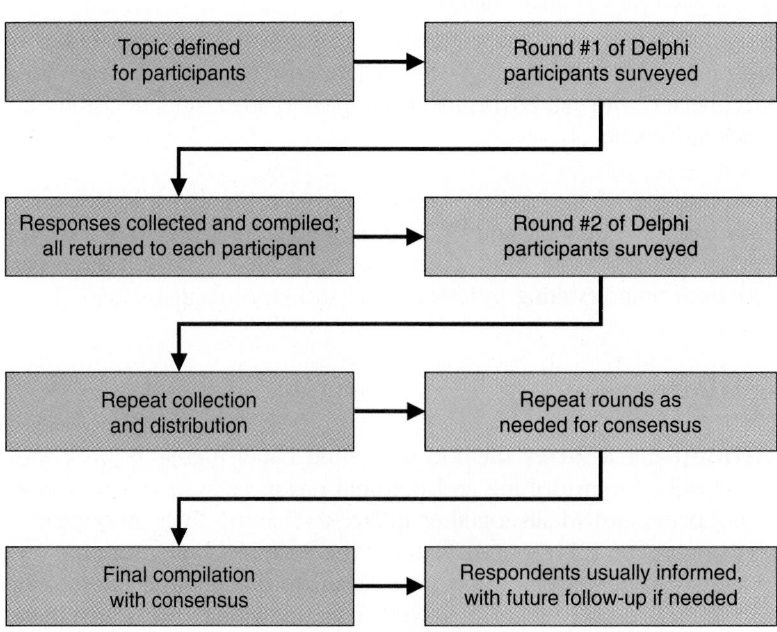
Topic defined for participants
Round #1 of Delphi participants surveyed
Responses collected and compiled; all returned to each participant
Round #2 of Delphi participants surveyed
Repeat collection and distribution
Repeat rounds as needed for consensus
Final compilation with consensus
Respondents usually informed, with future follow-up if needed

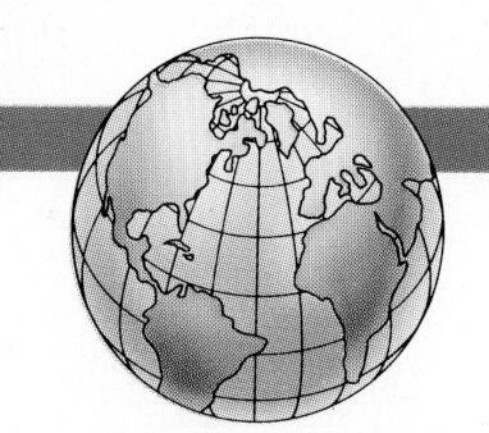

GLOBAL TRENDS

Making Decisions Asian Style

Although much has been written about models of decision making in Japan and among other Asian peoples, three behavioral characteristics in particular seem to influence the way Asians make decisions. These are *loyalty, accommodation,* and *honoring authority.*

Hitachi Ltd., the Japanese electrical and electronic manufacturing giant, has endorsed team decision-making concepts that date to the company's founding prior to World War I. The Hitachi corporate code of behavior places high priority on *loyalty* to the organization and has always used team decision making as a process for focusing loyalty. Thus most researchers readily agree that loyalty is the underpinning force in Hitachi's success.

Loyalty is also prized among employees in Korean firms. Lee Byung-Chull, founder of South Korea's largest *chaebol,* or family-run conglomerate, Samsung, wrote an employee policy in 1938 explaining that loyalty to the organization would be highly valued in all employees. Since that time, employees and managers tend to brainstorm or join together in small groups to consider most decisions. A similar pattern exists at Daewoo, Lucky-Goldstar, and Hyundai, other major Korean chaebols.

Japanese and Korean companies are linked through at least four generations of trade and manufacturing technology—much of this during the period of Japanese occupation of Korea. Although the Koreans, Japanese, and Chinese have distinct cultures, they are connected by a common social philosophy stretching back many centuries. In fact, this social philosophy has spread across Asia, extending to Indonesia and Malaysia, where intercultural migration has occurred.

Loyalty has fostered group behavior that seeks an optimal "consensus." However, consensus is an ideal that is seldom achieved. More often, Asians seek a form of *accommodation* in which dissent is minimized. Employees accommodate by avoiding confrontations, carefully wording their statements in meetings to prevent hurt feelings, and making "suggestions" more often than "decisions." When superiors recognize this accommodation, they praise employees for their contributions and "suggestions," often giving credit to or rewarding employees openly for their contributions.

Loyalty and accommodation exist in the shadow of *honoring authority.* Asians are far less democratic than the Western concept of "group behavior" implies; the two are not the same in Asian cultures. Most Asian companies are very hierarchical, and authority is clearly defined and defended. Consequently, subordinates are very careful not to offend a person of higher authority or greater age or someone in a position of trust. Group decision making allows individuals to become involved in important decisions and to make contributions, but at all times they must be careful not to offend.

These three interrelated patterns of behavior result in longer decision-making processes, compromises (i.e., accommodations), and lack of innovative changes. Researchers have consistently observed these results, yet they have also noted that decisions in Asian cultures solidify organizations, keeping conflicts minimal and misunderstandings rare.

Sources: "The Mountain Priest," *Fortune,* August 3, 1987, p. 42; Laurie Baum, "Korea's Newest Export: Management Style," *Business Week,* January 19, 1987, p. 66; Andrew Tanzer, "Samsung: South Korea Marches to Its Own Drummer," *Forbes,* May 16, 1988, pp. 84–89; and Dori Jones Yang, Stephen Hutcheon, and Joyce Quek, "Is Asia Breeding a Whole Pack of Tigers?" *Business Week Innovation 1990,* September 1990, pp. 152–155.

CHECKPOINT

- When brainstorming, what guidelines are helpful for making effective group decisions?
- Diagram the process of the nominal group technique (NGT) and explain how decisions evolve from that process.
- Explain the Delphi technique and contrast it with brainstorming and NGT approaches. In what situations would the Delphi technique be most useful?

THE ROLE OF MANAGEMENT SCIENCE

Behavioral decision making is complemented by sound quantitative methods. Brainstorming, NGT, and the Delphi technique presume "nonquantitative" value judgments and intuition, but managers often use information gathered through analytical research to generate responses in these group decision-making situations. *Quantitative analysis* is also used extensively to evaluate ideas generated through group processes, and in many organizational settings, problems are so complex that computational methods are essential to unravel problems and formulate their solutions. These issues constitute the mainstream of management science.

management science
In decision-making terms, a process of model building using quantitative techniques to resolve a problem.

The role of **management science** has been accelerating as new methods of information processing and computer applications rapidly become available, and management curricula typically contain several courses devoted to these topics. We will discuss these techniques and their importance for planning elsewhere in Part Two and for controlling in Part Five. For now, we can note that in decision-making terms, management science is the process of model building. Just as Boeing engineers built a model of the first B52, managers build models of problems. Then they test the models using scientific methods of inquiry and analysis.

Scientific inquiry begins by developing a model to simulate the problem. Unfortunately, managers can seldom create physical models as engineers do for airplanes; they must structure problems using mathematics. For example, a model of consumer behavior (researching a marketing problem) may use mathematical relationships (variables) for demand, product price, consumer income, and competitors' prices. These variables will be analyzed to determine how they affect one another and affect sales. Thus managers model the problem to answer a question, such as how much consumers might be willing to pay for products. Solutions to the problem can then be simulated to gain insight for making better decisions.

Similar techniques can be used for evaluating investments, manufacturing products, providing services, and hiring employees. Shell Oil Corporation uses a complex computer-based simulation technique for scheduling tanker ships on a global basis. Intel Corporation employs mathematical equations for maintaining quality control of microelectronic circuitry production. Hospitals use probability models for purchasing surgical supplies. These examples of management science rely on systems of variables (i.e., equations) that produce recommendations on which managers base their decisions. Variables are, in turn, formulated through algorithms. **Algorithms** are mathematical rules for finding unique solutions to well-established problems. These rules are very useful for making decisions under conditions of certainty because outcomes are known to exist and are mutually exclusive.

algorithms
Mathematical rules for finding unique solutions to well-established problems.

In many instances, there is not enough information available to determine either a unique solution or a probability. This is a condition of uncertainty, and techniques of management science have been extremely useful for guiding managers toward better decisions in uncertain environments. This is accomplished through methods of heuristics. The term **heuristics** is derived from a Greek word meaning "to find or discover." Heuristics uses procedures that lead one to systematically work

heuristics
A process of "learning" through which decision makers analyze ideas and "progress" toward a solution as ideas unfold.

through issues in an established model. "Learning" takes place in the heuristic model, so that when one condition exists, an alternative action is recommended. A chess game is heuristic because individuals never know how the game is going to unfold, yet for a given series of moves, a preferred countermove exists.

Decision making under conditions of uncertainty defies mathematical model building. However, as assumptions are developed, such as future scenarios from a Delphi round, decision makers implicitly use a heuristic approach to weigh decisions and refine their alternatives. For example, when Procter & Gamble introduced Pampers, market research managers sampled mothers with small children and made assumptions about the advantages of throw-away diapers compared with cloth diapers. P&G was facing uncertain conditions and was apprehensive about Pampers. The company initially underestimated demand and was overwhelmed with orders. However, armed with new information as the diaper markets changed, P&G adjusted their equations for producing and selling Pampers, and managers made better decisions to satisfy customers with improved products delivered in a timely fashion.[28]

Clearly, decision making has changed as managers utilize more sophisticated computational tools. Decision making has also changed as cultural attitudes about work and behavior in organizations have evolved. As we shall see in Part Three, group processes are becoming more refined. When we combine behavioral changes with advances in computational technology, we have tremendous capabilities to solve very complex problems. However, the process can be chaotic unless we approach decision making in a systematic manner. As we shall see in the next section, complex problems are best solved through a *rational* approach to decision making.

CHECKPOINT

- Discuss the importance of information science for decision making.
- How do algorithms differ from heuristics? Give an example of each in use by managers.
- Consider how a bookstore manager might resolve the problem of how many copies of a new novel to order. Will the decision be programmed or nonprogrammed? What information will be helpful in making the decision? Will a management science model based on algorithms or heuristics be more useful?

RATIONAL DECISIONS AND PROBLEM SOLVING

Rational decision making is a process involving several steps that lead managers toward optimal solutions. It identifies the right problems to solve and illuminates new opportunities. A rational decision-making model has evolved in practice that incorporates several distinct steps. Figure 5-7 shows this eight-step process.

rational decision making
A process of systematically analyzing a problem to find an optimal solution.

Step 1: Diagnose the Problem

It is essential to examine problems thoroughly, recognize *symptoms,* and identify *causes.* A medical analogy is useful in understanding this point. A good physician will systematically *diagnose* a patient's condition to determine the root cause of illness in order to strive for a cure rather than just treat superficial symptoms. For example, a patient with the symptoms of a bad cold may have a flu virus, an allergy, or perhaps a more critical, nonviral illness. If the physician jumps to a quick conclusion without

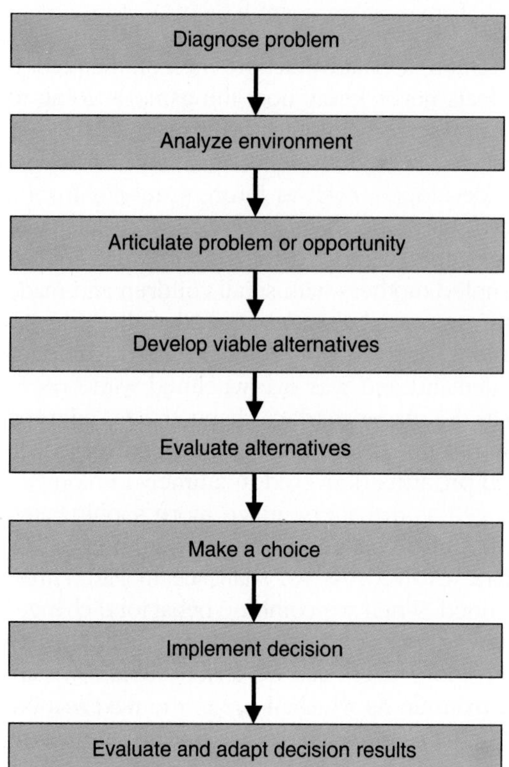

FIGURE 5-7 The Rational Decision-Making Process

proper diagnosis, the patient may be treated for the wrong illness, or the symptoms may be treated while the real illness is untended.

Problems in organizations are often as difficult to identify as medical ailments. Common symptoms of management problems are declining profits, escalating costs, employee absenteeism, poor-quality products, conflict, and employee stress. Frequently, however, there are no apparent symptoms, and managers must be on the alert to discover potential problems. Personnel managers, for example, track performance through formal periodic evaluations to detect early signs of poor employee performance. Quality control managers regularly monitor product performance. Market researchers gather information from customers to better understand the competition. Other diagnostic efforts range from political observations to machine maintenance inspections. (See Figure 5-8.)

Symptoms provide clues to existing or potential problems, and when they are diagnosed correctly, managers can accurately define the right problems to solve. The diagnostic process often leads to much more than problem solving. If an organiza-

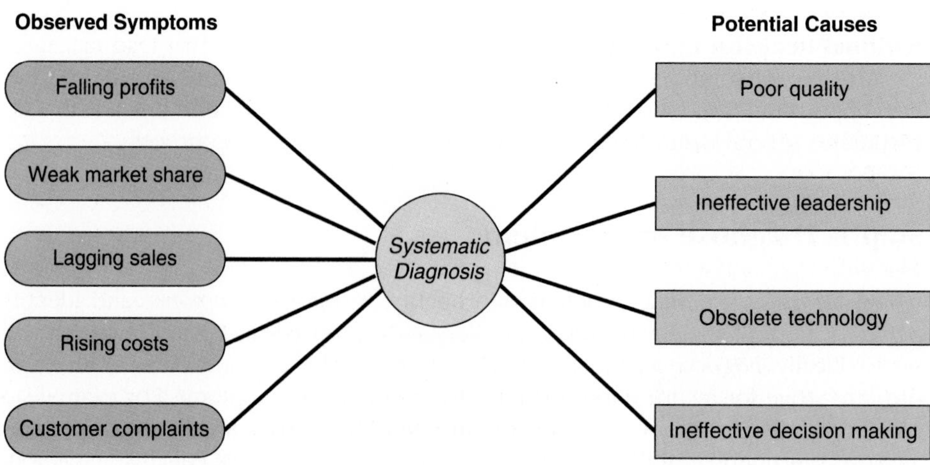

FIGURE 5-8 Diagnosis of Symptoms to Find Causes

tion has a good network of sensors (feedback reports, quality control checks, and market research data), it will also be able to uncover new opportunities, such as unmet consumer needs. Many opportunities surface during the environmental analysis, the next step in the process. For example, Xerox Corporation held an 80 percent share of the world market in office copiers from the mid-1960s until 1980. The company was content to manufacture great numbers of one successful model, but it had no method of evaluating potential competition. When Xerox started losing sales to Japanese manufacturers, its executives put more emphasis on sales, trying to hold an edge through price discounts and heavy advertising. Low sales, however, was not the problem. Xerox was weak in product research and development. By 1984, when its world market share had fallen to less than 45 percent, Xerox executives had identified the problem and set up a systematic intelligence network to monitor competition and the company's own research efforts. By 1991, Xerox had cut in half the resources and time required to develop new products and had regained nearly 60 percent of the world market share for office copiers.[29]

Step 2: Analyze the Environment

Managers should not automatically assume they have correctly identified the problem or opportunity after examining the symptoms. They should also evaluate environmental factors that could influence their diagnosis. For example, a company may be losing profits not because it is doing something wrong, but rather because an outside force has altered the competition. Deregulation of the airline industry during the 1980s led to a sudden lowering of fares and simultaneously helped incubate a number of small, highly competitive commuter airlines. Political changes can also create new problems or present new opportunities. For example, rigorous new legislation on hazardous waste disposal created problems for firms with huge quantities of hazardous materials. One view of this legislation was that government had imposed a new and costly burden on manufacturers. Another view was that government had created extraordinary opportunities for new methods of safe removal of hazardous waste. Those who saw the opportunity created new technologies for waste removal, and thus helped launch a profitable new industry.[30]

Constraints. Managers must consider internal and external limitations that might constrain their diagnoses as well as guide their decisions. Legislation, political changes, economic changes, consumer demand, foreign competition, new trade agreements, and many other factors affect both diagnoses and decisions. In addition to these external issues, managers face internal constraints, such as restricted capital, collective bargaining agreements, and prerogatives of top managers and owners. In the last instance, executives may simply not be aggressive, preferring a conservative course of action. At the other extreme, risk-taking managers may be extremely aggressive and endorse risky decisions.

Assumptions. Every organization has obvious constraints that influence the nature of its problems and limit solutions. As managers, we want to identify these constraints so we can make proper assumptions about what we can and cannot do. For example, money is invariably limited; we are seldom given a blank check to resolve a problem. Time is another constraint; many decisions must be made quickly. Information may simply be unavailable; managers often do not know what new products their competitors are developing until they are introduced into the markets. Other organizational resources may be lacking; it may be desirable to automate offices or computerize production, but employees may lack the skills to operate new technology. A complete *environmental analysis,* therefore, will establish constraints and assumptions to provide the groundwork for diagnosing problems and helping managers find solutions.

Step 3: Articulate the Problem or Opportunity

Perhaps managers have accomplished their most difficult task when they have correctly identified the problem or opportunity. This is particularly true in more complex situations such as long-range strategic planning (discussed in Chapter 7). To extend our medical analogy, doctors devote significant time and resources to identifying illnesses with the underlying belief that once they have found the *causes* of illnesses, solutions will follow. Managerial decision making is very similar. If profits slip and market share drops sharply, as happened to Xerox during the early 1980s, is it because the company is making a poor sales effort or because it has weak research and development? As noted earlier, Xerox initially blamed its decline on the wrong cause—a weak sales effort—when the problem was faltering R&D.

Even for a simple decision, such as purchasing a personal computer, it is not always clear *why* we are considering this option as opposed to hiring a typist to do word processing or using a hand calculator to solve equations. What problem are we trying to solve? Perhaps we are trying to better cope with a pressing issue, such as computational needs in financial management. But perhaps the computer is simply an ego satisfier or a coveted gadget. We cannot make our best decision in a masquerade. We must articulate the right problem before we seek a solution.

Step 4: Develop Alternatives

alternatives
Viable options from which managers can select a course of action to resolve a problem or take advantage of an opportunity.

A rational decision-making process focuses on developing *viable* options, or **alternatives,** from which managers can select a course of action. Because too many choices can be confusing, most managers avoid creating a laundry list of possibilities and instead focus on a few alternatives that can be reasonably evaluated. They also avoid jumping to conclusions before considering enough alternatives. For example, hospital managers faced with rising costs and more restrictive government payment programs have considered several solutions. Some have cut high-cost services and trimmed staff to contain costs. Others have sold out to corporations, such as Humana, that reduce costs through economic purchasing and wholesale stocking of supplies for hundreds of member hospitals and clinics. Still others have implemented policies that exclude patients who belong to groups with poor payment records, such as retired persons with only partial Medicare insurance coverage. A recent approach has been to form franchises, or groups of hospitals, that cooperate to buy bulk supplies, process insurance claims through centralized offices, and share local facilities.[31] These are several alternatives open to hospital executives.

Step 5: Evaluate Alternatives

If managers have done a good job of environmental analysis, as outlined in Step 2, they will have ample decision-making criteria for evaluating their alternatives. If they have not, they must develop decision criteria at this point. Managers can choose from an impressive number of decision-making tools, many of which are taught in business school courses about production, finance, and statistics. In Part Five, we discuss some of these tools. Using appropriate methods, alternatives are evaluated on three criteria: *sufficiency, feasibility,* and *realism.*

Sufficiency. An alternative is viable if it is sufficient to solve the problem identified or to exploit the opportunity envisioned. If an alternative does not meet minimum criteria for resolving the problem, it should be discarded. If none of the alternatives developed are sufficient, managers should look for new ones. Sometimes, however, the problem requires fast action, so an alternative recognized as insufficient is implemented as a "stopgap" measure. When managers make insufficient choices, they are said to **satisfice** (accept less-than-adequate measures) in the short run. For example, if there is a gas leak in a pipeline of an oil refinery, either it will have to be plugged up or the line will have to be shut down. Though essential at the time, neither option is a permanent solution. Management will have to find out what caused the leak and solve that problem.

satisfice
A decision-making behavior in which an individual chooses a satisfactory alternative, one thought to be adequate, though not necessarily the best.

Feasibility. Many alternatives that are intuitively feasible turn out to be impossible given the organization's resource constraints. As noted earlier, time, money, materials, human resources, and personality factors may limit a manager's choices. External forces such as legal restrictions, competition, politics, and the economy may also impose constraints. An alternative is feasible only if it can be implemented within the constraints faced by the company.

Realism. An alternative may be feasible yet unrealistic. Once again, an organization faces constraints that limit choices, and while an option may be feasible, it may not be realistic given the prerogatives of managers or some other limiting criteria. For example, RJR Nabisco was bought out by the Wall Street investment group, Kohlberg, Kravis, Roberts & Company. Interestingly, RJR Nabisco's management, led by President F. Ross Johnson, was the high bidder, but was rejected by stockholders and employees, who felt that KKR offered more realistic long-run strategies to make the firm a success.[32]

Step 6: Make a Choice

Ideally, a manager should make a decision that is optimal. As we have noted, however, constraints often lead to *satisficing*. If a problem has been accurately formulated and sufficient viable alternatives exist, then a manager should make a choice that is best under the circumstances. This will be the **optimal choice**—one that generates the greatest possible benefits with the fewest negative consequences.

optimal choice
One that generates the greatest possible benefits with the fewest negative consequences.

Often managers use quantitative and financial decision-making criteria to make "the most likely" decision under stated circumstances. A variety of decision-making methodologies exist but are beyond the scope of this text. It should be noted, however, that in maximizing decisions, managers are influenced by a tremendous amount of subjective information, including their own values and beliefs. What seems mathematically optimal to one manager may appear emotionally untenable to another. Optimality, therefore, is in the eye of the beholder.

This is reflected in the different decisions made by managers who have widely different personalities and prerogatives. For instance, a firm may be stereotyped as exploitative because top management chooses to endorse autocratic managerial policies or views labor as a combative force. In another firm, enlightened management may create a cohesive work environment through labor-management cooperation. Decisions throughout each firm will differ significantly. There is also a tremendous difference among individuals in their abilities to handle risk. Some managers are **risk averse:** they avoid situations with perceived risk. Others are **risk takers:** they are eager to take on high-risk problems in uncertain circumstances. Decisions taken at the higher levels of an organization reflect top-level managers' attitudes toward risk, and since these are the people who set the tone for the organization, subsequent decisions by lower-level managers reflect the same attitudes toward risk.

risk averse
Having an aversion to taking perceived risks, preferring instead to make decisions with a high degree of clarity.

risk takers
Those who have a propensity to pursue risks to resolve problems with uncertain outcomes.

Step 7: Implement the Decision

Few managers have the luxury of making decisions and leaving the task of carrying them out altogether to others. Most managers bear responsibility for their decisions and must become involved in implementing them. For example, James R. Houghton, chairman of Corning Glass Works, announced a strong commitment to improving quality at Corning in 1986. He then set up an internal training institute to educate the company's 20,000 employees in quality improvement techniques. The "problem" was how to improve quality at Corning, and the "decision" was to create a company-wide commitment to quality through education. This decision was selected from "alternatives" that included more forceful work rules, bonus incentives, and hiring quality consultants. Houghton chose to implement an *action plan* based on a five-year in-house education program with the objective of improving quality by 90 percent. By 1991, Corning Glass had achieved most of its quality targets ahead of schedule.[33]

Empowerment is also crucial and means giving employees sufficient authority and resources to carry out decisions. For group decision making, as noted earlier, empowerment is requisite. Corning was successful in its quality program not only because it had a viable action plan, but also because managers and employees learned to work with one another and were empowered with the responsibility for implementing their decisions.[34]

Step 8: Evaluate and Adapt Decision Results

The final step in the rational decision-making process is concerned with controlling activities that reinforce decisions. Once decisions are implemented, controls are needed to guide action toward desired results. This is, of course, essential for imple-

FIGURE 5-9 Buying a Business Computer: An 8-Step Decision Process

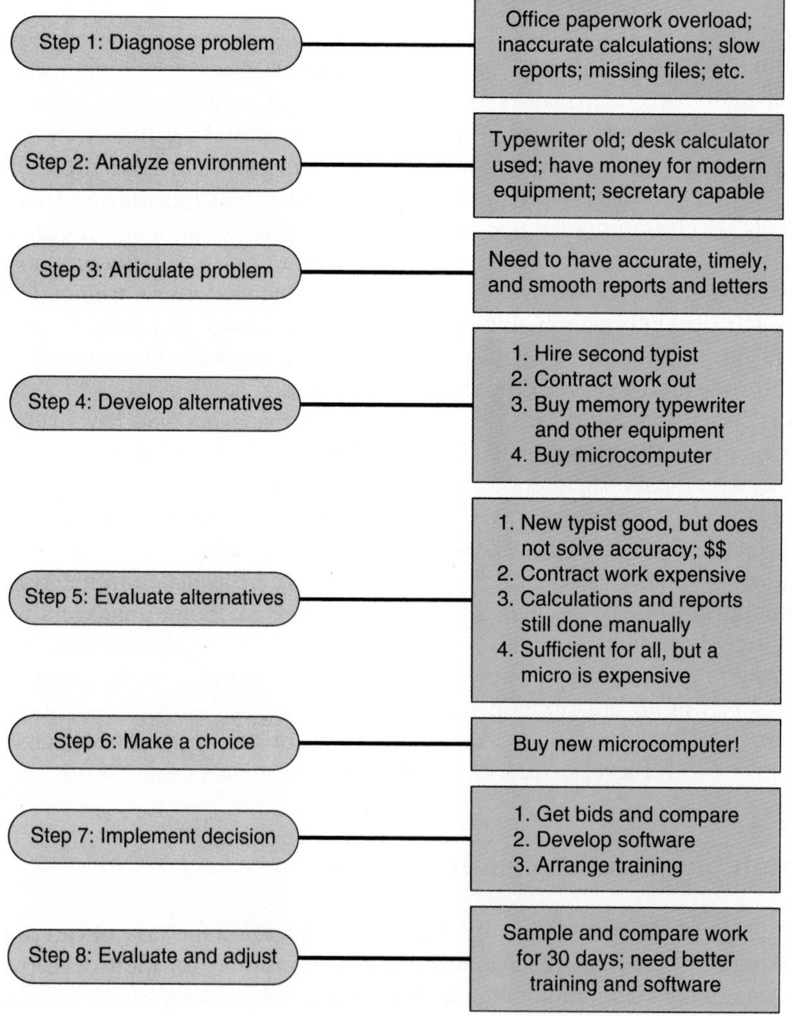

Step 1: Diagnose problem
Office paperwork overload; inaccurate calculations; slow reports; missing files; etc.
Step 2: Analyze environment
Typewriter old; desk calculator used; have money for modern equipment; secretary capable
Step 3: Articulate problem
Need to have accurate, timely, and smooth reports and letters
Step 4: Develop alternatives
1. Hire second typist
2. Contract work out
3. Buy memory typewriter and other equipment
4. Buy microcomputer
Step 5: Evaluate alternatives
1. New typist good, but does not solve accuracy; $$
2. Contract work expensive
3. Calculations and reports still done manually
4. Sufficient for all, but a micro is expensive
Step 6: Make a choice
Buy new microcomputer!
Step 7: Implement decision
1. Get bids and compare
2. Develop software
3. Arrange training
Step 8: Evaluate and adjust
Sample and compare work for 30 days; need better training and software

mentation; but effective managers use control and feedback mechanisms not only to ensure results but also to provide information for future decisions.

Illustrating a decision. Figure 5-9 illustrates a complete rational decision-making process for purchasing a computer. This is the type of decision made hundreds of times a day in thousands of organizations. When buying a personal computer, for example, we want to consider price, software availability, service support by the vendor, and perhaps its physical attractiveness. We are also concerned with the type of computing tasks to be done; thus the speed and performance of the computer will be critical. We might also be concerned about compatibility with other computers at work or school. Other factors that influence our decision might be the reputation of the vendor, favorable financing, and our emotional bias toward one brand or another.

CHECKPOINT

- What are the steps in a rational decision process? Create a flowchart of the decision-making process and explain what a manager does in each step.
- Why is it important to analyze both the internal and external environments when trying to identify the right problem to solve?
- Discuss the three elements of a "viable" alternative. They are sufficiency, feasibility, and realism.

TOWARD MORE EFFECTIVE DECISION MAKING

Our fundamental emphasis in business schools has been on teaching decision-making "tools" and "techniques" that are characterized by quantitative analysis. Perhaps this emphasis comes from our ability to teach factual information and to relate tools to procedures. But decision making is an art as well as a science, and our ability to teach the *art* of decision making is almost nonexistent. Nevertheless, several guidelines can help individuals understand the art of decision making.

Use Information Effectively

Few companies can run effectively without a good fact base. We need data and analytical capabilities to measure progress. Managers can, however, become so numbed manipulating numbers that they lose sight of why they are doing the analysis. For example, several years ago Merrill Lynch introduced its Cash Management Account (CMA) as a computerized investment system that would provide rapid transactions among brokerage, credit card, and banking services through a unified data base.[35] The Merrill Lynch CMA was meant to provide more timely information to customers to help them make investment decisions. For the first few months, however, CMA brokers overwhelmed customers with too many investment alternatives, each loaded with quantitative data. Customers were receiving nearly four times as much data as they were used to receiving, but the actual number of investment transactions was declining. Merrill Lynch solved the problem quickly by training CMA brokers to "manage information" so that they would artfully select data to reinforce investment decisions without generating an information overload.

Learning how to select relevant information and to use it reasonably is essential for timely decision making. Managing information so that it neither overloads people nor results in superficial diagnoses is the ultimate goal. A massive computer

ETHICS IN MANAGEMENT

Cadbury's Founder Set the Tone for Ethical Decisions

Sir Adrian Cadbury tells the story of how his grandfather, founder of the world-famous Cadbury Candies, solved two ethical dilemmas in 1900. It was the pinnacle year of the Boer War in South Africa, when black Africans were being slaughtered in a political contest between Great Britain and the Boers (settlers of Dutch descent) for white supremacy of that emerging country. Sir Adrian's grandfather bitterly opposed the war on humanistic grounds, going so far as to purchase a daily newspaper with a large circulation in Britain to voice his opposition. Unfortunately, the newspaper he bought was famous for publishing daily horse racing cards and setting "punter's odds," and Sir Adrian's grandfather also bitterly detested gambling. If he refused to print track cards and race results, circulation would drop, endangering the newspaper. He resolved his dilemma by continuing to print the racing sections because he felt it was essential to reach as many readers as possible with his war opposition messages.

The second ethical dilemma also involved the Boer War. Cadbury was given a royal commission to send boxes of candies to soldiers in South Africa. The commission promised a huge profit, more jobs for his factory workers, and world attention for Cadbury's, which at the time was only beginning to establish a reputation for British milk chocolates. Sir Adrian's grandfather also solved this problem in favor of his principles: he

model can spin off quantitative criteria for as many potential alternatives as we can create input for, but making a choice is still a human task.

Enhance Systems for Decision Making

Recent innovations in management reflect exciting changes in systems, human forms of organization, and joint endeavors that lead to improved performance. Practicing managers at every level are responsible for creating systems, not simply working within them. For example, researchers have found that when new computerized information systems are implemented, the pace of work increases and middle managers are pressed to make more rapid decisions about more issues. At Motorola, management addressed this problem by creating team decision making based on the concept of *quality control circles* whereby small groups are given the responsibility and autonomy to make work-related decisions without higher-level review or documentation.[36] This "system" change has redefined Motorola's organizational structure, how decisions are made, and how communication flows among management strata.

decided to send the candies, but did so at factory cost to avoid profiting from a war he opposed.

Cadbury Schweppes PLC has won notable awards since 1900 for corporate ethics, which Sir Adrian explains started with his grandfather's sense of public duty and continues today unchanged. One company rule—that it is best to tell the truth—often runs up against another—that it is best not to hurt other people. Consequently, there is no universal formula for solving ethical problems at Cadbury Schweppes. The company encourages group brainstorming on ethical questions, and managers are strongly urged to listen to employees who have complaints or information about potential ethical problems. In effect, Cadbury encourages a form of "internal whistleblowing" coupled to a decision-making process. Many similar well-run companies also have mechanisms for whistleblowing behavior by employees, including public forums, protected review processes, anonymous methods of being heard by top management through intermediaries, and hotlines within the company to quickly report potential problems.

Sources: Sir Adrian Cadbury, "Ethical Managers Make Their Own Rules," *Harvard Business Review,* Vol. 65 (September–October 1987), pp. 69–73. See also Janet P. Near, "Whistle-Blowing: Encourage It!" *Business Horizons,* Vol. 32 (January–February 1989), pp. 2–6.

Empower Those Who Must Implement Decisions

Participative decision-making systems, by definition, empower those who are involved in decision making, but unless everyone concerned in the decision is involved, empowerment may be restricted to small groups or selected individuals. Empowerment means not only including employees in decision making, but also ensuring that they are given both the resources necessary to implement decisions and the responsibility for getting the job done. The main benefit of empowerment is improved cooperation: those who feel empowered are more likely to *accept* and *understand* organizational decisions, even if they participated to only a limited degree in making the decisions.

As we shall see in Part Four on Leadership, although participation by employees in organizational decisions has become accepted in many excellent companies, nonparticipative systems based on managerial hierarchies are still more common. American, European, and Asian companies are not democratic forums. Consequently, empowerment through shared responsibilities and resource support systems is even more important.

Communicate Effectively

Decisions must be understood by those who carry them out as well as by those at higher echelons who must evaluate performance. Clear communication is crucial to gaining acceptance. Communicating expectations for performance, detailing decisions, and explaining changes and adaptations are all essential for organizational success. It is not enough for managers to simply accept that they must communicate clearly and effectively. The art of leadership and decision making demands that they develop a near-wizardry in oral and verbal communications.

Delegate Pragmatically

Leadership and motivation focus on the delegation of authority. Managers cannot evolve systems, communicate effectively, or empower employees if all decisions are made or vetoed by one dominant authority figure. Assuring timely and more accurate decision making at critical points in operations consists basically of shifting authority downward. Pragmatic delegation suggests that managers define who is best suited to make decisions on the basis of several criteria. People with experience in solving problems, who have access to information, and who are in the best position to implement decisions are the best candidates for decision-making authority.

Build on Strength

Effective decision making capitalizes on the strengths of individuals in given situations. For example, not everyone works well in group brainstorming sessions, but some individuals prefer making group decisions.[37] Still others express their creativity best in unstructured decision-making situations. Different managers seldom make similar types of decisions in similar styles of management, even under precisely the same circumstances. Learning how to choose the method of decision making that is most suitable is therefore extremely helpful. Learning how to empathize with others making similar decisions is essential to the art of management.

CHECKPOINT

- Discuss the advantages and pitfalls of having more information available for decision making. How would a manager best use the information at hand?
- Why is it important to gain subordinates' acceptance of decisions?
- What are the arguments for delegating decision-making authority?
- Some people enjoy group decision making, others do not. Reconsider the discussion of GE's storyboard brainstorming in light of your personal preferences, and then explain why you would or would not do well as a team member at a storyboard conference for making decisions.

AT THE BEGINNING OF THE CHAPTER, we introduced the concept of group decision making and described how General Electric has used the *storyboard,* a concept made popular by Walt Disney, to encourage creative thinking by team members assembled to solve a specific problem. At GE, some people were very uncomfortable working in a group brainstorming environment. Others got into arguments with their colleagues. But overall, the storyboard approach achieved what management hoped it would. For example, at GE's Erie, Pennsylvania, plant, one innovation resulting from the storyboard process was the design of an improved manufacturing process in which nine machines were used to complete a complex manufacturing process in sixteen hours. Previously, it took *twenty-nine* machines on-line for nearly *sixteen days* to complete the same process. As a result of this innovation, output per labor-hour increased 240 percent and accuracy 38 percent.

The program at GE did not achieve immediate success, however, because individuals who participated in it were discouraged by the bickering and arguments that erupted during group sessions. Several managers, accustomed to making unilateral decisions, felt that their authority was being undermined. GE improved the program by training managers to work better in groups and by counseling participants in ways to communicate constructively while avoiding conflicts.[38] ■

A SYNOPSIS FOR LEARNING

1. Describe how decision making is important to organizational success.

   Effective managers make decisions that reinforce organizational objectives, thereby improving performance through better allocation of resources, including people, materials, and capital. In making *programmed decisions,* which are well defined, a manager may rely on policies, procedures, or rules that lead to predictable results. *Unprogrammed decisions* depend on individual managers' judgment, experience, and creativity.

2. Explain the concepts of certainty, risk, and uncertainty in decision making. Then, discuss the Delphi technique for creative problem solving.

   Certainty is a condition of knowing the results of a decision before the decision is made. Risk is the situation of not being certain about the outcome of a decision, but having enough information to sense probabilities. Under conditions of uncertainty, managers have too little information to make an evaluation or to generate probabilities of risk.

3. Describe decision-making processes in brainstorming and nominal groups.

   Brainstorming and nominal group techniques help managers search for optimal solutions in situations where few rational models apply. Brainstorming is a group process without leadership or structure; participants enjoy the freedom of exploring solutions to problems without the restrictions of rules or procedures. The nominal group technique (NGT) provides a structure to group interaction so that individual suggestions are prominently displayed, discussed, and rank-ordered by voting; the process is repeated until a viable solution gains acceptance by the majority of group members. The Delphi technique is a survey method of polling selected panel members on well-defined problems. Delphi participants do not come together in personal meetings, and panel members can participate on a global basis with anonymity.

4. Explain the role of management science techniques for decision making.

   Management science is concerned with quantitative modeling of complex problems and solutions. Management science tools include a broad range of new computer-based applications that simplify management decision making.

5. Define and discuss a rational decision-making process.

   Rational decision making follows an eight-step process designed to provide managers with a method for unraveling complex problems in a systematic manner. The process begins with uncovering cause-and-effect relationships to diagnose a problem and concludes with obtaining feedback on performance results to make adjustments and to guide future activities.

6. Explore guidelines for making effective decisions as managers.

   Using information effectively is one way to reduce confusion and improve decisions because it is the quality of timely information that helps managers make good decisions, not the amount of information brought to bear on a problem. Managers can also improve their systems of decision making to achieve greater employee involvement.

SKILL ANALYSIS

CASE 1 The NASA Space Shuttle Launch Decision

To Launch or Not to Launch: That Was the Question

The final decision to launch the *Challenger* on January 28, 1986, rested on the coordination of hundreds of prior decisions made by thousands of contractors, subcontractors, and three space centers. Decisions were not only concerned with the ability of the rocket to fly but also with issues of cargo space, crew training, flight plan designs, schedules, experiments, and computer programs.

Data and decisions moved up through successive levels, and at each point in the succession, fewer people were involved in assessing increasingly reduced data summaries, adding their own particular views and concerns, and passing their evaluations and decisions up to yet another decision level. The Mission Management Team, the last in the chain of command, took over management 48 hours prior to the launch and encouraged launch officials at lower levels to report any new problems or difficulties. Unfortunately, these lower-level individuals had to report through the chain of command and, like a game of pass-it-on, information gets distorted as it passes up the hierarchy—often as a result of the reflected interests of bosses along the way. It was such a distortion, along with a number of other factors, that contributed to the disaster of January 28, 1986.

Various changes in NASA reflect the other factors contributing to the tragic decision to launch that day. Reorganizations in the agency's history included the development of a stronger headquarters team to coordinate efforts among field centers in 1961; a decentralization in 1963; a recentralization to integrate decision making and increase emphasis on safety in 1967 as a result of a tragic fire that resulted in the deaths of three astronauts; and finally, another reorganization in 1983 that reclassified the shuttle program from developmental to operational.

Such reorganizations were not only the result of the internal workings of NASA. They also reflected both the degree of financial support that could be garnered and the goals and agendas of U.S. presidents. On the heels of a time of great support through the Kennedy and Johnson administrations, when NASA was perceived as "an organism that was more responsive to its own internal technological momentum than to externally developed objectives," the Nixon administration called for more practical goals to provide tangible benefits to science, the economy, and national security. This shift from a technological focus to a more political one was followed by President Reagan's two 1982 policy priorities—to maintain U.S. leadership in space and to expand private-sector involvement and investment.

The shift in political tone brought NASA face-to-face with several new challenges: commercialization, meeting the needs of military and civilian agencies, developing private-sector activities, and meeting customer commitments. NASA was no longer its own customer; it had to serve the needs of the military and private industry. The primary stakeholders were now a close-knit network of NASA, Congress, the Department of Defense, and private industry. With the needs and priorities of commercial customers essentially driving the program, cost and schedule constraints received greater emphasis, and safety issues took a backseat as personnel were pushed beyond their endurance limits to meet deadlines. The organization moved from one dominated by scientists and engineers to one dominated by bureaucrats and administrators.

While the Kennedy and Johnson administrations provided NASA with its greatest period of support, the Kennedy administration was also responsible for opening up NASA to the public and moving the agency away from its emphasis on secrecy. With this shift NASA got an eager press. The benefits of media coverage were soon recognized, especially as space flights became more commonplace. Wornout notions of astronauts as fearless daredevils had to be replaced with new images, and contractors, performing 80–90 percent of NASA's design and development work, lobbied to promote their interests.

All these factors led to various changes. By the mid 1980s, a distinction was made between engineering and program management decisions. An engineer who had been with NASA since 1960 spoke about this change from years past: "At the beginning all the decisions were made at the lowest possible level. . . . It was simply inconceivable that one person could have thought something was wrong . . . and everyone else not know about it." Another engineer said, "People making the decisions are getting farther and farther away from the people who get their hands dirty." It was just such a distinction in decision-making responsibility that was ultimately responsible for the tragic decision to launch that fateful January in 1986.

In an evening telephone conference between Morton Thiokol, Inc., and the Kennedy Space Center, presentations of data were made by engineers expressing concern regarding seal integrity at particularly low temperatures. According to R. Boisjoly, a senior engineer on the project at MTI, the data supported a no-launch decision. At the end of the engineering presentation, Larry Mulloy of NASA asked MTI for a launch decision. Based on the engineering position, MTI recommended against launching. Mulloy then asked G. Hardy of NASA for his launch decision. While Hardy said he was "appalled" by MTI's recommendation, he said he would not launch over the contractor's objection. Mulloy then gave his views and concluded that the engineering data presented were inconclusive.

If NASA's earliest rules that forced contractors and the agency itself to prove it was safe to fly before a launch was authorized had been followed, Mulloy's statement about the inconclusivity of the data would have been enough to scrub the mission. However, this statement on the inconclusivity of the data seemed to prompt MTI Vice President Kilminster to request an off-line caucus to reevaluate the data. As soon as MTI was off-line, J. Mason, MTI's general manager, said, "We have to make a management decision." It was clear then that an attempt would be made by executive-level management to reverse the no-launch decision.

Two engineers, A. Thompson and R. Boisjoly, attempted to make themselves heard as the managers began a discussion among themselves. No one in management seemed to want to discuss the facts, and with cold and unfriendly looks toward the engineers, they struggled to make a list of data that would support a launch decision. A vote poll was taken by only the four senior executives present; engineers were excluded from both the discussion and the poll. Returning to the telecon, Kilminster read the launch support rationale and recommended that the launch proceed as scheduled. NASA accepted the launch recommendation without any discussion or any probing questions—the recommendation was consistent with their desires. In fact, NASA had placed MTI in the position of proving that it was *not* safe to fly instead of proving that it *was* safe to fly.

Case Questions

1. Decisions are intended to promote organizational success. What factors motivated MTI's decision to support a launch, and how did these contribute or detract from its success as an organization?
2. In what ways does this case demonstrate the rational decision-making process?

Sources: Roger Boisjoly, "Ethical Decisions—Morton Thiokol and the Space Shuttle *Challenger* Disaster," paper presented at the December 1987 meeting of the American Society of Mechanical Engineers; and R. Marx, C. Stubbart, V. Traub, and M. Cavanaugh, "The NASA Space Shuttle Disaster: A Case Study," *Journal of Management*, Vol. 3, pp. 300–18.

VIDEO CASE MVP Athletic Shoes: Decisions on a Shoestring

Harold Martin, president and CEO of MVP, decided to sell his race car business and establish a venture in athletic shoes, a field where three companies hold over 60 percent of the U.S. market. What type of decision making did Martin use as he developed a unique marketing approach to differentiate his products?

With $400,000 at stake, Martin was eager to break into the lucrative, but intensely competitive, athletic shoe market. He says, "I believed in myself, and I believed that just because there was a big guy there, that the David and Goliath story still existed." However, before deciding to enter the "sneaker wars," Martin studied the market. His research revealed that in the Michigan area alone, where his company chose to focus first, there were 634,000 students and each of those students bought about four pairs of shoes a year. With this information, Martin made some decisions about the product he wanted to offer and how he would go about offering it.

He decided to attack the market with $50-to-$60 leather athletic shoes personalized with college and high school colors and logos. By capitalizing on students' pride in their school and their desire to show school spirit, MVP's product appeared to have wide appeal. Martin's company also developed a creative approach to marketing its shoes. It arranged for a student club to sell the shoes, promising that for each pair sold, the school would receive $19. The money earned could support club and school activities.

One Detroit high school teacher whose marketing club has participated in this MVP program was enthusiastic about the approach not only because the school received significant income from it but also because his marketing students obtained practical skills in selling products that enhanced their classroom learning. What did MVP get in return? The money from shoe sales, of course. But it also got an eager sales force dispersing its sales message for free. Martin described the arrangement as "win-win."

But MVP is not content to operate only in the high school market. The company has taken its concept to corporations with the intent of selling them on the spirit of "belongingness" that MVP shoes represent. MVP has also approached retail sporting outlets to distribute college lines and contracted with national retailers to distribute a new "X" line, developed to exploit renewed public interest in the slain civil rights leader Malcolm X. In addition, the company has developed a line of Star Trek shoes for Trek fans.

How has Martin's strategy paid off? He maintains, "Every year to date, sales have pretty much tripled. We're expecting 1992 to be an on-track year for us." In fact, the thirty-five-person company expected to sell 150,000 pairs of shoes in 1992. But MVP's decision makers are also planning ahead. They are looking for expansion opportunities and new markets. Says Harold Martin, "We essentially, right now, have more business opportunity than we have dollars to match the opportunity, so we have to be very careful in our structure that we don't overposition ourself." Decisions on a shoestring? MVP has shown how to make decisions with shoestrings firmly in hand!

Case Questions

1. Do you think Harold Martin should have obtained more information before deciding to enter the highly competitive athletic shoe market? If so, what other information would you have recommended? If not, why not?
2. What specific steps of the rational decision-making process did Martin and his employees take in making decisions about the market and the product?
3. How would you classify Martin's decision-making environment? Why?

Sources: Richard Sandomir, "Top Athletes Are Wooed to Fill Big Shoes," *New York Times*, April 12, 1992, p. 33; Robert E. Carr, "Some Good News and Bad News for the Nineties," *Sporting Goods Business*, May 1991, Vol. 24, No. 5, p. 8; and Bob McGee, "A Really Big Shoe Story," *Women's Sports and Fitness*, March 1991, p. 31.

SKILL PRACTICE

THE ROLE OF INFERENCE AND OBSERVATION IN DECISION MAKING

Procedure

A. Read instructions and evaluate statements for the Sample Story (Time allotted: 8–10 minutes).
After you have read and understood the instructions, proceed with the four statements about the Sample Story. Circle the appropriate response: T, F, or ?. Then check your accuracy by looking at the appropriate answers printed beneath the statements. If you do not agree with the given answer, go back to the story to check.

B. Evaluate the statements about the Practice Story (Time allotted: 15–20 minutes).
Using the same instructions as for the Sample Story, proceed to read the Practice Story and evaluate the 15 statements that follow it. The instructor will provide appropriate answers for these 15 statements and the rationale behind these answers.

C. Discussion of nature of inferences (Time allotted: 15–20 minutes).
Consider errors you may have made in evaluating the statements in B. Why did these errors happen? Were the answers supplied by the instructor equal to or superior to your own? What is the concept of the "uncalculated risk"?

Test your skill in the area of inferences and observation by reading the Sample Story first. Then when the instructor indicates, read the next story and mark the most appropriate choice for the 15 statements that follow it.

Instructions

Read the following story. Assume that all the information presented in it is definitely accurate and true. Read it carefully because it has ambiguous parts designed to lead you astray. No need to memorize it, though. You can refer back to it whenever you wish.

Next read the statements about the story and check each to indicate whether you consider it "T," "F," or "?". "T" means that the statement is definitely true on the basis of the information presented in the story. "F" means that it is definitely false. "?" means that it may be either true or false and that you cannot be certain which on the basis of the information presented in the story. If any part of a statement is doubtful, make it "?". Answer each statement in turn, do not go back to change any answer later, and don't reread any statements after you have answered them. This will distort your score.

To start with, here is a sample story with the correct answers:

Sample Story

You arrive home late one evening and see that the lights are on in your living room. There is only one car parked in front of your house, and the words "Harold R. Jones, M.D." are spelled in small gold letters across one of the car's doors.

Statements About Sample Story

1. The car parked in front of your house has lettering on one of its doors. (This is a "definitely true" statement because it is directly corroborated by the story.) T F ?
2. Someone in your family is sick. (This could be true, and then again, it might not be. Perhaps Dr. Jones is paying a social call at your home or perhaps he has gone to the house next door or across the street.) T F ?
3. No car is parked in front of your house. (A "definitely false" statement because the story directly contradicts it.) T F ?
4. The car parked in front of your house belongs to a man named Johnson. (May seem very likely false, but can you be sure? Perhaps the car has just been sold.) T F ?

Now begin the actual test (the Practice Story). Remember to mark each statement by circling the right response in order—don't skip around or change answers later.

The Practice Story

A businessman had just turned off the lights in the store when a man appeared and demanded money. The owner opened a cash register. The contents of the cash register were scooped up and the man sped away. A member of the police force was notified promptly.

Statements About the Practice Story

1. A man appeared after the owner had turned off his store lights. T F ?
2. The robber was a man. T F ?
3. The man who appeared did not demand money. T F ?
4. The man who opened the cash register was the owner. T F ?
5. The store owner scooped up the contents of the cash register and ran away. T F ?
6. Someone opened a cash register. T F ?
7. After the man who demanded the money scooped up the contents of the cash register, he ran away. T F ?
8. While the cash register contained money, the story does not state how much. T F ?

9. The robber demanded money of the owner. T F ?

10. A businessman had just turned off the lights when a man appeared in the store. T F ?

11. It was broad daylight when the man appeared. T F ?

12. The man who appeared opened the cash register. T F ?

13. No one demanded money. T F ?

14. The story concerns a series of events in which only three persons are referred to: the owner of the store, a man who demanded money, and a member of the police force. T F ?

15. The following events were included in the story: Someone demanded money, a cash register was opened, its contents were scooped up, and a man dashed out of the store. T F ?

Source: Reprinted by permission of Richard E. Dutton.

6

Planning Concepts and Practices

OUTLINE

The Nature of Planning
- Formal and Informal Planning
- Why Planning Pays Off

Organizational Objectives
- Hierarchy of Objectives
- Types of Objectives
- Establishing Objectives

The Planning Hierarchy
- Board-Level Strategic Responsibility
- Strategic Planning
- Tactical Planning
- Operational Planning

Planning Roles for Managers
- Management by Objectives

Communicating Plans
- Policies/Procedures/Rules
- Programs/Projects/Budgets

Making Plans Effective
- Contingency Planning
- Comprehensive Planning

The Formal Planning Process
- Establish Objectives
- Evaluate Environmental Factors
- Articulate Assumptions
- Involve Management and Staff
- Develop Alternatives
- Stratify Plans
- Communicate Plans
- Develop Supporting Plans
- Implement an Action Plan
- Plan to Plan

Approaches to Planning
- Centralized Top-down Planning
- Decentralized Bottom-up Planning
- Team Planning

OBJECTIVES

- Define the planning function and explain how formal and informal planning differ.
- Describe the various types of organization objectives and how managers establish them.
- Explain management planning responsibilities and how they relate to different types of objectives.
- Discuss the different roles managers must assume in strategic planning and how MBO works.
- Describe the various ways plans are communicated and how managers document planning activities.
- Explain why contingency planning is so important.
- Identify the steps in a formal planning process.
- Contrast the three main approaches to planning.

FOR MORE THAN TWO DECADES, IBM has been one of the largest and most profitable companies in the world, yet few people know that most of the company's sales and profits come from foreign operations.[1] IBM Europe has generated nearly half of IBM's total profits since the late 1970s, and by itself the European division could be listed among the top 50 global firms with $28 billion in annual sales. This success may not continue without major changes because the new Europe has become a fiercely competitive market. IBM is still the dominant computer company in Europe, but as an American company, it must deal from a weakened position because of the declining value of the U.S. dollar, new rules for trade within Europe, and growing competition by aggressive Japanese firms.

Managers at IBM Europe, however, expect to survive short-term problems and prosper from long-term opportunities. Their confidence comes from having one of the best planning systems in the world. IBM Europe began planning for the post-1992 Europe in 1984. The company's finance managers created exquisite communication systems for monitoring currency markets and economic indicators. The IBM team instituted market research that spans Eastern and Western Europe, Scandinavia, and the Middle East. The company also set up research and development facilities positioned close to international competitors in Britain, France, and Germany. Long-range plans include new chip designs and new manufacturing processes based on research done jointly with innovative European companies. In order to achieve these objectives, management began forming strategic alliances with other European companies in the 1980s, and by 1991, they had created more than 200 new partnerships.[2]

As you read this chapter on planning, consider how companies like IBM Europe must constantly be on the alert for changes that could threaten their existence or provide extraordinary new opportunities. Planning is a continual process that helps managers ready their companies for changes, and often spearheads innovations that transform their industries and our societies.

Of the four primary functions of management—planning, organizing, leading, and controlling—*planning* is the most important. Planning provides a framework for organizing resources, structuring a firm, and controlling activities. Through the planning process, managers develop goals and objectives, and these are the criteria by which we judge organizational effectiveness. Plans do not evolve in a vaccum, even though we say "planning precedes all other activities." We need managers to do the planning and an organization for them to function in. Think of planning as part of a cycle of activities, the first step of which is to establish objectives and methods for reaching those objectives.

Long-range planning is called *strategic planning,* and each year managers at Ford, Xerox, the NFL, the Red Cross, and thousands of other organizations engage in strategic planning to establish viable objectives and to diagram organizational activities. Strategic planning is addressed in Chapter 7. Managers also make near-term plans that are *tactical* in nature, having a life span of about a year. For example, several years ago, IBM "strategically" planned to introduce a new line of high-speed business computers; "tactically," it introduced a new PC in 1988, an improved operating system in 1989, a network operating system in 1990, and a new computer work station in 1991 that incorporated these earlier features. In the immediate short run, managers have to do *operational planning,* which includes scheduling work, projecting labor requirements, and acquiring materials, capital, and technology. Tactical and operational planning issues are introduced in Chapter 8.

THE NATURE OF PLANNING

planning
One of the four major functions of management. It is the process of defining organizational objectives and then articulating strategies, tactics, and operations necessary to achieve those objectives.

Planning is the process of defining an organization's objectives and how it will achieve them. George Steiner describes the planning function as one in which managers must decide "what is to be done, when it is to be done, how it is to be done, and who is to do it."[3] A plan, therefore, is a navigational tool that maps out a destination and charts a course to get there.

An objective is the result desired at a future point in time. Most undergraduate students, for example, want to earn their degrees in exactly four years at college. Organizations such as the United Way set fund-raising objectives, and corporations like Turner Broadcasting and Citicorp have profit and sales objectives. These objectives cannot be reached without plans outlining activities that must occur to get things done. The March of Dimes organizes volunteers, schedules promotions, and develops programs for fund-raising events, all within a specific time frame for the annual drive. Turner Broadcasting and Citicorp have plans for new services, expansion into new markets, and hundreds of activities necessary to compete profitably.

Managers plan in order to make decisions *today* based on premises of what might happen in the future. We seek *direction* for current actions; we seek new *opportunities;* and we try to *solve* today's problems without creating new ones. The larger and more complex an organization is, the more difficult it is to establish workable plans, but even small enterprises operate in complicated environments. Effective planning reduces the guesswork managers face when making decisions.

informal planning
A process of intuitively deciding on objectives and the activities needed to achieve them without rigorous and systematic investigation.

formal planning
The process of using systematic criteria and rigorous investigation to establish objectives, decide on activities, and formally document organizational expectations.

Formal and Informal Planning

Planning has both formal and informal elements. Some managers, for example, seem to do little more than "react" to situations according to their intuition. Others follow a thorough process of investigation before they make decisions. **Informal planning** is planning based on an intuitive process. **Formal planning** is based on a rigorous method of investigation and decision making. Student term papers provide examples of both approaches. Some students seem to be able to write a paper without intensive planning. Others write from carefully planned outlines, rewrite and rewrite, and submit a final paper after careful proofreading. Occasionally, a paper written without such thoroughness is better than a formally planned paper, but not often. Whichever method is used, the fundamentals are the same. Both students want a good grade; both have to decide on a topic; both must submit similar exercises; and both must justify what they have written.

The fundamental nature of planning is no different for business executives making organizational decisions than for students writing term papers. Predetermined plans provide guidelines for future activities. These guidelines, called *planning premises,* account for limitations, such as time constraints and budget restrictions. Planning premises also provide clarity of purpose, such as a student's objective to obtain a high grade.

Even though we insist that formal planning is likely to lead to better results, we must acknowledge that managers rely heavily on their intuition. In the real world, most managers use their experience to guide them in planning decisions and leave formal planning details to subordinates. This is particularly true of senior executives. According to researcher Henry Mintzberg, "When the manager must plan, he seems to do so implicitly in the context of daily actions, not in some abstract process reserved for two weeks in the organization's mountain retreat. The plans of the chief executives I studied seemed to exist only in their heads—as flexible, but often specific, intentions."[4]

Mintzberg is not making a case against formal planning, only pointing out how many executives behave in practice. In fact, managers *do* plan, whether formally or informally, consciously or intuitively. Most managers who carry plans around in their heads are seasoned executives who have dealt with similar planning issues for many years. Mintzberg found that nearly all executives agreed that formal planning improves decision making and reduces errors. Moreover, the planning environment is becoming more complex as international commerce changes; intuition simply isn't sufficient to capture the essence of global affairs today. The counterpoint to Mintzberg's work, introduced in Chapter 1, is Fred Luthans's recent studies, which found managers to be more intensely involved in formal systems when supported with information technology.[5]

Increasing global concern for the environment has spurred many companies to think further and further ahead in their planning. This Sylvania Company engineer is testing an energy-efficient light bulb that will help consumers save on their electric bills, help utilities save on their new-capacity requirements, and—hopefully—help Sylvania win a greater market share.

Why Planning Pays Off

Formal planning models are tools for management. We use them to supplement intuition with sound analysis, for the planning process often helps us to discover opportunities or innovative ways to accomplish our tasks. For example, J. Edgar Broyhill, the grandson of the founder of Broyhill Furniture Industries, was revising the firm's marketing plans several years ago when he noticed that a large number of buyers were placing orders over the phone. This was not customary in the industry; furniture had traditionally been sold through elaborate showrooms. Nevertheless, sales information indicated a rising trend in telephone sales. Broyhill decided to create a telemarketing division with glossy catalogs and advertising placed in up-market publications such as *Architectural Digest* under the name "Edgar B Furniture Company." Within three years, Edgar B had topped $20 million in annual sales, prompting several competitors to reconsider their marketing strategies.[6]

Planning pays off in several important ways. Four planning payoffs are summarized in Exhibit 6-1 and discussed below.

The first payoff of formal planning is that it defines organizational purpose. The **purpose** of an organization is the fundamental reason it exists. Many firms lose sight of why they exist, and in the process lose sight of their customers and their objectives. General Portland Cement Company states, "We manufacture and sell cement, but we market concrete."[7] Portland's purpose is excellent because it not only

purpose
The reason a company exists; it is the fundamental rationale for being in business.

EXHIBIT 6-1	**Planning Pays Off**
Payoff #1	Knowing why we are in business; purpose of firm defined; articulation of major goals.
Payoff #2	Creating specific objectives and strategies to guide future activities successfully.
Payoff #3	Understanding environmental constraints, the competition, and critical factors, threats, and opportunities for future decisions.
Payoff #4	Providing alternatives for action; having preplanned options for contingencies.

identifies the company's product but also shows an understanding that customers buy the "utility" of the product—what it can be used for. Once a company knows *why* it is in business, it has a better idea of what it must do to succeed. Portland's production managers must ensure sufficient quantities of high-quality cement, and its marketing managers must help customers use concrete to their advantage.

The second payoff of formal planning is that it defines specific objectives for everyone in the organization. Not having objectives would be like trying to play a baseball game without bases; there would be no definition of progress and no way to tell when someone scored. Formal planning provides objectives and articulates them to everyone in the firm. For example, Michael Dell founded Dell Computer Corporation in 1984 as a nineteen-year-old premed student at the University of Texas, and he had two clearly stated objectives for his new venture selling PC's Limited. First, his firm would manufacture and sell a clone of the IBM PC at a price 40 percent below the competition; and second, it would guarantee every customer 100 percent satisfaction without question. Dell hasn't wavered from these objectives, and today nearly a hundred technicians answer customer inquiries, the company provides direct factory service, and there is a no-questions-asked return policy. Dell's PC clones were the first to sell for under $1,000, and this set the pace for the industry. The payoff was a $400 million business as Michael Dell, still in his twenties, headed into the 1990s.[8]

The third payoff of formal planning is the ability to define environmental constraints. Many things restrict our actions. When we consider the uncertainties involved in trying to plan for the future, we realize it is crucial to understand how we are likely to be affected by things to come. For example, when we decide to take a vacation trip by automobile, we rarely just "take off" for parts unknown. We study road maps, estimate mileages, and acquire all the information we can about expenses. Then we decide where to go and how to get there. We also try to envision what we will do if we run short of cash, the car breaks down, or any one of a number of other things happens. Astute managers try to identify events and situations that will limit their decisions, although even well-managed firms fall victim to unexpected circumstances. For example, U.S. defense contractors enjoyed huge sales volumes for weapons and supplies during the first half of 1991 when the so-called Gulf War with Iraq occurred. In September, however, following the failed Soviet coup, the U.S. defense budget was trimmed. In the meantime, Congress also set about to drastically reduce long-term strategic weapons.[9]

The fourth payoff of planning is that it provides alternatives. Good planning will identify preplanned alternatives so that if the primary plan doesn't work or if objectives become unattainable, managers can react quickly. Alternatives are formulated chiefly to avoid disasters, but they may also unearth new opportunities. Consider the auto vacation example. By studying a road map, you may discover interesting places to visit that you would have missed by merely focusing on a final destination. You will also be able to map out alternative routes in case your original plan hits a snag. An enterprise like Exxon is interested in discovering opportunities to improve sales and profits. It is also interested in avoiding disasters from unex-

GLOBAL TRENDS

Coca-Cola Company and Nestlé S.A. Brew a New Coffee

Switzerland's Nestlé S.A. has a reputation and brand image for its chocolate and coffee products that rivals America's Coca-Cola Company. Both have global marketing and distribution systems, and their international management cadres are respected for their planning acumen. Now Nestlé and Coca-Cola have joined forces to produce a product that will compete with Nescafé and Coke. Although the new product will carry the name Nescafé liquid canned coffee, the production and canning technology are Coca-Cola's. A new venture was formed in 1991, Coca-Cola Nestlé Refreshments Company, and located in South Korea to manufacture and distribute the canned coffee drink for Asian markets that include South Korea, Japan, and China.

The new venture is the result of several years of negotiation and careful planning by the partners to extend their product range into an instant coffee drink to substitute for their dry coffees and soft drinks. Plans call for initial introduction in South Korea, market expansion to Japan, and further joint ventures for distribution in China and other Asian nations. This incremental growth is expected to occur between 1992 and 1997, and if the product is successful, contingency plans exist for other drinks, including coffee milkshakes. Market tests are also going on to gauge the feasibility of a cold canned coffee sold through standard vending machines to U.S. consumers.

Source: Damon Darlin, "Coke, Nestlé Launch First Coffee Drink," *Wall Street Journal,* October 1, 1991, pp. B1, B7. See also "Famous Brands Combine Marketing Muscle to Satisfy Urge for Coffee-on-the-Go," *South China Morning Post,* October 5, 1991, Business Section, p. 2.

pected political changes. With global oil interests, Exxon has contingency plans for extracting crude oil from alternative sources in case a political crisis disrupts the firm's primary suppliers. Events such as the Persian Gulf War and political turmoil in Central America testify to the importance of having ready options.

The need for formal planning exists in every organization, and although the issues differ from organization to organization, the consequences of poor planning are similar. Companies that forget customer needs, misjudge the competition, and fail to understand their own limitations lose business and may end up bankrupt.

CHECKPOINT

- How does "informal" planning differ from "formal" planning and why is formal planning encouraged?
- Identify and discuss three reasons effective planning pays off.

ORGANIZATIONAL OBJECTIVES

organizational objectives
Performance targets or the end results that managers seek to attain through organizational efforts.

Every plan has the primary purpose of helping the organization succeed through effective management. Success is defined as achieving **organizational objectives.** These are performance targets, the end results that managers seek to achieve. Every company has a wide array of objectives that differ substantially at various levels within the organization. Consequently, there is a hierarchy of objectives that corresponds to strategic, tactical, and operational activities. There are also different types of objectives, such as those relating to sales, profits, human resources, and social responsibilities. Before we look more closely at the hierarchy and types of objectives, it is important to note that many books and research articles refer to objectives as "goals." This is largely a matter of semantics; either term will suffice, but "objectives" will be used here.

Hierarchy of Objectives

strategic objectives
Performance targets relating to long-term endeavors, such as growth, profitability, and the position of a firm in its industry.

tactical objectives
Medium-term performance targets for achieving limited results, such as annual sales, quarterly profits, or incremental changes in products or services.

operational objectives
Immediate short-term performance targets for daily, weekly, and monthly activities that, when attained, will reinforce tactical planning objectives.

There are three general levels in every organization, and each one has objectives that reflect management responsibilities at that level. Figure 6-1 illustrates this three-tier structure. At the executive level, objectives are **strategic** and relate to long-term planning issues such as the development of product lines and market expansion. Thus Coca-Cola has a diversified product line with Diet Coke, Cherry Coke, the "new" Coke, and the Classic. This array of products was introduced to satisfy long-term strategic objectives for expanded sales and greater profitability. Strategic objectives for the 1990s include rapid global expansion through even greater diversified product lines, as highlighted in Global Trends. Coca-Cola Company generated **tactical objectives** for producing these soft drinks, devising advertising programs, and structuring distribution systems. Very short run **operational objectives** reflect plans for dozens of activities from production scheduling to meeting monthly sales quotas.

Types of Objectives

Private businesses have *profit* objectives. Managers in the private sector have to define the income required to meet expenses and to generate profits. If profits fail to meet investors' expectations, a company may lose investors. Through planning, managers determine how much income is needed and what constitutes a reasonable profit. Managers also spend a great deal of time planning for costs and cash flow, even though they recognize how circumstances beyond their control can influence profits. For example, suppliers of parts and materials may alter prices, thereby increasing a firm's expenses. If energy costs, transportation expenses, or tax liabilities rise, that will affect cash flow and profitability.[10]

FIGURE 6-1 Hierarchy of Objectives

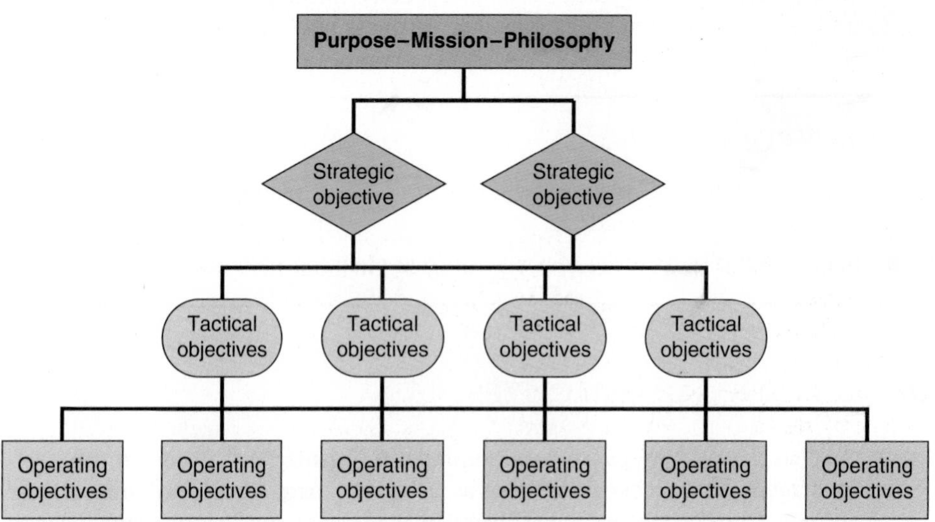

Growth objectives are those that define targets for increased sales volume, expanded markets, new products, or better services. For example, Apple Computer Company seeks to increase its sales of microcomputers during the 1990s by expanding *market share*. Currently, Apple holds 12.5 percent of the personal computer market. A half-percent increase (.5 percent) to a 13.0 percent share of the projected $300 billion market for the 1990s translates into an increase of $1.5 billion. Apple plans to attain that objective by introducing advanced products and innovative office software applications each year. However, Apple has also created an unusual partnership with its chief rival, IBM, to develop integrated computer systems with compatible software. Both companies seek growth through rapid scientific developments, shared through their joint innovations.[11]

Sometimes growth and profit objectives conflict. Profitability can suffer if a firm aggressively expands sales. It may lower prices to attract customers, but simultaneously have to increase expenses such as advertising. Texas Instruments, for example, mounted price-cutting campaigns and took huge losses in an unsuccessful attempt to expand its microcomputer sales. Profits plummeted, stockholders became restless, and TI withdrew from the personal computer industry.[12]

Another important objective is to maintain a certain level of *quality* for merchandise and services. One firm may consciously try to offer the best product in the industry; another may try to market an inexpensive product of limited durability. Both positions are equally viable in many industries. For example, there are inexpensive microcomputers with limited capabilities, yet highly sophisticated machines are also being sold at premium prices. The concept of quality is not necessarily related to price, even though price is usually a good indicator of quality. Another indicator is *intended use* by customers. Thus, to one person, a quality microcomputer means the best one available for less than $300; to another customer, that same item will seem like junk.[13]

Still other objectives are *philosophical*, reflecting a company's desire to support social programs, promote environmental protection, or improve the quality of life for employees, local citizens, or society in general. For example, General Mills has supported social programs for many years through a company foundation funded annually with 2 to 3 percent of pretax profits. The General Mills foundation matches contributions by employees to charitable agencies, underwrites grants to employees for education, makes direct grants to universities for scholarships and research, contributes to more than seventy community environmental campaigns, and supports health care for the elderly.[14] Philosophical objectives often reflect the personal interests of key executives or owners. Some of these people have strong personal commitments to ideals that influenced their careers. Philosophical objectives must be coordinated with the other objectives mentioned earlier and must take into account income, expenses, growth, investors' interests, social needs, and employees' expectations.

CEO John Akers of IBM and CEO John Scully of Apple Computer Company are now something that just a few years ago they probably never thought they would be: partners. IBM and Apple have long been rivals, but by 1991, the time had come for both companies to place the objective of corporate growth before the tradition of rivalry. The two companies are working together to develop integrated computer systems with compatible software.

Establishing Objectives

Organizations have multiple objectives that must be orchestrated to avoid conflicts. Just as profit objectives can directly conflict with growth objectives, social objectives requiring cash expenditures can be opposed by investors who want the highest possible financial returns. Setting company objectives is more complicated than making isolated choices in each category of objectives. Managers, for example, cannot define profit objectives separately from social objectives.

Well-defined objectives have several characteristics. They are *specific, measurable,* and *realistic,* and each has a definite *time period* for achievement.

- *Specific.* Objectives are expressed without ambiguity so that everyone will understand them. A statement that a company wants to "maximize profits," for example, is too vague. A more precise statement would be that the company wants to "make 7.5 percent net profit on sales."

- *Measurable.* Objectives are used to evaluate performance quantitatively. Employees want to be able to understand when they are making progress and when they are failing to meet expectations. Objectives should, therefore, be measurable and expressed in terms that relate to performance. A specific objective of "7.5 percent net profit on sales" is measurable and has a clear meaning to managers responsible for profits and losses. For shop-floor workers, an objective to "reduce product defects to 3.0 percent" is also measurable and meaningful.
- *Realistic and Challenging.* Objectives are meant to motivate employees to achieve results, so they must be realistic as well as challenging. Unrealistic expectations may only stymie progress. For example, if a company wants to produce "200 items per hour" and the production department knows this goal is realistic, then workers may try to achieve it. If the target is unreasonable, workers may become disgruntled and produce far less than they are capable of producing. Good objectives must also account for resource limitations; asking employees to produce 200 items an hour when they cannot get raw materials on time to do so is unreasonable.
- *A Defined Time Period.* Every objective should designate a certain time period to provide a frame of reference for performance expectations. An objective to achieve "7.5 percent net profit on sales" is specific and measurable, but it fails to state when this is to be achieved. A complete statement might be "to achieve 7.5 percent net profit on sales for 1994."

CHECKPOINT

- Define the hierarchy of objectives in a business organization.
- Identify types of objectives a company might pursue.
- What are the characteristics of well-defined objectives?

THE PLANNING HIERARCHY

Planning responsibilities are different for managers at each organizational level, and they correspond to the three levels of objectives. The emphasis an organization places on objectives will depend on its strategy, and its strategy is derived from its purpose. This relationship was introduced earlier and is also addressed in Chapter 7, Strategic Management. Tactical objectives are coordinated at middle-management levels and depend on strategic objectives. Operational objectives are defined in the short term and in direct relationship to tactical objectives. Tactical and operational objectives are treated in Chapter 8, Tactical and Operational Planning.

Board-Level Strategic Responsibility

The planning hierarchy, as Figure 6-2 shows, describes the delicate relationship between planning and decision making. Although we have specified three levels of plans and objectives, there is a fourth division of responsibility, which is assumed by the board of directors and CEO (represented on the board) acting as overseers of the firm's mission. This does not mean that an organization has only four levels of management, but that it has four general levels of responsibility. Board members are not "operating" managers; in fact, many of them are appointed from other organiza-

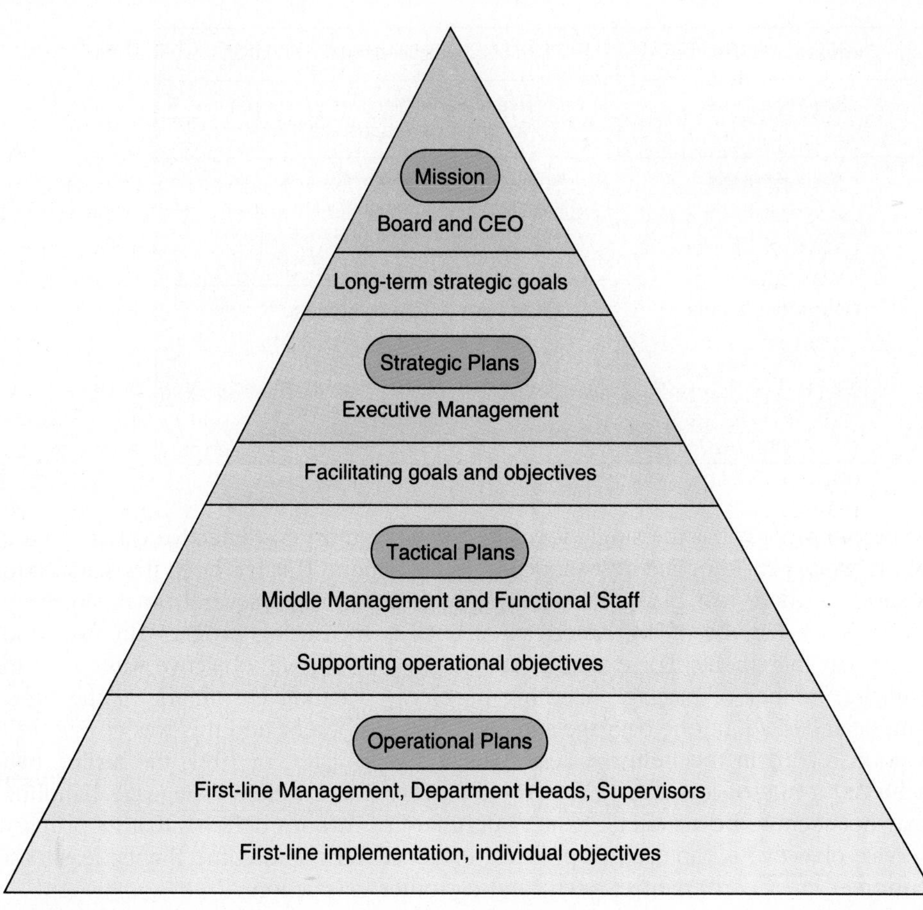

FIGURE 6-2 A Hierarchy of Planning

tions to serve as investors' representatives. They rarely intercede in operational decisions except to fulfill their responsibility to safeguard investors' interests. The *mission*—or the way in which an organization carries out its purpose—is at the top of the pyramid in Figure 6-2, to emphasize that although an organization's board is responsible for defining the mission, once that mission is established, the board and CEO subordinate their planning decisions to fulfill it.

Strategic Planning

The CEO, in conjunction with top-level executives, formulates long-term strategic objectives to reinforce the firm's mission. Figure 6-3 summarizes planning time horizons and emphasizes the difference between a company's mission and its strategic objectives. The mission clarifies organizational purpose and is written as if it will last forever. In contrast, strategic plans with long-term objectives are specified for a period of years. A five-year period is common for many companies, but circumstances dictate the planning horizon.

Mercedes-Benz, for example, took eight years to develop the S-class series of luxury automobiles. Launched in 1991, the S-class was conceived in strategic planning meetings in 1983. During the development period, Mercedes had to create nearly 200 new features, ranging from improved safety welds to a computer-assisted engine diagnosis system. Management determined nearly 80 percent of the S-class's quality standards through planning and testing that spanned six years before the company set up initial production engineering. Mercedes also spent more than a year training 6,000 employees to work on the S-class.[15]

In contrast, American Airlines is part of a rapidly changing industry in which several major companies have failed to survive a global shakeout in competition.

Purpose and Mission	Life of organization; no time horizon
Strategic Plans	Five-year plan; objectives expressed in long-term averages and trends
Tactical Plans	Annualized objectives; five-year plan is reduced to increments with definite and measurable performance targets; pro forma budgets used
Operational Plans	Short-term objectives with appropriate time horizons that match organizational needs: Sales incremented quarterly/monthly Production based monthly/weekly Cash flow based at least monthly

FIGURE 6-3 Conceptual View of Planning Time Horizon

American Airlines has the single focus of being the most cost-effective carrier in the world while providing the best service to its customers. This has been translated into a series of three-year plans, each having been transformed several times since the early 1980s. For the 1990s, American Airlines is measuring progress in two- and three-year increments. For example, at the end of 1989, one objective was to cut in half the number of baggage handling problems plaguing customers. At the time, American had about one baggage snafu per 150 customers, and this was considered a good record in the industry. Less than two years later, in 1991, the airline had achieved a rate of less than one error for every 300 travelers.[16] Baggage handling may not seem to be a strategic issue, but American Airlines believes that its primary service objective is captured in practical evidence such as on-time flights, least-cost customer fares, convenience, safety, and customer satisfaction.

Tactical Planning

Middle management is responsible for translating strategies into shorter-term *tactics*. Middle managers, defined in Chapter 1, include division heads, managers of functional departments such as research and development, and senior sales managers. Tactical objectives are also called *facilitating* objectives because they are formulated as performance targets that, once satisfied, reinforce and "facilitate" the firm's strategies. Tactical plans are often specified in one-year increments and expressed in budgets. Annual budgets are tactical planning documents used to articulate performance expectations and to track sales, production, profits, research expenditures, technology development, and many other activities.

Translating strategic plans into measurable tactical objectives is important because most strategic objectives are rather vague. American Airlines, for example, had a single growth objective to become the world's largest airline. That strategic objective was redefined in specific terms for managers, who were expected to expand the company's activities by 20 percent annually between 1988 and 1994. The airline achieved its comprehensive five-year objective by 1991 through route purchases and successfully bidding for European and Asian destinations. Mercedes-Benz wanted to translate its strategic objective of "the finest quality" into tactical safety achievements such as all-wheel antilock brake systems, fail-safe airbags, and reduced-skid cornering characteristics.

Most companies have strategic profit objectives, but these are usually vague and require tactical interpretation. A statement "to meet or exceed industry average profits," for instance, is too general, but a tactical objective "to achieve 8 percent return on equity for fiscal year 1993" provides a definite profit measure. Standard Oil of Indiana, for example, has a strategic objective "to preserve shareholders' capital." Although this provides no measure of performance, two annual facilitating objectives establish precise profit expectations. The first is "to increase earnings on an average of 10 percent a year," and the second is "to earn a return of 13 to 15 percent each year on shareholders' equity."[17]

Operational Planning

Operational planning is accomplished by first-line managers. They include department managers, shift supervisors, and individuals in charge of work groups. Operational planning is most concerned with budgets, quotas, and schedules. These are refinements of tactical objectives in which work is defined and results are measured in small increments. Time horizons for operational planning are very short; for example, weekly production schedules and monthly sales quotas come under operational planning.

Most plans at this level reflect operational cycles. If a heavy equipment manufacturer like Caterpillar Corporation identifies ten-day assembly cycles for earth movers, plans for manpower, materials, and production will be geared to a ten-day period. In high-speed production situations, such as electronic parts assembly, a cycle of one day or one shift is not unusual.

Operational objectives are narrow in scope, short-lived, and subject to sudden change. For example, to meet annual sales quotas, monthly sales increments are budgeted, but sales could fall short of quotas in one month, requiring a significant revision in the amounts budgeted for the following months to make up the deficit. Production plans are also notorious for variations due to equipment failures, absenteeism, disruptions in material deliveries, or one of many other reasons.

Operating plans at Allen Bradley—one of America's leading manufacturers of industrial automation control systems—reflect objectives for making quality products on a tight time schedule. Because the company's products are used by other manufacturers to monitor their production systems, it is essential to make quality instruments and to deliver them on time. One operational objective is to produce electronic control devices for motors at a standard rate of 600 units per hour. When this rate varies by more than 5 percent during any eight-hour shift, production supervisors are expected to adjust during the following shift. Another operational objective is to maintain weekly factory reject rates to below 3.5 percent of sales through quotas on scrap, rework, and defective workmanship.[18]

CHECKPOINT

- Contrast the responsibilities of board members, executives, middle managers, and first-line managers for planning.
- Explain how strategic, tactical, and operational plans differ.

PLANNING ROLES FOR MANAGERS

Strategic planning is a crucial responsibility of executives. They must deal with abstract ideas about the firm's future technology, energy resources, changes in productivity, and many other considerations. Strategic issues are inextricably linked with issues of society, the firm's industry, and the community in which the firm operates.

Executives must first of all account for profits and losses, but larger social issues often occupy much of their time and attention. For example, profits are viewed strategically in relation to stakeholder interests. In Chapter 1, we said that *stakeholders* are investors, customers, employees, local businesses, those relying on the firm's expenditures for their existence, and many others who are affected by its products,

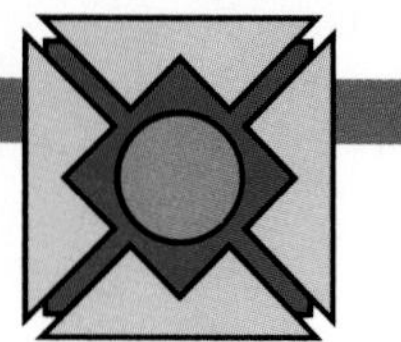

ETHICS IN MANAGEMENT
Corning's Community

Corporate activism at Corning, Inc., derives from the company's determination to be the fabric of its community. The company is headquartered in Corning, a town of 12,000 nestled among the hills and lakes of midstate New York. Since its founding, Corning has included social commitment to its community as a primary objective in its strategic planning. In 1914 Corning Glass Works helped launch the town's chamber of commerce; several years later, it financed a hotel and funded apartment complexes for workers. Today it also underwrites day-care centers, charities, and two small business development centers.

Corning's activism is formalized through its Corning Enterprises subsidiary, which is mandated to make community investments. This has resulted in a major cleanup campaign along state highways, political pressure that has rid the area of hazardous waste dumps, and cooperative efforts with city planners to improve playgrounds and parks. Corning's executives have also purchased and rehabilitated low-income housing, subsidizing local government efforts to raise the standard of living for economically disadvantaged families.

Corporate executives can also flex their muscles in somewhat controversial ways. Having decided that there was no place for "seedy establishments" in the town of Corning, management bought out several downtown taverns and converted an entire block to commercial stores. Also, it sponsored minority enterprises in the new commercial district, and then criticized local officials for not doing enough to improve social options and cultural diversity for minorities. Corning's opponents view this behavior as a form of corporate socialism, but the company maintains that its code of ethics would have no meaning if it were not implemented as part of its long-term plans.

Sources: Keith H. Hammonds, "Talk About Your Company Town," *Business Week,* May 13, 1991, p. 76. See also James R. Houghton, "Message from the Chairman," *Annual Report* (Corning, N.Y.: Corning, Inc., 1991), p. 2.

services, and operations. Executives monitor long-term profits and how they influence stockholder behavior, but they must also understand how their decisions affect other stakeholders. Society prefers healthy companies with full employment. The community wants stable or growing firms to support local enterprise. Employees want a safe place to work. Retirees want a profitable company to protect their pension incomes.

Middle managers are more concerned with the internal objectives of an organization. Their planning domain is defined by functional or divisional responsibilities. Plant managers, marketing directors, financial managers, and personnel administrators commonly focus on one-year accounting cycles. An external issue, such as the impact of the firm's performance on the economy, is not an immediate concern. Middle managers have their hands full with internal operations.

First-line managers, those at operations levels such as department heads and supervisors, have rather narrowly defined roles concerned with planning for weekly, monthly, or quarterly performance by their work groups. If we contrast the planning roles of top executives and first-line managers, several differences become evident. Executives spend as much as 70 percent of their time on long-term planning and as little as 8 percent on operational planning. First-line managers spend nearly 90 percent of their time on operational tasks and only a "trace" on long-term planning.[19]

The higher a manager is in an organization, the more he or she will deal with abstract concepts and a broader base of planning issues. The longer perspective required of top managers brings with it greater responsibility to more people for effective planning.

Management by Objectives

Because planning can be complicated, well-managed companies develop methods for systematic planning. These are processes that create accountability by the organization's managers for accomplishing their planning tasks. We take the opportunity in this section to introduce you to the most popular planning process, one that has been implemented in some form by a great many private and public organizations. It is called *management by objectives.*

Management by objectives (MBO) is a technique for involving employees at all levels in planning and controlling activities. MBO brings together superiors and subordinates to jointly define objectives and to control results. Managers have stratified planning responsibilities, as described in the preceding section, but MBO provides linkage between strata to improve coordination. At the heart of MBO is the philosophy that individuals are more likely to be committed to achieving objectives when they have actively participated in defining those objectives.

management by objectives (MBO)
A technique used in planning and controlling in which subordinates determine their objectives jointly with superiors and evaluation follows periodic monitoring and performance reviews.

MBO was first described by Peter Drucker in 1954 as a program to motivate employees to become personally interested in their work.[20] Since then, MBO has been adopted by many Fortune 500 firms, although it has been modified in most instances to accommodate differences in individual organizations. The MBO philosophy of participation is widely accepted, but the process itself is often controversial.

The MBO process. The MBO process begins with major strategic objectives articulated by senior executives, who then join with subordinates to formulate the next level of objectives. This process continues downward throughout the organization—at each level, superiors join with their subordinates to establish objectives that are consistent with, and reinforce, higher-level objectives. During the planning period, superiors and subordinates meet periodically to review performance and to redefine objectives. Four specific steps are involved in the MBO process:

1. *Determine objectives.* Managers meet with their employees individually to inform them of higher-level plans and to help them develop their own objectives. Ideally, this is a joint decision-making process, with employees encouraged to take a leading role by expressing their ideas.
2. *Specify action plans.* Realistic action plans are agreed upon by managers and their subordinates, and these are written down with sufficient elaboration for periodic review.
3. *Performance review.* Each planning cycle has a specific time frame, and managers periodically meet with their subordinates to review progress toward objectives. By systematically monitoring progress and reviewing plans, managers help subordinates fine-tune their efforts. Reviews should occur at least once each year, but can be more frequent.
4. *Correction and adaptation.* Corrective action is taken after each performance review. This can include changes in activities to achieve objectives or changes in the objectives themselves. At predetermined intervals, usually each year,

new objectives are established. These build on past results and changes in higher-level plans that provide planning premises for the next cycle in an MBO process.

Benefits and drawbacks of MBO. Proponents of MBO emphasize that participation encourages a more cohesive work environment and a stronger commitment to objectives by subordinates. Since results are conspicuous in MBO systems with frequent reviews, high-priority activities receive clear and purposeful attention. An important benefit of MBO is that better communication is achieved between managers at various organizational levels. This enhances collaboration and keeps subordinates better informed about plans and activities in other parts of the organization.

MBO systems also have some serious drawbacks. Many organizations are simply too complex to adopt MBO, which is itself a complex process. MBO also requires a tremendous amount of time and effort. Managers and subordinates must regularly meet, separately and together, to document plans, review performance, discuss corrective actions, and revise objectives, and the process tends to get bogged down in paperwork and schedules. To succeed, MBO requires a strongly committed top management and individual managers capable of working comfortably within a participative environment. When either condition is lacking, MBO can backfire. A poorly implemented MBO program will seem like a gimmick rather than a legitimate effort to improve participation.

CHECKPOINT

- From a stakeholder perspective, explain how managers are responsible to different constituents in setting objectives.
- Define the MBO process and the responsibilities of superiors and subordinates at every stage in the process.
- Contrast the advantages and disadvantages of MBO.

COMMUNICATING PLANS

Planning requires clear and effective communication at all levels before performance begins to mirror expectations. Objectives are written and plans are documented to give employees direction. Managers separate plans into two broad categories. **Standing-use plans** are those that are used on a continuous basis to achieve consistently repeated objectives. Standing plans take the form of *policies, procedures,* and *rules.* **Single-use plans** are those that are used once to achieve unique objectives or objectives that are seldom repeated. Single-use plans are communicated through *programs, projects,* and *budgets.*

standing-use plans
These are plans used on a continuous basis to achieve consistency in organizational activities; they include policies, procedures, and rules that can be repeated.

single-use plans
These plans are developed for unique activities and are seldom repeated exactly; they include programs, projects, and budgets.

policy
A standing-use plan that provides a general framework for decision making.

Policies

A **policy** is a standing-use plan that provides a general framework for decision making. Policies are concerned with many issues, as illustrated in Exhibit 6-2; they are meant to provide guidelines for behavior to ensure consistency over time. Policies are also instruments of delegation that alert subordinates to their obligations, but what a company policy says is not always how a company acts. The effectiveness of a firm's policies is shown by its track record and by the behavior of its managers. Stew Leonard, who is profiled in the Management Application, has an effective track record. He describes himself as a "simple milkman," but his Connecticut store grosses more than $100 million annually, making it the largest single dairy store in the world. Leonard's business is built on a mission statement with one policy that

EXHIBIT 6-2 Examples of Corporate Policy Areas

Major Objectives	Profitability targets and expectations for investment efficiency. Profitability trends, including returns to assets and equity interests. Dividend payments and commitments to stockholders. Growth of the firm through long-range technological/market innovations. Social responsibility for employee health and safety, public safety. Social considerations for ecology, pollution, employment, economy. Customer considerations, image of the firm.
Facilitating Objectives	Product development and research and development. Equal employment opportunities, affirmative action. Market penetration, new-customer development, foreign expansion. Advertising and promotion policies, pricing considerations. Cost containment, materials management, inventory, purchasing. Cash flow management, credit position, payables and receivables policies. Customer credit, financing of sales, collection. Production and quality control criteria.
Supporting Operations	Wage and salary administration considerations. Personnel management, hiring, training, promotion, termination. Layoffs and cutbacks, labor relations, grievances. Vacations, holidays, leaves, travel, employee theft, security. Performance appraisal, standards for work, absenteeism.

These are a few of the many areas in which corporate policies are drawn up to reinforce preferred behavior. Policies are used as guidelines to reduce risk in decision making and to help managers perform assigned tasks consistently.

permeates every decision made in his 600-employee store: "Our mission is to create a happy customer!" This policy is chiseled into a 6,000-pound rock that stands at the store entrance. Leonard calls it his "rock of commitment," and it has two rules: "Rule 1—The customer is always right. Rule 2—If the customer is ever wrong, reread rule 1." These are not glib remarks for public relations purposes. Stew Leonard lives by them, and he has 100,000 satisfied customers *every week* to prove it.[21]

Effective policy statements have three characteristics: They are *clear and understandable, stable over time,* and *communicated to everyone involved.* Stew Leonard's statement that "the customer is always right" is unambiguous, carved in granite, and prominently displayed for everyone to see.

Procedures

procedure
An explicit set of actions, often sequential in nature, required to achieve a well-defined result.

A **procedure** is an explicit set of actions required to achieve a well-defined result. Formal procedures provide specific and detailed instructions for the execution of plans. Often called "standard operating procedures" (SOPs), they prescribe preferred methods of performing tasks. Some procedures evolve through consistent application, and in turn provide guidelines for making *programmed* decisions; however, tasks that require a sensitive ordering of operations are covered by formal guidelines and are closely monitored.

Procedures commonly used in daily operations become *standing-use plans.* For example, bank tellers operate under policies that hold them responsible for cash and transactions, but these policies do not explain *how* to control cash and transactions. Therefore, procedures are developed with a definite sequence of money exchange and transactions recording to reduce errors. When a customer makes a deposit, the teller first compares deposit slip items against checks and cash tendered by the customer, then tallies the individual entries for a total deposit. This is done at a computer terminal or automatic calculator wired into the bank deposit system. The teller next checks the total on the deposit slip with the tally and, if they match, follows detailed procedures to record receipts, and give customers recorded copies of transactions.

MANAGEMENT APPLICATION

Stew Leonard—The Great American Milkman

Stew Leonard was a second-generation milkman with a home delivery route until 1968, when state highway construction forced him to relocate. This, coupled with the realization that home milk delivery was going the way of the buggy whip, led him to build a barnlike retail dairy store with glass viewing windows separating his customers from his milk cows. The dairy plant provides milk so fresh that the only way to get it fresher is to own a cow. After 26 additions, the small barn has become an eight-acre complex with more than 600 employees in Norwalk, Connecticut.

In a White House ceremony in 1986, Leonard received the Presidential Award for Entrepreneurial Achievement from President Ronald Reagan. His organization was also featured in Tom Peters's best-seller *A Passion for Excellence* as one of America's best-run companies. In the TV special "In Search of Excellence," Leonard's company was heralded as one of the nation's most innovative, along with Disney, McDonald's, and Apple.

Leonard's genius lies in making customers happy through quality service and innovative marketing. He says he wants to make customers say "Wow!" and then return to his store—again and again. Disneylike farm characters play music, perform, and mingle with customers. Children have close-up encounters with egg-laying chickens, milk-producing cows, and other animals. On any given day, the store is likely to feature a live band, free gifts, and ice cream for youngsters. Leonard and his family are also present every day, talking with customers, soliciting suggestions, and managing the business with one clear objective: to make customers happy.

Leonard's success depends on the sincerity of his mission and the attention to planning that results in what he calls "action-based policies." These include: "If you wouldn't take it home to your mother, don't put it out for customers"; "Only happy customers come back"; "A customer who complains is our best friend because we get the opportunity to improve"; "When in doubt, throw it out"; "Do it right the first time"; and "If you're training someone to be even better at your job than you are, you're one of the most valuable people in our company."

Leonard annually sells more of each item that he stocks than any other store in the world, including 10 million quarts of milk, 100 tons of cottage cheese, 800 tons of salad, 1,800 tons of poultry products, 1 million ice cream cones, nearly 3 million quarts of orange juice, 250 tons of butter, 5.6 million bananas, and 7.8 million ears of corn. These are a few of Stew Leonard's record-setting products for a record-setting family business.

Source: Courtesy of Stew Leonard.

Standard operating procedures are numerous in dangerous work areas, such as nuclear power plants. SOPs also simplify complex activities. Airline pilots need not memorize preflight checks because SOPs provide step-by-step guidelines. Similarly, doctors follow detailed surgical procedures to help ensure success. Good procedures provide a sequence of actions that, once completed, fulfill specific objectives, reinforce policies, and help employees achieve results efficiently and safely.

Rules

A **rule** is a *standing-use plan* that requires a specific action without variation. A procedure can evolve into a rule when the sequence of activities becomes mandated. Airline preflight safety checks fall into this category: A preflight safety check is mandated by law; the procedure has become a requirement to ensure passenger safety. Rules usually have a single purpose and are written to guarantee a particular way of behaving in a particular situation.

rule
A statement that tends to restrict actions or prescribe specific activities with no discretion.

We think of rules as restrictions because in practice most of them prevent us from doing something dangerous. Examples are rules against smoking in restricted areas, speed limits, and safety regulations that require workers to wear hard hats in dangerous areas. These rules leave little room for discretion. You either stop at a red traffic light or you don't; you can't stop "a little bit."

Programs

A **program** is a *single-use plan* comprising multiple activities orchestrated to achieve one important objective. Madison Square Garden, for example, has a $100 million renovation program that includes nearly fifty activities, all coordinated to be completed in 1995. When these activities are finished, the *program* will end. The program agenda includes new parking, electrical wiring, sound systems, renovation of rest rooms and common areas, safety improvements, and redesigned athletic equipment. One of the program's activities is to replace 1,300 low-priced seats at the top of the Garden with a two-tiered ring of 88 luxury boxes.[22]

program
A single-use plan with multiple activities that can be orchestrated to achieve one important objective.

Programs have several special features that set them apart in the planning process. They are like stories or stage plays in that they have clear beginnings and definite endings. Program managers are given scripts to follow that reflect a systematic completion of activities that culminate in fulfilled program objectives.

Athough we have said that programs are single-use plans, some types of programs are designed to be repeated. For example, universities develop academic undergraduate degree programs that are replicated by hundreds of students. Each student follows a format of courses that must be completed to satisfy degree objectives. In the sense that every student completes a degree program only once, it is a "single-use" plan; insofar as a degree program is replicated for many students, it is a "standing-use" plan. Most programs fall into the single-use category. NASA's Apollo program to land on the moon, once achieved, ended forever. Future NASA programs may build on the Apollo program's success, but they will have their own objectives.

Projects

A **project** is a *single-use plan* with a specific and uncomplicated short-term objective. Projects are similar to programs but distinguished from them in three important ways. First, projects are unambiguously planned with single objectives. The single activity to build luxury box seats for Madison Square Garden is a *project* within the larger scope of a *program.* Second, projects are not repeated. Unlike degree programs that are replicated, projects stand alone as single activities. Building a new employee parking lot is a project that will not be repeated. Third, projects tend to be accomplished in short periods of time. For example, building an employee parking lot may take only a few weeks.

project
A single-use plan with a specific short-term objective that is seldom repeated.

Budgets

budget
A plan transformed into quantitative terms (such as money or units) to allocate resources, articulate performance expectations in measurable terms, and provide control documents for monitoring progress.

A **budget** describes in numerical terms resources allocated to organizational activities. A budget also communicates performance expectations. By budgeting, managers identify resources, such as money, materials, human resources, and overhead support, allocated to an activity. Budgets also are clear statements of expected results expressed in measurable terms, usually dollars. We instinctively think "dollars" when talking about them, yet many budgets are expressed in other terms. Production budgets, for example, can be expressed in number of units produced. There are budgets for labor-hours, machine hours, inventory levels, computer time, customer credit, and many other activities. Marketing sales quotas are budgets used to express sales activity in both dollar and unit volume figures.

Budgets help to coordinate activities by providing specific information to monitor performance. They are used to control activities, track results, and restrain managers from misallocating resources. By having consistent measurement criteria, such as dollars, they provide excellent documentation that all employees can understand. Unfortunately, budgets are too often viewed only as restrictive controls, and can, in fact, become repressive. Used effectively, they are valuable management tools. Minnesota Mining and Manufacturing has consistently been ranked among the top five most admired corporations in America by *Fortune* magazine, and budgetary excellence has been cited as one of 3M's greatest assets. The company was singled out for "using its financial control system to encourage rather than curtail innovation and creativity. Numbers are used to set goals and measure performance rather than to deny expenditures or punish unmet expectations."[23]

Budget projections, called *pro forma budgets,* anticipate future results. These projections typically include a set of strategic budgets based on sales forecasts, and contain income statements, cash flow statements, and balance sheets. Strategic budgets are broken down into tactical budgets with annual projections for divisions or functional departments. Lower-level budgets describe in detail weekly, monthly, and quarterly activities, and provide the numerical information for operating schedules. A **schedule** is a commitment of resources and labor to tasks with specific time frames. Therefore, budgets and schedules reinforce each other to clarify expectations in measurable terms.

schedule
A commitment of resources and labor to tasks with specific time frames.

CHECKPOINT

- Explain the difference between standing-use and single-use plans.
- Describe the uses of policies, procedures, rules, programs, projects, and budgets.

MAKING PLANS EFFECTIVE

Planning is a process of looking into the future, and since the future is uncertain, so are plans. Plans must have a degree of flexibility built into them so that managers can adapt to circumstances. Policies are *guidelines,* procedures are *preferred* sequences for activities, and rules (although inflexible) can be *changed.* Few plans are so infallible that we can afford to take away management prerogatives. In fact, circumstances can change so drastically as to make the best-laid plan infeasible. Effective planning, therefore, will provide backup plans to take into account potential changes. This is called *contingency planning.*

Contingency Planning

A **contingency plan** is an alternative set of objectives and activities that can be implemented if and when circumstances change enough to make the preferred plan hopeless. This alternative plan will include contingency actions based on different sets of *planning premises,* and when these premises materialize, the new alternative plan is implemented, replacing the preferred one. Whereas flexibility assumes only that managers have some discretion for accommodating variations in circumstances, a contingency plan means sweeping change.

contingency plan
An alternative plan to replace the preferred plan if conditions change.

Planning premises are those considerations taken into account by managers that are expected to influence a company's objectives or its activities. Some of the most sensitive considerations are changes in government legislation, effects of tax regulations, access to raw materials, costs of resources such as energy, and the availability of personnel with the skills needed to accomplish an organization's work. Planning premises can extend to hundreds of factors that affect performance, ranging from high interest rates that can disrupt expansion plans to war in the Middle East that can affect oil supplies. Technological changes are particularly important because a firm's products or manufacturing processes can be made obsolete by rapid scientific changes. For example, researchers at the California Institute of Technology, working with a company called Synaptics, has made a breakthrough that will put supercomputer power into a single microchip costing a few hundred dollars. The chip is expected to become commercially available by 1995, and it could make IBM and Apple machines seem like antiques unless those companies respond with comparable technology.[24]

planning premises
Those considerations taken into account by managers that will likely affect plans or activities.

Contingency planning implies the development of alternatives for both expected and unexpected future events. Some considerations may seem farfetched now, but that's just the point. If we plan for only the expected, we can become extinct in the process. Several aeromedical research companies have started to plan working models of space colonies, major oil companies have plans for synthetic fuels, and the International Monetary Fund has a working model for a world currency.

Perhaps the most unnerving shift in planning assumptions concerns productivity and the rapid advancement of Japanese technology. For decades, most Americans assumed that we would remain the world leader in productivity and the superpower in technology. That assumption was shaken during the 1980s as U.S. markets were inundated with superior Japanese products. Although the Japanese have been our obsessive concern, they are far from our only competitors. U.S. manufacturing lags behind that of several other countries in such areas as microelectronics, robotics, base metals production, and consumer products.[25] Contingency planning takes into consideration as many factors as possible to establish alternative plans in a changing environment. As we shall see next, effective planning also requires a comprehensive effort.

The 3M company supports 6,000 scientists and engineers who add more than 200 products each year to the 60,000 it sells. Exceptional planning and careful budgeting ensure coordination for projects ranging from a new type of sandpaper to a Ganz Meter (shown) to test light reflection.

Comprehensive Planning

Comprehensive planning means involving an entire organization in systematic and formal planning that results in fully integrated objectives. Consequently, a preferred plan will include operating schedules, budgets, and projects closely tied to tactical plans, annual budgets, and programs. These, in turn, will be closely coordinated with long-term strategic objectives. In the event a contingency plan is implemented, it will be developed and communicated in a similar comprehensive manner. Comprehensive planning also relies on a formal system of performance checkpoints within the plan to reassure managers when things are going right and to alert them to take action when things are going wrong. Performance checkpoints constitute an early warning system for change.

comprehensive planning
The total involvement of an organization in systematic planning at all levels to integrate objectives and coordinate formal planning processes.

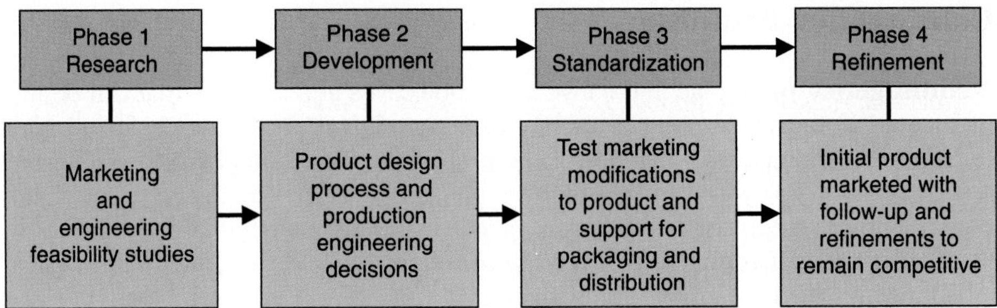

FIGURE 6-4 Digital Equipment Corporation's Four-Phase Product Plan

Digital Equipment Corporation (DEC) worked closely with Ricoh to develop a laser printer as part of DEC's strategy to become a technology leader in scientific computer equipment. The plan called for a scheduled three-year development process with four operational phases, shown in Figure 6-4. The research phase consisted of marketing and engineering feasibility studies. The development phase required product design and engineering decisions for production. During the product standardization phase, the printer was test-marketed, modified to meet market needs, and put into production for formal marketing. The fourth stage began after initial market introduction. During this refinement phase, the printer was continually improved with enhanced characteristics or variations on production and marketing to remain competitive. DEC used more than forty checkpoints in each of the four development phases to keep the laser project on track. During the second stage of development, for instance, DEC was surprised by Hewlett-Packard's introduction of a desktop laser printer. The HP breakthrough changed DEC's plans to design a similar model. Instead, the DEC printer was redesigned for manufacturing and engineering computing systems.[26]

In a recent study of several hundred major banks, Robley D. Wood and Lawrence R. LaForge concluded that banks that did comprehensive planning consistently outperformed banks that did not.[27] Profits were consistently higher and costs consistently lower in the comprehensive planning banks. The authors also noted that these banks had greater stability of customers, better track records for loan repayments, and higher earnings on investments. They were also able to forecast demand more accurately and react more quickly to market conditions.

An important advantage of comprehensive planning is its educational value. In the Wood and LaForge study, managers in banks that did comprehensive planning were better informed about potential changes and problems in their industry than managers in banks that lacked comprehensive planning. Bank executives felt that younger managers learned from being part of the formal planning process and were better prepared to handle decisions.

Our discussion of comprehensive planning and contingency planning boils down to the conclusion that *formal* and *systematic* planning is essential for every organization. We cannot keep corporate objectives tucked away in our minds (unless we like playing baseball without bases). Managers at all levels must be involved in the planning process, and the deeper a plan penetrates within an organization, the better that organization will be at adapting to new situations.

CHECKPOINT

- How does a contingency plan differ from flexibility in planning?
- Discuss how plans are integrated in comprehensive planning and why it is important to create a comprehensive planning document.

THE FORMAL PLANNING PROCESS

Formal planning is a systematic process. The most popular rational planning model lists four basic steps in the process. We will not try to reduce the formal planning process to "four easy steps," but instead will describe the process as it is used in complex situations. Figure 6-5 summarizes the process,[28] which consists of ten guidelines. These guidelines provide a *general* pattern of rational planning. They do not form a step-by-step procedure, yet the sequence approximates behavior in a formal planning environment. Let's briefly discuss each guideline.

Establish Objectives

Objectives must be established to define long-range operations. This is the task of strategic managers. Initially, objectives are communicated to tactical managers, who

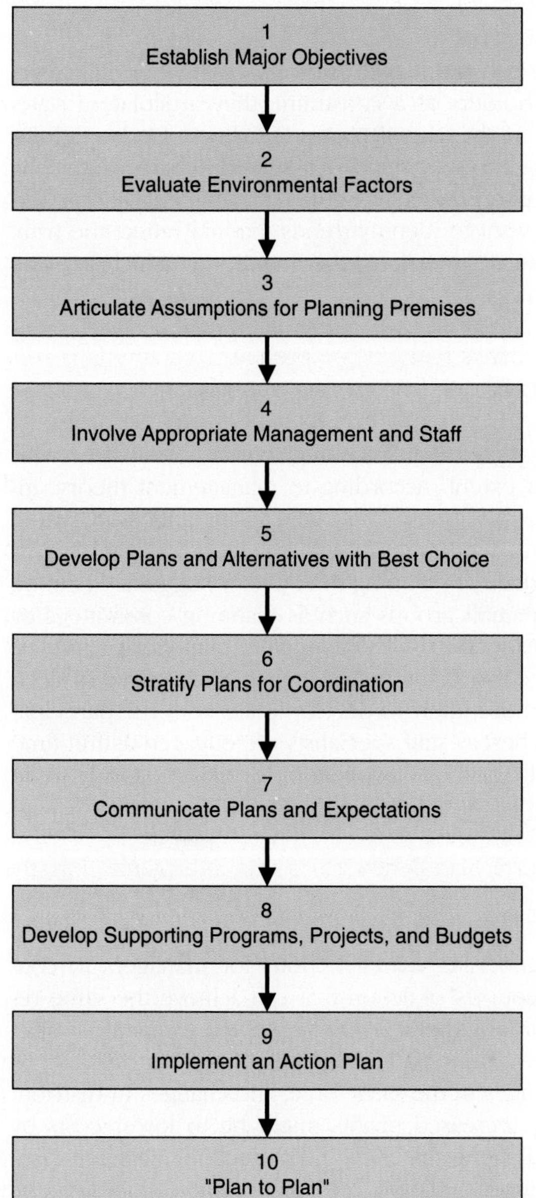

FIGURE 6-5 Guidelines in Formal Planning: A Ten-Step Process

then specify objectives for their subordinates. When managers find they cannot provide realistic tactical objectives that satisfy strategic preferences, strategies may be reconsidered. Reconsideration can also occur at operational levels as tactical objectives are broken down into short-term plans. The process of establishing objectives is a coordinated and comprehensive effort.

Evaluate Environmental Factors

Objectives are not determined in isolation. Managers must consider limitations on their decisions. These originate in both the internal environment of the firm and the external (political, social, cultural, and economic) environment. Internal influences include limited resources, capital, and skilled personnel. Examples of external influences are legislative constraints, high interest rates, and technological advances by competitors.

Articulate Assumptions

Assumptions tend to evolve from the constraint evaluation process. When managers identify profit expectations by shareholders as a constraint, they articulate a statement about how those shareholders might react if profits fall short of expectations. In other words, constraints are turned into statements of assumed behavior either by ourselves or by others. Managers want to predict probable operating conditions during the planning cycle, but they also want to identify trends that may affect the firm. These are discovered by asking "what if" questions, the answers to which provide managers with lists of planning premises.

Involve Management and Staff

Executive managers are inextricably involved in planning, but it is less clear who else should be involved and to what extent. According to management theory, involving a greater number of managers will result in better plans and more widespread acceptance of objectives. In reality, though, most managers are pressed for time, so fewer of them participate in formal planning than theory suggests. Planning is more often accomplished through small groups such as planning committees or staff planning specialists. Different leadership styles also affect planning processes. Most U.S. managers are inclined to be more autonomous than participative in decision making; consequently, they are more likely to develop plans with the participation of only a few other persons.[29] Whereas staff specialists are engaged as full-time planners, lower-level managers usually become involved in formal plans only in an adjunct way.[30]

Develop Alternatives

A successful planning process will generate several options for managers to consider. These options are alternative courses of action that can achieve the same result. Management's task is to decide among them. For example, if a company's objective is to increase profits, one option might be to increase sales. This can lead to decisions on pricing, promotion, changes in the sales force, and changes in distribution systems. An alternative route to increased profits might be to lower costs by trimming the work force or using substitute materials in production. Managers usually consider many alternatives for a given situation, but a *viable alternative* suggests a proposed course of action that is *feasible, realistic,* and *sufficient.* To be feasible, an action must not only be possible but also have a reasonable chance of success. To be realistic, the alternative must square with reality, such as complying with the law and conforming to the expectations of those who have to carry out the work. To be sufficient, the proposed activities, once accomplished, must fulfill their intended objectives.

Stratify Plans

Once alternatives are decided upon, a stratifying effect takes place. Starting at the top, policy statements express preferred objectives. At the tactical level, procedural directives reinforce objectives; programs and projects may also be developed at this level. At the lowest levels, operational plans reflect schedules and performance budgets. Stratification is the preliminary step in a systematic communication effort.

Communicate Plans

A great deal of communication must take place to get this far in the formal planning process, but as noted earlier, most managers are only involved in a limited aspect of planning. Plans are therefore documented to establish responsibilities, and planning documents are carefully distributed and explained to those who will be involved.

Develop Supporting Plans

Long-range plans are strategic summaries. At lower levels, progressively more detailed and specific documents define areas of responsibility and budgets. However, this guideline assumes more than mere documentation. It requires careful definition of "actions to be taken" and "controls" for monitoring progress. As noted earlier, DEC had many control points and required specific activities during its development of laser printers.

Implement an Action Plan

Many well-founded plans never get off the ground. It is important to consciously include *implementation* as a step in the planning process so that plans will be supported by management, resources will be committed, and people will act on decided courses of action. At the outset of this chapter, we said that the planning function was arguably the most important management function. It provides the framework for organizing, leading, and controlling. Organizing brings together human, material, and financial resources in a workable structure for implementing plans. Through effective leadership, managers convert resources into products or services by motivating employees to work toward established objectives. Controlling is the function of evaluating performance, measuring progress, and adjusting actions to ensure success.

Plan to Plan

Changes in the environment and in the organization subvert even the best plans. Obviously, long-range plans are most susceptible to change, owing to external influences. Annual plans are supposed to be less variable, but only a naive manager expects performance to match objectives perfectly. At the operations level, performance should be closer to expectations, but even here schedules are subject to many disruptions. Managers must therefore assume change and "plan to plan" soon after completing one round of planning decisions.

CHECKPOINT

- What is meant by evaluation of environmental factors?
- Identify three categories of assumptions that managers need to articulate when planning.
- What are "alternatives" and how are they used in a comprehensive plan?
- Explain why it is important to "plan to plan."

APPROACHES TO PLANNING

While the planning process describes how managers in most companies develop plans, there are three distinct *approaches* that describe who has responsibility for formulating plans. Each approach involves different managers, and each reflects a different philosophy of planning.

Centralized Top-down Planning

top-down planning
The prevalent approach to planning in which a centralized group of executives or staff assumes the primary planning responsibilities.

Top-down planning is the prevalent approach in small and highly centralized organizations. It is the traditional approach, embracing a philosophy of hierarchical authority in which strategic planning is first done by executives, tactical planning follows to reinforce strategic objectives, and operational planning is accomplished after tactical plans are in place. Previous discussions on planning roles for managers and the planning process reflect the centralized top-down approach because that is the most common practice in American companies.

The term *centralized* is used because planning responsibilities are assigned to a few executives at the organization's highest echelons. The term *top-down* is used because these executives assume the burden of establishing a firm's major objectives, writing policies, and communicating to lower-level managers expectations for formulating progressively more detailed plans. In larger, more complex organizations, executives charged with planning responsibilities have a planning department with staff experts who do most of the actual work. Major organizations that make use of formal planning departments include NBC, Edison Power & Electric, Ford Motor Company, Allied Chemical, and Citicorp. In each firm, staff planners are responsible for essentially every aspect of planning *except* making actual decisions; managers in operating positions, from the CEO down to a first-line supervisor, must decide what objectives to pursue and what activities to implement to fulfill those objectives.[31]

Decentralized Bottom-up Planning

bottom-up planning
An approach to planning in which authority to establish objectives and planning responsibilities is delegated to lower-level managers, who are expected to initiate planning activities.

Bottom-up planning is an approach that delegates planning authority to division and department managers, who are expected to formulate plans under the general strategic umbrella of corporate objectives. Companies using this approach have a planning staff, much like the planning department in a centralized top-down system, but the staff coordinates, rather than develops, plans. The term *decentralized* is used to emphasize that authority is pushed downward and throughout a company for independent planning initiatives. The term *bottom-up* is used to emphasize that planning decisions made at lower levels are aggregated at higher echelons to form a comprehensive plan. Lower-level decisions can be vetoed by executives, but it is more likely they will be reviewed by company executives and revised with the help of planning staff.

This approach involves more managers in planning, and it appeals to those who advocate participation in decision making. However, it is an effective approach only when company leaders truly believe in a philosophy of shared responsibility and have the organizational structure necessary to allow divisions and departments to function somewhat independently. General Motors, Procter & Gamble, IBM, and Teledyne Ryan have decentralized planning systems, but these companies are also organized with multiple divisions. At GM, the Pontiac Division operates independently of the Chevrolet, the GMAC, and the GM Truck Divisions, and acquired GM companies, such as Electronic Data Systems (EDS), are semiautonomous divisions within the GM family. Planning is carried out in each division, coordinated at GM's headquarters, and documented as a composite General Motors strategic plan.[32]

Team Planning

Team planning is a participative approach that relies on *task force* teams comprising managers and planning specialists temporarily assigned responsibilities for formulating plans. Westinghouse, Hewlett-Packard, Delta Airlines, Marriott Corporation, and Lockheed are a few of the major companies that endorse team planning, but many companies are moving toward it to encourage participation by more employees.[33]

team planning
A participative approach to planning whereby planning teams comprising managers and staff specialists initiate plans and formulate organizational objectives.

Each of these companies has designed a unique team system, but their planning activities are generally similar. Top management sets the process in motion with articulated strategies supported through executive planning committees. These executive committees comprise staff planners and managers who generate information for planning premises needed by lower-level teams. Guidelines are then drawn up by top management for division-level teams with the responsibility for formulating tactical plans. Division managers are often given a menu of strategic performance expectations, such as objectives for product development, market expansion, and financial results. Division teams coordinate their plans with strategic planning teams, and managers at both levels jointly determine the tactical plans to reinforce strategic objectives. Division managers in turn articulate these objectives and tactical plans to lower-level operating managers. Operating teams repeat the planning process, and the accumulated decisions are aggregated into a comprehensive company plan.

Team planning is not a compromise between the top-down and bottom-up approaches; it is the integration of the best features of both. The major top-down element is that as much information as possible is passed downward, together with guidelines for supporting the company's strategic objectives. The major bottom-up element is a commitment to participation by subordinates, who are given tremendous latitude for making planning decisions even though these decisions must be carefully coordinated with higher-level teams.

CHECKPOINT

- Describe planning responsibilities for a planning department in each of the three approaches to planning.
- How does team planning integrate the best of top-down and bottom-up planning features?

At the beginning of the chapter, IBM Europe was described as one of the company's most profitable and best-planned global divisions. We also noted that IBM's European management is confident of its long-term opportunities, and the company plans five to eight years into the future. Unfortunately, not all of IBM's divisions enjoy a similar planning mandate, and in late 1991, IBM's U.S. divisions announced layoffs of nearly 18,000 employees. The company also disbanded its personal computer software division, acclaimed only two years earlier as one of IBM's high-profile research and development units.

IBM Europe cut nearly 1,000 jobs, mainly in France, but this was viewed as an expected part of its long-term contingency plan to shift some aspects of marketing and distribution to several of the company's joint venture partners. Profits remained strong in Europe but dropped off sharply in the United States. These events prompted investors to question whether IBM executives were committed to a comprehensive corporate plan of action, and investment analysts concluded that IBM's American corporate cadre was beginning to suffer from marginal planning decisions made through a cumbersome bureaucracy. IBM Europe, however, seems to be setting a new standard in team decision making that has helped it become the company's leading division.[34] ■

A SYNOPSIS FOR LEARNING

1. Define the planning function and explain how formal and informal planning differ.

   Planning is the foremost function of management, the first in a cycle of responsibilities that determines what is to be done, when it is to be done, how it is to be done, and who is to do it. Planning is accomplished within the framework of the firm's *mission,* which defines its purpose through its products, services, and major objectives.

   Informal planning is an intuitive process. Formal planning requires rigorous investigation, careful definition of an organization's objectives, and well-defined activities to fulfill those objectives.

2. Explain management planning responsibilities and how they relate to different types of objectives.

   Responsibilities are related to a management hierarchy with strategic, tactical, and operational dimensions. These three strata represent the active managers below the board of directors. The board has the responsibility to support top management in instigating and fulfilling major objectives. Executives constitute top management, and they are concerned with *strategic* plans, which include long-term objectives and the strategies necessary to fulfill them. At the tactical level, middle managers break strategies into shorter time periods, translating major objectives into tactical plans and objectives. These typically are expressed in annual planning budgets with specific objectives. At the operational level, first-line managers and supervisors implement tactical objectives.

3. Describe the various ways plans are communicated and how managers document planning activities.

   There are *standing-use* plans that can be repeated and *single-use* plans that are seldom or never repeated. Standing-use plans are documented and communicated through *policies, procedures,* and *rules.* Single-use plans are documented and communicated through *programs, projects,* and *budgets.*

4. Explain why contingency planning is so important.

   A *contingency plan* is an alternative set of objectives and activities that can be implemented if and when circumstances change so drastically that the preferred plan is infeasible. Contingency planning is a vital responsibility for all managers.

5. Identify the steps in a formal planning process.

   A general pattern of planning includes these steps: (1) establish major objectives; (2) evaluate the environmental factors and the competitive issues that can affect the firm; (3) articulate assumptions; (4) identify and involve the proper managers; (5) develop alternatives; (6) stratify plans; (7) communicate and document plans; (8) determine programs, projects, schedules, budgets, and other activities necessary to accomplish documented objectives; (9) implement the action plan; and (10) immediately plan to plan.

6. Contrast the three main approaches to planning.

   The *top-down* approach is a method of centralized planning and reflects the hierarchical authority of most organizations. The *bottom-up* approach is a method of decentralizing planning authority. The *team planning* approach is a participative method involving as many people as possible at each level.

CASE 1 James J. Hill and the Great Northern Railway

SKILL ANALYSIS

James J. Hill was the last and greatest of the U.S. railroad builders. He started out in the shipping business, but recognized that the future lay with the railroad. In 1878, at the age of 40, he joined with a group of three other businessmen to take over the failing St. Paul and Pacific Railroad. Despite its grand name, the railroad actually consisted of just two short and poorly built lines within the state of Minnesota.

Hill's strategy was to take the railroad wherever there was traffic. He restored the profitability of the St. Paul and Pacific by building a line to the Canadian border to carry wheat from the rapidly expanding farmlands of Manitoba. Then he pushed the railroad west, to the farmlands of the Dakotas, the mines of Montana, and the timberlands of the Pacific Northwest. In 1893, Hill's railroad, renamed the Great Northern Railway, reached the Pacific at Puget Sound in the state of Washington.

The Great Northern faced intense competition in its westward movement. Its route ran between those of the Canadian Pacific and the Northern Pacific, both of which had government support. In contrast, the Great Northern was notable for not receiving any government land grants to subsidize its way. "Hill's Folly" succeeded brilliantly, however, because of Hill's superior planning.

Hill insisted on well-routed and well-built lines. "What we want," he said, "is the best possible line, shortest distance, lowest grades, and least curvature that we can build." To this end, he was prepared to invest heavily in surveying: for example, his employees spent three years surveying the Great Northern's route through the Rocky and Cascade Mountains in search of new and lower passes. Hill's policy of low gradients and gentle curves enabled his locomotives to haul heavier loads than those of his competitors. Once a route was chosen, Hill spared no expense on the actual construction, insisting on steel rails and stone bridges.

As a result, the Great Northern's operating costs were lower than its competition, allowing Hill to undercut their rates and still make a profit. Because of its low operating costs, the Great Northern survived the financial crash of 1893 and the ensuing depression, while the Northern Pacific and several other railroads were forced into bankruptcy.

Hill also tied the Great Northern into a larger transportation network. To reach the East Coast, he linked his lines with those of the Chicago, Burlington, and Quincy. He established a steamship company to carry grain from the Great Northern's Lake Superior terminal to Buffalo, New York. In 1902, he even launched the first of several large Pacific steamships.

Hill realized that the railroad's prosperity depended on the growth of the farming and mining communities it served. He actively encouraged settlement along the Great Northern's route, even sending agents to northern Europe to recruit immigrants. Hill took a special interest in agriculture, importing purebred bulls from Britain free of charge, distributing special wheat seed, and sending trains with exhibits and lecturers to show how agriculture could be improved.

Another of Hill's obsessions was keeping the Great Northern's cars full at all times. He was determined to fill the empty cars heading west to pick up timber from the Pacific Northwest. To that end, he sent agents to the port cities of Japan and China to investigate trade conditions and record all existing imports and exports. At the same time, he scoured New England, the mid-Atlantic states, and the South for potential exports to the Orient. Hill met personally with Japanese industrialists and persuaded them to try a shipment of long-staple American cotton.

Case Questions

1. What made Hill a master of planning?
2. What constraints did Hill face in building and operating his railway?
3. Suggest some policies Hill might have set for the Great Northern in order to achieve his objectives.
4. What kinds of contingency plans might Hill have needed when laying new track? Take into consideration rights of way, raw materials, labor, and weather.

Sources: The video segment from "The Entrepreneurs: An American Adventure," Vol. 3; Stewart H. Holbrook, *The Story of American Railroads* (New York: American Legacy Press, 1947); and David Mountfield, *The Railway Barons* (New York: W. W. Norton, 1979).

VIDEO CASE Club Med: Planning for Fun and for Success

Warm breezes. Sandy beaches. Carefree days. Balmy evenings. Tropical paradise. These phrases are enough to arouse in almost anyone the overwhelming urge to visit an exotic location where all worries and cares will vanish. One company that has long specialized in providing such a setting is Club Med. But Club Med has its own worries today because of a changing market.

Club Med, a global vacation and travel organization, was started in France over fifty years ago by a small group of friends who wanted to escape the rigors of urbanized Europe. They found unusual and isolated locations where they could camp out using war surplus tents and equipment. Soon "villages" were established for guests to enjoy a relaxing vacation, and Club Med became synonymous with good food, genuine attention to guests, beautiful settings, and well-equipped sports facilities. Capitalizing on this image, the company grew into a global organization. Club Med now operates on four continents with major customer groups from the Pacific, North America, and Australia as well as Europe. The company's current philosophy is similar to the founders' principles: "To provide a naturally beautiful setting for a vacation experience free from the rigors of daily life and monetary worries, with an emphasis on sports and friendship."

Club Med has always had a global marketing concept—one world, one product. However, after employees learned from guests that the North American consumer wanted something different, the company decided to restudy the market.

Managers identified some specific changes in the vacation consumer, which included: better-developed tastes and demands; increased career pressures; family responsibilities, including more diverse needs among family members; and financial responsibilities. In response to these changes, the company took some actions.

First, managers decided to continue their marketing research to determine an appropriate image for Club Med. They also decided to address competitive relations within the industry directly. Finally, they wanted to create a new image-oriented advertising campaign. In order to accomplish these objectives, Club Med used surveys, focus groups, and market studies. The company planned to repackage its product offerings while remaining true to its founding philosophy.

Club Med put its plans into action by developing a new message and new products. The company's message became "offer everything so you can do anything." It was a fully segmented message designed to appeal to the different target groups the company was trying to attract. The new product offerings were divided into different levels of vacation packages designed for these new target markets.

Case Questions

1. Explore the concept of "a product" in terms of Club Med's services, and describe how the company plans to refine or reposition its product in the North American market.
2. Identify the planning components in Club Med's management process using the "formal planning process" found in the chapter.
3. Describe Club Med in terms of its objectives, what it has gained from a systematic approach to planning, and where the company is headed.

Sources: Bernice Kanner, "Club Med Goes Luxe: Redefining Civilization," *New York,* June 17, 1991, Vol. 24, No. 24, p. 20ff; Claudette Covey, "Club Med Emphasizes Distinction Between Its Vessel and Villages," *Travel Weekly,* June 6, 1991, Vol. 50, No. 45, p. 52; and Dinah A. Spritzer, "Club Med Seeks to Broaden Image: Not Just a Singles' Paradise," *Travel Weekly,* April 22, 1991, Vol. 50, No. 32, p. 54ff.

CAREER PLANNING: STRENGTHS AND WEAKNESSES

SKILL PRACTICE

Introduction

Career planning is similar to organizational planning, and although we provide Chapter 21 as a special treatment on managerial careers, students can practice their planning skills here using career issues of interest to them.

Obviously, different occupations and professions require different personal strengths (skills, abilities, talents, etc.). The skills and abilities required for a particular line of work reflect the activities that are involved in the job, which, in turn, are largely dictated in the "raw materials" involved in the work. Broadly speaking, all jobs require dealing with one or more of four types of raw materials: things, data, ideas, and people. Exhibit 1 suggests some of the elemental job activities required for each of these raw materials.

Some jobs seem to require the ability to deal with only one type of material: bookkeepers work mostly with data, carpenters with things, philosophers with ideas, and salesclerks with people. Most jobs require the ability to effectively deal with at least two types of material. For example, *all* managers deal with people, but the controller also works with data, the vice president of engineering is heavily involved with data and things, and the vice president of marketing with ideas and data.

Individuals vary in their preferences and abilities for dealing with different types of work. These preferences and predispositions may be fundamental characteristics of personality that differentiate how people collect information (sensing versus intuition) and process it (thinking versus feeling). Some individuals are primarily oriented toward *things,* since they are drawn to the concrete and impersonal aspects of experience. Some people clearly prefer *ideas,* with their "focus on general concepts and issues." Others value the "personal and social needs of people," while still others like detail as it applies to a specific, immediate situation—that is, *data.*

Instructions

(*Note:* Steps 1 through 5 are to be completed *before* the class meetings.)

1. Each person should take four blank sheets of 8 1/2 × 11-inch notebook paper. Place a heading on each sheet for each of the four basic areas of:

   Things People Data Ideas

   a. On the first line of each sheet, write "Satisfying Skills." Beginning with Things, think of and list all of the things you can do really well with materials and objects. Think, especially, of skills that provide you with a deep sense of satisfaction when you exercise them. (Consult Exhibit 1—Four Categories of Job Activities—as a starting point.)
   b. When you have listed as many skills and abilities as you can think of for Things, move on to the sheets labeled People, Data, and Ideas. Repeat the process until you feel you have listed all of your really important skills and abilities in each area.
2. From your list of Satisfying Skills, *which* are the most important to you? On a fresh sheet of paper, make a list of your five most satisfying skills and abilities—those that you enjoy the most (be careful to retain the Things, People, etc., labels).
3. Choose either "a" or "b" below.
   a. For people who are *not certain* about their career interests: What types of careers tend to require your most important skills and abilities? Identify as many as possible before you select the one or two that seem to fit you best. Talk to people you know who do that kind of work. Look up some jobs in the *Occupational Outlook Handbook* or *Dictionary of Occupational Titles* in your university library or placement office. Pick up added information about how people get into this line of work. What education, training, and experience are you going to have to have? *Prepare notes* on your findings—*you will need these in step 5.* You are now ready to establish a *tentative* career objective. Consider the characteristics in Exhibit 2.
   b. For people who are *satisfied with career choices already made:* Where do you want to go in your career? What does it mean to you to "advance" in

EXHIBIT 1 Four Categories of Job Activities

Things	Here are some activities involving *things:* Move, manipulate, machine (saw, drill, finish, etc.), adjust, assemble, design, operate, handle, construct, arrange, inspect, clean, deliver, store, drive.
Data	Here are some job activities involving *data:* Compare, collect, copy, analyze, check, compile, organize, summarize, type collate, store and retrieve, classify, schedule, observe, diagnose.
People	Here are some job activities involving *people:* Counsel, assist, coach, teach, manage, persuade, interview, consult, advise, criticize, lead, communicate, request, encourage, sell, recruit, manage, arbitrate or mediate conflict, negotiate, speak in public, supervise, listen, help others to express themselves.
Ideas	Here are some job activities involving *ideas:* Create, compare, critique, publish, think about, argue, comprehend, decide, plan, interpret, define, establish goals, imagine, invent, synthesize.

EXHIBIT 2 Characteristics of a Good Career Objective

A good career objective is one that is:

Challenging: A good objective is one that you must stretch to achieve.

Realistic: While your objective should be challenging, it should also be one that you can realistically hope to achieve, given your strengths, weaknesses, needs, circumstances, values, problem-solving styles, and so on.

Measurable and Concrete: Establish a time target for achieving your objective. Phrase the objective in specific terms; for example:

Poor: I want to be an executive.
Better: I'd like to be a vice president of personnel within five years.
Best: I'd like to be a vice president of manufacturing of a medium-sized (200 to 500 employees) storm door company within twelve years. The position must pay at least $50,000 per year, and the company must place emphasis on quality manufacturing. Possibilities include . . .

Long Term: Your objective should represent a major career goal or milestone for you. You will probably want to think at least five to ten years into the future.

Relevant: Achieving your objective should be deeply satisfying because it fulfills your most central needs and requires the exercise of those talents and abilities you enjoy using most.

---

your field? For this activity, define advancement as "moving into a new position or redesigning your present job so that it requires you to use even more of your most important and satisfying skills." Prepare a statement of career objectives that fulfills the criteria in Exhibit 2. What would need to be done to make your goals really achievable? Do you need training or relevant experience? Are the opportunities realistically available in your present organization? In other organizations? Prepare notes for use in step 5.

4. Take the original four sheets (Things, People, Data, Ideas) and turn them over, then head up each sheet respectively: Weaknesses/Deficiencies—Things; Weaknesses/Deficiencies—People, etc., on the appropriate sheet. Consider these categories: Things I *do poorly;* Things I *would like to stop doing;* Things I would *like to learn to do well.* Which of these deficiencies are important to you *right now?* Which ones must you do something about first in order to begin moving toward your career goals? Select and rank-order the three most important ones on the paper where you listed *your most satisfying* skills.
5. Prepare a brief written plan showing how you plan to move toward your career objective. Include in it how you intend to deal with the weaknesses that stand between you and your objective.
6. The instructor will form groups of four to six persons each. Each person in the group has a maximum of eight minutes to describe his or her career goals and key strengths/weaknesses to other group members.
7. While someone is talking, other group members should provide some feedback: Is the plan clear and logical? Is the speaker aware and clear as to his or her most important strengths and weaknesses?
8. Instructors (in the last few minutes of the class session) may want to ask for a show of hands on:
   a. How many people found their greatest strengths (weaknesses) in each area: Things, People, Ideas, Data.
   b. How many found that their perception of their own strengths/weaknesses corresponded with the perceptions of others?

Other discussion of items still on the minds of the participants can be scheduled for a future class if the schedule permits.

Source: Roy J. Lewicki et al., *Experiences in Management and Organizational Behavior,* 3rd ed. (New York: Wiley, 1988).

7

Strategic Management

OUTLINE

A Strategic Perspective
- The Nature of Strategic Planning
- The Changing Environment of Organizations
- Strategic Shifts
- Social Responsibility and Strategic Issues
- Expectations of People in Organizations

Strategic Organization
- Corporate Strategy
- Business Strategy
- Functional Strategy

Formal Planning and Strategy
- Establishing the Mission Statement
- Focusing the Mission Statement
- Setting Strategic Objectives
- Formulating Strategies to Achieve Objectives
- Implementing the Strategic Plan
- Evaluating Performance and Reformulating Plans

Situation Analysis
- Industry Analysis
- Competitive Analysis
- Company Analysis

Master Strategies
- Growth Strategies
- Integration Strategies
- Diversification Strategies
- Retrenchment Strategies

Strategic Alternatives
- Growth
- Integration
- Diversification
- Retrenchment

Making the Strategic Decision

OBJECTIVES

- Describe the strategic planning process.
- Discuss the differences between the planning priorities of the corporate, business, and functional organizational levels.
- Explain how a strategic perspective influences management decisions.
- Describe the components of a situation analysis and examine the SWOT analysis for making business-level decisions.
- Identify and explain four classifications for master strategies.
- Explain the relationship between master strategies and strategic alternatives in terms of the four classifications for master strategies.
- Summarize the basic requirements for making strategic decisions.

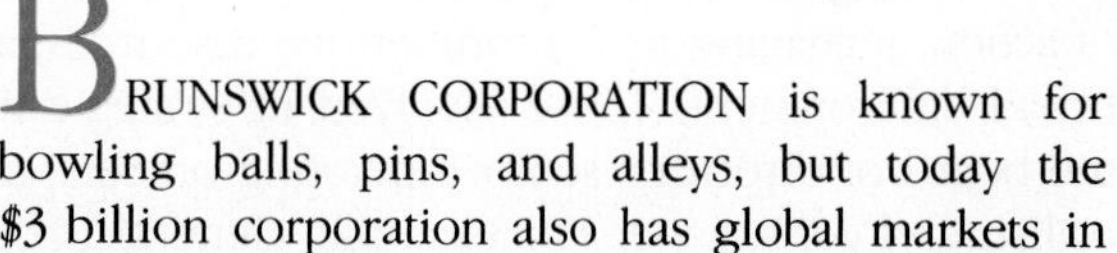

BRUNSWICK CORPORATION is known for bowling balls, pins, and alleys, but today the $3 billion corporation also has global markets in recreation, marine, defense, and industrial products. The company began producing billiard tables in 1845 with a half-dozen employees. Now it has more than 26,000 employees in five major divisions. During the early 1980s, Brunswick was not performing well and was the target of several takeover attempts. CEO Jack F. Reichert helped set a new strategic course, and now the company is positioned for growth in the 1990s.

Reichert explains Brunswick's success in terms of three S's: survival, strategy, and succession. The first task, to *survive,* followed hostile takeover bids in 1982, and Brunswick did so only through dramatic restructuring. It sold its Middle Eastern Health Care Services Division, a business Brunswick was uncomfortable with, trimmed nearly 25 percent of its employees, and rebuilt "winning divisions" by decentralizing management and giving shares of stock to every employee. Many mid-level and senior personnel lost their jobs when Brunswick eliminated five tiers of management, dropping from eleven to six levels between the CEO and line foremen. The remaining division managers and operating employees were given joint planning responsibilities; coupled with their new stock ownership, this motivated them to rebuild Brunswick into the highest quality producer in every market it served. Thus the second S, *strategy,* was long-term growth through quality. The third S, *succession,* was a commitment to Brunswick's people. In Reichert's words, "Of paramount importance is our people—their personal dignity, their pride in what they do, and the trust they have in their management."[1] Brunswick motivated its employees to provide quality products at a profit by making them investors and giving them responsibility for their own strategies.

Recall from Chapter 6 that a company serves many *stakeholders,* and in Brunswick's case, investors, employees, and consumers were consciously considered in the initial retrenchment and the company's long-term growth strategy. Brunswick's survivial, however, was not assured simply by trimming people and cutting losses to achieve a new strategic direction. As you read this chapter, consider how top management revived Brunswick.

A STRATEGIC PERSPECTIVE

Managers in executive positions have strategic roles that encompass long-range planning and complex decisions. Our introduction to planning in the previous chapter differentiated among strategic, tactical, and operational planning. At the strategic level of management, decisions are made that reach far into the future and encompass a firm's total activities. Tactical and operational plans and subsequent decisions are, as you will recall, more restricted and short-term in nature. In this chapter, we focus on strategic management activities, in particular, the planning and decision-making role of senior executives.

The term *strategy* implies long-range and broad-based considerations. It implies *change* and *uncertainty* because managers are often dealing with concepts and ideas that are novel or untried, but may in the near future be commonplace. Strategy also implies an organizational responsibility to contribute to society. In this era of increased international competition, many managers are preoccupied with revitalizing their firms to make them more productive and more profitable. Managers at multinationals have to deal with international competition and a variety of global associations with their firms and nations. Other managers are simply grappling with how to survive.

strategic management
The senior management responsibility for defining the firm's mission, formulating strategies, and guiding long-term organizational activities consistent with internal and external conditions.

Strategic management is the process of planning a firm's long-term course of action, managing its comprehensive resources, and fulfilling its mission within its broad environment. Those involved in strategic management include members of the board of directors, senior operating officers, and, in larger firms, planning specialists and consultants. For example, General Foods Corporation has strategic planning groups at the executive level consisting of staff specialists such as economists and forecasters who work closely with line executives like the chief financial officer, chief operating officer, and chief executive officer. At Procter & Gamble, planning teams are given strategic management responsibility at a lower division level. The P&G approach is to decentralize strategic decision making. Marriott Corporation is even more decentralized, with strategic planning and decision making pushed down three tiers to eight "business units."[2]

strategic planning
A disciplined effort to produce the fundamental decisions and actions that must be taken today to shape the long-term direction of an organization.

Strategic planning is a disciplined effort to produce the fundamental decisions and actions that must be taken today to shape the long-term nature and direction of an organization within its stated purpose and mission. As discussed in Chapter 6, those involved in strategic management define major objectives, develop strategies to accomplish them, and encourage lower-level planning that supports the firm's mission. Whether this is accomplished through a centralized cadre of executives or through a decentralized planning system is less important than fostering an attitude in managers to *think and act strategically*. Strategic managers do not have thick strategic plans tucked into their briefcases. Instead, they acclimate themselves to thinking strategically about where the organization is going, what major changes are likely to occur, and which major decisions must be made now to achieve their company's long-term objectives.

Among the most important questions strategic managers ask are: What products should we produce? What services should we offer? To whom should we offer these products or services? And what is our purpose for existing? For example, managers have introduced new products that have positioned their companies in new industries. In 1930, Du Pont was known for industrial explosives and construction materials, but then it introduced cellophane and moved into plastics. Other synthetic materials soon followed, including nylon and more than 200 different polyesters, and Du Pont was transformed into a plastics fabricating company. Soon after cellophane became popular, 3M Corporation, then a firm known for sanding abrasives, coated cellophane with an adhesive to create Scotch Tape, and the company repositioned itself as an innovator in films, adhesives, coatings, and sealers, including the recent Post-it notepads. Scotch Tape was initially designed in one-foot-wide rolls to seal cardboard shipping boxes. Then a marketing manager at 3M envisioned Scotch

Tape as a revolutionary product for home and office use, and 3M shifted its marketing efforts toward consumer goods.[3]

The Nature of Strategic Planning

Organizations exist to make contributions to society. An organization is a collective enterprise, a group of individuals that provides society with more than individual enrichment. If it fails to maintain its contribution to society, it can disintegrate. When an American automobile manufacturer stops providing customers with quality cars, customers buy cars elsewhere, perhaps from a Japanese company. If too many customers buy foreign cars, the American manufacturer can become bankrupt. If a church fails to serve its members, it will lose its congregation. And if a university no longer offers sound academic programs, students will transfer to other schools.

Thus when an organization no longer provides beneficial services or products to its stakeholders, society perceives little need for its existence. Strategy is concerned with the grand picture of how organizations serve society, and strategic planning is concerned with how organizations *intentionally and systematically* make decisions about products, services, customers, and human resources vital both to itself and to society.[4]

In their landmark book *In Search of Excellence,* Thomas J. Peters and Robert H. Waterman, Jr., note that managers of the best firms are adroit at planning, using the best information their firms can generate: "Show us a company without a good fact base—a good quantitative picture of its customers, markets, and competitors—and we'll show you one in which priorities are set with the most byzantine of political maneuvering."[5] Peters and Waterman are not advocating quantitative analysis; they are reporting a pattern of effective research coupled with innovative management among America's best firms. In fact, they observe that many disintegrating firms have relied too heavily on detached, analytical decisions at the expense of inquisitiveness and innovation.[6]

Several messages emerge from this and similar studies. First, intuition alone does not suffice for planning in a complex society. Second, analytical research is essential to enhance managers' ability to make good strategic decisions. Third, strategic planning is a blend of meticulous research and managerial verve to make better decisions. We should add that the process is also *future*-oriented, compelling managers to seek plausible courses of action *today* to assure the organization's future.

The Changing Environment of Organizations

Strategic managers must also bear in mind that an organization is part of a social system that includes many dimensions of economic, cultural, political, social, and business influences, as well as internal subsystems of work groups and social networks.[7] America is quickly changing from an industrialized to a "postindustrialized" society in which *information technology* is replacing mechanical technology. The trend is not limited to the United States. Other industrialized powers such as Japan, Germany, and France are also moving rapidly into the information age.

In 1950, only about 17 percent of United States workers were occupied in "information" jobs—creating, processing, and distributing information—but by the end of 1979, approximately 60 percent of U.S. workers were in information jobs. Forecasting into the 1990s, John Naisbitt and Patricia Aburdene in their best-seller *Re-inventing the Corporation* found that although information-related jobs would level off at about 63 percent of all jobs, corporations were already radically changing their composition of workers, reducing management levels, and redefining most middle-management roles.[8] Recall that Brunswick went from eleven layers of management to six, thereby streamlining its operations for the 1990s. Ford Motor Com-

MANAGEMENT APPLICATION

Marriott: Delegate and Hold Accountable for Results

Marriott Corporation has enjoyed a fivefold increase in ten years and is growing at a 20 percent annual rate in sales and assets. During the 1990s, the company expects to set new growth records and to be positioned as a global leader in the hospitality industry. To achieve their strategic objectives, Marriott's executives launched a massive restructuring that began in 1989.

At that time, the company was organized around three major strategic business groups: lodging, contract food services, and restaurants. Marriott had topped $6 billion in sales in 1988, and employed 200,000 people in twenty-six countries. The company was the world's leading in-flight caterer, supplying 150 airlines with 100 million meals a year. As one of the ten largest employers in the country, Marriott controlled the third-largest hotel chain. In addition to the Marriott hotels and resorts, the company operated more than 1,600 restaurants, including Big Boy, Roy Rogers, and Howard Johnson's. This was bolstered by the acquisition of Saga Corporation, a food service company with close to $1 billion in sales to universities, hospitals, and public restaurants.

In 1989, chairman J. Willard (Bill) Marriott, Jr., announced that the corporation was selling In-Flite, one of its most profitable divisions. He also announced a strategic retrenchment and divestiture in which Marriott would sell off all its restaurant assets, trim back its economy-level motels, and create a new portfolio of divisions based on new concepts in lodging. By 1991, Marriott was out of the restaurant and in-flight food service businesses and had only two strategic business units. These were focused on lodging and contract services.

Lodging now includes luxury commercial centers, resorts, cruise ships, the Marriott International Hotels, the new Courtyard and Fairfield chains featuring family and business suites, and unique four-star hotels in eighteen of the world's largest cities. Marriott has also

pany has cut two management levels, and TRW, Hewlett-Packard, and United Technologies have made similar reductions.

One reason for restructuring is that higher productivity is achieved with improved information systems and fewer but more highly skilled individuals. Significant improvements have been made in manufacturing through computer-integrated processes, which have changed fundamental work methods and management responsibilities. Robotics are now used in many repetitive jobs such as assembly-line welding and painting, and managers in these situations manage technology more than they do people. Research, marketing, and distribution services are also being restructured by information technology. Digital Equipment Corporation, for example, manages operations in thirty-five countries through 41,000 interconnected computers that link research, product development, marketing, distribution, and global finances. Citicorp and Banc One dramatically increased their market shares of

entered Eastern Europe, siting its first international hotel in Warsaw, Poland. The contract services unit includes Host International Management Systems; Saga Institutional Food Management for hospitals, universities, and convention centers; and Lifecare, an institutional long-term care system for the elderly.

Marriott is also a paradox in management. It is visibly run from the top by one man in a style that has changed little in sixty years. Bill Marriott, Jr., logs 200,000 miles a year with notebook in hand to jot down less-than-perfect details he observes in his business operations. Bill's father, J. Willard Marriott, Sr., read every customer complaint card for fifty-six years. Although a hands-on management style is very apparent, both father and son found out early on that trusting in good people was the only way to achieve great things. The company has a mission and a fifteen-point philosophy statement that has transcended time. The eleventh point is to "delegate and hold accountable for results."

Strategic planning was founded on that principle nearly fifty-three years ago, and Marriott's strategy is formulated by line managers in each business unit who are held fully accountable. Division and line managers create three-to-five-year plans, establish objectives and budgets, and coordinate these with senior corporate staff under a vice president for planning and business development. Acquisitions, entry into new markets, and international portfolio planning is the responsibility of a board-level finance committee headed by Bill Marriott. However, executives do not interfere with business-level line managers.

Marriott's corporate mission is "to have the best lodging services in the world." Each business unit is charged with becoming "(1) the preferred employer with the best management team, (2) the preferred provider, and (3) the most profitable." Specific growth objectives through the early 1990s are to continue at an annual 20 percent growth rate in both sales and earnings, but neither objective will be permitted to take precedence over Marriott's human resource commitment to employees and customers.

Sources: Carol Kennedy, "How Marriott Corporation Grew Five-fold in Ten Years," *Long Range Planning,* Vol. 21, No. 2 (1988), pp. 10–14. See also J. W. Marriott, Jr., "President's Letter," *Annual Report to Shareholders,* August 1991, pp. 2–3.

consumer banking and credit transactions through early adoption of automatic teller machines.[9]

Technological advances change organizations. Whenever these advances occur, the roles of all organization members—owners, managers, and workers—change. Organizational theorist Henry Mintzberg observes that for a given technology, there is a natural organizational structure that promotes harmony and productivity.[10] A large machine bureaucracy may be appropriate for mass production of automobiles, but it is a terrible model for a service organization such as a hospital. In high-tech firms like Digital Equipment Corporation that have mass-production requirements coupled with technical services, bureaucracies are giving way to consortia of small operating units, almost like companies within companies.[11] Marriott Corporation, described in the Management Application feature, is an example of a service company with a similar organizational philosophy.

Strategic Shifts

SWOT
A situation analysis that examines external factors and internal conditions of an organization to identify strengths, weaknesses, opportunities, and threats.

Strategic managers also must evaluate their organization's situation relative to industry shifts and competitive changes. They make these evaluations in order to formulate plans consistent with an organization's capabilities. Later in this chapter, we will describe the strategic planning process in which one important step is the *situation analysis.* A situation analysis is an examination of industry structure, economics, competitive forces, and other external factors coupled with an internal diagnosis of the organization to identify **strengths, weaknesses, opportunities,** and **threats (SWOT).** As we shall see, SWOT is extremely useful for discovering strategic "shifts" requiring managers to adopt new plans.

For example, the auto industry made a strategic shift into high-tech robotics during the early 1980s in response to pressing competition from foreign automakers. This shift in technology has had far-reaching implications. General Motors plans to close five major auto plants, reduce assembly workers by 20 percent, and restructure the corporation into more autonomous, smaller operating units. GM managers also expect total production to increase through the year 2000 and for the company to change from a five-to-one to a one-to-one ratio of skilled technicians to assembly-line workers.[12]

Social Responsibility and Strategic Issues

As noted earlier, an organization is perceived as useful only so long as it contributes to society. Companies that do not provide value to society are quickly weeded out. For example, in the biotech industry, approximately 500 firms emerged during the past decade with promises of exotic gene splicing medical enhancements, potential cures for cancer, and chemical solutions to environmental problems such as acid rain. Investors pumped several billion dollars into the industry. Unfortunately, only a few products have been developed, and these have had limited success. Genentech and Amgen, two entrepreneurial biotech research companies, have become successful by developing medical and laboratory diagnostic products, but barely two dozen of the remaining companies have come up with marketable products. Analysts expect half of all biotech start-up companies to dissolve or go bankrupt before 1998. Established firms such as Merck and Glaxo, two of the world's largest pharmaceutical companies, also have biotech products ranging from genetically enhanced chemicals for cancer treatment to agricultural additives that stimulate high-yield corn production. The public expects both large and small companies to provide society with *useful* products and services, and when Merck or Genentech have product failures, customers and investors become concerned.[13]

Expectations of People in Organizations

Strategic plans must also meet expectations of employees and managers. Recall from our discussion at the beginning of the chapter that at Brunswick concern for employees is a major strategic goal. The company took steps to make all its employees stock owners and to involve them in strategic decision making. In Chapter 4, we emphasized that developing human relations was a strategic consideration and that employees constituted a *stakeholder* group vital to an organization. All the people working for a firm have committed an irredeemable portion of their lives to its existence. Each employee has individual values, career aspirations, and social alliances within the firm that must be considered by management, and all employees benefit economically when an organization is successful. Therefore, all have a vested interest in a company's strategies.

Managers are distinguished from other employees in that they are held responsible for making decisions. Management strategist Charles E. Summer argues that managers live with a persistent dilemma emanating from the nature of strategic management. On the one hand, they are expected to make decisions, be innovative, and courageously drive the firm toward fulfillment of strategic objectives. On the other hand, they are held responsible for short-run profits, which can prevent them from taking risks or considering strategic changes.[14]

Hence managers often feel that it is safer to avoid change, reduce risk, and stick to familiar performance criteria than to consider new concepts and objectives. This has been called "*Titanic* Planning," a paradox in which managers become so dogmatically fixated on maintaining an unwavering course set by one stakeholder group, such as investors, that they fail to see an iceberg dead ahead. Recall that the owners of the *Titanic* wanted the ship's officers to steer a course that would set a transatlantic speed record, even though that would put everyone—owners, passengers, and crew—in danger. The owners disregarded the danger because they considered their ship unsinkable.[15]

The *Titanic* did sink, nonetheless, and everyone lost. The same thing can happen to a business. For example, R. J. Reynolds acquired Nabisco Brands, Inc., several years ago to create a juggernaut organization, RJR Nabisco. Management cut costs, reduced product research, and drove profits up to support a high stock price. Feeling unsinkable, RJR Nabisco's management tried to buy out investors and take control of their company, but instead found themselves ousted when Kohlberg Kravis Roberts (KKR) fashioned a $25 billion buyout. KKR was backed by employees, who felt the company had been poorly managed and that KKR had better strategic plans than RJR Nabisco's top executives. Other major firms, including Kraft, Bloomingdale's, TV Guide, Firestone, and CBS Records, have changed hands because of lack of confidence in management's ability to make their firms competitive.[16]

The absence of strategic growth and innovation is explained partially by a commitment to the status quo. Summer describes this *suboptimization* behavior as a concern for immediate tasks or sharply defined functional specialization that can suffocate growth and innovation.[17] Managers fall into the trap of avoiding risk, relying on their past successes rather than seeking opportunities for the future. Change, Summer notes, can disrupt continuity and threaten managers, who then behave rationally to protect their careers. The best plans, therefore, are plausible in terms of individual expectations and acceptable to those charged with implementing them.

From the strategic view of total human resource planning, all employees must have a satisfying place to work, with opportunities for growth and achievement. Peter Drucker suggests that although "happy" and "satisfied" employees are critical elements of success, it is the spirit of *performance* that separates outstanding companies from others.[18] Obviously, if employees view company strategies as personally threatening, they will not exert themselves to cooperate with management.

Often strategies are predicated on human resource planning. For example, Wal-Mart, headed until 1992 by America's richest person, the late Sam Walton, is ranked by *Fortune* as one of America's ten "most admired corporations." Wal-Mart achieved that reputation, along with more than $40 billion in annual sales, through a strategic commitment to people. Walton said that customers always come first, but that his 345,000 "associates" were a close second; investors ran a distant third. All employees are "associates" who benefit from profit-sharing plans, performance-based bonuses, and exceptional employee benefits—but most important, for the success of the company, they are involved in, and responsible for, plans and decisions from the stock room to corporate officers.[19] This philosophy of focusing strategies on human resources is translated into performance at many leading companies.

After building the largest retailing operation in the United States and retiring, Sam Walton came out of retirement to continue his self-piloted airplane hops to meet with his "associates" (nonmanagement employees) around the country. Walton's visits were not only inspirational; they were also an integral part of his human resource planning strategy. Walton believed that sales rely on associates who have "caught the spirit."

> **CHECKPOINT**
>
> - Describe how planning is accomplished in multilevel organizations through strategic planning teams.
> - Define strategic planning and identify three major questions that strategic managers must answer.
> - Explain how changes in technology, social systems, and expectations of stakeholders affect organizations.

STRATEGIC ORGANIZATION

Smaller organizations, and most entrepreneurial enterprises, have a simple strategic level of management. Recall that we illustrated a simple organizational structure in Chapter 6 with three levels of management. Strategic planning responsibilities were identified with the executive management level. This model is predominant because nearly 90 percent of U.S. companies have fewer than 500 employees and enjoy a simple structure of management.[20] Still, nearly half of all nonfarm employees work in major corporations where organizational structures are complicated. Strategic planning in these corporations is therefore also more complicated, and is usually subdivided into three distinct levels. As Figure 7-1 shows, these are called *corporate, business,* and *functional* strategy levels.[21]

Corporate Strategy

corporate-level strategy Also called the portfolio-level strategy, it concerns board-level decisions for acquisitions, mergers, major expansions, and divestitures that add to or reduce product lines.

At the apex of large organizations, board members and executives reshape the purpose of a firm by deciding what businesses to pursue. **Corporate-level strategy** is often called the *portfolio-level strategy* because board-level decisions are usually concerned with acquisitions, mergers, major expansions, and divestitures that add to or reduce product lines. Today this also involves setting up international operations and forming new enterprises through joint ventures with other corporations.

Acquisitions and mergers among well-known companies illustrate corporate strategy. Companies like Sears, Philip Morris, Coca-Cola, Citicorp, and Hospital Cor-

FIGURE 7-1 Three Levels of Strategy

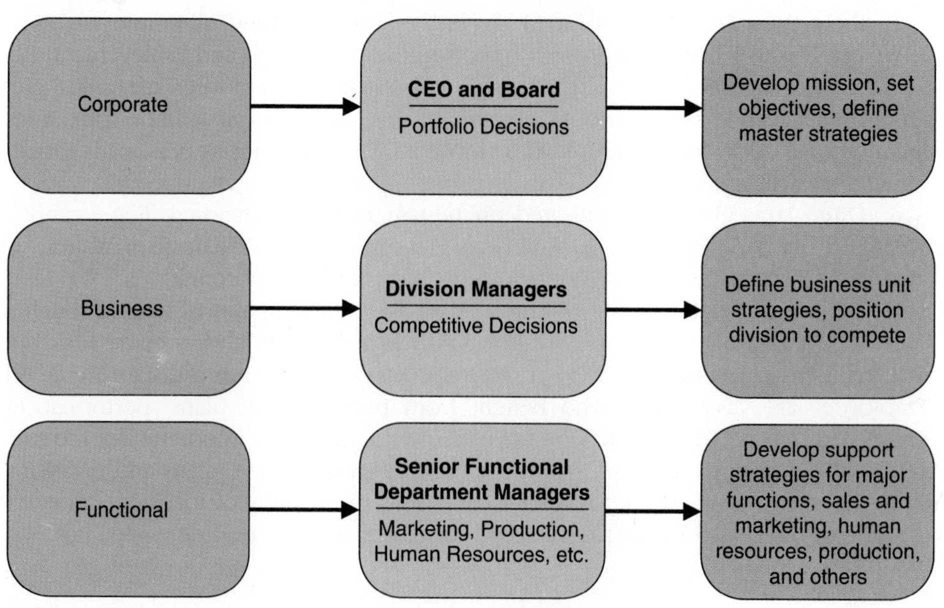

poration of America have acquired new product or service lines, added divisions, and in some instances altered their corporate purpose. For example, Sears had been a dominant merchandiser for nearly a century, but with the acquisitions of Allstate, Coldwell Banker, and Dean Witter, it became a financial giant in real estate, securities, and insurance. Johnson Wax, Johnson Worldwide Associates, Inc., and S. C. Johnson & Son, Inc., form a group of companies created by one family, each with products that were developed internally, without acquisition or merger, like Johnson Wax, Pledge, and Raid bug killer. But the Johnson family has also acquired divisions in bar coding, fishing equipment, recreational boating, and industrial ink-stamping, as well as a Wisconsin bank holding company, a Swiss bank, and a European diving equipment manufacturer.[22]

Business Strategy

Acquired companies become subsidiaries, and in many instances, sheer size requires companies to subdivide. Subsidiaries and divisions generate **business-level strategies** that focus on specific product lines or markets. Strategic managers are not concerned about portfolios but simply with how to compete in their respective industries. Strategic decisions at this level concern product development, technology, services, market expansion, and competitive positioning such as developing distinct brand images or becoming cost-price leaders. *Distinct competency* is important to business-level managers, who strive to achieve customer recognition by creating a company distinction such as a quality image or a technological advantage.

business-level strategies Managers focus on well-defined business lines or divisions of services to determine how to compete in their respective industries.

Coca-Cola and Pepsi Cola, both divisions of corporations that produce a variety of products besides soft drinks, compete directly with one another in this area to establish distinct competencies. Other corporations have separate divisions, each with a distinct competency and a mandate to compete effectively in one particular market. Examples are Rolls-Royce with automobiles, marine engines, and aircraft engines, and Ralph Lauren with sportswear, cologne, and fashion accessories. Business-level strategies also tend to focus on "market niches," such as Izod has in designer clothing and Kitchen Aid has in appliances.[23]

General Electric is credited with developing the first formal model of business-level strategic planning. Faced with a growing line of diversified products during the 1960s, GE restructured management to create a "family" of businesses, each having autonomy for its own decisions.[24] GE called these formal groups *strategic business units* (*SBUs*.) Today we say that a **strategic business unit** is a group of divisions or operations with compatible planning premises that compete in similar industries. Figure 7-2 illustrates the SBU concept.

strategic business unit (SBU) A major subunit or group at the strategic level of a large, complex firm. SBUs provide a focus on related services, products, markets, customers, or technologies to improve management and decision making.

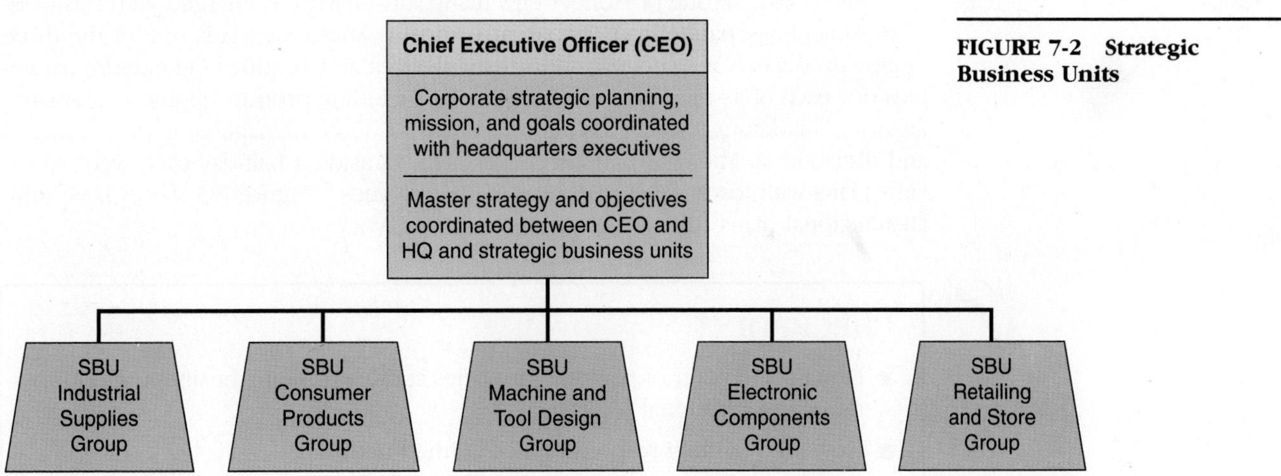

FIGURE 7-2 Strategic Business Units

FIGURE 7-3 Relationship of Functional and Business-Level Planning Activities

GE recentralized executives into a headquarters operation and redefined the top-management role as one of corporate-level portfolio planning. Each SBU was distinguished as a group of operating divisions sharing a common purpose. Divisions within an SBU therefore dealt with similar industrial and environmental planning issues, had similar production technologies, manufactured similar products, or competed in similar markets. In fact, GE's divisions often met several of these conditions. Its jet engine division, for example, served the same customers and competed with similar companies as its aerospace electronics division. These two divisions were grouped into one SBU, whereas home appliances, consumer products, electronic components, industrial motors, generators, and other product lines were grouped into several other strategic business units.

Functional Strategy

functional-level strategies Carried out by executives in functional areas, these strategies support business-level decisions to introduce new technologies, develop new products, open new markets, or implement functional action plans to help the firm compete effectively.

Subsidiaries and divisions are often too complex to have a single level of strategic decision making so they subdivide responsibilities into a third tier. Managers at this third level are concerned with **functional-level strategies,** or strategies that support business-level plans. Functional-level decisions include how to implement new technologies, develop new products, open new markets, expand into new facilities, and institute new human resource programs. Not all companies consider functional-level decisions to be strategic, and in Chapter 8, we explore functional management responsibilities as *tactical* issues. Many large firms do, nevertheless, require functional-level strategic planning systems that result, for example, in "marketing strategies" or "research and development strategies."

Micro Switch, one of Honeywell's many subsidiaries, is charged with business-level strategies separate from its parent company. Micro Switch is one of the three largest producers of switching and sensor devices and requires "integrating strategies" for each of its major functional activities, including product engineering, manufacturing, marketing, quality assurance, human resource management, procurement, and distribution. Micro Switch executives also set aside a half-day each week to review plans with lower-level managers and employees.[25] Figure 7-3 shows how similar functional plans relate to business-level endeavors.

CHECKPOINT

- Explain and contrast planning priorities at the corporate, business, and functional organizational levels.
- How are planning responsibilities defined in SBUs?

FORMAL PLANNING AND STRATEGY

Strategic analysis begins with a clear statement of purpose: the mission of the organization. With a well-articulated mission statement, managers determine major objectives. Recall from Chapter 6 that strategies are formulated through analysis to delineate actions an organization must pursue to fulfill those objectives. Although the formal planning process is similar for each strategic level we have described, different types of strategies will be employed to implement corporate-level, business-level, and functional-level objectives. Figure 7-4 identifies the general strategic management process.

Establishing the Mission Statement

Developing a mission statement is the process of clarifying the purpose of an organization in language that customers, managers, and employees will understand. A clear mission statement will crystallize the firm's long-term direction by answering: What is our business and what will it be?[26]

Some mission statements are one-liners like "to create a customer" or "to serve people," and although these may be appropriate as mottos, they are insufficient to clarify what an organization is about. The more informative, but still abbreviated, mission statements in Exhibit 7-1 illustrate how an organization can distinguish itself from other organizations.

Notice how clear the Monsanto Fund mission statement is. It specifies that the Fund is not merely a not-for-profit entity but, more importantly, a charitable trust established to promote corporate philanthropy for well-defined constituents. Control Data Corporation's mission is explained through its business strategy: applying the problem-solving capabilities of computer technology to select areas of society.

The mission statement of Hart, Schaffner & Marx initially seems vague, but once the company's nature is understood, it makes sense. HS&M executives are mandated to provide financial resources to 300 retailers and 50 operating units while manufacturing or licensing brand-name clothing for national distribution.

The USAA Group (United Services Automobile Association) is an insurance company that operates much like a cooperative or a credit union; customers are limited to policyholders, and policyholders are literally the corporate shareholders. Therefore, USAA defines its mission in terms of service to "members."

Each of these examples sheds some light on organizational character and how firms distinguish themselves from others. But many companies lack a clearly defined mission. It is common to hear corporate executives say that the mission of their firm is to "make money" or "survive." These statements say nothing about why a company is in business, why society should value its being in business, or how it intends to stay in business.

FIGURE 7-4 The Process of Strategic Management

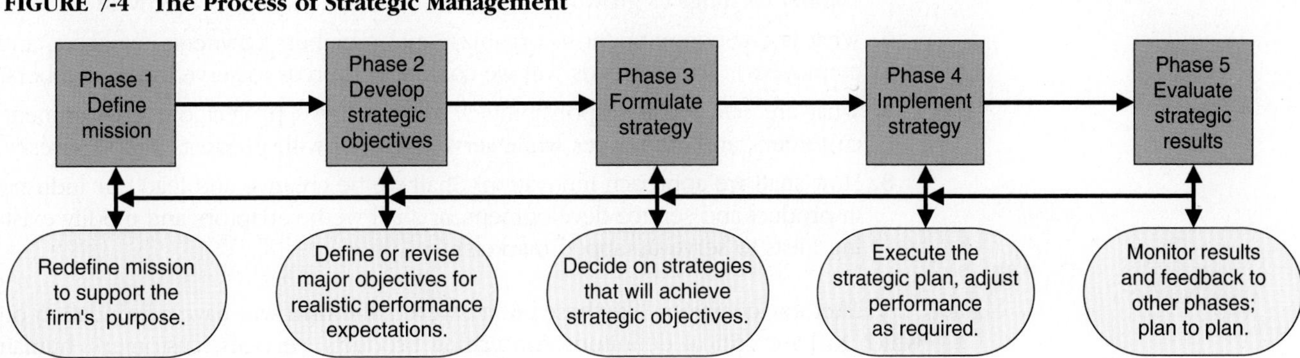

EXHIBIT 7-1 Selected Mission Statements

Monsanto Fund	"Monsanto Fund was created as a not-for-profit corporation. . . . The Fund was established to execute Monsanto's corporate philanthropy by contributing to tax-exempt organizations while providing services in the areas of education, health and welfare, youth activities, civic and community development and arts and culture." (Annual Report, 1987)
Control Data Corporation	"Control Data's business strategy is one of applying the problem-solving capabilities of computer technology, financial and human resources to those markets that have evolved from society's major unmet needs." (Annual Report, 1981)
Hart, Schaffner & Marx	"The Company, the most important resource for many apparel retailers, has a marketing strategy based on supplying quality apparel covering a wide range of prices and fashions. . . . We greatly value our relationship with the many retailers we serve and we strive to become more important to them by providing the best merchandise to fulfill the requirements of their customers. "The Company is able to offer diversified apparel fashions and prices through a prestigious array of brands, personalities and designers. These are very effective in appealing to different apparel markets and we enhance the saleability of our products by using a distinctive approach directed toward each market." (Annual Report, 1980)
United Services Automobile Association (USAA)	"At USAA we are optimistic about the potential of the future—both in terms of traditional values such as service and integrity, and in terms of modern technology. We are optimistic, too, about our nation's economic future and we're confident that we can continue to provide insurance and financial services second to none. . . . As always, service is USAA Life's number one objective. We strive to treat all policyholders equitably and to offer products that meet their needs." (Report to Members, 1988)

Focusing the Mission Statement

Mission statements are the result of answering many difficult questions about an organization's future. Some of the key questions are:[27]

1. What service or product do we offer to create and sustain a viable customer base? How are we serving society?
2. In which markets will we compete? How do we compete efficiently in those markets for products and services?
3. What is our technology? What should it be in the future? How do we ensure the most competent use of technological resources?
4. How do we define "quality"? Will we have a "high-value-added" image in a select market niche or a "discount" mass-market profile?
5. How do we define profitability? Will we seek a high return for shareholders, commit earnings to growth, or choose some mix of profit objectives?
6. What is our commitment to organizational members (owners, managers, and employees)? To what ends will we commit resources to serve these members?
7. What are our social responsibilities? How will we protect our environment, customers, and employees while serving society with products and services?
8. How shall we approach innovation? Shall we be creative and lead our industry in product and service development, or shall we be adaptors and modify existing ideas to serve uptapped markets?

After key questions like these are answered, the firm will have a foundation on which to base critical definitons concerning products, services, customers, human resources, and community responsibilities. Getting the answers to questions concerning the firm's mission is the crux of planning.

Setting Strategic Objectives

The mission statement is a framework for developing strategic objectives, and as you will recall from Chapter 6, these objectives should be clear, measurable, and expressed for a definite period of time. For example, Control Data Corporation's mission stipulates that it will develop special-purpose computer technology for "problem solving." CDC has elected not to build a full range of computers, but rather to concentrate on problem-solving applications in aerospace engineering and scientific environments. The company's strategic objectives for its five-year plan are to achieve a 15 percent annual growth in sales with state-of-the-art scientific work stations and to achieve quality improvements for 99 percent reliability.[28] Hart, Schaffner & Marx manufactures quality clothing. Hickey-Freeman, Jarmar, Christian Dior, Pierre Cardin, Cesarani, Jack Nicklaus, Playboy, and Johnny Carson are several of its menswear labels. Its women's labels include Baskin, Hannys, Chas, and deJong's. HS&M's main objective is to become the market leader in high-quality clothes, and to maintain investors' returns at or above industry averages with consistent annual dividends. HS&M is organized with business-level strategies so that each clothing line has competitive objectives for sales, profitability, and quality image.[29]

Formulating Strategies to Achieve Objectives

This third phase of the strategic planning process gives a blueprint for action. By **formulating strategies,** managers explain *how* objectives will be achieved. Formulating strategy, like setting objectives, takes into account information derived from the "situation analysis." Effective strategies address the following questions:[30]

formulating strategies
Strategies formulated by managers through their planning efforts to explain how the company will achieve its objectives.

1. How will the company respond to changing conditions such as new technology, shifts in consumer needs, competitive pressures, and economic factors? Through a situation analysis, managers will also be able to discover opportunities to pursue and threats to defend against.
2. How will the company allocate resources among its business units to support business-level and functional-level objectives while simultaneously preserving its financial integrity? In making such decisions, management will also rely on information derived from a situation analysis and the portfolio of businesses defined at the corporate level.
3. How will the company compete in its industry and in its markets to fulfill its strategic objectives? If it is organized around business and functional strategies, competitive strategies will be defined for each business unit.
4. Within each line of business, how will the company support strategies at the functional level? Answering this question will enable managers to coordinate functional activities to fulfill business-level and corporate objectives.

Strategies can include positioning the firm for growth through new products or new markets, global expansion, technological innovation, quality performance, cost-price leadership, and portfolio development. Brunswick Corporation, profiled earlier, has a strategy of diversifying its product line beyond bowling equipment to include recreation and industrial products, defense contracts, and leisure-time services. Coca-Cola has diversified into new products with diet and health drinks, juices, and twelve different soft drinks. We expand our discussion of how strategies are formulated later in the chapter.

Implementing the Strategic Plan

strategic implementation
The deliberate execution of strategies that achieve objectives through incremental activities defined in policies, programs, projects, budgets, procedures, and rules.

Implementation is the process of making things happen. It involves allocating resources through budgets, developing programs and projects that "activate" the organization, and articulating policies, procedures, and rules managers can use in guiding activities on a daily basis. **Strategic implementation** is the deliberate execution of strategies that achieve objectives through incremental activities defined in policies, programs, projects, budgets, procedures, and rules. Implementation may also require significant organizational changes, such as Brunswick's retrenchment or General Electric's restructuring into strategic business units.

Evaluating Performance and Reformulating Plans

The final phase in strategic planning consists of evaluating information gathered through control systems to ascertain whether plans are working as intended. The *controlling* function of management applied to strategic planning means evaluating performance toward strategic objectives so that corrective action can be taken where necessary. Corrective action may require adjusting performance objectives because of changes in circumstances, shifting to contingency plans, or fine-tuning strategies.

This phase of planning closes the loop and returns managers to the first phase of "defining the mission." In Chapter 6, we explained how the loop is closed by "planning to plan" because plans, once formulated, can quickly become obsolete. Commercial lending, for example, is unstable and highly speculative, according to the Bank Marketing Association. Nevertheless, BMA members had always attempted to develop long-term strategic plans—until 1990, when the junk bond market collapsed and the savings and loan fiasco required massive government intervention to bail out failing S&Ls. Commercial bankers suddenly found they had inadequate long-term planning premises to support their strategic lending programs or to forecast future capital requirements. BMA members therefore suspended long-term planning in favor of a series of short-term plans formulated to deal with a chaotic market. It may be several years before commercial lenders and credit specialists feel confident that long-term plans will not be made obsolete by circumstances.[31]

CHECKPOINT

- Describe the five-phase strategic planning process.
- Identify at least one essential question to be answered in each of the planning phases.

SITUATION ANALYSIS

situation analysis
An examination of industry structure, economics, competitive forces, and other external factors and internal conditions essential for strategic planning.

There are three major components of a **situation analysis.**[32] The first is an examination of industry characteristics related to a firm's products or markets. The second is a competitive analysis that evaluates a company's rivals and forces that could affect the nature of competition. The third is an internal diagnosis of the company that assesses its strengths and weaknesses and its ability to compete successfully. A situation analysis conducted at the corporate level identifies opportunities for changing a company's portfolio of business to complement long-term objectives. Used at the business level, a situation analysis reveals *strengths, weaknesses, opportunities,* and *threats* (SWOT) that affect performance. Detailed results from situation analyses provide functional-level strategists with planning premises related to operational ac-

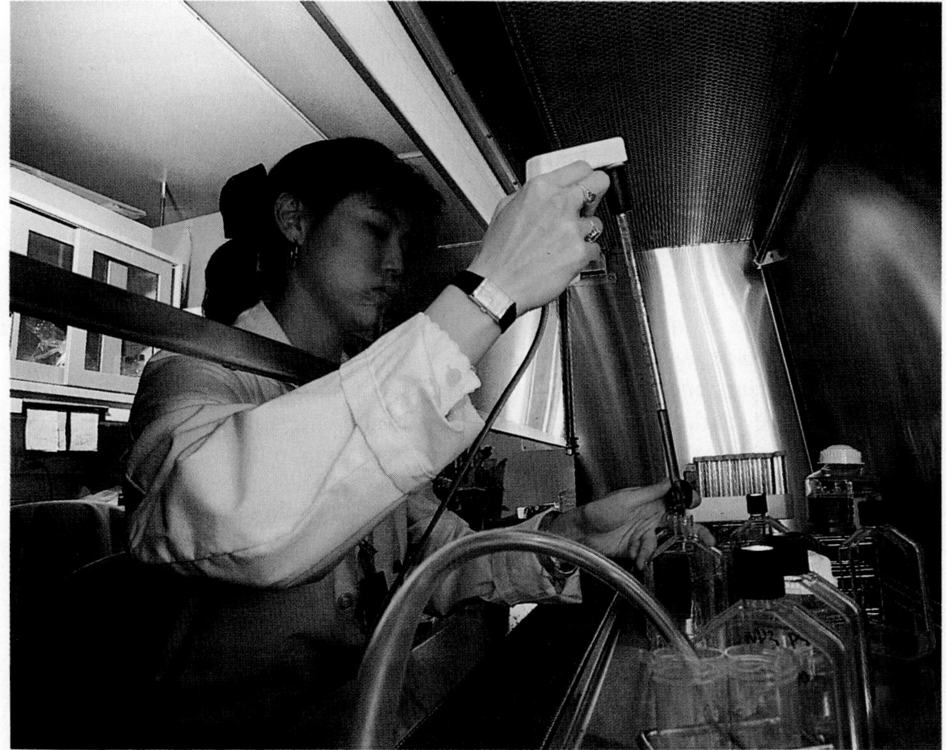

When Genentech, Inc., introduced t-PA, a heart drug, it could only guess at sales because no comparable product had ever been made or sold. With no market information on t-PA, no direct competitors for it, and no history of its use, Genentech had to do without two important aspects of a situation analysis—industry and competitive analyses—and rely on the strengths of its manufacturing and marketing skills. Eventually, Genentech produced only half of t-PA's projected sales and was forced to sell a controlling interest to Roche Holding, Ltd., the Swiss parent of Hoffman-La Roche Company.

tivities such as marketing, manufacturing, finance, human resource management, and technological development.

Industry Analysis

Strategists want to know several things about industries in which their firms compete. An industry analysis helps managers understand *how the industry is structured,* and if that structure is changing. For example, the cereal industry consists of twenty-one cereal producers, but three companies—Kellogg, Post, and General Foods—account for nearly 70 percent of sales in the U.S. cereal market. Each of these companies carefully analyzes the others, because small changes in products or in market shares can significantly alter their competitive strategies.[33] In contrast, the U.S. banking industry consists of more than 13,600 federal- and state-chartered banks. Of these, only about 20 have nationwide interests, such as Citicorp and Bank America; the remaining banks compete in local and regional markets. Incidentally, the number of major banks is declining as large banks merge to compete globally. The industry structure, therefore, is fragmented, with a few large banks operating nationally and globally and the majority emphasizing regional and local banking.[34] Strategists also want to understand consumer tastes, changes in buying power, and consumer preferences for industry brands. In addition, an industry analysis will help managers determine capital costs, material and labor costs, and economic trends that affect investment, interest rates, and stock prices for their company's competitors.

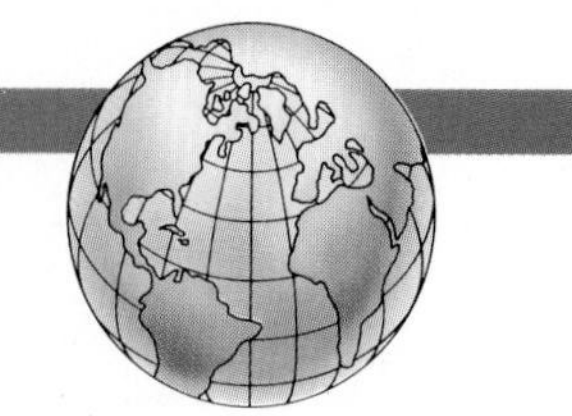

GLOBAL TRENDS

Watch Out Europe (America), The Americans (Europeans) Are Coming!

Strategic change has a special meaning for Europeans as the twelve Common Market members and the seven European Free Trade Association nations drop trade barriers and unite into a single competitive market. In effect, Western Europe will comprise nineteen countries with nearly 400 million consumers, and they will enjoy common trade conditions while buttressing trade resistance from nonmember nations. For American companies, the battle for markets after 1993 will be a decisive test of U.S. company strength. In the past, American companies have competed against a fragmented Europe, but the unification will create a $900 billion consumer goods market in Europe without barriers to trade among member nations. Companies from France will be able to do business in Germany, Great Britain, Italy, and a dozen other nations as easily as a U.S. company from Chicago does business in Detroit. But American firms in Europe will still be foreign companies facing the same, or stiffer, trade regulations.

How are American companies preparing for the challenge? The biggest and the best U.S. multinationals began in 1988 with a modest investment of about $2.4 billion to shore up their European operations; this figure rose to $19.7 billion in 1989, and $60 billion in 1990. Some U.S. firms are so well established in Europe that competition with European firms is not threatening. Coke and Kellogg are classic continental brand names, Ford and General Motors vie for the top spots in autos, and IBM and Digital Equipment dominate their European markets. Some companies, such as Colgate-Palmolive and AT&T, will remain strong even though challenged. Nevertheless, these and other U.S. firms are restructuring their corporations and anxiously searching out European acquisitions, joint ventures, and strategic liaisons to solidify their strategic market positions.

European firms are becoming galvanized to meet that competition and to expand their positions in the United States. While American companies are spending billions in Europe, the Europeans are spending even more in the United States to expand. So while U.S. multinationals are shoring up their operations in Europe, the Europeans are aggressively pursuing U.S. markets at an accelerated pace. Coke may be common in Europe, but Bayer Aspirin (a German brand) is just as common in America. Although GE and Westinghouse are well known overseas, Philips Electronics, British Petroleum (BP), Unilever, Nestlé, and Siemens are well known here.

Strategic planning on both sides of the Atlantic has changed in a fundamental way that will affect all future business decisions. No planning premises have been left intact. Not only are major shifts in consumer demand and competition taking place, but definitions of markets and consumers have changed. A U.S. division in France, for example, no longer competes against a French company in France for French customers; it now competes against French, German, British, Italian, Dutch, Austrian, Belgian, and Spanish companies for customers in those and several more countries. And while the United States is fighting for European markets, the Europeans are diving into U.S. markets with comparable strength.

Sources: "Will the New Europe Cut U.S. Giants Down to Size?" *Business Week,* December 12, 1988, pp. 54–58. See also Mark M. Nelson and Martin duBois, "Pact Expands Europe's Common Market," *Wall Street Journal,* October 23, 1991, p. A10.

Competitive Analysis

five forces model of competition
A systematic approach to evaluating a company's competitive position relative to its industry and economic power in society.

Strategic managers spend a great deal of time analyzing competitors to evaluate their own competitive strategies. One of the best approaches to making a competitive analysis is the **five forces model of competition** developed by Harvard professor Michael E. Porter. In Porter's model, depicted in Figure 7-5, all competition can be explained by the following five forces.[35]

1. *Positioning for competitive advantage.* Firms develop moves and countermoves to gain a competitive advantage over their competitors. One firm may go on the offensive to gain sales through aggressive low pricing, only to be countered by a rival who offers cash rebates and low-interest financing. This kind of competition has become common in the automotive industry. In contrast, competitors in the soft drink industry have jockeyed for market share through comparative taste tests, market strategies based on low-calorie diet drinks, and celebrity advertising. These are headline grabbers, but less dramatic positioning occurs daily in more businesses. For example, in 1988, Super Pampers, using a new high-absorbant polymer that improved the diaper and reduced manufacturing costs, were introduced by Procter & Gamble. Super Pampers forced diaper prices down and captured a larger share of the diaper market. Then in 1991, competitors showed evidence that Super Pampers were not biodegradable and sales shifted slightly toward P&G's rivals.[36]
2. *Threats of substitute products.* Competitors, by definition, offer close substitutes for one another's products. Soft drinks, beers, comparable automobiles, coffees, household detergents, and many other products have similar characteristics and are positioned in similar markets for identical customers. But strategic analysis must also consider substitutes with dissimilar characteristics. For example, while bottled soft drinks like Coca-Cola and Pepsi confront one another directly, powdered fruit drinks like Kool-Aid and Crystal Light attract their customers with low prices and sugarless fruit drinks.[37]
3. *Potential entry of new competitors.* Products with established brand names are seldom threatened by the entry of new competitors, but analysts cannot let their guard down if the capital required to enter their line of business is small. Campbell's and Heinz's soups, for example, are established brands, yet generic soups and private-label soups now compete equally with them because food processing is a relatively inexpensive production process. Conversely, the market for washing machines and dryers is controlled by a half-dozen companies, such as Maytag and General Electric, because the capital required to establish a

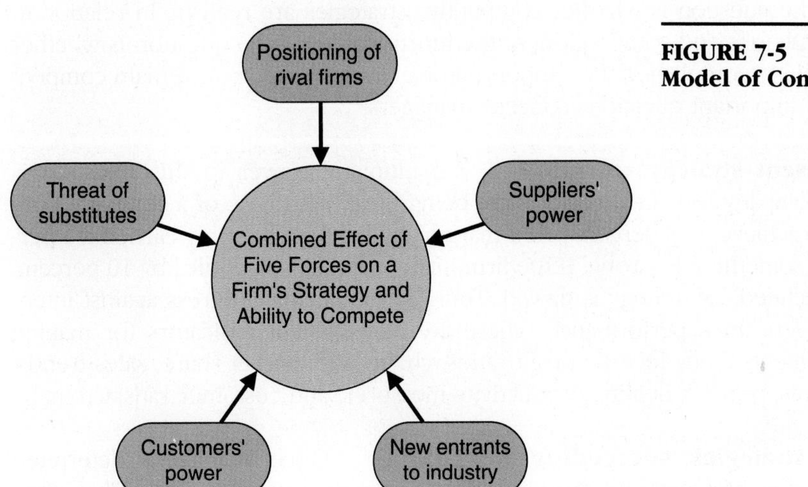

FIGURE 7-5 Five Forces Model of Competiton

cost-effective appliance line prohibits the entry of new firms. Entry can also be blocked if a company controls proprietary technology (patents, copyrights, and trademarks). Polaroid enjoys patent protection for its light-polarizing products, for example. Through competitive analysis, managers can evaluate other barriers to entry, such as licensing requirements, government-regulated services, access to raw materials, access to distribution systems, and scale economies of low-cost producers.

4. *Economic power of suppliers.* Suppliers influence competion by controlling raw materials, parts, supplies, and equipment needed by a company. If a firm must rely on a critical part, a disruption in supply can cripple production. For example, several essential semiconductor components required for VCRs are manufactured only in Japan. This has prevented some U.S. manufacturers who lack supply contracts from competing in the VCR industry. Powerful suppliers who control raw materials can also dictate prices, thereby affecting the cost structure of a purchasing firm. For example, petroleum companies dictate prices of resins used in plastics, and purchasing firms, such as Mattel Toys and Tupperware, are powerless to protest. When suppliers control products for which there are no readily available substitutes, they can also control the terms of sale, delivery schedules, and material quality.[38]
5. *Economic power of consumers.* The counterpoint to powerful suppliers is powerful consumers. When there are few consumers who buy in volume, they can squeeze prices and dictate terms of sale. This is true of domestic automobile manufacturers, who have strong bargaining positions with hundreds of small suppliers competing for orders. Huge retailers like K Mart and Wal-Mart can dictate prices, terms of sale, quality, delivery conditions, and product specifications to more than 18,000 suppliers. A competitive analysis will reveal the relative power of consumers and suppliers so that more effective purchasing strategies can be implemented to protect a company. For example, Wal-Mart does not have the ability to squeeze Procter & Gamble, which has comparable strength and bargaining power.

Company Analysis

The third component of a situation analysis is a self-assessment of the company. After completing an *industry* and a *competitive* analysis, managers examine the strengths and weaknesses of their own company to determine how well existing strategies are working. At the corporate level, the question is whether the company has created a portfolio of businesses that fit together to support corporate objectives. At the business level, the question is whether competitive strategies are realistic in relation to industry conditions and competition. At the functional level, the question is whether strategies have accomplished the supporting objectives necessary to remain competitive. Several important questions concern managers.[39]

Is the present strategy working? The ultimate answer to this question is whether a company feels its objectives are being achieved. If one of a company's objectives is to achieve an 8 percent profit margin and the firm has only earned a 4 percent return, something is wrong. If the firm intended to increase sales by 10 percent, but sales declined, its strategy is flawed. Thus, by measuring progress against intentions, managers track performance. There are many useful indicators for making these assessments. They include profit ratios, changes in market share, sales trends, cost structures, product quality, productivity measures, and customer satisfaction.

Why are strategies succeeding or failing? Once managers determine whether or not strategies are working, it is necessary to assess why. What went

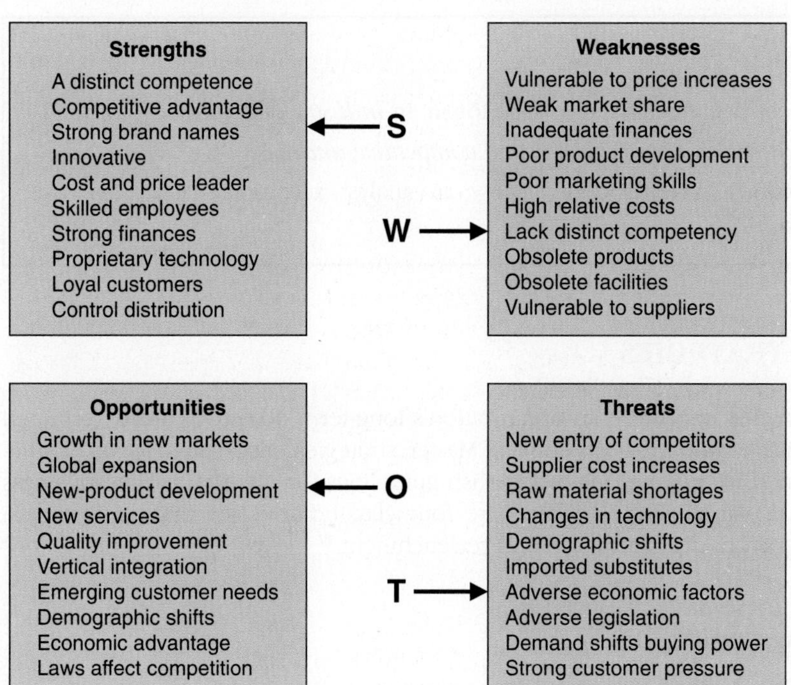

Strengths
A distinct competence
Competitive advantage
Strong brand names
Innovative
Cost and price leader
Skilled employees
Strong finances
Proprietary technology
Loyal customers
Control distribution
S
W
Weaknesses
Vulnerable to price increases
Weak market share
Inadequate finances
Poor product development
Poor marketing skills
High relative costs
Lack distinct competency
Obsolete products
Obsolete facilities
Vulnerable to suppliers
Opportunities
Growth in new markets
Global expansion
New-product development
New services
Quality improvement
Vertical integration
Emerging customer needs
Demographic shifts
Economic advantage
Laws affect competition
O
T
Threats
New entry of competitors
Supplier cost increases
Raw material shortages
Changes in technology
Demographic shifts
Imported substitutes
Adverse economic factors
Adverse legislation
Demand shifts buying power
Strong customer pressure

FIGURE 7-6 Components of the SWOT Analysis

wrong? What worked well? To answer these questions requires systematic probing into the reasons behind success or failure. By using information gained about the industry and competitors, managers can compare their company's strengths and weaknesses as the first two elements in a SWOT analysis. By examining *strengths,* they can discover untapped potential or identify distinct competencies that helped them succeed. By examining *weaknesses,* managers can identify gaps in performance, vulnerabilities, and fallacious assumptions about their existing strategies. Figure 7-6 illustrates all four components of a SWOT analysis.

Has the company taken advantage of opportunities? The third component of a SWOT analysis identifies *opportunities.* By using information gathered from industry and competitive analyses, managers try to identify opportunities for diversification into new markets, new products, or new technologies. Often hidden opportunities surface from a careful analysis.

Can the company avoid threats? The fourth component of a SWOT analysis identifies *threats* a company faces and whether its strategy provides an adequate defense against them. Once again, information gathered from industry and competitive evaluations is used to make the assessment. For example, the potential for new competitors to enter an industry poses a threat to sales; substitute products pose a similar threat. Global competition has accelerated both the number of firms in competition and the number of substitute products available in many fields. The obvious example of this trend is imported automobiles, but foreign competitors also enjoy substantial sales in U.S. markets for consumer electronics, semiconductors, chemicals, petroleum, minerals, clothing, and industrial supplies. Other threats emerge from economic conditions, such as rising interest rates and inflation, government regulations, and social changes. The critical question for strategists is whether the company is positioned well enough to avoid these threats, and if not, what strategies will be needed to counter them. When managers have completed the SWOT analysis and incorporated information from industry and competitive analyses, they have a comprehensive base of planning premises on which to formulate strategies.

CHECKPOINT

- What does a strategic analyst look for in an *industry analysis?*
- What are Porter's five forces in the *competitive analysis?*
- Using SWOT, briefly identify how an analyst accomplishes a *company analysis.*

MASTER STRATEGIES

master strategies
Also called grand strategies, these define in broad terms the long-term direction of an organization.

Master strategies to achieve an organization's long-term objectives are determined by *corporate-level planning* executives. Master strategies, also called *grand strategies,* are defined in broad terms to establish guidelines for managers at the business and functional planning levels. There are four classifications for master strategies: growth, integration, diversification, and retrenchment.[40]

Growth Strategies

growth
A growth strategy is the expansion of sales achieved either through marketing existing products more aggressively or through pursuing new products or new markets.

Growth is an expansion of sales activities, which can be achieved in several ways. First, a firm's existing products can be marketed more aggressively to increase sales volume. Second, existing products can be introduced to new markets by expanding into new territories. Third, products can be fine-tuned, or marketing strategies altered, to attract new consumer groups in existing markets. Fourth, new products can be developed to diversify a company's product line. All these are *strategic alternatives* that define *how* the master strategy will be implemented. Simply saying the firm

Goodyear Tire & Rubber company, which for years had insisted on exclusive dealerships, lost a lot of tire customers to multibrand discount outlets. After he became CEO of Goodyear in July 1991, Stanley C. Gault adopted a classic growth strategy approach to improve the company's sales: He announced that Goodyear would sell tires through Sears, Roebuck, and Co., one of the country's leading tire sellers, and through no-frills Just Tires stores. Goodyear would simultaneously increase its development of new products and boost brand advertising by a third. So far, so good—Goodyear had a profit of $90.1 million in 1991, compared to a loss of $38.3 million in 1990.

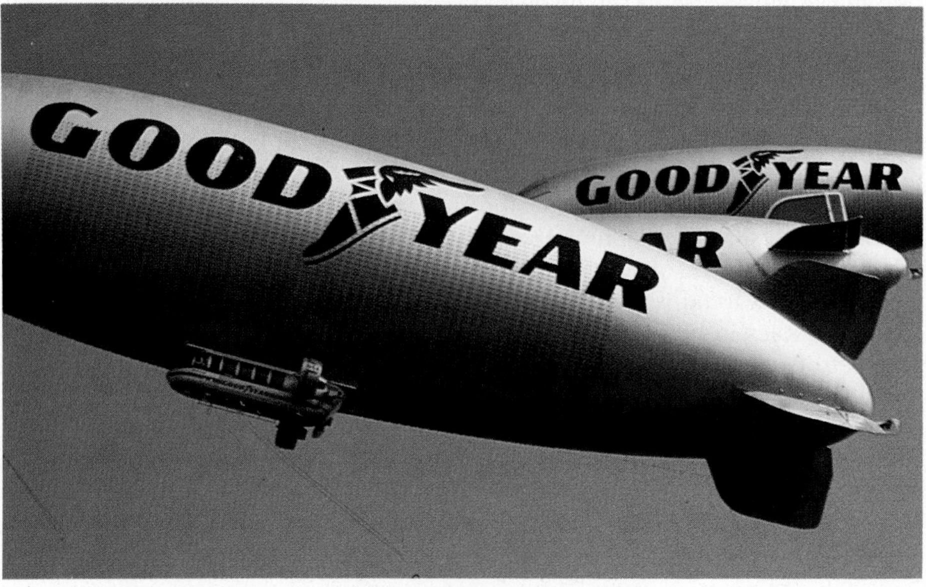

will "grow" is insufficient to guide organizational activities, but saying it will "grow through product innovation" can be translated into clearly defined activities.

Integration Strategies

Integration strategies occur when a company seeks to control activities in its chain of suppliers or distributors, or when it combines with another company to improve its competitive position. These strategies are usually interpreted as *portfolio* or *stabilization* plans. For example, corporate-level planners may seek a joint venture with another firm to bring together the marketing strength of one and the production strength of the other. Thus a firm with a recognized weakness in marketing could stabilize its competitive position through integration. Many companies also stabilize costs or ensure access to raw materials by integrating backward and acquiring their suppliers. Backward integration eliminates intermediary profits and secures sources of materials. At the portfolio level, acquisitions and mergers are pursued to enlarge the absolute size of a company or to reduce risks by having a variety of products or markets.

integration strategies
Companies integrate either backward or forward to stabilize supply and distribution lines, often reducing costs or securing raw materials or markets related to the firm's products.

Diversification Strategies

Diversification is the process of expanding into new markets, new products, or both. Many companies diversify to take advantage of opportunities, to deploy their assets more effectively, or to grow. Product diversification is a strategic alternative to the master growth strategy, but it may also be essential to replace products likely to become obsolete. The life cycle of a personal computer, for example, is very short since new models with enhanced attributes emerge about every ten months. The firm that fails to improve its product line or diversify in other areas may not last very long.

diversification
Expanding into new products, markets, or technologies to deploy a company's assets more effectively.

Nintendo, one of the most successful companies ever to market video games, relies on both product and market diversification. Nintendo has more than 150 game titles appealing to consumers with every degree of ability. Youngsters can play clever cartoon games or wrestle Hulk Hogan. More sophisticated games are available for those who want to direct an ice hockey game or challenge a championship golf course. The most popular are adult-level games with complicated sword-and-sorcery conflicts, fantasy strategies, and complex war scenarios. Nintendo has also diversified into TV cartoon shows, magazines, movies, syndicated game shows, and theme products such as T-shirts and toys.[41]

Diversification is sometimes seen as an end in itself. The value of conglomerate diversification as a strategy is suspect, however, because conglomerate profits have been consistently low. Several conglomerates have failed in recent years. RJR Nabisco, as noted earlier, was bought out and may be dismantled. Beatrice Foods, once one of the largest food conglomerates in the world, was disassembled following several years of poor profit performance. Although Beatrice Foods disappeared, many of its successful products were reformed into new companies, including International Playtex, Tropicana, Avis, Swift, Eckrich, and Beatrice Cheese.[42]

Retrenchment Strategies

Retrenchment is the process of falling back, of "regrouping" for a second chance to succeed. *Consolidation* is one retrenchment alternative, and it usually results from taking an overextended position. This temporary reversal of growth strategies can be accompanied by layoffs, plant closures, and organizational restructuring. Consolidation was the initial alternative chosen by Brunswick Corporation, discussed at

retrenchment
A strategy of "regrouping," usually through consolidation, to retreat from an overexpanded position.

the beginning of the chapter, to allow the company time to rebuild profitably. Another retrenchment alternative is *divestiture,* which means selling off divisions or subsidiary companies. By divesting poorly performing divisions, a company can improve its competitive posture and its profitability. By divesting good performers, a company can accumulate cash reserves for financing new growth strategies.

CHECKPOINT

- Describe four types of master or grand strategies.
- Why might management select each of these master strategies?

STRATEGIC ALTERNATIVES

Recall that master strategies do not exist apart from specific strategic alternatives. For example, when choosing to retrench, managers must be careful to plan how the retrenchment will take place and to what extent it will affect employees, investors, and customers. Exhibit 7-2 shows the relationship between master strategies and their alternatives. Strategic alternatives, which are described next, can occasionally apply to more than one master strategy.

Growth

concentration strategy
A strategy of trading on a distinctive competency to prevail in one product, market, or technology.

Concentration. A **concentration strategy** is one of trading on a distinctive competency to prevail in one product area, one market area, or one technology. Many companies focus on doing one thing well. Holiday Inn, Inc., builds and operates commercial hotels and motels with services designed for family and commercial travelers. McDonald's provides a family environment for fast foods with predictable quality and service. Anheuser-Busch primarily brews and sells beer.

Companies like these have developed a *distinctive competence,* one area of special ability that sets them apart from competitors, and use this distinct competency to concentrate on one growth strategy. For example, McDonald's is known for hamburgers, but its real product is good, clean, reliable customer service in low-cost fast foods. Anheuser-Busch brews beer. Even though Anheuser-Busch has entertainment parks (Busch Gardens), real estate ventures, and professional sports interests (the St. Louis Cardinals), its main business—accounting for about 90 percent of its revenues—is brewing beer.[43]

The fundamental logic behind a concentration strategy is to achieve a high degree of efficiency through a focal product or market. This strategy has dangers as well as obvious benefits. One of the dangers is that a company may become entrenched in a saturated market where growth is limited. Even worse, the company may become committed to an obsolete product.

Integration

vertical integration
A strategy to gain control of resources, supplies, or distribution systems that relate to a company's business.

Vertical integration. A **vertical integration** strategy is achieved by gaining ownership of resources, supplies, or distribution systems that relate to a company's business. In an effort to stabilize supply lines or reduce costs, a company will often integrate backward into suppliers or forward into distribution systems. By acquiring a supplier, it is able to eliminate an intermediary and gain access to materials it needs at a lower cost. A company may also want to solidify its supply lines. By inte-

EXHIBIT 7-2 Strategic Alternatives to Reinforce Master Strategies

Growth Strategies	*Concentration* is when a firm relies on a single product line, single technology, or single product-market combination. It tries to do one thing well; growth is through internal research and development.
	Market share is a growth of percentage share of a defined total market through aggressive marketing of defined products or services.
	Concentric diversification evolves products or services around the firm's primary product line or technology. It tries to provide an increasing range of activities without abandoning the firm's "distinctive competency."
	Conglomerate diversification is usually associated with mergers and acquisitions and is an effort to expand into new fields, technologies, products, or markets. The corporate portfolio is expanded, usually to seek financial benefits and profitability goals.
Integration Strategies	*Vertical integration* is an effort to control activities related to the firm's material sources or supplier channels. Forward integration is an effort to control market distribution channels for products or services. Goals include efforts to seek economic or market advantages, reduce costs, and gain access to needed technology or materials.
	Horizontal integration is an effort to consolidate competitors or reduce substitutes. Acquisitions are common as firms buy out competitors or expand facilities.
Diversification	*Product* expansion is developed through internal R&D, merger, acquisition, or joint venture to field new products in similar lines or dissimilar products that have sales or life cycles different from those of existing products.
	Market expansion is accomplished by geographic decentralization, proliferating sales locations, customer bases, or entry into international areas.
	Portfolio diversification underpins conglomerate activities of merger and acquisition to stabilize profits and earnings and reduce financial risks.
Retrenchment	*Consolidation* is a reversal of growth strategies (markets, products, or technologies) to "regroup," usually from an overextended position. Firms expect retrenchment to be temporary until they regain enough strength to pursue growth.
	Divestiture is the selling off of divisions or companies within a corporate group. It is common among conglomerates, which often seek to refine their portfolio of holdings for improved profitability.
Liquidation	*Liquidation* or termination, while not a retrenchment process, can be the ultimate result when retrenchment fails. Liquidation may be by selling the firm, filing bankruptcy, or simply closing.

grating forward, a firm acquires part of its distribution system, perhaps even its own customers. This, too, is a move to improve reliability, such as by owning the trucking system that previously delivered a company's products or by purchasing retail outlets that were previously customers.

Horizontal integration. **Horizontal integration** is an effort to consolidate competition by acquiring similar products or services. For example, a company may acquire a close competitor to expand its own product line and reduce competition. Clothing manufacturers and athletic shoe companies have consolidated their industries through buyouts of close competitors, and the banking industry has been substantially restructured by complicated acquisitions and mergers. If these strategies do not violate antitrust legislation, amalgamations are legal, and horizontal integration is common. Texaco, for example, bought Getty Oil, and Gulf Oil became part of Standard Oil of Indiana.[44]

horizontal integration
A strategy to acquire similar products or services in order to reduce competition or to improve the firm's product mix or market coverage.

Diversification

product diversification
A specific choice of growing by adding new products, either through internal development or acquisitions.

Product diversification. A **product diversification** strategy is achieved by expanding into new product lines, either through product development or acquisitions of products. Product development is probably the most common method of business diversification. Procter & Gamble has developed thousands of products, ranging from soaps to cake mixes, coffees to toilet tissues, and toothpastes to potato chips. The interesting characteristic of P&G's product diversification is that it maintains continuity in marketing for household goods sold primarily through supermarket channels.

market diversification
A method of growing by positioning existing products or services in new markets or for sale to new customers.

Market diversification. A **market diversification** strategy is accomplished by finding new markets and customer groups for existing products or services. Adding new markets is a straightforward growth strategy. The ability to sell a particular product to many different customers is the result of a marriage between engineering innovations and marketing skills. For example, Westinghouse sells light bulbs to a variety of customers. The same light bulb you purchase in a retail store is also bought by electrical contractors, federal purchasing officers, and wholesale industrial suppliers.

concentric diversification
A growth strategy achieved by developing new products or services that complement the company's existing line of business.

Concentric diversification. **Concentric diversification** is achieved by a developing products or services that complement one another to expand sales and a company's customer base. In this growth strategy, a firm remains close to its distinct competency.[45] Kodak has followed this strategy since its early years by offering not only an expanding range of cameras but also film, camera accessories, processing paper, developing chemicals, and photo-finishing services.

conglomerate diversification
A conscious effort to develop or acquire unrelated products, services, or technologies, thereby reducing the risk of being in one business subject to economic cycles or industry competition.

Conglomerate diversification. **Conglomerate diversification** is a conscious effort to develop *unrelated* products or services in unrelated markets. Conglomerates are more financially diversified than firms with product or market strategies. Organizations that have opted for a conglomerate profile usually have done so to avoid the risks associated with a single product or market. The motive for adding new companies or lines of products is financial. The most often quoted criterion for conglomerate expansion is that the new product (company or technology) will meet or exceed minimum standards for profitability.[46]

Conglomerates are created by buying entire companies or divisions. Since the early 1960s, the pattern has been for a stronger company to buy out another company that lacks the finances to operate efficiently. The acquired company usually has a distinct competency in products, markets, or technologies that is expected to become a high-powered asset once underwritten by the acquiring firm.

Retrenchment

internal consolidation
A form of retrenchment in which a company retreats to a more realistic operational position, reducing its costs and risks.

Internal consolidation. **Internal consolidation** is a form of retrenchment in which a firm retreats to a more realistic position where it can compete profitably. Retrenchment, as we said earlier, means to fall back and regroup; it does not mean to capitulate. Consolidation can be accomplished by shutting down plants, trimming personnel, and reducing the range of marketing activities to achieve cost savings. Corporate *downsizing,* as noted earlier, is a process of internal consolidation to improve productivity and reduce costs. It can be accomplished by implementing new technologies that replace labor-intensive operations. Chrysler is a prominent example of downsizing. At the the end of 1979, it employed more than 162,000 people, was overextended with nearly $1 billion of excess debt, and could no longer compete profitably in the automotive industry. Then, with huge loans and government

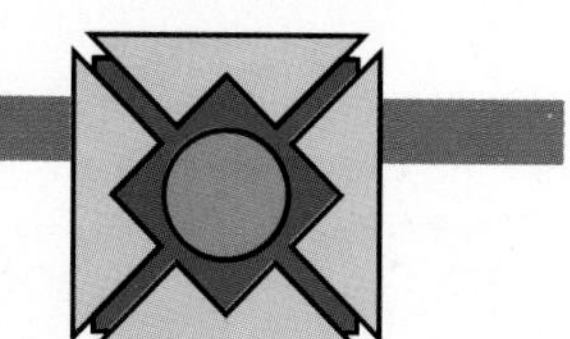

ETHICS IN MANAGEMENT

Acting in the Public Interest

Public utility companies across the country are actively helping customers to reduce their utility bills. Kansas City Power & Light, Southern California Gas Company, Alabama Gas Corporation, and Illinois Power Company are among the recognized leaders in social programs aimed at educating consumers to use energy more efficiently. In some instances, the utility companies actually provide money to needy customers for weatherization. Illinois Power, for example, has an assistance foundation for weatherization of homes. Alabama Gas Corporation trains disadvantaged teenagers to weatherstrip and insulate homes, then assists low-income customers who need these services.

Though it may seem perverse for companies to help customers spend less on their product, the companies will benefit in the long run from a strategy of energy conservation. Building a new utility plant is a huge project requiring massive capital funding. If this can be postponed through more efficient use of existing facilities, then everyone gains. Consequently, these public utilities are acting in the larger public interest, sacrificing some immediate income to preserve their strategic assets.

Source: "Utilities Recognized for Philanthropic Programs," *Public Utilities Fortnightly*, September 27, 1990, p. 9.

support, Chrysler shut down unproductive plants, built new ones with automated technology, reduced the number of its employees to 99,000, and began competing profitably with fewer but better-built car models. Within four years, the company had cleared its loans and regained peak production, although with a third fewer employees and nearly 40 percent fewer managers.[47]

divestiture The process of selling off divisions or subsidiaries that are either poor performers or do not fit well with the company's long-term strategic objectives.

Divestiture. **Divestiture** is the process of selling off divisions or subsidiaries to restructure a company around a smaller but stronger portfolio of businesses. Either a company will dispose of unprofitable business units to regain profit performance for the total enterprise or it will sell off a good division to bail itself out of financial trouble. Selling poor performers is the more likely option. Divestiture is often an attempt to cut losses and allow managers to focus their strength on potential winners. Another reason for divestiture is that a business unit doesn't fit into the company's overall portfolio. This was precisely the situation when Sperry Rand Corporation sold its Remington Electric Shaver division to Victor Kiam. Sperry Rand's portfolio of businesses was focused on computer hardware, industrial electronics, and office system equipment. Remington was an orphan division.[48]

liquidation The "final" option, liquidation is the decision to terminate a business in a systematic way through bankruptcy or a complete sale of the company.

Liquidation. **Liquidation** is the final option and means simply "to terminate." For a concentrated firm, divestiture and liquidation mean practically the same thing, but for a diversified company, liquidation may mean years of systematic restructuring. For example, before LTV filed for bankruptcy in 1988, the company had survived nearly two decades by periodically selling off divisions. One division, Braniff Airlines, was a healthy and profitable company when LTV sold it, and the sale generated sufficient cash to carry LTV through the mid-1980s.[49] Today liquidation is more likely to occur through a leveraged buyout or a friendly takeover when a struggling company is offered for sale.

CHECKPOINT

- What is a concentration strategy and what is meant by a firm's distinct competency?
- Describe two ways to grow through diversification.
- How do vertical and horizontal integration strategies differ?
- Define *retrenchment* and explain two retrenchment alternatives and how they help a company reposition itself.

MAKING THE STRATEGIC DECISION

Strategic management is primarily concerned with decisions that ensure the organization will be *effective,* which means "doing the right things." Of secondary importance is *efficiency,* which means "doing things right."[50] Therefore, strategic decisions are concerned with choosing a master strategy and a planned strategic alternative to achieve the organization's major objectives. *Administering* the strategy is important, but secondary to making the right choice of strategy.

Arriving at the right choice of strategy requires the strategist to evaluate each option to ensure it is *realistic* in relation to environmental constraints, *feasible* in relation to organizational resources, and *sufficient* in relation to accomplishing the mission of the firm. Managers review all the external environmental considerations (see Figure 7-7) to identify weaknesses in, or threats to, individual alternatives. They also carefully review internal considerations (see Figure 7-8) to identify critical shortcomings of potential strategies.

The reevaluation process answers many of the same questions posed earlier in the chapter, questions such as "What service or product do we offer to maintain a viable customer base?" and "What is our technological competence?" The chosen strategy will also be acceptable to most managers and employees. It will satisfy the constraints of economics, regulations, finances, human resource skills, and material resource availability. And it will not be detrimental to society.

Earlier in the chapter, we introduced a general strategic planning process (Figure 7-4). The model indicated a key decision point of choosing a strategy. In reality,

FIGURE 7-7 External Factors That Influence Strategic Decisions

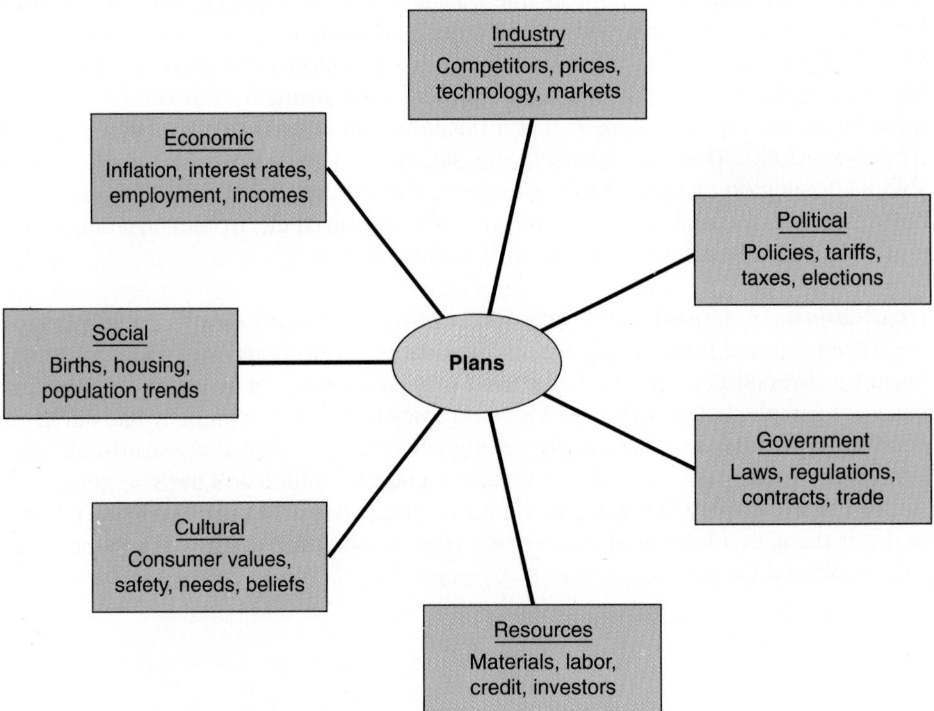

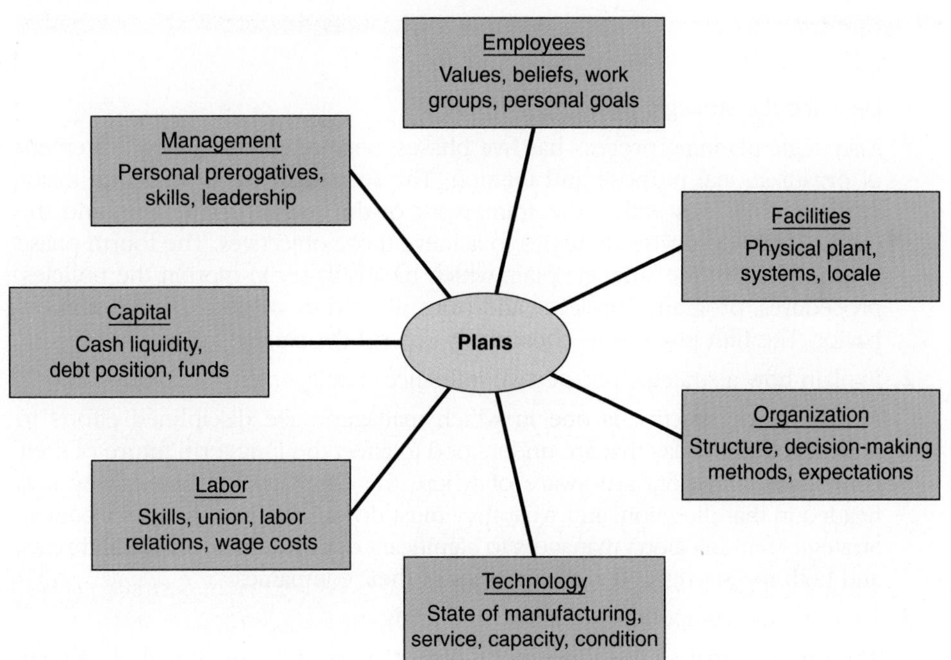

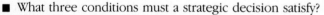

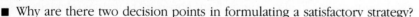

FIGURE 7-8 Internal Factors That Influence Strategic Decisions

there are two decisions. The first occurs when management selects a master strategy. The second occurs after the master strategy is reviewed to identify the specific strategic alternative to implement. Once both decisions are made, implementation can proceed, and the final stage in the process, control and evaluation, can take place.

CHECKPOINT

- What three conditions must a strategic decision satisfy?
- Why are there two decision points in formulating a satisfactory strategy?

STRATEGIC DECISIONS are well illustrated by the Brunswick Corporation example introduced at the beginning of the chapter. Initially, Brunswick decided to *retrench,* to regroup around potentially strong divisions with a *downsized* organization. To implement its retrenchment strategy, Brunswick divested itself of a profitable division, Middle Eastern Health Care Services. Brunswick made enough money on the sale to underwrite organizational change and a comprehensive new human resource program. Selling the health-care division was logical because, although it was profitable, it did not fit into the Brunswick portfolio of manufacturing sporting goods and industrial equipment. By cutting out unnecessary levels of management and implementing a human resource program, the company positioned itself for growth. Ultimately, its strategy was to grow through *concentric diversification.* Brunswick made a commitment to manufacture quality products that complemented its existing product line, staying close to its distinct competency in well-defined markets.[51]

A SYNOPSIS FOR LEARNING

1. Describe the strategic planning process.

   A strategic planning process has five phases, beginning with a clear statement of organizational purpose and mission. The second phase is to define major strategic objectives within the framework of the mission statement, and the third phase is to devise strategies to achieve those objectives. The fourth phase is to implement the strategic plan, which means to set in motion the policies, procedures, programs, projects, and rules needed to guide organizational behavior. The fifth phase is to consciously control the strategic plan.

2. Explain how a strategic perspective influences management decisions.

   A strategic perspective is one in which managers take disciplined efforts to make decisions today that are understood to affect the long-term future of their companies. Managers are aware of where the company is headed, why it is headed in that direction, and what they must do to keep it on a proper course. Strategic thinking alerts managers to significant opportunities, potential threats, and both the strengths and weaknesses of their companies.

3. Describe the components of a situation analysis.

   The situation analysis has three major components: an industry analysis, a competitive analysis, and a company analysis. Each of these prompts managers to investigate questions that help them formulate mission statements, objectives, and strategies to achieve objectives.

4. Examine the SWOT analysis for making business-level decisions.

   SWOT stands for *strengths, weaknesses, opportunities,* and *threats,* and can be used as a systematic analysis at every planning level. Employed at the business level, it is a method of looking into internal and external characteristics of competition. A company's strengths are internal factors that give it an advantage over other companies. Weaknesses are internal factors that put a firm at a competitive disadvantage. On the external side of SWOT analysis, opportunities arise from understanding changes in markets, products, or technologies and new opportunities can also emerge from government actions, changes in society, and global changes. Threats can come from external forces beyond the control of management.

5. Identify and explain four classifications for master strategies.

   Master strategies are devised by corporate-level planners to achieve long-term objectives and to provide an umbrella of guidelines for business- and functional-level strategies. Master strategies are expressed in broad terms and include growth, integration, diversification, and retrenchment. Strategic alternatives are the carefully articulated ways in which master strategies can be implemented.

SKILL ANALYSIS

CASE 1 Exxon's $2 Billion Strategic Fiasco

Few people remember Exxon's "Office of the Future" or its much-publicized division Exxon Office Systems (EOS). They both disappeared in 1984, but not before they lost $2 billion and ended the jobs of 8,000 people. EOS, heralded several years earlier as a contender capable of challenging IBM in business computers, became a record-setting strategic fiasco for Exxon.[52]

The initial strategy of EOS was to find the most innovative products in office equipment technology, acquire the best entrepreneurial firms in computer technology, and launch a frontal attack on the business systems industry. EOS was formed by a nucleus of QWIP, QYX, and Vydec acquisitions, and the mother company committed more money to the project than most competitors were grossing in sales each year. Unfortunately, Exxon's management had no clear plan and little understanding of the computer industry.

After acquiring the three entrepreneurial firms, EOS hired their three founders as consultants. These were young men on the rise who drove fast sports cars and preferred sports shirts and jeans to suits and ties. Nearly all their employees shared a similar social viewpoint, and they lasted only months in the suit-and-tie bureaucracy of EOS, whose top managers had been appointed from the ranks of near-retirement Exxon oil executives. EOS quickly became a mirror image of Exxon, steeped in process control with layers of management tucked away in field offices. Typical of large, established enterprises, EOS was expected to succeed through marketing, and management threw hundreds of millions of dollars into advertising. In fact, a technology-driven industry grows through innovation and product development, and Exxon unfortunately pursued neither. Exxon's first mistake, therefore, was to create an entrepreneurial firm run by risk-adverse corporate managers with objectives quite different from those embraced by high-risk innovators in competing firms.

EOS top management also turned over quickly. Exxon shareholders were led to expect profits and sales to leap past those of IBM, Xerox, and Burroughs, and when EOS lost money, heads had to roll. The last EOS division manager survived only a few months, the time he was allotted to "fix" the company just before the division was dismantled in 1984. His previous post had been manager of Esso Greece, about as far removed from office technology as one could get in the organization.

Exxon's view, when it still expected EOS to become the premier office systems company in the world, was that anything could be fixed with enough money. So more money was spent on more corporate managers, more salespeople, and more advertising. When stockholders asked about future plans, Exxon explained that it had no grand scheme or master plan for cementing the ventures, but was making all these investments to keep its options open. From the beginning, there was no well-thought-out strategic plan, and objectives for EOS changed according to the whims of revolving-door top managers. In the end, EOS was shut down quietly; a footnote in Exxon's annual report explained simply that some assets had been divested.

Some analysts blamed the demise of EOS on a cultural clash between entrepreneurs and professional managers with opposing objectives and expectations. Others said "oil men" couldn't run a "people business," one based on technology they knew nothing about. Still others believed that EOS implemented a de facto "global diversification" strategy before it had a distinct competency in a proven product line with which to diversify. And there were those analysts who believed that Exxon's managers foolishly superimposed oil industry planning premises on their competitive analyses for the computer industry. Ultimately, the question is: Did Exxon really expect to create a multi-billion-dollar company in a few years by throwing money into a venture only to keep options open?

Case Questions

1. Put yourself in the position of a strategic analyst. What do you think caused the demise of EOS?
2. What planning premises would you have proposed for EOS during the embryonic stage of the office systems industry?
3. Evaluate strategic alternatives for EOS at its inception. What might have been a winning approach to the office systems business?
4. From Exxon's corporate perspective, was office systems a logical business for diversification? Suggest alternative businesses that might have fit better with the firm's distinct competency.

VIDEO CASE The Vermont Teddy Bear Company: Strategically Marketing Teddy Bears

Nearly everyone has had the pleasure of owning a cute, cuddly bundle of synthetic fur known as a teddy bear. The appeal of teddy bears to many ages and classes of people makes the market for teddy bears very lucrative indeed. One small company, the Vermont Teddy Bear Company, has discovered how important it is to position its product strategically and to reach the customer with this information.

The Vermont Teddy Bear Company began as a modest business whose owner sold handmade teddy bears from a pushcart. From these humble beginnings, the company has grown to a multimillion-dollar business that ships an average of 400 bears a day. Prosperity did not come easily, though. For the first two years, business was downright "bearish," John Sortino, the president of the company says. "We weren't doing very well at all financially until 1990, when we had a meeting . . ." What was decided at that meeting eventually changed its fortunes.

At that 1990 meeting the Vermont Teddy Bear Company decided to advertise on the radio and to use a toll-free 800 number for taking orders. The initial ad that aired on a single New York station declared, "The friendly, accommodating folks at the Vermont Teddy Bear Company are waiting for your call right now. Toll-free . . ." Today the company advertises on thirty stations in five cities across the country, using a toll-free number that permits it to maintain direct contact with its customers. In fact, because the radio ads are done live, the company can also control demand.

Another important part of the company's successful marketing strategy is its advertising pitch offering 100 percent American-made teddy bears guaranteed for the life of the owner, for an average selling price of $55. The bears are "so Vermont," in fact, that their joints are made from recycled Ben & Jerry Ice Cream containers (another well-known and prosperous Vermont company).

Have the Vermont Teddy Bear Company's strategic planning and marketing paid off? Here's what the president said: "One year, eight months ago, we had three incoming lines, and today we have twenty incoming phone lines. Our phone bill used to come in an envelope and now it comes in a UPS box." Not only does the phone bill come in a UPS box, but so do customer orders.

Case Questions

1. Does the Vermont Teddy Bear Company have a distinctive competence? What do you think it is?
2. What functional strategies do you see the company using?
3. What other elements of strategic planning and management would you recommend that the company's managers employ? Why?

Sources: Don Anderson, "When Is a Small Business Ready to Invest in a Toll-Free 800 Number?" *American Salesman,* July 1991, Vol. 36, No. 7, p. 6ff; Brian Y. Rivette, "The Key to 800/900 Numbers," *Direct Marketing,* April 1991, Vol. 53, No. 12, p. 28ff; "The Ultimate Bear Market," *The Economist,* September 29, 1990, Vol. 316, No. 7674, p. 66; and Michael J. Major, "800 Number: Once a Specialty, It's Now Almost a Necessity," *Marketing News,* May 28, 1990, Vol. 24, No. 11, p. 6.

SKILL PRACTICE

SITUATIONAL ANALYSIS FOR A HEALTH-CARE FACILITY

Instructions for the Analysis

1. Participants will be divided into small groups of four to six members, depending on the class size. In each group, the instructor will designate one focal activity of a strategic situational analysis (e.g., industry analysis). Each group will have a spokesperson. (Time allotted: 5 minutes.)

2. The group will utilize the case scenario and chapter material to prepare a brief outline of the most important points of the analysis. Participants are encouraged to list points beyond the case from general knowledge of the health-care industry or environment. (Time allotted: 15 minutes.)
3. Reassemble as a class. Group spokespersons report their findings. These can be listed on flip charts or blackboards, or simply discussed at the discretion of the instructor. (Time allotted: variable.)
4. Discussion. Participants should state the major problem (or opportunity) from the case, critique the case strategy, and offer alternative strategies based on the situational analyses. (Time allotted: 15 minutes.)

Scenario for Analysis

Lincoln Memorial Hospital is a community hospital with about 250 beds serving a midwestern city with a population of nearly 60,000. The hospital became part of a chain of corporate-owned health organizations after a decision in 1991 that allowed LMH to be acquired. The board of directors was somewhat bitter over the decision to "sell out," feeling they had been forced into the situation by federal Medicare guidelines that set a pattern for payment programs.

Medicare legislation during the 1980s was aimed at reducing hospital costs by generating new government-defined rate systems and controls. These changes resulted in many hospitals being forced to deny operating privileges to doctors whose surgery rates exceeded those guidelines. This was no reflection on the physicians involved, but the Medicare mandate had created an absolute flat-rate system that forced hospital administrators to reduce high-cost services.

Some hospitals continued to charge the high rates and put the financial burden on the patient to pay the excess over flat-rate guidelines. Others cut services to reallocate hospital resources to high-cost, high-rate services. Many hospitals, weakened by rising costs and stiffer controls, faced insolvency, and chose to be acquired by one of the national hospital chains. These chains reduced costs through group purchasing, economies of scale, and operational efficiencies.

Before LMH was acquired by a major chain, it faced an uncertain future and huge financial losses from several problems. First, 35 percent of the hospital's revenue came from major surgical and intensive care services. For a community hospital, these represented very high costs, and with a growing population eligible for Medicare, demand for these services would increase. Second, more serious illnesses require extensive diagnostics, and LMH's radiology and laboratory facilities would have to be expanded. Third, the cost of liability insurance for doctors, nurses, and the hospital had increased rapidly.

The hospital board of trustees was concerned that if they maintained LMH as an independent facility, costs would outrace income, with the result that patient services would have to be curtailed or eliminated and some patients might have to be turned away. They also cited rising capital costs and difficulty in acquiring loans for expansion in a weak economy.

Hospital management wanted to consolidate services, reduce staff, and subcontract ancillary services such as radiology and laboratory diagnostics. The hospital director also felt LMH and similar hospitals in nearby communities could generate "shared services" for expensive capital needs. For example, no local hospital could afford a $1 million CAT scan facility, but four hospitals sharing the cost for a mobile CAT scan made such a purchase feasible. Consolidation, however, meant fewer jobs.

When the board announced its decision to sell out, members justified their decision on economic grounds. They cited high capital costs and the inability to restructure hospital loans to meet cash flow requirements. In addition, they pointed out that the American health-care industry was changing toward profit-based chain operations because an acquiring corporation could write down assets, thus gaining tax advantages, and then use the corporation's financial power to leverage favorable loans or float significant development bonds.

8

Tactical and Operational Planning

OUTLINE

The Nature of Tactical Planning
- Tactical Planning Periods
- Tactical Planning Considerations

Marketing: Tactical Planning Requirements
- Developing the Marketing Plan
- Developing the Marketing Program

Production Planning
- Strategic Production Plans
- Tactical Production Planning
- Factors in Production Planning

Human Resources and Tactical Planning
- Tactical Considerations for Human Resource Planning
- Responsibilities for Human Resource Planning

Financial Management and Tactical Planning
- Profitability

Bridging Gaps Across Functional Lines

Operational Planning
- Importance of Operational Planning
- Operational Planning Activities
- Operational Planning Linked to the Planning Hierarchy

OBJECTIVES

- Describe the nature of tactical planning and related managerial roles.
- Define the key elements of a marketing plan and a marketing program.
- Explain production planning and how it relates to marketing projections.
- Describe human resource planning from a tactical perspective.
- Discuss the responsibilities of financial managers in tactical planning.
- Describe operational planning responsibilities and the critical task of scheduling.

THE QUESTION of how to succeed in business is most often answered by saying "guarantee customer satisfaction," but savvy managers add to that phrase "in a cost-effective manner." At Tenneco, one of the nation's largest diversified companies, the concept of customer satisfaction is stressed in its commitment to provide quality products and services, and the concept of cost effectiveness is emphasized throughout its planning processes.[1] Tenneco has billion-dollar divisions in natural gas transmission, shipbuilding, farm and construction equipment, packaging, minerals, and automotive accessories. Its $1.7-billion-a-year auto parts division produces shock absorbers, brakes, mufflers, tailpipes, and many more components through its Monroe, Walker, and Tenneco Brake lines, and these are sold to major automotive companies, parts wholesalers, and retailers.

Tenneco relies on quick-response planning to changes in sales forecasts for tactical adaptations at each plant. The company integrated its production, marketing, personnel, and financial planning functions into coordinated business systems that could adapt to changes efficiently. Monroe shock absorbers and accessories and Walker mufflers and tailpipes can be manufactured in small batches of 100 to 300 parts (rather than thousands), and production orders can be set up to run in a matter of hours (versus days). Weekly sales forecasts—rather than quarterly projections—drive the planning system, and timely decisions on materials, purchases, scheduling, and cash management keep costs to a minimum.

As a result, Tenneco's auto parts division has reduced unit costs while improving overall quality. Consequently, profits remained strong throughout 1991 and into 1992 when the auto industry suffered losses. As you read this chapter, consider how *functional-level planning,* like that at Tenneco, reinforces corporate and business strategies. Also consider how first-line managers, such as production foremen, devise *operational plans* to support higher-level plans.

This chapter focuses on tactical and operational planning that encompasses decisions in marketing, production, finance, and human resources. We follow the three-tiered model of planning—strategic, tactical, and operational—illustrated in Chapter 6. Figure 8-1 shows a foundation of that model. It excludes the three strategic levels explored in Chapter 7 because, in reality, only very large companies have multi-tiered strategies. Most companies have an organization similar to that shown in Figure 8-1, where *tactical planning* is the responsibility of middle management and *operational planning* relates to activities and tasks at the lowest managment level.

THE NATURE OF TACTICAL PLANNING

tactical planning
The transformation of strategies into medium-term objectives and activities usually implemented by middle managers in functional roles.

In **tactical planning,** middle management transforms strategies into more specific medium-term objectives. For example, G. D. Searle, a large pharmaceutical company, developed NutraSweet and obtained FDA approval to market the chemical sweetener in 1981. Searle's corporate-level strategy was to create new industrial and medical products that complement a product line of more than 600 medicines and pharmaceutical ingredients used by food and drug manufacturers. When marketing became feasible in 1981, the first year's objective was to position NutraSweet as the only sugar-free sweetener in the diet soft drink industry. Searle failed to achieve that objective because the public—and major soft drink companies—were not ready to accept a chemical sweetener. Searle's managers had also relied on industrial sales tactics to introduce the product, such as making technical sales presentations to purchasing managers at soft drink companies. Over the next several years, Searle switched tactics and developed its own advertising program to generate consumer acceptance. Nationwide TV ads were aimed at convincing the public that a sugarfree

FIGURE 8-1 Hierarchy of Plans

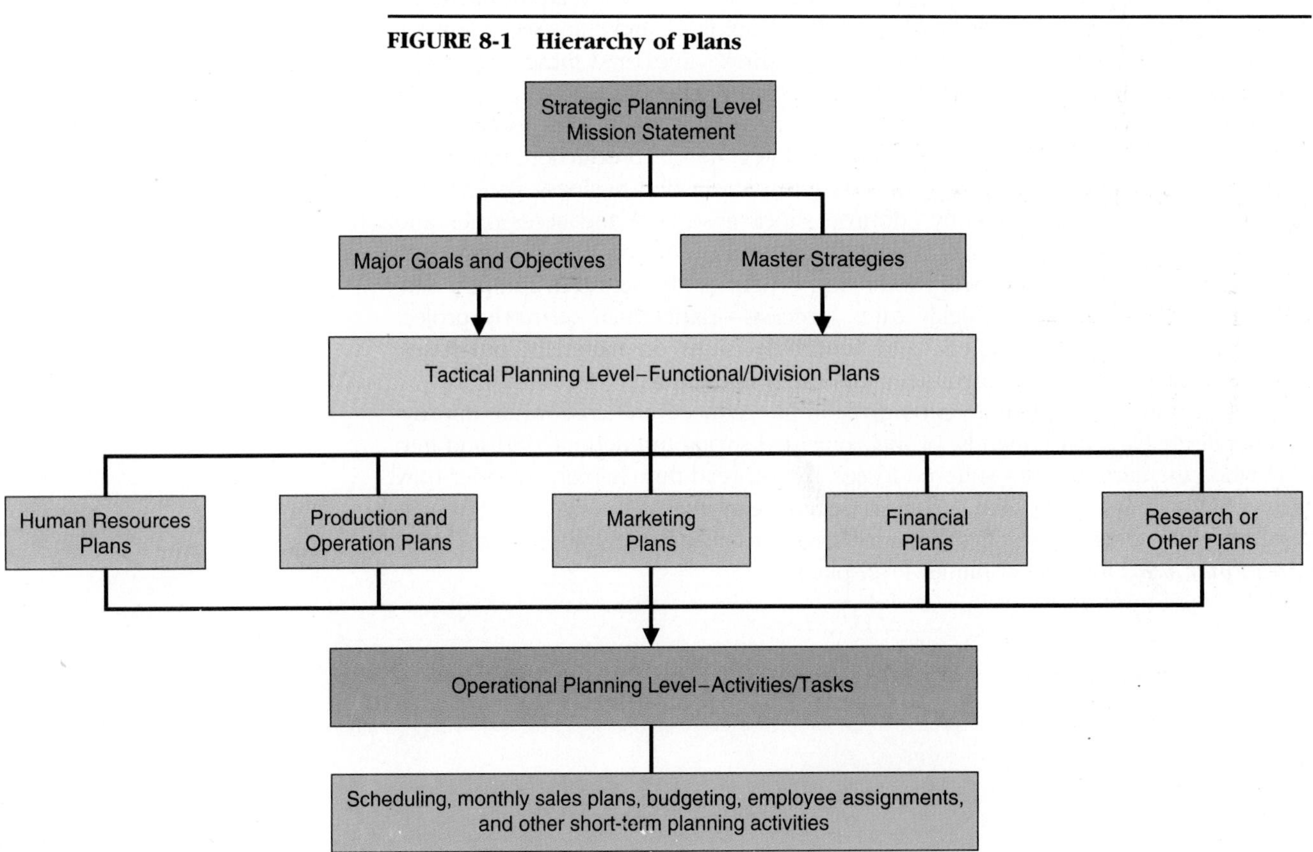

sweetener was both good-tasting and safe. PepsiCo and Coca-Cola began using NutraSweet exclusively, and sales exploded to $600 million annually.[2]

Tactical Planning Periods

We noted in Chapter 7 that strategic plans are expressed in time periods of several years; a five-year planning horizon is popular. Tactical plans are much shorter, often expressed in annual increments of one calendar or one fiscal year. In the Nutra-Sweet example, initial marketing objectives were specified for 1982, respecified for 1983, and substantially revised annually through 1989.[3]

Tactical plans do not have to be tied to a one-year time frame, but because they are associated with *annual budgets,* this is convenient. As we noted in Chapter 6, budgets provide quantified expectations and a clear allocation of resources. Because tactical objectives need to be specific, annual budgets at division and department levels are common. Actually, tactical plans are often longer than one year, even when they are budgeted in one-year increments. For example, Pillsbury outlined an eighteen-month market test phase before introducing Soft Breadsticks to the market.

The plan had two intermediate tactical stages; a twelve-month trial period in a test market, and a six-month marketing research period to determine whether the product would sell nationwide. Independent budgets were established for each test phase, and seven different departments had specific tasks to complete in each budget period. Product development managers, for example, had to test several different combinations of ingredients, and consumer behavior analysts had to gather data on consumer perceptions of the new product. Other managers were concerned with advertising, packaging, competition, pricing, and manufacturing requirements.[4]

Shorter time periods are also possible in tactical planning. Fisher-Price toys are test-marketed in six-week increments to coincide with high-volume sales seasons. The company also coordinates manufacturing and sales campaigns for six-month intervals on the assumption that most toys go through a short product life cycle. Reebok International altered the structure of the sporting shoes industry by establishing tactical planning periods based on seasonal needs. Before 1986, Reebok was a little-known manufacturer in an industry dominated by Nike, but Reebok intro-

Reebok has successfully used tactical planning techniques to challenge Nike's dominance of the sporting shoe and apparel markets. Most effective has been Reebok's adjustment of its product offerings to meet consumers' seasonal needs.

duced four different shoes that year, several more in 1987, and a line of ten models in 1988. Subsequently, Reebok implemented a tactical plan for seasonal specialization and the company has become a strong competitor to Nike, with comparable market value.[5]

Tactical Planning Considerations

Manufacturing firms have four major tactical planning functions: *marketing, production, human resources,* and *finance.* In addition, they may have specialized departments in supporting roles that develop tactical plans. For example, a manufacturer may have product engineering, distribution, credit, consumer service, and purchasing departments. In some instances, companies are large enough to also have separate departments for information systems, market research, plant and facilities, and others in supporting roles. Service organizations, such as banks, hospitals, and insurance companies, have similar planning functions, except that production is replaced by *service operations* and support activities such as engineering and distribution are unnecessary.

CHECKPOINT

- Describe how management responsibilities differ in strategic, tactical, and operational plans.
- Identify and discuss several tactical planning considerations for managers in the functional roles of marketing, production, human resources, and finance.

MARKETING: TACTICAL PLANNING REQUIREMENTS

Strategic marketing objectives provide a foundation for tactical marketing activities. Recall from our discussion in Chapter 7 that a master strategy is first defined (e.g., *growth*) and then clarified through a strategic alternative (e.g., *concentric diversification*). Once a strategy is formulated, responsibilities for making each component of the plan work are delegated to tactical managers. Thus a concentric diversification strategy to develop new products requires a marketing plan for reaching consumers with these new products. Marketing plans that have a strategic foundation are based on answers to the following questions:

1. Why will customers buy our products or services? Price? Quality? Brand image? Convenience?
2. What is our product or service profile within the industry? Price comparability? Performance profile? Quality image?
3. What are our options for distribution? Wholesale? Retail? Field sales representatives? Licensed distributors? Mail order?
4. How will we promote products or services? Aggressive mass media advertising? Demonstrations? Point-of-sale displays?
5. Who is our primary customer? Do we have a unique market niche?
6. Who are our potential customers? How do we define them?
7. What is the expected life cycle of our product or service? Will it have a long life or will it soon be obsolete? What will replace it?

8. Who are our competitors and what are they doing? Are we threatened by strong competitors?

Answers to these questions are derived from a *situation analysis,* precisely the same analysis developed for strategic planning and discussed in the previous chapter. Marketing managers are either directly involved in the strategic process or have ready access to the results of the strategic situation analysis. Recall that these results pertain to *industry, competitive,* and *company analysis,* and marketing managers adapt that information to develop their marketing plans.

A **marketing plan** defines customers, sales forecasts, and market positioning to support strategic objectives. The first element of the plan, defining customers, requires managers to segment their markets according to *customer scenarios.* The second element is to formulate *sales forecasts* based on these customer scenarios and information gained through a situation analysis. The third element focuses on *positioning* products or services in specific markets where sales forecasts indicate there are opportunities. The marketing plan usually is one of the *functional-level strategic plans* explained in Chapter 7. When a company does not have three strategic levels (see Figure 8-1), the marketing plan is treated as a tactical plan, but one that can cover several years. This is merely a matter of semantics; to avoid confusion, simply remember that a marketing plan will be formulated and exist at the highest level of marketing. It provides a broad scope of what marketing is expected to accomplish.

marketing plan
Managers develop marketing plans to support strategic objectives using customer scenarios to position products or services in markets according to well-documented sales forecasts.

To implement the marketing plan, a **marketing program** is created. This addresses *product characteristics, pricing decisions, promotional activities,* and *distribution channels.*[6] Figure 8-2 illustrates the relationship between a marketing plan and a marketing program.

marketing program
A marketing program addresses specific product characteristics, pricing decisions, promotional activities, and distribution channels.

Developing the Marketing Plan

Once a corporate or division strategy is established, marketing managers work closely with staff planning experts to develop each element of the marketing plan. Much of this work is highly specialized, requiring market research analysts, consumer behavioral scientists, economists, and product designers to help develop the plan. Line managers from sales, production, finance, and human resources departments have crucial roles in this stage of planning because they have firsthand knowledge of consumers, product characteristics, company finances, and employee skills. The next several sections of the chapter describe how the elements of a marketing plan are developed.

FIGURE 8-2 Relationship Between Strategic Marketing Plan, the Sales Forecast, and the Marketing Program

customer scenario
A customer scenario describes a group of prospective buyers with common needs who are expected to respond similarly to a marketing program.

Customer scenarios. A **customer scenario** describes a group of prospective buyers who have common needs and who will respond similarly to a marketing program. Customer scenarios are derived through market research that subdivides large markets with diverse needs into *market segments* so that a cohesive plan can be formulated on product characteristics, pricing, promotions, and channels of distribution. For example, Campbell Soup developed a canned nacho cheese sauce with three distinct flavors to match consumer tastes of Americans in the West, Southwest, and East. The nacho cheese sauce made for eastern consumers is bland, the sauce made for western consumers has a zesty taste, and the sauce made for southwestern consumers is laced with chili peppers.[7]

Customer scenarios combine information from dozens of sources to try to describe a reasonable market segment. Personal characteristics, such as male or female, married or single, and couples with or without children, provide information on shopping habits. Demographic and economic information on age, education, income, profession, home ownership, race, lifestyle, and recreation habits can help explain demand for new products. Other information includes how certain consumers buy products, where they shop, and how they perceive certain types of products and services.

Armed with information about potential customers, marketing managers evaluate industry trends and competition to forecast sales. These are estimates of potential sales that are contingent upon the company's ability to provide products or services in the quality and quantity needed. Thus a full evaluation of information derived from a situation analysis is crucial for creating a marketing plan.

sales forecast
A sales forecast is an estimate of expected sales for a specific time period related to target markets.

Sales forecasts. A **sales forecast** is an estimate of expected sales for a specific time period related to target markets. Thus a sales forecast will provide a numerical base for projecting income derived from sales of products and services to distinct consumer groups. For example, Wilson Sporting Goods managers develop long-term forecasts for golf clubs, tennis rackets, and basketballs based on scenarios of potential buyers for each product line. These long-term forecasts are broken down into annual and seasonal projections, which are important for marketing managers. Wilson golf clubs, for example, sell well during the spring and early summer, and marketing managers need to understand these fluctuations during the year as well as annual sales patterns. By watching seasonal sales and compiling information on trends in their industry, marketing managers will be able to forecast sales in successive seasons and years more accurately.

Sales forecasts are expressed in measurable units (number of sales, tons of product, hours of service, number of clients, and dollars). When a manager has only one product to concentrate on, forecasting is simply a matter of comparing the product's performance with that of direct competitors. Budweiser beer's marketing managers compare their beer to Miller's, Stroh's, Coors, and a few others to estimate changes in sales. Managers in retailing, however, have to estimate sales based on perhaps several thousand items, then compile the volumes for all stores in a chain for regional and corporate sales forecasts.

A sales forecast provides a focal point for tactical planning throughout the firm. In manufacturing firms, production planners use sales forecasts to derive objectives for production, engineering, purchasing, and inventory. Human resource planners employ them to develop labor profiles, skills projections, training objectives, and employee support programs. Finance managers rely on them to plan capital expansion, operational budgets, and cash management programs.

In service organizations, sales forecasts are just as critical, but they are often referred to as "merchandising plans" or "annual billing projections." Hospitals provide services that must be forecast accurately. For example, a hospital near Tampa, Florida, an area faced with a growing population of retirement-aged people, will have to plan on expanded critical care services, extended care facilities, cancer units, and

Until recently, nonalcoholic beers have not figured very prominently in the sales forecasts of the major beer producers. However, although nonalcoholic beer accounts for only 1 percent of the beer market, sales have tripled in the past three years and business analysts now believe that this share could grow to 10 percent by the late 1990s. Anheuser-Busch, Miller, and Coors have all entered the market, but none has a commanding share yet.

cardiac units. A hospital in metropolitan Baltimore, serving a younger population, will have to plan for emergency care, maternity care, and family services.

The differences in marketing between hospitals and manufacturers are obvious, but the fundamental process of developing a sales forecast is the same. Hospitals must understand what services are needed and how many people will need them. Manufacturers must understand what products are in demand and how many people will buy them.

Positioning. **Positioning** is the act of targeting specific products or services to specific markets. Although the need for this seems obvious, many companies squander opportunities by haphazardly trying to sell everything to everyone. Simply unleashing a product on the general public is not a marketing strategy. Making a conscious effort to position products or services to create market niches is.

positioning
Positioning is the act of targeting specific products or services to specific markets.

Firms in the microcomputer sector have been jostling one another for several years to establish strong market niches. Major market segments are home users, hobbyists, small businesses, schools, technical-scientific users, and larger firms employing networked office systems. Leading companies vying for shares of these markets include Apple, IBM, Compaq, AT&T, Digital Equipment, Zenith, Hewlett-Packard, Toshiba, NEC, and AST Research. Recent entrants with MS-DOS systems (i.e., so-called IBM-compatible) have combined to dominate the market. These "clones" actually had 50.6 percent of the U.S. market by 1991.[8]

Few microcomputer firms try to compete in all market segments. Most try instead to position specific products in specific markets. Although it has the size and strength to enter more markets than other companies, even IBM has positioned its Personal Computer (PC) in a focal niche for business and professional applications. IBM has avoided a "game" image and therefore, the home hobbyist market. Apple Computer is in some of the same markets as IBM, but is a leading innovator with a strong home-hobbyist niche. Apple has also established a strong position in education through innovative software.[9] IBM developed microcomputers a few years after Apple, and introduced the PC first to its business clientele, branched into professional environments, and then developed markets in higher education. Thus each firm serves a distinct clientele in well-differentiated markets.

Other companies, like Tandy Corporation with its TRS series, entered the hobbyist market. Digital, Hewlett-Packard, and Xerox zeroed in on technical and scientific markets in a premium price sector. These firms have positioned their products well, but some companies have not. During the early 1980s, for example, Texas Instruments decided to mass-market a low-end microcomputer at discount prices. It jumped into the home and game markets with fast-paced advertising aimed at young people and novice users. Although TI sold a lot of computers, it also created a mindset among consumers that its products were cheap toys. Despite an advertising blitz, TI lost millions and withdrew from the PC market.[10]

Positioning, then, is crucial for several reasons. Without a position, defining a company's market share and potential sales is at best erratic. Without good positioning, consumers become confused about the product and the firm's image may become one of promiscuous bobbing in and out of markets to make money rather than to provide quality products and good service.

Product life cycle. A **product life cycle** describes the stages a product goes through in the marketplace: introduction, growth, maturity, and decline.[11] Although the life cycle concept is not a specific part of the market plan, it is an important planning consideration. A life cycle is the span of viable demand for a product or service from inception to demise, as Figure 8-3 shows. At each stage in its life cycle, a product or service will require a unique blend of marketing activities to remain competitive. These activities are defined in the *marketing program* described later, but first we will examine the four life cycle stages. They are:

product life cycle
A product life cycle describes the stages a product goes through in the marketplace from introduction to decline.

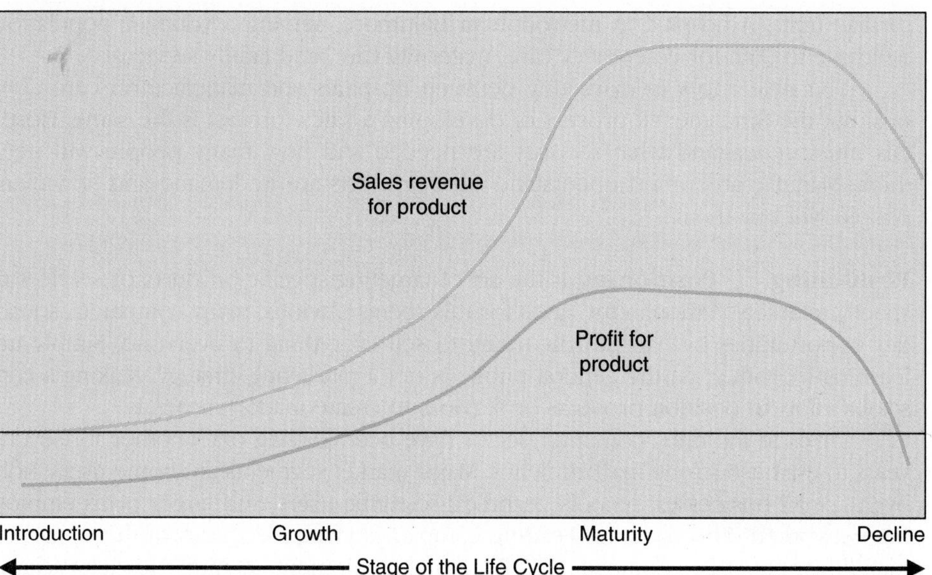

FIGURE 8-3 The Product Life Cycle

Introduction stage. This is the initial introduction of the product to its markets. Sales tend to be slow during this stage, and a company may have to take huge losses to gain consumer acceptance. The tactical challenge for marketing is to win awareness for the product. At this stage, advertising, pricing tactics, and distribution focus on gaining rapid recognition of the product. For example, when Cabbage Patch Kids dolls were introduced in 1983, Coleco spent more money on advertising than on production. During the late summer of 1983, sales representatives called on department stores, gave away dolls to TV personalities, offered special advance sales in women's magazines, and placed the dolls in toy stores at discounted prices. Sales were slow for the first few months after the dolls were introduced.[12]

Growth stage. The growth stage arrives when sales begin to rise at an increasing rate. Companies can expect their highest profits during the growth stage because sales are strong enough to manufacture products in huge quantities at low costs. Later in the growth stage, competitors will be attracted by profits. Growth will continue after the rapid entry of new products until the market is saturated. The challenge for marketing at this stage is to attract consumers while the company still has a competitive advantage and to create a distinct image or brand. Coleco's Cabbage Patch Kids reached peak sales during the 1983 Christmas season with an all-out publicity campaign. This included air time on the *Today* show, a life-size Brooke Shields Cabbage Patch Kid, and donations to children's hospitals that received international attention on the *Bob Hope Christmas Special.*

Maturity. The maturity stage is a period of slow growth or stabilization in a saturated market with many competitors. There are ample substitutes for the product, and competing companies fight for one another's customers. The challenge for marketing is to attract customers away from competitors and to balance prices with costs while continuing to make a profit. The Cabbage Patch Kids dolls enjoyed a growth market for only one year. When the 1984 toy season opened, there were similar dolls and substitutes, such as Kenner's Strawberry Shortcake, and the market became saturated.

Decline. The decline stage is the beginning of the end. Sales drop off sharply and profits are made only through cost reductions. The challenge for marketing is to harvest sales without adding costs, to reduce or eliminate advertising, and to hold prices at profitable levels until the product no longer has any market value. For the Cabbage Patch Kids dolls, this stage occurred just after Christmas 1984, and Coleco

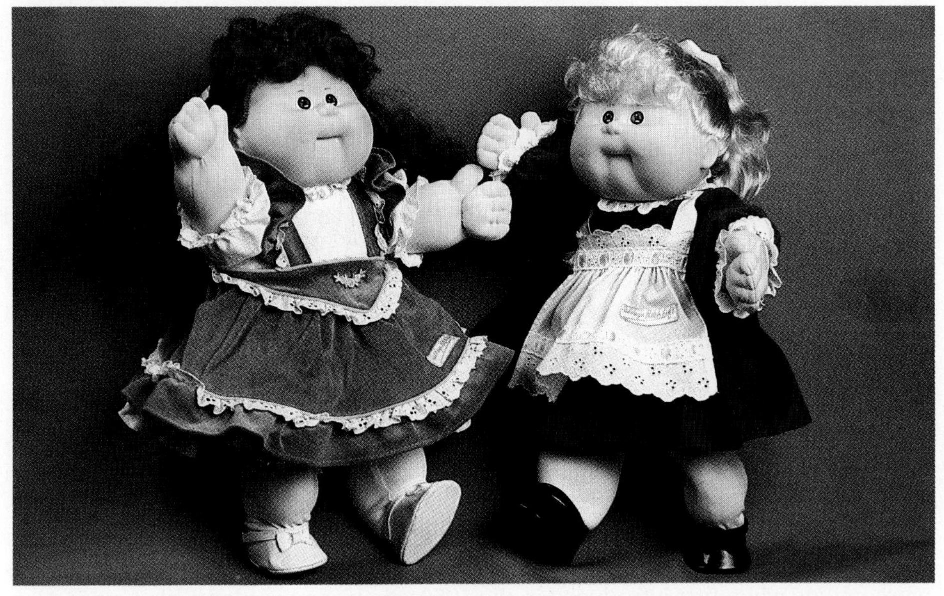

When the market for Cabbage Patch Kids dolls and competing dolls became saturated, prices for all dolls dropped. Sales for the Cabbage Patch Kids stabilized during the mid-1980s, then plummeted. The dolls seem to be poised for a comeback in the mid-1990s.

began manufacturing only with advance retail orders. Advertising was eliminated, prices were reduced to clear inventory, and the company let the dolls quietly fade into history. The Cabbage Patch Kid doll was typical of many toys, such as Star Wars laser swords and Rubik's Cube, with short life cycles. Other products may have life cycles of several decades or more. When 8-mm home movies were introduced in 1950, for example, it was ten years before there was a growth market, yet the leader in 8-mm film and cameras, Kodak, abruptly withdrew from the market in 1980 when VCR sales began to accelerate. Laser discs now have a major share of VCR markets.[13]

Developing the Marketing Program

A marketing program, as defined earlier, is designed to implement a *marketing plan.* Marketing managers formulate activities that coincide with the life cycle, the consumer scenario, and the strategic positioning of products and services. Programs are usually budgeted annually and evaluated for their effectiveness each year. Exemptions to this include seasonal fashions and toys that require very short-lived programs aimed, for example, at the Christmas market. In many instances, programs can also extend into years, such as Pepsi Cola's plan to challenge Coca-Cola in the soft drink market. Figure 8-4 illustrates the four elements of a marketing program.[14]

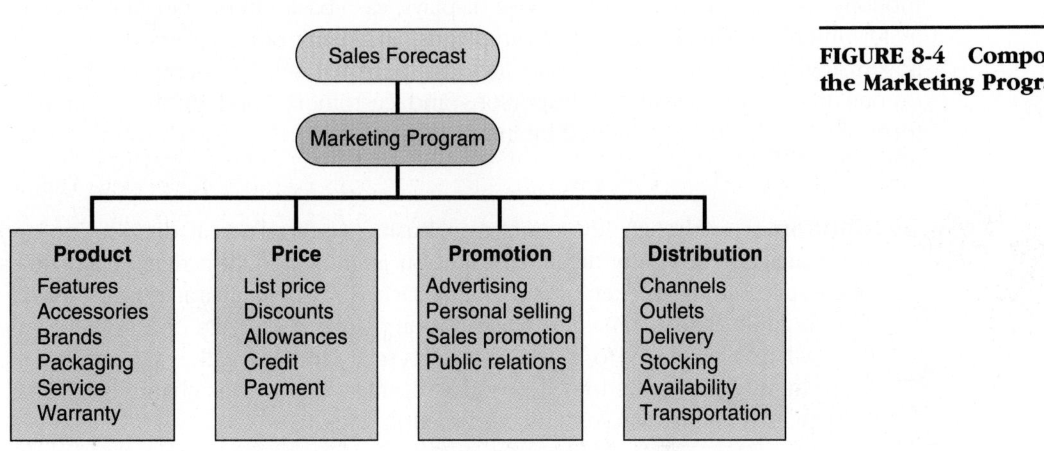

FIGURE 8-4 Components of the Marketing Program

Product characteristics. The concept of a product includes its physical characteristics, features, accessories, brand name, packaging, service and warranty, and usefulness. A Rolex watch, for example, has most of the standard operating parts of any other quality watch, but it is also made with exceptional quality control so that a lifetime warranty can be given. Several models have jewels for numerals, several others have diving indicators and accessories, and all Rolexes are packaged in expensive boxes. Other watches are made less expensively and priced, boxed, and sold through less specialized stores. Marketing managers often work with design engineers to develop product characteristics that reflect customer expectations. They are also involved in planning how to inform customers of product characteristics and how to take advantage of them.

Pricing. Products and services are priced according to life cycle influences. Tactical pricing is developed in tandem with positioning. Of course, pricing options must be defined in order to develop sales forecasts, but most pricing decisions are determined by examining the competition.

New products differentiated in some way from their competitors can often generate a price premium, but such premiums rarely last. Because Polaroid cameras were unique when first introduced in the 1950s, they commanded a high price. Now they sell for much less than most single-lens reflex cameras. Sophisticated hand-held calculators sold at high prices in the mid-1960s: A calculator costing $5.99 today sold for $89.99 in 1968. In less than two years, the prices of compact disk players plunged from $1,000 to under $200 as competitors proliferated. Once new competitors emerge, a firm can no longer claim to be unique nor can it charge premium prices.

The reasons for price changes are not as important as how market planners consciously choose pricing tactics. Again, a product with differentiated values for consumers can command a premium price, and a firm may choose to sell the product at that premium until forced by competition to lower prices. This is called *skimming,* a tactic that Coleco chose for its Cabbage Patch Kids dolls. In contrast, a firm may choose to set a nonpremium price to establish a strong market share that will dissuade competitors or to *penetrate* a market through very high sales. Wal-Mart consistently uses penetration pricing to capture retail sales from its competitors.[15]

Quality plays an important role in setting prices. For example, Panasonic and General Electric maintain premium prices for their VCRs, relying on quality improvements to distinguish their products. Other companies, such as Emerson, make VCRs to sell at discount or through mail-order catalogs at low prices. Prices can also be used to imply quality, such as prestige prices for Christian Dior men's clothes and Estée Lauder perfumes.[16]

Promotional tactics. Promotional activities significantly influence the image consumers have of a firm and its products. Promotion is often equated with advertising, but actually advertising is only a small part of the promotional mix. Tactical promotions also include point-of-purchase displays, cash-back offers, special offers such as low-interest financing, giveaway campaigns, and many other efforts distinct from advertising. Promotional tactics also include "personal selling"—emphasizing one-on-one interaction between salespersons and customers—and public relations, a form of free advertising obtained by introducing newsworthy issues into the promotional mix.[17]

Distribution. Although few courses in business schools treat distribution and logistics management in any detail, distribution is an important activity. Companies can often successfully market products that lack distinctive characteristics by distributing them in a unique manner. Distribution planning answers questions of *how* the firm will get products to market and *where* customers will make purchases. There are hundreds of ways to sell products besides the obvious channels of distribution such as retailing, wholesaling, and catalog sales.

Frito-Lay relies on a form of "rack jobbing" to market snack foods through a widespread network of route distributors. We noted in Chapter 6 that Frito-Lay has a customer-oriented strategy of service with a 99.5 percent on-time delivery objective. Effective distribution has made this relatively undifferentiated product line of snacks highly successful.[18]

Franchising is a major category of distribution that may be the fastest-growing segment of business in America. McDonald's was built on franchising and a marketing philosophy of clean stores in convenient locations. Other well-known franchises are Jiffy Lube, 7-Eleven, and Red Carpet Realty, but there are literally hundreds of products and services that owe their success to franchising with exquisite distribution systems. A few recent entrants are Merle Harmon's "Fan Fair," Julie Brice's "I Can't Believe It's Yogurt," and corporate-owned ARCO "am/pm markets."[19]

Distribution emphasizes physical placement of businesses. Holiday Inn Corporation locates hotel facilities at arterial traffic centers like airports, vacation spots, and business travel hubs. In the photocopying business, a California firm called Kinko's locates all its copy centers within walking distance of college campuses. Distribution can also be defined by how sales are controlled. IBM and Apple license dealers in carefully selected areas. Hewlett-Packard exercises tight control over distribution offices, and PC Limited is a factory-direct system bypassing intermediaries.

CHECKPOINT

- Describe a marketing plan and a marketing program, and contrast the two.
- What is a customer scenario and why would it be important to you if you were responsible for developing a marketing program?
- How would you use a sales forecast to help plan product improvements and promotional activities?

PRODUCTION PLANNING

Production planning is concerned with manufacturing quality products in the right quantities for delivery to customers at the right time. Production and marketing objectives must be orchestrated because they are interdependent; production managers must understand how marketing programs will be implemented, and marketing managers must understand how products will be made and delivered to their customers. Sales forecasts and marketing objectives affect production plans, yet the reverse is also true. Production is subject to constraints that affect not only how much can be manufactured but also how much can be sold.

production planning Managers in production planning are concerned with manufacturing quality products in the right quantities for delivery to customers at the right time.

Strategic Production Plans

Master strategies, such as for growth and diversification, partially depend on a company's production capabilities; plans to manufacture a great new product or to expand sales to new customers will be hollow if a firm does not have the necessary production capacity. At the same time, strategies drive production plans for long-term changes in technology, production processes, and product development. From a strategic production planning viewpoint, managers evaluate a firm's *aggregate capacity.* The **aggregate capacity plan** establishes the maximum feasible output that can be manufactured and delivered during a strategic planning period. It takes into account major changes in technology, such as process changes away from labor-intensive assembly to automated assembly systems, raw material supplies, purchas-

aggregate capacity plan This establishes the maximum feasible output that can be manufactured and delivered during a strategic planning period

ETHICS IN MANAGEMENT

Marketing Skills at Levi Strauss Help Solve AIDS Support Group Problems

Levi Strauss has long been considered a model for corporate involvement in community activities, and it donates millions of dollars to combat social problems ranging from AIDS to illiteracy. In 1990, for example, Levi Strauss distributed more than $7 million, about 2.5 percent of its pretax earnings. The corporation may be making its most important contribution, however, through its people, who are encouraged to become involved in social programs. The company backs these efforts with time-release programs and donation of corporate assets and facilities.

One such effort involved Robert Hanson, Levi's youthwear advertising manager, who normally spends his time convincing kids to wear Levi's as they bop around malls or ride skateboards. Hanson became aware of Bay Area efforts to provide help to AIDS patients, and he noticed that a San Francisco support group called the Shanti Project was doing a terrible job of attracting patients to its AIDS center. He felt that *pro bono* marketing (literally, marketing for the public good) could benefit the group.

Hanson helped the group devise a marketing plan with specific goals and support activities to reach out to its clientele. Clients included both heterosexual and gay patients and family members of all ages and both sexes. To create a marketing program that would bring these people together in a mutual support environment was a tremendous challenge that involved Levi's advertising team, company training specialists, counselors, and office staff members. They initially focused on center-sponsored seminars, the first called "The Courage to Care: Healing Yourself to Help You Care Better." Today seminars and counseling deal with many related topics, such as working with neurologically impaired AIDS patients and dealing with death.

Robert Hanson's project is unique, but the commitment is not unusual at Levi Strauss, where several hundred employees are involved in community activities. Hanson's pro bono marketing effort shows how valuable good business skills can be in addressing social problems. The Bay Area Shanti Project is successful today because such skills were brought to bear—and because a company and its people chose to be concerned.

Sources: Jon Berry, "Pro Bono Marketing," *Adweek's Marketing Week*, March 25, 1991, pp. 18–19; and personal correspondence with the Shanti Project, November 1991.

ing and inventory capabilities, manufacturing and storage facilities, and human resources required in production. Sales forecasts and strategic marketing plans are important for coordinating long-range production requirements with master strategies.

In terms of tactical planning, the strategic *aggregate capacity plan* determines how medium-range planning will be formulated.

Tactical Production Planning

Strategic aggregate capacity plans are translated into annual production plans. These are sometimes called capacity plans or production budgets, but to avoid confusion, we will use the term *production plan*. A **production plan** specifies the planned volume of each product to be manufactured consistent with marketing plans for projected sales during a planning period.[20] The production plan also describes annual production quotas and budgeted resource allocations that are the basis for operational planning decisions.

production plan
A formal production plan specifies the planned volume of each product to be manufactured consistent with marketing plans for projected sales during a planning period.

Figure 8-5 depicts a simplified model of the production plan. Notice that forecasted sales establish the requirements for *finished goods inventory,* the number of items that must be ready to be delivered when sales are expected. The finished goods inventory, in turn, establishes required production levels specified in the production plan, and the production plan then becomes the basis for operational decisions. In tactical terms, this implies an annual cycle of preplanned activities, but because customer demand is seldom the same month to month, annual plans must conform to *seasonal patterns of demand* that alter the requirements for finished goods inventory.

Retail stores, for example, have three or four heavy sales seasons, the busiest being Christmastime. The December sales volume at Sears and J.C. Penney's is nearly quadruple that of any other month, and for certain types of products, such as toys, the December volume is six times that of any other month. Firms dependent on construction, such as those in lumber, structural steel, and insulating products, reach peak sales in early summer. Resort services (skiing, golfing, boating, camping) and agricultural suppliers (farm equipment, fertilizers, commodities) have two or three peak months each year when they make more than 80 percent of their annual sales. Companies that support these industries face similar fluctuations. For example, farm loans almost always precede farm revenue by many months. Consequently, banks face a heavy agriculture loan service demand early each year, with payback periods later in the year.[21]

Production planning, therefore, requires more than an annual estimate of sales with production broken down into convenient increments; weekly or monthly pro-

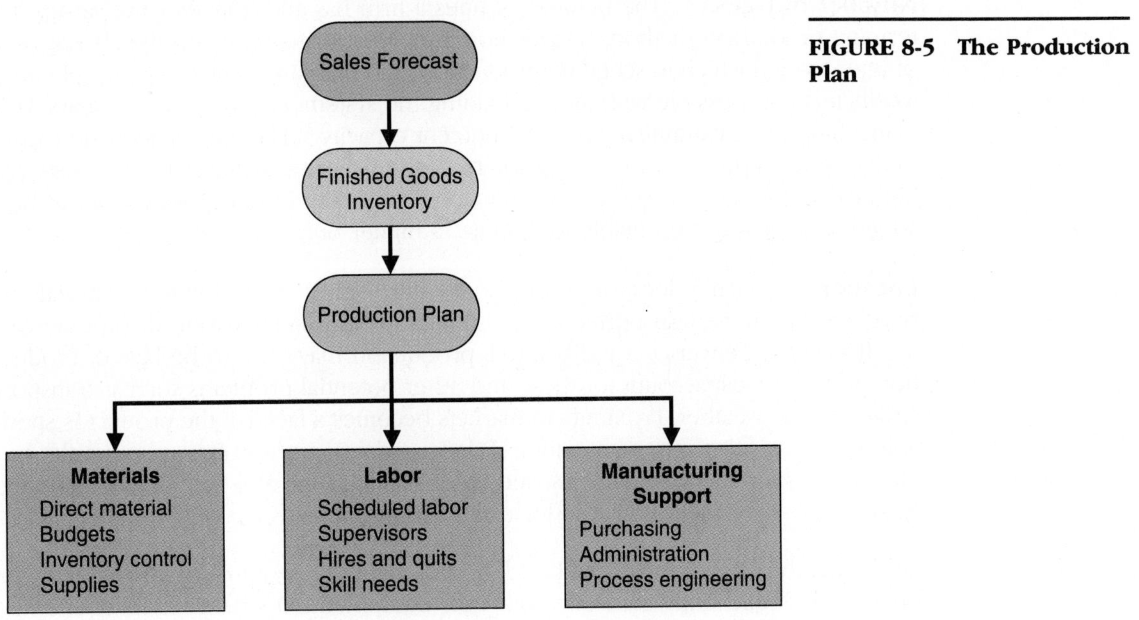

FIGURE 8-5 The Production Plan

duction levels with similar quotas can result in serious inventory shortages as sales fluctuate, changing the demand for finished goods inventory. Service organizations face similar changes in demand, and their *operations plans*—the service equivalent to production plans—show similar variations. Johns Hopkins Medical Center in Baltimore, for example, has peak seasons for maternity care, virus treatment, cardiac care, and emergency orthopedics. Community hospitals located near universities are pushed to capacity toward the end of each semester and have fewer patients during summer vacation.[22]

Factors in Production Planning

Production is subject to many constraints that limit production capacity and influence plans. Planners evaluate several critical factors of production in much the same way marketing managers evaluate customers and markets. A brief review of these production factors follows.

Facilities. Facilities include buildings, materials management capacity, energy resource configurations, the number of production lines available, and the location of facilities and their proximity to materials or markets. Facilities are necessarily limited in size and number; therefore, companies always have a ceiling on how much production they can achieve at any given time.

Materials management. Production systems must be capable of handling raw materials and finished goods. If a firm lacks handling equipment or storage capacity, production lines can outrun the company's ability to provide basic materials and supplies. Materials account for approximately 40 percent of production costs; consequently, poor materials planning can seriously affect profitability.[23]

Energy resources. Energy is usually a strategic issue, but how it is used in plant operations is also important. For example, a manufacturer can choose between electrically or pneumatically powered tools; in an area where electricity is expensive, this choice can be critical. Heating and cooling systems can use natural gas, fuel oil, electricity, or a combination of resources. Also, different choices for scheduling machines, improving production processes, and running multiple shifts can affect the total energy resources used.

Number of lines. The number of lines a firm has and how they are set up determine production methods in the short run. Most firms have an inflexible system of lines around which to schedule production, and planning is necessary to schedule as efficiently as possible without overloading the system. For the past few years, U.S. plants have been running at about 80 percent capacity.[24] Planning at reduced capacity is just as important as planning for high-end capacity because start-up costs are high each time a line is put into production. Unless the level of production justifies added costs, it is not profitable to operate at higher output rates.

Location. Facility location must also be considered because when materials or products have to be transported long distances, much can happen to disrupt deliveries. If material deliveries are disrupted, production may have to be halted. Production planning must account for these and other potential problems such as transport strikes or bad weather. Proximity to markets becomes a factor if the product is spoilable or sensitive to excess handling. Food products are an obvious example, but electronic components, chemicals, and other products are also sensitive to shipping. Proximity to customers is crucial for service industries.

Technology. A company with older equipment that requires more maintenance operates less efficiently than one with new equipment. Operator-based equipment

MANAGEMENT APPLICATION

Spokes Bicycles: College Grad Applies Textbook for Success

When Jim Strang opened his first bicycle shop in 1986, he had already spent a year planning the new venture. Jim was convinced that if he applied management principles learned in college, the shop would be a success. A recent business school graduate and a veteran of collegiate racing, Jim worked briefly after graduation in a Washington, D.C., area bike shop. There he had the opportunity to compare actual business practices with textbook prescriptions.

"Theory and reality were miles apart," Jim said, "and it seemed to me that there were a lot of really neat things in the textbooks that managers could use to make a business succeed. But they were not doing these things in the real world. I mean, nobody seemed to plan anything. Talking about quality service was just so much talk. Inventory control meant buying as cheaply as possible, and salespeople were hired at the lowest wages. I made up my mind that good business theory could be applied to succeed."

By early 1989, Jim Strang had not only opened a store in Alexandria, Virginia, that was grossing $1 million in sales, but had expanded to a second store in Arlington that had even higher sales. He was featured in Silvia Porter's *Personal Finance* magazine and on the cable-TV news program *USA Business News* for his unusual commitment to customer quality.

"I planned everything, and I still do," Jim explained. "I wanted my vendors and bicycle suppliers to be my friends, and we have a great understanding: I pay for quality, get correct orders, and control my inventory and costs so that I have nothing in my stores that I wouldn't use myself. I hire the best people I can find and we all love the business. We're family, and so are our customers."

Jim feels that his success comes from applying innovative methods learned from his college textbooks coupled with a personal commitment to make things happen. For example, he read about "just-in-time" inventory control, a feature of Japanese management for assuring quality material and production control. "I use JIT," Jim said, "not because it's a buzzword, but because it works. I get the best supplies on time and in the quantities needed without waste or huge storage costs, and I can pass these savings on to customers."

Jim tenaciously plans and revises his plans using innovative computer spreadsheet applications and forecasting techniques. "Most small business owners think planning is a waste," he explained. "After all, it takes a lot of time. But through planning, I find out more about my competition and customers than most guys know who have been in business for a decade."

Source: Personal communication to author.

like standard lathes requires set-up time. Set-up time refers to the time needed for operators to shut down a machine, reconfigure it for a new job, test-run a few items, and then prepare for actual production. Newer computer-assisted systems have more accurate machinery with automated procedures that reduce set-up time and eliminate many errors associated with manual systems that rely on the skills of individual operators. The technology of purchasing systems, inventory control systems, and logistics also influences production plans. Recent innovations in computer-integrated manufacturing solve this problem by networking support systems with production systems.[25]

Distribution systems. Production managers must plan for a flow of products that satisfy customer expectations. An excellent on-time record often provides a competitive edge. If marketing has developed an excellent sales record but receives only partially filled orders or late deliveries because of production snags, the whole firm pays with reduced sales and a tarnished image.

Quality. An emphasis on quality in production planning often results in smaller production runs, more hands-on quality control, and greater contact with customers. If higher quality is crucial to remaining competitive, production may have to abandon large-batch production runs—which typically create more rejects—in favor of small-batch runs. But such a switch may not cure quality problems without a quality assurance system that enhances quality performance. Even though smaller quantities of items can be controlled better, a firm may have to put more resources into quality testing, and will certainly have to respond to customer expectations.[26]

CHECKPOINT

- Describe the roles of quality and quantity in production planning.
- What factors would be most important for manufacturing if your company made toys? What similar factors would be important to a service, such as an accounting firm?
- How would technology influence your decisions for aggregate production planning?

HUMAN RESOURCES AND TACTICAL PLANNING

Human resource planning is generally concerned with people joining and leaving organizations. Strategically, the firm is concerned with long-term systems for recruiting, training, evaluating, compensating, and providing benefits to employees. In the short run, managers are concerned with obtaining and retaining qualified employees to meet operational needs. During the tactical time frame, managers must determine what skills their company needs and how to attract employees with those skills.

Tactical Considerations for Human Resource Planning

Tactical considerations for human resource planning are closely associated with marketing and production plans because these influence employment levels and skills required of workers. Exhibit 8-1 illustrates the tactical objectives of human resource planning.

EXHIBIT 8-1 Tactical Objectives in Human Resource Management

Area of Management	Objectives for Planning Period	Actions Required in Planning Period
Personnel Director	Improve coordination with functional departments. Articulate regulations, federal codes, and EEOC/AA goals.	Schedule manpower meetings. Hold short periodic seminars and management development (MD) programs.
Recruitment and Selection	Fulfill employment and skills requirements of departments and divisions. Provide labor market forecast and reassignment capacity.	Develop skills inventory in-house, cross-reference labor supply/skills, upgrade place/test data.
Compensation and Benefits	Coordinate technical needs with skills/employment. Offer competitive wages and salaries. Revise pensions according to federal mandates and cost-of-living index.	Do job analysis and job evaluation. Set up joint task group for planning on technical and skills needs. Commission labor study.
Labor Relations	Improve labor-management relations, reduce turnover by 10 percent. Reduce avoidable accidents by 12 percent and lost time by 8 percent. Prepare collective bargaining data prior to contract negotiations.	Review grievances and hold supervisory meetings to improve relations/safety. Post safety standards, hold safety orientation sessions for new workers, and enforce safety rules.
Affirmative Action	Comply with federal code on minority, sex, age, and handicapped employment. Retain and advance all qualified personnel. Improve timeliness of discrimination investigations.	Hire minorities to match labor market mix. Set up task group with production and marketing managers for equal opportunity compliance. Establish program of worker release time for training/counseling.
Training	Set up management development program for superiors and staff. Upgrade skills for semi- and unskilled workers. Coordinate high-tech skills with strategic production expectations.	Schedule MD programs to coincide with slack time. Use cross-training for new technology. Propose program by midyear on robotics planned online beginning 3rd quarter.

The planning process starts with management's determination of what skills are needed. The next step is to decide where the firm stands in terms of existing skills and employment. If there is a gap between the two, plans to make adjustments in human resources must be developed.

needs assessment review
A process of matching projected activities with projected employment requirements.

Needs assessment. The first planning step, a **needs assessment review,** is a process of matching projected activities with projected employment requirements. If a company has done a good job setting up personnel systems, managers will be able to define employment needs on the basis of past reports of production and marketing activities. Questions that must be answered include how many employees are needed for projected production and sales activity, how many are likely to quit, how many will be released, and how many will retire during the planning period. An action plan resolves this matching process to define recruiting, training needs, and compensation levels.

wage and benefit management
Usually the responsibility of specialists in the field, wage and benefit management in planning terms is the professional planning and control of compensation and employee benefits.

Compensation planning. Compensation is concerned with **wage and benefit management.** Compensation systems are seldom revised in the short run, but there are constant fluctuations in wages and benefits in response to the ebb and flow of employment. Production and marketing activities may require substantial changes during a tactical planning period, such as peak-period hiring, overtime scheduling, planning for layoffs, and scheduling around vacations. These can have serious cost effects on production, and if wage and benefit systems are not managed well, a company may be unable to attract the human resources it needs. For firms that have incentive plans or variable piece-rate systems, compensation can be a complicated planning responsibility.

Labor relations. Tactical plans also address collective bargaining issues in union environments, which can be quite complicated. Aside from actual union contracting, managers are responsible for effective relations with all employees to enhance the quality of work life. The following changes in employment can disrupt labor relations and are constant concerns of planners.

Layoffs and recalls. These stem from changes in production and marketing tactics. If a firm develops a stable production system, layoffs and employee recalls will be minimized. But when labor costs become a focal issue, as during a recession, the pressure to trim employment increases. Employees may be laid off, and then, when production picks up again, recalled. Being laid off is a traumatic event for most workers, so layoffs and recalls should not occur without careful planning.

Reassignments. Personnel often need to be reassigned to meet short-term production requirements. From a planning perspective, reassignments should never be capricious. In organizations with strong unions, reassignments may be impossible.[27] Reassignments occur in the short run for two reasons. First, they are made to cope with unexpected personnel needs in other areas. Second, they are purposely made on a widespread basis to minimize aggregate changes in employment or to hold down labor costs.

Scheduling. Schedule changes are short-term adjustments in how human resources are to be used to meet competitive and economic pressures. Some firms create four-day work weeks or split-shift schedules to alter patterns of operations. Others schedule vacations for all employees during the same period so plants can be entirely shut down. By shutting plants, a firm has to sell off excess inventory without replacement, but at the same time it avoids labor and fixed costs.[28] Numerous other tactical adjustments deal with pension changes, wage freezes, concessions in contracts, training, and personnel programs aimed at meeting short-term objectives.

Responsibilities for Human Resource Planning

Responsibility for human resource planning is shared between line managers in operational positions and staff specialists in human resources. As we shall see in Chapter 12, staff specialists are those experienced in personnel administration, wage and salary administration, counseling, labor relations, and corporate training. They complement and support line managers, who are individually responsible for human resources in their operational areas.

Planning responsibilities for scheduling, budgeting, production, marketing, and support activities in human resources must be assumed to a great degree by operating managers. Supervisors focus on scheduling and potential disruptions such as absenteeism, illnesses, and accidents. Middle managers coordinate human resource needs, monitor compensations, and implement training programs. Higher-level line managers, such as division managers, are responsible for creating the systems within which their subordinates can function effectively.

CHECKPOINT

- Explain how human resource planning is accomplished to provide the needed people with appropriate skills for various departments throughout the firm.
- How would you develop and use a needs assessment for recruitment and selection of workers?
- Why are human resource managers concerned with layoffs, recalls, reassignments, and scheduling?
- If you were a manager in marketing, production, or information systems, what responsibilities would you have for human resource planning?

FINANCIAL MANAGEMENT AND TACTICAL PLANNING

The tactical planning picture would be incomplete without a broad view of financial planning tactics. Corporations often find their plans tempered by the short-range expectations of investors and stockholders, who focus on earnings with little regard for managers' concerns with human resources, production, or marketing. Financial planners must satisfy investors while accounting for revenues, costs, profits, capital expansion, and cash flow. They must also take into consideration other stakeholders who are affected by the company's financial performance. Figure 8-6 illustrates these relationships. Financial budgeting was discussed in Chapter 6, and financial controls will be introduced in Chapter 17, so we will only briefly examine financial planning responsibilities here.

Profitability

A firm must remain profitable and solvent, regardless of its purpose or its strategic objectives. Every manager involved in financial planning knows that profitability influences the firm's ability to generate capital. In a recessionary period, for example, money is usally tight and stockholders are more sensitive to changes in a firm's performance. Financial considerations therefore intensify. A recession is likely to

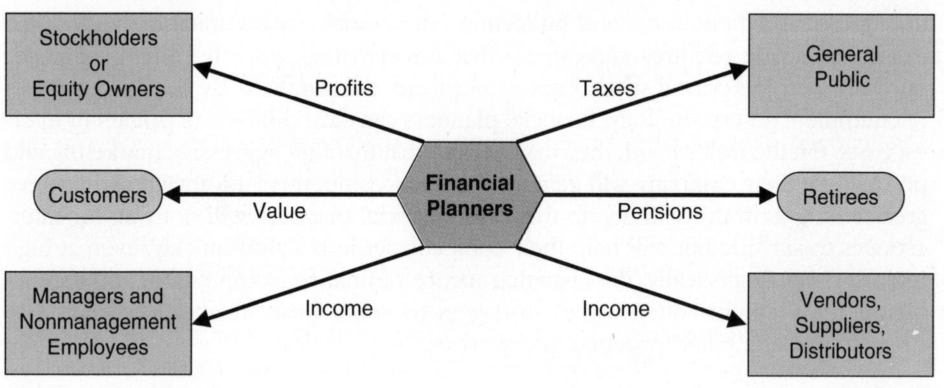

FIGURE 8-6 Organizational Stakeholders of Concern for Tactical Financial Planning

Nabisco Biscuit, which makes Oreo and Fig Newton cookies and Ritz and Triscuit crackers, shows how financial and tactical planning work hand-in-hand. While parent company RJR Nabisco has been busy cutting costs during the last three years, Nabisco Biscuit has actually increased spending by 20 percent to enlarge its sales and customer service staff. Nabisco Biscuit's different approach to financial planning was prompted by its different approach to tactical planning: The company has organized its selling completely around the store manager/client, a tactic that has more than doubled Nabisco Biscuit's operating profits.

dampen sales, compress prices, and lead to increased costs. Some of these costs are associated with higher material prices and labor changes, others with more aggressive marketing or more intensive services. During a growth period in a healthy economy, financial planners concentrate on acquiring capital for new plant and equipment and on underwriting the costs of increased production and sales. Higher total compensation for labor, larger material orders, and greater overhead require careful advance budgeting to protect the company's liquidity.

Recessionary downturns. During a recession, a company is hammered from both sides as expenses increase and revenues decrease. These factors, coupled with more trepidation on the part of investors and creditors, are menacing because they mean a company may be unable to attract the capital necessary to fulfill its objectives. Since recession is usually a short-term phenomenon, financial managers must tactically plan how to best use limited financial resources—that is, they are concerned with redeployment of financial resources rather than with strategic change. Redeployment involves budgeting cash flow, reducing costs, and postponing debt-based purchases.

Product and market growth. When a company grows, adds to its product line, or diversifies into new markets, tremendous costs are incurred long before sales are generated. Strategic growth requires long-term capital outlays, and when a company is simultaneously faced with technological changes, these expenditures can put the entire organization at risk. At the tactical level, financial managers are involved with timing capital expenditures and budgeting operational costs. Capital expansion, for example, usually requires substantial debt underwriting, and the timing of major purchases can be critical when interest rates vary substantially. By timing purchases of equipment and technology, financial planners can save millions of dollars in interest costs. On the other hand, they may believe that through aggressive marketing and production, their company will gain a substantial competitive advantage and achieve greater long-term profitability. In that case, financial planners will not wait for interest rates to subside but will help their company get into action quickly, even at high interest costs. Realistically, the changing nature of finance, competition, and technological requirements often forces managers to subordinate financial objectives to strategic marketing and production objectives.[29]

CHECKPOINT

- How is a financial planner involved with profit planning and budgeting with managers in other functional areas of marketing and production?
- When economic conditions change, either toward recession or toward growth, what influence do these changes have on financial planning in the short term?
- How does a financial manager plan for capital expansion when a firm is expanding into new products and markets?

BRIDGING GAPS ACROSS FUNCTIONAL LINES

If managers could plan for their individual operating units independently of one another, there would be little need for "bridging gaps," but this is impossible. Each operation or functional unit is like a puzzle piece that must fit with others to make a complete picture. Each provides a subset of plans and objectives that must be synchronized to reinforce the common objectives of the organization.

Bridging gaps between divisions is a matter of reconciling differences to ensure harmony. Theoretically, it is the task of executive managers to pull organizations together, yet realistically it is the responsibility of all managers to consciously foster congruence and harmony. The planning process cannot be random or carried out in isolated divisions. All parts must fit nicely together. Marketing objectives must be reflected in production planning, personnel with the right skills must be available at the times needed, and operations must be funded to ensure solvency.

One way of bridging gaps is to develop formal planning procedures that stabilize relationships between managers both vertically and at peer group levels. A formal planning process, as described in Chapter 6, provides consistency in daily operations and a forum for exchanging information among managers with diversified interests. Decisions are outlined and communicated through formal planning, and when a team approach to planning evolves, performance expectations are more clearly articulated to lower-management levels.

Before turning our attention to operational planning, we should recognize that tactical planning can involve more than marketing, production, human resources, and finance. These are the mainstream considerations, but in manufacturing, for example, other departments are involved in planning, such as research and development, process engineering, maintenance, information systems, public affairs, and various administrative functions. In service organizations such as hospitals, specialized planning is needed for radiology, nursing services, surgical and medical departments, research, laboratory services, and many other areas. In each instance, coordination is required among functional managers to offer tactical guidelines for operational planning.

CHECKPOINT

- What responsibilities do middle managers have for coordinating their individual plans with others?
- Why must plans be synchronized, and what departmental managers might be involved in this process?

GLOBAL TRENDS

GE's Joint Venture with FANUC of Japan: Going Global the GE Way

When the history of GE's globalization efforts is written, the company's joint venture with FANUC, Ltd., of Japan may serve as the prologue. GE Fanuc Automation Corporation was formed in December 1986 to meld the strengths of each company, and by the end of 1988, GE Fanuc had become the premier company serving American industry with industrial robots and computer numerical control (CNC) devices.

This strategic move was inspired by conditions at both companies. During the early 1980s, GE had become overextended in their ability to provide service and technology to U.S. automakers. The company found itself trying to guarantee factory overhauls, yet without the expertise or technology to support an active marketing plan. Demand outpaced supply, and GE stretched itself too far to compete effectively. During the same period, FANUC had gained world recognition as the best manufacturer of CNCs and robotic controls, but the Japanese company lacked the marketing capabilities to go global. The joint venture allowed the companies to open a new automation plant in Virginia, merging GE's marketing power with FANUC's quality engineering. Within a year, GE Fanuc captured a leading share of U.S. sales and was positioning to market in both Europe and Asia.

During the three-year start-up period, managers found themselves in a planning transition unlike any they had previously experienced. Engineers on the manufacturing floor had to develop plans compatible with the Japanese approach to efficient, high-quality production. This meant that U.S. managers could no longer produce "to stock" or get away with "some rejects." Production objectives were 100 percent quality, on-time delivery, and no excess inventory or waste. Incremental planning each year, coupled with new processes and total involvement of all employees in planning, helped create a GE Fanuc sys-

OPERATIONAL PLANNING

operational planning
Operational planning occurs at the lowest management levels and focuses on specific performance objectives for immediate results.

Planning at the lowest organizational echelons is called *operational planning.* **Operational planning** focuses on specific performance objectives expressed in monthly, weekly, or daily task requirements. It is planning for the shortest time periods conducted by first-line managers or task groups who are closest to daily operations. They often deal with activities and problems of immediate concern.

Production supervisors, for example, are apprehensive about sudden rush orders, flu bugs that keep workers home, machine breakdowns, poor weather that holds up supplies, and a host of other considerations that can wreak havoc in their schedules. Sales managers tend to work in monthly time frames, but they have the same sense of immediacy about planning issues. Generally, operational planning is concerned with tactical planning issues, but expressed in shorter increments with more specific and immediate performance expectations. The following is a summary of operational planning issues.[30]

1. *Objectives* are stated in unambiguous and precisely measurable standards of performance. Production may have standard numbers of units of product per

tem that gives customers guarantees of 100 percent quality. Today the company is the low-cost producer in robotics, with defect rates less than 1 percent.

Marketing programs also evolved into a series of annual planning scenarios for reaching domestic customers with a small array of robotic products. Rather than diversify into many products, the company concentrated on making a few products to the best specifications. Marketing programs emphasized the quality of GE Fanuc's selected innovations and hands-on customer service.

During this time, GE's CEO Jack Welch introduced an aggressive management philosophy that required all of GE's divisions and subsidiaries to implement human resource development programs to meld cultural differences of Asian, European, and American partners. For GE Fanuc, this meant becoming a "multilingual and multicultural" company positioned as a global enterprise. Today subsidiaries of the GE Fanuc venture are located in Europe and Japan, and they comprise American, Japanese, and European workers. Everyone is bilingual, many employees are skilled in several languages, and all have been trained in the GE philosophy of quality workmanship for exceptional customer service.

GE Fanuc is one of the nearly 500 divisions, subsidiaries, and operating units that make up GE: together, they represent 298,000 employees and $60 billion in sales. GE's commitment to major developments in technology and in human relations has earned it the title of the "Harvard of Corporate America." The company has exquisite strategies that are implemented through tactical human resource development systems, financial management, quality production, and extensive marketing systems.

Sources: "World Games," *Monogram*, Vol. 66, No. 1 (1988), pp. 1–9. See also Thomas A. Stewart, "GE Keeps Those Ideas Coming," *Fortune*, August 12, 1991, pp. 41–49.

hour, day, or week. Marketing is usually concerned with sales quotas. Personnel may schedule and control for a certain number of employment interviews.

2. *Operating* plans must reflect devision-level expectations for performance standards such as machine-hours, man-hours, and product defects.
3. *Budgets* are used in operational planning, less as cash controls than as translations of planned objectives into common denominators for performance. Operational budgets may be expressed in monetary terms, but more often they reflect physical measures of units produced or sold.
4. *Time* management is perhaps the core issue for first-line managers. They must obtain performance results in restricted periods of time.
5. *Coordinating* operating unit objectives with others is a pervasive activity to ensure coordination of scheduled performance.

Importance of Operational Planning

Operating managers seldom recognize that they are consciously planning; they feel as if they are simply supervising operations. Thus scheduling and budgeting may not seem like planning activities to them, and an elaborate formal process like that described for strategic planning will appear unnecessary. Most effective managers do, however, follow a formal, if simple, planning process. They may set aside time each week to meet with their employees, and using feedback they receive from recent activities, they plan ways to make improvements.

Such meetings occur in most well-run organizations. In participative environments, they form an integral part of first-line managers' jobs. The *team approach* to planning introduced in Chapter 6, for example, can bring together managers and employees on a weekly basis to go over production or marketing reports, discuss machine scheduling or sales efforts, and preview expectations for the next planning period. Several different group approaches can be adopted, but the point is to create a constructive planning process that will yield benefits described below.

Problems defined. A conscious effort to think into the future and involve employees in the process will allow potential problems to surface. At first, a think tank approach yields insights into current problems only, but with experience, participants start asking "what if" questions that lead to identifying future problems. Once potential problems surface, the group can start working on creative solutions.

Alternatives developed. Managers will find that if they encourage participation and open communication, employees will offer innovative suggestions to solve potential problems. This process has been formalized into programs such as *Quality Control Circles (QCCs), People Involvement Programs (PIPs),* and *Total Approach to Productivity (TAP).*[31] OCCs, PIPs, and TAPs have one common characteristic: They are group efforts by employees to identify and solve problems. This is the essence of planning.

Productivity improvement. Operational problems usually concern efficiency issues, such as how to serve customers better or how to improve quality and performance, but quality and productivity issues are rapidly becoming focal considerations.

Improved teamwork. Making a group activity out of planning improves group cohesion. It also reduces tension between people and helps clarify individual roles. In well-devised operational planning activities, individuals from different work groups that have interrelated tasks are brought together to plan and coordinate their activities. For example, an assembly line may have several work centers, each one receiving products from work groups behind it in the assembly process and passing on products to groups ahead of it. Peformance by a group ahead in the assembly process depends on performance by groups behind it. By bringing together representatives of these groups, the entire assembly process may be improved. This is an important aspect of *empowering* employees with responsibility for their jobs and task results.[32] Bridging occurs as individuals who must work together come together, and others who interface with the work group or otherwise influence operations are brought into planning discussions. For example, a production department may bring in materials procurement clerks, recruiters, and quality control inspectors to help the department plan production schedules.[33]

Operational Planning Activities

schedule
A time-phased series of activities to be performed to achieve specific and measurable objectives.

Most operational planning activities are concerned with schedules. A **schedule** is a time-phased series of activities to be performed to achieve a specific and measurable objective. Production managers have *master production schedules* that specify all orders to be filled during a production cycle. A production cycle typically is for one month. During this month, a company may have several hundred orders to schedule and each order may require the performance of twenty or thirty operations in several departments.

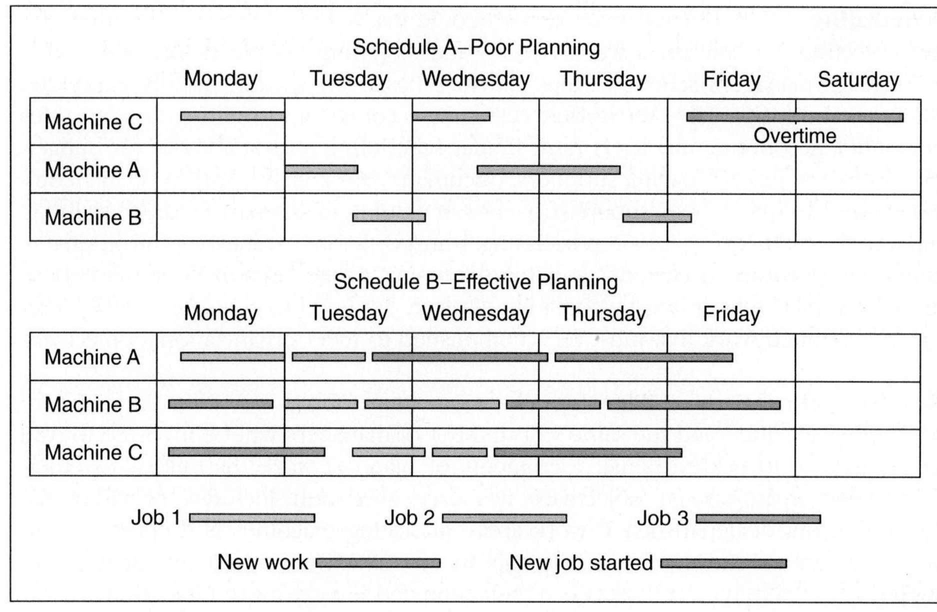

FIGURE 8-7 Improved Scheduling in a Machine Department

A special *production control* department in each production area creates a master schedule; then first-line managers in each work area schedule their workers and machinery to fulfill their responsibilities as outlined in the master schedule. Supervisory work schedules are usually set up for each week. An example of this is shown in Figure 8-7, where one week's work consists of several "jobs" assigned to work groups on three machines. To illustrate how careful planning can improve productivity, there are two schedules in Figure 8-7. Schedule A is inefficient compared to Schedule B because it sequences work poorly. Schedule B required more thought to set up, but it results in "uncommitted time" toward the end of the week when the following week's production can be started. A company with several work groups able to follow Schedule B for several months would save a lot of money and be able to manufacture more products in a shorter period of time.

Managers in production areas constantly schedule work for their employees, and the mark of a good manager is that work is accomplished on time. Yet, a company also expects its managers to achieve high productivity, good quality, and efficient use of resources. Figure 8-8 summarizes these tasks as well as the responsibilities for resource allocation and productivity planning. **Resource allocation** is the planned use of facilities, equipment, materials, energy, cash, and supplies during a budget period. **Productivity planning** is paying conscious attention to quality, costs, and work processes to improve resource allocation while enhancing performance.[34]

resource allocation
The planned used of facilities, equipment, material, energy, cash, and supplies during a company's budgeting period.

productivity planning
The conscious attention to quality, costs, and work processes to improve resource allocation while achieving higher total company performance.

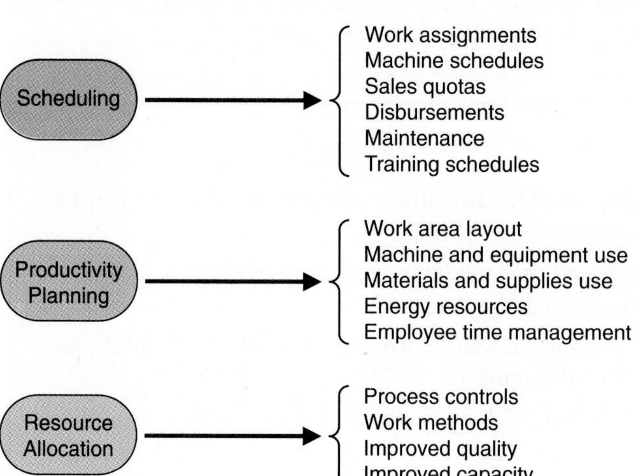

FIGURE 8-8 Primary Planning Tasks for First-Line Managers

Scheduling. Production managers schedule manufacturing work by setting output objectives, usually on a weekly basis, and assigning people to predetermined tasks. Sales managers schedule sales activities based on quotas, usually expressed monthly, and assign sales territories, customer accounts, and training tasks to sales personnel. Accounting managers have similar scheduling responsibilities for budgeting, preparing payroll, paying suppliers, documenting expenses, and so on. Scheduling extends to many other supervisory tasks, including maintenance, safety, training, recruiting, credit management, purchasing, transportation, inventory control, quality control inspections, packaging, and housekeeping. Large organizations have hundreds of similar scheduling responsibilities, each designed to achieve a small increment of planned work that must be accomplished to meet organizational objectives.

Resource allocation. Planning allocations of resources occur in parallel with scheduling activities, and the same vast number of managers will be involved for the same reasons: to achieve small increments of planned work that, taken together, help meet organizational objectives. Resource allocation includes providing an efficient layout of departmental work areas, allocating machines and equipment to tasks, conserving energy, using materials in cost-effective ways, avoiding waste in supplies, and helping employees use their time and energy more efficiently.

Productivity planning. Perhaps all good management practices are meant to improve productivity. Effective scheduling and efficient resource utilization certainly improve performance. Productivity planning, however, has a more specific meaning. For example, whenever managers consciously attempt to improve quality, they also reduce scrap, reduce the time and materials needed to make a product, improve the capacity of machines and equipment, and make work more efficient, thereby simplifying tasks and reducing costs. Similar productivity planning can occur throughout an organization. New computer applications in accounting, for example, are productivity enhancements.

Operational Planning Linked to the Planning Hierarchy

We began this chapter by saying that strategies, tactics, and operational activities must be linked by systematic plans. We have ended with operational planning, which focuses on immediate, short-term objectives involving people in daily activities. When companies achieve these operational plans, their accumulated results satisfy tactical plans related to functional responsibilities at middle-management levels. When tactical plans are well defined and coordinated, they reinforce higher-level strategic objectives. This vertical linkage is crucial to an organization's effectiveness. Horizontal coordination is also essential to bring together marketing, production, human resource, and financial resources in a comprehensive plan.

CHECKPOINT

- Describe operational objectives for first-line managers involved in production, marketing, human resources, and finance.
- Explain how operational planning might be accomplished by managers in personnel administration and data processing.
- Explain how first-line managers schedule activities and why scheduling and operational budgeting are important.
- From a human resource perspective, how do managers establish new planning processes to enhance productivity?

As WE CONCLUDE THE CHAPTER, recall the opening discussion about PepsiCo's battle to reposition its soft drink line and become an equal contender with Coca-Cola. The Pepsi-Cola division seemed to achieved this objective in 1988, only to have Coca-Cola recapture market leadership by 1991. Nevertheless, Pepsi-Cola proved that through a series of tactical plans, it could compete domestically and globally with Coca-Cola. Each of its plans was designed to make incremental progress toward the strategic objective of equal market share.

The company had to improve its research and development, diversify its product line in diet drinks, change its packaging designs, and modernize its bottling technology. Marketing tactics were developed each year for a variety of ads and promotions that were so effective that Pepsi-Cola had to increase production by more than 40 percent in less than a decade. This growth had to be financed through a series of carefully planned capital expansion programs during the period 1978 to 1986, when it was difficult to attract investors and high interest rates made debt financing expensive. The success of PepsiCo was the combined effect of achieving a succession of plans articulated through strategies, translated into incremental tactical plans, and implemented through effective operations.

While Pepsi-Cola relied on celebrity advertising, including spots by Michael Jackson, Ray Charles, and M. C. Hammer, Coca-Cola continued to reinforce its mystique as the world's most extensive American distributor of soft drinks. The closest Coca-Cola came to celebrity advertising was to approach opera star Luciano Pavarotti for a European endorsement. Coca-Cola, however, quietly added new markets, increased distribution, and diversified its product line to include fruit juices, health drinks, and diet colas.[35] ■

A SYNOPSIS FOR LEARNING

1. **Describe the nature of tactical planning and related managerial roles.**

   Tactical plans usually cover one year, though they may run longer or shorter to fit the needs of the particular business. In tactical plans, managers define activities to complement strategic objectives. Middle managers decide on annual objectives, express them through budgets, and break down major tasks into controllable activities to be accomplished.

2. **Define the key elements of a marketing plan and a marketing program.**

   A marketing plan outlines functional objectives and the activities needed to implement them in support of major strategies. The marketing plan in a diversified company is called a "business-level strategic plan," but for a smaller firm, the marketing plan is a functional plan that breaks down the strategic plan into marketing activities. A marketing program details specific tasks in developing product characteristics, creating price scenarios, formulating advertising and promotional activities, and refining distribution channels.

3. **Explain production planning and how it relates to marketing projections.**

   Production planning starts with a solid sales forecast. Then an aggregate production plan is formulated for each tactical planning period. With a clear idea of total sales expected, production planners can formulate a plan for meeting demand in the most cost-effective way. The sales forecast determines objectives, and production capabilities determine aggregate production schedules. Together, they define tactical activities.

4. Describe human resource planning from a tactical perspective.

   Human resource planning is concerned with people joining and leaving organizations. Tactical human resource objectives are to meet organizational needs with skilled personnel, provide the training required for operational success, and coordinate with other managers the assignments of people to accomplish their tasks. These objectives are achieved through periodic "needs assessments" based on strategic plans and proposed activities in functional areas such as marketing and production.

5. Discuss the responsibilities of financial managers in tactical planning.

   Most financial planning is viewed as strategic, but financial planners have to be involved with tactical and operational planning so they can match resources with organizational needs. During a tactical planning period, financial planners are concerned with profitability, cash flow, and budgeting expenditures so that annual marketing and production objectives will be met. They also interact with other managers to formulate plans consistent with financial limitations imposed by the company and by the economic environment.

6. Describe operational planning responsibilities and the critical task of scheduling.

   Operational planning focuses on immediate activities and performance objectives. Planning activities include three categories of responsibility: scheduling, resource allocation, and productivity planning. Most first-line managers participate in carefully designed operations budgets and schedules for labor, materials, and overhead. Scheduling concerns affect production managers, accounting managers, and training supervisors, among others.

SKILL ANALYSIS

CASE 1 Cow-Milking Technology Attracts Genetic Engineers

A Swedish company, Alfa-Laval, holds nearly 50 percent of the world market in automatic cow-milking machines.[36] Machines used in milking technology—those that scientifically separate cream from milk and water from oil—are among the most sought after purchases in genetic engineering and biotechnology research. The future seems quite promising for Alfa-Laval, but because it is a low-tech and old-line engineering firm, management needs to make a lot of changes to enter the lucrative new market of biotechnology.

Alfa-Laval designed separators years ago to enhance milking operations, then found that, with some minor modifications, the equipment could be used for separating water from oil. This new process led to design modifications for a centrifugal separator that could separate edible protein from plants. The firm then attempted to enter the brewers' market with separators that remove yeast particles from beer. All these activities spanned several decades and represented an earnest attempt to extend the life cycle of basic milking equipment.

Trying to enter the brewers' market had been a major step for Alfa-Laval. The firm had hoped for a surge in sales, but the brewers were not interested. After this major setback, the centrifugal separator was accidentally tested for research use by genetic engineers. Suddenly the firm had new fields to plow.

Alfa-Laval was not ready to actively market its product in 1983, when the genetic market opened up. It had recently gone through several intense years of diversification, which had created a rather confused array of company services and products. The firm also had a lot of "fat" in executive ranks, with some 300 executives at headquarters. After a rather drastic upheaval, Alfa-Laval reorganized and began trimming its ranks. Its strategic plan was simple: become a high-tech company by using the fundamental products it already had, and then couple computer technology with engineering resources to "reposition" itself in the biotech equipment industry. The planning horizon included a two-step action plan, with 1986 penciled in for "real volume production of genetic materials." By 1990, the firm expected to have a solid market share in biotech equipment.

Alfa-Laval also purchased two American "gene-tech" research and development firms before 1990. These acquisitions gave its workers hands-on engineering experience and an inside track on marketing expertise. The firm then purchased interests in several European companies and developed a licensing arrangement for some key equipment. It aimed its U.S. sales pitch at drug manufacturers, such as Eli Lilly & Company, that used separators in hormone production.

To finance this move, Alfa-Laval began selling off companies and operating divisions that no longer matched the strategic profile of a high-tech company. However, the milking machine division was considered a bread-and-butter business that had to be retained. Production planners demonstrated how the firm could enter the high-tech era in milking through computerization, something they realized during a group planning session. Before the meeting, there had been serious concern about keeping the low-tech milking equipment, which basically sold in saturated markets. During the meeting, management discovered that by linking computers to milking controls, one farmer could handle 300 cows rather than 25 a day, as well as complete the milk-processing treatment with improved quality control.

After the firm test-marketed the computer-assisted separators for milking (the same separators as those used in biotech), word leaked out to cheese makers that Alfa-Laval had a system that could boost productivity by nearly 300 percent. Thus the firm found itself in another high-demand market. Buffeted by so many swiftly moving events, executives at Alfa-Laval began to doubt their ability to control their company. Most of their innovations had occurred during a few brief years, after half a century of producing milking machines. Alfa-Laval's engineers were unprepared for the biotech revolution, executive thinking was still mired in old-line technology, and the firm's finances were insufficient to underwrite rapid growth. Consequently, although the company was able to bring its innovations to market and enjoy rapid growth in its sales, it also suffered serious cash-flow losses. These losses were the result of unforeseen expenses for specialists in biotech engineering, high-cost research, and new capital expenditures. Ultimately, before the company could establish its biotech product lines in profitable markets, it was forced to sell these product lines to several European companies.

Case Questions

1. Explain the life cycle concept and illustrate how it influenced product development at Alfa-Laval. In what period of the life cycle are automated milking machines? Computerized milking operations?
2. Discuss the concept of developing customer scenarios for marketing. In this case, what customer profile would you describe for each of the following three products: (a) mechanical milking machines, (b) computer-assisted milking systems, and (c) centrifugal separators?
3. Briefly describe planning roles in terms of (a) finance, (b) production, (c) personnel, and (d) marketing.

VIDEO CASE EuroDisney: Mickey Goes French

In Spring 1992, Mickey, Minnie, and the other familiar Disney characters sported French accents as EuroDisney opened for business. Located just 20 miles outside Paris, the new multibillion-dollar entertainment complex raised a few French eyebrows—some French were put off by what they called "hamburger culture"—as Disney readied itself for business. Plenty of operational planning and building preceded opening day as Disney and its French partners prepared to bring the European market a little taste of Mickey mania!

The facility includes the usual features found in Disney's other theme parks, such as Main Street U.S.A., Fantasy Land, and Adventure Land. Guests at EuroDisney are treated to activities, shows, and rides much like those in the U.S. parks. Getting ready to handle an estimated 11 to 13.5 million visitors annually demanded that Disney executives pay tremendous attention to operational and tactical details.

To get those millions of people to the entertainment complex, the French government extended a commuter line from Paris out to the park, and a special EuroDisney stop for France's high-speed train will eventually be constructed. Making operations at EuroDisney smoother was only part of the total package that Disney negotiated for this project.

Disney put up an astonishingly small amount of money—about $140 million—for the $4 billion project. Buyers of a special EuroDisney stock offering contributed the rest of the financing. Disney owns 49 percent of the equity and earns a 3 percent fee for managing the entire project. The company gets an additional 7.5 percent in royalties for use of the Disney name.

Since marketing the Disney name was crucial to the successful debut of Mickey in Paris, Disney took no chances. It prepared a marketing blitz to entice the French and other Europeans to visit EuroDisney. A special store selling EuroDisney T-shirts and souvenirs was started prior to the park's grand opening. A house-sized model of Sleeping Beauty's Castle was sent on tour throughout Europe, including stops in several Eastern European countries. Opening-day ceremonies for EuroDisney were expected to be covered on European-wide television, providing the park with two hours of essentially free publicity in prime time. All these marketing activities were designed to ensure that the European love affair with Mickey Mouse progressed beyond the fantasy stage. Especially responsible for fulfilling that fantasy were the thousands of employees hired by EuroDisney. Disney was just as thorough in its operational details here as it was in other areas.

The squeaky-clean image and strict dress code mandated by the company stirred up a controversy when EuroDisney recruited in London. The company is very exacting about its employees' clothing and appearance. One job seeker complained, "What's unfair is they ask you to take your nose ring out. It's the smallest one I've got, and are they that strict?" But Disney is adamant about how its employees look because employees are part of the image the company is trying to project. Long hair, beards, mustaches, and large earrings have no place in that image.

This great attention to details has contributed to Disney's global success. In all areas of its operations, Disney, which also has a park in Japan, does not risk making a mistake. Its coverage of each aspect of operations ensures that Mickey, Minnie, and the other Disney characters will continue to be part of the global culture.

Case Questions

1. What were some key elements of Disney's marketing plan and program?
2. How did Disney plan for the "production" of its product at EuroDisney?
3. What type of human resources planning did Disney employ in opening EuroDisney?
4. What role did financial planning play in the EuroDisney project?

Sources: Michael Williams and Terry Ilott, "Disney Puttin' on the Blitz," *Variety,* March 2, 1992, Vol. 346, No. 7, p. 1ff; Beth Kobliner, "Next Stop: EuroDisney!" *Money,* March 1992, Vol. 21, No. 3, p. 155ff; and "Riding Out EuroDisney's Razzamatazz," *Marketing,* February 27, 1992, p. 16.

DEVELOPING A TIME PLAN

SKILL PRACTICE

Introduction

Managers and books on managing frequently stress the importance of scheduling work and people to perform that work. One critical aspect is often missing in this effort: We often fail to schedule our own time and energy wisely. Our time is our scarcest resource. It is not endless and it is *not replaceable.* We *can* make more money; we *cannot* make more time!

Some people seem to be able to take on one more project and still get everything done on time. Others have relatively little to do and still have difficulty judging priorities and getting tasks done on schedule. The difference between these two groups of people is usually one of *recognizing and acting on priorities.* Not *all* our activities are of equal importance, so we can benefit from better planning based on a system of priorities. The three-tiered system of categories described here is helpful.

Often people use the phrase "as soon as possible" in their requests. This is *not* helpful because it does not specify when something *really* needs to be done, and all assignments *do* have a real deadline. It is far more effective to state specifically when something needs to be done—and sometimes stating *why* that is the target is also helpful. Knowing real deadlines also helps us decide what priority (level of urgency) is appropriate.

Our bodies also have personal (unique) time rhythms. Some people are very alert and productive in the morning hours, others during the aftenoon, and still others during late afternoon and evening. Look back on your own activity patterns. When are you most effective during a twenty-four hour period? Is this fairly consistent for you over a period of time, say six months or more? When do you usually take on your *toughest* jobs (assuming you have some flexibility in scheduling work)? Would you do things differently if you had *more* flexibility?

Another way to look at time planning is to view all work in *two* dimensions: importance and urgency. Not all tasks are urgent. Think of some tasks you are doing *right now.* Place them in the diagram below:

Importance

Urgency		High	Low
	High		
	Low		

Source: Adapted with permission of the Publisher from Travers, "Supervision: Techniques and New Dimensions," Copyright 1987, Prentice-Hall, Inc.

CATEGORY/PRIORITY	DESCRIPTION OF ITEM
I (Top)	Urgent directives, changes in high priorities, crisis conditions. (Such work should receive attention within 24 hours.)
II (Moderate)	Continuing projects, changes in sequencing of earlier "moderate" projects, new work with no clear priority preassigned. (Such work should receive attention within 5 days.)
III (Low)	Incidental assignments. "For Your Information" material, copies of memos where others are the principal actors, general reading material. (Such work should receive attention within 5 to 30 days.)

Instructions

1. Take some time to mentally review the tasks you have committed yourself to do for one week starting with *today.* (approximately 5 minutes)
2. Enter those commitments on the schedule that appears below. (Note the rectangles do not necessarily equal 30-minute time blocks.) Enter *specific* times where an appointment or deadline is firm. There will probably be other deadlines that you have agreed to that you can't recall right now. Add these items as you think of them throughout the rest of today. (approximately 20 minutes)

A Sample Planning Calendar

TIME	Monday	Tuesday	Wednesday	Thursday	Friday	Saturday	Sunday
7 A.M.							
8:00							
9:00							
10:00							
11:00							
12:00							
1 P.M.							
2:00							
3:00							
4:00							
5:00							
6:00							
7:00							

3. Review your entries. Which ones are important? Which ones are difficult and mentally demanding? Place an "I" beside those entries that are important, and a "D" beside those that are demanding. (approximately 5–8 minutes)
4. Review the entries that you have marked with a "D." Can any of those be moved to a time when you usually are at your best? If so, try to arrange this. (Note those entries that have been moved for this reason.) (approximately 5–10 minutes)
5. Your instructor will randomly select people from the class a week from today to give a brief report on how their week went. Special emphasis will be paid to Important and Demanding events, especially those events that you were able to move to a more effective time period.

Xerox Redefines Its Purpose and Plans for the 1990s

Under the guidance of founder Joseph C. Wilson, Xerox was the hot growth company of the 1960s. Wilson acquired exclusive world rights to inventor Chester F. Carlson's xerographic process and changed the way people work. By 1966, the company dominated the copier market and had made the name "Xerox" synonymous with photo reproduction. Wilson's singular strategy was to make Xerox equipment the best in the world. Because of its tremendous growth, he also established financial controls and clear lines of authority.

Wilson handed the CEO's baton to C. Peter McColough, who drove Xerox to become one of the nation's most profitable companies during the 1970s. A Harvard M.B.A. who had managed the recruitment and training of Xerox's remarkable sales force, McColough transformed management structure by recruiting executives from big-name companies. He diversified Xerox by acquiring new companies, many of them in the insurance, real estate, and investment fields. He also took Xerox global with acquisitions or corporate ventures in Canada, Japan, Mexico, and the United Kingdom.

The bright gleam of McColough's speedy success faded quickly. Although at first his organizational reforms produced good results, eventually they made Xerox too bureaucratic. Management became preoccupied with achieving financial objectives rather than with creating innovative, high-quality products. Also, McColough's diversification strategy had no planned direction other than to add businesses with potential short-term profits. Haphazard diversification of the corporate portfolio sorely complicated decisions about future growth plans. Meanwhile, major competitors—Eastman Kodak, IBM, NEC, Ricoh, and Canon—submarined Xerox's products and grabbed a hefty part of the copier market.

When David T. Kearns became the company's third CEO in 1982, Xerox was in serious decline, no longer dominant in the copier market and uncompetitive in personal computers and network communications. Management was top-heavy, and bureaucratic inefficiencies had reduced planning to a series of disjointed decisions. By 1987, however, Kearns had begun to turn the firm around. Xerox earned $465 million that year, well below record-setting earlier years, but total revenues were up by 60 percent over 1982, to $12.9 billion. The company's return on equity was 9.5 percent, only about half that achieved in its best year, but Kearns had positioned Xerox for the long run with a strategy of quality product development and a commitment to excellent planning.

A quality strategy had been essential. When Kearns took the reigns as president and CEO, the major Japanese competitors had a 40 to 50 percent cost advantage in copiers. In Kearns's view, Xerox had not realized the severity of its poor-quality problems because the bureaucracy had obscured flaws. He implemented a crash program aimed at quality planning that included eliminating 15,000 jobs—many in higher management—and introduced shop-floor quality team planning systems. He also trimmed purchasing, reducing the number of vendors from nearly 5,000 to fewer than 400. This was a significant change strongly resisted by purchasing managers who were convinced that thousands of vendors locked in competition had kept prices down and quality up. Kearns proved otherwise. With a small staff and good planning, Xerox achieved a 99.2 percent quality record in 1987 (less than 1 percent defects) compared to a 92.0 percent record four years earlier (8 percent defects).

By 1991, when Paul A. Allaire became the new chairman and CEO of Xerox, Kearn's plans were paying off. Allaire built on this success by strengthening the company's human resources and its global strategies. Under Allaire, minority recruiting was stepped up and performance-based promotions opened the door to higher-level management positions for minorities and women. Today 20 percent of the company's managers are minorities and 30 percent are women. As chairman of the global-consolidated Xerox Corporation, Allaire emphasized Xerox's mission as a "document processing company" and determined that quality and product innovation would drive the company into the twenty-first century. Document processing is defined clearly by Xerox as equipment, systems, software, and support technology required in business offices and information processing. In order to concentrate on this mission, many of the company's diversified services had to be sold—a process Kearns started in the late 1980s when he divested the company's interests in auto insurance and global casualty underwriting. Allaire has closed down or sold divisions involved in real estate development, and although Xerox maintains extensive real estate holdings and financial investment services, these are not allowed to interfere with the strategic thrust in document processing.

Looking back on the 1970s and early 1980s, Xerox executives concede that despite periods of robust profits, the firm had lost its direction and was indecisive about its role. The new approach for the 1990s builds on the distinct competency of Xerox technology in document processing to focus on office systems, electronic printers, networks and software, and the reprographic quality Xerox can assure customers. Xerox won the Malcolm Baldrige National Quality Award in 1990, a signal to the world that the company had regained its winning form. And for 1991, Xerox was able to report to stockholders a return on assets of 14.6 percent, nearly double the average rate achieved during the 1980s. Gross revenue exceeded $18 billion—a record for Xerox—and profits were $605 million. Its overseas affiliates in Asia and Europe were equally profitable.

Allaire attributed much of this success to changes initiated by Kearns to empower employees with decision-making authority. Allaire has taken the empowerment concept two steps further in 1992 by establishing a planning and decision-making system that relies on management teams at each level of the organization and by creating an "executive team" to share the office of president. Instead of having one person as president, Xerox has a "presidental team" consisting of six top executives who divide responsibilities for global marketing and strategic portfolio management. Nine new product divisions were also created, each with a group vice president responsible for one of the company's focal categories of business. Major strategies are formulated at the top and reinforce the company's product focus and quality commitment. Division-level managers drive the business-level group strategies and coordinate tactical planning systems below them. Middle and first-line managers are expected to work closely with their employees to implement operational action plans through management teams and self-directed work groups. Consequently, there is a new intensity at Xerox to revive the entrepreneurial culture of its founder through focused planning systems and motivated employees who are empowered to control more of their activities.

Case Questions

1. Describe and contrast the planning system that existed at Xerox during the 1970s and the one that exists now. Explore potential advantages and disadvantages of both planning systems.
2. Identify and explain the three major strategies employed by Xerox during the tenure of its three chief executive officers.
3. Explore the quality issues discussed in the case. How would an 8 percent defective parts and components ratio affect profits, and why would having fewer vendors lead to improved quality performance?
4. In making a competitive analysis, what issues would you want to have developed if you were chairman of Xerox? What competitive factors are most important to help Xerox reach its objectives during the 1990s?

Sources: John A. Byrne, "Culture Shock at Xerox," *Business Week*, June 22, 1987, pp. 106–110; Joel Dreyfuss, "What Do You Do for an Encore?" *Fortune,* December 19, 1988, pp. 111–116; Gary Jacobson and John Hillkirk, *Xerox: American Samurai* (New York: Macmillan, 1986), pp. 1–4, 29; Kenneth Labich, "The Innovators," *Fortune*, June 6, 1988 pp. 50–56, 60, 64; "Xerox Emerges as the Document Company: President's Message to Shareholders," *Xerox Annual Report*, March 8, 1991; Suein L. Hwang, "Xerox Forms New Structure for Printer, Copier Businesses, Creates New Office," *Wall Street Journal,* February 5, 1992, p. B6; and Amanda Bennett, "Firms Run by Executive Teams Can Reap Rewards, Incur Risks," *Wall Street Journal*, February 5, 1992, pp. B1, B5.

9

Organizing: Bringing Together People and Resources

OUTLINE

Why Organizing Is Important

Division of Work
Potential Problems of Specialization
Horizontal Job Specialization
Vertical Job Specialization
Job Enlargement
Job Enrichment
Balancing Specialization for Productivity

Bureaucratic and Organic Structures
Bureaucratic Structures
Organic Structures
Bureaucratic and Organic Structures Critiqued

Contingency Theory and Organizational Structures
Age and Size
Technology
The Technological Imperative
Environmental Contingencies
Power and Personal Attributes in Management

Informal Structures Within Organizations
Costs and Benefits of Informal Structures
Managing Informal Structures

Evolution of Organizations
Phase 1: Creativity
Phase 2: Direction
Phase 3: Delegation
Phase 4: Coordination
Phase 5: Collaboration

Service Organizations in Perspective
Characteristics of Service Organizations

OBJECTIVES

- Discuss why organizing is an important management function.
- Explain the concepts of job enlargement and job enrichment.
- Describe and contrast bureaucratic and organic structures.
- Explain the environmental factors that influence organizational structure.
- Discuss the nature of informal patterns of organizational structures.
- Examine how firms grow and change in dynamic environments.
- Describe the characteristics of service organizations.

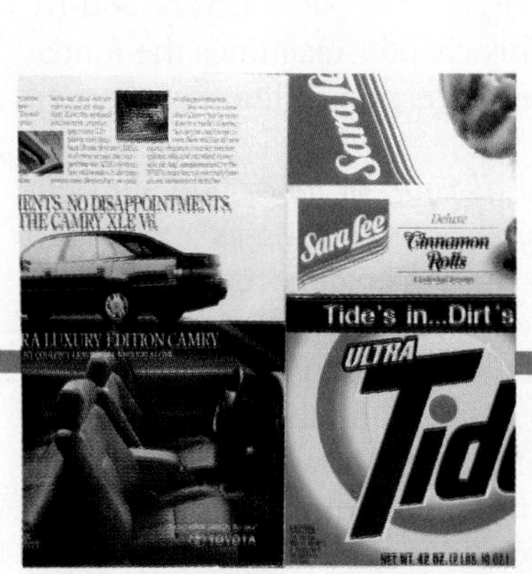

SAATCHI & SAATCHI Advertising Worldwide began to globally reorganize its business in 1991 to create a more *centralized* company.[1] At first glance, the new centralized structure seems illogical both because more and more of the company's clients are international companies and because other service businesses—banks, securities brokers, and competing advertising companies—are rapidly *decentralizing* operations. A decentralized firm, as we shall see later in this part of the text, tends to set up subsidiaries or semiautonomous divisions where lower-level managers have greater operational authority. In contrast, a centralized structure consolidates authority under key senior executives at the home office. With more international clients, why would Saatchi want to centralize?

Saatchi's global shift can perhaps be explained in terms of its clients. The company's client list includes Procter & Gamble, Sara Lee Corporation, British Airways, and Toyota Motor Corporation, among others that range from European rock stars to Asian high-tech semiconductor manufacturers. Most of these clients operate major international divisions in dozens of countries. Sara Lee, for example, markets retail desserts and confectioneries in such far-flung places as the People's Republic of China, Brazil, Spain, Great Britain, and Israel. Toyota and P&G have operations on four continents, and British Air has direct service to fifty-three countries with linked airways to eighty more. Saatchi is expected to handle advertising for these clients in their domestic and overseas endeavors, and if the company were to maintain local service for each client, Saatchi would need more than 300 foreign offices. Many of these offices might require only one or two employees, while core business centers in London or Tokyo would require a substantial staff.

Saatchi apparently decided that such a global effort would result in corporate disintegration and major coordination problems. Also, a client like British Air would be better served by having its global interests handled by one responsible account team working closely together. During the 1980s, Saatchi had followed the trend toward decentralization with affiliates and offices throughout Europe and Asia. The agency is now reorganizing to have executive account teams headquartered in the United States who have global experience and the freedom to travel extensively. Technology played an important role in Saatchi's decision. With advances in telecommunications and network computer systems, Saatchi will have around-the-clock, on-line service to clients and account teams throughout the world.

organizing
The function of gathering resources, allocating resources, and structuring tasks to fulfill organizational plans.

Managers *organize* as a natural extension of their planning efforts. As previously stated, planning provides organizational objectives and a framework for accomplishing those objectives. **Organizing** is the function of gathering resources, allocating resources, and structuring tasks to fulfill organizational plans. Consequently, management must determine what tasks must be done, who is to do them, and who will make decisions about those tasks.[2] As we shall see, many circumstances affect how organizing takes place. Saatchi's management, for example, was influenced by a rapidly expanding international clientele that required a team to provide closer client services. That requirement affected the entire organizational structure and responsibilities of the company's managers and staff. This chapter examines the fundamental concept of organizing, focusing on managerial responsibilities concerned with human activity.

Organized human activity results from a logical *division of labor* and a system of *coordination*. We typically think of these two aspects of organizing as applying to large, complex organizations, but they are applicable to any group activity. Organizing has three dimensions. First, the organization itself has a form—a configuration that describes the management hierarchy and formal channels of communication. Second, through the process of organizing, tasks are defined and individual jobs are structured. Third, a philosophy of organization influences how coordination is achieved. We begin by describing why organizing is important, examine the concept of division of labor, then address the three major considerations of the organizing function. In a concluding section, we describe particular organizing issues for service enterprises.

WHY ORGANIZING IS IMPORTANT

Effective organization of both human and material resources ultimately increases productivity. This is done through synergism, whereby an organization's members, who combine their efforts to collectively accomplish tasks that would far exceed the simple sum of their individual efforts. Synergy is achieved through the integration of specialized tasks. Specifically, effective organizing provides the following benefits:[3]

1. Clarity of individual performance expectations and specialized tasks.
2. Division of work that avoids duplication, conflict, and misuse of resources, both material and human.
3. A logical flow of work activities that can be comfortably performed by individuals or groups.
4. Established channels of communication that enhance decision making and control.
5. Coordinating mechanisms that ensure harmony among organization members engaged in diversified activities.
6. Focused efforts that relate to objectives logically and efficiently.
7. Appropriate authority structures with accountability to enhance planning and controlling throughout the organization.

As you have learned, management *effectiveness* means doing the right things, whereas *efficiency* implies doing things right. Organizing benefits both. Effectiveness is improved by obtaining the right resources and organizing management and employees to work together toward organizational objectives, and efficiency is improved by using the most productive combinations of material and human resources.

At the core of organization is the *division of work* to logically design tasks and clarify individual performance expectations. Division of work is the fundamental force in industrialization that describes how organizational work is to be accomplished.

> **CHECKPOINT**
> - How does organizing complement planning?
> - Why is organizing concerned with coordinating both people and resources?

DIVISION OF WORK

Organizations divide their labor into specialized tasks to improve productivity. They have done this through history, but Adam Smith was the first to coin the term *division of labor* in *The Wealth of Nations,* written in 1776. His famous example of making pins is worth repeating:

> One man draws out the wire, another straights it, a third cuts it, a fourth points it, a fifth grinds it at the top for receiving a head; to make the head requires two or three distinct operations; to put it on is a peculiar business, to whiten the pins is another; it is even a trade by itself to put them into the papers.[4]

Smith showed that ten specialists, each working on one task to complete a pin, produced 4,800 pins per day, but that when the same number of men worked individually to make a complete pin, they produced only 200 pins per day. Figure 9-1 shows the task components and the derived specialized jobs for pin making in Adam Smith's time. Improved productivity of pin making resulted from task specialization, but several elements of organizing, taken for granted today, also evolved.

specialization
The planned division of work into individual tasks that can be repeated efficiently.

standardization
Making work uniform throughout repeated use of similar methods, machines, and materials to achieve similar and predictable results over time.

Specialization is the planned division of work into individual tasks that can be repeated efficiently. The process of planning these tasks is called *work simplification,* which means breaking down work into its most common elements, such as Adam Smith's ten jobs for making a pin. As employees repeat a task, they become better at it. Using similar methods, machines, and materials repeatedly hones their abilities, and the work becomes standardized. **Standardization** means uniform work with predictable results. Managers must also be concerned with matching employees to tasks according to their abilities. Assigning tasks to individuals best suited

FIGURE 9-1 Specialization

Task Components

Individual Pin Maker:

- Makes wire for pins
- Draws wire and smooths
- Cuts wire for each pin
- Points each pin
- Grinds heads for each pin
- Makes heads
- Attaches heads to pins
- Buffs and paints each pin
- Packages approved batches
- Boxes for shipment to customer

Diffused Specialties

Wire Maker:	batches wire
Straightener:	stretches and smooths wire
Cutter:	cuts wire pins to proper lengths
Pointer:	points pins
Grinder:	grinds pins for head assembly
Assembler:	attaches heads
Finisher:	buffs and paints
Inspector:	checks products
Packager:	puts pins in sized packets
Boxer:	boxes packets for shipment

for them enhances utilization and increases efficiency. In pin making, for example, one individual may be much better at grinding pin points than at packing.

Specialization suggests expertise in a narrow range of tasks in complicated circumstances. Surgeons, lawyers, engineers, and scientists attain high degrees of specialization in extremely complex and challenging occupations. Specialization implies that individuals can physically perform a limited range of tasks efficiently and can psychologically juggle a limited number of skills. By becoming expert and then coordinating results with other experts, employees achieve excellence and productivity.

Potential Problems of Specialization

Managers cannot approach organizing without some apprehension about the effects of specialization on people. It is difficult to envision a life of packing pins every day. Boredom, fatigue, and emotional burnout can occur if the job is so dehumanized that people become mere biological counterparts to their machines. So while specialization is essential, excess specialization can create problems.

These potential problems can take several forms. Employees may become so fatigued by monotonous work that any productivity gains achieved through specialization are canceled out by absenteeism, resignations, strikes, and labor disputes. But productivity losses need not be so obvious. Employees may simply become alienated from their jobs, take longer breaks, become cynical about management, resist innovation, or become incapable of adapting to circumstances.[5] Therefore, it is essential to organize individual jobs so that potential problems are minimized while the benefits of specialized tasks are maximized. This is called *work design*.

work design
The process of structuring individual jobs, integrating them within work groups, and making work efficient and interesting.

Work design is the process of structuring individual jobs, integrating them within work groups, and making work efficient and interesting. For example, managers at Walt Disney World fill 1,100 different jobs with more than 25,000 full-time and part-time employees each year, and they do it through a philosophy of organization that makes each person important. Walt Disney once said, "You can dream, create, design, and build the most wonderful place in the world . . . but it requires people to make the dream a reality."[6] He believed that if an organization was anything, it was its people. Jobs are carefully designed for specialized work, ranging from street sweepers on Main Street to actors playing Mickey Mouse or Pluto, but they are also made as interesting as possible. For example, all employees are expected to help define their own tasks, to bring individuality to each "role," and to make suggestions for improving their "performance."

The Disney organization is unique, but many of the concepts it uses in organizing people are applicable to most other firms. As we look closer at organizing, and later in Chapter 11 at individual job design, these concepts will become clearer. The important point here is that every organization must design jobs and make them both productive and interesting. Among the more notable authors who have researched and written about these issues are Chris Argyris, Warren Bennis, Frederick Herzberg, Rensis Likert, and Douglas McGregor.[7] These scholars have produced a significant body of literature about leadership, a topic that we discuss at length in Part Four, but we note here a fundamental conclusion from their research: Although formalization of work through specialization is essential, *behavioral* relationships must complement one another to ensure cooperation and enhance job satisfaction. The critical question is how to organize work without creating an organizational pathology of behavioral dysfunctions. We will discuss concepts of organizing with this question in mind.

Horizontal Job Specialization

horizontal job specialization
The result of dividing complicated tasks into simpler jobs or operations, reducing the scope of tasks.

Horizontal job specialization results from dividing complicated tasks into simpler jobs. Adam Smith's example of pin manufacturing is the classic illustration of how the *scope* of a task is reduced by narrowing the breadth of workers' activities. Pin

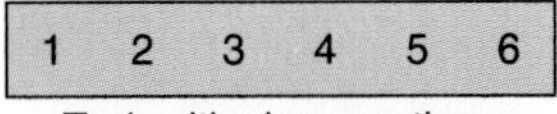

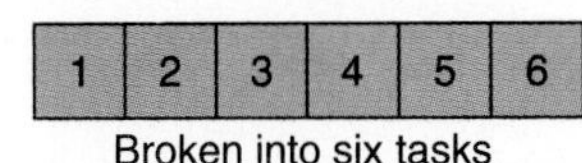

FIGURE 9-2 Horizontal Job Specialization

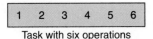

making was broken down into logical divisions of work and individual performance was sharply defined and standardized. Figure 9-2 shows how one task with six operations is divided into six individual tasks, each one coordinated with the others. Horizontal job specialization applies equally to a group of tribal hunters in Borneo who assign different individuals the tasks of stalking, killing, skinning, and cooking meat and to a corporation such as ITT with worldwide operations to coordinate.

Vertical Job Specialization

Vertical job specialization results from delegating responsibilities for tasks and decisions to subordinates. Thus the *depth* of a job becomes shallower as subordinates assume decision-making burdens previously shouldered by the superior. As organizations evolve from small entrepreneurial firms into large complex enterprises, new tasks emerge that require further subdivision of work. A small shopowner such as a tailor who makes men's clothes may initially measure clients, purchase materials, make suits, and sell them, as well as run the entire business. As the business grows, he may hire apprentices and train them to specialize in making parts of each suit. The tailor will then do less tailoring and more overseeing of others' work. As the business further expands, the tailor will become so engrossed in management decisions that he will need an organization of salespersons, craftsmen, and support staff. This process is typical of any growing firm. As management jobs become too burdensome, there is a downward reassignment of tasks and authority, as Figure 9-3 illustrates.

vertical job specialization The result of delegating responsibilities for tasks and decisions to subordinates, thereby compressing the depth of tasks.

In this figure, the organizational tasks of designing, making, and selling have been horizontally specialized, and the *depth* of each job has been reduced to exclude decision making that vertically differentiates tasks. For example, when Victor Kiam bought Remington Products, Inc., the firm that makes Remington Electric Shavers, in 1981, there were 480 employees in one Bridgeport, Connecticut, plant. Kiam as CEO ran the business with six senior executives in production, sales, engineering, and staff support positions. Now, Remington has more than 2,000 employees and 80 senior managers with more sharply defined responsibilities.[8] In Remington's engineering section, there are several departments for product development, product design, and quality assurance, each responsible for products such as the Lektro Blade Razor and the Remington Pool Alarm.

FIGURE 9-3 Vertical Job Specialization

Job Enlargement

job enlargement
An organizational development technique for combining two or more tasks into one, usually at one level of skill, to add variety, reduce boredom, or improve efficiency in work.

Job enlargement is the process of combining tasks to create a new job with broader activities. It is concerned with the breadth of work. Boredom and dissatisfaction are combated by adding more operations to a given task. Employees perform a wider range of tasks, but without vertical integration of decision making. Job enlargement is the antithesis of specialization.

In manufacturing, for example, two specialized job classifications have evolved called "machine operators" and "machine set-up technicians." For a production run of automobile bumpers, a metal-pressing machine will be set up by a technician who rigs the machine and makes adjustments to conform to design specifications. Then a machine operator who has no part in the set-up procedures runs the machine to make bumpers. In many companies, these two jobs are being combined so that machine operation and set-up tasks are components of one person's job.

Similar job combinations have been implemented in many companies, particularly when improved technology and training make it possible for workers to be more efficient. At Firestone, for example, machine operators skilled at running rubber vulcanizing equipment also perform their own quality control tests with computerized monitoring equipment. At Pacific Bell, sales representatives also train new employees and conduct market research as consumer consultants. In each instance, jobs have been enlarged to challenge employees by expanding the breadth of their activities. The result has been satisfied employees who are more productive. There is, however, the danger of enlarging a job too much. Too many managers, in their enthusiasm to improve productivity (or cut costs), have added job activities that become stressful, and the result is lower-quality work with reduced productivity.[9]

Job Enrichment

As discussed earlier, specialization is necessary for a firm to grow, but it can create problems such as boredom, fatigue, and stress. If carried to extremes, vertical job specialization pigeonholes subordinates into decision-making roles that are isolated and emotionally deadening. To combat the problems of overspecialization, jobs are often *enriched*.

job enrichment
The vertical combination of tasks that increases one's duties and responsibilities; job depth is enhanced to improve job satisfaction.

Job enrichment is the process of expanding a person's responsibilities so that the work becomes more challenging and satisfying. Specialized tasks are expanded in *job depth* to include greater decision-making responsibilities. Individual jobs are enriched by combining vertical relationships, so that machine operators monitor and correct their own mistakes, for example, instead of being monitored by inspectors and having their own errors corrected by other operators. This gives employees greater autonomy for controlling their work and making decisions.[10] They become more than workers as they share in decisions about *how* to perform tasks and *what* tasks should be accomplished.

Job enrichment often occurs through a process of reorganizing management responsibilities. At Aluminum Company of America (Alcoa), for example, four layers of executive management were dissolved and their responsibilities reassigned. Top management appeared to take on far-reaching duties by having Alcoa's twenty-five business group heads report directly to the chairman, but the reverse occurred: The twenty-five group executives assumed greater top-management strategic management authority, and they were also expected to coordinate many lower-level functions. These managers, in turn, delegated more responsibility to lower-level managers, and first-line managers developed work teams giving their employees authority over many daily decisions. Du Pont also abolished several management layers, reducing executive positions by nearly 50 percent in 1991. This reorganization required remaining managers and employees to share more decisions. At Du Pont, the change was accomplished through job enrichment programs that retrained employees to make decisions about budgeting, purchasing, and other activities previously carried out by middle managers.[11]

Enrichment programs do not have to be all-embracing efforts at company reorganization. More often, they are accomplished by redefining individual jobs and group activities. Clerical duties, for example, can be redefined so that typists' work includes making decisions about correspondence, arranging travel, or coordinating data processing. Work activities can also be grouped, and a team of employees can be given responsibility for managing its activities. These are called autonomous work groups and are discussed thoroughly in Chapter 11.

Balancing Specialization for Productivity

Henry Mintzberg believes that "job enlargement pays to the extent that the gains from better-motivated workers in a particular job offset the losses from less than optimal technical specialization."[12] Jobs enlarged to extremes, as noted earlier, can create problems: Overloaded employees may perform poorly or quit. People also vary in their abilities and preferences to handle enlarged jobs. Some prefer the clarity of simple tasks, whereas others like diversification. Striking the right balance becomes even more crucial with job enrichment because some employees try to avoid decision making, preferring instead to work in less demanding positions, while others enjoy the responsibility of making decisions and are eager to assume greater leadership roles.

Job organization has come a long way from the simple division of labor observed by Adam Smith, yet experts have very few solid suggestions about *how* to design jobs or *when* integration of tasks will be beneficial. We do know that enlargement and enrichment concepts coupled with careful analysis of job design are crucial for assuring productivity. We also know that before a job enlargement or job enrichment program can be developed, managers must account for individual differences among their employees and for circumstances peculiar to their company. For example, union collective bargaining agreements may prevent combining jobs. The ultimate rationale for improving jobs is to improve the quality of work and productivity in the work environment.

Organizing and designing jobs have come to be synonymous with *quality of work life,* known by its acronym *QWL,* and QWL programs have become synonymous with productivity improvement efforts. **Quality of work life** is the concept of making work meaningful for employees in an environment where they are motivated to perform and satisfied with the results of their work.[13] This is a version of personal *improvement,* a concept discussed in Chapter 2. The behavioral implications of this discussion will be treated in Part Four, on leadership.

quality of work life (QWL)
The concept of making work meaningful for employees in an environment where they are motivated to perform and satisfied with their work.

CHECKPOINT

- Define and explain specialization and standardization.
- How is work design related to organizing people and resources?
- Contrast horizontal and vertical job specialization.
- Discuss how jobs are enlarged and enriched.

BUREAUCRATIC AND ORGANIC STRUCTURES

bureaucracy
A form of organization in which activities are rationally defined, work is divided unambiguously, and authority is formalized through prescribed skills and responsibilities.

Formalized organizations, particularly in the public sector, tend to be labeled *bureaucracies.* A **bureaucracy** is a form of organization in which activities are rationally defined, division of work is unambiguous, and managerial authority is explicitly vested in individuals according to skills and responsibilities prescribed for their organizations. "Organic" implies a flexible entity, one "full of life." As polar extremes, both stereotypes may be unrealistic; they simply differ by degree of *standardization*.

As organizations grow, new jobs are created and relationships become more complex as organizations grow. To reduce confusion, individual and group tasks are formalized during the growth process, with the result that jobs become more narrowly defined and tasks more standardized. Standardization may also result from management policies and legal mandates ranging from safety procedures to equal opportunity laws. Laws and rules impose constraints and lead to internal policies and procedures to guide management decisions. Policies and procedures do not necessarily impose constraints, but when combined with technological requirements, they do lead to standardization and greater bureaucracy.

Bureaucratic Structures

As we saw in Chapter 2, the German sociologist Max Weber coined the word *bureaucracy*.[14] He has been credited (or discredited) with creating an organization form that has dominated Western civilization during the twentieth century, one that is inflexible, formal, coldly rational, and dehumanizing. Weber, however, created nothing; he merely described and put a name to what he saw in European organizations at the turn of the century. Today we recognize five characteristics of modern bureaucracies.[15]

1. *Fixed and official jurisdictions of authority.* Activities are governed by rules and regulations that fix decision-making parameters, align specific duties, and strictly define command privileges.
2. *Firmly established rational chains of command.* Graded levels of authority are structured in an absolute hierarchy with a narrow span of control over subordinates. It is the positions that are defined, not the individual roles within them. Therefore, vacancies are filled by individuals who meet defined criteria; positions are not redefined to suit individual characteristics.
3. *Quantified and thoroughly documented information.* Nearly everything is reduced to writing in bureaucracies. Decisions and conferences are recorded, files are maintained, and allocations are quantified, which creates complex administration systems.
4. *Supposition of expertise.* Because positions are filled by individuals who have met defined criteria, it is assumed that people at each skill level have expertise. Selection for employment, then, is based on job skills; promotions are made according to job criteria rather than personal attributes.
5. *Management is technically scientific.* Although the art of management is recognized as important, managers of bureaucratic organizations rely on rules and procedures. This reliance leads to the assumption that once managers learn administrative processes, they will have the technical knowledge for managing organizations.

chain of command
A vertical line of authority between successively higher levels of management, unbroken and direct, linking each stratum in the hierarchy of management.

span of control
The effective number of subordinates who report to a superior in a given work environment.

Two specific attributes mentioned under characteristic 2 should be explained: *chain of command* and *span of control*. A **chain of command** is the unbroken line of authority between the lowest and highest positions in an organization. It is the description of rank-ordered authority, and in a bureaucracy, there is a presumption that a subordinate will seek direction, communicate decisions, and take orders directly from an immediate superior. A **span of control** is defined by the number of subordinates one manager supervises. In a bureaucracy, the assumption is that an optimal span of control can be unambiguously determined by rationally studying how work is performed and what decisions must be made by the manager. Bureaucracies typically have narrow spans of control whereby managers supervise few subordinates. This results in many levels of management in which little authority is delegated. In contrast, a wide span of control exists where fewer managers supervise many employees, which is a feature of team-managed environments.[16]

Organic Structures

In the classic 1966 article "The Coming Death of Bureaucracy," theorist Warren Bennis heavily criticized bureaucracies and proposed that we create *organic* organizations.[17] According to Bennis, we have outgrown our need for a rational form of organization modeled on machine efficiency and explicit, inflexible lines of authority. In this view, Weber's ideal of a rational organization was a response to the "irrational" world of work of the Victorian age, when employees labored under capricious managers and subjective rules. Formalized organizations brought order and provided employees with protection.

In contrast, Bennis believes today's world of rapid change, complex technology, and diversified knowledge requires flexible patterns of organization. In his view, bureaucracies are ill-adapted to the evolving management philosophy of humanistic values with democratic ideals. In place of bureaucracy, Bennis has proposed flexible organizations, with executives as coordinators and employees organized according to their personal skills. His article heralded the arrival of organizations based on groups of projects rather than on stratified authority. As we shall see in Chapter 10, many of these changes are taking place, but bureaucracies have not disappeared. To the contrary, the sheer size and complexity of contemporary organizations often lead to greater rationalization.

Bureaucratic and Organic Structures Critiqued

Milestone research by Tom Burns and George Stalker illustrated that bureaucratic structures are preferred in stable environments and mature industries, but that when the environment is uncertain or an industry is experiencing rapid change, bureaucracies are ineffective.[18] Burns and Stalker concluded that *mechanistic* forms of organization such as bureaucracies are too inflexible and too burdened with impersonal rules to be effective in dynamic environments.

In contrast, they found that *organic* organizations appear to be quite adaptable to change. Managers in such organizations are comfortable with individual decision making and informal patterns of communication. They also work with few rules and procedures, and thus have great latitude for making decisions. Yet too much latitude, particularly in large companies, can result in chaos. Burns and Stalker concluded that where adaptability and speed of innovation are essential, the organic form of organization is superior, but that in stable environments and in organizations so complex as to need careful coordination, the bureaucratic approach is superior.

If we view bureaucratic and organic structures as models at opposite ends of a continuum, then organizations in more or less stable environments are more likely to be bureaucratic, whereas those in more or less unstable environments are more likely to be organic. Few organizations are likely to be totally bureaucratic or totally organic. Most organizations have a natural tendency to formalize jobs and authority to improve predictability of managerial decisions and results of operations. Consequently, a company's primary operations tend to conform to bureaucratic processes, but in other areas of a firm, such as a research design department, work may require creativity and people are more likely to resist bureaucratic conformity. In these environments, organic—informal or loosely structured—relationships are common. In strategic management positions where executives interact with an uncertain outside world, behavior is likely to be more fluid because structured rules and procedures could seriously handicap these executives in their duties.

Sheer momentum of growth often makes companies too bureaucratic, and decision making becomes mired in rules and procedures. Compaq Computer Corporation, for example, was known during the 1980s as a highly innovative company that could react quickly to market changes. As Compaq grew, however, management became highly structured with a great deal of standardization and a rigid reporting system—in effect, a form of bureaucratic stagnation developed that led to lagging sales and unprofitable operations. In late 1991, Compaq made major organizational changes, eliminating about 1,400 people in unnecessary positions, including five top managers, and giving managers and employees greater latitude to make decisions without having to go through a complicated chain of command. Compaq's new CEO, Eckhard Pfeiffer, described the company's old management structure as unfocused, bogged down, and too slow to respond to change. With a smaller staff and a leaner organization, Pfeiffer expects managers to pursue innovations and emphasize individuality, thus regaining the responsiveness the company was once noted for.[19]

As described in the next section, there are many circumstances that influence how a company's structure evolves. However, Mintzberg has provided a conceptual model of the prevailing structure in complex organizations.[20] Shown in Figure 9-4, this model organization has five parts, each one capable of evolving independent patterns of behavior. The strategic apex is likely to be organic and relations among top managers will be highly interactive; the technostructure and support staff at

FIGURE 9-4 Major Components of Organizations

Source: Henry Mintzberg, *Structure in Fives: Designing Effective Organizations* © 1983, p. 11. Adapted by permission of Prentice-Hall, Inc., Englewood Cliffs, N.J.

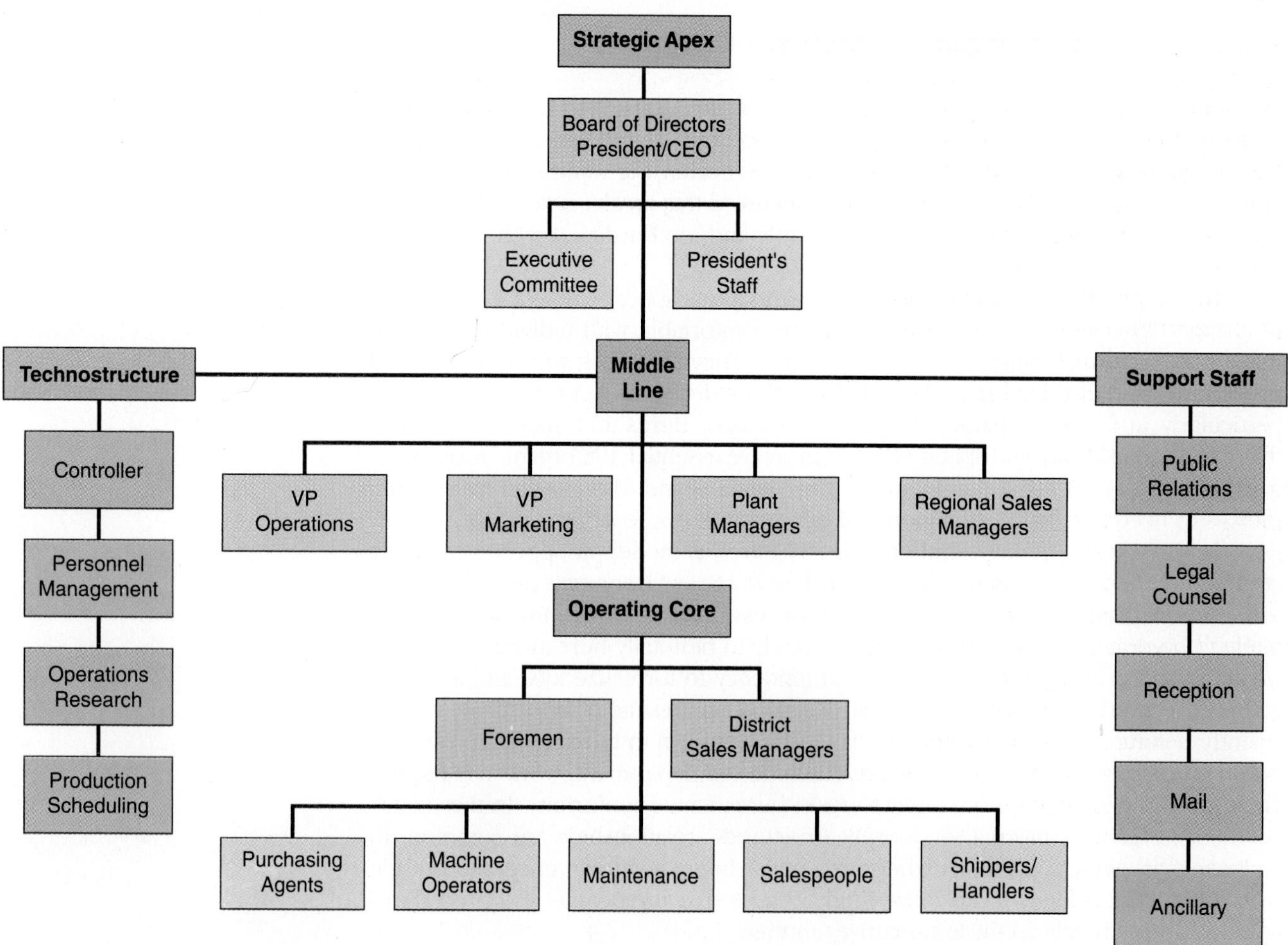

lower levels may become organic if left to their own devices, but will often be drawn toward bureaucracy if managers in the operating core and middle-line positions are bureaucratic.

Ultimately, a successful organization will evolve a structure that provides the best framework for quality and productivity. There are too many variables in a complex society to say that any one form of organization is best. The driving force of specialization will shape jobs and define tasks. Standardization is the natural result of our tendency to strive for stability, and as Compaq discovered, there is the danger of stifling creativity and responsiveness in the process. On the other hand, the humanistic values and democratic ideals Bennis alluded to are countervailing forces that can reduce the risk of bureaucratic stagnation without endangering the benefits of a well-coordinated organization.

CHECKPOINT

- Identify and discuss the five characteristics of a bureaucracy.
- How would you explain the concept of an organic structure?
- In what circumstances might bureaucracies be beneficial?
- Discuss advantages and disadvantages of bureaucracies and organic structures.

CONTINGENCY THEORY AND ORGANIZATIONAL STRUCTURES

Contingency theory implies that organizations must be capable of adapting to situations under various circumstances. The notion of "one best design" for most companies is discarded in favor of "design based on contingencies." Researchers have categorized contingency factors into four basic concerns: the organization's *age and size,* its *technology* and that of the industry, *environmental forces* that influence decisions, and the *power and personal attributes* of the organization's executives.[21]

Age and Size

The longer an organization has existed, the more formalized its behavior is likely to be. With age comes standardization of systems and procedures; it follows that older established organizations in both private and public sectors reflect bureaucratic decision making.

The age of the industry is just as important as the age of individual firms within it. A new electric utility company, for example, will structure itself to be similar to other electric utility companies. In retailing, construction, steel, and autos, company structure tends to follow industry norms. Newer high-tech industries, such as microcomputers, have few presumptions for forming organizations.

The size of an organization influences its structure in several ways. Small utility companies, for example, may not imitate the bureaucratic style of larger cousins even though they are often drawn toward the prevailing design. Instead, smaller firms with less complex management relationships may be quite informal. A small college, for instance, may be able to register students in classes without elaborate procedures, whereas a large university requires complex procedures.

Size and age of organizations usually define the need for more or less elaborate control systems. The larger the firm, the more elaborate the system needed for control; hence, the more complex its administration. Older firms, particularly in

ETHICS IN MANAGEMENT

Italian Company's Ads Go Even Further Out on a Limb

Controversy has never been a stranger to advertising campaigns. Although the basic traditional purpose of advertising is to promote and sell a product, some companies have used in their advertising campaigns themes or images that don't seem to have much to do with promoting specific products. In effect, instead of drawing attention to products, the companies draw attention to social issues or to themselves—as social crusaders or as spokespeople for the environment, for example. This approach to advertising has met with mixed reactions. Some people believe that companies do us all a service by trying to raise social awareness of important issues while selling a product. Others feel that the companies are exploiting these issues.

Nevertheless, many companies have won praise for effectively combining their advertising campaigns with company initiatives to increase public awareness about issues such as the environment, human rights, and education. Ben and Jerry's Ice Cream, for example, advertised and sold the Peace Pop with the promise to donate 1 percent of sales revenues to the causes of world peace and human rights. Russell Athletic Company advertisements prominently featured the tag line "Stay in School" in the hope of reminding the high school and college-age consumers of their activewear products that a good education includes more than knowledge of a basketball court or a baseball diamond.

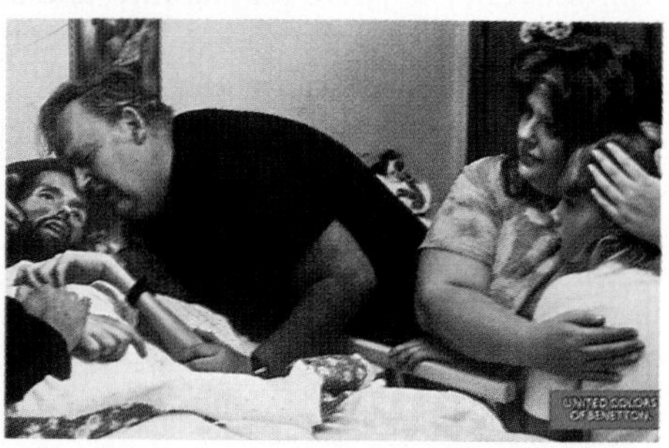

Enter Benetton Group of Italy, one of the world's most visible marketers of upscale casual clothing. Benetton executives claim that their company wants to go beyond presenting social issues *and* selling products in their advertising: they want to present *only* social issues. Benetton's 1991 and 1992 United Colors of Benetton advertising campaigns featured photographs of such subjects as the blood-soaked corpse of a Mafia hit victim, a priest kissing a nun, a dying AIDS patient surrounded by his family, and a crowd of refugees desperately swarming onto a ship. Not surprisingly, these images have generated controversy among ad executives and the public.

older industries, develop more elaborate relationships with more differentiated and specialized administrative tasks. Hierarchies grow with specialization, and since authority becomes more sharply focused with differentiation, these firms evolve toward bureaucracy, a consequence that Compaq may have experienced.

Departmentalized organizations make systematic efforts to replicate standardized patterns of work. Management wants predictability across departments and stability within them. McDonald's worldwide chain of fast-food restaurants was initially a small, rapidly changing organization, but today virtually every process and most operations are standardized. Rules, procedures, job descriptions, uniforms, restaurant design, prices, servings, and so on are formalized and replicated in nearly every McDonald's location.

The company's creative director, Oliviero Toscani, has said that the sole intention of Benetton's United Colors campaign is to increase worldwide attention to important social issues. Critics of the campaign say that Benetton is exploiting these issues and that the company is out to shock people to get itself noticed and to hype its products. While Toscani concedes that some of the images are shocking, he says that selling products was never Benetton's point. "Everybody uses emotion to sell a product. The difference here is that we are not selling a product. We want to show, in this case, human realities that we are aware of."

One factor that seems to have helped Benetton's case for sincerity is the company's reliance on in-house creative managers, rather than an advertising firm, to develop the original ideas for the United Colors campaign. Not only were the original ideas homegrown, but most of the photographs used in the earlier ad campaigns were taken by Toscani himself. While many people continue to question Benetton's sincerity and motives in its social-issue advertising, the vast majority of the magazines Benetton regularly advertises in say that they will continue to run the ads, which seem to bear out Benetton's claims in at least one respect: An *Advertising Age* poll in February 1992 found that the ads *do not* influence 82.7 percent of the company's target age group (18- to 34-year-olds) to shop Benetton.

Sources: "What's New Portfolio," *Adweek's Marketing Week,* April 9, 1990; p. 52; Alison Fahey, "Benetton's Latest," *Advertising Age,* February 11, 1991, p. 16; Gary Levin, "Benetton Brouhaha: $60M Campaign Ignites More Controversy," *Advertising Age,* February 17, 1992; p. 62; and Adrienne Ward, "'Socially Aware' or 'Wasted Money'? AA Readers Respond to Benetton Ads," *Advertising Age,* February 24, 1992; p. 4.

Technology

Before we can discuss how technology influences structure, we need to understand the meaning of technology. **Technology** is the total accumulation of tools, systems, and work methods used collectively to transform inputs into outputs. One way to think of technology is to divorce knowledge and behavior from the work process. This leaves "instrumentation," the equipment and physical process of work, as technology.[22] Accountants, for example, can use a pencil or a computer to work out budget calculations, and the results will be similar. However, computer technology requires fewer accountants with greater skills; therefore, the way work is organized will differ significantly.

technology
The total accumulation of tools, systems, and work methods used collectively to transform inputs into outputs.

In a classic study, Joan Woodward identified three distinct categories of technology in modern industry, each defining a different trend in structure. Her three categories of *unit, mass,* and *process* production also describe a general pattern of change as a company or industry grows.[23]

Unit production. Woodward observed that most new enterprises start with a customized service for a select clientele. Units or small batches of products or services are emphasized rather than mass production. In some instances, companies make it their business to customize products through a unit or small-batch process. Henry Ford began by producing a single customized race car; mass production came much later.

Unit production is nonstandard, often informal, and indicates a close system of individual control in management. Owner-managers usually have a hands-on style of decision making. They are involved in most aspects of the company, and employee specialization is not sharply defined. Frequently, employees work independently, and middle managers supervise many subordinates in diverse jobs. Woodward noted that small-batch operators had an average of twenty-three production workers for each manager in contrast to sixteen workers for each manager in mass-production systems. Thus, in unit or small-batch systems, flatter organizations with fewer layers of management exist.

Mass production. Mass-production technology is characterized by formalized work. Specialization is the rule, and there is rigid separation of formal authority for decision making. In stereotypical assembly-line mass production, labor is subdivided, work is interdependent, and there are a great number of management controls. Work is entrenched in formal methods and well documented through job descriptions. Technical equipment may be sophisticated, but job specialization reduces work to simple, easily replicated tasks.

Mass-production technology makes possible the kind of fine-tuned operation with emphasis on efficiency that is crucial when a company is producing thousands of like items for customers. Company success is often predicated on mass-production techniques that make it the low-cost competitor. For example, Ford began to turn around its manufacturing program after a disastrous 1982 sales year when the Honda Accord was positioned against the Thunderbird and captured half

The Steinway grand piano is produced today much the same way as it was more than a century ago. Steinway craftspeople shape each piano component, fashion each sound board, and even laminate rich blends of hardwoods for the piano casement.

Source: "From Pianos to Planes to Pacemakers," *Fortune,* March 28, 1988, p. 43.

of Ford's domestic market. Management attributed disaster to inefficient mass-production techniques and a proliferation of Thunderbird "options" that added more than $1,000 to the sticker price of each car. The 1982 Thunderbird had 69,120 options compared with 32 for the 1982 Honda, and even though the Honda had a 25 percent import duty, its full retail price was lower than the manufacturing cost of the Thunderbird.[24]

Mass production is the basis for the "machine bureaucracy" Warren Bennis saw as a cold and dehumanizing work environment that alienated employees. Woodward also found that mass-production systems stifled individuality and were so stressful that workers often became hostile toward their work and one another. In a machine-paced environment, rules and procedures dictate activity and make workers feel exploited. A tighter span of control by more managers over fewer workers is necessary to moderate conflicts, and this results in taller organizations with many layers of management.

Process production. Companies that require continuous production use a process technology that converts materials into homogeneous and undifferentiated products. Examples are chemical production, petroleum refining, and beer brewing processes. The difference between process systems and mass-production technology is automation. Mass production relies on interdependent assembly-line mechanisms, whereas process production relies on continuous conversion of materials through automatic systems. Mass production ties many less-skilled workers to repetitive machine-paced tasks. Process production uses fewer higher-skilled individuals to control more sophisticated technology. Thus technicians monitor equipment, maintain processes, and control systems that perform the conversion tasks.

In technologically advanced firms, taller organizational structures are being replaced by flatter ones. Compare Figures 9-5 and 9-6 to see the differences. In flatter structures, fewer technicians make more decisions on a wider variety of issues and work more autonomously.

Process organizations tend to have more people gathered at the strategic apex than are found in the executive suites of mass-production firms, but their roles differ significantly. Process executives include a cadre of specialists who make decisions that affect the entire production system. Executives in mass production and in process environments have similar responsibilities, but in mass-production companies, a more complicated hierarchy of middle managers implements decisions. The process hierarchy has fewer middle managers with broader responsibilities.

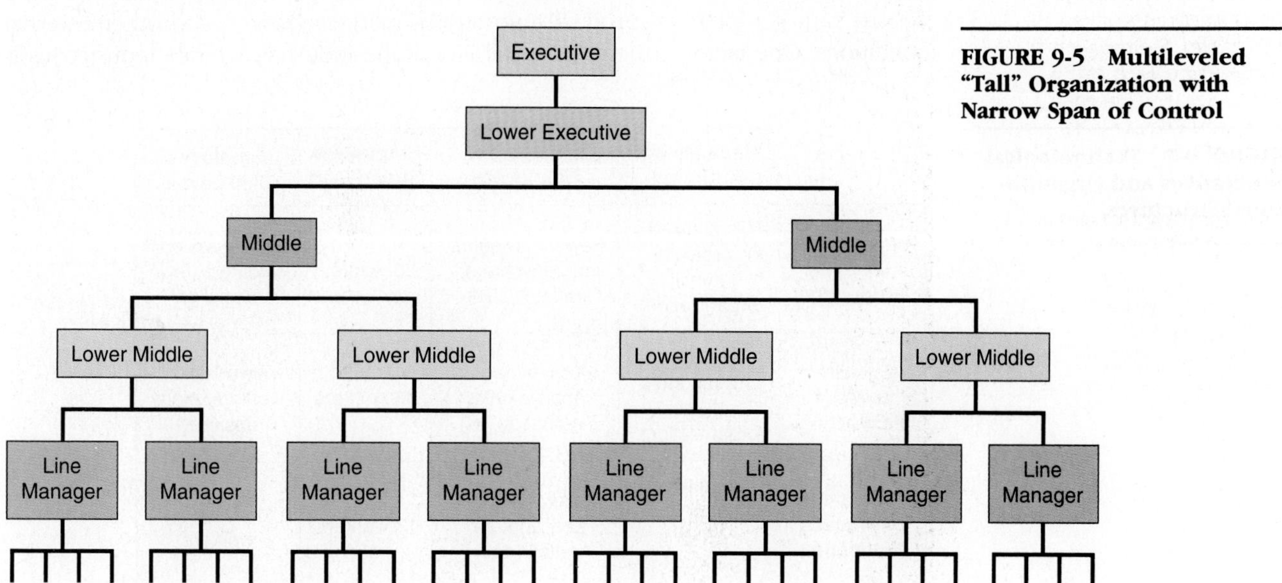

FIGURE 9-5 Multileveled "Tall" Organization with Narrow Span of Control

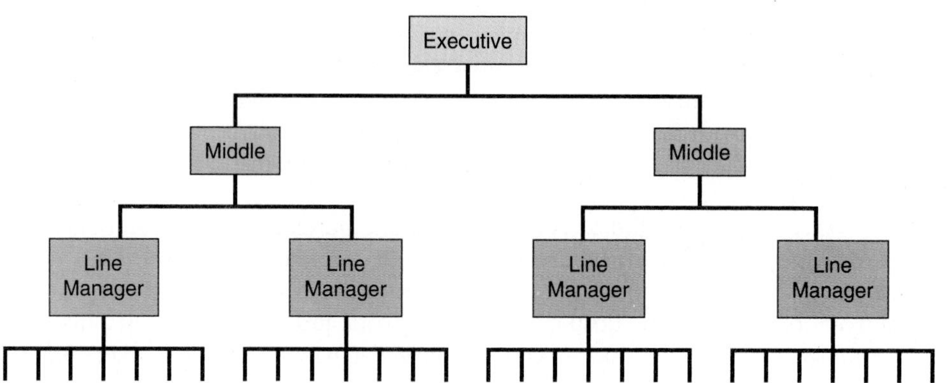

FIGURE 9-6 "Flat" Organization with Few Levels and Wide Span of Control

The Technological Imperative

technological imperative The concept that an organization's structure and relationships among its members are often dictated by the technology employed.

Joan Woodward's studies, together with research by Henry Mintzberg and others, define what is called the **technological imperative**. Simply put, this means that technology often dictates the structure of the firm. Small-batch operators who expand toward mass-production techniques therefore have to expand middle management, tighten span of control, and strive for greater formalization. Mass manufacturers in the process of automation have to reduce the number of middle managers, enhance strategic echelons, and emphasize more highly skilled supervision at all levels. Figure 9-7 summarizes these relationships.

Mintzberg concludes that "the more regulated the technical systems, the more formalized the operating work and the more bureaucratic the structure of the operating core."[25] By "operating core," he means the focal activity of the firm, such as factory operations in manufacturing. Mintzberg also says that automation will transform bureaucratic organizations into organic structures with fewer production employees and more sophisticated technical specialists. Information technology, therefore, is an important factor that is rapidly changing organizations, affecting not only the operating core but middle management jobs as well.

Environmental Contingencies

Our discussion of age, size, and technology implied that there are potentially many environmental factors that influence organizational design. Several of these are concerned with competition, product innovations, market changes, and other external conditions. One factor is the relative stability of the industry. A stable industry leads

FIGURE 9-7 Technological Imperatives and Organizational Structures

	Management Authority	Managers to Employees	Employees Supervised	Employee Skill Levels
Small-Batch or Unit Production	Centralized, organic (small organization)	Fewer managers, more workers; ratio: 1 to 23	23 workers	Many skilled workers, few unskilled
Large-Batch or Mass Production	Stratified, bureaucratic (large organization)	More managers and workers; ratio: 1 to 16	48 workers	Fewer skilled workers, many unskilled
Automated or Process Production	Decentralized, organic (large organization)	Fewer managers and workers; ratio: 1 to 8	13 workers	Many skilled workers

GLOBAL TRENDS
Mitchell Cotts Chemicals

Rising from the rubble of World War II, British manufacturer Mitchell Cotts Chemicals has become a world leader in agricultural and industrial chemicals. Until the 1980s, however, the company's rate of growth was not spectacular, nor was it a major competitor in the emerging markets of Africa and the Far East. Then in 1985, Mitchell underwent a transformation that led to a three-year period of growth that nearly matched the previous forty years' achievements. Mitchell Cotts Chemicals won the Queen's Award for Export Achievement, and by 1988 had opened markets in the former Soviet Union, the People's Republic of China, Rwanda, Central Africa, and Ecuador. By 1991, the company had expanded sales to forty countries, including the United States.

This breakthrough in growth occurred when management transformed its marketing and logistics systems through information technology. Before the change, marketing and product distribution systems relied on brokers and field offices whose growth depended largely on personal sales activity and the physical transportation of products through a logjammed system. Customer orders, purchasing, transportation, and billing generated mountains of paperwork. Under the old system, a sales order written in Egypt, for example, would have to go through six offices and might take six weeks to be delivered from Muirfield, England. Today, less than half as many field personnel are needed to process more than double the sales volume the company had in 1988.

Information technology made the difference. Today, with the stroke of a few keys on an office computer, sales information from almost anywhere in the world can be transmitted to one of five manufacturing plants on three continents. Using electronic mail, sales orders take less than two minutes to be transmitted and confirmed. Major customers have on-site terminals for twenty-four-hour service. For the cost of a telephone call, Mitchell Cotts managers can send hundreds of pages of crucial firm-specific information on products, costs, schedules, and services via satellite to virtually any part of the world in just seconds.

Equipped with a portable facsimile machine, an engineer in Trincomalee, Sri Lanka, for example, can send a two-page sales invoice to Britain in thirty-six seconds. A broker in St. Louis, Missouri, can use a telex machine to schedule an order in Ecuador in less than a minute. Recently, a customer on a flight from Sidney, Australia, made a conference call linking himself with his office in Washington, D.C., and a project engineer in Toronto, Canada.

For Mitchell Cotts Chemicals, marketing and administration technology is now approaching the level of efficiency found in their automated production facilities. Serving customers has become as much a process technology as manufacturing.

Source: Personal communication with Mitchell Cotts Chemicals, UK.

to a more bureaucratic structure. This was the situation in telecommunications, and before the breakup of AT&T, the company had evolved into an entrenched bureaucracy. Subsequent to the breakup, AT&T reorganized its core divisions around semiautonomous strategic business units.[26]

Another environmental factor is relative complexity. More complex environments result from market diversification and changes in consumers, world competition, and geographic locations. The Gillette Company, for example, manufactures and sells more than 800 products in 200 countries, and because personal grooming varies so much among world cultures, Gillette cannot simply replicate its U.S. products or management system. Instead, Gillette has set up autonomous subsidiaries in more than two dozen overseas locations, and each subsidiary organizes to match local conditions. In Western Europe, Gillette plants are heavily unionized and reflect a mass-production technology, whereas in Japan, the Gillette plant is nearly totally automated, reflecting a process technology. In contrast, a Gillette facility in Nigeria is labor intensive with little sophisticated technology.[27]

In addition, when markets become complex, *decentralization* of authority is essential to control distribution systems. Decentralization is the process of giving more authority to lower-level managers in more diversified roles. This is discussed at length in Chapter 10, where we introduce several major designs for organizations. It is important here to recognize that managers must be able to adapt quickly to local conditions and competition. On the other hand, complex strategies, such as those discussed in Chapter 7 on strategic planning, often require executive control of crucial decisions. This influences managers to *centralize* many decisions. These apparently conflicting forces result in four general models of organization, shown in Figure 9-8 and summarized below:

1. *Decentralized bureaucratic organizations* standardize systems and skills to provide replication of marketing systems in complex but stable market environments.
2. *Decentralized organic organizations* develop field specialists who have authority over divisions. Systems and skills are not standardized. Therefore, such companies have a cadre of highly trained managers with authority to react to unpredictable market situations.
3. *Centralized bureaucratic organizations* standardize work processes and systems. These are the classic pyramid structures, with many layers of management that formalize behavior within a tight chain of command.
4. *Centralized organic organizations* cannot standardize processes, systems, or behavior. These include young entrepreneurial firms in rapidly changing markets or those with rapidly changing technologies; microcomputer firms and software manufacturers are recent examples. Managers must maintain close control, but uncertainty and environmental dynamics preclude standardization.

Cultural issues. Organizations depend on the individual values of their employees, and companies are changing to conform to new human values. Today this means a propensity for participative management and greater independence for all employees. As noted earlier, bureaucratic guidelines are softening to allow greater joint decision making, and managers are expected to organize teams in which employees take responsibility for directing their own work. At American Airlines, for example, CEO Robert Crandall holds round-table discussions and encourages execu-

FIGURE 9-8 Organizational Types in Four Environments

Source: Henry Mintzberg, *Structure in Fives: Designing Effective Organizations* © 1983, p. 144. Adapted by permission of Prentice-Hall, Inc., Englewood Cliffs, N.J.

	Stable	Dynamic
Complex	Decentralized, bureaucratic (standardization of skills)	Decentralized, organic (mutual adjustment)
Simple	Centralized, bureaucratic (standardization of work processes)	Centralized, organic (direct supervision)

tives to challenge directives, debate strategies, and argue for their points of view. Crandall ridicules conformity and rewards creative thinking, and managers are expected to instill this behavior throughout the organization. Between 1980 and 1991, American's fleet more than doubled and its employment grew from 43,000 to 105,000 people, yet the company's management cadre increased barely 12 percent because more decisions were being made by employees and lower-level managers.[28]

Our culture is producing more highly educated people who seek challenge and growth in their occupations. Individual jobs are therefore being redesigned to enrich human endeavor. Two opposed forces are at work in contemporary organizations. One, specialization, pulls people toward well-defined and more standardized jobs. The other, individualism, pulls them away from standardization and toward greater freedom of choice. The combined influence of education, cultural changes, and personal expectations is pushing managers to redesign individual jobs while encouraging greater employee participation. As mentioned in Chapter 1, one of management's greatest challenges is to *empower* employees, and this translates into fewer bureaucratic controls, more individuality, and an environment that is conducive to creative decision making.[29] Tom Peters, a noted management writer, also points out that in our changing culture, more women are coming into management ranks, and women are much more comfortable than men in team relationships. Peters believes that women are rapidly changing the organizational environment by empowering employees to participate in work decisions.[30]

Economic and legal aspects. As the economy changes, markets become disrupted. As international competition increases, stability decreases. With changes in inflation or unemployment, labor markets, personal expectations, consumer tastes, demand, and many other factors also change. These conditions have dramatically undercut assumptions about appropriate behavior in organizations. Decentralized bureaucracies, as Chrysler used to be, have evolved into more centralized and organic enterprises.

Legal considerations have historically constrained organizations and helped shape authority. During the past few decades, proliferating legislation has complicated organizational decision making. In turn, this has led to greater standardization. The Equal Employment Opportunity Act, for example, created standardized hiring and promotion criteria, and the Environmental Protection Act has prescribed standard practices for hazardous waste disposal. Many similar regulations also encourage standardization, thus becoming a counterforce to human preferences for greater individuality.

Power and Personal Attributes in Management

All organizations, regardless of their size, age, or technology, are influenced significantly by their executives. This is also an age of *imposed prerogatives*—a period in which external power struggles often dictate managerial style. In 1987, for example, management at United Airlines was beginning to settle into a new organizational structure that included a new name and parent company called Allegis. In fact, Allegis was a holding company that had recently bought Westin Hotels, Hilton International, and Hertz, among other companies, before launching a strategy for a new image for the renamed airline. Executives entrenched in their own management style presided over a centrally controlled organization that was positioned to buy and sell companies like playing checkers. But a small group of outsiders, investors who owned little stock yet were "very active shareholders," goaded Allegis into a massive reorganization. Allegis disappeared as a separate entity; Westin Hotels, Hilton International, and Hertz were sold; and today United Airlines is once again an autonomous airline. In similar instances, outsiders—those not involved directly in operating management, such as investors, bankers, and influential board members—

have forced a reorganization of Gillette and imposed decisions on management at Media General.[31]

Researchers have also found that external power blocks often induce takeovers and mergers. These so-called corporate raiders have forced managers to substantially change their organizations, to embrace new innovative technologies, and often to accept new management strategies in an effort to thwart takeover bids. When managers refuse to embrace change and instead elect to fight takeover bids through financial maneuvering, they often lose. This was what happened in the $25 billion buyout of RJR Nabisco in 1988. Following a period of reduced profits that affected the company's stock prices, RJR Nabisco executives sought to buy out the corporation, but external bidders with promising new strategies were more attractive to stockholders. RJR Nabisco's executives simply countered with high stock price bids, and lower-level managers and employees lined up behind KKR (the external bidder) because it promised to reorganize the firm's divisions and implement decentralized strategic planning systems.[32]

Entrepreneurial companies, often targets of acquisition, are initially organic in form and manner. Once acquired, they are suddenly vested with the acquiring firm's corporate structure and culture. This usually means a sudden forced change to formalized structures that bureaucratize the organization.[33] Many managers, and too frequently the firm's founders, cannot accommodate this sudden transformation to a formalized structure of authority. For example, Mitch Kapor, Lotus Corporation's charismatic founder, and the creater of LOTUS 1-2-3, walked away from his firm citing an oppressive environment tempered by rules and regulations he found stifling.[34]

On a positive note, many of America's most successful companies have benefited from prerogatives of talented managers. Apple Computer's CEO, John Sculley, reorganized the company around new manufacturing technologies and strong marketing efforts based on self-managed work groups. At GE, chairman Jack Welch redefined the corporate culture based on fewer layers of management and greater autonomy for lower-level managers and their work groups. Roy Vagelos, CEO of Merck, streamlined the giant pharmaceutical company into hundreds of independent operations, each based on joint team efforts and shared responsibilities. As a result, Merck has been named four times during the past eight years by *Fortune* as America's most innovative company. And Robert Crandall of American Airlines, as noted earlier, has inspired a sense of individuality among employees while encouraging joint decisions.[35]

CHECKPOINT

- If there is no "one best way" to organize a company, what are the factors that influence organizing decisions?
- Define and contrast unit, mass, and process technologies.
- What is the technological imperative described by Mintzberg?
- Describe external factors that influence how an organization is structured.

INFORMAL STRUCTURES WITHIN ORGANIZATIONS

informal structure
A shadow structure that exists apart from the formal organization, resulting from personal interactions, sentiments, and social activities.

Informal structures are *shadow* organizations that evolve through the personal interactions, sentiments, and social activities of individuals. They form intricate patterns of influence beyond the rigid lines of formal organizational charts. Informal organizational structures are not written down, they do not have job titles or formal descriptions of authority, yet they are often more influential than formal structures of

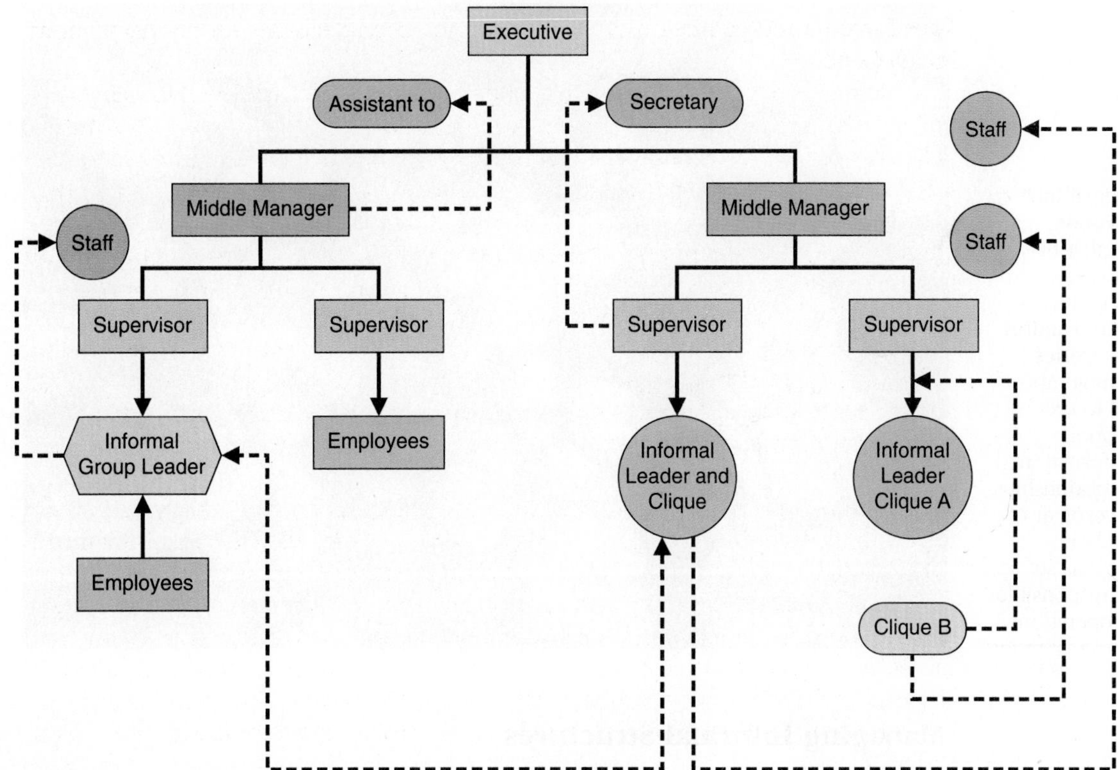

FIGURE 9-9 Informal Associations and Patterns of Information in Organizations

authority. Formal structures can be completely circumscribed by these shadow structures.

It is not unusual, for example, for a payroll clerk to have more influence on how payroll schedules are met than the supervising payroll manager. Newly matriculated freshmen recognize the importance of informal organizations, and one of the first things they do is seek advice from other students on how to beat the registration system or how to get into closed classes. Even after talking with official advisers, students seek peer advice on how things really work. Since informal relationships are shadowy, they are not easily illustrated, but Figure 9-9 shows lines of influence between individuals who typically do not show up on an organizational chart.

Costs and Benefits of Informal Structures

Informal structures influence patterns of behavior and can either usurp or support management authority. This implies possible benefits and the equal likelihood of costs. On the cost side, workers can band together into informal groups and settle into work routines somewhat less productive than management desires; productivity suffers, and there is also an implied dilution of formal authority. Rumors may become more believable than facts. Workers may rally to informal leaders and resist change. Their power diffused, managers may have great difficulty enforcing policies.

On the benefit side, cohesive informal groups result in predictable behavior and performance. Mutual support by members may also ensure fluid communications, enhance socialization, and provide a sense of group identification. Informal group leaders gain status, although without rank, which can help satisfy employees' needs for leadership. The last point is important because employees who sense a lack of leadership usually turn to their co-workers for support. Most organizations seem to have many employees with leadership abilities to whom other workers turn for advice.

John Mackey, founder of the twelve-store Whole Foods Market chain, claims that his company is "based on love instead of fear." Whole Foods, based in Austin, Texas, features "health-food" type groceries in a supermarket setting. Above all, Mackey has tried to create a formal organization that is completely informal in manager-employer relationships. Emphasizing empowerment of his 1,300 "team members" (employees), Mackey has set up departmental teams responsible for all of their own operations.

Managing Informal Structures

Managers who try to suppress informal relationships risk having workers unite against them in retaliation. If, instead, they encourage cohesion, managers may make their own work easier. By encouraging informal group leaders who constructively enhance group efforts, managers gain allies rather than enemies. Given current trends toward greater work participation, a coalition between key workers and managers, even if informally accomplished, intensifies behavior directed at achieving organizational objectives. In cohesive work groups that include managers, workers will be more receptive to authority.

An example of management-encouraged cohesive groups is the Lawton, Oklahoma, plant of the Goodyear Tire and Rubber Company. Goodyear managers urged workers to form work groups among themselves, and 164 teams evolved to "self-manage" shop-floor tasks. They assumed responsibility for scheduling, purchasing materials, quality control, hiring new employees, and controlling other team activities such as discipline among members. As a result, absenteeism dropped to less than 1 percent from nearly 6 percent, production improved, and so did quality. Managers became involved as members of each team, but this did not impede informal team activities; managerial roles changed to emphasize support and counseling rather than directing employees' work. Inclusion of managers as team members is important to provide coordination among teams and throughout the company hierarchy. It is not enough to give employees responsibilities in an unstructured environment. That borders on abdication of authority. Goodyear made the transition systematically by involving employees in decisions while endorsing their constructive efforts to work in cohesive teams. Many other companies have simply loaded responsibilities on employees, creating confusion through a void in leadership.[36]

The ultimate goal of managing informal structures such as shop-floor work teams is to shift toward an organic form of organization. This allows greater flexibility for self-management by those who actually perform operating tasks, and it encourages informal group leaders to assume greater roles among their co-workers. Thus rigid lines of formal authority are softened to bring more people into the decision-making process. Managers find their roles altered to include greater responsibilities for coordinating teams, helping employees make constructive decisions, and resolving problems.[37]

CHECKPOINT

- What is meant by a "shadow organization"?
- Discuss the benefits and costs of the informal structures that evolve among work groups.
- How might managers use informal organizations to improve performance?

EVOLUTION OF ORGANIZATIONS

Our discussion focuses on complex organizations, but most organizations are rather small. The Small Business Administration reports that about 52 percent of all hourly paid workers in the private sector are in firms with fewer than 500 employees. Nearly 90 percent of all U.S. firms have fewer than 100 employees; 79 percent of those have no more than 5. A few very large firms, about 3 percent of all businesses, employ huge numbers of people.[38] Because so many small firms exist, Chapter 20 is devoted to entrepreneurship, but growing firms, large or small, face structural problems during their evolution. This evolution creates greater numbers of employees, complex relationships, and several critical periods of change. Larry E. Greiner has identified a growth model with five phases of change corresponding to a range of development shown in Figure 9-10.[39]

Phase 1: Creativity

When an enterprise is created, it usually makes or sells a product or service through the personal efforts of a few individuals. Young firms are small and relationships are informal. Management is not concerned with delegation of authority; in fact, owner-managers may "be" their organizations. As firms grow, they add employees and confront the first crisis of organizing. Greiner identifies this crisis as one of leadership in which owner-managers are too overworked to manage operations. In some in-

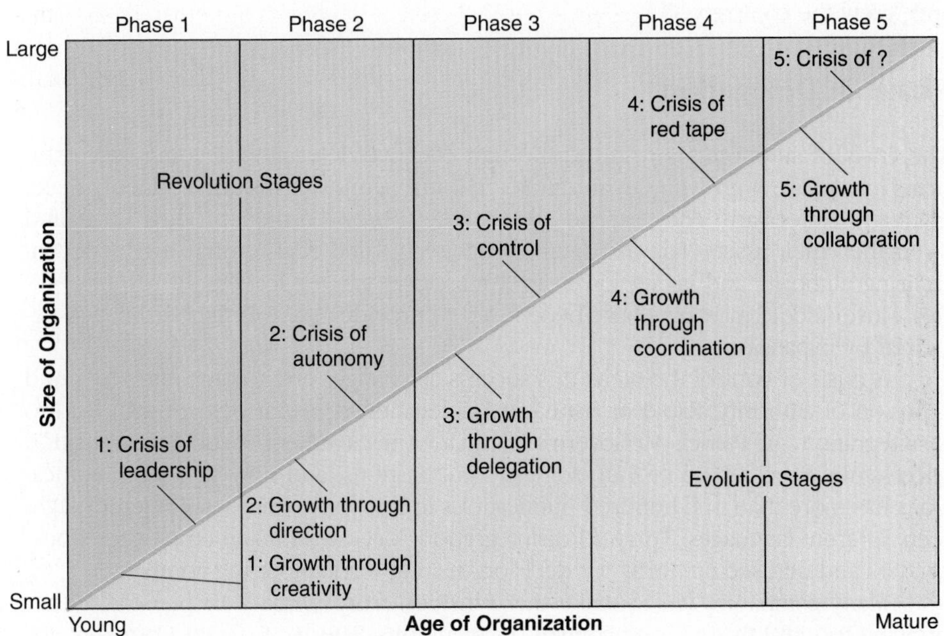

FIGURE 9-10 The Five Stages of Growth

Source: Reprinted by permission of the *Harvard Business Review*. An exhibit from "Evolution and Revolution as Organizations Grow," by Larry E. Greiner (July–August 1972). Copyright © 1972 by the President and Fellows of Harvard College; all rights reserved.

stances, owners may want to grow, but not to the extent of losing touch with their entrepreneurial roots. For these individuals, there may be no crisis. Ben & Jerry's Homemade, Inc., profiled in Management Application, illustrates the point.

For firms that are growing rapidly, there is a leadership crisis because many entrepreneurs are unsuited for managerial roles. Many firms do not survive this leadership crisis because their owners fail to hire and organize a cadre of managers capable of helping their enterprises grow. Bill Rogers, the only four-time winner of both the Boston and New York marathons, lost his $9 million active sportswear business, his home, and most of his assets when his two-year-old company was liquidated in 1987.[40] Rogers had tried to manage his growing company by himself, and the job overwhelmed him. Later that year, Bill Rogers Sports Wear was restarted by Odilon Cormier, an experienced manager, who brought Rogers back into the company as a member of a small management team. Subsequently the company grew and profited, and was positioned for rapid expansion during the 1990s.

Phase 2: Direction

As formalization occurs, centralized management develops a "functional" structure of responsibilities. Top management still controls the firm, but functional specialists are added in accounting, marketing, production, personnel, and other areas. A management hierarchy evolves, even though the firm may still be relatively small.

A crisis of autonomy develops as the firm grows and a formal hierarchy solidifies. The centralized management structure created to bridge the leadership gap constrains expansion. Lower-level managers seek greater authority, but too often top managers are unwilling to delegate it. Their initial strength as hands-on leaders becomes a serious weakness in later growth stages Patrick McGovern, founder and CEO of the $300 million IDG Communications, turned a one-magazine company into a corporation with sixty-five independent divisions. His first publication, *Computerworld,* was a struggling weekly for nearly a decade before McGovern launched *PC World, Macworld,* and *CD-ROM Review*. With four successful magazines, McGovern and his staff continued to hold a tight rein on operations, requiring regular reports from all managers, scheduling frequent meetings, and making most operational decisions. Reflecting on how his business grew, McGovern said that initially he had sowed self-doubt in his people, which showed up in less crisp decision making and low morale. However, once he "empowered" his managers with authority and showed them he had faith in their ability to work independently, they took control and "grew the company."[41]

Phase 3: Delegation

The crisis of autonomy is resolved through effective delegation, leading successful firms into phase 3 growth. Organizations that manage this transition suddenly make giant strides forward. They expand their markets, broaden their product lines, and strengthen their assets. Top management has reconciled decision making by decentralizing authority and giving lower-level managers greater leadership responsibilities. More middle managers have been hired to provide the vertical coordination required by expansion.

A crisis of control threatens this success as changes are accompanied by rapid diffusion of authority. Rapid or haphazard delegation is precarious and can lead to disintegration. In Patrick McGovern's company, management made this transition successfully from a base of four domestic publications, and now IDG Communications has more than one hundred publications in thirty-six countries written in eighteen different languages. To avoid disintegration, McGovern made employees stockholders and diffused authority for decision making throughout the company.

Many companies fail to make the transition from phase 2 to phase 3, either growing too rapidly or losing control of operations. The W. T. Grant Company, for example, became the second-largest retailer in the United States by 1973, but was bankrupt by 1974. Grant opened 700 new stores between 1968 and 1973, more than doubling its number of locations to 1,200, but it also had a succession of three CEOs during that period, and managers found themselves trying to control twice the resources and employees they had before expansion. Grant's failure was blamed on a complete breakdown in operational controls.[42] News Corporation, the company that owns Murdoch Magazines, faced a similar crisis in 1991. Murdoch published *Automobile, European Travel & Life, Mirabella, New Woman, New York Magazine, Seventeen, Soap Opera Digest,* and *TV Guide,* among other magazines. Several of Murdoch's titles were highly profitable, but most new titles were losers, draining the company of its resources. The company expanded Murdoch's product line so rapidly that it could not control its acquisitions or develop a stable management structure. Consequently, a majority of Murdoch's publications were put up for sale with the intention of regaining control over a limited number of well-managed publications.[43]

Phase 4: Coordination

If an organization survives the control crisis, it will face coordination problems. A firm in this phase is usually operating in a mature market—growth has slowed, competitors are established, and technology is relatively stable. Management roles are standardized early in this stage with formal systems and channels of communications. The firm focuses on efficient use of resources and greater rationalization of formal procedures. In short, it develops a bureaucratic profile.

In this stage, a coordination crisis develops, often accompanied by too much "red tape." Such a crisis is akin to organizational paralysis; managers are so bogged down in procedures that they cannot coordinate their efforts. Avoiding paralysis requires redefining authority to instill innovation and adaptability in jobs and management systems. As noted earlier in the chapter, bureaucratic methods may be appropriate if the company is in a stable industry, but more frequently, companies face stiff competition in rapidly changing industries that require adaptability. Survival requires flexible organization and management decision making that is responsive to competition.

After deregulation of the telecommunications industry, AT&T had a cumbersome bureaucracy that hampered its competitiveness in the new environment. Management met this challenge by streamlining the company, making it competitive once again. Similar transitions have occurred at Coca-Cola Company, Xerox, and ITT.[44] Unfortunately, there have been notable failures at this stage. Pan American World Airways was America's flagship airline, but it became crippled by management systems that were neither responsive to consumer needs nor adaptable to the deregulated environment of the 1980s. In 1991, after a brief period of bankruptcy, the company and its assets were bought and soon liquidated by Delta Airlines.[45]

Phase 5: Collaboration

Greiner suggests that many corporations are entering a phase of collaboration as a result of actions taken to counter red tape and paralysis of phase 4. Thus new organizational forms are becoming visible, many with participative systems of decision making. Mutual goal setting and employee work groups are emerging in these organizations through programs such as MBO and quality circles, and labor and management are collaborating on mutually beneficial labor contracts. Many American firms use integrated team management to foster innovation while avoiding the "paralysis syndrome."[46]

Perhaps there is a sixth phase in our future; we are only now beginning to understand phase 5 attributes that were considered radical changes only a few years ago. What the future will bring is largely a matter of speculation, but researchers have found several trends emerging. As information technology changes, for exam-

MANAGEMENT APPLICATION

Ben & Jerry's: Forever Young

Ben & Jerry's Homemade, Inc., which ranks second in the premium ice cream business behind corporate giant Pillsbury (Haagen-Dazs) and ahead of Kraft (Frusen Gladje), refuses to grow old. Marking its fifteenth year in 1993, Ben & Jerry's Homemade, Inc., began in a renovated Burlington, Vermont, gas station. Today it grosses more than $60 million. Founders Ben Cohen and Jerry Greenfield refer to themselves as "weird" and "funky," and in fact look more like middle-aged dropouts in shaggy jeans and T-shirts than successful businessmen. They don't want to be any different than they are, nor do they want to grow up. Yet they are astute managers with a genuine sensitivity to the needs of their employees.

Jerry Greenfield prefers the title "Undersecretary of Joy," and his employees do not laugh at this self-description. To the contrary, when addressing a plant meeting of 150 workers, he recently proposed a "Joy Committee" to bring more fun and humor to the workplace, and employees applauded. Greenfield's ultimate goal is to have an organization of happy people, employees not merely satisfied with their jobs but eager to work because their work allows them to be creative.

Naturally, Ben & Jerry's Homemade has its share of crises, but they are greeted by an unusual response. For example, when production fell short of peak orders, the alarm sounded, and everyone came together to get the product out. Even Ben and Jerry did a stint, wiping containers and emptying garbage. Jerry recognized that the pressure fatigued workers, so he hired a masseuse to give them massages during breaks.

Innovation extends to the once-monthly staff meetings, held in a plant

ple, better-educated workers are integrating automation into semiautonomous work groups. This creates "work cells" or small groups that do a multiplicity of tasks, moving companies further away from assembly-line mass manufacturing. In affluent societies, people want to work fewer hours and enjoy more leisure, with the result that more companies are hiring temporary workers and part-timers. Also, information networks, rapid travel, and telecommunication systems allow many people to work at home or in their own offices far from the physical facilities of their companies. All these trends are redefining authority structures and how work is coordinated.[47]

CHECKPOINT

- Define and discuss the five stages of organizational evolution.
- Each stage is accompanied by a potential crisis. Discuss these crises and how managers can overcome them.

receiving bay. During these meetings, production stops so that all employees and managers can attend. The events resemble town meetings rather than corporate staff meetings. Coffee, cider, and doughnuts are served, communication is open, suggestions are taken seriously by managers, and recognition awards are announced.

Ben Cohen and Jerry Greenfield realize that professional management is essential to succeed, but they reject the idea that the company or its people must become "old" or stifling in the process. Consequently, the theme is to remain "forever young," a slogan that appears on T-shirts and hats. On the company's tenth anniversary, employees designed their own T-shirt that read: "Be 10 again!" This unique philosophy extends to product development and marketing at the company where superpremium ice cream features flavors such as Dastardly Mash, Cherry Garcia (named after rock star Jerry Garcia of the Grateful Dead), and Heath Bar Crunch. The company also launched a marketing campaign several years ago to protest the huge U.S. defense budget. Called the "1% for Peace" project, the company earmarked 1 percent of sales proceeds during 1990 to a nonprofit peace foundation. Profits from a special ice cream called Rain Forest Crunch go to a fund to help save the Amazon rain forest. Also, the company donates nearly 7.5 percent of pretax profits to a nonprofit foundation that supports causes that range from helping the homeless to AIDS research.

Ben Cohen and Jerry Greenfield view their business as a vehicle for helping resolve social and environmental problems, and the best way to do so is to have a strong, successful enterprise. This has meant a transition in organization whereby more highly capable managers have been brought into the company to head marketing, production, finance, and other key functions. The founders, however, not only require executive capabilities in their managers but also a similar strong commitment to social responsiveness. They are also expected to be able to roll up their sleeves and work with employees as team members involved in the company's vision.

Sources: Erik Larson, "Forever Young," *Inc.*, July 1988, pp. 50–62; "The Peace Pop Puzzle," *Inc.*, March 1990, p. 25; and Alan Deutschman, "Inside Scoop," *Fortune*, March 12, 1990, p. 130.

SERVICE ORGANIZATIONS IN PERSPECTIVE

Service organizations are becoming more prominent, both domestically and internationally. In the United States, more people are finding employment in service organizations than in manufacturing, and in many advanced European and Asian societies, service companies are rapidly outgrowing manufacturing companies. Some of the fastest-growing service organizations are banks, financial chains, recreation developments, and retirement centers. Other that are growing rapidly are research centers like the National Science Foundation, not-for-profit organizations like the March of Dimes, and professional organizations like the National Association of Accountants, as well as churches, government agencies, and thousands of small firms ranging from beauty salons to tax consultants.

Growth has been rapid in service organizations in societies with established industrial economies and strong education systems. This does not mean that industrialized countries are losing their manufacturing base. Rather, a shift has occurred whereby nations with advanced technologies are better suited to an information age

The United Way of America scandal of early 1992 brought to light many interesting questions about how not-for-profit organizations are—and should be—managed. By February 28, 1992, allegations of mismanagement and extravagant spending had forced United Way of America President William Aramony to resign. Many people feel that Aramony was simply behaving and spending like the CEO of any large organization as large as the United Way. Aramony himself claimed that he needed certain perquisites to get his job done. However, other people believe that because the United Way operates on donations Aramony should have tried to get by with minimal expenditures.

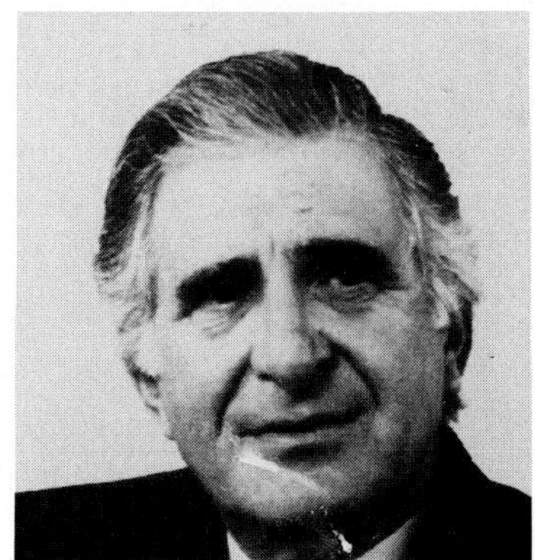

with scientific and knowledge-based industries, whereas developing nations are better suited to expand into manufacturing systems, particularly those based on mass-production techniques.[48] As a result, many business students will find themselves working in service organizations after graduation.

Characteristics of Service Organizations

Large service organizations differ little from those modeled by Joan Woodward for large manufacturers. In fact, most large service firms typify the model of a bureaucracy engaged in mass production. Labor is highly differentiated, work is standardized, procedures are formalized, and systems are steeped in documentation. These firms also tend to have many levels of authority stratified in hierarchical chains of command; fourteen to sixteen levels is not uncommon. However, many large service organizations are now going through "downsizing" transitions similar to those undergone in manufacturing over the last decade. In this chapter, we have included examples of service companies, such as major airlines, advertising agencies, publishers, software development firms, and retailers, that have successfully reorganized to become competitive. We have also provided examples of service companies that have failed to address their organizing problems. Service organizations, however, do have characteristics that set them apart from standard models in manufacturing.

Characteristics such as technology and environment may influence the structure of service organizations more than size and age. In organizations that offer professional services, bureaucratic values collide with personal values of professional staff in key positions. Public accounting firms, universities, hospitals, and scientific research firms are examples of service organizations where bureaucratic formalities are likely to clash with professional preferences for informality or autonomy. When this occurs, it is unclear how the structural architecture will develop. For example, Hospital Corporation of America, a large company, superimposes management practices similar to those used in manufacturing on its hospital facilities. There are physicians on HCA boards of directors, but executive positions are occupied by financial, marketing, and administrative managers, much as they are at GM or IBM. In contrast, independent hospitals are more likely to have physicians in joint decision-making roles with hospital administrators. At HCA, formal business procedures, rational job descriptions, and chain-of-command decision-making processes are emphasized, whereas most independent hospitals encourage an informal, collegial organization among physicians and administrators.[49]

Research shows that as operations in service companies become technically complex, work becomes more difficult to standardize and organizations tend to be molded by the ideologies of professionals. There are more informal lines of authority, rules and regulations are less rigidly applied, and adaptability is more highly valued than operational efficiency. When work is not technically complex, however, it is often standardized, and when a service industry matures (phase 4 growth), company structures often become mirror images of one another, standardizing their systems and operating procedures. Banking, insurance, and large public accounting firms are visible examples. Professional ideologies in these cases are replaced by administrative systems often emulating rational bureaucracies.[50]

CHECKPOINT

- What are some of the similarities and differences between service companies and manufacturers?
- Explain the technology of a service company such as an insurance firm.
- How does not-for-profit status affect organizational structure?

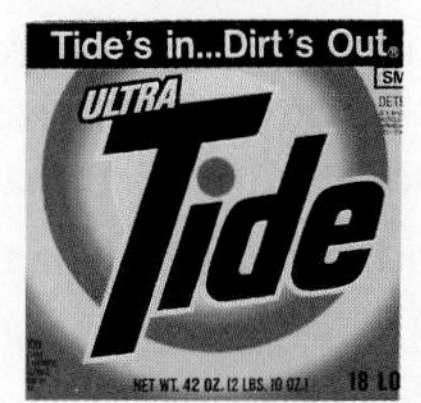

AT THE BEGINNING OF THE CHAPTER, we saw how Saatchi & Saatchi, a global advertising firm, has begun to reorganize as a centralized company. This unusual move was necessary to improve client service by creating global executive account teams. The reorganization is feasible because telecommunications and network computer systems allow the company to maintain coordination of its global interests. Saatchi will become less bureaucratic and account teams will become more responsive to client interests because they will have the expertise to serve select clientele. Its staff, however, will need to think globally and have extensive skills to work in a multicultural company.

A SYNOPSIS FOR LEARNING

1. Discuss why organizing is an important management function.

Good organizational skills are essential for managers to bring together people and resources productively. Organizing jobs clarifies individual performance expectations and focuses effort on the tasks needed to accomplish the company's objectives. Well-organized companies define authority, create a logical division of work, and allocate resources efficiently. Organizing also produces a logical flow of activities and establishes communication channels for decision making and control. An essential aspect of organizing is to develop a structure for a company that coincides with its technology and work environment.

2. Explain the concepts of job enlargement and job enrichment.

Job enlargement is the process of combining tasks to create a new job with broader activities. The goals are to reduce job boredom and mental fatigue, relieve stress, and make jobs more interesting for employees. Job enlargement does not expand a person's decision-making authority, only the activities associated with the job. Job enrichment is the process of expanding decision-making authority so that individuals have greater responsibility for their jobs and the results of their work. Its aim is to increase the depth of a job.

3. Describe and contrast bureaucratic and organic structures.

Some characteristics of the stereotyped bureaucracy are: (1) a fixed and official jurisdiction of authority; (2) a firmly established rational chain of command; (3) quantified and thoroughly documented information; (4) a supposition of expertise whereby positions are filled according to skills rather than personal attributes; and (5) a technically scientific management process. The bureaucracy is viewed as inflexible, formal, coldly rational, and dehumanizing. In contrast, the organization is conceived to be flexible, devoid of fixed lines of authority, responsive to change, and overseen by managers attentive to individual needs.

4. Explain the environmental factors that influence organizational structure.

The age of a company, or an industry, influences organizational structure. The size of a company influences the degree of formal systems needed to control it. Perhaps the most influential factor is a company's technology. Other environmental influences are legislation, politics, economics, competitors, and changes in information technology.

5. Discuss the nature of informal patterns of organizational structures.

Formal structures are those with established rules, procedures, and channels of communication, clear lines of decision-making authority, and well-defined jobs. Informal structures are shadow organizations that evolve through personal interactions, sentiments, and social activities of individuals working in proximity. These informal relationships create patterns of behavior that influence decision making and alter formal management authority.

6. Examine how firms grow and change in dynamic environments.

   Most companies go through several stages of development. Entrepreneurial firms start with a creative stage in which they are often headed by one person who "is" the company. The enterprise grows and reaches the direction stage: The founder must turn to other managers to shoulder some of the decision-making responsibilities. The third stage of growth is called delegation because managers must find ways to diffuse authority as the company diversifies into new product lines and new markets. The fourth stage, coordination, suggests a transition away from bureaucratic paralysis toward more flexible and adaptive forms of organization. The fifth stage, collaboration, is characterized by participative systems of decision making, with collaborative goal setting, employee work groups, and integrated team management to encourage innovation.

7. Describe the characteristics of service organizations.

   Service organizations provide people with intangible benefits. Service firms sell results, perceptions, or images to customers or clientele, often through the personal efforts or expertise of professionals. Not-for-profit service organizations serve a public constituency and therefore must account carefully for resources and results. This can lead to formality in procedures and authority structures; however, most service firms are profit-oriented, requiring a customer-service relationship with adaptable and responsive managers.

SKILL ANALYSIS

CASE 1 Organizational Response to High-Tech Changes

Monsanto Corporation is one of many established firms that emerged as an innovator during the 1980s. For nearly half a century, Monsanto made and sold commercial chemicals, but today its products span biotechnology, plastic fabrications, and food processing systems based on mechogenetics, the use of genetically manufactured products to improve food processing and preservation. Changes in product development, research, and global operations at Monsanto were prompted by the oil crisis of the 1970s. Until then, the company had been structured around functional specialization in marketing and production for oil-based chemicals and plastic products, but the oil shortages threatened Monsanto with the loss of its primary raw material, and rising oil prices endangered the company's profits. Monsanto responded by turning to research and restructuring its entire organization to pursue new product innovations. The following is an excerpt from a *Fortune* article about the change:

> The company devised a clever way of altering its culture to facilitate the change. It began investing in Biogen, Genentech, Cetus, and Genex—all start-up biotechnology firms. Then it invited scientists from some of these outfits to company headquarters to train Monsanto employees. . . . The next step was to finance biotechnology projects inside the company. Monsanto tripled its basic research budget and is building its own research park near St. Louis. To further expand R&D, Monsanto formed joint ventures with the biotechnology firms.
>
> Not quite what you would have expected from an old-line chemical company. The point is that technological sophistication is spreading, and as it spreads, it becomes harder and harder for companies that don't join in to maintain a competitive edge. The merging of technologies—electronics and mechanics, for example, or biotechnology and food processing—has created the potential for much faster change in industry after industry.[5]

The thrust of the article was that organizations must change not only their strategic outlook on industry but also their organizations in order to be responsive and adaptable. Another excerpt from the same article focuses on this point:

> The most difficult challenge may be creativity and the people who embody it. Companies that have mastered high-speed management try to keep the mental light bulbs on by establishing small teams to design, manufacture, and market new products. Whatever they're called—entrepreneurial groups, independent business units, skunkworks—these teams remove the bureaucratic straitjacket from product development. . . . To be successful, independent business units must be small, hardworking, and preferably located somewhere away from the normal corporate premises.[52]

Change did not come easily for Monsanto. Before 1972, the firm had prided itself on being a stable company in the petrochemical industry. Oil and its resin-based raw materials were relatively secure for American manufacturers. The 1973 oil crisis forced Monsanto to recognize its vulnerability, and management made a commitment to change the company's direction and scope of business interests. Still, bureaucratic traditions were so firmly in place that the company seemed paralyzed for several years. It was not until 1983 that significant change began to take place.

In early 1984, the "skunkworks" for R&D appeared. This was an ad hoc group of research scientists who were allowed to pursue research projects with little management intervention or control. They spearheaded several dozen new project ideas and helped the company set up joint ventures with other companies, like Biogen and Genentech, to bring together petrochemical and biogenetic technologies. New products and market research laboratories were brought on line, and Monsanto expanded into the sports markets with equipment, plastics, and Astroturf. It also produces medical supplies, equipment, surgical accessories, and building materials. In addition to complicated biotech chemicals, Monsanto has made innovations in a wide range of consumer products.

During the process, the company's structure has flattened. There are fewer middle managers but more technical specialists, and the breadth of operations has expanded, with division managers in charge of more than a hundred product lines. Even so, much of the innovation has come from joint ventures with smaller firms physically separated from Monsanto, and global marketing and distribution are accomplished through autonomous subsidiaries located on four continents.

Case Questions

1. Identify and discuss the environmental factors that influenced Monsanto to change structurally. In your answer, explain how the technological imperative has altered the firm.
2. Explore why it took Monsanto more than a decade to soften its bureaucratic lines sufficiently to launch new projects. Why must such a firm set up physically remote independent operations to assure creativity and innovation?
3. Discuss the case issues in terms of Bennis's once-futuristic forecast of an "end to bureaucracies." Could Monsanto have continued to succeed in its historic chemical market within a bureaucratic framework? What organizational factors are important today? Support your answers.

VIDEO CASE Success at Any Price? Organizations Face Changes

Of all the resources an organization has at its disposal, the most important and potentially the most fragile is human resources. What happens to an organization when its human resources find themselves working more and enjoying it less?

The victims of corporate downsizing and restructuring during the 1980s were not only those who were laid off from their jobs. Employees who remained with the organization were also affected. These people now find themselves burdened with a heavier workload and troubled by uncertainty about their futures. And even in organizations that have not downsized and restructured, employees face stress from the escalating demands placed on them by a dynamic, complex and increasingly competitive marketplace. The problems of stress manifest themselves in various ways.

A new study by the Northwestern National Life Insurance company has disclosed that 70 percent of American workers say job stress causes them frequent health problems. Also from the same survey came the startling fact that 70 percent of respondents believe that stress has made them less productive on the job. Says a Northwestern representative, "I think we're headed on the road toward *karoshi,* what the Japanese call death by overwork. . . ." In fact, the price of all this strain to American business is estimated by some experts at $150 billion a year in health costs and lost productivity.

Job stress cuts across all economic and career lines. For example, an estimated 40,000 attorneys leave the legal field every year. One former executive with a $100,000-plus salary chucked his position to run a neighborhood grocery store. Bill Parcells, the super-successful coach of the New York Giants, left the football team at the peak of his career. However, many authorities now believe that job stress is even greater for workers further down the organizational ladder who are under extreme pressure to produce and who have little control over their work. One worker says, "Well, there's stress all the time, you know. We have to think about the bosses looking for their production."

An organization can take steps to reduce workplace stress. Some companies have set up gyms and fitness facilities and offer programs to help fight stress-related illnesses. A corporate stress consultant provides some other suggestions. She says it is important to acknowledge how stressful a job can be and to recognize the stress points. She also says that as a society we need to clarify our values. Americans have always tended to think that working really hard most of the time will make both them and their families happy. However, studies have shown that providing for closer relationships and connections to others is instrumental in keeping people healthy and happy. The same expert suggests that organizations need to think about new ways to work. Working smarter rather than longer and providing for more employee control over the work situation can go a long way toward reducing stress.

Success often does have its price, both for individuals and for organizations. To capture all the benefits associated with effective organizing, managers need to recognize the problems related to workplace stress and take steps to reduce its likelihood.

Case Questions

1. What are some of the problems associated with stress, both for individuals and for organizations?
2. What specific organizing activities can contribute to reducing the amount of workplace stress? How?
3. Which would be more likely to create workplace stress—bureaucratic or organic structures? Why?

Sources: Alan Farnham, "Who Beats Stress Best—and How," *Fortune,* October 7, 1991, p. 71ff; "Relieving Workplace Stress," *Occupational Hazards,* April 1991, Vol. 53, No. 4, p. 38ff; Joan M. Lang "Career Burnout," *Restaurant Business Magazine,* March 1, 1991, Vol. 90, No. 4, p. 131ff; and Robert E. Lindberg, "Creatively Coping with Job Stress," *Association Management,* October 1990, Vol. 42, No. 10, p. 80ff.

SKILL PRACTICE

SAVE THE TREES: A GROUP ADVERTISING EXERCISE

Introduction

Teams of four to eight persons will be formed to work independently on an advertising poster. Each team will be given instructions about how to organize its work, and when it has completed a poster, a team spokesperson will present the finished product. Team members will be asked to respond to several questions about how they completed the assignment.

Team Organization

Three types of teams will be organized as noted below. (approximately 5 minutes)

- **Formal teams:** A manager will be appointed by the instructor, and the manager must in turn appoint employees responsible for creative writing, art, and marketing. More than one employee can work on the same task, depending on the group size.
- **Informal teams:** Members of these teams will be required to select a group leader and spokesperson to coordinate group activities, but no specific tasks will be assigned. Group members must determine how work is to proceed.
- **Self-managed teams:** Once formed, these teams will be given no instructions about organization or election of formal or informal group leaders. They are completely responsible for determining what to do and who is to do it.

The Project

Each team must develop a poster to illustrate an environment theme to "save the trees." Assume that groups work for an advertising agency hired by an environmentalist group to design the poster, write a catchy expression to urge the public to support a movement to control deforestation, and suggest a marketing strategy to use the poster and the expression in advertising. (approximately 20 minutes)

Team Reports

Each group will be asked to present the finished poster (roughly drawn with an expression and outlined marketing strategy). The posters should be displayed, taped on the wall or on flip charts. Then teams will address the following questions: (approximately 20 minutes, depending on class size)

1. How were decisions made concerning poster art, expressions, and the marketing plan?
2. What contribution did each member make to the final product?
3. How did team members decide who had responsibility for each phase?
4. Each member should respond to the following questions: Were you comfortable with your assignment or would you have preferred doing a different task? How do you feel about the group's ability to coordinate work? Were other group members sensitive to your ideas? How were you encouraged (or discouraged) to participate?

Discussion

After giving each team member time to make brief answers to the questions above, the instructor will invite opinions about individual preferences for types of group organization. (time is variable)

1. Would students have been more comfortable with one type of group? Why?
2. Which group process seemed most efficient?
3. Which group seemed to have the most creative poster? Why?
4. Which group seemed to get the most fun from the exercise? Why?

10
Organizations in Transition: Structural Evolution

OUTLINE

Departmentalization
- Functional Pattern
- Product Pattern
- Geographic Pattern
- Customer Pattern

Matrix Management
- Behavioral Implications of Matrix Management
- Matrix Evolution and Potential Problems
- A Matrix Perspective

Authority
- Traditional and Emerging Views of Authority
- Accountability: Balancing Authority and Responsibility
- Line and Staff Authority

Delegation of Authority
- The Spectrum of Delegation
- Reasons for Delegating Authority
- Barriers to Effective Delegation
- Toward More Effective Delegation

Centralization versus Decentralization
- Factors That Influence Decentralization
- The Leadership Dimension
- Information as an Environmental Imperative

Organizational Culture
- Culture in America's Most Admired Firms
- Culture Transforms Systems
- Changes in Organizational Relationships
- Effects of Participation
- Redefined Ownership Structures

OBJECTIVES

- Describe how organizations departmentalize to improve coordination.
- Describe matrix organization and its implications for management.
- Explain how authority is being transformed in today's organizations.
- Describe why managers delegate authority and barriers that often prevent them from doing so.
- Identify factors that influence centralization and decentralization.
- Explain what culture is with respect to organizations.

LIZ CLAIBORNE, the company, lost Liz Claiborne, the creative genius, who retired after a stellar career in fashion as the most recognized designer of women's clothes in the world.[1] With husband and partner Arthur Ortenberg, Liz Claiborne started her company in 1976 on the premise of making fashionable clothes for women at affordable prices. At the time of her announced retirement in 1989, Ms. Claiborne's company was selling more than 500 different clothing and accessory items for women and men through 3,500 merchandisers on four continents. Gross sales of $1.2 billion in 1988 topped the industry for brand-name designers. Yet with the retirement announcement, Liz Claiborne's stock price tumbled because investors were uncertain whether the company could survive without its founder. Liz Claiborne, Inc., however, did not become a billion-dollar company on the strength of one creative design genius.

As one of only three women CEOs in the Fortune 1000, Liz Claiborne also had organizational genius. She developed a core of thirty-one designers, each supported by a cadre of enthusiastic fashion specialists. Today the company has semiautonomous operating divisions in each major line of merchandise, ranging from perfumes to retail stores. Liz Claiborne designed the company around a "culture" of individual expression and independent control, and her transition from CEO to retirement was as well planned as one of her best fashion lines. Consequently, Liz Claiborne, the company, entered the 1990s with an efficient organization positioned to grow and continue its founder's pattern of success. As you study this chapter, consider how organizations organize, grow, and deal with transition periods to ensure a competitive posture in their industries.

In this chapter, we present several ways managers structure their companies to achieve growth. As a company expands, for example, authority has to be delegated to more managers who develop new products or new markets. As American companies become more involved in international business, their structures become more complicated (this was briefly discussed in Chapter 3 on international management). We also address how companies encourage innovation through "new-venture units," a method of empowering employees to break away from the restrictions of their corporate jobs to pursue new ventures. We conclude the chapter by looking at organizational models emerging out of high-tech industries. These are called "matrix organizations," and as we shall see, new technology is spearheading changes in the organization of work and managerial authority.

The previous chapter introduced concepts of organizing and emphasized that as companies grow, patterns of activities and decision making change. Activities are grouped into specialized departments, and decision-making authority is delegated to managers with expertise relating to activities within those departments. This is called *departmentalization,* and we begin our presentation with this topic.

DEPARTMENTALIZATION

departmentalization
Logical grouping of work activities based on expertise, products, markets, customers, or projects to enhance planning, leading, and controlling.

decentralization
Dispersal of authority through delegation that gives successively lower-level managers greater decision-making responsibility.

The term *departmentalization* is often confused with decentralization, but the two are not synonymous. When an organization uses **departmentalization,** a horizontal grouping of specialized activities is attained. When an organization uses **decentralization,** decision making is vertically altered, with more authority delegated to lower levels of management. We will discuss decentralization separately later in the chapter.

Departmentalization is a pragmatic segmentation of a company's activities when growth requires more people doing more things. It is usually linked with functional authority, such as creating departments in marketing, production, and accounting. However, as we shall see momentarily, there are several ways to departmentalize a company. Departmentalization relies on specialization, which is the core determinant of organizational structure. As organizations grow or become complex, they need more specialists involved in a wider range of activities. As more people are hired, more managers are needed to control more narrowly defined activities. These points are emphasized by Pradip N. Khandwalla, an organizational researcher:

> The more specialized the tasks performed by individuals, the more likely they are to be grouped together by areas of specialization to permit effective supervision.
>
> The greater the similarity in the kind of work performed by individuals and in their norms and values related to work and to interpersonal relations, the greater the probability of their being grouped together for maintaining morale.
>
> The more diversified the demand for a service within an organization, the more likely it is that individuals providing that service will be grouped together to facilitate access to them.[2]

span of control
Also called the *span of management,* it is the number of subordinates who can be effectively supervised given the type of task, technology, and environment of work.

unity of command
The concept that a subordinate should report to only one superior or receive only one set of directions from one superior at one time.

There are several other reasons for organizing employees into specialized groups. As mentioned in the previous chapter, an important consideration is **span of control** (number of people effectively supervised), also called *span of management.* If tasks are interdependent, management under one supervisor with compatible skills can widen the span of control and improve coordination. **Unity of command,** individuals reporting to only one superior rather than several, is also enhanced by departmentalization; confusion is avoided when orders come from only one person rather than several. Through departmentalization, management can ensure unity of command, and when departmentalization is coupled with effective span of control, the organization becomes more productive.

There are four approaches to departmentalization, each based on a different way of grouping specialists. These approaches are called *functional, product, geographic,* and *customer* patterns of organization.

Functional Pattern

functional pattern An approach to departmentalization based on grouping people according to their skills and expertise, giving them authority within their areas of expertise.

A **functional pattern** of organization is created by bringing together people with similar skills and expertise, and then giving them authority for those expert activities. An accounting department, for example, is created by grouping managers and employees with skills in accounting tasks, such as cost control, payables, receivables, and MIS/EDP. In a large firm, each of these specializations may become individual departments and be grouped together under a functional executive, such as the vice president for finance. Production control, quality control, purchasing, and similar activities may be individual departments under a functional executive in manufacturing. Figure 10-1 illustrates these relationships.

Horizontal coordination is improved by having functional groups because managers can then focus their attention on specific objectives. Production managers are able to concentrate on manufacturing, marketing managers on sales objectives, and other departments on their particular activities. In a small company that has not segmented its activities, a few managers may be able to tackle all these responsibilities concurrently. In a functionally organized firm, each manager's job is redefined according to his or her expertise. The company benefits from more efficient decision making in each department, and morale is improved because individuals with similar professional training are working together. Moreover, employees are likely to be more productive when they share similar values and work attitudes. Nonbusiness organizations may use similar functional patterns. Hospitals, for example, usually group their primary departments under "Services." Universities are organized according to schools or colleges, such as those in business and arts and sciences.

Although functional departmentalization has several important advantages, it also has disadvantages. Cohesiveness and leadership compatibility often create organizational blinders; the work group makes decisions according to narrow, specialized viewpoints. A functional organization is conducive to growth in earlier stages of change, but enterprises become burdened by strict functional lines in later growth stages. For example, when a firm expands into new markets or develops a wide range of products, functional managers are overwhelmed by the diversification. Westinghouse passed through this crisis during the 1940s when management faced building hundreds of different electric motors, weapon assemblies, aircraft and shipboard wiring systems, and a range of consumer goods from light bulbs to power

FIGURE 10-1 Functional Pattern of Departmentalization

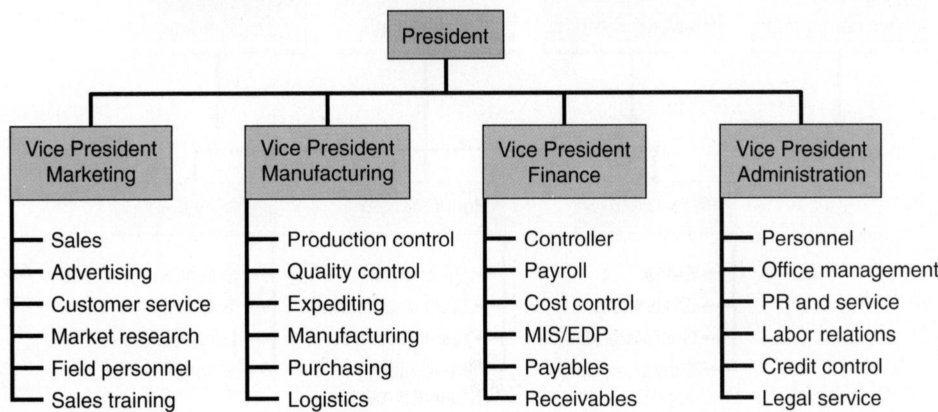

generators. One production system or one marketing office could not handle the diversified interests, and consequently, Westinghouse reorganized along multiple division lines. Functional departmentalization was the first step in the process that led to an organization based on *product* lines.

Product Pattern

product pattern
An approach to departmentalization based on grouping people according to an organization's products or services, with functional activities relocated under product or service divisions.

Before Westinghouse became departmentalized, Alfred Sloan guided General Motors away from a functional structure to one based on product lines. This occurred in the 1930s when functional authority was relocated under division managers of distinct product groups. This is called the **product pattern** of organization. Other firms made similar design changes when the burden of managing multiple products and services became too great for a functional structure. Procter & Gamble built its entire merchandising empire on logical product groups.

Figure 10-2 illustrates the product pattern, which has become one of the most common structural designs in diversified companies. The chief advantage of this pattern is the intense focus achieved for particular groups of products or services. Product organization also allows concentrated decisions that do not operationally affect other products. For example, if a Procter & Gamble product—perhaps a detergent—is in trouble, it can be easily dropped without affecting operations pertaining to hand soaps, paper products, or foods. A new product, such as Pringle's Potato Chips, can be introduced by P&G without detracting from activities in other product lines, and if Pringle's were to be dropped, it would not affect other divisions.

A critical difference between functional and product patterns is that in a company organized on product lines, functional department managers are in *subordinate* positions under senior product or division managers. Three of these positions are shown in Figure 10-2.

One of the primary benefits of a product pattern is that division employees—from the division's vice president down to its most junior person—focus exclusively on products or services within that division; activities in other divisions may go completely unnoticed. This concentration of energy improves operational efficiency within each division. Yet such intensity can also create problems if employees become so narrowly focused that they lose sight of broader organizational

FIGURE 10-2 Product Pattern of Departmentalization

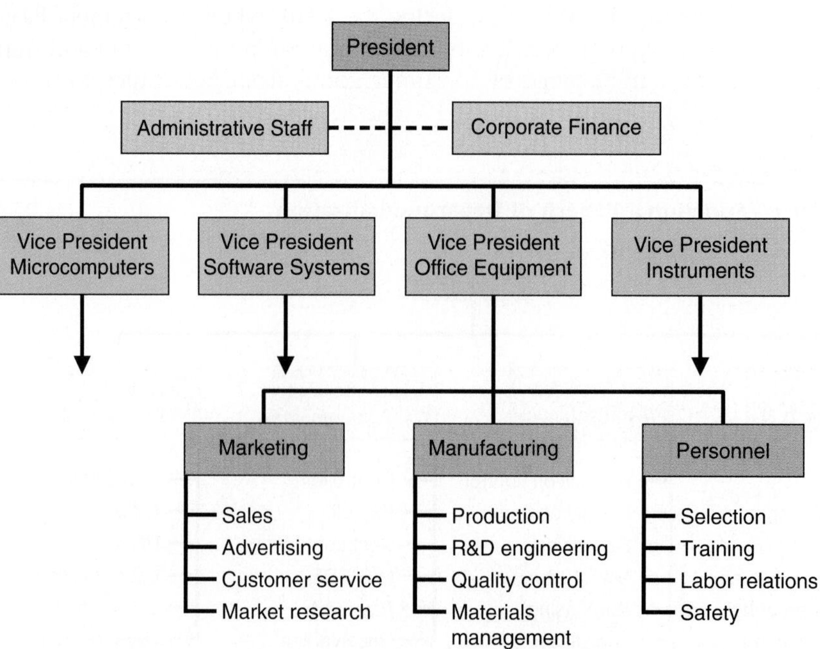

objectives. This is called *myopic behavior,* and it is not unusual for divisions to compete against one another because employees view "their" division as an independent company. Another major drawback of the product pattern is duplication of functional activities within each group. This can be an expensive organizational pattern, although the extra costs are usually offset by the enhanced coordination and efficiencies achieved by concentrating activities under one product manager.

Geographic Pattern

Territorial expansion creates a system of authority based on local control and decision making called a **geographic pattern.** Organizations must be able to cope with differences in local customs, laws, and consumer needs. In southwest Texas, for example, consumers like spicy foods, so Campbell's soups for that region are made with local chili pepper seasoning. In several areas of Los Angeles, there are concentrations of Hispanics and Asians, so Sears stocks clothing styles and colors reflecting Hispanic and Asian tastes in its L.A. stores. Field managers must have a defined territory small enough to manage, yet large enough to accommodate growth. Companies involved in international operations are sensitive to territorial patterns of behavior and find geographic patterning of management authority essential.

geographic pattern
An approach to departmentalization based on territorial control and localized decision making, with functional activities subordinated to geographic divisions.

Few companies are dominantly patterned along geographic lines, but diversified firms often have substantial geographic departmentalization at lower echelons. Figure 10-3 demonstrates the concept with marketing responsibilities distributed territorially in a product-patterned firm. These territories are labeled with compass points, but actual markets are segmented in more complicated ways. In metropolitan centers like New York, sales territories might be confined to several large office buildings. Many "mega-center" buildings have greater working populations and more individual organizations than many small cities. In contrast, a salesperson in the rural South may cover a dozen cities in several states.

An example of a geographically patterned organization is the U.S. Department of State, which has embassies, consulates, and foreign offices all over the world. State Department offices are organized with territorial responsibilities delineated first, and functional support activities then clustered according to geographic divisions. A

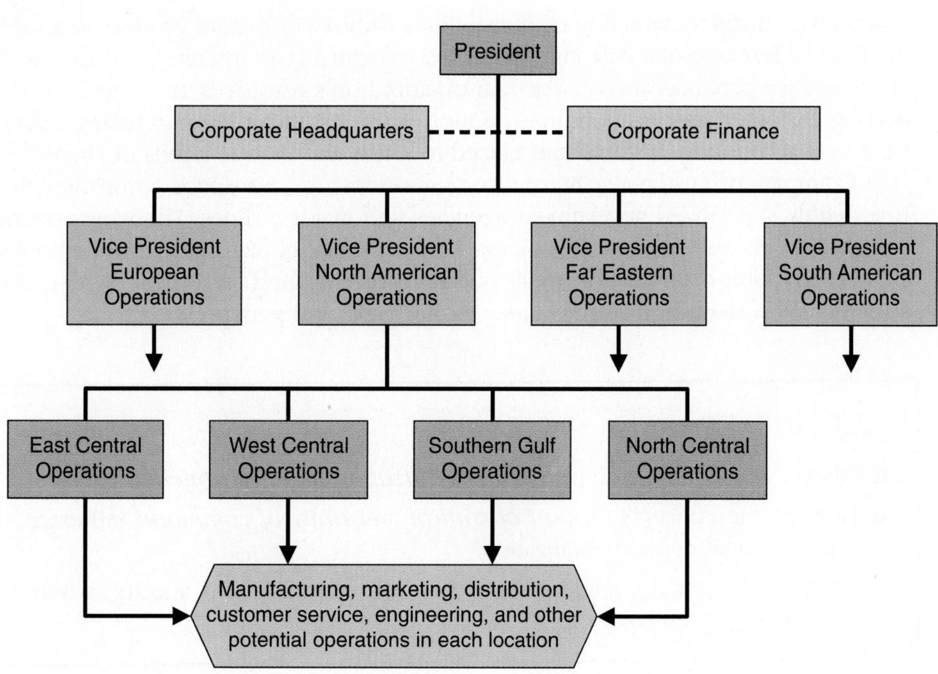

FIGURE 10-3 Geographic Pattern of Departmentalization

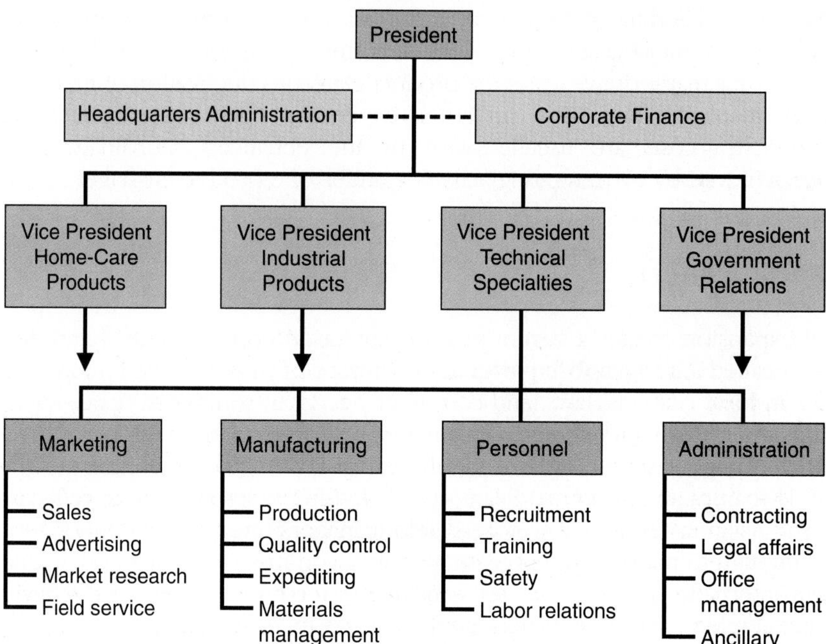

FIGURE 10-4 Customer Pattern of Departmentalization

growing number of businesses are following this example, replicating domestic products and services overseas. Caterpillar has manufacturing and distribution divisions in Canada, Europe, the Far East, and several other major foreign locations. Coca-Cola Company has become a world distributor by replicating bottling and distribution services in various countries.

Customer Pattern

customer pattern
An approach to departmentalization based on well-defined customer groups whereby employees and activities are focused on unique needs of clientele.

Many firms choose to organize according to the type of customers they serve. This is called **customer pattern** of organization. For example, an automobile manufacturer has several different types of customers requiring subdivisions of marketing skills. Domestic cars are sold to dealers, private businesses (fleet sales), car rental firms, and a variety of government agencies. Figure 10-4 illustrates a customer organization with distinct marketing responsibilities within a dominant product structure. The major advantage of a customer-patterned structure is an intense focus on customer needs for products and services. An organization's resources are rallied around meeting customer specifications, and support activities, including purchasing, advertising, and accounting, become specialized to satisfy the unique needs of clients.

Examples of customer-patterned organizations are aerospace companies that serve highly specialized government agencies and major airlines. Publishers define special divisions for college textbook markets, high school materials, juvenile books, and perhaps adult materials. Hospitals often organize around customer (patient) services such as pediatrics, maternity care, cardiac care, and geriatrics.

CHECKPOINT

- Discuss and contrast the terms *decentralization* and *departmentalization.*
- How do the concepts of *span of control* and *unity of command* influence organizational departmentalization?
- Identify the four dominant patterns of departmentalization and the advantages and disadvantages of each.

MATRIX MANAGEMENT

The evolution of organizational structures has resulted in a hybrid structure called the *matrix*. The matrix retains the functional structure, so that employees with similar expertise are grouped together in administrative units, but they work on assignments within a product or process structure, so they focus their efforts on narrowly defined projects. This type of system is known by various names, such as *project, cell,* or *matrix management,* and companies that use the hybrid structure refer to it as a *matrix organization.*

In a **matrix organization,** teams are formed on a temporary basis to manage a project or complete an activity within a company's existing structure. At the center of matrix management is a combination of specialists gathered from a number of departments to form autonomous operating units under the leadership of a project manager. The project manager may be hired from outside or be reassigned from an internal position. Figure 10-5 depicts a matrix organization in which there are two chains of command. One is vertical, linking employees in production, engineering, materials, personnel, and accounting with their functional departments. The other is horizontal, linking the same employees with their project.

matrix organization
An approach to organizing work based on forming temporary teams from the ranks of existing employees that are responsible for completing well-defined projects.

Matrix teams are drawn together to tackle specific problems or to work on well-defined projects. For example, American Cyanamid, a manufacturer of industrial and agricultural chemicals, has formed matrix teams to develop new synthetic products, research new fertilizers, and market new herbicides. Xerox used matrix teams to create desktop publishing software and a new integrated office system. Hughes Aircraft, ITT, TRW, Texas Instruments, Caterpillar, Avco, Boeing, and Lockheed use matrix techniques extensively.[3] In each instance, the matrix teams will exist until they complete their assigned projects. Then they will disband and team members will return to their functional departments or be reassigned to new projects.

Many companies have a hundred or more matrix teams operating simultaneously. Each new assignment pulls together a different group of personnel from a variety of departments. In many instances, the team includes individuals hired specifically for the project. Members of matrix teams usually face a series of recombinations and adjustments that can make life exciting or distressing. For example, an engineer at Hughes Aircraft may spend two years at White Sands Missile Range in New Mexico working on a NASA project, then spend four months on a company project in Saudi Arabia, and then join a team in the South Pacific to resolve a technical problem for one of Hughes's clients. If the engineer is somewhat adventurous and likes to travel, this lifestyle can be exciting. On the other hand, if the engineer has a family or dislikes globe-hopping, these periodic moves can be distressing.

Sometimes reassignment simply means redefining individual jobs without physically moving personnel. This can be done when work is not location-specific. Major accountant firms, for example, can assign projects to their auditors or management consultants without uprooting employees, just as advertising agencies can assign projects to teams who remain at their desks even though the clients are across the country or overseas. Most matrix teams, however, require some travel and probably relocation for extended periods of time.[4]

Behavioral Implications of Matrix Management

Matrix management creates a number of unpredictable situations for employees. Behavioral problems associated with matrix teams include career disruptions, changes in authority relations, role conflict, and stress generated by travel or relocation.

Career planning. Matrix structures typically create dual career ladders. One career track is in the employee's functional department; the other is in the employee's technical field or profession. A matrix assignment detracts from departmental oppor-

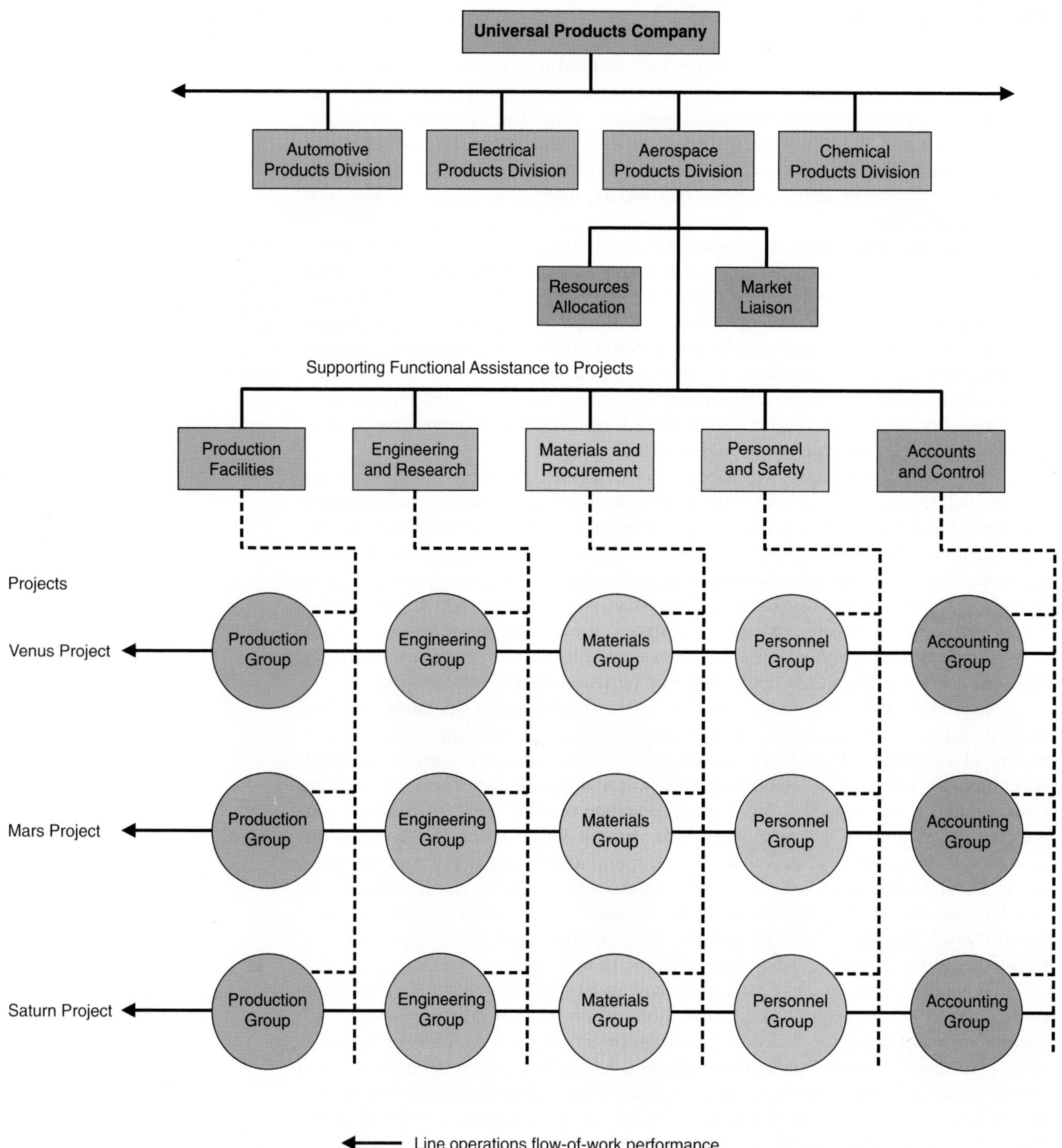

FIGURE 10-5 Reassignment in a Matrix Organization

tunities because the employee is seldom involved in mainstream departmental activities while serving as a team member. However, an employee's technical career is enhanced through diversified assignments and challenging field work. Team members, therefore, often find that career advancement and promotions are limited while they are temporarily assigned to projects, yet their enhanced technical expertise can make them more valuable employees and good candidates for more challenging project assignments.[5]

Demarcation of authority. Because employees assigned to matrix teams report to two bosses simultaneously—the department manager and the project manager—their loyalties may be split. Managers often have no clear notion of where their authority begins or ends in team assignments, and team members may become confused when conflicting directions come from their two managers. To resolve this situation, companies must clarify authority for each manager and communicate to employees what the lines of demarcation are for decisions.[6]

Role reassessment. Traditional job descriptions are inadequate to express work expectations for employees assigned to matrix teams. This problem is particularly acute for employees who report to two bosses. One answer is to write a new job description for each assignment, expressing performance expectations and employee responsibilities as a team member.[7]

Spatial orientation. If an employee is physically relocated, a host of problems crops up, including the need to maintain two houses, travel extensively, adjust culturally to new environments, and revise social networks. These problems can be addressed on two levels. First, organizations can formulate policies clarifying length of assignment, adequate compensation, and job security. Second, they can set up support systems, such as training, counseling, and relocation assistance, to alleviate tensions associated with temporary assignments.[8]

Matrix Evolution and Potential Problems

Matrix management began in large aerospace firms and involved teams of engineers and scientists working on technical projects. Today matrix teams are found in hospitals, marketing firms, universities, banks, insurance companies, and many other types of organizations. However, there are no organizations entirely structured by matrices. Traditional patterns of authority still define management hierarchies; matrices are supplemental and temporary refinements within the organization.

Large-scale projects, like NASA's space station project, cannot be managed in traditional ways. Matrix teams provide the means for accomplishing program objectives by creating grids of matrices (matrices within matrices) under a superstructure of a coordinating agency (NASA).

Matrices have evolved in companies where the complexity of product-market relations requires more focused attention on smaller, more manageable operations. They have also evolved in response to technological changes that require intense focus on new-product development, market research, or new methods of manufacturing. These needs can be met through permanent forms of organization, but matrix teams achieve results more rapidly and efficiently. Most research concludes that matrix management techniques are essential for amassing resources and personnel from many independent organizations. However, the management of matrix teams creates several problems.[9]

Dual accounting and control. Matrices within traditional forms of organization maintain separate accounting and records; one set of budgets and accounts relates to the matrix project, and the other relates to existing company operations. Budgets and resource allocations become not only confusing but also subjects of contention between managers in both arenas.

Coordination and information processing. Traditional reporting procedures are modified, and information processing serves two distinctly different types of operations. Matrix teams need specialized information in remote locations; the information needed for corporate operations reflects established models. This can lead to confusion and coordination problems.

Dilution of power. Two-boss systems create a separation of authority that affects employees, resources, and facilities. This situation is confusing to the specialists who move between teams and home-based departments. Managers also experience problems because their power is diluted and their authority over resource decisions is ambiguous.

Myopic objectives. Many groups that operate under matrix systems become semiautonomous and in the process lose sight of total organizational objectives. Teams focus narrowly on project results, and ironically, the better they do this, the greater the likelihood of their becoming myopic about organizational needs.

A Matrix Perspective

All these difficulties raise the question of whether matrix management is really superior to more traditional patterns of departmentalization. Advocates argue that "matrix" is merely a convenient label for changes taking place in organizations that require temporary units and flexibility in management. Rosabeth Moss Kanter, author of the best-selling management book *The Change Masters,* says that American firms are being transformed in the direction of innovation and internal entrepreneurship.[10] This movement, she suggests, is concerned with tapping the creativity of individuals within organizations, encouraging collaborative thinking, and engendering greater risk taking.

Kanter admits that matrix organizations can be frustrating because managers constantly have to juggle resources and authority; however, she believes that these interdisciplinary efforts are valuable because they focus people across departmental boundaries on results.

Many examples support Kanter's view. Allied Corporation created teams to investigate the market potential of shelved ideas in commercial chemicals. Among ideas that had been collecting dust for years, research teams found commercially viable suggestions for new chemical alloys, metal treatments, and new technologies. Subsequently, Allied extended its matrix management concept by incorporating several of these teams and underwriting new ventures. Security Pacific Corporation, a bank holding company, formed service and customer teams to target their efforts on special forms of investments. The result was several new ventures staffed by permanent employees.[11]

The matrix, or multifunctional project team, has become common in American corporations, and it is rapidly influencing how firms organize their tasks. In the future, organizations are likely to be more flexible and to emphasize smaller, integrated group processes. If this prediction proves accurate, collaborative organizations will dominate our culture in the early twenty-first century.

CHECKPOINT

- Define matrix management and the two-boss system of organizational structure.
- What are the major advantages of the matrix management system to a company and to an individual?
- Discuss four major problems associated with matrix management that companies must resolve.
- Argue for or against matrix management as a means of engendering creativity and innovation in organizations.

AUTHORITY

Organizational social systems are affected by, and have a direct influence on, *authority*. This is a recurrent theme that was addressed in Chapter 15 on decision making and Chapter 9 on the fundamental concepts of organizing. **Authority** is the right to make decisions within predetermined boundaries sanctioned by an organization. Often this is a legal mandate, such as the authority vested in a judge or a law enforcement officer; but in business, it is more often a form of *institutionalized* responsibility delegated by owners to senior managers, further delegated to lower-level managers, and, in many instances, subsequently delegated to individual employees and work groups.

authority
The right to make decisions within predetermined boundaries sanctioned by an organization, often taking the form of legal or institutionalized responsibility.

Traditional and Emerging Views of Authority

In the traditional models of organization, the extent of an individual's authority is based largely on his or her position within the hierarchy of management. Consequently, "position" and "authority" are almost synonymous in their implications for decision making. Positions of authority are like rungs on a ladder, and we aptly view this as *scalar authority*. We also tend to think of authority in a chain relationship and refer to position power in terms of *unity of command*.

Scalar authority. All of us accept the notion of hierarchical authority; we have come to expect it in organizations. Since we also prefer order and clarity in our lives, we expect managerial authority to be ordered and clear. We want formal reporting channels to be unambiguous. A scalar chain of authority provides this clarity. In the **scalar chain,** there is a direct linkage between each level of management from bottom to top in an organization. We have many metaphors in our culture to illustrate it. Thus, we speak of "climbing the ladder of success" and reporting up the "chain of command." Scalar authority means that we report to someone who in turn reports to someone else; there is no ambiguity about who reports to whom.

scalar chain
The concept of a clear, unbroken line of authority derived from unambiguous delegation throughout the management hierarchy.

ETHICS IN MANAGEMENT

Technology Opens Doors for Women at Siemens

Although women come up against stiff obstacles to advancement to the upper echelons of management, some are finding a new route to high-paying careers in technical positions. Specifically, women who understand information systems (IS) and are capable systems analysts are moving ahead rapidly in corporate positions.

PCs and IS management are great equalizers, according to women executives at Siemens Medical Systems and Chemical Bank of New York. Joanne Witt, the senior technology analyst at Siemens, was promoted rapidly during the six years after she entered the corporate world. She found that in the IS field results are more important than gender, and a systems analyst who can solve corporate problems will reap the rewards. At Siemens, information technology is crucial to research and development, operations controls, and marketing, and Witt found that she had a keen interest in solving these types of systems problems.

Doreen Rubin, senior technology officer at Chemical Bank, is responsible for microcomputing, and although she finds the route to upper management blocked, she believes it is because of stereotypes held by top management regarding staff MIS, rather than because of sex stereotypes; few men have been promoted out of staff positions to fast-track general management jobs. There seems to be an internal battle between advocates of mainframe systems and advocates of microcomputers. Mainframes still dominate, even though micros are popular among lower-level managers. Top managers are schooled in mainframe systems and therefore promote managers with similar views, who are generally older men. According to Rubin, future careers for women hold exciting growth opportunities in microcomputing and software development.

Witt agrees with Rubin, believing that all avenues in this field are open to women, but at Siemens there is a barrier, common in most companies, preventing staff technicians from "crossing the line" into executive management. For Witt, that is not an uncomfortable situation because, she says, success in her field is spelled out in software applications and end-user satisfaction. Information systems are gender-free, and because women are often at ease in IS development situations requiring patience and long hours of concentration, she feels that women can find rewarding careers in the information field.

Women are also enjoying public honors in the IS field. In 1992, the Association for Systems Management gave its highest honors to Dorothy Yetter, chief information officer for the County of San Mateo, California, and Judy Andrews, business development manager at Texas Instruments. Both were cited for their leadership roles in information systems development.

Sources: Kristi Coale, "Women Making Gains in IS Sphere," *Infoworld*, March 9, 1992, pp. 53–54. See also Alice LaPlante, "Retraining Staff Is Crucial to a Shift to Information Management," *Infoworld*, February 17, 1992, p. 52.

unity of command
The concept that a subordinate should report to only one superior or receive only one set of directions from one superior at a time.

Unity of command. While scalar authority implies a direct reporting relationship, **unity of command** means that each person should report to only one superior. Subordinates should not have more than one superior telling them what to do. We expect only one person at a time to be in charge; therefore, when someone other than our immediate superior gives us an order, we tend to resent it. If authority is to be accepted, it must be clear who has it.

Realistically, an absolute chain of authority and unambiguous reporting channels are rare today. They may exist in some highly disciplined military units, but in practice most reporting channels are "soft" and employees answer to or work with several senior managers.

Shared decision making and teamwork. We must recognize the changes taking place in Western organizations to understand how managerial roles and authority are changing. For example, during the early 1980s, GE's chairman, Jack Welch, was considered a tough CEO who wielded his authority and expected corporate managers to reinforce a rigid chain of command. He held managers fully responsible for decisions and resisted employee involvement in those decisions. Yet by 1990, Welch had transformed himself into a strong advocate of participative team management. In 1990, *Financial World* named Welch CEO of the year, and today he is considered a visionary. GE managers and their employees are encouraged to accept greater independent decision-making authority, and "old-school bosses who yell and scream" have been rapidly weeded out.[12] Welch has been singled out by the business press, but CEOs of many organizations—including those listed by *Fortune* as among America's most innovative companies—have aggressively pursued team management.[13] Consequently, organizations are being redefined to conform with a redistribution of authority based on *shared* decision making and *teamwork*.

Accountability: Balancing Authority and Responsibility

Authority, whether in a team environment or in a rigid chain of command, means being held accountable for results. Those receiving the authority must therefore also be given the means, tools, and control over decisions to effect results. This is not a matter of semantics, but of managerial *behavior* sanctioning those who have been given authority for their work.

Unfortunately, many managers *say* they are delegating authority, form participative teams (such as quality circle work groups), or tell employees they are responsible for their decisions—and then disenfranchise subordinates in practice. There are two general ways this happens. First, a senior manager may formally announce that a subordinate or work group has certain authority, but then continue to interfere with operations or veto decisions; the process of delegation subsequently fails. For example, Frank Lorenzo, the former chairman of Texas Air, *said* his managers were responsible for their own decisions, yet he was notorious for making spot decisions overruling anyone at any time on any issue.[14] Second, a senior manager may formally delegate authority to the extent of giving subordinates or work groups complete autonomy, but provide little or no support for them; this is an act of abdication that creates a leadership vacuum. Stephen Jobs, a brilliant entrepreneur, gave employees wide-ranging freedom at Apple Computers when he headed the company. However, he provided very little leadership support, thereby creating a chaotic work environment in which employees lacked direction.[15] In either situation, authority is unsanctioned, so neither subordinates nor their work teams can reasonably be held accountable for results. In addition, they usually become confused, frustrated, and unproductive.[16]

Line and Staff Authority

Departmentalization often focuses on achieving coordination between *staff* and *line* activities. **Line managers** directly concern themselves with primary operations of the firm, whereas **staff managers** usually concern themselves with support or advisory activities.[17] In a manufacturing firm, production and marketing managers are

line managers
Line managers concern themselves with the primary operations of a firm and have direct authority for operational results.

staff managers
Staff managers concern themselves with the support and advising activities that reinforce line operations, but do not have direct authority for operational results.

line; accounting, data processing, and purchasing managers are usually considered staff. In a hospital, X-ray and personnel specialists are in support roles, and their departments are subordinated to medical and surgical services, which are the hospital's line functions.

Distinctions between line and staff are not always so clear. A data processing manager in a university, for example, holds a staff position, but a data processing manager in a computer software company holds a line position. A finance officer may be considered staff in manufacturing but line in a bank. So professional classifications do not necessarily define functional roles or authority in organizations. In each of the organizational patterns discussed earlier, functional departments were shifted downward to support departments, further confusing the distinction between line and staff. The distinction is important, however, because decision-making activities differ significantly between line and staff managers.

Distinguishing between line and staff. Specialists in many fields find themselves in staff positions where they act as expert advisers to line managers. Corporate attorneys, for example, often act as personal advisers to company executives. Economic advisers, affirmative action officers, and strategic policy experts often have similar positions. They are called **personal staff** because, as expert advisers, they provide special services or advice related to unique responsibilities within their fields. Personal staff specialists do not make decisions; the line managers they advise make decisions. Yet, they often have tremendous influence on those decisions because of their expertise and because they have access to key individuals and sensitive information.[18]

personal staff
Expert advisers who provide special services or advice related to particular responsibilities such as legal affairs, economic consulting, or affirmative action.

staff assistants
Assistants and advisers to line managers who directly support operational activities but do not become involved in those decisions.

Staff assistants provide direct support to line managers, and they are usually concerned with operational tasks. Unlike personal staff, who are experts and hold positions directly related to the professions in which they are educated, staff assistants take responsibility for a broad range of tasks required to support operations. In a manufacturing company, for example, a staff assistant to the vice president for production may handle much of the office correspondence, prepare draft reports, oversee records, help schedule meetings and trips, and provide a liaison with union representatives. Some staff assistants have duties that limit them to clerical and office activities, and many of these assistants are appointed to these positions based on their experience in secretarial jobs. Others have duties that make use of their personal skills, such as in public relations or customer relations. Still others find themselves assigned to various projects, such as assisting with a new foreign office or researching a capital improvement budget.

Personal staff and staff assistants are seldom considered managers in the sense of having decision-making responsibilities for functional activities. There are "staff managers," of course, such as personnel managers, market research specialists, and payroll accountants. These positions and their departments are addressed momentarily. Personal staff, however, do find themselves in managerial roles. Large companies often need teams of specialists and, consequently, several economic advisers or attorneys may be grouped together. As these teams evolve, they may develop internal structures with someone in authority for assignments or team activities. In contrast, staff assistants rarely find themselves in managerial roles. Even when several assistants work together, a line manager will remain in authority; yet, like personal staff, staff assistants can be extremely influential because of their accessibility to key people and their involvement in operational activities.

Staff departments. Staff departments are common in larger firms, and how they are positioned in the hierarchy to support line management activities depends on the pattern of organization. As shown earlier, in a functionally patterned organization, staff support activities have a chain of command within the functional specialization ranging from operational to executive levels. In the product-, geographic-, and customer-patterned organizations, staff departments are subordinated to division

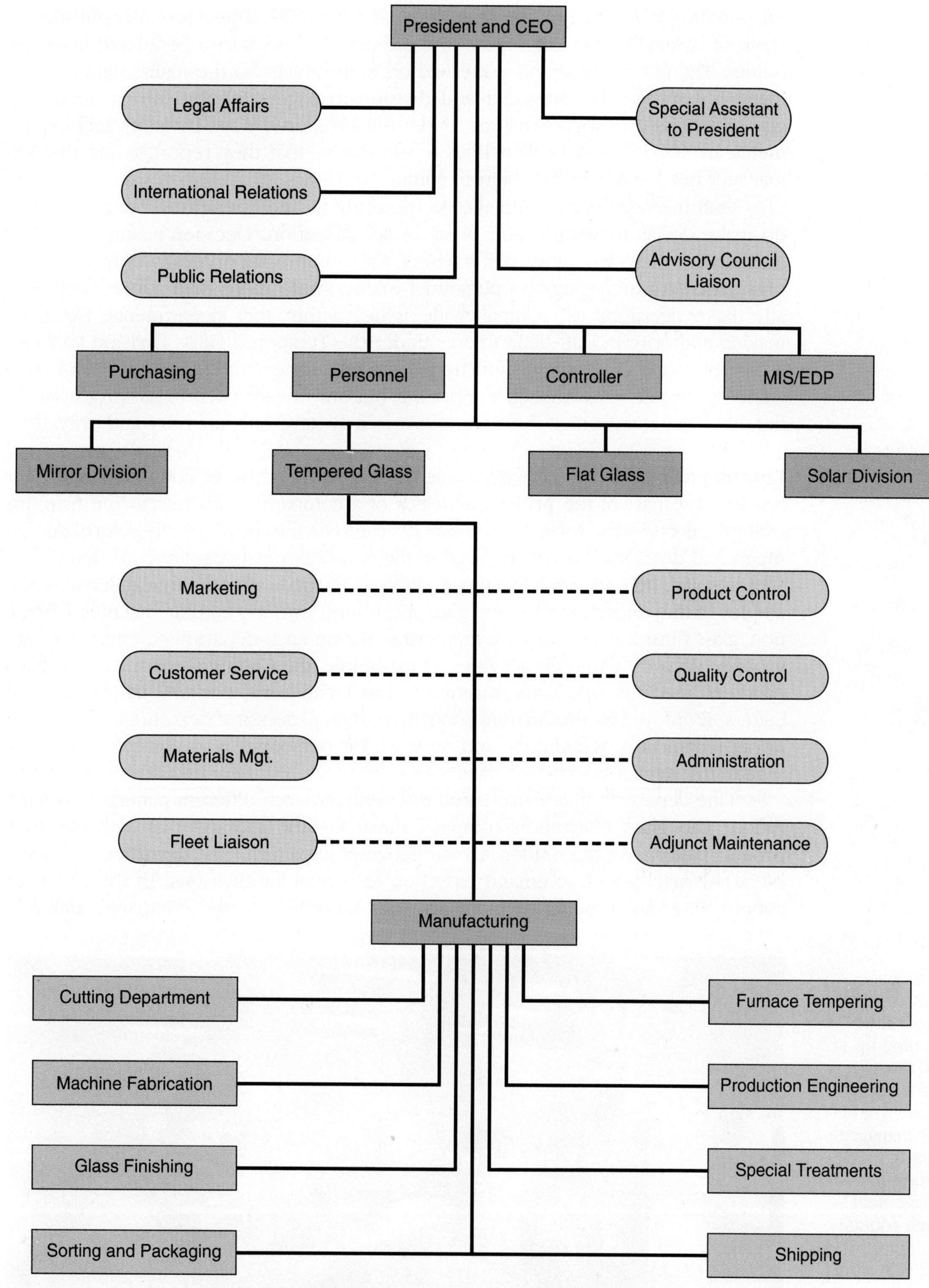

FIGURE 10-6 Line and Staff Relationships in a Glass Fabrication Firm

line managers; staff departments are also positioned lower in the hierarchy.[19]

Figure 10-6 illustrates a variety of line and staff relationships in a glass fabrication firm. Notice that the president and CEO has "personal staff"—for legal affairs, international relations, and public relations—in executive support roles. These personal staff are not in the chain of command. At the next level, staff departments exist for purchasing, personnel, the controller, and MIS/EDP. These are also outside the chain of command, yet employees in these departments have operational responsibilities. The glass company is patterned on its products, so the main chain of command is between the president and division managers for the mirror, tempered glass, flat glass, and solar divisions. Under the Tempered Glass Division, staff departments are shown with broken lines to emphasize that they report to the division manager but are not in the chain of command.

Staff managers may not make decisions about line operations, but clearly they do make decisions within their areas of specialization. Decision-making authority also varies widely. Executive staff advisers, for example, theoretically only *advise* the president, yet purchasing and personnel managers do more than advise; they actually make decisions on companywide issues within staff departments. Decision-making authority in staff departments under the Tempered Glass Division will vary according to the department's function. Marketing, for example, may have substantial authority for sales, advertising, and pricing, but only for tempered glass products. On the other hand, customer service employees may have only advisory authority.

Line departments. Line departments exist in the chain of command, and their activities are part of the primary activities of a company. A manufacturing firm, for example, is concerned with conversion of materials into products; therefore, departments and divisions directly involved in the conversion process are considered line. In a hospital, line activities are those involved in medical and surgical services. Examples of line departments in the glass fabrication firm are cutting, machine fabrication, glass finishing, and furnace tempering. Within each department, employees are grouped according to their activities. For example, the Cutting Department has glass handlers, machine operators, machine setup technicians, packers, inspectors, and cutters. Employed in Production Control are data processing personnel, expediters, layout technicians, schedulers, and sales liaison personnel who control production scheduling activities.

Line departments are structured differently in each different pattern or organization. The glass fabrication company illustrates the hierarchy of activities in a product-patterned organization. In the geographic pattern, line departments form a hierarchy or chain of command based on territorial subdivisions. In the customer pattern, line departments segment activities according to the company's different

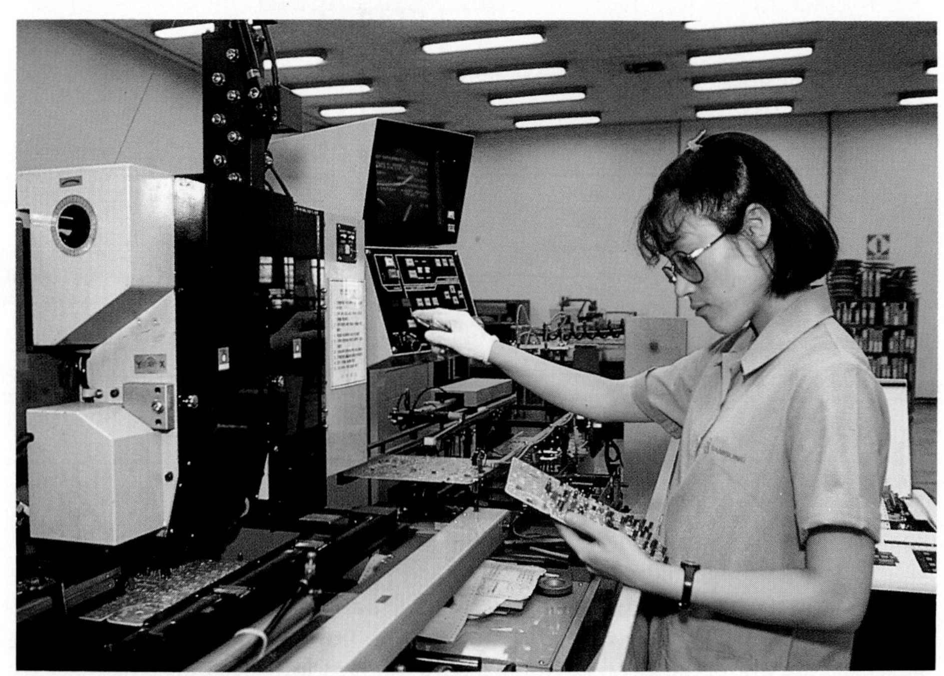

Like other Korean *chaebol* (conglomerates), Samsung has recognized the massive new market potential opening up in the ruins of the Cold War. The company has taken the lead in increasing its productivity and efficiency. Samsung's managers have proved particularly effective at reorganizing line production and management departments. Although robots are displacing many line employees, Samsung is avoiding layoffs by training first-line managers and workers for new positions—a program that greatly enhances morale. At the same time, the company has streamlined its staff operations. Samsung staff managers now meet less frequently and compile fewer reports, forcing immediate, direct communication.

customer classifications. In each instance, workers are organized in line departments to galvanize operational activities, not to focus on specialized functional activities.

Line and staff departments develop in response to growth. As a company expands, it becomes departmentalized so that line and staff activities can be separately clustered in departments. As departmentalization increases, there is also a greater need for coordination between line and staff personnel, and with more departments, there is usually greater decentralization of authority. These two forces, departmentalization and decentralization, require more middle managers with abilities to coordinate diverse groups and to control operations.

Clarifying line and staff authority. Management faces ongoing difficulties resolving line and staff responsibility. On the one hand, organizations need staff experts to deal with special issues such as government regulations, employment activities, safety, pensions, environmental protection, litigation, quality assurance, information systems, and finances. Few companies can rely solely on line managers to handle these responsibilities. On the other hand, as more staff managers are brought into an organization, decision-making authority becomes dispersed and the potential for misunderstanding increases. There are five areas of concern: *encroachment, infringement, ambiguity, perceptual differences,* and *concurrent authority.*

- *Encroachment* is associated with staff managers who either take it upon themselves to make decisions about operational issues or unintentionally encroach on line authority by influencing decisions by the weight of their expertise. A staff cost accountant, for example, might go beyond his or her role as an "adviser" to make decisions that change resource allocations for line departments.
- *Infringement* implies a conscious effort to usurp line authority or overrule line managers' decisions. When this is done maliciously, conflict between line and staff managers is certain. At times, however, staff specialists are expected to intercede. An affirmative action officer, for example, is required to review employment and promotion decisions and to intervene, changing decisions that violate federal or state laws on equal opportunity and affirmative action.
- *Ambiguity* in staff roles can result in lack of accountability for decisions by both line and staff managers. At one end of the spectrum, this means simple misunderstandings about who is responsible for certain tasks. At the other extreme, it means that both line and staff managers defer decisions, creating a chaotic work environment.
- *Perceptual differences* that arise from incompatibilities between staff and line managers based on education, age, and experience can create conflicts. Managers with different backgrounds are likely to come up with very different solutions to the same problem, and often a manager in one category resents involvement by someone in the other category.
- *Concurrent authority* exists when members of line and staff groups have joint authority for decisions. This can occur, for example, when research engineers have a voice in production methods or staff MIS officers work jointly with line managers to develop computer-based information systems. Concurrent authority has the potential for producing conflict or misunderstandings.

Preventing problems in these areas is a matter of structuring authority in staff and line positions. If staff accountants are in advisory roles, for example, then it should be clear that they have only limited authority to assist and advise line managers about resource allocations. A labor relations specialist, however, may have contractual authority to arbitrate grievances between employees and line managers. In a clearly structured organization, credit managers are authorized to veto sales; quality control managers have the authority to halt production lines; and safety officers are expected to enforce work rules. If credit managers can only refer suspect sales back to a sales manager, a quality control manager needs the permission of a line manager to interfere with production, or a safety officer is only allowed to point out work rule infractions, authority becomes muddled.

Encroachment, infringement, and ambiguity are more probable potential problems when an organization relies on participative teams for operational decisions. At Procter & Gamble, product development teams commonly include these staff specialists in addition to line operating personnel from production, sales, distribution, process engineering, and materials management. Also, the groups can call on others, including legal advisers, safety experts, and advertising specialists, to sit in on decisions.[20] Group decisions are subsequently made, but the extent to which line and staff employees contribute to those decisions is vague. Chapter 11 addresses group processes in greater detail. In the next section of this chapter, we describe how proper delegation of authority can help resolve many of these problems.

CHECKPOINT

- Describe institutionalized authority and how accountability for decisions can be assured.
- What are the main differences between line and staff managers in terms of decision-making authority?
- Discuss and contrast line and staff departments, and explain their positions in an organizational hierarchy.
- What are the common problems associated with line-staff authority and how can they be reconciled?

DELEGATION OF AUTHORITY

delegation
The process of partially distributing authority to subordinates for making decisions or performing tasks.

Many line-staff conflicts can be minimized by proper delegation of authority. **Delegation** is the downward dispersal of formal authority to make decisions. Therefore, when we speak of "proper" delegation, we mean formal authority that is vested in line and staff managers for effective decisions and accountability.[21]

Delegation of authority has evolved by necessity. To many smaller businesses, the process of delegation means the same thing now that it did 200 years ago—a method of getting help for overworked owners. In larger companies, however, delegation means transferring specific authority to managers for highly specialized tasks.

The Spectrum of Delegation

The spectrum of delegation defines the degree of management decision-making authority. Minimum delegation creates a situation in which management seeks only advice from "personal staff advisers." At the other extreme is thorough delegation of authority whereby lower-level managers or work groups have autonomy to make decisions. Figure 10-7 illustrates six strategic points of delegation along this spectrum, each with different degrees of authority. [22]

- *Personal Assistance.* At one end of the spectrum, minimum authority is delegated. Subordinates act solely as advisers. They may influence decisions, but they do not participate in decision making.
- *Participative Assistance.* Subordinates have a voice in actual decision making, but this is only a "degree of participation," not "equal participation." At this

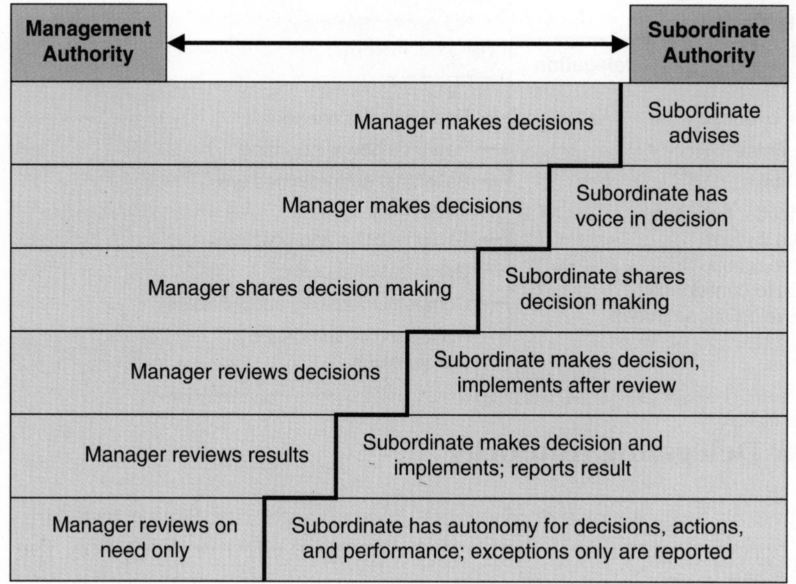

Management Authority
Subordinate Authority
Manager makes decisions
Subordinate advises
Manager makes decisions
Subordinate has voice in decision
Manager shares decision making
Subordinate shares decision making
Manager reviews decisions
Subordinate makes decision, implements after review
Manager reviews results
Subordinate makes decision and implements; reports result
Manager reviews on need only
Subordinate has autonomy for decisions, actions, and performance; exceptions only are reported

FIGURE 10-7 Degrees of Delegation Along the Spectrum of Authority

point on the spectrum, subordinates are involved in decisions where their expertise is needed, and they may advocate positions, but they do not actually participate in making decisions.

- *Joint Decision Making.* Shared responsibility for making decisions between superiors and subordinates is not uncommon. At this midpoint on the spectrum, subordinates have crossed the line that separates "advising" from "decision making." Often, decisions made in this context derive from group behavior. Committees are used extensively for joint-task decisions, and superiors may consider recommendations from subordinates or work together with them to reach consensus.
- *Subordinate Decision Making.* Greater delegation occurs as subordinates are given positions and commensurate responsibility for independent decision making. The formal positions that are created are either in staff or line management, and the people in those positions have appropriate authority for making decisions without the direct participation of superiors.

  There are two general models of management behavior for decision making as subordinates accrue authority. A manager may retain the right to review all decisions by subordinates prior to implementation, or may choose instead only to be informed periodically of decisions. The first model is delegation with a string attached. Subordinates make decisions, but because their superiors review them, subordinates may be asked to reconsider their decisions. The second model implies a more sweeping transfer of authority.
- *Autonomy in Decision Making.* The greatest formal transfer of authority occurs when subordinates are autonomous within legal and ethical limits. Senior managers are informed of results through periodic reporting procedures, but otherwise their subordinates succeed or fail within a general framework of full accountability.
- *Near-Abdication.* There is no real delegation beyond autonomy; managers who go beyond this point on the spectrum abdicate! Unfortunately, some managers think that once they have delegated authority, their subordinates must bear the full burden of success or failure. But, as noted earlier, no manager can completely avoid responsibility. If we assume that every organization has a clear line of authority, then no manager is ever completely free of accountability for his or her employees' behavior.

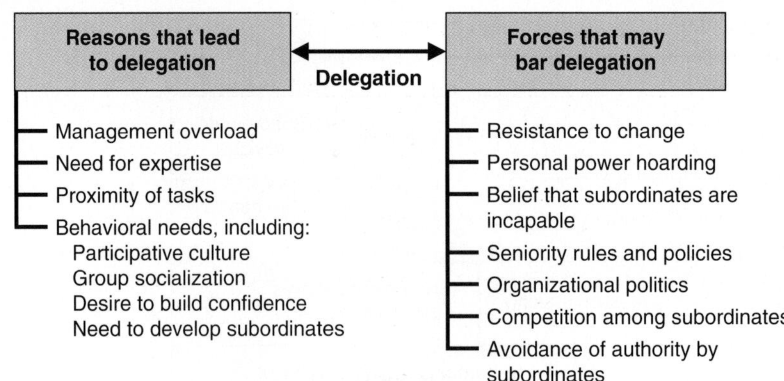

FIGURE 10-8 Factors That Influence Delegation

Reasons for Delegating Authority

We have touched on the reasons that managers delegate authority. Figure 10-8 summarizes these reasons, together with the barriers that retard effective delegation. The reasons for delegation are:[23]

- *Managerial Overload.* If managers have too much work, they need assistance. This is the classic model of delegation, in which a general but limited transfer of authority relieves operational pressures.
- *Need for Expertise.* This is the most common reason for delegating authority in complex organizations. Specialization is needed in so many situations that no one person can successfully handle decisions across the breadth of a firm.
- *Proximity of Tasks.* A fundamental reason for delegating authority is to situate managerial control as close as possible to activities. First-line managers' proximity to tasks suggests a logical transfer of authority to ensure timely decisions at operational points.
- *Behavioral Needs.* Managers often delegate authority to create a psychological climate of cooperation. We all want to feel important to our organizations, to believe we are making a contribution. We feel part of the process when we have contributed to decisions that affect us. Consequently, managers find they can motivate subordinates more effectively by bringing them in on actual decision-making situations.[24] Also, by identifying individuals with leadership potential and offering them the opportunity to expand their responsibilities, managers develop these people for future leadership roles.

This is only an introduction to the behavioral topics pertaining to delegation and decision-making authority. Chapters 14 and 15 expand on behavior and leadership concepts.

Barriers to Effective Delegation

We have discussed delegation as if all managers *willingly* relinquish some of their authority. Generally, this is *not* true. Managers, in fact, tend to hoard authority and strongly resist giving it up. Some business owners hold on to authority so tightly that they destroy their companies by making decisions that experts would have handled better. In large organizations, managers often control decisions so closely that they throttle their employees. The halls of defunct organizations echo with such catch phrases as "It will get done faster if I do it myself," "Subordinates lack the experience to do the job right," "I don't have time to train these people, I need performance."

Despite the element of truth in these catch phrases, they are shortsighted. As work piles up and problems go unattended, managers who "didn't have time" to train others eventually run out of time to do anything effectively. Then they *really* have no time to train their employees and can count on little support from those employees when they desperately need it. Managers and owners who did not have the patience to encourage subordinates to share in decisions discover in a crunch that the people under them not only are unaccustomed to making decisions but also shy away from authority when it is finally offered to them.

Another barrier to effective delegation is stereotyping. General managers often view functional experts as rather narrow specialists who lack the ability to handle broader issues of leadership. There is no logical reason for this view because decision-making and leadership qualities depend more on individual characteristics than on technical expertise.

There are other barriers to effective delegation. Organizational politics often block delegation. Union seniority rules may prevent the promotion of capable employees. Co-workers can pressure peers to resist authority. Competition between managers leads to power hoarding. And many subordinates refuse to accept authority because they do not want the added responsibility.

Toward More Effective Delegation

Two fundamental elements of effective delegation are *clarity* and *sufficiency*. First, managers must clarify in their own minds why they are delegating authority, and then they must make it plain to subordinates what authority is being delegated. Second, managers must delegate sufficient authority for subordinates to be able to accomplish what is intended without abdicating responsibility for the results.[25]

Clarity means that managers must be explicit about how they expect their subordinates to make decisions. If subordinates are to have advisory authority, then both they and their superiors should clarify the boundaries of that authority and agree on how decisions are to be made. At the other extreme, if subordinates are supposed to act autonomously, then managers must articulate their expectations and resist the temptation to intervene.

clarity
Managers must be explicit about how they expect subordinates to make decisions and the extent to which subordinates have authority to make decisions.

Actually, these polar extremes do not present problems for management nearly as often as the intermediate degrees of authority. The demarcation noted earlier between advisory situations and participative management is real, but where the role of adviser ends and that of decision maker begins is elusive. If it is important to be clear about expectations, it is equally important to reinforce them with consistent behavior. Managers cannot set up participative systems for making decisions and then overrule subordinates' decisions. Clarity of delegation is essential to provide subordinates with decision-making parameters, but it is also crucial to define boundaries of behavior for superiors.[26]

Sufficiency means balancing authority with performance expectations. Managers cannot be held accountable for decisions they are only superficially involved in. If managers hire advisers, they cannot expect them to be accountable for decisions.

sufficiency
Subordinates can only be held accountable if they have sufficient authority to make decisions relating to activities for which they are responsible.

For example, a plant manager recently complained that he was no more than a "glorified clerk," a whipping boy of the company's president. When asked why he felt this way, he said that although he apparently had profit-and-loss responsibilities for millions of dollars' worth of production, he couldn't hire a janitor without clearing it with the president. A review of some of the plant manager's decisions revealed that although he had tremendous authority to make production and marketing decisions, his decisions were often overruled. Because almost any of his decisions could be vetoed, he could not reasonably be held responsible for profits and losses.

We cannot generalize about sufficiency; it has no objective measurement because situations and individuals vary. Yet intentions must be clear between superiors and subordinates. Both must understand the extent of their authority and accountability.

CHECKPOINT

- Why do managers delegate authority?
- Identify key points along the spectrum of delegation.
- Identify several crucial barriers to delegation that managers must overcome.
- Why are clarity and sufficiency important for effective delegation?

CENTRALIZATION VERSUS DECENTRALIZATION

centralization
The concentration of decision-making authority at top levels of management with little delegation to others.

An organization resorts to **centralization** in order to permit one individual or a group of senior executives to retain decision-making authority. Little delegation occurs in a centralized organization, and lower-level managers have limited discretion. An organization is *decentralized* if decision-making authority is widely delegated to lower-echelon managers. Subordinates then have greater latitude and a certain degree of autonomy. Whether a firm is centralized or decentralized depends on actual decision-making *behavior,* not on the extent to which the firm appears to be one or the other on an organizational chart. Several factors tip the scales toward more or less decentralization.

Factors That Influence Decentralization

When companies grow, they need more managers, and as our world becomes more complex, the need for specialists increases. Consequently, decision making becomes more complicated, and more reasons develop to decentralize, among which the following are most important.[27]

Size and age. Larger organizations have more employees working in more diversified jobs that require more managers to coordinate activities. These managers are expected to assume decision-making responsibilities to free executives to concentrate on strategic issues. Older companies tend to develop more routine patterns in decision making that allow lower-level managers to broaden their spans of control. This can result in "downsizing," or reducing the number of managers, as described in Chapter 9.

Complexity. Organizations of almost any size can become complex, requiring specialized knowledge and decision making. Product or service diversification will influence management to delegate more authority to specialists, but even firms with single products or services can operate in complex markets, such as those involved in government contracting. Some face complex legal problems imposed by government regulations, such as those promulgated by the Food and Drug Administration. In these instances, elaborate management systems may evolve.

Need for adaptation. A need for speedy decisions at lower-management levels and greater latitude for adaptation will influence firms to decentralize. For example, in dangerous situations, a lower-level manager may not have the time to seek advice or approval before taking action. Merck & Company delegates substantial authority to line managers in manufacturing who work with hazardous materials and are responsible for workers' safety. Marketing managers in field situations also tend to accrue greater authority to compete more effectively against local rivals.

Need for innovation. Centralized authority, particularly in larger firms, implies less scope for individual initiative. Structured environments can stifle creativity. Innovative companies constantly strive for new products, new services, and more productive methods of accomplishing their objectives. Companies seeking to be competitive must unshackle their people and encourage new and often risky ideas. Delegation, with more autonomous control over operations, is essential to nourish innovation. For example, 3M executives encourage managers to allocate up to 20 percent of their time to original work.[28]

The Leadership Dimension

Innovation, complexity, size, age, and need for adaptation encourage or discourage decentralization, but these factors can be understood only in the context of a company's leadership. Regardless of how authority is officially delegated, executives can diffuse or hoard it, thereby centralizing or decentralizing decisions. Although a decentralized structure is theoretically superior in large and more complex companies, it is not a panacea; many organizations thrive under the centralized control of exceptional leaders.

Many firms have achieved success through the wizardry of their leaders. William C. Norris spearheaded Control Data Corporation to prominence, John McCoy revolutionized electronic banking at Bank One in Ohio, and H. Ross Perot created Electronic Data Systems through his strong character. Organizations, then, are often reflections of their top-echelon managers; regardless of their size or complexity, decision-making authority conforms to the style of leadership at the top. [29]

Organization charts do not reveal how leaders behave. Sun Microsystems, for example, is organized around its computer hardware and software divisions, and a block chart of management would look very much like the "product" organization described earlier. However, Sun's president, Scott McNealy, has hired senior division managers who are described as hard-driving individualists capable of creating riots

John Deere and Caterpillar, makers of agricultural and construction equipment, have long been guided by similar philosophies of decentralization. Both companies sell hundreds of products in more than 100 countries. Field managers and dealers in all of these countries are given substantial responsibility for decisions and suggestions at many levels of company operations. Here, Deere and Caterpillar equipment are loaded for export to Europe.

at management meetings. Carol A. Bartz, promoted by McNealy to head his Federal Systems Division, describes herself as someone who "avoids airy-fairy stuff" and "moves at breakneck speed," challenging any management directive and ready to go to war with IBM, Hewlett-Packard, or DEC. She demands the same drive from her staff and regularly tells her boss and other executives to stay out of her way.[30] Bartz is a take-control executive, but she is also considered to be one of Sun's most capable managers. In contrast to Bartz, Sandra Kurtzig, founder and CEO of ASK Computer Systems, hires capable senior staff, quietly delegates authority, and prefers a team approach for making executive decisions. Kurtzig, who is featured in the Management Application box, is recognized as America's leading woman entrepreneur and top woman CEO.[31]

Norris, McCoy, Perot, Bartz, and Kurtzig are all unusually talented people who manage quite differently. Several are outspoken individualists who prefer to make unilateral decisions, directing the work of their companies. Others quietly encourage executive team building and delegate authority for many decisions. Yet all are remarkably successful and respected by their managers and employees.

Information as an Environmental Imperative

Our age of rapid technological development requires managers to redefine organizational efforts and their roles in a high-tech society. Perhaps the most sensational characteristic of this era is the pervasive impact of information systems on decision making. Information is the basic element for making decisions, and delegation is rationalized when managers have better information to base decisions on. Therefore, as patterns of information change, they influence patterns of decision making.

Widespread implementation of information systems creates two conflicting forces in most organizations. On the one hand, middle and first-line managers armed with data bases, terminals, microcomputers, and so forth have rapid access to an exceptionally large pool of information. With these tools, they can monitor and control operations far better and with less analytical assistance than previously. On the other hand, information systems tend to be controlled through large-scale, centralized operations. Paradoxically, as access to, and dissemination of, information prompts greater decentralization of decision making, concentration of information prompts management to centralize many decisions.

Figure 10-9 illustrates these apparently contradictory forces. Although both work simultaneously, they seldom affect the same areas of an organization similarly. For example, improved information systems allow first-line managers in manufacturing to monitor operations better on the plant floor (decentralization), whereas computer-based data systems make it possible for upper-echelon managers to generate manufacturing schedules (centralization). Either way, this technology alters decision structures and authority.

Information systems are generally reshaping firms toward centralized activities. Banks, for example, process information more efficiently through centralized data systems than through branch operations. Similarly, team sales efforts are frequently more effective than those of individual representatives. Computer-aided design and computer-aided manufacturing systems (CAD/CAM) are replacing decentralized control decisions at the shop level. When CAD/CAM is coupled with global information networks for marketing, the result is an extraordinary recombination of decision making and control.

Some organizational activities are being combined and centralized to improve synchronization. John Deere & Company, for example, has collapsed all its management positions in product engineering and manufacturing into one executive position to better synchronize product design with manufacturing processes. After recognizing that design teams seldom understand production needs, Quantum Corporation, a major Silicon Valley producer of computer disk equipment, required its

MANAGEMENT APPLICATION

Sandra L. Kurtzig—America's Leading Woman CEO

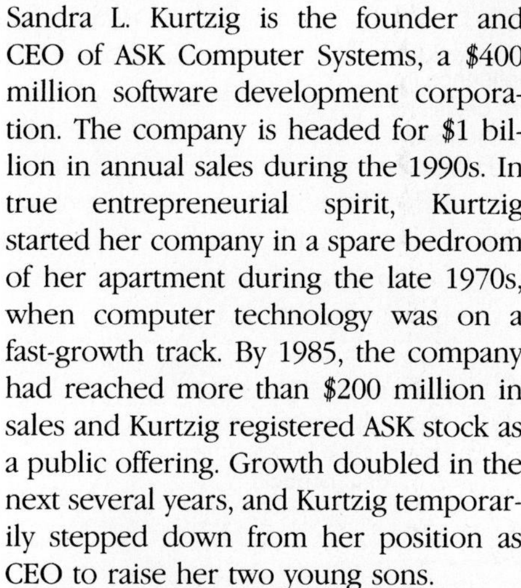

Sandra L. Kurtzig is the founder and CEO of ASK Computer Systems, a $400 million software development corporation. The company is headed for $1 billion in annual sales during the 1990s. In true entrepreneurial spirit, Kurtzig started her company in a spare bedroom of her apartment during the late 1970s, when computer technology was on a fast-growth track. By 1985, the company had reached more than $200 million in sales and Kurtzig registered ASK stock as a public offering. Growth doubled in the next several years, and Kurtzig temporarily stepped down from her position as CEO to raise her two young sons.

She left the corporation to be managed by a team of executives who had been like family to her during ASK's early rise to success. During their tenure, management ranks increased nearly threefold and the nature of the organization changed. By the end of 1989, a bureaucracy had taken shape, and the company was expanding through external acquisitions. Unfortunately, ASK's performance and earnings suffered, so Kurtzig stepped back into the CEO's chair to take control. She immediately reduced the work force and management ranks both at ASK and at its $112 million acquisition, Ingles Corporation, a data-base software company. Kurtzig also tore down the bureaucratic walls, replacing twelve executives with a team of three hand-picked managers.

Although she was always a no-nonsense chief executive officer, Kurtzig built her company on the strength of good employees who could be relied upon to make many of their own decisions. That sort of behavior has returned to ASK, and, according to Kurtzig, the company's employees, departments, and divisions are beginning to "bond" once again. Named woman entrepreneur of the decade by the Association of Collegiate Entrepreneurs in 1989, Sandra Kurtzig has also left her mark on other companies. While away from ASK Computers, she founded a publishing company and the popular *Entrepreneurial Woman* magazine. She also established business networking systems for other women aspiring to become entrepreneurs, and she continued to be active in software engineering. She is the only woman in the nation to head a technology corporation the size of ASK Computers.

Sources: Maria Shao, "25 Executives to Watch: Sandra Kurtzig," *The 1991 Business Week 1000,* August 1991, p. 72. See also Sandra L. Kurtzig, "Meeting the Entrepreneurial Challenge," keynote address to the International Conference of the Association of Collegiate Entrepreneurs, March 12, 1989.

designers to get involved in the manufacturing development process. Eastman Kodak Company introduced new technology for Kodachrome and 70mm film production through a program that encouraged hourly workers to design much of their own equipment. Kodak's program resulted in a high degree of automation, not only in production, but also in purchasing, materials control, and quality assurance—all

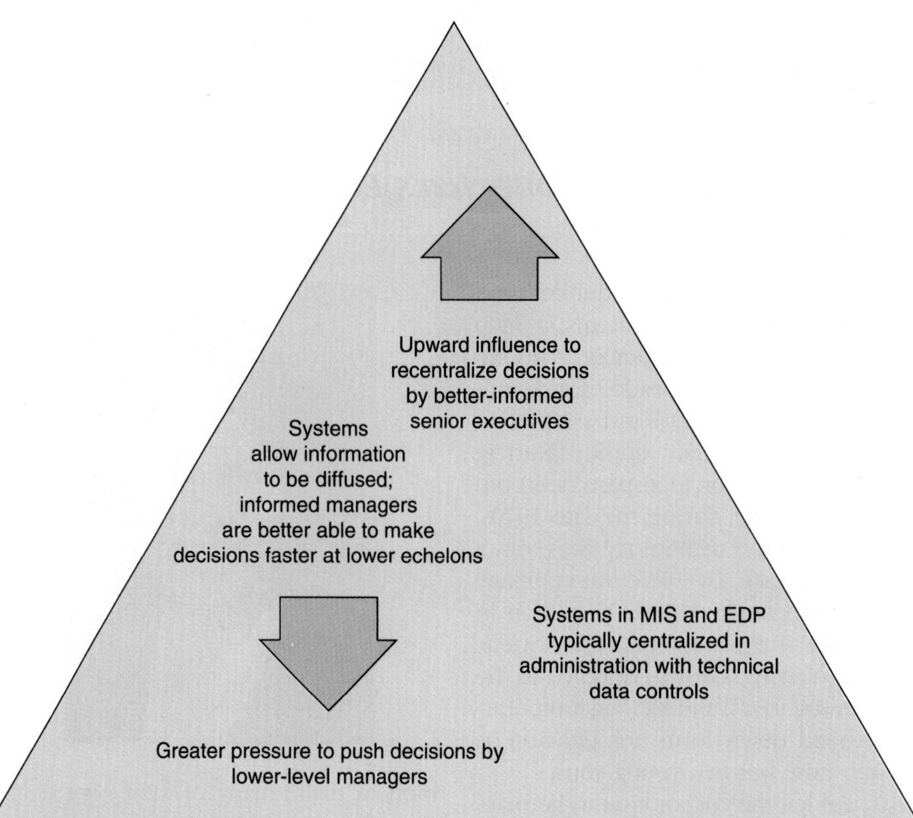
Upward influence to
recentralize decisions
by better-informed
senior executives
Systems
allow information
to be diffused;
informed managers
are better able to make
decisions faster at lower echelons
Systems in MIS and EDP
typically centralized in
administration with technical
data controls
Greater pressure to push decisions by
lower-level managers

FIGURE 10-9 Influence of Information Systems on Organization Structure

based on advanced information systems. More important, because Kodak's employees were given authority for controlling these systems, several levels of middle management were no longer needed to make decisions or oversee automated operations.[32] These contradictory forces can create organizational problems for a company. Information systems such as those employed at Kodak decentralized authority, but many middle-management and staff positions were eliminated in the process. This is a recurring controversial issue, one we address at some length in Chapter 19 on Information Systems Management.

CHECKPOINT

- Identify and discuss four factors that influence decentralization.
- How do leadership and personal management style influence structural changes in management authority?
- How are information systems affecting decision making?

ORGANIZATIONAL CULTURE

culture
A shared set of values and beliefs that determine patterns of behavior common to groups of people; corporate culture refers to patterns of behavior based on shared values and beliefs within a particular firm.

There is a strong association between the structure of an organization and its *culture* because authority is influenced by the patterns of behavior, values, and beliefs shared by organizational members. In any organization, **culture** is the shared language, events, symbols, rituals, and value systems of its members working together in a system affected by its environment. Defined more clearly, culture is: "A system of shared values (what is important) and beliefs (how things work) that interact with a company's people, organizational structures, and control systems to produce behavioral norms (the way we do things around here)."[33]

It is important to emphasize that a corporate culture does not evolve apart from the environment in which a company finds itself operating. Consequently, values and beliefs shared by employees are influenced by prevailing patterns of authority, technology, the nature of the work itself, social affiliations within the company, the philosophy of leadership endorsed by management, and many other considerations. Most of these factors are not static, and consequently, the company's culture is constantly changing. Shared values and beliefs of organization members, in turn, influence environmental factors. The result is a dynamic organizational system that may encourage decentralization or recentralization, affect strategies for departmentalization, influence how authority is delegated, and determine relationships among managers and their employees. Let's look at several examples of corporate culture, and then examine how culture affects organizational systems.

Culture in America's Most Admired Firms

Merck & Company has earned the title of America's "most admired corporation" four times in the annual *Fortune* survey that began in 1978. Only a few other firms have been among the top ten companies consistently. They include Herman Miller, 3M, Rubbermaid, and Wal-Mart. The survey polls 8,000 executives, directors, analysts, and consultants, who are asked to evaluate firms on eight key attributes that constitute a company's corporate culture. These attributes are innovativeness; quality of management; value of long-term investments; ability to attract, develop, and keep talented people; quality of products or services; financial soundness; community and environmental responsibility; and effective use of corporate assets. Merck has invariably been ranked among the top three companies in nearly every category. Recently, Merck was cited as the company most admired by its employees. When the stock market tumbled as 1991 drew to a close (the Dow Jones suffered its fifth-largest loss ever), Merck's stock price had an unprecedented surge based on the company's innovations in cardiovascular drugs and a new anticholesterol fighter called Mevacor.[34]

Conspicuously missing from the most-admired lists are companies that are often cited as examples of American ingenuity and management—IBM, Coca-Cola, AT&T, Citicorp, Apple Computers, and General Motors. Although we have cited these

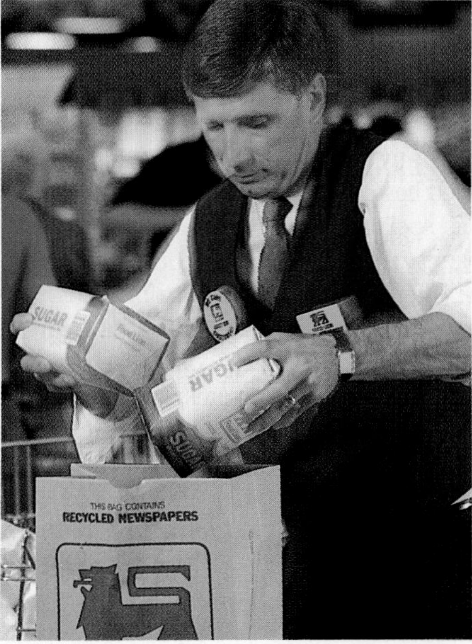

Many management leaders make a point of regularly participating at different levels of their organizations. This kind of hands-on corporate cultural exchange not only helps close the "trust gap" between employees and managers but also lets higher-level managers themselves see what lower-level managers and employees must contend with. U.S. Hyatt President Darryl Hartley-Leonard got a firsthand look at his company's commitment to service by working as a doorman in Chicago. Food Lion CEO Tom Smith recently demonstrated two-handed grocery bagging at one of his company's supermarkets.

companies as examples in this textbook for particular reasons, each of them has had serious enough shortcomings to keep it off *Fortune's* list. IBM has been found lacking in innovation and, because of this, has seen its market position in the United States weaken. Apple has experienced disruptive reorganizations and has been plagued by questionable management of corporate assets. GM has been trying to reorganize for years, but has not lived up to expectations as America's leading automaker. Coca-Cola has been viewed as a company with entrenched management unable to change with the times, and the company's minority hiring practices have been criticized. Citicorp and AT&T have cumbersome internal organizations that are viewed as unresponsive to consumer markets.[35]

A pattern has emerged to separate the best companies from those that do not quite measure up to society's expectations. Companies that consistently demonstrate a commitment to quality management and good human relations are held in high esteem; these are the primary attributes of a strong organizational culture with an innovative and committed work force.[36]

Culture Transforms Systems

America's most admired companies have undergone evolutionary changes that have resulted in tremendous differences in how they are organized. Internal cultural changes have transformed social systems, redefined authority, and altered basic philosophies of doing business. These points would be obvious perhaps if we could break down culture and examine its component parts, but we can only understand culture by its results. The following passage may provide some insights:

> Strange things happen at the best plants. Workers complain about machines being idle for too long and then fix them on their own to reduce downtime. A plant manager smiles approvingly when he encounters the head of the janitorial crew dictating a letter to the manager's own secretary.
>
> The fanciest conference rooms are sometimes found not in the administration building, but inside the plant, for workers to use when meeting with foremen. . . . The best-run factories don't look alike when you first walk into them. Stepping into GE's spanking new dishwasher plant, an awed supplier said recently, is like stepping "into the Hyatt Regency." By comparison, stepping into Lincoln Electric's 33-year-old, cavernous, dimly lit factory is like stumbling into a dingy big-city YMCA. . . . But it isn't too much to say that, in general, trust has replaced strife, and communication has been substituted for confrontation. In most well-managed plants, workers now get frequent reports on plant profits, product quality and cost, the competitive situation, and other subjects—information that wasn't normally released to them before.[37]

Both Lincoln Electric and General Electric are well thought of, and although their physical environments differ, their social systems and cultures are quite similar. Each has created exceptionally high standards for quality products and services. Each has socialized its employees so that everyone is a quality inspector. In each company, workers can stop production lines until parts are free of defects. Workers control line speeds in conjunction with management systems. GE and Lincoln Electric have restructured authority so that group decision making involves managers and employees. Also, each company has invested in human resources through training, improved reward systems, and an enhanced quality of working life.

Lincoln Electric has been a leading manufacturer of arc welding equipment for nearly half a century, and the firm relies on its "Million Dollar Employees" for its continued success. Lincoln's employees earned this title through innovations that saved the company more than $1 million in operating costs. Lincoln's employees are also well rewarded. In a good year, machine operators can earn as much as $80,000 from bonuses based on their level of work. Employees like being part of the Lincoln Electric family and rarely see themselves as simply working for a company.[38]

Changes in Organizational Relationships

From a social-anthropological viewpoint, the best-managed organizations have broken away from the conventional wisdom that authority should emanate from a rigid hierarchical system to adopt more open and flexible systems. William Torbert, a researcher and theorist in organizational behavior, suggests six characteristics of companies that have made this transition:[39]

1. Organization members from top to bottom share assumptions about the larger purposes of the organization.
2. There are organizational norms of open disclosure of information, conciliatory support, and open communication.
3. Individuals evaluate the effects of their own behavior on others in the organization, as well as the effects of the organization on its environment.
4. Organizational members are encouraged to find unconventional solutions to conflicts.
5. A deliberately chosen structure, unique in the experience of the participants, supports changing values and a social system of beliefs with commitment over time.
6. Role differentiation and interpersonal relations have a horizontal instead of a vertical emphasis.

Clearly these six characteristics do not explain all the differences between the best- and the less-well-managed firms, but there is strong evidence of a pattern among the more successful companies. This pattern includes a propensity to reallocate power and redefine authority according to values of group participation, quality performance, and equitable relationships. Chapters in Part Four on leadership address these concepts thoroughly, and Chapter 11 expands the theme of participation to the design of jobs and work groups. Here we are interested in how culture affects the way companies are structured. We examine two topics: the effects of participation and new methods of ownership.

Effects of Participation

Participation is a vertical change that pushes decisions deeper into the organization. Consequently, cultural changes that encourage greater involvement by employees will result in more decisions being made at successively lower levels in the company. Notwithstanding trends toward recentralization noted earlier, participation tends to flatten out organizations. Executive echelons may expand to include more managers in strategic decisions, but fewer middle managers are necessary to coordinate operational decisions, because in a participative system, these decisions are delegated to first-line managers and their employees.

Participation programs have become more common and more formalized in companies committed to the new style of shared leadership. Formal programs, which are known by many names, can be referred to generally under the umbrella phrase: improvement of *quality of work life (QWL).* The implication is that as more employees become more involved in their work, work satisfaction—and presumably work quality—increases substantially.[40] Terms used for QWL programs include *quality circles*; *production*, *product*, and *productivity teams*; *employee involvement efforts*, and *labor-management councils.* Companies that have found QWL programs particularly fruitful include Ford, Corning Glass, IBM, Motorola, Merck, Westinghouse, John Deere, GE, and DuPont.[41]

Some of the companies noted above, and many others, have QWL programs that were created in collaboration with labor unions. These programs are often more complicated to implement because unions require that terms of manager and worker participation be spelled out—for example, how work teams will be constituted and how decisions will be made. Nevertheless, there are many successful QWL programs in hard-core unionized companies, among them Jones & Laughlin Steel, Bethlehem Steel, TRW, Cummins Engine, and Alcoa.[42] Productivity has improved in each of these companies through better-quality products or services, and because collaboration between union members and managers has reduced adversarial relationships. In addition, many companies seek out innovations by using participative techniques to tap the entrepreneurial spirit of employees. Evidence of hierarchical change is found in the proliferation of so-called *skunkworks* and *new-venture units*.

Skunkworks. These are small, autonomous teams of individuals insulated from corporate activities so they can generate new ideas. They often evolve without formal authority or even spring up surreptitiously. Figure 10-10 illustrates the concept. Skunkwork units are distanced from the formal structure, not only physically, but also in terms of reporting responsibilities. They are entrepreneurial efforts existing outside authority channels.

IBM used this technique to develop its first personal computer. "Big Blue" formed a research team and moved it to an isolated spot in Florida where team members were shielded from corporate affairs. They had no mandate other than to "innovate" in the microcomputer area. Many other high-tech firms are also taking individuals and teams out of corporate harness in an effort to encourage innovation. NCR, 3M, Genentech, Monsanto, Convergent Technologies, Boeing, and Hewlett-Packard are a few that sponsor out-of-channel activities that defy traditional hierarchical authority. The skunkworks have generally been quite successful, and include notable new products such as IBM's PC and Boeing's 757 aircraft.[43]

New-venture units. NVUs are volunteer teams charged with speedy development of new products in a shielded environment apart from other operations. The

FIGURE 10-10 Engendering Innovation by Creating Free-Form Subunits: "Skunkworks"

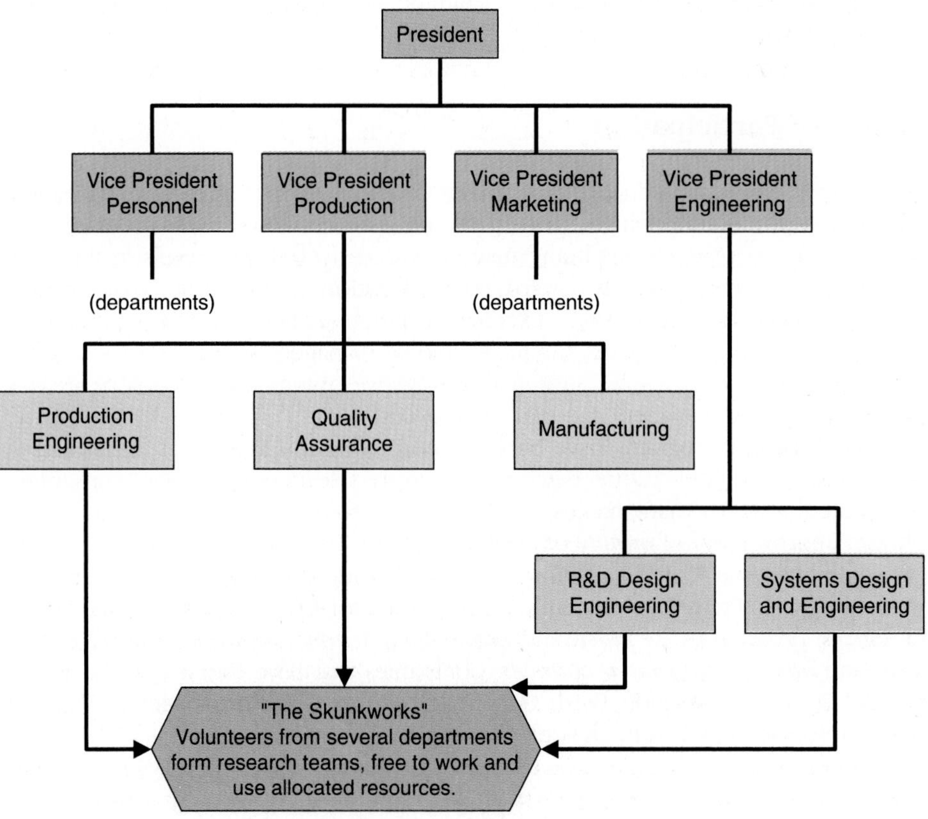

rationale for NVUs is that isolated teams with formal budget support but without the restraints of mainstream administrative responsibilities can concentrate their energies on new ideas. Research at M.I.T. has shown that a leading cause of new-product failure in large divisionalized firms is management's preoccupation with current operations that leaves too little time and resources for properly developing innovations. By using NVUs, these same large companies can encourage entrepreneurial verve without upsetting their other operations. Formal NVUs are common at 3M, where they accounted for 25 percent of the increase in company operating profits during the 1980s.[44]

From an organizational perspective, new-venture units represent substantial changes in hierarchical authority and decision making. NVUs are participative teams working autonomously, almost like small companies within their parent organizations. The teams are expected to be innovative, and their managers are expected to encourage risk taking. The teams set their own objectives, make planning decisions with a reasonable degree of privacy, and have few constraints on how they organize their work. If they are successful in coming up with a new product, team members may return to their original operating units, but the trend is for the NVU itself to remain separate and to continue to work on new projects. We shall explore NVUs more fully in Chapter 20 on entrepreneurship because they are a way to create new business enterprises.

Redefined Ownership Structures

Cultural expectations that have influenced greater employee involvement in company decisions have also encouraged employee ownership. As we shall see in Chapter 12, various incentive programs, such as profit sharing, have also resulted in employee ownership. Ownership usually takes the form of holding equity through common stocks. Merely buying stock, of course, does not affect company structure. However, in this section, we describe a model that is a purposeful transfer of company stock to employees, one that does generate an employee-owned, highly participatory system. In addition, we briefly address new forms of equity ownership beyond direct employee involvement that have also altered authority structures.

ESOP companies. An **Employee Stock Ownership Plan (ESOP)** is a program designed to transfer stock ownership to employees through a formula that shares increases in profits with employees. Formulas differ from company to company, but the object is the same: to increase employee ownership in, and commitment to, the organization. ESOPs are created in such a way that corporate stock is sold to employees by existing owners—in effect, existing owners "sell out" to the company's employees. If the sellout formula is based on growth or profitability and the company is highly successful, the completed transfer takes place rapidly. Consequently, employees become highly motivated to improve performance so they can reap the rewards of their efforts.[45] This is the most common form of ESOP adopted by existing companies. New enterprises often set up ESOPs at their inception, reserving a percentage of stock for the founders and then making a transfer to employees of new shares issued on the basis of performance.

Employee Stock Ownership Plan (ESOP)
A program designed to transfer stock ownership to employees through a formula that shares profit increases with employees.

As owners create *equity rights* for employees, they also create a *duty* for employees to share in decisions affecting their company. The result is that authority structures often shift toward more democratic processes. For example, in 1988, ComSonics, a Virginia manufacturer of electronic components for cable television, completed the total transfer of corporate stock from its original investors to its employees. The president and founder of ComSonics, Warren Braun, no longer holds common stock in his corporation—the employees own all common stock issued—but Braun remains the CEO. His role is similar to that of other CEOs, except that employee groups make new-product decisions, review jointly with top management

ComSonic's financial performance, and work in a participative environment to guide the company's future. Top management cannot determine policies, veto decisions, or launch new programs without employee ratification. Braun wanted to create an employee-owned company before retiring, and as that time nears, his shareholding employees have elected several board members and designated a successor for a smooth leadership transition.

research and development limited partnership (RDLP) A legal partnership of limited life that allows public and private organizations to contribute resources to a separate organization that operates independently for a specific purpose.

RDLPs. Another recent innovation in ownership is the **research and development limited partnership (RDLP).** An RDLP is a legal partnership that allows public and private organizations to contribute resources to a separate organization that operates independently for a specific purpose. It has a limited life that ends when the purpose is accomplished. RDLP partners can be individuals, other partnerships, corporations, universities, or any legal entity, including a government agency.

RDLPs can be formed for all sorts of interesting enterprises, from putting a communications satellite into orbit to commercializing a new hybrid rose. RDLPs have also become popular in Europe, as illustrated in the Global Trends feature. RDLPs are common in the United States in the semiconductor industry. Normally, RDLP members are intense competitors, but they join together to accumulate the expertise and underwriting necessary to tackle huge projects that no member could take on alone. The Semiconductor Research Corporation (SRC), for example, has twenty-three members, including IBM, Honeywell, Digital Equipment, and Hewlett-Packard, who will all share in the benefits of SRC research.[46]

RDLP ventures may be short-lived or last for a number of years. The crucial ingredient is a joint effort unrestrained by traditional authority systems. Smaller RDLPs have evolved for "low-tech" and "no-tech" projects such as developing a new barbecue sauce, creating a franchise network for videodiscs, and writing educational software for elementary schools. Several universities have formed partnerships with business firms, bringing together research assets and business acumen.[47] Because these joint efforts involve executives and organizational partners with substantially different interests, management authority is often shared through an executive team. Hierarchical authority is less apparent than a system of contractual obligations and predetermined responsibilities. RDLPs tend to adopt the matrix management process, in which authority is based on assignments. Consequently, RDLPs resemble systems of consortia.

Joint ventures and alliances. Recall from Chapter 3 on international management that many new alliances are being created by companies that are "going global." The most popular vehicle for doing this was shown to be the *joint venture,* where two or more companies invest together to set up a third venture. Genencor (a U.S. company researching biotech enzymes) and Siemens (a German company known for medical equipment and electronics) created Seicor Corporation to pursue fiber optics for medical imaging technology. Joint ventures also are common in domestic alliances. Dow Corning, for example, is a joint venture of Corning Glass Works and Dow Chemical.[48] Service businesses are equally likely to form alliances. Hyatt Legal Services is an association of attorneys that operates like a commercial franchise. Also, many doctors have reorganized into group practices and cooperatives called *independent practice associations* (IPSs). Still others have joined *health maintenance organizations* (HMOs), which are consortia of physicians, insurance companies, and medical clinics that provide fixed-fee care to subscribers.[49]

In each of these new forms of organization, reporting relationships and decision-making authority differ substantially from those found in hierarchical organizations. Some operate under team management; others have dual executives appointed by joint venturers or corporate boards; and still others have a form of decentralization similar to fast-food franchising, where local owners control a majority of operational decisions. Many of these organizations have also adopted matrix management systems. Regardless of the type of structure chosen, the main point is

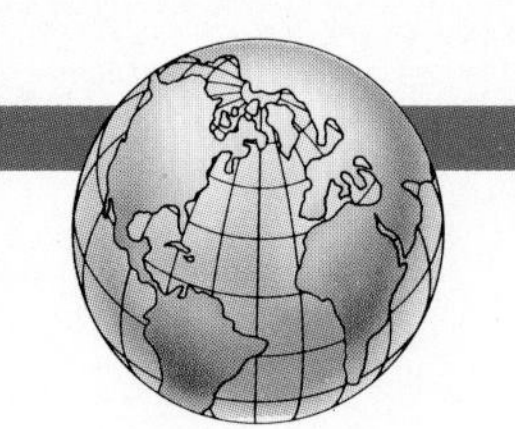

GLOBAL TRENDS

Eureka—The European Research Consortium

EUREKA began in 1985 as a collaboration of companies from twenty-one countries, including the EC members, Scandinavian nations, and the United States. Like the huge U.S. RDLPs, EUREKA was started in response to fast-growing Japanese research activities in preemptive information and telecommunications technology. Unlike many other programs, EUREKA is focused on application technology such as laser equipment, fifth-generation computing methods (called artificial intelligence), and automated production techniques.

The consortium completed its first major project in 1987 on the Eurolaser manufacturing technology, which is now shared by all members of EUREKA. In 1989, it brought on-line a proprietary welding process that can be used in space through remote distancing controls. In 1990, it launched ten projects on information technology (IT), and by 1991, there were 214 total EUREKA projects involving more than $3.8 billion in budgeted research funds.

Each project has a lead "participant company" that brings together a global research team. The Eurolaser project, for example, was led by Ferranti Industrial Electronics of the U.K., with primary participants from Germany, Finland, Spain, and Denmark. The major IT project is headed by Bull-Honeywell, which is itself a joint company formed between Honeywell (U.S.) and Groupe Bull (France). Siemens, a German firm that is one of the world's largest diversified electronics companies with 330,000 employees, heads twenty-eight projects, including a megaproject on fifth-generation computing technology.

Managers have not fully come to grips with the projects and organizations they have created. The projects are "matrices" of participants drawn from private industry, government research laboratories, universities, public and private financial institutions, and joint ventures that may include less visible members from Middle East investment groups, North America, and Japan. People assigned to work on projects usually are employees of participant organizations, but they need not be. In many instances, project leaders subcontract work to nonmember organizations or license technology from competing companies. However, all project participants are temporary—assigned for the budgeted life of the project or some portion of R&D—and they come from diverse backgrounds and cultures. The Eurolaser project had people representing seventeen ethnic groups speaking twenty-one different languages. Consequently, there is little formal authority structure, and decision making often emulates the behavior of project managers and their lead companies.

Sources: Cooperative R&D in Industrial Competitiveness (Washington, D.C.: Office of Productivity, Technology and Innovation, 1987), pp. 1–2; Timothy M. Collins and Thomas L. Doorley III, *Teaming Up for the 90s: A Guide to International Joint and Strategic Alliances* (Homewood, Ill.: Business One Irwin, 1991), pp. 166–169; and "Active Promotion of High Technology and Scientific Development," Association Route des Hautes Technologies, Sophia Antipolis, France, June 10, 1991, p. 79.

that traditional structures based on fixed positions of authority are being abandoned in favor of flexible and more participative systems. As these organizations grow in number, and as more companies become involved in global alliances, traditional hierarchical authority will become less important. Looking forward to the next chapter where we address the concepts of participation and group endeavor, cultural issues and the resulting evolution in organization structures provide the foundation for major changes now taking place in how we work in the Western world.

CHECKPOINT

- Define the concept of corporate culture.
- Why are some companies esteemed while others are less well thought of?
- What effect does participative decision making have on organizational structure?
- Explain the concept of a "skunkworks," and discuss how these new-venture units are influencing organizational structures.
- Discuss new forms of ownership and how these are affecting organizational decision-making authority.

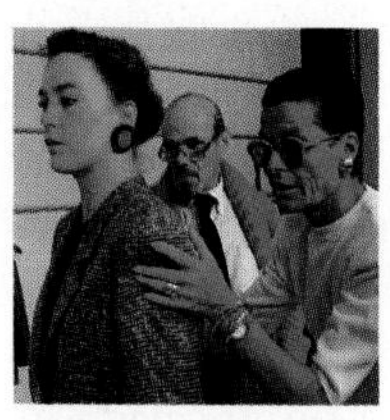

AS WE CONCLUDE THIS CHAPTER, it is appropriate to return to the opening scenario of Liz Claiborne—the company and the successful woman who founded it. Recall that when Ms. Claiborne announced her retirement, investment analysts were concerned that the company might not survive her withdrawal. Currently, the company has thirteen separate divisions with offices or distribution facilities in every state in the United States and in Europe and Asia as well. Contrary to popular belief, one person, even a fashion genius such as Ms. Claiborne, cannot single-handedly manage a $2 billion corporation with global markets. Realizing that, Claiborne earlier restructured her company with divisions focused on "product lines aimed at customer groups." Women's casual fashions, women's business clothes, young men's fashions, sun-and-surf wear, perfumes, and metropolitan retailing are among the divisions headed by second-tier professional managers. Corporate headquarters is organized with functional specialists in marketing, finance, human resource management, legal services, and administrative services. Although the company misses Liz Claiborne's personal touch, she created a soundly organized corporation that is surviving quite well without her. ■

A SYNOPSIS FOR LEARNING

1. Describe how organizations departmentalize to improve coordination.

   Departmentalization is the horizontal grouping of activities. This grouping is normally accomplished through a functional pattern of organization in which personnel with similar technical skills and capabilities are gathered in separate departments. Departmentalization by product, geographic territory, and customer can emerge as companies grow.

2. Describe matrix organization and its implications for management.

   A matrix organization is a temporary formation of teams or projects using personnel drawn from existing departments. A matrix creates a two-boss system: a person assigned to a matrix team reports both to a project manager within the matrix and to his or her functional department supervisor. Matrix management systems permit results to be achieved rapidly and efficiently.

3. Explain how authority is being transformed in today's organizations.

The traditional view of authority is that it is an absolute right derived from ownership to make decisions and direct subordinates in their work efforts. This viewpoint is still customary in most Western organizations, but another view of authority is emerging because today's employees expect to be treated with respect for their abilities, to make many of their own decisions, and to guide their own work. Thus, greater participation is being encouraged among employee work groups in many organizations. In addition, managers are finding that although they may possess the formal authority vested in their positions, it is the degree of acceptance by their subordinates that determines whether or not they will have the power to lead.

4. Describe why managers delegate authority and barriers that often prevent them from doing so.

Delegation is the downward dispersal of authority to make decisions, and it can occur through a partial distribution of authority to individuals or to work groups. The most common reason for delegation is to relieve managers of part of their work load, but in complex organizations, most authority is vested in individuals because of their particular expertise and capabilities. Authority is also delegated to place decisions in the hands of those in closest proximity to sensitive tasks and to speed up decisions when time is of the essence. Delegation is also done to help less-experienced subordinates develop their management skills, to encourage participation, and to help build confidence among employees. Among the barriers to delegation are resistance by managers who enjoy the power of controlling decisions and rejection by employees who do not want additional responsibility. Some managers resist delegating because they do not believe their employees are capable of making decisions. Finally, competition among subordinates to gain power often thwarts management from relinquishing authority.

5. Identify factors that influence centralization and decentralization.

Centralization and decentralization relate to the vertical organization of management authority. In a centralized firm, a single executive or a small cadre of executives controls the majority of decisions, delegating little authority to lower-level managers. Decentralized firms have more managers with greater authority diffused to lower operational levels.

6. Explain what culture is with respect to organizations.

Organizational culture is the shared language, events, symbols, rituals, and value systems of the organization's members. The result is a pattern of behavior that affects work, organizational relationships, perceptions of authority, and employee expectations. These expectations span the scope of human activity to include such things as compensation, benefits, and compliance with socially accepted norms (i.e., environmental protection). Management tries to develop a culture that encourages innovation, reduces conflict, and ensures a high degree of satisfaction among employees so that they want to remain with the organization and be productive members of it.

CASE 1 Martin Marietta: Matrix at a Price

SKILL ANALYSIS

By the end of 1991, events in Eastern Europe and the former Soviet Union had led to major reductions in U.S. military expenditures. Contenders in the 1992 presidential race were more concerned with the domestic economy than with the dangers of global warfare. Consequently, aerospace companies that relied on government spending found themselves with few new projects and the likelihood of large budget cutbacks and layoffs. By early 1992, an unusual number of aerospace engineers were unemployed after the government trimmed defense spending.

The experience of one aerospace engineer, Gary McAlister, was typical. The thirty-four-year-old McAlister was employed by Martin Marietta, a company involved in the MX missile program and military weapons launch systems. For more than seven years, he had been a "fast-tracker," working on glamor projects as a mechanical engineer, but the industry cutbacks led him to consider making a major career change. McAlister had been caught in the same situation twice before: once in 1986, when the MX program was pared back by Congress, and again in 1988, when presidential election jitters had forced budget cuts in aerospace. In both instances, he was among the 25 to 30 percent of project engineers his company laid off. Most displaced engineers were later rehired when government funding was reinstated, but McAlister felt as if he had been on a roller coaster.

The first time he was let go, McAlister felt despondent about losing his job. The substantial salary increase he received on returning eased the pain. The second time, he had a better perspective. By then, he had concluded that engineers working on aerospace projects were being moved around like part-time help, while engineers in production positions—those unattached to projects—were seldom laid off.

Even though McAlister recognized that anyone caught up in matrix management and company projects could be reassigned, shifted around, or terminated, he found being attached to projects exciting—he made a lot of money, traveled extensively, and enjoyed challenging assignments. For example, in 1984, he had been assigned to a component design team in Denver. Nine months later he was on temporary assignment in New Orleans. After six months there, he was back at his desk in Colorado, but almost as quickly sent to Washington, D.C., on a "lobbying team." In 1988 and 1989, he had temporary assignments in Europe and Asia. Then in 1990, he was part of a civilian "tech-team" supporting U.S. forces in the Middle East.

During his interlude of unemployment in 1986, McAlister actively interviewed with other firms, assuming his job at Martin Marietta was permanently gone. But he wanted to stay in aerospace, and no new job in that field materialized. Unemployment compensation was insufficient to sustain the lifestyle he had become accustomed to on an engineer's pay, and his savings were drained, so he was happy to be rehired by his old company. He thought his career was back on track, and by 1988, he once again felt secure in his job. By this time, McAlister was married and he and his wife had bought a home on the outskirts of Denver. His wife had a good position in Denver, and project assignments were less alluring to McAlister. So he determined to apply for a transfer to production engineering where his schedule would be stable and his position permanent. After the Gulf War ended in early 1991, he got the transfer.

Once in his new post, McAlister found himself being treated almost like a new college graduate rather than a seasoned engineer. His new work group was close-knit, and he wasn't part of it. Even after several months, he was still being treated like an outsider. McAlister also found the work extremely boring. The designs his group were working on seemed unrelated to specific results, and there was no sense of accomplishment in a day's work. When work slowed, his co-workers simply made sure they "looked busy" by drawing cartoons or designing "nonproducts." Nevertheless, McAlister was assured that his group would be insulated from any cutbacks, and indeed, when several minor layoffs occurred, production engineers were not affected. In contrast, a number of project engineers were laid off.

When the aerospace budget cutbacks occurred later that year, it became obvious that positions in government-funded military projects were again very unstable. Nevertheless, they were still exciting, and McAlister was despondent about staying in a production department. He reflected on his situation and realized that during his nearly seven years with the firm, he had made few friends, seldom enjoyed close relationships with co-workers except on projects, and had not seen his career rapidly move forward.

He saw two options. First he could stay in the production post, and "tough it out," draw a good paycheck, and doodle when work slowed. Eventually, his seniority would get him into position for promotions. Or he could return to aerospace design on projects and, with his current seniority, probably avoid future cutbacks. His wife suggested a third option: get out of aerospace and go into something that would permit a "normal" and "secure" lifestyle.

Case Questions

1. Discuss the advantages and disadvantages of working as a team member on aerospace projects like McAlister's.
2. From a company standpoint, what are the advantages and disadvantages of matrix management? Explain in terms of the case.
3. How would you view a career in a matrix environment? Do you think your views would change as you got older?

VIDEO CASE How Telecommuting Is Changing Organizational Relationships

Will anthropologists look on our society as having come around full circle when they discover that once again people are working out of the home? Working from the home was once practically the only means of employment. However, the advent of the Industrial Revolution in the late eighteenth century all but eliminated the "cottage industry" form of business. Paid employment for work done at a location other than home became the rule, not the exception. But the rules are changing! More and more employees are being encouraged by their employers to perform their work at home and to telecommute rather than physically commute. Telecommuting, working away from the office, is possible only through the technology of computers and telecommunications.

The *Telecommuters Handbook* estimated that in 1991 there were some 5 million Americans who did some of their work at home. And this number will undoubtedly grow in the future. What lies behind this return to the "cottage" to work, and what impact will telecommuting have on organizational relationships?

More and more corporations are turning to telecommuting to meet traffic and air-pollution restrictions. A pilot project run by the state of California, which has the nation's worst traffic and air-pollution problems, found that telecommuting did indeed lead to savings in energy and decreases in pollution. Moreover, the study showed that telecommuting employees were more productive. Says an official from the California Telecommuting Project, "Employee effectiveness over the two-year pilot was 9 percent greater for the telecommuters than for the noncommuters." Officials were so impressed with the results that California is considering legislation to promote telelcommuting. But some corporations aren't waiting for government incentives to encourage employee telecommuting.

Pacific Bell has the nation's largest formal telecommuting program. As of early 1991, the company had 1,500 official telecommuters, including some who worked out of satellite offices. One executive explained the company's satisfaction with the program this way: "Most of the employees, by a big majority, who telecommute feel that they are more productive, less stressed out. They get more control over their lives. What is equally significant is the vast majority of their bosses feel the same way." The importance of telecommuters to Pacific Bell's organizational operations became even more evident after the devastating earthquake in 1989 in Oakland and San Francisco. Highway commuting was a nightware, and Pacific Bell found that it was able to restore normal business operations much faster than other companies did after the earthquake because of its use of telecommuting. In fact, many companies are now including telecommuting in their disaster preparedness plan.

Another California company that has begun telecommuting is Apple Comuter. When Apple wanted to build a new research and development facility on a site in Cupertino, California, city officials worried about the problems associated with increased traffic. Working together to solve the problems, Apple and the city came up with a list of solutions, including telecommuting. Says Apple's transportation manager, "It expands the opportunities for employees to do their work in a unique way."

Telecommuting presents challenges as well as advantages. Managers who are used to equating work output with employee attendance must change their focus. Says one expert from New Ways to Work, "Telecommuting really requires you to learn to manage by measuring results and outcomes and not paying so much attention to whether the person is physically right in front of you." As corporations experiment with telecommuting and other new ways of performing work, managers will have to learn how to adapt to the demands created by the changes occurring in organizational relationships.

Case Questions

1. What organizational relationships do you see changing as the result of telecommuting? Why will these relationships change?
2. How will our current views of authority and delegation have to change to accommodate the practice of telecommuting?
3. What type of organizational culture would find telecommuting an acceptable way of performing work? Why?
4. Why do you think the bosses at Pacific Bell felt as positive about the telecommuting situation as the telecommuters themselves?

Source: Cheryl Currid, "Workers Warm to Telecommuting—Middle Managers Stay Cold," *Infoworld,* March 16, 1992, Vol. 14, No. 11, p. 59; Cheryl Currid, "Telecommuting Has Yet to Assimilate into Corporate Culture," *Infoworld,* February 10, 1992, Vol. 14, No. 6, p. S74; Francis Kinsman, "Home Sweet Office," *Accountancy,* November 1991, Vol. 108, No. 1179, p. 118, and J. A. Young, "The Advantages of Telecommuting," *Management Review,* July 1991, Vol. 25, No. 7, p. 19ff.

SKILL PRACTICE

THE RESTLESS ENGINEER

Introduction

Do our occupations tend to "create" our professional personalities, *or* do our professional personalities (work-related skills and abilities) predetermine our occupational choices?

Careers differ from jobs in that careers have a *pattern* of related jobs. There is a sequence that reveals a plan by the career holder. A series of jobs can be held that shows no connecting pattern or relationship. There is an old saying: "If you don't know where you're going, any road will take you there."

As time passes and circumstances change, dynamic organizations change also. Employees—especially professional employees—should be ready to reevaluate whether they want to stay in their changing organization, move to another firm, or leave their present career for a new one.

Instructions

Read (review) the case: "Martin Marietta: Matrix at a Price," at the end of this chapter.

The instructor will form several groups of four or five people. Each group will have thirty minutes to discuss and decide the following:

1. What can you tell about Gary McAlister's views of his career in aerospace thus far?
2. Assume that the matrix structure is *not* a problem for McAlister. Is there something he can do to find a better fit for his talents/goals in an organization?
3. McAlister states he sees two options (mentioned at the close of the case). Are there other options for him? What are they? (List in order of long-run career value to him.)

Each group should elect a spokesperson to report that group's conclusions to the entire class.

11

Organizing Jobs and Groups

OUTLINE

Antecedents of Change Affecting Jobs and Work Groups
Technology
Social Forces

The Nature of Jobs
Group Technology
Job Variations

Job Design
Core Job Dimensions
The Job Characteristics Model
A Strategy for Effective Job Redesign
Job Design in Perspective

Groups and Group Processes
Types of Groups
Benefits of Group Membership

Characteristics of Groups

Group Development
The Four-Phase Model
Implementing the Development Process

Group Decisions
Individual versus Group Decisions
Empowering Groups—Concluding Comments

OBJECTIVES

- Describe how technology and social forces affect employees' jobs.
- Explain how the range and depth of jobs are changing.
- Describe the job characteristics model and explain how it is used in job design.
- Identify and contrast the primary types of organizational groups.
- Explain group norms and cohesiveness and how they affect performance.
- Describe how work groups develop into mature teams.
- Explain group empowerment in terms of decision making.

HERMAN MILLER, INC., has been making creative furniture since 1923, and among its many awards is its ranking as America's No. 1 furniture company by *Fortune* magazine.[1] A major reason for the company's success is its participatory work environment. Chairman Max DePree is a strong advocate of encouraging bottom-up initiatives, teamwork, and reinforcing a corporate culture in which employees are committed to the company's success.

To DePree, human relationships are born of shared ideas and value systems. The company encourages an environment of mutual responsibility in which employees share the rewards of success through stock ownership, bonus plans, and profit sharing. Individuals describe their jobs as team efforts, and they work toward mutually shared team objectives that create an organizational family.

Herman Miller has produced furniture designs that are considered works of art. Its Eames lounge chair has changed the way we think about chairs. The ergonomic lounger, the culmination of years of teamwork by craftsmen and shop-floor technicians to redefine how furniture can best fit the human body, was exhibited in New York's Museum of Modern Art. By encouraging project teams, DePree has solidified an internal social system for furniture making at Herman Miller, with group efforts aimed at collective results rather than individual efforts aimed at selective results.

The group theme has special meaning at Herman Miller in terms of corporate responsibility for environmental protection. Through a variety of management and employee initiatives, the company has found ways to recycle leather, vinyl, foam, office paper, phone books, and lubricating oil. And furniture design engineers have worked successfully with domestic woods from nonendangered species of trees rather than use precious hardwoods from the world's tropical rainforests.[2]

Herman Miller is a company committed to solving problems through team efforts. In turn, the corporate family is a composite team that shares in the success of its members' efforts. As you read through this chapter, consider how our cultural values are changing the way we organize work, define jobs, and combine the resources of talented people into energized work teams.

Organizations are dynamic social systems that must constantly adapt as people's values change, technology advances, and work processes are redefined. The formal structures studied in Chapters 9 and 10 are like book covers, and the complex human relations and activities within those structures are like chapter and verse. These relations and activities describe an organization's culture, defined at the close of Chapter 10 as the collective values and beliefs held by an organization's membership. Herman Miller's corporate culture, for example, can be described by its participative environment and employee involvement in defining how their teams will work and the results they will try to achieve. Other organizations might be described in terms of their bureaucratic rigor or emphasis on hierarchical authority.

Every organization has a unique culture, and although this culture is difficult to describe clearly, it determines how employees' jobs are defined, whether they work individually or in teams, and how their work is supervised by managers. Our chapter begins by addressing the antecedents of today's work environment and how the concepts of jobs are changing. Then we examine the nature of jobs and the process of redesigning them to accommodate ongoing changes. The latter half of the chapter is devoted to group processes and team building because today collective efforts are replacing narrowly defined jobs by individuals working on isolated tasks.

ANTECEDENTS OF CHANGE AFFECTING JOBS AND WORK GROUPS

As we saw in the previous chapter, delegation of authority alters individual and group responsibilities. We also emphasized in Chapter 10 that cultural changes have permanently altered how decisions are made about an organization's tasks. We want to focus our attention here on *technology* and *social forces* that are reshaping our expectations about human relations at work. Rapid advancements in technology and fundamental changes in society are the two primary categories of events having the greatest influence on how jobs are defined and work is accomplished. Consequently, they are forcing managers to reconstrue their ideas of authority and to redefine their organizations.

Technology

Perhaps it is not overly dramatic to say that greater technological changes have taken place in our society during recent decades than ever before in history. As Figure 11-1 shows, more than 80 percent of all scientific discoveries and nearly 90 percent of all applied technology breakthroughs in human history have occurred during the last several decades.[3] This conclusion is not surprising since more than 85 percent of all scientists who have ever lived were alive in 1970, and the volume of scientific literature has doubled since then. We get some idea of the present information explosion when we realize that nearly 1,000 new books in the English language are published each day; that is more than the annual number of books published a century ago. In addition, computer applications will quintuple the rate of information dissemination before the end of the century.[4]

Technological change has shifted the burden of work away form human endeavor to energy-based work systems. In this century alone, we consumed half of all the energy consumed during the past 2,000 years. We doubled our production of goods since 1970 and accelerated the rate of resource utilization to meet the needs of a world population that itself will double in about thirty-five years.[5] The sheer number of innovations requires incredible changes in organizations and work meth-

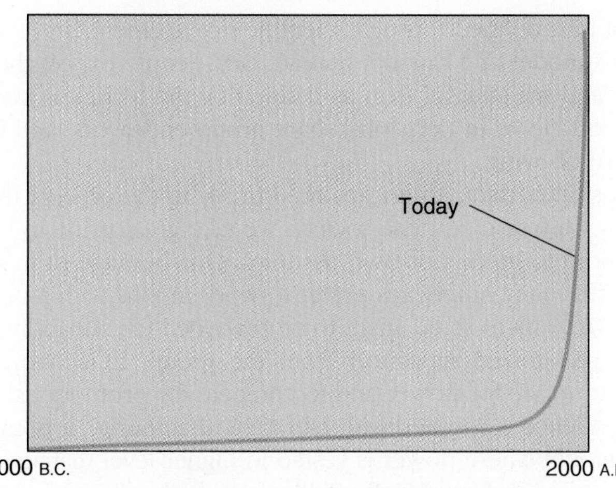

FIGURE 11-1 Technology Explosion in the Late Twentieth Century

Source: D. Bruce Merrifield, *The Measurement of Productivity and the Use of R&D Limited Partnerships: A Productivity Update* (Washington, D.C.: Office of Productivity, Technology and Innovation, 1991), p. 2.

ods. Robots have become common in manufacturing. Computers are used to control operations and to enhance professional services such as financial modeling. Telecommunications allows us to shop electronically, send facsimiles around the world, and bank at home. Advances in agriculture, engineering, chemicals, and physics have resulted in huge changes in human productivity.[6]

People today are using new technologies that, although they did not exist a short time ago, will be rapidly replaced. The implications of this scientific surge for organizing work are tremendous. For example, many production jobs, including human welders, glass blowers, and weavers, have become obsolete. Other jobs have become more complicated, but require fewer people to accomplish—fewer bank tellers using electronic systems to conduct transactions, fewer accountants armed with software performing calculations, and fewer physicians accessing expert data bases to make complex diagnoses. The nature of work has changed as human endeavor and technology are being integrated into *systems of jobs*. More important, with technological advances, employees have greater responsibility for performing their jobs.

Social Forces

Some of the most startling changes are taking place among human beings. Our social systems and personal expectations concerning work and relationships have changed. Family structures, for example, have altered to accommodate dual-career marriages, thereby redefining roles for both men and women at home and at work. In Western societies, women have finally begun to occupy higher positions in economic, political, and social systems. Laws now help protect employees from discrimination due to a variety of reasons. The Americans with Disabilities Act, for example, not only helps all handicapped employees secure their jobs, but also protects the rights of employees who have tested positive for the AIDS virus.[7] There have been compelling changes in attitudes toward work, the status of minorities, government, education, parenthood, retirement, and sex; relationships at work have therefore changed. Organizations find that they must provide more services to attract and retain employees. Many firms, for instance, have tuition assistance programs to help employees advance their careers. Others provide pregnancy leave and child care as job-related benefits. And policies on sexual harassment have redefined work relationships, particularly those between managers and employees.[8]

Education, opportunities for advancement, family priorities, appropriate social interaction, and harmony with management are just a few of the social factors that employees now consider important on the job.[9] All these issues seem remote from

Frederick Taylor's concept of jobs defined through scientific management, and they have no place in Max Weber's model of a rational bureaucracy. People expect their work to be more interesting and meaningful than as defined by the technical mandates of a job. They want to participate in decisions, share group endeavors, and be rewarded with a high standard of living.

Finally, and perhaps most important, Americans hold firmly to the precept that individualism is the keystone of a free enterprise society. We take great pride in being individuals with the freedom to guide our own destinies. Our heritage of independent decision making makes many Americans prefer to work in jobs with a high degree of personal freedom. We want to stand apart, to be rewarded for our individual accomplishments, to be recognized separately from the group. In economic terms, self-interest motivates us to vie for power and to compete for promotions.[10]

When this fierce independence is coupled with hierarchical authority, it is easy to accept a decision-making model where power is vested in higher-level managers. Americans have always resisted the ideology that the collective membership of an organization is more important than individuals. This conclusion does not seem to support an emphasis on group participation—the so-called Japanese management style now being adopted by American companies that mandates collective behavior, such as decision making by consensus and a commitment to the organization rather than to the individual.

Nevertheless, many U.S. corporations are pushing ahead with team development and altering authority to accommodate group decision making. In the process, American jobs are going through a social transformation that employees find difficult to accept. If we ignore the label *Japanese-style management,* however, and accept the evidence of good results, the commitment to teamwork makes good sense. In the next section, we focus on the nature of jobs and how they are redesigned to accommodate technological and social changes.

CHECKPOINT

- Describe how technological and social changes affect jobs and employees' responsibilities for how work is accomplished.
- Explain the dilemma created in organizing work by the contrasting ideologies of individualism and collectivism in U.S. companies.

THE NATURE OF JOBS

job
The synthesis of related task activities to be performed by a single employee.

A **job** is the content of work, the synthesis of related task activities that a single employee is responsible for performing. The synthesis of tasks into jobs and of jobs into work groups provides the building blocks of an organization. The nature of jobs has evolved along with the growth of organizations; as ways of redefining authority have changed over the years, jobs and relationships among jobs have also changed.

The concept of a wage-paying job is relatively new in human experience, becoming sharply defined only with the rise of factories during the industrial revolution. For thousands of years before that, people filled predetermined roles based on their social class. The upper class did not work; "jobs" were the domain of the lower classes. Between these two extremes were people who worked only when they found it absolutely necessary. Unlike the vast middle class of wage earners today, the middle class of preindustrial Western societies consisted of entrepreneurs, merchants, and adventurers who were often barred by caste systems from assuming roles in upper-class society and viewed wage-paying jobs as the lot of serfs.[11] Today many entrepreneurs, merchants, and adventurers still come from middle-class backgrounds, but then so do the majority of wage earners. However, jobs are no longer defined today in the same terms that they were in the past.

In the early days of industrialization, workers were not well differentiated from their tools and machines. Jobs were described rigidly by the work to be performed, such as cloth weaving, parts assembly, or coal mining. Skilled workers were treated differently from unskilled laborers; they were groomed through apprenticeships to become tradesmen such as stonemasons, carpenters, and silversmiths. Throughout the evolution of jobs, however, job definitions have focused on two dimensions of task performance: *job range* and *job depth*.[12]

Job range is concerned with the horizontal *scope* of tasks an employee is expected to perform. Recall from Chapter 9 how the job range can be expanded through *job enlargement* as a way of reducing the boredom and fatigue associated with highly repetitive jobs consisting of severely limited tasks. Early assembly-line jobs had a narrow range. Until recently, many white-collar jobs—those of secretaries, clerks, bank tellers, and bookkeepers, for example—were similarly limited. Improved technology and the grouping of jobs into teams have expanded the range of many jobs. Thus job enlargement is more than merely loading more tasks into a job description; it is intertwined with changes in how work is accomplished. In addition, through cross-training and job rotation, workers diversify their activities, thereby enlarging the total scope of their jobs. **Job rotation** is periodically shifting into complementary jobs with similar skill levels, and this occurs more often today than in the past as team members shift to temporary roles or substitute for one another.

job range
The horizontal scope of activities expected within a specific job.

job rotation
Periodic temporary assignment to jobs with complementary skills.

Job depth is concerned with the relative responsibility employees have for making decisions about their jobs. Changes in job depth alter the authority employees have for accomplishing their tasks. Recall from Chapter 9 that *job enrichment* is a method used to change job depth in order to give employees more individual freedom over decisions related to their work. Redefining jobs to give them greater depth has become an important facet of motivating employees because it makes work more satisfying. With the present emphasis in organizations on developing more work teams, job enrichment methods are in extensive use.

job depth
The relative responsibility employees have for decisions about their task activities and jobs.

The workers who assembled this Airbus Industrie airplane know a great deal about job range and job depth. Because Airbus is a European consortium supported by the French, British, German, and Spanish governments, different parts for each airplane are manufactured and assembled in different countries and collected for final assembly in Toulouse, France, Airbus's headquarters. Work teams with rotating worker responsibilities at each plant handle a wide range of skilled procedures. In addition, each worker is expected to show a great deal of individual responsibility for decision making and skill enhancement in areas that range from shop-floor assembly techniques to fluency in several languages.

Group Technology

group technology
The combination of several jobs into one that integrates job activities through new technology or redefined work processes.

Group technology is a term used to explain how several sets of operational tasks are combined to be performed by one person or a small team. Instead of having many people doing specialized jobs, a few people skilled in several jobs perform a variety of activities.[13] The concept is generally applied to manufacturing examples, where new technology allows employees to do more tasks efficiently. As jobs expand to include more complex technology, fewer people are needed to control more tasks. Consequently, grouping technology together is an incremental change along a spectrum leading to fully automated production systems. Employees involved in group technology are skilled and "manage" their technology as often as they perform functional tasks. A simple example of group technology is shown in Figure 11-2, where four previously independent jobs are merged into one more responsible position. The job has greater scope (more activities), but also greater depth (more control over decisions such as quality inspection).

Consider the example of a GE plant where washing machines are manufactured through highly automated process technology. Washers are assembled in a series of continuously moving computer-controlled assembly lines. A handful of trained technicians set up computerized production runs, monitor progress, and intervene only to correct errors or adjust the machinery. Most of the machinery is automated and controlled by a few technicians who adjust robotic welders and assemblers rather than do the work themselves. The result is more predictable and higher-quality work with fewer variations in performance.[14] As group technology expands toward automation, it means not only fewer jobs but also that existing jobs will require knowledgeable employees who can use advanced technology.

Group technology can also be applied to office systems and professional jobs, although the term is not commonly used in these instances. Secretaries who used to work with a standard typewriter, for example, often had their hands full just typing correspondence and filing papers. They may have had related responsibilities, such as reception duties, answering phone calls, making copies, and dealing with outside printers for making brochures and replicating reports. If an office was busy, all these duties may have required several secretaries and support clerical staff. Today office

FIGURE 11-2 Job Enrichment through Redesign for Group Technology

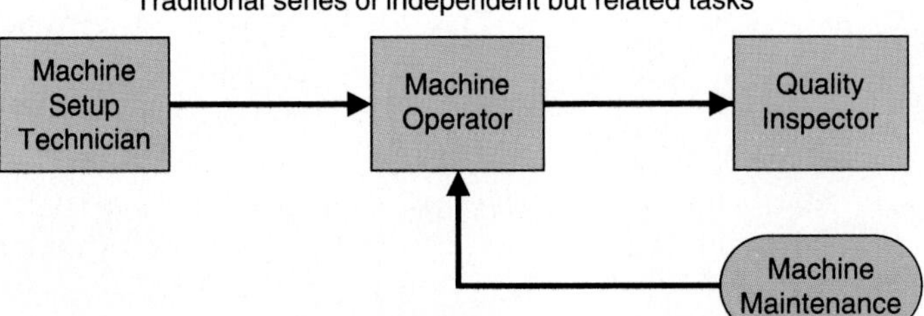

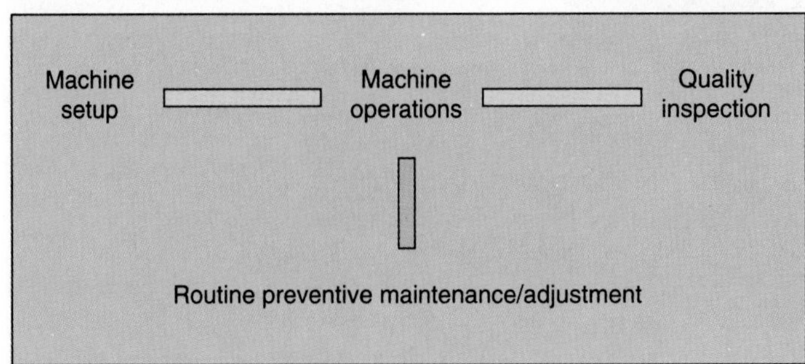

technology is capable of collapsing most of these activities into one work center. Armed with desktop publishing systems, facsimile machines, and networked telecommunications, secretaries can write, print, copy, transmit, and file professional-looking correspondence while electronically linked to other offices and data bases worldwide.

Group technology is the result of both job enlargement and job enrichment to redesign jobs, and it is being employed by many companies striving to improve their productivity. Apple's Macintosh manufacturing system is characterized by a series of "production cells," each having grouped tasks performed by small expert teams of technicians. Honda America's plant in Marysville, Ohio, is structured entirely on group technology. Ford Aerospace has used group technology to create design and engineering cells, integrated marketing teams, combined purchasing and inventory management centers, and office systems.[15]

Job Variations

The conventional concept of a job presupposes full-time employment in one physical location belonging to an organization. But this is changing as full-time employees find themselves working alongside part-timers and "temporaries," and many employees work at home or in private offices away from their organizations. Although technology has had a role in these changes, it is the combination of social forces mentioned earlier that has most directly influenced these new patterns of work.

Contingent jobs. Part-time and temporary workers have always been used to fill labor shortages during peak seasons. In agriculture, for example, seasonal planting and harvesting are often accomplished by short-term migrant workers, and employers who hire these workers minimize their wage costs by avoiding the overhead of full-time employees. Organizations hire temporaries and part-timers primarily to match employment levels with seasonal employment needs, but having flexible staffing patterns also allows companies to respond quickly to competition. In addition, many companies hire contingent employees to work on short-term projects such as special aerospace design contracts.

Today organizations of every size in nearly every type of business use part-time and temporary employees. For some time, universities have been contracting with instructors to teach one course or for one semester, banks have been hiring "temps" during peak periods and to cover vacations by tellers and clerical personnel, and retailers have been contracting with agencies for temporary and part-time workers during peak sales seasons such as Christmas. Now manufacturers are adopting this practice on a significant scale. Apple Computer, for example, fills one of every six jobs with temporaries. This allows the company to rapidly alter employment levels—up to one-sixth of its total labor force—in response to changes in market conditions and production needs.[16] Du Pont, AT&T, Northern Telecom, Mobil, Whirlpool, and National Steel also make extensive use of part-time and temporary employees, although most companies with collective bargaining agreements are forced to limit these jobs. As an alternative, companies hire out work normally accomplished in-house to firms that use temporaries and contract workers almost exclusively. Hired-out work can range from project engineering to mail-room operations employing contract workers who range in skill from engineers with Ph.D.'s to untrained manual laborers.[17]

Over one million people are in the temporary work force, and their ranks are growing by nearly 20 percent annually. Many of these individuals gain employment through temporary agencies and job shops (contract service companies).[18] An extension of this trend is the filling of executive positions with experienced senior managers. The preferred term applied to this practice is "employment of *interim executives,*" but it is also known as "rent-a-boss" or "lease an executive." Interim

MANAGEMENT APPLICATION

Home Offices Transcend Space and Time

Home offices used to be limited mostly to self-employed individuals, but businesspeople are finding them perfect for putting in extra hours or for escaping the problems of commuting to the office. In fact, productivity has increased dramatically among businesspeople working in home offices, and most find working at home far more satisfying than fighting traffic, paying for expensive parking, and elbowing through crowds.

Today's home office can have practically every convenience of a formal corporate suite, and being away from the company office is not a serious barrier for many people. A PC equipped with word-processing and spreadsheet software is ideal for doing financial or operational analyses as well as for writing reports. With a modem, a copier, and a facsimile machine, you can tap into data bases, communicate worldwide, and do much of the impersonal work required of managers—usually better and faster than you could in corporate quarters.

Bill Donohoo handles sales and corporate planning for Gibson Group, Inc., from his home in Huntington Beach, California. This might not sound unusual until you know that his corporate offices are in Cincinnati, Ohio. Regardless of Donohoo's physical location, he would spend most of his workday on the phone to clients and the remainder on reports and paperwork. Charlene Weiss supervises eighty field managers, all working out of home offices for the National Opinion Research Center (NORC). NORC is based in Chicago; Charlene Weiss is in Fountain Hills, Arizona, and David Swinford, a New York-based human resource consultant, runs his business from home offices in Vail, Colorado, and Switzerland.

For well under $10,000, a home office can be set up that includes excellent equipment, furnishings, and a communications system. The same office in a commercial building would cost at least double that amount. In fact, it is their low costs that make home offices attractive to many smaller firms. For example, Tradenet, Inc., a Boston software company that services brokers in the oil industry, set up home offices for its officers in preference to locating them in expensive corporate offices, thereby saving capital and operational costs.

Home offices have their drawbacks. Those who work at home have no opportunities for personal collaboration or socialization with co-workers, which is why they often schedule a day or two each week at the company office. Instead of begrudging the commute to work, they find these trips rejuvenating. Home offices can also be a problem if family activities intrude on work. Moreover, companies find it harder to evaluate performance, track working hours, and manage benefits for employees working at home. Employees working at home also have difficulty separating personal and business expenses (for example, allocating utilities costs) to meet IRS reporting requirements. Since a standard forty-hour workweek is not scheduled at home, keeping track of time for those paid by the hour is also difficult. Nevertheless, the concept of organizing work is changing, and "office" no longer means proximity to company activities.

Sources: Sarah Glazer, "Setting Up an Office at Home," *1988 Inc. Office Guide,* pp. 28–32. See also Laura L. Castro, "Managers Declare Independence to Run Businesses from Their Personal Utopias," *Wall Street Journal,* September 5, 1991, pp. B1, B4.

executives are hired to fill temporary vacancies created by illness or retirement, and these executives often work for many months while a firm searches for a permanent employee. Temporary executives are also brought in to supply expertise for specific projects. Many companies find that interim executives can instigate changes without being constrained by career considerations. Organizations that regularly use interim executives include Comsat, Maxwell Communications, Space Systems/Loral, and GTE/Contel.[19]

Shared jobs. Another, less common type of temporary and part-time employment is job sharing, the practice of splitting one full-time job between two or more people. Job sharing is a desirable alternative to full-time employment for certain people and companies.[20] Working women who want to spend more time with their children often find that employers are willing to let them share a job. By doing so, the company gains a valuable employee without adding a permanent position to its job roster. Many shared jobs are created when companies cut full-time positions. Instead of terminating one employee, companies negotiate half-time employment for two workers with comparable skills whose full-time jobs were both at risk. Also, many retired people are hired into shared positions to accommodate their wishes for a reduced workload; employers gain experienced employees at substantial savings because they usually can avoid paying into retirement funds and Social Security.

Telecommuting. Working at home or away form the office is rapidly becoming a common practice among white-collar workers whose jobs do not have to be performed inside the walls of the organization. **Telecommuting** is a term derived from the practice of allowing employees who use computer technology to work at home and receive a salary or contracted payment for predetermined tasks.[21] Recall that in our opening scenario on Herman Miller, Inc., we noted that the furniture maker's designers are encouraged to work away from their offices to broaden their contact with the outside world. The designers also find that this allows them to create at their own pace without restricted schedules and to avoid rush hour commutes.

telecommuting
The practice of allowing employees to work at home or in other locations away from the organization; usually associated with job tasks that can be accomplished with computers and telecommunications.

Because it is feasible for so many occupations, telecommuting is becoming popular among companies of every size. IBM encourages software engineers to work away from the office, where they can feel more creative and minimize interference from meetings, phone calls, and social conversations. Toys "R" Us executives, including CEO Charles Lazarus, spend a majority of their time with suppliers or customers; the company has equipped them with computerized home offices and portable units so they can stay in touch while attending to field business with clients and vendors. And Christopher Leinberger, managing partner of Robert Charles Lesser & Company, a Beverly Hills real estate company, oversees sixty employees in Atlanta, Washington, D.C., Newport Beach, and Beverly Hills from his ranch near Santa Fe, New Mexico. The growth in telecommuting parallels the growth in computers and telecommunications. If the trend continues, experts predict that by the turn of the century nearly 20 percent of the U.S. work force will be telecommuting.[22]

CHECKPOINT

- Describe how jobs have been conventionally defined and how job range and depth are changing today.
- What is group technology and how are jobs being redesigned around new technologies?
- Define and contrast alternatives to institutional jobs, including contingent jobs, job sharing, and telecommuting.

JOB DESIGN

job design
The process of combining tasks into a well-defined job to be performed by each employee.

The process of **job design** is concerned with defining jobs by synthesizing tasks to be performed by each employee. This can occur when a growing organization requires new jobs; when technological changes create a need for employees with particular skills; and when companies alter their organizational structures, thereby combining tasks or downsizing the work force. Because organizations are in a constant state of change, the process of job design is often called *job redesign,* and there are formal guidelines that we will address momentarily to help managers implement job redesign programs.

Many companies face major design (or redesign) efforts when circumstances force management to make strategic changes in their organizational structures. For example, IBM announced that it would trim employment by eliminating nearly 20,000 jobs between 1992 and 1994. The initial impact of this statement was a sharp reduction in IBM's stock price because investors mistakenly assumed that the company was about to implement massive layoffs. In fact, IBM has launched a systematic restructuring, and most employment losses will occur through job changes. Positions are being eliminated, technology is being grouped, and management authority is being redefined to accommodate a downsizing effort through attrition. Similar strategic changes have been announced recently by Lotus Development Corporation, Allied-Signal, McDonnell Douglas, Digital Equipment Corporation, and General Dynamics; each expects between 10 and 14 percent staff reductions.[23] These strategic changes by major corporations make headlines, but most job design efforts occur through annual job reviews that result in subtle job changes throughout an organization. Since managers must periodically reevaluate their own positions and those of their employees, the process of job design is a substantial part of every manager's professional responsibilities.

Core Job Dimensions

The process of job design focuses on five core dimensions, each of which has a set of conditions that must be addressed to formulate a concise new job description. These core dimensions also provide the fundamental guidelines for analyzing jobs during strategic redesign programs. During periodic job reviews, managers can make improvements by altering one or more of the five core dimensions:

1. *Skill variety*—the extent to which a job requires different skills. If a job demands little skill, it may not be challenging to an employee. In contrast, a job requiring an employee to use wider range of skills in a variety of activities will usually be more challenging and satisfying. A TV newsperson who only reads stories on the air uses few journalistic skills. By also covering news events, writing stories, and coordinating video films, this person will use different skills in a variety of situations.
2. *Task identity*—the extent to which an individual can identify with the results of his or her work. Highly specialized jobs are often low in task identity because employees perform segmented tasks without seeing the finished product. When several operations are combined, or when a team works together to complete a set of tasks, employees recognize the results of their efforts and have greater task identity.
3. *Task significance*—the extent to which an employee perceives his or her job to be important to the company, co-workers, and customers. Employees will feel better about what they do when they know their jobs are meaningful to others. Employees who have difficulty perceiving the importance of their jobs are generally less motivated than those who readily understand the value of their work.

Rubbermaid's product development team has always enjoyed a sterling reputation for innovation and an incredible output of new products. However, the team recently won its company's special praise for introducing the Sidekick—the first environmentally correct lunch box for the grade-school set. Much of the team's success can be attributed to effective job design, particularly in the core job dimension of task significance: At Rubbermaid, the product development team, not the accountants, is responsible for ensuring that there is a minimum of 12 to 14 percent return on assets used to develop a new product.

4. *Autonomy*—the extent to which an employee can make decisions about his or her job. When employees have few choices about work methods, tools, performance criteria, or schedules, they may feel harnessed to a job rather than in control of it. Employees who have substantial latitude for scheduling their work and for choosing materials, tools, and work methods feel more involved in their jobs.
5. *Performance feedback*—the extent to which an employee receives information about the results of his or her efforts. Some jobs, such as teaching and scientific research, are low in feedback. The results of these jobs are often difficult to identify, even after many years. Other jobs, such as nursing and product engineering, have high feedback. Employees will be more highly motivated if they receive positive feedback, and they will perform better when told of ways to improve.

The Job Characteristics Model

Effective managers do not alter jobs haphazardly. Instead, they approach the process systematically to ensure good results. This is particularly important during strategic redesign efforts and when a company implements broad job enrichment programs. One paradigm for accomplishing this is called the **job characteristics model (JCM),** which provides a conceptual framework for identifying activities, relationships, and responsibilities synthesized into a job by analyzing the five core job dimensions. The JCM was developed by J. Richard Hackman and Greg R. Oldham as a predictable way to achieve four results: (1) *high work motivation,* (2) *high-quality performance,* (3) *high job satisfaction,* and (4) *low absenteeism and turnover*. When used correctly, the JCM will improve both the quality of working life for employees and organizational productivity.[24]

job characteristics model
A conceptual framework for identifying activities, relationships, and responsibilities using core job dimensions that influence job design and redesign decisions.

The relationship of core job dimensions to work results is shown in Figure 11-3. The degree to which a job includes these core dimensions determines *critical psychological states* for employees, and the combined effect of the psychological states influences work results. Also illustrated in the figure is an *employee's need for growth*. This is an important consideration because not all individuals have the same career objectives, so changing their jobs can be threatening or stressful. For exam-

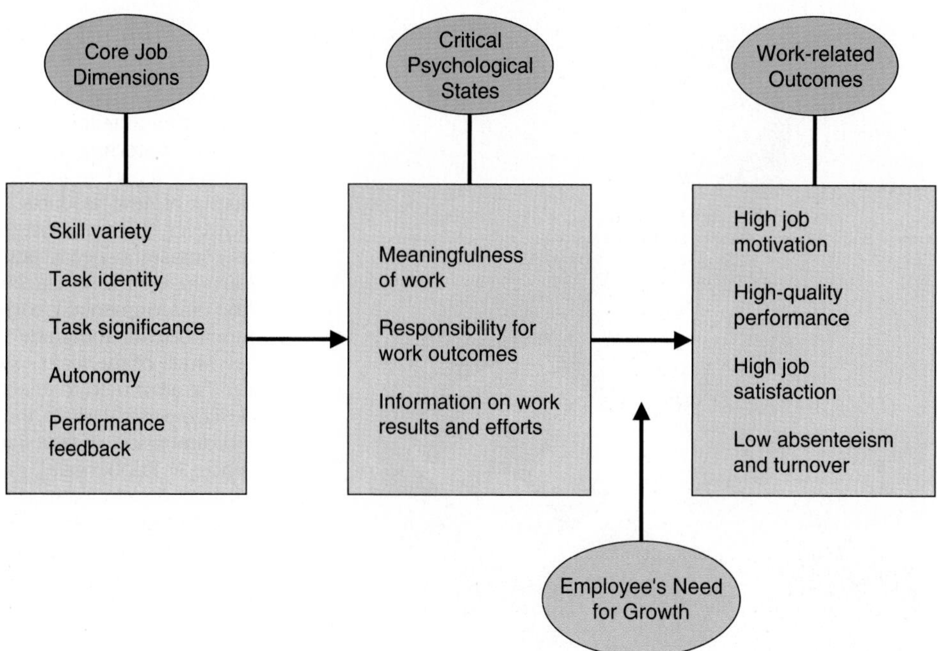

FIGURE 11-3 The Job Characteristics Model

ple, someone who is highly motivated to work autonomously under challenging circumstances will probably relish having an enriched job with tremendous responsibility; another person in the same job may find such responsibility overburdening. To take another example, if a job is enlarged by adding skilled tasks, the employee who enjoys learning new tasks and the variety associated with the enlarged job will be highly motivated to perform well, while another employee may find the enlargement a chaotic and meaningless ordeal.

The JCM suggests that managers approach job design logically by first analyzing their employees, the options for redesigning their jobs, and how the core dimensions will affect performance. Managers then can work with their employees to identify how changes in core dimensions will improve psychological states. Once the changes are implemented, they monitor performance to ensure expected results are being achieved. If the anticipated results do not materialize, or if the employee cannot be reconciled to the job changes, the redesign process is repeated. When companies face major redesign programs, such as those envisioned by IBM, a strategic plan is required to replicate the JCM process.

A Strategy for Effective Job Redesign

Figure 11-4 identifies eight steps required in a thorough strategic plan for job redesign. It appears to be complicated, yet each step is an essential element to ensure an effective program.[25] The importance of following a planned strategy becomes apparent when you consider the potential disasters associated with indiscriminate job redesign efforts. IBM, Lotus, General Dynamics, and other companies noted earlier are restructuring thousands of jobs affecting tens of thousands of employees and their families. These individuals face disrupted careers through termination or new job responsibilities, and the companies risk major disruptions in their operations.

Step 1: Identify need. Some reasons for job changes are fairly obvious, such as technological innovation. Symptoms of organizational problems, such as high turnover and absenteeism, are less obvious, but still signal a need for change. Social changes, competition, the evolution of individual careers, cultural values, and many other factors can induce changes in jobs. Managers have to monitor these environ-

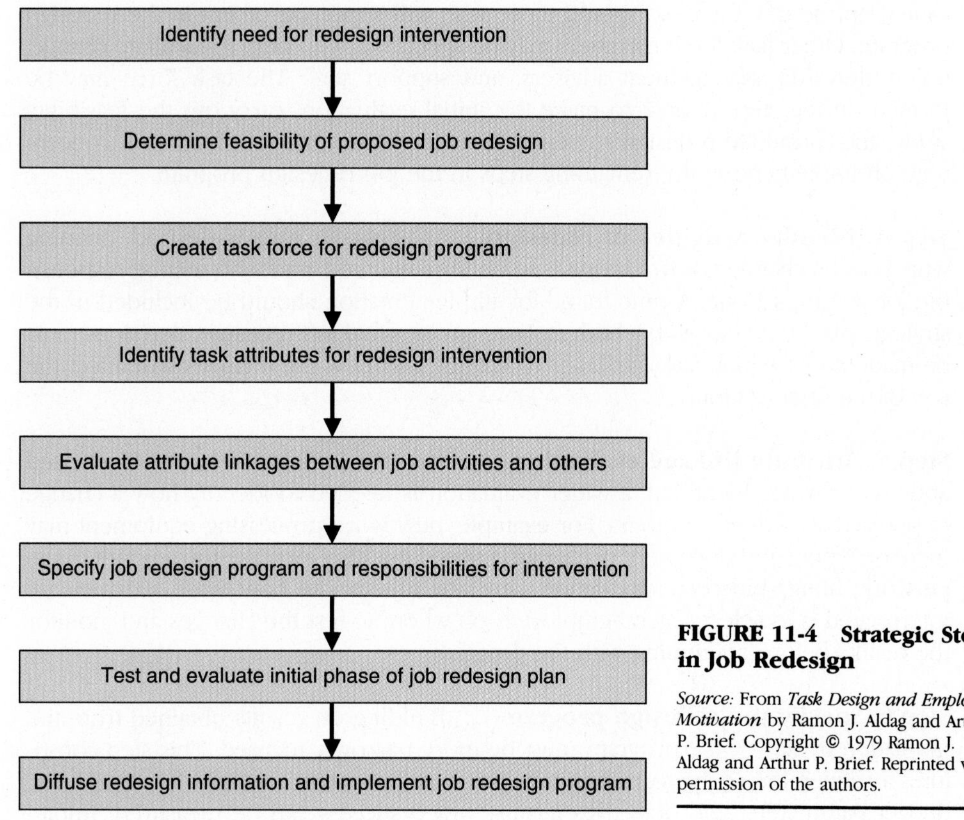

Identify need for redesign intervention
Determine feasibility of proposed job redesign
Create task force for redesign program
Identify task attributes for redesign intervention
Evaluate attribute linkages between job activities and others
Specify job redesign program and responsibilities for intervention
Test and evaluate initial phase of job redesign plan
Diffuse redesign information and implement job redesign program

FIGURE 11-4 Strategic Steps in Job Redesign

Source: From *Task Design and Employee Motivation* by Ramon J. Aldag and Arthur P. Brief. Copyright © 1979 Ramon J. Aldag and Arthur P. Brief. Reprinted with permission of the authors.

mental signals to identify when jobs need updating or job processes require modification. There are many methods used for monitoring, ranging from simple *job analyses* to complex audits conducted by teams of human resource consultants. Regardless of the methods used, the objective is to address core job dimensions to derive *job inventories* for each position.

A **job analysis** is conducted by systematically identifying tasks, skills, physical requirements, and duties specific to an individual job. This can be expanded by considering social and psychological dimensions described by the JCM. The findings of a job analysis are used to create a **job inventory** that describes task activities and attributes related to each job. A secretary, for example, may be expected to type at a certain speed, take shorthand, file, greet visitors, and operate certain office equipment. Some secretaries may be required to handle classified government documents, speak a foreign language, use sophisticated computer office systems, and supervise other workers.

job analysis
A formal method of identifying tasks, skills, physical requirements, and duties specific to an individual job.

job inventory
A descriptive list of task activities and attributes for a job derived from a thorough job analysis.

Step 2: Determine feasibility of redesign. Managers may be considering necessary job changes, but before they implement them, they must determine if the changes are feasible. For example, computer-based office systems have become common, so office staff may be expected to become skilled in word processing. There is no doubt that information technology is important for office productivity, but many employees find new methods difficult to accept. Consequently, when a company buys new office equipment, employees must learn to work with it. Yet merely changing job descriptions and holding employees responsible for learning new methods may be infeasible. The change may require carefully planned training programs and expert consultation for those involved, and in some instances, employees may simply be incapable of learning or accepting the job changes.

Step 3: Create a redesign task force. It is important to form a task force for the redesign program. Employees whose jobs will be redesigned should be represented on the task force; so should those who will supervise others in the redesign program. Other task force members may be specialists who help to facilitate change, union stewards, management advisers, and support staff. The task force may be formed during steps 1 or 2 to make the initial evaluation, carry out the feasibility study, and formulate redesign strategies. If formed later, the task force will concentrate on implementing the remaining steps in the job redesign program.

Step 4: Identify activities of redesign. A strategic plan is devised, defining what is to be changed, how change is to be implemented, and who will be responsible for getting it done. A time frame for implementation should be included in the strategic plan, together with a budget. In terms of actual job redesign, decisions must be made about which task attributes to change and how the changes will affect the rest of the organization.

Step 5: Attribute linkage evaluation. Once the initial plan has been devised and task activities identified, a wider evaluation is needed to identify how a change in one activity will affect others. For example, new word processing equipment may increase typing and document preparation speed but also increase the amount of paperwork, filing, and correspondence. One way to evaluate how these activities are interrelated is to select several employees on whom to test the changes and monitor the results before continuing with the program.

Step 6: Specify the redesign program. Building on results obtained from the evaluation in step 5, the program must be more narrowly focused. This step constitutes a refinement of the formal plan by documenting program activities, time lines, budget parameters, and objectives against which success can be measured. Implementation follows from this stage of planning.

Step 7: Evaluate. At critical control points, the task force evaluates progress and suggests adjustments to each job and to the program. For example, when training office staff in new word processing systems, these employees may be interviewed at several points during the training program to ensure that they are adapting as expected to new methods. Using the JCM, the task force also evaluates how employees are responding to the social and psychological aspects of their jobs. Objective results of job performance are monitored to validate company expectations for work improvements.

Step 8: Diffuse. Job redesign is usually not attempted in a comprehensive manner but implemented through a few individuals and small groups. For example, a company with several hundred offices scheduled for new word processing systems will initially introduce the changes to a few offices. As results are gathered on these initial efforts, the redesign program will be fine-tuned in anticipation of wider implementation. Progressively more individuals and groups will be included in the change process. Rapid diffusion is generally not possible, and even where it is, most companies prefer to commit the necessary capital and resources incrementally to avoid costly errors.

Job Design in Perspective

Up to this point, we have described job design (and redesign) in terms of individual positions. Because jobs are the fundamental building blocks of an organization, they comprise the focal activities that must be managed. As we shall see in the next section, however, jobs cannot be treated apart from immediate work groups that include other jobs affected by changes. More important, with the trend toward team development, jobs are more closely related to one another, so rather than consider each job as a set of isolated activities, management must think of all jobs as components of the collective work environment. Groups and group processes, therefore, are as important considerations as individual jobs.

> **CHECKPOINT**
>
> - Describe the core dimensions for evaluating jobs and how they affect the psychological states and work results of employees.
> - How is the job characteristics model used in job design and redesign programs?
> - Briefly describe job redesign process and explain why a planned program is necessary.

GROUPS AND GROUP PROCESSES

A **group** consists of two or more individuals regularly interacting with one another to pursue one or more common goals. In business organizations, groups are formed with members who complement one another, each having different skills or jobs that are needed to accomplish a shared purpose.[26] As we shall see in a moment, groups may be formal or informal, and they can be formed purposely by management or allowed to develop spontaneously as individuals come together for mutual benefit. However, a group is not a mere gathering of individuals—a common purpose must unite the participants.

group
Two or more individuals regularly interacting with one another in pursuit of one or more common goals.

Types of Groups

Companies organize **formal groups** around related jobs and technologies; they are created by authority and have defined purposes and reporting relationships. Formal groups become part of the organizational structure; examples are departments, work groups within departments, project teams, committees, and task forces. Formal groups are more narrowly defined as *command groups* and *task groups*.[27]

formal group
Created through formal authority, a formal group has defined purposes and reporting relationships.

A **command group** is permanently fixed within the organizational hierarchy and has formal authority within the chain of command. It represents a predetermined cluster of jobs or positions with a defined structure and purpose. A company's board of directors meets these criteria at the pinnacle of an organization's hierarchy. Departments and work groups within departments are also command groups. An accounting department, for example, may have several work groups with separate authority for payroll, sales receivables, and payables.

command group
A permanent group with jobs clustered within a formal structure that reports through the chain of command.

A **task group** also has formal authority, but it is distinguished from a command group by having selected members who work together to complete a particular task, which, once completed, may terminate the group. Consequently, membership in task groups is often temporary and includes different individuals under a variety of circumstances. Members of committees, project teams, and task forces are designated for their potential contributions to group assignments, and although they have formal leadership (committee chairs, project managers, etc.), they rarely report through the organization's chain of command on a permanent basis.

task group
A formal group with selected members who work together on focused tasks; a task group is seldom permanent and rarely reports through a chain of command.

Informal groups are created by their members without formal authority to pursue mutual benefits and interests. Informal groups serve many important purposes, such as satisfying members' social needs, providing forums for expressing employee grievances, and creating an affiliation to achieve goals beyond those defined in formal work groups. There are two types of informal groups: *interest groups* and *friendship groups*.[28]

informal group
Created by their members without formal authority for the purpose of pursuing mutual interests or satisfying social needs.

interest group
An informal group that comes together to pursue specific objectives of interest to its members.

An **interest group** consists of people who join together to attain a specific group objective. The group may elect a leader or spokesperson, but this is not necessary. An interest group within an organization has no place in the organization's hierarchy. For example, employees may affiliate to support a charity such as the annual March of Dimes fund drive, or to pursue a social program such as Save the Trees. Employees may come together to pressure the company to institute changes, such as creating a smoke-free environment. In organizations that lack formal channels for reviewing grievances (i.e., no labor union representation or appointed employee spokespersons), employees may form advocacy groups to challenge unfair work rules, pursue allegations of sexual harassment, or challenge management decisions about employee pay and benefits.

friendship group
Developed spontaneously by employees with similar characteristics or needs to affiliate socially.

A **friendship group** develops spontaneously among employees with similar characteristics or common interests for social interaction. Friendship groups' purposes are implied by their actions rather than consciously expressed, and they have neither leadership nor status in an organization. However, they can be influential because members tend to create very close social affiliations that affect their perceptions of work and their behavior. For example, office employees may cluster as groups, going to lunch together, meeting daily for coffee breaks, and jointly pursuing social activities such as holding birthday parties for one another or organizing company picnics. These groups satisfy members' social needs, and because members often become very close to one another, friendship groups can be a force in their companies. Employees with similar ethnic or racial backgrounds, for example, tend to congregate together, and through their shared values, they implicitly influence organizational policies.

Benefits of Group Membership

People belong to groups for many reasons. Often it is the logical pattern of work that determines formal groups, and as described earlier, jobs are clustered to achieve predetermined objectives. Similar functions or expertise, such as sales or accounting, lead to proximity of groups of employees with similar responsibilities or skills. This was discussed in Chapter 10, where we explained different types of organizational structures. Here we are concerned with the *psychological* benefits of groups and why employees are attracted to join them. These include security, power and influence, social affiliation, self-esteem, achievement, and self-development.[29]

Security. Belonging to a group helps insulate members from capricious actions by other individuals or pressure exerted through formal company mandates and management prerogatives. Formal work groups and informal interest or friendship groups are forces within an organization that other groups and managers take into consideration when making decisions. The voluntary nature of an informal group implies a commitment by its members to stand by one another. The assigned nature of department and work groups does not carry the same connotation. Consequently, the security enjoyed by employees in a formal group depends on the perceived commitment by its members to remain united.

Power and influence. Individuals working alone seldom have as much leverage to influence decisions as groups. Groups can often bring significant pressure to bear for changes in company practices. Groups are also more powerful to force compliance with social standards and values. Groups can demonstrate their power and influence in simple situations—for example, by showing a united front in support of an employee who was unjustly fired—or they can issue challenges on significant issues—for example, by insisting that the company conform to equal employment and affirmative action guidelines.

Social affiliation. Informal group membership and the psychological commitment to formal work groups solidifies affiliations among members. By becoming a group member, an individual enjoys regular interaction, friendship, and the opportunity to contribute to group goals. People enjoy being accepted by others, and through their social interactions, they gain friendly feedback on their accomplishments or constructive criticism on their shortcomings. Most important, groups provide individuals with companionship.

Self-esteem. Being an accepted group member provides a sense of self-esteem. Individuals are recognized as important, competent, and worthy by other group members. Groups also support their members and reinforce their perceptions of self-worth as they contribute to group activities. Status *in* a group and status *of* that group add to the personal satisfaction members feel with their jobs and organizations. Although work groups may not enjoy any status apart from their functions, membership in groups such as honor societies, professional organizations, and boards of directors carries tremendous prestige.

Achievement. Many command and task groups are formed with the purpose of combining talented individuals into teams that can achieve far more together than those individuals could working alone. Informally, employees cluster within their work groups to generate highly productive teams. By doing so, they may accomplish spectacular results, and often reap commensurate rewards. If bonuses are tied to performance, for example, a team can outperform the same number of employees working independently, teamwork will evolve, either formally or informally, to pursue larger bonuses. In addition, group achievement brings an increased sense of accomplishment that has psychological rewards for each team member.

Self-development. Work groups are vehicles for sharing information and expanding the skills and knowledge of individual members. Consequently, by joining groups, employees can improve themselves and develop both professionally and psychologically. New employees not yet accepted into work groups find themselves confined to the perimeters of their formal job descriptions. They do not readily participate in group activities, express opinions, or utilize their skills to be creative; group members only cautiously include them in their discussions and provide little constructive feedback on their performance. Once accepted into their work groups, employees break through the formal boundaries of their job descriptions, share their feelings, use their skills more thoroughly and productively, and enjoy a reciprocal relationship with other group members.

CHECKPOINT

- Define and contrast formal and informal groups, and explain the primary types of groups that exist in each category.
- How do employees benefit from group membership?
- Explain how organizations benefit by developing effective groups.

CHARACTERISTICS OF GROUPS

Groups of every size ranging from small teams to entire organizations have social, psychological, and sociotechnical properties that affect performance. The result is a "chemistry" of group behavior. Social properties are derived from the interaction of members and how the group behaves as a whole. Individual behavior within groups constitutes the psychological context of work. Thus a particularly influential employee who is unhappy can affect the work attitudes of others in the group, and two employees who cannot get along can make other group members disagreeable. The sociotechnical system of the group evolves out of technological work methods and how members integrate those methods into their group behavior.[30] These three properties of groups—social, psychological, and sociotechnical—influence how they perform. The reverse is also true: Group performance influences individual behavior, social processes, and how technology is implemented. Collectively, these properties constitute a certain *group psychology*. Although there is as yet no clear explanation of how group psychology evolves, several important characteristics of groups are known to be influential.

Leadership structure. Formal groups have mandated positions of authority and a prescribed structure. Departments have heads, work teams have supervisors or team coordinators, projects have managers, and committees have chairpersons. If these positions are filled by individuals capable of performing in leadership roles, ideally they will be accepted as leaders by group members. To be accepted, leaders must possess attributes that members perceive as critical to representing group interests, embody group values and be able to defend them against other groups, and satisfy group expectations for sharing information and coordinating activities without creating conflicts.[31]

Unfortunately, many individuals who acquire authority over groups lack the qualities of leadership necessary to gain group acceptance. Without an accepted leader, the group breaks down; the chemistry doesn't work and coordination, communication, or synthesis fails. If group members have strong bonds, they may reject formal leaders in favor of "informal" leaders who emerge from the group by virtue of their leadership capabilities. The result can be a tightly knit group that performs well, but that develops an adversarial relationship with management.

Informal groups seek out leaders from among their members. Because informal groups are not recognized in a company's organizational hierarchy, adversarial relationships over group leadership seldom arise. Conflicts can arise between management and the group, though, and if the informal leader is a belligerent spokesperson, these conflicts can be serious. Figure 11-5 illustrates some of these issues. The important point is that informal leaders only enjoy power as long as they adequately represent their group's interests. Consequently, a belligerent spokesperson who remains in control usually signifies that the group expects belligerent behavior. Similarly, a congenial spokesperson who fosters a cooperative en-

FIGURE 11-5 Leadership and Authority in Formal and Informal Groups

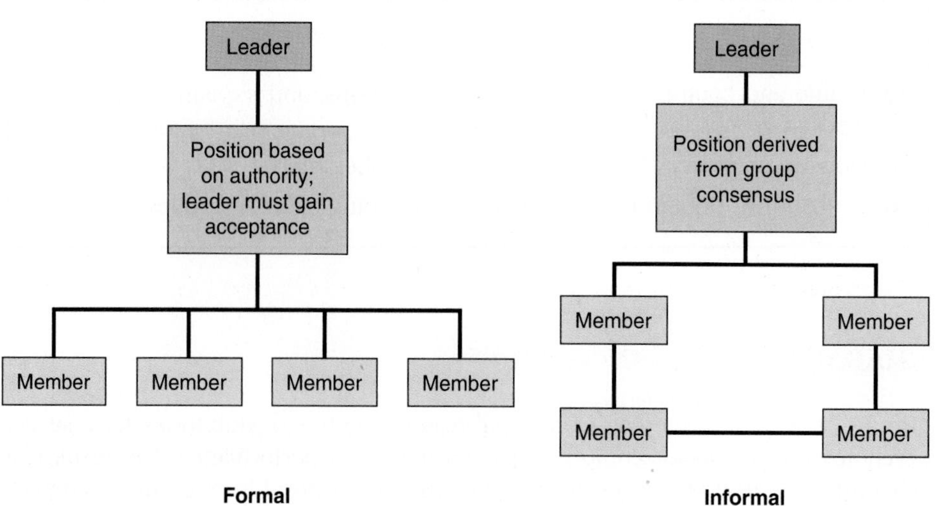

vironment with other groups and management tends to validate corresponding group behavior.[32]

Group objectives. Formal groups have two sets of objectives.[33] The first, called **manager-assisted objectives**, are derived from the primary purpose for which the group was formed. They may be formulated by management and reinforced by a group leader who has formal authority; or in a participative environment, they may be jointly determined by managers and members of the work group. (Group decision making is addressed later in the chapter.) In either instance, the group must be willing to accept the manager-assisted objectives as meaningful or conflicts will erupt between group members and the organization's management and the group will either not perform up to expectations or will become subversive.

manager-assisted objectives
Derived from the purpose of the group, these objectives may be expressed by management or jointly developed with employees.

The second set of objectives, called **group objectives**, are determined by group members and their collective behavior and can be defined in terms of *group achievement* and *group maintenance*. Group achievement may mirror manager-assisted objectives if members accept the objectives formulated by management. But most groups develop their own achievement targets through actual practice, and these can either fall short of or exceed management's expectations. The end results of work activities usually provide accurate clues about a group's achievement intentions. Group maintenance depends on members' expectations about the benefits of holding the group together. They include the degree of internal affiliation expected by members, social and security benefits derived from remaining within the group, and rewards derived from contributions to group efforts by individual members. If being committed to the group or contributing to group efforts fails to satisfy members' expectations, the group may dissolve into a mere gathering of individuals working in proximity to one another.[34]

group objectives
Objectives developed by group members that relate to task achievements and maintenance of the group; they can be purposely created or they can evolve through group behavior.

Group norms. An important characteristic of group psychology is how group members develop **group norms**, or informal standards of conduct that all members are expected to follow.[35] Norms may include work standards such as pace and quality of work and length of work breaks. They may also apply to patterns of communication such as use of jargon, whom to speak to and whom to ignore, and when to remain quiet. Other standards relate to attitudes toward supervision, company policies, and peer relations.

group norms
Informal rules of conduct and patterns of behavior that all group members are expected to follow.

Most cohesive work groups have established patterns. Assume, for example, that office staffers have a formal workday that starts at 8:00 A.M. and ends at 5:00 P.M., that they have an official ten-minute coffee break in the morning and another in the afternoon, and that their lunch hour runs from noon to 1:00 P.M. Typically, staff workers will arrive at 8:00 A.M. and pour themselves a cup of coffee, spend the first fifteen minutes of the day talking about personal experiences and socializing, take a twenty-minute coffee break, and stop working ten minutes before noon to get ready for lunch. They usually go through a similar pattern in the afternoon, so that at 5:00 P.M., most workers have one foot out the door. Thus the "formal" expectations of employers are superseded by "informal" patterns of behavior established by employees. Where this pattern exists for only a few employees, however, it is not the result of group norms but of individual behavior. Group norms imply that most, if not all, members of a recognized group behave similarly. In the example, a majority of office employees would have to follow this pattern of work for it to become the "office routine," and new employees would be expected to conform to it.

Group cohesiveness. The extent to which employees are attracted to their group and feel compelled to stay in it is called **group cohesiveness**. Cohesiveness is crucial for reinforcing group norms. If the group is highly cohesive, its members will more rigorously adhere to norms. Individual members will bend to dominant peer pressure to avoid being ostracized by the group. This is how groups change in-

group cohesiveness
The extent to which employees are attracted to their group and feel compelled to stay in it.

dividual behavior. Less cohesive groups reflect less peer pressure and therefore have more flexible group work norms.

Cohesiveness is a two-edged sword. Cohesive groups tend to have strong group loyalty, a sense of internal security, stable membership, and commitment by members to common objectives. This can be beneficial to the organization if the group's work standards are high and its objectives support organizational objectives. If, however, group objectives oppose organizational objectives, the cohesive group becomes a powerful adversary. If its work standards are low, for example, a cohesive group will constrain growth and productivity. When companies need to institute change, cohesive groups must be convinced to change as a group because then group pressure will quickly bring the majority of members into line.[36]

Groups have tremendous influence on organizations and how organizational objectives are fulfilled. Managers must handle them skillfully. Usually, managers prefer cohesive groups, but whatever the type of group, managers must ensure that group work norms are high and that group objectives support those of the company. One way to encourage positive results is to create group decision-making processes that enhance positive and cohesive behavior.

CHECKPOINT

- What are the factors that influence group psychology?
- Contrast formal and informal group leaders and how conflicts arise over leadership, manager-assisted objectives, and group objectives.
- How do group norms influence individual and group behavior?
- Define group cohesiveness and describe its advantages and disadvantages to both an organization and the group's members.

GROUP DEVELOPMENT

Developing effective groups involves much more than creating departments or forming employee teams. It requires a systematic process of cultivating team confidence, cohesion, and synergy among co-workers to perform as effective groups. This implies that groups will be empowered by the process to participate in decisions with their managers and in many instances to make decisions for themselves. Groups exist at every organizational level and in every type of organization, but the focus of this section will be on activities that include nonmanagement employees. Groups formed with employees are commonly known as *work groups*.

work groups
Small formal teams of co-workers who, together with their managers, share tasks and responsibilities for well-defined segments of work activities.

Work groups are small teams of co-workers who share tasks and responsibilities for well-defined segments of work. As noted earlier, work groups (also called *work teams*) usually include managers and can include staff specialists who have a direct bearing on the group's activities. They range in size from three or four employees to as many as twenty, and they are formal, meaning they have an authority structure and recognized decision-making responsibility. Managers of work groups have supervisory roles that develop in concert with their groups' activities. Specifically, managers may be officially charged with directing group activities, but as groups mature, managers' roles are transformed by group expectations to encompass coaching, advising, and supporting their teams. Groups become effective only if managers make this transformation away from a "directive" use of authority. Consequently, developing work groups begins with reeducating managers to accept new roles in an environment where work and decisions are shared.[37]

Long before Japanese management practices became popular as models for group endeavors, and long before buzzwords like "quality circles," "self-managed

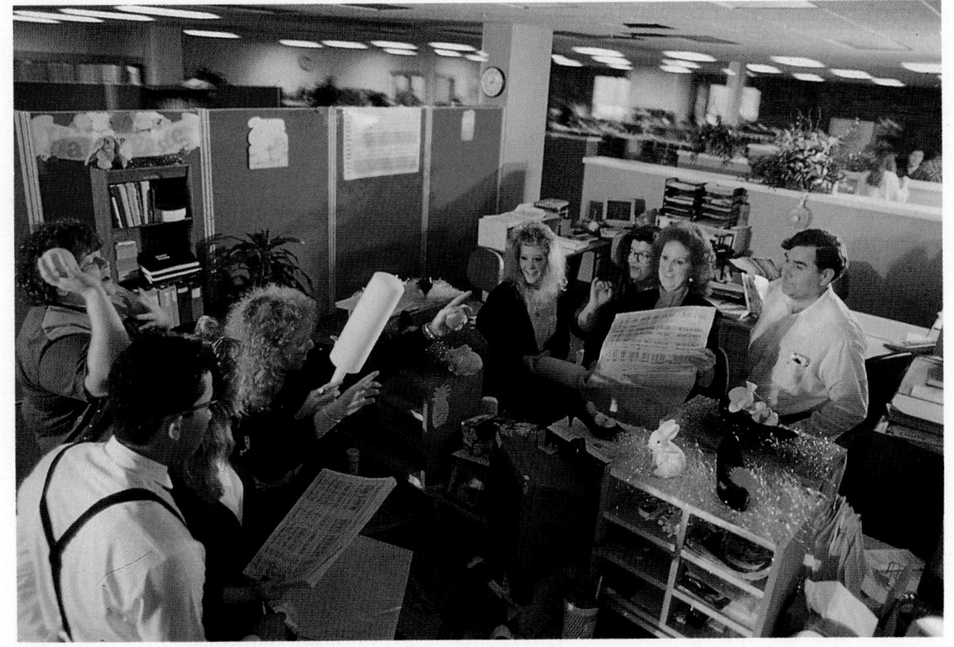

Chaos in the workplace? Hardly. These Tranzact Systems employees take their "play" seriously. The eight-year-old company, based in Homewood, Illinois, audits and pays freight bills for companies that shift these operations to outside suppliers. Hit hard by recession in the 1990s, Tranzact is using various techniques to streamline operations and lift the quality of work. These techniques include play—intended to help employees build new self-managing team systems.

work groups," and "consensus decision making" crept into management jargon, American management experts and leading U.S. companies were implementing team-building techniques.[38] Although Japanese companies embraced these concepts more rapidly than most U.S. companies did, more than half of all Fortune 500 corporations now have participative work teams.[39] The most common model used in group development is the four-phase process shown in Figure 11-6.

The Four-Phase Model

All groups fall into one of four phases of development. A newly formed group is in phase 1, where members are just beginning to know one another and are striving to find common ground for further development. At the other extreme, the mature

FIGURE 11-6 Four Phases of Group Development

Phase	Mutual Acceptance	Decision Making	Motivation	Control
Relationships among members	Mistrust Aloofness	Open communication Developing knowledge about members	Cohesiveness Cooperation	Sanctions are communicated Status system is understood
Task and problem-solving functions	Searching for objectives and mission	Problems and roles identified Tasks assigned	Helping each other Sharing information	Abilities and skills fully used Problem solving
Level of Maturity	Low ⟵	⟶	⟶	High

group of phase 4 is a cohesive team whose members trust the group to meet their social and professional expectations. Between the extremes are various degrees of development, ranging from open communications at the lower border of phase 2 to a high degree of cohesiveness and information sharing at the upper border of phase 3. A summary of the four phases follows.[40]

- *Phase 1: Mutual Acceptance.* Group members are aloof and apprehensive about working closely together. Initially, they tend to shield themselves from one another and behave independently. As the group develops during this phase, barriers start to come down and members begin to learn about one another, to define group objectives, and to identify how the group will be led.
- *Phase 2: Decision Making.* Members have learned to accept one another, to communicate openly, and to trust one another in a participative decision-making environment. They tackle task-related problems as a group, and as they progress through phase 2, they assume greater decision-making responsibilities consistent with the company's particular philosophy of empowering work groups.
- *Phase 3: Motivation.* The group becomes a cohesive team during this phase and progressively matures into a competent decision-making body. Many groups do not progress beyond phase 3, or they languish for years as "maturing teams" while attempting to resolve internal difficulties. The degree to which a team achieves greater results depends on complex circumstances, including company support for continued growth, effective leadership within the group, members' capabilities, technological constraints of the task environment, and the relative benefits members perceive they are gaining from their contributions.
- *Phase 4: Control.* Groups in this phase have matured. Their interests are fully aligned, the leadership issue has been resolved, group objectives have been accepted and internalized by group members, and each person is contributing fully to group maintenance and task activities. The term *control* is used to emphasize that the group has established norms and sanctions in place to perpetuate group interests and to defend those interests against outside influences or disruptive individuals.

Implementing the Development Process

In most organizations, employees already work in close proximity to one another and have informally harmonized their interests or progressed through the early stages of group development. In these circumstances, organizations will not have to start from scratch to cultivate group behavior. Therefore, as a prelude to implementing group-building programs, companies must evaluate existing group behavior for several important characteristics.[41]

The first characteristic to identify is what phase of development the group of employees falls into in the four-phase model. The second is the group leader, and whether that person will support a group development program. The third is the membership profile, including who is included in the group, who is exempt, and why this particular profile exists. The fourth is a description of the group's operating environment, including its existing and foreseeable activities, sociotechnical properties, and relationship to other groups. After obtaining these answers, management has a baseline for defining a development process.

Although the details of development programs are beyond the scope of this book, there are several points to bear in mind. Group development programs often take years to implement. In fact, the initial stage of evaluation may take months and necessitate bringing in teams of outside consultants. If the organization is confronted with rapid changes, such as increasing competition, new technology, or recessionary staff reductions, management may have its hands full just trying to develop the baseline needed to launch a program.[42] Once initiated, the program will attempt changes only among a few groups, then monitor their progress for several months. This is a period when managers must be trained to make the transition to new roles and employees must be encouraged to support program changes. Intervention consultants often spearhead this phase of the development program, and one of their most important tasks is to transform groups into decision-making bodies.

CHECKPOINT

- What are work groups and how are they involved in decision-making tasks?
- Explain the four-phase development model, distinguishing the key features of work groups in each stage.
- Describe activities that are important for implementing a development program.

GROUP DECISIONS

In the 1960s, research by the Tavistock Institute in Great Britain showed that when employees could make group decisions about work and when individual members felt they were contributing to group decisions, productivity increased.[43] Tavistock researchers also found that increased job satisfaction was associated with group problem solving. More recent studies of Japanese management systems dramatically underscore these points.[44] Still, we should be cautious about concluding that group processes by themselves solve organizational problems.

Individual versus Group Decisions

There is no definitive support for the superiority of either group or individual decision making. Actually, it may be less important to resolve this question than to recognize how complicated the issue is. Generally, when problems demand innovative solutions or original insights, individual decisions are superior to group decisions. Also, when time and technical constraints suggest urgency, personal decision making is more expedient. On the other hand, when problem solving demands a diversity of skills and viewpoints, group decisions are usually superior. And group decisions are better when there is a need for broad-based acceptance.[45]

Studies of Japanese management indicate that culture has a tremendous influence on the workability of group processes. Even though the United States is experiencing an extraordinary change in organizational philosophy that is moving us toward participative systems, we are a long way from endorsing a culture based on conciliatory group processes. The following section summarizes the advantages and disadvantages of group decisions.

Advantages and disadvantages of group decisions. Group decisions have certain advantages compared to individual decisions in several important situations.[46]

- *Need for Diverse Information.* Because of the increasing complexity and specialization of organizations, the resolutions to many problems are beyond the capabilities of one individual. A group comprising knowledgeable individuals from diversified backgrounds can provide the expertise to tackle complex problems.

ETHICS IN MANAGEMENT

No Golden Parachutes for Middle Managers

Downsizing and "rationalizing" company structures endear top management to their stockholders. Wall Street applauds CEOs who take the difficult steps of reducing company bureaucracies, implementing highly productive team environments, and replacing human endeavor with technology because these strategies can turn a company around and make it more competitive and profitable. America's smokestack industries were once considered the primary targets of turnaround strategies, but that myth exploded in the wake of so-called demassing by IBM, Lotus, Chase Manhattan, Citicorp, General Electric, and Eastman Kodak. Less publicized staff reductions have occurred in nearly all the Fortune 500 companies through job redesign, increased automation, and downward shifting of the burden of decision making to employee work teams.

The course of restructuring has eliminated 3.4 million industrial jobs over the last decade, and in the service sector, where job opportunities seemed to be increasing in the 1980s, company failures, mergers, and reorganizations are having a similar effect. Approximately half of the largest commercial banks have merged, with subsequent staff reductions; six of the nation's largest ten airlines have either gone bankrupt or been bought out, with huge job losses; and employment in the entire telecommunications industry has shrunk by 12 percent, starting with AT&T's global reorganization. The most telling statistic, however, is that while middle

- *Need for Alternative Solutions.* Most problems have more than one possible solution. Individuals tend to focus on a single solution or a narrow range of options, but groups tend to generate a wide variety of alternatives. In situations where there is uncertainty or a high degree of risk, such as in long-range planning, the richer array of choices provided by groups can be especially valuable.
- *Need for Broad-Based Acceptance.* Nearly all decisions are more easily accepted by those who participated in making them. When an organization has to make particularly sensitive decisions in areas such as job redesign, the group that makes those decisions will furnish a base of needed support.
- *Need for Effective Communication.* Many decisions result in complicated programs, new projects, changes in jobs, and confusing new processes. Communicating these decisions to employees can be more stressful than making them. Information sharing during group processes reduces misunderstandings and ambiguity and ensures that information will be disseminated more effectively.

managers make up only between 5 and 8 percent of the nation's work force, they account for 17 percent of all dismissals in recent years.

The core dilemma for most middle managers is how to be the driving force of change in their companies while knowing that if the changes are effective, they will be endangering their own careers. Middle and lower-level managers are the ones expected to build autonomous work teams, to empower employees with a large share of their own decision-making authority, and to reduce the company's dependence on formal management controls. They are expected to cheerfully redistribute job responsibilities, thus reducing their own numbers, to enable their companies to accomplish more with less human endeavor.

Top executives who successfully downsize and show increased profits are richly rewarded with huge bonuses, and those who try but fail often have "golden parachutes"—multimillion-dollar compensation packages and benefit guarantees—to soften their downfall. Because of the political sensitivity of layoffs, there are job outplacement programs, extended unemployment insurance, and retraining to partially soften the blow of being fired for blue-collar workers and wage-based white-collar employees. Seniority systems and collective bargaining agreements help ensure that the first brunt of cutbacks will be felt by younger and less-experienced employees, who are often able to switch into other fields. Middle managers and staff, however, usually find themselves on the wrong end of pink slips with no golden parachutes. As a group, they are older and less mobile than other employees, so few middle managers can make parallel career changes. And those who remain employed have more to do and less authority to do it; they are running scared.

Sources: Anne B. Fisher, "Morale Crisis," *Fortune,* November 18, 1991, pp. 70–72, 76, 80; "New R&R Doesn't Give Executives Any Rest," *Wall Street Journal,* December 13, 1991, p. B1; Richard W. Hallstein, "Team Unbuilding," *Training & Development Journal,* June 1989, pp. 56–58; and Max Messmer, "Strategic Staffing for the '90s," *Personnel Journal,* October 1990, pp. 92–97.

Critics of group decision making point to several drawbacks. The most frequent criticism is that group decisions are inferior to decisions made by one well-informed individual. There is an old clichè that the camel is the result of a committee trying to design a horse. That may be trite, but some less-than-optimal results do emerge from group decisions. Let's review several of the more serious concerns.[47]

- *Compromised Results.* Group cooperation is often more valued by members than effective performance. This preference can lead to poor compromises in order to preserve group harmony. Too wide an assortment of options can strangle group deliberations and force a weak majority resolution. Compromise behavior may also thwart innovation.
- *Dominant Behavior.* Groups can become power platforms for individuals who champion particular viewpoints and overwhelm others by dominating group activities. Or group decisions may reflect filibustering rather than genuine participation. In either instance, group effectiveness is reduced and the potential benefits of group decision making are lost.

- *Conflict.* If groups are improperly constituted, conflict among members may outweigh cooperative endeavors. Then creative individuals may withdraw or suppress their ideas to avoid ridicule.
- *Untimely Decisions.* Group decisions always take longer than individual decisions. One individual can make a decision faster than two because the pair must exchange ideas and agree on a decision. When groups are large and composed of people with diverse interests, quick decisions may be impossible. In situations that demand timely action, decisions are better left to individuals.
- *Uncertain Risk Factors.* The research is not clear about whether groups tend to make riskier or more cautious decisions. Conventional wisdom supports the contention that groups are more conservative, but reliable research shows that, in some cases at least, cohesive groups tend to recommend more risky decisions, apparently because of group solidarity and internal group security.
- *"Groupthink."* Group members can reinforce one another's illusions about the importance or invulnerability of their collective efforts. Thus they can lose touch with reality.[48]

Empowering Groups—Concluding Comments

The critical feature that sets a group apart from a gathering of individual employees is the group's participation in decisions. While most employees working as individuals rely on managers to make decisions for them, groups are involved in deciding what tasks to perform, how they will be accomplished, who is to do them, and how the group will support team decisions. Although groups do much more, and individual members see many other benefits to teamwork, the essential attribute of an effective group is being *empowered to participate in decisions*. The most elaborate development programs conducted by top consultants will fail if an organization resists making the necessary changes to empower groups.[49]

There are, however, two cautions worth repeating. First, management cannot abdicate its responsibilities; delegation has its limits, and work groups cannot operate in a vacuum of planning, leadership, or control. Second, even if highly autonomous work groups evolve, managers will not have less to do, but more. Their roles will be substantially redefined, so that instead of directing work activities and making decisions for employees, they will be coaching, teaching, supporting, counseling, and participating as team members in leadership positions.[50]

In conclusion, we must emphasize that cultural values, beliefs, ethics, social transitions, and new technologies have been altering our society. Early in the chapter, we discussed how individual perceptions of jobs are changing and how employees no longer perceive authority to be an absolute right of ownership. Consequently, organizations are making genuine efforts to restructure authority, redefine jobs, and empower groups. These are all fascinating aspects of a society in transition, but they can be difficult to manage. Nevertheless, employees have become exuberant about working in more harmonious surroundings based on participative groups, and managers have become more adroit at working within systems that encourage group processes. We are not losing our individuality so much as gaining respect for individual contributions to group activities.

CHECKPOINT

- Explain the predevelopment evaluation process and why it is important.
- Briefly describe the advantages and disadvantages of group decisions.
- Describe group empowerment and how management roles change with group development.

HERMAN MILLER, INC., introduced at the beginning of the chapter, has been a leading company in effective group development. Recall that chairman Max DePree emphasizes "covenantal relationships" and "shared ideas" in an environment of mutual responsibility.[51] Managers at Herman Miller have not shifted their responsibilities to employees, and employees are not free to do whatever they please, but there is *mutual* sharing of decisions and group responsibilities. In DePree's estimation, both his managers and their teams work harder now than they did in a more structured hierarchy because shared responsibilities require much more interaction, patience, and commitment from everyone. Managers had to accept "covenantal" roles rather than contractual roles, thereby learning to listen to employees, support their creative efforts, and provide the leadership necessary to reinforce group objectives and task activities. ■

A SYNOPSIS FOR LEARNING

1. Describe how technology and social forces affect employees' jobs.

   New technologies are rapidly changing how work is accomplished. This is most obvious in the replacement of many human endeavors by computers and robotics, but it is also apparent in improved processes and engineering innovations that redefine jobs. The transformation is taking place in service organizations as well as in manufacturing, so that electronic banking is as common as robotic assembly lines. Jobs are no longer strictly defined in terms of human endeavor, but rather in terms of the technological environment and how people use new tools and processes. Social trends such as dual-career families, compelling changes in minority status, better education, and changes in retirement patterns have influenced the nature of jobs and organizations.

2. Explain how the range and depth of jobs are changing.

   Job range relates to the breadth of tasks accomplished by an employee, and job depth relates to the responsibility an employee has for directing his or her work. Technological advances, together with sociotechnical advances such as grouping technology processes with work teams, have vastly expanded the job range; more can be accomplished by fewer people working with new tools and methods in highly productive teams. Because of the changes in organizational culture and new social forces at work, employees expect more freedom, greater responsibility, and more meaningful tasks. As a result, group efforts prevail in more than half of America's leading companies, and employees throughout these organizations have greater decision-making responsibilities.

3. Describe the job characteristics model and explain how it is used in job design.

   The job characteristics model is a conceptual framework for understanding the activities and relationships that exist in a job situation. It identifies core dimensions of jobs and how those dimensions are likely to change. Managers use the JCM to evaluate core dimensions in terms of how they affect psychological states of employees. Once they understand employees' psychological states, managers are in a better position to understand work-related outcomes associated with the job being studied. Employee profiles are also evaluated in the JCM to establish people's relative needs for growth, and then job design (or redesign) efforts are undertaken to benefit both employees and their organizations by improving the total job configuration.

4. Identify and contrast the primary types of organizational groups.

   Groups are either formal or informal. Formal groups exist within the organizational structure, their formal leadership is usually determined by the company, and they have specific work objectives. Informal groups develop apart from the formal organization, often spontaneously, and are not recognized in the organizational hierarchy. Formal groups consist of command groups, such as departments and work groups, and task groups, such as project teams and committees. Informal groups include interest groups, whose members affiliate for a specific purpose such as supporting charities or reviewing grievances. Friendship groups are informal associations that satisfy members' social needs by meeting regularly for lunch, for example, or attending sporting events together.

5. Explain group norms and cohesiveness and how they affect performance.

   Group norms are informal standards of conduct that all members of a group are expected to follow. These norms usually take the form of sanctions for or against work rules, expressions of personal behavior, and patterns of work. Cohesiveness is the extent to which employees feel attracted to their groups and compelled to stay in them. A highly cohesive group can be very influential in establishing its own work norms, pressuring the company for changes, and controlling individual members' behavior.

6. Describe how work groups develop into mature teams.

   Work teams do not merely come together and instantly achieve high productivity. To the contrary, they often take years to solidify into mature teams with effective leadership, stable internal status relationships, and competence at controlling work and group activities. They often start out as immature groups whose members distrust one another, remain aloof, and only tentatively search for common ground and objectives on which to build stronger relationships. As they develop, communications become open, the group starts making collective decisions, and members discover the benefits of group security and interdependence. With further development, they become cohesive work teams with a high degree of cooperation and sharing of problems, tasks, decisions, and information.

7. Explain group empowerment in terms of decision making.

   Empowerment is the process of entrusting work groups with significant control over their tasks as well as their membership, work methods, and work-related decisions. It requires managers to relinquish tremendous authority to their groups, then provide the necessary leadership to support group efforts. Part of the empowerment process is training managers to exercise leadership as coaches, counselors, and participating team members.

SKILL ANALYSIS

CASE 1 Tapping the Talent of Good People at Colgate-Palmolive

Colgate-Palmolive, one of the top five consumer-products companies in the world, has quietly built a success record on the strength of its policy of having talented people work as responsible teams. According to CEO Reuban Mark, however, this has often been an elusive objective. Considering the company's global operations and its diversity of interests, Mark explains that team development efforts are a continuing challenge that will extend into the next century.

Colgate operates in more than fifty countries worldwide and derives 64 percent of its revenues from sales outside the United States. Sales offices, manufacturing, and distribution facilities are spread across four dozen cultures among peoples speaking twice that many languages. Consequently, the corporate policy of holding employee teams responsible for work-related decisions may be easily accepted in one location and rejected or ridiculed elsewhere. To address this problem, Colgate has implemented many different programs under local management control.

In Turkey, for example, Colgate uses professionally produced videotapes and local trainers to educate managers about empowering employees to make team decisions. Then managers are expected to develop work teams, designing both jobs and group roles for employees who respect chain-of-command authority. In the People's Republic of China, employees enjoy the harmony of working together in groups, but long-established cultural values constrain them from making outright decisions. They prefer to consult with managers, expressing their ideas as cautiously worded suggestions, thus avoiding forcing anyone to "lose face." Because the Chinese seemed eager for productivity bonuses, Colgate initiated a program of incentive pay for managers and their employees based on group sales. As a result, employees rapidly developed into cooperating teams where informal norms and group pressure became more important than formal authority relationships.

In Venezuela, Mexico, Malaysia, and Pakistan, Colgate has entered into partnerships that include local businesses and government organizations. In Mark's vernacular, the company does not just "drop off an American with a boatload of toothpaste" and expect business to boom, but forms a local business around the company's products and technology. It is then up to local managers to motivate, coach, and lead employees. Great successes have been scored in Singapore, Thailand, and European countries where employees have adopted team methods and managers have shown their willingness to share decision making. In less-developed South American countries, more traditional patterns of work exist.

To overcome cultural barriers, Colgate introduced a global strategy that is meant, in Mark's words, "to allow those leading the local entity to feel they are controlling their own destiny." That strategy is based on hiring talented people and giving them the opportunity to share not only in decisions but also in company ownership. Employees at almost every level throughout Colgate have stock or stock options, except in countries where laws prevent the practice (e.g., the People's Republic of China). This program began in the early 1980s and has shown good results.

The greatest productivity changes have occurred in several U.S. operations where Colgate employees have forged new work relationships. In Fremont, Ohio, for example, where the company makes its Hill Pet Products line, productivity gains nearly double the U.S. standard have been recorded every year during the past decade. Employees at the Fremont facility have been involved in work team programs since the late 1970s, and Colgate introduced new process technologies several years ago, further enhancing the subsidiary's record. Under a flexible manufacturing system (FMS) that uses small groups of employees to control this integrated technology, fewer people make more products with less supervision than in previous years. FMS process technology uses specially designed computer-assisted machinery that automatically produces small batches of products, then sorts, moves, tracks, and stacks them with a minimum of human effort. Some machinery can be programmed to automatically set up for different products or custom orders, and then, through data links, precisely account for operations and transmit information to management.

When a similar type of technology was introduced in one of the company's northern Illinois plants, results were poor. The Illinois employees had been working in teams, but under a collective bargaining contract. When the company introduced automation, union shop stewards objected to the changes unless the company would guarantee job protection. Shop-floor workers, recognizing that many jobs might be lost, saw little reason to change their work habits to implement the new systems. Managers, too, took note that the use of integrated technology and work teams in other plants had "flattened" the organization, eliminating a number of management positions. Consequently, lower-level managers also resisted the changes and did little to encourage work team development.

Case Questions

1. Describe how employees in different cultural environments might be motivated by Colgate's efforts to develop work teams. What benefits of working as teams might they perceive as important?
2. The FMS implemented successfully at Colgate's Fremont, Ohio, plant illustrates what concept of work? Explain the benefits of this concept.
3. Why has the company had excellent results with group development and new work methods in some situations and very poor results elsewhere? What factors influenced these different outcomes?

Sources: Based on "Top Products for Less Than Top Dollar," *Business Week,* October 25, 1991, pp. 66–68; and Reuban Mark, "Partnerships Will Be the Thrust of the 1990s," *Fortune,* March 26, 1990, p. 32.

VIDEO CASE Self-Managed Work Teams: A Concept Catching Fire

Who needs a boss? While the concept of working without a boss has guided Japanese corporations for a long time, many American companies are just now beginning to experiment with "boss-less" work groups. These self-managed work teams are taking over many of the responsibilities traditionally assigned to a supervisor. Although the supervisor's job has not been eliminated, it has changed in focus. One company that has enjoyed resounding success with this approach is Rockwell Tactical Systems, a division of Rockwell International.

The Hellfire missiles manufactured at a Rockwell Tactical Systems plant outside Atlanta played a critical role in the Gulf War. Using the on-target Hellfires, Apache helicopters blasted holes in the Iraqis' radar defenses so Allied bombers could launch surprise attacks on Baghdad. High-tech but not high-expense, the $20,000 Hellfire missiles did their part in the war won with technology.

A short time back, in 1988, the Hellfire factory was losing money. The parent company, Rockwell Systems International, an extremely profitable enterprise, decided to take drastic action to turn around its Tactical Systems division.

General manager Paul Smith was sent to a week-long seminar on the teachings of Edward Deming and the Japanese style of management Deming inspired. Smith came back a convert. He says, "They were talking just to the kind of problems we were having, and that was improving our quality, getting the cost down." So Smith implemented some changes in the way the plant was managed. Instead of supervisors calling all the shots on the shop floor, the work force was divided into self-managing teams composed of ten to fifteen workers.

The work groups were put in charge of deciding on acceptable quality within their group. One early decision made by the teams was to use new assembly machines to reduce the number of defects in the circuit boards being produced. After the new machines were brought in, the number of circuit boards without defects climbed to close to 100 percent. Says one Rockwell employee, "If I've got an idea that will make something better, something like that, we all discuss it."

Another example of the workers' new self-management was a decision made in one of the assembly areas to close for two weeks because the group determined there were not enough orders to operate economically. The Rockwell workers are willing to take this kind of initiative because a percentage of any cost savings is passed back to them in the form of a bonus. In 1990, this "gainshare" program amounted to $1,000 per worker.

Has this "boss-less" approach worked? At this particular division of Rockwell, employment has dropped from 2,100 workers to 1,300, yet missile production and profits are up. At least at this Hellfire plant, the concept of self-managed work teams has caught fire!

Case Questions

1. Is the approach used at Rockwell Tactical Systems similar to group technology? Why or why not?
2. Using the job characteristics model, describe how the use of self-managed work teams may have contributed to the success of Rockwell Tactical Systems.
3. Would self-managed work teams be appropriate for all organizations? Why or why not?

Sources: Stephen S. McIntosh, "Empowered Teams: Creating Self-Directed Work Groups That Improve Quality, Productivity and Participation," *HRMagazine,* December 1991, Vol. 36, No. 12, p. 11ff; Bob Hughes, "25 Stepping Stones for Self-Directed Work Teams," *Training,* December 1991, Vol. 28, No. 12, p. 44ff; Stephen S. McIntosh, "Self-Directed Work Teams: The New American Challenge," *HRMagzine,* September 1991, Vol. 36, No. 9, p. 9ff; and Richard Wellins and Jill George, "The Key to Self-Directed Teams," *Training and Development Journal,* April 1991, Vol. 45, No. 4, p. 26ff.

JOB CHARACTERISTICS

SKILL PRACTICE

Introduction

We have all been in work situations where things went well. Tasks were completed on time, co-workers seemed compatible and pleasant, supervisors were available and appeared pleased with our work. We had a sense of well-being and generally looked forward to going to our place of work. During these times, we felt important to our organizations and probably were getting compliments on work well done by our co-workers and supervisors.

On the other hand, most of us have been in situations where things were going poorly. Assignments were viewed as a "chore" rather than a challenge, and we were not happy with the quality of our own efforts. Our supervisors were unhappy about our work, and probably told us about it. It seemed clear to us, and to others, that we were not performing up to par.

Instructions for the Exercise

Take a sheet of paper and, thinking first of a *positive* work situation, describe the factors that were present at the time that accounted for your good performance.

Next, on the back of that sheet of paper (or on a separate sheet), think back to the situation when you were performing *poorly*. Describe the factors present at the time that accounted for your poor performance. (You may wish to review the statements made in the Introduction above.)

You will have approximately *eight to ten minutes* to write down the factors for good and poor performances.

The instructor will form small teams of four to six persons to discuss and compare these two sets of factors. Each team should prepare a joint list of four or five of the most critical factors to be discussed in class or submitted as a written exercise. Use Figure 11-3, *The Job Characteristics Model,* to compare these factors with the "core job dimensions" described in this chapter and the resulting "psychological states" that influenced performance.

12

Staffing and Effectively Managing Human Resources

OUTLINE

Major Factors in Human Resource Management

Human Resource Planning
- Human Resource Objectives
- Assessing Internal Resources
- Determining How to Accomplish Objectives
- Monitoring Progress
- Forecasting and the Planning Function

Recruitment and Selection
- Nonspecialized Internal Recruitment
- Specialized Internal Recruitment
- Nonspecialized Outside Recruitment
- Specialized Outside Recruitment
- Selection
- Selecting Managers
- Assessment Centers

Orientation, Training, and Development
- Orientation Programs
- Purposes of Orientation
- Training and Development

Compensation and Benefits Management

Employee and Labor Relations
- Employee Relations
- Labor Relations

Performance Evaluation
- The Rationale for Employee Evaluations
- Methods of Evaluation
- Performance Evaluation in Summary

Transfers and Terminations

OBJECTIVES

- Describe the function of human resource management.
- Define management responsibilities for human resource planning.
- Explain the process of recruitment and selection in organizations.
- Describe orientation, training, and development programs.
- Discuss compensation management and benefits management.
- Summarize the roles of staff specialists and line managers with respect to employee and labor relations.
- Discuss the importance of effective performance evaluation systems.
- Discuss the concepts of transfer and termination.

FOR OVER TWO DECADES, the Blackfeet Indian Writing Company has produced high-quality pencils, pens, and other writing instruments and provided Blackfeet Native Americans with a stable, decent living.[1] The company, which is 80 percent owned by the Blackfeet tribe, was founded in Browning, Montana, in 1971. Included in BIWC's mission statement is one of the company's main reasons for existence: "to help Blackfeet Indians pull themselves up by their own moccasin strings." BIWC's customer base has grown steadily and now includes over 350 major American businesses like IBM, Boeing, Eli Lilly, and General Motors.

Most Americans are not aware of the deplorable economic conditions that continue to cause despair on Native American reservations. Unemployment is common; on the Blackfeet reservation, it has often hovered between 40 and 80 percent. However, BIWC has been a model of job creation by employing people from the reservation community to produce high-quality goods for American business.

One of the most difficult problems BIWC faced at its outset was the lack of a labor pool with industrial experience. This problem is rooted in the Native American lifestyle, which, with its strong respect for individual differences, is simply not compatible with traditional assembly-line work. In fact, many Blackfeet have held jobs off the reservation, but most return to Browning because they lack the skills needed to advance in a commercial environment.

After a year of high employee turnover, BIWC received assistance from the Small Business Administration in 1972 to establish a work environment suited to the company's employees. The solution to BIWC's human resource problem and tribal unemployment was to structure a work environment where the prosperity of the firm was predicated on the prosperity of employees working together. Seeking to balance the importance of teamwork with respect for the uniqueness of each employee, the company instituted a thorough group training program supplemented by individual counseling. Employees participate in an incentive program providing production bonuses. In addition, BIWC trains and promotes managers from within the company, which keeps morale high. The result: Over the past twenty years, quality and productivity goals have been surpassed time and time again. Although the company remains relatively small (with slightly more than 100 employees), it has created opportunities for increased expertise, job advancement, and better pay for the Blackfeet people. They have a sense of pride and ownership in the business and in their careers. Just as important, BIWC has become a model for other small businesses.

In this chapter, we discuss human resource management, often called the function of *staffing*. This is the process of acquiring and retaining the skilled human resources needed to accomplish organizational objectives in a timely fashion. We also examine managers' responsibilities for training, compensation, employee and labor relations, and performance evaluation. Because many of these issues are common concerns for organizing and leading, this chapter serves as a transition from the general function of organizing to the personal function of leading, a topic covered in Chapters 13 through 16.

In all but the most capital-intensive organizations, people are the prime determinants of productivity. In this age of extraordinary technological change, we sometimes forget to distinguish between tools and their users. Technological advances are crucial for success, but it is people who galvanize knowledge, skills, and technology into effective performance. A s we reach new horizons in technology, we encounter new challenges in managing human resources.

MAJOR FACTORS IN HUMAN RESOURCE MANAGEMENT

We study *human resource management* from both the "personnel specialist" and "operating manager" perspectives. The term *personnel*—along with *employee relations* and *manpower management*—is often used interchangeably with *human resource management*. Personnel and its substitute terms, however, are most precisely used to refer to the specialized duties of personnel administration. Human resource management is a broader term; it includes responsibilities for personnel, as well as the responsibilities of operating managers for effective use of human resources. **Human resource management** is the sum of activities required to attract, develop, and retain people with the knowledge and skills needed to achieve an organization's objectives.[2]

human resource management
The sum of activities required to attract, develop, and retain people with the knowledge and skills needed to achieve an organization's objectives.

Thus human resource management encompasses recruitment, selection, training, compensation management, labor relations, benefits management, performance evaluation, discipline, grievance handling, counseling, and career development. Many of these activities are relegated to personnel specialists, but everyone responsible for subordinates is involved in them.

The composition of an organization rarely stays the same for long. As companies grow, they add employees, and as older employees retire, younger replacements are hired. As companies adopt new technologies, they hire employees with the necessary technical skills or train existing employees. Also, in our society, most employees change companies rather frequently. These shifting situations require managers to pay constant attention to staffing. Figure 12-1 illustrates the major activities for human resource management, which are summarized below.[3]

Human resource planning. Managers plan for future human resource needs, including the types of skills and number of employees required to fulfill organizational objectives. *Human resource planning* is the process of forecasting employment requirements and determining available external resources within relevant labor markets in order to decide when, why, and in what numbers employees will be needed in the future. Strategically, managers establish long-term plans for fulfilling human resource needs. At operating levels, line managers plan short-term work schedules, replacement, and training.

Recruitment and selection. Staffing begins with *recruitment,* the process companies use to locate qualified job candidates, entice them to apply for openings, and maintain a labor pool of potential employees. *Selection* is the process of choos-

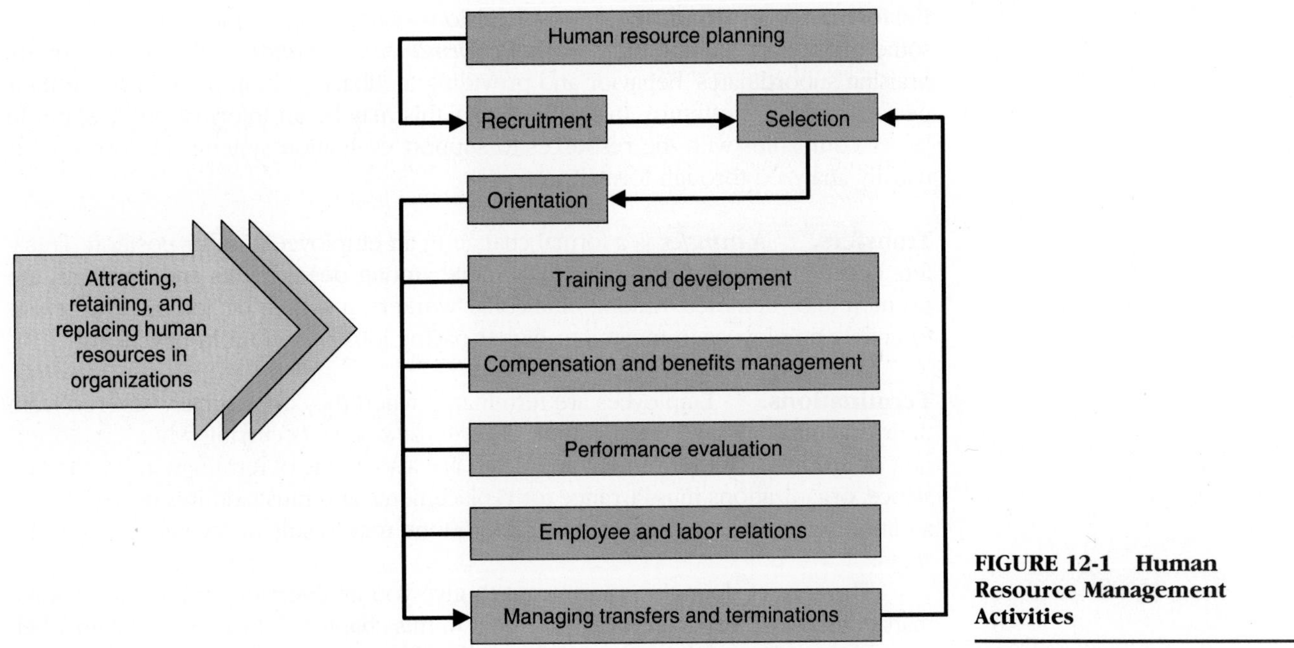

FIGURE 12-1 Human Resource Management Activities

ing new employees from the applicant pools through evaluation, testing, screening, and interviewing. Recruitment and selection are the responsibilities of personnel specialists, but operating managers are responsible for job specifications and they often make actual selection decisions.

Orientation. New employees must be inducted into organizations. *Orientation* is a process of indoctrination to familiarize employees with company policies, safety codes, objectives, and work expectations. Orientation may also include technical training to acquaint newcomers with specific work conditions, equipment, and processes. Effective indoctrination programs incorporate a human relations element, permitting newcomers to become familiar with their co-workers and supervisors.

Training and development. Most organizations differentiate between training and development. *Training* programs are usually associated with "vocational teaching" of specific job skills for nonmanagement employees. In contrast, *development* programs prepare employees for advancement or prepare managers for expanded responsibilities.

Compensation and benefits management. *Compensation management* includes wage and salary determination, raises, and similar monetary issues. Operating managers deal with compensation at the individual level by recommending raises or tracking data for bonuses. *Benefits management* is a multifaceted area of personnel specialization that deals with pensions, insurance, workers' compensation, dental plans, educational benefits, vacations, and a variety of "fringes" such as sick pay, recreation, health care, maternity leave, day care, and use of company vehicles. Although they are called *fringes,* the term is misleading because today benefits account for nearly 35 percent of total compensation.[4]

Employee and labor relations. *Employee relations* consists of efforts by a company to help individuals resolve personal problems and improve their performance, and also addresses situations such as safety and health that concern all employees. *Labor relations* is a field of specialized management concerned with collective bargaining and maintaining relationships between an organization's management and legally constituted employee unions or associations.

Performance evaluation. Most decisions concerning employees are based on some method of judging their work. *Performance evaluation* is the process of appraising subordinates' behavior and providing feedback to help them improve their performance in the future. In smaller firms, this may be an informal process, but in larger companies with the resources to support evaluation systems, performance is usually analyzed through formal processes.

Transfers. A *transfer* is a formal change in an employee's job or position. Transfers occur in several ways: individuals move among departments and divisions, are promoted, or demoted. Among blue-collar workers, a system of "job bidding" exists to enable employees to move into higher-paying jobs or retrain in new skills.

Terminations. Employees are terminated when they are formally severed from their organizations. We usually think of *terminations* as occurring when employees quit or are fired, but retirement and death are also forms of termination. In each instance, organizations must arrange for replacements and must administer benefits. In addition, economic and competitive conditions may result in layoffs or plant closures.

These brief definitions are meant to give you an overview of human resource management. We expand on each element in this chapter so that you will gain a better understanding of the responsibilities of staff specialists and line managers.

CHECKPOINT

- Define human resource management as a dimension of both personnel administration and line management.
- Briefly define the primary factors in human resource management.

HUMAN RESOURCE PLANNING

The first major consideration in human resource management is effective human resource planning. According to William F. Glueck, at the strategic level, "Human resource planning focuses on *developing an integrated set of personnel policies and programs to achieve the human resource and organizational objectives*."[5] In contrast, at the operating level, managers are concerned with planning for periodic replacements, transfers, promotions, and other changes in employment to maintain an effective work force.

human resource planning Planning for future personnel needs, skills, labor changes, and related issues (such as compensation and retirement).

Human resource planning is also an integrating process that defines internal needs and explores external sources for personnel during a company's future planning period. Its main objective is to ensure that the organization is neither understaffed nor overstaffed. Staffing requires that employees with appropriate skills be placed in the right jobs at the right times. For example, during the early 1980s, there was a major expansion of oil drilling in the Middle East following a decade of oil embargoes and disruptions. Exxon is highly regarded for its expertise in oil exploration. In 1981, Exxon planned a ten-year program for opening as many as thirty-three oil operations, but management realized that it had insufficient site engineers. The Abu Dhabi site in Saudi Arabia, for instance, required nine field engineers, and Middle Eastern laws prescribed that engineers had to have five years' experience to be licensed to work. To open thirty-three more sites would require at least a hundred new engineers. However, college recruits would not immediately qualify, and older engineers with families were reluctant to go into the field. Consequently, Exxon launched a five-year recruitment campaign among new college graduates to

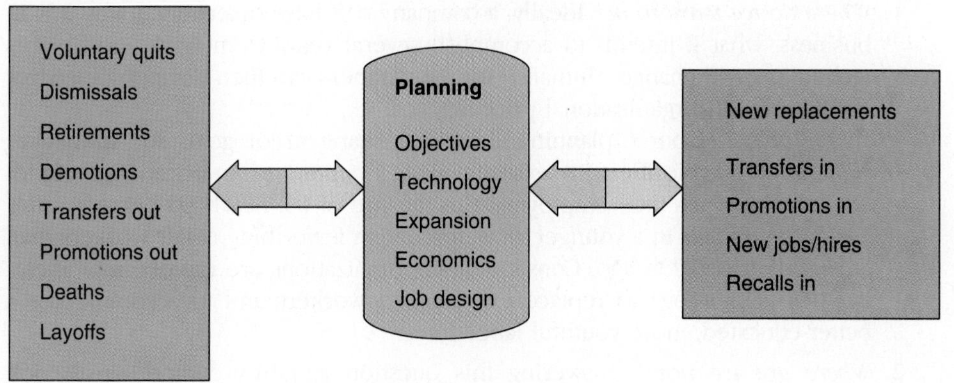

FIGURE 12-2 Dimensions of Human Resource Planning

build an organization capable of expansion by the early 1990s. Management patiently built a cadre of engineers that spearheaded major expansion projects in 1990 and 1991.[6] Figure 12-2 illustrates the relationship of internal and external factors that organizations must manage to ensure proper staffing.

Successful organizations have strong human resource planning systems. For example, Quebec-Telephone, recently recognized by Canada's Association of Human Resource Professionals as the nation's best company in human resource management, has a comprehensive strategic program for human resource planning based on three branches of activities: internal manpower planning, employee career planning, and external human resource availability.[7] The company, a subsidiary of GTE, had a tenfold increase in productivity between 1970 and 1988, achieved by ensuring that employees became progressively more skilled at more sophisticated jobs. Employees enjoy rapid career advancement, and few of them have to be replaced except for natural attrition such as retirement.

Success at Quebec-Telephone is partly attributable to an internal "manpower planning system" consisting of teams of managers that carefully coordinate company objectives, such as technological expansion programs, with requirements for employment. Its success is also attributable to "employee career planning," a system of internal programs for developing employees' skills and helping them achieve personal objectives. Recognizing that some employees will quit, retire, or turn out to be untrainable, the company supplements its internal programs with a task force that monitors external sources for available new employees. The result is a comprehensive planning effort that identifies human resource needs and meets those needs through effective recruitment and development programs.

Figure 12-3 illustrates the components of human resource management that constitute a progressive planning system. Four of the five components are based on answers to planning questions; the fifth, *implementation,* comprises daily activities defined in the plan. Human resource planning, then, is resolved by answering four questions:[8]

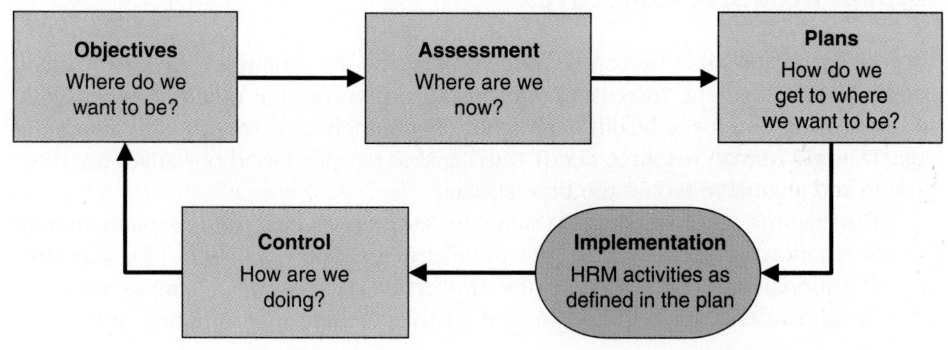

FIGURE 12-3 The HRM Process

1. *Where do we want to be?* Ideally, a company will have determined why it is in business, what it intends to accomplish several years from now, and how its technology will change. Human resource planners can then develop objectives consistent with organizational priorities.

   Human resource planning also helps shape major goals and influences organizational priorities. For example, only 5 percent of American workers today remain in full-time employment to the age of 65; nearly 95 percent retire early. This results in a younger work force with fewer blue-collar workers than we had a generation ago. Consequently, organizations are rapidly implementing new technology to replace experienced workers and to accommodate a better-educated, more youthful labor force.[9]

2. *Where are we now?* Answering this question requires comprehensive job analyses to determine current work methods, as well as to evaluate employees on a wide scale to determine their skills, attitudes, and behavior in the work environment. If, for example, a company expects to automate production through computer-integrated manufacturing systems, managers must have recognized the current limitations of using conventional work methods. But they must also realize that automating will mean fundamental changes in the types of skills needed by employees.

3. *How do we get to where we want to be?* Once we know where we are and have defined where we want to be, we must determine how to get there. This requires developing strategic programs for hiring, training, and replacing employees. For example, as a company automates production, it will need to set up programs for attracting electronics engineers, information systems technicians, and managers capable of supervising a more technically sophisticated work force. It may also have to establish plans for retraining existing employees, terminating those whose skills are no longer needed, and revising compensation systems to compete for the right people.

4. *How are we doing?* Once management has devised its plans, those plans must be implemented. *Implementation* is the actual conversion of plans into results through daily activities. For every action taken to implement a plan, there must be a reciprocal controlling action to judge effectiveness. Thus human resource planners develop systems for monitoring performance to ensure that progress is being made toward objectives. For example, if plans call for hiring robotic engineers, a schedule for recruiting will be established with budgets for hiring costs and compensation. As recruiting occurs, managers will compare hiring objectives with actual results to determine how to adjust their recruiting program.

These four critical questions summarize the human resource planning process, but they do not cover all the planning activities. In the next few sections, we discuss planning activities in more detail and show why managers in all organizations must address human resource requirements.

Human Resource Objectives

There are many possible human resource objectives—for example, improving safety, stabilizing employment, increasing job satisfaction, enhancing quality performance, and improving employee health—but the most compelling objective is to match the organization's human resource needs with capable people. Good objectives are measurable and attainable within the time allotted.

For example, a university that wants its students to become computer literate (an organizational objective) must have the instructors and equipment to accomplish this educational aim. Let's assume the university decides on a simple program whereby all students are required to take a survey course in computing. If the university knows how many students it will have, it can calculate how many instructors it needs, the number of class sections to schedule, and the cost of the program. Planners must also define skills needed and depending on how the program is designed, instructors may have to be literate in several programming languages and be experienced with certain types of computers.

The parallel between a university computer literacy program and manufacturing or service industry needs is easy to see. A manufacturer in the midst of installing a computer-aided manufacturing system (CAM) would require operators, technicians, and maintenance personnel. A hospital that is expanding services for cardiac intensive care would require specialized physicians, nurses, and support personnel. In each instance, what people to hire, with what skills, and when to hire them are essential planning questions.

Assessing Internal Resources

Determining "where we are now" is partly done by assessing current human resources. In our example of a computer literacy program, personnel specialists carefully review existing faculty members' qualifications, match those against needs, and determine whether there is a skills gap that may prevent the university from offering the desired courses.

A skills assessment is only one of several considerations. For example, the university may have skilled faculty, but not in the department designated to implement the computer literacy program. Similarly, a manufacturer may have skilled engineers, but find that they are working in design departments or field research instead of in production, where they are needed. Like faculty members in different departments, engineers cannot be easily transferred to areas where they are most needed because this might disrupt employees' careers. Yet transfers are often feasible, and provide new opportunities for employees.

One method of assessing human resources is through a **skills inventory,** which is a data base detailing each employee's qualifications, education, interests, and career aspirations. Using a skills inventory file, managers can locate employees who fit vacancy needs or who have potential for development. This low-cost search-and-sort system for internal recruits benefits employees by giving them preferential access to new job opportunities. One of the strengths of Quebec-Telephone Company's human resource system discussed earlier is its career development program. A primary feature of this program is the "career data base," through which most positions are filled by existing employees.

skills inventory
A data base detailing each employee's qualifications, education, interests, and career aspirations.

Human resource planning focuses on staffing positions, but determining "where we are now" also requires assessing attitudes, behavior, and performance. These may not always be objectively measurable, yet managers can reasonably assess them with behavioral science techniques such as performance reviews (discussed later in the chapter), questionnaires or interviews, and assessment programs provided by consultants.

Organizations can also trace patterns of behavior such as absenteeism, turnover (resignations and dismissals), grievances, poor workmanship, and accidents. Comparing these data over time (monthly or annually) as well as with data from similar organizations will give managers important clues about the state of the organization's internal human resources.

Determining How to Accomplish Objectives

Once the company has defined its objectives, it must decide how to accomplish them. Large organizations usually have specialized personnel staff to implement complex programs aimed at achieving company objectives. They have access to in-

ETHICS IN MANAGEMENT
The Language of Layoffs

"Firings" are humiliating to employees and "layoffs" imply the company is in trouble, so managers have created some obfuscating terms to disguise their decisions to reduce company employment levels. Unfortunately, many of these terms hide from public view what is going on in the boardroom.

General Motors, for example, announced that between 1992 and 1995 it would have to "downsize" the corporation to regain its competitiveness against aggressive foreign automakers. "Downsizing" is supposed to indicate that a company is reducing its bureaucracy and eliminating layers of management. However, GM is closing factories and cutting jobs among blue-collar, white-collar, and management employees. At the same time, it has increased the corporate bureaucracy by adding another executive layer to manage acquired companies like EDS and Hughes Aircraft. GM will eliminate 74,000 jobs, the equivalent of the population of a small city. Is it possible that "downsizing" is too benign a term for such a large-scale action?

Shortly before Pan American closed its doors for good in 1991, it announced a "scaling down" of operations. This began with a huge sell-off of routes to the six major cities in Europe. Flight crews were "furloughed" and jobs for overseas ground crews and support staff were "relinquished." The scaling down continued with Pan Am's sale to Delta of its commuter airline with hubs in Boston, Washington, and New York. Although 60 flight crews were transferred to Delta, several hundred jobs, including ground crew and support staff positions, were termed "redundant" and disappeared. When Pan Am finally, and abruptly, ceased operations, there was no term offered to describe the fate of nearly 20,000 employees suddenly without jobs.

Other organizations have come up with other terms. IBM referred to a "rationalization" to achieve productivity, while Xerox simply announced it was "letting some people go." Several universities have used the phrase "budget reduction mandates" to announce the elimination of faculty and staff positions. And companies in the aerospace and defense industry favor the explanation "implementing a work force reduction." The prize for euphemism would probably go to Bank of America for eliminating 14,000 jobs through a "release of resources."

Unfortunately, employees are often confused by this rhetoric and unprepared for their sudden ouster. It is difficult to believe that these people find comfort in being told that they were not "fired" or "laid off"—just "released as a resource," "rationalized," "furloughed," or "relinquished."

Sources: Alex Taylor III, "Can GM Remodel Itself?" *Fortune,* January 13, 1992, pp. 26-29, 32-34; James Ott, "Delta Faces Fight to Regain Lost Shuttle Passengers," *Aviation Week & Space Technology,* September 9, 1991, pp. 35–36; Alan Murray and David Wessel, "Torrent of Layoffs Show Human Toll of Recession Goes On," *Wall Street Journal,* December 12, 1991, pp. A1, A8; and "Gee Thanks Boss—What a Lucky Break!" *Business Week,* January 27, 1992, p. 41.

formation to diagnose their options and the expertise to supervise HR programs such as Exxon's effort to establish a strong cadre of oil field engineers. Nevertheless, even large organizations are sometimes faced with human resource crises emanating from corporate problems or changes in strategic objectives.

For example, GM and IBM announced plans for major employment reductions in 1992 to permanently change the size and scope of corporate operations. These "downsizing" efforts were handled by the companies in substantially different ways. GM announced major plant closings that would result in sudden and sweeping staff reductions. IBM targeted 20,000 positions for 1992 and presented a three-phase plan: During phase one, attrition from quits and retirements would trim employee ranks; in phase two, the company would offer attractive bonuses for voluntary quits and early retirement; and in phase three, IBM would retrain employees in unneeded jobs to fill other positions in the organization, both domestically and overseas.[10]

Organizations large enough to afford professional staff can support formal programs and perhaps endure temporary financial problems to solve long-term problems. Many smaller firms, however, simply cannot afford to retain human resource staff. Firms large enough to support one personnel specialist may expect that person to handle everything from orientation of new employees to strategic planning. Implementing new programs in these companies is therefore the responsibility of line managers, most of whom are inadequately trained in human resource management. Recent downsizing at the *Record* newspaper of Hackensack, New Jersey, for example, was accomplished by handing all employees sealed envelopes one morning in the editor's office. Those employees who were being retained opened the envelopes to find new passwords for their computer terminals, and those who had lost their jobs were summarily dismissed with the message that they no longer had access to the terminals.[11]

Managers always prefer to have clear objectives and systematic methods of reaching those objectives. This is particularly important in the area of human resources, where decisions affect not only individual careers and family livelihoods, but also the company's resources and its reputation among customers, lenders, and investors. Secondary economic effects are also felt in communities when companies alter employment practices by either expanding or contracting and redefine how work is accomplished by acquiring new technologies and more skilled personnel.

Monitoring Progress

Human resource planning is incomplete if management has not established programs for evaluation and control. Many of the same techniques used to assess "where we are now" can be used to monitor "how we are doing." There is a clear advantage to using the same techniques because they provide comparative and consistent data over time. Many firms, however, lack either the data or the expertise for assessment. These firms often hire consultants to intervene periodically to make program assessments. A better solution is to hire consultants to teach managers how to assess and monitor programs.

During a restructuring at Xerox, for instance, 2,500 programming positions were targeted for elimination in 1992, but the company avoided layoffs by implementing a closely monitored program of attrition. By monitoring the number of employees who quit or retired, Xerox was able to recruit or retain the necessary skilled employees and at the same time to reduce its total employment level. Through its monitoring system, Xerox identified future positions that would have to be filled through recruitment or internal transfers, thereby providing valuable information to human resource planners.[12]

Forecasting and the Planning Function

Ensuring that the right number of people with appropriate skills are employed at the right time to fulfill organizational objectives requires accurate forecasts of employment needs. **Human resource forecasting** is the process of estimating future demand for employees, based partially on anticipated demand for future products or services, and partially on future expectations for productivity improvements, techno-

human resource forecasting The process of estimating future demand for employees, based partially on estimated demand for products and services, and partially on productivity, technological changes, and social changes.

EXHIBIT 12-1 Forecasting Human Resources Over Time

	Short Term (Operational Planning Period)	Long Term (Strategic Planning Period)
Demand	Replacement for authorized employees, changes, layoffs, turnover, retirement, deaths, transfers, and promotions.	Replacement patterns plus growth from products and services, new technology, social factors, new skills requirements, competition, demographics of workers.
Supply	Promotions, transfers, census changes, job redesign, recalls, local labor available, market and competition, economic factors.	Short-term supply cycles and group redesign, population shifts, labor market demographics, competitive nature of labor markets, education, employee expectations, and economic trends.
Needs	Net new employees required and available, new skills, and time lines for recruitment.	Periodic cycles and trends for net new census for long-term human resources that affect current decisions.

logical changes, and socioeconomic changes.[15] Exhibit 12-1 indicates the importance of forecasting over the short term and the long term.

The forecasting process begins with an understanding of the company's objectives for sales, profits, and technological changes. Unless strategic managers provide human resource planners with accurate estimates of company activities, employment planning is impossible. Once they have an accurate estimate, planners can determine the number of employees needed with the appropriate skills and qualifications.

Planners must also have company information on finances and budgets to forecast compensation and related costs of maintaining a work force. If there are financial constraints on hiring new employees, planners may consider training programs to fill higher-level positions—usually a less expensive alternative.

Another consideration that influences forecasts is labor union contracts that mandate how management can hire, terminate, or replace employees. Unions can also restrain decisions to introduce new production techniques or, alternatively, encourage changes in work methods that improve productivity. In either instance, forecasts of human resource needs will change. Planners must also consider characteristics of existing employees. For example, a company with an aging work force may expect an increase in the number of retirees and thus an increase in its need to recruit replacement employees. In addition, forecasters must also account for labor supply—the availability of candidates for employment in the labor market. Regardless of forecasted needs, if there are insufficient candidates for employment, management cannot implement recruiting programs.

CHECKPOINT

- Describe human resource planning as both a strategic and an operational management responsibility.
- What are the four main questions the planning process must answer in relation to human resources?
- Discuss the relationship between organizational objectives and human resource forecasting.

RECRUITMENT AND SELECTION

The personnel function is most closely associated with recruiting and selecting new employees. The purpose of **recruitment** is to provide sufficient qualified candidates for employment. Nonmanagement employees without unusual skills are often recruited locally through newspaper advertisements or internal company transfers. Managers and skilled employees usually must be recruited through more complicated and expensive methods. Effective recruitment will provide a pool of candidates from which to hire employees. Selection, as we shall see momentarily, is the process of choosing employees from the recruitment pool.

recruitment
The process of attracting qualified applicants to an organization through activities such as advertising and campus visitations.

Recruitment and selection rely on job analyses that provide job descriptions for each vacancy. **Job descriptions** are written statements specifying what jobs involve in the way of duties, qualifications, and responsibilities. Detailed job descriptions include wage or salary information, skill levels, qualifications for operating equipment, responsibilities for supervision, and requirements such as security clearances or physical work limitations. Personal characteristics may also be specified if it is important to select people who can work in unusual circumstances such as traveling extensively or taking overseas assignments.

job description
A written statement of expectations and duties related to a specific job. It may also include the particular responsibilities and personal characteristics needed to fulfill job assignments.

Nonspecialized Internal Recruitment

Many firms prefer to *hire from within* by filling vacancies through promotions and reassignments. Job postings on bulletin boards are typically used to attract employees to bid for nonspecialized openings. Internal hiring benefits employees by providing advancement opportunities and companies by motivating workers.

Internal hiring is inexpensive compared to external recruiting, and is appreciated by employees, but the system has drawbacks. Selection tends to favor employees with the greatest seniority rather than those with the best qualifications. In some instances, labor agreements require that senior employees be given priority consideration for new openings. Internal recruitment also prevents fresh talent from entering the firm. On balance, though, internal hiring is beneficial because it helps stabilize employment and develops a stronger commitment by employees to their organizations.

Specialized Internal Recruitment

Hiring managers and specialists is difficult, and selection is based more on ability than seniority. Companies that prefer internal recruitment for these positions must be able to support development programs and be prepared to encourage the career aspirations of their employees. A skills inventory, as discussed earlier, simplifies recruiting and gives managers insights about employee career expectations. An example is illustrated in Exhibit 12-2.

Candidates often have the potential for promotion to more responsible positions but lack the necessary skills or experience. Consequently, many large companies maintain training and development programs to improve employees' skills or to help them gain the experience necessary for promotion. Most companies, however, are too small to spare the resources to implement such programs, so they resort to outside recruiting to fill important positions.

Nonspecialized Outside Recruitment

Outside recruitment is normally done in local labor markets composed of people who are unemployed or in the process of changing jobs. Because companies experience ebbs and flows in their needs for operating personnel, local labor markets are

EXHIBIT 12-2 Skills Inventory Employee File

Employee Name: ______________________ **Department:** ______________
ID # ______________ **Soc. Sec. #** ______________ **Date Hired:** ______________

Job Classification	Date Rated	Experience to Date	Skills Data	Comments
Primary:				
MIS Manager and Programmer	1/89	2 yrs. DP ops. 3 yrs. Asst. Mgr. 4 yrs. Mgr.	B.S. degree COBOL, APL. RPG.	Rated as excellent
Secondary:				
Computer Integration Systems	Not rated	NC institute training	20 hrs. in job seminar	Rated on NC computer
Other:				
Software Engineer	—	2 programs sold to Boston firm	MS DOS and Graphics	Royalty shared with firm

Interests:
An avid ski competitor who has shared design of computerized ski training program.
Taking courses in electrical engineering to become qualified in systems relating to robotics.
Long-term goals expressed in research and design of software and integrated production graphics programming.

dynamic. Advertising usually attracts the bulk of job hunters, but most companies also have a continuous flow of walk-in applicants. Walk-ins seldom apply precisely when openings occur, but the promising candidates among them are sometimes hired in anticipation of future openings. Once again, only larger firms can afford this luxury.

Applicants also come from local state employment offices, veterans' referral services, or through the recommendation of existing employees. The last type of referral results in few hirings, but companies consider employees hired this way to be highly reliable. After all, people put their own reputations on the line when they suggest candidates.

Finally, operational jobs are occasionally filled through ads in trade journals or through conferences. Nurses, for example, are actively recruited through nursing magazines and regional job fairs.

Specialized Outside Recruitment

Professionals and managers are often recruited through professional publications, college placement offices, and reputable agencies. This is different from other recruiting efforts because there is no local labor market for specialized individuals; firms may have to recruit nationally to find key executives and specialized personnel.

Most organizations tailor recruitment programs for each category of applicant. College recruiting, for example, is aimed at pooling talent for entry-level technical and managerial positions. Each year recruiters visit selected schools to attract a sufficient number of candidates for available openings. Some companies recruit at schools with reputations in particular fields, such as accounting or engineering. Yet if a company needs unusual talent, such as genetic engineers, its recruitment effort may become international.

Recruiting executives is expensive and time-consuming. It is usually done through executive search firms, advertising in newspapers such as the *New York Times,* personal contacts, and professional associations. Candidates for executive positions are usually employed and must be enticed to change organizations. Sometimes competition becomes so fierce that people are virtually pirated away from

When Joe and Cathy Joe Linn received job offers from Microsoft Corporation, they were undecided about making the move from Virginia to Seattle. Company recruiter Carrie Tibbetts located a home within half a mile of the office, promised a flexible work schedule, and even discovered a karate instructor to replace the one the couple would have to leave behind. The Linns accepted Microsoft's offer. Why did Tibbetts pursue the Linns so aggressively? "They're very smart," she says. Selecting and hiring have high priority at Microsoft. Every year company recruiters visit 137 campuses. In 1991, to fill 2,000 positions, Microsoft received over 12,000 résumés and interviewed 7,400 candidates. Observes senior vice president Jeff Raikes, "You can't hire bad programmers and get great software."

their companies by lucrative offers. This level of recruiting is far different from advertising a job vacancy.

Selection

The purpose of **selection** is to fill positions with the best people from available candidates, and to do so in a timely manner. Figure 12-4 illustrates a general model for selecting employees. It begins with an *application* that provides comparable information on candidates, serves as a formal request for employment, and becomes part

selection
The process of choosing and hiring employees from among those candidates recruited for the organization.

FIGURE 12-4 General Model for Personnel Selection

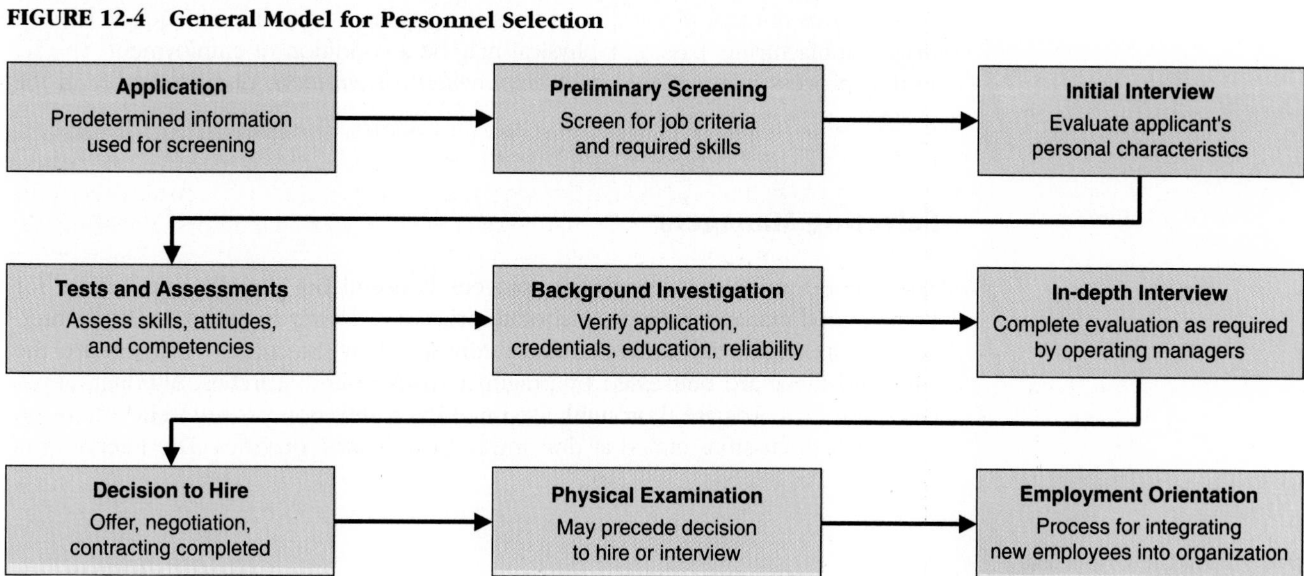

of the permanent record of those hired. *Preliminary screening* then creates a slate of qualified candidates.

Initial interviews reduce the applicant field to a manageable number of individuals. Interviewers gain personal insights into characteristics not apparent on a candidate's job application and applicants gain insights into the organization. During this process, the applicant, the employer, or both may decide that the candidate is not right for the job.

Many organizations require formal *testing,* but it is not always essential for selection. Tests for operating personnel focus on skills, such as typing ability or operational competency. Skill tests may be mandatory for a job rating, and are common in civil service systems. Psychological and personality tests may be necessary when the position requires a security clearance or is otherwise sensitive. Most tests are designed to evaluate whether candidates will fit into an organization. In the past few years, however, disputes have developed over some tests, such as pre-employment drug tests and AIDS screening tests.[14]

Companies also make *background investigations* to check the candidate's truthfulness on the application. What applicants say they can do and what they can actually do are often quite different. It is not unusual to find outright lies on application forms—more than half have misleading information about candidates' qualifications—and, of course, there is no such thing as a "bad résumé." In response, many organizations conduct background checks on candidates for skilled jobs and managerial positions, and some organizations even require lie detector tests. But phone-call requests to references for elaboration on a candidate's abilities can be misleading; hand-picked references are unlikely to reveal anything controversial about an applicant. Harvey Mackay, a multimillionaire entrepreneur and author of the best-selling book *Swim With the Sharks Without Being Eaten Alive,* interviews everyone who applies for work with his company. During the interview, he picks up the names of the candidate's acquaintances, prior bosses, or co-workers. These are the people Mackey calls for insights, not the person's references.[15]

Mackey's practice of interviewing all candidates is unusual. Personnel specialists, not CEOs, usually conduct interviews for nonspecialized positions. Nevertheless, in small companies and professional organizations, candidates often find themselves being interviewed by several key managers, top executives, or even owners.[16] Interviews with management committees are not uncommon. An important part of the selection process, the *in-depth interview* can consume much time and effort. Only a few applicants reach this stage, and a so-called interview may stretch into several days of on-site assessment.

Decisions to hire are made at the end of in-depth interviews or a short time afterward. If the job offer is accepted, an employment contract is signed. For specialized positions, contracting can be complex and often includes stock options, bonus agreements, and job security clauses. Also, many organizations require *physical examinations* to establish health records and provide data for insurance. When a position involves unusual physical tasks or is in a sensitive environment such as food or drug manufacturing, passing a physical may be a condition of employment. The selection process is completed with *employment orientation,* discussed later in the chapter.

Selecting Managers

The general model for selecting employees is useful but not always adequate for finding good managers; a more elaborate process is usually required. In-depth interviews of potential executive managers conducted by executive managers are the rule, and these are buttressed by pragmatic background searches. Although applicants' track records are thoroughly examined, the selection process relies more on exuberant discussions aimed at drawing out candidates' qualities. The interviewers try to discover if a candidate has the interpersonal skills, leadership abilities, and emotional stability, in addition to the technical expertise, to meet the organization's standards for the position.

Assessment Centers

Many large companies use assessment centers to evaluate management candidates. At an **assessment center,** structured exercises probe the decision-making behavior of candidates under conditions that mirror actual work conditions. Applicants may be given individual tasks or placed in simulated work groups charged with solving complicated problems. One frequently used method is called the *in-basket exercise.* Candidates are allotted an hour or so to cope with a variety of memos, telephone calls, reports, and materials typically handled by employees in these positions. The in-basket is usually overloaded to put the candidate under tremendous stress. This process was introduced at AT&T during the late 1960s, and it has become a preferred means of assessing managerial potential at Merrill Lynch, IBM, GE, and other prominent companies.[17]

assessment center
A method of evaluating employees—usually managers—by conducting exercises, simulated work situations, tests, interviews, and psychological testing to determine skills and managerial potential.

Other assessment center techniques are role-playing incidents, management games, and group problem-solving exercises. In each instance, candidates are presented with a decision-making dilemma and asked to resolve it. For example, Merrill Lynch simulates a stock transaction office and has candidates respond to a series of rapidly placed inquiries from clients (roles played by company employees). They are then evaluated on how they handled inquiries, advised on securities, and resolved conflicts purposely created by the role players. Candidates may also be asked to make a formal presentation explaining their decisions and conduct during the assessment period. A panel of evaluators rates all the candidates and makes selection recommendations.[18]

Assessment center programs are conducted by specialists and are expensive to maintain. Consequently, few American organizations use them except to screen candidates for critical positions. In contrast, Japanese companies throughout the world conduct elaborate hiring programs. The Toyota plant near Georgetown, Kentucky, screened 90,000 applicants for 3,000 openings and required thorough assessment testing for even the least important job. All applicants at the Nissan Truck Plant in Smyrna, Tennessee, must endure forty hours of pre-employment training and assessment. Similar methods of screening and selection prevail at Sony, Panasonic, Mitsubishi, and other notable Japanese companies where the philosophy is to invest heavily to find the right employees, thereby reducing the costs of making employment mistakes and having to terminate poor workers.[19]

CHECKPOINT

- Describe and contrast specialized and nonspecialized recruiting.
- How does recruitment for most operational jobs differ from recruitment for managerial or specialized positions?
- Describe the purpose of selection. Who makes selection decisions?
- Discuss how assessment centers are used in evaluating candidates.

ORIENTATION, TRAINING, AND DEVELOPMENT

Orientation is the process of introducing new employees to their new jobs and the organization. The orientation process often includes initial training, but as we shall see in a moment, training is an ongoing program to enhance employees' skills, whereas orientation is a one-time event. Development programs, also described momentarily, are broad-based efforts that are usually directed toward preparing managers for higher-level promotions and responsibilities.

Orientation Programs

orientation
A formal indoctrination program that introduces new employees to their job responsibilities, co-workers, and work environment.

Orientation is a formal program of indoctrination to introduce new employees to their job responsibilities, co-workers, company policies, and work environment. Too few organizations have actual orientation programs; in most instances, employees simply sign employment agreements and are told when and where to report to work. Orientation is left to co-workers or supervisors, who may do little more than explain where restrooms are located and when to take a lunch break. Effective orientation programs involve weeks or months of "break-in" duties, classes, and initial training.

Orientation is composed of two elements. The first involves merely pointing out the location of amenities, telling new employees how to fill out benefit forms, and explaining what is expected in terms of reporting, leaving work, parking, and eating lunch. The second is a process of socializing new employees, easing them into new work groups, and fine-tuning their job-related expectations. Socialization may also involve establishing a mentor relationship with another employee whereby the new person learns "how things usually get done" in the work environment.[20]

Purposes of Orientation

There are several benefits of conscientiously including new employees in the organization through a formal orientation program:[21]

- *It develops realistic job expectations.* New employees often have inaccurate work expectations. Even people experienced in their professions must gain a fundamental understanding of their new organization and "how things really work" because every organization has unique cultural values, group dynamics, networks of co-workers, styles of leadership, and governing policies. In fact, the chief purpose of orientation programs is to provide information about job expectations. The informational process has evolved in many firms to include psychological development and sociological integration into work groups.
- *It improves productivity.* Properly orientated new employees will get "up to speed" quicker and perform at higher-quality levels than those not given such training. Thus, although formal orientation programs are costly, they are cost effective because they improve total productivity.
- *It saves time and effort.* Formal orientation programs reduce the time and effort required of supervisors to train new employees. Instead of asking line managers to indoctrinate employees—a task they may handle haphazardly—orientation ensures systematic and efficient induction without imposing on line operations. Well-indoctrinated employees create fewer problems because they are aware of procedures and job expectations.
- *It improves employment stability.* Turnover is very heavy during break-in periods because new employees typically lack self-confidence and suffer from anxiety about their jobs. Properly oriented newcomers are eased into their positions, and therefore are more likely to stay in the job.
- *It reduces conflict.* New employees are rarely integrated into established work groups without some conflict. One form of conflict is hazing by veteran employees to force new recruits to conform to existing work practices. Another is an attitude that keeps new employees at arm's length until they prove themselves. In extreme cases, where the new employee's sex, race, or ethnic back-

ground differs from that of established workers, orientation helps to promote a smooth integration.

Training and Development

Organizational training can involve huge expenditures as companies strive to keep employees abreast of changes in technology and productive in their jobs. **Training** usually refers to efforts to upgrade employees' skills or focus on work-related topics beneficial to both employees and the company. Training clerical staff on word processors, for example, may involve periodic classes on new systems, new software programs, or specific applications using computers such as generating reports. In contrast, **development** is intended to provide general knowledge about theoretical concepts, to enrich organizations through improved human resource programs, and to sensitize managers to their responsibilities.[22] Although these distinctions are somewhat arbitrary, there is a sense that training is narrowly defined with short-term programs targeted to nonmanagement employees, whereas development is a process, targeted to managers with long-term implications for organizational changes.[23]

training
Instruction for specific job skills, usually associated with nonmanagement employees.

development
Programs focused on leadership, productivity, and organizational issues, often associated with management.

A good example of corporate commitment to training and development is Motorola, Inc., where the annual T&D budget exceeds $44 million, or 2.4 percent of the company's total payroll.[24] Motorola has nearly 800 full-time training specialists and contracts with more than 300 outside consultants to provide 40,000 employees with nearly 600 programs each year. At one end of its training spectrum, the company holds half-day sessions on job safety. At the other extreme, Motorola underwrites employee education through universities for postgraduate degree programs leading to M.B.A.s and masters degrees in engineering and electronics fields.

On-job training. Organizations favor programs such as *on-job training (OJT)* for teaching employees operational skills. This type of training is given while the employee is working; it is much like serving an apprenticeship. Skills upgrading is accomplished rapidly, and employees benefit from associating with co-workers while gaining actual hands-on experience.

Off-job training. In contrast to OJT, off-job training methods remove employees from their work environments for concentrated programs. These can be course work at local colleges, in-house seminars by experts in particular fields, or classes held in other organizations. Thus a company that wants its engineers trained in computer programming might pay for formal college courses, bring in consultants to train the engineers at corporate training facilities, or send engineers to a computer service company to be trained. In addition, training may be acquired through professional associations and educational conferences.

Especially in larger organizations, the personnel come from a variety of cultures. As part of Hewlett-Packard's development efforts, King-Ming Young manages the company's diversity programs, which use videotapes on cultural issues to help employees learn to understand and appreciate one another's different backgrounds.

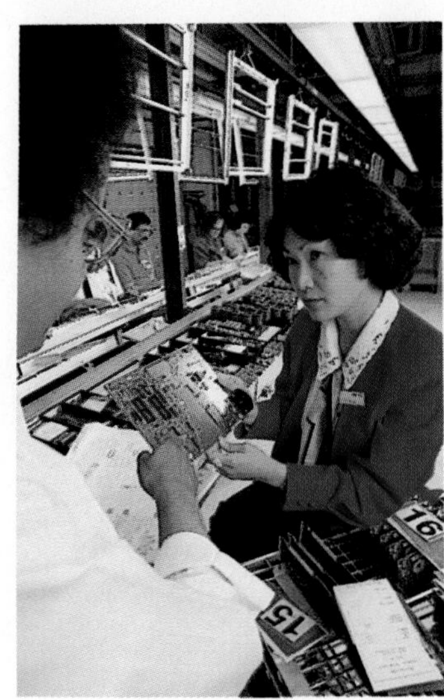

Vestibule training. Vestibule training is a form of intense education held in proximity to the actual work environment. For example, engineers might literally move to a "vestibule" area near their offices to sharpen their skills on new equipment set aside for training. A parallel to this is college laboratories for learning language, science, or computer skills.

Institutional training. There are many forms of training and, of course, many subjects and reasons for it. The federal government's Job Training Partnership program, for example, allocates $4 billion annually to help unemployed and unskilled youths gain job-related skills.[25] Private companies involved in this program set up institutional training programs and do actual training. Some larger corporations have their own accredited university programs, such as the General Motors Institute. Others hire professional staff for one- or two-year periods to conduct intensive in-house training. IBM, for example, requires first-line and middle managers to attend several days of course work each year on supervision. The company spends almost $900 million annually on education, nearly two-thirds of it on first-line managers and non-management employees who complete 5 million student-days a year—about twelve days per employee—in formal training sessions. On any given day, 18,000 IBM employees are receiving formal training in an exceptional range of topics from basic reading literacy to quality control engineering systems.[26]

Management development. Development programs targeted to managers represent long-term efforts to ensure continuity of an organization's leadership. Most companies do not have "management positions" but rather positions in which managers develop careers. Usually, companies induct college graduates into entry-level positions, such as sales or accounting, then help them fashion careers consistent with their abilities and interests. Development programs for younger managers typically have a two-pronged approach: the first trains them for a task specialization, and the second develops their leadership abilities.

A company needs to educate young and inexperienced managers to perpetuate its culture and to be prepared for promotion into leadership roles. Development programs ensure that there will be an infusion of fresh talent for responsible positions, and well-run programs will accentuate innovative behavior. Four common types of development programs for managers are:[27]

- *Formal Training.* This involves classroom exercises coupled with actual field assignments. Classes may cover sales methods, performance evaluation, decision making, motivation techniques, employee disciplinary procedures, management of on-the-job safety, and the technical aspects of particular positions. Field assignments may consist of controlled exercises in simulated situations or actual work with colleagues who act as coaches, often called *mentoring.*
- *Off-Job Formal Training.* Many organizations send managers to training institutes or enroll them in seminars and programs conducted by universities or training institutes. The American Management Association (AMA) is one of many professional organizations serving thousands of firms with development courses and seminars.
- *Job Rotation.* A company may not initially groom management trainees for a particular task but rather rotate them through several positions. Airlines tend to assign trainees to jobs at several locations during their first two years of employment before allowing them to take stable positions. Experienced employees may also be rotated or reassigned, but this usually means formal promotion into permanent positions.
- *Development Positions.* Some firms assign less experienced managers to work temporarily as assistants to more experienced managers. Subordinates in these posts perform a wide variety of staff tasks. Although their decision-making authority is usually curtailed, working with an experienced manager gives them a model for development. Sometimes younger managers are temporarily assigned to committees and task forces so they can develop a broader appreciation for organizational activities.

CHECKPOINT

- Discuss the benefits of a formal orientation program.
- What are the differences between training and development programs?
- Describe three different methods of training employees in job-related skills.
- Discuss how development programs prepare managers for greater responsibilities.

COMPENSATION AND BENEFITS MANAGEMENT

compensation management The management of wages and salaries, including raises, bonuses, and monetary incentives.

Compensation management is concerned with wages and salaries, pay raises, and similar monetary issues. The most visible part of the employment contract, compensation is the monetary exchange for employees' performance. The objectives of a compensation system are to reward employees equitably and to provide an inducement for attracting and retaining good employees. Figure 12-5 shows the relationship of compensation to other personnel activities in an organization.

Compensation is complicated and requires specialized knowledge to manage effectively in any sizable company. Many attorneys and personnel staff focus their careers on compensation issues ranging from the simple process of paying employees to formulating corporate compensation policies in compliance with government regulations. Addressing compensation management is beyond the purpose of this book, but it is important to recognize how managers are involved in determining financial benefits for their employees.

The fundamental concern is structuring employees' base pay, and this is accomplished through strategic planning for wage and salary systems. Closely associated with direct base pay are merit pay and various bonus incentives that supplement employee earnings. Very few American companies lack incentive and bonus systems, which today are often coupled to performance objectives, profitability, or company growth. In addition, pay is affected by external economic conditions such as inflation; consequently, most pay systems are fine-tuned for "cost of living" changes. Although personnel specialists are directly responsible for managing compensation systems, line managers find themselves making most decisions on pay raises, bonuses, recommended promotions, and incentive payments. In addition to these "direct" compensation issues, managers are also responsible for "indirect" compensation, including paid time off (for example, for vacations and sick days) and assignments that carry premium wages, travel pay per diem, or opportunities for overtime and holiday pay.[28]

Since employees are more motivated when they feel the company's compensation policies are fair and fairly administered, managers need to be able to assure their employees that the pay system is *equitable* and decisions affecting all aspects of the compensation package are responsible. Maintaining equity, or internal consistency, in employee compensation implies more than "paying equals for equal work." It means rewarding employees fairly for their "inequalities," such as exceptional performance or superior skills. This is where bonuses, incentives, promotions, preferential assignments, and wage premiums become useful, but managers must remember that any decision affecting employee compensation has to comply with numerous laws, employee expectations, and collective bargaining agreements in unionized environments.

benefits management The management of pensions, insurance, workers' compensation, dental plans, educational benefits, vacations, health care, and other "fringes" important to employees.

Benefits management is the management of pensions, insurance, educational benefits, vacations, and a variety of fringe benefits ranging from dental plans to maternity leave. Benefits are often monetary in nature—such as workers' compensation and paid vacations—and therefore associated with compensation. Many others,

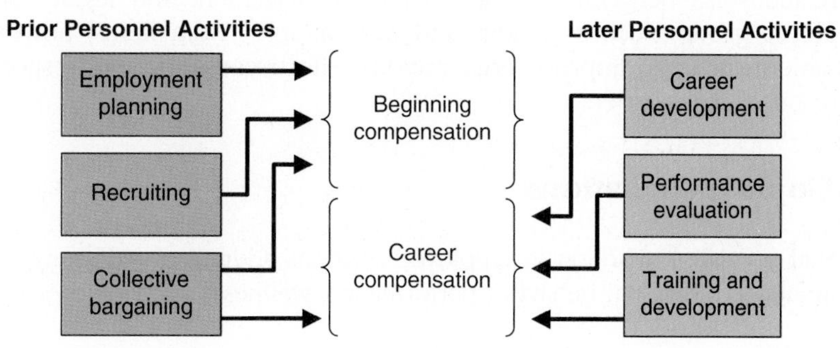

FIGURE 12-5 Relationship of Compensation to Other Personnel Activities

Source: From *Personnel: A Diagnostic Approach,* Third Edition, by W. F. Glueck and G. T. Milkovich. Copyright © 1982 Business Publications, Inc. Reprinted with permission.

however, do not involve money but enhance the quality of life of employees. These include bereavement leave, maternity leave, release time for education, company-supported child care, and employee assistance programs such as drug rehabilitation, counseling, and family counseling.

With an aging work force and the majority of people retiring early, retirement systems and preretirement counseling are an important area of benefits. Du Pont, for example, is one of many excellent companies that provide older employees with preretirement counseling, retraining for retirement-based occupations, and courses in financial planning to help them solidify their investments for financial security.[29] Child care has also become a sensitive benefits issue, since most families now have dual-career parents. American Express, Eastman Kodak, Xerox, Bausch & Lomb, IBM, Honeywell, and many other companies have on-site corporate child-care facilities and liberal leave policies for parents who must stay home to care for infants.[30] Perhaps the most controversial and most expensive benefit is employee health care. Because health care (Medicare, Medicaid, and other services) consumes nearly 40 percent of the federal budget, it is one of the most sensitive issues for congressional action.[31] However, corporations are not waiting for a government solution to the problem of accelerating health-care costs but are searching for innovative solutions of their own. Adolph Coors, for example, pays workers in cash for any savings the company derives from reduced health-care expenditures, and the Bank of Delaware and Southern California Edison pay bonuses to employees who follow prescribed fitness programs or comply with preventive medicine measures.[32]

Although compensation and benefits management constitute a specialized field within the purview of personnel administration, operating managers are inextricably involved in the daily operations that influence employee behavior and subsequently affect employee compensation and rewards. Also, because compensation is so complicated and benefits have become such a sensitive issue, they are focal points for government legislation and collective bargaining agreements.

CHECKPOINT

- Explain compensation management and the responsibilities of staff personnel managers and line managers in this area.
- What employee benefits have become common in most large organizations?

EMPLOYEE AND LABOR RELATIONS

Employee relations are closely associated with compensation and benefits, and these are often coordinated through one office. Labor relations addresses many of the same issues, but is a discipline concerned with union workers and others in legally recognized associations. Thus it is useful to define **employee relations** as a field that helps employees resolve personal problems and improve their performance in contrast to **labor relations,** which is a field concerned with activities arising out of relationships between an organization's management and legally organized employee groups such as unions and associations.[33] Both fields, however, have the same mandate to improve organizational effectiveness through responsible human resource management.

employee relations
A field of activities to help employees resolve personal problems and to improve their performance.

labor relations
Activities concerned with relationships between an organization's management and legally recognized unions and associations.

Employee Relations

Staff specialists working in employee relations address a wide range of issues that influence individual behavior, performance, wellness, safety, and peace of mind. In companies lacking staff specialists, line managers or small-business owners are responsible for employee relations. Consider the following points:[34]

- *Safety*. Companies are responsible for maintaining a safe work environment, one that complies not only with regulatory guidelines but also with employee expectations for protection in the course of their work. Consequently, management imposes work rules, ensures safety monitoring, trains employees, and provides safety attire and equipment to minimize risks.
- *Health*. Employees are becoming increasingly aware of the health risks associated with certain tasks, such as biological hazards, mental stress, and physical impairment. Therefore, companies confront two imperatives: they must eliminate or minimize health hazards on the job; and they must help employees remain healthy. Employee relations focuses on the second imperative by offering wellness and fitness programs, counseling, advice on preventive health measures, and rehabilitation programs.
- *Sexual Harassment*. Although sexual harassment is a major concern for company policymakers, it is employee relations personnel who must resolve harassment complaints at the individual level. Policymakers define sexual harassment, but it is managers who must provide a channel of communication for grievances and procedures for disciplining offenders and enforcing standards of conduct. One way to do this is through a company ***ombudsman***, a neutral party appointed, or elected, to investigate grievances and resolve problems—when possible, in confidence. Another approach is to set up a committee with the authority to investigate complaints and recommend disciplinary actions.[35]
- *Substance Abuse*. Companies have to be concerned with drug and alcohol *abuse* by employees that leads to *impaired* performance or *maladaptive* behavior, thus putting other employees at risk through safety infractions or work-related conflicts. Companies can resolve these problems through discipline or termination measures, but many companies choose instead to use employee assistance programs for treatment, rehabilitation, and counseling in order to help individuals and retain valuable employees.[36]
- *Employee Conflicts*. Quite often, employees have personal conflicts with their co-workers that require attention beyond intervention by their immediate supervisors. Actually, the conflict is often with a supervisor. Companies handle these problems through staff specialists trained in conflict resolution or by referring employees to outside specialists. Conflicts can range from easily resolved minor misunderstandings to complicated problems such as discrimination complaints. Family problems, mental stress, and other personal problems can also create conflicts at work or affect employee performance. These are often handled through employee assistance programs, career counseling, and family support programs.[37]

Employee relations extends to many areas beyond those listed above; in fact, the field takes in most human resource activities. For example, safety and health programs include policy mandates, insurance administration, subsidized benefits such as fitness memberships, training and development, and tangible compensation such as workers' compensation payments and paid sick leave. Many employee relations activities have intangible benefits for both the employee and the organization. These include improved performance by employees who complete substance abuse programs, commitment by employees who are supported by their organizations through assistance programs, and improved family relations that result in productive employee behavior. From a general viewpoint, employee relations means a pervasive effort by managers to improve organizational effectiveness by addressing individual employee needs and expectations.

MANAGEMENT APPLICATION

Helping Parents Cope with Dual Responsibilities

Companies are trying harder to help employees resolve personal and family problems with specialized counseling, flexible scheduling, and a variety of employee assistance programs. At Avon Company, for example, a new mother faced a tough choice between quitting to take care of her child or finding full-time child-care services. The prospect of being away from her child most of the time was too much to bear, but as a career manager in line for an executive promotion, she did not feel she could simply walk away from Avon. The company's human resource department resolved the problem by helping her design a part-time position working three days a week. The new position kept her benefits intact and ensured continuity in her career plans.

At Hallmark Cards, Inc., managers are taught how to be better parents through counseling and intervention training courses. The Hallmark program is designed for managers who find that their business roles conflict with their parental roles. For example, one young executive who had climbed the corporate ladder quickly did so because he was an aggressive competitor who thrived on work pressure. He set rigid objectives for himself and his employees, demanded punctuality and attention to detail, and followed challenging agendas for sales growth. But unfortunately, he carried these values home, and neither of his two children could live up to "the boss's" expectations. Consequently, he found his family drifting further and further away from him, until the stress began affecting his work behavior. Fortunately, Hallmark's employee assistance program helped him recognize the problem and provided family counseling. Today he is able to shift between work and parental roles without stress.

Similar programs exist at United Airlines, where parents of small children are singled out for special family assistance. According to a UA spokesperson, "An employee can't expect to work all day in a technical environment and make major decisions, then go home to a toddler and turn into Mr. Rogers." Executive women face similar challenges switching between work and home roles. Many of UA's cadre of young woman executives hold M.B.A. degrees and are "take charge" managers at work. As competent professionals, they make decisions and control the cadence of their work environments, but the same take-charge attitude at home can lead to conflicts with husband or children. UA's response is to bring managers together in classrooms where they role-play to sharpen their professional skills and differentiate them from their personal expectations.

Sources: Sue Shellenbarger, "Parental, Managerial Roles Often Clash," *Wall Street Journal*, September 12, 1991, pp. B1, B4; Barbara Hetzer, "A Foot in Two Worlds," *Advertising Age*, Vol. 62 (March 25, 1991), p. 30; and Gabriella Stern, "Young Women Insist on Career Equality, Forcing the Men in Their Lives to Adjust," *Wall Street Journal*, September 16, 1991, pp. B1, B2.

Labor Relations

The concept of labor relations is historically one of adversary relationships between business owners and their employees. This adversarial relationship existed long before the industrial revolution, but the factory systems of the eighteenth and nineteenth centuries polarized the groups into two general castes: those who did the work (labor) and those who told others what to do (management).

Foundations of labor relations. Until the 1930s, managers exploited workers, and factory conditions were horrendous. Child labor laws often went unenforced. There were few safety rules, long working hours, no pay standards, no job protection or employee benefits, and no recourse for workers to resolve grievances. Any attempt by employees to band together to protect themselves or to collectively seek redress for wrongs was viewed as criminal conspiracy. Occasionally, company managers with enlightened viewpoints sought to help employees, and in rare instances, employees were allowed to form unions to pursue limited activities.[38]

Then in 1932, Congress passed the Norris-LaGuardia Act, which declared that all employees had a legal right to join unions. A few years later, in 1935, Congress passed the National Labor Relations Act, commonly known as the Wagner Act. The Wagner Act guaranteed employee rights to organize and bargain collectively. It also created the National Labor Relations Board (NLRB) to investigate unfair labor practices. Government subsequently passed further legislation setting national standards for minimum wages, child labor, the workweek, the right to strike, and rules for arbitrating disputes.

By 1947, more than 35 percent of all nonfarm workers were unionized; this was the peak of union membership in the United States. Unfortunately, union activity became as violent as company-instigated antiunion activity had once been, and government responded in 1947 with the Labor-Management Relations Act, usually called the Taft-Hartley Act.[39] Under Taft-Hartley, unions and companies had to conform to strict rules for bargaining, mediating disputes, honoring individual employee rights, and resolving strikes.

Since 1947, labor relations and working conditions have improved, and the percentage of nonfarm workers in unions has declined. Today only about 16 percent of nonfarm wage earners in the private industrial sector are unionized. However, in the public sector, nearly 33 percent of all employees belong to unions or employee associations established under labor relations laws. Those represented include teachers, firefighters, public safety workers, air traffic controllers, municipal workers, and college professors. White-collar professional associations also exist and, like public-sector groups, are experiencing an annual growth trend of about 3 percent.[40]

Union activities.[41] The fundamental reason employees join unions is to gain some control over their work environment. Consequently, unions focus on issues that most directly affect an employee's livelihood. Through collective bargaining, they seek appropriate compensation for their members. Compensation usually means higher pay, but it also includes compensation systems that ensure equity between pay grades, policies concerning skill qualifications, and established guidelines for rewards, penalties, promotions, demotions, and resolving pay disputes. Popular news stories focus on pay issues, but equally important in contract bargaining is resolving job security issues such as how employees can be disciplined or fired, grievance procedures, training opportunities, protection under seniority guidelines, and working conditions. Union contracts also address benefits, such as life insurance, holidays, vacations, bereavement, maternity leave, child care, and pensions.

Management activities.[42] Each point in a collective bargaining agreement noted above represents a management activity. Some of these are specialized, such as administering a health insurance system or managing pension funds. Others are generalized so that personnel specialists and line managers are jointly responsible for them. Besides managing compensation systems, these issues include making decisions that affect employees' training, skills, promotions, assignments, and opportunities for growth; enforcing disciplinary rules; honoring grievances; and resolving

At GM's Lordstown (Ohio) plant, management and UAW Local 112 have formed a unique partnership to enable Lordstown to become the automaker's first North American plant to operate twenty-four hours a day. The joint goal: to manufacture 450,000 vehicles a year. Union members have overwhelmingly agreed to work four ten-hour shifts a week without overtime. Why the cooperation? One big reason is that, instead of firing workers, GM agreed to rehire 1,500 who had recently been laid off at another plant. Explains one union member at Lordstown, "We've matured, both labor and management. Now most of us on both sides have kids in college, and if we screw up, they won't still be there."

conflicts. In addition, many issues require union and management cooperation, such as maintaining a healthy work environment, promoting quality performance, and enforcing safety regulations.

Labor relations specialists spend most of their time working with union representatives and line managers to effectively administer the collective bargaining contract. Few people outside an organization realize how much work occurs on a daily basis with respect to labor relations. What outsiders see are the highly publicized contract negotiations and disputes that end in mediation or legal arbitration. These activities often engage an organization's entire labor relations staff, but the actual negotiation and reconciliation of bargaining issues are handled by senior executives and their legal representatives.

Perhaps the most important responsibility for labor relations personnel is "preemptive" human resource management. Historically, this has meant taking actions that will prevent unions from organizing company employees. From this viewpoint, management is cautioned to implement job security measures so that employees do not feel threatened. For example, the company may institute a grievance procedure or a disciplinary code so that employees will be treated fairly by management. Some companies pay employees high wages to disarm potential claims by union organizers that they can win wage concessions or establish employee relations programs to improve the quality of working life. A more appropriate view, however, is that preemptive human relations management is a total commitment to improving the organization's effectiveness by helping employees to improve themselves, develop interesting careers, and enhance their work environment.

In the next section, we explore performance evaluation, which is one of the specific ways in which managers help employees improve their performance while monitoring their behavior. As we shall see, performance evaluation is an important tool for employee relations and labor relations managers.

CHECKPOINT

- Describe the concept of employee relations and several of the more important programs that exist to assist employees.
- Explain the primary activities of unions and comparable responsibilities of labor relations managers.
- What is meant by the term *preemptive labor relations?*

PERFORMANCE EVALUATION

The process of assessing employees' work and behavior, and then giving them constructive feedback to improve their performance, is called **performance evaluation**.[43] Performance evaluation occurs informally on a continual basis as managers supervise work and observe employees. Managers are expected to keep employees abreast of how they are doing and to communicate in such a way that employees are motivated to perform effectively. Formal performance evaluation, however, is a more specific task whereby managers periodically appraise employees using guidelines that result in a record of each employee's behavior.

performance evaluation The process of appraising subordinates' behavior and providing feedback to help them improve their performance.

The Rationale for Employee Evaluations

Formal evaluations provide records useful for comparing performance among all employees. Mangers can therefore judge each employee's progress over time or assess the contributions of a work group. Assessment records are most often used to make decisions about assignments, training, raises, bonuses, and promotions. They are also used to evaluate how well the company and its managers are making human resource decisions. For example, following the grounding of Exxon's oil tanker the *Exxon Valdez* off Alaska, investigators concluded that the accident was caused by human error and questioned whether the company had effectively used performance appraisals to determine the ship captain's alcohol abuse–related behavioral problems. Exxon's records revealed it knew of the captain's problem and also was aware that senior officers on the *Valdez* were not significantly experienced in the maneuvers required to operate a ship of that size in those waters.[44] Appraisal systems are used by AT&T and Control Data Corporation to spot personal problems such as telephone operator cynicism and computer programming errors caused by stressful workloads.[45] On a positive note, PepsiCo uses performance appraisals to rate contributions by managers to the company's growth and profit objectives.[46]

Methods of Evaluation

There are many formal methods of assessing employee performance, and although most organizations design their own evaluation instruments, the general methods described below are the most popular. These methods are used in similar ways: to periodically assess and document performance. Consequently, most employees have an "annual review" by their managers who "score" their performance and place the evaluations in their personnel records.[47]

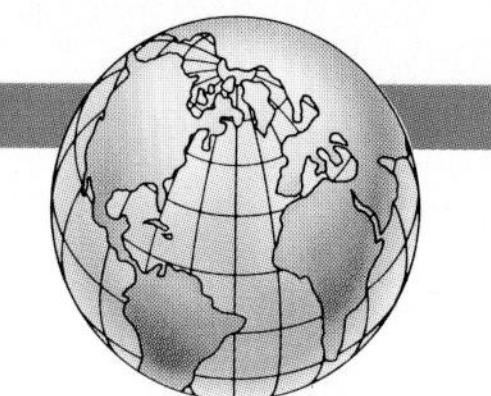

GLOBAL TRENDS
Labor Relations in Europe

Labor relations in Europe are distinctly different from labor relations in the United States. American managers working in multinational companies are often stunned by the contrast in laws and find they must radically alter the way they make decisions regarding employees.

In Britain, for example, the Trade Union Council, representing a majority of all unions, has a consultative role with government and with its industry counterpart. Together they influence national labor policy and act as a strong centralized control over national laws that restrict company practices. When British workers are laid off, for instance, they can remain unemployed (and "on the dole") almost indefinitely. Therefore, it is often less costly for the nation to keep people employed, even when they are not needed. The consequence is that individual managers seldom fire individual employees. Labor unions in Britain are national coalitions, and they have a history of nationwide strikes that are beyond the control of any one company. Hiring is regulated by unions, and job assignments are made according to trade union rules, not company directives. Also, few collective bargaining agreements in Britain can be enforced in court. Both British companies and unions, it seems, can cheat on contracts without legal intervention.

The Swedish model of labor relations reflects Sweden's tightly regulated labor laws and national unions, and this model has been adopted in France, Germany, and the Netherlands. In all these countries, a company can fire an employee for good cause, but cannot shut down a plant or eliminate jobs without incurring government sanctions. Union contracts often include government as a third party, and wage bargaining has historically been a national political issue. In Sweden, workers cannot remain unemployed longer than fourteen months. Soon after a person becomes unemployed, government specialists try to place the worker in a new job. If no suitable job is available, the worker is either retrained or assigned to public-sector duties.

Checklists. The simplest method of evaluating performance is for raters to check statements on a list that describes subordinate behavior. Checklists comprise adjectives and short phrases that can be checked (yes) or ignored (no). They may have as few as a half dozen items or as many as several hundred. Once completed, an employee's checklist is compared against a master list to determine the employee's performance rating. Although checklists have been used for years, they are not very effective because items cannot always be answered "yes" or "no" and some of them are irrelevant to the job being evaluated. And although each item theoretically carries the same value, in reality some are more important than others. One way to overcome this disparity is to weigh each item. If twenty items are used, for instance, raters could distribute 100 points among the items with limits between 0 and 10. A checked item would carry the assigned weight (points) for summation, thereby providing a more realistic score.

Graphic rating scales. One of the most widely used evaluation instruments is the graphic rating scale. Many students are familiar with the graphic rating scales used for teachers' evaluations. A typical scale has at least minimum, maximum, and midpoint values, but the number of values can range from three to ten. Raters circle the one value that best describes the behavior of the person being evaluated, the

Southern European countries—Spain, Portugal, Greece, and Italy—have "political" trade unions. Union officials are often more involved in running for public office than in labor administration, and they can represent extremist groups of the right or the left. Therefore, managers often find themselves negotiating with government leaders over employment issues.

How a dispute is resolved depends more on the politics of company manangers than on existing laws; any laws that do exist are enforced capriciously. For example, none of these countries has a distinct child labor law but there is an "understanding" that children should not work in dangerous circumstances. Yet children are regularly exempted from school to take jobs, and many become trade apprentices before they reach thirteen.

With the restructuring of Western Europe into the European Community, a new body of labor law is taking effect. Based on a "social charter" (a resolution passed by the European Parliament in late 1991), a European commission will be able to make laws on working conditions for companies in all member countries. This commission will consist of labor union representatives, industry representatives, and parliamentary appointees.

Several facts suggest the task that confronts them. Prior to 1992, only six EC nations had equal employment regulations, only five had child labor laws, and only three had passed legislation on employee privileges such as maternity leave. Most national unions had some understanding with industry representatives on these issues, but they took the form of a nonbinding social contract. European management and union representatives, therefore, face an interesting future with many changes anticipated in labor relations.

Sources: "European Social Legislation: Union Comeback," *The Economist*, November 23, 1991, p. 81; "Labour Law: Kicking the Corpse," *The Economist*, July 27, 1991, p. 56; and "Survival of the Fittest Bit," *The Economist*, September 21, 1991, p. 61.

midpoint value indicating an "average" rating. Also, there may be an extra category at the end called "not applicable." Although graphic rating scales are easy to use, they have distinct shortcomings. For example, scales with midpoints offer raters an easy escape from thinking. Raters simply check off the "average" score for most items. Evaluators also tend to distribute item ratings between high and low in such a way that the end result is an overall "average" rating. Another problem associated with graphic rating scales is referred to as the **halo effect** (or halo error). A halo effect occurs when a rater's evaluation is skewed negatively or positively by a limited number of traits. For example, an employee may be rated as "intelligent, practical, industrious, skillful, loyal, determined, disorganized, and emotionally cold" and end up with an evaluation that rates him or her as a below-average employee because of the last two traits only. The tendency to rate everyone in the middle can be partly overcome by using an even-numbered scale (four or six points) without a midpoint. However, it is difficult to overcome a halo effect on graphic ratings because the evaluator's intentional and accidental biases are very awkward to monitor.[48]

halo effect (halo error) Positively or negatively skewing an individual's evaluation on the basis of a limited number of traits.

Behaviorally Anchored Rating Scales. A technique called the Behaviorally Anchored Rating Scale (BARS) adds a vital dimension to the concept of rating scales.[49] BARS focuses on *what employees should do* rather than on their personal characteristics, thus relating job performance to job responsibilities. Each BARS has categories for evaluation such as "supervision" or "initiative," and within each category example statements describe what constitutes "excellent," "average," and "unacceptable" performance in sample incidents. Points are assigned to ratings for excellent, average, and unacceptable (such as 0, 5, and 10), and raters choose a behavioral description that best fits the person being evaluated. Points are then tallied, and managers can compare an employee's appraisal score with a master list or with the individual's previous appraisals. Exhibit 12-3 provides an example of a BARS evaluation with two categories on which a shop supervisor is rated. There may be as many as twenty categories in a BARS evaluation.

BARS is a far more complicated process than indicated here. For it to work effectively, it is essential to have a participative system in which behavioral statements are developed among employees and managers who are familiar with the position being evaluated. Further, the statements derived for each item can change over time, which weakens long-term comparability. BARS is time-consuming, yet this method is far superior to checklists and graphic rating scales.[50]

Essay appraisals. The most difficult method of evaluation—and the one requiring the greatest subjectivity—is the appraisal. Managers write a brief open-ended essay on each subordinate, explaining his or her strengths, weaknesses, behavior, and performance. Although essay appraisals have no set format, most systems provide evaluators with predetermined criteria and guidelines on which to base their comments. Essays are useful for evaluating executives, who usually occupy positions that permit few direct comparisons. For example, if a company has only one labor relations manager, other managers asked to assess that person's performance cannot draw on comparative data or ratings from comparable positions for making judgments. The disadvantages of the essay appraisal are that raters may be inarticulate or lack the time and composure to write effectively; raters may write volumes on one

EXHIBIT 12-3 BARS Evaluation for Production Supervisor

	(10 = Excellent; 5 = Average; 0 = Unacceptable. Circle one.)	
Leadership	a. Supervises work and subordinates without conflict, encourages a cooperative environment, and promotes a sense of enthusiasm. Motivates employees through positive reinforcement, yet is fair and decisive. Exceptional leader committed to job.	10
	b. Has a high degree of integrity, elicits a purpose of high-quality work through proper performance standards. Understands and supports organizational objectives, balances those objectives with proper discipline. Average performance to expectations.	5
	c. Is more concerned with impressing superiors than ensuring quality work. Not a motivated leader; resorts to threats and intimidation to meet output requirements. Unacceptable performance.	0
Initiative	a. Works extremely well without supervision, carries responsibility well. Imaginative and creative individual who finds new ways to solve complex problems, thereby enhancing performance and the value of the firm. Exceptional initiator and innovator.	10
	b. Works well with expected supervision, is responsible and has the expected skills to carry out assigned tasks. Is not an innovator but implements new ideas well. Average performance to expectations.	5
	c. Lacks imagination and initiative. Does not take independent responsibility and reacts only to close supervision. Unacceptable performance.	0

or two characteristics, but neglect others; and the essay is difficult to validate because it is necessarily subjective.

MBO models. More complex appraisal techniques have evolved with the acceptance of management by objectives (MBO). MBO, as described in Chapter 6, is a participative approach to planning that requires joint formulation of objectives between superiors and subordinates. Performance evaluation brings them together again, this time to evaluate results. Under MBO, results are judged in terms of joint objectives written down during the first stage in a planning cycle. Appraisals can take the form of essays, graphic rating scales, BARS statements based on the joint objectives, or simply mutual agreement between the two people as to how well the employee has met those objectives. Through the evaluation process, the MBO cycle is renewed, with more refined objectives and clarification of performance expectations established for the next evaluation period.

Performance Evaluation in Summary

There are dozens of performance evaluation models with several hundred different techniques and applications. Because organizations differ tremendously, no single technique is universally accepted. Large companies generally use several techniques, each selected for its advantages in evaluating particular employee groups or management echelons. There is no perfect appraisal system because each technique requires human interaction and subjectivity. In fact, researchers have discovered that almost all employees whose performance has been evaluated are convinced their superiors know very little about them or what they do.[51] This does not imply that performance evaluations are useless, but only emphasizes how important it is for managers to be well-versed in appraisal techniques.

CHECKPOINT

- Define performance evaluation and a manager's responsibilities for assessing employee performance.
- Why are performance evaluations important and how are they used for decisions about employees?
- Identify and briefly explain the advantages and disadvantages of the most common methods of appraisal.

TRANSFERS AND TERMINATIONS

Reassignment of a person within an organization to fill a vacancy is called a **transfer**. Some transfers are intended to honor employee preferences for working in different jobs, training in new skills, or changing work location. The purpose of others is to accommodate shifts in a company's work; for example, workloads may change so that employees in some departments are idle, while those in other departments are overloaded. People are also transferred within job rotation systems to further their development or to cross-train them in new jobs.

transfer
A transfer is a formal change in an employee's job or position to satisfy employee preferences or to accommodate organizational shifts in resources.

In addition, transfers alleviate boredom and revive burnt-out employees. For example, a machine operator who has been doing the same repetitive work for a long time might be transferred to a technical maintenance department where the work is nonrepetitive and has a different physical cadence. A secretary might be transferred from one office to another that is very different, even though the required skills are similar. Lateral transfers like these can rekindle employees' enthusiasm because they get to work in different surroundings, perhaps with different equipment, and certainly with different people.

Promotions are a special class of transfer. They are the most significant way to reward outstanding performance as well as to provide continuity of leadership. An extraordinary amount has been written on promotion in U.S. organizations; it is the premiere measurement of successful performance in this country. That does not always hold true for other countries, where seniority or social status more often dictate opportunities for advancement.

Terminations are generally seen as the opposite of promotions, but this is an inaccurate perception; the opposite of promotion is *demotion*—a downward transfer of an employee to a position with less status, perhaps lower pay, and less responsibility. Demotion also occurs when a nonpromotable employee is moved aside to make way for a more promising individual—again, this is not a termination.

termination
Employees are terminated when they are formally severed from the organization through retirement, death, resignation, or dismissal.

Terminations occur when employees are fired, furloughed, or laid off, or when they resign, retire, or die. Actually, firings account for relatively few terminations; more employees quit than are fired. This usually benefits the employee, who may find a better position elsewhere or one better suited to his or her personal characteristics. When poorly performing employees quit, it also benefits the company. When good employees leave, the company suffers, yet managers who perform "exit interviews" with departing employees often discover problems that can be resolved to improve the company's performance. Resignations often occur simply because employees want a lifestyle change. Some geographic areas, for example, attract people seeking to relocate; during the past two decades, many people from the Northeast have moved to jobs in the Sunbelt states.

Layoffs and furloughs occur mainly because of decreased demand for products and services, but new technology, competition, and unstable economic conditions also lead to reductions in employment levels. "Downsizing," addressed earlier, presents personnel problems because it seriously disrupts careers and family incomes.

Another form of termination is retirement. Because of the aging population in most Western societies, retirements require companies to recruit aggressively for capable replacements. In affluent societies, more employees retire early, intensifying the competition for qualified employees.[52] Finally, many employees die or become permanently disabled, and although it seems gruesome to address this issue, staff personnel specialists cannot ignore the fact that nearly 25 percent of the working population will terminate through death or illness before reaching retirement age.[53]

Even during a recession, a number of companies find ways to avoid firing employees. In the view of such companies, layoffs are simply bad business. For example, in 1991, earnings at Fort Worth's Baldor Electric dropped 16 percent. Management did not respond by passing out pink slips. Explains CEO Roland Boreham, with layoffs "you have a lot of training, experience, and skill going out the door, as well as company loyalty."

Consequently, plans must be made to provide timely replacements. Specialists in benefits management also have to address the issues of retirement income, medical and disability insurance, and family survivors' benefits.

CHECKPOINT

- Explain how transfers benefit both employees and their organizations.
- How do voluntary resignations occur, and why can they be beneficial to employees and their organizations?
- Briefly describe terminations other than firings and resignations that are important for managers to address.

WE SAW IN THIS CHAPTER'S OPENING EXAMPLE that the Blackfeet Indian Writing Company had to resolve the problem of recruiting and keeping employees whose lifestyles and employment experience were not compatible with assembly-line manufacturing practices. New BIWC employees take part in a training program that both emphasizes teamwork and provides individual counseling to help determine and reinforce each employee's contribution and goals. Granting production bonuses and appointing managers from employee ranks help keep productivity, quality, and morale high. Now a well-established business particularly famous for its Blackfeet Indian Pencil, BIWC has exceptional human resource programs to help employees with a history of few opportunities—a problem that persists on many Native American reservations. ■

A SYNOPSIS FOR LEARNING

1. Describe the function of human resource management.

   Human resource management is concerned with providing the needed people with the appropriate skills to ensure an organization can meet its objectives. The human resource management function includes planning future personnel requirements as determined by growth, decline, changes in skills, changes in technology, employee resignations, transfers, retirements, and promotions. Thus human resource managers are engaged in recruitment, selection, orientation, training and development, compensation and benefits management, performance evaluation, effecting transfers, and controlling terminations.

2. Define management responsibilities for human resource planning.

   Human resource planning is focused on long-term future employment requirements influenced by technology, leadership, organizational structure, and sociocultural changes. In the short term, it concentrates on identifying recruiting needs, upgrading employee skills through training and development programs, and controlling the ebb and flow of employees as a result of terminations, layoffs, and transfers.

3. Explain the process of recruitment and selection in organizations.

   Recruitment is the process of attracting a pool of qualified candidates for organizational positions. Nonspecialized job recruitment involves locating applicants for jobs mainly characterized as unskilled or low-skilled. Specialized recruitment for positions requiring higher-level skills or management abilities may be either internal or external. Selection is the decision-making process of hiring employees.

4. Describe orientation, training, and development programs.

Orientation is the process of inducting new employees into organizations. Through formal orientation programs, newly hired employees are introduced to their tasks, the work environment, co-workers, company policies, safety rules, and supervisors. Training programs are designed to upgrade job-related skills. Development programs attempt to provide general knowledge about theoretical concepts, improve work relationships, and sensitize managers to their responsibilities.

5. Discuss compensation management and benefits management.

Compensation management deals with wage and salary administration. Personnel specialists manage compensation, develop systems of pay and rewards to attract and retain qualified employees, and assist line managers in deciding on raises, bonuses, and incentives affecting wages and salaries. Benefits management deals with retirement programs, unemployment insurance, Social Security, medical and dental programs, vacation scheduling, and holiday planning. It also includes employee programs for drug rehabilitation, family counseling, and child care, as well as bereavement and maternity leaves.

6. Summarize the roles of staff specialists and line managers with respect to employee and labor relations.

Employee relations is a field concerned with helping individual employees perform better, enjoy their work, and resolve personal problems. Consequently, staff specialists and line managers have equally important roles in improving organizational effectiveness. Staff, however, have specific responsibilities for programs relating to such areas as employee fitness, family assistance, and substance abuse counseling. They are also responsible for subsidies and opportunities such as tuition assistance, skills upgrading, career counseling, and preretirement planning. Labor relations constitutes a highly specialized field based on laws relating to collective bargaining and contract administration. Executives are directly involved in union-management negotiations, but it is the labor relations specialist who administers contracts, deals with grievances, and works with unions on problems such as discipline. Operating line managers often find themselves in the middle of labor-management grievances, and they are also responsible for honoring contract terms such as compensation and employee assignments.

7. Discuss the importance of effective performance evaluation systems.

Effective performance evaluation systems offer meaningful assessments of employee behavior and performance. They are properly documented for decisions on compensation, promotion, transfers, discipline, and terminations. Managers at every level who supervise subordinates are responsible for performance appraisals and for providing feedback and guidance to employees on their behavior and performance. Because so many decisions are based on performance evaluation, it is one of the most important management responsibilities.

8. Discuss the concepts of transfer and termination.

A *transfer* is the reassignment of an employee within the organization. Transfer may be lateral or horizontal. Demotions are also transfers. *Termination* is the permanent severance of an employee from the organization. Terminations may result from employee resignation, retirement, disability, or death. Also, the company may terminate employees through layoffs, downsizing reorganizations, plant closings, and firings.

CASE 1 Nine-to-Five

SKILL ANALYSIS

"There are very few companies that really care about their people. . . . They get so wrapped up with . . . the products and the markets that they don't really consider how it's going to affect the people. . . ."[54]

The result of poor or ineffective management of human resources is almost certainly a dissatisfied work force and, consequently, high absenteeism, an increase in errors (sometimes intentional), low productivity, and resistance to change. In the film *Nine-to-Five,* a comedy tribute to office clericals of America, three women oppressed by a smarmy and uncaring boss end up devising an outrageous scheme of revenge and show just how high the costs of unconcern for the work force can be. Though kidnapping the boss and implementing changes in his absence is an unlikely scenario in the real world, the film demonstrates the negative results of a lack of concern for workers and the positive results of a number of human resource interventions.

The boss, Mr. Hart, was originally trained by one of his own staff and has rapidly moved up the hierarchy to the position of vice president. Between issuing memos to maintain a very sterile work environment (no plants, family pictures, or even coffee cups on worker desks permitted), demanding coffee from "the girls," firing an employee for speculating about his earnings, threatening others with dismissal, taking full credit for ideas and proposals generated by a staff member, promoting a new man over a female supervisor with long experience and expertise, and chasing his secretary around while suggesting to the office that they are having an affair, Hart is defrauding the company. His behavior eventually takes its toll on three of the women in his employ, and as they vent their feelings over drinks at a local bar, they imagine a number of ways they could get revenge.

The following morning, one of the women (Lily Tomlin) inadvertently puts rat poison instead of an artificial sweetener in the boss's coffee (the boxes look the same except for the small skull and crossbones). She discovers her error when she hears that Hart is unconscious and has been rushed to the hospital, though she doesn't know that, in fact, Hart just fell out of his chair and bumped his head; he never drank the coffee. Hart, however, finds out about the mistake and his attempt to blackmail the women provides them with an unintended opportunity to realize some of their fantasies of revenge. Held at gunpoint and trussed up with cord and chain, Hart is kept captive while the women try to obtain proof of his fraud.

In the almost six weeks of his incarceration, the three women find it fairly easy to run the office in his absence (no one really wants to talk to him face-to-face anyway), and since Hart's secretary (Dolly Parton) can write his signature better than he can, the women decide to implement a number of changes. Starting small with a memo announcing that workers are now permitted to display personal objects on their desks, they soon move to bigger changes. The work environment is modified to permit wheelchair access, dingy gray lockers are painted bright yellow, an open modular work-area plan replaces the rows of desks, and the time clock is removed. Workers are provided opportunities for flexible working hours, and job sharing and day-care and drug rehabilitation programs are implemented.

Then Hart reappears on the scene, holding one of the women (Jane Fonda) hostage with a gun in his pocket. He has already covered his fraudulent tracks, and plans, once he's called the police, to "put a stop" to the changes. However, the opportunity to exercise his power is lost when he hears that the chairman of the board has arrived to meet with him and he has to turn to the women for support. Flustered and impotent, Hart (enduring the blessings and hugs of a reformed alcoholic staff member) follows behind the chairman, the women, and an entourage of head-office staff as they view the changes that have resulted in a 20 percent increase in office productivity. The chairman is impressed with the innovations and rewards Hart with an appointment to Brazil ("I need a man like you on my team"). Hart is less than enthused, but the chairman is not a man who takes no for an answer. The women are delighted, not only about their innovative success in the workplace, but also because they will no longer be oppressed by the tyrannical Hart. Hart appears to be about to receive his just desserts.

Case Questions

1. In what ways do the positive and negative aspects of the case reflect your own work experiences? How would various human resource interventions have made your experiences more positive?
2. Discuss the case in terms of the four questions that need to be resolved in human resource planning.

VIDEO CASE Private Lives Away from the Job—Not So Private Anymore

Where should an employer's rules and controls end? Does a boss have the right to dictate what employees do on their own free time? In managing their human resources, how far should managers be allowed to go in mandating acceptable on-the-job and, more important, off-the-job behavior? These difficult human resource management questions are being raised by employers and employees alike.

To reduce expenses, many companies are not employing people they think might get sick or injured because of activities they engage in off the job. Janice Bone, formerly a payroll clerk at Ford Meter Box in Wabash, Indiana, was fired because she smoked at home, away from the job. Says Ms. Bone, "When they tell me I'm being terminated because of nicotine, I'm just very surprised and wonder, you know, 'What is this? What's going on here?'" The company explained that insurance costs were the main reason for its policy of not allowing smoking on or off the job. Experts suggest that for each employee who smokes, corporations must pay about $300 more per year. As a result, many companies now are implementing no-smoker policies.

One of the first to establish such a no-smoker policy was Ted Turner's Turner Broadcasting System. The vice president of administration at TBS stated, "It saves us on hospitalization, medical costs. [Mr. Turner] just thought, with smoking being, you know, bad for the employee, bad for the environment—passive smoke—that he just wanted a totally smoke-free company." The Turner policy extended to employees who smoked at home. Although TBS has never fired anyone for violating the policy, Shaw conceded that some elected to leave the company rather than stop smoking.

Some companies rule out employee drinking off the job. At Best Lock Corporation of Elwood, Indiana, Daniel Winn was fired because he had a few drinks at a bachelor party. Says Winn, "If a person has a problem with drinking, he obviously needs help. If he doesn't have a problem, I still don't see why it would, in any manner, you know, come between him and his job performance." A real estate company in Atlanta forbids its employees to take up *any* dangerous activity. The company specifically lists skydiving, mountain climbing, riding a motorcycle, and driving a race car as prohibited activities. This policy came about after an employee had a motorcycle accident and the company's insurance premiums went up 18 percent.

Although these examples of controlling employees may seem unfair or unjust, there is nothing in the U.S. Constitution that gives employees a right to privacy vis-à-vis their employers. "Employment at will" is the legal principle that permits employers to set rules about all kinds of off-duty behaviors. According to this doctrine, if employees do not like the rules that employers establish, they have the option of quitting. Also, employment at will means that employers can fire or not hire for almost any reason except race, religion, sex, age, disability, or any other characteristic explicitly protected by law. The job of managing a company's human resources has become more complex in light of the realities of the privacy issue.

Case Questions

1. What areas of human resource management do employee privacy matters influence? How?
2. If an organization chooses to implement rules about off-the-job behavior, how could it do so most effectively?

Sources: David S. Hames and Nickie Diersen, "The Common Law Right to Privacy: Another Incursion into Employers' Rights to Manage Their Employees," *Labor Law Journal,* November 1991, pp. 757–765; Maria Shao, Zachary Schiller, and Walecia Konrad, "If you Light Up on Sunday, Don't Come in on Monday," *Business Week,* August 26, 1991, p. 68ff; and Jane Easter Bahls, "Checking Up on Workers," *Nation's Business,* December 1990, p. 29ff.

SKILL PRACTICE

OSHA TRAINING GUIDELINES: DEVELOPING LEARNING ACTIVITIES

Although the Occupational Safety and Health Administration holds employers responsible for training employees in safety procedures, during the first decade of its existence, the agency issued no guidelines about what constituted proper or adequate training. Employers were liable nonetheless. During the Reagan administration, OSHA finally published training guidelines. The following evaluation of them is by the editors of *Personnel Manager's Legal Report.*[55]

OSHA's model consists of seven steps: (1) identifying training needs, (2) determining the content, (3) preparing instructional objectives, (4) developing learning activities, (5) conducting the training, (6) evaluating program effectiveness, and (7) improving the program.

Common Sense

Although they are often camouflaged by unnecessary jargon, the guidelines are based in commonsense notions. First, identify dangers and those workers exposed to them. Second, develop activities that let workers learn, without exposing them to danger. Third, monitor the training to make sure it is doing the job required.

Developing Learning Activities

These activities allow employees to learn and to demonstrate the acquisition of the desired skills and knowledge. As with any document that covers thousands of different situations, the guidelines are somewhat vague as to how this should be done. In general, two points should be remembered. First, training should simulate the actual jobs as closely as possible. Second, the employer should have some way of observing whether the employee has acquired the desired skills and knowledge.

How a company will enforce these guidelines depends on the nature of the job. Yet they clearly anticipate that classroom-oriented instruction will precede exposure to processes too complex or dangerous to allow hands-on experimentation. OSHA recommends that trainers develop step-by-step activities that allow employees to learn concepts or skills. Lectures, role-play, demonstrations, self-paced instruction, charts, diagrams, manuals, slides, films, transparencies, videotapes, or simply blackboard and chalk are all satisfactory, if they adequately relate to the necessary skills and provide means for testing proficiency.

Conducting Training

OSHA's guidelines do offer specific advice on how companies should conduct training, but they do present training objectives. Training should involve three steps: (1) an overview of the material to be learned; (2) an explanation of how each specific item of knowledge relates to the ultimate purpose of the training; and (3) an explanation of how each specific skill relates to the individual employee.

Steps 2 and 3 relate to employee motivation, and the guidelines suggest five ways to develop it: (1) explain to employees the objectives of instruction; (2) ask questions or give a short quiz before beginning the training session; (3) explain to employees that they will be tested following completion of the training session; (4) preview the main points to be presented; and (5) point out the benefits of the training—for example, employees will be better informed and therefore able to work at less risk.

The guidelines also state, "An effective training program allows employees to participate in the training process and to practice their skills or knowledge." Among the ways that employees can become involved in the training process are "by participating in discussions, asking questions, contributing their knowledge and expertise, learning through hands-on experience, and through role-playing exercises."

Evaluating program effectiveness. The guidelines suggest that a plan for evaluating training sessions be designed at the time course materials are developed, and not as an afterthought. An evaluation program will be deemed adequate if it determines the amount of learning achieved and whether on-the-job performance has improved.

Improving the program. If the evaluation indicates that the training is inadequate, it may be necessary to revise the program. Prior to revision, employees and administrators should be asked: (1) What material in the program was already known and, therefore, unnecessary? (2) What material was confusing or distracting? (3) What material was missing? (4) What did the employees learn and fail to learn?

The employer should also ask: (1) Was the job analysis accurate? (2) Was any critical feature of the job overlooked? (3) Were all deficiencies of knowledge or skill included? (4) Was material already known by employees omitted? (5) Were instructional objectives stated clearly? (6) Did the instructional objectives state standards of acceptable performance? (7) Did the learning activity simulate the actual jobs? (8) Was the learning activity appropriate for the kinds of knowledge and skills required on the job? (9) When the training was presented, was the organization of the material clear? (10) Was the proper motivation provided? (11) Were employees allowed to participate actively in the training process? (12) Was the employer's evaluation of the program thorough?

Suggested Exercises

One of the many training areas is vehicle operation. Most of you can appreciate the need for driving safely—traffic accidents are responsible for a great many fatalities in the United States—so put yourself in the position of a novice driver and address the following:

1. Outline a vehicle training program using OSHA's seven-step process.
2. How would you explain and implement "motivational aspects" of the program in terms of OSHA guidelines?
3. What objectives would you specify, and how would you measure the success or failure of the training?

Tucker: The Car of the Future Today

Preston Tucker's car had beautiful looks, safety windows, speed, economy—everything the American people wanted. "The car of the future today." But dreaming up the car turned out to be a lot easier than making the dream come true.

Tucker was certain about what people wanted. A postwar survey indicated that more than 80 percent of Americans polled put a new car at the top of their list of desires, so he was assured of demand. The fact that this car was so different in so many ways made it competitive with other cars available. In fact, Tucker was so convinced of the value of his innovations that he expected them to revolutionize the car industry. History shows us that his ideas did have a substantial impact on car design, but in the late 1940s, getting financial support for his ideas and realizing them in production would take a lot more than dreaming.

During the Great Depression of the 1930s, automobiles were a luxury. Then, with World War II, raw materials were requisitioned for producing tanks, guns, and other military equipment, so few new cars were produced. By the time World War II ended, however, Americans were ready for some fun and a better life—and for many of them, that included a new car. The long years of depression and war and the scarcity of cars had increased demand.

The response by most auto manufacturers was to offer superficially updated 1941 model cars. Some people may have thought that this reflected a lack of effort or creativity, but there were other factors involved. Steel and other materials required for production had been heavily utilized by the war effort and consequently were in short supply. Services such as machining, tooling, and casting were demanded by many businesses eager to provide goods for a suddenly increased market. Changes in design required changes in equipment and production, the building of new models, testing, and specialty engineers—all expensive. For the small manufacturer, competition with the "Big Three" was an added factor. The Big Three not only had greater access to needed resources (vendors were more likely to offer products or services to an established company than to an untested one), but their large-scale production facilities and huge market share (the Big Three had 47,000 dealerships compared to the 6,900 of Hudson, Nash, Packard, and Studebaker combined) made them particularly powerful adversaries.

Undeterred by these factors—or perhaps never truly cognizant of them—Tucker sought financial support for his dream. His initial responses were not positive, and it is uncertain whether he was even taken seriously at the start. The responses he received tended to be along the lines of: "Forget about it. You've got no chance." But Tucker was not a man to easily abandon a great idea, and certainly not on the basis of the negative opinions of a few. Recognizing the power of advertising, he publicized the Tucker car in a widely sold magazine of the time. Public and dealer response was instant and strong.

Because of this overwhelming response, Tucker was able to obtain initial financing through the sale of dealerships. (The price of a dealership was $4,000; Tucker hoped to start with 3,000 of them, knowing that buyers would be reluctant to buy a car not easily serviced.) He managed to lease a plant from the War Assets Administration (WAA) that consisted of 16 buildings on 475 acres, including one building reported to be 73 acres in size—the largest building under one roof in the world! It was a "sweet deal" and there were those who challenged it, but ultimately Tucker won the right to keep the plant. Tucker also attempted to acquire a steel plant to ensure a continual supply of steel for production, but his bids were disallowed. It was suggested that the government had manipulated the bidding process (and that it did so to protect the Big Three, who would have to match Tucker's design innovations), but this never became entirely clear.

These were not the only problems Tucker faced. More financing was required, and for this he required strong stock sales. But for stock to sell, there must be some assurance of a good product (and Tucker didn't have one yet) and good management. Good management meant management that was known and proven. Tucker was neither known nor proven in the auto industry, so someone else, preferably from Detroit, had to be hired as chairman of the board to ensure stock sales. An ex-Ford/ex-Plymouth executive was hired for this role. Unfortunately, while Tucker saw him as window dressing, the new chairman had every intention of being fully in control. This difference in perception was to create problems later.

A prototype was also needed, and because of the pressure to raise money and meet other deadlines, the prototype design schedule was tight. While Ford took about nine months to develop a prototype model, Tucker had to do it in sixty days. The immediate problem was the lack of clay to build the model (again, it was suggested that the Big Three were influential here), and the builders were forced to move directly to metal. But that problem was minor in comparison with the design problems. Very few of the latter were solved in the prototype development phase; shortcuts were taken and substitutions made to meet the premier deadline.

The premier event drew more people than were invited or expected. The Tucker prototype proved so inadequate that the unveiling was delayed; Tucker used every tactic in the book to stall while mechanics tried to unlock wheels, stop up oil leaks, and attend to all manner of problems behind the stage curtain. Amidst band fanfare and the parading of beautiful cars, the car was finally unveiled in June 1947; it was, however, more "look" than substance. In fact, the car was not operational.

The design problems didn't end with the development of the prototype. Problems that couldn't be solved in that stage presented challenges later. It was some time before an operable Tucker car was taken out to tour the road, and the car that finally did ride the streets was not entirely the one initially publicized in that first feature article. The movable fender-and-light construction that was to better light the street when turning corners had been abandoned when it was found that the fenders were unsafe. The original transmission design didn't work when tested, so a transmission scavenged from another car was substituted. The originally planned engine turned out to be years from a realistic production model, so the design had to be modified. Preston Tucker's response to such problems was often a "You can work it out" or a "Who can look me in the eye and say it can't be done?"

While designers, engineers, and mechanics worked to solve these design problems, Tucker himself was out promoting the car. (It would later be charged that the money he spent on promotion—especially since little was required to bolster product enthusiasm—might better have been allocated to solving the design and production problems). Meanwhile, the board made its own decisions about appropriate ways to alter designs and solve production problems. The board's decisions, based variously on cost, time, and resource concerns, were not particularly welcome among Tucker's original and loyal team. The unilateral manner in which these decisions were made, which was contrary to Tucker's participative decision-making style, did not help to make them popular. After employee efforts to discuss issues with the directors failed, Tucker returned to make his own stand, only to find that there were extreme limits to his corporate control.

Fortunately, not all the news was bad. As the board moved to reorganize production to their own requirements, the Tucker team worked on developing an engine that was more in keeping with the original design. A helicopter engine was adapted for use in the car; modifications resulted in performance acceleration from zero to 30 mph in 3.5 seconds, zero to 60 mph in 10 seconds, and zero to 80 mph in 15 seconds—and the car was clocked at speeds of over 100 mph. With the success of the modifications, Tucker returned production to original specifications (though not without some negative board reaction). The promises of speed, rapid acceleration, and good mileage (well over 20 mpg) were all achieved in the final design. Several innovations were also built into the design. These innovations included interchangeability of seat covers, matching luggage, popout windows and padded dashboards, disc brakes, and an independent suspension system.

But such successes did not end Tucker's problems. The fact that the car had been publicized long before a prototype was built or a car actually manufactured resulted in both the public and the government becoming suspicious. It is not clear to what degree the Big Three and government may have been conspired against Tucker, but in June 1947, the Securities and Exchange Commission (SEC) canceled the proposed stock offering for reasons of incomplete information disclosure. The delay prevented Tucker from meeting the deadline for acquiring $15 million in assets that was a condition of his agreement with the WAA. The deadline was extended, and by September 1947, two months after the public stock offering was made, $15 million worth of stock had been purchased.

Tucker and his wonder car received high-profile attention in the media, but the tone of that attention began to shift from positive to negative. In mid-1948, a Republican senator announced that investigations had been made into the Tucker Corporation and allegations of nonpayment and collusion between the chief WAA negotiator and Tucker were made. In the fall of 1948, a popular radio commentator (one whom Tucker had previously denounced in relation to issues surrounding the plant acquisition) claimed possession of a secret SEC report that charged that the Tucker car was nothing but a scheme to defraud the American public. Such claims were repeated and enlarged in other news media, and as the negative publicity grew, Tucker Corporation's stock price fell.

In October 1948, Tucker and a number of his associates were indicted by the SEC on several charges, including mail fraud and conspiracy. A trial followed, and again, it is difficult to sort out the truth from embellishments and falsehoods. The film made of the Tucker story represents the charges against Tucker as manufactured, and shows Preston Tucker making a highly charged speech about American ideals and how these were at risk. Tucker did attempt to produce a dream car for himself and for the American people; Tucker cars did, in fact, exist. In reality, as in the film, Tucker was exonerated of all charges, but the Tucker Corporation was dead.

Case Questions

1. Discuss how the organizational structure helped or hindered Tucker Corporation. How were contingency factors involved?
2. Comment on the degree of centralization/decentralization in the Tucker Corporation.
3. What forms of power are evidenced in the Tucker case, to whom are they attributed, and how well were they accepted?
4. Comment on group dynamics and decision making in the Tucker Corporation.

Sources: Lucasfilm, *Tucker: The Man and His Dream,* Paramount Pictures, 1988; and Trudy Versor, *The Tucker Corporation: A Management Case Study* (Englewood Cliffs, N.J.: Prentice Hall, 1989).

13

Motivation: Productivity Through People

OUTLINE

The Nature of Motivation
- Motivation Defined
- Understanding the Definition

Motivation and Human Endeavor
- Assumptions of Motivation Theory
- Approaches to Motivation Theory

Content Theories
- Maslow's Hierarchy of Needs
- Alderfer's ERG Theory
- Herzberg's Two-Factor Theory
- McClelland's Acquired-Needs Theory

Process Theories
- Expectancy Theory
- Self-Efficacy
- Equity Theory
- Goal-Setting Theory

Reinforcement Theory
- Learning and Operant Conditioning
- Organization Behavior Modification
- Implications for Management
- The Controversy Over OB Mod

OBJECTIVES

- Define the concept of motivation and discuss its implications for productivity.
- Discuss and contrast the three major approaches to motivation.
- Describe content theory and the concept of perceived needs for motivation.
- Explain process theory and the concepts of expectancy and equity.
- Describe reinforcement theory and issues fundamental to operant conditioning, and discuss the controversy about the ethics of motivation and behavior modification.

DELTA AIR LINES has a reputation for motivated employees who participate in organizational decisions and, through various bonus and incentive plans, hold substantial company stock. Delta has been characterized as having "good-ol'-boy management" and a "happy family of employees."[1] One of the airline's strengths is employees who are loyal and highly motivated. Employee compensation is the highest in the U.S. airline industry, and because Delta's productivity is also the highest, bonuses and benefits based on profits have been exceptional. Delta is strong financially, ranked first in profitability and operating efficiency, and is America's third-largest carrier; it is the fifth-largest carrier worldwide.

Still, Delta's managers and employees have been criticized for placing too much emphasis on "being family" and too little on discipline and control. These criticisms, recorded in Federal Aviation Administration reports, followed investigations of a series of recent incidents. Between 1987 and 1991, Delta pilots twice landed their flights at the wrong airports; a flight crew turned off an airplane's engines while in flight, nearly crashing the plane; and a Delta flight was involved in a near-collision over the North Atlantic. In August 1988, a Delta Air Lines 727 crashed at Dallas–Fort Worth, killing thirteen people.

The FAA concluded that each incident resulted from slack management practices. It noted that there was no evidence of either unprofessional behavior or purposeful negligence by flight crews, but stated that cockpit operations were not controlled closely enough, leaving too many decisions to pilots. Delta contested the FAA's conclusions, and in 1991 was exonerated by a National Transportation Safety Board finding that the Boeing 727 aircraft that crashed had structural flaws.

Nevertheless, Delta agreed that its management control over operations had become too loose. Subsequently, the airline introduced new programs to improve pilots' accountability and to bolster their training. Delta's executives, however, felt that their flight crews were highly motivated by the empowerment process that let them make many of their own decisions. Chairman Ronald Allen said that being nice to employees, paying them well, and giving them significant responsibilities were not signs of "good-ol'-boy behavior," but enlightened management.[2]

Leading others in the pursuit of organizational objectives is one of the most challenging roles of managers, and motivating people to achieve preferred results is a crucial part of that leadership role. This chapter introduces vanguard theories of motivation and discusses their implications for managers. We do not attempt a comprehensive view of something so encyclopedic as motivation, nor do we presume to offer pat answers to the question of how to motivate people. Instead, this chapter describes a variety of approaches to motivation, and alerts you to some of the misleading information and ideas about it.

THE NATURE OF MOTIVATION

Motivation is without doubt one of the most universal concerns of human endeavor. It is a buzzword of industry, a term constantly used by management, a conspicuous aspect of education. Motivation seems inextricably related to organizational performance; we are convinced that highly motivated individuals working "smarter" are more productive both quantitatively and qualitatively. Thus productivity is achieved by having an organization of highly motivated individuals.

Motivation is, nevertheless, one of the most misunderstood human phenomena. We must assume that human beings have been concerned with motivating others throughout history. Neanderthal parents surely watched their children waste time throwing rocks into a stream and asked, "How do we get them to do something useful?" Little has changed since then; we raise the same kinds of questions today. As managers, we ask, "How do we encourage employees to work better and be more creative?" Although this question has been investigated by an extraordinary number of people, we still have few definitive answers.

Motivation Defined

motivation
The concept of behavioral change or result of influence that alters an individual's performance.

In broad terms, **motivation** is the stimulus of behavior. It consists of all the forces that cause a person to behave in certain ways. These forces come from within the person, from other people who interact with that person, and from the person's surroundings. As managers, we need to know how people are motivated and what stimulates their behavior so we can determine its form, direction, intensity, and duration.[3]

Defining motivation is difficult, and as we shall see later, theorists differ sharply in their explanations of why and how employees are motivated to work. For example, some writers explain motivation by economic rationality; they view human beings as goal-directed, intent on avoiding pain and seeking pleasure, and therefore responsive to threats and rewards. Others suggest that motivation is a subconscious psychological process evolving out of personality, background, environment, and

FIGURE 13-1 The Basic Motivation Behavior Sequence

Source: Adapted from David A. Nadler and Edward E. Lawler III, "Motivation: A Diagnostic Approach," in J. Richard Hackman, Edward E. Lawler III, and Lyman W. Porter (eds.), *Perspectives on Behavior in Organizations* (New York: McGraw-Hill, 1983), p. 69.

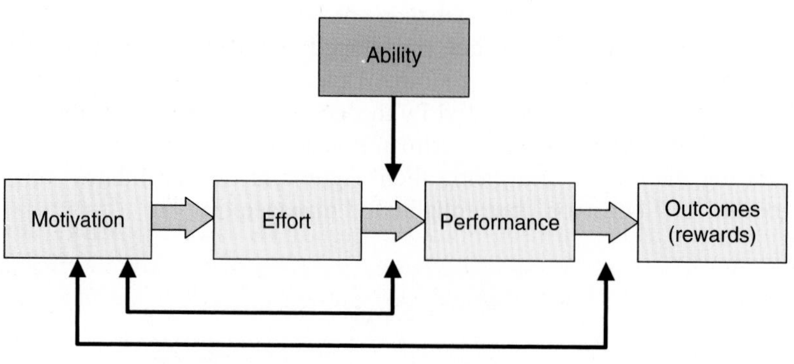

cultural factors. Still others believe motivation is a conscious process that results from individuals making choices about what they will and will not do in a given situation.[4]

You will recall that we defined management earlier as the "ability to get things done through others." Figure 13-1 shows a basic model of motivation as the process of getting things done by motivating people. Note that outcomes follow performance, which rely on effort and ability, and are in turn influenced by motivation. How employees are stimulated to behave, then, determines the direction, intensity, and duration of their efforts, which subsequently affect organizational results.

Understanding the Definition

One characteristic of motivation is that it can originate within a person. We can generate our own momentum for doing or not doing something. In Chapter 2, this idea was introduced as a premise of the *human relations movement*. The theme is emphasized by Jack Welch, CEO at GE, where he has implemented corporate-wide programs to encourage creative behavior in employees who are empowered to work through self-directed teams. GE believes that employees find greater self-esteem and satisfaction with broad responsibilities as team members.[5] Thus, through internally generated stimuli, people become motivated. Internal factors are called *intrinsic* motivators.

The second characteristic of motivation is that in an organizational environment work-related behavior is influenced by external enticements. These include rewards, such as pay and promotion, and threats, such as disciplinary action and ridicule. These externally generated stimuli are called *extrinsic* factors of motivation.

The third characteristic of motivation is that it is *situational*. Behavior can seldom be explained apart from the environment in which it occurs. In group situations, our performance is influenced by the people around us; it is also influenced by the process of work, the tools we use, and the company's technology and organization. These are facts often overlooked by those who blame poor American productivity on individual workers. American workers have been criticized for "losing the work ethic," "being soft," and "caring only about payday and the hell with performance."[6] Clearly some employees fit these descriptions, but to generalize about workers in any country in this manner assumes that they are unaffected by working conditions, leadership behavior, technological change, or other important considerations that constitute the work environment.

The fourth characteristic of motivation is that individual abilities and responses to stimuli vary widely, so finding "pat answers" to what motivates individual employees is difficult. At Johnson & Johnson, for example, there are 166 divisions, and company presidents vary widely in age and background. J&J's chief executive Ralph Larsen says it is impossible to expect the same behavior from a division president who is a fifty-four-year-old Texan with a background in marketing as from a thirty-five-year-old Harvard-trained executive with a Wall Street mentality. Consequently, Larsen gives his executives lots of latitude and expects them to do the same with *their* managers. Managers, Larsen explains, cannot be distracted by the process of management itself. They must be free to pursue success in their own ways and within their capabilities.[7]

Individual differences affect performance, but it is not always the less-capable employees who perform poorly. Many employees with the knowledge, skills, and talent to do excellent work often perform below expectations, and less-capable employees often perform exceptionally well. The most important lesson to be learned from the study of motivation theory is that explanations of behavioral variations are seldom simple. It is not enough to say that an able employee doesn't want to work; we have to understand the individual and how environmental forces influence his or her work behavior.[8]

CHECKPOINT

- Define motivation and state how different theorists explain it.
- Describe intrinsic and extrinsic factors of motivation.
- Why must we consider individual ability in terms of motivation?

MOTIVATION AND HUMAN ENDEAVOR

As emphasized throughout this text, many factors influence productivity, but human endeavor is central to it. Managers at every level in all organizations are concerned with two elements of human endeavor: people's *ability* to perform assigned tasks, and the *effort* they exert. Both can be influenced by managers, negatively as well as positively. Poor management practices can antagonize employees, interfere with their ability to work, and stifle innovation. In contrast, enlightened management practices can nourish performance and stimulate employees to use their abilities and make efforts to excel.

Assumptions of Motivation Theory

We need to recognize several fundamental assumptions about the nature of work and how human beings perceive their responsibilities. These assumptions were voiced by Douglas McGregor and introduced in Chapter 2. As you may recall, McGregor identified two approaches to management, Theory X and Theory Y.[9] *Theory X* is the historic approach, which assumes that workers are lazy, prefer to be directed, avoid responsibility, have little ambition, and must be forced—perhaps even threatened—to do their jobs. Managers who operate under Theory X assumptions are autocratic, control-oriented, pessimistic about human nature, and distrustful of their subordinates. McGregor strongly opposed Theory X assumptions and proposed *Theory Y,* an approach to management that assumes work is natural and that workers prefer to be challenged, are committed to their jobs, and want to achieve worthwhile results. Managers who operate according to this view believe that every individual has the ability to be creative, to be part of an innovative environment, and, under reasonable circumstances, to accept responsibility without force or threats. All contemporary motivation theories integrate McGregor's assumptions, but we still do not have one undisputed theory about motivation or how managers stimulate behavior.[10]

content theory
The management theory usually associated with motivation that focuses on helping individuals fulfill their needs and improve their performance through behavioral techniques and enhanced job satisfaction.

process theory
The motivation theory that focuses on individual attitudes, thoughts, and preferences to understand and influence personal performance.

reinforcement theory
A theory of motivation that explains behavior in terms of consequences learned from past experiences that teach individuals what to do to avoid pain and to gain pleasure.

Approaches to Motivation Theory

Theorists approach motivation from three general perspectives. **Content theory** focuses on human needs or desires that are internalized and give impetus to individual behavior. **Process theory** examines employee behavior in terms of job satisfaction related to perceived rewards (or lack of rewards) that instigate behavior. **Reinforcement theory** is based on the concept of *operant conditioning,* in which individuals, having learned from the past, develop patterns of behavior to control future consequences.

These three approaches are not mutually exclusive; proponents of one are not necessarily opponents of the others. They are best viewed as complementary, each providing us with insights about human behavior that can help us motivate others toward effective performance. Each theory offers clues about individuals and why they work or avoid work. Definitions of the three approaches to motivation are given

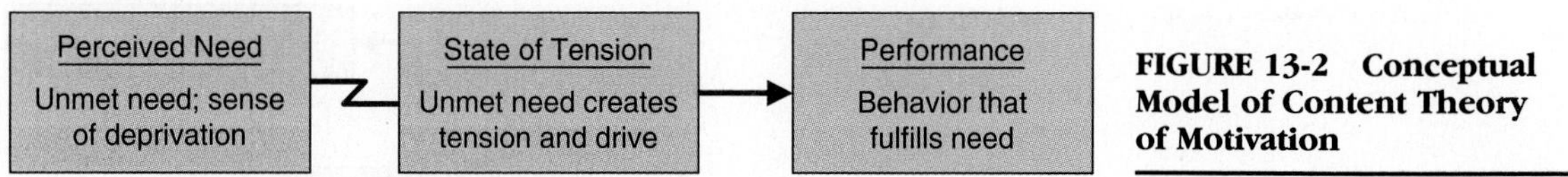

FIGURE 13-2 Conceptual Model of Content Theory of Motivation

here to provide a focused comparison of terms. The remainder of the chapter will expand on each approach, introducing the leading proponents and theories.

CHECKPOINT

- Explain the two elements of human endeavor that affect motivation.
- Describe the fundamental assumptions of motivation theory.

CONTENT THEORIES

All individuals have psychological and physiological needs that prompt them to act to fulfill them. Content theorists study how managers can motivate employees by helping them fulfill their needs. A physiological need, such as hunger, may motivate a person not only to find a job but also to do distasteful work and be obedient to oppressive orders. A psychological need, such as the desire for self-esteem, may motivate a person to do exceptionally high-quality work or be creative.

From the viewpoint of content theory, understanding motivation consists largely of recognizing patterns of needs and then encouraging behavior that results in satisfying them. The crucial characteristic of content theory, illustrated in Figure 13-2, is that unmet or deprived needs result in a state of tension that motivates individuals to act to satisfy the deprivation. Motivation, however, is not so simple. Both physiological and psychological needs are multifaceted concepts confounded by individual values. One hungry person might resort to garbage collecting under an oppressive boss, while another would prefer starvation and a third would steal food before taking a demeaning job. People's value systems vary tremendously.[11]

Another factor affecting motivation is change in individual needs. What motivates an individual one day may have little meaning the next. Hunger may impel us to work, even at the most unpleasant jobs, but once it is satisfied, we need a different reason to continue in the job. We will work hard one day and do little the next, and as we grow older and our social priorities change, so will our attitudes toward work and rewards. However, motivating needs do not seem to be random or chaotic. Research has shown that patterns of behavior emerge in work environments that provide us with clues about how to motivate others and, consequently, manage more effectively.

Maslow's Hierarchy of Needs

Perhaps the most often cited content theory is the **hierarchy of needs** developed by Abraham Maslow and introduced in Chapter 2. Maslow believed that people are motivated to fulfill one of five categories of unfulfilled needs, focusing first on lower-order needs, then ascending to higher-order needs.[12] Figure 13-3 illustrates Maslow's hierarchy. From lowest to highest order, the five categories are:

hierarchy of needs
The progressive categories of needs set forth by Maslow that he suggested motivate human behavior when they are deemed unfulfilled.

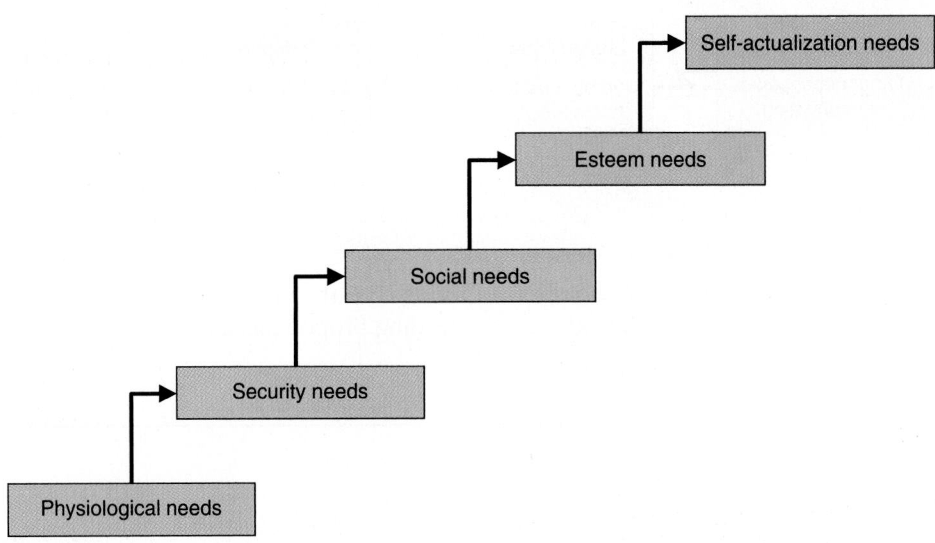

FIGURE 13-3 Maslow's Hierarchy of Needs

1. *Physiological needs:* biological or physical needs, including food, water, air, shelter, and sex.
2. *Security needs* (also called *safety needs*): reasonable freedom from fear or threat of loss in such matters as personal safety, job security, economic maintenance, instability, and the capricious actions of others.
3. *Social needs:* the need for love, affection, and a sense of belonging.
4. *Esteem needs:* self-esteem, respect by others, recognition for accomplishments, and prestige.
5. *Self-actualization needs:* self-fulfillment, personal growth, creativity, and other such needs that can be met only by the individual.

deficit principle
A crucial aspect of Maslow's theory of motivation based on human needs that suggests an unsatisfied need becomes a focal motivator, while a satisfied need no longer influences an individual's behavior.

progression principle
Abraham Maslow's concept that successively higher-order needs in his hierarchy of needs are not active motivators until lower-order needs are fulfilled.

Unmet needs in any of these five categories will potentially motivate behavior, but needs that are already satisfied will not. Maslow called this the **deficit principle:** The state of tension triggered by the perception of being deprived of a need fosters an urge to change behavior to fulfill that need. From example, when people are hungry, they will work for sufficient money to buy food, but once they have satisfied their hunger, some other unmet need must motivate them to work.

A second element of Maslow's theory, the **progression principle,** states that the hierarchy defines a step-by-step process in which lower-order needs are recognized, met, and replaced by higher-order ones. For example, once a lower-order need such as hunger is satisfied, an unmet need at the next level will take precedence. This may be job security—a safety need. Once this need is satisfied, a social need will prevail, and so on. Therefore, individuals are not only motivated to fulfill unmet needs, but also to fulfill those needs that are most powerful to them at the time within a ranked order of priority.

Maslow's theory suggests that managers should identify the needs that preoccupy workers so they can better understand why individuals will or will not work and focus on the rewards that stimulate desired behavior. In recessionary periods of high unemployment and restricted wages, many workers will be concerned about lower-order needs such as earning sufficient money to pay bills and retaining their jobs. In prosperous times, when they do not anticipate threats to their incomes or jobs, workers will place greater emphasis on social interaction and self-fulfillment needs.

The message for organizations is that they should first provide employees with wages sufficient for food and shelter, then with reasonable job protection, health programs, and safety. With lower-order needs addressed, management can seek to provide a satisfactory physical and social environment in which to work, and then strive to provide rewards or recognition that reinforce self-esteem. Enlightened managers will recognize and support workers' needs at the highest level by providing opportunities for advancement, encouraging personal development, and creating an environment where employees can explore their individual talents and dreams.

There are several problems with Maslow's theory. Although the progression principle suggests a systematic approach to satisfying needs from the lowest to the highest levels, research has provided little evidence that such a steplike hierarchy actually exists. Nor has research confirmed the deficit principle, which says that unfilled needs systematically motivate behavior.[13] Moreover, there are sufficient exceptions to the theory to arouse caution. Why, for example, have outstanding artists tenaciously pursued their creative work to the detriment of their health and security? What impels someone to risk death for an ideal? ("Give me liberty or give me death!") Less dramatically, why do some employees strive for excellence even in low-paying jobs?

In general, however, Maslow's work provides insight into the nature of motivation and how needs and desires tend to influence our actions. Besides giving us a convenient window through which to view human nature, his hierarchy has stimulated research on motivation and led to important changes in how managers view human endeavor. It has also given managers a personal understanding of their own needs and the potential of those needs for stimulating behavior.

Alderfer's ERG Theory

In response to reservations about Maslow's need hierarchy, psychologist Clayton Alderfer presented an alternative theory based on three levels of needs: *existence, relatedness,* and *growth.*[14] Initials from the three need categories provide the name **ERG theory,** which suggests behavior is driven by the urge to fulfill one or more of these needs. Existence needs are those that address physiological and safety needs, which are satisfied by material objects, thus collapsing much of Maslow's two categories into one. Relatedness needs encompass safety needs satisfied by the presence of other people and group security together with love and social esteem needs. Growth needs comprise the highest level for self-esteem and self-actualization.

ERG theory
A theory of motivation in which a person's behavior is driven by the urge to fulfill one or more of existence, relatedness, or growth needs.

Although Alderfer agreed with Maslow's general model, he disagreed on the five categories and how they were defined. Alderfer's three-stage model is a refined perspective. He also agrued that several needs could motivate behavior simultaneously and that a step-wise progression was not necessary. Therefore, unmet needs remain important as motivators, but multiple reasons can exist to influence behavior. Alderfer also argued that people could regress, returning to a lower-order need when sufficiently incited by the reoccurrence of an unfulfilled need.

Alderfer's ERG theory has intuitive appeal as an important enhancement to Maslow's general need hierarchy. It is easy to understand, has clear categories of needs, and minimizes the controversy over progressive importance of higher-order needs. Both Maslow's and Alderfer's work, however, is difficult to research or test, and although most observers support the principle that unfulfilled needs are motivators, few have found organizational applications to reinforce how these needs lead to particular types of behavior.[15]

Herzberg's Two-Factor Theory

In the late 1950s, Frederick Herzberg introduced his **two-factor theory** of motivation, which posited that employee satisfaction is achieved mainly through changes in job content.[16] According to Herzberg, satisfaction depends on the work itself (intrin-

two-factor theory
A motivation theory developed by Frederick Herzberg that defines hygiene factors generally associated with dissatisfaction and motivation factors generally associated with satisfaction.

MANAGEMENT APPLICATION

Helping Employees Increase Their Self-Esteem at Cincinnati Milacron

Cincinnati Milacron, Inc., has gone through two major transformations during the twentieth century. Fifty years ago, the company had a reputation as a machine tool manufacturer with smoke-filled factories and a taskmaster environment. During the early 1970s, management changed Milacron's name from Cincinnati Machine Tool & Die, and repositioned the company to manufacture robotic machine tools. Although the new facilities looked like a modern factory, the working environment resembled the earlier assembly line. Today the company is being transformed into a sophisticated manufacturer of high-tech robotics and production systems using information technology. At the same time, the way work is accomplished at Milacron is also changing.

A new plant in Cincinnati is experimenting with two-person assembly teams, each of which is responsible for the complete assembly of each new machine tool. The team prepares the IC control circuits, wires the machine, assembles its parts and accessories, installs it at the customer's site, and teaches customers how to operate it. There are no time cards or supervisors, and each team has total responsibility for quality. Employees taking part in this experiment say that they feel involved in the work they are doing for the first time in their careers. Now that they are no longer being told what to do and how to do it, and when to start and to stop work, they feel good about themselves, their work results, and the company.

Source: Bob Davis and Dana Milbank, "If the U.S. Work Ethic is Fading, Alienation May be the Main Reason," *Wall Street Journal,* February 7, 1992, pp. A1, A4.

sic satisfaction with the job), recognition, achievement, promotion (advancement or growth), and other factors having to do with the inherent nature of work.

The two-factor theory evolved when Herzberg and his associates realized that job satisfaction and job dissatisfaction were influenced by different and distinct sets of variables. Through interviews with thousands of workers, technicians, and managers, Herzberg's team identified certain factors associated with satisfaction and separate factors associated with dissatisfaction.[17]

Company policies, for example, were often sources of dissatisfaction, and personal achievements were often cited as sources of satisfaction. Herzberg categorized factors associated with dissatisfaction as *hygiene factors* and those associated with satisfaction as *satisfier factors*. See Figure 13-4.

hygiene factors
In Herzberg's two-factor theory, those potential dissatisfiers that can be troublesome if not properly managed, yet are factors having little motivation potential.

Hygiene factors. **Hygiene factors** relate to the work environment or the job context. These include company policies, pay, guidelines for administration, rules affecting job security, physical surroundings, and the nature of supervision.

In Herzberg's view, management must improve or control hygiene factors to reduce dissatisfaction. Hygienic management is much like brushing your teeth: It reduces the likelihood of problems and prevents trouble. Management must prevent poor salaries, restrictive work rules, autocratic supervision, job insecurity, unpleasant work surroundings, and other factors that can lead to dissatisfaction. However, by

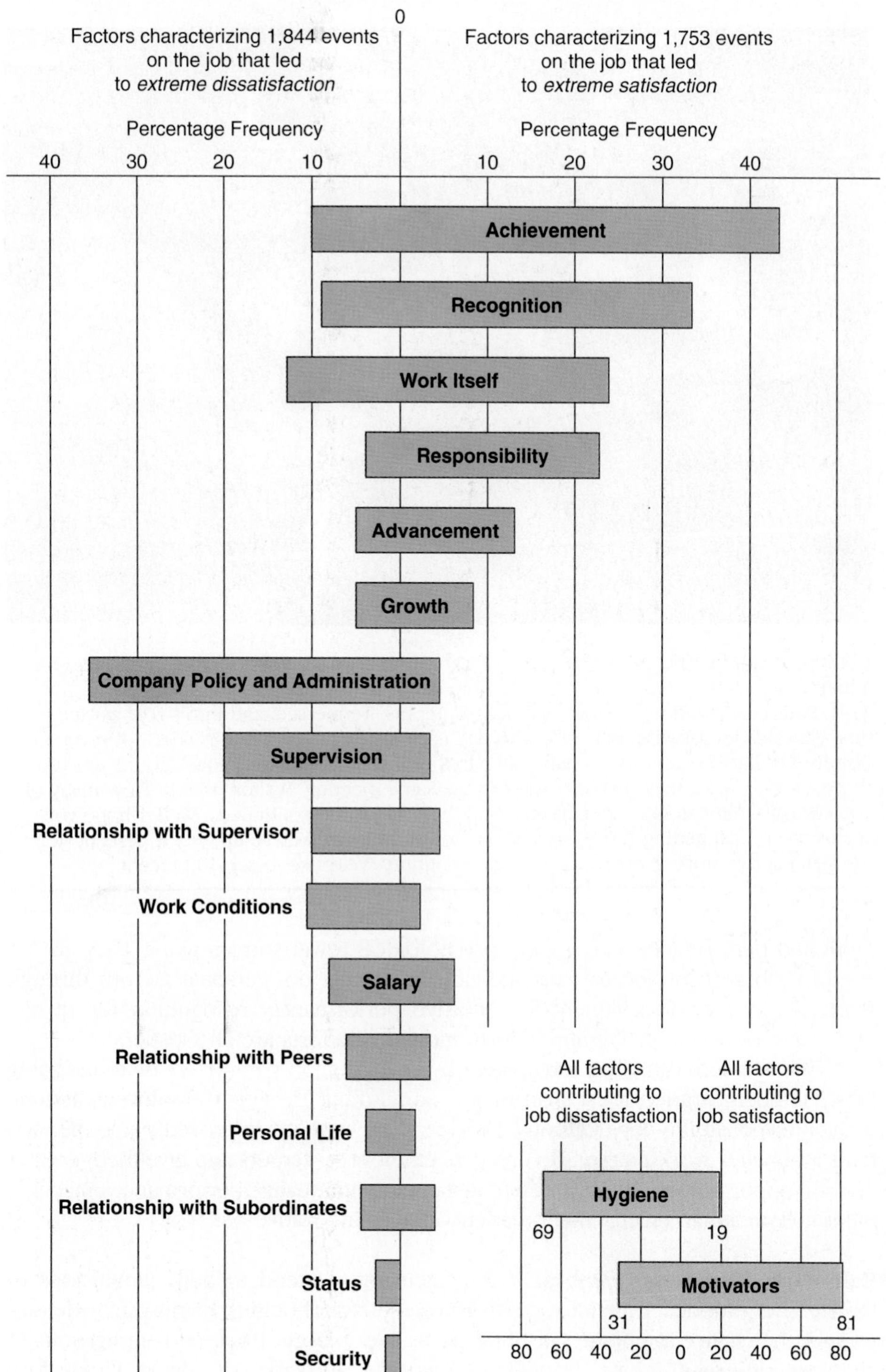

FIGURE 13-4 Herzberg's Research Findings on Hygiene and Satisfier Factors

Source: Reprinted by permission of the *Harvard Business Review*. An exhibit from "One More Time: How Do You Motivate Employees?" by Frederick Herzberg, issue September/October 1987. Copyright © 1987 by the President and Fellows of Harvard College. All rights reserved.

merely preventing trouble, managers do not necessarily enhance performance; they may only lessen the risk of employee dissatisfaction. Providing equitable salaries, for example, may avoid dissatisfaction, but that does not mean that employees will be satisfied with their jobs or motivated to perform better.

satisfier factors
Motivating factors associated with job content, achievement, recognition, and intrinsic rewards, including promotion.

Satisfier factors. Herzberg believed that satisfaction was an entirely separate dimension from dissatisfaction. **Satisfier factors** lead toward higher worker morale,

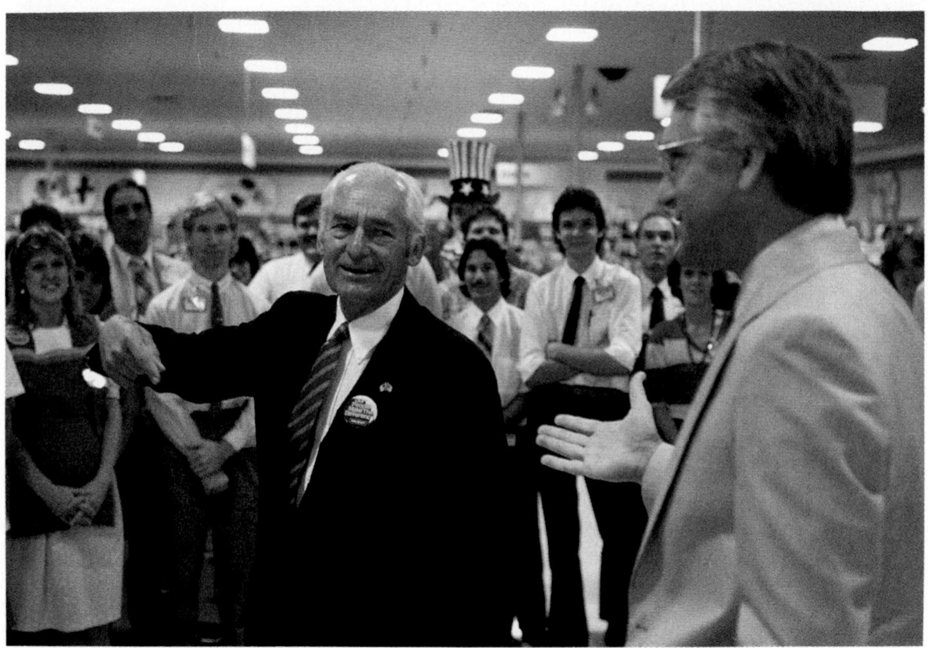

Until his death in 1992, Sam Walton, chairman of America's biggest retailer and universally admired as a master motivator, liked nothing better than visiting his Wal-Mart stores. In 1991, Walton showed up at store 950 near Memphis, Tennessee, and in his role as Number-One cheerleader asked employees, who had each just received a bonus check of several hundred dollars because unaccounted-for loss of inventory was very low, "Could you use those checks? Were they helpful?" Later in the same meeting, Walton asked, "How many of you own Wal-Mart stock?" After most raised their hands, he continued, "Well, I hope you realize we're just getting started. But we've got to improve. You're up over 8 percent [for the year] at this store. I wonder if you can continue. We'd like to see 10 percent."

motivated performance, and greater psychological rewards from work. They are related to job content and to what individuals actually do. Personal growth through work, a sense of achievement for effective performance, recognition for quality work, and advancement stemming from individual efforts are all satisfiers.

Management can affect job content by changing job parameters or redesigning jobs. Herzberg argued for a plan of job enrichment in which employees assume greater responsibility for decisions. Managers can develop improved personnel systems and better work methods to enhance employees' careers and give them greater growth opportunities. By rewarding sustained high-quality performance, management will create an environment that encourages innovative behavior.

Balancing Herzberg's factors. Managers must attend to both dimensions of the Herzberg model. They must control hygiene factors, and they must provide employees the chance to pursue satisfier factors. This concept has broad applications in all types of organizations. Madeline Cartwright, principal of Blaine Elementary School, was one of the ten people named to the 1991 "The Best of America" list by *U.S. News & World Report.* Blaine is located in a drug-ridden inner-city Philadelphia neighborhood. An African-American from a poor background, Cartwright had come up through a similar system. When she became principal, she eliminated restrictive policies and unnecessary disciplinary codes. She challenged students to achieve, stabilized teaching salaries, and enhanced job security. Grades soared, teacher turnover lessened, and self-esteem grew.[18]

Herzberg's theory provides a framework for instituting changes that reduce potential problems and increase potential benefits. Cartwright addressed "content" changes of student and teacher roles, thereby enriching the organizational environment.

McClelland's Acquired-Needs Theory

acquired-needs theory A theory developed by David C. McClelland that proposes people develop a profile of needs through life experiences.

The **acquired-needs theory** proposes that people develop a profile of needs that influence behavior. These needs are learned through life experiences. The acquired-needs theory was formulated by David C. McClelland during the 1960s on the basis of research on human potential and personality done by John W. Atkinson. Atkinson had hypothesized that everyone enjoys an "energy reserve" that can be tapped to fulfill personal goals, and that there are three basic human orientations derived from individual personality profiles.[19] McClelland found that people were not born with these orientations or needs but learned them. Employees bring to organizations a lifetime of learned needs that influence their behavior, but organizational circumstances further influence these needs. McClelland's three acquired needs and examples of related behavior, illustrated in Figure 13-5, are:[20]

- *Need for achievement:* a person's desire to be independent, to accomplish complex tasks, and to resolve problems.
- *Need for power:* a person's desire to influence or control behavior in others, to compete, and to exercise authority.
- *Need for affiliation:* a person's desire to associate with others, to form friendly relationships, and to avoid conflict.

McClelland's theory proposes that everyone has all three needs or orientations but that one will dominate and affect the individual's behavior. Employees with high achievement needs enjoy challenges and thrive in highly stimulating environments. They are best suited to situations where independent responsibility and autonomy prevail. McClelland also argues that achievers require clear and adequate feedback on their performance results. One implication of this theory is that achievers are not always the best managers because organizations are based on diffused authority and group responsibilities. Achievers are, however, often the most creative persons in organizations. Recognizing this, General Mills screens employees for characteristics that suggest whether they will work better on teams or independently on creative problems, and managers are trained in techniques to make the best use of everyone's talents. People high in achievement needs are often groomed for autonomous positions requiring independent initiative.[21] Many achievers feel uncomfortable in structured organizations and break away to start their own businesses. McClelland's theory often associates achievement needs with entrepreneurship.[22]

"Power," as McClelland uses the word, does not imply dictatorial behavior. It suggests a sense of responsibility for controlling others and for influencing subordinates' behavior. Power-oriented managers are comfortable with executive decision making and competitive situations; power-oriented employees seek advancement and aggressively assume responsibility for controlling work activities.

Affiliation needs reflect a desire for social interaction. People with high affiliation needs prefer friendly, participative work environments where the quality

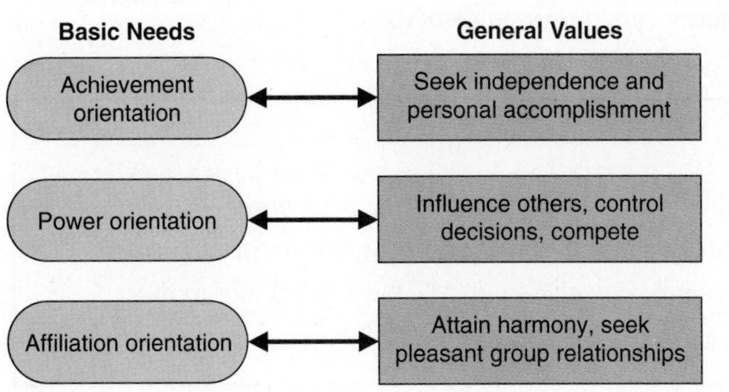

FIGURE 13-5 McClelland's Acquired Needs and Related Values

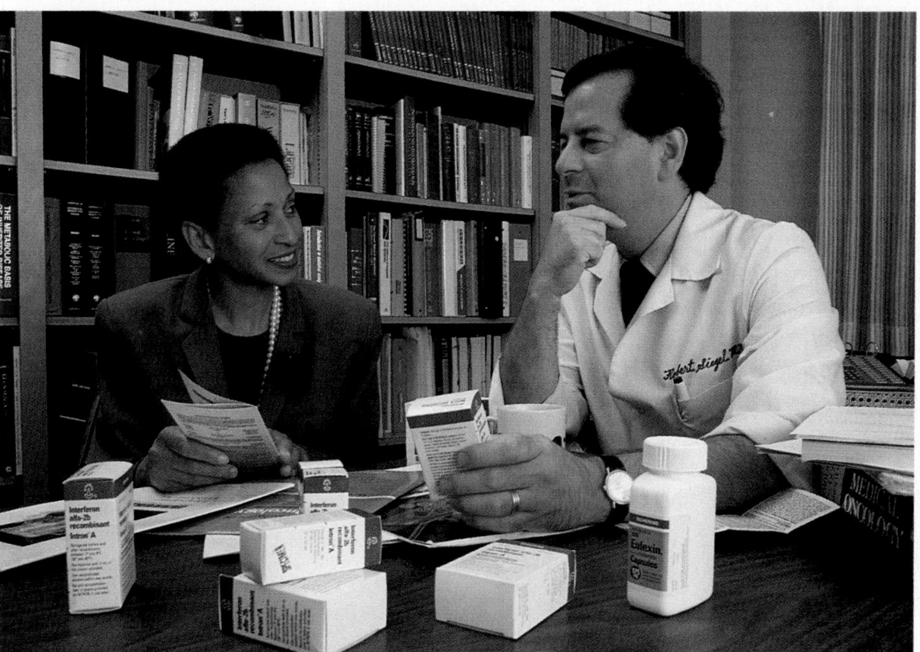

High achievers, such as this Schering-Plough salesperson, do well in sales positions because such jobs provide relative freedom, personal responsibility for outcomes, immediate feedback on performance, and the opportunity to take moderate risks.

of group interaction is more valued than creativity and the ability to influence others. They are also successful as integrators, bringing together departments and workers with diverse interests, coordinating interdependent tasks, and helping to resolve conflicts. Few affiliators are happy in line management and executive positions, where emotionally difficult decisions must often be made, such as disciplining employees and enforcing policies. Their propensity to solidify friendships conflicts with the need to put effective decisions ahead of social compatibility.[23]

Working on the premise that these needs evolve through a learning process, McClelland conducted experiments to try to alter them by placing individuals in different circumstances. He specifically tried to enhance participants' achievement needs by moderating power relationships and encouraging creativity in situations requiring independent actions. McClelland was successful in altering people's orientation, but found that when his participants returned to their previous environments, they reverted to previous patterns of behavior. McClelland concluded that for individuals already strongly set in their ways, matching work and career environments is crucial, and that people established in organizations undergoing rapid change require counseling and education to help them adapt to new circumstances.[24]

In summary, content theories are concerned with motivating employees by addressing their needs. Each theory defines human needs differently, but all agree about managers' responsibilities for influencing behavior by fulfilling those needs. Collectively, content theories have provided a foundation for research to discover how employees react to different organizational stimuli, and this research has led to a branch of motivational theory called *process theory*.

CHECKPOINT

- In terms of content theory, what factors influence behavior?
- Describe Maslow's theory and the deficit and progression principles.
- How does Herzberg's work correlate with Maslow's need hierarchy?
- Discuss McClelland's approach to motivation and his categories of needs.

GLOBAL TRENDS

Nissan Challenges the Japanese Status Quo for Motivating Employees

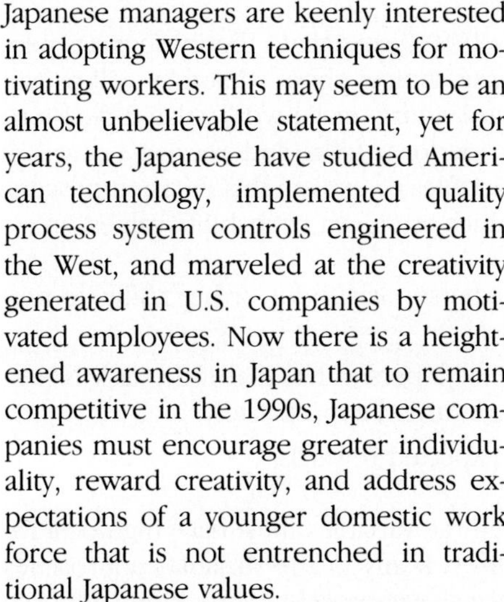

Japanese managers are keenly interested in adopting Western techniques for motivating workers. This may seem to be an almost unbelievable statement, yet for years, the Japanese have studied American technology, implemented quality process system controls engineered in the West, and marveled at the creativity generated in U.S. companies by motivated employees. Now there is a heightened awareness in Japan that to remain competitive in the 1990s, Japanese companies must encourage greater individuality, reward creativity, and address expectations of a younger domestic work force that is not entrenched in traditional Japanese values.

Older Japanese workers and most senior managers still adhere to those traditional values, including the concept of lifetime employment, respect for hierarchical authority, loyalty by employees who are expected to work without complaint for fifty to sixty hours a week, and a seniority system that rewards employees with raises or promotions based almost solely on their length of service. Younger workers reject these practices. Instead, they expect to have opportunities for advancement based on their performance, want a voice in their companies' practices, and are likely to change jobs or seek promotions outside the seniority systems.

Recognizing these trends, Nissan has begun to disrupt its internal seniority system by actively recruiting employees and experienced managers from other companies. The company has also begun to promote employees based on performance, to introduce individual bonuses for innovations, and to encourage risk-taking behavior. According to the Japan Institute of Labor, these changes are becoming widespread among many leading Japanese companies. Other changes noted by the institute are a move away from consensus-building rituals toward individuality, pay systems that recognize fast-track performers, and new incentives to recruit and retain good employees. These incentives tend to focus on career development, such as providing opportunities for overseas sabbaticals, training in Western management techniques, and postgraduate educational subsidies. But they also include greater autonomy, preferential assignments, and recognition for employees with outstanding performance or new ideas. Old notions of unswerving loyalty and rigid seniority—both tied closely to risk-avoidance behavior—are rapidly being replaced by a youthful wave of upheaval in which individuals seek opportunities and companies seek to motivate employees toward greater risk-taking behavior.

Sources: Masaya Miyoshi, "Competition, Cooperation, Interdependence," *Speaking of Japan,* Vol. 11, No. 115 (1990), pp. 20–24. See also "Japan Encourages Its Young," *The Economist,* August 10, 1991, p. 55.

PROCESS THEORIES

Content theories emphasize people's perceived needs. In contrast, process theories emphasize that employees make decisions about how they will perform at work. They are viewed as making conscious and subconscious evaluations of contemplated actions and the consequences of those actions. In other words, personal expectations of outcomes associated with performance are critical for determining how employees will be motivated. If they expect and want rewards for doing work, they will do it. If they expect and value recognition for certain behavior, then they will decide to behave accordingly. These rudimentary examples emphasize that process theory views individuals as decision makers who weigh the advantages and disadvantages of their behavior.

Expectancy Theory

expectancy theory
A theory concerned with motivation that suggests people make conscious decisions about their behavior based on expectations of outcomes.

Introduced by Victor Vroom during the early 1960s, expectancy theory suggests people not only are driven by needs but also make choices about what they will or will not do. **Expectancy theory** proposes that individuals make work-related decisions on the basis of their perceived abilities to perform tasks and receive rewards.[25] Vroom established an equation with three variables to explain this decision process, as Figure 13-6 shows. The three variables, which are given probability values, are:

- *Expectancy:* the degree of confidence a person has in his or her ability to perform a task successfully.
- *Instrumentality:* the degree of confidence a person has that if the task is performed successfully, he or she will be rewarded appropriately.
- *Valence:* the value a person places on expected rewards.

Because the model is multiplicative, all three variables must have high positive values to imply motivated performance choices. If any of the variables approaches zero, the probability of motivated performance also approaches zero. When all three values are high, motivation to perform is also high.

Thus, when you believe you are able to accomplish a task, your self-confidence will lead you to assign a high value to *expectancy*. When you also believe that once you have accomplished the task successfully, your reward will be commensurate with your achievement, you will assign a high value to *instrumentality*. Finally, if you consider the reward to be important, you will assign a high value to *valence*.

A low value assigned to any variable will result in a low score, thus a low probability of motivation to perform the task. For example, assume that you feel certain you can perform (expectancy of 1.00) and that you will receive the associated reward (instrumentality of 1.00), but you are indifferent to the reward (valence of 0.50). When multiplied, the result is low ($1.00 \times 1.00 \times 0.50 = 0.50$), which could be interpreted as "indifference."

To see this more concretely, let's assume that two students are quite capable of doing A work (high expectancy values) and both are studying for their final exams in management. One student has a B average in the course, the other an A− average. Assume that a strong A on the final will give the B student an A for the course. Will this student study hard for the exam? The answer depends on the values the student

FIGURE 13-6 Expectancy Model of Motivation

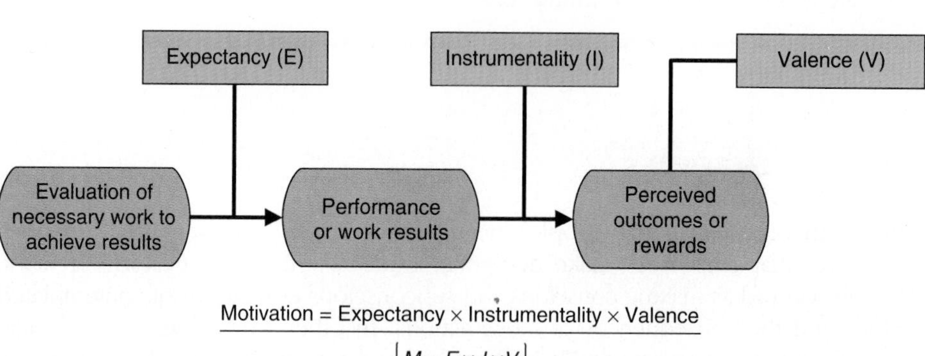

assigns to the two remaining factors. Although expectancy is high, we do not know how much faith the student has that the professor will award him an A for the course. Even if he believes an A is a good possibility (high instrumentality), he may feel that passing the course with a "decent" grade is all that matters (low valence), and go out for pizza instead of studying. Now the A− student may feel confident that if she studies, she can easily get an A for the course (high instrumentality). If that matters enough to her (high valence), she will study while the B student is out for pizza.

Of course, the issue is rarely so simple as whether to study for an exam or go out for pizza because most actions have multiple outcomes. Good performance may enhance promotion opportunities, support merit pay raises, and generate recognition and higher self-esteem. But an individual may make a trade-off when high performance that enhances rewards also leads to alienation from co-workers. In McClelland's terms, an individual high in affiliation needs will not risk alienating co-workers solely for a chance at promotion. Someone with a high need for power, however, may be willing to risk friendships for the chance to be promoted.

The implications of expectancy theory for managers have been emphasized in research by David A. Nadler and Edward E. Lawler III. Figure 13-7 shows their expanded model of expectancy. Their suggestions are summarized in the discussion below.[26]

Determine what outcomes each employee values. The first step is to find out what stimulates each employee, what rewards and outcomes he or she values. Nadler and Lawler suggest that managers can discover this by asking employees what they want from their jobs and by observing their behavior. More complex methods include analysis by consultants who correlate patterns of past behavior with reward structures.

Determine what kinds of behavior are desired. Skilled managers will not try to motivate workers until they themselves have set performance goals. Once they have defined performance objectives in measurable and observable terms, they will be able to determine what is expected by workers.

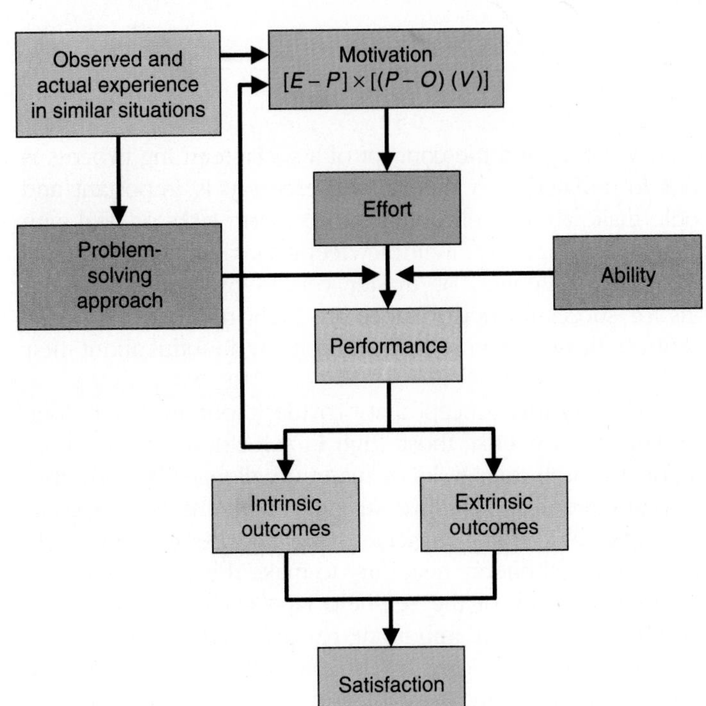

FIGURE 13-7 Simplified Expectancy Theory Model of Behavior

Source: David A. Nadler and Edward E. Lawler III, "Motivation: A Diagnostic Approach," in J. Richard Hackman, Edward E. Lawler III, and Lyman W. Porter (eds.), *Perspectives on Behavior in Organizations* (New York: McGraw-Hill, 1983), p. 75.

Asked by IBM to develop a new midrange computer, project director Tom Furey set clear expectancy goals for workers. Says Furey, "It had to be quick, so we bet the entire schedule that we could build the processor on the first pass. If we had been wrong, we'd have been dead wrong, and that would have been it for IBM in the midrange computer business." Everyone involved shared the same goal—to introduce a machine that would lead the market by 1991. Adds Furey, "We had a lot of resistance to change, but eveyone was so inspired by that simple goal that they never stopped." As a result, his team brought out the As400 in a record-breaking twenty-four months. Since its introduction four years ago, the As400 has been crucial in making IBM competitive in a critical market segment.

Make sure desired levels of performance are attainable. Expectancy theory requires that individuals be reasonably certain they can achieve the performance levels expected of them. If expectations are set too high, even the most enticing reward will be ineffective. Employees must be convinced that what is asked of them is feasible before they can become excited about potential rewards.

Link desired outcomes to desired performances. Managers must link rewards and other desired outcomes explicitly to preferred performance expectations. The linkage must be clear, well communicated, and reinforced with examples that build credibility. If rewards are extrinsic, such as bonuses, then managers must implement concrete and well-publicized payoffs. If rewards are intrinsic, such as self-esteem, then managers must create recognition factors that are obvious and equitable.

Analyze the total situation for conflicting expectancies. Considering the differences in perception among employees and the likelihood that people with different needs will be working together, it is nearly impossible to establish a reward structure that will satisfy everyone consistently. Monetary rewards that motivate one person may be a low priority for another. Esteem may motivate some individuals, but be little valued by others. Therefore, every reward system should seek to minimize negative factors and emphasize positive ones.

Make sure changes in outcomes are large enough. Unless the desired behavioral changes are trivial, rewards cannot be trivial. Since most efforts to change behavior and motivate performance are significant, managers who institute trivial rewards will only elicit employee ridicule.

Check the system for its equity. Rewards must be differentiated so that excellent performers receive more than good performers, and good performers more than poor performers. Here managers have to discard the notion of equality, unless they want all employees to do precisely the same task at precisely the same level of performance. As Nadler and Lawler suggest, equity is not equality, but fairness. The equity issue has resulted in important changes in relations between managers and employees—a topic we explore next.

Self-Efficacy

Closely related to expectancy theory and the concept of a social-learning process is *self-efficacy.* Although not formulated as a theory, **self-efficacy** is important and refers to judgments people make about their abilities to perform tasks or deal with perceived problems.[27] Individuals high in self-efficacy feel strongly that they can accomplish these tasks, take on challenges, or master certain problems. In other words, their expectations for successful performance are high, reinforced by their own self-assurance. In contrast, those low in self-efficacy remain doubtful about their capabilities.

self-efficacy
The judgments people make about their abilities to perform tasks or deal with perceived problems.

There are two implications of this concept that provide important psychological dimensions for expectancy theory. First, those high in self-efficacy are likely to put forth even greater effort to fulfill their tasks or master challenges because they have made a personal commitment and believe strongly in themselves. Second, those low in self-efficacy may give up trying to tackle many tasks because their self-doubt prevails, draining the personal energy necessary to make the commitment.

Dale Carnegie courses and many of the self-help tape and correspondence courses are designed on this concept. More important, research has found that people can be successfully trained to achieve higher levels of self-efficacy either through persuasion techniques or by helping them to establish patterns of achievement in difficult situations. Consequently, thousands of employees at companies such as Ford Motor Company and Corning Glass and athletes in both the NBA and NFL are being trained in self-efficacy.[28]

Perhaps the most important aspect of this training is the results attained through improved employee performance. Recall from Chapter 1 that we emphasized the role of *total quality management (TQM)*. TQM is a comprehensive approach to improving performance by generating a strong commitment by everyone in an organization to believe in their ability to do quality work. Self-efficacy training has provided one of the vital means for achieving TQM, and because it has been successful, companies like Compaq, First Chicago, Tenneco, and American Express have adopted similar techniques.[29] At Compaq, for example, initial results of achieving higher quality have reinforced employees' confidence in being able to improve performance, and subsequent efforts have led to even better quality. Therefore, objections to management cries for quality improvement have quickly dissolved, and resistance to new techniques or processes is minimized.

Equity Theory

Equity theory is concerned with individuals' perceptions about how fairly they are treated compared with their peers. One of the most sensitive issues in management is equity in rewarding workers' performance. Equity means fairness; motivationally, it means employees' perceived fairness of rewards or treatment at work. Perception of equitable rewards is an important link between performance and satisfaction. This is illustrated in Figure 13-8.

equity theory
A theory of motivation that suggests individuals modify their behavior based on perceptions of fair treatment and equitable rewards.

The primary research on equity theory was done in 1963 by J. Stacy Adams, who showed that perceived inequities lead to changes in behavior.[30] When individuals compare their rewards to those given to others doing similar tasks and feel inequities exist, they will react in one of the following ways:

- *Increase* their performance and work to justify higher rewards when they perceive a positive inequity—when their pay, for instance, seems too high by comparison with others.
- *Decrease* their performance and work to compensate for lower rewards when they perceive a negative inequity—when their pay, for instance, seems too low by comparison with others.
- *Change* the compensation they receive (usually when they perceive that rewards are too low) through legal or other action, or by inappropriate behavior such as misappropriation or theft.

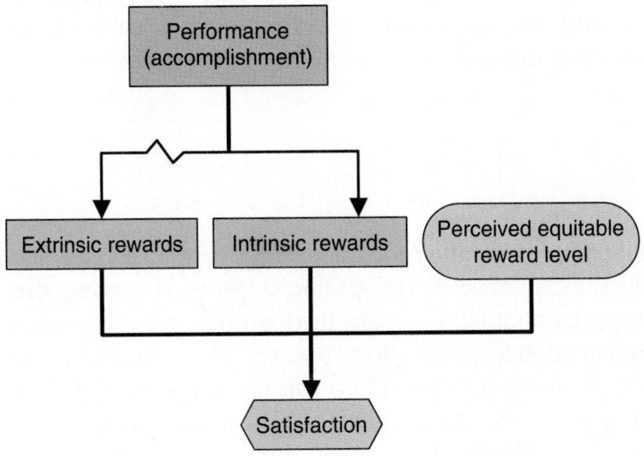

Performance (accomplishment)
Extrinsic rewards
Intrinsic rewards
Perceived equitable reward level
Satisfaction

FIGURE 13-8 Model of the Relationship of Performance to Satisfaction

Source: Edward E. Lawler III and Lyman W. Porter, "The Effects of Performance on Job Satisfaction," *Industrial Relations,* 7 (1967), pp. 20–28. Reprinted with permission.

- *Modify* their comparisons—for example, by persuading low performers who are receiving equal pay to increase their efforts or by discouraging high performers from exerting so much effort.
- *Distort* reality and psychologically rationalize that the perceived inequities are justified.
- *Leave* the inequitable situation—by quitting the organization or by changing jobs or careers—because they think inequities will not be resolved.

Inequities arise out of many different situations, and they occur in promotions, benefits, work assignments, job ratings, employee recognition, transfers, and the nuances that can make a job pleasant or unbearable. Many of these are emotionally charged, ranging from racial problems to sex discrimination. On a daily basis, even minor managerial decisions can lead to perceived inequities. Most equity issues, however, concern money. For example, merit pay raises often create inequities. Although merit pay is supposed to be an additional reward for exceptional performance, merit pay systems often distort pay relationships and create bitter comparisons among employees. A merit raise that changes the base wage rate may seem justified when awarded, yet a change in the base rate is magnified if all employees subsequently get across-the-board percentage raises; the merit employee gets the same percentage increase, but realizes an even higher wage level because the percentage is based on a higher base rate.

Merit pay illustrates another equity problem. Typically, a company puts aside a limited amount of money for merit pay or allocates only a set number of merit increases. Thus, in an organization with a hundred capable workers and only ten merit awards, ninety employees will be passed over for the merit increase. Conceivably, twenty or thirty other people could be performing meritoriously, but since there are only ten awards available, they will not be recognized. The merit awards, then, may motivate the ten best employees while irritating twice or three times as many.

The psychology of equity issues is insidious because it matters little what managers believe is fair and equitable—equity and fair play are in the minds of those affected.[31] Since human beings are not robots, there will always be differences in rewards for pay, promotion, status, recognition, and so forth. Moreover, even if all employees were given precisely the same rewards, there would still be inequities, because it is just as unfair to treat unequal employees equally as it is to treat equal employees unequally.

Consider a situation in which two people who work as computer programmers have equal experience and education and came to work for the firm simultaneously. If one is a man and receives a higher wage than the other, who is a woman, we would suspect sex discrimination. But if after we looked at their performance reviews we discovered the man's performance was rated superior, we might change our mind and acknowledge that his higher wage was justified by his better results. If, however, they had the same performance reviews, there would be a strong case for inequity. But what if the man and woman are paid exactly the same even though their performance evaluations show that one does better work than the other? Here again, an inequity exists.

Goal-Setting Theory

goal-setting theory
The process of generating commitment to tasks so that individuals have direction to their efforts with realistic expectations for success.

Expectancy theory, equity, self-efficacy, and the fundamental concept of process motivation are rooted in individual goals. Edwin Locke advanced the **goal-setting theory** as the process of generating commitment to tasks through psychological incentives for individuals who seek direction for their efforts and realistic expectations for achievements.[32] Much of what has been presented here on process theory demonstrates this concept, and in Chapter 14 on leading, goals are presented as fundamental to understanding how managers influence behavior in their employees.

Setting goals is a cognitive process by which individuals consciously think about what they want to achieve, define their tasks, and set about a fulfill their goals. In Locke's viewpoint, employees will not be motivated to perform a particular task unless they consciously know what it is they want to accomplish. Locke also emphasizes that people need to accept these goals as sufficiently important to exert the effort needed for success. By directing employees toward specific and attainable goals, managers create a robust effort of focused activity, but in order to maintain commitment, management must also provide commensurate rewards and appropriate feedback.

Locke also found that participation in goal setting by those involved in the work process resulted in higher achievement levels than when goals were assigned.[33] Employees who become participants become emotionally involved not only in setting goals but in defining how they should be achieved. When this argument is extended to organizing tasks, the concept of team management stands out, a point emphasized in Chapter 11 on group behavior. However, we also noted that not all employees work well in groups or enjoy participation, and it is equally true that organizational goals and individuals do not always coincide. Therefore, although process theories and goal-setting behavior have much to recommend them, they cannot stand apart from other concepts of motivation.

CHECKPOINT

- Describe process theory and state how it differs from content theory.
- Explain the model of expectancy theory and how expectations are related to performance.
- Explain how self-efficacy affects behavior and can reinforce the concept of total quality management.
- Define equity theory and possible reactions to inequities by employees.

REINFORCEMENT THEORY

In contrast to content and process theories, which explain behavior in terms of needs and conscious decisions about work, reinforcement theory is based on the idea that behavior results from consequences. Behavior in reinforcement terms is closely associated with consequences *learned* from past experiences. Reduced to its simplest concept, a child who has been burnt when touching a hot stove will in the future avoid touching hot stoves and be cautious around all stoves. Similarly, a child who has been consistently praised by parents for helping with housework will expect to be praised in the future when helping. Theorists recognize similar characteristics in adult behavior and suggest that employees can be motivated through a reward-and-punishment system that reinforces desired performance. Those working in the reinforcement field do not deny that individuals have needs and make their own decisions about their behavior, but maintain that it is more important to understand the reality of how environment influences behavior.[34] Figure 13-9 shows the general relationship of consequences and subsequent behavior.

Learning and Operant Conditioning

operant conditioning The process of reinforcing behavior through positive or negative consequences to condition future behavior.

At the core of reinforcement theory is **operant conditioning,** the idea that we learn through experience what to do or not to do to gain rewards or to avoid unpleasant consequences. Perhaps the most widely read and quoted researcher in this

FIGURE 13-9 Conceptual Model of Reinforcement Factors and Motivation

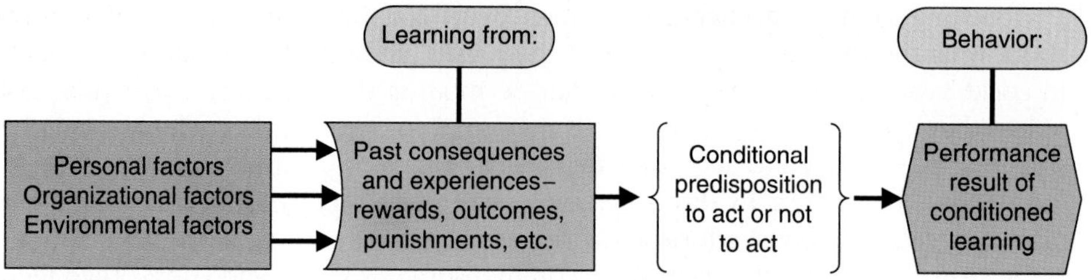

area is B. F. Skinner, who believes that reinforcement concepts are sufficient to explain all human behavior.[35] The term *operant conditioning* first appeared in the writings of the English philosopher Herbert Spencer more than a century ago, but it was E. L. Thorndike who gave substance to the concept of operant conditioning in 1911 by postulating the *law of effect,* which says that people tend to repeat behavior associated with pleasant outcomes and to avoid behavior associated with unpleasant outcomes.[36]

The logic of reinforcement theory is simple, and its advocates point out that evidence abounds throughout human history that all human beings adhere to its tenets. We learn from touching a hot stove, and we understand what is meant by electric shock after sticking a finger into a light socket. Whether or not we accept the morality of operant conditioning, we cannot avoid it. Parents reward children for good behavior and admonish them for inappropriate behavior. In education, we invoke the law of effect by awarding grades for various levels of performance. By understanding how operant conditioning works, we gain insight into how and why people behave as they do. We learn to recognize environmental stimuli and probable responses, thereby improving our ability to predict behavior.

Organization Behavior Modification

Organizations make use of operant conditioning through commissions, raises, methods of recognition, bonuses, promotions, demotions, dismissals, reprimands, and a variety of other positive and negative consequences that employees associate with work-related behavior. Performance guidelines, performance evaluations, orientation, and training programs are also used to condition employees' behavior.

organizational behavior modification (OB Mod)
The process of changing human behavior by influencing individuals through such methods as operant conditioning.

The conscious application of operant conditioning is called *behavior modification*. Extended to management, it is called **organizational behavior modification (OB Mod)**. Most OB Mod researchers focus on positive reinforcement to influence behavior and strengthen the future probabilities of desirable behavior. Milestone research was conducted at Emery Air Freight during the early 1970s, when the company took pioneering steps to apply operant conditioning to motivating changes in employee performance.[37] Emery used positive reinforcers for a three-year period to improve customer service, freight delivery systems, scheduling, and other personal services. The company saved an estimated $3 million in those three years, while improving performance in its experimental work groups by impressive margins.

Emery's initial positive reinforcers were praise, formal recognition, time off, and reassignment to pleasurable tasks for employees who improved their performance. These lost their reinforcement value after a while because employees came to see them as manipulative. Still, the experience at Emery illustrated how operant conditioning techniques can be applied in work environments.

Implementing OB Mod is a matter of choosing among four major strategies, or combining elements from them, to systematically reinforce desirable behavior while discouraging undesirable behavior.[38]

1. *Positive Reinforcement.* Rewards or other positive consequences are used to stimulate desired behavior and strengthen the probability that it will be re-

peated. Positive reinforcers may be primary or secondary. Primary reinforcers have direct beneficial consequences; they include food, water, and shelter. Secondary reinforcers bring pleasure, and may include money, promotion, and praise.

2. *Negative Reinforcement.* This strategy (also called *avoidance learning*) uses unpleasant consequences to condition individuals to avoid behaving in undesirable ways. When unpleasant consequences result from undesirable behavior, individuals learn to systematically change their patterns of behavior. In work environments, training, safety warnings, orientation sessions, and counseling alert employees to the negative consequences of undesirable behavior.
3. *Extinction.* The withdrawal of all forms of reinforcement is used to extinguish undesirable behavior. For example, an employee who picks fights and is appropriately punished by the manager may continue the behavior because of the attention it brings. By ignoring or isolating the disruptive employee, the manager withholds attention, and therefore the motivation for fighting.
4. *Punishment.* Punishment is the historic method of reducing or eliminating undesirable behavior. Organizations provide ample examples of the use of this strategy: docked pay for tardiness, suspensions, dismissals. In terms of reinforcement theory, punishment is not coercive unless it is meted out unfairly. It is crucial to differentiate between coercion, which is abusive, and punishment, which may be ethically and lawfully administered. Managers find punishment has a rather narrow range of benefits because it only reinforces what should not be done; it does not give employees clues for desirable behavior.

Implications for Management

Operant conditioning may not always be a consciously applied strategy, but just as parents attempt to modify their children's behavior through daily guidance, managers try to change their subordinates' behavior through rules, regulations, directions, incentives, and a host of subtle clues that fit one of the dominant strategies just presented. However, a conscious formal program with behavioral objectives suggests an entirely different pattern of management.

Programs relying heavily on negative reinforcement or punishment are unlikely to be popular. Nor are managers apt to appreciate having to apply these strategies. Extinction, a long-term strategy, is typically difficult to implement because managers are expected to resolve problems immediately. Therefore, most OB Mod programs have an underlying strategy of positive reinforcement. At PepsiCo, CEO D. Wayne Calloway has made a determined effort to alter how people behave toward one another. He noted that several years ago a typical response to a mistake would be "You dummy, how could you do that?" but today it is "Gee, that made sense at the time."[39]

Procedures for using positive reinforcement have been suggested by several researchers, but all generally follow the process of OB Mod intervention illustrated in Figure 13-10 and developed by Fred Luthans and Robert Kreitner.[40]

- *Identify* behavior that is desirable and undesirable. Initially, managers are more likely to focus on undesirable behavior because problems tend to trigger their attention.
- *Measure* consequences and monitor behavior over a reasonable period of time to identify what might be causing or sustaining behavior. By ascertaining how desirable behavior is stimulated, managers enhance their chances of developing a program of behavioral modification.
- *Analyze* patterns of continued behavior that require modification. Analysis should give managers insight into individual differences in behavior. If it also

At General Electric's Answer Center in Louisville, Kentucky, ten "coaches" record the more than 14,000 telephone queries from potential appliance buyers and do-it-yourself fixers answered daily by 200 GE agents. The supervisors then replay selected parts of the conversations to the agents to help them improve the quality of their communication with the public. As measured by outside survey companies, "silent monitoring" has resulted in 96 percent Answer Center customer satisfaction. Another positive outcome: GE often does not have to send repair people to fix products under warranty.

results in an inventory of positive reinforcers, the next step in the process—intervention—will be greatly simplified.

- *Intervene* through a systematic strategy of changing behavior. Monitoring will improve managers' control over the change process by validating how and why behavior changes occur. Intervention may require outside professional help or a long-term commitment to training.
- *Evaluate* both effective and ineffective strategies. During the evaluation process, cost and benefit trade-offs that moderate or accelerate programs may become apparent. Organizations often try to emulate successful programs in other firms, but comparisons may be significantly different because circumstances and work environments vary widely among organizations. Evaluating circumstances is therefore as important as monitoring behavioral consequences.

FIGURE 13-10 Pattern of OB Mod Intervention

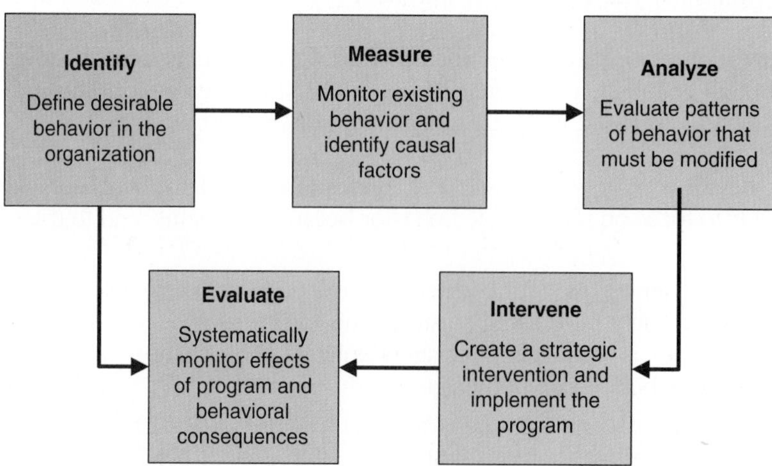
Identify
Define desirable behavior in the organization
Measure
Monitor existing behavior and identify causal factors
Analyze
Evaluate patterns of behavior that must be modified
Intervene
Create a strategic intervention and implement the program
Evaluate
Systematically monitor effects of program and behavioral consequences

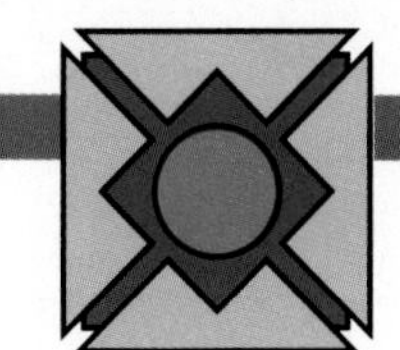

ETHICS IN MANAGEMENT

Redirecting Behavior at General Electric

More than just a quality improvement program or an effort to increase productivity, GE's comprehensive human resource training system is designed to permanently redirect employee behavior toward a common vision of striving for perfection. Located near Crotonville, New York, GE's Management Development Institute (MDI) has been called the greatest effort to change behavior since the Cultural Revolution. CEO Jack Welch instigated the MDI concept as part of his corporate strategy to reposition GE's 500 business interests into high-growth global markets as premiere quality leaders. Hiring top business school professors and tapping industry consultants and specialists, MDI provides multiple tiers of intense training and development in areas ranging from fundamental business problems in supervision to creating strategic global alliances.

GE managers are expected to work for about six months in a new position before attending the institute so they will have time to acclimate themselves to management responsibilities or, if they are newcomers to GE, to assimilate company expectations. When they are assigned to development training programs, they begin with a "starter kit" of more than eighty problems to study. Working in groups led by consulting facilitators, participants are expected to resolve these problems. Most importantly, they are expected to do so through an almost aggressive form of problem-solving behavior. There are no barriers to voicing opinions, no boss-employee structures, no limits to creativity or imagination. The expected result is simply to find the best answer and to defend it.

One specific program called Work-Out, also conceived by Welch, forces managers into high-stress decision-making roles where they face critical problems and have to devise creative solutions. Participants are formed into teams, presented with problem situations, and then told to find solutions. They are given all the technical and information assistance they need, but few guidelines. The stark reality of a no-holds-barred pressure situation was compared by one manager to taking a bath in ice water. Many managers find themselves behaving in ways they never did before. "When you've been told to shut up for twenty years, and someone tells you to speak up—you're going to let them have it," explained one newly promoted manager. Another manager, also promoted after years with GE, said, "I was wringing wet within half an hour."

The GE program currently serves more than 3,000 company managers each year and expects to soon double that number, drawing participants from outside organizations. More than 50,000 employees have now been involved in these programs. Although it is too early to assess the results, participants strongly agree that the system works. They have some apprehension, however, that their individual values have been restructured to conform to a "company line" that may be great for GE but has high personal costs.

Sources: Janet Guyon, "Culture Class: GE's Management School Aims to Foster Unified Corporate Roles," *Wall Street Journal,* August 10, 1987, p. 29. See also Thomas A. Stewart, "GE Keeps Those Ideas Coming," *Fortune,* August 12, 1991, pp. 41–45, 48–49.

The Controversy over OB Mod

Although a growing body of evidence suggests that OB Mod programs work, they are quite controversial.[41] Some people question whether we have the right to control another person's behavior. The most common response to this criticism is that control is natural from the time we are born. We all live in a Skinnerian world of operant conditioning in which we are constantly responding to circumstantial consequences (jumping back when we accidentally touch a hot stove) or to intended stimuli (slowing down when we drive past a police car). Consequently, managers have the responsibility to control behavior; those who refuse to do so are ignoring their responsibilities.

Critics of OB Mod also question the use of operant conditioning to alter people's behavior on the grounds that these techniques infringe on free will. They argue that managers can accomplish the same objectives through improved communication processes, training, and other nonintervention programs that respect human freedom while encouraging individuals to modify their behavior for their own welfare. Advocates of OB Mod reply that organizations are, by definition, systems of control in which individuals agree to behavioral parameters. Thus, when employees accept jobs, they are fully aware of the control that will be exerted to accomplish objectives in the collective environment.

OB Mod and other dimensions of motivation theory will continue to stir controversy. Most arguments about motivation revolve around what degree of control is needed to accomplish organizational objectives and how individual rights and human dignity are to be protected.

In conclusion, there is the important question of how well versed managers are in any motivational technique. Certainly, some managers are educated in the concepts of OB Mod or the nuances of behavioral intervention, but most managers have neither the educational background nor the experience to implement complicated behavioral techniques. Consequently, companies that introduce new systems of incentives or programs aimed at changing employee behavior must be careful not to create a manipulative environment that results only in ridicule. As we shall see in the next chapter, resolving these problems is partly a matter of having effective, well-trained, and capable leaders in management positions.

CHECKPOINT

- Describe how learned consequences are related to reinforcement theory.
- What are operant conditioning and the law of effect?
- Discuss OB Mod in terms of positive and negative reinforcers.
- Argue for and against OB Mod intervention by managers.

RECALL from the beginning of the chapter that Delta Air Line's chairman Ronald Allen defended his company against the charge of having sloppy "good-ol'-boy" management by saying Delta has enlightened managers who try to motivate employees to take individual initiative. Allen did agree with FAA authorities that Delta's pilots may have been allowed to make too many decisions, yet he defended the company's policy of encouraging high expectations for performance, and then rewarding employees who perform up to expectations with high pay and bonuses. In addition, Delta rewards employees intrinsically through recognition systems, work autonomy, and long-term career development programs. The result is an organization of motivated and loyal employees. ■

A SYNOPSIS FOR LEARNING

1. Define the concept of motivation and discuss its implications for productivity.

   Motivation is the process of stimulating employees to perform better in the pursuit of organizational objectives. It results partly from a conscious process of influencing persistent and constructive behavior by addressing individual needs and reinforcing activities that enhance employee satisfaction, partly from work-related behavior initiated by the individual through self-generated drives, and partly from environmental factors. When employees want to perform better and are better satisfied with their results, organizational productivity will improve through higher-quality products and services.

2. Discuss and contrast the three major approaches to motivation.

   The three major approaches to motivation are *content, process,* and *reinforcement* theories. Content theorists argue that motivation comes from within an individual via needs and desires that can be consciously addressed by managers. Process theorists argue that behavior is the result of expectations about work and rewards; employees decide how to behave on the basis of their perceptions of relationships between work, rewards, and the importance of rewards. In contrast to content and process theories, which focus on people's perceptions and needs, reinforcement theory is based on conditioning people to respond to the consequences of their behavior.

3. Describe content theory and the concept of perceived needs for motivation.

   Psychological and physiological needs motivate individuals to act to fulfill them and seek satisfaction. Content theorists study how managers can motivate employees to fulfill perceived needs. In content theory, understanding motivation consists largely of recognizing patterns of need and then encouraging behavior that results in satisfying those patterns.

4. Explain process theory and the concepts of expectancy and equity.

   Process theory emphasizes that employees make decisions about their work performance. Personal expectations of performance outcomes are critical for determining how to motivate employees. Expectancy theorists believe that individuals make work-related decisions based on their perceived abilities to perform tasks and to receive rewards, both of which are influenced by how important the tasks and rewards are to the employees. Equity theorists study individuals' perceptions about how fair their treatment is compared with their peers' treatment.

5. Describe reinforcement theory and issues fundamental to operant conditioning, and discuss the controversy about the ethics of motivation and behavior modification.

   Reinforcement theory proposes that people learn from past experiences to behave in ways that lead to rewards and avoid punishments. Operant conditioning implies a consistent replication of consequences (rewards or punishments) for behavior so that we become conditioned to them in similar circumstances. Organizational behavior modification (OB Mod) is the process of using reinforcement methods to alter work-related behavior. The controversy involves purposeful efforts to modify behavior by managers. Some managers may be incapable of making constructive modifications, and their efforts may be manipulative, which is ethically negative.

SKILL ANALYSIS

CASE 1 Building Relationships in the Best Companies

Herman Miller, the furniture maker in Zeeland, Michigan, has a reputation for unusual designs, award-winning furniture, and highly motivated employees (see the chapter-framing story for Chapter 11.) To bolster that reputation, the company has made a strong commitment to protecting the environment through employee-led public support programs and campaigns to reduce industrial waste. Now Herman Miller has stopped using all wood from tropical rain forests where endangered species such as rosewood are rapidly disappearing. Consequently, the company's designers are concentrating on commercially available woods for office desks, chairs, and accessories. Employees talk with pride about working for Herman Miller, and they take greater pride in trying to extend the environmental concept to using new production methods and fewer materials in furniture making and to producing quality products with less waste.

At Merck & Company, one of the nation's largest pharmaceutical firms, chairman Roy Vagelos speaks to applauding students at top universities about the wonderful discoveries being made in medicines and drugs at his company. Unlike many other companies in the industry, Merck has a reputation as a cost-effective producer of drugs and is the most admired corporation in the United States. Top scientists from competitors and top graduates from Harvard, Yale, and MIT are lured to Merck, and once hired, they rarely leave. This is no surprise to industry analysts, who ask rhetorically: "Why wouldn't anyone want to work for the best company in the world?" One policy that makes Merck so good is that all managers are compensated and rewarded for their ability to hire and retain top-notch employees. Motivated managers and a very high employee retention rate, coupled with Merck's excellent reputation result in continued improvements in the company's work environment and its profile of innovations. The results, in turn, reinforce Merck's reputation and staff motivation.

Levi Strauss has a global reputation for quality products, and even in those countries where "yankees" are pointedly asked to "go home," Levi's jeans are one Yankee product that is enthusiastically prized. The company's marketers never receive a rude welcome, either at home or abroad, and they have no trouble touting their products. Employees at Levi Strauss are encouraged to be innovative, and the company's most recent new product, Naturals, resulted from employee experiments with natural cotton fabrics that needed no chemical dyeing process. The Naturals are a line of cotton jeans made of natural fibers whose color doesn't fade but intensifies with age. The company's designers reaped a comfortable bonus for their work, but more important, they joined a company elite who are recognized for their contributions through public awards. Levi's marketers, who do not have the opportunity to spur unusual product development, get strong reinforcement from company executives for establishing strong ties with retailers. The company expects marketing representatives to build lasting relationships, and they are compensated for repeat sales and long-term patronage. Executives also spend much time on the shop floor with production employees, just being sociable and listing to what their people have to say. Consequently, employees feel that their work is important and that what they have to say is heard and appreciated.

Merck, Herman Miller, and Levi Strauss lead their industries and are among the most admired companies in America. Each company has an unusual reputation for quality products, excellent managers, and motivated employees—who seldom aspire to work anywhere else.

Case Questions

1. Describe how each company in this case has developed intrinsic and extrinsic motivators to enhance performance.

2. Explain how rewards in each company might be viewed by individuals who, in McClelland's terms, are power-, achievement-, or affiliation-oriented.
3. Identify and explain the needs that are being met by managers in each company. What are the implications for expectancy theory as related to employee perceptions in each company?

Sources: Susan Caminiti, "The Payoff from a Good Reputation," *Fortune,* February 10, 1992, pp. 74–77; Gordon Bock, "Merck's Medicine Man," *Time,* February 22, 1988, pp. 44–45; and Edwin M. Epstein, "The Corporate Social Policy Process: Beyond Business Ethics, Corporate Responsibility, and Corporate Social Responsiveness," *California Management Review,* Spring 1987, pp. 99–114.

VIDEO CASE The Daddy Track

Home. Office. Balancing the demands of the two has become a lot more difficult for women *and* men. As more and more women have gone into the work force, men have had to pick up some of the duties at home. Men are finding out what working women have long known—that home and family responsibilities and office responsibilities often conflict. Balancing these demands satisfactorily can be next to impossible, and people often must sacrifice family time, career time, or some of both. What happens to working dads when they opt for spending more time with their kids and less time fighting their way up the corporate ladder?

American men have always been programmed to believe that they could not make it on the fast career track and be a strong family man at the same time. Achieving success in corporate America demands hard work and long hours. In fact, as one executive recruiter stated, "the fact of life is that—and my firm represents 1,250 major corporations in the United States—the fact of life is that senior executives cannot accommodate easily and for any length of time the [career] track and the 'Daddy track' or the 'Mommy track.'" The pressure to get the job done is strong, and getting on the dual track—one track career and the other track parenthood—only slows down career advancement. "The traditional perception in senior management is that anyone, any man who would want to . . . take time out from [his] job to take paternal leave can't really be that serious about [his] career," says one dad who did take time off from his job as a bond trader when his first child was born. In fact, many men are faced with what James Levine from The Fatherhood Project calls "the invisible dilemma"—the conflict between work and family and the steps men feel compelled to take to hide it.

Yet a national survey conducted during the summer of 1991 showed that 70 percent of male respondents said they would accept a slower career path in exchange for more family time. Many men would be willing to give up promotions to have more time to spend with their kids. However, most companies do not provide any paternity leave at all. The government has not mandated it, and fewer than 20 percent of big- and medium-sized companies offer unpaid time off for working fathers. American business is only slowly beginning to recognize the dilemma of working fathers.

One organization that has made progressive strides toward reducing the conflicts between the workplace and the home is the Du Pont Company. Du Pont feels that it can be more competitive in the marketplace by helping its employees cope with the stresses and realities of day-to-day life in the 1990s. The company has been conducting research on the issues of families and work for over six years and has discovered that employees want company understanding of office-family conflicts and also flexible work schedules. "Our men tell us, increasingly, they want the flexibility to be with their families. They're still committed to their careers, but they need to be with their kids." However, even at Du Pont, all has not gone smoothly in allowing men and women to choose less demanding career paths. There has been resistance, primarily at the middle-management level, which fears it may lose control over employees allowed to take the parent track. Yet top-management commitment remains very strong. Says one Du Pont official, "I think the most important thing is to be connected to what it is your people and your company want. I think if we neglect that, we're building our business enterprise on sand. We need to understand the complex lives people lead today. We need to offer the flexibility to allow them to lead that life and, at the same time, contribute to the company." Perhaps companies will allow working men and women to choose the path they want to take in the future.

Case Questions

1. Can innovations like the "Daddy track" motivate employees? If not, why not? If so, how?
2. Explain the motivational benefits of the "Daddy track" from the point of view of the content, process, and reinforcement theories.
3. What is the Du Pont Company doing to meet the needs of its employees?

Sources: Keith H. Hammonds, William C. Symonds, and Robert Barker, "Taking Baby Steps Toward a Daddy Track," *Business Week,* April 15, 1991, p. 90ff; Dyan Machan, "The Mommy and Daddy Track," *Forbes,* April 16 1990, p. 162ff; and Joseph A. McKenna, "The Daddy Track: A Road-Condition Report," *Industry Week,* March 5, 1990, p. 11ff.

SKILL PRACTICE

WOMEN AS MANAGERS: THE WOMEN AS MANAGERS SCALE (WAMS)

Introduction

Stereotypes influence our thinking even when we have increasing amounts of specific information at our disposal. The use of stereotypes makes our thinking patterns "easier" and faster because it lets us bypass many details about real people and events. Our minds prefer to deal in categories rather than in actual cases. Consider: Southern Baptist preacher, Boston banker, forest ranger, female taxi driver. These are *categories,* not actual people, yet when asked for characteristics of any of these labels, people produce a long list of attributes, both positive and negative.

Instructions

The following items represent an attempt to assess the attitudes people have about women in business. The best answer to each statement is your *personal opinion.* The statements cover many different and opposing points of view; you may find yourself agreeing strongly with some of the statements, disagreeing just as strongly with others, and perhaps uncertain about others. Whether you agree or disagree with any statement, you can be sure that many people feel the same way you do.

Using the numbers from 1 to 7 on the rating scale, mark your personal opinion about each statement in the blank that immediately precedes it. Remember, give your *personal opinion* according to how much you agree or disagree with each item. Please respond to all 21 items.

RATING SCALE

1 = Strongly Disagree
2 = Disagree
3 = Slightly Disagree
4 = Neither Disagree nor Agree
5 = Slightly Agree
6 = Agree
7 = Strongly Agree

_______ 1. It is less desirable for women than for men to have a job that requires responsibility.

_______ 2. Women have the objectivity required to evaluate business situations properly.

_______ 3. Challenging work is more important to men than it is to women.

_______ 4. Men and women should be given equal opportunity for participation in management training programs.

_______ 5. Women have the capability to acquire the necessary skills to be successful managers.

_______ 6. On the average, women managers are less capable of contributing to the organization's overall goals than are men.

_______ 7. It is not acceptable for women to assume leadership roles as often as men.

_______ 8. The business community should someday accept women in key managerial positions.

_______ 9. Society should regard work by female managers as valuable as work by male managers.

_______ 10. It is acceptable for women to compete with men for top executive positions.

_______ 11. The possibility of pregnancy does not make women less desirable employees than men.

_______ 12. Women would no more allow their emotions to influence their managerial behavior than would men.

_______ 13. Problems associated with menstruation should not make women less desirable than men as employees.

_______ 14. To be a successful executive, a woman does not have to sacrifice some of her femininity.

_______ 15. On the average, a woman who stays at home all the time with her children is a better mother than a woman who works outside the home at least half time.

_______ 16. Women are less capable of learning mathematical and mechanical skills than are men.

_______ 17. Women are not ambitious enough to be successful in the business world.

_______ 18. Women cannot be assertive in business situations that demand it.

_______ 19. Women possess the self-confidence required of a good leader.

_______ 20. Women are not competitive enough to be successful in the business world.

_______ 21. Women cannot be aggressive in business situations that demand it.

Once you have responded to an item, do not change your answer.

Now go back into the chapter and read the section titled "Equity Theory." After reading this section, review your responses to the survey. Would you change any of your answers? (Do not change any at this time.)

Your instructor will divide the class into small groups of three or four persons each. Your task as a group is to come up with a mutually satisfactory set of responses to the questions you answered earlier as individuals. You will have only *thirty-five minutes* to do this, so the groups must work as rapidly and sincerely as possible.

Source: L. H. Peters, J. T. Terborg, and J. Taynor, "Women as Managers Scale (WAMS)" (ms. no. 585). *Journal Supplement Abstract Service* (APA), 1974.

14

Leadership: Influencing Behavior for Excellence

OUTLINE

The Leadership Process
- Defining Leadership
- Leadership Power and Influence
- Leadership Acceptance
- Reciprocal Leadership Processes

Leadership Traits

Leadership Styles
- A Basic Model
- System 4 Management
- Choosing a Leadership Style
- The Managerial Grid

Contingency Leadership
- Fiedler's Contingency Theory
- House's Path-Goal Theory
- Implications of Path-Goal Leadership
- The Vroom-Yetton Theory
- The Hersey and Blanchard Life Cycle Theory

Multicultural and Transformational Leadership: Current Challenges
- Managing in a Multicultural Environment
- Transformational Leadership
- Leadership in Perspective

OBJECTIVES

- Explain leadership and behavioral relationships in organizations.
- Identify and discuss traits and characteristics of effective leaders.
- Describe and contrast major theories on leadership. Discuss the Blake and Mouton Managerial Grid.
- Discuss how motivation and leadership are interrelated and explain the role of decision making in effective leadership.
- Describe the multicultural environment and transformational leadership as critical management issues.

ROBERT HORTON, managing director of British Petroleum, is turning his company around through dynamic leadership.[1] British Petroleum had been a plodding giant, losing enough money every day to feed a tenth of London's population. After being sold to private interests, BP management began repositioning its $56 billion in assets and expanding into profitable markets.[2]

In 1986, BP gained a controlling interest in Standard Oil Company of Ohio and sent Horton to Cleveland to run the company. Within two years, Horton had reversed huge losses, expanded sales, and reorganized management. He won acclaim from employees for being an inspired and motivated leader.

In 1988, Horton was recalled to London as BP's chief executive. What he found was a hollow company devoid of leadership, long on useless debate, and crippled by inefficiency. BP was the world's third-largest publicly traded oil company, but it was in decline. Horton concluded that the company's problem was not lack of oil or money, but unmotivated employees led by uninterested managers. His first move was to trim BP's headquarters from 2,400 to less than 1,400 managers and staff. Those who remained were carefully evaluated for potential leadership skills.

Horton then selected a seven-person team, mainly younger managers, to "learn how the real world operated." The team talked with experts in management education like Peter Drucker and top-notch executives, including Jack Welch, chairman of GE, and John Akers, CEO of IBM. Team members visited hundreds of companies and viewed first-hand how many of BP's global divisions were being operated. Horton's team then sat down with BP's top executives and redefined the company's organization. They eliminated 80 of the 86 corporate committees, pushed spending decisions down into the company's structure, and began building a participative environment. Horton introduced a program for nearly all employees to discuss change, cooperative work methods, and goal-directed leadership.

Feedback from BP's people shows that by 1992 they believed Horton was sincere about creating a sense of "empowered leadership" in everyone working at the company. One executive said, "What this is all about is the simple belief that our people know more about their jobs than their bosses and their bosses' boss."

THE LEADERSHIP PROCESS

Leadership is one of the most important elements of management. We have all experienced behavioral relationships with leaders, and many of us have been in leadership roles ourselves. Yet describing the leadership process can be very difficult. Management researchers, however, have succeeded in identifying patterns of leadership behavior that provide some insight into how managers influence their employees. In this chapter, we present the work of prominent researchers and the better-known models of leadership as they relate to personal interactions between managers and their subordinates in formal organizations.

Defining Leadership

leadership
The process of influencing others to behave in preferred ways to accomplish organizational objectives.

Leadership is the process of influencing other people to behave in preferred ways to accomplish organizational objectives. Robert Blake and Jane Mouton explained leadership as the managerial activity that maximizes productivity, stimulates creative problem solving, and promotes morale and satisfaction.[3] Although many researchers, historians, and philosophers have tried to explain how great men and women have persuaded people to follow them in their endeavors, we are still searching for an unambiguous definition of leadership. The definition offered here emphasizes a *process of influencing behavior,* a *stimulating effect* on group and individual performance. The basic process of leadership is shown in Figure 14-1. Exactly how this process works is unclear, but in centuries past, theorists believed leaders were born with the gift of persuasion. Although most reputable theorists today no longer subscribe to the belief that "leaders are born," they recognize that some individuals have more potential than others as influential leaders. They also recognize that leadership skills can be learned. Consequently, leadership studies focus on developing these skills in managers to improve organizational effectiveness.

In today's sprawling organizations, leadership implies a system of inequalities in which superiors influence subordinates and modify or redirect behavior in groups to satisfy a wide variety of objectives. Often those objectives are personal, such as the individual needs discussed in the previous chapter. More frequently, they are social, such as the need for harmonious conditions at work.

Focusing on a system of inequalities in which there are many individuals involved with varied objectives does not yield a satisfactory definition of leadership. Researchers who have examined hundreds of leadership studies conclude that there are almost as many definitions as definers.[4] Leadership remains an enigma, yet one common thread among the definitions is that it is a social-influence process.

Leadership Power and Influence

The social nature of leadership is explained in terms of the *influence* one person has over others. Recall from Chapter 10 that formal authority vested in managers creates a source of power. Based on this source of power, superiors influence subordinates, directing their efforts toward fulfilling organizational objectives. Our discussion in Chapter 10 then went on to distinguish how authority is structured and

FIGURE 14–1 Leadership: A Basic Process

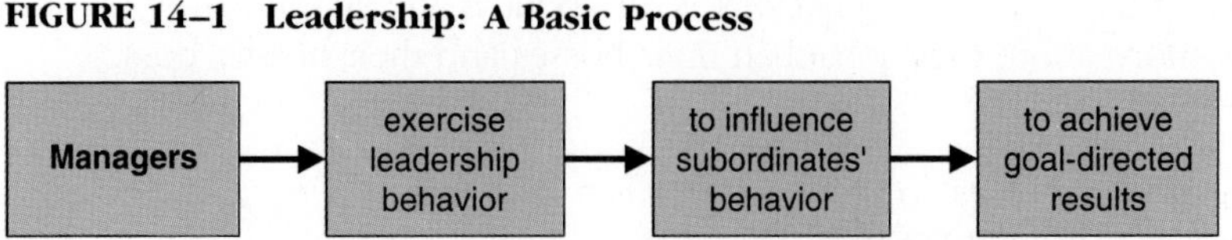

delegated to different degrees, allowing subordinates more or less participation in making decisions. Now we need to distinguish between the terms *power* and *authority* as they relate to leadership and the ability of managers to influence behavior.

As we saw in Chapter 10, *authority* is the culmination of formal rights, duties, and responsibilities associated with a position of management. In contrast, **power** is the "force" or ability to influence others, and in an organizational context, that means the ability to influence behavior to accomplish preferred results. As we shall see, power can exist separate from authority, and although authority may be a source of power, it is only one way that managers can be influential. Power (and therefore influence) is defined according to five sources. These are summarized in Exhibit 14-1 and described below.[5]

power
The ability to influence others' behavior to accomplish preferred results.

Legitimate power. Also called *formal authority,* **legitimate power** is the right to manage based on the concept of property rights. Business owners are presumed to have a legitimate right to command employees, and if owners delegate authority, they also delegate some degree of property rights to command. These prerogatives are less clear in complex organizations, where diversified stock ownership is separate from management, and in public organizations such as schools, where the owners are the taxpayers. Essentially, though, managers act in proxy positions representing owners, and the power of these proxy positions diminishes as companies become larger and authority becomes more widely diffused.

legitimate power
Also called *formal authority,* it is the right to manage derived from delegation based on ownership or property rights.

Expert power. Many people are powerful because they are experts in their fields. In their case, having a position of authority is unnecessary to influence other people. Nevertheless, managers who have the technical skills, education, or competency to influence behavior augment their legitimate power with **expert power.** The critical point is that employees recognize this expertise and are willing to be influenced by a person they perceive as having superior knowledge or ability.

expert power
The ability to lead others and influence behavior based on perceived expertise or special knowledge.

Referent power. The ability of someone to generate in others a sense of personal respect and admiration is called **referent power.** We say that these leaders have *charisma,* and consequently, we feel comfortable listening to their advice or devoting ourselves to their ideas. Abraham Lincoln is remembered as an intensely sensitive man who was burdened by the Civil War, yet was able to inspire others to do great things. John F. Kennedy's image as a charismatic, youthful, cavalier president persists thirty years after his death. Martin Luther King, Jr., remains the champion of civil rights whose ideas continue to influence thousands of people. Unfortunately, Adolf Hitler and Saddam Hussein also qualify as charismatic leaders. Although we deplore the results of their leadership, we must recognize their referent power. The ability to inspire allegiance does not imply a beneficial use of that power.

referent power
The ability to generate in others a sense of admiration and devotion; often associated with charisma.

Coercive power. Based on the ability to instill fear, **coercive power** is the capability to punish or withhold rewards, thereby inflicting pain. Fear of physical harm is of little concern to most employees in the civilized world because we have devel-

coercive power
The capability to punish, rather than reward, or to withhold rewards to influence preferred behavior; power based on fear and force.

EXHIBIT 14-1 Power Sources in Organizations

Legitimate	Stems from authority of ownership and delegated responsibilities.
Expert	Depends on perceived skills and appropriate expertise in tasks.
Referent	Charismatic power derived from the ability to create devotion and allegiance.
Coercive	Relies on force and fear of reprisals, both physical and economic.
Reward	Includes compensation, promotion, esteem, expectations, and recognition.

oped safeguards and legal penalties to prevent such abuse. Managers can, however, inflict punishment through disciplinary rule, reprisals such as withholding pay raises, and psychological pressure such as public ridicule or humiliation.

reward power
The ability to influence behavior by controlling rewards in a positive, motivating way.

Reward power. Because people work for gains, managers can influence employee behavior with **reward power.** Gains include rewards such as pay raises, bonuses, and economic benefits, but they can also be praise or recognition for quality work, career opportunities, promotions, and subtle means of psychological reinforcement that make the work environment pleasant. Recall from Chapter 13 that we emphasized the power of rewards to motivate behavior, either through reinforcement (operant conditioning) or through expectations (expectancy theory).

Leadership Acceptance

Although managers have the potential to be influential through the legitimate power associated with their positions of authority, subordinates often behave indifferently, resisting managers' efforts to influence them. Indifference to the other four power sources is also common. No source of power has meaning if employees refuse to *accept it* as meaningful. You cannot induce someone to work for a raise if money is not important to that person, nor can you coerce someone with a threat if he or she thinks you lack the ability to carry it out.

Chester I. Barnard wrote about acceptance in 1938. He suggested that the extent to which orders are obeyed and workers perform rests on the degree of *acceptance* by workers of a manager's authority.[6] In this view, influence is not the result of the degree of authority passed downward, but instead a function of acceptance from the bottom up. Influence, then, rests with subordinates.

zone of indifference
A concept articulated by Chester Barnard that implies a range of acceptance by subordinates to orders with few objections. Beyond the zone, subordinates are no longer indifferent and object to orders.

Barnard used the term **zone of indifference,** shown graphically in Figure 14-2, to illustrate his concept. In his view, each subordinate perceives how far a manager can go when issuing orders. When managers ask subordinates to do something that falls routinely within this zone, they have no problem accepting the order. However, when subordinates perceive an order to be outside the zone, they are no longer indifferent and may refuse to carry it out. The range of acceptance depends greatly on a subordinate's perceptions, a manager's ability to gain acceptance, and the particular work environment.

Barnard's zone is flexible. A manager can broaden it—thus encouraging greater acceptance by employees—by becoming more skilled, better liked, more ad-

FIGURE 14-2 Conceptual Model of Barnard's Zone of Indifference

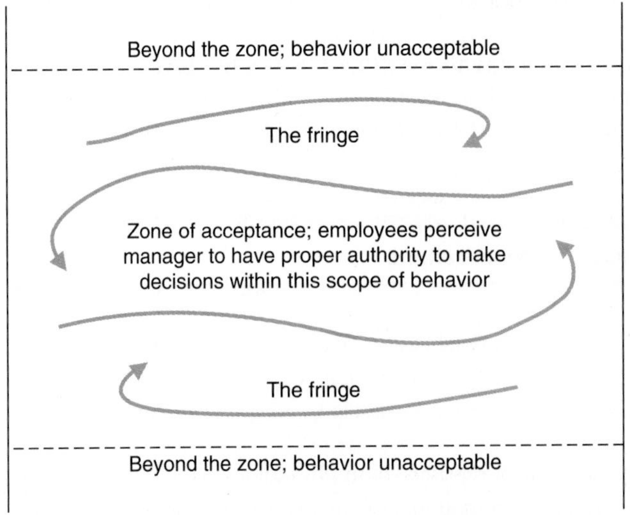

mired as a charismatic leader, or better able to provide rewards. A manager can quickly narrow the zone by losing credibility or becoming less able to provide expected rewards. For example, Edwin L. Artzt, chairman of Procter & Gamble, is getting mixed reviews for his behavior. After becoming CEO in 1990, Artzt introduced a no-nonsense style of command that often extends to outright rudeness. He has ridiculed top division managers in public and "taken apart people limb from limb" over minor faults, according to a top P&G manager. Artzt, who calls his approach "combat conditioning," expects his managers to be equally aggressive. He has revitalized P&G, improved profits, and expanded rapidly into new foreign markets. He has also created new career opportunities, promoted more employees, improved compensation and benefits, and instilled new pride in a company that was faltering. Some managers have left P&G, others avoid Artzt or merely tolerate his behavior, but many strongly support him, citing his contributions and expertise.[7]

Mismanagement shrinks the zone of acceptance. Consistently asking employees to do more than expected (to work outside the zone) will increase their resistance to authority. They will then become less tolerant of all management directives. Similarly, flaunting authority can annoy subordinates and shrink the zone. Also, anytime an employee feels harassed or imposed upon, the zone shrinks.

Reciprocal Leadership Processes

If the essence of leadership is influencing others, then leadership is impossible without followers. Gary Yukl has pointed out that influence between leaders and followers does not move in one direction, but is reciprocal.[8] At any given moment, the leader or the follower may be either the "agent" or the "target" of influence, though in business situations the agent will usually be the higher-ranking individual. Yukl has refined the explanations of the five sources of power into three broad categories that depend on an individual's (1) position in an organization, or *position power;* (2) personal attributes and relationships with others, or *personal power* (the same as referent power); and (3) ability to influence political processes in the organization, or *political power.* Exhibit 14-2 lists some of the components of these three basic sources of power.

The idea of the reciprocity of power and influence points out the dynamic, rather than static, nature of leading. The components of the three basic sources of power are always in flux, and the effective manager can draw on each of them as necessitated by the power relationship. At the same time, the follower must be willing to be influenced. In effect, therefore, leadership status is earned through an *ex-*

EXHIBIT 14–2 Components of Power in Organizations

Position Power	Formal authority Control over resources and rewards Control over punishments Control over information Control over workplace environment
Personal Power	Expertise Friendship/loyalty Charisma
Political Power	Control over decision processes Coalitions Gaining participation of opponents Institutionalization

Source: Adapted from Gary Yukl, *Leadership in Organizations,* 2nd ed. Copyright 1989, p. 14. Reprinted by permission of Prentice Hall, Englewood Cliffs, N.J.

change relationship that exists between leaders and the subordinates they seek to influence. As this relationship develops, either a growing and fruitful leader-follower association is cultivated, or a deteriorating relationship unfolds wherein managers have little influence and employees have little interest in their performance.

Although good leader-follower relationships and subordinate acceptance are necessary elements of leadership, they do not provide adequate explanations of it. A growing body of research illustrates that descriptions of leadership must take account of individual situations and contingencies. Mike Ditka, head coach for the Chicago Bears, is known for his absolute command of the football field, yet in private life, he is portrayed as a supportive individual who goes to great lengths to accommodate others' opinions. Football Hall of Famer Mel Blount, reknowned for his apparent cruelty as a Pittsburgh Steeler quarterback, has a second career working with disadvantaged children as a counselor, and today his reputation is one of patience and gentle persuasion.[9] Situations and circumstances often dictate behavior.

As we shall see, behavioral science helps us to understand when leadership is effective and when it is not, and how people behave in various circumstances. In the next few sections, we will explore leadership *traits* and leadership *styles*–two distinctly different approaches taken by behavioral scientists to help explain how managers exert influence.

CHECKPOINT

- Explain why leadership in organizations implies a system of inequalities.
- Differentiate between power and authority.
- Identify and explain the five primary sources of managerial power.
- How does acceptance theory reverse the influence process?
- What is the exchange relationship between superiors and subordinates?

LEADERSHIP TRAITS

Individuals become leaders by demonstrating their capabilities for eliciting results-oriented actions—not, as many people believe, by being born to a particular culture, race, creed, or sex, or by possessing a unique blend of personal characteristics.[10] Few contemporary theorists disagree with these conclusions, yet only a half century ago, in Nazi Germany, leadership was thought to be the right of a superhuman race. Even today in America, we revere our TV heroes for their physical prowess and our heroines for their beauty, revealing our propensity to believe physical attributes are related to leadership ability. Many of us also cling to archaic biases about sex and race roles for leaders and subordinates.

In trying to isolate traits common to many leaders, researchers have focused on performance rather than on personal characteristics. The need for achievement, expressed as a desire for occupational success and responsibility, is high on this list. Self-assurance, or a feeling of competency in problem-solving situations, is another common trait. Intelligence—the effective use of judgment, reasoning skills, and creative abilities—is yet another. Decisiveness is also regarded as an important factor. Finally, supervisory skill in managing the functions of planning, organizing, directing, and controlling is crucial.[11]

Some argue that these behavioral traits broadly define the entire management function and therefore have little value for differentiating effective from ineffective leadership. Proponents of this viewpoint suggest that managers attain their status in organizations only after influencing others and effecting changes, so successful lead-

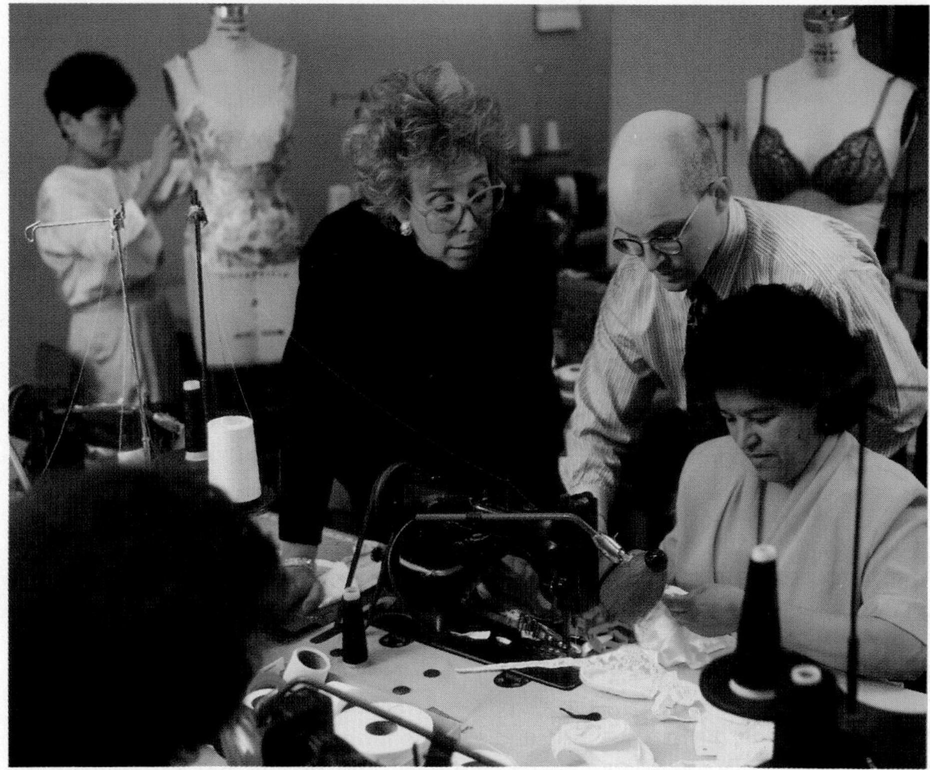

In our culture men have traditionally been seen as dominant, aggressive, objective, independent, forceful, and competitive, while women have been stereotyped as passive, emotional, dependent, accepting, and compliant. Despite the feminist movement, leadership expectations still generally tend to mirror the male model. However, Warnaco's Linda Wachner, at forty-six the only female CEO of a Fortune 500 industrial company, is the image of a forceful, decisive, aggressive leader. Perhaps it is because she breaks the stereotype that some have attacked her leadership style. Complains one executive, "A lot of people have been run over by Linda. She will do anything, *just anything* to get to the bottom line." Tough boss Wachner's reply to such critics: "I just want people to be good, and I apply an enormous amount of pressure to get everybody moving this company in the right direction. I know I push very hard, but I don't push anyone harder than I push myself."

ers are also successful managers, and the "traits" noted earlier are common to most of them. Opponents of this viewpoint counter that many managers simply "manage" assets or resources, and although they may be responsible for subordinates, their status and promotions are not predicated on their skill in human relations. True leaders attain that status without regard for formal authority; they become leaders through their ability to influence employees to achieve successful results.[12]

CHECKPOINT

- Describe and contrast personal traits and results-oriented traits of effective leaders.
- Explain several traits common to most effective leaders.

LEADERSHIP STYLES

Leadership styles are patterns of behavior observed over time in similar circumstances among leaders with similar performance profiles. Before we look at several models that categorize leadership styles, it is important to point out that a style is seldom consciously selected the way you would select a dish from a menu. Students, however, tend to conclude that "menus" do exist with distinct and mutually exclusive options for leadership behavior, and the research models that we will discuss have not dispelled this notion. A controversial and common conclusion is that there is "one best style" of leadership, even though there is no exact evidence supporting it. Most people cannot change their lifelong patterns of behavior or adapt their value systems to conform to a perceived style preference.

A Basic Model

Leadership studies conducted at Ohio State University and the University of Michigan during the 1950s led to a basic model that explained leadership behavior through its relation to work and employees.[13] Two general leadership orientations were identified. **Task orientation** describes a style in which managers control rather than encourage employees to perform tasks. Managers with a task orientation emphasize work results, responsibilities, and standards. **Employee orientation** describes a style in which managers are concerned for employees and emphasize motivation, social cohesion, and participative decision making.

task orientation
Management style emphasizing control of, rather than encouragement of, employees' work, focusing on work results, task responsibilities, and work standards.

employee orientation
A style of management that emphasizes motivation, social cohesion, participative decision making, and a concern for employees.

These two orientations are illustrated by the four-quadrant model in Figure 14-3. Managers with a low concern for people and tasks (lower left block) have little regard for either employees or work results; they simply abdicate leadership. Managers with a low concern for people and a high concern for tasks (lower right block) are called "directive." Managers with a high regard for people and low concern for tasks (upper left block) are labeled "supportive." And managers with a high concern for both people and tasks (upper right block) are termed "participative" because they act democratically and encourage participative behavior.

Several terms are used to explain the two basic leadership orientations. The Ohio State model refers to task orientation as *initiating structure,* a propensity by managers to direct subordinates to attain task-oriented results; and to employee orientation as *consideration,* a propensity by managers to gain employee trust and encourage behavior to achieve results. Other popular terms for these dimensions are *production* and *people* orientations.

Research that evolved from the Ohio State and University of Michigan studies during the early 1960s indicated two general correlations between results and leadership styles. Managers with an **autocratic leadership** style seemed to have less success with employees; their subordinates accomplished tasks within reason, but they were likely to resist efforts to improve performance. Organizations with autocratic managers had more absenteeism, greater turnover, and more employee grievances. In contrast, **supportive leadership** styles resulted in more cohesive work groups, more productive organizations, and fewer problems associated with turnover, absenteeism, and grievances.[14]

autocratic leadership
A directive style of leadership with power centered in one or a few key individuals; autocratic leaders typically focus on tasks, centralize personal power, and have a low concern for people.

supportive leadership
A style of leadership that encourages employees through motivation techniques and acceptance.

democratic leadership
An approach to leadership that involves employees in decisions through group efforts and team-building techniques.

Researchers discovered later that **democratic leadership**—involving employees in decisions—not supportive behavior, led directly to the dramatic results

FIGURE 14-3 Two-Dimension Leadership Model

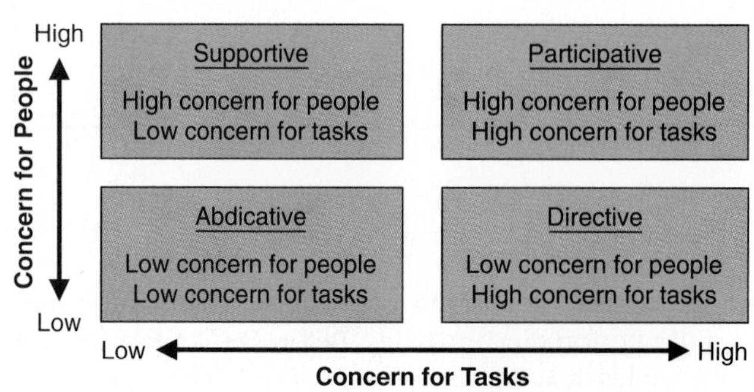

noted above. Hence a high regard for employees was not in itself sufficient to generate successful results. Researchers also found that any conclusion that there was "one best" leadership style in all places and circumstances was inappropriate. For example, democratic leadership was often considered weak and ineffective in the armed forces, whereas supportive leadership was rated highly effective in working with office staff.

These early research efforts raised several questions. The most obvious was whether one style of leadership was generally more effective than others. Another question was whether the use of a four-quadrant model rather than a continuum oversimplified leadership. A third concern was the extremely emotional "task versus employee" and "production versus people" terminology. Humane terms such as *participation, social cohesion,* and *mutual trust* were favored over mechanistic terms such as *task* and *production output.* According to Bob Allen, CEO at AT&T, leadership encompasses many responsibilities, some humane and some mechanistic. He believes in the need for decisive behavior when faced with personal decisions, yet prefers "to create ambiguity" to allow other managers to make decisions according to their own characteristics. Allen does expect AT&T executives to be results-oriented and to drive toward achievement goals, but at the same time he expects them to treat employees with dignity and to behave ethically.[15]

System 4 Management

Many of the problems associated with polarized concepts of leadership styles are resolved by modeling leadership behavior on integrated variables. Rensis Likert proposed the best-known integration model, now called **System 4 Management.** Figure 14–4 provides a schematic summary of Likert's four systems.[16]

System 4 Management
Developed by Rensis Likert, it is a description of four approaches to leadership taken by managers, ranging from autocratic to participative. Likert believes the one best way to lead is through "System 4 participation."

Managers in System 1 are autocratic and rely on so-called traditional structures of authority for decision making. Formal authority and rigid chain-of-command processes underscore human relations, with little or no interaction between hierarchical levels.

Managers in System 2 are benevolent but still at the autocratic end of the leadership continuum. Decision making is structured along hierarchical lines, but a mellowing of relationships allows for productive interaction between levels.

Managers in System 3 are consultative and tend to include subordinates in decisions. Their behavior falls short of allowing a fully participative system, but they seldom make decisions unilaterally. Systems of communications are more open, and subordinates are brought into the problem-solving process.

Managers in System 4 have a fully participative style of leadership. They rely on team-building approaches rather than stratified methods of organization. Managers in System 4 emphasize group decisions and supportive relationships without making performance trade-offs. System 4 management is strongly supported by Likert as one in which high-performance goals and strong commitments to results are paramount to team success. In his view, participative management encourages acceptance of decisions while providing for broad-based support of collective goals and objectives.

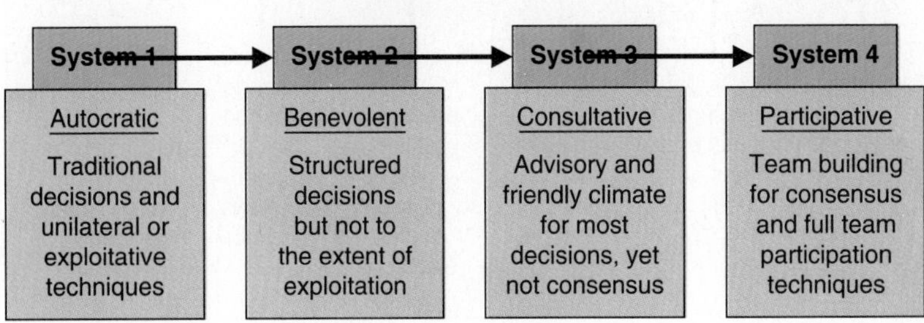

FIGURE 14–4 Likert's System 4 Management

Although a significant amount of research supports System 4 as the preferred leadership style,[17] few organizations, managers, and employees can realistically assume the psychological responsibilities of a fully participative system requiring consensus decision making. For example, at Copeland Corporation, both managers and union employees recently rejected efforts to implement participative management techniques. The company, an Ohio-based manufacturer of air-conditioner compressors and 200 other electromechanical products, had experienced a decade of decline and was on the verge of shutting down several plants. Management decided it needed a new approach to leadership to turn the company around: team decision making and shop-floor quality task forces composed of supervisors, technicians, and employees. However, lower-level managers, who had long worked under an authoritative—though friendly—system of making independent decisions, appealed to top management to reconsider the proposal. Employees and their union representatives were also uncomfortable with shared decision making and work teams. Consequently, when union members voted on the new leadership initiatives, they defeated them.[18] Eventually, new quality control techniques were adopted, but plant leadership methods remained virtually unchanged.

Recent management studies comparing Japanese to Western methods of leadership reinforce belief in the superiority of System 4 because it resembles the phenomenally successful Japanese model.[19] But the Japanese culture relies heavily on harmonious group processes. The Western perspective on leadership has quite different cultural underpinnings. Even American organizations that have adapted Theory Z (introduced in Chapter 2) retain many characteristics of an authority-based system of leadership. This does not diminish the importance of Likert's ideal System 4; it only points out the difficulty of adopting it in Western culture.

Choosing a Leadership Style

Figure 14–5 illustrates a continuum of leadership behavior that implies managers can pursue a leadership style that best fits their employees' expectations. In reality, experienced managers usually become defensive about the notion of "choosing" a leadership style from a continuum. In their view, this is unrealistic for adults whose values and personalities are relatively fixed, and who are often limited by other

FIGURE 14–5 Continuum of Leadership Behavior

Source: Reprinted by permission of *Harvard Business Review*. An exhibit from "How to Choose a Leadership Pattern" by Robert Tannenbaum and Warren II. Schmidt, issue May/June 1973. Copyright © 1973 by the President and Fellows of Harvard College; all rights reserved.

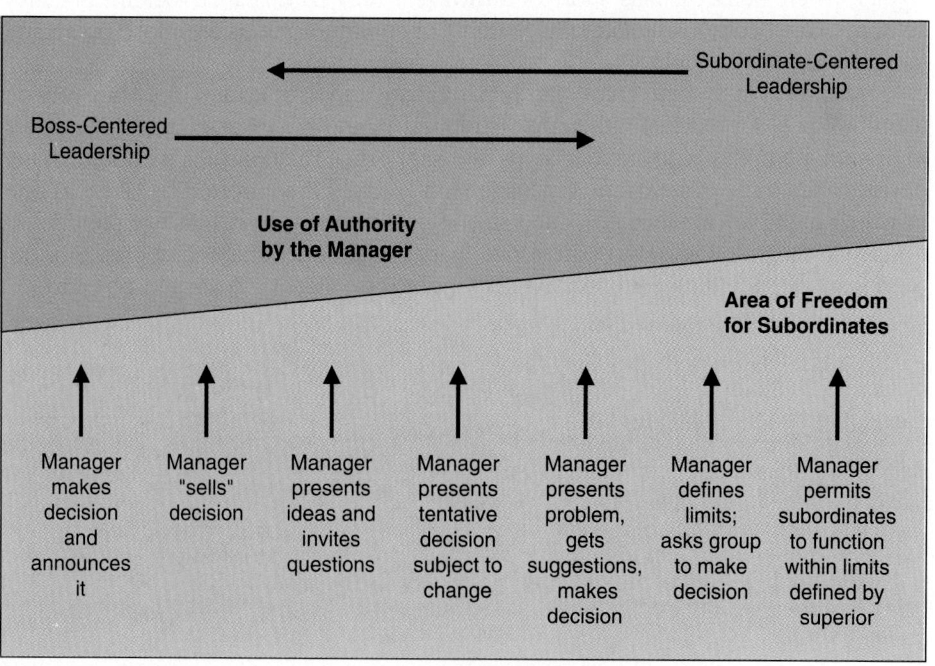

forces to a narrow range of behavior in a given situation. Research shows that five critical factors influence leadership patterns.[20]

1. *Expectations of Superiors.* Since rewards, promotions, and most outcomes are controlled by higher-level managers, their expectations influence lower-level managers' leadership styles.
2. *Expectations of Subordinates.* Management effectiveness is ultimately determined by how well subordinates respond to leadership efforts. If managers exceed subordinate expectations, either by being too authoritarian or too conciliatory, subordinates will be less responsive to their efforts.
3. *Task Structures.* As discussed in earlier chapters on organizing, the operational environment influences work methods and leadership. Machine-paced assembly lines permit few opportunities for participatory decision making, whereas collegial environments allow quite a bit.
4. *Organizational Culture.* Policies and organizational mandates restrict or encourage a given style of leadership. Cisco Systems of Menlo Park, California, a maker of computer network systems, has successfully created a culture that encourages all of its employees to be leaders and problem solvers. Cisco CEO John P. Morgridge maintains that this is not so much a matter of choice as of necessity. In order to keep overhead low and stay lean in a highly competitive environment, Cisco subcontracts many of its basic manufacturing requirements to other companies. Most similar companies have primarily production and manufacturing personnel, with a smaller number of computer scientists and engineers for design and development. In contrast, only one-quarter of Cisco's staff of 619 are production and manufacturing workers, and these workers are strategically placed to participate in every phase of product design and development.[21]
5. *Peer Expectations.* Peer pressure universally shapes behavior, beliefs, and leadership styles. Managers who would like to pursue more participative methods

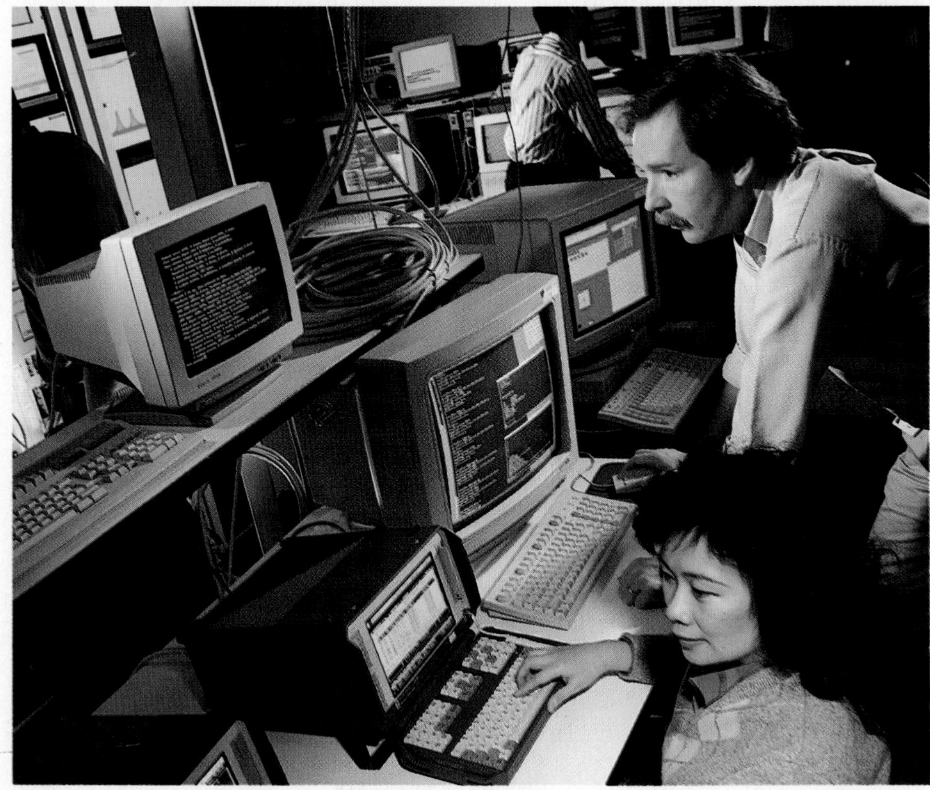

California-based Cisco Systems, a computer network maker, keeps production costs down by subcontracting many basic manufacturing functions and encouraging its staff to develop leadership skills. Explains David Ring, vice president of manufacturing, "Everyone here is a problem solver. Our job is not simply to put products together and get them out the door but to figure out how to do it better."

may be restrained by their perceptions of how authoritarian peers view such behavior. To protect themselves, conciliatory managers may adopt more authoritative behavior. Of course, peer pressure can also influence autocratic managers to adopt participative methods.

The Managerial Grid®

Managerial Grid
An organizational development model created by Robert Blake and Jane Mouton that is based on a matrix of values between 1 and 9 for two primary variables explaining a manager's orientation: concern for production and concern for people.

Developed by Robert Blake and Jane Mouton, the **Managerial Grid** is a framework of leadership that describes five management styles. Each style is identified by a set of coordinates on the two dimensions of *concern for production* and *concern for people.* Blake and Mouton propose "one best approach" to leadership that maximizes a concern for both production and people, a view consistent with Likert's System 4 Management.[22] Figure 14–6 presents the Grid®, republished as the Leadership Grid in 1991.

The two dimensions in Blake and Mouton's Grid are *attitudinal* in character and therefore are to be distinguished from the *behavioral* dimensions identified in the research originating in the Ohio State study. The horizontal dimension, concern for production, reflects a manager's focus on operational tasks. The vertical dimension, concern for people, indicates a manager's perception that interpersonal relationships are important. A value between 1 (very low) and 9 (very high) is assigned for each dimension, resulting in a pair of coordinates that identifies a pattern of leadership behavior.

Many companies use the Grid Seminar as a training program to improve leadership and to attain an optimal pattern of behavior that will reinforce task objectives and interpersonal relations. For example, General Electric evaluates both managers' and employees' perceptions each year as a way of monitoring progress in supervisory training programs. Ideally, training will help GE first-line managers to become more productive while developing supportive relationships with their employees.[23]

Although there are eighty-one possible styles of leadership, Blake and Mouton define five sets of coordinates as benchmarks. These provide reference points for the development of programs to alter patterns of leadership behavior.[24]

Impoverished management. At the lower left point in the Grid is a 1,1 style, called *impoverished* because it denotes minimum effort to get work done as well as

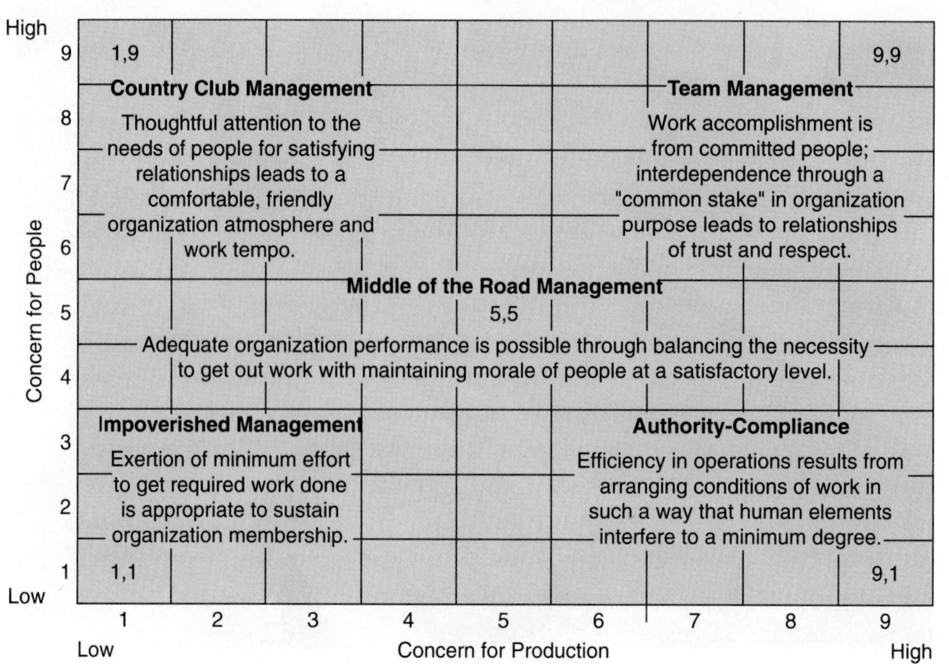

FIGURE 14–6 The Leadership Grid®

Source: The Leadership Grid® figure from *Leadership Dilemmas–Grid Solutions,* by Robert R. Blake and Anne Adams McCanse, p. 29 (Houston: Gulf Publishing Company). Copyright © 1991, by Scientific Methods, Inc. Reproduced by permission of the owners.

minimum effort to sustain and support organizational members. The manager scoring 1,1 has little regard for work or people.

Authority-compliance. The 9,1 position reveals a very high regard for efficiency and operational results. The manager at this position maximizes production by exercising power and authority unilaterally, exacting obedience from subordinates. In the extreme interpretation of this set, subordinates are regarded as irrelevant.

Country club management. This, too, is an extreme orientation, but at 1,9 there is a high regard for people, not production. Managers with a 1,9 orientation concentrate on meeting employee needs, assuming that happy people working in a friendly, satisfying environment will automatically produce operational efficiency; task requirements and production are systematically ignored.

Middle of the road management. This middle-of-the-road orientation at 5,5 is a suboptimal compromise in which managers attain adequate results by exercising limited authority, balancing the needs of employees with the needs of production. It is a noncontroversial position reflecting a least-risk style of leadership.

Team management. The 9,9 orientation is Blake and Mouton's ideal approach to leadership. Work is accomplished through teamwork so that operational results are maximized while a satisfying work environment in which employees can fulfill their needs is provided. Managers at this position exercise authority with the full acceptance of their integrated teams to achieve maximum productivity through a committed work force.

Clearly a 9,9 orientation represents a philosophy of leadership that is most effective. It is also rarely found among individual managers or as a pattern of leadership in organizations. Nevertheless, it is a valuable ideal, and in Blake and Mouton's view, a team management style provides the best possible means of achieving high productivity.

CHECKPOINT

- Identify the two dimensions and four quadrants of the Ohio State and University of Michigan model.
- Describe decision-making behavior in Likert's management model.
- Identify and explain critical factors that influence leadership behavior.
- Describe the five benchmark coordinates in the Managerial Grid.

CONTINGENCY LEADERSHIP

In contrast to theorists who emphasize "one best" leadership style, contingency theorists believe that circumstances require adaptive leadership behavior. **Contingency leadership** is based on the theory that work is best accomplished when managers determine how to behave toward subordinates in each situation. Several contingency theories are described in this section.

contingency leadership
An approach to leadership that suggests the most effective management behavior depends on circumstances.

Fiedler's Contingency Theory

Fred Fiedler's contingency theory, the first to be introduced, described successful leadership as a direct result of matching managers' styles with situational variables.[25] Fiedler grouped situational variables into three areas of concern:

MANAGEMENT APPLICATION

Rome tried ruling its empire with two Caesars twice. One coalition led to pitched battles between armies loyal to each leader, and both co-consuls were killed in the process. The other coalition succeeded, but behind the scenes, one Caesar ruled while his partner kept a low administrative profile. Now several major American companies are trying the team approach, naming as many as five executives to the executive suite.

Xerox Corporation's chairman, Paul A. Allaire, named four senior executives to join him in a committee replacing the company's president in 1992. Microsoft Corporation put a trio in charge, also in 1992, and in the previous year, American Telephone & Telegraph, Eastman Kodak, and New York Life Insurance set up executive teams to replace top management. In each instance, there is still one chief executive officer, but there is no obvious heir apparent waiting to take over the helm. The crucial question is whether team members can work together under these conditions without conflict.

The teams were formed to speed up decision making and to foster collective problem solving for complex strategic management issues. Periodically, the official chairmanship of the group rotates to a different member, but individual titles and other trappings of office have disappeared. Allaire explained Xerox's effort as essential to keep his global organization intact because one person can no longer shoulder the full range of executive responsibilities of an operating president.

Although the companies are optimistic about their new executive teams, similar efforts at General Electric, GTE Corporation, and Citicorp led to turf battles and intense confrontations. Power sharing by Citicorp's three-man executive team was described as a thinly disguised competition for the top spot. That effort subsequently failed, and Citicorp has reverted to a traditional one-person CEO. At GE, the effort was called a horse race that ended with a leadership void; the executive team was replaced by Jack Welch, a CEO who has the reputation of being one of corporate America's strongest leaders. GTE reverted to a traditional management hierarchy after observers noted that it was in a "zero-sum game" where one of the team members expected to emerge triumphantly.

Like the Roman experience nearly 2,000 years ago, American efforts may have mixed results. In some instances, team management may end in drawn battle lines, while in others, it may achieve cooperation.

One question that remains unanswered is what will be the role model for corporate leadership. Another is whether the teams will become so preoccupied with resolving their own coordination problems that they will compromise decisions rather than making tough choices. And who will be accountable? The ultimate question is: Can these executives and their employees accept power sharing?

Sources: Amanda Bennett, "Firms Run by Executive Teams Can Reap Rewards, Incur Risks," *Wall Street Journal,* February 5, 1992, pp. B1, B5; Suein L. Hwang, "Xerox Forms New Structure for Printer, Copier Business, Creates New Office," *Wall Street Journal,* February 5, 1992, p. B6; and Joann S. Lublin, "Companies Form Teams to Expedite Decisions," *Wall Street Journal,* December 20, 1991, p. B1.

- *Leadership-Member Relations.* If group members respect the manager and also feel a personal attachment to him or her, formal authority will be less important to accomplishing work. This goes further than acceptance theory by implying a friendly relationship. Fiedler believes leader-member relations to be the most important situational variable.

- *Task Structure.* If tasks are highly structured with formal guidelines and well-defined expectations, such as on assembly lines, authority will also be formalized and managers and employees will both prefer a more directive style of leadership. If tasks are unstructured, such as in creative research labs, managers and employees will expect a more conciliatory style of leadership.
- *Position Power.* The position power of leaders is influenced by organizational culture, the formality of management hierarchy, and the type of work environment. Therefore, the values and beliefs of employees and managers, as well as top management's philosophy of leadership, will partially determine what style is acceptable.

When Mickey Drexler became president of the Gap Inc., he had a firm idea of what the specialty clothing chain could be. What Drexler wanted he communicated in one word: Simplify. By this he meant not only the merchandise itself but also how the company did business. Executives who resisted Drexler's message were fired. In their place Drexler hired managers who understood the new order: to speed up production of new, more wearable products (clothes Gap designers would themselves want to wear) and pull nonmovers rapidly. Melvin Jacobs, chairman of the Saks Fifth Avenue department store chain, says of Drexler's strategy, "The Gap is a huge success, while retailers around the world are struggling like crazy."

Fiedler recognized that managers develop a dominant style of leadership early in their careers, and it changes very little over time. In his view, this predisposition to one style of leadership is strongly grounded in personality, and although some marginal change in behavior is possible, a significant change is unlikely. This conclusion has strong implications for staffing managerial positions. When there is a mismatch between a manager's predisposed leadership style and the situation, that manager may have to be replaced by someone more closely attuned to situational demands. If the mismatch is not severe, however, a leader's style may be sufficiently changed through management development.

Fiedler's model is controversial but has prompted important research about how situational variables influence behavior. The greatest controversy concerns his conclusion that since situations and leadership styles vary widely, no one best style of leadership exists. An impressive array of research is aimed at refuting Fiedler and supporting the "one best" school of thought championed by Blake and Mouton, Likert, and others.[26]

Equally impressive research supports Fiedler's proposition that different styles fit different situations, and a good match between leadership style and circumstance leads to better organizational results. This proposition has led to two additional hypotheses. The first is that task-oriented leadership is more effective in situations where control is high (high task structure) and in uncertain situations where control is needed. The second is that relation-oriented leadership is better in situations requiring less control and for tasks that are less structured. The inescapable implication is that managers will never quite meet leadership expectations where situations tend to vary greatly or organizational changes are taking place.

House's Path-Goal Theory

The **path-goal theory** is a contingency approach that holds managers responsible for influencing employees to work for rewards linked to specific tasks. This theory is identified with Robert J. House, who published his research in 1971.[27] It is contingency based, but also inextricably related to expectancy theory. Like expectancy theory, it emphasizes that people want to benefit from their efforts and assign probabilities (expectancies) to behavior that will result in desired outcomes. The path-goal theory builds on expectancy theory, stating that leaders identify desired outcomes (rewards) and then lead others toward attaining them (paths toward fulfillment).

path-goal theory
A contingency approach to leadership that holds managers responsible for influencing employees to work for rewards linked to specific tasks.

Specifically, subordinates will be motivated to behave in ways that lead to rewards or that help avoid unpleasant outcomes. For example, at the Prudential Insurance Company, top management announced several years ago that managers would be expected to improve opportunities for women and minority employees and would be held accountable for promoting them through merit-based performance systems. Prudential managers would either encourage promotions and be rewarded with higher bonuses or fight the system and suffer the penalty of lower

GLOBAL TRENDS

Shanghai Vacuum–Contrast in Leadership Values

Shanghai Vacuum, once a subsidiary of America's General Electric, has begun to produce color TVs, the first in the People's Republic of China. Although this alone marks a milestone in progress, one that the United States passed thirty years ago, managers at the Shanghai plant are trying to emulate current Western management standards in every way.

Managing director Xue Wenhai is among the company's elite–managers who have been educated in North America and Europe and have worked for the GE alliance in Western markets. Wenhai is pushing for a complete market approach to decision making. He says, for example, "The enterprise should have a free hand to say what and how much it produces . . . and if this happens, the 'iron rice bowl' will be broken." (The "iron rice bowl" was Mao's expression for the policy of lifetime security for all workers.) Wenhai has educated his employees in basic production and marketing aspects of business and says that every one of them can tell you exactly what they produce, how this is accomplished, and where the products will be sold. But, he adds, they have no idea of the cost of production or the meaning of productivity. Raw materials, workers' salaries, and how the company is charged for services and taxes are factors controlled by central government or regional agencies.

Nevertheless, the Shanghai plant is determined to create a sense of employee accountability through its own accounting system, which measures contributions by employees and rewards them for excellence through "informal" awards, personal recognition, and extra holidays. Management cannot, however, alter employee wages or determine promotions without government approval, and employees are often transferred to other companies by regional agencies. Consequently, leading in a Chinese plant can be frustrating. While managers like Wenhai understand how important it is to motivate employees and give them incentives, they must also conform to political mandates and local customs that discourage individuality, status symbols, and special attention. Company executives, for example, earn enough to purchase decent cars and live in better-than-average housing, yet most shun these status trappings, preferring instead to live in simple cooperative apartments and ride bicycles to work. The profit motive is not a priority with them because excess earnings bring ridicule and, sometimes, direct retaliation by government agencies.

Sources: "Has Capitalism Won?" *Asiaweek,* March 13, 1992, pp. 49–52. See also Kunio Yoshihara, "After Communism, What Next?" *Far Eastern Economic Review,* October 1991, p. 28.

bonuses. The result has been implementation of more than 750 individual action plans focused on high-potential women and minorities. These have not been arbitrary plans to fill quotas; managers have to demonstrate viable methods of developing these subordinates for promotion, and candidates for promotion must prove capable. Company goals are clear, and managers have created well-defined paths for goal attainment.[28]

Figure 14–7 depicts elements of expectancy theory as "intervening variables." The path-goal model shows a causal relationship between leadership and these intervening variables to modify performance toward satisfying organizational objec-

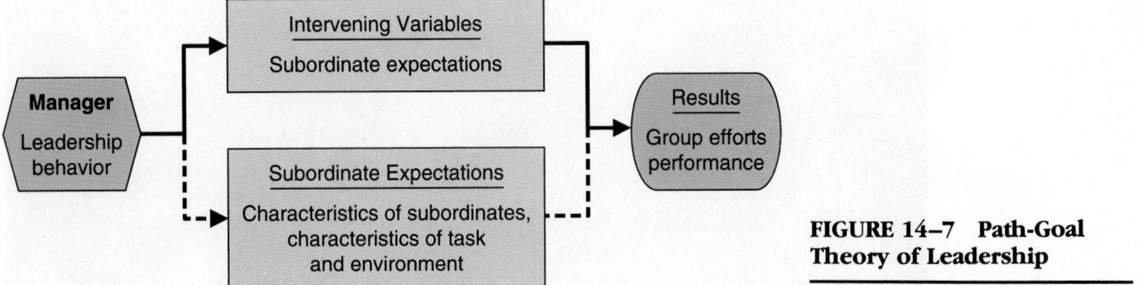

FIGURE 14–7 Path-Goal Theory of Leadership

tives. "Results" are equivalent to the expectancy notation of "valence" or perceived outcomes, with the added dimension of actual subordinate performance. The path-goal model includes situational moderator variables (called "subordinate expectations" in the figure). They include characteristics of subordinates and characteristics of the task environment.

Path-goal theory addresses two complicated issues: First, how to deal with employee expectations, and second, how to ease constraints imposed by the work environment. In House's words, "The motivational function of the leader consists of increasing personal payoffs to subordinates for work-goal attainment, and making the path to these pay-offs easier to travel by clarifying it, reducing roadblocks and pitfalls, and increasing the opportunities for personal satisfaction en route."[29] It follows that certain kinds of leadership behavior will motivate workers to expect better results because of leadership behavior will motivate workers to expect better results because of leadership support, and other kinds of leadership efforts will thwart performance by dampening expectations for rewards. These conclusions are explained by four major categories of leadership.[30]

Supportive leadership. This style considers subordinate needs and supports a friendly climate at work. When work is tedious or boring, supportive leaders ease frustrations and make tasks more tolerable, thereby influencing more productive performance. However, when work is pleasant and the environment enjoyable, supportive leaders have little effect on performance or satisfaction.

Directive leadership. This behavior reflects authority, rules, policies, and a formal organization. Subordinates follow specific guidelines and traditional patterns of decision making. When tasks are unstructured and roles ambiguous, directive leaders are effective because subordinates perceive that closer supervision and more directed leadership will increase their opportunities for success. In other words, uncertain or unstructured work environments make employees apprehensive. However, when subordinates know their jobs and feel confident about performing well, directive leadership is viewed as an imposition.

Participative leadership. Participative leaders emphasize team-building relationships and results can be similar to those of directive leadership. In unstructured and ambiguous situations, participative leadership enhances performance and satisfaction. However, unlike directive leadership, participative methods also enhance satisfaction when work is tedious, boring, or otherwise unpleasant. When work is structured and subordinates have a clear understanding of their jobs, however, it is not clear whether participative leadership affects performance.

Achievement-oriented leadership. This style of leadership sets challenging goals, encourages innovation, and emphasizes confidence in subordinates. It is particularly important when subordinates have to perform nonrepetitive tasks in ambiguous circumstances. When tasks are repetitive and clear, achievement-oriented leadership has little or no effect on performance or satisfaction.

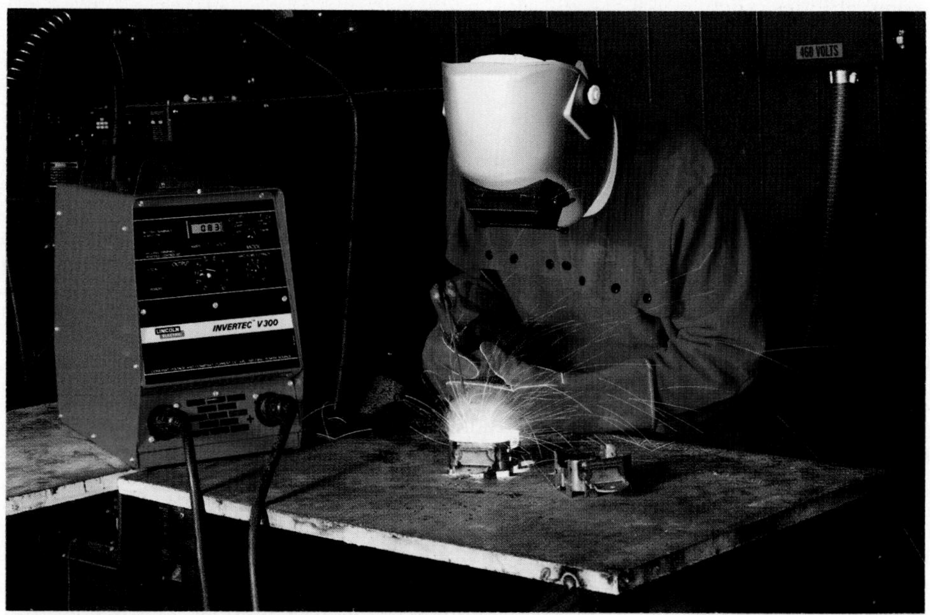

Lincoln Electric Company offers an outstanding example of path-goal leadership. Because employees have no base wage but are paid according to actual production results, they are highly motivated to find new ways to improve performance. Lincoln managers are responsible for encouraging employees to become more productive. In turn, employees expect supervisors to help them increase productivity. Managers seldom "direct"; instead, they improve work methods and production systems and encourage employees to create high-quality products, such as the refrigerator shown here. In this way, management also helps employees reach higher income and bonuses.

An illustration might clarify these points. Assume a group of college students charters a student organization called the Association of Collegiate Entrepreneurs (ACE). The student leaders expect a faculty adviser to take a leadership role and help them develop their club. An experienced faculty adviser could easily write the charter, structure the objectives, and suggest a number of activities, but one who did this would be trampling on the concept of student participation. Instead, the faculty adviser should patiently encourage students to develop their own charter, devise objectives, and develop activities. If the charter the students come up with is unsatisfactory, the faculty adviser must counsel them to modify it rather than dictate what the charter should contain. If the students' objectives are somewhat muddled, the adviser must find a way to show them how they will benefit from a clearer set of objectives (raise expectations). If the proposed activities do not satisfy those objectives, the adviser must help students develop activities (new paths) that do. In this situation, an effective leader recognizes situational constraints, such as the loosely structured university environment, and takes into account personal limitations, such as the students' lack of experience.

Implications of Path-Goal Leadership

The implications of the four scenarios of path-goal leadership are uncertain because of intervening variables that prevent a generalization about appropriate leadership in all situations. Task characteristics, for example, are only partially accounted for in any of the four scenarios. These include the degree of formalization in an organization, mandates of authority, the physical structure of the tasks, and the interpretation of task responsibilities. The second variable, characteristics of subordinates, is addressed more clearly and includes employee needs, personality traits, and subordinates' abilities to accomplish tasks. Thus personal needs (such as for esteem), personal abilities (such as skills), and personality traits (such as desire for achievement) all modify leadership requirements.

House's work has become a focal point for research on contingency leadership. The path-goal theory was one of the first attempts to integrate motivation and leadership systematically. This alone has added to our understanding of why subordinates respond to certain types of leadership in given circumstances, but the model has several drawbacks. It is complex and difficult to apply in practical situations. It has also been criticized as being weakly based on expectancy concepts that rely heavily on the premise that managers consciously choose their style of leadership, a point vigorously debated.[31]

The Vroom-Yetton Theory

Victor Vroom, known for his work in expectancy theory, teamed up with Phillip Yetton to provide an alternative view for contingency leadership. The **Vroom-Yetton model** proposes that managers consciously adapt their leadership behavior to suit the different types of decisions they face.[32] For example, when a complex decision requires the involvement and acceptance of workers, they are more likely to implement a participative decision process and to adopt a consultative style of leadership. In the midst of an emergency or when a timely decision is demanded, managers are prone to a directive style of leadership.

Vroom-Yetton model
A theory of leadership that suggests conditions that influence subordinates to participate in various ways in decision making.

Vroom and Yetton are convinced that managers are more adaptive than Fiedler and other theorists suppose, and therefore that they consciously choose a style of leadership. Most models view leadership style as the primary factor influencing decisions. Vroom and Yetton turn the process around, proposing that it is the type of decision demanded that influences the leadership style.

Since no extensive research on the model has been done, it has been neither validated nor refuted, but if it does hold up, several conclusions can be drawn. If leadership decisions can be identified, for example, then managers' behavior can be correlated with them to improve performance. Management development programs can teach more successful leadership methods, leading to higher-quality decisions and a more productive work environment. But as noted, this assumes the type of decision needed can always be identified. Figure 14–8 illustrates the Vroom-Yetton model as a decision tree based on answers to seven diagnostic questions. As a manager progresses through the questions, yes-or-no answers will determine alternative routes toward one of twelve outcomes. Each outcome defines an approach to leadership noted in the figure.

Unfortunately, the Vroom-Yetton model suffers from many of the same flaws as other contingency models. It proposes a complex set of variables that are difficult to define and analyze. It also assumes managers can consciously choose a leadership style, a moot point. Finally, it has been criticized for not adequately accounting for subordinate behavior in terms of personal needs, personality traits, or decision-making capabilities.

The Hersey and Blanchard Life Cycle Theory

Paul Hersey and Kenneth Blanchard put forward another contingency model, the **life cycle model,** based on the maturity of subordinates.[33] Their premise, illustrated in Figure 14–9, is that managers adopt one of four approaches to leadership depending on both *relationship* and *task* dimensions. The two dimensions of the Hersey and Blanchard model are similar to those in the Ohio State and University of Michigan studies discussed earlier. Leadership is described by a bell-shaped curve with four modes of leader behavior: *delegating, participating, selling,* and *telling.* Each is dependent on the maturity of subordinates.

life cycle model
An approach to leadership in which managers adopt behavior to coincide with the maturity of subordinates; the four behavior modes are delegating, participating, selling, and telling.

A. Does the problem possess a quality requirement?
B. Do you have sufficient information to make a high-quality decision?
C. Is the problem structured?
D. Is acceptance of decision by subordinates important for effective implementation?
E. If you were to make the decision by yourself, is it reasonably certain that it would be accepted by your subordinates?
F. Do subordinates share the organizational goals to be attained in solving this problem?
G. Is conflict among subordinates over preferred solutions likely?

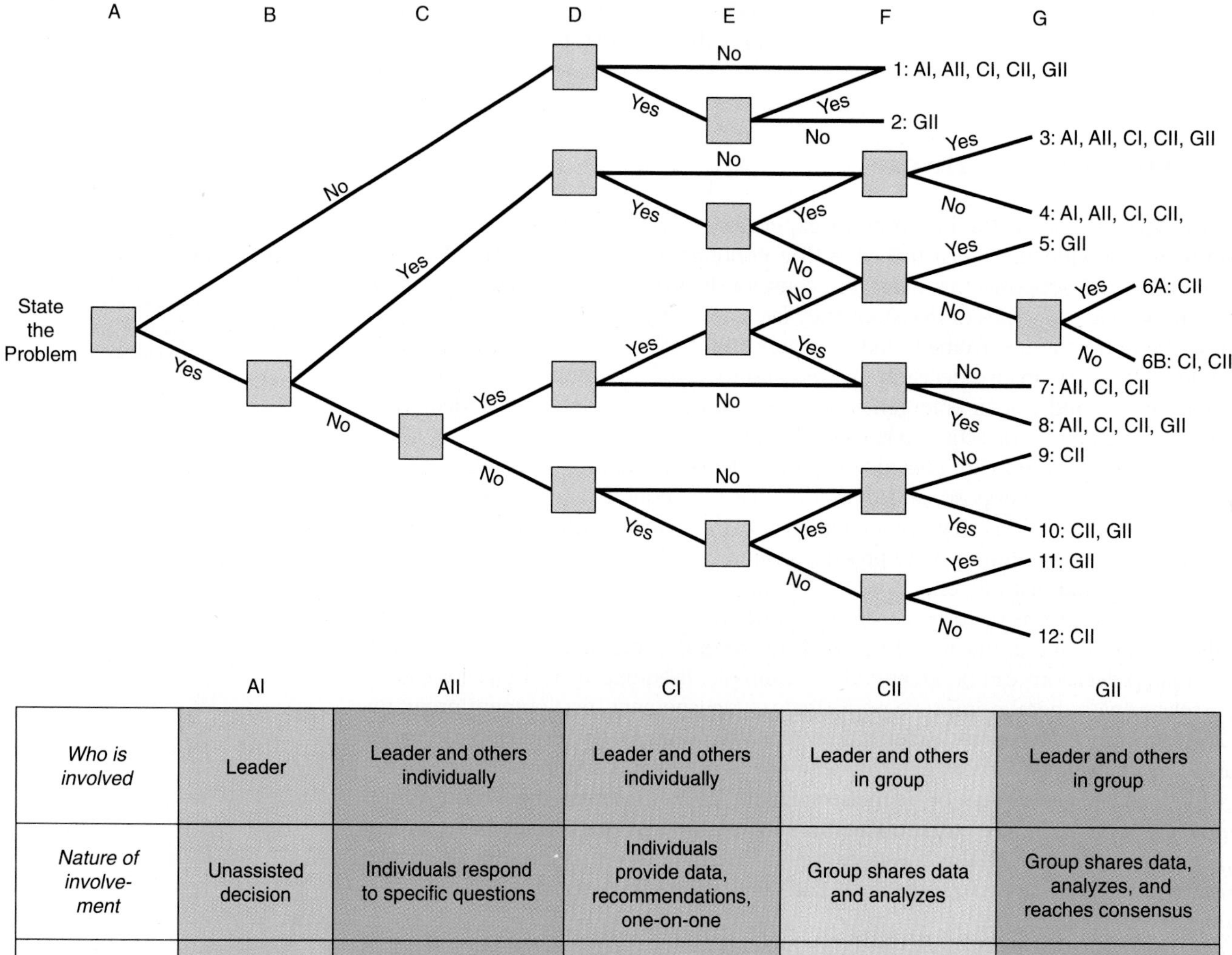

	AI	AII	CI	CII	GII
Who is involved	Leader	Leader and others individually	Leader and others individually	Leader and others in group	Leader and others in group
Nature of involve-ment	Unassisted decision	Individuals respond to specific questions	Individuals provide data, recommendations, one-on-one	Group shares data and analyzes	Group shares data, analyzes, and reaches consensus
Who makes decision	Leader	Leader	Leader	Leader	Group

FIGURE 14–8 Vroom-Yetton Decision Tree Governing Group Problems–Feasible Set

Source: (upper half) Reprinted from *Leadership and Decision-Making* by Victor H. Vroom and Philip W. Yetton, by permission of the University of Pittsburgh Press. Copyright © 1973 by the University of Pittsburgh Press. (lower half) Copyright © 1976 by Kepner-Tregoe, Inc. All rights reserved. Reprinted with permission of Kepner-Tregoe, Inc., a Princeton, N.J.-based company specializing in operational and strategic decision making.

Delegating. Managers adopt a low-profile style that provides little support and little direction for subordinates, who are given the responsibility for carrying out plans. Subordinates, or followers, are at a high maturity level and are willing and able to take responsibility. They are confident and neither need nor want direction or support.

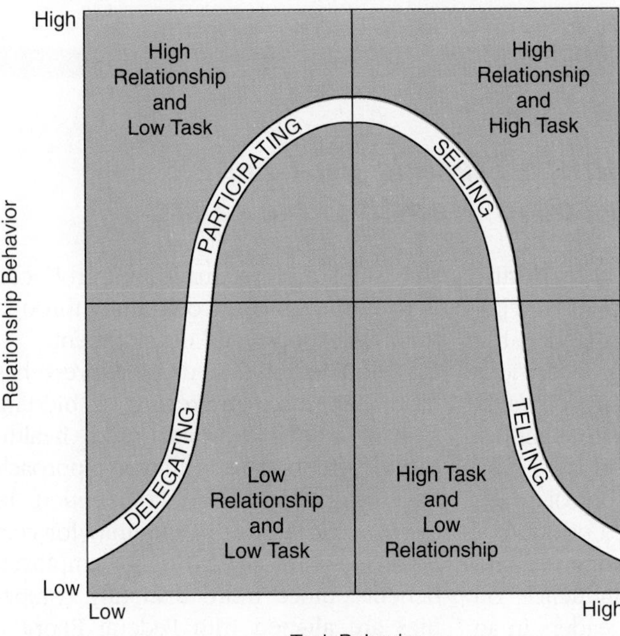

FIGURE 14–9 Hersey and Blanchard's Life Cycle Approach

Source: Paul Hersey and Kenneth H. Blanchard, *Management of Organizational Behavior: Utilizing Human Resources,* 5th ed. Copyright 1988, p. 182. Adapted by permission of Prentice Hall, Englewood Cliffs, N.J.

Participating. Managers with work groups at this moderately high maturity level face a motivation problem. Subordinates are capable but lack the confidence to take full responsibility for performing expected tasks. Managers are most effective in this situation by participating with their subordinates, supporting their efforts to carry out plans. These employees want support, not direction.

Selling. Managers with subordinates at this level of maturity adopt a selling style of leadership. They try to get workers to "buy into" desired performance. Subordinates at this level are willing but not necessarily able to take responsibility for carrying out plans. They need support and want to accept responsibility, but they also require some direction.

Telling. Managers must assume maximum responsibility for subordinates, who lack both the ability and the willingness to carry out plans. Workers at this lowest level of maturity cannot take responsibility and have not matured in the sense of being prepared for responsibilities. Because of this insecurity, they expect direction and may view supportive behavior as permissiveness.

To understand the life cycle model, one must know what Hersey and Blanchard mean by *maturity.* They do not rely on age or seniority to define it, although these may be factors. Rather, the authors' concept of maturity relates to job ability and psychological willingness to assume task responsibilities. In terms of job ability, maturity means having the skill, knowledge, experience, and confidence to perform necessary tasks. Psychological maturity means having the intrinsic motivation, or willingness, to accept responsibility.

Figure 14–10 shows the relationship between leadership behavior and subordinates' profiles in the life cycle model. Leadership stems from understanding the dominant group profile of subordinates. It is based less on types of decisions than on characteristics of employees. The life cycle model is not static; group lev-

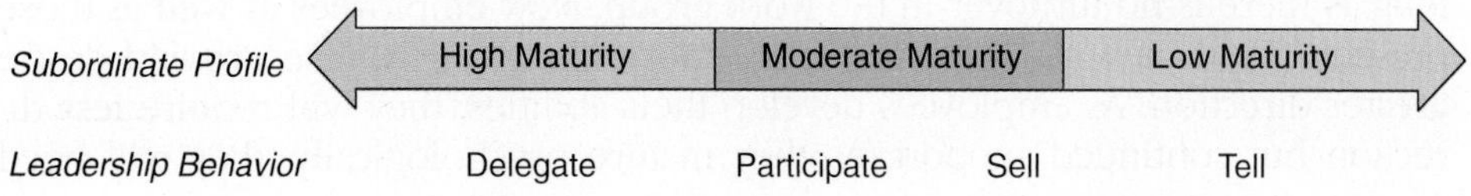

Subordinate Profile — High Maturity | Moderate Maturity | Low Maturity

Leadership Behavior — Delegate | Participate | Sell | Tell

FIGURE 14–10 A Life Cycle Continuum of Leadership Behavior

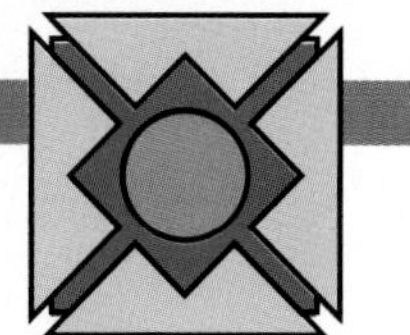

ETHICS IN MANAGEMENT

Executives at Reliance Electric and FedEx Take the Lead on Lower Health-Care Costs

John C. Morley, CEO of Reliance Electric Company in Cleveland, Ohio, has a reputation as a charismatic team leader, but one who can make tough decisions when the chips are down. Fred Smith, founder of Federal Express in Memphis, Tennessee, has a reputation as a fast-acting entrepreneur who controls decisions through a consolidated position of authority. Both men are admired, and both are exerting their influence on other community business leaders in an attempt to solve the health-care crisis.

"As executives," Morely explained, "we have an opportunity to work in our own communities to take control of the cost and quality of care provided to our workers through the application of sensible, old-fashioned market principles." Smith formed a consortium of business leaders and was more direct in his explanation, saying that they would break the back of soaring health-care costs.

In Cleveland, Morley has applied business techniques to help physicians and hospitals form a cooperative community group to make health-care providers "competitive." In his view, managers have experience with competition and know how to survive in tough markets, so they can help build a competitive profile for health care. The Cleveland effort is directed at creating quality assurance programs, cost-effective controls, sound planning, and a marketing system for health care. But most important, Morley intends to create an environment of "transactional leadership" whereby effective business leadership skills are systematically introduced into the health-care community through training, support, and development.

In Memphis, Federal Express has taken the lead in creating a bidding system among hospitals and health-care providers. This "pull-type" approach has instigated intense competition in the local health-care community for corporate contracts covering employee benefits. Since more than fifty companies are aligned with Federal Express, these corporate contracts represent a huge portion of the local market and income to the providers. The result has been an immediate cost reduction for corporate health care in Memphis, and a system-wide reduction of health insurance costs for everyone. When Federal Express originally instigated the bidding system in early 1991, most hospitals simply ignored it, but when corporate business was contracted out to the one hospital willing to meet quality standards at reduced costs, virtually every Memphis hospital became involved.

The approach in Cleveland has had similar results: improved care, better services, lower costs, and competitive pricing. Unlike Memphis, which experienced a "shock effect," Cleveland has experienced the effects of what is called "private leadership gone public."

Sources: John C. Morley, "The Cleveland Health-Care Experiment," *Wall Street Journal,* February 10, 1992, p. A16. See also Julia Flynn Siler and Susan Garland, "Sending Health Care into Rehab," *Business Week,* October 25, 1991, pp. 111–112.

els of maturity will change over time and leaders will have to adjust their styles to reflect changes in subordinates' expectations. Maturity is bound to increase so long as there is no turnover in the work group. New employees as well as those presented with new tasks, however, are more likely to feel insecure and desire greater direction. As employees develop their abilities, they will require less direction but continued support. As they mature psychologically, they will need less support. As both ability and willingness to take responsibility increase, subordinates will require less support and less direction.

Hersey and Blanchard's arguments are intuitively appealing but have been criticized. Opponents say the life cycle model ignores situational variables such as personality characteristics and formal organizational authority. They also point out that a group may be composed of individuals with differing levels of maturity, thus complicating its capacity to respond to a common leadership approach. In addition, critics say the life cycle model does not distinguish between types of tasks and reasons for insecurity, but equates an insecure worker faced with an easy task with a secure worker confronted with a difficult task.[34]

The life cycle theory does provide several genuine benefits for more effective management. It is easy to understand, and it suggests several alternatives for management behavior that emphasize the need for adaptive leadership. This approach also supposes that managers can influence both employees and the work situation by building up subordinate skills and confidence.

CHECKPOINT

- Describe Fiedler's three groups of situational variables and how his model explains managerial behavior.
- How does House's path-goal theory combine contingency and expectancy concepts to guide leadership behavior?
- Trace a decision through the Vroom-Yetton model to describe a choice of leadership style, and then describe why the choice would be most effective.
- Explain how the life cycle model relates "maturity" of subordinates to task and relationship behavior to describe four approaches to leadership.

MULTICULTURAL AND TRANSFORMATIONAL LEADERSHIP: CURRENT CHALLENGES

Throughout the text, we have emphasized that many changes are taking place in society, and these changes are transforming the business environment. Summarizing these changes, we find many things to concern managers. Educational levels for most workers are rising, technology is rapidly becoming more sophisticated, and there is a pronounced emphasis on ethical behavior within our organizations. Also, decision-making processes are changing as companies become more involved in participative environments with integrated team systems. In addition, we mentioned that organizations are becoming more culturally diversified, both domestically through broader-based employment of minorities, and globally through strategic alliances with companies from other nations. Collectively, these changes present a pressing challenge for managers to acclimate themselves to their *multicultural environments,* and in the process to stimulate even greater changes in their organizations by becoming what management theorists call *transformational leaders.* We will address these issues separately and conclude this chapter with a summary perspective on leadership.

Managing in a Multicultural Environment

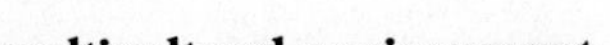

multicultural environment Refers to an organization that has employees from diverse cultural backgrounds or that has relationships with customers and other external constituents who represent diverse sociocultural interests.

A **multicultural environment** refers to an organization with employees from diverse cultural backgrounds. A complete definition must also include organizational relationships with customers, suppliers, community constituents, government leaders, investors, and competitors who represent diverse sociocultural interests. Cultural diversity is explained by the composite profile of individuals, including their sex, race, ethnic, age, and religious characteristics. Therefore, a multicultural environment is explained by the differing values of people working in organizations and their relationships with external constituents who often have divergent characteristics and interests.[35]

Leadership responsibilities become extremely complicated in multicultural environments because managers must abandon stereotypes of individuals, models of performance expectations, and assumptions about values employees hold toward their work and lifestyles. Research shows, for example, that women neither manage like men nor expect their male counterparts to manage as they would. A woman manager is more likely than a man to develop a coöperative style of leadership, facilitating dialogue and encouraging cooperation rather than clutching authority and favoring unilateral decision making. Male employees tend to sanction leadership behavior that conforms to expectations for so-called male characteristics such as decisiveness. They seldom sanction similar behavior in a female manager, but expect her to conform to so-called female characteristics such as conciliation.[36] Unfortunately, even though research findings like these can put to rest many misunderstandings about how men and women perceive leadership roles of women, they also can prompt stereotypes that women are less effective managers and less assertive decision makers. These stereotypes result in a "glass ceiling," the invisible barrier created by perceptions and biases that prevents women from being promoted to higher-level management positions.[37] Research also shows, however, that male and female managers do not differ in personal leadership qualities—only in their manner of leading. Consequently, there is no reason to believe that either women or men make superior managers.[38]

Stereotypes and biases in relation to black managers are notorious, but an Afro-American culture has emerged with strong leaders and role models who have begun to break down color barriers in the business world. In particular, black entrepreneurs have established themselves as capable managers with successful, growing corporate interests. Many have come from the ranks of professional sports, including Dave Bing, a former NBA star who is chairman of Bing Steel, Inc., and Julius Erving ("Dr. J"), formerly a basketball player with the Philadelphia 76ers and now a principal investor with former black investment banker J. B. Llewellyn in the Philadelphia Coca-Cola Bottling Company. Their successes are complemented by black executives who hold positions as presidents or group vice presidents in major corporations such as Xerox, AT&T, Motorola, and TLC Beatrice. But blacks, like women, are underrepresented in management positions and face significant obstacles in being accepted in the business world on their individual merits.[39]

When black managers supervise white employees, or when blacks deal with white customers, there is often blatant racial antagonism.[40] White employees tend to hold the perception that black managers are inferior until the managers "prove" their leadership abilities. Blacks who have risen to their managerial positions through affirmative action face resentment and are often hampered by uncooperative employees. Consequently, many black managers cannot be as effective as their white peers simply because they get little support from their employees. Those who succeed usually do so by being exceptionally capable and also by having the unusual ability to draw together workers from diverse backgrounds into effective work groups. In that sense, successful black managers may be far more effective at multicultural management than white managers.[41]

Managing in a multicultural organization involves dealing with people with many characteristics other than being female or African-American, but the space limitations of a management principles text do not allow us to address this subject in detail. The brief examples of women and blacks in management positions are meant to encourage students to seek out books and articles dedicated to specific cultural diversity issues.

Here we address several broad issues relating to leadership in culturally diverse companies.[42] Regardless of their own backgrounds, managers must develop an appreciation of individual differences among their employees, peers, and superiors. These individual differences are not always extreme—such as male versus female, black versus white—but are often subtle—such as differences between single working women and married working women with children. Expectations and priorities for work, benefits, and scheduling differ significantly between young men in their first jobs and men nearing retirement.[43] Language differences between Hispanic and Asian-American workers may result in different patterns of communication. Other subtle differences in values may exist between employees brought up in urban centers and those brought up in rural environments. Most Americans identify with their ancestral roots, and therefore tend to retain social and religious values reinforced through family and community relationships.

Consequently, appreciating individual differences is necessary to gain an understanding of how to communicate with employees, develop cohesive work groups, and become alert to potential problems when people with diverse interests work together. It is also necessary to structure incentive programs, reward appropriate behavior, discipline inappropriate behavior, and recognize those individuals with potential for advancement. In multicultural environments, recognizing individual contributions by developing individual incentive pay systems has been found useful. Also, accommodating individual problems such as parental child-care responsibilities or dual-career schedules can be accomplished through flextime programs, home office work arrangements, or job-sharing programs. These were discussed in Chapter 12. In contrast, developing integrated work teams, discussed in Chapter 11, can help draw employees together, thereby minimizing perceptual differences among people by focusing their efforts on cooperative goals. By creating an interdependent work environment, managers can forge team efforts that take priority over differences in personal values or characteristics.[44]

Transformational Leadership

Managing in a multicultural environment requires a pervasive change in organizational behavior. Instead of merely making adjustments in leadership behavior to accommodate diverse interests, managers must build new foundations of behavior to *transform* their organizations. This requires a new way of thinking about human resources. Although this requirement is vital, it is not a complete explanation of transformational leadership. **Transformational leadership** is the ability of leaders to make profound changes, to introduce new visions for their organizations, and to inspire people to work toward achieving those visions.[45]

transformational leadership
The ability of leaders to make profound changes, introduce new visions for their organizations, and inspire people to work toward achieving those visions.

The transformational perspective contrasts sharply with nearly everything we have previously said about management and leadership because in those presentations we emphasized *transactional* responsibilities. For most managers, transactional leadership is concerned with the daily management of resources and employees to achieve organizational objectives. Transactional behavior is therefore crucial, but it assumes a relatively stable environment or one of incremental change and adjustment. Transformational behavior, in contrast, assumes a fundamental change in the organization and where it is heading.[46]

Companies consistently ranked among America's best also consistently have had strong transformational leadership. During the past decade of fierce global competition, leaders who have been most noticed are those capable of redirecting their organizations toward *total quality management.* Most of these chief executive officers and their companies appear in this text and include Roy Vagelos of Merck & Company, Richard Ruch of Herman Miller Furniture, Robert McDermott of USAA Insurance, Jack Welch of General Electric, Don Petersen of Ford Motor Company, and the late Sam Walton of Wal-Mart. Each of these contemporary CEOs made an unusual commitment to change the fundamental culture of their organizations to focus on *continuous quality improvement* without compromise. Each had a strategic vision of change. Welch, for example, transformed GE from a plodding company making electric appliances and light bulbs into an innovative global corporation involved in telecommunications, aerospace technology, and diversified electronic systems. Walton redefined retailing as a comprehensive customer-driven industry. Petersen quietly turned Ford around from a poor-quality manufacturer to the best (and most recently, the most profitable) American automaker.[47]

Historically, the giants of industry have been the transformational leaders capable of mobilizing their organizations to pursue new dreams. These visionaries have created new industries, spearheaded technological revolutions, and often altered the course of behavior in society.[48] The achievements of Thomas Watson, Jr., Steven Jobs, and Martin Luther King, Jr., will not be forgotten for generations. And as we watch organizations such as General Motors and Caterpillar struggle with transactional problems or listen to presidential candidates whose agendas are mired in transactional modifications to existing problems, we await leaders who will step forward with new visions.

The new visions require *charismatic* leaders who exert extraordinary influence over others, commanding loyalty to new ideas and inducing performance by others to carry them out. Transformational leaders also have an unusual ability to create *intellectual stimulation*. They foster new ideas, encourage new ways of solving problems, and establish new agendas for their organizations by their own actions or by inspiring their employees. And the transformational leader is capable of managing organizational dualism whereby group endeavors—often in multicultural environments—are championed, yet individual differences are appreciated. Consequently, transformational leaders are capable of developing cohesive organizations through teamwork while maintaining personal relationships with employees, encouraging individual contributions, and helping employees to resolve their personal problems.[49]

Leadership in Perspective

The theories and models put forward to explain leadership behavior do not agree on how managers influence subordinates.[50] Some are concerned with behavior presumed to be associated with situational contingencies, but the relevance of situational contingencies is hotly debated. Others focus on personality traits or characteristics that differentiate effective leaders from ineffective leaders. Still others explain leadership in terms of subordinates' expectations and subsequent decisions that affect their behavior. And recent theories emphasize transformational leadership processes as distinguished from transactional considerations. The fact that these theories and models disagree on how managers influence behavior is less important than the things they have in common.

All the models emphasize that leadership skills can be learned. With the exception of those that claim the individual characteristics of leaders constrain behavioral change, most theories emphasize that managers can adapt and improve their skills. This suggests that a company might employ a skills approach to leadership that focuses on improving the interpersonal relationships of managers and their subordinates. Such an approach would nourish individual initiative while plausibly satisfying individual needs. Leadership research systematically emphasizes that employees are increasingly better educated and technologically skilled as knowledgeable workers. Consequently they are capable of solving complex problems and sharing responsibility for decisions. Expectations for leadership behavior are moving away from command relationships based on authority toward supportive behavior and team-based participation. Finally, leadership theories take into account the duality of organizational work whereby individual prerogatives cannot be allowed to subvert group priorities, yet individual contributions, needs, and differences are appreciated.

CHECKPOINT

- Describe what is meant by a multicultural environment, and explain how effective leaders address problems in these environments.
- How does transactional leadership differ from transformational leadership, and how are organizations affected by both?

AT THE BEGINNING OF THE CHAPTER, we described how Robert Horton, managing director of British Petroleum, set about to alter the fundamental nature of his organization. Early in his career, Horton developed the necessary skills to be an effective transactional leader who was able to manage resources and encourage people to perform well. Consequently, he was able to reposition Standard Oil of Ohio as a competitive company and to stabilize its operations. In his role as BP's managing director, he has become a transformational leader intent on realizing a new vision for the company through comprehensive changes that draw people together in participative systems. One of his highest priorities is to synthesize the interests of BP employees who come from diversified backgrounds on four continents, and he intends to do this by creating teamwork focused on organizational goals. Yet Horton takes a personal interest in the needs, attributes, and problems of his individual employees.[51] ■

A SYNOPSIS FOR LEARNING

1. Explain leadership and behavioral relationships in organizations.

Relationships between leaders and subordinates are critical for explaining how leaders behave. Leadership implies a system of inequalities in which superiors influence subordinates and direct behavior in groups to satisfy a wide variety of individual, organizational, and social objectives. Leadership behavior must account for human relationships as well as for task relationships.

2. Identify and discuss traits and characteristics of effective leaders.

Individuals become successful leaders by demonstrating their capability for eliciting results-oriented actions from subordinates. Effective leaders tend to be achievement-oriented and confident of their ability to perform well, solve problems, and influence others to perform well. They are relatively intelligent and capable of making effective judgments, have strong reasoning skills, and are often creative. The most effective leaders also skillfully apply management techniques to plan, organize, and control work.

3. Describe and contrast major theories on leadership. Discuss the Blake and Mouton Managerial Grid.

The Ohio State University and University of Michigan model consists of a two-dimensional grid—"concern for people" and "concern for tasks"—and four primary approaches to leadership—"abdicative," "directive," "supportive," and "participative." Likert's refinement of the model, *System 4 Management,* identifies similar behavioral sets ranging from "autocratic" to "participative."

Blake and Mouton's *Managerial Grid* combines the Ohio State and University of Michigan model and Likert's four systems of behavior into a nine-by-nine matrix encompassing a broad range of leadership behavior.

Fiedler's *contingency theory* suggests that successful leadership results from matching managers' styles, which are grounded in personality and thus hard to change, with situations. There is no one best approach to leadership, but rather an optimal approach in each situation. Robert House's *path-goal theory* links this contingency approach to expectancy theory by specifying that a leader's responsibility is to increase subordinates' motivation to perform work by providing a path, or a direction, for accomplishing tasks that leads to expected rewards. The path-goal model adds to participation or team building a dimension called "achievement-oriented leadership."

The *Vroom-Yetton model* incorporates expectancy theory of motivation into a formal decision-tree analysis. Managers adapt their behavior according to a systematic analysis of the task environment and leader-subordinate relationships. This model proposes that it is the type of decision that influences leadership style rather than the other way around.

The *Hersey and Blanchard life cycle theory* is conceptually similar to Fiedler's theory. However, Fiedler based his theory on personality characteristics and situational variables, while the life cycle model focuses on the "maturity" of subordinates, defined as the experience, skill, and ability to perform a task combined with the psychological willingness to assume responsibility. Managers adopt one of four approaches to leadership, ranging from delegating to telling, according to both the nature of the task and a group profile of the maturity of subordinates.

The Blake and Mouton Managerial Grid has two dimensions, each with nine points that create a matrix of coordinates. One dimension is the manager's degree of "concern for people," and the other is his or her degree of "concern for production." In each dimension, a scale value of 1 implies least concern and a scale value of 9 implies maximum concern. Therefore a 1,1 orientation, suggests little concern for either people or production (impoverished management). At the opposite extreme, a 9,9 orientation indicates a fully participative approach to leadership that seeks to attain both maximum satisfaction for employees and maximum work results (team management). Other benchmarks on the grid are a 1,9 orientation, which implies a low concern for tasks and a high concern for employees (country club management); and a 9,1 orientation, which suggests a high concern for production with little regard for subordinates (authority-obedience management).

4. Discuss how motivation and leadership are interrelated and explain the role of decision making in effective leadership.

The common assumption of leadership models is that leadership is a process of influencing subordinates to perform well in exchange for something they value. Likert's System 4 model assumes there is "one best way" to lead—through participation—implying that, in general, subordinates want to be involved in decisions and will be more productive when they have a voice in directing their work. Blake and Mouton propose that leadership behavior must be matched to subordinates' expectations.

Both the Vroom-Yetton model and the path-goal theory are explicitly based on the expectancy theory of motivation. According to Vroom-Yetton, leaders model their behavior in concert with organizational expectations for performance and employees' expectations for rewards, whereas the path-goal theory proposes that leaders clarify a direction of effort for work that leads to rewards subordinates perceive as important.

Contingency theories encompass a wide range of motivational elements, including content needs of employees, perceptions of job satisfaction, perceptions of task requirements, and the interaction required between superiors and subordinates. These theories take a situational approach, incorporating both human and task elements of the organizational environment. Leadership consists of motivating employees to fulfill organizational goals while satisfying their personal expectations for participation.

5. Describe the multicultural environment and transformational leadership as critical management issues.

As organizations become more culturally diversified, managers must acclimate themselves to changes taking place in their work groups. Cultural diversity is explained by the profile of individuals working for the organization, including their sex, race, ethnic, age, and religious characteristics. Within this framework, organizational leaders are concerned with providing appropriate opportunities for minorities, reconciling differences in behavior among their employees, and, most important, transforming their organization into multicultural enterprises devoid of stereotypes and unproductive biases.

Transformational leadership addresses the human resource issues of managing a multicultural organization, but it also encompasses a philosophy of leadership whereby leaders are able to make profound changes, introduce new visions for their organizations, and inspire people to work toward achieving those visions. In contrast to transactional leadership, which focuses on incremental changes or adjustments in relatively stable environments, transformational leadership is the process of making fundamental changes in where an organization is headed.

CASE 1 Tune in to Management from Mars

SKILL ANALYSIS

Watch out for the Japanese, and stay abreast of developments in Germany, but learn management from Mars—not the planet, but Mars, Inc., the $12 billion American multinational. So goes the advice of people who have worked for the Mars family, which owns one of the most obscure corporations in the world.

The company was founded by Forrest E. Mars, Sr., in 1923, when, as a schoolboy, he began making Milky Way candy bars. Today Mars has more than 1,000 products in a dozen product lines sold on 5 continents in nearly 150 languages. It is a family-owned business five times larger than arch-rival Hershey Foods Corporation, and second only to the Swiss conglomerate Nestlé SA in combined international markets. Mars is famous for M&M's, Snickers, Milky Way, Twix, Skittles, Bounty, and Starburst Fruit Chews, but few people know that it leads all competitors in pet foods, including Whiskas, Expert, Pedigree (formerly Kal Kan), Bowser, and Kitty. The company is Number 1 in parboiled rice (Uncle Ben's) and ice-cream novelties (Dove Bars and Rondos), and it makes 25 percent of all the candy and snack foods consumed in the United States.

Mars, however, is managed with a headquarters staff of only 51 people—5,000 fewer than companies with comparable products and markets. With 28,000 employees worldwide, productivity per employee based on gross sales is twice that of Nestlé and three times better than food industry averages. How the Mars family has achieved this is the stuff myths are made of, and much of what is known about Mars has quietly slipped out over a half-century of business. The Mars family does not give interviews, allow company studies, or invite attention. Yet it is known to hold several axioms sacred.

Bureaucracy is anathema. Consequently, writing memos is against company policy, and everyone, including family members, is addressed by first name. Meetings take place only as needed, and there are no private offices. The founder's two sons, Forrest Jr. and John, and his daughter, Jackie, share simple desks in an open office area with their headquarters staff. There are no reserved parking places for anyone; bonuses are the same for everyone, including family members; and status is a dirty word. All Mars people make their own photocopies, handle telephone calls without secretaries, and clean their own work area.

Mars employees have always been called *associates,* and everyone from the company president on down punches a time clock and earns a 10 percent bonus for consistently arriving on time. Employee compensation is the highest in the industry, but executive pay is the lowest. Everyone is on a step-increase system, getting the same annual pay adjustments as everyone else. All employees and managers are cross-trained and rotated among five to seven jobs. Vice presidents have worked in every functional area, including shop-floor production, quality assurance, marketing, and human resource management. Most have also held positions in at least two foreign posts, where they are paid exactly the same salaries and benefits.

Lacking "office suites," managers are immersed in an open communications environment. Whether in Indonesia, Japan, or Mexico City, the pattern of work is the same as at Mars' Virginia headquarters. A senior manager's desk is located at the center of a cluster of managers who report to that manager. Beyond this circle are other managers or staff work areas forming similar clusters. Consequently, when something has to be said, it requires nothing more than speaking across one's desk. All offices are near plant operations, and employees have access to managers and managers to employees.

Cleanliness is an obsession and quality control a compulsion at Mars. The "M" on M&M's, for example, must be perfectly placed on every piece, and the slightest flaw in the appetizing squiggle of milk chocolate on a candy bar will prompt managers to discard the entire batch. Floors, desks, and machinery are cleaned and polished regularly, and plant conditions are monitored for bacteria levels; every Mar's plant is cleaner and safer than the best family kitchens.

Since success is measured by "return on assets" rather than by investors' earnings, every company asset—from office telephones to production equipment—is maintained in top condition. Family members—though billionaires—all fly commercial class, take no dividends other than their share of bonuses, and reinvest all profits in the company. Employees say they enjoy outstanding health and benefit coverage, excellent retirement benefits, and when business is booming (as it is in most years), they can earn in bonuses the equivalent of ten to fifteen weeks' pay.

On the downside, family members have been known to explode in anger over minor quality flaws or mistakes. They make no bones about being in control. Few employees quit Mars, but violating a safety standard, quarreling with another employee, or failing to maintain a clean workplace can result in immediate dismissal. And, yes, the quickest way to lose a job at Mars is to talk to anyone outside the company about the company. This unique and consistent management style, even though harsh in some ways, commands respect and nearly total commitment by everyone in the Mars planetary system.

Case Questions

1. Describe Mars' management in terms of expectancy theory and the life-cycle approach to leadership.
2. How can the Mars family command allegiance from employees and run a global corporation with so few executives and such simple operations?

3. Describe how Mars' employees are motivated and identify which motivating factors are missing at the company.

Sources: Joel Glenn Brenner, "Planet of the M&M's," *Washington Post Magazine,* April 12, 1992, pp. 11–19, 24–26. See also Craig J. Cantoni, "Quality Control from Mars," *Wall Street Journal,* January 27, 1992, p. A12.

VIDEO CASE Southwest Airlines' Strong-Arm Leader: Herb Kelleher

In the dogfight being waged over America's skies, one company is flying high with the industry's top profits for 1991. Southwest Airlines, the Dallas maverick, enjoyed its nineteenth straight profitable year. The company also had the best complaint record of any major airline in 1991, according to the Department of Transportation. Even Southwest's competition reluctantly acknowledges the airline's success. An executive with American Airlines states, "Southwest has found a very interesting point in the value curve. . . . They produce a very simple product and then they deliver with high quality what they promise and they do so at a very low price." Much of the company's accomplishments can be attributed to its feisty, unpredictable, and somewhat whacky chairman, Herb Kelleher.

Kelleher keeps his company on top by knowing what direction he wants to go in and never allowing the company to stray from that direction. He states, "We understand what we're doing. We understand that we do it very well, but we're also humble enough to realize that if we attempt to ape what somebody else is doing and if we attempt to compete on their turf we probably can't do it as well as they can." Southwest's strategy has always been to appeal to a niche market of short flights between thirty-three cities in fifteen states. The airline offers less service in return for a cheaper ticket. There are no meals, no seat assignments, no luggage checked through, and no big-ticket tickets. Paying an average fare of $56, Southwest's customers appear to be satisfied. The company assuredly has found a formula for delivering customer value at a good profit.

Although Southwest doesn't provide a lot of the amenities that other airlines offer, it makes sure that its customers are treated well and courteously and that they have fun while on Southwest. "We're like friends, the employees and the customers," remarks a skycap. Another Southwest employee states, "It's kind of casual. You get up there, put everybody on a plane, have a good time with them, socialize with them, get them on board, get them ready to go, and make them happy." It's all part of the corporate culture that Kelleher has created, which reflects his own brand of humor and individuality. For example, when Sea World was scouting for its official airline, Kelleher had one of Southwest Airlines' Boeing 737s painted to look like Shamu the Killer Whale, one of Sea World's best-known performers. The airline won hands down the prize of being named Sea World's official carrier. Southwest's director of corporate development explains the company's unusual corporate culture this way: "Humor not only is a great learning tool, but humor is also a great stress tool, and this is an organization that has fun while we work."

Herb Kelleher's latest adventure occurred in settling a dispute over rights to the slogan "Just Plane Smart," which both Southwest and Stevens Aviation were using. Both parties wanted to avoid a costly and drawn-out lawsuit, so, says Kelleher, "They suggested that we arm wrestle for the right to the slogan, and in a P.S. they said 'we want to tell you that our chairman bench-presses a Cessna every day.'" As any good leader would do in rising to the challenge, the sixty-one-year-old Kelleher went into training to meet his thirty-seven-year-old opponent.

So how did Southwest's strong-arm leader, "Smokin' Herb Kelleher," fare in the aviation sporting event of the decade? "Killer Kurt" Herwald of Stevens Aviation vanquished Kelleher, winning the match—called "Malice in Dallas"—*and* $10,000 for his chosen charity. In a surprise decision, however, Herwald announced that Southwest could continue to use the slogan in exchange for a $5,000 contribution to the Ronald McDonald House! Herb Kelleher may have lost the arm-wrestling contest, but his airline continues to dominate the skies.

Case Questions

1. Is Herb Kelleher a leader? If not, why not? If so, how does he demonstrate leadership?
2. What role does a leader play in influencing corporate culture? How has Herb Kelleher done this?
3. Can Herb Kelleher be called a transformational leader? Why or why not?

Sources: Bridget O'Brian, "After All, Concerns' Strong-Arm Tactics Don't Settle Dispute," *Wall Street Journal*, March 23, 1992, p. B3D; Charles A. Jaffe, "Moving Fast by Standing Still," *Nation's Business*, October 1991, Vol. 70, No. 10, p. 57ff; and David A. Brown "Southwest's Success, Growth Tied to Maintaining Original Concept," *Aviation Week and Space Technology*, May 27, 1991, Vol. 134, No. 21, p. 75ff.

SKILL PRACTICE

LEADERSHIP PERCEPTION

Leadership involves influencing others to alter their behavior in constructive ways to support organizational endeavors. Managers in leadership roles benefit from a certain degree of authority delegated to their positions, but their actual *influence* depends on one or more power sources. It also depends on their subordinates' acceptance of them as leaders and the reciprocal relationships that evolve. In this exercise, you are asked to work in small teams to identify people who are influential and to describe why they are able to exert influence.

Team Deliberation

Teams of three or four individuals will be formed to work together. Each team will identify two influential people whom class members are likely to know and be able to talk about. People to consider may include politicians or government leaders, business people, social activists, public opinion leaders, and local people known to students. Develop a profile of these choices that includes:

1. Your perception of their power source for influencing others.
2. Their style of leadership defined according to one of the theories discussed in the chapter.
3. Their perceived reciprocal relationships with subordinates. (Time = 10 minutes)

Preliminary Report

Each team will report through a spokesperson its two choices and its profiles of these leaders. The instructor will list the selections and the whole class will vote to select the three most influential people identified. Each of the leaders selected must have a different power base and different subordinates or constituents. (Time = 6–8 minutes)

Team Evaluation of Leadership Issues

Then each team will reconvene to prepare a profile on each of the three leaders selected by the class, addressing the following points:

1. Evaluate each person's perceived power base and describe how other bases may come into play.
2. Describe each person's leadership in terms of one of the leadership theories discussed in this chapter, supporting your perceptual comments with leadership concepts.
3. List individual or group feelings (all that apply) about whether each of the selected leaders could influence you (individually or as a group) to want to follow and perform. Explain why or why not.

Final Team Report

Each group's spokesperson will report group findings, and these will be summarized on a blackboard or chart. (The instructor may appoint someone to do this or ask the group spokesperson to make the list.) (Time = 10–15 minutes)

Discussion

Be prepared to defend your answers and to question other groups' responses. The ultimate point of this exercise is to reveal any pattern of consensus about leadership profiles, styles, traits, or behavior. If no pattern is discovered, why are there divergent viewpoints? How do the three leaders selected stack up against theory? Is there one best way to manage? If so, how and why?

15

Managing Change and Conflict

OUTLINE

OBJECTIVES

- Discuss the concept and nature of organizational change.
- Explain the process of change and major approaches to effect change.
- Discuss organizational development and intervention techniques.
- Describe types of conflict within organizations.
- Discuss methods of resolving conflict while enhancing healthy competition.
- Relate stress to organizational productivity and personal health.
- Explain how organizations and individuals within organizations can manage stress.

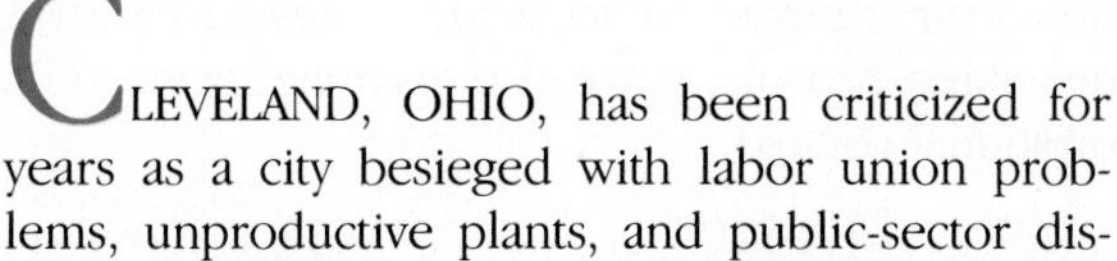

CLEVELAND, OHIO, has been criticized for years as a city besieged with labor union problems, unproductive plants, and public-sector disputes involving "slowdowns" and "no-show protests" by city employees. On the positive side, the Cleveland area has several of the most innovative companies in the nation. Now the city's public housing authority is demonstrating how a civil service agency can join the ranks of outstanding organizations.[1]

The Cuyahoga Metropolitan Housing Authority was one of Cleveland's most troubled agencies until 1990, when changes were introduced to make civil-service employees more responsible for their work. The agency had 600 field employees who maintained buildings housing more than 17,000 families, but work was shoddy and tenants complained bitterly about having to wait six months for such minor repairs as fixing leaky faucets. Buildings were littered, covered with graffiti, and becoming very rundown. Broken windows and faulty wiring created safety risks. Strict union rules forced management to assign overtime on a seniority basis, and employees observed union job demarcations to a fault. An electrician, for example, would not pick up litter because that was someone else's job.

In 1990, the housing authority put in place a program of systematic changes that began addressing the housing authority's problems. By 1992, the seniority system had been abandoned in favor of a task assignment system created jointly with employees. All workers became eligible for overtime, and those with the best work records went to the top of the list. Cooperation replaced demarcation disputes as crews were allowed to assign tasks among themselves. Training was initiated with the creation of a "model apartment" used for upgrading employee skills, and joint problem solving was initiated through employee teams with supervisory participation.

These efforts paid off in fewer tenant complaints, quicker resolution of maintenance problems, and major improvements in building cleanliness. Work crews cleared litter, cleaned off graffiti, and added new landscaping. The housing authority has earned a reputation for efficiency and quality. The change process has not been easy, however. Union representatives and managers have had bitter confrontations, some employees have transferred out of the agency, and supervisors feel disenfranchised by the empowerment of employees.

Organizations continually adapt and change. For some, change is slow and subtle; for others, it is rapid and obvious. Managers are emphatically involved with change, adaptation, and innovation to improve organizational performance. In fact, the single most important challenge for managers is to achieve change constructively.

Change also implies disruption; the cliché that "just when you get used to doing something one way, someone changes it" contains a good deal of truth. Change can be disruptive and stressful; it can lead to conflict. Nonetheless, it is essential in a progressive organization.

In terms of the four management functions, change is a critical element in *planning,* as organizations redefine objectives and propose new strategies for attaining them. Change can be examined in terms of *organizing* because it often involves redefining authority structures and the nature of work. It is primarily studied in conjunction with *leading* because change often means a redefinition of leadership relationships. Finally, change is related to *controlling,* as managers adapt to circumstances to keep their organizations viable.

In this chapter, we first discuss the nature of change and then how managers handle sensitive changes in their organizations. A vital part of the chapter concerns how to minimize conflict while achieving constructive change. Because change can be anxiety-provoking, we also examine stress and how it can be managed in an organizational context.

THE NATURE OF ORGANIZATIONAL CHANGE

Organizational change cannot be defined in simple terms because it can occur across a broad spectrum—an industry-wide revolution in technology—or narrowly—a refinement of one individual job description. Managers rarely take a wide view of change, and they often fail even to admit that it is needed. Realistically, most organizational changes occur only when managers are under pressure to make them.[2] The impetus for change is usually a heightened sense of dissatisfaction or an outright crisis, as Figure 15-1 shows. Without this impetus, most people tend to resist upsetting the status quo. Michael Beer, an organizational development analyst, explains the nature of change thus:

> Crisis provides the motivation to change. It sufficiently raises dissatisfaction with the status quo to overcome resistance caused by the costs of change to organizational members. These costs are the pain of change itself which may threaten individual or group identity, sense of competence, power, status, pay, and even job security. These costs can be felt at all levels of the organization.[3]

If change is resisted until there is a crisis, it follows that few organizations experience smooth change processes. Change seems to induce an erratic pattern of behavior in most instances. What Beer has indicated is that organizations can operate for years making continuous but subtle changes that are insufficient to make a real difference, and then suddenly reach a point when dissatisfaction erupts into a phenomenal change process. This was the pattern in the automotive industry. For years

FIGURE 15-1 Impetus to Change

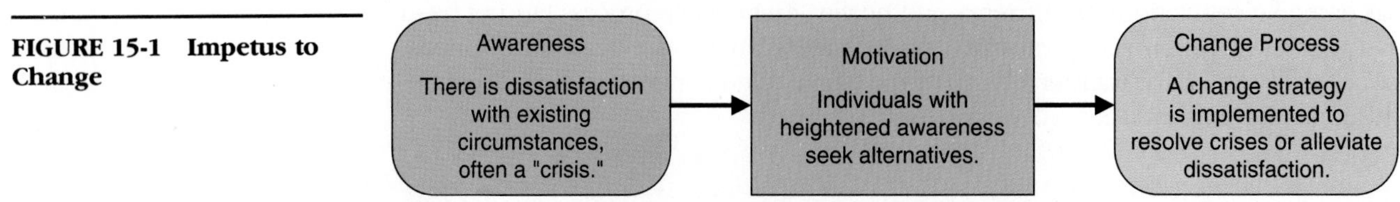

U.S. automakers inched forward with product alterations, cosmetic changes, and periodic flashes of brilliance. Then long-built-up pressures exploded, shattering the industry. Foreign competitors moved in, taking huge shares of the markets; energy shortages decimated consumer demand for large cars; and shoddy products became headline news. Consequently, auto manufacturers instituted strategic changes such as organizational realignments, new technologies, new processes, new auto designs, and rapid marketing adaptations. Many of these changes began a decade ago and are only now beginning to show results.

Change also causes apparent contradictions. For example, Gradall Company, an Ohio manufacturer of construction equipment, hired high-salaried CAD/CAM engineers just as it was terminating nearly half its work force. Workers who were aware that the company had suffered losses could not easily reconcile the trade-off between production employees and high-priced systems engineers.[4]

Forces Influencing Change

External conditions may influence a company to change more than internal situations. New technology, for example, leads to changes in skill requirements for production workers, which in turn signal new management systems with commensurate changes in leadership. Technology that alters products or services also alters financing and facility requirements. In addition, technological changes may require new marketing techniques as well as purchasing and communication systems, with each setting off a chain reaction of behavioral adjustments.[5]

Competitive pressure spurs management to adapt or suffer marketing losses. Only a few years ago, for example, Compaq Computer Company was the rising star of the personal computer industry. Then in 1990, clone systems began challenging Compaq's markets, and to survive, the company had to drastically cut prices. Consumer expectations fostered change from the demand side: Compaq found that customers wanted bargain prices coupled with reliable products. Before the company could react sufficiently, however, Packard Bell Electronics—a company that was virtually bankrupt in 1985—had rushed past Compaq to the Number 3 position after IBM and Apple by marketing PCs through discount outlets like Circuit City and consumer buyers' clubs. Incidentally, Packard Bell, once a top competitor in U.S. television sales, had become so bureaucratically entangled in financial manipulations that it failed in the early 1980s, then sold out to new owners who repositioned the company in personal computers.[6]

Other factors that contribute to competitive pressure and influence change include changes in competitors' product quality, new services, safety performance, pricing, and new distribution systems such as discount outlets. Economic conditions affect everything a company does, from capital expansion to hiring employees. Politics and legislation can lead to pervasive changes in company operations, hiring processes, and employee benefits. Finally, sociocultural trends such as nuclear power (or pressure to abandon it) and public concern for the environment can redefine a firm's fundamental philosophy about how it operates in society.

Internal considerations that may influence a company to change include labor relations, employee problems, intraorganizational conflict, and a variety of financial ailments. The more intense the situation, the more likely change will occur. The massive downsizing and layoffs that began rippling through companies like IBM and GM in early 1992 were the direct result of several years of disastrously low profits and skyrocketing costs.[7] When intensity increases, managers "react," often instigating change through scare tactics or induced discomfort. Caterpillar Corporation made tremendous changes by cutting its labor force, introducing new production techniques, and creating a strategic thrust to regain its competitive posture through a corporate-wide drive for high quality. Sales began to rise and the company announced good profit margins in 1990, but too many rapid changes and too many employee cuts resulted in a massive strike late in 1991 that stretched into 1992. Caterpillar found itself temporarily paralyzed.[8]

Even intense situations can be controlled with good planning. USAA, a San Antonio insurance and financial services company, for example, faced major competition from companies four times its size. In 1987, CEO Robert McDermott announced a complete corporate restructuring that included new computerized technology, training for more than 800 employees in new telecommunications systems, and pay-for-performance systems based on client service for all field claim adjusters and customer representatives. McDermott also reassured employees that their jobs would be secure and the change process would be well planned over a five-year period. By 1992, USAA had implemented these and many more changes, had risen to a top-ten position in the insurance industry, and had gained a reputation as one of the best-managed companies in America.[9]

Climate for Change

For change to take place successfully, those affected must be psychologically willing to make the effort. Although the initiators have a heightened sense of dissatisfaction with the way things are, others who will be affected may not recognize change is needed. Thus an automotive executive who realizes that robotic welding machines are essential to maintain competitive production costs must convince welders and their union leaders of that fact. Several key assumptions illustrate management's responsibility for establishing the proper climate for change. Edgar H. Schein offers the following observations.[10]

1. Any change process involves not only learning something new but also unlearning something that is well integrated into the personality and social relationships of the individual.
2. No change will occur unless the motivation to change is present. Inducing that motivation is often the most difficult part of the change process.
3. Organizational changes in authority structures, processes, and systems occur only through individual change by key members of organizations.
4. Change involves altering attitudes, values, and behavior. The unlearning of present responses can initially be painful and threatening.
5. Change is a multistage process, a complex cycle of behavioral modification that requires a systematic approach.

Schein's assumptions are concerned with how large organizations cope with significant changes, but the issues are the same with small groups or individuals. His first point emphasizes that we must relinquish our strong commitment to established patterns of behavior in order to change. His second point emphasizes that the benefits of change are often hard to see by those most affected; welders replaced by robots are not going to feel enthused about robotics' potential for raising corporate profits. His third point is that change comes only through personal leadership. His fourth point concerns the psychological dimensions of behavior. Finally, his last point assumes a cycle of sensing, communicating, adapting, and controlling behavior. For these reasons, initiating can be extremely difficult. Even slight changes may be disruptive if managers fail to generate the proper climate before attempting them.

The Change Process

There are several change models, but nearly all of them are based on a simple paradigm developed by Kurt Lewin. His model is illustrated in Figure 15-2 and consists of the following three-stage process:[11]

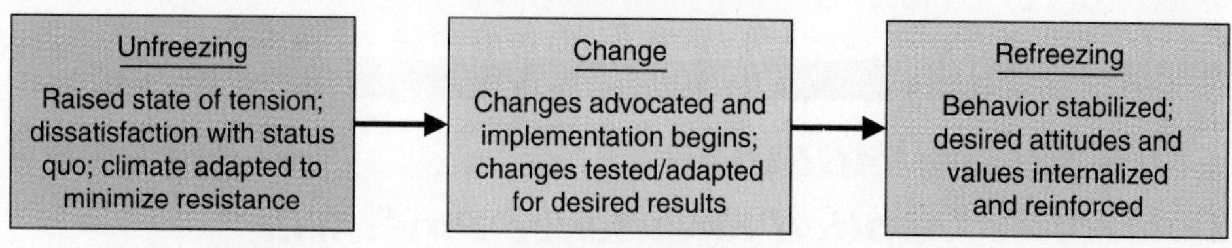
Unfreezing
Raised state of tension; dissatisfaction with status quo; climate adapted to minimize resistance
Change
Changes advocated and implementation begins; changes tested/adapted for desired results
Refreezing
Behavior stabilized; desired attitudes and values internalized and reinforced

FIGURE 15-2 Three-Stage Change Process

Source: Based on Kurt Lewin, "Group Decisions and Social Change," in G. E. Swenson, T. M. Newcomb, and E. L. Hartley (eds.), *Readership in Social Psychology* (New York: Holt, Rinehart & Winston, 1952), pp. 459-473.

1. *Unfreezing.* In stage 1, an unfreezing process convinces individuals that present conditions or behavior are inappropriate. As noted earlier, critical events or managers can raise anxieties so that people stop defending the "old ways" and begin seeking alternatives.[12] Individuals contemplating change must also believe that it is safe to relinquish established values and behavior before change can proceed.
2. *Change.* In stage 2, new behavior is developed and change is effected through a conscious process as individuals seek to resolve the anxieties that surfaced during stage 1. Change is achieved in one of two ways: Either individuals systematically scan the environment for new ideas and then implement a choice, or they emulate others who have made similar changes successfully.[13] In the first instance, change is planned. In the second, an imitation process evolves, perhaps by trial and error.
3. *Refreezing.* In stage 3, preferred behavior is stabilized. This can be a long process, requiring patience and commitment. People are unlikely to adjust immediately to significant changes.[14] Most are more likely to "try on" changes before actually "buying" them. They will test whether the changes are congruent with their ethics and beliefs and will need confirmation that the new methods actually work. Whenver there is change, everyone is so sensitive to results that even a trace of doubt will trigger a retreat to the safety of the old behavior. Recognition and reinforcement are necessary to refreeze the new, preferred behavior.

The process in perspective. Lewin's model is concerned with psychological adaptation to changes that modify personal behavior. If employees view changes as unjustified, the adaptation process may fail to take place. Although conceptually simple, the process can be extremely complex in practice. Difficult interpersonal relationships, uncommitted leaders, inflexible authority structures, corporate politics, and many other factors can thwart change. That is why organizations often hire skilled consultants to facilitate the change process.[15] We address the consulting issue later in this chapter.

Change and Ethical Issues

The very nature of change requires managers to accept roles as change agents. Lewin's stage 1 has the potential for creating anxiety or stress. Inducing others to become dissatisfied may be dangerous and unethical. For example, a company president who announces to employees that there will be widespread layoffs unless the firm makes sweeping reforms raises the anxiety level of employees. If the president then uses this heightened anxiety as leverage in bargaining with the employees' union to win wage concessions, there may be good cause to question his or her ethics. If the firm is honestly faced with severe losses requiring cost reductions, the president may have a valid argument, but if inventory costs are out of control or sales are down because of poor marketing, frightening workers into wage concessions rather than solving the real problem is unethical.

When consultants are called in, disruptions can occur. Consultants have no vested interest in the organization. Unlike managers, they do not have to experience the pain of discarding old habits or the stress of introducing new expectations.[16] The

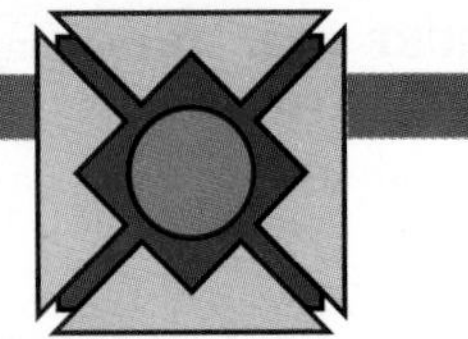

ETHICS IN MANAGEMENT

Polaroid's "Applied Knowledge Pay": Will Employees See Reward or Manipulation?

While companies are shrinking their work forces, they are also trying to hold on to their best employees and to increase productivity by using fewer people to get more accomplished. One of the techniques being employed by executives and consultants is to change compensation systems to so-called skill-based pay. The concept of skill-based pay is that while wage rates are kept stable, or perhaps even reduced, employees get the opportunity to earn bonuses based on their results. If they raise productivity, they earn incentive wages. Although this is not a new twist (Frederick Taylor introduced incentives at the turn of the century), the notion of "skill-based rewards" sounds new.

Polaroid Corporation, for example, has not achieved a significant increase in sales or profits since the mid-1980s, and to counteract this stagnation, the company introduced a skill-based system known as *applied-knowledge pay (AKP).* Employees are rewarded both for the skills and knowledge they apply at work and for their individual contributions to team goals. AKP is linked to changes in individual behavior—specifically to work on teams—and employees can achieve a higher AKP wage level (i.e., a higher wage increment) by upgrading their skills. The company believes these changes will motivate employees to achieve higher productivity and a stronger sales record.

Employees at Polaroid, however, are mum about the program, and similar efforts at other companies have had only short-lived faddish appeal. Although it is too early to tell if Polaroid's plan will work, successful programs based on pervasive compensation changes are those that were developed and nourished for the long run, not just to turn around sluggish performance. Disgruntled employees of many companies—many of them now out of work—point out that similar pay schemes were part of a series of manipulative changes attempted by management, and that these changes were made without really empowering employees to guide their own destinies. Consequently, there was no change in leadership or in employee attitudes—except, perhaps, an increased cynicism about management.

Sources: "New Ways to Pay," *The Economist,* July 13, 1991, p. 69. See also Brian O'Reilly, "Preparing for Leaner Times," *Fortune,* January 27, 1992, pp. 40-47.

refreezing stage is as critical as the unfreezing stage because once again values and attitudes are being modified. If handled improperly, the refreezing process can regress to brainwashing.[17] To continue the wage concession scenario, suppose a firm truly has overly high wage costs and hires consultants to solve its problem. If after the consultants effect the necessary wage changes management continues to make dramatic pronouncements about high wage costs, employees may become paranoid about their future. Such an environment is repressive, and neither the company nor its employees are likely to benefit.

Managing change and controlling subsequent behavioral adaptations are critical responsibilities. Managers cannot wait for the right conditions to emerge to take action. Instead, they must initiate change. Several approaches to change are discussed in the next section.

CHECKPOINT

- Discuss how technology, competition, and internal factors such as labor relations and employee expectations influence change.
- Describe five assumptions that create a climate for change to occur in an organization.
- Identify and explain the three-stage change process.

MANAGING ORGANIZATIONAL CHANGE

Change occurs in all organizations as they grow, consolidate, introduce new products, pursue different customers, adapt to new technology, and compete in a society that is itself changing. Many changes are small ones that occur in the normal course of daily affairs. These constitute adjustments to keep the enterprise focused on its objectives. Others are substantial changes that can permanently reshape the company. Between these extremes, there are considerable variations in the types of changes that occur and the attention required by managers to implement them. Consequently, how change is managed depends on the *type* of change taking place, its potential ramifications, and, as we shall see, the *approach* top management endorses to implement change.

Types of Change

As a convenience, managers think of changes in two broad categories: those that are *incremental* and those that are *strategic*. Each category is further refined as being *anticipated* or *unexpected*.[18]

incremental change An adjustment that can be implemented within the existing framework of operations.

Incremental change. Small changes with little risk occur regularly. These **incremental changes** are adjustments that can be implemented within the existing framework of operations. A marketing manager, for example, might introduce a new advertising campaign aimed at repositioning products in new markets; or a production manager might train employees to work with computer-assisted machinery, thereby changing how work is accomplished. Most incremental changes can be anticipated by organizations that plan systematically and are careful to stay abreast of industry and social trends. Managing change in this environment is described as *tuning* or *adapting* to circumstances. Successful organizations have planning systems to help managers, for example, tune their marketing programs or adapt their production techniques to new customers, products, or technologies. They have good human resource planning to address incremental changes necessary to recruit, develop, and retain employees. Similar planning processes exist for any functional or operational area.

Managers can be surprised by unexpected events, and when these occur, implementing even small changes can be stressful. This situation is described as *reactive change* because managers are forced to react to something they failed to anticipate, often because of poor planning or because the company has become too myopic to recognize its own shortcomings. Unexpected events can also occur in the form of government legislation, revolutionary changes in technology, and social factors. For example, consider how many organizations and people were affected by the breakup of the Soviet Union. Although the breakup and the new political confederation that came out of it had major ramifications, there were also many small changes managers in thousands of organizations worldwide had to adapt to. To offer

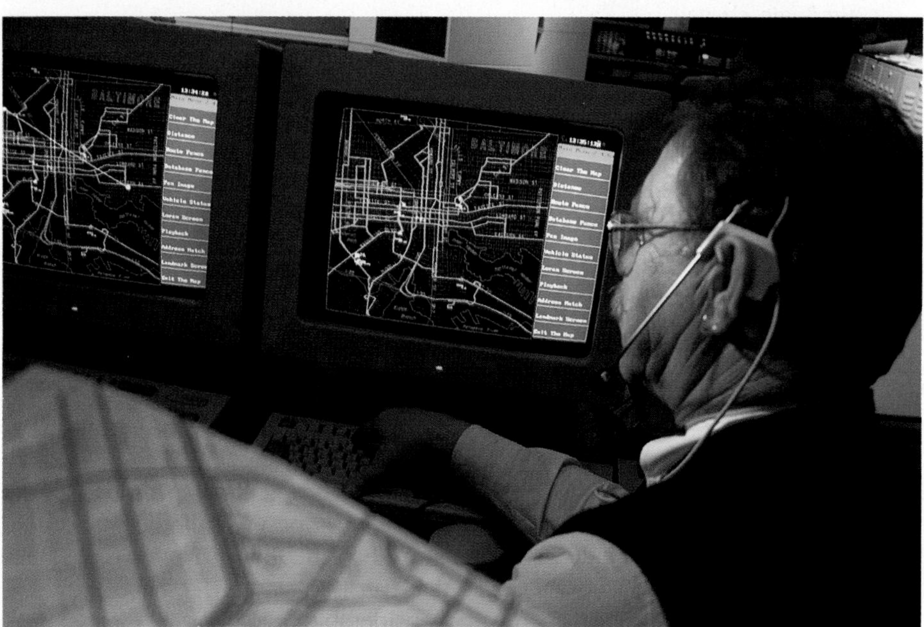

In the aftermath of the cold war, most U.S. defense contractors are counting on "defense conversion" as a way of restructuring for survival in the wake of large defense cuts. Explains Richard A. Linder, president of Westinghouse Electronic Systems, "We're leveraging our defense technology and expertise into other areas." For Westinghouse, a major producer of defense radar and electronic warfare gear, conversion means producing systems to control air traffic, track buses, and protect homes. Massive corporate restructuring efforts have had low success rates historically. However, most defense contractors are betting that they can make the transition by venturing, as Westinghouse Electronic has done, into related technologies. Still, says Katherine Gillman, a senior associate at the Office of Technology Assessment, "I don't see how we're going to avoid some pain." Indeed, despite its efforts, Westinghouse Electronic Systems was forced to fire 3,000 workers in 1991.

one example, Olympic teams previously known as "Soviet" had to reorganize based on the new eleven-member Commonwealth of Independent States, changing team members' alliances, funding, and representation for the 1992 Olympics. The teams also had to adapt to new titles, uniforms, coaches, and competition. Other countries had to adapt to new competition from a number of new independent nations.[19] Obviously, reactive change can be rather complex, if not chaotic.

strategic change
A major effort that redefines an organization, its objectives, or its methods of doing business.

Strategic change. Major changes that redefine the organization, its objectives, or its methods of doing business are called **strategic.** When strategic changes are anticipated, they can be systematically implemented. Specialists in change techniques call this type of change "frame bending," or *reorientation,* because although the organization redirects its efforts, it does not change its fundamental business frame of reference.[20]

PepsiCo, for example, decided in 1990 to reshape its Kentucky Fried Chicken subsidiary. PepsiCo changed the subsidiary's name to KFC, committed hundreds of millions of dollars to reposition KFC in the fast-food market, and replaced the subsidiary's executive staff. In an effort to expand rapidly on a global scale, KFC dropped the down-home image (the "Colonel's" picture disappeared from all packaging); put in new operating systems for supply distribution, food preparation, and management; and created an expanded product line of menu items. At the operational level, KFC's managers followed a planned program of incremental changes ranging from training in food preparation and delivery to new marketing efforts such as packaging chicken snacks for sporting events. A year later, KFC had turned around. After nearly a decade of losses and falling market share, KFC registered a 9 percent growth rate and a 28 percent increase in profits.[21]

Strategic change can also be *reactive,* the result of major unexpected events. Reactive strategic change can pose significant problems for an organization. In many instances, companies must make changes in their fundamental business concepts in order to survive. Because these changes are so severe, they are called "frame breaking," implying that the organization must construct a new frame of reference for its long-term purpose.[22]

The breakup of the Soviet Union led to improved relations between the new coalition of nations headed by Yeltsin and the United States. This produced major reductions in defense projects and military weaponry, which led to huge cuts in defense spending. In response, Boeing, Lockheed, General Dynamics, and other major U.S. aerospace and defense contractors resorted to immediate short-term survival solutions, such as employment cutbacks. But top management at these firms also began laying the foundations for repositioning their companies in commercial markets with nondefense products.[23] Although it may be years before these companies achieve this transformation, managers are intensely involved now in redefining their organizational frame of reference.

Approaches to Change

Characterizing change as either incremental or strategic is a broad generalization. How changes are implemented is also framed in broad generalizations to reflect different philosophies of change behavior. Convenient terms have evolved for three general approaches to change: *top-down, bottom-up,* and *participative* methods. These approaches are illustrated in Figure 15-3; they parallel the organizational approaches to planning studied in Chapter 6.

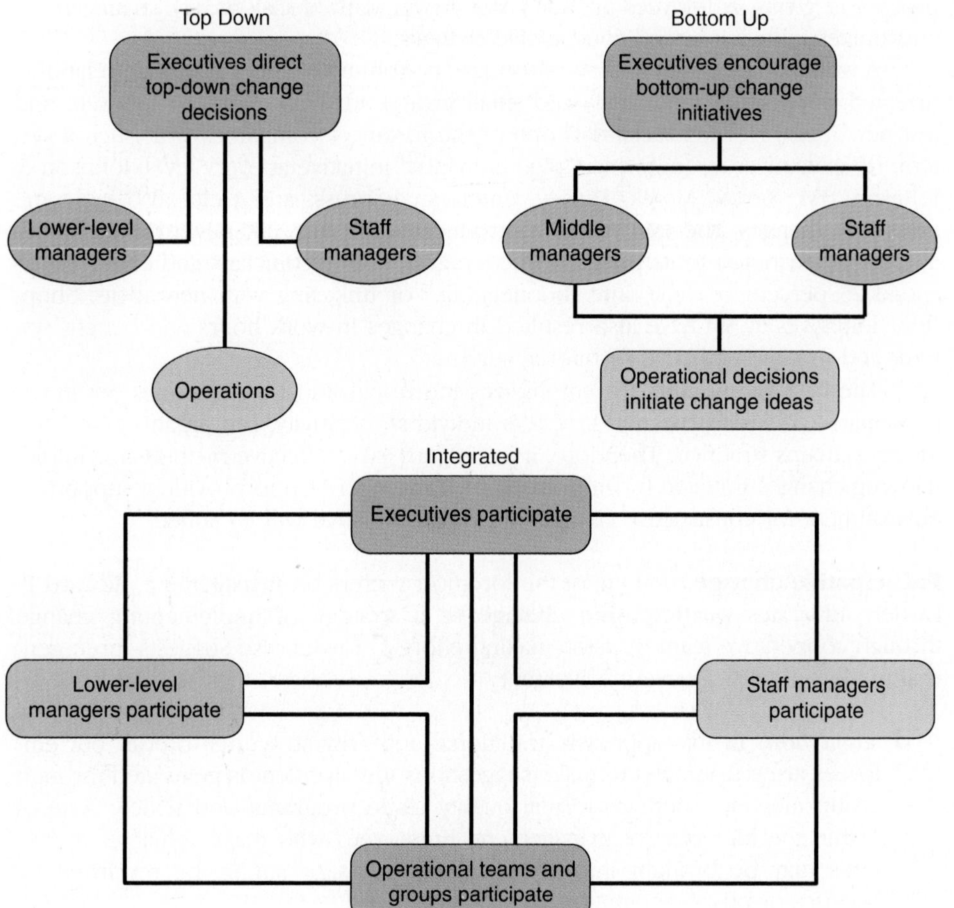

FIGURE 15-3 Approaches to Change

top-down change
The traditional approach to change that emphasizes unilateral decisions by superiors who direct how organizational change is to occur.

Top-down change. In Western societies, decisions have traditionally been made at higher levels and articulated downward. **Top-down change** strategies follow similar patterns of authority. A few key executives make decisions without involving lower-level managers and without necessarily "softening up" the organization first. This process is not always considered onerous. In many organizations, executives are expected to "captain the ship," and this expectation includes directing how changes are to be implemented.[24]

Strategic changes usually justify a top-down initiative, and executives are held accountable for these decisions. Lee Iacocca gained fame for his massive reorganization of Chrysler Corporation, and Jack Welch became prominent in the news when he spearheaded GE's move into aerospace communications. Welch has become known as a master change strategist. When GE sold its Small Appliance Group and diversified into hundreds of household products, only the highest-placed company executives were included in plans for what turned out to be a major shift in the fundamental GE business philosophy.[25]

The top-down approach has the advantage of being a rapid and efficient way of implementing major changes. Also, because only a few executives with broad-based authority are directly accountable, changes that require comprehensive efforts can be introduced as policy directives carrying tremendous weight. A top-down approach can be disruptive, though, particularly if employees and managers at lower ranks are not prepared to accept a directive style of leadership.

bottom-up change
An open environment for change where employees are encouraged to take independent action, initiating or recommending organizational adaptations.

Bottom-up change. At the other extreme, change may be instituted at the lowest organizational level. The **bottom-up change** approach assumes an open environment for change where employees are encouraged to take the initiative. Decisions relating to corporate strategies remain focused at the highest echelons, but responsibility for initiating operational changes is shifted downward. Through the process of giving employees greater control over daily decisions, top management encourages innovations and constructive changes.

A well-managed system that encourages bottom-up changes is human-relations-oriented, supporting individuals and small groups in their efforts to innovate and test new ideas. Hewlett-Packard is one of the foremost companies with such a system. HP executives strongly encourage individual initiative at every level. Johnson & Johnson, 3M, Xerox, Merck, Disney, American Express, and Delta also welcome grass-root changes. The 3M Company introduces more than 200 new products annually, a feat attributed to its policy of encouraging R&D technicians and engineers to spend 25 percent of their time "bootlegging," or tinkering with new ideas. Shop-floor initiatives at 3M have also resulted in changes in work hours and benefit systems and in new methods of janitorial service.[26]

The bottom-up approach emphasizes individual initiative, but does not imply participatory decision making. It fosters individual creativity, but organizational authority remains stratified. Therefore, if a company lacks effective methods for implementing changes initiated by employees, or if managers fail to provide a supportive environment for constructive change, individual initiative will be stifled.

participative change
A strategy of implementing change through cooperative efforts, team decision making, and group initiatives.

Participative change. One of the foremost writers on management, Edward E. Lawler, advocates **participative change** as a strategy of implementing change through cooperative team decision-making efforts.[27] Lawler also suggests three general models of participative involvement:

- *Suggestion.* In this approach, traditional authority structures prevail but emloyees are encouraged to make suggestions. Involvement is generated through group meetings, perhaps formal quality circle programs, and review systems within the hierarchy of management. Employees who make valuable suggestions may be brought into the change process or simply be rewarded by bonuses or other recognition.

- *Job involvement.* Lawler builds on Frederick Herzberg's concept of job enrichment for this approach. Although a traditional hierarchy of management may prevail, individuals control how work is accomplished. Even if a company has no formal parallel structures such as quality circles, team performance is emphasized, along with skill-based rewards and personnel policies that support individual growth and development.
- *High involvement.* This descriptive label by Lawler implies an egalitarian approach to involvement. Individuals make decisions about work methods, have input to strategic decisions, and often serve on formal task forces to resolve major business issues. The organization may be traditionally structured, or it may be designed around business units and work teams. It is more likely that work teams will parallel functional management structures, but in any case, team skills are emphasized.

Lawler believes that simply choosing to implement change strategies through "participation" is too vague to work. A definite approach must be fashioned, but if it does not mesh with existing practices, the change to participation may be extremely disruptive. Nevertheless, tremendous benefits can be reaped from widespread involvement of employees. The process itself opens many topics to constructive debate, and sensational ideas can emerge from collaboration. Commitment follows consensus, and although complete consensus is seldom achieved, merely moving toward it increases support by employees.

The management style of General Motors Corporation's president John H. Smith, Jr., is strictly top-down. Only three weeks after he became chief operating officer in April 1992, Smith compacted the company's money-losing three-unit North American auto operations into one unit. (Two months earlier, Smith's boss, Chairman Robert C. Stempel, had said that the reorganization would take two years.) Smith also wasted no time in trimming the fat from GM's white-collar ranks, offering early retirement to workers over fifty. The offer's deadline: June 1, 1992, less than two months after Smith took over. Next on his agenda is making lower levels of management accountable. Says Lehman Brothers analyst Joseph Phillippi about Smith's hands-on approach, "He'll call the guy [who is responsible] himself and want a three-minute answer immediately." In instituting these radically swift changes, Smith is acting on the nearly universal perception that if the ailing automaker is to survive, radical measures are needed.

Choosing an Approach to Change

Managers can consciously choose one of the three approaches to change, but their choice will be influenced by many complex variables. Recall from Chapters 13 and 14 that employees are motivated by many different circumstances and that managers must adopt a leadership style that is congruent with employees' expectations and their work environment. Likewise, managers must choose an approach to change that is congruent with employees' expectations and that takes into account the complexities of motivation and leadership issues. An added dimension is that change itself is often a matter of adopting new patterns of leadership. This is the dominant theme of organizational development, a topic we will soon address. The important point here is that managers can successfully implement a change program through one of the three approaches only if that approach is acceptable to employees who are involved with, or affected by, the changes.[28]

The top-down approach remains important for strategic initiatives, and in Western cultures, managers are expected to take leading roles in making most decisions. If an organization has nourished a strong, centralized style of management, this approach will be congruent with employees' expectations. The bottom-up option is realistic in those companies that have developed employees' expectations for independent problem solving and that have support systems encouraging individual initiative. Participation requires an environment that favors collaboration and team building. Recall from Chapter 11 that a team-building environment is created through organizing techniques focused on restructuring individual decision-making authority and job responsibilities to foster constructive group behavior.

During the early 1970s, the concept of team building began to be recognized as an effective way to involve employees in decisions and to gain their support for making changes. By the early 1980s, about one in twenty U.S. employers had started to use self-managed teams to implement operational changes. This did not mean, however, that entire organizations operated through participative teams, only that some departments or small divisions had created environments in which teams could function effectively. By the early 1990s, more than one in five U.S. employers had introduced team management processes, and in some instances, entire plants

GLOBAL TRENDS

The Clash of Traditional Values and Reality in Asia

For many Asian companies, economic growth has been tremendous, but it has absorbed all available management talent, and those who do manage find that their methods clash with employees' expectations. Consequently, major changes are taking place in Asian companies both to attract managers and to alter how work is accomplished. These changes are not being felt in Japan, where there is a strong record of effective management, but in the fast-growing economies of South Korea, Taiwan, Hong Kong, and Singapore.

In these economies, businesses were traditionally owned and operated by family members or carefully selected executives who reflected the owners' values. Employees were wage-earning cogs in the family business machinery; they neither participated in nor expected to become part of those businesses' decision-making processes. Managers had all the authority and made all the decisions. This tradition is still adhered to in many firms today. However, with economic growth, Asian businesses have become inextricably involved in global trade, and many of their younger managers have been trained in Western or Japanese management.

Ng Pock Too, for example, is CEO of Sembawang Group, a Singapore shipyard and construction company that only a few years ago was still small enough to be run by the family. Now that the company is involved in multinational sales and ocean freight systems, however, Ng needs two dozen competent senior managers in addition to his supervisors and field managers. He cannot find enough managers, and because there is a management shortage in Singapore, his best people rarely stay for long. More important, Ng himself was educated in North America, and he brought to the company a preference for open management with expectations for team involvement by

supported the concept. Researchers expect the upward trend to continue, but clearly managers cannot arbitrarily select the participative approach without having a compatible work environment.[29]

At Chrysler Corporation, for example, Lee Iacocca has created a legacy of strong, central decision making; this was noted earlier. Nevertheless, one of Chrysler's oldest and dingiest plants in New Castle, Indiana, operates almost entirely through self-managed teams.[30] Not long ago the New Castle plant had a reputation for resisting any management initiative and its workers were accused of purposely impeding changes. Today time clocks no longer exist, shop-floor employees assign their own tasks and correct production problems, and joint labor-management committees review hiring decisions, oversee technical changes, and participate in planning decisions. As a result, the plant has been cleaned up, absenteeism has plummeted to less than 3 percent from more than 7 percent, and the plant is among the quality leaders in the corporation.

Managing Resistance to Change

Managing change is primarily concerned with managing *resistance to change*. That has been implied throughout this and preceding chapters. Recall that in the change process attitudes must be "unfrozen" before constructive change can occur. Then, af-

managers. Since few local managers—including Ng's own family—endorse this style of leadership, Ng faces two major challenges: how to find and develop managers who can work in a more open, participative system; and how to change employees' expectations about their work and job responsibilities.

In Taiwan, Nelson Chang heads a computer company founded by his father. Chang, now 38 years old, was educated in New York, and is typical of the new breed of Asian managers. He has created self-managed work teams, introduced extensive human resource training programs, and implemented incentive-based compensation systems for everyone. This behavior has clashed both with the Chang family tradition of tightly held hierarchical control and with employees' expectations for a strong, almost feudal style of leadership.

Multinational companies going into Asia, such as Procter & Gamble and Unilever, find that they must provide extensive training for local managers. P&G contracted with Hong Kong University for a three-year program to train more than 100 Chinese managers in fundamental business practices. Unilever committed nearly $800,000 to a one-year program for managers in Indonesia. IBM Singapore has replicated its U.S. management development system, and because the system is so good, the company's young managers are rapidly hired away by other firms. This trend is pervasive in Asia. Since further growth will be impossible without people capable of working with new technology and with new methods of management, both managers and their employees must learn to accept major changes in fundamental methods of doing business.

Sources: Ford S. Worthy, "You Can't Grow If You Can't Manage," *Fortune,* June 3, 1991, pp. 83-88. See also "P&G in China: A Management Challenge," *South China Morning Post,* January 28, 1992, p. C1.

ter the change is introduced, attitudes are "refrozen" to reinforce behavior preferred in the new situation. But then, when the next change occurs, these patterns of behavior must be overcome to make way for yet another new preference. Consequently, employees caught up in a rapidly changing environment can feel victimized by contradictions. If the change process is handled poorly, they may become cynical and feel manipulated by management.

Resistance to change is a pervasive problem because few people accept change without a rationale. Some situations require a forceful approach that justifies unpleasant tactics. For instance, integration of the public schools during the late 1950s and early 1960s was a tremendous change in organizational relationships, and without dramatic tactics—including the use of armed guards to enforce court orders—school integration might not have been accomplished. In most situations, however, change is more subtle and managers can choose far less traumatic methods to overcome resistance to it. Here is a summary of six of these methods:[31]

- *Education.* Communicating with employees through an educational approach is advantageous when people need additional information to accept and implement change. It can, however, be time-consuming.
- *Participation.* Building on the participative approach to change, managers can reduce tension and improve cooperation for implementing needed changes.

People who are involved tend to be committed. However, this can also be a time-consuming process.

- *Facilitation.* Often managers cannot overcome resistance without outside assistance. Facilitation is the process of bringing in specialists to intervene in constructive ways to make change go more smoothly. (See the discussion of organizational development in the next section.)
- *Negotiation.* A common method of reducing resistance is negotiation between those seeking change and those resisting it. This policy is not uncommon in unionized environments and often ends in a compromise agreement. If negotiations are constructive rather than adversarial, mutual agreements and cooperative behavior should result in smooth change processes.
- *Manipulation.* This is not advocated as an explicit strategy; nevertheless, managers who manipulate employees often get results. The earlier discussion on ethics in change behavior illustrated how dangerous this strategy is, yet it regularly occurs.
- *Coercion.* A straightforward use of authority overcomes resistance simply by dictating change. Coercion is the least acceptable form of change management, though there are many situations where force is expedient. For example, changes mandated by new laws require enforcement tactics by management; coercion takes the form of disciplinary action when individuals resist such legal changes as equal rights and affirmative action.

As we shall see in the next section, these methods of managing resistance to change are important elements in organizational development programs. If we compare the polar extremes of coercion and participation, we find that changes can be implemented using these approaches, but often with unpredictable results. Figure 15-4 shows this comparison: Coercion may ensure employee compliance with changes, but it does not ensure acceptance, and resentment may hinder the successful implementation of the changes. On the other hand, participation may ensure employee acceptance of changes, but because employees are empowered to make decisions about the changes, results may differ significantly from those expected by management.

FIGURE 15-4 Coercion versus Participation

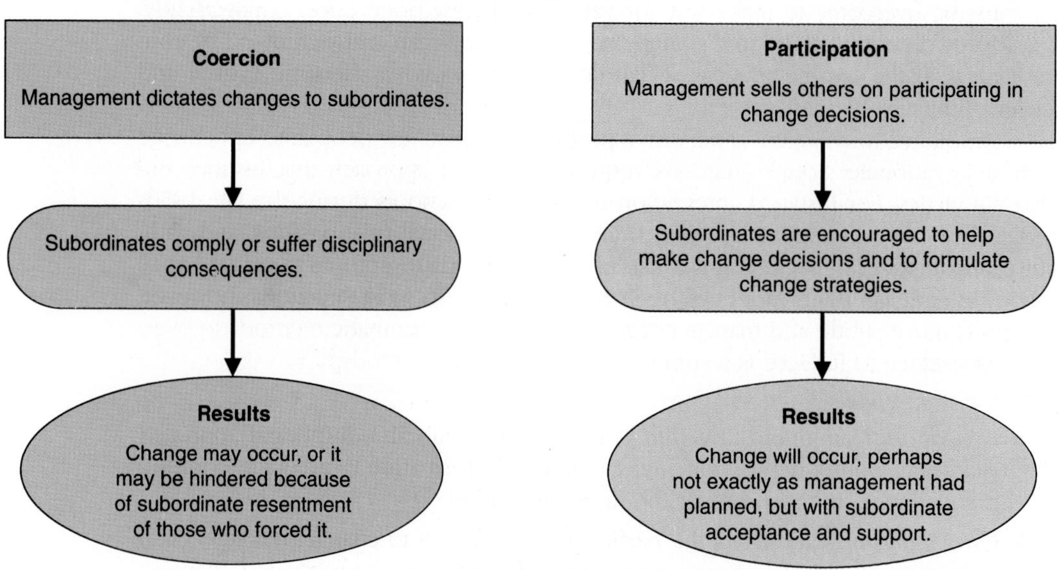

CHECKPOINT

- Describe the types of changes that occur in organizations and how managers respond to them.
- Define and contrast top-down, bottom-up, and participative approaches to change.
- Discuss how managers can overcome resistance to change.

ORGANIZATIONAL DEVELOPMENT

organizational development (OD)
The process of changing organizations through behavioral science techniques such as consulting, intervention to improve performance, leadership, and decision-making systems.

Much of what we have explored so far in this chapter relates to the field of organizational development. Wendell L. French and Cecil H. Bell explain **organizational development (OD)** as an effort to renew organizational processes by emphasizing cultural change patterns and by working with individual managers and teams.[32]

OD has been debated as a formal field of study. In one view, it is the application of intensive educational programs aimed at modifying managerial behavior toward more participative decisions and leadership.[33] Others avoid the term *OD,* preferring to refer to intervention consultants involved in these changes as "culturalists."[34] Whatever they are called, consultants who become involved with organizations almost always change processes, work methods, jobs, structures, or patterns of behavior. They are expected to intervene, and if not to resolve specific problems, at least to act as catalysts for constructive change.

Assumptions for Intervention

French and Bell provide a comprehensive view of OD intervention and why changes in managerial behavior tend to improve organizational effectiveness. At the heart of OD is the assumption that nearly everyone can contribute much more to the attainment of objectives than current organizational practices permit. The authors suggest that individuals have untapped energies that are often throttled by outdated ideas of authority and leadership. They also conclude that employees will be more cooperative if involved in team decisions.[35]

According to French and Bell, several conditions are critical to the success of OD programs. First, key people need to understand the value of behavioral intervention and become involved in the OD effort. Second, top management must actively support OD programs by committing resources and encouraging lower-level involvement. Third, OD programs must be continuing, long-term efforts if they are to enable participants to experience successful changes. Fourth, an action research model that systematically provides diagnostic activities, information gathering, and articulation of plans must be followed. Finally, participation by managers and employees as team members is critical.[36]

These assumptions provide a framework for intervention. The underpinning objective of OD is to expand participation through team-building techniques, as Figure 15-5 illustrates. The success of OD intervention techniques, however, is debatable. As noted earlier, nearly one in five U.S. companies has sought to implement a team-building system, yet fewer than one in ten actually report having these systems in place. OD intervention specialists report having made a significant difference in slightly less than 50 percent of their consulting assignments—although these have included notable successes at IBM, Lockheed, Texas Instruments, Motorola, and many other organizations.[37] The success with self-managed work teams at Chrysler's New Castle plant described earlier resulted from a two-year intervention program by

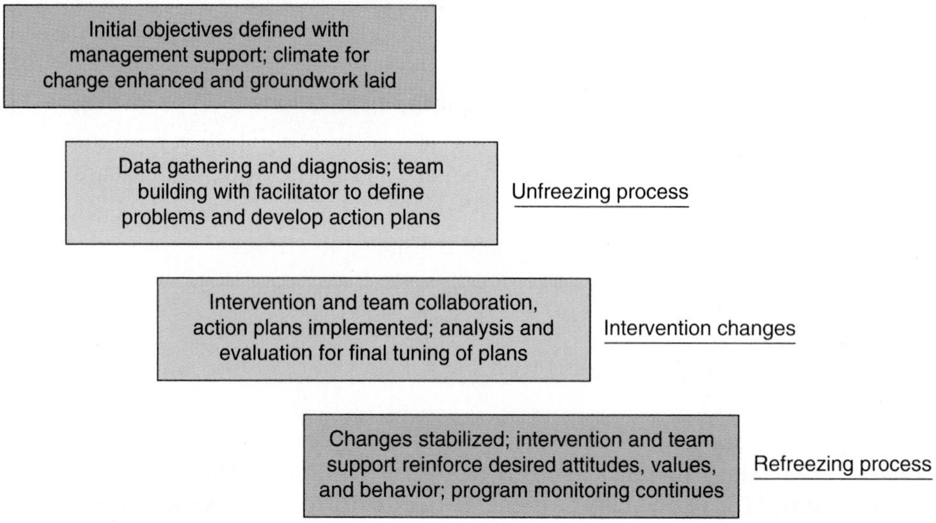

Initial objectives defined with management support; climate for change enhanced and groundwork laid

Data gathering and diagnosis; team building with facilitator to define problems and develop action plans — Unfreezing process

Intervention and team collaboration, action plans implemented; analysis and evaluation for final tuning of plans — Intervention changes

Changes stabilized; intervention and team support reinforce desired attitudes, values, and behavior; program monitoring continues — Refreezing process

FIGURE 15-5 General Process of OD Intervention and Team Building for Change

private consultants who systematically redefined the entire work environment with the cooperation of union officials and plant employees.

OD Intervention Activities

There is a rapidly expanding list of activities by OD consultants. Some of the most notable are:[38]

- *Diagnostic activities.* Data are collected and analyzed using methods such as questionnaires, interviews, structured observations, group meetings, and operational information. Evaluations of individual, group, and organizational effectiveness are then made.
- *Team-building activities.* Consultants use diagnostic methods to enhance team performance. These include activities helping members to improve work methods, refine tasks, modify decision-making processes, resolve conflicts, and improve communication. A compelling rationale for team building is to encourage members toward consensus decision making.
- *Survey feedback activities.* Information derived from diagnostic investigations provides a rich assortment of insights, which consultants structure for reports and seminars and further refine for use in workshops and team development interventions to facilitate constructive changes.
- *Intergroup activities.* Closely associated with feedback and team-building techniques are strategies for resolving differences between work groups. An extension of this is third-party peacemaking, whereby consultants act not only to resolve dysfunctional conflicts but also to improve the general climate of cooperation through behavioral modification techniques.
- *Education and training activities.* Perhaps the most common form of intervention is to provide education and training. Consultants package seminars aimed at resolving social problems, dealing with cultural changes, improving leadership skills, and enriching individuals within organizational settings.
- *Technostructural activities.* Consultants help define tasks, improve skills, restructure management systems, and revise reporting relationships. Given the assumptions of OD, most intervention activities are concerned with decentralizing power and increasing participation.
- *Process consultation activities.* Consultants focus on group dynamics and organizational processes to recommend improvements. These activities include ef-

When William Donlon became CEO of Niagra Mohawk Power in 1988, the giant utility was reeling from problems involving two nuclear power plants. Says Donlon, "The whole system just wasn't working any longer. It was apparent to me that we had to change." He moved swiftly. By 1991, the company had twenty new senior staffers. An outside management consultant reassessed the functions of the company's 11,000 workers and suggested millions of dollars' worth of productivity savings. Donlon listened and divided Niagra into four virtually autonomous units. He instituded a new incentive plan giving managers and officers bonuses up to 35 percent of their salary for meeting performance goals. The results of this makeover: Profits have soared, while customer complaints to the Public Service Commission have dropped 27 percent.

forts to improve communication, alter intergroup cooperation, introduce conflict resolution techniques, and encourage career development programs.

A Strategy for OD Intervention

Intervention activities are selected to resolve certain organizational problems, but as noted earlier, comprehensive changes in leadership are often necessary. These major changes require a strategy for OD intervention. The most popular strategy is based on the Blake and Mouton Managerial Grid, which was described in Chapter 14 as one of the prominent leadership models. Recall that the Grid® has a horizontal axis for plotting a "concern for tasks," and a vertical axis for plotting a "concern for people." Also recall that Blake and Mouton advocate an ideal approach to leadership, called a 9,9 team orientation, in which managers maximize their concern for both people and tasks through a fully implemented system of participation. Consequently, an OD strategy based on this model has this ideal orientation in mind as an objective to work toward.

The intervention strategy is implemented through a six-phase program that may take years to complete. Intervention techniques described above are employed systematically in the following phases:[39]

- *Phase 1.* Using diagnostic means such as interviews or surveys, existing patterns of leadership and expectations for leadership are identified.
- *Phase 2.* Through education programs, consultants help participants learn to work in a team-building environment.
- *Phase 3.* Using team-building activities, intervention specialists help managers learn how to develop work teams and to apply techniques for intergroup problem solving.

MANAGEMENT APPLICATION

Entrepreneurial Mentors Help Women Succeed

Organizational development, team management, change strategies, and most other "big-company" concepts have little meaning for the independent businessperson. The entrepreneurial sole proprietor has no organization to develop and no team members to bring together. Small partnerships and closely held companies, which make up more than half of all enterprises in the United States, have few employees to be concerned about. For these entrepreneurs, the prevailing challenge is surviving in a highly competitive world.

The concept of "team support" that underpins OD programs, however, has its countepart in *entrepreneurial networks,* which are loose associations of personal assistance created through social contacts. These networks are particularly crucial for women entrepreneurs, who are less apt to join traditional business or social organizations, such as Rotary, Kiwanis, Jaycees, and Lions Clubs, that give entrepreneurs access to professional and community contacts. Consequently, women find themselves isolated in the business world with limited access to external support systems.

This is changing, however, through efforts by women entrepreneurs to band together in networks and help one another through *mentoring*. Mentoring is perhaps the fastest-growing trend in "team support" concepts. Because successful mentors have themselves gone through years of isolation, they can empathize with others who need an external support system. Women who seek help often find mentors through the Small Business Administration or regional networks of entrepreneurs that are the equivalent of business clubs and fraternities. Informal mentoring occurs at network meetings where network members gain access to others who can advise them on their business problems. Formal mentoring takes this concept further: One successful woman takes a personal leadership role in helping a new business owner start, nourish, and grow her venture.

Mentoring is the two-person team concept in action. It helps reduce the alienation and stress that most women experience in business, and it provides support for solving the problems any new entrepreneur faces. Established mentors also provide a personal successful role model. Although mentoring among small-business owners and networking among entrepreneurs are activities seldom associated with organizational development concepts, they produce remarkably similar results.

Sources: Wendy J. Meyeroff, "Follow the Leader," *Entrepreneurial Woman*, December 1991, pp. 56-59. See also "Networks in Action," *The Small Business Advocate,* October 1991, p. 2.

- *Phase 4.* Working systematically from higher echelons downward, management teams are developed with the long-term objective of implementing the team concept throughout the organization.
- *Phase 5.* Through periodic interventions and reinforcement efforts, OD specialists help managers to overcome resistance to change and to establish participation in a comprehensive manner.
- *Phase 6.* Team processes and participative behavior are stabilized, or "frozen," through continued intervention counseling. It may take years of effort to resolve conflicts, educate employees, and establish new patterns of behavior.

Although this strategy may sound simple, it is quite complex and involves everyone in the organization. Because most organizations have diversified functions, and people with equally diversified interests and values, the Grid® strategy is only a framework for developing a carefully prepared program of intervention activities. Also because of these diversified characteristics, OD change programs can be extremely stressful to participants. Consequently, many conflicts occur that the consultants must help resolve. Ultimately, however, a successful program will culminate in comprehensive teamwork that minimizes organization conflict.

CHECKPOINT

- Discuss the concept of organizational development (OD).
- Explain how diagnostic activities occur in an OD intervention program.
- Describe an OD intervention strategy as a framework for change.

CONFLICT IN ORGANIZATIONS

Ironically, management theorists are at odds with one another over the nature and definition of conflict. They also disagree on how to manage it. In this section, we examine viewpoints on conflict and types of conflict that exist in organizations.[40]

Traditional view. A negative connotation of conflict is undoubtedly the most widely held viewpoint. In this traditional definition, conflict in organizational relationships implies discordance or irrationality. Proponents of the traditional view argue that every conflict leads to mistrust, poor communication, and lack of cooperation. They believe that conflict must always be stopped as soon as possible.

Behavioral view. Behaviorists argue that conflict is an inevitable consequence of group and organizational behavior. Because it cannot be eliminated, proponents argue, it must be accepted. This results in a paradox: Conflict can lead to problems and dysfunctional behavior, but it can also be beneficial as a provocation for moving groups to adopt new methods of work or innovations. In the behavioral view, conflict should be encouraged as a way of broaching carefully protected issues that need airing and resolution.

Interactionist view. A refinement of the behavioral view advocates assimilating conflict when it is beneficial and discouraging it when it is dysfunctional. The critical problem, of course, is how to make the distinction. Proponents of the interactionist view suggest that an unusually harmonious environment is not conducive to growth because it makes individuals overly tranquil. In the three-stage change process reviewed earlier, change is motivated by anxiety. Consequently, where tranquility prevails, little change will occur. If the organization is successful, a pleasant environment may be appropriate, but if the company is stagnating, tranquility is dangerous. Creating anxiety will be necessary to instigate changes.

An emerging view. During the early 1980s, a preoccupation with Japanese management techniques led to a reevaluation of conflict management. The Japanese recognize that individual imperfections make conflict inevitable, but feel that it is inexcusable not to control it. In contrast, they see harmony and tranquility as inherently good. These values are highly regarded for individual and group behavior in all Buddhist cultures.[41]

As a result of exploring the foundations of Japanese management, an emerging viewpoint in well-managed U.S. firms is that harmony is crucial to team building and that intervention techniques should be used to resolve conflicts. Also, the constructive anxiety that is a prerequisite of change need not come from conflict but can occur through healthy competition.

Conflict Defined

The approaches to conflict are not as far apart as they may seem. The critical difference lies in how conflict is defined. Stephen P. Robbins proposes a definition to help reconcile these differences: "We can define conflict to be a process in which an effort is purposely made by A to offset the efforts of B by some form of blocking that will result in frustrating B in attaining his goals or furthering his interests."[42]

Robbins's definition adds a special meaning to conflict by suggesting that it is a purposeful activity. Other researchers differentiate conflict from competition by explaining **conflict** as a purposeful interference by one party that blocks or frustrates another. **Competition** in this view is not purposeful interference.[43]

conflict
An effort by one party to purposely interfere with another's ability to perform or attain objectives, thereby creating tension and discord.

competition
A contest between two or more parties to attain a singular reward or to secure advantages and resources, but not to the extent of deliberate interference by contenders.

Once conflict and competition are differentiated, the historic paradox of finding both costs and benefits in conflict ceases to be a problem. We can easily accept organizational competition while disavowing conflict. Individuals can still disagree and try to "outrace" others, but do so without interference. Managers can vie for budget resources, debate priorities, or contend for promotions in a competitive spirit.

Types of Conflict

Managing conflict begins with an understanding of situations in which it can occur. Before looking at the actual management side of conflict, we present four distinct types of conflict.

Conflict within the individual. Individuals bring to organizations a variety of possibly conflicting roles that often do not coincide with prescribed work roles. For example, an accountant may have a managerial role in addition to a professional accounting role. Simultaneously, he or she may be a spouse and a parent. If the accountant comes to work worried about marital problems or a sick child at home, how effective will he or she be at work? The reverse is also true: What happens to domestic life if the accountant brings home pressures from the job?

The prescribed role is defined in terms of a set of expectations in a given situation. The accountant has prescribed roles at work and at home, but when the two vie for the same mental space, interference can distort behavior.[44] Figure 15-6 shows several possible roles and conflicts.

Role conflict can also lead to ethical dilemmas. Lockheed Aircraft executives were involved in bribery in Japan to try to land a major contract. While they were doing all they could to secure favorable contract terms, they crossed the line of competition by interfering with competitors to block bids. A reverse example is the engineer for Hooker Chemical Company in Buffalo, New York, who found it ethically impossible to follow company guidelines for chemical waste disposal and forfeited his career to oppose corporate practices at the famed "Love Canal."[45]

Role conflict is not usually so sinister. Most of the time it simply means people become so preoccupied with roles beyond their prescribed work role that they fail to concentrate on the job. As a result, they make mistakes, become inattentive to safety rules, or behave unpleasantly toward others. Sometimes they just daydream and do less effective work.

Conflict between individuals. Perhaps the most common form of conflict is between individuals. Several of the many ways this can occur are illustrated in Figure

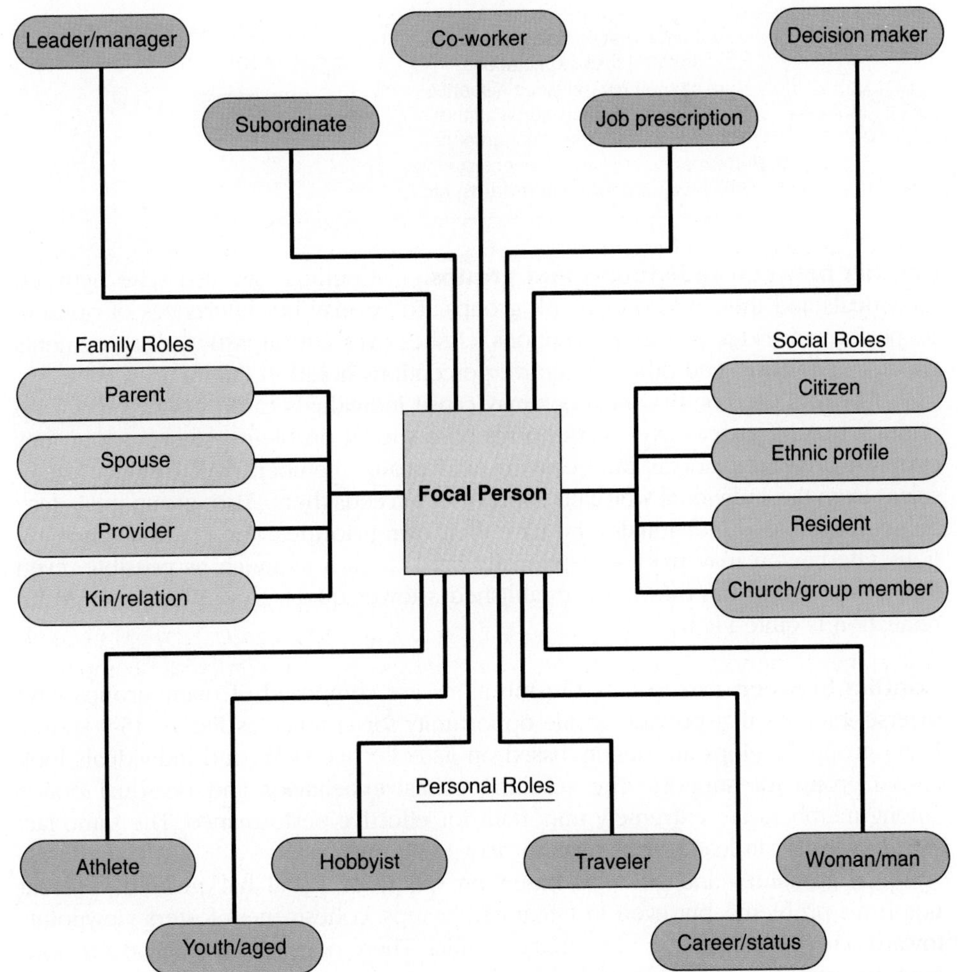

FIGURE 15-6 Potential Roles and Role Conflict

15-7. So-called personality conflicts are often unresolved role-conflict situations in which two individuals disagree over perceived role expectations. These cause frequent problems between superiors and subordinates because managers are charged with altering behavior, which means altering job expectations.

Potential conflicts between managers also emerge when they vie for limited resources, but actual conflict erupts only when one person deliberately interferes with another to gain resource advantages. Healthy competition can be maintained as long as interference is prevented; it can even result in vigorous allocation hearings that improve decision making.

Jeffrey Pfeffer cites power politics as a primary source of organizational conflict. He refers to this as the law of political entropy and suggests:

> Given the opportunity, an organization will tend to seek and maintain a political character. The argument is that once politics are introduced into a situation, it is very difficult to restore rationality. Once consensus is lost, once disagreements about preferences, technologies, and management philosophy emerge, it is very hard to restore the kind of shared responsibility and solidarity which is necessary to operate under the rational model.[46]

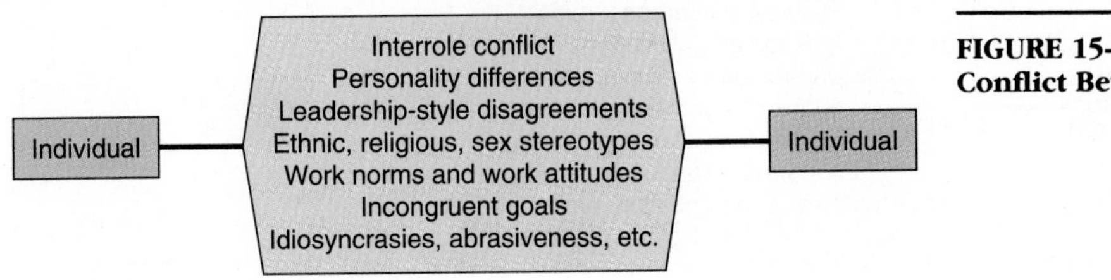

FIGURE 15-7 Potential Conflict Between Individuals

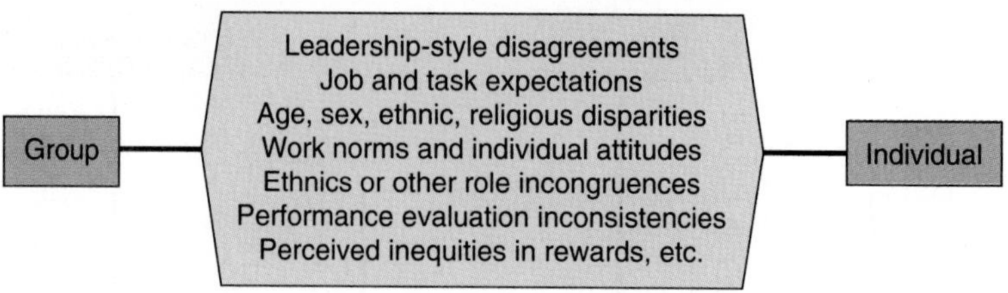

FIGURE 15-8 Potential Conflict Between Individuals and Groups

Conflict between individuals and groups. Conflicts can also arise between individuals and their reference work groups. These may be differences of opinion on performance due to role perceptions, clashes over ethical issues, disagreements about work norms, and other disruptive perceptions noted in Figure 15-8.

Any of these conflict situations may cause individuals to be isolated in group settings, but differences over work norms pose special problems. Most work groups establish unwritten norms for behavior, and group members will distance themselves from the individual who falls short of or exceeds them. Also, group goals may be unacceptable to individuals who have their own priorities. For example, an ambitious salesperson may work exceptionally hard to earn as much as possible, even though the group has informally established a lower quota. In this instance, group retaliation is quite likely.

Conflict between groups. Organizations are composed of many groups with diverse interests that provide ample opportunity for conflict, as Figure 15-9 shows. Every group develops an identity based on its collective tasks, and individuals look to the group for support. The resulting cohesive behavior and personal bonds among members are extremely important for effective performance. The same factors, however, can lead to polarization between groups.

Group values and attitudes based on ethnic or racial backgrounds present notorious problems, but even in integrated groups, cohesiveness fosters viewpoints toward other groups that tend to create conflict. There does not have to be a serious issue to evoke trouble; often one group merely wants to be different or stereotypes other groups in derogatory terms. Staff and line departments wrestle with this problem because of age, education, pay, and status differences.[47]

Interdependence—when one group's efforts affect another's performance—can also produce intergroup conflict. When coupled with proximity of group tasks, as in assembly-line situations, it is especially likely to create friction.

Various groups have different objectives that often conflict. Cost accountants, for example, are expected to keep costs down without sacrificing operational effectiveness. Research and development engineers are expected to experiment, which often leads to unpredictably high expenditures. Accountants and research engineers are each committed to different objectives that, if unreconciled, can lead to conflict. In another example, production managers prefer stable production schedules and predictable patterns of work, but sales managers must satisfy customers who often make purchases in unpredictable patterns.

Other causes of conflict. Individual and group conflicts may arise for a number of other reasons. Several of these issues are worth mentioning.

FIGURE 15-9 Potential Conflict Between Groups

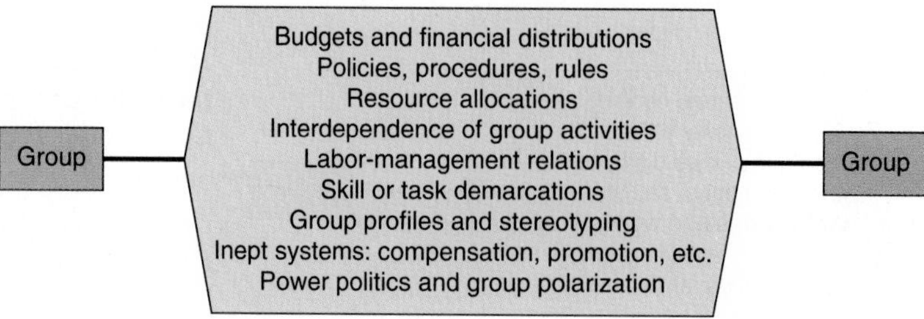

An organization that has inept control systems or poor communications is apt to be permeated by ambiguity. Employees in these uncertain environments are forced to guess at performance expectations and obliged to interpret change rather than accurately learn about it from management.

Leadership styles may be at odds with employee expectations, a particularly sensitive issue today. Other causes of conflict include poor systems of personnel selection, capricious compensation decisions, inequitable work assignments, and inconsistent promotion policies. Obviously, sex and racial bias problems vex managers, and other highly visible personal or group differences challenge them to find sensible ways to avoid conflict.

CHECKPOINT

- Describe the traditional, the behavioral, the interactionist, and the emerging views of conflict.
- Describe the causes of conflict within individuals, between individuals, between individuals and groups, and between groups.

MANAGING CONFLICT

Managers must stimulate healthy competition while reducing undesirable conflict. The initial problem is how to defuse potential problems before they become actual ones. The following is a summary of commonly used resolutions.[48]

Creating excess resources. Conflict over resources can be avoided if management provides more than sufficient resources. This may sound trite, but think how many labor-management disputes have been settled by granting huge wage increases to avoid confrontations. Many nonunion organizations have paid high wages to prevent unionization. Such excess resources are often underwritten by consumers, who pay higher market prices for goods and services.

Conflicts can and most often do lead to divorce in international joint-venture projects. One happy marriage that has survived more than thirteen years is that between Ford and Mazda. The two car makers cooperate on new vehicles and exchange technical, marketing, and financial expertise. Their relationship has not always been easy, but over the years the partners devised stratagems to resolve differences. For example, they often called in a third party, Sumitomo Bank, to mediate disputes, suggest ways out of logjams, and function as a neutral listener for both sides.

Integrating or buffering. Work groups that rely on one another can avoid conflict by creating buffers or by integrating tasks. For example, assembling electronic circuit boards is usually accomplished in two operations: One group assembles components and another tests circuits. Workers who test rely on an even flow of assemblies from the other work group; when the flow is uneven, testing is disrupted. On the other hand, when testing gets behind schedule, assembly components jam up. Managers can resolve this problem and avoid conflict by integrating the tasks—that is, by making assembly and testing one department or two components of an individual job description.

Another solution is to buffer the two operations. Buffering means separating operations so that logjams in one are not immediately felt in the other. For example, a safety stock of circuit boards can be made in one area. These become in-process subassemblies stacked up between work areas, used to feed work to the next group. Many manufacturers employ this tactic, but it is an expensive solution because it increases inventory and handling costs.

Another technique buffers human beings rather than materials. For example, a sales liaison committee with representatives from marketing, production, distribution, and purchasing can help coordinate interdependent activities and thus improve relationships among these groups. Or individuals can be appointed to act as personal liaisons between sensitive groups or operations.[49]

Creating superordinate goals. Group cohesion is enhanced by focusing activities on great causes. A superordinate goal is one that is more important than any individual goal that exists under normal circumstances. People band together for causes that eclipse their individual needs. Sensitive social issues such as civil rights, environmental protection, and consumer safety are good examples. Intragroup conflict is defused by intense concentration on greater issues.

Group competition is one way to achieve this in organizations. Sales contests, group production awards, safety awards, and recognition systems that reward group productivity help focus group members' energy on collective goals. If competition polarizes group behavior, however, it can lead to intergroup conflict.

Resolving interpersonal differences. Personal disagreements and role conflicts are bound to occur, at least occasionally, but managers can avoid unnecessary problems by assigning incompatible individuals to jobs that minimize opportunities for interference. Training, counseling, and OD intervention processes may also help resolve role conflict and friction. Good personnel selection processes, equitable compensation systems, and fair promotion policies can prevent many conflicts to begin with.

Group problem solving. Conflict can be resolved through participative groups in which decisions are discussed by the individuals who are affected by them. Some groups are in fact organized specifically to confront problems or debate differences. This can be beneficial as long as facilitators do not let the process degenerate into a win-lose situation.

Management Reactions to Conflict

An important part of managing conflict is applying the right tools at the right times. Managers may react to conflict issues in ways that either resolve or inflame them. Four common reactions are:[50]

Dominance. The autocratic response is to impose authority and simply force others to cease and desist from their conflict. This response is misguided in most organizational situations because it tends to suppress conflict rather than resolve it. The manager may then become a target of the initial antagonists.

Avoidance. Instead of dominating, managers may pretend problems do not exist. This strategy is equally misguided, yet several forms of it are common. Stalling by "studying the problem" is equivalent to turning a blind eye to the situation in the hope that it will resolve itself. Another form of avoidance is to set up such complex grievance procedures that employees will be reluctant to pursue them. Such responses seldom solve problems and often breed contempt.

Smoothing. Smoothing is a diplomatic plea for empathy. In many situations, it effectively calms the disputants, but it can also be an ineffective way to avoid resolving conflict issues. If the conflict issue is simply one of misunderstanding, however, smoothing may be an appropriate response.

Compromise. Resolving conflict by compromise is a weak solution because it assumes both sides will be happy to gain something when, in reality, both are more likely to be unhappy about losing something. Collective bargaining agreements are by definition compromises, but because both parties know compromise will occur, they take extreme positions with the idea of giving up only enough to win. Compromise tends to produce solutions that satisfy no one and merely postpone conflict until the next bargaining round.

Encouraging Competition

The best management solution to conflict is to eliminate or minimize opportunities for interference between conflicting parties. This may be done through rules, procedures, policies, or penalties for infractions. It may also be done preventively, by encouraging competition within predetermined guidelines for constructive debate and healthy rivalries.

From the viewpoint of involved employees, there must be some payoff beyond the satisfaction of "running a good race." Athletes compete for the psychological rewards of self-esteem and personal achievement, but they also compete for rewards, and often for monetary compensation. Employees can be rewarded with bonuses, prizes, formal recognition, and other positive motivators.

Managers must resign themselves to the fact that employees will often disagree about everything from work rules to nuclear defense systems. Their challenge is to generate a climate in which healthy debate can occur. Here again, participative groups can be beneficial by rejuvenating organizations through job rotation programs, job enrichment efforts, and change strategies for realigning group processes. The critical points, however, are to resolve conflict through problem-solving methods and, when possible, to use preventive techniques to reduce the risk of dysfunctional conflict situations.

Managing conflict can be challenging, but it can also be stressful. Just as change creates anxiety, so do tension and conflict create anxiety. In the next section, we address the closely related subject of *stress* and its implications for effective management.

CHECKPOINT

- Discuss the conflict resolution techniques of dominance, avoidance, smoothing, and compromise.
- Explain the advantages and disadvantages of joint problem solving and shared responsibility for resolving conflicts.

stress
Associated with tension and anxiety, stress can be destructive both physically and psychologically, but it is also essential for life.

distress
The destructive dimension of stress, which exceeds the normal tension associated with healthful living and threatens an individual physically or psychologically.

eustress
The constructive dimension of stress, which is essential for a healthy mind-body response to life.

Any demand made upon us, whether physical or psychological, creates stress. **Stress** is associated with tension and anxiety. In extreme cases, it can lead to death due to related illnesses such as heart attacks. A more appropriate term for extreme stress is **distress.** Although it can be destructive, stress is a natural consequence of being alive.

In an organization, the goal is to maintain productive levels of stress while avoiding the destructive consequences of distress. This means that individuals must be challenged without being pushed beyond endurance. To be healthy, a person must maintain a balance of activities without creating an overload. Too little stress, too sedentary a lifestyle, and too few opportunities for exercising the mind and body lead to unhealthy imbalances. Balanced systems with constructive stress levels create **eustress,** or stress that creates a healthy mind-body response to life.

All forms of exercise are stressful. The body is forced into tense performance that alters body chemistry, accelerates blood flow, activates vital heart muscles, and increases oxygen distribution through the blood supply. Mental activities such as examinations, debates, and problem solving are also stressful—and incidentally, the psychological response to mental and physical stress is quite similar. However, we all have different coping abilities and limitations for mental and physical activity. When stressed, each person adapts in his or her unique way.

Nature of Adaptation

general adaptation syndrome (GAS)
The psychophysiological (mind-body) reaction that is a natural mobilization and recovery process to stress stimuli.

When we are stimulated by physical or psychological phenomena, our bodies respond through two physiological systems. The nervous system adjusts bodily functions, including heartbeat, blood pressure, digestion, breathing, and muscle tension. The hormonal system creates adrenalin and converts cholesterol to steroid hormones and protein to energy. Through these changes, the body systematically mobilizes in what is called the **general adaptation syndrome (GAS).**[51]

GAS has three stages. The first, or alarm, stage is a sudden psychophysiological (mind-body) reaction as the body mobilizes in response to mental stimuli and prepares for action. In the second stage, resistance, the body expends energy or takes action. During the third stage, exhaustion, the body and mind can no longer endure these expenditures and must either rest or collapse.

Figure 15-10 illustrates an adaptation sequence in which stress overload prevents recovery, as the mind or body fails to adapt normally. Figure 15-11 shows a sequence of emergency mobilization, in which prolonged resistance leads to exhaustion. Figure 15-12 illustrates a normal mobilization process where optimal stress is achieved and the mind and body recover normally.

FIGURE 15-10 Unremitting or Overload Stress in the Three-Stage Model

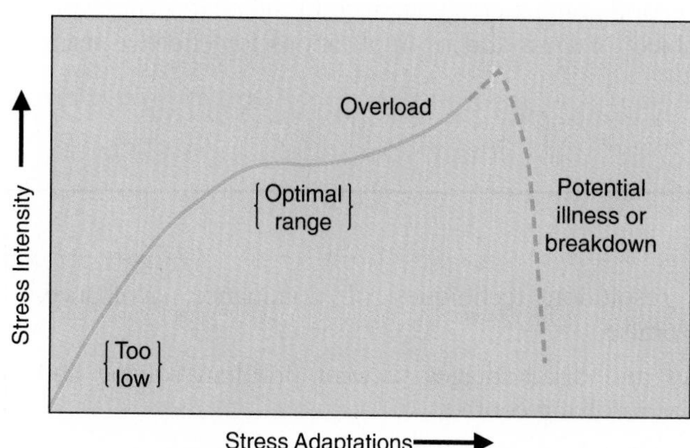

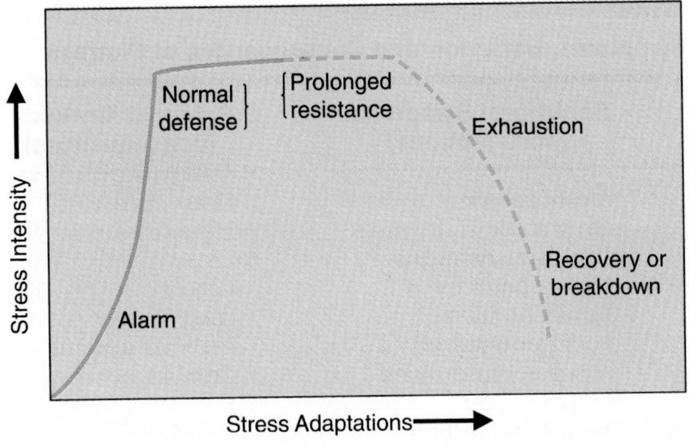

FIGURE 15-11 Emergency Adaptation and Potential for Exhaustion

Maladaptive results can occur at either end of the spectrum. During the alarm stage, the body may be insufficiently healthy to mobilize. For example, a person who has led a sedentary lifestyle may be unable to take the shock of sudden physical action because of weak heart muscles. Faced with a crisis, the heart may simply fail. At the other extreme, a person may be able to mobilize but not to return to normal; again, a heart failure may result.

Distress may also result in maladaptive behavior. When faced with an alarm, some individuals escape by mentally blocking out reality. Others escape through drug or alcohol abuse. Still others become tense and violent. Symptoms of maladaptive behavior include cynicism, excessive smoking, sleep disturbances, sexual dysfunction, and appetite disorders. Exhibit 15-1 summarizes these consequences.

A psychological consequence of distress is *burnout*. This is a serious consideration for management because burnt-out individuals pull their organizations down with them. Unfortunately, such employees are often written off as office deadwood when, in fact, they may be suffering from a serious illness. Individuals who are burnt out frequently do not understand why or when they became this way. All they know is that they cannot pull themselves together anymore; they may even have given up trying. A similar symptom in retired people is called *rustout*. In either case, people have lost direction and feel useless.

Stressors

Many events in life are stressful. Some of these are happy events, others are sad ones. Getting married and getting divorced are equally high on the stress list. Being hired or fired is another such pairing. Physical emergencies, accidents, serious illnesses, and strains are stressors, but so are challenging tasks, opportunities, sporting contests, and other enjoyable activities.

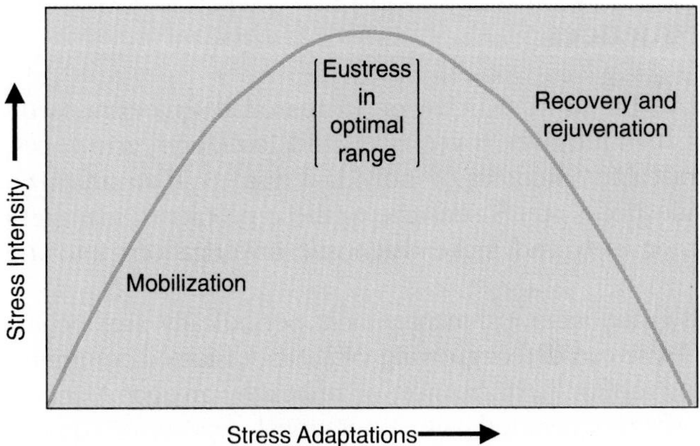

FIGURE 15-12 Healthy Mobilization, Well-Managed Stress, and Normal Adaptation

EXHIBIT 15-1 Common Symptoms, Behavior, and Consequences of Distress

Physical Symptoms (early warnings)	Behavioral Symptoms (maladaptions)	Potential Illnesses (consequences)
Appetite disorders	Alcohol abuse	Heart disease
Weight change	Drug abuse	Hypertension
Gastrointestinal disorders	Cynicism/arguments	Ulcers
Skin disorders	Violent behavior	Cancer
Muscle tension/aches	Family problems	Lung disease
Exhaustion/fatigue	Poor performance	Diabetes mellitus
Increased accidents	Absenteeism/tardiness	Criminal behavior
Nervous disorders	Employee theft	Family breakup
Loss of energy	Sexual dysfunction	Suicide
Increased headaches	Withdrawal/isolation	Job/career loss
Impatient/tense	Work sabotage	Psychological disabilities
Depression	Burnout/rustout	

Many stressors are unrelenting; they accumulate over time and go unnoticed until illness occurs. Daily hassles at work, task boredom, role conflicts, career constraints, unpleasant social relationships, work overloads, child-care problems, and financial problems build up and contribute to unhealthy stress levels. Organizational stressors might include poor lighting, high noise levels, unpleasant temperatures, persistent squabbles with co-workers, constant travel, and group pressures.[52]

Persistent high stress levels are dangerous for several reasons. First, the subtle changes they make in life and work can go unnoticed by the individual affected. Second, the relentless nature of stress may prevent normal adjustment; individuals may not have the opportunity to decompress and give their minds and bodies a chance to unwind. Third, unrelenting stress may damage the body or mind little by little until, with bodily wear and tear, the system snaps.

Stressors seldom apply to everyone in the same way with the same intensity. Some individuals like living in the "fast lane." They thrive on high-energy situations. People who fit this description are called Type A personalities. Others prefer less frantic circumstances and predictable work environments; they are called Type B personalities. Type A people are time-driven and often earn the label of "workaholics." Type B people maintain a less frenzied pace. Neither type is better or worse off than the other; they are simply different.

There are several implications for managing stress when individuals and organizations differ in their stress profiles. For example, a boring work environment will be stressful for Type A employees, who need higher-level activities, while rapid organizational changes may rattle Type B employees. Managers must consider work schedules, career development, assignments, delegation of authority, promotions, and other elements of human resource management to assure healthy conditions.

Symptoms and Consequences

Many symptoms of stress are visible in work behavior. Increased absenteeism, tardiness, strikes, work stoppages, high turnover, low-quality work, accidents, grievances, and employee theft are all traceable outcomes of individual distress. If an organization has human resource evaluation systems sensitive to these problems, managers can detect changes in behavior early and make diagnostic investigations into the causes of stress.

To audit individual and group attitudes, management periodically uses behavioral evaluation techniques. These can detect growing cynicism, distorted communications, inept decision making, erratic performance, or unhealthy anxiety. Management also uses survey information coupled with operational reports on quality performance to uncover stress problems. These investigations can also show management where a healthy environment is reinforcing effective behavior. Other methods of investigation include physical examinations and nutritional evaluations for employees.[53]

CHECKPOINT

- Define and contrast the concepts of distress and eustress.
- Identify the main symptoms of organizational stress in work groups and discuss how managers can improve stress assessment processes.

MANAGING ORGANIZATIONAL STRESS

Several guidelines can generally help improve stress management. First, individuals must be able to recognize stressors and understand their consequences. Second, organizations must develop prevention techniques as well as techniques for resolving distress. Effective stress management often includes a blend of training programs, counseling, company-sponsored wellness facilities, and evaluation systems that follow these guidelines.

Organization-Level Stress Management

Managers are primarily concerned with improving their work environments to minimize distress. Several methods are used in stress management:[54]

- *Task redesign.* Individual tasks can be redesigned to improve the balance between individual and organizational expectations. This makes it possible to assign tasks that use people's abilities without overloading them.
- *Environmental change.* Specific changes in the environment can be achieved through techniques such as flexible work schedules, improved decision making, and employee involvement programs.
- *Physical change.* Physical characteristics of the workplace can be improved to alleviate stress. These include noise levels, oppressive temperatures, poor lighting and ventilation systems, unsafe conditions, congestion, and awkward methods of work.
- *Career development.* Training and counseling can enhance individual self-concepts and provide career guidance. This helps prevent burnout, and when employees near retirement, preretirement planning helps prevent rustout.
- *Support systems.* Managers can encourage employees to become involved in physical fitness programs, diet plans, and wellness techniques. They can also encourage their organizations to sponsor these programs.
- *Role analysis.* Role conflict and role stress can be reduced by clarifying individual role expectations. This requires a systematic evaluation process that defines roles while articulating expectations.
- *Social support.* Managers can improve social support within work groups by improving group communications, combating alienation, and assuring emotional support for those who need it.
- *Team building.* Managers are particularly concerned with building team efforts toward productivity through congruent goals, integrated work norms, and harmonious behavior. Stress is reduced by removing threats in working relationships and by supporting team achievements.

Individual Stress Management

Although organizations can develop systems and programs that support stress management objectives, it is ultimately the individual who must take the initiative in managing stress. The following suggestions have been found helpful:[55]

- *Set realistic deadlines.* Rather than trying to accomplish more in less time, establish priorities with realistic expectations. Achieving results with adequate challenges but without overload is important.
- *Say "no" constructively.* Some people cannot say "no" to any task handed to them. Saying "no" constructively does not mean being obstinate; it means being able to refuse to take on too much work or to spread yourself too thin.
- *Avoid maladaptive reactions.* Running away from a problem can relieve stress, but the form of escape is important. Resorting to drugs and alcohol, for example, is more harmful than facing tough issues squarely.
- *Do not let problems fester.* Stressful situations that mobilize the body are normal, but permitting overload to continue is unhealthy. You must relieve stress by resolving the situation that created it.
- *Exercise regularly.* A healthy person is better able to cope both physically and psychologically with a distressful situation. Consequently, regular exercise is important, but it should be a form of exercise you enjoy.
- *Maintain a proper diet.* Although individuals vary in their nutritional needs, proper food intake helps people to avoid many of the physiological problems associated with stress.
- *Relax and decompress.* Since stress is a natural part of life, the mind and body are continuously adapting to it. But both must have periodic rest to adjust to normal. Work breaks and lunch periods provide opportunities to get away and decompress. A brisk walk in the fresh air couples exercise with psychological relaxation.

CHECKPOINT

- Discuss three ways organizational stressors can be managed to prevent individual and group problems.
- Identify and discuss three ways individuals can reduce the risks associated with stress-related diseases.

AT THE BEGINNING OF THE CHAPTER, we described how the Cuyahoga Metropolitan Housing Authority in Cleveland, Ohio, succeeded in rejuvenating itself. It did so by *empowering* employees to work in teams, control their schedules, and make decisions about work priorities. Change was effected through self-managed work groups, and conflict between the city and its employees was significantly reduced. Many of the techniques described in this chapter for change and conflict resolution were employed by the housing authority. In the process, stress was reduced between housing authority tenants and the agency. Looking to the future, the director of the housing authority expects greater changes, but only through an incremental program that allows civil service employees to implement changes at their own pace.[56] ■

A SYNOPSIS FOR LEARNING

1. Discuss the concept and nature of organizational change.

   Change implies disruption, but for an organization to progress, constructive disruptions are essential. Managers must encourage change to improve organizational performance. As change occurs, it is important to have in place a system that assures a smooth transition from old to new methods, technologies, or expectations.

2. Explain the process of change and the major approaches to effect change.

   Change in Lewin's model is a three-stage process. The first, *unfreezing,* consists of making employees aware that change is necessary. The second, the *change* stage, consists of introducing new methods and motivating employees to adapt to them. The third stage, *refreezing,* is the process of stabilizing changes made in the second stage by reinforcing desired behavior.

   There are three approaches to change. In the first, called *top down,* higher-level managers dictate what they want changed and use their authority to implement it. In the second approach, called *bottom up,* higher-level managers only encourage change; actual change is initiated by lower-level employees. The third approach relies on *participatory* management to encourage teamwork for suggesting and implementing change.

3. Discuss organizational development and intervention techniques.

   Organizational development (OD) is an effort to renew organizational processes by emphasizing cultural change patterns and by working with individual managers and work teams. OD is an intense educational approach to effecting change, usually by having consultants work with managers and workers to alter patterns of behavior. One method of intervention, *team building,* encourages participation by creating decision-making teams.

4. Describe types of conflict within organizations.

   First, role conflict occurs within an individual when one role (e.g., parent) interferes with another role (e.g., employee) so that the employee fails to perform well at work. Second, conflict can occur between individuals, such as through personality differences or debates that one person must win at another's expense. Third, conflict between individuals and groups occurs when one employee is isolated from the work group, purposely disrupts group work, or rejects group norms. Fourth, conflict can exist between groups, such as between line and staff departments or between functional departments.

5. Discuss methods of resolving conflict while enhancing healthy competition.

   A conflict over resources may be resolved by creating excess resources for the competing groups. A conflict between individuals or groups may be resolved by a buffer, which can be physical separation or an individual who acts as a counselor or a negotiator. Resolution may be achieved by integrating conflicting parties through cooperative work patterns or liaisons among groups that tend to have misunderstandings. Personal intervention techniques, such as career development programs, are often used to resolve role conflict.

6. Relate stress to organizational productivity and personal health.

   Stress is essential to accomplish anything, and a certain degree of stress exists in every job. When employees endanger themselves physically or psychologically with excessive strain or anxiety, however, they undergo *distress*. A healthy level of stimulation is called *eustress,* which is the effective mobilization of an individual mentally and physically.

7. Explain how organizations and individuals within organizations can manage stress.

It is ultimately the individual who must take the initiative in recognizing and managing stress. Such practices as setting realistic deadlines, exercising regularly, and eating properly will help the individual cope with and respond appropriately to stress. However, organizations can do much to prevent and resolve distress. Training programs, individual employee counseling, and on-site wellness facilities are just some of the ways companies can effectively manage employee stress.

SKILL ANALYSIS

CASE 1 The Kirk Stieff Company: Changing with the Times

The Kirk Stieff Company of Baltimore has been desperately trying to adapt to modern times over the past fifteen years. The company was formed in 1979 when two long-established silversmiths, the Stieff Company and Samuel Kirk and Son, merged. Wild fluctuations in the price of silver bullion, however, almost immediately upset the company's plans for the future. While Stieff and Kirk were closing their deal, the price of silver doubled to $10 an ounce. It continued to rise to nearly $50 an ounce before sliding back to the price of $10. At the same time, changes in the American lifestyle eroded the company's customer base. No longer did every newly married couple aspire to expensive silverware, which accounted for half of Kirk Stieff's sales.

By the early 1980s, the whole silver industry was in a slump. Kirk Stieff's heavy debt load—a legacy of Stieff's purchase of Kirk—made the situation even more precarious. The company laid off one hundred people, but that did not solve underlying problems. By 1983, the company was in crisis. That year the entire silverware market fell by 45 percent, and Kirk Stieff lost one-third of its net worth.

The company's history and the nature of the silver business did not predispose Kirk Stieff to change. The company prided itself on a long tradition of excellence and hand craftsmanship. Many of the techniques Kirk Stieff uses today—hand engraving and chasing, for example—remain the same as they were when Samuel Kirk and Charles Stieff founded their companies in 1815 and 1892, respectively. New apprentices can only hope to become master engravers or master chasers after five to seven years of training. Even the products change remarkably slowly. One of the company's best-selling silver flatware patterns was introduced by Samuel Kirk in 1830.

Given the weight of tradition and the naturally slow rhythms of the industry, it was difficult for Kirk Stieff to respond to its changing environment. In 1984, Chairman Rodney Stieff went outside the company to appoint a new president, Pierce Dunn. Dunn, in turn, recruited other managers who were prepared to break with the traditions of the silver industry.

Patrick Diaz, the new chief financial officer, overhauled the accounting department to provide managers with timely, relevant information—a new departure for Kirk Stieff. As a result of his efforts, company managers found that profits on some large accounts were really much smaller than everyone had assumed. They also discovered that many retailers were making more money on Kirk Stieff's products than the company was.

Johanna O'Kelley was appointed the new vice president for marketing. Not especially fond of silver or of Kirk Stieff's traditional products, O'Kelley set out to develop innovative product lines for the company. One of her ideas was a silver kaleidoscope filled with semiprecious stones. Pierce Dunn felt that ideas like O'Kelley's kaleidoscope fit Kirk Stieff's niche. Thus, for several years, Kirk Stieff attempted to produce and sell goods of exceptional quality for a small group of discerning clients who seemed willing to pay a premium price.

Two of the most important changes Dunn made at Kirk Stieff were to streamline the company's production processes and to cut manufacturing costs. Dunn reorganized the factory into production cells that cut across department lines. Before this change, each production job passed through each department. With the new manufacturing system, the small group of people who made up the production cell were solely responsible for taking a particular product from start to finish. Cell members worked together to solve production problems. For the kaleidoscope project, for example, the company assembled a team of four workers to manufacture the kaleidoscopes. After electing a team captain, the workers developed a cost- and time-efficient system for manufacturing their product. The use of cells effectively reduced inventory, improved quality, and accelerated production.

While some of the changes made at Kirk Stieff during Dunn's tenure helped streamline operations, the company's attempt to appeal to an exclusive market was not very successful. In 1990, Kirk Stieff management decided to accept a buyout offer from Lenox, Inc., the well-known American maker of chinaware, crystal, jewelry, and many other heirloom and gift products.

Now, Kirk Stieff is benefiting from the knowledge that Lenox—itself an old, well-established business based on craftsmanship—has acquired in markets very similar or even identical to Kirk Stieff's traditional markets. New Kirk Stieff managers are making decisions with more speed and market information than ever before.

For example, the silver kaleidoscope project was terminated after experiencing disappointing sales activity; only 150 items were sold in the year of introduction. In general, the strategy that Kirk Stieff's niche was in the production of unusual goods of exceptional quality at premium prices was not producing the desired results. Kirk Stieff managers now believe that the market for such products—discerning customers willing and able to pay premium prices—is actually much smaller than originally estimated.

Under the company's new president, James Solomon, Kirk Stieff has accelerated its emphasis on new products as a means of growing the business. As of 1992, the company has had very good success with its strategy of designing thirty new products for each new introduction in pewter, silverplate, and stainless steel. Kirk Stieff managers now perform extensive, careful market review and analysis before and after each product introduction to measure required return ratios, customer demand, and product performance. Solomon says that the combination of new products and reorganization has helped to create a very positive, forward-looking atmosphere at Kirk Stieff.

Case Questions

1. According to Michael Beer, managers delay making changes until there is a crisis. What caused the crises at Kirk Stieff? What happened as a result of these crises?
2. In many ways, Kirk Stieff's business is a relic of the past. How do you think the traditional nature of silversmithing affected the company's approach to change?
3. Which kind of strategy did Kirk Stieff managers use under Pierce Dunn and to what extent did they try to involve employees? What are some successful and unsuccessful aspects of this strategy? Which kind of strategy is Kirk Stieff managers using now under James Solomon? What is the main difference between the two strategies?
4. What kinds of conflict and stress do you think the changes at Kirk Stieff caused? Consider both managers and employees in your answer.

Sources: Jesse Glasgow, "Kirk Stieff Weathers Cloudy Times by Making Its Own Silver Lining," *Baltimore Sun,* October 22, 1988, pp. B16-B17; and direct communication with James E. Solomon, president, and William F. Sample, Jr., controller, the Kirk Stieff Company, April 27, 1992.

VIDEO CASE Is This a Life?

Nationwide, the average commuter travels about forty-five minutes a day to get to a job. What happens when that commute is half as long as the workday itself? What types of stresses and conflict does that put on an individual or on a community? Can people learn to cope?

In one community in California—Moreno Valley, about seventy miles east of Los Angeles—most of the adult residents commute to their jobs. Some one-way commutes of 70 miles from Moreno Valley take around two hours, but some Moreno Valley residents commute 110 miles each way and are on the road six hours a day. One of Moreno Valley's most popular businesses is Children's World day care, open from 6:00 A.M. to 6:30 P.M. There are many parents who need the whole twelve and a half hours of care for their children. Says the Children's World's director, "[Parents] talk about having to get their children, and they still have to go home and prepare dinner and get the children ready for bed, and if they have older children, they have to make sure the homework's done." One commuter admits, "You'll find a lot of talk about family problems that start because of the commute, and it's hard, but I think if you just—you need to get a mindset that this is what you have to do to have an affordable home and a nice home and you just cannot afford to live in Los Angeles."

Why do Moreno Valley residents put themselves through such agony? As the older Los Angeles suburbs became more and more expensive, middle-class parents had to move farther and farther away from their jobs to get an affordable decent-sized house. The community didn't even exist when the 1980 census was taken, yet the middle-class push into the desert has made it one of the fastest-growing cities in the nation in the 1990s. The priest at the Moreno Valley Catholic church says, "The people want to have a small-town atmosphere. They came out because they liked the quiet out here away from the booming metropolis and now it's booming."

Still, the community survives somehow, and so do its residents. The grinding daily commute to faraway jobs may make for a tough life, but most of the commuters feel they made the right choice and accept the necessary sacrifices.

Case Questions

1. What impact do you think long commutes have on the people who have to make them? Consider both the impact on their job performace and the impact on their personal lives.
2. What can organizations do to help employees who endure long commutes?
3. How can people who must commute long distances manage their stress?

Sources: John Huey, "New Frontiers in Commuting," *Fortune,* January 13, 1992, Vol. 125, No. 1, p. 56ff; Jeffrey S. Zax, "Compensation for Commutes in Labor and Housing Markets," *Journal of Urban Economics,* September 1991, Vol. 30, No. 2, p. 192ff; Jeffrey S. Zax and John F. Kain, "Commutes, Quits, and Moves," *Journal of Urban Economics,* March 1991, Vol. 29, No. 2, p. 153ff; and Bruce H. Smith, "Anxiety as a Cost of Commuting to Work," *Journal of Urban Economics,* March 1991, Vol. 29, No. 2, p. 260ff.

SKILL PRACTICE

SITUATIONAL ANALYSIS FOR A HEALTH-CARE FACILITY: PUTTING TEAMWORK TO WORK

Background for Exercise

Students are frequently required to work in teams to solve problems, but they have little experience in teamwork. Consider how education works. Students attend classes as individuals, are tested individually and awarded individual grades, and then move on to different courses with different students to repeat the process. They seldom interact educationally. Consequently, when asked to form teams and work together on joint projects, students find themselves in unfamiliar situations, with unfamiliar team members, yet they are expected to perform (and be rewarded) as groups.

This exercise is meant to explore the anxieties students have to resolve in this situation and to show them how they can more easily form teams. The exercise is a team effort whose objective is to bring to the surface problems experienced in forming teams and working in a group environment.

Instructions for the Analysis

1. Prior to forming groups, students are asked to review the text section on stress and to consider their personal anxieties about working as members of teams. They are to write down on 3-by-5 cards one primary concern they have about working as team members. The statement should be in the form: "I would be particularly concerned with . . . ." Then on the reverse side of the card, they are to write a recommendation in the form: "I can resolve this by . . . ." (Time allotted: 15 minutes)
2. Participants are divided into small groups of five to eight members. Each group has a "facilitator," who may be appointed by the instructor if no one volunteers. The facilitator is to be an impartial coordinator who accumulates responses (see Step 3) and marks them down on large flip charts, a summary page, or a blackboard.
3. Each facilitator collects the response cards from his or her group. The instructor collects the cards by groups and redistributes them at random to other groups. Then the group facilitators pass out cards to group members, who read and list the "anxiety concerns." Then the "resolutions" are also read and listed. (Time allotted: 10 minutes)
4. The facilitator asks group members to prioritize the "anxiety list," either by polling members, having them vote, or asking them to brainstorm. (There is no set requirement.) Team members may discuss the list or add to it, but the priorities should be assigned efficiently. (Time allotted: 10 minutes)
5. Team members review the "resolutions" to the priority list of anxieties and indicate the best choices. Do not add new resolutions at this time, but rely on the response cards for potential solutions. (Time allotted: 10 minutes)
6. As a final exercise, each team member should be polled for potential new resolutions to the highest-priority anxiety. Then each team decides on the best idea and states why this idea successfully addresses the priority anxiety. (Time allotted: 15 minutes)

Discussion

The instructor asks each facilitator to present each team's priority list of anxieties and recommended resolutions. These can be posted (if listed on flip charts) or summarized on a blackboard. If time permits, the instructor can lead a general discussion on the anxieties and proposed resolutions. (Time allotted: 20 minutes)

The entire exercise, including the general discussion, requires one hour and twenty minutes. If classes are shorter, the time allowed for each part of the exercise can be reduced, the students can be asked to prepare cards in Step 1 before class, or the general discussion can be held during a subsequent class period.

16

Toward More Effective Communication

OUTLINE

The Communication Process
- The Basic Communication Model
- Making the Process Effective

Organizational Communications
- Formal Channels of Communication
- Informal Channels of Communication
- Reconciling Formal and Informal Communications

Interpersonal Communication
- The Leadership Dimension
- How Attitudes Affect Communication

Cross-Cultural Communication
- The Importance of Language
- A Perceptual Framework for Cross-Cultural Communication
- Attributing Meanings Accurately

Barriers to Effective Communication
- Semantics
- Obfuscation
- Noise
- Listening
- Screening
- Jaundiced Viewpoints
- Stereotyping

Overcoming Barriers to Effective Communication
- Toward More Effective Communication
- Improving Organizational Communication

OBJECTIVES

- Describe the communication model and the roles of senders and receivers.
- Identify and discuss communication problems in organizations.
- Explain how perceptions and attitudes mold communications.
- Explain how communication problems occur for managers working in a cross-cultural environment.
- Describe barriers to effective communication and how they affect organizational performance.
- Describe how managers can ensure more effective communications.

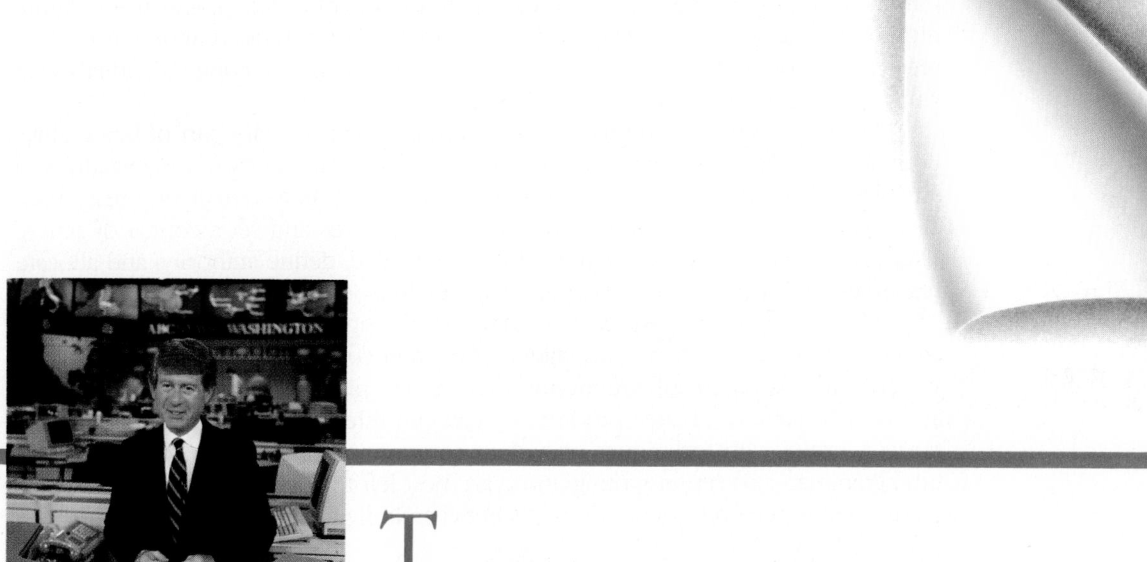

TED KOPPEL, host of the late-night ABC news program "Nightline," is an effective communicator who has mastered the art of selling others on the worth of being involved in an active information exchange.[1] Koppel interviews government officials, diplomats, scientists, and entertainers, stroking their egos by asking incisive questions and being an attentive listener. He sells his guests on the idea that he is after the truth by creating a communications atmosphere of fairness and genuine concern for their opinions, and he sells his viewers on the idea that his program can be trusted to pursue answers to newsworthy questions by giving guests the freedom to express themselves.

The recipient of more than twenty awards for journalism and leadership in news coverage, Koppel is one of the few television investigative reporters who does not threaten guests with his style of interviewing. Instead of forcing them to answer embarrassing questions, he persuades them to respond to issues, eliciting information by concentrating on their ideas and building an exchange of opinions among guests. Koppel rarely speaks more than his guests, and he interrupts only when necessary to keep the conversation focused. In his view, asking open, nonthreatening questions promotes understanding of the issues and enlightens viewers. As you read this chapter, consider how Ted Koppel's approach to communication stimulates an exchange of information by guests and a sense of confidence by viewers in his leadership in news coverage.

Whenever individuals speak to one another, there is a chemistry that works either to draw them closer together or push them further apart. Managers must try to pull their employees together and create a climate of cooperation. Effective communication strengthens organizations by promoting relationships, reinforcing goal-directed behavior, and helping to create a bond of confidence among individuals who work together. *Communication is the essence of leadership.*

From a process perspective, communication is a necessary part of being alive. From an organizational viewpoint, it is what we do as members of organizations to articulate plans, organize efforts, coordinate activities, and control progress. Managers exchange planning information to form objectives and set a course of action. They also communicate expectations for performance, define authority, and allocate resources, and when they do these things, they function as leaders.

In this chapter, we explore the nature of managerial communications and examine some of the problems managers have when communicating with employees. We also discuss a general communications model, pitfalls of poor communication, and how to achieve greater productivity through effective communication. We are not concerned with techniques of written communication, such as sentence structure, grammar, and report writing; those are best left to specialized courses. Our focus is on interpersonal communications between individuals in group environments.

THE COMMUNICATION PROCESS

communication
The interpersonal process of sending and receiving messages through symbols or gestures.

From a managerial perspective, **communication** is the process of exchanging information in a way that achieves mutual understanding between two or more people about work-related issues. By "communication," we mean that the individuals involved have established a reasonable understanding of one another's feelings or ideas. If we define communication in this way, it suggests a psychological process of sharing information to achieve a common understanding between ourselves and others. In fact, this definition reflects the Latin root for the word, *communicare*—"to make common."[2]

Communication, then, is the process of sharing meanings. It involves our total behavior, from uttering words to making subtle physical gestures that enhance what we have to say. Exactly how we share meanings is difficult to analyze. When speaking, writing, or sending electronic messages, we encode information from a unique perspective. Our intended message is packed with our own perceptions of the world around us. We evaluate our receiver's viewpoint from this perspective and make assumptions about how our message will be received. Moreover, we speak, write, and transmit information in a complex environment with many possible distractions.

Language is the medium of interpersonal communication preferred by leaders, and the spoken word is the essential and most natural form of language. We string together complex thoughts, express ideas through complicated sentences, and consciously expect others to receive and react to our messages. Managers must do all this within the context of a technical work environment. They must also communicate with many individuals whose backgrounds, attitudes, and perceptions may differ widely. Because nearly everyone misuses language in one way or another, there is ample opportunity for communication problems.

Managerial communication implies much more than effective use of language. Managers' attitudes toward workers, how managers embellish words with actions, and how employees perceive superiors are also part of the chemistry of communication. Since we all interpret the words and actions of others from our own unique perspective, managers must be conscious of individual perspectives, communicate in ways that ensure proper interpretation, and strive for a collective understanding by their employees.

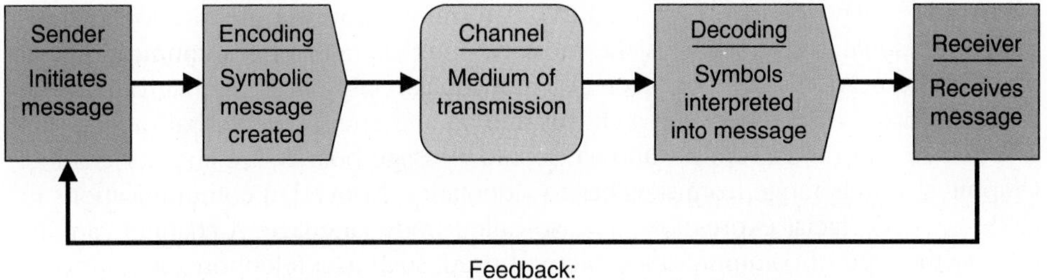

FIGURE 16-1 The Basic Communication Process

The Basic Communication Model

Figure 16-1 illustrates the basic communication model. The process of communication requires a full cycle of events from sender to receiver and back to sender. A common misconception is that communication is over once a sender has encoded a message and transmitted it. In fact, simply encoding and transmitting is merely "broadcasting"; no common understanding is assured. The complete cycle of communication consists of encoding a message by a sender, transmitting it through a medium, decoding the message by a receiver, and then authenticating receipt and understanding of the message by a receiver through feedback.[3]

encoding
A message is encoded by a sender, who uses symbols, words, pictures, or gestures to formulate the message content.

Encoding. A sender is the source of information who **encodes** a message by using symbols, words, pictures, or gestures. Anyone who initiates communication does so from a perceived need to share information or feelings. This need may be little more than a desire to have social contact, or it may be an important need, such as teaching someone how to perform a certain task. The encoding process is crucial to ensure that an intended receiver understands what is being transmitted. Improper encoding can distort a message and confuse the receiver.

The method of encoding partially depends on the channel of communication you choose. For example, if you decide to speak privately to another person—this channel is known as *personal oral communication*—you then choose language, structure your statement, amplify its meaning with physical symbols, and further embellish your message with facial expressions. The tone of your voice will also add meaning to the message. Some managers are very effective at personal oral communication. Peggy Eddy, for example, the CEO of Creative Capital Management, Inc., in San Diego, believes that her success is directly related to her ability to motivate employees through close, personal talks with them. Eddy often spends most of her working day talking with employees who are invited into her office just for "friendly chats," not necessarily because there are problems to discuss. In the process, she discovers potential problems or employee frustrations and is able to address them before they become crises. This style of communication is a way of avoiding what Eddy calls a "seagull style" of management where one "swoops in, dumps orders, demands and commands, and then swoops out."[4] Although personal discussions with employees are time-consuming, Eddy prefers them because she can reinforce messages with facial gestures, hand movements, and close eye contact.

Consider the question "How do you like your job?" If asked by a manager of an employee and accompanied by a warm smile, it could be taken as encouragement. If asked by the same manager of the same employee and accompanied by a raised eyebrow and a certain aloofness, it could mean "You aren't cutting it here; shape up if you want to keep your job." Properly encoding a message is therefore crucial to ensure a clear understanding of its intended meaning.

channel
A medium of communication between sender and receiver; the method of delivering a message.

Channel. The **channel,** or medium, determines how communication is transmitted. Personal conversation is the most obvious channel of communication, but oral communication can be between two individuals, one sender and a group, or between groups (such as between a chorus and an audience). The verbal media, such as letters, memoranda, reports, and electronic message boards, are another channel. Graphic channels range from sketches to videotapes. Nonverbal communications include gestures, facial expressions, and so-called body language. A channel can also refer to the type of communication method used, such as a telephone, a microcomputer, a textbook, or the mail.

The choice of channel is critical in the communication process. For example, it would be awkward to ask, "How do you like your job?" through a memo. How could the employee understand the manager's meaning, and how could the employee respond? Then again, if this question were rephrased so that the employee were also asked to suggest ways to improve the job, a letter or questionnaire might be appropriate.

Channel selection may involve a combination of media. An employee questionnaire, for example, might be followed by short, personal conversations between managers and subordinates. A new safety rule might first be communicated in company newsletters, graphically illustrated with posters, and then reinforced through meetings. This method is often used by firms when dealing with critical issues such as a new policy requiring employees to wear safety glasses in hazardous areas.

To effect major changes, companies frequently find it necessary to structure complicated networks of communication channels. For example, management at Georgia Power launched a comprehensive communications program in 1989 to better inform employees of company activities. The program was prompted by a survey that revealed only 4 percent of Georgia Power's employees could correctly identify the company's major objectives. In addition to existing media that included a weekly newsletter, a monthly employee magazine, and plant bulletin boards, management created a daily telephone newsline with recorded messages, a quarterly magazine for employees' families, a bimonthly video news program, and a computerized system of news with monitors in 100 company locations. More important, the company launched its Vision 2000 campaign to improve company communications during the 1990s. This began with a new image using various colors and logos for Vision 2000 messages, a competition among employees to write articles for the weekly newsletter, weekly meetings between managers and their employees, communications seminars for managers, and the formation of employee "focus groups" to study ways in which the company could improve performance. By 1990, nearly 70 percent of Georgia Power's employees could correctly describe corporate objectives. In 1991, the company introduced a program called "Everybody Has a Customer" to further enhance employee understanding of company expectations for performance. Management expects that 90 percent of its employees will have a comprehensive understanding of company objectives and operations by 1993.[5]

decoding
A message is decoded by a receiver, who interprets symbols, words, pictures, or gestures to give them meaning.

Decoding. The **decoding** process consists of unraveling symbols. Receivers interpret messages, and in so doing, give them meanings. Decoding is the receiver's perceptual assessment of the language, gestures, and context of the sender's message. The receiver also implicitly evaluates why the sender is trying to communicate, and perhaps searches for hidden meanings in the choice of channel.

Decoding cannot occur properly if the receiver is given an unclear message or if communication is attempted in a confusing manner. Employees have difficulty understanding their benefits, for example, because too often benefits such as insurance plans are written in confusing legal terms. When they are orally explained by benefit specialists, they can sound just as confusing.

Consider this clause in an employee retirement plan: "The party-in-interest includes fiduciaries, as well as relatives of and business interests controlled by the plan sponsor. Transactions between a plan and parties-in-interest are generally prohibited." When a personnel specialist was asked by an employee what "party-in-interest" really meant, the specialist replied, "The plan or its controlling interest who has a fiduciary duty as sponsor of the plan, or the principal or his or her beneficiaries, but also other business interests."[6] The employee left the personnel office more confused than when she went in.

Even simple messages can be decoded improperly. If a supervisor comments, "Great job . . . you think smart," in a noisy environment, the message could be received as "Get Bob . . . you stink, Art." Most of us can recall similar misunderstandings. The solution is to consciously communicate, without noise or other interference, in a way that gives the receiver every opportunity to hear and decode a message clearly. When decoding results in a clear and correct understanding of a message, communication is conceptually complete, but the only way to be certain of this is to verify the understanding through feedback.

Feedback. The process is not over until communication completes a full cycle back to sender. **Feedback** occurs when a receiver responds to a sender's message with an understandable return message. This may be in the form of a simple acknowledgment, or it may be an answer or elaboration. The feedback response may surprise the sender, who then will reply to clarify the initial message. For example, in response to the question "How do you like your job?" (said with a raised eyebrow), a new employee may answer with trepidation, "I like it okay. But why do you ask? Am I doing something wrong?" The manager, shocked at this response, may say, "No, no. You misunderstand. You're doing just fine. I just though I'd check. We really haven't had the chance to talk."

feedback
Reports, performance information, results from operations, and other data routed back to planners and decision makers to enhance future decisions or correct deviations in performance. In communications, a response or acknowledgment that a message has been received and understood.

Feedback is essential to clarify and reinforce the commonality of shared information, beliefs, or values. It is the link between receiver and sender that ensures effective communication. Without feedback, you have a one-way communication process. Feedback makes possible a two-way process, reversing the sender and receiver roles so that information can be shared, recycled, and fine-tuned to avoid ambiguity.[7]

Making the Process Effective

Management scholar Peter F. Drucker views the communication process from the receiver's perspective. He believes that communication is the act of receiving information, of perceiving language and gestures within a total environment; the spoken word has no meaning apart from the receiver's cultural and social interpretation of it. Drucker explains his views in the following passage:

> It is the recipient who communicates. The so-called communicator, the person who emits the communication, does not communicate. He utters. Unless there is someone who hears, there is no communication. There is only noise. The communicator speaks or writes or sings—but he does not communicate. Indeed, he cannot communicate. He can only make it possible, or impossible, for a recipient—or rather, "percipient"—to perceive.[8]

To be a good communicator, then, you have to initiate messages clearly, encoding them carefully and choosing appropriate channels for transmission. However, you must also be a good listener. You cannot be an effective communicator unless you are both an able transmitter and an able listener. The challenge for managers is to improve the likelihood that their messages will be received and understood, while being receptive to messages sent to them by others.

CHECKPOINT

- Explain how communicating is a process of sharing information to achieve a common understanding between two or more persons.
- Describe the basic communication model and the sender's and receiver's roles in conversation.

ORGANIZATIONAL COMMUNICATIONS

Organizational communications are concerned with how information flows within the formal structure of a company, how managers use information, and how informal communication takes place among organizational members. The general model of communications is also applied to activities that involve organizations with outside constituents such as customers, investors, lenders, suppliers, and others in society potentially affected by a company's operations. Consequently, in addition to internal systems of communication, organizational communication includes public relations, marketing, purchasing and procurement, shareholder relations, and community relations. Communication responsibilities related to specific activities are best left to courses and textbooks in those areas. Here we will address topics related to internal communication systems.

Internal communication systems are often described in terms of *managerial communications,* and research has focused on how effective managers are in their communication roles. Recall from Chapter 2 that Henry Mintzberg identified the *informational role* as one of the major responsibilities of all managers. Studies of top executives reveal that they spend, on average, more than 90 percent of their time communicating; the average time spent daily by all managers is about 81 percent.[9] Furthermore, about 75 percent of all communications by managers are described as "face-to-face." These include personal conversations with other managers and employees, meetings, committees, and forms of speeches such as making oral announcements, giving instructions to work groups, and leading group discussions. About 10 percent of communication time is spent on the telephone, and the remaining 15 percent involves writing messages (directives, notices, and memoranda), transcribing reports, and using information media such as facsimile machines or electronic mail. Figure 16-2 summarizes managerial communication activities.

Patterns of communication evolve in organizations between managers and their subordinates, among peers, and between individuals and their superiors. These patterns are affected by how organizations are structured. Recall from Chapters 9 and 10 that we described hierarchical relationships and authority in terms of formal structures but also emphasized that every organization has an informal structure.

FIGURE 16-2 Managerial Communication Activities

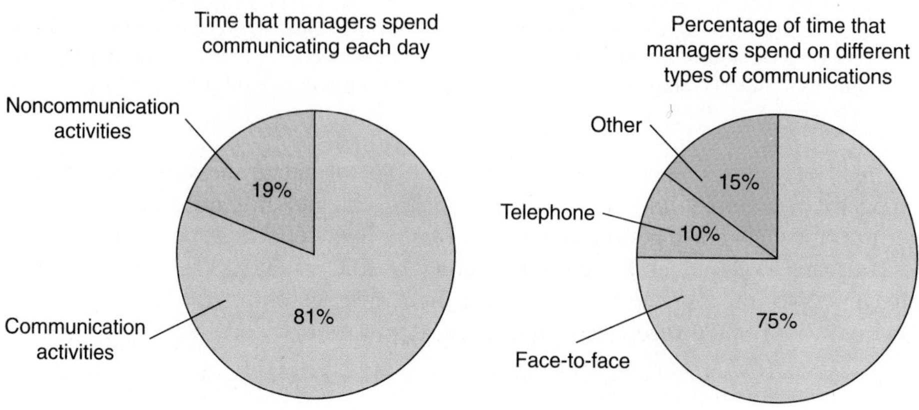

Communications in organizations can follow patterns based on these formal structures or they can evolve spontaneously through informal relationships. We will refer to the informal communication system as the *grapevine*.

Formal Channels of Communication

Formal communication channels are determined by the structure of management and formal reporting systems. Every firm prescribes who reports to whom and what forms these communications will take. For example, monthly sales reports may be required by sales managers, who must pass them directly to regional sales directors; or weekly job assignments may be required of first-line production managers, who must post them for their department's employees. Plans, as we saw in Chapter 6, follow hierarchical patterns established by the formal authority structure. Traditional top-down planning systems stress a communication process in which strategic objectives are articulated by executives, who then approve tactical plans and budgets drawn up by middle managers, who break the approved plans down into short-term operational plans for first-line managers, who in turn articulate performance expectations to nonmanagement employees. Progress reports related to these plans reverse this pattern so that communication flows upward. Most other official forms of communication conform to this vertical reporting system.

formal communication channels
The reporting relationships determined by the structure of management through which prescribed messages are sent.

Because communicating is a pervasive activity in all organizations, we have discussed it throughout the text in terms of planning systems, structures of authority, delegation, work-team formation, motivation, and leadership. Also, it will be an important part of later discussions of the controlling function and information technology. However, we can gain insights into the workings of organizational communication systems here by distinguishing three categories of formal communications: *downward, upward,* and *horizontal* communication channels.

Downward communication. Messages and information communicated by managers to their subordinates is called **downward communication**. This channel of communications was described in the previous section in our brief review of a traditional planning hierarchy, but it encompasses more than executives communicating objectives, providing information about strategic performance expectations, and encouraging behavior by subordinates congruent with the company's objectives. There are many other forms of downward communication at nearly all organizational levels. For example, first-line managers instruct employees through directives and procedures about work methods, rules, job expectations, and task activities needed to accomplish organizational objectives. Also, managers must assign work, define schedules, and control tasks for which they are responsible. In each instance, a manager's position of higher authority requires articulation of official messages, and circumstances will require the use of a variety of official media.

downward communication
Messages and information initiated by superiors to subordinates, usually in the form of directives.

Downward communication is a necessary feature of every organization with some form of hierarchical authority, but that does not mean that communications must be "authoritative" or onerous. For example, the Walt Disney Company has a very well defined hierarchy of management with clear definitions of authority. Managers are held accountable for their roles as communicators, yet they are encouraged to establish good relationships with employees (called "cast members") so that conversations are friendly and official documents, such as plans, become interesting "scripts" to follow.[10] Of course, managers occasionally must exert their authority to enforce rules or to discipline subordinates, and they often find themselves taking authoritative actions to resolve conflicts.

Upward communication. Messages and information initiated by subordinates for superiors are called **upward communication**. Employees report on activities, work progress, and problems they are having with their jobs. They also communi-

upward communication
Messages and information initiated by subordinates for their superiors, usually in the form of reports.

cate upward through channels devised to air grievances, solicit suggestions for productivity improvements, and provide responses to management inquiries.[11] Much upward communication is predetermined to keep superiors advised on work progress and potential operational problems. For example, cash flow reports, sales activity reports, and production reports communicate performance results routinely through formal information systems.

Effective companies also develop systems that encourage an upward flow of information not prescribed in reporting procedures. For example, at Hewlett-Packard, managers are encouraged to mingle with employees and be sociable so that employees will consider them approachable. The H-P effort—known as "managing by wandering around (MBWA)"— has become popular at Bell Labs, Humana Hospitals, and GE, and other companies where employees have ample opportunities to express their viewpoints or make suggestions.[12] An interesting form of upward communication has evolved through the use of interactive computer systems for electronic brainstorming. In this *groupware networking,* employees gather in a conference room equipped with interconnected terminals or log on to remote terminals to participate in meetings. During the sessions, participants enter comments, complaints, or suggestions on their terminals anonymously. Dell Computer, Inc., Marriott Corporation, and J. P. Morgan Company are among a growing number of companies using groupware networking to encourage candid communications.[13]

horizontal communication
The process of exchanging information between peers at any organizational level, usually to coordinate activities.

Horizontal communication. A lateral or **horizontal communication** process exists between peer managers, departments, and co-workers. Effective systems of horizontal communication are essential to ensure coordination of activities and to avoid misunderstandings. In Chapter 10, we discussed how staff and line managers

How close are companies to using video equipment to communicate in place of face-to-face meetings? Not very. At present the technology is simply too expensive. For example, PictureTel's complete video-room system costs almost $20,000. But desktop machines, when developed, should double industry sales by making videoconferencing easier. The critical missing piece is a single-chip codec (a special computer that sends video signals over phone lines) to replace the expensive five-chip codeces now used. With such a chip in place, prices could fall as low as $1,000. Then, predicts Steve Fischer, manager of applications development at U.S. West Communications, "people who shy away from technology will find personalized videoconferencing as easy to use as a public telephone." And when that happens, industry watchers promise, videoconferencing systems may be found on every executive desk next to the PC, phone, and the fax machine.

can become isolated from one another, creating confusion among employees. Quality control staff, for instance, may communicate production standards and intercede with operations to ensure quality manufacturing without communicating with line managers responsible for the work. Horizontal channels of communication, such as a quality control team or an established process for joint reporting of quality problems, ensure that information will be shared.

The ultimate goal of these peer-level communication processes is to improve coordination. For example, when Donald Petersen was CEO of Ford Motor Company, he introduced department- and division-level task force planning teams that comprised representatives from line and staff positions in several functional areas. Ford design teams were among the first task force teams assembled, and they included design engineers, production engineers, purchasing officers, personnel administrators, quality control staff, market researchers, and customer service specialists. At the executive level, Ford introduced task force teams with executives and United Auto Workers representatives.[14]

Informal Channels of Communication

Every organization has an informal structure, which we referred to in Chapter 9 as a *shadow network* of relationships. The **informal channel of communication** is the unsanctioned personal network of information among employees. It is commonly called the *grapevine* because, like a grapevine that sends long leafy runners shooting off in many directions, the informal network is often expansive and carries information in many different directions. The influence exerted through this network often circumvents official processes and disrupts formal authority.

informal channel of communication
The unsanctioned personal network of information among employees fostered by social relationships and friendships.

Keith Davis, who has researched informal communications extensively, suggests that informal information is neither vertical (flowing upward or downward) nor horizontal (flowing between peers or across departmental lines). Rather, it flows up and down hallways, in and out of offices, around water coolers, over transoms, and between friends and colleagues. A message can begin its journey at any point in the organization and end up everywhere.[15]

In Figure 16-3, several grapevine routes are illustrated. The single-strand model indicates the most direct route for informal messages, often passed through a chain of trusted associates. In contrast, the gossip route implies a chaotic process in which almost anyone is capable of passing along information to almost anyone else—the proverbial rumor mill. The probability chain suggests a selective network

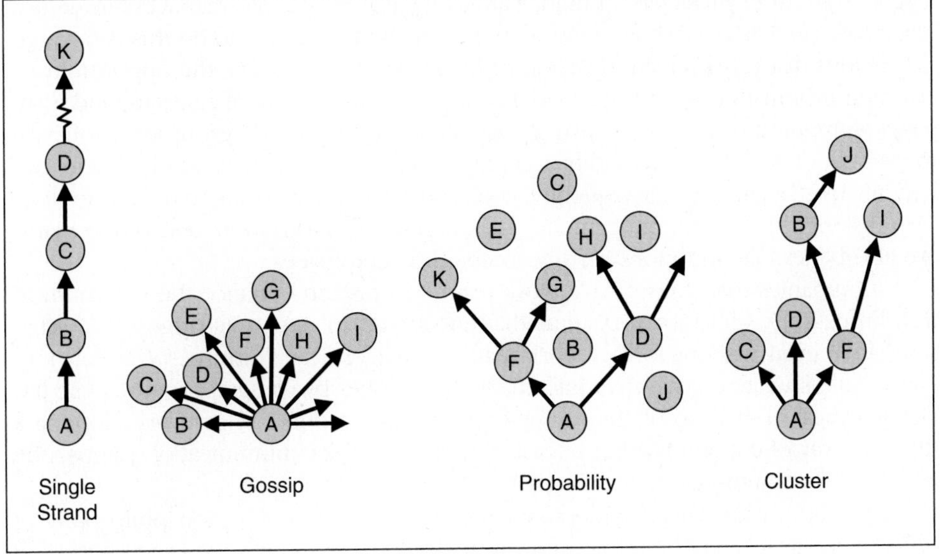

FIGURE 16-3 Types of Grapevine Chains

Source: Reprinted by permission of the *Harvard Business Review*. An exhibit from "Management Communication and the Grapevine" by Keith Davis (September–October 1953). Copyright © 1953 by the President and Fellows of Harvard College; all rights reserved.

defined by co-worker relationships or proximity. The cluster system is even more selective, often depending on purposeful exchanges of information among influential individuals or groups.

Managers sometimes send messages through the grapevine intentionally to instigate behavior by subordinates without having to officially communicate with them.[16] For example, a division manager at a San Diego aerospace firm knew he was going to have to lay off a number of engineers following serious budget cuts that resulted from NASA's temporary suspension of aerospace projects after the explosion of the space shuttle *Challenger* in 1986. The division manager did not want to announce these layoffs to a large number of employees without warning, so several weeks before they were scheduled, he casually let his chief engineer know. During a gym workout, he simply said, "There's been a lot of talk upstairs about the shuttle tragedy. People are running scared about NASA contracts, and there is no way we won't have tremendous cuts. This one's going to be deep and long." The chief engineer repeated these remarks, with some embellishment, to several of his top people, and within two days, everyone in the company expected major layoffs. When the layoffs were officially announced two weeks later, they affected fewer people than employees had anticipated, so rather than being stunned by the announcement, most employees felt relieved that so few jobs were lost.

Hard-line managers who believe that informal communications only result in unsubstantiated rumors and erroneous information try to stifle the grapevine, but research has shown that nearly 75 percent of information passed along informally is accurate.[17] Consequently, the informal communication process is a potent force in every organization, and attempts to restrict it only foster employees' beliefs that their managers cannot be trusted.[18] Admittedly, the 25 percent of information that is inaccurate can create serious problems, but managers should not attempt to suppress the system on this account. Instead, they should be alert to potential misunderstandings and try to reconcile discrepancies between formal and informal communications.

Reconciling Formal and Informal Communications

Team development and participative decision making help create an environment where managers can reconcile problems stemming from having two communication processes operating simultaneously. Information can be contradictory and confusing when formal and informal channels address the same issues. Because employees are more likely to believe information received from close friends and influential colleagues than from managers in higher authority, it is crucial for managers to defuse inaccurate rumors and reinforce accurate information. One way to do this is through discussions that rely on team decision making.[19] Participants have the opportunity to question information, search for evidence to support or refute allegations, and instigate communications on their own. As discussed in Chapter 11, group decisions are more believable and more readily accepted by employees than decisions made unilaterally by managers.[20] Consequently, communications that come out of group decision making, such as announcements, memoranda of clarification, and action plans, are also believable and more readily accepted by employees.

Companies that do not have work team systems can enhance the communication process through formal systems that encourage an open exchange of information. Also, even without formal work teams, managers can nurture social relationships that stimulate constructive information exchanges by using approaches like the Hewlett-Packard method of "managing by wandering around." However, adopting a different way of communicating often requires changing communication philosophy and, therefore, authority relationships.

An authoritative management system reflects a communication philosophy of inflexibility. In this environment, rigorous top-down communicative processes result

MANAGEMENT APPLICATION

Making Informal Communication a Positive Force: Bush Industries

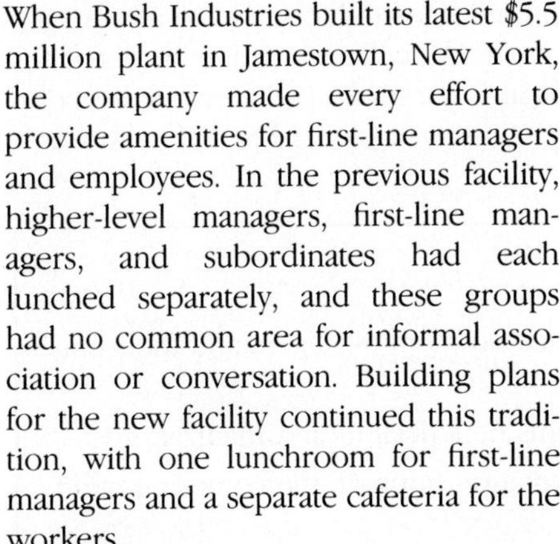

When Bush Industries built its latest $5.5 million plant in Jamestown, New York, the company made every effort to provide amenities for first-line managers and employees. In the previous facility, higher-level managers, first-line managers, and subordinates had each lunched separately, and these groups had no common area for informal association or conversation. Building plans for the new facility continued this tradition, with one lunchroom for first-line managers and a separate cafeteria for the workers.

Meanwhile, the firm's president, Paul Bush, worked to achieve wide participation in plant decisions through the introduction of quality circle teams. He and his executives put a great deal of effort into the leadership project, but when the new plant opened, managers and plant workers found that they had no place to hold informal team gatherings other than the rather stark workers' cafeteria or the intimidating managers' lounge.

Within two weeks the walls came down and the cafeteria was transformed into a "common room" where workers and managers could meet or take a break. A new arrangement of chairs and tables created a comfortable environment. Plaques and awards appeared on walls, company newsletters and popular newspapers and magazines were made available, new bulletin boards were devised by plant employees, and soothing music was piped in. The "commons" became a popular place immediately; even executives took their coffee breaks there. All Bush employees were encouraged to take breaks together, and team meetings became commonplace. Within months, the "commons" became the focal gathering place in the plant.

Several executives felt that more was accomplished in that room than through formal office meetings. The vice president for human resources commented, "It's a vehicle, a form of communication in itself, where a VP can bump into a secretary or a maintenance man and ask 'Hey, how are you doing?' and then get a straight answer. The room is conducive to candor, and you wouldn't believe the insights one can gain by just hanging around the coffee machine."

Source: Personal communication with Paul Bush, president, and Robert Liguori, vice president of human resources, Bush Industries, Inc.

in broadcasts, not conversations, and directives, not information sharing. Directives pass downward and the free exchange of information is stifled, so that employees have few opportunities to contribute ideas to their company. Reversing the process through a comprehensive system of open communication, however, is not necessarily better. At Kroy, Inc., a Scottsdale, Arizona, company, financial problems led to rumors of a shutdown. Management recognized that the company had a communications problem fostered by a rather inflexible formal reporting system. In a bold strategy, Kroy's executives had every office door in the company removed, and the CEO announced that Kroy was now committed to totally open communication. Unfortunately, after an initial period of disbelief when nearly all conversation became guarded, employees and managers responded with a burst of enthusiasm that became chaotic. People were communicating about everything all the time, and this not only distracted them from their work, but also caused important information to get lost in the noise. Management nevertheless stuck to its new philosophy, but altered its strategy so that systematic meetings and group discussions could engender constructive exchanges of useful information.[21]

The requirements for shared information and joint decisions necessarily thrust people into open communication processes. The resulting relationships can range from consultative to consensual, as discussed in Chapter 10. Formal lines of communication in these open systems link vertical levels of management while fostering horizontal cooperation through team activities. Consequently, a philosophy of management—and therefore a philosophy of communication—that strives to achieve cooperation through vertical and horizontal integration will reduce the potential for misunderstanding while increasing the potential for accurate and constructive communication.

CHECKPOINT

- Describe how communication takes place between managers and their employees in formal organizations.
- Why are informal communication systems beneficial to an organization?
- How does a philosophy of shared information improve the communication environment?

INTERPERSONAL COMMUNICATION

interpersonal communication The personal interaction between individuals that involves their perceptions during a dialogue in which specific meanings are attached to messages.

Most communication is "interpersonal" in the sense that people are involved in an information-sharing process, but there are many forms of communication, such as computer-generated reports, that are impersonal. **Interpersonal communication** is the personal interaction between individuals that involves their perceptions during a dialogue in which specific meanings are attached to messages. Interpersonal communication connotes a personal relationship in which symbols (words, phrases, and numbers) are used to create messages and behavior (physical gestures and voice intonations) gives specific meanings to messages.[22] A computer-generated report rarely conveys the perceptions of its originator (if there is an originator), so although a message is sent by the report, its meaning is either sterilized or left to unassisted interpretation.

Written messages can be forms of interpersonal communication. The symbolic nature of words combined with appropriate punctuation can convey powerful perceptions and meanings; novels and poems by gifted individuals prove this point. Most written organizational communications, however, do not convey the perceptual meanings personal dialogue does. Reports, letters, memos, budgets, and computer printouts have beneficial uses, but managers in their roles as leaders must be concerned with conveying meanings.

The Leadership Dimension

Leadership is accomplished largely through interpersonal communication. Managers' communication skills are therefore important components of the leadership process. Robert Lengel and Richard Daft address the leadership dimension in terms of identifying managerial problems and then selecting the appropriate media for communication.[23] The authors describe this selection process as a crucial skill necessary for managers to be effective communicators, and they characterize the choices available for communication in terms of *media richness*. Figure 16-4 illustrates the concept.

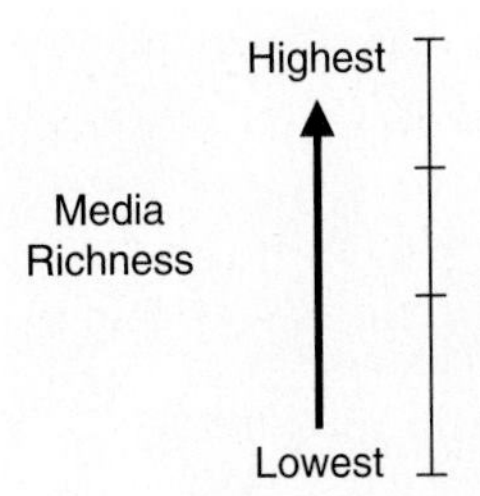

FIGURE 16-4 Media Richness Hierarchy

Source: Robert H. Lengel and Richard L. Daft, "The Selection of Communication Media as an Executive Skill," *Academy of Management Executive,* Vol. 2 (August 1988), p. 226. Reprinted by permission.

media richness
The capability of a given form of communication to convey information.

Media richness is the capability of a given form of communication to convey information. At the lowest level, media are considered *lean* because they convey only limited and impersonal information. They do not contain information on the attitudes, perceptions, or emotions of senders that give meanings to messages, and they cannot easily induce feedback response from a receiver. Indeed, these impersonal media may have no specific senders (computer reports can be generated through programs that assimilate information from data bases) and no specific target audiences (advertising flyers can be mailed to almost anyone, anywhere, for any reason). At the highest level of richness, media convey messages and meanings through multiple information clues, symbols, gestures, and the give-and-take of conversation that constantly alter senders' and receivers' perceptions. Between these extremes, forms of written and interactive media provide a variety of choices. The telephone, for example, is a relatively rich medium because callers can express emotions and solicit immediate feedback from receivers. A personal memorandum—if skillfully written—can convey emotion, but without sender-receiver interaction, a memo provides no opportunity for immediate feedback.

Lean media are generally cost-effective and thus are often very efficient ways to disseminate routine information to a large number of people. For example, a computer-generated price list can be automatically distributed through a data-base mail system to thousands of customers, or a safety bulletin can be photocopied and distributed to hundreds of employees along with their paychecks. These are effective uses of lean media. However, a computer-generated message announcing layoffs and sent to employees is an ineffective use of media and its coldness may significantly damage employee morale. Important nonroutine issues should be handled through rich media. A manager can fire an employee over the telephone, but the telephone is a poor substitute in this situation for a face-to-face conversation. Rich media can also be misused. Routine performance reports such as monthly sales summaries, for example, are not efficiently communicated through personal conversations. Such conversations would require people to repeat long lists of data and to explain all sorts of statistical information, which would not only be terribly boring but would also be too complicated to understand.

Effective leadership, of course, includes activities and skills far more complicated than selecting media. The process of matching appropriate media to circumstances, however, is a necessary requirement for effective communication, and effective communication is, in turn, a necessary requirement for effective leadership. Citicorp has developed a unique blend of media to communicate corporate ethics to its 90,000 employees. Using a board game with flash cards that identify ethical dilemmas faced by managers, players compete in teams to resolve the dilemmas and earn points. As the game progresses, the teams are cast in roles at successively higher levels of management to face ever-more-complex problems. The game is supplemented by case analyses, simulated incidents, and discussions led by a consultant. The process stimulates teamwork, but more important, it conveys a tremendous amount of comprehensible information about corporate ethics through an intense exchange of competitive ideas.[24]

Microsoft founder William H. Gates III encourages every employee to log on and share ideas via electronic mail, even sending them directly to him. Says one manager, "You can get mail from Bill G. any time. If you're intimidated by that, Microsoft is not for you." Besides electronic mail, Microsoft keeps open as many channels of information as possible. One recently hired manager came upon a group of programmers discussing software bugs while playing volleyball in their bathing suits in the hallway. And to cement their bonds, Microsoft employees have developed a language all their own. For example, in Microspeak, "flame mail" means electronic mail that is biting or emotional; "hardcore" means to be serious about work; "bandwidth" is the measure of someone's intellect; "nonlinear" is out of control; and "random" is illogical.

How Attitudes Affect Communication

attitude
A predisposition to respond favorably or unfavorably to objects, persons, and concepts.

An **attitude** is a predisposition to respond favorably or unfavorably to objects, persons, and concepts.[25] The critical word is *predisposition*. We learn from past experience, and our predisposition to respond is affected by all the elements of our past and present environments. Our cultural frame of reference predisposes us to act in certain ways in certain situations, our attitudes are tempered by our personal standards, work, and aspirations, and ingrained values influence our perceptions of how we respond to others. Figure 16-5 summarizes a few of the factors that interact to form our attitudes.

Because people have different attitudes, all messages conveyed through all media are interpreted (decoded) according to the unique perceptual frame of reference of each receiver. Managing the interpersonal communication process, therefore, depends on the ability to accommodate diverse attitudes. Equally important, managers must understand how their own attitudes affect their relationships with other members of their organizations.[26] When we have had less than pleasant experiences with certain individuals, we tend to limit our association with them. If we continue to have unpleasant experiences, we put greater distance between ourselves and these individuals. Our attitudes toward them become negative, and consequently, our predisposition to communicate with them declines. Managers who

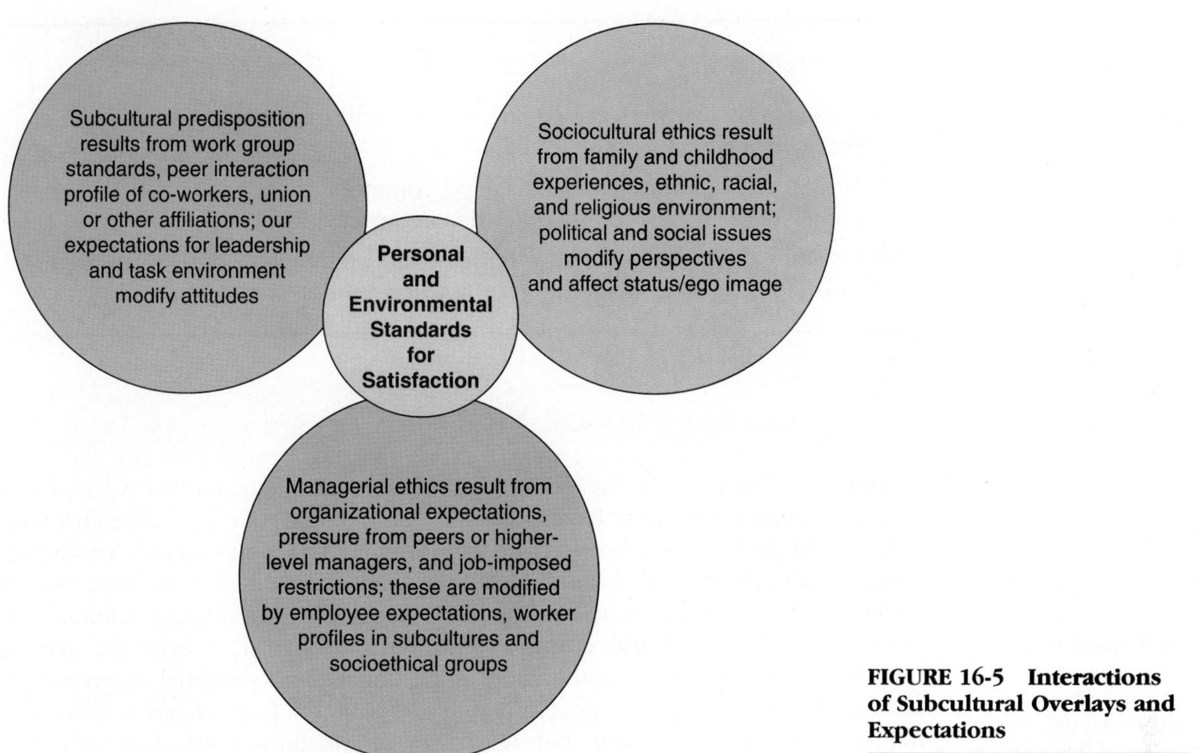

Subcultural predisposition results from work group standards, peer interaction profile of co-workers, union or other affiliations; our expectations for leadership and task environment modify attitudes
Sociocultural ethics result from family and childhood experiences, ethnic, racial, and religious environment; political and social issues modify perspectives and affect status/ego image
Personal and Environmental Standards for Satisfaction
Managerial ethics result from organizational expectations, pressure from peers or higher-level managers, and job-imposed restrictions; these are modified by employee expectations, worker profiles in subcultures and socioethical groups

FIGURE 16-5 Interactions of Subcultural Overlays and Expectations

maintain a sense of aloofness, either from their peers or from their employees, create patterns of *dissociation* that impede communications. When those managers attempt to communicate, their intended audience is predisposed to block reception or to distort the message. It is clearly to the benefit of managers to create an atmosphere of *association,* in which other members of the organization are predisposed to interpret their messages without distortion.[27]

Creating patterns of association is crucial to the development of teamwork. In Chapter 11, we stressed the importance of group cohesion as an antecedent to creating harmonious work teams. Association, and therefore group cohesion, is enhanced through communication behavior that is congruent with team members' expectations about leadership roles of their managers. This does not necessarily mean that groups need to behave democratically or that managers must structure communications in a congenial manner. Cohesive teams can exist in an autocratic environment such as a military combat squad or in a collegial environment such as a self-managed work group. At one extreme, team members expect their leaders to take command and to be decisive; consequently, combat team leaders will structure their communications to complement subordinate expectations. At the other extreme, team members expect to participate in decisions; therefore managers of self-directed work teams encourage a democratic style of communication in which information is shared through a cooperative process of team interaction.[28]

At any point along the spectrum of teamwork, perceptions by team members determine what pattern of communication will be complementary. Communication behavior that violates this expected pattern will result in communication failures, distorted messages, or conflict. A combat squad leader, for example, cannot suddenly stop giving orders in the field to hold a meeting to decide what the team should do next. Neither can a manager of a self-directed work group start dictating work assignments when team members are accustomed to making those decisions.

The point for managers is that, whether communicating with other individuals or with group members in a team environment, their communications must be structured to accommodate their audience's attitudes and predispositions.

CHECKPOINT

- Explain why interpersonal communication skills are crucial for being an effective manager.
- How does the richness of media affect communication, and why is it important to select media according to the circumstances?
- Describe how attitudes affect interpersonal communication. How do predispositions engender dissociation or association?

CROSS-CULTURAL COMMUNICATION

cross-cultural communication The process of communicating with people of different cultures who have substantial differences in assumptions and behavior that influence language usage, perception, and attribution of meaning.

Organizations are rapidly expanding their global operations, and as we noted in Chapter 3, recent changes in Eastern Europe, Asia, and the redefined states that once made up the Soviet Union have created extraordinary new opportunities for international development. Globalization also brings unprecedented challenges, one of which is for managers to learn to cope with the complexities of cross-cultural communication. **Cross-cultural communication** is distinguished from the general model of interpersonal communication by encompassing substantial differences in assumptions and behavior by people of different cultures. This process is also called *intercultural communication,* but regardless of the term used, communicating across cultures implies there will be problems associated with language, perception, and attribution of meanings.[29]

Effective cross-cultural communication involves both transmitting messages that are understood as intended and accurately understanding messages that are conveyed back. To communicate effectively in global business situations, managers must be able to communicate in a language familiar to those involved, encoding messages so that misunderstandings are minimized and decoding messages to accurately interpret their meanings.

The Importance of Language

English is becoming the language of international business, but it may be several generations before it is a common second language in foreign cultures. Even then, it is likely to be used only by those who are involved in international business or employed by companies with strong connections to English-speaking nations. Managers working overseas will still have to deal with operational employees who have only a rudimentary understanding of English, sell products to customers who do not speak English at all, and live in societies where most people have no desire or reason to use the English language. Consequently, learning a second (or third or fourth) language is a high priority for managers working for global companies right now, and as global business accelerates, the importance of being multilingual will increase dramatically.

Even managers in global companies who are home-based must recognize the importance of having foreign language skills. In the United States, when we speak about "global" operations, we typically think of a U.S. company like IBM operating overseas, but globalization has attracted many foreign companies to the United States. For example, more than 500 Japanese companies have substantial business operations in the United States, including Honda, Nissan, Sumitomo Bank, NEC (Nippon Electric Company), Itoh, and Sony, and each has contingents of Japanese executives. Although these managers are fluent in English and conduct business in this country in English, their native language is Japanese, and (like Americans who work overseas) they continue to think and to attribute meanings to messages based on

GLOBAL TRENDS

Going Beyond Berlitz

As more U.S. companies go global, American managers are finding that they must learn foreign languages. Knowing a foreign language is a good beginning, but it does not prepare managers for misunderstandings due to attributing unusual meanings to words and phrases.

Several years ago, for example, when Chevrolet was preparing to export its mid-sized Nova to Mexico, company executives failed to recognize that *Nova* in Spanish translates into "It won't go." Chevrolet suspended marketing efforts for the car. The 3M Company had been successfully selling Scotch tape in Japan for years when sales suddenly dropped off sharply. Company executives could not figure out the cause until a clerk in 3M's Tokyo office explained that a recent ad slogan that said "it sticks like crazy" came across to the Japanese as "it sticks foolishly." In Taiwan, the ad slogan "Come Alive with Pepsi" translated into "Pepsi brings your ancestors back from the grave."

Colloquial English can lead to major problems in Asian countries when translated exactly. For example, a businessman trying to conclude an important contract in Beijing departed from a meeting with a friendly nod and said in perfect Chinese, "See you later." To the Chinese, that meant he would return shortly to continue the discussion. They waited, he didn't come back, and the infuriated Chinese ended negotiations. Writing things down can be equally troublesome. An American, eager to impress Chinese buyers with his firm's four-year experience in China, described his company in a communiqué as an "old friend." The Chinese characters he used for "old" literally meant "bygone," with the connotation of "former." The Chinese concluded that the American firm wanted no more trade with China.

Communication problems in Europe can be as serious as those in Asia. Mars Candy, for example, sells M&M's throughout Europe, but has a special problem in France. There is no ampersand in the French language, nor do the French use apostrophes; consequently, "M&M's" is nonsense and unpronounceable in French.

Products brought into the United States can create equally unpleasant problems. For example, an imported Vodka, marketed through a Belgium firm with Icelandic connections, was labeled with a skull-and-crossbones logo and sold under the name Black Death. In Icelandic and several Baltic languages, the words for "black death" connote "a good strong drink" and the skull-and-crossbones logo conveys the image of an alcoholic drink that has a "free wild taste." Officials at the U.S. Health Agency and U.S. Bureau of Alcohol, Tobacco and Firearms were enraged. They pointed out that the skull-and-crossbones logo means "poison" to Americans, and that in English "Black Death" refers to the bubonic plague.

Sources: René White, "Beyond Berlitz: How to Penetrate Foreign Markets Through Effective Communications," *Public Relations Quarterly,* Summer 1986, pp. 12–16; Eric N. Berkowitz, Roger A. Kerin, Steven W. Hartley, and William Rudelius, *Marketing,* 3rd ed. (Homewood, Ill.: Irwin, 1992), pp. 615–617; and Laura Bird, "New Vodka Sold as Black Death Riles Regulators," *Wall Street Journal,* April 3, 1992, pp. B1, B4.

their native language. The Japanese are not alone in having substantial U.S. interests. By 1990, foreigners owned 12 percent of U.S. industry outright and had significant investments in an additional 21 percent of American companies. Approximately 90 foreign countries have business interests in the United States, and although we have been especially sensitive to Japanese activities, French, German, Dutch, and British investments are actually higher.[30] Many of these foreign interests have managers based in the United States who—like American managers based overseas—must deal with domestic workers and customers, and live among citizens, who neither speak their language nor see any reason to learn it.

Language difficulties are more noticeable among American managers working in foreign cultures than among foreigners working in the United States because fewer Americans are likely to know a foreign language. Learning a second language, however, is beginning to be emphasized for American managers. Du Pont, Eastman Kodak, Citicorp, and General Electric are a few of the companies that have established foreign language training programs for their managers. Berlitz International, the leading company in foreign language training systems, had a 50 percent increase in U.S. corporate clients between 1985 and 1989. However, contracts with Berlitz by European companies to teach English during that same period more than doubled; and English classes account for 64 percent of Berlitz's total business.[31]

By 1992, the number of U.S. corporations with foreign language training programs doubled from the figure for 1988, but the emphasis on English by foreign interests increased equally.[32] Just as important, many leading American companies introduced programs to train foreign national employees in English. Procter & Gamble established a "P&G College" for developing cross-cultural language skills; PepsiCo, Raychem, and Colgate-Palmolive have cross-cultural internship programs for both domestic and foreign employees; and American Express has inaugurated a global management exchange program that allows young managers from different countries to swap places for eighteen months.

Managers actively involved in foreign operations—either Americans assigned to overseas units or foreign nationals assigned to U.S. units—have fewer language difficulties than managers who engage in foreign trade while remaining home-based. Those with foreign assignments often have foreign language skills and are purposely trained in multicultural management, but those who only periodically travel overseas or do business from a domestic base often have no foreign language skills and not much knowledge of foreign cultures. Their international experience is comparable to that of the occasional tourist. Consequently, they struggle to communicate, necessarily relying more on foreigners to use English than on their own translation abilities. Too often, communication breaks down or critical misunderstandings occur because even though the words used may be recognizable, subtle differences in usage convey unintended meanings.[33]

A Perceptual Framework for Cross-Cultural Communication

Understanding the words of a foreign language is important, but insufficient to encode messages that can be understood. Receivers decode both verbal and nonverbal information in a message from their own perceptual frames of reference. They attribute meanings to messages that take into account gestures, facial expressions, and voice inflections, and ascribe their own cultural connotations to how words and phrases are used in the message context. Misunderstandings occur when the encoding process fails to account for these perceptual and nonverbal factors, and often the fault lies with the encoder, who holds false assumptions about the communication process. Some of these false assumptions are:[34]

- The other person sees the situation the same way you do.
- The other person is making the same assumptions you are.
- The other person is (or should be) experiencing the same feelings you are.
- The communication situation has no relationship to past events.

- The other person's understanding is (or should be) based on your logic, not on his or her feelings.
- The other person is the one who has the "problem" or does not understand the logic of the situation.
- Other cultures are changing and becoming more like your own culture; therefore, the other person is becoming more like you.

Research on intercultural relationships shows that in only a few instances are any of these assumptions accurate, and that in most instances, they are all wrong.[35] People from different cultures—even those who are neighbors—rarely see a situation in the same light, and they make different assumptions about language and nonverbal expressions. For example, the Japanese have sixteen definitions for the word "no," but when coupled with facial expressions such as raised eyebrows, or when spoken softly or given nuances through body movements, the word has literally thousands of possible meanings.[36] People from different cultures do not experience similar feelings because their attitudes, priorities, and cultural predispositions influence their feelings. In China, for example, most conversations begin with a *lubricant phrase* such as "I'm sorry, but . . . " or "Excuse me, may I . . . " or "This may not be important, but . . . ." Whether speaking Chinese or another language, the practice of using an apologetic opening is a common way the Chinese set the stage for a cooperative exchange of information. Ironically, they rarely say "thank you" or "you're welcome," and there are no common words in Chinese for either phrase. Consequently, when buying something in China, a customer may be politely greeted by a sales clerk with "Excuse me, may I help you?", but when the sale is completed,

---

Motorola, Inc., has been moving aggressively in Asia's flourishing telecommunications and semiconductor markets, building thirteen factories in nine countries. To run its Asian empire, the corporate giant is using Asian managers and local technicians and engineers. But Motorola is also relying on sending the right messages out, some of them nonverbal. For example, when the company built its $400 million Silicon Harbor complex in Hong Kong in 1990, the building was situated so that water—symbolizing wealth—surrounded it on three sides and mountains—symbolizing power—ringed it. Says Tam Chung Ding, president of Motorola's Asia-Pacific semiconductor division, "This office has about the best *feng shui* (good luck) in Hong Kong."

the customer will be handed the change abruptly without the slightest word of thanks or gesture of gratitude.[37] Chinese feelings and logic prevail, not the foreign customer's.

Negotiation is a characteristic of many cultures, and in Greece, Italy, and much of the Middle East, negotiation is emotional and loud and involves highly visible gestures. Even a friendly discussion with a street vendor can take on the appearance of a confrontational debate in Greece, where participants toss their heads, wave their hands, and shout terms and conditions. They also emphasize points through personal contact; it is not unusual for a Greek or an Italian to grab a visitor's arm to draw attention to something or to emotionally embrace an acquaintance when meeting. Americans, in contrast, are likely to maintain their distance or stiffen uncomfortably in such encounters.[38]

Finally, other cultures may be changing, but there can be no presumption that they are becoming more like ours. Recent changes in Eastern Europe, for example, have fostered nationalistic sentiments and the return to values and cultural conventions deeply rooted in these people's past. American standards and values are not necessarily appreciated in other societies, so cross-cultural business relationships can become substantially strained unless American managers make a conscious effort to understand the receiver's perceptual frame of reference and to avoid false assumptions when encoding messages.

Attributing Meanings Accurately

Because we have our own unique set of perceptions, and because people of other cultures can make the same encoding mistakes or false assumptions we often make ourselves, we are just as likely as they are to decode messages incorrectly. The same rules for encoding apply to decoding, with the added dimension that the receiver must provide sufficient feedback to acknowledge the message and communicate an understanding of it.

Ideally, receivers of cross-cultural messages have a sufficient appreciation of the sender's culture to be able to respond with unambiguous language and gestures. Realistically, most people who find themselves in a foreign country do not have the depth of cultural conditioning needed to respond in this ideal manner. Even those who speak the foreign language fluently are rarely able to abandon their native patterns of behavior. Consequently, Americans respond with American gestures and voice intonations, the French respond in their unique way, the British in theirs, and so on. It is good to remember that foreigners appreciate efforts to "fit in to" their frame of reference. In China, using slightly apologetic "lubricating" phrases is admired; in Italy, a slight touch to the arm or shoulder enhances reception; and in Britain, a soft tone of voice coupled with language that includes a few additional adjectives or adverbs is respected. More important, these gestures motivate the foreign person to listen carefully and to try to grasp the meaning of your response.[39]

CHECKPOINT

- Describe communication problems that occur for managers working in a cross-cultural environment.
- What are some of the main complications that must be resolved when encoding messages for someone from another culture?
- Why is it important to try to "fit in to" another person's cultural frame of reference when communicating with that person?

BARRIERS TO EFFECTIVE COMMUNICATION

Managers in local domestic companies and diversified global corporations have similar communication problems. Those working in multicultural environments certainly have more complications to resolve, but the interpersonal communication process is equally important in any organization. In the preceding sections of this chapter, we touched upon several important communication problems. Here we will address the fundamental nature of those problems and how they become barriers to effective communications.

Semantics

semantics
The nature and meaning of words and phrases and how they are used in the context of messages.

Semantics is concerned with the meaning of words and phrases and how they are used in the context of messages. One of the fundamental problems in management is semantic errors: creating misunderstandings by the indiscriminate use of words. As a rule, speakers try to use words that are common enough for everyone to interpret in approximately the same way. Managers speak constantly, and their audiences are employees who must interpret this verbal information and act upon it in a predictable manner. But words do not have consistent meanings, even among people with similar cultural backgrounds who work together in a domestic company.

Many things affect how we interpret the words we hear. As we noted earlier, communicating in a foreign culture requires recognizing that perceptual frames of reference unique to that culture affect the meanings people attribute to words when encoding and decoding messages. When we look at how the English language is used on a daily basis in U.S. culture, we also discover a variety of attributed meanings. The educated adult in daily conversation uses approximately 2,000 words selected from the nearly 600,000 words in the English language. Of those 2,000 words, only about 500 are employed frequently, and these 500 common words are used to communicate more than 14,000 different meanings. Even more astonishing, we have the ability to weave these few simple words into conversations with more than 110,000 different interpretations.[40]

In addition to interpretation problems, semantic problems from the use of "shop talk" or jargon can become barriers to effective communication. Jargon is a specific vocabulary created and used by people who belong to the same profession or work closely together and therefore share a common frame of reference; technical language used by attorneys or engineers is an example. Another type of jargon is used by people of the same cultural and social background or people with the same sex, ethnic, and racial characteristics; for example, slang expressions such as "rap" are associated with a particular ethnic group. While jargon often improves communication among reference group members, it raises barriers for everyone outside the group. Consider the following passage condensed from an explanation of how computerized voice mail systems work:

> The audiotex makes use of an IVR and data manipulation through an LAN so that speech-to-text inputs provide digitalized options for deciphering through voice recognition and text-to-speech transmission.[41]

This passage says, roughly, that a prerecorded message created through an "interactive voice response" system (software) can be created on a "local area network" (interconnected computers). Then a human caller who activates the system over the telephone will hear a response generated by the system from the prerecorded data.

Technical jargon does not have to be this complicated to create semantic barriers. The abbreviation *OB* means *organizational behavior* to management professors, but to physicians, *OB* refers to *obstetrics*. Also, common terms are given unusual meanings by specific groups. *Shark repellent* means exactly what the words say to a sailor, but in corporate finance, the expression refers to a tactic designed to discourage outsiders from trying to take over a company. New words also slip into special vocabularies, such as *doable* (a term that evolved from aerospace engineering meaning that something can be done) and *suits* (a slightly contemptuous reference to company staff managers and professionals).

Managers who want to be understood must avoid semantic errors, but this does not mean they should abandon technical terms or jargon. To the contrary, when used with the appropriate reference group, jargon can enhance communications. The point is that managers must consciously identify their intended audience and consider how those individuals will interpret the information they want to convey. When they are unsure about the audience or when they are addressing more than one group, managers can enhance understanding by using plain terms and concrete words that reduce misinterpretations. There is seldom any reason to seek to impress others with abstract terms with complicated meanings. In addition, managers can develop a predictable pattern of using words so that employees will attach consistent meanings to them.

Obfuscation

obfuscate
Literally, "to cloud an issue," *obfuscate* implies a purposeful attempt by one person to confuse another through the use of perplexing language.

Obfuscate, which certainly is not a concrete word a manager should use, means "to cloud the issue." The word *obfuscate* illustrates precisely the sort of language managers should avoid. Why use a confusing term when a more common one is available? When we obfuscate, we muddy our meanings and confuse listeners.

Obfuscation is used for two reasons. Some people unintentionally use confusing language and accidentally create misunderstandings. Others intentionally swamp their audiences with perplexing language. This willfully malicious use of language is a game of "one-upmanship" that might be fun as a parlor exercise but is deadly in management.

Managers employ a more subtle form of deliberate obfuscation when they issue vague and confusing directives to cover their own inadequacies. This is called a "snow job," and it is a defensive form of communication. Most of us have resorted to this practice to protect our egos. Some managers unconsciously make a habit of it, and are subsequently ridiculed. When managers deliberately try to confuse their employees, they are considered malicious and can cause bitter conflict.[42]

Noise

noise
A communication killer; interference, static, or distractions that cripple clear transmission or reception of information.

Noise disrupts communications. When we hear static on the radio, we become upset because our attention has been diverted from the program we want to hear. Static is called *interference* because it garbles and confuses communications. There are two types of static that interrupt oral communications between individuals: physical noise that drowns out words and perceptual noise that distorts meanings.

Physical noise. Many messages are lost because a receiver's attention has been diverted. Managers usually communicate in busy surroundings. Telephones ring, secretaries enter with messages, or subordinates buzz around. In factories, noise from machinery can be distracting. In offices, the noise may come from typewriters or printers.

At Transamerica Occidental Life Insurance Company, managers attempt to orient new employees through formal programs held away from the work environment. Comfortable rooms with training equipment, congenial seating arrangements, and privacy are provided for small-group orientation sessions. Transamerica's oper-

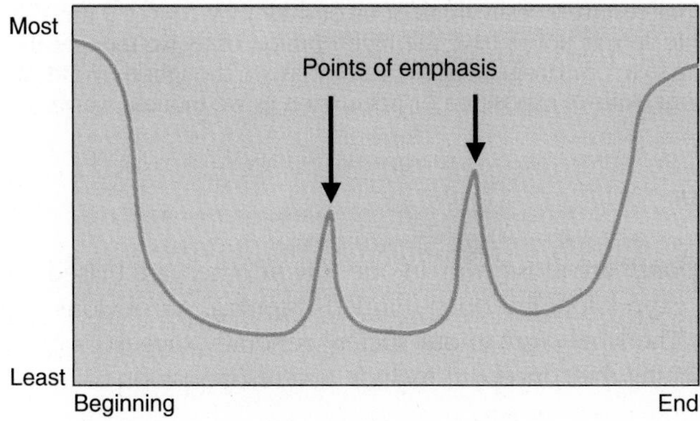

FIGURE 16-6 Receiver's Listening Curve

ating managers are also trained in how to conduct classes, including how to reduce unnecessary noise. Specifically, they are alerted not to conduct training with coins in their pockets because unconsciously rattling a pocketful of change distracts listeners' attention. They are also counseled to avoid tapping their fingers on desk tops.[43]

Perceptual noise. The second type of static is **perceptual noise,** which is distortion of meaning and selective filtering of messages through a personal frame of reference. People develop mental roadblocks that impede effective conversation. As noted earlier, cultural habits, beliefs, personality traits, and attitudes influence frames of reference. Sometimes people simply tune out mentally and actually do not hear what is being said. Most people cannot focus their attention for long, so although they hear what is being said, they do not consciously register the full content of the message. Figure 16-6 shows the pattern of attention for most listeners.

perceptual noise
A distortion of meanings and selective filtering of messages created by a receiver's personal frame of reference and attitude.

Listening

Listening is more a management than an employee problem.[44] Superiors tend to listen less to what subordinates have to say than vice versa. When superiors speak, the authority vested in them is usually sufficient to gain at least minimum attention from most workers, but subordinates lack this edge. Recently many leading companies have developed training programs to improve managerial listening skills.[45]

For example, General Electric's New Manager's Program, taught at the company's Management Development Institute in New York and at major overseas locations including Great Britain, West Germany, the Netherlands, Singapore, and Brazil, has a specific course on listening. The course content includes awareness training for "actively hearing" what others have to say, reducing noise and interference to improve communication, and developing better communication habits through skits, role playing, and team presentations. Results from employee surveys over a four-year period confirm that communication between managers and employees has improved significantly and that productivity and motivation have been enhanced by the managerial training program.[46]

Screening

Screening is a process of guarding against certain information. Usually, it is a subconscious process of blocking information—an automatic defense mechanism that acts to shut off hard-to-take criticism and other unpleasant messages. It can also be a conscious effort to filter messages or to manipulate information to one's benefit. The subconscious process, called *perceptual selection,* occurs when people need to protect their egos by remaining ignorant of unpleasant facts. The following quotation taken from research on perceptual communication problems illustrates the point:

screening
A subconscious blocking of information to avoid unpleasant facts; also, a conscious and deliberate filtering of messages to manipulate information to one's benefit.

When we find out what our receivers really think of us or how they convey a message, we often get angry. People appear not to have the high opinion of us we thought they did. They do not find our style of management as pleasant as we thought they did. We are not as competent in our skills of exposition or persuasion as we thought we were.[47]

Jaundiced Viewpoints

People with *jaundiced viewpoints* are those who, in one way or other, are biased. Biases create barriers to free expression and open-minded listening. An obvious and extreme example is bigotry. The label *bigot* in our society generally suggests a racial bias, but here we are broadening the concept to include severe opposition to others of different culture, race, creed, color, or sex.

polarization
A jaundiced viewpoint in which a person interprets information in extreme—black and white—contexts.

Communications theorist William V. Haney has identified two particular forms of jaundiced viewpoints: *polarization* and *frozen evaluations*.[48] **Polarization** occurs when a person has a strictly black-and-white opinion on everything that happens in an organization. A slight variation in productivity is viewed as a serious breakdown in efficiency; an employee's minor disagreement over an inconsequential point is proclaimed insubordination; a slightly distorted message is subversion. Haney suggests that "One of the most destructive forms of polarization is the pendulum effect—the escalation of conflict. It thrives on overreactions. Regrettably, the easiest, the most dramatic, and the most infantile response to opposition is absolute counteropposition."[49] As Figure 16-7 shows, polarization assumes no middle ground or shades of behavior or relationships.

frozen evaluation
Assumption of "no change," in which a person shuts out information, thereby protecting the status quo and avoiding the threat of having to alter values or beliefs in a changing world.

The **frozen evaluation** is an assumption of "no change." It is a naive belief that the work environment or some other phenomenon is now the way it was in the past and the way it should be in the future. Of course this attitude impedes progress and hampers change. It also shuts out incoming information that could help a manager adapt in an ever-changing world. The frozen evaluation is a rationale for not listening. Managers caught up in this mentality are often passed over for promotion and generally ignored because constructive communication with them is often impossible.

A classic example of frozen evaluation occurred during the period 1976 to 1981 in the computer industry when Apple Computer Company brought to market its personal computer systems. Steven Jobs, co-founder of Apple who at the time was an outspoken folk hero, made bold announcements concerning the entire computer industry and the future of information technology, including: "The personal computer is the bicycle of this century, improving human endeavor a hundred-fold . . . ," "Our technology will redefine how we work, and, soon, a ten-year-old will be using his personal computer at home to do school papers and science projects . . . ," and "The personal computer will change forever the process of education." In response, IBM managers, together with a majority of people in the business of making typewriters and huge mainframe computers, labeled the Apple computer a "toy" and a "fad" that attracted "strange enthusiasts" and "kids who are mesmerized" by electronic gremlins chasing one another. Consequently, the computer industry continued to build huge mainframes until Jobs and several adventurous entrepreneurs like him had sold several million personal computers, proving Jobs's bold claims. Today with perfect hindsight, managers admit to "not listening" to signals in society, to Steven Jobs, or to their own customers. Perhaps this type of jaundiced viewpoint re-

FIGURE 16-7 Polarizing Decisions

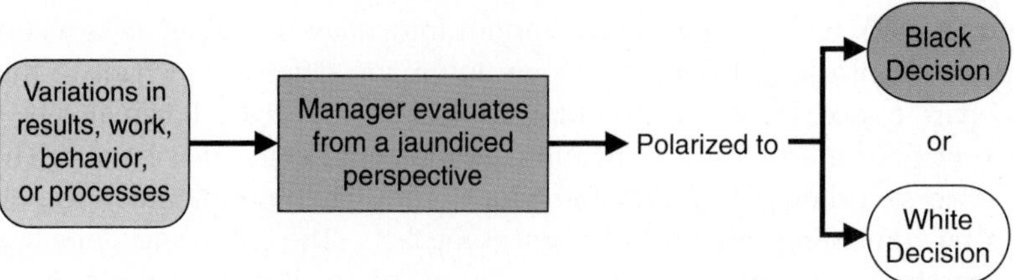

peats itself regularly. When Jobs, as head of NeXT, Inc., came back with a computer system he said would revolutionize the nation's educational system by redefining how we structure the learning process, IBM, Xerox, Prime Inc., and DEC announced layoffs, not visions for a new age of technology. While Jobs was optimistically talking about innovations in computer technology, they were blaming their financial losses on poor economic conditions.[50]

stereotyping
The belief that certain people have attributes based on group characteristics such as sex, race, and ethnic origin that make them superior or inferior.

Stereotyping

Stereotyping is the belief that certain people have attributes based on their group characteristics that enhance or impede their abilities to perform effectively; racial, sexual, and ethnic characteristics are common categories. Stereotyping is a kind of "shorthand" thinking that makes work easier because it allows us to neatly compartmentalize ideas and attitudes for quick reference. But strong preconceptions can make managers lose sight of unique opportunities and ignore potentially good ideas from individuals.

Thinking in shorthand leads to talking and acting in shorthand. Managers often talk down to employees they have categorized according to some profile of their reference group. Worse yet, they may exclude them from conversations because they assume everyone in their reference group is incapable of making a contribution. When an individual does not fit the stereotype, managers shy away, distrusting someone who appears to be unpredictable.

Some shorthand thinking is inevitable, and stereotyping can be helpful to identify trends in society or patterns of behavior among employees, but more often stereotyping is counterproductive because putting people into convenient categories ignores their individual contributions. It is particularly counterproductive in *multicultural environments* where employees come from many different backgrounds.

Overcoming sexual stereotyping to improve opportunities for capable women is one of the most sensitive issues in multicultural management. A number of books and book-length reports point out that although women hold more than 40 percent of all jobs in the United States, less than 1 percent of these jobs are in senior management. Only 0.5 percent of CEOs are women, most of them founders of their own enterprises.[51] This imbalance is attributed to a "white male system" of organizational management with value-loaded stereotypes of women (and other minorities) that perpetuates discrimination. Organizational discrimination is seldom deliberate, and most men who are part of the system individually support women's rights. However, the "system" is replete with masculine job titles, executive men's clubs, and expectations for managerial behavior modeled on long-standing patterns of male dominance.[52] The white male juggernaut is a "no-peer" world in which men can be one-up (or one-down) but never equal. In their managerial roles, men often feel they have no choice but to establish themselves as "one-up," and relegate all others to positions at least one-down. In contrast, research shows that women are more comfortable as peers, and in leadership roles they tend to facilitate behavior among subordinates rather than direct them. Consequently, two stereotypes have evolved, creating a gender gap in which men and women are trapped by systems of values that neither has been able to change substantially.[53]

Shortly after becoming the new head of Baxter International's Canadian unit, Michelle J. Hooper was invited to join the Young Presidents' Organization, a predominately white male club. At her welcome dinner, a member joked that it was nice that Hooper was a woman, and it was even better that she was black, but it would have best if she were disabled too. His remarks were greeted by uneasy silence, until Hooper broke the tension by laughing at the joke. Hooper is no newcomer in dealing with the issues of race and gender. Her promotion in 1988 elicited grumblings about the job going to a person with little management experience. Recalls Hooper, "One of the first questions I got was whether I was making the decisions or whether someone else was. The answer was that I made them."

CHECKPOINT

- Describe how each of the barriers to effective communication creates problems between managers and their employees.
- In terms of communication, what are some of the important problems facing managers in a multicultural environment?

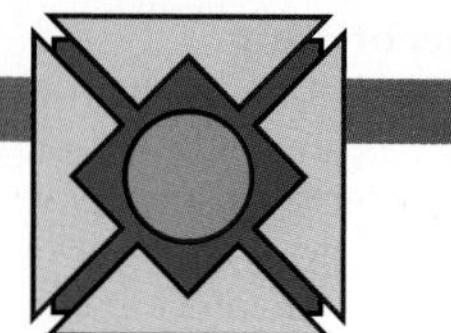

ETHICS IN MANAGEMENT

Bad News Unwelcome: Mum's the Word at American Express

Executive managers at the Optima Card Division of American Express were cleared of any wrongful behavior after auditors discovered $24 million in hidden losses because the managers, it seems, knew nothing of the trouble. The losses had been quietly concealed at lower levels, often by youthful fast-track managers reluctant to tell their bosses how poorly the card division was performing during its first several years of operations. Ironically, a few of these lower-level managers were fired, not for poor performance, but for failing to communicate accurately with upper-level management.

Killing the messenger who bears bad news, although a fabled practice in ancient Egypt, has a modern interpretation as many younger managers in corporate America find themselves jobless after telling their bosses things those bosses do not want to hear. During recent years of downsizing and corporate cutbacks, consultants and researchers have noted that when "tough top managers" are expected to turn around ailing companies, one aspect of that task is to impose a form of "corporate McCarthyism," actively suppressing any criticism or dissent." Consequently, people clam up for fear of losing their jobs, and higher-level managers don't hear about problems until they become full-blown crises. Then someone has to pay the price for what often appears to be a cover-up.

Fortunately, many companies provide their newly hired managers with initial training to help reduce barriers to communication between individuals and their superiors, and American Express, to its credit, tries to instill a sense of active listening in all its managers through leadership development programs. Yet research shows that the information environment for newly hired managers is often intimidating even in the best-managed companies. Younger managers simply lack the necessary sense of security to be candid with their superiors. Problems may reflect badly on a boss, and like the messengers of Egypt, subordinates often find it safer to say nothing or to tell the pharaoh how well he is doing rather than sound the alarm.

Sources: Janet Barnard, "The Information Environments of New Managers," *Journal of Business Communication*, Vol. 28, No. 14 (1991), pp. 312–423; Sandra L. Kirsch, "When Management Regresses," *Fortune*, March 9, 1992, pp. 157–158, 162; and "Get Me Mail Order," *Fortune*, March 9, 1992, p. 153.

OVERCOMING BARRIERS TO EFFECTIVE COMMUNICATION

empathy
The conscious effort to understand another person's viewpoint or to psychologically adapt to the other's frame of reference.

A general prescription exists for treating most communication problems: It is *empathy*. **Empathy** is the conscious effort to understand another person's viewpoint, to psychologically adapt to the other person's frame of reference. Effective listening begins with empathy. Many employees are less skilled in communications than their managers or feel too intimidated by the superior-subordinate relationship to speak freely. Therefore, managers must adjust to the level of their employees, not in a condescending manner, but in a spirit of cooperation that encourages communication. This is called *adaptive listening*.

Managers should also confirm that they hear and understand what the speaker is saying. This can be accomplished through gestures, by stopping periodically to retrace vital points, or by paraphrasing points to ensure that the messages being received are the same as those being sent.

Managers must also attempt to recognize biases, jaundiced viewpoints, and obfuscation, in employees as well as themselves, so they can reduce these barriers to communication and concentrate on the meanings of messages. Environmental noise can be managed by systematically planning communications under controlled circumstances, such as finding a quiet place to talk or taking an employee to lunch when there is a need to discuss something important.

Perceptual noise, like polarization and frozen evaluations, is very hard to manage. Managers must try to recognize these perceptual problems in employees and keep them from distorting information in the organization.

Managers can address the problem of semantic confusion by using more concrete words and phrases in their conversations. Reinforcement is crucial, and paraphrasing or summarizing what they think they have said is often an excellent way to clarify their receivers' understanding. Examples are another great clarifier.

There are two basic considerations for effective communication: Senders must want messages received and understood, and receivers must want to listen and understand. Both must be willing to engage in a free exchange of information while factoring out biases and perceptual barriers that led to misinterpretations. Exhibit 16-1 summarizes ways to manage the communication killers.

Toward More Effective Communication

In this chapter, we have moved through a series of discussions aimed at one objective: to alert you to ways to avoid miscommunication. We have examined communication problems, particularly the critical communication barriers, and discussed how they are related to differences in perceptions. We have also emphasized that empathy can go a long way toward improving communications. Once a person has this empathic viewpoint, there are additional ways to enhance the communication process.[54]

Develop a conversational tone and demeanor that reinforce your key points. Good eye contact helps to gain and retain attention for both persons. You cannot easily be distracted when you are concentrating on eye contact with your receiver. If you choose to use gestures to dramatize meanings, do not employ so many that you distract attention from the message.

Structure your messages for the greatest impact with the least risk of being misunderstood. Concrete words used in simple contexts help to clarify a message. Semantic problems arise when managers use a lot of abstract words. Abstract

EXHIBIT 16-1 Managing the Communication Killers

Semantic confusion	Be clear and concise in your communications; avoid jargon.
Obfuscation	Use common words; do not "blow smoke."
Physical noise	Find a quiet environment; do not introduce noise yourself.
Perceptual noise	Get your listener's attention; reinforce your message through repetition.
Poor listening	Focus on the sender; actively give and take during communication.
Jaundiced viewpoints	Be aware of personal and cultural biases; avoid polarized and frozen viewpoints.
Stereotyping	Do not oversimplify situations and individuals; adapt personal attitudes to the needs of others.

words carry too many meanings for us to be able to assume the receiver is hearing the same thing we think we are saying.

Don't "blow smoke." Obfuscation is wasted effort. Have the message clear in your own mind before you attempt to convey it. Don't pretend to knowledge you don't have, and if you are wrong about something, acknowledge it instead of trying to cover up your error. You will not gain your subordinates' respect by insisting you know things you don't and are always right.

Avoid noise whenever possible. If you can adjourn to an office or a conference room to have a conversation, do so. Then avoid interruptions so your message will have a strong chance of being heard and understood. Don't tap your fingers, shuffle your feet, jingle change, or ride a squeaky chair while you are conversing.

Do not polarize a conversation. We often find ourselves involved with others who are geared up for a fight, but confrontation seldom leads to improved communication or closer associations. Although confrontation is a prescribed method of therapy for resolving some forms of conflict, here we are concerned with daily communication behavior between managers and employees. When confronted, do not automatically "fire back." As a general rule, patience is more successful than retribution in solving misunderstandings. There are times, however, when a firm stand is required, particularly if you are being tested by others.

Listen carefully. Consciously focus your attention on what is being said to you and how it is being said. Shake off perceptual noise such as stereotyping, concentrate on the speaker, and actively respond. Paraphrase what you think you heard. This repetition of the content of the message acts as confirmation of your understanding and also gives the sender the opportunity to clarify points. The sender should make some gesture of reconfirmation to your response. Such give-and-take allows a message to be confirmed, clarified, reconfirmed, and mutually understood. Other methods can be used for reinforcement or for important messages that require documentation. Bulletin boards are great places for less important announcements, such as work assignment changes, company picnics, and reminders. Directives and formal notices are useful for important messages such as policy changes on overtime or vacation scheduling. Signs and posters convey work rules well or reinforce safety standards. Committees and group meetings are ideal media for mass personal conversations. Then there are the two standbys in business communication: the telephone and the memo.

Develop communication behavior that is congruent with attitudes of your receivers. Managers sometimes have to adapt their personal attitudes toward others or toward tasks to ensure effective performance. If they strive for association and attraction between themselves and employees, they stand a greater chance of gaining acceptance of goals and control over behavior in the work environment. Figure 16-8 illustrates the relationship of attitudes to communication.

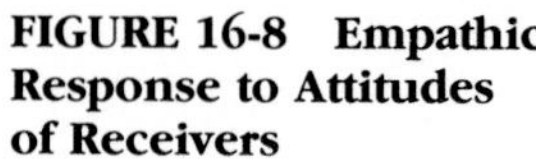

FIGURE 16-8 Empathic Response to Attitudes of Receivers

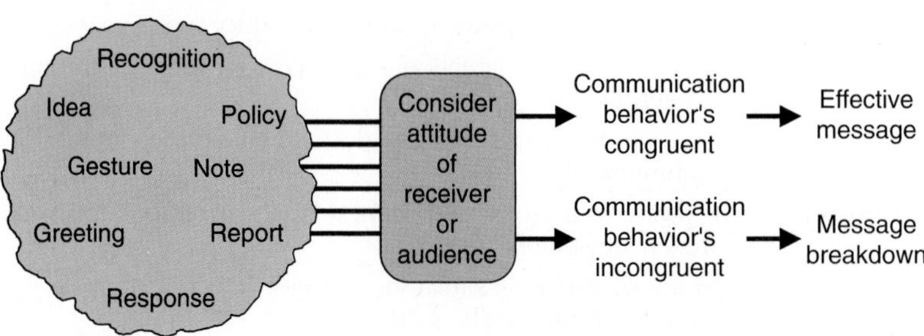

Improving Organizational Communication

Becoming more effective by improving interpersonal communication skills will subsequently improve an organization's communication environment, but there are additional considerations. These involve company policies and programs. As a conclusion to the chapter, we describe three groups of activities that can improve organizational communication.[55]

Gaining feedback from employees. Although managers can individually solicit feedback from their employees, information can also be systematically gathered from employees through surveys, consulting interventions, exit interviews, and suggestion programs. Employee surveys can be conducted periodically using questionnaires to study opinions about changes, leadership, work methods, technology, motivation, and many other sensitive issues. Surveys are very useful when it is important to have candid answers from all employees as a group. Also, surveys can be directed to specific employee groups such as middle managers, women, men, minorities, employees in specific divisions, or those in certain age brackets. Responses from surveys help managers understand prevailing trends or group attitudes, and often they can identify potential problems such as patterns of discrimination or sexual harassment—issues individuals often find difficult to talk about to their superiors.

Consulting interventions involve contracting with specialists to conduct surveys, study work methods, facilitate changes, introduce special training and development programs, or provide counseling. In addition, human resource programs such as conducting exit interviews can provide the organization with vital information. An exit interview is the final interview, usually conducted by a personnel specialist, with a departing employee who may have quit, retired early, or been fired. The point of the interview is to discover problems the employee perceived as important during his or her tenure with the company. Another type of program known generally as a "suggestion system" is a means of encouraging employees to put forward constructive ideas for organizational improvements or for innovative products and services. Often these programs provide employees with monetary awards for suggestions that are adopted, and they are usually highly publicized as a means of reinforcement and motivation.

Many adaptations of programs used to gather information or solicit responses from employees are possible. Electronic mail systems have enhanced the process, allowing rapid accumulation of information and extensive analysis of data. An added benefit of these efforts is that employees are drawn into the communication process and, consequently, become more involved in organizational affairs, often effecting changes or influencing decisions.

Improving training and development. In addition to the obvious purposes of well-devised training and development programs, organizations benefit from the information process that goes on in every form of education. Recall that we described earlier in the chapter how Citicorp uses its *ethics game* to encourage dialogue among employees. The company's game not only helps inform employees about ethical issues and gives them practice in resolving ethical dilemmas, but also creates an atmosphere for open debate and constructive criticism about these issues. Similar benefits can be realized through job training, technical skills upgrading seminars, company-sponsored travel to professional conventions, development meetings, and innovative programs such as teleconferencing or simulation exercises.

Media enrichment. Companies have a wide choice of media to enhance the communication environment. Most companies can develop a variety of media to enhance organizational communications. Recall from an earlier section in this chapter that media were ranked according to their "richness," some being relatively impersonal, and others being rich in personal contact. We noted that because an impersonal medium such as a computerized report was "lean" in communication content, it could be a valuable tool for disseminating information to a large number of employees. We also noted that although a "rich" medium such as personal conversation permits the highest degree of information exchange, it can be very inefficient and time-consuming. A mix of media, therefore, is most effective in raising the level of communication throughout a company. This mix might include monthly meetings with employees, use of focus groups for problem-solving or brainstorming sessions, newsletters to employees, bulletins and posters, and computer-generated documents. Managers can also do things like occasionally walking around and talking with employees (managing by wandering around) or regularly inviting employees into their offices for informal chats (the open door policy). Finally, they can send birthday cards to employees and their family members, sponsor picnics or parties, or hold "retreat" meetings in fun places away from work.

CHECKPOINT

- How does empathy help resolve communication problems? Explain other means of improving interpersonal communications.
- Describe how managers can improve organizational communications, and identify some of the innovative ways they can encourage employees to become involved in the information-sharing process.

A complementary approach to communication is one of Ted Koppel's strengths as an interviewer, as we noted in our opening discussion of "Nightline." He encourages guests to speak candidly about a topic while patiently listening to what they have to say. Koppel rarely speaks more than his guests, seldom interrupts, and frequently paraphrases their points to clarify issues or emphasize them for the TV audience. When guests disagree or when the conversation becomes a confrontation, he regains control by saying something like "Forgive me, were we not talking about . . . ?" or "I understand your concern for . . . , but shouldn't we focus on the facts?"[56] Instead of badgering guests or becoming a party to confrontations between them, Koppel is more likely to buffer differences. His approach keeps conversations focused and helps to clarify points for viewers. ■

A SYNOPSIS FOR LEARNING

1. Describe the communication model and the roles of senders and receivers.

   The communication model comprises four components: encoding, channel selection, decoding, and feedback. It is the responsibility of a sender to encode information, selecting words, symbols, phrases, or appropriate gestures to form a clear message. Then a channel is chosen to transmit the message. This channel may be a telephone, memo, conversation, computer printout, or other medium. Next, a receiver must decode the message, interpreting what he or she hears or sees and giving meaning to the message. Finally, a receiver provides recognition—feedback to the sender acknowledging that what was sent was received and understood.

2. Identify and discuss communication problems in organizations.

Organizations have two categories of communication problems. The first stems from "interpersonal" relationships in which managers and their employees share information about work, objectives, and activities. Interpersonal problems result from poor semantics, physical and perceptual noise, stereotyping, filtering, obfuscation, polarization, jaundiced viewpoints, and divergent attitudes. The second category of problem originates in "organizational" relationships and the patterns that emerge between strata and among different departments and functions. When formal communication channels are vague or when managers misuse them, crucial information about company activities is ineffectively communicated or not communicated at all. Poorly defined horizontal channels between departments and peers or staff and line managers also lead to communication problems.

3. Explain how perceptions and attitudes mold communications.

Communication is more than words. Communication enhancements, such as body language, give clues that help listeners interpret the words. People have perceptual barriers that prevent them from hearing and interpreting messages correctly—a different perspective from that of the communicator, internal distractions and preoccupations, a tendency to filter out unpleasant information. Attitudes, or predispositions to respond in certain ways to certain people and ideas, also affect people's interpretations of communications. Managers who communicate clearly and identify and adapt to the attitudes of their employees will develop in their subordinates a willingness to listen and cooperate toward attaining mutual goals.

4. Explain how communication problems occur for managers working in a cross-cultural environment.

Language differences present obvious difficulties in exchanging messages, and sometimes the same words have different meanings in different cultures. Encoding and decoding messages can also be difficult because the nonverbal information associated with communication significantly affects how meanings are conveyed by senders and interpreted by receivers, and this type of information—gestures, eye movements, facial expressions, voice inflections, and physical touching—differs from culture to culture. Managers working overseas face these issues daily and become effective communicators only if they come to understand them. Managers who work from a domestic base and only trade or travel overseas have even greater difficulties because they are seldom able to gain an appreciation of foreign cultures and the difficulties of communicating to the people from those cultures.

5. Describe barriers to effective communication and how they affect organizational performance.

There are several important barriers to effective communication, including semantic differences, physical noise, perceptual noise, and screening. People also polarize information and have frozen evaluations. Stereotyping is the belief that certain people have attributes based on group characteristics such as sex, race, and ethnic backgrounds that make communication strained. Biases often lead to deliberate blocking of information, filtering, or manipulation of meanings.

6. Describe how managers can ensure more effective communications.

From an interpersonal perspective, managers can become more empathic toward their employees by recognizing differences in attitudes, values, and personalities. By being active listeners and repeating messages, clarifying meanings, and giving constructive feedback, managers enhance their relationships with employees. Organizational communications can be improved through programs such as employee surveys, exit interviews, "managing by wandering around," employee suggestion systems, and training and development efforts. Management can also enrich company media with newsletters, meetings, social gatherings, and innovations such as simulation games.

SKILL ANALYSIS

CASE 1 Confusion at Heritage Furniture

Bob Anderson was determined to improve plant efficiency. As vice president of Heritage Furniture, he was concerned about poor quality and a 12 percent rate of return of merchandise by customers. He also knew that he had a problem with his plant manager, Don Rogers, who was difficult to communicate with. Several attempts to discuss problems with Rogers had ended in buck passing, accusations that "purchasing" had bought cheap veneering materials, "maintenance" couldn't keep tools in good condition, or "his people" just didn't care.

Anderson arranged an early evening dinner in a private conference room for his plant managers and key personnel. After dinner, he encouraged an open exchange of information.

In response, Gene Brock, a foreman in charge of veneering table tops, admitted that the company was producing too many tables of unacceptable quality. He explained that because his crew was trying to push too much production through the system, they were apt to make mistakes. However, he blamed most of the quality problem on poor materials and cheap veneers.

Next, a quality control manager, Fred Grimes, said that the veneer crew was doing sloppy work. He pointed out that more than half the rejects were for bumps and scratches put on by the workers. He also blamed Brock's people for "slopping around with the glue" that was used in veneering, smearing it on table surfaces and thus marring finishes.

Brock snapped back, "What do you expect from my people? These guys are half-literate, labor-grade people getting zilch for pay. They are expected to crank out production with junk for materials. But you guys are the experts, so tell me how to solve the problem?"

Anderson interrupted. He noted that there were indeed too many handling errors, but it was not quality control's responsibility to tell a foreman how to improve workmanship. Admittedly, materials were not always good, but poor veneer was supposed to be weeded out by inspectors.

A usually quiet plant supervisor, Ray Gardner, then spoke up. "Mr. Anderson, do you really want to know what the problem is?"

"I want the answers," Anderson said, "even if they are painful."

"Well, the first problem is that you fellas up higher in the company don't really listen to us," Gardner said. "We've reported time and time again that materials were getting worse, and the truth is, the veneers are not all that good. We've said that two saws are just about worn out, but the only answer I've ever gotten back is that as long as they're running, use them. Those saws are shot. We've also sent up reject reports showing problems with paint, with repair parts, and with poor handling methods, but I've never heard one word of concern from you fellas."

Grimes supported the point. "We've rejected products only to be told to pack them anyway. I get the idea no one's interested in quality, only how much product we can ship."

Anderson had seen many of these reject reports and had asked his plant manager about them, but Rogers had always assured him that most of the problems were due to poor workers. The explanation had sounded reasonable because the workers were low-paid and unskilled, but Anderson now realized that Rogers had been careful not to pass on bad news.

Anderson said, "I'm going to take action on everything I hear. That's a promise. But why do all these rejects keep occurring? In spite of poor materials, can't we motivate our people to watch for defective products and stop them from being shipped?"

"Sure we can," Gardner answered, "but everyone has to believe the company really gives a damn, and right now that isn't so."

After the meeting broke up, people were still talking in groups on their way to the parking lot. When Anderson stopped the plant supervisor near his car and thanked him for his candid response, he got an even bigger shock.

"I wasn't candid, Mr. Anderson; I just touched the surface," Gardner said. "No way would anyone say what they felt in there. You want some truth about our place? Well, you said we have 12 percent rejects, right? No way. We're shipping twice that much of junk product. I can't read or write, so I don't know about the figures, but I been here a long time, and I tell you, we screw up a lot."

"Ray, everyone respects you," Anderson replied. "Tell me confidentially why I don't hear about these problems."

"Mr. Rogers will say what you want to hear. He's going to tell you we shipped the numbers you wanted. That's it; that's all I should say."

Case Questions

1. Identify the various types of barriers to communication used by individuals in the case.
2. Identify and discuss attitude problems and perceptual aspects that affect working conditions at Heritage.
3. How could Anderson improve communications between Rogers and himself? Between Rogers and his first-line managers? Between first-line managers and workers?

VIDEO CASE College Campuses Debate Politically Correct Communication

Political correctness—politically correct thought—politically correct communication. These words are igniting a bitter debate on college campuses. In the ivory towers of academia, the intellectual freedom to express and explore ideas has long been assumed to be a sacred right and obligation. Now, however, sensitivity over what is or is not politically correct (PC) is creating an atmosphere of outrage from two viewpoints: those who see PC as part of the struggle to eliminate racism and sexism and those who condemn it as the new McCarthyism.

The whole issue of political correctness arose when a group of journalists a couple of years back decided to define what was and was not politically correct usage in their dictionary of cautionary words and phrases. Some words and phrases that seemed perfectly innocent in everyday usage can appear offensive on occasion. For example, the journalists' dictionary advised avoiding the phrase "Dutch treat" since it implies that Dutch people are cheap.

On college campuses the issue of political correctness has raised some difficult questions. "The question has become at what point does politically correct thinking change the university from a marketplace of ideas to a center of intellectual intimidation and censorship?" asks Jackie Judd of ABC news.

Some academics believe that political correctness limits their intellectual freedom to exchange ideas. One professor stated that "what you have is a collapse of a real belief that language can help convince someone else or alter opinions or find the truth, and a real culture of forbidden questions." These people say that restrictions have gone so far that "certain ideas are too dangerous to even discuss . . . on college campuses today, among militant special interest groups. . . ." A Berkeley University newspaper editor contends that writing an article about these issues is as "dangerous as manuevering through a minefield." She says, "Whenever we think we're doing the right thing and using the right word, inevitably it's not quite the 'right' word or we could have done something 'different' or 'better.'" Another person said, "PC demands a conformity to thoughts, words, and symbols."

Those academics who endorse political correctness in communication see it as a way to eliminate racism and sexism on college campuses. One professor puts it this way: ". . . in a plural society, in a multicultural society, in a diverse society, the very fragile fabric of such a society demands that we have sensitivity to everybody. . . ." Attempts at political correctness have been made nationwide on college campuses ranging from state universities to the Ivy League. At Smith College, students learned that calling someone pretty or ugly was an offense called "lookism." At New York University, law students refused a hypothetical case assignment about lesbian motherhood because it might offend the gay community. However, PC advocates say that being politically correct is more than using the proper words or phrases. It means providing more than one view of history or literature or another topic. One individual asserts that "a liberal education in contemporary times in the American society, which is a multicultural and a pluralistic society, demands that you have education that responds to such a society."

So the debate over political correctness on college campuses will continue to rage, both sides firm in the belief that the other group is destroying the very foundations of a sound education. It is an argument that will not be easily resolved.

Case Questions

1. What impact could using politically correct communication have on people's perceptions and attitudes? What impact might non–politically correct communication have on perceptions and attitudes?

2. What steps for improving communication would you suggest to address some of the problems that the advocates and critics of political correctness have identified?

Sources: "Sensitivity Facism: Imposed Legality of Political Correctness on College Campuses," *National Review,* April 27, 1992, Vol. 44, No. 8, p. 1; John M. Ellis, "The Origins of PC," *Chronicle of Higher Education,* January 15, 1992, Vol. 38, No. 19, p. B1ff; Courtney Leatherman, "AAUP Statement on the 'Political Correctness' Debate Causes a Furor," *Chronicle of Higher Education,* December 4, 1991, Vol. 38, No. 15, p. A23ff; and Joan Wallach Scott, "The Campaign Against Political Correctness: What's Really at Stake?" *Change,* November–December 1991, Vol. 23, No. 6, p. 30ff.

SKILL PRACTICE

PERCEPTIONS

Perceptions influence our patterns of communication and how we interpret information we hear and see. Our perceptions are shaped by our personalities, friends, situations, environmental backgrounds, cultures, and hundreds of daily events and experiences. It can be fun to explore differences in perceptions.

In this exercise, we explore only a few perceptual points, although students may introduce many more as the exercise gets under way. We focus on colors, shapes, and numbers.

Instructions

Each student should jot down key words as quickly as possible in response to the instructor's comments. After each round, be prepared to explain what came to your mind following each comment. Four comments by the instructor and your responses should take about 20 minutes.

One student may be asked to summarize key word responses on the board for each of the instructor's comments.

Discussion

Marketing managers and advertisers know that customers are influenced by perceptions, as this exercise suggests. You will be asked to react to a product-packaging scheme presented by the instructor that builds on your earlier reactions.

Leadership at GM and Honda: Contrasting Styles

It seems that whenever a new cadre of managers takes the helm at GM, before long another new cadre emerges with a new program for turning the company around. In the chapter-framing story for Chapter 2, we saw how in 1992 a management "coup" by GM's executive committee took control of the company to accelerate changes. Just prior to the coup, however, CEO Robert Stempel had announced an entirely new program of global management. Stempel had just begun to implement team-style management techniques through two new top managers—one in charge of North American operations, the other in charge of foreign operations. The coup changed all that. Within a matter of months, the North American executive, Lloyd Reuss, who was officially GM's president, was ousted by GM's board of directors. The board simply explained that GM had not moved quickly enough in the right direction and that it was time to speed change.

GM's new president, Jack Smith, is said to have the board's blessing for introducing Stempel's original program of restructuring coupled with a strong commitment to build team management systems. Stempel, although still CEO, is said to be in a backseat position while Smith is in charge of operations. What this means to GM workers, however, is not clear, and most employees seem to believe the recent changes at the very top of the organization, along with a number of replacements among key executives, are just one more stumbling effort that has little chance for success.

Darlene Fiorillo, a GM employee, describes how employees feel. She says, "Down on the floor, you can see the operation, and you know how it's supposed to be done. Up there, upper management's saying, 'Nah, nah, we can do it cheaper and more efficient if we do it our way.' So these people up there are calling all the shots and are not experiencing what really needs to take place on the floor. And they really don't care, because they're thinking 'short-term dollars and cents, it looks real good,' and we're down here on the floor thinking 'Long term, it's our job.' Plus we want to give a person exactly what they bought: a perfect vehicle for the price. Any auto worker will tell you that."

It is interesting that employees seem to be thinking long term but believe that management is thinking short term. This idea is echoed by other GM workers, who comment that management is more interested in saving six or seven seconds on making a car than making it right. Consequently, defects are often pushed on through the system—not by the employees, but by supervisors, who are themselves pushed by higher and higher levels of management. Some employees feel disenfranchised by the recent downsizing of GM, which was coupled with major cost-reduction tactics and a harder push for more production. With GM trimming its size, fewer employees are being trained for promotions or new jobs, and few say they see any great evidence of the team management program at the shop level. Top GM managers are insulated from employees, and only a few of them are ever seen on the shop floor.

In contrast, employees at the Honda plant in Ohio find themselves eating in the same cafeteria as the company executives, talking with them in parking lots open to everyone, and training with them in the same company seminars. At any time, an employee can call the plant manager directly and talk about problems or make suggestions. And most often, first names are used in conversation. Soni Tron, a production-line worker for Honda, explained how she sat down next to the company's president for lunch one day and suggested a plan for an employee assistance program. The president listened, and the program was implemented. Sandy Johnson, another production worker at the plant, explained how it is to work with the plant manager, Ed Buker, who answers his own phone calls. "If you've got trouble," she says, "all you have to do is say, 'Hey Ed, we've gotta meet with you.' He'll say, 'No problem.'"

The differences between GM and Honda are not due to "American" versus "Japanese" management practices, but rather to fundamentally different views of leadership. Both plants are managed and operated by Americans who were trained domestically and are mostly from midwestern backgrounds. However, Honda began with a fresh approach to training employees in quality management and team participation. Mark Russell, a Honda paint shop employee, says, "Honda's thing is, the guy on the line is the gut professional on his job, and he knows what is best for that process at the time. He knows how to make it better." Another Honda employee, assembler Calvin Thomas, adds, "You give us an opportunity to have a say-so, and we can do a good job."

At Honda, production workers, maintenance personnel, office staff, and many others are part of design teams, process trouble-shooting teams, and quality control teams. They have a "say-so" backed up by managers at every level who are themselves team members. When employees are initially hired, they are thoroughly trained in work-group techniques and in their production jobs, and once they demonstrate their willingness to be part of the team environment, they are moved into responsible team positions. Every employee is encouraged to learn more, to work for promotions or changes, and to work at a pace that ensures quality products. The company underwrites extensive training and development for employees who wish to take part. Thus, Honda workers feel they have secure jobs with few career constraints.

One explanation of this was put forth by an eight-member group during a discussion with *Fortune* editors. The employees said Honda treated them as mature individuals responsible for their jobs and their decisions, while in other automotive jobs they had held (most had worked at other plants before they came to Honda), they were treated as immature and incapable of learning new techniques. The group explained that employees no longer had to be told what to do, only sold on new ideas occasionally or given the opportunity to come up with their own solutions to problems. Consequently, they feel motivated by their involvement in work and their group decisions, rather than being motivated entirely by how much they are being paid to do what management expects to be done.

Compensation for managers and employees is a hot issue in both companies. At GM, employees feel the huge top-executive rewards are far out of balance with executives' contributions. And that feeling is echoed by employees at Chrysler and many other U.S. corporations. Employees at the shop-floor level, although paid well themselves, cite the millions of dollars awarded to executives under contractual stock options, deferred salaries, and various bonus plans as a slap in the face at a time when thousands of operating employees are losing their jobs. Executive salaries at GM for the top two tiers of managers are, on average, more than double those of Honda executives, and when coupled with stock options and incentives, the differential is nearly four times as great. Honda executives still do very well, but their compensation does not seem out of line to employees. American workers are keenly aware of large executive compensation packages and point to them as evidence of poor management decisions and inadequate board-level controls.

A GM employee summarized his feelings about the company by explaining, "To General Motors, you're a number. You're number 7795. This department needs a body, that department needs a body; they send the short person up to the horse-collar line where everything is way up here, and they'll take some long tall person and stick him down on the frame line or in the pit. And then they get hurt." One Honda employee summarized the situation this way: "Depending on how a person's treated and how he's trained, anybody can achieve."

Case Questions

1. The case illustrates extreme viewpoints. Every employee at GM is not dissatisfied and unmotivated, just as every employee at Honda is not ideally satisfied or similarly motivated. There are, however, distinct differences in the patterns of management styles and employee attitudes between the two companies. Explain what you believe are the primary motivators at GM and at Honda, and how they differ.
2. Why are executive compensation, decisions about spending, and strategic acquisitions such sensitive issues to employees? Explain how you would feel in such a situation, whether in an automotive plant or in any other kind of company.
3. Describe GM and Honda leadership profiles in terms of the life-cycle theory of leadership. Where do the employees fit in the life-cycle model in each company, and if you believe there is a difference, why does it exist?
4. How does the team concept affect "situational variables" that might exist at each company, and why do both companies want to implement a team approach?

Sources: Myron Magnet, "The Truth About the American Worker," *Fortune,* May 4, 1992, pp. 48–51, 54–58, 59–60, 64–65; "Executive Pay," *Business Week,* March 30, 1992, pp. 52–58; Alan Bryman, *Charisma and Leadership in Organizations* (Newbury Park, Cal.: Sage, 1992), pp. 103–104; and Alex Taylor III, "The Road Ahead at General Motors," *Fortune,* May 4, 1992, pp. 94–95.

17

The Controlling Function

OUTLINE

The Concept of Controlling
Planning and Controlling
Open and Closed Systems

The Control Process
Feedback and Feedforward
Controllable Variables
Steps in the Control Process

Types of Controls
Steering Controls
Yes/No Controls
Postaction Controls
Integrating Different Types of Controls

Controlling Responsibilities
Deciding What to Control
Setting Standards and Measuring Results
Reporting
Corrective Actions
Toward Effective Control

Controlling Performance
Benchmarking—Setting High Standards
Production and Operation Controls
Human Resource Controls
Marketing Controls
Financial Controls

Budgets
Types of Budgets
Budget Variances and Flexibility in Control
Responsibility Centers
Budgeting in Not-for-Profit Organizations

Behavioral Control in Organizations
Management Audits
Social Audits
Behavioral Assessment Controls

OBJECTIVES

- Explain how planning and controlling are coordinated.
- Describe the process of controlling operations.
- Describe three major types of controls and their purposes.
- Explain how managers implement effective control systems.
- Describe production and operation, human resource, marketing, and financial controls.
- Describe how budgets and responsibility centers improve control and accountability.
- Explain the concepts behind management and social audits.

DELL COMPUTER CORPORATION battles competition through lower prices, lower costs, and rapid response to customer demands.[1] In 1992, when nearly every other computer manufacturer struggled with recession-ridden markets, Dell expanded. As the industry leaders announced layoffs and financial operating losses, Dell opened East European markets, increased U.S. sales, and chalked up strong profits. For fiscal 1992, Dell's revenue grew by 63 percent to $890 million, and by the end of the calendar year, it was expected to reach a billion dollars. Net income rose by 87 percent, and shareholder earnings were up 55 percent. Yet Dell's prices dropped by more than 17 percent across its entire product line of personal computers and network work stations.

Success at Dell Computers is attributed to effective internal controls on operating costs, high-quality service, and support for customers. Since it was founded in 1983 by Michael Dell, the company has followed a fundamental rule: Ensure value for customers. Managers have a complementary expectation to spend money only on activities that add value to customer purchases. That means, within reason, avoiding luxuries and unjustified expenditures. Managers fly on economy fares, many have reconditioned office furniture, and Dell recently replaced $400 "nice-to-have" speakerphone systems with "functional" $80 sets. Manufacturing facilities, like office spaces, are not uncomfortably spartan, but they are cost-effective. The company can respond to customer orders so rapidly that it needs only a two-week inventory; in contrast, IBM has a sixty-day inventory stockpile. Consequently, Dell needs very little storage space, and when things change in the computer industry, Dell can react quickly without worrying about having to unload an aging inventory.

The company has introduced a new product or major product modification every three weeks, and it has built a reputation for providing on-site service to customers within twenty-four hours. It now promises customers a four-hour response on all new sales. Because these are value-added activities, Dell does not skimp on costs. The company receives more than 5,000 customer calls each day, and Dell customer representatives have exquisite communication equipment and are well-trained. Information on technology, suppliers, and competitors is continually updated. Dell Computer Corporation is considered a pacesetter in customer service and technical support.

controlling
The management function of monitoring performance and adapting work variables to improve results.

Controlling is concerned with monitoring organized efforts, comparing progress with planned objectives, and making the necessary decisions to ensure success. This chapter discusses managers' responsibilities to control operations and direct organizational performance toward achieving objectives. As noted in previous chapters, however, no single function of management can be isolated from the others. Planning, the first function, begins the process by establishing objectives. Next, organizing assembles resources needed for pursuing those objectives. Leading provides the dimension of supervision. Controlling completes the process and links organizational efforts with planned objectives. Peter Drucker defines controlling as:

> The management function that aims to keep activities directed in such a way that desired results are achieved. Monitoring of performance is the starting point of all control. In case performance deviates from what is expected, corrective action must be taken to get the process back on track.[2]

THE CONCEPT OF CONTROLLING

To "keep activities directed," as Drucker notes, managers need accurate and timely feedback derived from systematic monitoring of activities. Feedback alone, however, is insufficient to ensure control. Managers must also evaluate performance against desired results, which means they need standards. Standards allow managers to compare actual results to expected results to determine what corrective action, if any, is needed, and how to improve performance when possible. Figure 17-1 shows the control process, and emphasizes the three key components of controlling: having standards, measuring performance against standards, and taking corrective action when appropriate. As we shall see, this process takes place in concert with an organization's plans.

Planning and Controlling

Conceptually, controlling is as simple as the illustrated relationship, but in reality, it is a complex process. A synthesis of coordinated activities must be created among departments and managers to reinforce planned objectives. Controls complement plans to achieve this synthesis at all organizational levels. At the executive level, strategic objectives have strategic controls. For example, a major objective of market growth will have control benchmarks for sales, market share, and relative competi-

FIGURE 17-1 The Controlling Function: A Conceptual View

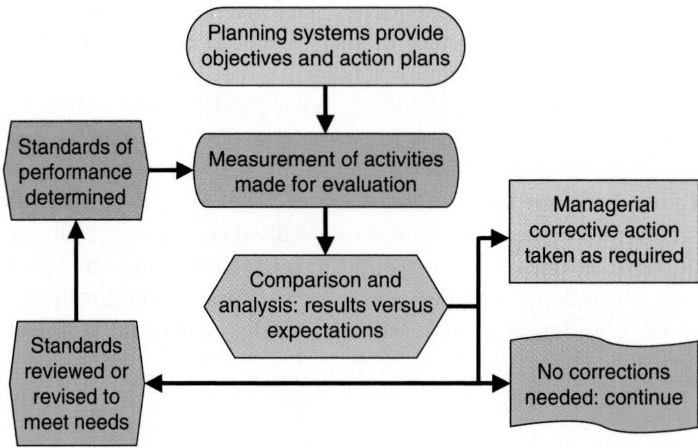

tive strength. The most obvious strategic objective, profitability, will have financial targets expressed in specific time periods. Other strategic controls reflect major objectives in social responsibility, asset management, human resources, and technological progress. Executive controls include monitoring techniques for evaluating competitors, economic conditions, financial trends, market behavior, technological advances, and a variety of social conditions.

Managers at tactical levels such as division heads are concerned with more restricted controls that match their planning responsibilities. These often reflect functional performance expectations in production, marketing, finance, and human resources, among other areas. Control systems at this middle-management level are pivotal for coordinating lower-level operational activities as well as for collecting information used at higher levels by strategists.

Operational controls are perhaps more obvious than others because first-line supervisors spend a relatively greater amount of time controlling a firm's activities than other managers do. First-line supervisors monitor daily work, adjust task activities, and report results. Operational control activities focus on sales, production scheduling, purchasing, inventory control, logistics, maintenance, and cash flow. The many examples of operational controls range from simple responsibilities such as inspecting work to complex responsibilities such as monitoring equal opportunity programs. Controlling is a process of adapting behavior to satisfy plans, but information derived from control systems also gives managers insights into planning. The link between planning and controlling is illustrated in Figure 17-2.

FIGURE 17-2 Linkage Between Planning and Controlling

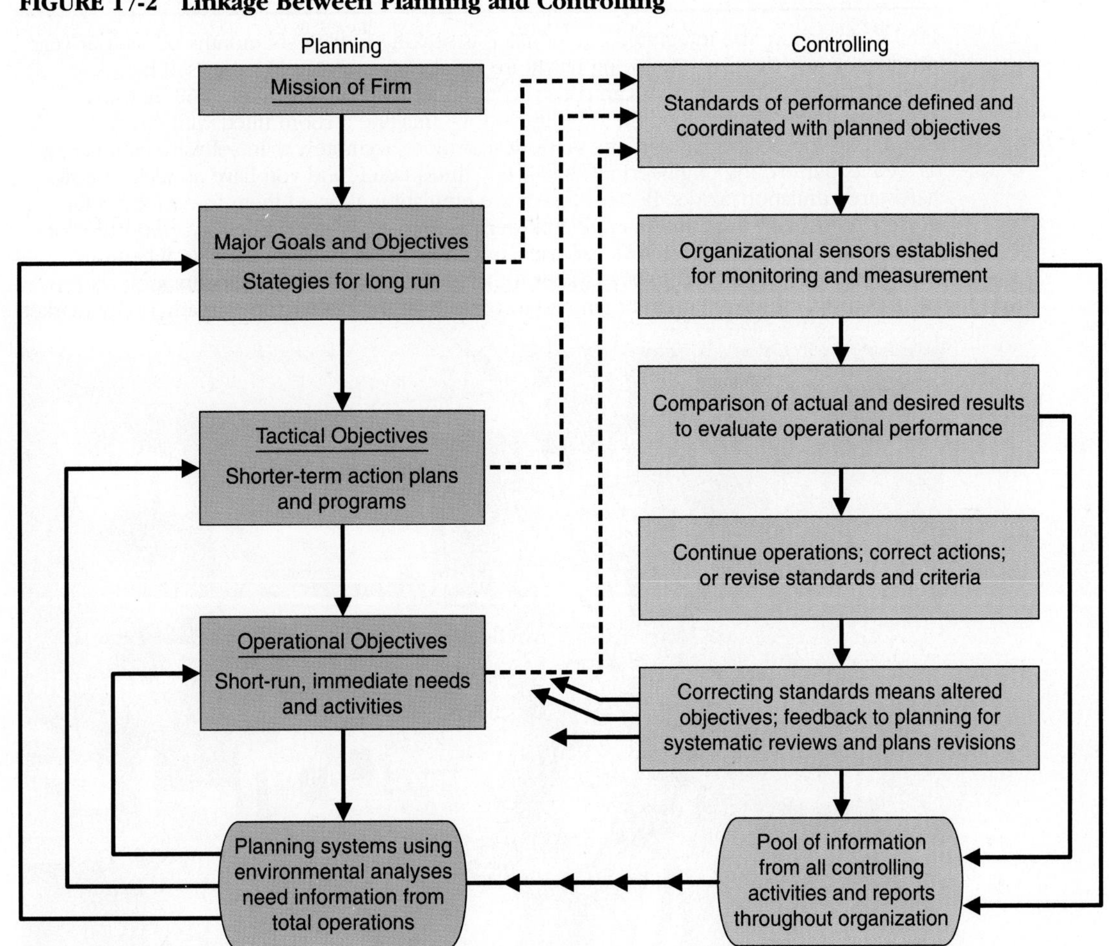

Open and Closed Systems

open system
A control system in which managers intervene to set standards, monitor performance, decide whether results meet expectations, and take corrective actions.

closed system
A control system that can be substantially operated without management intervention once standards are set; monitoring and corrective actions are performed by the system technology.

Although managers are responsible for performance, automation and information technology have resulted in systems that relieve managers of the work associated with controlling activities. These are called *closed systems,* in contrast to situations where managers are actively involved, which are called *open systems.*

An **open system** is one in which managers actively intervene to make decisions. They set standards, monitor performance, judge comparative results, and personally take corrective actions. A purely open system without automation support is like a coal furnace heating system whose temperature is controlled by manually stoking the fire or adjusting heating vents. In contrast, a purely **closed system** is like an automatic air-conditioning system whose heat sensors (thermostats) continuously monitor temperature and switch the system on or off to maintain predetermined room temperature standards.

In reality, few systems are totally open or closed; people still have to set their home thermostats and occasionally perform maintenance. At John Deere & Company, for example, engineers set up production machines for making tractor engine parts, run test products, check them for accuracy, then adjust their setup calculations. After operators begin production, engineers return periodically to test samples, adjusting the machines to meet production standards. This is an open control system where managers actively intervene. John Deere has, however, converted most of its operations to computer-controlled production in which machine setup processes, monitoring, and adjustments are accomplished through information programs and electronic sensors. These are closed control systems where managers do not intervene except in emergencies.[3] Figure 17-3 compares the two systems.

Intel Corporation, the integrated circuit giant, is seeking to trim six months off its four-year production schedule by employing hardware emulation, a technology devised by Quickterms Systems, Inc., that can construct a model chip such as Intel's 468 by using programmable chips pretending to be transistors. Imagine a room filled with circuit boards that mirror the performance of the 468's design more accurately than software simulations as well as performing engineering tests 30,000 times faster, and you have an idea of how hardware emulation works. Because hardware emulation allowed them to perform a far greater number of tests, Intel's engineers were able to catch many bugs *before* production started. Compare this with Intel's experience with its previous chip, the 386: When one error was discovered by consumers after the chip was in the field, engineers took six months to fix the problem and then had to replace all the faulty chips already in the market.

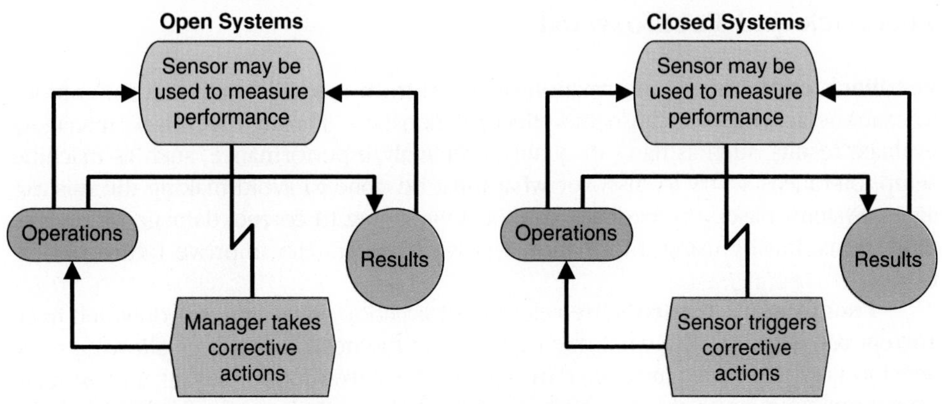

FIGURE 17-3 Open and Closed Control Systems

The two types of control processes reflect fundamental differences in management philosophy. For example, an organization may be characterized as having a hands-on philosophy in which managers are expected to scrutinize behavior. In this instance, open control systems will predominate. In another organization, management may endorse a system of arm's-length control. In this situation, closed system methods will emerge.

Technology often dictates one type of control process or the other. For example, police are expected to personally control busy intersections during rush hours and when events such as football games create traffic jams. A computerized system would be unable to restrain overanxious fans rushing from a football parking lot; human judgment is required. On the other hand, gasoline is refined at Phillips Petroleum through a process that is almost totally automated. Monitoring equipment continuously evaluates quality factors such as octane ratings, chemical impurities, and product viscosity. The system also controls line pressure, flow rates, and dozens of minute operations. Chemicals are produced at Mobil, Texaco, and Chevron through similar automated processes. A handful of technicians can operate a massive petroleum refinery or chemical plant, perhaps being called on to intervene only when sensors alert managers to potential problems requiring human judgment.[4]

CHECKPOINT

- How are controls related to plans to provide guidelines for monitoring performance?
- Describe the general control model and decisions that managers are responsible for making.
- Contrast open and closed systems and a manager's responsibilities in each type of system.

THE CONTROL PROCESS

The human body, together with its sensors and adaptors, is a control system. Think about your body and you will realize that your senses act as control devices to hear, smell, see, feel, and taste elements of the environment. The nervous system triggers body functions based on sensory perception, and either we make conscious decisions to take action or the body automatically adjusts to circumstances. For example, we may sense a hot stove when we get too close, and intentionally back away, but if we accidentally get too close, the body will automatically recoil. Although organizational systems are unlikely to become as sophisticated as the human body, the process of controlling organizational activities is quite similar.

Feedback and Feedforward

feedback control
The use of information from recently completed operations to learn how to improve performance or to avoid repeating mistakes.

feedforward control
The use of information to project what might occur in the future, thus allowing managers to take preventive measures.

Feedback controls use information obtained from recently completed operations to examine activities for cause-and-effect relationships. Through feedback, managers evaluate results, such as flaws in quality, and analyze performance, such as machine setup tolerances, to try to discover what must be done to avoid making the mistake again. Systems based on feedback cannot do anything to correct damage or reverse past events, but by using information wisely, managers can improve future performance.

Feedforward controls use relevant information, including that obtained from current results, to project what might happen in the near future, thus allowing managers to take preventive measures. In organizations, we monitor results and evaluate operations to uncover clues about potential problems. Perhaps the feedforward element of controlling is not emphasized enough as we teach the conventional wisdom of measuring results. It is the incremental measurement of performance that allows a compilation of information so that we can learn from small mistakes to avoid bigger ones. Eventually, we learn to recognize early indicators of potential problems and adjust rapidly.

At Corning Glass Works' television glass tube factory, for example, huge gas furnaces melt raw materials into molten sheets for fabricating the funnel-shaped backs of TV tubes. Improper heating can cause bubbles to appear in the glass, and a single bubble the size of a pinhead can destroy the product. Bubbles also occur when Corning Glass receives poor raw materials from suppliers. Therefore, employees inspect the fabricated tubes and inform furnace operators and purchasing managers about every defective product. This *feedback* information prompts actions such as adjusting furnace temperatures or negotiating with suppliers for higher-quality materials. Furnace operators also know from past experience that heat variances will increase the probability of bubble faults, and consequently, they are careful to check furnace temperatures before treating TV tubes. Corning's inspectors also sample incoming materials to ensure they meet specifications, thereby reducing the likelihood of producing faulty TV tubes. These are *feedforward* control methods.[5]

Controllable Variables

Managers are primarily concerned with decisions about *controllable* variables while being alert to uncontrollable factors that can influence results. Managers must be aware of uncontrollable circumstances, develop the skill to orchestrate controllable factors, and make decisions that improve their probabilities for success. Federal Express, a recent winner of the prestigious Malcolm Baldridge National Quality Award, succeeds by exquisite shipping and cost controls, but the company has lost money on international operations and subsequently withdrawn from several European markets. The reason given by management is inability to control shipping schedules while struggling with currency fluctuations that affect costs throughout European operations.[6]

Consequently, managers focus on controllable variables, yet devise systems that account for uncontrollable factors. These are incorporated into a control process that, if effective, will provide feedback and feedforward information to correct mistakes and prevent future problems when possible.

Steps in the Control Process

An effective control process provides managers with timely and useful information that can be used in making corrections or planning decisions. Whether a system is open or closed, four fundamental steps are required: setting standards, measuring performance, comparing results to standards, and taking corrective action when necessary. A discussion of each follows.

Establishing standards. Managers are responsible for setting *performance standards* that are specific objectives against which results can be compared. Performance standards reflect expected and planned results of organizational activities. Even the best automated system cannot determine what is required. Standards must be predetermined, and as long as technology is imperfect and human endeavor varies, performance will fluctuate. Effective standards are therefore rarely absolute but are realistic expectations for performance.[7] For example, a sales quota is a target objective for periodic comparison of actual and expected results. Sales will seldom match quotas, but a quota provides direction.

Standards must also be expressed in meaningful terms and be measurable. A sales quota can be stated in dollars, units sold, number of customers served, or in several other ways. Whatever the criterion, it should be a meaningful measurement of sales activity that is applied consistently over time. For example, a firm operating in a volatile industry such as music videos may discard quotas based on sales dollars in favor of quotas based on number of video recordings sold. An uncertain market like music videos generates fierce competition and unpredictable pricing behavior. Thus a "dollar" quota has little meaning, but a quota based on unit sales is realistic. Similarly, an ideal standard for quality control in manufacturing would be "zero defects," but that is unrealistic. Instead, a standard that reflects improvement in quality expressed as a lower percentage of rejects may motivate workers toward attainable results.[8]

Measuring performance. Once performance standards have been established, progress must be monitored in quantifiable terms. This is where open and closed systems are differentiated. In situations where a repetitive process exists, such as

Because such new products like Newton, a kind of electronic filofax, will not be available until 1993, Apple Computer has to depend on existing products for growth. This means that its Macintosh Hardware Division has to produce Macs more quickly and cheaply. General Manager Fred Forsyth's 1993 production goal is to get new products out every six months rather than every year. To accomplish this objective, Forsyth has carved up his division into small, workable units. Not only does each unit control its own budget, but its engineers have a say about which products to start up or stop. Says Forsyth, "They actually kill their own products now."

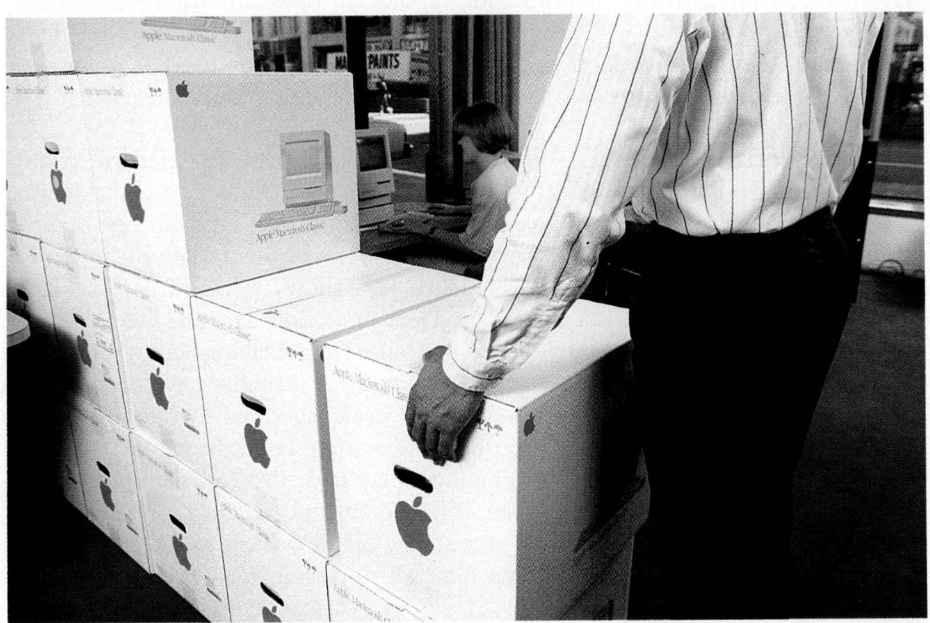

gasoline refining, automatic sensors may be used to monitor operations continuously. Home thermostats and barometers are continuous sensors. In open control situations, managers may periodically check to ensure compliance with standards. Sampling tests of water purity and circuit tests of electrical equipment are examples.

Statistical sampling procedures are often used in open systems where inspectors select items for test and measurement. A few products may be randomly chosen from a large batch and subjected to rigorous evaluation against predetermined criteria. Then the entire batch is either accepted or rejected on the basis of test results of the sample.

Criteria for measurement must be appropriate, and actual measurement decisions must be realistic. In the manufacture of color TV sets, for example, it would be appropriate to test for color sensitivity under normal operating conditions and realistic to accept color performance within a reasonable range of variation. It would be inappropriate to test color sensitivity under extraordinary circumstances and impose exacting color standards on low-priced sets.

Comparing results. Measurement data have little meaning unless they are compared to standards. For example, in 1991, Chrysler's chairman Lee Iacocca announced a target cost-reduction program to trim $3 billion by the end of the year. Part of the program was a $1.2 billion reduction in costs attributed to production-line defects, yet existing records of defects were only estimates and therefore provided ambiguous standards for meaningful comparisons.[9] In contrast, Ford Motor Company selected Motorola to provide microprocessors for automotive power train electronic systems starting in 1992 because Motorola proved through comparative data that it could deliver high-quality components. Motorola's 88000 microprocessor was being manufactured with a defect rate of 6,000 per million units in 1986 (0.6 percent), but incremental quality enhancements demonstrated that it could produce at less than 40 defects per million units by 1992 (0.004 percent). The company's standards for comparison are prior-year defect rates, and comparisons are made almost daily with statistical controls that monitor results.[10]

If performance matches standards, we may reasonably assume there is no need for adjustment. Most standards, however, are targets with ranges of acceptable outcomes. Comparisons therefore take into account acceptable deviations within a predetermined tolerance range. Figure 17–4 illustrates a control chart with range data. Management predetermines the upper and lower limits as acceptable deviations in performance results. Control charts are reports that accumulate results and display performance patterns using statistics and graphics. In open control systems, deviations beyond range limits will prompt managers to take corrective actions. Closed systems are often designed on statistical control charts, but used in computer-assisted systems with sensors to trigger adjustments when deviations occur.

Taking corrective action. The conclusive reason for having effective control systems is to take corrective action to raise performance results to acceptable standards. Corrective action is based on informed decisions, derived from first comparing actual and planned results and then evaluating reasons for deviations. In the Falconer Glass Company control chart, as Figure 17-4 shows, performance has fallen below acceptable standards, but there is no clear indication why this has happened. The responsible manager must investigate the cause before taking action. In fact, the outcome could be attributed to a number of causes. A machine may have failed, a substitute operator may have been doing poor work, lightning may have caused a power outage, or materials needed for the job may have been defective.

A manager who simply blames employees for poor productivity without careful analysis will destroy a control system. In the Falconer Glass Company control chart, the huge deviation on 12/2 (the second day of the week) was traced to a faulty machine used for edging glass. The machine was repaired, and production was re-

Control Charts and Boundary Control Limits

Falconer Glass Company

Work Center: Glass Fabrication — Machine Number: 360-A

Date: week of 12/1 - 12/7 — Shift: 1st

Day	12/1	12/2	12/3	12/4	12/5	12/6	12/7
1/2"- 4 edge	88	74	78	92	44		
1/2"- 2 edge	42	30	66	28	82		
1/4"- 4 edge	86	98	104	122	136		
1/4"- 2 edge	204	102	218	214	164		
Total sq. ft. @ std.	420	304	466	456	426		
Mean/wk. = 414.4							
Variance/wk.	+5.6	−110.4	+51.6	+41.6	+11.6		
Standard: 440							
Variance/standard	−20	−136	+26	16	−14		

Monthly Chart: Productivity/sq. ft

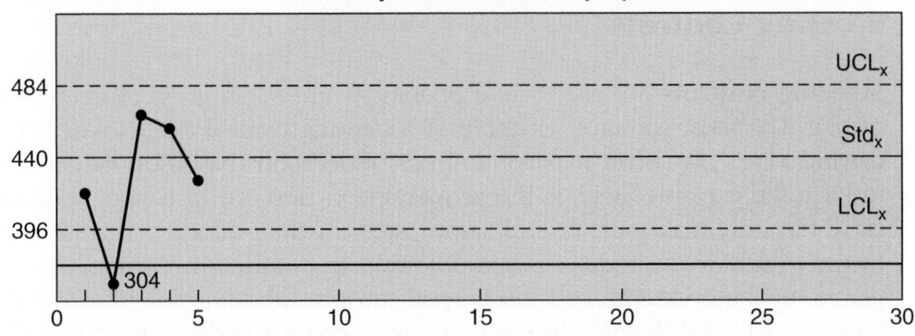

Monthly Chart: Variances to Standard and Week

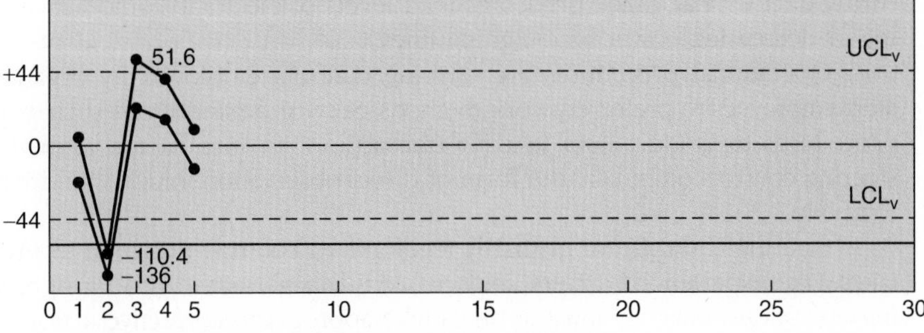

FIGURE 17-4 Control Charts and Boundary Control Limits

stored the next day. Before the machine problem was discovered, however, the supervisor in charge had blamed two operators for doing poor work, an accusation that led to a formal grievance against the supervisor.[11]

Taking appropriate corrective action is necessary, but controls by their very nature create tension that can lead to inappropriate decisions. They tend to have financial overtones, with standards set in accounting terms. Many managers view the entire process as unpleasant and restrictive, and thus may not always be motivated to push budget numbers, meet quotas, and satisfy profit and loss imperatives.[12] But managers must find ways to motivate their subordinates to take appropriate corrective actions that are backed up by workable systems and plausible standards of performance.

CHECKPOINT

- Describe how feedback and feedforward processes influence decisions.
- Why do managers distinguish between controllable and uncontrollable variables?
- Describe the steps in the control process and managers' responsibilities in each instance.

TYPES OF CONTROLS

The process we have been discussing is a conceptual framework for control. Management theorists have identified three types of control that lead to different decisions. These are *steering controls, yes/no controls,* and *postaction controls.*[13]

Steering Controls

steering controls
Controls used to adjust behavior or operations, such as correcting the speed and direction of a car.

Steering controls are used while operations are in progress to keep activities on course. The most common example of a steering control occurs when a person is driving a car. The driver makes hundreds of decisions based on mental evaluations to keep the car on course, at the proper speed, and out of danger. Craftsmen who build furniture make similar evaluations, steering their efforts and adjusting their activities to achieve a predetermined objective. In petroleum refining, automation replaces human endeavor, and mechanical sensors substitute for human judgment in keeping crude oil flowing through a refining process at the correct speed and temperature. Similarly, electric power generation is monitored through a system of measuring devices that gauge predetermined levels of electricity, automatically increasing or decreasing power for outgoing lines.

Operational procedures are steering controls employed by organizations to alert employees to preferred work methods. Service organizations such as banks use procedures to guide tellers in daily transactions. In manufacturing environments, steering controls often take the form of direct observation, much like driving an automobile.

Steering controls are primarily feedforward controls designed to prevent mistakes. Like experienced drivers, experienced managers have good insight into guiding operations, but they must at times take appropriate corrective actions. Even experienced drivers can stray into oncoming traffic and cause accidents.

Yes/No Controls

yes/no control
A screening technique that yields a "yes" or "no" (go or no-go) decision at selected checkpoints in an operation.

go/no-go controls
Another term for "yes/no controls," go/no-go controls have fail-safe standards dictating absolute corrective action or no action.

Practicing managers have another term for **yes/no controls: go/no-go controls.** Corrective action dictated by this type of control is rather obvious: either "go" or "stop." Corrective action can go only one way or the other, like turning on or off a light switch. These controls are used as fail-safe methods in critical operations, and can be incorporated into steering procedures at specific points to modify operations. Students who have sketched flow charts in computer programming exercises will recognize the use of go/no-go options as controls.

A common example of these controls is the commercial airline preflight checklist that incorporates critical go/no-go options. If an oil gauge indicates low pressure or a radio fails, the preflight check will stop, and so will the flight.

Yes/no controls are also used as delimiters for management decisions. For example, department managers may have discretionary use of funds to buy supplies costing up to $1,000. Beyond that amount they must obtain higher approval. Salespersons may be able to accept credit charges up to a certain amount and then need approval. Safety inspectors may be able to shut down operations under certain conditions. Yes/no controls usually leave little room for doubt about what action managers must take.

Postaction Controls

Statistical control procedures have strong postaction elements because many statistical evaluations are made using samples of results. **Postaction controls** permit comparisons of actual results with standards "after the fact." Deviations from standards are analyzed and corrective action is taken to avoid similar mistakes in the future. With improved methods of monitoring, results can often be evaluated very rapidly; some computer-assisted quality control systems monitor operations as soon as they are completed. Consequently, when postaction controls provide rapid feedback, they become very useful to enhance steering controls.

postaction controls
Systems that periodically monitor results "after the fact," comparing actual performance with standards to prompt corrections and thus avoid repeating mistakes in the future.

Organizations with sophisticated information systems are able to maintain rapid-response controls, but most postaction controls are devised as periodic reports. These often stem from existing formal reporting procedures, such as using budget documents or cost accounting methods to track performance. Quality control inspections using sample tests on selected products are good examples of postaction controls. Products found to be defective are rejected, but more important, if patterns of defects are discovered, entire production runs may be rejected. Banks use monthly loan activity summaries to evaluate patterns of risk in the number and types of loans processed. If the resulting risk profile is higher than a bank wants to maintain, fewer high-risk loans are made in the coming period. Monthly sales activity summaries have similar uses, and the Nielsen television rating system samples households periodically to identify viewer preferences as well as programs that should be discontinued.[14]

One reason that The Gap, Inc., can maintain high quality and low costs is that it designs its own clothes, selects its own materials, and maintains close ties with its manufacturers. The result: The company's 200 quality control inspectors work inside factories in forty countries to ensure that specifications are met at every point in the production process. In addition, a $75 million automatic distribution center near Baltimore will ultimately allow the The Gap to stock its New York stores daily rather than three times a week.

Integrating Different Types of Controls

Steering, yes/no, and postaction controls are convenient labels for studying elements of control in the total process. Figure 17-5 presents an overview of these three types of control and how they are used. Rarely is one type of control employed in isolation. In fact, managers seldom formally differentiate between types of control but choose controls based on answers to the following questions:

1. What controls are needed to ensure performance expectations?
2. What are the critical control points for monitoring operations?
3. Who is capable of measuring performance and making corrections?
4. Is an operation critical enough to justify the costs of controls?

Managers may not clearly articulate these questions when developing control systems, but they explicitly answer them. For example, a preflight check for a commercial airline is a result of recognizing that this control is necessary to ensure public safety. The actual preflight checklist defines critical control points and what is to be monitored. Flight crews have been assigned the responsibility for these control

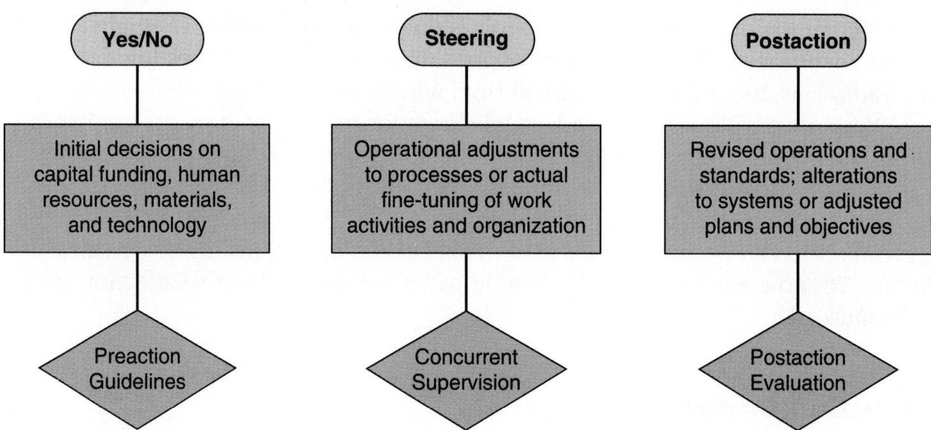

FIGURE 17-5 Relationship of Types of Control to Activities

checklists because they are ultimately responsible for flying the aircraft. Other personnel, such as ground crews, will have control lists as well. Preflight checks coupled with a rather extensive array of other controls are expensive, but the costs are justified by the high risk of failure if controls are neglected.

The yes/no controls used in preflight checks are only one component of the controls employed for a commercial flight. Others are activated during and after the flight. Anyone who has glanced inside a cockpit knows that it contains many instruments. Few of these are needed to actually fly a plane; most are steering controls for monitoring flight operations. Postaction controls include pilot debriefing sessions, evaluation of information from in-flight recorders, and reports on schedules, costs, maintenance, and other elements of airline operations.

Even the best controls cannot guarantee success. Planes crash, and when they do, even more stringent controls are inaugurated. Tenacious attention to detail is essential, but it is also very expensive. For operations that are less critical than an airline flight, managers trade off a certain level of error for cost savings. Harmonizing organizational priorities for cost effectiveness and for maintaining control is one of the tougher responsibilities of managing.

CHECKPOINT

- Explain how steering controls are used in a product assembly plant.
- Identify examples of yes/no controls in a service firm and in a government agency.
- How are reports used in postaction controls for quality assurance?

CONTROLLING RESPONSIBILITIES

Managers must motivate employees while monitoring performance and often instituting unpopular control techniques, and, as just noted, they must also harmonize diverse interests. Both managers and employees may view the controls with some trepidation. Control is an exercise of authority, and many of the techniques employed can be tedious and stressful.

Deciding What to Control

Since managers cannot possibly control everything, they must decide what operations are essential to control. Some activities require close supervision, others need only periodic examination, and still others can be ignored. For those that must be tightly controlled, managers have to determine critical control points. **Control points** are places or times selected during operational activities for testing, sampling, or measuring progress. For example, Lockheed Corporation uses *acceptance sampling*—a statistical control for accepting or rejecting products—at forty-three points during the assembly of a commercial aircraft passenger cabin. Windows, for instance, are tested to ensure that they will meet pressurization standards. If they fail the acceptance tests, assembly work stops until they pass. After they pass, interior cabin walls are put into place and fastened. These are tested for proper seams and rivets. After walls pass, overhead panels are assembled and tested, and so on until the cabin is finished.[15]

control points
Designated places or times during operational activities to measure progress, sample results, or test products.

Manufacturing companies set up controls to monitor production output, resources (materials, labor, and capital), and marketing operations (sales, credit, and distribution systems). Examples of controls are man-hour efficiency reports, inventory control reports, monthly cost and expenditure reports, ratios used for measuring asset and labor productivity, profitability ratios, and market growth statistics. Controls are also developed for periodically measuring the physical results of production, sales, human behavior, and financial management.

Some firms control processes. For example, hospitals must control procedures for giving medications. Chemical manufacturers use process controls for combining and producing complex medications. And we have even developed controls to monitor human biological processes; a pacemaker attached to the human heart monitors heart rhythms and activates to prevent the heart from stopping or slowing down.

These examples illustrate how important it is to make conscientious decisions about what to control. Once these decisions are made, points of control must be established that ensure adequate monitoring without disrupting operations. Sampling procedures are instituted at control points in manufacturing to evaluate quality without slowing performance. Figure 17-6 is a conceptual diagram of control points in a process conversion system.

A useful way to select control points is to locate them where change takes place. For instance, when a batch of soup is mixed, a sample is drawn and tested just before the mixture is put into cooking vats. Then temperature checks are made while the soup is being processed. When the soup is transferred from vats to distribution canning processes, another sample is tested. Once canned, sample cans are drawn for inspection. This process occurs at each point of change until shipments leave the factory. Most control points that monitor performance during production—or some other operation, such as surgical procedure—are designed to signal managers to continue or stop action. If everything is proceeding properly, action continues; if not, the system is halted until corrective action is taken.[16]

Another way to select control points is to locate them at the most important or most critical parts of operations. Classic **ABC inventory systems** follow this method. **A items** are imperative for operations and thus are closely monitored; **B items,** having less importance, are less closely controlled; and **C items,** which can be readily replaced or substituted, might not be controlled systematically. A items are typically expensive and justify expensive controls, but if an inexpensive item is crucial to operations, it too may be rigorously controlled. At the other extreme, C items are almost always inexpensive and can be replaced rapidly if shortages develop, so any expense for control is difficult to justify.[17]

ABC inventory systems
A formal method of classifying materials according to their importance and cost.

A items
Materials and parts imperative to operations that seldom have substitutes and therefore require extremely close control.

B items
Materials and parts that are important and require close control, but can be replaced even though costly.

C items
Materials and parts that have many substitutes and are usually inexpensive to purchase and store; C items are not closely controlled.

Setting Standards and Measuring Results

Managers must determine what standards of performance are satisfactory. As noted earlier, standards must conform to organizational objectives. They are generally related to output, expense, or resource controls, and as we shall see in Chapter 18, the fundamental rationale behind all standards is to *improve quality*. More output of production, for example, requires fewer rejects and a higher-quality manufacturing

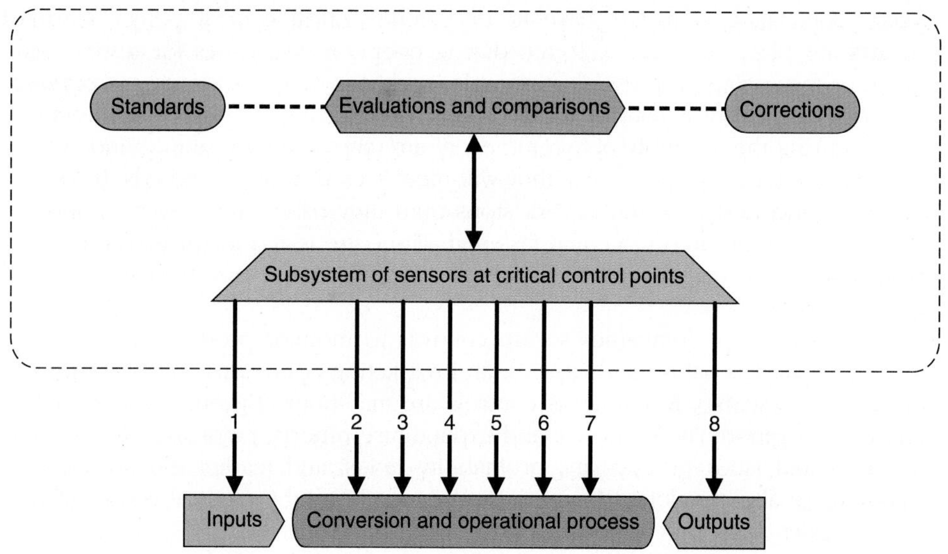

Control Points

1. Input controls, initial resource decisions (human, material, capital, etc.).
2. Operational and facilities precontrols (maintenance, machinery, capacity, etc.).
3. First subsystem of operations completed (preassembly inspections, etc.).
4. Second-stage operations at change points (products or minor subassemblies completed and transferred to advanced work station).
5. Midpoint manufacturing inspection (quality control, off-line testing, cost evaluations, scheduling evaluations, etc.).
6. Subassembly quality assurance and organizational monitoring (same as #5, and may be repeated several times at any critical change point).
7. Final inspection and postaction control evaluations on entire production process (all elements of operations evaluated appropriately for future operations or corrective actions and feedback).
8. Finished goods inventory controls, market distribution system evaluation, postaction feedback monitoring on consumer behavior/acceptance, credit, costs, profitability, and productivity analyses.

FIGURE 17-6 Control Points in a Process Conversion System

process. Lower expenses result from fewer mistakes, better management, and more efficient operations. And higher-quality services mean fewer resources will be required to obtain the same results.[18]

As an example, the Inland-Fisher Guide Division of GM produces automotive seat covers, and prior to 1991, it took seventy-one days for a seat cover to be completed, counting the time from fabric production to final assembly. The company identified more than two dozen points during production that created problems, most resulting from poor quality such as improper scheduling, delays in yarn shipments, mistakes in fabricating products, and machine breakdowns. New standards were set at each point, starting with a target of reducing the seventy-one-day cycle to a thirty-one-day cycle by the end of 1991. Individual department standards included reducing machine failures, defects, and scheduling mistakes by monthly percentage increments. By June—six months short of the target deadline—the company had achieved its thirty-one-day cycle with a 56 percent increase in products that met high-quality specifications.[19] Services are more difficult to measure, yet MBNA America, Inc., the nation's fourth-largest bank credit card issuer, defined quality customer service on fourteen points that included answering telephone inquiries, maintaining on-line computer processing during transaction hours, and being able to process customer inquiries efficiently. The bank set standards that required every phone to be answered within two rings, computers to be up 100 percent of the time during working hours, and customer inquiries to be answered within an hour. This required new equipment, training for 5,000 employees, and incentive systems to motivate everyone to accept the new performance standards. Within a few months, the bank had accomplished its objectives through periodic checks and rapid feedback to employees.[20]

The most effective standards are those concerned with *feedforward,* and as noted earlier, these are preventive measures. Feedforward standards are also called **initial controls** because they are measures designed to guide managerial decisions that affect future activities. In the personnel selection process shown in Figure 17-7, initial controls influence decisions at each critical point in the hiring procedure. Similar controls are used in purchasing materials, making capital funding decisions, and adopting new technologies.[21]

initial controls
Preventive control measures to guide managers in resource allocations and other decisions such as hiring, purchasing, and capital funding.

Actual measurement of results is often left to staff specialists, who can deal with data more expertly than line managers, and without disrupting work. For example, cost accountants are responsible for accumulating expense data, comparing actual to standard results, and developing appropriate reports. With rapid implementation of computers, theses analyses are becoming instantaneous, or "real time," allowing nearly constant reporting.

Staff managers in accounting, MIS, quality control, engineering, and other areas bring expertise to organizational controls, but in many instances, line managers are responsible for direct measurement. For example, only supervisors can make performance evaluations, which are often subjective. Similarly, compensation management for wages and salaries, skills development processes, personnel upgrading, and discipline require the judgment of supervisors.

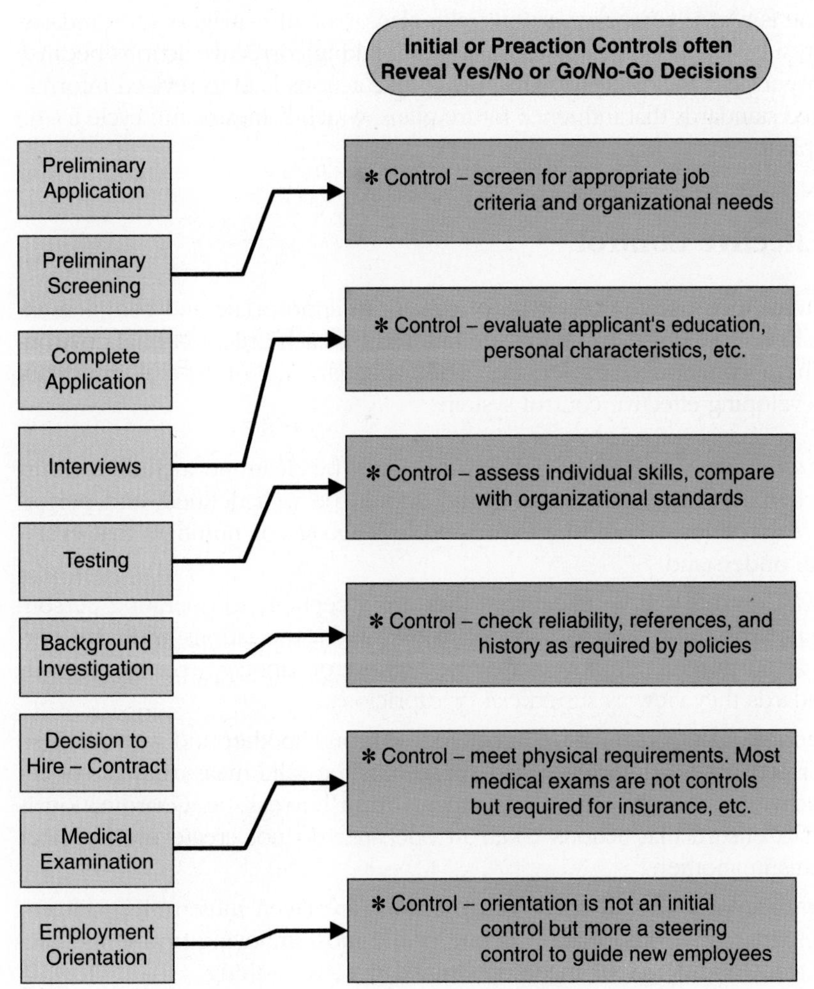

FIGURE 17-7 Initial Control Points in Personnel Selection

Reporting

Reports must have value to those who receive them. Reports that are well designed provide managers with timely and relevant information without overloading them with extraneous data. Some organizations are parsimonious with information; others generate excessive reports. In either case, managers are likely to be poorly informed and make poor decisions.

Real-time reports represent a quantum leap in communication because activities are continuously monitored and status reports are instantly available. Inventory control is one area where real-time systems have wide application. Computers can store data on inventory stock, update files with new purchases or issues, describe locations of stock, assimilate price and cost information, and provide a rich assortment of reports, including ones about stock status, orders, and vendor analysis. When a part is issued—sold or transferred to production—on-line computer programs automatically update stock status.

To be useful in developing effective control systems, reports must communicate sufficient and accurate information to the people responsible for taking corrective actions. Good reports are joint productions of staff experts and operating managers. Those who request reports must define what information is needed; those who create reports must be expert at accumulating and analyzing the information requested.

Corrective Actions

The firing line is where corrective actions take place. Not all managers set standards or evaluate results, but they all are responsible for taking corrective actions because it is the manager's job to solve problems. Corrective actions lead to revised information or revised standards that influence future plans, which brings us full cycle to the stage of preplanning.

Toward Effective Control

Effective systems incorporate every type of control in appropriate and complementary relationships. Though such systems are tailored for each organizational environment, they have common characteristics. Following is a list of several important points for developing effective control systems.[22]

- *Understandable.* Standards of performance must be clear and include measurable criteria. Management responsibility should be well defined, and performance expectations should be expressed in language or numbers that everyone can understand.
- *Justified.* Controls will be effective if they are acceptable to operating personnel. Standards must therefore be plausible, and expectations must be perceived as purposeful. Employees may well ignore or sabotage control methods or standards they view as superficial or capricious.
- *Coordinated.* Controls must be integrated with one another and with plans so that corrective actions make sense. Criteria must be valid measurements of desired activities, and prescribed adjustments must be realistic. Coordination is crucial to ensure that actions taken in one area do not create even greater problems in another.
- *Accurate.* Reports on which corrective actions are taken must reflect diligent analyses. Inaccurate information is one of the most annoying problems managers face. Good decisions made on faulty data solve nothing.

- *Timely.* Information must be available to managers when they need it for making decisions. The attraction of real-time systems is rapid access to information, and with technological advances such as new production techniques and computer systems, the risk is that operating systems will outrun control capabilities. Controls must keep pace with technology.
- *Realistic.* Control systems must achieve intended purposes without being excessive. Excessive controls can result in oppressive monitoring that suffocates employee behavior and costs more than expected savings.
- *Acceptable.* Controls must be acceptable to employees as appropriate means of improving organizational performance. Good controls establish boundaries of behavior without throttling initiative; the standards are attainable and the evaluation methods foster harmony, not cynicism.

Although control systems may meet all these criteria, controlling is a process of evaluating decisions that ultimately affect future operations. Consequently, control decisions have an implicit risk factor. If we also consider that most controls involve sampling rather than comprehensive monitoring, it is safe to say that managers will make mistakes. Performance will not always be precisely on target: controls will not always be appropriate; and managers will not always make correct decisions. The process of control is therefore concerned less with being correct all the time than with never being completely wrong at any time.[23]

CHECKPOINT

- Explain the criteria organizations use to decide what to control.
- Describe effective standards for operational controls.
- What characteristics are essential to effective measurement of work?
- Discuss how reports are used by managers to make decisions.

CONTROLLING PERFORMANCE

Controlling performance begins at the top of an organization with a strategic umbrella of objectives and plans. Without sound objectives, even the most exquisite control systems have little practical value. Consequently, as we examine performance controls, keep in mind the connection between planned objectives and controls. We begin with the concept of *benchmarking,* a technique used to define performance objectives. Then we describe how controls are used in the major functional areas of an organization.

Benchmarking—Setting High Standards

Benchmarking is the process of searching for the best results achieved by other companies, then developing performance standards to achieve similar results. An organization will define benchmarks for common functions, such as marketing, or for specific work practices, such as automated inventory control.[24] Unlike a "competitive analysis," discussed in Chapter 7, which is used to evaluate close competitors within a distinct industry, benchmarking is a process of defining what is called "best-in-class" performance results by any organization in any industry.

benchmarking
The process of searching for the best results achieved by other companies to define objectives and to develop organizational standards for achieving similar results.

Benchmarking is not restricted to strategic, tactical, or operational issues, but is used to develop standards for nearly any task. For example, Procter & Gamble has studied how American Express handles customer billing and collection because American Express is considered among the "best-in-class" in this activity. Meanwhile, American Express has emulated General Electric's training programs, 3M has created benchmarks for warehousing and distribution systems based on systems at Hershey Foods, and Hewlett-Packard has set new standards for sales management based on Merck & Company's methods. Researchers have identified as many as 300 benchmarking categories, and in each instance, there are two or three companies with outstanding performance results. For instance, American Express and MCI excel in customer account services, IBM, Merck, and Procter & Gamble excel in sales management, and Helene Curtis and Microsoft are considered the best in marketing. Some companies stand out in several categories. Westinghouse, for example, is among the best-in-class for automated inventory control and quality process control, and GE heads the list for robotics and training.[25]

The interesting aspect of benchmarking is that managers from a particular organization often find themselves studying methods used in a company outside their industry group, and because this company is not competing against the managers' organization, it will freely share information about its operations. Motorola, which is best-in-class for production design and engineering technology, learned how to implement a top-notch purchasing system from Sysco, Inc., a perishable-food distributor. Ford designed its quality process system after its managers studied quality practices at twenty-three organizations, including MEI Quasar, Merck, and Wal-Mart. Companies benefit from benchmarking by discovering what performance levels are possible and by learning how others have achieved them. Managers can capitalize on both of these benefits by working with companies outside their own industries, whereas competitors would not share information with one another.[26]

Strategic benchmarking provides insights into measurable standards related to major goals such as profitability, capital asset management, market and product development, and growth. Although these are valuable considerations, benchmarking is most useful for identifying areas for improvement in production and operations management, marketing, human resource management, and finance. Within each of these areas, benchmarking targets specific tasks for improvement, such as inventory control, sales, training, or cash-flow control. Although benchmarking is an extremely useful technique, managers must also consider internal data, industry trends, and competitors' performance to develop appropriate standards and controls. In the following sections, we describe some of these controls and how they are used in specific functional areas.

Production and Operation Controls

Manufacturing is the prime focus for production and operation controls. Hospitals, banks, insurance companies, universities, government agencies, professional sports clubs, airlines, and many other organizations must address quality assurance, asset management, and operational processes such as scheduling.[27] Production and operations management is addressed in Chapter 18, so our comments here will be limited to illustrative controls concerned with managing operations. Instead of explaining the mechanics of these controls—topics addressed in specific courses in production, purchasing, and cost accounting—we will describe why the controls are important and how managers use them.

Controlling payroll costs. Production workers represent 74 percent of all employees in manufacturing organizations, and their payroll expenses account for 64 percent of total payroll costs. In service organizations such as the Travelers Insurance Company, operations payroll costs are even higher.[28] Consequently, small changes in scheduling, employment levels, or employee efficiency can result in

ETHICS IN MANAGEMENT
Motorola Wants Suppliers That Deliver on Promises

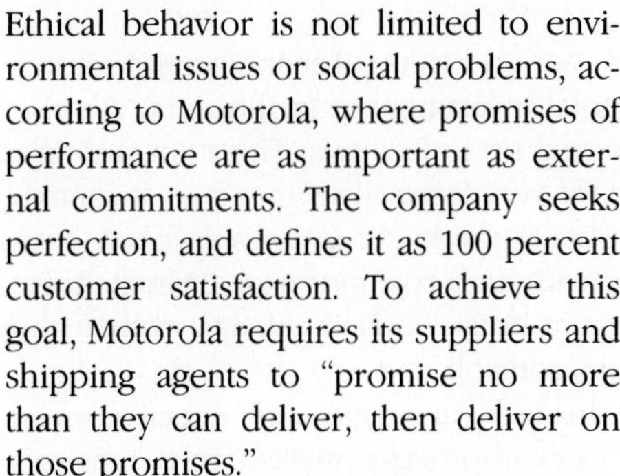

Ethical behavior is not limited to environmental issues or social problems, according to Motorola, where promises of performance are as important as external commitments. The company seeks perfection, and defines it as 100 percent customer satisfaction. To achieve this goal, Motorola requires its suppliers and shipping agents to "promise no more than they can deliver, then deliver on those promises."

One example of Motorola's commitment is its standards for contract carriers who deliver company products to customers by sea van, rail, and trucking routes. Ideally, carriers will deliver on time 100 percent of the time, without shipment damage, and ensure that customers are satisfied with their service. This standard is rarely met, yet Motorola has implemented extensive control systems to pursue the ideal.

The company spends up to a year investigating contract carriers, evaluating their quality records, on-time performance reports, standards of conduct for employees, training systems, and safety records. Once carriers are contracted, Motorola sets up a monitoring system that formally evaluates delivery criteria every three months. Performance is analyzed for on-time delivery, losses or damages to shipments, claims made by customers, billing accuracy, and customer service. Motorola maintains an office of supplier contracting that contacts the company's customers on a regular basis to rate carriers on more than two dozen quality service criteria. They ask, for example, whether the customer was provided with correct invoices, if the carrier delivered materials safely, how carriers answered complaints or inquiries, and whether carrier personnel were courteous.

Motorola's staff also visits carriers as least monthly to discuss ways to improve quality performance. When possible, they provide training and support services to jointly raise standards of performance. Should a problem occur, Motorola's staff gets involved as members of a team that also includes carrier staff to find solutions. Things do go awry every so often, but the company tries to avoid repeating mistakes through creative problem solving. This includes personnel training, distribution system refinements, improvements for equipment maintenance and repair, improved scheduling, and cost-effective materials-handling programs. Meetings are also set up among carriers, Motorola staff, and customers to examine ways to improve services. This not only leads to innovations, but also enhances communications with customers and builds better relationships with them.

Sources: Peter Bradley, "Delivering on Promises," *Purchasing,* August 15, 1991, pp. 79–81; Ted Holden, "Guilty! Too Many Lawyers and Too Much Litigation. Here's a Better Way," *Business Week,* April 13, 1992, pp. 60–65.

tremendous cost savings. At Chevron Canada, for example, operations employees process 165,000 complex transactions each month, totaling more than $1 billion in annual revenues. Employees are responsible for 300 products sold and delivered to 28,000 customers at 50 distribution points. In 1992, these transactions were efficiently handled by 200 employees, yet only five years earlier, the company required nearly twice that number of people to handle 25 percent less business. Moreover, errors occurred in 10 percent of all transactions. Chevron introduced an information system based on one used at Lucky Stores, Inc., a California retail chain, to reduce transaction errors to a target of less than 1 percent. The information system included control data on twenty-four criteria, each benchmarked to improve customer service. The company also implemented new scheduling controls to reduce employee idle time during slow periods and to ensure customer service during peak periods. Training occurs during slack work hours, and every employee is evaluated on performance skills. As a result, operational payroll costs have declined annually by nearly 9 percent as a percentage of total costs.[29]

Controlling inventory costs. The total year-end value of manufacturing inventories in the United States is 168 percent of total investment in facilities. Put another way, inventory costs are $168 for every $100 tied up in facilities. This comparison is unusual, yet it emphasizes that companies have very large investments in inventory, and a control system that shaves a few percentage points off inventory expense can more than offset interest expenses associated with high-cost mortgages. Yet manufacturers will negotiate frantically to get a 1 percent break on facility loans while losing ten times that amount through poor inventory control.

Many excellent companies understand this and have developed effective inventory control systems. Hewlett-Packard has a work-in-process production control system that monitors the flow of materials, and over a five-year period, H-P has increased production by 29 percent while decreasing inventory handling expenses by 320 percent.[30] At Adolph Coors, stocks of beer brewing ingredients and case-loaded finished goods inventories are monitored using bar code scanners. Every inventory item can be traced using the bar codes, and ideally, Coors wants to reduce "static" inventory to zero—no materials or finished goods standing idle. During a three-year program, the company has halved the time for idle stock material and achieved an almost continuous flow of finished goods from brewing to distribution.[31]

Controlling material costs. Although inventory is a significant part of material costs, many other expenses are also included in the total cost of materials used in production and operations. Figure 17-8 illustrates that 52 percent of all controllable expenditures are related to materials, and this figure is representative of 85 percent of all U.S. manufacturers.[32] The cost components are direct purchases of inventory and supplies, materials-handling equipment, materials warehousing, labor required for materials handling, and purchasing costs. Materials controls are focused on reducing purchasing costs, eliminating faulty materials through inspections and statistical sampling techniques, and reducing warehousing, equipment-handling, and labor costs through systems that allow materials to be delivered directly to points of production rather than to intermediate storage areas.

As shown in Figure 17-8, every dollar saved through more effective controls over purchasing or incoming materials is worth about $10 in new sales. Consider a firm with a product that sells for $100. If it has a 10 percent profit margin, it realizes $10 from each sale. To double profits to $20, sales would have to double, all other things being equal. If, however, material costs were 50 percent of shipped value and were reduced only 20 percent, profits would double to $20. A dollar saved in materials is high-powered money and more profitable than a dollar received from new sales.

Controlling technology costs. In many instances, new information systems are providing the means to reduce payroll, inventory, and material costs. A new information system, however, is also costly. Engineers and accountants have devised models for evaluating purchasing decisions for computers and software development, topics that are addressed in Chapter 19, but as a general rule, managers must consider the benefits achieved from new technology against the equipment price and operating costs. Control systems are being rapidly developed to monitor infor-

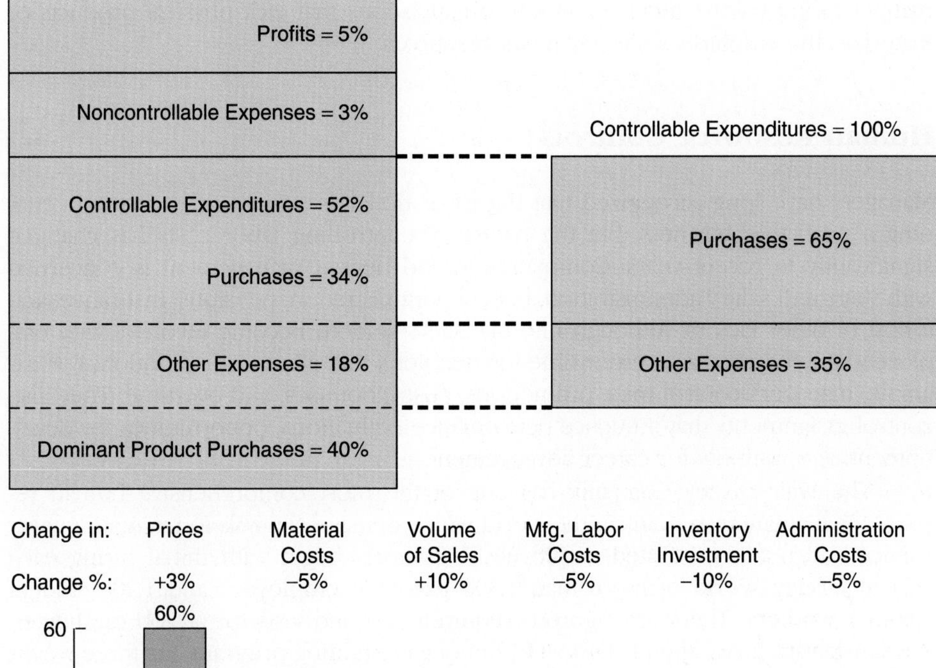

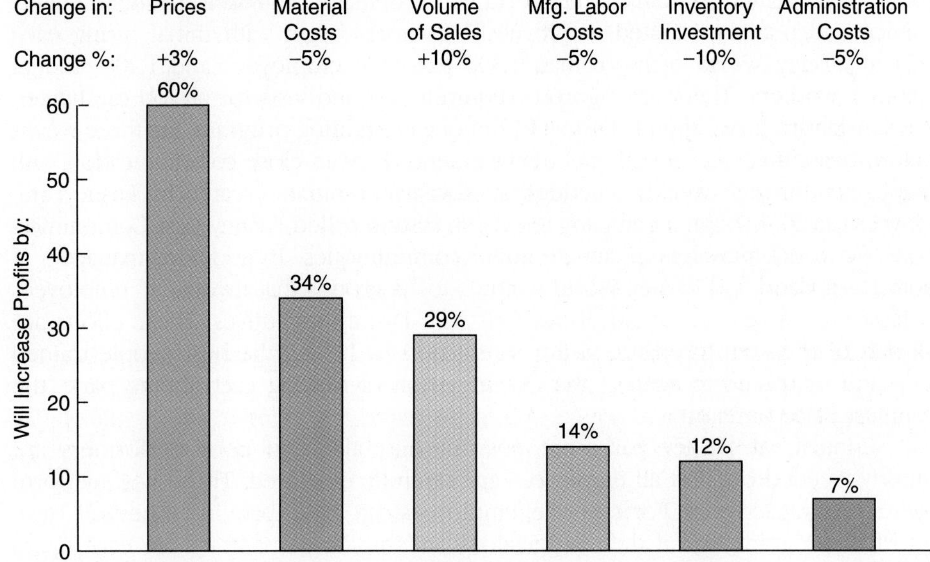

FIGURE 17-8 Profit Impact and Relative Importance of Cost Controls

mation system usage, such as on-line computing time and capacity utilization (i.e., the percentage of time the system is used as intended). Also, there are qualitative controls such as "system audits" that question whether computers are used productively or misused because they are convenient.[33]

Controlling technology also requires evaluation of manufacturing equipment, such as capacity utilization. This is a control measure that registers the actual time a machine is used in production and compares that with the total time available for the machine to be used. During an eight-hour shift, for example, a particular machine might be 100 percent utilized if it is operated for seven hours. The one lost hour would account for time required to set the machine up, make operator adjustments, and clean up after an operation. Therefore, if a machine is utilized for only five or six hours, there is room for improvement. Perhaps this can be accomplished with more efficient setup procedures, better operator training, or improved work scheduling. Companies develop controls to monitor capacity utilization that identify reasons for inefficient results.

Categories of production and operation costs described are the major areas that concern managers, but there are many other specific costs to consider. These include energy utilization, maintenance, distribution expenses, health and safety considerations, and administrative overhead associated with operations. In many organizations, these costs can be more important to control than in a durable-goods manufacturing environment. In service organizations that lack physical products or materials, the emphasis shifts to human resources.

Human Resource Controls

Managers have long recognized that the labor dollar is an important factor in running a profitable business, but the nature of controlling labor costs has changed significantly in recent years. Compensation and benefit management is concerned with wage and salary administration, benefit administration, pensions, insurance, and a host of other factors. Although line managers seldom become involved with employee benefits, they are responsible for decisions that affect compensation. For example, managers control most promotions, raises, bonuses, and overtime. They also control assignments that influence performance evaluations, opportunities for development, and visibility for career advancement.

The Walt Disney Company has one of the most comprehensive human resource management systems in the world with extensive controls to maintain quality service and retain motivated employees.[34] Controls begin with initial hiring each year at Disney World of more than 1,500 part-time employees and 1,200 student summer workers. There are rigorous requirements and tests for all job candidates. Those who are hired attend "Disney U," an on-site training program, for three weeks before becoming "cast members." Management keeps in close communication with employees through weekly meetings, audiovisual seminars created by Disney employees (aired through a company television system called Disney Cast Communications Network), newsletters, and frequent communiqués. In addition, managers at both Disneyland and Disney World conduct focus groups that involve all employees at least once a year in candid discussions with Disney executives. These efforts are all part of a system to ensure visitor satisfaction by having the best people trained well and motivated to achieve the Disney vision of making each theme park "the happiest place on earth."

Controls at Disney parks are not onerous, although poor performers are quickly weeded out and all employees are carefully evaluated. Those who perform well are rewarded well. For example, employees can participate in Disney's "I Have An Idea" program, and if their suggestions are implemented, they can earn up to $10,000 in bonuses. At the same time, the company conducts employee opinion polls and collects information on employee behavior through "guest comment forms." These are reviewed during monthly employee meetings, and they are supplemented by periodic performance evaluations. Slightly more than 60 percent of all management positions are filled through internal promotions based on progress reports, training results, and peer-group evaluations. Finally, when an employee resigns or is fired, managers conduct an exit interview to determine why that person did not fit into the Disney organization.[35]

Effective control of human resources usually involves less glamorous work than suggested by the Disney example. It does not have to be unpleasant, but it is often difficult and includes the sometimes tedious daily procedures of scheduling, monitoring work results, and documenting performance. Control activities focus on reducing defective products or ineffective services, improving on-time records for sales, distribution, and customer service, lowering labor costs through improved use of technology or training, and improving employee productivity through better work methods or team development efforts. Control techniques also track employee-related problems. For example, safety reports and lost-time accident records provide insights into work-related problems or dangerous conditions that affect employees. Reports on absenteeism, grievances, turnover, and disciplinary problems help managers evaluate patterns of work, employee satisfaction, and situations that impede performance.

Marketing Controls

Most controls in marketing concern sales and service records. Although sales personnel are stereotyped as free-wheeling and somewhat autonomous individuals, they are often held more accountable than their peers in production. Sales volume is certainly the main concern of marketing controls, and consequently, it is vital to maintain good information about sales personnel, patterns of sales, market trends, competitors, and customer preferences. Actual performance is compared against sales quotas, industry ratios, market expectations, sales forecasts, and previous performance records. The importance of sales controls cannot be overemphasized because data collected on marketing underpin future marketing plans. In turn, marketing plans drive production schedules and set in motion plans for purchasing, materials controls, financing, and personnel recruiting.

For example, at Nucor Steel, CEO Ken Iverson spends a half day each week personally typing sales information into the company's computer. This is unusual behavior for a company executive, but Nucor is an unusual company, run with a corporate staff of about twenty people and generating more than $800 million in annual sales at minimills located in four states. Iverson's rationale for handling sales reports personally is, "By keying in the numbers, you're forced to look at every figure for every week. That's the value."[36] American Airlines completely revamped its air fares and structure of customer services in 1992 in response to industry competition that had created very complicated ticketing systems. Citing customer dissatisfaction with the airline industry pricing system and costly errors in passenger ticketing, American Airline's parent company, AMR Corporation, announced a simplified fare system at substantially reduced prices. AMR's chairman Robert L. Crandall explained that the old system was not only too complicated to understand but also almost impossible to control. Consequently, American's managers were often surprised by marketing results under the old system, where revenues sometimes fluctuated wildly, competitors often reacted to price changes with strange discounts, and ticketing agents seldom knew whether flights would be half empty or overbooked. Under the new system, global fares are well defined, reservation systems are simplified, and management has fewer marketing variables to contend with.[37]

Marketing controls also provide feedback on a variety of cultural and social conditions affecting organizations. For instance, changes in sales often mirror changes in consumer tastes and preferences. Close tracking of sales reveals patterns of growth or decline, demographic shifts, and subtle changes in consumer shopping. For example, many products initially sold only in department stores are now marketed through inexpensive catalogs; convenience stores have altered the pattern of food purchasing; and shopping centers draw customers away from downtown locations. These kinds of changes have far-reaching effects on a company's internal operations. The Sharper Image was so successful selling expensive gifts and novelties that Tiffany's, Saks, and Neiman Marcus—exclusive retailers hurt by Sharper Image and similar high-end catalog companies—began direct-marketing campaigns to select customer groups. In turn, the Sharper Image began opening boutiques in select mall locations. Other companies, such as Nestlé and Sunkist, have expanded their product lines, repackaged traditional coffees and food products, and entered the catalog business. And Sara Lee, a company founded on wholesale distribution of desserts, now has more than 600 retail outlets in fifty countries.[38]

Financial Controls

Marketing information offers a rich assortment of data for planning, but typically it is the conversion of these data into financial terms that interests top management. Financial controls are largely *activity controls* that express sales, production, purchasing, and personnel results in convenient dollar terms that everyone understands. A

GLOBAL TRENDS

Du Pont Looks Toward Compliance with European Quality Standards

Concerned that it could lose the entire European market, Du Pont is preparing to join the ranks of more than 10,000 companies that have become registered with International Standards Organization 9000, known in Europe simply as the ISO 9000. "Registration" requires meeting rigorous quality standards for company performance, manufacturing safety, environmental compliance in production and disposition of materials, and customer service. There is nothing in the United States to compare with this European system of quality standards.

Although being unregistered does not legally bar a company from competing in Europe, ISO 9000 registration means that a company has been subjected to a year-long investigation, that it can meet or exceed international quality standards, and that it supports social standards for environmentally safe operations.

ISO 9000 evolved from the British Standards Institute (BSI) model for controlling exportable products, which was first introduced through a royal charter in 1931. The ISO was set up in 1946, and in 1979, the European Community (EC) refined the standards and designed the registration process as "9000." Nearly 800 European companies apply for registration each month; fewer than 100 companies are accepted for study, and barely half of those succeed in gaining registration.

Once registered, a company is recertified every three years, but it can lose its certification more quickly if its quality standards fall. The ISO monitors performance every six months through comprehensive evaluations. In effect, ISO 9000 registration is tantamount to international recognition of quality.

There are standards for nearly 200 engineering and environmental criteria, 125 organizational considerations, and 50 management measurements. Highly reputable consultants are chartered to make the evaluations, including Lloyds Register Quality Assurance (LRQA). One of LRQA's techniques is to interview a company's customers, and for a major manufacturer, this can mean months of investigation covering as many as 3,000 clients. Unfortunately, the United States ignored the ISO mandate until 1986, when the Department of Commerce formally recognized the need for internationally accepted quality standards that would solve the problems of shoddy exports and exports to Third World countries made only to exploit consumers.

Du Pont is one of the few U.S. companies now rushing to adopt these global standards. Only about 130 other U.S. companies have ever applied for recognition under ISO 9000, and barely a dozen have achieved it. Several of these are long-distance telecommunication companies that realized they had to win registration to access European markets. Several more are microelectronics firms with major European interests. U.S. companies in the auto industry, metal manufacturing, and aerospace are not yet positioned for compliance. They could be among the first victims of a unified European Community that expects tight quality control for trade.

Sources: Carolyn V. Woody and Robert A. Fleck, Jr., "International Telecommunications: The Current Environment," *Journal of Systems Management,* December 1991, pp. 32–36. See also Mike Moyer, "Targeting EC 1992 Standards," *Quality,* March 1992, pp. 37–38.

In focus groups, parents suggested that Sears lower prices, have more sales, sell name-brand clothing for kids, and devise better ways to prolong the lifetime of children's clothing. Sears's answer: Kid Vantage, a program that offers shoppers over seventy brand names, a frequent-purchase card to track spending and gain discounts, and Sears WearOut Warranty, which replaces kid's clothes for free if they wear out while the child is still the same size. Says one mother who bought new clothes for her children recently at Sears, "I saved the tags because the snow clothes will get battered. There's a good chance they'll wear out."

common misconception about financial controls is that they are used primarily by financial managers for financial purposes. To the contrary, operating managers in well-managed firms understand and use these controls to make more effective decisions.[39] For example, tracking monthly profit ratios helps to identify high-activity periods when people must be hired in production and sales. Financial controls are equally valuable for operational decisions and financial management decisions. Generally, there are two categories of financial controls: *financial statements* and *financial ratios.*

Financial statements. The two most widely used financial statements are the balance sheet and the income statement. The **balance sheet** is a position statement that reflects the particular status of a firm on a given date. Balance sheets are customarily prepared quarterly, semiannually, and annually to provide comparable data on the general condition of the company with respect to assets, liabilities, and owners' equity. The **income statement** summarizes operating results and the relationship between revenues and expenses for a certain period of time. Income statements are usually prepared quarterly, semiannually, and annually. They are also called *profit-and-loss statements* because they are used to calculate net income while providing a summary of how profits or losses occurred.

balance sheet
A financial statement or position statement that summarizes a firm's assets, liabilities, and net worth at a certain point in time.

income statement
Also called a *profit and loss statement,* the income statement is a financial summary of revenues and expenses with calculations for profits (or losses) and resulting taxes on operational income.

Companies use many more financial statements to summarize information and to evaluate performance. These are beyond the scope of this text, but together, they provide managers with periodic reports on activities ranging from line-item purchasing costs to major capital improvements. With increased use of information systems, operational data can be accumulated almost instantaneously, and financial reports can be prepared very quickly. Data can also be used more effectively to simulate operational scenarios and analyze results from automated controls such as machine utilization or inventory systems. Software programs such as spreadsheets and integrated office systems permit a wide range of customized reports that can be made available to managers rapidly and transmitted globally through electronic media. Consequently, managers have access to a tremendous amount of information to help in planning and controlling their activities.[40]

financial ratios
Computations of selected data used to analyze performance, track company results over time, and compare companies to one another.

Financial ratios. Selected information, mainly taken from balance sheets and income statements, is used to develop financial ratios. **Financial ratios** are computations that allow comparisons of company results over time within the organization, compare data between companies, or compare company results to industry averages. For example, *net profit margin* is the result of dividing net profit after taxes (in actual dollars) by sales (in actual dollars). This provides a ratio expressed as a percentage of net profit to sales. With this ratio, managers can compare current results with those of prior periods—or with those of other companies with wide differences in sales volumes—without having to juggle huge dollar figures or do complicated mathematics. Ratios are used to assess the immediate position of the company, how the company has changed over time, or the relative strength of a company within its industry.

The concept of ratio analysis is better understood by examining several of the most common ratios. Because most students will study ratio analysis in depth in accounting and finance courses, we will only touch on them here. Exhibit 17-1 gives examples of these ratios using hypothetical data to illustrate the required calculations. Categories of ratios and their purposes follow:

- *Liquidity ratios* are used to assess a company's ability to meet its short-term obligations and remain solvent. Lenders are keenly interested in these ratios because they provide clues about how a company can meet its cash expenditures such as loan payments.
- *Leverage ratios* indicate how a company finances itself. Various control ratios, such as a *debt ratio,* show the relative percentage of financing obtained through debt and through equity investments.

EXHIBIT 17-1 Financial Ratios for Solarflex Window Manufacturers

Liquidity Ratios	Current Ratio	$= \frac{\text{Current Assets}}{\text{Current Liabilities}}$	$= \frac{11{,}965}{3{,}611}$	= 3.31
	Acid Test	$= \frac{\text{Current Assets} - \text{Inventories}}{\text{Current Liabilities}}$	$= \frac{4{,}285}{3{,}611}$	= 1.19
Leverage Ratios	Debt-to-Net-Worth	$= \frac{\text{Total Debt}}{\text{Net Worth}}$	$= \frac{13{,}873}{26{,}461}$	= 0.52
Coverage Ratios	Times-Interest-Earned	$= \frac{\text{Earnings b/Int. and Tax}}{\text{Interest Charges}}$	$= \frac{6{,}935}{1{,}664}$	= 4.2 times
Profitibility Ratios	Gross Margin	$= \frac{\text{Gross Margin on Sales}}{\text{Sales}}$	$= \frac{10{,}965}{34{,}386}$	= 31.9%
	Net Profit Margin	$= \frac{\text{Net Profit after Taxes}}{\text{Sales}}$	$= \frac{3{,}554}{34{,}386}$	= 10.3%
	Return on Equity	$= \frac{\text{Net Profit after Taxes}}{\text{Net Worth}}$	$= \frac{3{,}554}{26{,}461}$	= 13.4%
	Return on Assets	$= \frac{\text{Net Profit after Taxes}}{\text{Total Assets}}$	$= \frac{3{,}554}{40{,}334}$	= 8.8%
Operating Ratios	Inventory Turnover	$= \frac{\text{Cost of Goods Sold}}{\text{Average Inventory}}$	$= \frac{23{,}421}{5{,}662}$	= 4.1 times

- *Coverage ratios* illustrate a company's ability to accommodate finance and interest charges. Bond-rating analysts assess financial risk in part by examining a firm's coverage ratios.
- *Profitability ratios* relate different profit information to sales, net worth, or assets. These ratios give managers important insights for making decisions related to sales activity, financing, or asset management.
- *Operating ratios* are used to judge a firm's effectiveness in operations, such as how well it manages inventory.

Ratios do not prove anything by themselves; their usefulness lies in the comparisons they permit. For example, the current ratio should be above 1:1, indicating the company has short-term assets that are at least equal to short-term liabilities. Yet a high ratio of, say, 4:1 is not necessarily good if it is out of line with industry averages of, say, 2:1. A high ratio could then mean that the company is mismanaging its assets by allowing too much cash to sit idle, holding too much inventory, or allowing accounts receivable to accumulate uncollected.

Ratios are valuable because they provide consistent measurement among firms, across industries, and over time. By converting raw data into ratios, managers factor out differences in company size, sales levels, and other hard-to-compare characteristics. For example, a computer manufacturer with a gross profit margin of $20 million on $400 million in sales has a gross margin of only 5 percent. A competing firm with $20 million gross profit margin on $100 million in sales is much stronger with a 20 percent gross margin. Had only gross sales dollars been compared, the first company with $400 million in sales would have seemed stronger; had net sales dollars been compared, the companies would have seemed equal. The lower 5 percent gross margin does not necessarily mean the large firm is doing poorly; it may be having problems, but it may also be growing by aggressively offering low prices that compress profits.

Although our description of financial statements and ratios is necessarily brief, it should illustrate that financial information requires interpretation. Even sophisticated analyses compiled through highly reliable information systems will be valuable only to the extent that data can be understood by managers and used to improve their decisions. In the final section of this chapter, we will introduce several of the more sophisticated methods used by managers.

CHECKPOINT

- Describe the most important factors to control for managers with production or operations responsibilities.
- What are some of the control methods used by managers with respect to human resources?
- How are marketing controls used to improve organizational performance?
- Explain how managers use financial statements and ratios to analyze performance in areas other than financial management.

BUDGETS

budgets
Plans expressed in commonly understood numerical terms such as dollars or units that serve the reciprocal purpose of providing measurable standards for controlling operations, expenses, and performance.

Budgets are plans expressed in schedules of expenses, income, sales, production units, and other activities that can be reduced to numbers and have the reciprocal purpose of providing measurable performance control standards. Well-developed budgets provide managers with the means of quantifying performance expectations and monitoring progress toward objectives.[41]

Types of Budgets

Although most budgets are prepared in financial terms, they are used throughout an organization for both operational and financial control. Those budgets expressed in nonmonetary terms may have disguised names, but they are still budgets. A weekly quota that projects 10,000 units in sales is called a sales quota, but it is a budget. The sales quota is translated into dollars (10,000 units x $2.00 = $20,000), which will show up on financial statements. The sales staff will monitor performance in terms of units sold, and the accounting staff will monitor the dollar value of sales revenue. This illustrates two main types of budgets: *operating budgets* and *financial budgets.*[42]

Operating budgets. Recall from the previous section on financial controls that one of the major planning and control documents in any organization is the income statement. An income statement has three primary sections of information: revenues, expenses, and profits. These sections constitute the most common types of operating budgets. Specifically, there are revenue budgets, expense budgets (also called *cost budgets*), and profit budgets. In addition, companies use activity budgets to monitor operating efficiency.

revenue budget
A budget derived from sales data and used to evaluate the effectiveness of marketing efforts.

A **revenue budget** is derived from sales data and is used to evaluate the effectiveness of marketing efforts. Sales results are compiled from individual offices or departments and recorded on income statements. Actual revenue is compared to planned revenue, and when unacceptable variances occur, management is prompted to take corrective action. Supplemental budgets also help managers make better decisions about their marketing efforts. For example, an official price list is a budget, but because prices are negotiated, discounted, or changed through sales promotions, actual prices can vary substantially from list prices. Budgeted revenues, therefore, can be substantially different from actual revenues generated. Other budgets include data on consumer credit, quality defects, bad debt allowances, and account collections.

expense budget
A budget that identifies specific operational costs to evaluate how efficiently a firm's resources are being deployed.

An **expense budget** identifies a specific category of operational or administration cost to evaluate how efficiently a firm's resources are being deployed. There are hundreds of different costs that can be budgeted, but the most common are variable operating expenses, such as labor, materials, and direct operating overhead, and relatively fixed expenses, such as rent, current interest on debts, R&D budgets, and administrative salaries.

profit budget
A budget that consolidates revenue and expense information to identify planned net income and to record actual results.

The **profit budget** consolidates revenue and expense information to identify planned net income. The budget is used to record revenues and expenses, and then calculate the net difference between them to identify profits or losses. This can be complicated if a company includes tax expenses, allowances for certain credits or deductions, and adjustments to income or expenses. The point of a profit budget, however, is to create a record of relative income and expenses and how profits are affected by variances in the individual budget items.

activity budget
Usually expressed in nonmonetary terms, an activity budget is used to plan and control operational tasks.

An **activity budget** is used to plan and control operational tasks, and although a company can convert activity data into monetary terms, the activity budget is typically expressed in nonmonetary terms. Consequently, results from activity budgets seldom show up on financial statements except indirectly. For example, manufacturers use activity budgets to measure machine utilization, specified as a percentage of real time (or actual time) that a machine is in use. This is measured against expected use of the machine during a certain time period. When a variance occurs, management is alerted to potential problems such as poor scheduling, faulty materials, or poor workmanship. Activities such as labor hours, packaging, warehousing, expediting orders, credit collection, inventory usage rates, purchase order times, and maintenance schedules can be specified using hours, units, percentages, and other appropriate criteria.

Financial budgets. Managers use financial budgets to help them *gain access to and control* productive assets. This means much more than merely obtaining the cash necessary to buy tangible objects. The critical point is to "gain access to" assets. Consequently, companies can lease equipment, use debt leveraging to purchase facilities, deploy their retained earnings for purchases, or pursue creative means of financing such as time-sharing with other firms for information systems. Cash is, of course, one essential asset required for "transactions," but there are many financial instruments available to managers. Therefore, managers are concerned with effective planning to gain access to assets, and then with efficiently controlling their use. These dual responsibilities are accomplished using *cash budgets, financing budgets,* and *capital expenditure budgets.*

A **cash budget** documents actual receipts and disbursements from revenue and expense data, tracks payments made for capital expenditures, and identifies cash required to remain solvent. Unlike expense budgets, which include depreciation, accruals, and deferred items, cash budgets get to the bottom line of projecting cash receipts and expenditures. Consequently, when a company projects its cash flow needs and finds that it will come up short, managers must decide how to find more money, reduce expenses, or curtail capital expenditures. Cash budgets are useful because they reveal cash flow patterns and identify potential problems such as huge payments for equipment purchases that might be reduced by leasing.

cash budget
A summary budget that shows actual receipts and disbursements from all sources to identify cash required to remain solvent.

A **financing budget** is derived from cash flow projections and capital expenditure plans to identify how assets can be financed. Financing budgets reflect decisions about structuring an organization's finances, including loans, leases, credit lines, use of revenues (cash and receivables), deployment of retained earnings, private investments, stock equity, bond income, and other financial resources.

financing budget
A budget derived from cash flow projections and capital expenditure plans to identify how assets can be financed.

A **capital expenditure budget** is used to document strategic decisions for purchasing facilities, equipment, technological processes, and other resources that represent long-term investments. For example, installing a computer-assisted manufacturing system requires major investments in hardware, software, training, and engineering, and perhaps a significant initial loss in productivity as the system is being implemented. This entire process represents a capital expenditure project that must be financed, and a small change in loan interest rates may result in huge cash expenses. Also, cost components such as expenditures for personnel training, engineering, or software development may be difficult to control and require sophisticated capital budgeting techniques.[43]

capital expenditure budget
A budget document used to make strategic decisions about facilities, equipment, technological processes, and other assets that represent long-term investments.

Budget Variances and Flexibility in Control

Every budget has specific projections that are used as standards, but actual results rarely coincide with these planned projections. The difference between actual and planned results is called **budget variance.** The fact that actual results do not match planned results, however, is not as important as how much variance is acceptable. Consequently, managers must determine a range of variance that will meet performance expectations. Some activities require very close tolerances, such as manufacturing parts for a space shuttle; slight variances can lead to disaster. Other, less critical activities may have broad tolerances, such as sales performance in a highly competitive environment.

budget variance
The difference between budgeted results and actual results used to analyze unacceptable variations, causes, and potential consequences.

For example, if weekly sales revenues for a particular office are projected at $20,000 and that office generates only $18,000, it has an unfavorable variance of

$2,000 or 10 percent. The question is whether this variance is justified. A control process will permit managers to evaluate past sales in similar periods and factors that affect sales such as consumer demand, competition, or pricing decisions, and then decide what corrective action to take, if any. The variance may be acceptable because prior experience shows that sales vary in any given week by as much as 20 percent. On the other hand, if the office generates a favorable variance of $24,000 in sales, management may want to determine what that office is doing to achieve such high sales.

Budget controls, therefore, take into account potential variances that are often derived through statistical methods. By comparing budget performance over time, managers statistically estimate future budgets and their variances. This process introduces a certain degree of flexibility and defines decision-making criteria for intervention. In addition to using statistical methods, managers also evaluate the costs and benefits of intervention. A tight budget variance on sales performance may not be reasonable, even if it is statistically sound, if the cost of taking corrective action outweighs the benefits. On the other hand, the risk of not having an extremely tight variance on a life-threatening activity may justify very high costs. Also, managers must consider whether the situation is controllable. If profits are falling because of extremely high interest rates, managers may be able to do little more than cope with the situation until economic conditions improve. To sum up, taking corrective action is warranted when the budget variance is more costly than the corrective action, when it is consistent with the risk involved, and when the situation itself is controllable.

Responsibility Centers

responsibility center
A work group, department, or division of a company with budgetary controls focused on relevant and controllable activities.

A **responsibility center** is a work group, department, or division of a company with budgetary controls focused on controllable activities. Managers are held accountable for decisions that affect their budgets in the four types of centers shown in Figure 17-9. These are *cost centers, revenue centers, profit centers,* and *investment centers.*[44]

cost center
A work unit where managers are responsible for controllable expenses, but not revenues, profits, or investments.

Cost centers. Also called *expense centers,* **cost centers** hold managers responsible for controllable expenses generated through work activities. Managers in cost centers are not responsible for revenues or investments, and performance is evaluated in terms of budgeted cost standards and variances. Most production departments are cost centers.

Quality assurance, manufacturing departments, and maintenance units are budgeted on expense criteria. Administrative departments, support services, and functions such as purchasing are cost centers. Although every company activity ultimately affects revenues and profits, managers of cost centers are primarily concerned with maintaining cost-effective operations.

FIGURE 17-9 Responsibility Centers and Their Objectives

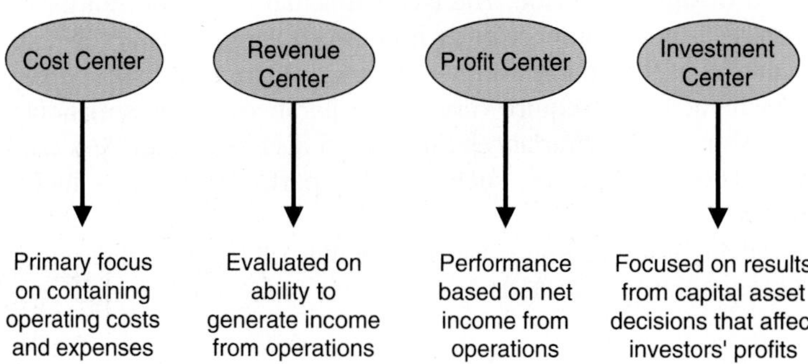

MANAGEMENT APPLICATION
Yoplait Profits Through Accountability

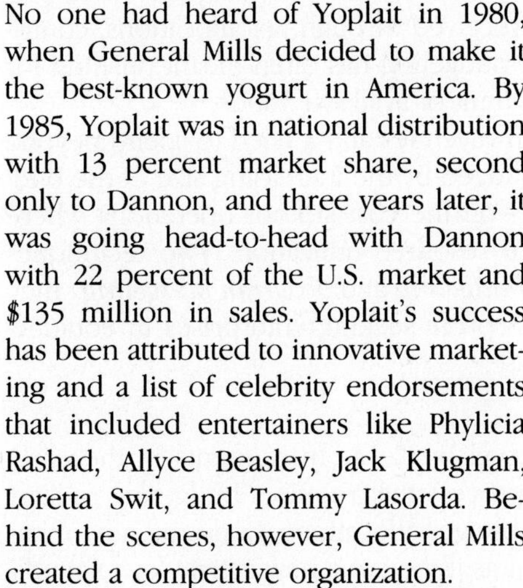

No one had heard of Yoplait in 1980, when General Mills decided to make it the best-known yogurt in America. By 1985, Yoplait was in national distribution with 13 percent market share, second only to Dannon, and three years later, it was going head-to-head with Dannon with 22 percent of the U.S. market and $135 million in sales. Yoplait's success has been attributed to innovative marketing and a list of celebrity endorsements that included entertainers like Phylicia Rashad, Allyce Beasley, Jack Klugman, Loretta Swit, and Tommy Lasorda. Behind the scenes, however, General Mills created a competitive organization.

Marketing was divided into responsibility centers for advertising, public relations, research, and sales. Early success in gaining market recognition prompted a similar system of accountability for manufacturing and distribution to create new flavors of yogurt, manufacture to very high standards requiring 100 percent natural ingredients, distribute fresh yogurt to thousands of grocery markets daily, and control customer billing with better than 99.4 percent accuracy. Accountability was fostered throughout the Yoplait division with budget and performance controls linked to specific responsibilities.

Departmental and functional activities were networked through planning systems and rigorous performance standards that were coordinated as cost and revenue centers. In a system developed by the Yoplait team, profit responsibility was allocated to most divisions according to their contribution to growth.

Sources: "General Mills," *Review,* GM quarterly report, 3rd quarter, 1987, p. 2; General Mills, *Annual Report,* 1990, pp. 1–2; and "The Yogurt Market," *Growth Through Acquisition* (Battle Creek, Mich.: General Mills, 1984), pp. 2, 6.

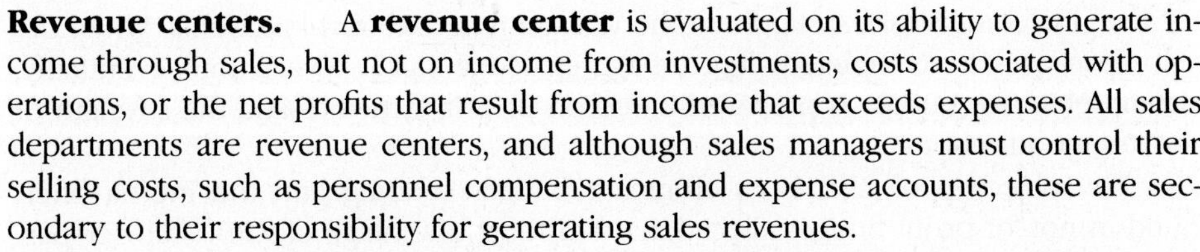

Revenue centers. A **revenue center** is evaluated on its ability to generate income through sales, but not on income from investments, costs associated with operations, or the net profits that result from income that exceeds expenses. All sales departments are revenue centers, and although sales managers must control their selling costs, such as personnel compensation and expense accounts, these are secondary to their responsibility for generating sales revenues.

revenue center
An organization unit that is evaluated on its ability to generate operating income, but not income from investments or costs or profits from operations.

Profit centers. A **profit center** is held responsible for both costs and revenues, and performance is evaluated in terms of the net difference between income and expenses. Marketing departments, for example, have revenue centers (sales offices) and cost centers (advertising, market research, customer services, etc.). Marketing managers are accountable for profits resulting from the combined operations of revenue and cost centers. Managers in this situation are said to have "P&L responsibilities" (i.e., profits and losses), and include those concerned with division-level marketing, production, or operations.

profit center
An organization unit that is held responsible for both costs and revenues; performance is evaluated in terms of the resulting net income.

Investment centers. An **investment center** focuses on effective management of capital assets. Managers of profit centers who are also responsible for their capital equipment and facilities are in control of investment centers. Budgetary controls include revenues, expenses, and investment criteria that measure the effective use of assets. These criteria include asset financing methods and costs, depreciation, capacity utilization, asset deployment, and value created from assets, such as operating profits and retained earnings. Performance is evaluated in terms of company earnings, net worth, and investor dividends.

investment center
An organization unit whose managers are held responsible for capital expenditures and the structure of investments.

Budgeting in Not-for-Profit Organizations

Although not-for-profit organizations such as government agencies and the Red Cross can adapt responsibility centers to their services, budgets for profits and investments are inappropriate for these organizations. Their method of budgeting is to ascribe values for benefits, then control the costs of providing those benefits. Because their services are exempt from market forces, benefits are subjective and performance is difficult to measure. Funds are received through tax allocations, contributions, and limited forms of revenue. Thus budgeting has often meant pushing for maximum allocations while spending to the limit of available funds.[45]

This results in a perpetual constraint on revenues and a need to spend beyond income limitations. Value is therefore often judged by the increasing size of the budget, and budget controls consequently focus on the cost side of operations where objective standards can be used to measure resource utilization. Two techniques have evolved to accomplish this: *zero-based budgeting* and *program budgeting*. Incidentally, both techniques are widely used in profit-seeking enterprises in conjunction with traditional forms of budget controls.

zero-based budgeting (ZBB)
A process that requires budgeting to start from scratch rather than build on previous budget allocations.

Zero-based budgeting. Initially developed by Texas Instruments in the early 1970s, **zero-based budgeting (ZBB)** is a process that requires budgeting to start from scratch rather than build on previous budget allocations. Consequently, managers are required to justify each budget item as if it were a new activity or expenditure. This eliminates the assumption that because a budgeted item was funded in the past it is to be funded in the future. ZBB has been implemented with excellent results at many for-profit firms, including Westinghouse, Xerox, and Ford Motor Company, and during the late 1970s, it was widely adopted by federal and state governments.[10]

ZBB represents a change in budget philosophy in that lower-level managers become responsible for careful budget decisions. ZBB starts with budget requests from operating departments called *decision packages,* with individual line items justified in writing. For example, if a manager requests a word processor, it must be justified as a necessary purchase. Theoretically, everyone and everything must be justified, including salaries, supplies, phone expenses, and travel accounts. When decision packages are completed, they are aggregated at higher levels, until, eventually, a comprehensive budget is prepared based on priority activities and the strength of line-item justifications.

The objective of ZBB is to eliminate budget padding and the inertia often found in not-for-profit budget allocations. A distinct advantage of ZBB is closer participation and improved communication between managers at all levels. However, ZBB creates extra paperwork and it is a time-consuming process because managers often write wordy justifications. In practice, zero-based budgets are tempered by common sense, so that starting at "zero" does not mean having to justify every pencil or note pad, but rather sensible decisions about expenses.

program budget
A method of separating budget criteria so that allocations are tied directly to programs or projects rather than to functional departments or operating units.

Program budgeting. A **program budget** is one that allocates resources directly to a program or project rather than to functional departments. The federal government began using program-based budgets sparingly during the 1950s, when the Rand Corporation developed program budgeting techniques for use by the Department of Defense as a way of concentrating control. Since then, program budgets have become popular because they allow expenses and revenues to be associated with well-defined activities. Managers gain greater control over resources allocated to these activities while being held accountable for performance. NASA space projects, for example, have been individually budgeted, controlled, and evaluated with separate funding that, once allocated, is not affected by changes in other program areas.

Program budgets require managers to consciously plan activities and justify expenses. Once budgets are in place, political infighting is minimized because reallocations between programs are unlikely. However, some managers dislike the system because it pits programs against one another for funding. Consequently, low-priority programs may be scrapped to avoid having several programs weakly funded. Many hospitals, for example, have "unbundled" services such as pediatrics, critical care, surgical procedures, radiology, and laboratory testing so that specific budgets can be tied to services as if they were independent programs. The result is better accountability, and when the cost of a service cannot be justified, it may be discontinued, with the hospital contracting for it in the private sector. Similar "privatization" of public activities has evolved in government for many activities that do not justify program costs.[47]

CHECKPOINT

- Explain how operating and financial budgets are used and how they differ in their use of information.
- How are responsibility centers able to separate accountability for different organizational activities?
- Describe how zero-based budgeting and program budgeting are used in not-for-profit organizations.

BEHAVIORAL CONTROL IN ORGANIZATIONS

Human resource controls were introduced earlier in the chapter as important for improving individual and group performance. Controlling behavior also requires periodic evaluation of *performance systems.* As a conclusion to this chapter, we describe methods of evaluating management systems and assessing organizational activities in behavioral terms.

Management Audits

The purpose of any audit is to evaluate an organization and ensure that its performance is adequate. The **management audit** uses predetermined criteria to evaluate behavior through surveys, interviews, and observations by audit teams. The teams, which may include outside consultants, peers, and employees, appraise how managers plan, make hiring decisions, conduct performance reviews, assign personnel, and help subordinates develop their work-related skills. For example, certified public accountants are evaluated by the Association of Independent Certified Public Accountants (AICPA) on as many as 151 guidelines documented in the AICPA's Professional Standards procedures. CPA peers are assigned, often each year, to evaluate member firms, and the results are compiled for confidential evaluation reports and recommendations to member CPAs.[48] The management audit resembles an accounting audit. Both follow prescribed procedures to collect information on critical criteria, use techniques for evaluating deviations in results, and use external examiners to ensure objectivity.

management audit
A method of appraising leadership behavior through surveys, interviews, and observations of managers, often employing evaluation teams of peer managers, consultants, and employees.

Management audit results are expressed in performance terms that can be objectively measured. For example, a leadership component reflects patterns of decision making and draws inferences about how the firm can improve by altering managers' leadership styles. A productivity component measures traditional results like quality defects and labor turnover, but it also relies on customer feedback and information gathered from employee surveys to evaluate potential for behavioral changes and organizational relationships. The latter are determined by examining changes in patterns of grievances, work group productivity, and team benchmarking of quality improvements.

A "clean" audit that establishes what is being done well is just as valuable as an audit that unearths serious problems because it reinforces effective performance and motivates employees to continue their high-quality performance. Most audits, however, provide insights into problems that need attention, and managers benefit by understanding how performance can be improved through such programs of leadership training as team-building processes.

Social Audits

social audit
Evaluation of organizational activities that have a significant influence on social responsibility and external relationships.

A **social audit** evaluates how well managers are meeting their social responsibilities. Most social audits focus narrowly on the firms's role in product safety, environmental protection, consumer rights, community service, and management ethics. They are also used to periodically monitor quality of life inside the organization, including employee benefits, working conditions, affirmative action programs, work climate, opportunities for employee growth, and support systems such as health care and child care.[49]

Social audit responsibility exists at three levels: the society of humankind, the community external to an organization, and the collective human resources inside an organization. Figure 17-10 shows that the value of an organization depends on the value it adds to these constituent groups.

Humankind. The most abstract audit asks: Is the organization benefiting the world by its existence? When Chrysler Corporation was in danger of going under in the 1970s, it was rescued by government-guaranteed loans because the public did not want to see a major American automaker (and thousands of jobs) disappear. In contrast, deregulation of the airline industry resulted in fierce competition that left many airlines bankrupt. The demise of Pan American in late 1991 did not arouse public concern in the same manner as Chrysler's crisis, and there was no outcry that society would suffer from another airline failure.[50] However, many jobs were lost and many investors were hurt by Pan Am's bankruptcy.

FIGURE 17-10 Value of Firm to Society

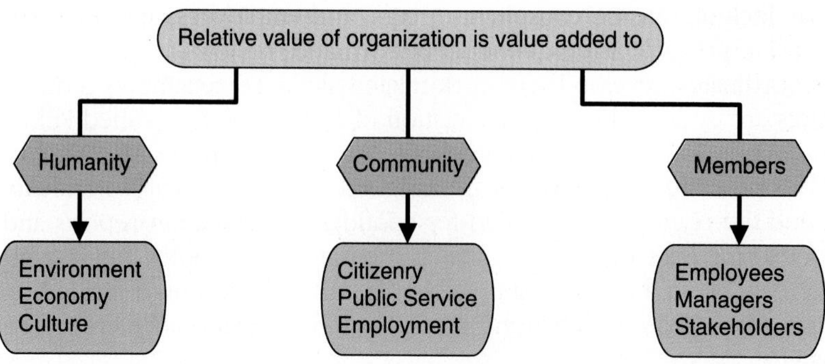

Community. At the local level, social audits are concerned with performance that enhances economic development, creates jobs, enriches lifestyles of citizens, and protects the ecological environment from undue harm. Audits also examine how companies support cultural opportunities, the arts, and charities. The question to answer is whether the organization returns value to its community constituents. One method of determining this is through benchmarking, as described earlier, using comparable standards for social behavior by an organization and its leadership.

Organization. At the organizational level, the social audit can be far-reaching, including such minor issues as cleanliness of the work environment and such major issues as pension benefit administration. Audits may be concerned with human relations, career training, physical fitness, mental health, counseling problem employees, and minority opportunities for advancement. The important question to answer is whether an organization is providing value for its members.

Behavioral Assessment Controls

As described earlier, managers use performance evaluations to assess individual behavior and to provide feedback. When these evaluations are designed effectively and applied consistently, they provide continuity among organization members and enrich communications between managers and their employees. Behavioral control is also enhanced by periodic assessments through organizational development (OD) intervention (described in Chapter 10) and periodic evaluations of individuals and groups within job categories.

Intervention. Intervention usually requires professionals from outside an organization to evaluate needed changes and implement change programs. OD and behavioral modification programs were discussed in Chapter 14. From a control standpoint, they constitute methods of assessing performance or focusing on behavioral issues such as team formation and productivity enhancement.

Differentiation and integration. Paul Lawrence and Jay Lorsch have suggested that in order to assess individual needs and change, it is first necessary to differentiate roles and how these roles are integrated into organizations.[51] Essentially, the concept is that a person working in one situation will face different problems regarding work schedules, rewards, and skills than a person working in another situation, even though both people have similar job descriptions. Sales representatives, for instance, deal with an external world of volatile markets requiring unstructured decisions, and performance varies substantially among salespeople. Production managers tend to work in regulated environments requiring structured decisions, yet the composition of their work force and the relationships they develop with employees affect performance results. Organizations can differentiate individual roles by using psychological testing, periodic assessment tests with groups of employees, comparison reports on group activities, and benchmarking between organizations.

CHECKPOINT

- How does a management audit improve control over performance?
- Describe how social audits help focus organizational activities on constituent interests within an organization and outside it.

As THE OPENING SCENARIO on Dell Corporation emphasized, controlling a company is a comprehensive effort to ensure efficiency and effectiveness. Dell's management has been able to focus on major issues such as international competition and market development without losing sight of minor considerations such as efficient office systems and well-managed cost controls. Capital expenses for equipment and office systems, for example, are as closely controlled as global prices for millions of dollars' worth of computer systems. And the company keeps in touch with its customers through very well developed marketing research and control methods.[52] ■

A SYNOPSIS FOR LEARNING

1. Explain how planning and controlling are coordinated.

Control mechanisms complement plans at all levels. Strategic objectives have strategic controls; for example, a company will plan to achieve a certain level of profits by meeting annual sales objectives, and management will use interim financial statements and performance ratios to monitor profitability. At division levels, tactical controls focus on plans in functional activities, such as production, marketing, human resources, and finances, with more specific and shorter-term objectives. At the operating level, activity controls are designed to monitor immediate results, such as quality control sampling of work-in-process and tracking of daily work schedules.

2. Describe the process of controlling operations.

Controlling is the process of keeping activities directed toward desired results. It begins with predetermined standards of performance, developed in plans, that provide clear and measurable objectives. Organizational activities are then monitored through control systems that measure results and activities.

3. Describe three major types of controls and their purposes.

Steering controls are used to fine-tune most organizational activities on a daily basis. First-line managers make numerous subtle adjustments to steer work activities. Operating procedures are steering controls that provide guidelines for performance while helping managers check work progress.

Yes/no controls, also called *go/no-go controls,* are fail-safe methods of avoiding problems in situations where no tolerance for error exists. These controls require managers to take one of two actions: Stop whatever is going on or go ahead as planned.

Postaction controls are comparisons of results "after the fact" with predetermined standards. Most marketing and financial reports are postaction controls whereby managers analyze past performance to make decisions about future plans and activities.

4. Explain how managers implement effective control systems.

Managers must first decide what to control. Some activities require controls too expensive to justify them; others require controls without regard for costs. When what is to be controlled is determined, standards are developed that can be measured consistently and are acceptable to employees who must use and understand them. With effective standards, organizations can implement monitoring systems capable of accurately evaluating performance and recording results. Through the monitoring process, comparisons are made between actual results and standards, and when variances occur, management is prompted to take corrective action. Taking action, however, means taking corrective actions that are understandable and acceptable to employees.

5. Describe production and operation, human resource, marketing, and financial controls.

   Production and operation controls focus on the daily activities of converting materials into products or performing services for customers. In manufacturing, production controls monitor schedules, inventory, human and material resources, quality, equipment utilization, maintenance, shipping and handling, and production methods. Operation controls in service companies are not concerned with products, but otherwise are similar to controls used in manufacturing. They monitor asset utilization, supplies, schedules of services, work processes, quality performance, and all cost factors.

   Human resource controls center on employing the correct number of people with appropriate skills and abilities to achieve organizational objectives. Human resource managers also control employee wages, labor costs, compensation systems, pension plans, insurance, and training systems.

6. Describe how budgets and responsibility centers improve control and accountability.

   Budgets have dual purposes, for planning and controlling activities, and by having budgets that set reasonable planning standards, companies can more accurately forecast expected results. Accountability is enhanced when budgets are not used as absolute rules for performance but rather as guidelines for expected results, and when flexible budgets address "controllable" items. Managers cannot be held responsible for results over which they have no control—thus the concept of responsibility centers where work activities and results from operations are specifically tied to the nature of the organizational unit. Consequently, organizations have cost centers, revenue centers, profit centers, and investment centers, and managers in each type of center are accountable for relevant budget activities under their control.

7. Explain the concepts behind management and social audits.

   Management audits are "system" evaluations that address broad patterns of leadership or management behavior. Instead of focusing on individual behavior and performance results, these audits are designed to give an organization insights into how human resource systems are working, relationships between managers and their employees, and the profile of performance across the organization as compared to past performance or as benchmarked to other companies. The social audit examines whether the company is responsive to environmental and social issues, whether it is supportive of community constituents, and whether it provides value for its members through internal social programs and an appropriate work environment.

SKILL ANALYSIS

CASE 1 Andrew Carnegie: "Watch the Costs and the Profits Will Take Care of Themselves"

Andrew Carnegie emigrated from Scotland to the United States in 1848 as a teenager. In the four short years following his arrival in this country, he rose from a menial job in a textile mill to messenger boy and then telegrapher with O'Reilly's Telegraph, and finally to personal secretary and telegrapher to Tom Scott of the Pennsylvania Railroad.

Even while he was working fourteen-hour shifts for the textile mill, Carnegie took a night class in double-entry accounting. His twelve-year stint with the railroad, however, was the real inspiration for his obsession with controlling costs. The railroads pioneered the use of cost accounting in the United States. The sheer size of their operations forced managers to keep careful records and then use those records in making operating, personnel, and investment decisions.

In 1872, Carnegie took $250,000 he had made on his investments and built a modern steel mill outside of Pittsburgh. The railroads were converting from iron to steel rails, and Carnegie believed that the demand for steel would only continue to grow. He revolutionized the iron and steel industry by bringing together all the processes—smelting, forging, rolling, cutting, and founding—in one location. Later he integrated vertically, buying quarries, mines, and coke smelters to ensure his supply of raw materials.

Most importantly, however, Carnegie applied the lessons he had learned at the railroad and imposed a system of strict cost accounting. Traditionally, mill owners had balanced their books only once a year, figuring their profits by dividing total expenses by total output. Before the year was up, they did not even know if there was a profit!

Carnegie established a series of checkpoints with scales and weighed every scrap of material going into and coming out of each process. He kept detailed records on each worker and reviewed the weekly cost sheets personally, no matter where he was at the time.

These records allowed Carnegie to compare the performances of different employees and different processes. He based all his personnel and operating decisions on these data, consistently choosing the quicker, cheaper alternative. His goal was to be the industry's high-volume, low-cost producer.

More often than not, Carnegie's cost-based decisions defied industry traditions. For example, Carnegie was a proponent of "hard driving." That is, he ran his equipment and men full out, around the clock, to increase productivity. Hard driving pushed the output at one of his furnaces from 13,000 to 100,000 tons per year. In contrast, the British tradition was to coddle furnaces to prolong their life span as much as possible. Hard driving burned out furnaces quickly, but Carnegie's data showed that the lower cost per ton produced more than compensated for the need to buy replacement equipment.

The rapid speed of Carnegie's operations became one of his trademarks. Materials were rushed from one process to the next. For example, at Carnegie's mills, molten steel from the blast furnace was poured into molds on moving flatcars; these cars carried the newly formed ingots directly to the rolling mill. This eliminated stockpiles of ingots awaiting further processing. The warm ingots required less reheating at the rolling mill.

Although Carnegie lacked a scientific understanding of steelmaking, his cost data consistently pointed the way to the latest technology. He appalled his competitors by scrapping equipment while it was still good in order to replace it with state-of-the-art machinery. He once ordered a manager to tear out a three-month-old rolling mill because a newer design would reduce costs by a cent or two per ton.

He also applied the latest in scientific techniques to purchasing decisions, hiring a chemist to measure the iron content of the various ores on the market. He found that an ore's reputation—and price—was unrelated to its actual iron content and changed his purchasing patterns accordingly.

Carnegie's relentless efforts to cut costs worked. Over the course of his career, from 1872 to 1900, he drove down the cost of producing a ton of steel from $56 down to $11.50. Low costs enabled Carnegie to undersell the competition and still make a profit. He was the unquestioned leader of the industry when he chose to retire to a life of philanthropy.

Case Questions

1. Describe how Carnegie applied the four steps of the control process.
2. Of the three types of controls, which did Carnegie himself use? What role would the others have played in his operations?
3. The world has changed dramatically since Andrew Carnegie's day. What kinds of controls do contemporary steel makers use that Carnegie ignored?

Sources: Video segment from "Entrepreneurs: An American Adventure," vol. 4; Robert Sobel and David B. Sicilia, *The Entrepreneurs: An American Adventure* (Boston: Houghton Mifflin, 1986), pp. 156–164; and Harold C. Livesay, *American Made: Men Who Shaped the American Economy* (Boston: Little, Brown, 1979), pp. 113–125.

VIDEO CASE Grounded Pilots—Age Controls in the Airline Industry

Imagine that you're in a commercial airliner 39,000 feet above the earth and a serious emergency arises. Who would you want to be at the controls of that plane? Undoubtedly, most of us would choose someone with many years' experience, a clean bill of health, and an excellent flight record. Well, if a pilot is sixty or over, no matter how experienced, healthy, or remarkable that person's flying record may be, he or she won't be at the controls. The Federal Aviation Administration mandates that commercial airline pilots retire at the relatively young age of sixty. Is this age restriction the best approach to controlling safety in the airline industry?

The FAA's "Age 60 Rule," which has existed for thirty years, prohibits anyone sixty years or older from sitting in the front of the cockpit as pilot or co-pilot of any commercial airliner carrying more than thirty passengers. The agency's concern is safety. It defends its use of the Age 60 Rule by citing a 1983 study that found that pilots in their forties and fifties had much lower accident rates than pilots in their sixties. However, as critics have pointed out, this study had nothing to do with airline pilots. It focused on private pilots, who had much less training and were flying much smaller planes. Also, critics say that the study was biased against older pilots to begin with because of the way that flying time was calculated. In fact, pilots challenging the Age 60 Rule had the study's accident rates recalculated and found that the accident rate for active pilots in their forties and fifties was *higher* than that for pilots in their sixties and that pilots in their seventies had the lowest accident rates of all. Nevertheless, FAA officials continue to defend the Age 60 Rule. One administrator said, "You must draw the line somewhere for safety reasons and you must apply it fairly across the board."

With more than one million U.S. passengers taking off and landing in commercial airliners every day, safety would seem to require experienced captains with exceptional skills and reflexes. Yet, in 1990, 700 experienced commercial pilots were grounded because they had reached age sixty. In 1991, 800 more were forced out, and in 1992, another 1,000 were compelled to retire. A number of experienced pilots have been challenging the FAA's mandatory retirement age. Says one captain, a pilot for thirty-seven years and about to reach age sixty, "It's almost a paradox because I feel I'm reaching the peak of my professional capabilities; and physically, I'm working probably as hard, if not harder, than I even did ten years ago to maintain a good physical profile." In fact, when a concerned group of thirty older captains put themselves through a series of physical and psychological tests far more extensive than those the FAA requires for younger pilots, they were all certified fit to fly by a panel of experts. Yet the FAA has refused to make a single exception to the Age 60 Rule. Pilots who have reached sixty and wish to continue their flying careers with commercial airlines have only one option under FAA rules: to take a back seat in the cockpit as flight engineer. And most of those pilots resent being forced into the "back seat."

Case Questions

1. How do mandatory age restrictions attempt to control performance?
2. What other types of human resource controls could you suggest for ensuring safety in the airline industry?
3. What are the positive attributes of the FAA's Age 60 Rule as a control tool? What are the negative aspects?

Sources: Doug Petersen, "Report Suggests Ending Mandatory Retirement Ages," *Nation's Cities Weekly,* February 24, 1992, Vol. 15, No. 8, p. 12; Richard O. Reinhart, "Training for Obsolescence: Age 60 Retirement," *Business and Commercial Aviation,* June 1990, Vol. 66, No. 6, p. 76ff: and "Still There for the Axing at Age 60," *Flying,* September 1989, Vol. 116, No. 9, p. 26.

SKILL PRACTICE

EXERCISING CONTROL OVER PERSONAL FINANCES

Creating a personal budget is similar to the planning process for any organizational budget, and exercising control over one's personal finances is similar to challenges faced by managers in controlling operating budgets. Recall that a control process has four steps: setting standards, monitoring performance, comparing results with standards, and taking corrective actions. Using these steps and the information presented below, student teams will establish personal budgets for class discussion.

Guidelines

Assume that a recent graduate has a nice position earning take-home pay of $18,000 a year ($1,500 per month). The graduate has been working for several months and feels a need to develop a personal budget. The graduate lives in a major suburban area where rent ranges from $300 to $2,400 a month. He or she needs a car to drive into the city to work—a distance of twelve miles. The graduate has only begun to look for furniture and wants to replace the car, which was a present when he or she first went away to college. Other considerations include basic necessities, social activities, clothing, and plans for a vacation in about seven months.

Instructions

1. Six groups will be formed, three assigned to create a personal budget for a young single woman and three that will focus on a young single man.
2. Each group will define how monthly income will be allocated as budget items with estimated expenditures. Explain why these are standards.
3. Each group will develop a monitoring system: How will the individual keep track of budgeted expenses?
4. Introduce flexibility into the budget and explain what acceptance variance is and how that variance can be corrected.
   (Allow twenty to minutes for these activities.)

Discussion

Each group will elect a spokesperson to describe the categories of expenses and amounts allocated. A second student from each group will summarize categories on a blackboard or flip chart as they are described.

When all six group budgets have been quickly listed, each group spokesperson will describe how that group intends to monitor its budget and what will be done about variances.

(Allow twenty to thirty minutes for presentation and discussion.)

As an alternative, student groups can be asked to present a written budget during the next class period with explanations of monitoring and corrective actions to be taken when variances occur.

18

Production and Operations Management Control

OUTLINE

OBJECTIVES

- Discuss how improved quality enhances productivity.
- Explain design, product, and service and use controls.
- Describe how PERT and CPM are used in production control, and the concepts of SQC, SPC, and cellular systems.
- Describe materials controls and inventory management.
- Describe and contrast EOQ, MRP, JIT, and statistical process controls.
- Explain how integrated systems using MRP II and JIT are complementary.

COMPAQ COMPUTER CORPORATION has three manufacturing centers, each coordinated with one another and serving global customers through a system the company calls "world-class quality" management.[1] The primary facility is at the company's Houston headquarters; the second facility is in Singapore; and the third is in Erskine, Scotland. The two foreign plants together produce 75 percent of the company's products, and the Scottish plant—Compaq's newest—is responsible for 60 percent of all Compaq personal computers, portables, and desktop systems. The Scots are also setting the standards by which Compaq claims its place as a world-class quality company.

Compaq Scotland has an enlightened system of manufacturing and management that includes a fully integrated quality system of purchasing, inventory, and process manufacturing based on *just in time (JIT)*. JIT is a system of buying just enough materials to fill orders, delivering materials directly to production in time to be used, and manufacturing products just in time to meet orders. Ideally, it eliminates raw materials and finished goods inventory to achieve the most efficient flow of production without waste.

JIT is only one part of Compaq's integrated system, which combines *cellular manufacturing, manufacturing resource planning (MRP II),* and *autonomous work teams (AWTs)* in an environment for *total quality management (TQM)*. Production cells are work centers coordinated through sophisticated computer control processes, and MRP II is a comprehensive planning and scheduling process. By integrating these two types of processes with JIT, Compaq has achieved one of the best "on-time" records with the fewest defect rates. AWTs represent the company's approach to leadership, focusing on participative teams, and TQM is the philosophy of a pervasive commitment to quality improvement throughout the organization. These are at the heart of Compaq's human resource systems, and they have resulted in one of the most productive, customer-driven organizations in the world.

These terms may seem confusing now, but they represent several of the most important concepts fundamental to effective *operations management*. In this chapter, you will be introduced to terms and concepts that seem to focus solely on production systems. However, organizations that provide services as well as those that manufacture products integrate technology and human endeavor in the quest for quality performance.

Production and operations management (POM) is concerned with how organizations use their resources to achieve the highest-quality performance, which, in turn, ensures the greatest productivity. Quality and productivity are therefore inseparable concepts. Although we study POM as a technical field and examine how technology, processes, and systems are created in the POM environment, it is not the "tools" but the improved performance that results from using those tools that is important.[2] Consequently, we study production and operations management to understand how managers develop effective systems that help their organizations flourish in a complex, rapidly changing world.

THE QUALITY-PRODUCTIVITY CONNECTION

productivity
The relationship of combined inputs such as labor, materials, capital, and managerial verve to outputs such as products or services; the summation of performance that results in more efficient utilization of resources.

Productivity is on everyone's mind today as the media keep reminding us that foreign competitors are outproducing Americans. **Productivity** is not a matter of producing the greatest number of products, but of providing customers with the greatest number of *quality* products at the lowest possible costs. Figure 18-1 provides a conceptual view of the quality concept.

Satisfying customer needs is the ultimate mandate of organizations and therefore a primary concern for control. Profit is a result, not a goal, of quality performance, and those companies that best satisfy customer needs with reliable products and services are often the most profitable.[3] Our discussion focuses on managerial decisions that encourage total quality control.[4]

The Quality Concept

quality
The concept of doing things better, not just more efficiently.

In absolute terms, **quality** implies error-free, totally reliable products or services. Quality in the real world, however, is relative; it exists in the eye of the beholder. Customers measure a product's quality by how well it fulfills their expectations at a given price.[5] Figure 18-2 illustrates this relationship.

From a producer's standpoint, quality reflects a conscious decision to manufacture inexpensive or expensive products, and also to make things that work. Profitability problems and low productivity do not stem from attaching lower or higher price tags, but from making poor-quality products that do not work. Poor quality results in lost sales, recalls, a tarnished brand image, costly repairs, warranty losses, scrapped materials, wasted time, and many other expenses for the company. Quality problems can come from substandard materials, erratic supplies, careless purchasing, poor workmanship, design faults, or management blunders.[6]

Quality problems also affect product safety and reliability, and can lead to legal costs and huge losses in customer sales. This is often a very sensitive issue for service organizations, such as hospitals, where substandard performance can have life-threatening consequences. Most service organizations can control quality through processes similar to those used by manufacturers to improve purchasing, materials, safety, human resource performance, and reliability.

Total Quality Management (TQM)

total quality management (TQM)
The comprehensive approach to quality by everyone in an organization to provide customers with reliable products and services.

Total quality management (TQM) means a comprehensive approach to quality by everyone in an organization to provide customers with reliable products and services.[7] An ideal TQM perspective is one that encourages all employees—from executives to janitors—to be responsible for improving quality on a continuous basis. TQM is a strategic concept that must be implemented by top management and ingrained in the culture of an organization. Until recently, this has not been a common theme in the United States or Europe, yet it was adopted as far back as the 1950s in

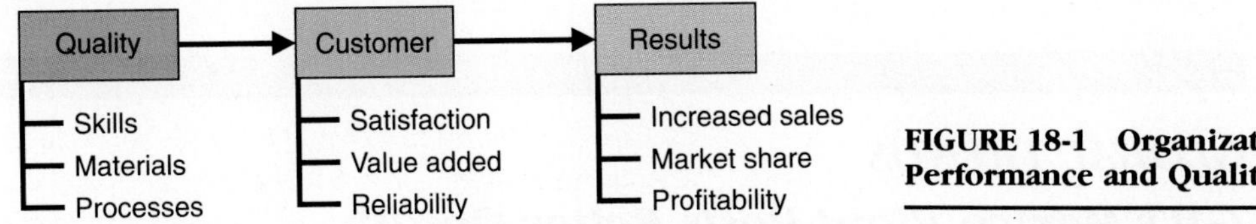

FIGURE 18-1 Organizational Performance and Quality

Japan. Subsequent to Japan's international success, Western companies have recognized the value of a quality commitment and have begun in earnest to create TQM cultures. Prior to this movement, the predominant view concerning quality in Western cultures was to control operations through specialized staff specialists and inspectors who performed a surveillance function.

Ironically, the concept of TQM originated in the United States through the vision of engineers such as W. Edwards Deming, whose message fell on deaf ears in his own country but was received enthusiastically in Japan. Deming's message was that improved productivity is the result of improved quality, and quality requires a total and systematic approach to excellence by an organization. As an engineer, he reinforced his philosophy with carefully designed quality control and management systems that helped transform Japanese industry.[8]

Although the term *TQM* has become common only recently, the underpinning concepts of quality management have been evolving for years. Deming focused on manufacturing controls, and while quality management was only reluctantly adopted in the United States during the 1960s and 1970s, a number of excellent American companies were early proponents. These companies are recognized for their quality products and services, and they have been among the nation's leading organizations for several decades. General Electric Corporation has consistently been rated by peer companies at or near the top of its industry. It has implemented TQM practices in most of its plants and earned a reputation for reliability. Merck and Company has been ranked the best in chemicals and pharmaceuticals for a decade or longer. Also ranked among the top half dozen firms in the United States for quality products are Boeing Aircraft Corporation, Eastman Kodak, 3M, and Hewlett-Packard. Service-oriented firms among the quality winners include J. P. Morgan and Dow Jones. At Dow Jones, publisher of the *Wall Street Journal* and purveyor of business and technical services, TQM from the lowest strata to the boardroom has been a strategic goal for several decades.[9]

The Productivity Concept

If quality is a way of managing, then productivity is the result of effective quality management. Traditionally, productivity has been concerned with greater quantities of output; thus measurements of productivity have centered on units of output with-

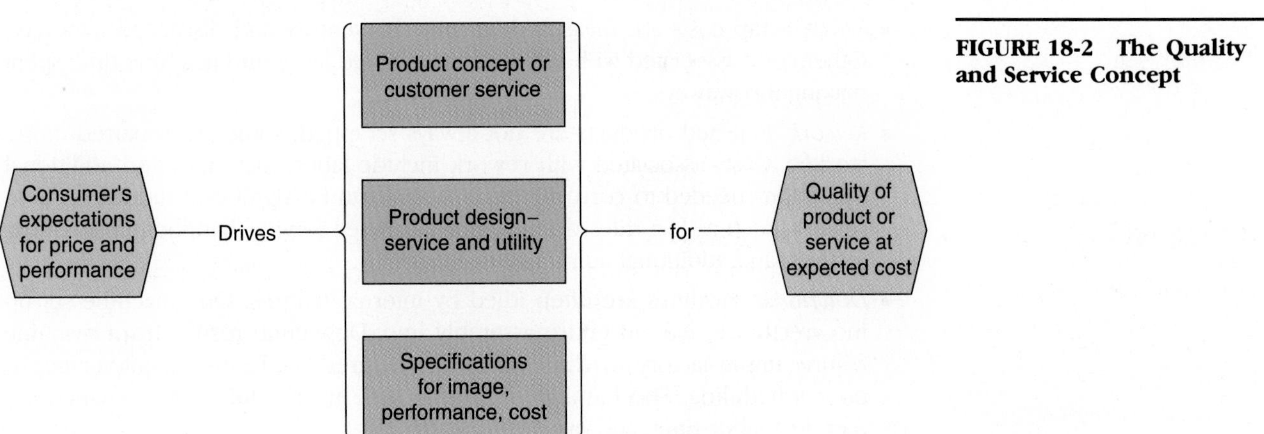

FIGURE 18-2 The Quality and Service Concept

GLOBAL TRENDS

GM's Mexico Plant Posts Better Quality Record Than U.S. Units

Ramos Arizpe, Mexico, a town 200 miles south of the Texas border, is the location of General Motor's automotive plant with the highest quality rating in the corporation's North American system. Industry studies found that the Ramos Arizpe plant only had 86 in-process defects per 100 cars compared to an average of 158 for all GM plants and 140 for the entire automotive industry. This represented an 80 percent improvement between 1987 and 1991. During the same period, the Mexican plant reduced warranty claims by more than 65 percent.

Today GM's Ramos Arizpe plant assembles Buick Century and Chevrolet Cavalier models for the U.S. and Canadian markets. With the North American Free Trade Agreement expected to be phased in during 1993 and 1994, Mexican imports are projected to increase dramatically. Meanwhile, GM has been trimming production in the United States and taking a close look at plants in Oklahoma City and Ste.-Therese, Quebec, as candidates for downsizing. GM's union workers fear wholesale job losses due to shifts in production to Mexican plants. Citing cheap Mexican wage rates, union leaders claim GM manufactures in Mexico to create cost advantages. However, the quality record of the Ramos Arizpe plant has saved more money in warranty work and recalls than the total wage differential between U.S. and Mexican workers.

Conventional wisdom suggests that manufacturing in a country where most workers are undereducated and unskilled would result in poor quality. The Ramos Arizpe experience proves otherwise, and GM's success is not an isolated case. Ford's Escort plant in Hermosillo, Mexico, was ranked third-lowest in the world in automotive defects in 1987, and although the Japanese auto industry has recaptured the top ten slots on a global basis, Ford's plants in Mexico continue to outperform their U.S. counterparts. Nissan Motor Company will open a plant

out attention to *good* units of output. The most common measurement accounts for labor efficiency as output in units per labor-hour.[10]

Enlightened managers search for productivity standards that identify salable, good-quality products and services in relationship to all relevant inputs, including labor, capital, materials, and energy. We can better understand these points by examining the costs of poor productivity. These include:

- *Scrap.* Scrap costs are measured in ruined inventory and discarded materials. Other costs associated with scrap include wasted labor and machine time spent making throwaways.
- *Rework.* Rejected products are not always scrapped; some are repaired or reworked. Costs associated with rework include labor, materials, and additional operations needed to correct defects. There can be significant hidden costs in rework, such as lost sales due to poor customer service, handling costs of defectives, and additional administrative costs.
- *Downtime.* Facilities are often idled by internal failures. One machine set up incorrectly can halt an entire assembly line. Downtime results from machine failure, unsatisfactory machine setup procedures, ineffective maintenance, or poor scheduling. Specific added costs include unscheduled maintenance, repair, lost labor time, and overhead.

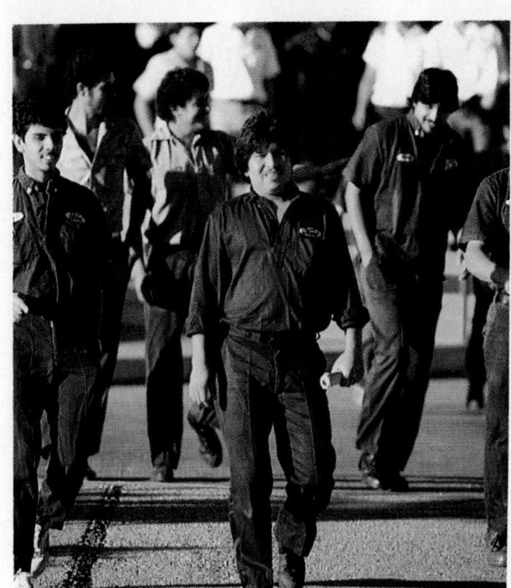

Workers leaving Ford's plant in Hermosillo, Mexico, at the end of their shift.

near Guadalajara in 1993, and Mercedes-Benz is building a plant just south of the Arizona border. Volkswagen has been in Mexico for several years with engine parts plants, and it opened a full production plant in 1992 to complement its other plants in Argentina and Brazil.

GM attributes its success in Mexico to a team management system coupled with new assembly processes based on manufacturing cells. Employees work in groups and are cross-trained in multiple skills related to cell activities. Each employee is formally trained for several job-related skills, and then upgraded on the job for self-directed quality control activities. Nissan trains its prospective employees for several months before it formally hires them, and selected employees are sent to Japan for hands-on experience in Japanese plants. Ford has replicated its "Quality is Job One" program in Mexico, and employees who pass the seven-week course receive diplomas and quality skills ratings.

Sources: Stephen Baker, "If You're Lucky, Your Next Car Will Be Made in Mexico," *Business Week/Quality,* October 25, 1991, pp. 72–73; "Quality: Job #1 South of the Border," *Ford's Way* (Detroit: Ford Motor Company, 1991), p. 14; and "The New World's Newest Trade Bloc," *Business Week,* May 4, 1992, pp. 50–51.

- *Yields.* Poor controls result in wasted materials. These are not scrap from defects but actual waste generated by poor use of resources. For example, when parts are stamped out of sheet metal, there are wasted "cutoffs." By using good layout patterns and accurately stamping out parts, raw materials can be better utilized with less waste. In addition, innovative uses of waste materials can lower disposal costs.
- *Disposition.* Discarded products and waste must be disposed of. Even reworked items require management analysis and decisions on whether to scrap any or all of them. Costs associated with physical disposition include materials, expensed labor, overhead, and physical handling. For many sensitive products such as chemicals, paints, and explosives, disposal costs can be nearly half the initial cost of making the product.[11]

Costs Associated with Quality

Quality costs are incurred before manufacturing begins as well as during production and after products are sold. Many are hidden costs not traced specifically in traditional accounting systems. Several of the most obvious costs associated with quality are:

According to the Software Engineering Institute, which rates Pentagon contractors' software development processes, Hughes Aircraft's ground systems group deserves to be ranked first. The group not only has a reputation for being able to solve the most complex problems but also delivers its contract ahead of schedule and below budget. To eliminate the basic causes of problems, the group employs statistical tools developed by W. Edwards Deming.

- *Incoming materials.* Product failures, scrap, and rework can result from poor materials. Controlling the quality of incoming materials can be costly because it requires inspection, sorting, returning unacceptable materials, and extra administration. There are also sizable costs associated with having insufficient supplies or overstocking to prevent shortages.
- *Purchasing.* Purchasing must analyze utilization rates, fluctuations in production, seasonal sales, and maintenance requirements. Quality purchasing done diligently minimizes errors in ordering and ensures cost-effective procurement. Unfortunately, purchasing managers seldom have adequate support systems to do a quality job.[12]
- *Inventory.* Costs associated with poor inventory control are notorious. They stem from excess or short inventories, disruptions in shipments, mishandling, and outright losses. In manufacturing parlance, inventory losses are *shrinkage* and are usually difficult to trace.
- *Warranty and service.* After products are sold, there are costs of servicing defectives and honoring warranties. These activities are directly related to quality and can be captured in accounting documents. However, accounting models tend to limit costs to direct wages and replacement parts. Other costs—such as indirect overhead, capital financing costs applicable to warranty and service, and losses in future sales—are ignored.

Social and Human Costs Associated with Poor Quality

If poor quality leads to poor resource allocation, waste, scrap, and misused human effort, then U.S. society suffers from a general accumulation of these problems. This is the implicit assumption in political debates about national productivity and comparisons between ourselves and foreign competitors. Excessive waste in material and

EXHIBIT 18-1 Costs Associated with Poor Quality and Poor Productivity

Material scrap	Shipment disruptions
Wasted rework	Warranty and service expense
Machine downtime	Excess inventory holding costs
Poor yields	Capital waste
Expensive disposition	Social and environmental costs
Vendor rejects	Safety and reliability risks
Excess purchasing expense	

human resources has serious implications for our environment as well because it results in entropy. Entropy is the process of using resources in such a way that their previous natural mass is nonrecoverable; when a tree is cut down, it cannot be replanted, nor can burnt wood be recovered for other uses. In recent years, society has become more aware of the amount of damage being done to the environment. Jeremy Rifkin, a writer and lecturer concerned with environmental issues, writes, "Our lives are bound up in constant repair. We are forever mending and patching. Our leaders are forever lamenting and apologizing."[13] The message is that everyone would benefit from less mending and repairing. Doing it right the first time conserves resources and human effort. Exhibit 18-1 lists the costs of poor quality and poor productivity.

CHECKPOINT

- Discuss quality from a consumer's perspective.
- Explain how quality and productivity are related.
- Identify and discuss costs associated with poor quality.

CONTROLLING FOR QUALITY AND PRODUCTIVITY

The quality-productivity connection provides a framework for examining techniques of control in greater detail. Effective quality control systems monitor operations at many different stages. They provide vigilance in purchasing, influence product design, signal needed changes in manufacturing processes, reveal gaps in human resource skills, and alert managers to shortcomings in leadership. They can also stimulate managers to study new methods and new technologies that can lead to innovations in both products and services.

Design Controls

Research engineers responsible for new products are concerned with materials, perceived quality required by customers, safety characteristics, and reliability standards. Quality engineers complement designers by helping to coordinate plans with design application and monitoring progress toward new-product development. For example, at Data General, project leaders for new computer hardware and software designs are responsible for all phases of engineering, from initiation of designs to market introduction.

The integration extends to marketing research specialists, who provide the connection between customer needs and production. Thus companies develop new-

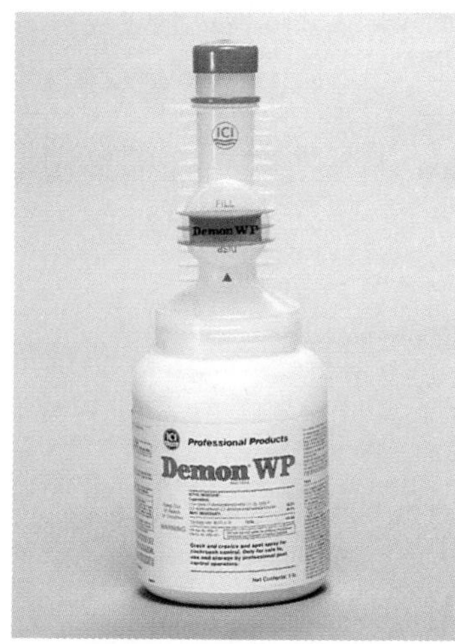

Integration of engineering responsibilities is now used by large companies, such as GM, IBM, 3M, and Apple. These companies have discovered that they can develop new projects faster and more successfully by including people from other disciplines on their design team. Smaller companies are learning the same lesson. For example, when ICI Americas, Inc., wanted a new dispenser of roach insecticide, designer Peter Bressler requested that a team be assembled from various ICI Americas' departments, including purchasing, materials, quality assurance, and marketing. Explains Bressler, "We insisted on getting everyone involved in the process together very early. We didn't want to design something, then throw it over the wall to the engineering and supply departments, only to find out later that they couldn't make it." The result: ICI's user-friendly Demon Dispenser.

product designs by harmonizing marketing and engineering expertise. A total quality control concept evolves in which a wide range of personnel who are empowered with decision-making responsibilities in design, production, and marketing cooperate to influence product development.

Product and life cycle analysis. This kind of control requires market analysis, a competitive (or industry) analysis, forecasting, and customer evaluation. The product must be assessed for image, reliability, functionality, appearance, serviceability, and operational cost to consumers. R&D engineers will have one part of this responsibility; market researchers another; and perhaps specialists such as psychologists yet another. If a team approach to control is taken, small groups of these experts will be empowered to monitor products and services and recommend appropriate changes to extend their life cycles.

Materials control and purchasing. Characteristics of materials to be used in manufacturing must be studied, their availability must be assured, and the reliability of suppliers under consideration as primary sources for materials must be evaluated. Adequate materials of the right kind and price must be available for production. Quality material control also encompasses systems for handling materials before, during, and after production.

Production control. Well-designed, cost-effective products may never get off the ground because of production limitations. Designers come up with exceptional new ideas all the time that a firm simply is not equipped to produce. Therefore, production control managers and shop-floor engineers must be brought into the design process to ensure that the firm is working on feasible projects.

Special needs. There are many special considerations that affect product design. For example, new products may require changes in market distribution systems. Some may need special handling because they contain sensitive materials. Materials used in production may be subject to legal constraints such as EPA regulations. Unusual equipment may have to be purchased. Labor union constraints may prevail, or additional capital may be required. A total commitment to quality requires that these and other issues that affect products, design characteristics, and methods of manufacture be resolved early in the design stage.

Product Controls

Historically, the notion of quality control was identified with control and inspection of the physical product, but this is only a small part of the picture. Product control for quality requires in-plant controls from the point of purchase to end-use field controls related to customer service. Note that there is a difference between product control and production control. **Product control** is concerned with reducing costs associated with poor quality and unreliable products, whereas **production control** is concerned with controlling the manufacturing process. The following discussion focuses on product controls.

product control
Product control is concerned with reducing costs associated with poor quality and unreliable products.

production control
Production control is concerned with controlling the manufacturing process.

Inspection and testing. Companies evaluate products at strategic points during manufacture to determine whether work and materials conform to standards. Inspection and testing require specialized skills for spotting problems and directing corrective action. Most U.S. firms train a select cadre of inspectors to perform these tests and make inspections, which include:[14]

- *Acceptance sampling.* Inspections may occur on receipt of raw materials, at critical points when subassemblies are completed, during manufacture after important processes, and prior to shipment when products are finally completed. Sampling data are used to make cost-effective evaluations on larger numbers of items, to accept or reject entire batch runs called *lots.*

- *Detailed inspections and tests.* These are performed on every finished product to sort out substandard items or identify inadequate processes. In some instances, close surveillance and careful testing methods are used because there is no room for error. Medicine is a good example.
- *Control sampling.* Periodic tests are done to detect significant variations in production processes or workmanship. Control charts are often used to compare performance deviations, but added control samples may detect early problems with machines, worn tools, bad parts, poor work flow, or personnel problems.
- *Quality rating inspections.* These procedures are used to classify processes or products with differences in quality. For example, eggs can be graded into several classifications according to size and color; oranges are also sorted for several characteristics. In lumber production, one processed tree yields a small proportion of high-grade wood useful in furniture manufacturing, medium-grade wood used in construction, and by-products for plywood fill or pulp.
- *Qualification testing.* Products are tested for performance to determine reliability criteria and safety features. Testing is also done to rate product capabilities. This occasionally takes the form of destructive tests, such as crashing cars to study accident characteristics. Drugs are tested in laboratories and clothing samples are tested for flame resistance.
- *Accuracy inspections.* Comparative tests by inspectors or instruments are only as accurate as the testers of their equipment. Therefore, inspectors and instruments must be periodically evaluated. For example, calibration equipment is used to evaluate and correct deviations in test instruments. Inspectors are evaluated in laboratory settings to sharpen their skills.

Sensory evaluations. Quality cannot always be determined by technical standards and test results. Intangible characteristics of products or services may influence perceptions about quality.[15] Consumers judge the quality of many products according to color, image, smell, taste, and other sensory perceptions. Controlling quality in terms of sensory criteria is subjective and difficult. Sometimes this is done with simple sensory tests during production, such as taste tests by panels of experts or visual judgment evaluations. Other times comparison reviews are needed. These use preferred samples—such as swatches of fabrics with high-quality designs as the standard against which samples from production are judged.

In one type of sensory evaluation, market researchers employed by coffee manufacturers designed tests, surveys, or experiments to document what consumers want or expect from their coffee. They learned that coffee drinkers value aroma, taste, color, caffeine content, ability to reheat, consistency, and labels like "Colombian" and "mountain grown." Consumers were also influenced by packaging, container shapes, and perceptual factors, such as the notion that "fresh ground" is better than instant coffee. Since many of these perceptions were created in consumer minds by market promotions, the researchers were actually monitoring the effects of their company's promotional strategies.

Sensitivity analysis. Beyond field investigations and experiments, analysts must monitor subtle changes in consumer preferences. For example, coffee tests continue long after the product is established to detect consumer shifts toward low-caffeine blends, relative changes in preferences for instant blends or certain types of grinds—anything that might signal a major change in product needs. The introduction of automatic coffee makers, for instance, created a buying surge in drip and automatic coffee-maker blends.

Competitors' quality. Market analysts, engineers, and a host of other managers monitor the quality standards within an industry to assess subtle differences in competitors' products and services. It is not uncommon for a company to buy competitive products and then perform rigorous inspections and tests to compare them with the company's own products. Technical products such as microcomputers, earth movers, and machine tools are often "backward engineered" to assess competing products—and to learn how to make them. Backward engineering consists of tearing down a product to its last bolt, then documenting its restructuring.

Service and Use Controls

Service to customers does not end with a sale. After-sale service is a crucial part of quality management. If product quality is poor, or if something goes wrong with delivery and installation, the added costs to cover repairs and warranties can be huge. Quality costs of repair and replacement across ten major U.S. manufacturing sectors averaged about 5.8 percent of total sales revenues during the 1970s. Warranty costs in U.S. durable manufacturing averaged nearly 6 percent of sales annually during the early 1980s. This record is improving, but only slowly. J. M. Juran, one of the gurus of industrial quality training, estimates that the costs of poor quality attributed to customer complaints, product liability lawsuits, redoing defective work, and products scrapped exceeds 20 percent of sales.[16] These costs rival or surpass the average profitability in many industries.

Controls on service and use extend from monitoring customer support to feedback on warranties for production and design changes. Few of these activities are the responsibility of shop-floor manufacturing; marketing managers and customer service field representatives usually supervise quality control for after-sale service. As part of the TQM process, marketing and customer service staff play leading roles not only in gathering data after sales but also in determining what is required by customers before products or services are planned. When this part of the process fails, results can be disastrous. Research shows, for example, that nearly 35 percent of all customer returns can be attributed to marketing service errors, another 10 percent to shipping and installation errors, and about 5 percent to improper use by customers. That represents approximately half of all warranty claims. Consequently, a company could manufacture a perfect product, but lose as much as half its sales through warranty problems connected to customer service and sales.[17]

Interplak, a division of Bausch & Lomb that manufactures expensive dental instruments, improved sales from $5 million to $120 million between 1985 and 1990. The company's success is attributed to its strong after-sale service and follow-up program whereby every regional sales office is expected to interview 98 percent of dentists—those who buy Interplak as well as those who do not—to evaluate product reliability and consumer requirements. Consequently, Interplak has identified new products and introduced new methods of improving oral hygiene to both dentists and home markets. Stanley Works, the 140-year-old Connecticut company reputed for its quality tools and hardware, found itself losing business to cheap overseas manufacturers in 1982. Stanley launched a major TQM effort with marketing and customer impact teams who gathered information about product design and customer needs through focus groups, field testing, and cooperation with retailers. By 1991, Stanley had regained its competitive position through fully guaranteed quality tools.[18]

Figure 18-3 illustrates the relationship of quality to service and use controls. Several important issues that managers must consider are:[19]

- *Packaging and delivery controls.* These ensure customer satisfaction, safety, and service. Package design is important not only for product image but also for protection against hazards such as tampering, moisture, spoilage, and theft.

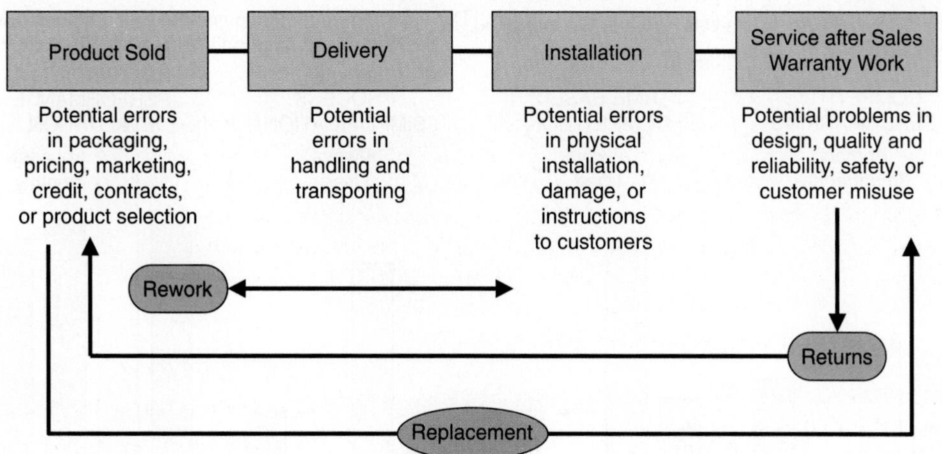

FIGURE 18-3 Service and Use Controls

Package designs must also provide accurate and useful information to customers through responsible labeling. Improper labeling, such as claiming that a product is "fat free" when it isn't or writing confusing instructions in fine print, have led to major lawsuits and recent government investigations of companies in pharmaceuticals and food processing. The average cost of packaging and handling durable goods in U.S. manufacturing is about 22 percent of total costs, and the legal costs associated with mislabeling and improper packaging are estimated as between 7 and 9 percent of total costs.[20]

- *Transportation and storage costs.* To determine the best methods of shipment with the least damage to goods, packing and handling techniques are tested and alternative modes of transportation are evaluated. Storage facilities are evaluated for safety and capacity, and customer facilities are checked because most customers have limited handling equipment.
- *Installation service controls.* Quality control of installation is critical in reducing customer misuse. Many customers associate product quality with quality installation and after-sale service, expecting companies not only to honor warranties but also to provide continuing service.

Contrasting Approaches to Controlling Quality

The attention given to managing quality is a sensitive issue because comparisons between international competitors are inevitable. Politicians in the United States focus on how we are doing (or where we are lacking) in productivity compared to the Japanese, and when the economy is sagging or unemployment persists, debates over U.S. competitiveness can become extremely heated. Productivity in the United States, in absolute terms of labor efficiency, is the best among all industrialized nations. That is to say, more products are made with fewer labor-hours in the United States than in any other country as measured by dollar-value costs. However, that measure does not take into account relatively higher costs in the United States resulting from warranty service, defectives, and customer returns. These combine to lower productivity, and raise prices, which gives many Japanese companies a competitive edge. Consequently, the heart of the controversy is whether the United States can compete on quality standards to regain its global leadership.[21]

There are five primary criteria that provide cross-cultural comparisons of quality management. These criteria are shown in Figure 18-4, and represent categories in which many specific methods are used for quality control. We have introduced several of these methods in this section and will describe more as we progress through the chapter. From a management perspective, the five criteria provide measurable

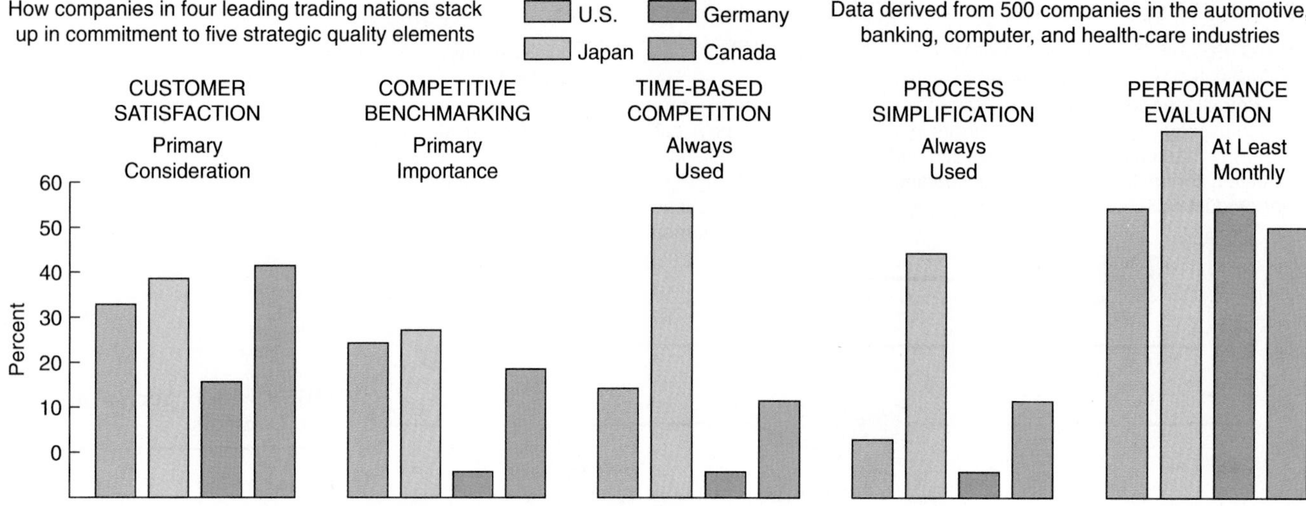

FIGURE 18-4 Comparing Quality Cultures

Source: Data courtesy Ernst & Young, American Quality Foundation. Reprinted from the October 25, 1991 issue of *Business Week* by special permission. Copyright © 1991 by McGraw-Hill, Inc.

comparisons, and as the figure illustrates, there are several glaring differences between Japan, Canada, Germany, and the United States.[22]

Customer satisfaction. Canadian companies emphasize customer satisfaction more than companies from the other nations, although Japan also has a very good record in this category. This result would not surprise Canadian consumers, who expect, and get, excellent service from retailers, wholesalers, and primary manufacturers. The level of support for warranties is outstanding. The United States, although better than Germany in this category, lags behind both Canada and Japan. If the data used here were broken down for the various industries—automobiles, banking, computers, and health care—the U.S. profile would be far worse in automobiles and health care, where fewer than 10 percent of consumers are satisfied; but the best in computers by a very large margin.

Competitive benchmarking. Benchmarking was described in Chapter 17 as an important method of controlling performance by comparing organizational results against those of another company with the best record on any operational criterion or activity, ranging from job training to scientific research and development. German companies tend to ignore benchmarking with other companies (or other nations), but Japanese companies have a strong reputation for studying their competitors. Many Japanese firms have used benchmarking to outrace their competitors and "set the cadence," thus becoming benchmark targets themselves. U.S. and Canadian firms, although lagging in this category, have embraced the concept of formal benchmarking and are rapidly gaining ground on their international competitors.

Time-based competition. The concept of compressing the time it takes to complete an operations cycle is only beginning to gain attention outside of Japan (the clear leader in this category). Time-based competition means creating an efficient production or service cycle measured from the time a customer order is received until it is filled (product delivered or service completed). Those companies that can "deliver the goods" quicker will be more cost effective and enjoy a much better relationship with their customers. As we shall see later in the chapter, time-based control objectives are becoming important strategic considerations in Western firms.

Process simplification. Once again, Japan excels, and Canada does very well, while the United States and Germany struggle with transforming work processes. As noted in the opening scenario, Compaq Computer has high-quality production standards, in part due to "cellular" manufacturing systems and efficient management of materials, but the company also has autonomous work teams with well-trained employees who are extremely efficient. These are several of the components of a simplified process that results in high quality and efficient operations.

Performance evaluation. All four countries strongly emphasize performance evaluation systems. This is the traditional approach to quality control whereby products, services, and individual employees are monitored, tested, observed, and rated for results. Nevertheless, Japanese companies do better than their counterparts in other countries. The United States would rank higher on this scale if we were to exclude health care, where performance evaluation is suspect.

The comparison of these four countries illustrates why the Japanese have such a strong quality profile, but it also shows that an individual company must do more than focus on one or two isolated criteria to compete effectively. If a company concentrates on traditional performance evaluation measures, it may enjoy only incremental improvements. Having a good grasp of performance evaluation is necessary, but not sufficient, to establish a total quality management system.

CHECKPOINT

- Describe how design controls are used to improve product reliability.
- Contrast different types of inspections used in product control.
- Why are service and use controls important to TQM?
- How do quality cultures differ in the four countries profiled?

PRODUCTION AND OPERATIONS CONTROL

Concerns about quality and productivity are most commonly associated with the manufacturing process. The term *production control* is used in manufacturing to refer to the management of the actual shop-floor conversion process. We emphasize *operations control* as well because the responsibilities and many of the procedures used in a production environment are quite similar to those used in service organizations. In hospitals, banks, merchandise retailers, and research firms, there are many complicated activities, and most require careful sequential scheduling. Most of the quality controls described in the previous section for production also apply to services, such as controlling Citicorp's banking transactions or United Airline's passenger services.

Scheduling and Gantt Charts

A widely used scheduling technique is the *Gantt Chart,* named for its inventor H. L. Gantt (see Chapter 2). Around 1910, he developed a graphic progress chart depicting sequential tasks that has since become a standard in many industries. Figure 18-5 illustrates a Gantt Chart used in making beveled mirrors. It begins with initial operations such as moving stock glass from inventory and ends with loading trucks for shipment. A similar pattern, using different terms, could be used to trace the steps in preparing for an airline flight or scheduling an auditor's activities for a public accounting firm.

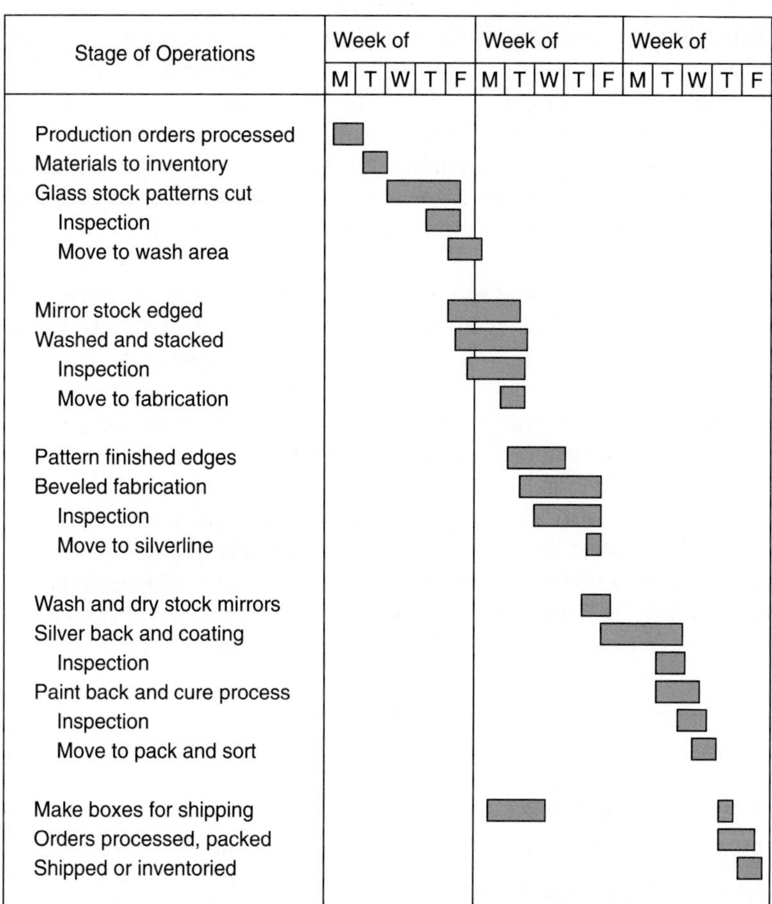

FIGURE 18-5 Gantt Chart Used for Producing Beveled Mirrors

Gantt Charts are inexpensive and require little expertise to use, but they are limited as control devices. Performance variations can be visualized on the charts, but reasons for variations are not distinguished. Costs are seldom tracked by physical flow measurements, nor do charts clearly identify quality problems. Nevertheless, Gantt Charts are used by organizations of every size because of their simplicity, and they can be designed on computer spreadsheets or used with complex data bases for rather sophisticated operational sequencing.

Network Scheduling: PERT and CPM

program evaluation and review technique (PERT) A network model that identifies sequential events necessary to complete a project while defining activities that individually lead to the next event.

critical path method (CPM) A network scheduling technique for planning and controlling operations (usually projects) based on critical time increments to complete defined tasks.

Network scheduling is the name given to techniques of time-phased models that trace sequential operations. Two of the most noteworthy scheduling models are **program evaluation and review technique (PERT)** and **critical path method (CPM).** PERT breaks down complex projects into sequential operations called *activities*, which occur within *events,* which, in turn, define completed steps within projects. Both models allow managers to trace a *critical path,* which is the longest and most pessimistic route to complete a project.

PERT resulted from research by the U.S. Navy, Booz-Allen and Hamilton Company, and Lockheed Aircraft Company in 1957 to develop a control system for engineering the Polaris Missile Project. CPM was developed by Du Pont Company in 1959 for improving engineering controls, specifically for very large industrial projects requiring many months or several years to complete.[23]

PERT and CPM are used in similar circumstances to control projects or production systems where unique aspects of operations can be sequentially identified. Each operation, or event, has a definite beginning and end, but no specified time for completion. However, each set of activities within an event has forecasted completion times. Managers can therefore identify events, track the time required to complete all the activities within each event, and use graphs charting activities to monitor project performance.

Network systems such as PERT and CPM trace various paths along which project events take place. The most direct path is the most optimistic forecast of completing a project in the shortest time possible without deviations. The least direct route—the critical path—is the most pessimistic, and it indicates to management the outer boundary for completing a project. The model also provides managers with alternatives that, if taken, must be evaluated. In this way, managers control a project's progress and stay alert to performance deviations. Figure 18-6 illustrates a simple CPM model.

Network models are used generally for complex and nonrepetitive projects. Examples are building a highway or developing a new missile system. The two models, however, have been used quite effectively in design research, maintenance scheduling, and job-shop production systems by companies such as Chrysler, Hughes Aircraft, Lockheed, Tandem Computers, and Boeing Company. PERT and CPM typically require customized computer programs and expert planning based on accurate information. Consequently, most applications are found in large companies involved in complicated projects, yet construction companies use CPM models to delineate sequential operations and to identify time-phased activities by subcontractors for electrical wiring, plumbing, window installation, roofing, and interior finish work. A modified form of PERT is used by Price Waterhouse to sequence field activities by consulting teams.[24]

In-Process Operational Controls

The two network systems provide planning for operational activities and controls for complex sequencing, but in most production systems, the critical control points occur during the conversion process. Companies like Kodak have as many as fifty oper-

FIGURE 18-6 Simplified CPM Network for Constructing a House

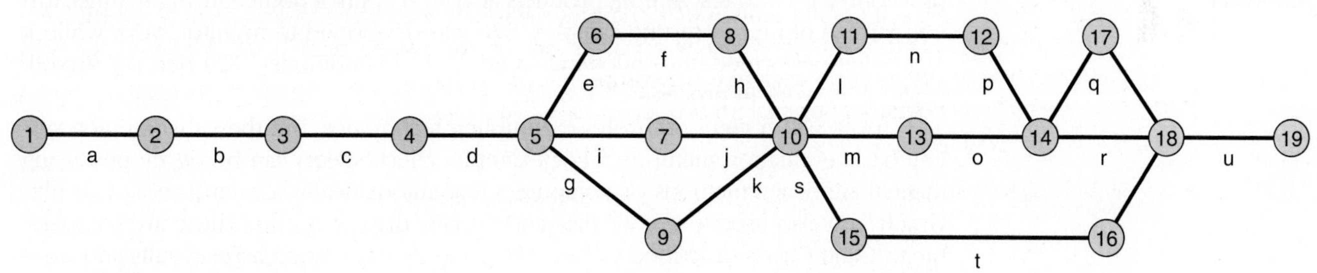

CPM = 75 Days

Activity	Time (days)	Prior Activity
a. Permits and surveys obtained	14	none
b. Grade land and compact soil	2	a
c. Foundations set and cured	7	b
d. Construction framing completed	16	c
e. Chimney and vents roughed in	2	d
f. Roof subcontracted, installed	4	e
g. Plumbing subcontracted, roughed in	5	d
h. Electrical subcontracted, roughed in	5	f
i. Furnace and air conditioning installed	2	h
j. Insulate and complete subfloors	3	g, h, i
k. Exterior bricked	6	g, h, i

Activity	Time (days)	Prior Activity
l. Windows and doors installed	3	k
m. Drywall and interior paneling	8	l
n. Kitchen cabinetry and rest rooms complete	4	m
o. Undercoat sealing and painting	3	m
p. Finished carpentry and trim	12	o
q. Finish plumbing and appliances	3	n
r. Finish electrical and fixtures	4	o, p, q
s. Exterior concrete walks and drive	2	k
t. Landscape subcontracted	4	s
u. Clean and present for inspection	2	r

ational activities required for manufacturing a camera, but once defined, the process is relatively stable. The challenge is to be able to monitor quality of work and status of activities at each control point to minimize in-process defects or errant performance. This is accomplished in three ways: by using *statistical quality controls, statistical process controls,* and *cellular systems.*

statistical quality control (SQC)
A method of analyzing deviations in manufactured materials, parts, and products.

Statistical quality control (SQC). The objective of monitoring work during the operational process is to discover performance problems quickly and then to correct them or halt operations. **Statistical quality control (SQC)** is a method of analyzing deviations in manufactured materials, parts, and products, thus ensuring the highest-quality results while minimizing costs. As noted in the previous section, these costs include scrap due to defective work or materials, rework to correct errors, disposition of rejects, idled labor due to scheduling delays, and warranty costs or lost customers.

SQC utilizes information derived from in-process monitoring systems to calculate critical measurements. For example, heat sensors linked to computers and installed on Ford Motor Company's automobile assembly lines scan weld joints on auto bodies. This procedure registers thousands of bits of data on weld temperatures and metal "hot spots" that can cause weak joints. SQC programs display these data in graphic distributions, perform statistical calculations to identify welds that could be weak, and then generate instantaneous reports on potential defects. SQC uses probability data, distributions, and mathematical measures of deviations (e.g., standard deviations and analyses of variance) that compare results against specifications. If the deviations are unacceptable, SQC will run further analyses, then "flag" the problem on the operator's computer terminal or, in extreme cases, activate an alarm to prompt management to take immediate corrective action.[25]

statistical process control (SPC)
A method of collecting information and analyzing results during operations to improve quality and in-process performance.

Statistical process control (SPC). As a monitoring system, **statistical process control (SPC)** is a method of collecting information and analyzing results during operations. SPC does not necessarily use complex statistical techniques, and when sophisticated calculations are used, it is common to refer to the monitoring system as an *SPC/SQC system.* Initially, SPC was simply an extension of standard inspection procedures used to test sample products at critical control points during manufacturing. Instead of merely testing samples, SPC was developed to monitor work while it was being performed, thus allowing—under ideal conditions—100 percent surveillance of all work-in-process.

Most SPC systems still rely on sampling techniques, but they also employ several basic evaluation methods.[26] For example, check sheets can be developed using manual clipboard methods or computers that automatically scan and record results. Graphs are also used to record data and visually display results. These are comparable to Gantt Charts described earlier. SPC control charts summarize results and compare them to performance standards, using various methods ranging from simple numerical counting (e.g., number of units produced per hour compared to number of units scheduled) to statistical comparisons (e.g., analysis of variance for actual versus specified work tolerances). More complicated methods of evaluation use histograms, cause-and-effect diagrams, and Pareto charts. *Histograms* are visual displays of distributions and summarize statistics such as means, deviations, and variances. *Cause-and-effect diagrams* record results and use established data to calculate probabilities for likely causes of performance deviations. *Pareto charts* rank problems or defects according to their frequency of occurrence, thereby emphasizing patterns of deviation.

SPC can be implemented in even the smallest organization with inexpensive technology and a little imagination. For example, Burke Industries, a company in California that manufactures roofing materials, uses a video camera linked to a microcomputer to scan rolls of material for flaws.[27] As the material comes out of a heat bonding process, the camera sends to the computer pictures that are translated

MANAGEMENT APPLICATION

SPC at Crown Cork and Seal Company

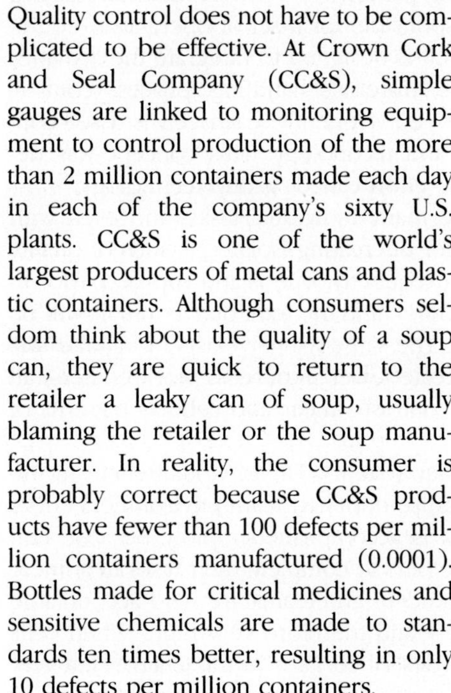

Quality control does not have to be complicated to be effective. At Crown Cork and Seal Company (CC&S), simple gauges are linked to monitoring equipment to control production of the more than 2 million containers made each day in each of the company's sixty U.S. plants. CC&S is one of the world's largest producers of metal cans and plastic containers. Although consumers seldom think about the quality of a soup can, they are quick to return to the retailer a leaky can of soup, usually blaming the retailer or the soup manufacturer. In reality, the consumer is probably correct because CC&S products have fewer than 100 defects per million containers manufactured (0.0001). Bottles made for critical medicines and sensitive chemicals are made to standards ten times better, resulting in only 10 defects per million containers.

Can cylinders are formed in a press, stamped with stress rings and ridges that make them very strong, then seamed. End pieces (can bottoms and tops) are stamped out on presses, ridged for strength, and edged in such a way that they can be crimped to the cylinder to form the can. These parts are treated in various ways, and cans are shipped to customers with their bottoms attached (tops are attached after the cans are filled).

The company must provide high-quality cans to ensure proper sealing and product safety (e.g., soup can lids that fit tightly and can withstand the extreme heating and cooling processes used in food processing). Consequently, CC&S requires cylinders and end parts to meet specifications to within 1/10,000th of an inch. This is accomplished in some plants with mechanical gauges that measure critical dimensions of parts as they complete each activity in the manufacturing process. In other plants, electronic gauges scan parts with electrical impulses, sending the information to a computer for instant analysis. The company is experimenting with lasers for use with extremely critical production, allowing measurements to specifications as close as 1/100,000th of an inch.

The company's SPC monitoring system is now able to monitor standards better than production machinery can make the parts. Now CC&S management feels it can meet any customer's standards with room to spare. But the company's rigorous standards and its use of SPC pay dividends in other ways. Prior to installation of the monitoring systems, inspection of can parts was accomplished manually, and it was only possible to test small samples. This took more than an hour for each production run on each shift, and because the company was testing only samples, more defective products escaped detection, eventually resulting in high scrap costs and large numbers of products returned by customers. After SPC was installed, the time required to analyze production runs fell to four minutes and continuous monitoring of all parts became possible. Consequently, simple and inexpensive systems have saved the company huge sums of money and have increased quality control productivity by nearly 600 percent.

Sources: Kevin Parker, "Better Ends by SPC Means," *Manufacturing Systems,* March 1992, pp. 28–32. See also "Interferometer Gives CNC Machines Laser Precision," *Quality*, March 1992, p. 51.

into surface patterns. These are continuously compared against a specified pattern stored in the computer memory. When a defect is noted, the computer activates a buzzer alarm. It is also linked to a simple mechanical "tape thrower," a machine that shoots a piece of gummed red tape onto the material at the defect point. A machine operator then stops the line long enough to identify the flaw and cut away the defective portion. The entire system was implemented at a cost of $20,000, and it saved the company $70,000 in its first year of operation by efficiently identifying defective materials and reducing scrap.

manufacturing cell
An integrated process of related activities based on group technology that includes individuals or autonomous work teams responsible for a set of operations, equipment utilization, and product quality.

Cellular systems. Unlike SPC and SQC, which are systems based on technology, cellular systems are based on organizing patterns of work. A **manufacturing cell** consists of autonomous work teams responsible for a set of operations, equipment utilization, and product quality. Each cell is designed to integrate the activities of machine setup, production, maintenance, materials handling, process control, quality control, and personnel assignments.[28] Consequently, each cell is a self-contained system that brings together people and technology. This concept was described in Chapter 11 as a team development effort called "group technology."

In traditional, linear systems, there are many individual tasks, and even with excellent in-process controls, there is a danger of creating isolated islands of quality rather than an integrated quality system. Consequently, one island can be performing extremely well while another is doing poorly, and the total quality result will be no better than the weakest link in the chain. The same danger exists in cellular systems, but the concept of using cells is to create fewer in-process work centers, all with *independent* operations.[29] Figure 18-7 contrasts linear and cellular patterns of operation.

There are many benefits to using cellular systems. The obvious benefit in human relations is a motivated work force because enriched team environments have replaced repetitive and isolated tasks. Work is accomplished rapidly because employees are not standing around waiting for others to complete their tasks in a linear sequential system. Because work is interdependent and teams are held accountable for results (not activities), quality is a priority and therefore very high. When cells are used in conjunction with MRP II or JIT (described later in this chapter), a very high quality, rapid-response system is created.

Companies that have organized production using cells include the highly productive GM Truck and Bus division, Hewlett-Packard, Compaq, Xerox, Allen-Bradley, GE Fanuc, and Eastman Kodak. American Express Travel is one of many service organizations that use cell clusters focused on "groups" of integrated activities.[30] In each instance, customer service has been improved and the cycle time to produce (or to perform services) has been sharply reduced. For example, BASF Corporation can now respond to customer orders with delivered products in as few as three days instead of the nearly four weeks it took before the company implemented production cells.[31]

Production and operations control is a complicated discipline that involves organizing work, utilizing new technologies, creating systems of accountability, and coordinating operational activities. However, it is not an isolated discipline that exists apart from other functional activities such as marketing, purchasing, and financing. As we shall see in the following sections, manufacturing and service organizations are moving toward comprehensive integrated systems.

CHECKPOINT

- How are Gantt Charts, PERT, and CPM used to schedule and control operations?
- Describe SQC and SPC, and explain how they are used together to improve quality and productivity.
- What is the concept of organizing using manufacturing cells, and how does a cellular system benefit a company?

Linear Operations

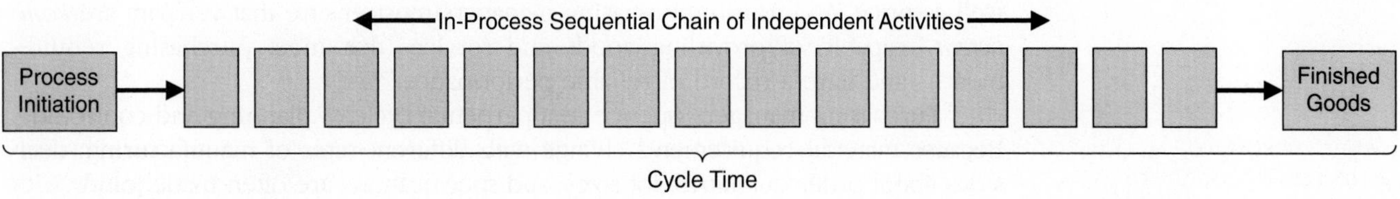

Cellular Operations

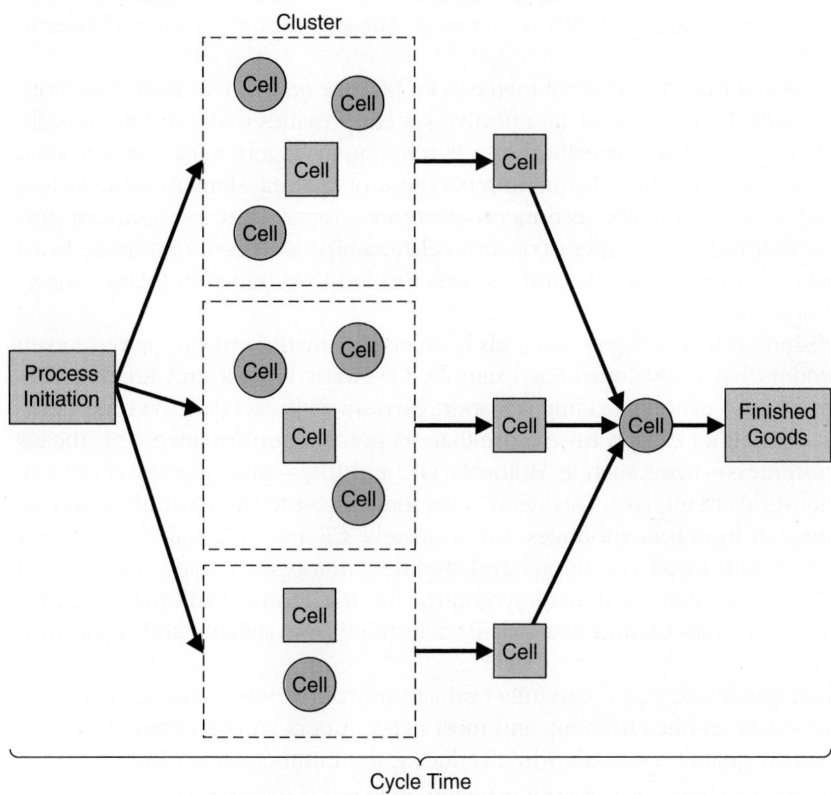

FIGURE 18-7 Linear and Cellular Patterns of Operation

MATERIALS CONTROL

Quality and productivity depend on adroit purchasing, including diligent vendor analysis coupled with careful inventory control. As we mentioned in Chapter 17, costs associated with purchasing and materials control often approach 50 percent of total costs, and controllable costs in manufacturing range up to 64 percent in some industries. Therefore, a marginal change in material cost can significantly alter profits.

Purchasing

Purchasing is the acquisition of needed goods and services at optimal costs from competent, reliable sources.[32] Note the four components of this definition. First, goods and services must be purchased in the correct *quantities* needed in production. Second, they must be ordered at the correct *time* to meet operational require-

purchasing
The acquisition of needed goods and services at optimal costs from competent, reliable sources.

ments. Third, they must be purchased at *optimal cost,* a component that includes quality, terms of purchase, and associated services such as conditions for delivery as well as price. And fourth, purchasing managers must ensure that vendors are *competent*—capable of providing goods and services that meet purchasing requirements—and have a record of reliable performance.[33]

Purchasing managers operate in a perpetual cycle of planning and controlling. Because material requirements change with different rates of manufacturing, decisions about order quantities, lot sizes, and specifications are often made jointly with engineering and production managers. Several systems have evolved to help managers make these decisions. In the United States, statistical decision models based on economic order quantity (EOQ) prevail, though a more advanced system called material requirements planning (MRP) is common. These topics are explored later in this chapter.

Conventional materials control methods emphasize *quantity* of materials more often than *quality.* In this context, an effective system provides necessary items without excesses, on time, and to specifications. Purchasing managers must take into consideration a number of critical factors to meet these objectives. Many of these factors are discussed in the next major section, on inventory control. Here we note that purchasing responsibilities most often concern relationships with *vendors,* those firms that sell parts, supplies, materials, and services needed in production, plant maintenance, and operations.

Establishing reliable supply channels is crucial for manufacturers because even the best vendors have problems. For example, CF Motor Freight and Roadway Express are two of the nation's leading transport carriers with excellent on-time delivery records, yet neither can promise more than 95 percent performance. This means that their customers—firms such as Motorola, GE, and IBM—must plan on 5 percent of freight deliveries being late. This delay represents a cost to the customers and often the danger of inventory shortages. Unfortunately, CF and Roadway drivers must contend with erratic road conditions and weather, unforeseen traffic delays, and many other problems that are difficult to control. Their customers still make a determined effort to evaluate CF and Roadway to determine how reliable and responsive they are.[34]

Purchasing managers also carefully evaluate primary vendors that supply parts, materials, or subassemblies to them, and most major American corporations are imposing very high quality standards while reducing the number of vendors they deal with. Xerox, for example, has rewritten quality material standards to reduce defective parts by 90 percent. Consequently, many vendors unable to meet quality specifications have lost their contracts with Xerox. The number of vendors with Xerox contracts in 1991 was approximately 500; five years earlier, Xerox dealt with nearly 5,000 vendors. Digital Equipment trimmed its vendors from 9,000 to 3,000, and Texas Instruments dumped 8,000 vendors in three years, reducing their suppliers to 14,000 companies.[35]

Most purchasing managers are plagued by daily problems of unusable materials, shortages, unpredictable prices, and defective parts or assemblies that disrupt company operations. During the past six to ten years, leading U.S. companies have implemented rigorous *vendor quality surveys* to systematically rate suppliers before negotiating purchase contracts. Exhibit 18-2 lists the more common considerations in a quality survey.

Specific survey questions relate to the vendor's handling of equipment, maintenance record, production methods, and quality control procedures. It is not unusual for a purchasing company to send an expert team to investigate a vendor's work methods, labor relations, manufacturing technology, service support systems, and human relations practices. These on-site visits coupled with survey data provide purchasing managers with very thorough profiles of their vendors, but this is an expensive process. Those companies with limited budgets or less-rigorous requirements for vendors still should take into account four important considerations. These are:[36]

EXHIBIT 18-2 Vendor Quality Survey Considerations

Management: Policies for quality control, leadership philosophy, structure of organization, commitment to quality, and indoctrination of employees.

Quality control: Quality planning (materials, inventory, work-in-process, finished goods, packing and shipping, usage, field service), quality roles for staff engineers and line managers, and roles for employees.

Quality coordination: Organization, order analysis, subcontractor controls, quality cost analysis, corrective action, in-plant coordination, and nonconformance disposition.

Design controls: Reliability factors, caliber of product specifications, systems in use, engineering controls, and development techniques.

Manufacture controls: Physical facilities, maintenance, production capacity, process capability, caliber of planning, product identification, special processes, and traceability.

Purchasing: Procedures, specifications, vendor relations, cost analysis, materials coordination, and management support.

Inspection and test: Measurement controls, instruments, laboratories, special tests, and calibration processes.

Information systems: Facilities, procedures, effective use of reports, and data resources coordination.

Personnel: Motivation for quality, orientation procedures, performance controls, training provided, skills, and stability of labor relations.

Quality results: Performance factors attained (on-time records, defective materials records, back orders to customers, price and cost records, lead times and stability), self-use of product, prestigious customers, stability of subcontractors, and value analysis.

Source: Adapted with permission from J. M. Juran and Frank M. Gryna, Jr. *Quality Planning and Analysis,* 2nd ed. (New York: McGraw-Hill, 1980), pp. 232–233.

- *Price and cost variations.* Competing vendors are compared on changes in material prices, discount policies, order-lot cost variances, and credit policies. Vendor profiles can chart performance for any one vendor as far back as available information allows.
- *Quality differences.* Comparisons of material quality are based on inspection reports, in-process reports on material flaws, and accumulated information from warranty services or controlled sampling techniques.
- *Service characteristics.* Invoice statistics are developed on lead times, delivery rates, full or partial shipments, back-order problems, and other similar issues. Vendors' refund policies for defectives and response to problems in serving purchasing firms may also be evaluated.
- *Product reliability.* Purchased materials or subassemblies may be sampled and subjected to rigorous testing. This is an extension of the traditional inspections of incoming materials. Sophisticated techniques for evaluating product reliability before accepting shipments have begun to emerge.

These are only a few of the many control challenges purchasing managers face. Some others are analyzing efficiency of purchasing activities, questioning chargeback systems for vendor failures, and working with accountants to ensure timely payments that take advantage of price discounts.

CHECKPOINT

- Discuss why purchasing managers must avoid making procurements solely on the basis of low-price criteria.
- Name four problems associated with vendors and discuss why companies should conduct vendor analyses.

INVENTORY CONTROL

inventory control
The management of incoming materials and supplies, work-in-process inventory, and finished products.

Unlike materials management or purchasing, which are activities focused primarily on incoming materials and components, inventory control is concerned with the total flow of physical production from procurement to shipping finished products. **Inventory control** is the process of ensuring adequate stocks of materials and supplies used in production, managing the flow of partially completed products or components called *work-in-process*, and overseeing finished goods ready for market.[37] In the past, these activities were independent; management of incoming materials was the responsibility of purchasing, work-in-process was controlled by production, and finished goods were coordinated through marketing.

Today managing inventory requires integration of the activities concerned with establishing an effective flow of physical materials prior to, during, and after the production process.[38] Therefore, companies need well-conceived systems—often made possible by information technology—for effective inventory control. These systems are based on *economic order quantity (EOQ), materials requirements planning (MRP),* and *just-in-time (JIT)* models. Before we look at these models, we need to be clear about the objectives of inventory management.

Because purchasing inventory is a large expenditure, managers are expected to maintain cost-effective inventory levels. Also because work-in-process and finished goods inventory represent idle cash, managers are expected to create the most efficient flow of physical inventory. Finally, because all inventory requires storage facilities, handling equipment, and employees to maintain and move materials, inventory represents a major capital investment. Thus managers must find ways to minimize inventory expenditures and related overhead costs.

These objectives translate into several focal activities. First, purchasing materials at optimal prices and quantities reduces expenditures. Second, reducing inventory stock levels (ideally, having no idle stock at any point in the system) minimizes costs. And third, having an efficient flow of work reduces overhead and capital investments. In the past, inventory controls were keenly focused on operating costs (material prices, purchasing costs, labor expenses, and overhead associated with inventory handling). Today the TQM philosophy has superimposed a system of *quality objectives* onto the entire process.[39] Consequently, managing for quality first will help managers attain their cost and efficiency objectives.

Economic Order Quantity (EOQ)

economic order quantity (EOQ)
A mathematical model for determining the optimal quantity of materials or inventory to purchase based on inventory usage, carrying costs, and purchasing costs.

Economic order quantity (EOQ) is a formula, used widely in the United States, that minimizes inventory ordering and holding costs. This mathematical relationship has intuitive appeal because it unambiguously specifies the quantity of inventory. When EOQs are calculated, precise orders are placed, accounting is simplified, and inventories can be mathematically defined. Unfortunately, calculating EOQ can be an immense task for firms with thousands of inventory items.[40]

Exhibit 18-3 illustrates an easy-to-use version of the EOQ formula. It provides an optimal quantity needed for ordering materials, but its effectiveness depends on how accurate the data are for four variables: monthly usage, order cost, unit cost, and carrying cost.

- *Monthly usage* is determined from production records and forecasts of quantities of items consumed in the production process. Computer-based systems track inventory and calculate historic use rates, adjusting for patterns of production usage and demand.
- *Order costs* are allocated as an average of total costs associated with purchasing. This method yields an average cost per purchase order that is often too simplistic because orders for various items can substantially differ in complexity and costs of processing information.

EXHIBIT 18-3 Economic Order Quantity (EOQ)

An EOQ formula is used to determine optimal quantity for material purchase orders by evaluating inventory carrying costs in relation to costs accrued in ordering materials. The model assumes a continuous demand at a fixed rate over a given period of time, usually one year.

The general formula is:

$$EOQ = \sqrt{\frac{2 \times \text{Annual usage} \times \text{Order cost}}{\text{Unit cost} \times \text{Carrying cost}}}$$

Using monthly data:

$$EOQ = \sqrt{\frac{24 \times \text{Monthly usage} \times \text{Order cost}}{\text{Unit cost} \times \text{Carrying cost}}}$$

Where

EOQ .... Unique optimal order quantity
Monthly usage .... Number of units issued and used
Order cost .... Fixed average order cost in dollars
Unit cost .... Estimate of unit price in dollars
Carrying cost .... Decimal percentage of inventory value

Example:

Given an item with monthly usage of 200 units, a unit cost of $1, a fixed order cost of $10, and a carrying cost of 25% of inventory value, then:

$$EOQ = \sqrt{\frac{24 \times 200 \times 10}{1.00 \times .25}}$$

$$EOQ = 438 \text{ items}$$

- *Unit costs* are determined from actual prices, but EOQ calculations precede actual orders—often by several months—so unit prices are estimates. If vendors change, prices increase, or higher-priced substitutes are ordered, unit cost information becomes unreliable.
- *Carrying costs* are expressed as a percentage of inventory. This method applies an estimated portion of operating overhead to all inventory. Since inventory levels vary, values for inventory items with different characteristics such as bulk numbers, depreciation, shelf life, spoilage, and security can become complicated.

Limitations and benefits of EOQ. Even if all variables can be exquisitely determined, there are several problems with the EOQ model. It focuses narrowly on optimal order quantity; there is no calculation for quality of materials. It also ignores vendor behavior, on-time delivery performance, and special service considerations such as handling and packaging. In addition, the model requires enhancements to account for price discounting, safety stocks needed, and special handling problems. Perhaps the EOQ model's most serious liability is its lack of accountability for capital and facility costs.

Despite these limitations, companies that have implemented the EOQ model have realized substantial savings and made tremendous improvements in inventory management. The model's mathematics force managers to evaluate use rates, carrying costs, order costs, and commodity prices, and this analysis has led to improved inventory control.

Statistics in Inventory Control

The limitations of the EOQ model have led to more complicated methods of calculating inventory requirements. Statistical inventory methods based on probability models are used to estimate individual variables like use rates and inventory demand such as the likelihood of stockouts. These are only two of many ways statistical procedures greatly enhance management decisions.

ABC inventory system
A formal method for rank-ordering inventory and matching cost-effective controls to items with relatively different values.

ABC inventory controls. The simplest use of probabilities has been in the **ABC inventory system**, which identifies different types of inventory in rank order to achieve cost-effective controls.[41] Because purchasing managers decide on perhaps thousands of items each month, it makes sense to use different methods of inventory control for different types of items. *A items* are typically expensive, difficult to stock, and essential, with few substitutes. Tight control and careful analysis are needed to ensure maintenance of a sufficient inventory of these critical items. *B items* are less important; expensive perhaps, but with ample substitutes or sources of supply. Control is essential, but by using probability models for aggregated *B* materials and doing careful, periodic ordering, managers can contain the inventory costs of these items. *C items* are usually relatively inexpensive, abundant, and easy to stock. Periodic sampling of stock, prices, and use rates is sufficient to maintain adequate inventory controls. When mistakes are made, *C* items can be replenished rapidly at little additional cost. *A* and *B* items warrant greater controls to avoid critical production problems or unusual added costs for procurement.

Safety stock. Probabilities are used to estimate the margin of extra stock needed to avoid stockouts due to variations in use rates, production demand, or delays in vendor deliveries. One of the limitations of employing EOQ is overcome by calculating a safety stock factor for each type of purchase. By utilizing data-base information, a probability program can recognize subtle changes in inventory requirements and provide information for timing orders better or changing their quantity.

Perpetual inventory controls. Perpetual inventory control systems use statistical control techniques to provide continuous accounting of stock items. Purchase orders, receipts, issues, and other transactions affecting stock levels are accumulated to update stock status. Early systems used index card files and manual updating to track each transaction. Now integrated information systems automatically record transactions, providing managers with real-time information. It is even possible to have *paperless purchasing* by linking inventory data-base systems through computers that electronically transmit orders to contracted vendors.

Reorder points. In each of the statistical models, *reorder points* are identified according to a formula that accounts for the type of inventory, the safety stock required, and projected use rates determined through a system such as perpetual inventory control. A reorder point is the critical inventory level that triggers an order. Every inventory control system has a reorder point, but in statistical models, it is predetermined and considered fixed in the short term. In the EOQ model, it is redefined each time EOQ is calculated. In more sophisticated models, such as materials requirements planning (MRP), reorder points depend on intricate production schedules.

Materials Requirements Planning (MRP)

materials requirements planning (MRP)
A computer-integrated process of coordinating master production schedules, purchasing, inventory control, and resource allocation based on projected orders.

Materials requirements planning (MRP) is a production planning and inventory control system that uses forecasts of customer orders to schedule manufacturing and manage materials. MRP incorporates EOQ, perpetual inventory control, and statistics to provide a coordinated system for purchasing materials, scheduling various activities of production, and meeting projected customer orders.[42]

MRP requires two levels of demand forecasting: *independent demand,* which is a projection of actual customer sales, independent of a company's capabilities and its existing inventory; and *dependent demand,* which is the calculation of resources needed to produce the components and parts required to assemble finished goods. Thus dependent demand is an assessment of a company's capabilities that helps managers decide what to produce and what resources are needed to meet scheduled output. Managers use sales forecasts to project future sales, and then assess their company's existing inventory and capabilities to generate internal demand estimates for planned production and resource requirements. In the MRP model, resources include raw materials, supplies, labor, parts, components, and equipment for every stage of production.

An MRP program begins with a master schedule of planned production that uses sales forecasts to determine the quantities of finished goods required in definite time periods. Final demand is translated into sequenced production schedules. MRP explodes the final product into component parts, item by item, and then generates a production schedule for each component. Bills of materials are prepared from schedules with precise projections for procurement. Figure 18-8 illustrates the process.

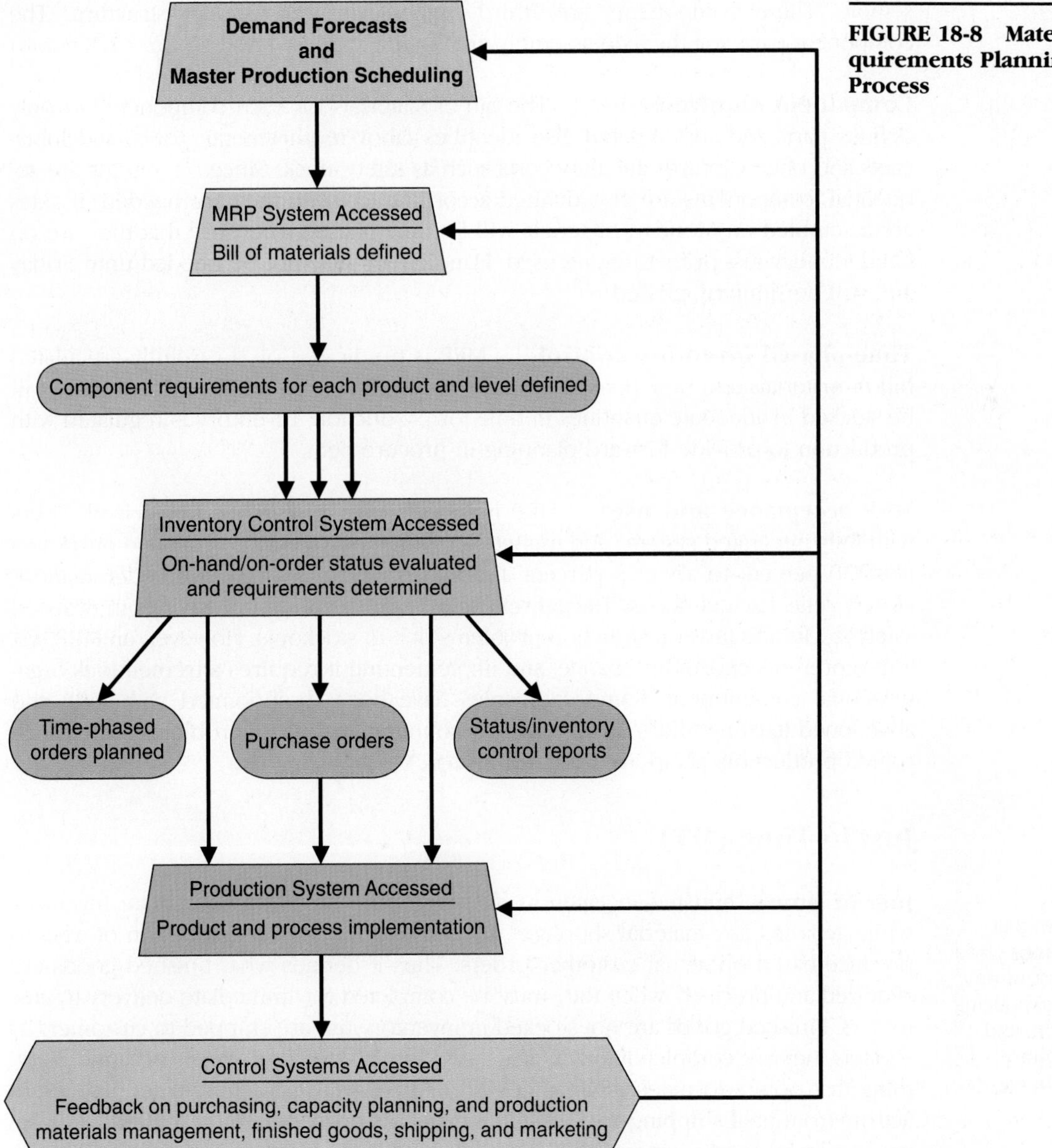

FIGURE 18-8 Materials Requirements Planning (MRP) Process

Master production scheduling. Master schedules are projected for short-term periods, such as several weeks or months, and may be based on forecasts or on actual customer orders. Each schedule is typically segmented into weekly production requirements. If a firm makes bicycles, for example, there may be a weekly output target of 100 "ten-speed, 26-inch, woman's touring models." The finished bicycle is the "major" assembly, called in MRP the *highest level* in the product structure.

Bills of materials. These are developed from major assembly specifications and identify component parts, subassemblies, and supply items required. For example, several hundred items are required to make one bicycle. A bill of materials starts with an "exploded" three-dimensional drawing of a bicycle identifying one frame, two wheel assemblies, one seat, one yoke, one handle bar, and so on. MRP will also identify the total number of each of these components required to meet weekly output targets. Thus an output of 100 bicycles will need 200 wheel assemblies, 100 frames, and 100 gear assemblies. These components needed in final assembly are "second highest" in the product structure and will be exploded into detailed drawings. A wheel assembly ready to bolt to the frame is further refined into its component materials: a tire, rim, a certain number of spokes, nuts, washers, and an axle assembly. These components are "third highest" in the product structure. The component parts for the axle assembly are "fourth highest." And so on.

Component requirements. The bill of materials for each component not only defines parts and supplies but also identifies labor requirements, tools, and lubricants and often captures ancillary costs such as safety stock. Since operations are sequential, components are also defined according to *when* they are needed. If axles are assembled on Monday, materials will be time-phased to ensure that they are on hand Monday just prior to being used. Handle bars may not be needed until Friday and will be similarly phased in.

Time-phased inventory control. MRP is predicated on a carefully articulated bill of materials and time-phased inventory control that ensures individual parts will be stocked in adequate quantities in time for production. Inventory is regulated with production to provide forward planning in procurement.

MRP acceptance and use. MRP has been both praised and criticized. Users with fully integrated systems and trained personnel have reduced past-due purchases from 30 percent to about 3 percent and have found that quantities ordered more closely reflect actual needs. These firms have realized substantial savings in reduced safety stocks and fewer production problems due to stockouts. However, an MRP system represents enormous change, and implementing it requires a tremendous organizational commitment. Some companies have been disappointed with MRP and abandoned it, citing MRP's limitations in accounting for quality problems such as disrupted production, scrap, rework, and defects.[43]

Just in Time (JIT)

just in time (JIT)
A comprehensive system that seeks to eliminate inventory by purchasing materials just in time for use in production, producing just in time for shipment, and shipping just in time to meet customer orders without errors or quality defects.

Just in time originated in Japan as a management system to eliminate inventory while avoiding any material shortages. JIT begins with an exact definition of what to produce based on actual customer orders. Thus it defines what finished goods are required and precisely when they must be completed for immediate delivery to customers. Finished goods are not stocked in inventory but are shipped to customers as soon as they are completely manufactured. JIT is called a *pull system* because everything that occurs to meet a customer's order starts with an actual order, and every activity from final shipping back to initial materials procurement is "pulled" into the process by customer orders.[44]

The ideal JIT system delivers customer products on time and in the exact quantities ordered. Tracing the process backward, a shipping department will receive finished products just in time to send them out, production will schedule manufacturing just in time to fill the orders, and all materials and supplies required in manufacturing will be delivered to production just in time to be used. Furthermore, in order to have materials and supplies arrive precisely on time *at their point of use,* vendors must deliver exact quantities needed according to precise orders received through purchasing. If all these conditions are met, there will be no raw material or supplies inventory, no storage or safety stock, no "buffer" stock sitting idle during the manufacturing process, and no finished goods inventory. Richard J. Schonberger, who has written extensively on JIT, explains:

> The ideal of zero inventory by means of one-at-a-time continuous delivery from supplier to user is a pipedream—in Japan as well as here. But relentless attack upon delivery lot sizes and relentless search for ways to overcome the freight economies of full truckload and carload lots is a Japanese approach that we can and should emulate.[45]

Schonberger emphasizes that JIT is a way of thinking that transforms activities throughout a company. In contrast to MRP, JIT is customer-driven and reverses the entire decision-making process. Although MRP and JIT both require detailed master schedules, accurate bills of materials, and excellent procurement systems called *time-phased operations,* they are fundamentally different in other aspects. MRP is a *push system,* with all production and inventory activities based on demand forecasts, not actual customer orders. Therefore, materials are purchased and stored according to projected production schedules, manufacturing creates a stock of finished goods, and customer orders are filled from finished goods inventories. Figure 18-9 contrasts these push and pull systems.

JIT evolved in conjunction with Toyota's *kanban system,* a term that means "moving card." **Kanban** is a manual inventory control process that uses scheduling cards prepared when orders are received to pull work through production with maximum efficiency.[46] These cards list manufacturing activities, scheduled back through the system with parts requirements and dates and times each activity is to be

kanban
An inventory system based on scheduling cards prepared for each order and used in production to track progress and alert management to problems.

FIGURE 18-9 Work Flow in Pull (JIT) and Push Systems (MRP)

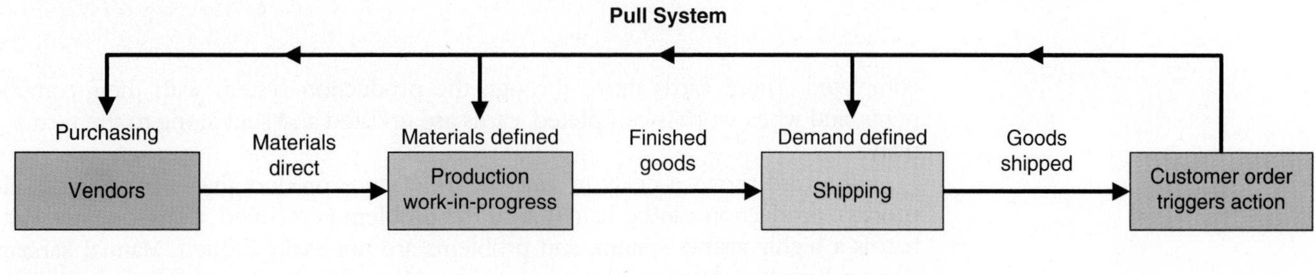

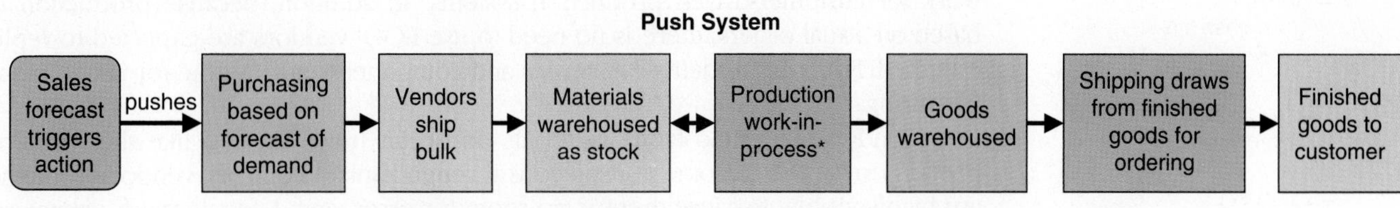

* Production work-in-process draws on warehoused materials as needed; the bi-directional arrow (◀▶) designates this back-and-forth relationship.

ETHICS IN MANAGEMENT

Du Pont and AT&T—Quality Leaders for Mother Earth

Techniques used in quality control for manufacturing are ideal for use in environmental protection programs. Although "factory" activities carry the popular connotation of dirty work that adds to our pollution problems, companies like Du Pont and AT&T demonstrate that "steel-cold concepts" of statistical process control and number-crunching statistical quality control analyses are the best means of solving environmental problems.

Like most companies, Du Pont initially addresses its environmental compliance responsibilities through white-collar staff specialists during the 1970s. These specialists remained at a distance from shop-floor quality control activities until 1987, when Du Pont announced the strategic goal of slashing manufacturing wastes and hazardous waste disposal problems by 35 percent by 1990. Compliance staff found solutions in SPC/SQC methods, bringing together shop-floor quality engineering techniques and compliance administration.

Du Pont saves more than 15 million pounds of plastics annually by recycling them in manufacturing rather than dumping them into landfills. Air pollutants have been reduced to emission standards far better than those mandated by the Environmental Protection Agency.

The company has also discovered methods to eliminate defective hazardous materials by substituting raw materials and educating suppliers in safe inventory procedures. Through electronic purchasing, Du Pont has reduced wastepaper to a trickle, and by using new packaging designs, the company has cut in-process material wastes by nearly 40 percent.

Du Pont began by identifying priority problems using existing information from quality control systems and materials management data bases. Compliance staff worked with cause-and-effect and Pareto chart analyses that statistically revealed where major problems occurred. Then, using in-process SQC monitoring techniques, the com-

completed. These cards move through the production system with their components, and when work is completed, cards are updated and sent along to the next activity.

If a card shows a delay in status or a defective product that disrupts work-in-process, production can be halted until the problem is rectified. Consequently, kanban is a highly visible system, and problems are not easily hidden. Manual kanban systems have been replaced by computer-based systems, but the process remains the same. JIT incorporates kanban techniques and has emerged as the conceptual framework for customer-driven production systems. In addition, because production is based on actual orders, there is no need to use EOQ; vendors are expected to replicate the JIT process to deliver materials and components just in time for use in manufacturing.

Vendor delays and faulty materials do occur, however, and like the work-in-process errors that become conspicuous through kanban controls, vendor problems are highly visible. Because there is no room for error, any defect in work or materials can be costly; shutting down an assembly line idles workers and disrupts the entire flow of work. Instead of "hiding" costs with safety stock or buffers that allow production lines to continue (and therefore mask problems), JIT managers bear the

pany began reducing waste materials through improved quality standards for production. Tying together shop-floor information-based monitoring systems with air-quality standards, Du Pont identified ways to reduce emissions. And using vendor evaluation systems linked to JIT purchasing requirements, the company initiated controls over incoming hazardous materials.

AT&T set up strategic TQM teams to attack problems with toxic waste and air quality hazards. Using Pareto diagrams and statistical data bases, AT&T's teams quickly identified ozone-destroying chlorofluorocarbons (CFC) in thirty-five plants that make fiber optic cable and various parts used in telecommunications equipment.

The most prominent problem discovered was a paint process used on cable and cable drums that emitted toxins into the air. AT&T eliminated the problem with an improved treatment process and a nontoxic paint. Air-toxic CFC was reduced 55 percent through a pilot SPC program, and in 1990 alone, the company saved 60 percent in manufactured waste products through an in-line SQC monitoring system.

Du Pont and AT&T discovered that by integrating quality systems and staff compliance activities, they could make major quality improvements that far exceeded regulatory guidelines. Also, both companies realized huge savings through quality improvement efforts. Most companies have similar means at hand to accomplish environmental quality objectives because purchasing, materials management, inventory control, and integrating manufacturing control activities result in exactly the same information and techniques needed in compliance management.

Source: Emily T. Smith, "Doing It for Mother Earth," *Business Week/Quality,* October 25, 1991, pp. 44–46, 49; Emily T. Smith, "Why AT&T Is Dialing 1-800-Go Green," *Business Week/Quality,* October 25, 1991, p. 49; and Eric E. Dwinells and Julianne P. Sheffer, "Hazardous Materials Require Integrated Information Systems," *APICS—The Performance Advantage,* March 1992, pp. 30–31.

costs as necessary penalties for discovering problems. Then, of course, they must solve the problems, and as they do so, quality is improved and costs are permanently avoided. The fact that JIT makes problems conspicuous is an important feature of the system. Since problems anywhere in the system—from vendor errors to customer warranty services—become immediately apparent, the pressure for quality performance is extraordinary.[47]

Recent examples of JIT used in U.S. firms offer rather stunning evidence of its potential. For example, Matsushita Electric Industries (MEI) purchased Quasar, an Illinois television manufacturer, and made tremendous improvements by implementing JIT methods. Prior to acquisition, the firm made well-designed TV sets with competitive quality, but Quasar had, on average, 130 in-process defects per 100 TV sets produced—more than one defect per set. Although many of the defects were small and required only minor rework, costs drove the firm's profits down significantly. In fact, warranty costs due to defective sets returned by consumers rivaled net profits. After MEI acquired Quasar, JIT was instituted, and within two years, the in-process defect rate fell to 5.1 defects per 100 sets. Within four years, the defect rate was down to 3.2 per 100, productivity had increased by 30 percent, and warranty costs had fallen to one-tenth of the pre-acquisition level.[48]

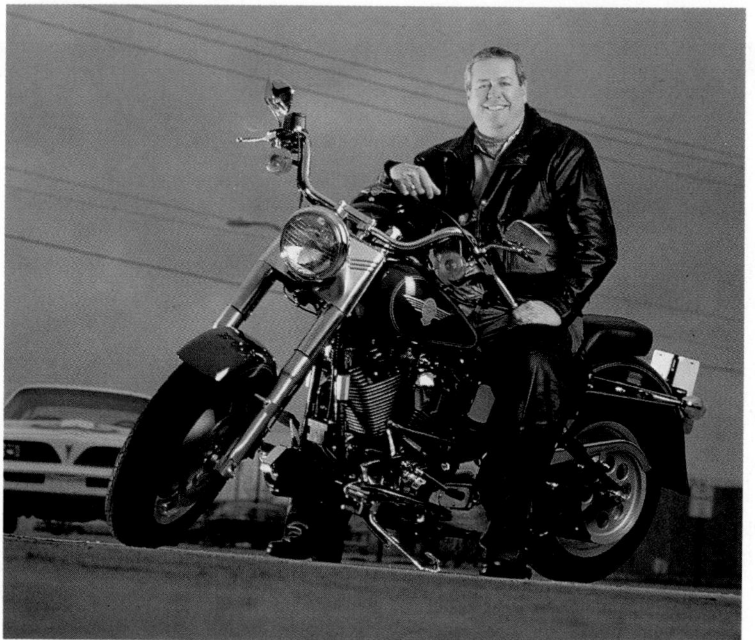

In the mid-1980s, Harley-Davidson, Inc., dropped 200 of its 320 suppliers. To cut their own costs, the survivors were sent to classes in just-in-time inventory management. Says Harley's manufacturing manager, Gary E. Kirkham, "We buy 50 percent of the dollar value of our motorcycles from suppliers. So improvements we made [internally] only got us halfway."

Another study compared American and Japanese firms in the air-conditioning industry. All Japanese manufacturers and all but one small U.S. manufacturer were included in a three-year intensive study of room air conditioners. Japanese firms had assembly-line defect rates that were, on average, *70 times lower* than those for U.S. firms. The worst U.S. firm had a failure rate nearly 1,000 times higher than the best Japanese firm. The worst Japanese firm had a failure rate only half that of the best U.S. firm. Underpinning the Japanese success was a commitment to manufacturing the highest-quality product. In U.S. firms, managers counted on sufficient inventories to overwhelm huge numbers of defects.[49]

Today JIT is being adopted by many companies in North America and Europe, and the result is rapid improvements in quality. Nevertheless, the Japanese have made JIT a pervasive practice, while Western companies are only beginning to make the transformation. The major differences between Japanese and Western production systems are summed up by Schonberger: "Japanese industry produces small quantities *just in time* . . . while Western industry produces massive quantities *just in case.*"[50]

CHECKPOINT

- Describe how decisions about inventory differ when inventory is controlled by purchasing managers and when it is controlled by production managers.
- Describe EOQ, MRP, and statistical controls used in inventory.
- Although JIT focuses on inventory, it is considered a general approach to management. Explain why.

INTEGRATED MANUFACTURING SYSTEMS

integrated manufacturing system
A system that includes plans and controls linking together all organizational activities to ensure quality performance.

When the concept of inventory control was introduced at the beginning of the previous section, it was emphasized that today many companies require an integrated manufacturing system. An **integrated manufacturing system** is one that includes plans and controls linking all organizational activities, thus ensuring an effective operational process from initial purchasing to final delivery of goods to customers. Under the subject of inventory control, we also describe EOQ and MRP, techniques that are independent of other organizational activities. JIT was introduced in the section on inventory control because it emphasizes the elimination of inventory, yet JIT is an integrated manufacturing system. In this section, we will introduce an integrated system called *manufacturing resource planning (MRP II),* address elements of both MRP II and JIT systems, and then describe how MRP II and JIT can work together.

Manufacturing Resource Planning (MRP II)

manufacturing resource planning (MRP II)
A comprehensive planning system that encompasses production resources and activities of MRP plus financial, capital, and marketing resources and activities.

Manufacturing resource planning (MRP II) is a comprehensive planning system that encompasses the production resources and activities of MRP plus financial, capital, and marketing resources and activities throughout the company.[51] MRP II should not be confused with MRP. MRP II is an integrated manufacturing system, whereas MRP is focused on materials and inventory control. MRP II emphasizes planning and controlling a firm's total resources, not just production and materials management activities; it includes calculations for cash flow, capital financing, energy costs, and profitability. In addition, MRP II incorporates a competitive analysis, after-sale service requirements, and marketing factors such as pricing, distribution, and promotional activities.

MRP II is a strategic management system coupled to operational controls in production, marketing, and finance. Since it requires an integrated information system for calculations and decision-support activities, it is used mainly in large companies that can afford the necessary computer systems and staff. For example, IBM created its own version of MRP II during the early 1980s, but it did not have a fully integrated system operating until 1989. Even then, the company had to introduce new methods of information processing for specific uses in functional areas such as marketing and production control.[52] Corning Glass Works, GM-Delco Electronics, GM-Hughes Aircraft, Lockheed, Martin Marietta, and Rockwell International employ MRP II. Advanced computer technology, however, is beginning to make MRP II a feasible option for smaller organizations, but like larger firms, these smaller ones must have parallel quality control and inventory systems because MRP II does not account for quality factors such as defective materials, scrap, rework, warranty costs, or design flaws.[53]

MRP II is a *push* system. It is not driven by a mandate to minimize inventories, as the JIT *pull* system is, so companies must intentionally seek ways to reduce inventory independent of MRP II controls. Like JIT, MRP II is a time-phased planning process used to synchronize manufacturing events and functional activities. MRP II is activated by strategic market forecasts that result in detailed simulations. Based on projected sales (demand), these simulations provide scenarios for each functional activity and each manufacturing event, ranging from materials procurement to shipment of finished goods. Management, however, decides on how to use the scenarios to run the company.

Specifically, management can elect to "produce to the forecast," which means manufacturing exactly the number of items projected to be sold at some future point in time. These products become finished goods inventory, and if production is well planned, they will remain in stock only briefly before being shipped. Management may instead decide to "produce to performance," which means that if the company expects to have defective products, marketing errors, or inaccurate demand forecasts, it makes and stores a safety stock of finished goods. Another consideration is that the company's suppliers may not have good performance records (late orders, flawed materials, disruptions due to shutdowns or labor disputes, etc.), so management will stock extra materials "just in case" and maintain a finished goods safety stock. These decisions result in excess finished goods, work-in-process, and materials, but they help the company avoid shortages and delays in customer orders.

MRP II was initially designed for use in a "batch production" environment, and it is very effective for project management where demand can be defined in discrete numbers and production can be planned well in advance of sales. (Job shop, batch, mass assembly, process, and project technologies were addressed in Chapter 9). For example, Digital Equipment Corporation uses MRP II for manufacturing minicomputer systems. Because orders for these computers are relatively small (compared, for example, to "mass-assembled" PCs), and because customers plan acquisitions long before required delivery dates, demand can be effectively defined. Digital's managers can therefore use MRP II to orchestrate their organizational activities.[54]

Repetitive manufacturing common in mass assembly systems used to manufacture personal computers or automobiles relies on economic demand forecasts, and MRP II is less effective here than in project or batch environments. Retail demand and inventory requirements can fluctuate substantially, thereby eroding the accuracy of MRP II simulations. One answer to this problem has been to improve MRP II systems so that more rapid simulations can be generated to give managers time to adjust manufacturing schedules. Another solution has been to set up manufacturing in small lot sizes (e.g., make fewer numbers of each model of a car to reduce the risk and cost of holding excess inventory). This adaptation incorporates the fundamental rule of JIT—to reduce inventory by producing small orders exactly to customer needs rather than producing to stock. Such a hybrid system is difficult to manage, however, because MRP II is predicated on pushing production through a system based on simulated forecasts.[55]

MRP II and JIT as Complementary Systems

Although MRP II is designed to push production, thereby creating inventory stock, and JIT is a technique to pull production, thus eliminating inventory, the two systems are not diametrically opposed. Both have advantages, and can be used jointly to complement each other.

MRP II has the advantage of being an effective planning instrument, and it is a technique that fully integrates organizational activities. MRP II also has evolved into an elegant information system where calculations can be performed with a high degree of reliability. Its effectiveness, however, rests on the accuracy of simulated information, vendor reliability, and separate attention to quality assurance. JIT has the advantage of being a sound philosophy that drives a company toward quality objectives based on continuous improvement. It is a system that strives to meet customer needs through perfect performance and elimination of waste. As a pull system, JIT does not require forecasts or advance planning; accurate orders initiate JIT activities. However, companies using JIT must have exceptional control over quality, vendor relations, and manufacturing processes.

Each system works best in different manufacturing environments. MRP II is optimal in batch production systems, and JIT is most effective in repetitive manufacturing systems. However, most companies operate somewhere between these extremes with mixed assembly lines and variations on batch and repetitive processes. Managers in these firms have difficulty implementing either MRP II or JIT. By combining the systems, however, some companies have realized substantial benefits.

Eastman Kodak, for example, endorses the JIT philosophy and ranks its strategic objectives as coinciding with JIT quality improvement standards. Kodak seeks to eliminate finished goods inventory by pulling all orders through its system. Focusing on achieving 100 percent customer satisfaction, Kodak's repetitive manufacturing system is geared up to meet orders in exact quantities exactly on time. Thus operations flow backward through the system, driving fifty individual subgroup activities. Kodak's vendors are expected to be JIT suppliers who can deliver quality materials on time directly to production areas. This ideal is rarely realized, but by working with vendors to devise JIT/MRP II systems and to educate vendor's employees in the JIT philosophy, Kodak succeeded in reducing on-hand materials by 74 percent during the 18-month period following introduction of the system in 1990. Lead times became shorter, finished goods inventory was reduced, waste was lower, and work-in-process declined by 40 to 70 percent. Most important, product quality improved by 86 percent. MRP II was modified to integrate activities and to provide a networked information system. Instead of operating as a push system, MRP II was reversed to coordinate activities based on the JIT pull process.[56]

Future Directions for Integrated Systems

As we conclude the chapter, it is important to recall that many different techniques are used to control quality and productivity. Integrated operations processes are being designed to incorporate these techniques into comprehensive systems. Specifically, new-product design procedures, statistical process controls, statistical quality controls, on-line (paperless) purchasing, materials management systems, inventory controls, and new methods of production control such as coordinated work cells are becoming operational components of combined JIT/MRP II strategic systems. Financial decisions, such as capital expenditures, are being made to help eliminate unnecessary equipment and facilities, thus improving efficiency and the productive use of investments. Accounting systems are being redesigned to capture costs associated with quality problems. Finally, it is being recognized that profitability results from total quality management (TQM) achieved through integrated systems based on objectives for continuous productivity improvements.[57]

CHECKPOINT

- Describe MRP II as an integrated manufacturing system and state how it differs from MRP.
- Contrast JIT and MRP II, explaining their advantages and benefits.
- Will integrated systems replace techniques such as EOQ, SQC, SPC, MRP, PERT, and CPM? Support your answer for each technique.

AT THE BEGINNING OF THE CHAPTER, we emphasized that Compaq Computer Corporation has a global organization with a fully integrated system of manufacturing and management. Compaq's system was explained as one built on JIT concepts and implemented using MRP II, with workers organized in autonomous work teams (AWTs) that manufacture computers through a cellular production process in a corporate environment committed to total quality management.[58] When these terms were introduced in the opening scenario, they probably had very little meaning for the reader, but as we end the chapter, the reader should understand they are the foundation stones of Compaq's successful bid to be recognized among the world's quality leaders. ■

A SYNOPSIS FOR LEARNING

1. Discuss how improved quality enhances productivity.

   Productivity is measured by a ratio of output to the total resources a company uses to create that output. Higher quality translates into higher productivity because companies use fewer resources to provide manufactured products or services to customers.

   The costs of poor quality are defective products that must be reworked, serviced, or replaced; wasted materials; inefficient use of human resources and facilities; and excess inventories that add to capital overhead. From a social viewpoint, low-quality products result in wasted natural resources, unnecessary costs of disposition, and safety problems. Higher quality and productivity significantly reduce costs for companies and society.

2. Explain design, product, and service and use controls.

   Design controls are used to improve product reliability and reduce costs. Product controls include acceptance sampling to ensure high-quality manufacturing, tests of finished products to ensure reliability, and accuracy tests of both inspectors and their equipment to improve quality and product control systems. Service and use controls (such as field warranty checks, installation evaluations, and consumer surveys) focus on after-sale results.

3. Describe how PERT and CPM are used in production control, and the concepts of SQC, SPC, and cellular systems.

   PERT and CPM, two network control systems, are used to plan and control complex projects that require complicated sequential operations. PERT maps out the sequence of events necessary to complete a project. It identifies the sequence and activities required for each event to graphically show how work is to proceed and the time required to complete each event. CPM is similar to PERT, but identifies alternative routes for scheduled events and then estimates a "critical path"—the longest period of time and sequence of events required to complete a project. SQC is the mathematical process of evaluating performance results using various calculations and methods to provide management with decision-making information. SPC is a system of monitoring and analysis of manufactured components, parts, or products during the production process. In contrast to these techniques, cellular systems reflect a reorganization of work processes away from sequential chains of activities toward clusters of interrelated task activities.

4. Describe materials controls and inventory management.

   Materials controls are concerned with efficient purchasing to provide to production when needed materials with the correct specifications in the right quantities. Inventory controls are concerned with receiving, storing, handling, and transporting three types of inventory: raw materials and parts to be used in production, work-in-process inventory that represents partially made or assembled products, and finished goods that are ready to ship to customers.

5. Describe and contrast EOQ, MRP, JIT, and statistical process controls.

   EOQ is a model used to reduce costs associated with ordering and holding incoming materials. MRP is a computer-based system of scheduling purchasing and production in an integrated model. JIT is a management approach that eliminates inventory and defects by providing materials and parts directly to manufacturing points without intermediate stocking or warehousing. JIT also requires that precise quantities of materials be delivered without faults. Thus any deviation in delivery or quality will disrupt production. However, JIT eliminates the capital costs of inventory and requires—ideally—perfect quality performance.

6. Explain how integrated systems using MRP II and JIT are complementary.

MRP II is a push system that is activated by sales forecasts and management decisions about when and how much to produce for finished goods inventory. It also is a process that integrates all company functions through an elegant information system that incorporates materials, production, inventory, and quality controls. JIT is a pull system, and as a philosophy of manufacturing, it establishes the objective of 100 percent quality driven by the need to produce exactly what a customer needs exactly when it is needed. JIT is activated by actual orders, not forecasts or decisions by management based on probability scenarios. Consequently, JIT pulls work through a system and integrates all activities back through a complete operations process. When MRP II and JIT are used together, a strategic system evolves that is driven by customer orders and a commitment to total quality management, but that also has the sophistication of a fully integrated technology and precise controls.

CASE 1 Controls in Computer Manufacturing Plague Managers

SKILL ANALYSIS

A marketing shakeout in home computers occurred during 1990 and 1991 as many marginal firms failed and several were bought out by larger firms as major manufacturers took a dominant lead in sales. One of the smaller companies caught in this shakeout faced bankruptcy in 1992 even though it had several years of excellent sales and growth. At its peak in 1989, this firm had a nationwide network of outlets with $180 million in sales, and from a marketing standpoint, the future looked exciting. But business turned sour quickly when major players in the computer industry aggressively positioned themselves with new high-quality products and lower prices.

The company's managers and stockholders could not believe that disaster came so quickly, and when bankruptcy was apparent, there were several heated discussions. Some managers blamed workers, others blamed the poor quality of materials, and still others said that subcontractors were passing rejects. Stockholders blamed management, and retailers were unhappy with design engineering. All that was certain was that in spite of very good early sales, the firm's microcomputers had not kept up with customer expectations or remained competitive with the industry. Too many rejects were being rushed out of the factory; upgrade and peripheral designs seemed to be stalled or inadequate.

Closer inspection revealed several specific quality problems. In-process defects the previous year were more than 227 per 1,000 units. Reasons for this included (1) defective casings and chassis with misaligned parts requiring substantial rework, (2) defective chips and electronic components requiring replacement in about 8 percent of sold units, (3) poorly constructed cable assemblies that required rework or replacement in 12 percent of units sold, and (4) assorted rejects of assemblies due to workmanship errors and handling mistakes.

Reports presented to the stockholders showed that most of these defective parts and subassemblies were purchased from outside vendors. Costs for materials and vendor chargebacks were estimated at 9.2 percent of total costs of operations. Meanwhile, the firm made up replacement pins and cable connectors that were unaccounted for in production summaries. Although managers did not itemize workmanship errors, they estimated that in-plant costs of materials and scrap were 3 percent of total costs. They pointed out that this was not excessive, but vendor problems were huge. The firm apparently maintained large safety stocks to assure smooth production runs.

Stockholders were unimpressed with this explanation and accused company executives of trying to find scapegoats among vendors.

One influential stockholder who also owned several retail computer stores pointed out design faults. He said the firm's computers had small screens, a compressed keyboard, and limited operating characteristics that would not support mainstream software. The combination of these factors, he noted, led to substantial discounting by retailers, and this in turn had put pressure on the firm's representatives to further discount to retailers in order to move its products.

The vice president countered this criticism by arguing that the firm's product was supposed to be a low-end, low-priced home computer and should not be expected to compete head-on with big office systems. He further implied that several vendors were exploiting the market with high prices and low-quality materials.

Another stockholder at the meeting was also a supplier of some of the electronic parts used by the firm. Enraged by the top manager's position, he threatened a lawsuit that would hold them all personally liable for mismanagement. He blamed design faults, but also noted that warranty replacement costs and service modifications absorbed far more than the explicit costs showed by management. Where was their quality control? Where was their concern for customers' design needs? The meeting ended with charges and countercharges leading nowhere.

Case Questions

1. What questions would you ask management about quality costs and production losses if you were a stockholder? What costs are associated with these issues?
2. Identify and discuss the apparent vendor and purchasing controls the firm might have employed to reduce losses and improve quality.
3. Discuss the design and warranty problems. Are these quality issues real, or was the vice president's perception reasonable?
4. How would you evaluate customer needs in the home computer market?

VIDEO CASE Are the Japanese Really Better Workers?

The image of American workers took a beating in early 1992 as Japanese politicians called U.S. employees lazy. Have American workers really lost the work ethic, as Japanese Prime Minister Kiichi Miyazawa claimed? The truth, as Japan's own labor ministry finally admitted, is that by some measures U.S. workers are more productive than their Japanese counterparts.

In fact, according to the Bureau of Labor Statistics, American workers are the most productive in the world. Japanese workers are only 77 percent as productive as Americans. They ranked fifth, behind France, Italy, and Germany. However, the Japanese are increasing their productivity much faster than American workers are and could catch up within a few years. One reason for the lag in U.S. productivity is that many U.S. factories still use turn-of-the-century management techniques.

Since 1987, when Motorola started its drive to improve productivity, the payoffs have been big. A Motorola vice president explains, "Reducing [product] defects by 150-fold over the five-year period has resulted in a manufacturing cost savings within Motorola of $2.2 billion." In 1991, 3,000 Motorola employee teams worldwide competed for the company's gold medal for the most effective idea to improve productivity.

Other American manufacturers, though, have a long way to go to improve productivity. A management expert from Cornell University says that organizations need to eliminate layers of management that slow down decision making. He also believes that "there is still this negative labor-management attitude that we had 15 years ago. It's getting better, but I believe that managers have more control, and it is more a management problem than it is workers on the floor." Too many U.S. managers still make unilateral discussions about work without employee input and then expect employees to fall into line.

Many American managers are learning from observing Japanese production lines, like the one at the Honda plant in Marysville, Ohio. Here workers come together to solve production problems and any worker has the power to stop the production line if he or she sees a problem arising. General Motors' newest division, Saturn, adopted this and other Japanese management techniques when designing its new factory in Tennessee. American managers are starting to recognize what it will take to stay ahead of the Japanese.

Case Questions

1. What are some of the reasons for the declining level of American worker productivity? How could production and operations management controls be used to combat the decline in U.S. productivity?
2. What role does quality play in productivity? How can American companies achieve high levels of both productivity and quality?

Sources: Marc Levinson, "America's Edge," *Newsweek*, June 8, 1992, p. 40ff; Ed Rubenstein, "The Lazy American?" *National Review*, February 17, 1992, Vol. 44, No. 3, p. 16: and Annetta Miller, "Are We Really That Lazy?" *Newsweek*, February 17, 1992, p. 42ff.

IN SEARCH OF THE PERFECT TERM PAPER

SKILL PRACTICE

Quality control is often difficult to grasp for students who have little experience and cannot relate to manufacturing systems. However, many of the concepts introduced in this chapter are fundamental to succeeding in any situation. This exercise is designed to give you the opportunity to see how the concepts can be used in a situation familiar to you: writing a term paper. The objective is to devise a system that gives you the best chance for a perfect grade for a term paper.

Instructions

Assume your task is to write a ten-page term research paper and you have a definite deadline. This date is known at the beginning of the semester, and it falls near the end of the semester. Your subject can be anything on management, but you must have adequate academic references, present a clear problem or issue, and draw relevant conclusions supported by research.

The instructor will form teams of no more than five students who have twenty minutes to complete the exercise. Each group will work as a team to address the exercise questions listed below. Once finished, a spokesperson will summarize the team's recommendations, with a time limit of five minutes for each presentation. (The instructor may alter these instructions.)

Exercise Questions

1. What are the most frequent causes of poor term paper grades? List these causes and why they occur.
2. To eliminate the problems associated with poor term papers, what control criteria must be established and how will progress be monitored?
3. How do criteria, control points, and methods your group has selected coincide with in-process controls and the philosophy of total quality management?
4. Is a term paper assignment a form of "push" or "pull" process? Explain your answer.

19

Management and Information Systems

OUTLINE

Management of Information
- The Nature of Information
- Management Requirements for Information
- Information Systems

Management Information Systems (MIS)
- The Nature of MIS
- Management Information Services
- The Role of Integrated MIS

Types of Information Systems
- Transactions Processing Systems (TPS)
- Office Automation Systems (OAS)
- Decision Support Systems (DSS)
- LAN, Distributed Computing, and Client/Server Systems (C/SS)
- Expert Systems (ES)
- Artificial Intelligence (AI)

Organizational Issues for Information Technology
- Changing Patterns of Communication
- The IS Transition for Organizations
- Problems Related to IS Technology

OBJECTIVES

- Describe different requirements for information by managers in organizations today.
- Explain the components of an MIS and why it is a service within a company.
- Distinguish between the types of information systems and their organizational uses.
- Discuss how information technology has changed human relationships in organizations.

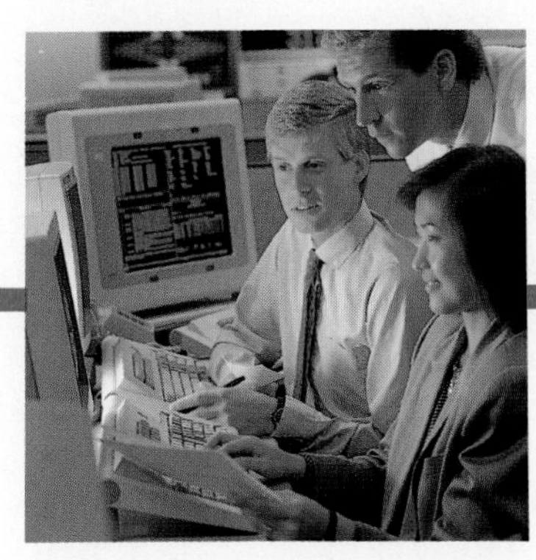

THE TRAVELERS CORPORATION thrives on information. Known for domestic insurance, the company is a global enterprise with financial and real estate interests that rival its insurance empire. For Travelers—and any other company, in services or manufacturing—effective information results in better decisions, more efficient customer service, and higher profits.[1]

Travelers also realizes that managing information resources is a strategic responsibility, not an adjunct duty of staff specialists, and it requires managers to address *hardware, software,* and *people.* Too often, managers focus on either hardware systems or software applications while ignoring the human side of information technology, and Travelers managers were no exception. When centralized mainframe computers were introduced to the business world in the 1960s, Travelers was one of the first-round buyers. When microcomputers began to be mass-produced in the early 1980s, Travelers again was a big buyer. When spreadsheet software was developed, Travelers readapted its entire system. And when *area networks* with integrated work stations and software came to market, Travelers embraced the technology. Information technology at Travelers was redefined five or six times in less than twenty years. Each change was often stressful for employees.

Today The Travelers Corporation is planning yet another changeover, but this one begins with its people. *Client/server* computer systems—a term coined to capture the notion of designing systems based on information and applications that end users (people) need—begins with defining individual or departmental information requirements and then identifies software and hardware that can meet those needs. The problem, however, is how to provide systems for thousands of individuals equipped with microcomputers working on hundreds of different types of problems.[2]

Finding an answer to this problem is currently one of the most pressing priorities for the information industry. At issue is the fundamental question of how to manage information resources, and that implies creating a system that allows employees to use those resources effectively. For Travelers, the answer must integrate the power of central mainframe computers with the benefits of individualized and flexible desktop work stations. Such a system does not yet exist.

This brief history of events at The Travelers Corporation illustrates how critical it is not only to manage information effectively but also to have an organization that is adaptable to new technologies. The field of information science, whose birth was a revolution in itself, has been subject to constant and often revolutionary changes. Because information resources are constantly changing, methods of managing those resources quickly become outdated. In fact, the sheer pace of technological change means that whatever is described in this chapter may be superseded by events before it is published. Nevertheless, we can benefit by understanding the nature of information and how organizations strive to use this effectively.

MANAGEMENT OF INFORMATION

information
In systems terminology, the result of thoughtful analysis and communication of data in a form useful to recipients.

data
Raw information and facts, figures, and results that become source inputs for analyzing activities, events, and circumstances.

Information is the result of thoughtful analysis and communication of data in a form useful to recipients. **Data** are the raw materials from which information is derived. The distinction is important because data can be generated by the ton without producing much useful information, and managers need information, not data, to make effective decisions. By sorting through data and analyzing which data are important at the time, managers can make more timely and accurate decisions. Too often managers have data thrust upon them, which creates confusion and overload. Therefore, managing information is a critical requirement in any organization.

The Nature of Information

Now that there are computers capable of manipulating millions of bits of data in a few seconds, people can be overwhelmed by verbiage, symbols, and statistics. Although we focus on *information systems* that involve computer technology, we must recognize that information can also be generated in our minds and communicated with paper and pencil. How we create information is important—and will be discussed—but the nature of useful information is independent of how it is created. Useful information is characterized by its quality, which is assessed by five characteristics: *accuracy, verifiability, completeness, timeliness,* and *relevance.*[3]

accuracy of information
The degree to which information is error-free.

Accuracy. Managers need accurate information to make effective decisions. **Accuracy of information** is the degree to which it is error-free. Some information is precise, such as the amount of cash a company has on hand. Other information can be inexact, such as market estimates for future sales. Marketing managers make decisions based on information provided to them by analysts, who obtained the information from market data such as surveys, economic projections, and sales records. If analysts give managers inflated information, the company may produce too many items, hire too many people, and spend too much money. A pessimistic forecast, of course, has the opposite effects.

verifiability
The extent to which information can be traced to its source and its accuracy determined.

Verifiability. Decision makers must be able to verify the accuracy of information they use. **Verifiability** is the extent to which information can be traced to its source and its accuracy determined. For example, if analysts have projected a 10 percent increase in sales, a marketing manager may question how this figure was derived. The analysts then verify their projections by explaining how survey market data were used to create the forecast. Also, they may indicate a degree of confidence by noting, for example, that similar methods used in similar circumstances have proved 95 percent accurate. In many instances, information can be precisely verified. For example, auditors use sales receipts and accounting records to verify costs, revenues, and profits. However, too often managers use impressive computer printouts that seem reliable, yet are based on fallacious data. Managers call them "GIGO"—garbage in, garbage out.

Completeness. Information may be accurate and verifiable, yet insufficient. **Completeness of information** is the degree to which it is sufficient to support decisions, addressing key issues without omissions. Since information is expensive, managers also must decide how much information is cost effective. For example, market analysts might be able to supply sales projections with a 90 percent degree of accuracy at a reasonable cost, but to attain a 95 percent degree of accuracy, they might have to spend more in the process than would be justified by the better forecast. The analyst's first priority, however, is to ensure the information is free of omissions. Thus the failure to include information about competitors in a sales projection might invalidate the entire report.

completeness of information
The degree to which information is sufficient to support decisions, addressing issues without omissions.

Timeliness. Although some problems require immediate attention, others can be addressed in a more leisurely manner. **Timeliness of information** refers not only to having accurate and complete information, but also to having it at the right time. A great advantage of computer-based information systems is their ability to quickly analyze, store, retrieve, and transmit information, but managers must ensure that the information is provided to the right person when needed. For example, a sales projection for July probably is needed by production and marketing managers in May so they can plan their activities. If an unexpected change occurs—such as a price rise by a major competitor—that information should be transmitted immediately. Strategic sales forecasts that project changes two or three years ahead might be sent through channels quarterly.

timeliness of information
The concept of not only having accurate and complete information, but also having it at the right time.

Relevance. **Relevancy of information** refers to its appropriateness in helping managers make decisions. An overload of information creates confusion. Just as extraneous data can overwhelm car drivers, unrelated information can overload managers. For example, when sales managers are trying to schedule activities for the coming month, they do not want to spend time studying three-year strategic forecasts. An analyst who buries monthly sales projections in a two-inch-thick strategic forecast confuses managers instead of helping them make decisions.

relevancy of information
Appropriate information that helps managers make decisions without creating an overload.

Management Requirements for Information

Managers at all levels need decision-oriented information, but the type required differs at each organizational stratum. In Chapter 5, we discussed how management decisions differ from one level to the next. Specifically, senior executives in strategic management roles make *nonprogrammed*—abstract and unstructured—decisions; first-line managers in operational roles make *programmed*—concrete and structured—decisions; and middle managers in tactical positions make less concrete decisions than those made by operating managers, but also less abstract decisions than those made by executives.

Information required for strategic, nonprogrammed decisions is difficult to delineate because strategic decisions address long-term issues and involve uncertain future events. Executives require information about competitors, society, government, politics, resources, financial markets, economics, and their company's future capabilities. These are data that are extremely difficult to obtain with a high degree of reliability; often managers must be satisfied with probabilities.

Middle managers' tactical decisions typically focus on time periods of one year or several quarters. They are concerned with resource allocations, near-term trends in sales, and annual operating profits. Information required for these decisions can be reasonably well defined. They include current sales records; competitors' products, prices, and promotional activities; estimates of near-term economic factors; and

The brokerage firm of Charles Schwab & Company has invested in information technology since 1979. Its technology has enabled it to collect extensive data about customers, which it uses in management decision making. For example, in 1988, Schwab studied 27 million American households. One thing it learned from the study was that investors wanted objective financial advice. Schwab's response: Its Financial Advisory Service, which identifies for investors the financial planners who will work on a fee basis only, and therefore have no incentive to push certain investments on their clients.

performance results. However, middle managers also make less structured decisions requiring special information such as how to alter working conditions to improve quality performance.

Decisions made by operating managers are usually routine, well defined, repetitive, and have immediate effects on organizational activities. Information for programmed decisions can be gathered through feedback on existing activities. For example, operating managers base work-related decisions on performance reports that track scheduled activities and budgets, identifying variances in results that alert them to take action. Figure 19-1 illustrates the type of information managers at different organizational levels need to make decisions.

FIGURE 19-1 Information Needed by Different Levels of Managers to Make Decisions

Executive Management

Strategic

Unstructured information environment.
Decisions are often unprogrammed and data are abstract.

Middle Management

Tactical

Less well-defined information environment.
Decisions by middle managers can be structured or unstructured, but reliable data are often available.

Supervisory Management

First-line Operations

Well-defined information environment. Decisions are structured and relate to immediate operations, and data are often concrete.

Information Systems

A *system* was defined in Chapter 1 as a group of interrelated parts working together to achieve a common result. An **information system,** therefore, is a group of interrelated parts working together to provide useful information to decision makers.[4] System components include *hardware, software, people, procedures,* and *data.* These components, in turn, have many different configurations. We will discuss several types of information systems later, but we begin with a brief description of the components, graphically displayed in Figure 19-2.

information system
A group of interrelated hardware, software, people, procedures, and data combined to provide useful information to decision makers.

Hardware. Using the terminology of our computer age, information system **hardware** is the physical equipment employed to input, store, retrieve, and output data. A computer-based information system generally uses a keyboard to input data, a central processing unit (CPU) to store and retrieve data, and a printer to generate output. New technology has been developed to enhance hardware; for example, optical character readers scan written or graphic data, converting information for computer use; storage has progressed from floppy disks to laser-generated compact disks; bar-coding equipment is now commonly employed in stores and factories to read coded information on products; and digital voice synthesizers transcribe vocal information into stored data. Output hardware has evolved from simple printers based on mechanical typewriters to digital video imagery called *virtual-reality technology (holography).*[5]

hardware
The physical equipment employed to input, store, retrieve, and output data.

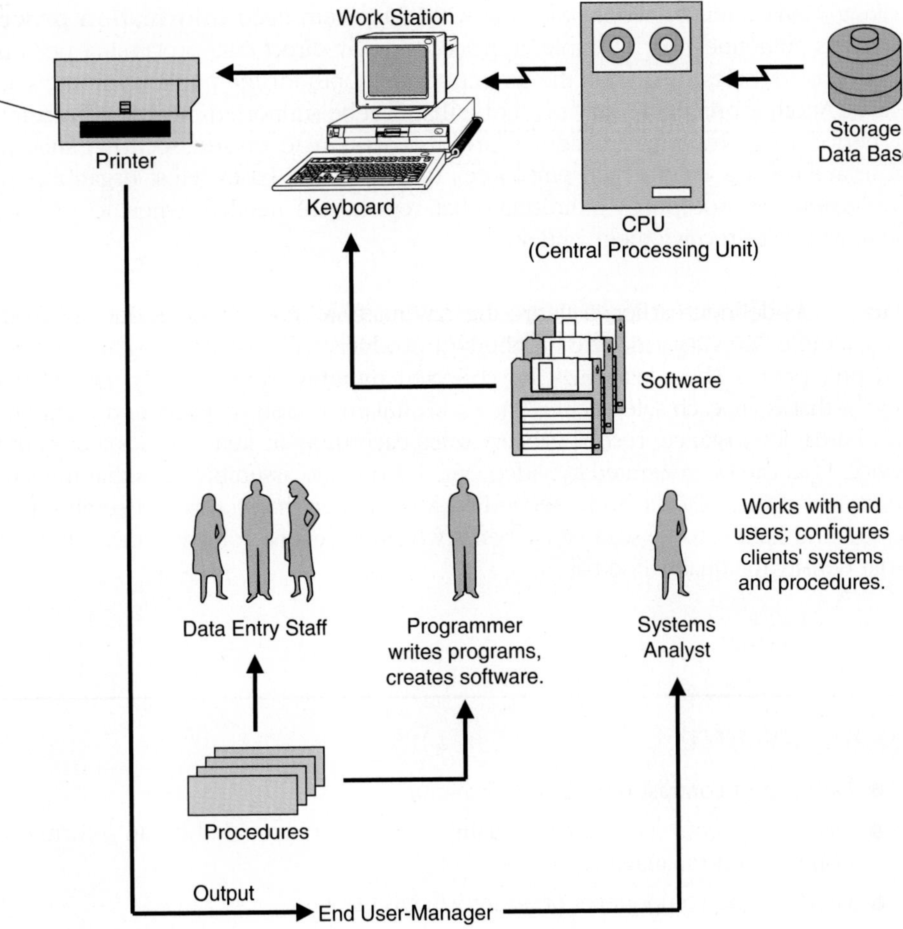

FIGURE 19-2 Components of an Information System

software
The means for driving hardware and controlling an information system.

information procedures
Guidelines for using a system and providing required information that is accurate, verifiable, complete, timely, and relevant.

For about twenty years, bar codes have been a staple at supermarket checkout counters, among other places. Ordinary bar codes spell out the universal product code, which, after being fed into a computer, informs a cash register how much to charge for an item. Now, however, Symbol Technologies has developed a two-dimensional bar code that is capable of storing about a hundred times more information. For example, a hazardous waste company can use it to encode emergency instructions onto toxic waste drums, enabling workers to clean up any leak from such drums instantly. Or a manufacturing company can improve production on an assembly line by using robot arms with scanners attached to read the 2-D bar codes on parts.

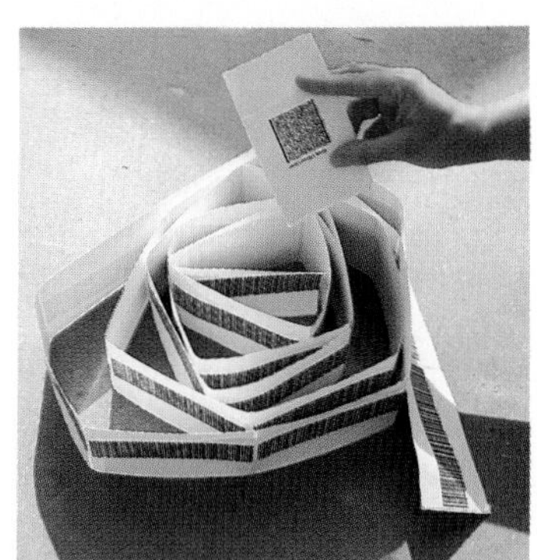

Software. Hardware can accomplish nothing by itself. **Software** is the means for driving hardware and controlling an information system. Software programs direct hardware activities to read and store data in understandable formats, retrieve it, and transform it into useful information. Software developed for early computers created languages such as FORTRAN and COBOL that allowed computer programs to customize data processing. During the 1980s, software development focused on using many different artificial computer languages to create *applications,* including such popular programs as Lotus 1-2-3 and WordPerfect. The 1990s may be the decade of scientific advances in software such as enhanced computer-aided design systems, fiber optic voice translation, and interactive global work stations.[6]

People. We have not yet developed an information system that works without people. In fact, the more sophisticated the system, the more likely it will need experts to use it. Several categories of people are involved in information systems. Data-entry personnel are responsible for putting data into, and extracting information from, computer-based systems. Data processing managers are responsible for directing the use of systems, preparing reports, and transmitting information to decision makers. Systems analysts configure hardware and software into a system designed to provide the information required in an organization. Programmers create the software defined by a systems analyst to make the system work. End users—recipients of information—are also part of the system because they identify what information is needed, when it is needed, and in what form.

Procedures. Recall that useful information must be accurate, verifiable, complete, timely, and relevant; simply generating data is insufficient for effective decision making. Consequently, people working within a system need **information procedures** as guidelines. For example, a procedure may direct data processing personnel to provide sales reports on the tenth of each month for the previous month's activities. Another procedure may prescribe that data be supported by verified receipts or performance reports. Procedures are also written to ensure security, such as those authorizing only certain employees to access data bases. Most organizations have extensive procedures indicating what reports are needed, when to prepare them, who is to receive them, and so on.

Data. As defined earlier, data are the raw material information is derived from. For example, sales data include numbers of products sold, the dollar value of sales, and unit prices. These data may be collected monthly, weekly, daily, or in "real time"—that is, as each sale occurs. Bar codes linked to cash registers and computer data bases, for instance, record grocery sales each time an item crosses a scanning device. Data can be generated by video cameras on auto assembly lines that transmit hundreds of bits of data every second to a computer that controls assembly processes. And light sensors scan fabric being woven to record color variances and material density for quality control.[7]

CHECKPOINT

- Define and contrast data and information.
- Discuss the concept of useful quality information provided by an information system to managers.
- Describe the components of an information system.

MANAGEMENT APPLICATION

Pensoft, Inc., Hopes to Make Sales Management a Bit (or Byte) Easier

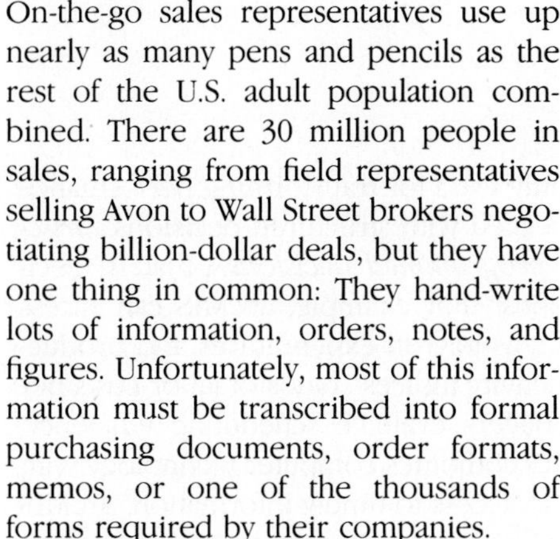

On-the-go sales representatives use up nearly as many pens and pencils as the rest of the U.S. adult population combined. There are 30 million people in sales, ranging from field representatives selling Avon to Wall Street brokers negotiating billion-dollar deals, but they have one thing in common: They hand-write lots of information, orders, notes, and figures. Unfortunately, most of this information must be transcribed into formal purchasing documents, order formats, memos, or one of the thousands of forms required by their companies.

Pensoft Corporation, a new software company in San Jose, California, wants to change all that with its Pen-PC. The Pen-PC is an electronic tablet that a person can scribble on freehand with a special pen that looks and feels like a common ballpoint. The tablet can be designed for almost any type of order blank or format, and hundreds of pages of data can be stored, downloaded, or transcribed electronically through a "collector" hooked to a company computer.

The Pen-PC has Japanese competitors, and Hewlett-Packard is also getting into the race with similar products and hand-held appliances such as electronic notebooks and scheduling systems. Sales, however, have been disappointing. When the pen systems first came to market in 1991, estimates were for sales in excess of 200,000 the first year; actual sales were barely 75,000. Competitors dropped prices from around the $4,000 range to under $3,000 in 1992, but still the market did not develop as expected.

Price does not seem to be the problem. Instead, H-P analysts and NEC market researchers believe customers are not yet ready for pen systems and other exotic productivity tools. The task, analysts say, is to educate company managers about the value of using the instruments, not to excite salespeople about the fancy features. What the pen systems do best is unscramble scrawled and often illegible handwriting, position items in proper places on forms, and transform input into clean, crisp print. Preprogrammed forms also alert writers to information they have missed and incorrect entries, thereby reducing errors.

Sales may be more promising among doctors, a market the companies admit they have not cultivated, yet one with a brisk sales potential. Doctors, it seems, like the idea of writing prescriptions and hospital orders on electronic tablets that will unscramble their notoriously illegible scrawls for pharmacists.

Sources: Kathy Rebello, "The Pen-PC Market Is Moving Half Steam Ahead, *Business Week,* March 30, 1992, pp. 82–83; Robert D. Hof, "Information Appliances Turn HP On," *Business Week,* March 22, 1992, p. 89; and Ron Winslow, "Desktop Doctors," *Wall Street Journal,* April 6, 1992, pp. R12–14.

MANAGEMENT INFORMATION SYSTEMS (MIS)

The concept of a **management information system (MIS)** is use of total information resources in a way that will enhance managerial decisions, provide monitoring capabilities, and ensure accurate and timely performance feedback. The acronym *MIS* is also used for *marketing* and *manufacturing* information systems, indicating narrower definitions, but construing MIS as a *management* tool is more appropriate because it transforms data into useful information to support managers in every area

management information system (MIS)
A service that uses total information resources in a way that enhances managerial decisions, monitors activities, and ensures accurate and timely performance feedback.

of specialization. Therefore, MIS is not a system in the same sense that a decision support system or an expert system is. Instead, it is the *process* of ensuring that information resources are effectively used. In many organizations, the term *MIS* has been replaced with *IS,* an acronym whose meaning evolved from *information systems* to *information services.* Consequently, MIS may be appropriately defined as an organizational service, while IS carries a broader connotation of total management of all information resources within an organization. MIS is nevertheless a significant part of the total service.[8]

The Nature of MIS

Management information systems are commonly used for transforming performance control data into information most often associated with structured decisions. *Structured* decisions were previously defined as *programmed decisions*—that is, decisions based on predictable patterns of activities.[9] For example, an MIS can access data from transaction processing systems, such as payroll expenditures and production output reports, and calculate labor productivity indices (ratios of labor costs per unit of output). This information helps managers evaluate scheduling efficiency, work methods, and resource utilization. An MIS combines computer technology with efficient control models to give managers rapid access to timely information. An MIS also provides traceability—audit trails, history files, and validation procedures—with greater reliability than do slower periodic reports passed through the management hierarchy. The net result is better decision making by managers who are better informed about organizational activities.

data base
A pool of raw data stored in such a way that parts of it can be selected, changed, used in calculations, and transformed into useful information for end users.

The cornerstone of an MIS is a data base. A **data base** is a centralized pool of raw data stored in such a way that parts of it can be selected, changed, used in calculations, and transformed into useful information for a wide variety of users. The data base resembles an information warehouse in that it is compartmentalized, with bits and pieces of data marked and stored electronically for easy retrieval. Through a combination of large data bases and powerful computers, an extraordinary number of different reports can be generated for a great number of people. MIS typically uses centralized data bases and software managed through specialized staff in an IS department. The IS staff help managers by generating reports, analyzing data, and networking company systems for a combined information systems capability.

Although clearly beneficial, this vast capability can be costly to a company because the easy access to data tempts managers to call up too much information. This problem can be resolved if managers clearly understand the dual nature of MIS. First, information is a resource that can be misused, just as raw materials can be purchased inappropriately or energy can be used inadvertently. Second, MIS is a service providing information through IS departments, and end users are internal "clients" using this service.[10] MIS clients, however, seldom have to pay for the service they receive. Free service is part of the controversy over misuse of information resources because MIS departments—like other departments—have limited budgets and personnel. When something is free, managers behave like most people, taking all they can get. Consequently, many companies experience runaway MIS costs.

One solution to this problem is to create a buyer-seller relationship between end users and the IS department. McDonald's Corporation has done this.[11] From the company's information center in Orlando, Florida, information is provided to more than 2,800 end users around the world, among them other departments, staff offices, and individual managers from the CEO to field sales managers. For each end user, McDonald's provides free (off-budget) MIS services, such as standard reports and transactions processing. When additional services are provided, end users are billed through a transfer procedure that deducts the cost for those services from the buyer's budget. A similar budgeting process at United Missouri Bank in Kansas City resulted in a 60 percent reduction in reports and computer printouts; many bank employees found they could either do without the information or create it themselves on their PC work stations.[12]

Management Information Services

As a service, MIS offers strategic managers nonroutine information for long-range planning. It also provides executives with performance reports and statistical analyses. Strategic services differ from those provided to middle managers, who, as you may recall, need information that focuses on near-term results and operations. Much of this information is based on well-defined models of cost accounting, production control, and sales activity reports. At the operational level, rapid feedback is required; ideally, MIS collects data in real time to give first-line managers instantaneous activity summaries. From a control standpoint, MIS is valued for providing to line managers fast, accurate, and timely information called *routine performance, exception, on-demand,* and *predictive* reports.[13]

Routine performance reports. These scheduled performance summaries include purchasing summaries, quality control reports, production output summaries, periodic sales activity reports, credit summaries, and a vast number of traditional accounting reports that have been automated. For example, a typical sales summary contains sales volume, units sold, numbers of orders completed, and changes from previous periods.

Exception reports. These reports are generated only when performance deviates from predetermined standards; their purpose is to alert management to the problem. In automated systems, exception reports are triggered much the way a circuit breaker is by an electrical overload. For example, when automated quality control equipment records defects on an assembly line, it triggers a warning and documents vital information on assembly procedures, enabling managers to quickly identify and resolve the problem. In most organizations, exception reports supplement rather than replace routine performance reports. As their name implies, they report variations in results.

On-demand reports. These are occasional reports that managers request. For example, purchasing managers can call up stock status reports, ask for an update on outstanding orders, or request a listing on vendor prices. Production managers may call up a report listing all maintenance performed on a particular machine. Personnel may ask for special rosters sorted by employee profile data such as age or sex.

Predictive reports. These reports are used in planning, when managers want answers to "what if" questions based on simulated conditions. MIS personnel employ analytical software to forecast future conditions, ranging from economic indicators to technological changes. The concept of an MIS must be expanded here to include the integration of economic, technological, and behavioral forecasting methods. Predictive reports are valuable because they allow managers to simulate what might happen if they initiate different decisions such as changing product prices or entering new consumer markets.

The Role of Integrated MIS

Although the fundamental role of MIS is to provide managers with information for decision making, there are more complicated uses of MIS; simple transaction reports are at the low end of a continuum of activities. At the other extreme are integrated operational activities. Recall that the definition of MIS emphasizes that it is the effective use of total information resources. Consequently, an effective MIS integrates information from TPS, OAS, and other specific types of systems to create unusual information capabilities. In Chapter 18, we described a number of these capabilities, including integrated production and operations systems such as MRP III, various computer-assisted on-line quality control techniques, inventory control models, materials management systems, capacity planning methods, and marketing systems.

In the future, MIS is expected to play a vital role in creating the "automated factory" where a few highly skilled technicians will operate very sophisticated technology. That technology is evolving today in so-called flexible manufacturing systems where information systems drive robotic machines. One example of this is **computer-integrated manufacturing (CIM),** a method of automating groups of processes and coordinating all related activities from processing initial customer orders to expediting final deliveries. CIM is also linked to subsystems, such as *computer-assisted design (CAD),* where products and processes are engineered, and administrative systems, where customer orders, credit, billing, and collections are controlled.[14] Figure 19-3 illustrates the primary manufacturing components of a CIM system.

computer-integrated manufacturing (CIM)
A process using information resources to integrate activities required for a complete manufacturing system.

CIM cells run entirely by computer-controlled devices, including advanced robots. Materials are brought on-line through automatic storage and retrieval systems (AS/RS), and work-in-process is moved between cells using automated guided vehicles (AGVs). Human intervention is minimized, and these automated activities are recorded together with intricate details on inventory usage, quality performance, order tracking, scheduling variances, and progress reports. Then information is sent to various subsystems such as inventory control and cost accounting data bases, where MIS processes instantaneous reports so that managers can control activities in their respective areas of responsibility.[15]

No system has been engineered to operate without human intervention, and the effectiveness of a CIM depends crucially on how well information systems can be managed; an exotic computer has little value unless directed to perform a function within a system of activities. Consequently, a CIM process is feasible only with effective operational control systems and highly skilled personnel to monitor them and to correct technical problems. At the strategic level, a CIM requires expert systems analysts to plan and design these integrated processes and managers capable of using information resources effectively.

In order to capture the essence of these responsibilities, the phrase *IS management* is being used in place of MIS. The connotation of **IS management** is that

IS management
The concept of responsibility by all managers for the management of integrated information systems.

FIGURE 19-3 Computer-Integrated Manufacturing (CIM) Work Flow and Critical Control Points

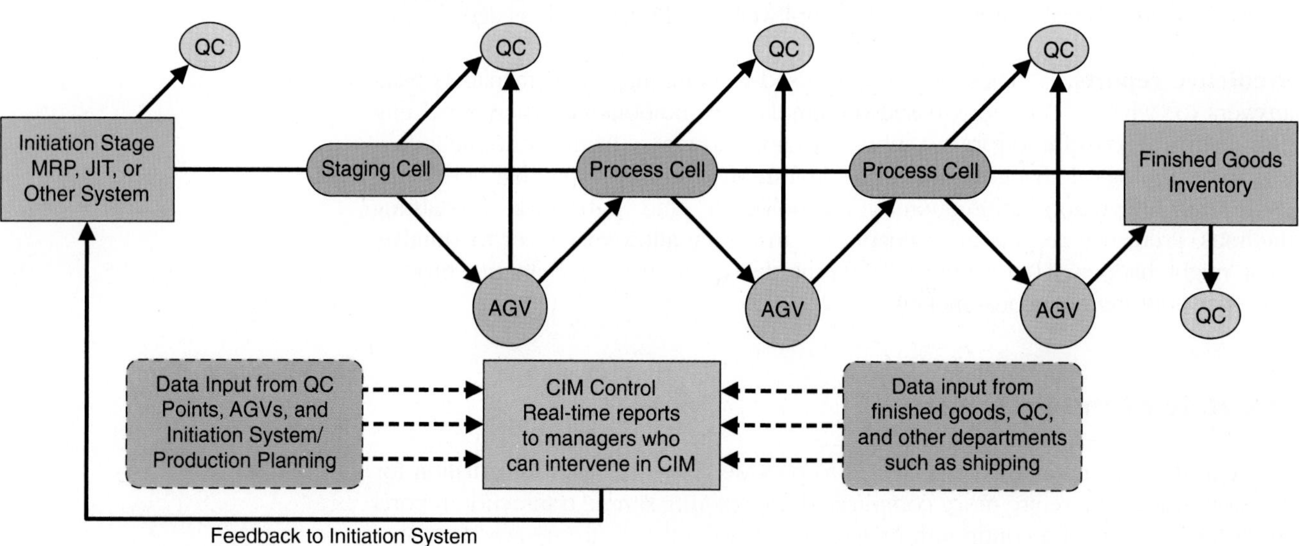

managers in every functional area and at every organizational level are responsible for information systems, not just specialists trained in information technology.[16] Therefore, future managers will be involved in integrated information systems management regardless of their field of specialization.

CHECKPOINT

- Explain how information is created and provided to managers in MIS.
- Describe information as a resource to be managed and MIS as an organizational service.
- How have integrated MIS redefined managerial responsibilities in all areas of an organization?

TYPES OF INFORMATION SYSTEMS

Although all information systems have similar categories of components, there are several types of systems, each with unique characteristics and each designed for specific uses. These are summarized in Exhibit 19-1 and discussed below.

Transactions Processing Systems (TPS)

The first information system to be computerized during the 1960s dealt with an organization's daily transactions. **Transactions processing systems** evolved as natural extensions of accounting activities, using computers to record, sort, and process data more efficiently than could be done by hand. TPS were also called *electronic data processing (EDP) systems,* and they were usually managed by a company's accounting department.[17] These systems created tremendous improvements in the computer's productivity when data were repetitive and calculations were simple. For example, computerization of payroll systems allowed rapid collection of labor hours, accurate calculations of customer billings, and automatic preparation of payroll checks. Production departments used TPS to track manufactured parts and record

transaction processing system (TPS)
Also called *electronic data processing (EDP),* a TPS is configured to handle repetitive data and programmed calculations for efficient transactions and report summaries, not to handle decision-making support information.

EXHIBIT 19-1 Characteristics of Information Systems

System	Orientation	Typical End User
Transactions processing system (TPS)	Repetitive transactions of structured information.	Operational: electronic data processing staff.
Office automation system (OAS)	Task productivity improvement in office and white-collar jobs	Operational: clerical staff.
Decision support system (DSS)	Information access of data base management for distribution use; schedules for management analyses.	Executives and middle managers: independent decisions and analyses, control documentation, and self-regulated reports.
Client/server system C/SS	Centralized data base with distributed but proprietary applications.	Departmental work groups and cell team users.
Expert systems (ES)	Knowledge-based decisions using stored information and expert logic.	All managers: rapid analyses and decisions provided to managers for solving unstructured problems.

costs, and as software evolved, applications were created for other repetitive tasks such as inventory control.

Today transactions processing systems are well established. They are distinct from other information systems because they are not specifically used to assist managers with decisions. TPS simply streamline data efficiently, providing accurate and timely transactions. A common misconception by managers outside this system is that information produced through a TPS should be useful to them in making decisions, but TPS results are oriented toward efficient transactions; not decision-making reports.[18]

Office Automation Systems (OAS)

office automation system (OAS)
Designed to improve productivity, an OAS is meant to reduce clerical work and increase the efficiency and effectiveness of office administration.

Office automation systems comprise information technologies designed to improve office productivity. Although they may help managers make better-informed decisions, their main purpose is to reduce the clerical burden of office administration. Included in office information technology are computer work stations configured for word processing, electronic mail networks, telecommunications equipment, electronic file systems, and support equipment such as facsimile (fax) machines. With computer systems linking company purchasing offices and suppliers, paperless purchasing has also become feasible. This requires an agreement between a company and its supplier to place orders by electronic transmission instead of sending typed purchase orders by mail. In sophisticated purchasing systems, orders are placed automatically whenever reduced inventories trigger a "buy order," and suppliers respond with electronic billing.

electronic data interchange (EDI)
A process that allows information with predetermined formats to be exchanged electronically between end users.

By integrating word processing, purchasing, and billing systems, OAS led to advances in marketing, such as telemarketing, interactive banking, and a new field called *electronic data interchange.* **Electronic data interchange (EDI)** is a subsystem of OAS that allows information with predetermined formats to be exchanged electronically between end users. Companies introduced EDI systems for paperless purchasing, but EDI utilization has been most apparent in situations where timely information is vital or huge reductions in paperwork can be realized. The IRS introduced a form of EDI with electronic tax filing, in which standard tax forms can be downloaded from a filer, then transcribed by the IRS into a hard-copy form. Blue Cross/Blue Shield of Massachusetts has introduced an EDI system—one of the first in health care—in which patient information can be electronically transferred between health providers (hospitals, doctors, clinics, etc.) and BC/BS for immediate processing. This simplifies patient records and admissions procedures, rapidly initiates insurance coverage, and efficiently handles billing, while eliminating mountains of paperwork.[19]

Among the latest advances in office automation systems is integrated telecommunications. AT&T has developed prototypes of voice and image transmission through video telephones, and although these systems are not generally available for commercial use, they are employed extensively within corporate communications networks for teleconferencing. U.S. Sprint has also developed a voice-activated system that electronically traces a caller's voice, matching a voice print with customer records to verify that a long-distance call is being made by an authorized credit card holder.[20] Soon office managers will be able to trace, verify, and record long-distance calls, update telephone billing, and control credit card use with OAS.

Decision Support Systems (DSS)

decision support systems (DSS)
Systems based on stand-alone microcomputers or work stations that allow independent application or access to central data bases to support management decisions. Also called *executive support systems (ESS).*

Decision support systems (DSS) allow managers to access central data bases without direct assistance of information systems staff. By employing application software, managers can do their own analyses and create their own reports. With the spread of microcomputers and desktop work stations, DSS have become popular. For example, a securities analyst can call up a client's account, access stock market information, tap into network data bases, simulate investment transactions, and perform a variety of portfolio evaluations without disturbing colleagues or using expensive mainframe computers. However, this puts greater responsibility on individual managers to learn applications and to use information resources effectively.

New software from Adobe Systems may finally make the paperless office a reality. Adobe has developed a technology called Carousel, which instead of printing files on paper, renders them readable on other computer monitors. Carousel accomplishes this task by creating a "universal" document that can be viewed on a number of different types of computers. Thus a company that installs Carousel throughout its organization would be able to circulate large documents like employee policy manuals via disk or distribute the data on a computer network. Unlike the widely used American Standard Code for Information Interchange (ASCII), Carousel will also be able to handle graphics and photos as well as various typefaces.

DSS as management tools. Decision support systems are also called *executive support systems (ESS)* when they are configured to support the unstructured decisions typical at higher management levels. For example, a decision support system used by Chase Manhattan Bank allows managers to retrieve data on commercial loans, then analyze the effects of interest rates on profits. By applying hypothetical interest rates to different categories of loans, Chase executives can study how changes in their loan portfolios and interest rates are likely to affect bank revenue. At Ernst & Young, consultants perform financial risk analysis on clients' accounts and investments. And at Chemical Bank of New York, executives run disaster simulations on personal computers, evaluating physical facilities for risk of fire, earthquake, and flood damage.[21]

Most DSS systems are constrained by their small memories and limited data storage capacities. They also tend to be slow compared to powerful mainframe systems. Although several computers can be linked to share information, most systems are designed for individual applications. Therefore, when large amounts of data such as company payroll records require processing, mainframe systems are more effective.

Despite these limitations, DSS are tremendous tools for helping managers make better-informed decisions. The individuality of DSS also allows managers to work after hours—at home, on airplanes, or in hotels—at their own pace. With the rapid growth of telecommunication systems, managers can also access electronic mail networks on a global basis.[22]

Decision support systems and associated software are becoming very sophisticated, and advanced systems may soon make "stand-alone" DSS obsolete. Figure 19-4 shows how these information systems developed slowly from their mechanical beginnings.

LAN, Distributed Computing, and Client/Server Systems (C/SS)

As companies equipped people with more personal computers, pressure mounted for "linkage" within departments to share common information. At the same time, companies realized that a network of computers could share printers, software, and data storage, resulting in huge cost savings. Consequently, the concept of *network computing* was born. A network is driven by a central device called a *file server* that allows individual work stations to access centralized software, retrieve or store data, and send information to printers or electronic bulletin boards.[23] A **client/server system (C/SS)** is a network that allows distributed computing among network users, yet retains full access to a central mainframe file server. Although the concept seems simple, true client/server systems are only beginning to emerge. In order to understand how a C/SS works, it is necessary to understand the concepts of a *network* and *distributed computing.*

client/server system (C/SS) A network that allows distributed computing among network users, yet retains full access to a central mainframe file server.

LAN. The most common form of network is a **local area network (LAN).** LAN is depicted in Figure 19-5. This is a system of interconnected hardware, software, and communication devices linking various work centers together for shared information activities.[24] LANs can be used in decision support system roles, but they are more often employed to access central file servers, which run faster, store more

local area network (LAN) A system of interconnected hardware, software, and communication devices, linking various work centers together within an organization so that information can be shared.

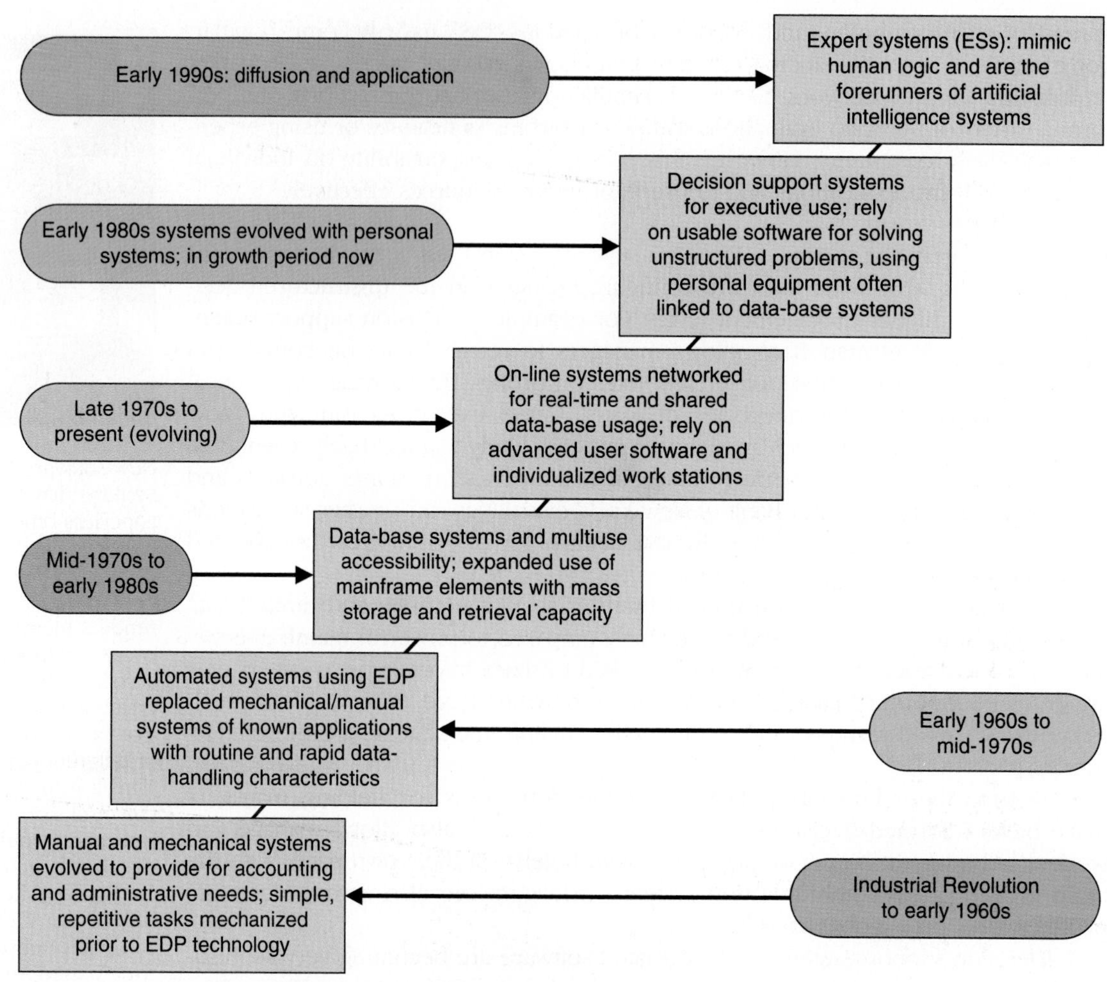

FIGURE 19-4 Evolution of Information Systems

FIGURE 19-5 Local Area Network (LAN) Using Shared Data Base of System Network Software for Multiuser Service

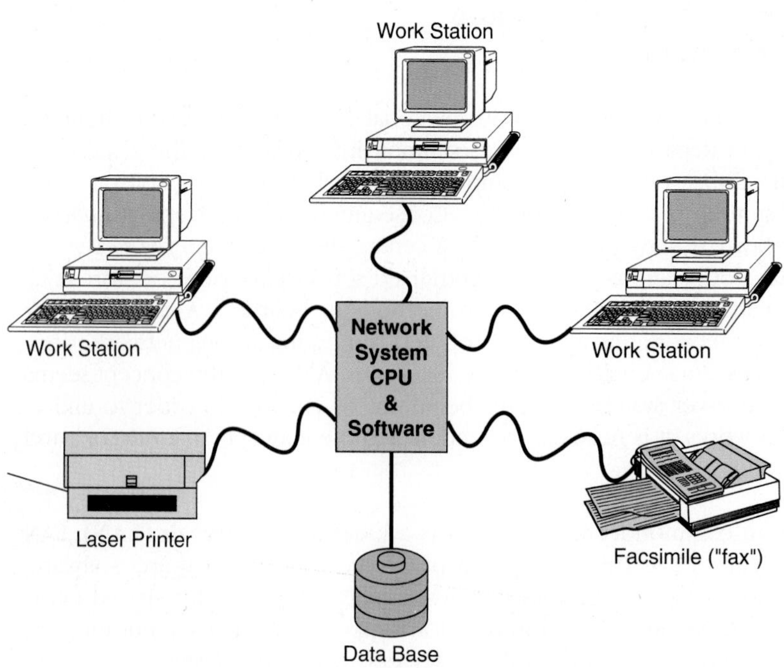

data, and accommodate more powerful software than a single PC. Thus a person can do efficient transaction processing or access vast amounts of information rapidly on a network that would otherwise be impractical on a PC. Networks are also used for interoffice communications, and information can be moved among users to improve coordination.

A LAN also allows employees to work privately on different tasks at their individual work stations while sharing common data and central software. For example, a purchasing clerk can work at one station processing orders while another employee is preparing a report on vendor price changes at another station. Still another employee can check inventory status at a third station while the purchasing manager is analyzing the purchasing budget at a fourth station. All four people will be using the vendor data base simultaneously without interference because the LAN file server rapidly (in microseconds) allocates software and data access time to the various users.

Distributed computing. What an LAN does not do is allow applications to "move off" the file server; software cannot be downloaded to or legally copied at individual work stations, and data storage is securely maintained in a central repository. The LAN does allow distributed computing. **Distributed computing,** also called *distributed processing,* is the decentralization of information processing work from a central computer to multiple work stations. This extends the power of the central mainframe by adding work stations, and it also relieves the workload of a centralized staff by shifting much of the actual processing work to other employees. Consequently, a networked purchasing office like the one in the example given above will process its own orders, do vendor and price analysis, and generate its own reports. In a centralized system without networks, purchasing would have to request all this work from the central staff, and then wait for hard-copy reports and printouts to be routed to them.[25]

distributed computing
Also called *distributed processing,* it is the decentralization of information processing from a central computer to multiple work stations.

Distributed computing and LANs have clearly improved organizational productivity by enormous margins. They have revolutionized how work is accomplished and brought many important benefits to society. For example, while mainframe systems are used for airline flight reservations, airlines have LANs at airports to control schedules, passenger lists, fares, and maintenance. LANs are also used to process payrolls, revenues, expenses, and personnel schedules. In manufacturing, mainframes are used for major tasks such as MRP III and JIT processing (described in Chapter 18), but LANs are used to distribute processing for customer order tracking, purchasing, production and quality control, and administrative functions such as payroll, cash management, personnel scheduling, and dozens of other activities. Engineers access mainframe data, but do their own computer-aided design work on LANs, and communications staff use LAN distributed systems to control PBX telephone networks, telemarketing activities, and teleconferencing.

Client/server system (C/SS). A client/server system is an extension of network and distributed computing concepts. However, a C/SS goes much further than sharing access between a central file server and distributed work stations. A true C/SS allows applications to "move off" the mainframe so that software and data are not merely shared but actually decentralized. In this type of information environment, software and data are no longer controlled as proprietary assets held in a central file server and accessed only with appropriate authority by end users. A C/SS, by definition, allows any person with a work station to communicate with any other person with a work station.

There are two severe constraints on implementing a C/SS in its pure form. First, the technology exists but is limited to "hard-wired" systems. LANs are physically wired together, limiting the number of devices that can be linked together and limiting how far away they can be from a file server. Second, allowing applications to move off the file server threatens software and data security. Mainframes can be secured by electronically locking-out access (or locking up data and software), but a C/SS allows access to almost anyone. Unlike the LAN illustrated earlier, which is based on a "ring" of devices with a central file server, the C/SS is based on a "bus" system without a central controller. A bus's spread is limited today by the technology of hard-wired systems, but with advances in telecommunications, wires will soon disappear and this constraint will be eliminated. A C/SS bus system is shown in Figure 19-6.

Nevertheless, many companies are implementing C/SS with methods to maintain security. At the beginning of the chapter, we noted that The Travelers Corporation is developing such a system. The company distributes software applications to its users, but maintains data security and sensitive communications through a tier of controlled file servers. Chevron introduced a C/SS for sales and marketing functions by using PC-based LANs that process more than 165,000 transactions each month. Chevron has more than 200 users, including transactions clerks, managers, and marketing analysts. Data and processing are distributed, but the software is centralized. And Barclay's Bank has introduced a layer of file servers using minicomputers that replicate selected mainframe software and data for specific banking functions such as commercial lending and money transactions. The bank then uses LANs tied to its minicomputers to distribute processing.[26]

These examples disguise the progress C/SS represents. Most analysts believe C/SS technology will not become common until 1997, and then only if security and access problems have been resolved. They point out that in 1992 the average LAN had only seven users in common work groups, and by 1994, the number should rise to fourteen, but that these numbers hardly represent the concept of C/SS as an information system for interactive computing throughout an organization.[27]

FIGURE 19-6 A Bus Network with Open Systems Linkage

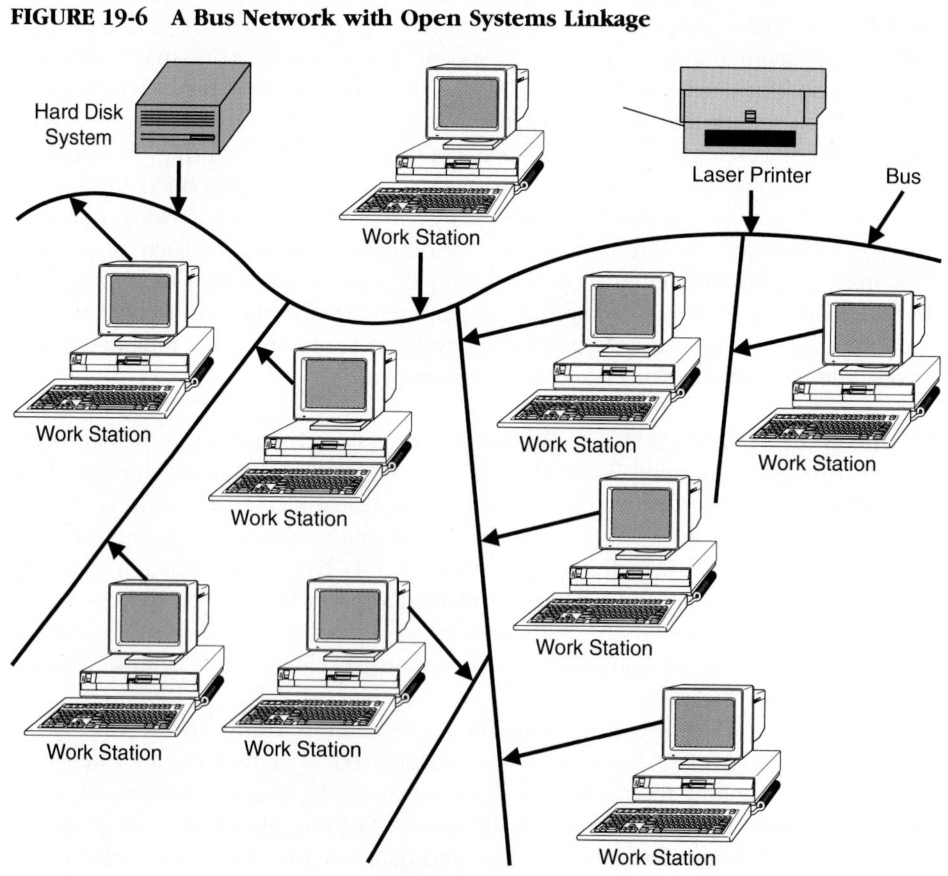

Expert Systems (ES)

Expert systems (ES) mimic the thinking of human experts by using models of expert decisions and the extensive knowledge stored in their data bases.[28] Although ES programs are still in their infancy, breakthrough programming by major computer firms has already created operating systems that perform analysis and monitoring activities as their human creators would. The heart of an ES is its ability to pose "if . . . then" questions and computer-generated solutions. Some programs actually create programs of their own. Westinghouse has an ES called PDS that is an integrated computer program within the steam turbines Westinghouse manufactures. PDS operates continuously to monitor turbine performance and generates recommendations to management for maintenance and repair. American Express uses ES to automatically analyze credit applications and to monitor customer credit card spending limits. XCON, a Digital Equipment Corporation program (eXpert CONfigurer), is a product design system that combines information from salespersons, customers, engineers, production managers, and financial managers to suggest new-product innovations.

expert systems (ES)
Software programs that are capable of mimicking the human thought process by using extensive human knowledge stored in complex data bases.

The major constraint of expert systems is that "if . . . then" scenarios are limited to information put into the system by human beings. Computers still do not "think"; they only process information. Expert systems are, however, able to access huge amounts of data and hundreds of separate data bases, with extraordinary speed to create new amalgamations of information. These new configurations of information are self-generated, and this unusual feature of ES is what differentiates it from other systems.

Artificial Intelligence (AI)

Although not a system, **artificial intelligence (AI)** is concerned with computing technologies that will allow machines to emulate the way a human brain processes information. When AI reaches this stage of development, machines will be able to accomplish tasks previously believed to be the exclusive domain of human intelligence.[29] Expert systems form a subset of artificial intelligence, but differ from AI in that ES engineers have already succeeded in creating programs that at least mimic some human actions, whereas AI engineers are still striving to make a humanlike breakthrough. Nevertheless, the rate of change in technology is extraordinary, and fifth-generation AI technology may be a reality by the turn of the century. An international research group that includes American, Japanese, and European members has mounted an unprecedented research effort aimed at creating AI in usable applications by the early 1990s. The group, called the Institute for New Generation Computer Technology (ICOT), expects to have an AI model tested before 1994.[30]

artificial intelligence (AI)
Fifth-generation computer technology that enables computers to emulate human brain processes for problem solving.

AI and ES are *knowledge-based* systems in which computer technology is used to make the knowledge that is implicit in the behavior of decision makers explicit in machine-usable form. By codifying knowledge as patterns of decisions made by experts, they permit managers to learn from, and replicate, great decisions. For example, doctors can search medical data bases containing thousands of diagnoses to find the one whose list of symptoms matches a patient's, identifying the patient's illness. These expert systems use stored knowledge to improve decisions, but they are not artificial intelligence. Although some researchers casually refer to advanced systems as having artificial intelligence, the current generation of computers can only claim to be fast, provide clear transmission of information, and manipulate a tremendous amount of stored knowledge; they cannot substitute for human intelligence.

AI, when it evolves, will be able to engage in "error learning," just as human reasoning does. The machines used in AI will understand natural language and replicate commonsense decisions through an extremely powerful process of scanning stored information. No existing system is even close to doing this, even though some

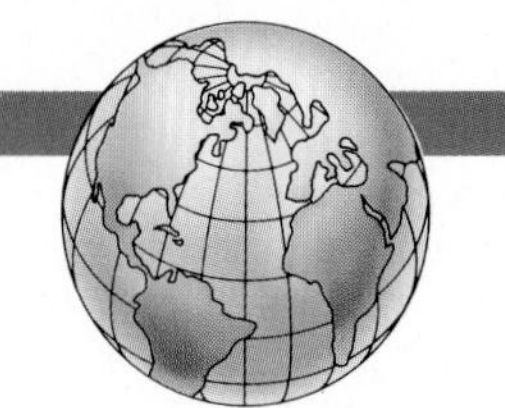

GLOBAL TRENDS
Matsushita Makes Neuro-Fuzzy Appliances

Although artificial intelligence is still a futuristic concept, appliance manufacturers in Japan make their machines mimic human logic. Matsushita Electric Industries (MEI) uses expert system concepts to generate *fuzzy-logic* microwave ovens that simulate a cook's judgment, setting temperatures according to sensory feedback. The latest MEI oven monitors air temperature, food texture, and moisture content to trigger electronic controls with minute adjustments in timing and heat levels.

MEI uses fuzzy-logic to control washing machines so that wash cycles, water heat, and spinning speeds are adjusted in predetermined ways to match types of clothing. The manufacturer claims its washing machines and clothes dryers perform much better than human operators, who only guess at machine settings and walk away; the MEI machine is sensitive to hundreds of settings and continuously monitors laundry. The technology is also embedded in camera processors to improve automatic focusing features, trigger light-sensitive flash-photo equipment, and operate shutter speed and aperture controls.

These "smart" appliances are just a few of the more than 2,000 experimental home and office mechanisms being developed by MEI. The company envisions rapid growth in small-appliance expert systems, ranging from kitchen food processors to home security systems. The cornerstone of the technology is its neuro-fuzzy logic controllers. Instead of responding to yes-no, on-or-off digital commands, the fuzzy system can respond with "sort of" and "maybe, but let's see" actions based on if-then logic programming. The next step in technology development is the use of neuro-networks that can "learn" from preprogrammed expert data and their own accumulation of inputs from sensory preceptors.

In addition to use in home appliances, the technology is being designed for applications in CD equipment, robot equipment, navigational aids, and anti-crash automobile sensors. Experimental versions are being developed for holographic imagery that can replicate a kitchen-size room with sensors that adjust images for people who walk through the holograph, perceiving reality where none exists.

Source: Jacob M Schlesinger, *"Get Smart,"* Wall Street Journal, October 21, 1991, p. R18.

advanced systems can accomplish amazing things. For example, one of ICOT's systems can read and translate 25,000 words a minute from English to Japanese, and it can rationally restructure language into appropriate contexts. A working prototype of AI, however, is likely to require capabilities many times faster and have the ability to concurrently assimilate dissimilar language relationships and concepts.[31]

British researchers are working on artificial intelligence technology that emulates the human senses. They are linking computer programming to human nervous systems in an effort to transfer human electrochemical responses to electromechanical devices.[32] This emerging fifth-generation technology, when integrated with artificial intelligence, may lead to *cyborgs* (human-computer hybrids). However, the early practical uses of these systems will most likely be to replace human limbs and to enhance medical rehabilitation technology.

As hardware systems are being developed to meet these engineering requirements, parallel biotechnical research is trying to unravel how the brain actually processes information.[33] Artificial intelligence will not be feasible until both the hardware engineering and the biotechnical brain processes are thoroughly understood. Only then will it be possible to develop application software, and it will be several years before workable models reach organizations. The socialization required to cope with this technology will take even longer. Still, people now in college will see these developments in their lifetimes. They will be called upon to lead their organizations through the transition from fourth-generation microelectronic computing to fifth-generation artificial intelligence.

CHECKPOINT

- Explain how TPS and OAS evolved and how they are used today in organizations.
- What are the major benefits of a DSS for managers?
- Describe client/server systems, how they facilitate distributed computing, and problems of managing these systems.
- What is an expert system, and how does it differ from artificial intelligence?

ORGANIZATIONAL ISSUES FOR INFORMATION TECHNOLOGY

Applications of information technology are important as management tools, but with each advance in technology, new issues emerge. Some of these issues lead to beneficial changes in organizations, but some create difficult problems. Rapid acceptance of microcomputers, for example, brought computing power to everyone's desktop, but as we saw earlier, this has resulted in tremendous pressure for client/server systems that bring software and data security problems. In this final section, we briefly address similar issues related to changes in organizational communications and social relationships and problems unique to information technology.

Changing Patterns of Communication

Technological advances such as use of fiber optics and satellite transmission have simplified communications. Global long-distance telephone and facsimile systems link overseas offices of multinationals as if they were across town. Electronic mail, an interactive process of exchanging information through computer terminals, allows entire data bases to be downloaded through telecommunication networks. And local area networking creates an information-sharing environment among select users. In each situation, information exchange processes are enriched; managers have in their hands vast new information resources and can transmit enormous amounts of information to other people. At the same time, they become more isolated at their PCs or work stations. The computer is a form of remote communication that does not require human interaction. Thus, social relationships dissolve in organizations equipped with LAN systems and electronic message boards.[34]

On the other hand, companies have realized immense benefits from using advanced forms of communication. One of these is *computer conferencing,* whereby a network links individuals through interactive computers. These networks can be restricted to one organization or have global subscriptions. For example, the Department of Defense has several internal networks. One, restricted to its Research Projects Agency, links together selected scientists, government officers, military agencies, and research institutions. By using special passwords, network members can exchange research through conferences that have several hundred people on-line simultaneously. Similar organization-based conference networks are used in nearly every Fortune 500 company, major university, and government agency. These so-called dedicated networks restrict use to subscribers, but network members may also belong to more comprehensive general networks linking different organizations. For example, NASA operates SPAN (Space Physics Analysis Network), connecting hundreds of government agencies and more than 2,000 private companies, like General Dynamics and Teledyne-Ryan, that have contracts with NASA. BITNET ("Because It's Time" Network), currently has more than 5,000 organizations in 82 countries. Other networks with commercial subscribers include GTE Telenet and TYMNET. Home networks such as PRODIGY have also become popular.[35]

An extension of computer conferencing is *videoconferencing,* which connects members through computer-integrated television systems. Compact television cameras transmit video data into broadcast systems controlled through computers, allowing members to switch among members during a conference for live TV pictures. It is like having a telephone conversation with television, but with the added dimension of interactively connecting people at the speed of light. The latest innovation (which will probably be replaced by yet more advanced methods before the ink is dry on this book) is called *groupware communications.* The concept of groupware is that it enables people to "meet" much like a committee meets, but to do so through electronic networking that allows instant exchange of notes, memos, or comments. Participants do not have to meet together physically to converse, so groupware members can be anywhere in the world.[36] As we saw in Chapter 10, this is a form of *telecommuting* that allows employees to work at home or in remote offices, restricted only by time schedules and office protocols.

This brings us full-cycle to where we began: with the problem of distancing or "disassociation" that threatens human relationships. Managers cannot adopt new information technologies without conscientiously addressing how these technological changes will affect the behavior and social fabric of organizational relationships.

The employees at this Boeing meeting are using groupware. Boeing concluded from a study it conducted on the cost-saving advantages of groupware that this software decreased the time needed to complete team projects by an average of 91 percent. One project, which would have normally taken a year, took only thirty-five days, including fifteen electronic meetings.

The IS Transition for Organizations

Many applications of information technology did not exist until fairly recently, yet we have rapidly become socialized to their uses. Banks, for example, have made credit card transactions commonplace through electronic transfer of information. Credit card consumers, initially amazed that they could buy something without writing a check or paying cash, now take plastic money for granted. Direct dialing and credit card calls are the result of information technology; few people miss having to place long-distance telephone calls through an operator. We have become socialized to these applications, and a similar socialization is occurring in organizations where word processing systems are rapidly replacing typewriters and robotics is no longer a futuristic technology.

Still, rapid diffusion of information technology has not significantly altered patterns of decision-making behavior. Strategic decisions are still made by committees of managers poring over reams of paper reports. Financial decisions, even when supported by computer analyses, are still largely a matter of personal intuition. Marketing studies still rely on individuals who churn out reports on consumer surveys. This does not mean that information technology is a neglected force, but that managers who are educated in computer applications tend to be young staff technicians, not operating managers or executives.[37] Organizations have yet to create an information culture, yet the transition is taking place.

Perhaps the most significant transition is to distributed computing, a concept discussed earlier. Distributed computing has expanded with the use of LANs, and also, as we saw earlier, LANs can be networked vertically through modified client/server systems. These broader networks that host LANs are called ***wide area networks (WANs),*** and although they are not pure client/server systems, they diffuse information processing and alter organizational relationships.[38] Figure 19-7 illustrates how networks can be layered and connected to external communication systems such as BITNET or TYNENET.

These changes in information technology have prompted a new concept in organizational structure. Called the **cluster organization,** this new structure will involve groups of people working together to solve business problems, manufacture products, or serve clients.[39] Some clusters will be temporary teams—much like project teams in matrix organizations—that come together for a specific task and disband when it is completed. Information and communication systems will enable these teams to be geographically dispersed and operate autonomously while maintaining close ties to the organization. Other clusters will be permanent teams—

cluster organization
An organizational structure based on work groups that work together to solve problems, manufacture products, or serve clients.

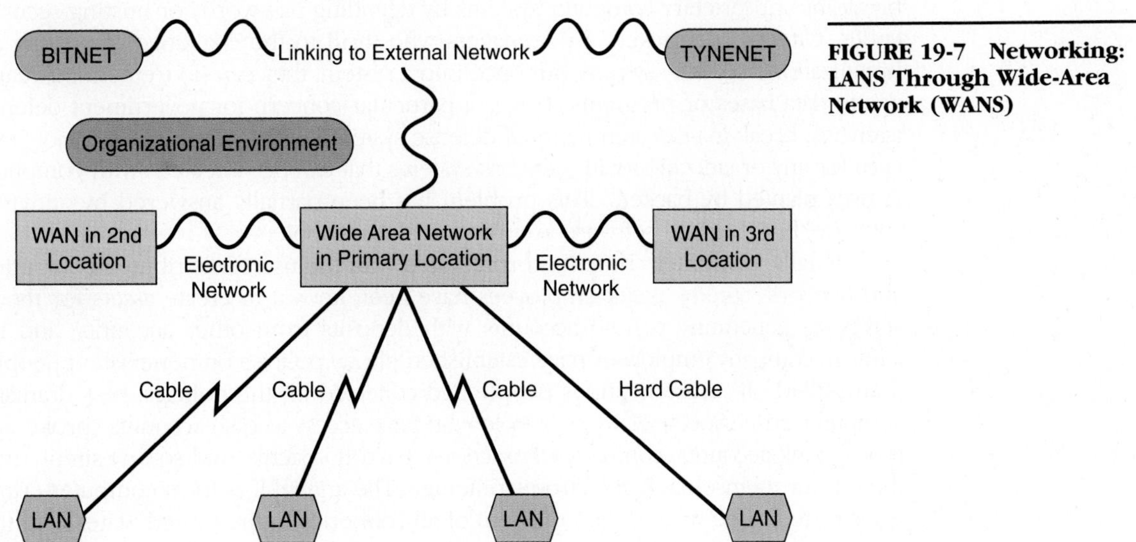

FIGURE 19-7 Networking: LANS Through Wide-Area Network (WANS)

much like manufacturing cells in a CIM process—whose members have complementary skills and carry out activities defined by their functional specialty.

The cluster organization is intuitively appealing because it helps resolve the problem of organizational disassociation created by distributed computing and remote-entry telecommunication systems. It also has a sound conceptual basis in team-building situations. Consequently, leading computer hardware manufacturers are building systems to accommodate WAN and LAN systems specifically designed to work with software developed for clustered work centers. The NeXT computer system is described by the company as an interactive team-based system for computing, Hewlett-Packard is experimenting with network architecture that would link hundreds of clusters into integrated systems of up to 35,000 individual users, and Lotus Development Corporation and Digital Equipment Corporation are making a joint effort to develop systems for "families" of work groups that would allow team members to work on one program or spreadsheet simultaneously.[40]

Problems Related to IS Technology

In addition to the important problem of social distancing, managers must address several problems peculiar to information technology. One of the most prominent issues is software security, as we noted earlier, the lack of effective security has constrained development of client/server systems. Unfortunately, software can be pilfered very easily. Unlike a $30 book that may cost $80 to photocopy, a $700 software program can be copied quickly onto floppy disks costing as little as $2. Wherever there is access to software, pilferage is almost assured. Those who copy the software may not do so for the purpose of selling it for a profit, but merely to configure their own work stations without incurring the cost of a formal site license. Nevertheless, it is thievery that deprives the developer who owns the software copyright of appropriate revenues, and this problem has not been satisfactorily resolved.[41]

Theft of software for the purpose of repackaging it and selling it is called *piracy*. Software pirates are rare in the United States or Europe, where copyright laws are recognized and violators are prosecuted, but piracy is a significant problem in almost all developing countries, which neither subscribe to international copyright laws nor have the capabilities to enforce such laws.[42] Piracy in the Asian countries of Taiwan, Thailand, South Korea, and the People's Republic of China is notorious, and many pirated software programs find their way back to North American markets through mail-order and discount outlets.

Another significant problem is access security. So-called hackers regularly break into proprietary computer systems by decoding passwords or busting security codes. Often these hackers are teenagers who thrill to the challenge of beating an organization's security system, but once into a system, they can do tremendous damage to data bases or programs. This is a particular concern for government defense agencies; break-ins threaten national defense system integrity. It is also a major concern for any organization with network systems that can be "infected" with computer viruses planted by hackers. This problem has been partially answered by antivirus software, but data and software security remains a problem.[43]

Finally, computer crime has proliferated with the use of distributed computing and network systems. Bank employees have been known to create assets for themselves by generating private accounts with deposits from other accounts, and insurance company employees have established phony policies on nonexistent people, then "killed off" these fictitious people and collected on the policies. Less dramatic computer crimes occur daily as people who have access to cash accounts (brokerage funds, bank accounts, company transactions, payroll systems, and so on) simply "tap the till" for themselves by electronic pilferage. The annual loss from computer crime is estimated to be greater than the sum of all robberies in the United States, and the prosecution rate for offenders is among the lowest for any crime category.[44]

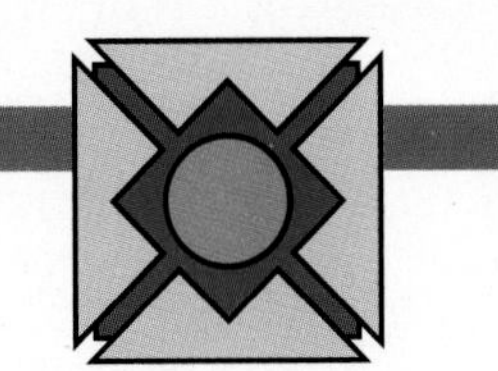

ETHICS IN MANAGEMENT

High-Tech Makes Cheating Easy

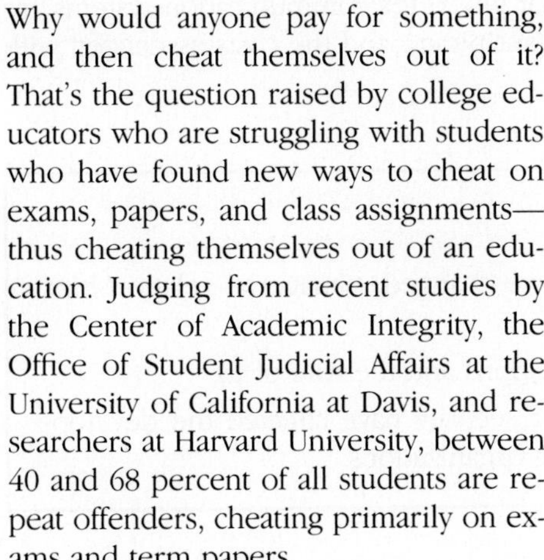

Why would anyone pay for something, and then cheat themselves out of it? That's the question raised by college educators who are struggling with students who have found new ways to cheat on exams, papers, and class assignments—thus cheating themselves out of an education. Judging from recent studies by the Center of Academic Integrity, the Office of Student Judicial Affairs at the University of California at Davis, and researchers at Harvard University, between 40 and 68 percent of all students are repeat offenders, cheating primarily on exams and term papers.

The controversy is focused less on student behavior—though that is a major concern—than on the information technology that makes cheating so easy. For example, students equipped with calculators and electronic memo pads can bring to exams answer sheets and class notes. Getting caught is a low risk because students can punch a memory erase button and destroy the evidence if necessary. Copies of exams and answer keys are also showing up on Walkman tapes and portable CD players.

More insidious is the ease with which vast data bases can be replicated on school computers, term papers copied on disks or distributed through network systems, and entire manuals electronically mailed between universities. Electronic bulletin boards allow students to rapidly share information or download copies of term papers. Instructor manuals that publishers send to professors are finding their way onto CD-Rom data bases or network systems, and with advances in optic scanners, no document is secure from reproduction. Publishers' test banks are commonly prepared on floppy disks, and these have become so popular that opportunistic students in California are replicating the disks and marketing them at huge profits.

Access to data bases has also prompted commercial interest by companies that sell CD disks containing complete biographies, short story plots, essays, and critical commentary on the most often assigned novels, plays, and poems. Students can therefore copy professionally prepared documents with the command of a keystroke, or they can cut-and-paste selections using software that automatically arranges an outline, spell-checks for errors, and corrects grammar. Once an essay or term paper has been prepared, it can be disguised for sale to other students by using an electronic thesaurus to alter words and syntax. Consequently, electronic plagiarism has now reached epidemic proportions.

Professors at MIT are fighting back by designing their own code-breaking software to detect language patterns among groups of term papers and exams and randomly restructuring exam questions for unpredictable patterns of answers. But the best solutions are low-tech—pop quizzes, oral exams, and spontaneous class exercises or cases.

Source: William M. Bulkeley, "High-Tech Aids Make Cheating in School Easier," *Wall Street Journal,* April 28, 1992, pp. B1, B11.

Companies address many of these problems by periodically upgrading all software and altering code systems for all data bases. However, this solution makes it necessary to retrain employees in new software methods. A company with a centralized mainframe environment and minimal distribution computed can upgrade and alter systems cheaply enough; for example, replacing an aging software program with an upgraded version on a mainframe may cost a company only a few thousand dollars, while a sophisticated high-end CAD/CAM system may run to only $30,000. However, if a company with a thousand desktop computers wants to upgrade a relatively inexpensive $200 program, the total cost is $200,000, and configuring multiple work stations with expensive software could mean exorbitant costs.[45] Consequently, advanced uses of information technology such as independent processing on WAN or LAN systems, the adoption of new methods such as client/server systems, and the development of true interactive computing or global telecommunication systems are all severely restricted by user pilferage, blatant piracy, and the costs associated with maintaining security.

CHECKPOINT

- Describe how information systems have changed managerial relationships and social behavior in organizations.
- Discuss the concept of cluster organizations and the role of IS.
- Explain how problems with computer security have affected the development of information systems in today's organizations.

AT THE BEGINNING OF THE CHAPTER we described how information systems have evolved at The Travelers Corporation. Travelers' most recent effort has been to introduce client/server systems, yet the company is concerned about maintaining effective use of its centralized software and data management capabilities while encouraging a distributed processing system. After reading this chapter, you should be keenly aware of the challenge implementing such a system represents. Thousands of individuals will be affected by the new system, and Travelers must consider the sensitivity of its data; security for a financial services and insurance firm is crucial. Nevertheless, if Travelers can make the system work, it will have extraordinary benefits for employees and clients through distributed computing and efficient communication processes. ■

A SYNOPSIS FOR LEARNING

1. Describe different requirements for information by managers in organizations today.

   Executives require information to support unstructured decisions related to strategic planning. Much of this information is derived from external sources, and it relates to economic, political, social, and competitive issues. General networks and telecommunication systems that access public data bases, bring together geographically dispersed offices, and provide industrial information are therefore important to executives. Middle managers have less abstract decisions to consider, though these decisions are not concrete and programmed like operational decisions. Therefore, middle managers require information that can be used in statistical models, such as predictive reports, and information derived from operating summaries. Decision support systems—once thought of as executive tools—have become important for middle managers, who use data from operating summaries to simulate near-term conditions and model alternative decisions. Operating managers need immediate feedback on activities, and are concerned with concrete, programmed decisions. Ideally, information systems provide them with "real-time" reports.

2. Distinguish between the types of information systems and their organizational uses.

   Transaction processing systems (TPS) record, sort, and process data that require repetitive calculations. TPS are most efficient when large amounts of data must be processed, such as payroll checks, and data are used to create various reports for managerial controls over transactions. Office information systems (OAS) are designed to improve office efficiency using electronically integrated tools such as word processors, facsimile machines, data storage and retrieval systems, and applications tailored to forms and filing. OAS seldom generate new data, but provide efficient ways to organize information for better productivity. Decision support systems (DSS) allow managers to access central data bases, selectively using and analyzing information without direct assistance by MIS staff. Managers use applications software to create their own models of data analysis and reports. DSS are valuable tools because managers can work privately and at their own pace without resorting to expensive centralized MIS projects. Client/server systems (C/SS) are based on networks of work stations that are themselves linked to broader networks. The C/SS concept is to load software and data "off-system" to local independent users, giving them the computing power and breadth of access currently restricted to central systems. Expert systems (ES) mimic the thinking of human experts by using models of expert decisions and stored knowledge. ES programs use logical if-then arguments to compute probable solutions to organization problems. ES are valuable because they can access prodigious amounts of information and perform extraordinary analyses faster than is humanly possible, but they do not create or think in human terms. Artificial intelligence (AI) involves computing technologies that allow machines to emulate the way a human brain processes information. AI is not yet a reality, but when it evolves, it will be able to engage in "error-learning" processes similar to those human reasoning engages in.

3. Explain the components of an MIS and why it is a service within a company.

   The five components of MIS are hardware, software, people, procedures, and data. Consequently, merely having an exotic array of machinery does not constitute a system, nor does any other component or incomplete combination of components. Too often the "human" element of the end user is ignored when designing a system, and the result is an expensive grouping of technology with exquisite capabilities that is of little use to the person (or purpose) for which it was designed. This is such a problem that MIS has begun to transform itself as a field into a "client service," designing services for human users and designing systems in conjunction with their end users. This is a major change in MIS philosophy, and with its acceptance has come a pervasive change in relationships and how MIS are organized and managed.

4. Discuss how information technology has changed human relationships in organizations.

   The act of distributing information resources and altering responsibilities for computer processing has led to disassociation as individuals become isolated at their work stations. This trend is most notable where various forms of telecommunications allow remote "meetings" and activities such as teleconferences or network electronic communications that eliminate the need for human interaction. On the other hand, the efficiencies generated by these systems have improved company and global communications. In addition, new systems called "groupware" allow people to work jointly on single programs, thereby helping to bring work groups together and improve their coordination. PCs, however, have made people and teams more autonomous, and new organizational structures are evolving around team concepts. One of these, called "cluster" organizations, involves consolidating team-based work cells or activities around common responsibilities and information centers.

SKILL ANALYSIS

CASE 1 Blake Realty: Leveraging Information

Blake Realty is a progressive home and commercial real-estate brokerage firm in southern California with six branch offices. The company has expanded rapidly under its founding broker, Ken Blake, but lately, growth has been hampered by problems of too much paperwork and inefficient customer transactions. Blake decided to automate his office systems and bought twelve microcomputers. Each office was given two systems. One was dedicated to office work and word processing to prepare house listings, closing papers, contracts, and correspondence. The second system office was connected with the other offices by telephone modem to share a common data base on property listings, bank and mortgage lending rates, and transactions related to sales.

For several months, the systems worked well, and Blake was pleased with the improvements in office productivity. His sales staff, however, were not happy with the systems. The data base provided them with a tremendous amount of information, but most of it was in "raw" form. They still had to calculate mortgages and taxes for clients and hand-write sales contracts and agreements (even though final documents were printed on the office system). Company administration, such as accounting, payroll, and sales commissions, was still done manually. Upon meeting with his managers, Ken heard a number of complaints, and consequently, he hired a consultant to analyze his business operations and resolve the issues.

The consultant concluded that Blake Realty had moved too fast in buying hardware without properly deciding what information services were needed. The first task was to identify the problems and types of information services the company needed. What the consultant found was:

- Salespersons needed applications that calculated mortgage payments, taxes, investment criteria, rental data, and other information related to buying decisions needed for client relations.
- The data base was updated by "batch" only as hard copy of sales contracts and listings were typed into the system. An on-line interactive process of directly updating sales and listing data was needed.
- Errors occurred in contracts and other customer records because documents were still prepared in writing by salespeople, then transcribed by a clerk using word processing. Ideally, a sales data base would provide accurate document preparation, validation, and record keeping without involving several people in each transaction.
- Offices would be linked together through one shared system that ensured rapid updating and easy access to information on listings and sales without delays or errors.
- All transactions would provide accounting information for calculating sales commissions, payroll, and summary financial reports.
- Much information could not be computerized, such as letters from clients, lender information, appraisal reports, and insurance documents. Therefore, a way had to be found to copy, file, and transmit this type of information efficiently.

Case Questions

1. For each problem or information service identified, suggest a category of information system needed and explain its characteristics.
2. Describe how a decision support system would help the broker with client relations.
3. What type of information processing is needed for those documents and correspondence that cannot be computerized?

VIDEO CASE Dreams to Reality: Advances in Computer Graphics

The line between reality and illusion is dissolving. Advances in computer graphics are now making it possible to create artificial three-dimensional worlds—worlds that are complete and believable, although they exist only in the mind of the viewer and the heart of the computer. Known as *virtual reality* (VR), this new technology uses pictures and sounds to wrap around the viewer's senses. VR allows you to imagine a place and step into it, to dream a dream and fly through it.

Jonathan Waldern, a thirty-one-year-old computer scientist in England, has launched one of the first companies to mass-produce virtual reality systems. He says, "The goal of virtual reality is simple. It's total submersion, complete detachment from reality." Waldern's system, like most VR systems, uses stereoscopic images projected onto tiny screens inside a helmet worn by the viewer. A powerful computer generates the graphics and sounds needed to convince the viewer he's in another world, and motion sensors in a special glove worn by the viewer allow him to begin interacting with whatever he sees. New imaginary vistas are opened up.

Virtual reality is also being used to re-create distant *real* worlds. At the NASA-Ames Research Center in California, virtual reality techniques were employed to convert two-dimensional electronic pictures sent back from the *Viking* orbiters into a three-dimensional model of the planet Mars. Thus NASA geologists and astronauts are able to explore other planets without ever leaving Earth.

More down-to-earth applications of virtual reality are also available. Detailed models of city landscapes made possible by VR allow urban planners to redesign streets and neighborhoods without lifting a stone. Architects can use the wonders of VR to show buyers what their new home or building will look like before the first brick is laid.

The most promising applications for virtual reality are in the area of medicine. Current techniques for positioning radiation beams in cancer treatment are painstakingly slow and potentially dangerous. Professor Frederick Brooks, one of the pioneers working in virtual reality, has been testing a VR system that takes traditional CAT scan images and turns them into a three-dimensional model of the patient's body. This system would allow doctors to plan their method of attacking the tumors on the virtual patient before dealing with the actual patient.

Case Questions

1. What is virtual reality? What makes it possible?
2. Do you see any areas where managers might be able to utilize VR systems? If so, what? If not, why not?
3. What are some of the potential drawbacks of virtual reality?

Source: Christopher Barr, "Virtual Reality Goes Mainstream," *PC Magazine,* April 28, 1992, p. 31ff; Glenn Rifkin, "PBS Series Will Stroll into 'Virtual Reality,'" *New York Times,* April 1, 1992, p. C7; Harvey P. Newquist, "Virtual Reality's Commercial Reality," *Computerworld,* March 30, 1992, p. 93ff; William F. Zachmann, "Virtual Reality in the Real World," *PC Magazine,* March 17, 1992, p. 107; and Banjamin Wolley, "Larger Than Life," *New Statesman and Society,* August 30, 1991, p. 36ff.

SKILL PRACTICE

TOO MANY PAGES

Introduction

Our need for voluminous amounts of information, coupled with our ability to rapidly produce printed documentation, is drowning readers in a sea of paper. Some have called this problem "information indigestion."

The U.S. Navy is currently grappling with this very problem. A Navy cruiser may carry up to 26 tons of technical manuals with operating and maintenance instructions for its complex weapons systems. Each ton of paper that a ship has to carry means one ton less is available for fuel, ammunition, and other supplies.

Even if well-indexed, a large manual requires considerable technical knowledge on the part of the user to find the information required to perform a maintenance function. Often two or three manuals have to be accessed simultaneously during a maintenance task. Only a couple of pages may be needed from each manual, but the entire manual must be carried to the work location. Updating these manuals is another major problem. Either the entire manual must be reprinted and distributed, which can cost millions of dollars, or new pages must be printed and distributed. These changed pages must then be manually posted by sailors throughout the Navy. What the Navy needs is an economical alternative to paper technical manuals. This alternative must act like a book and cost like a book, take up less space, provide more aid to the user, allow the user to interact with it faster, and reduce the update burden. There are millions of pages of technical manual documentation currently in existence. Any computer system that would replace them must be capable of digitizing this documentation at a cost of only pennies per page. It must produce an image that looks like a technical manual page, including foldouts and pictures. And it must allow the user to access any page in a manual at least as quickly as it can be accessed in the paper documents.

Instructions

- Small teams will be formed by the instructor with four to six members in each one. Each team will be part of the Super Tech Consulting Corporation. Thus the teams will be Super Tech One, Super Tech Two, and so on. (10 minutes maximum)
- Each team should consider the problem the Navy faces with modernizing its bulky manuals. Consider the five key characteristics: accuracy, verifiability, completeness, relevance, and timeliness. Teams should also consider MIS, DSS, Expert Systems (ES), and Teleconferencing.
- Teams should brainstorm the problem for 20 minutes, then scan the ideas generated and select the three that are considered by team members to be the most promising. These three should be ranked. (10 minutes)
- The instructor will ask one person from each team to present their top three ranked recommendations to the class and will make comments on the optimum solution, given realistic constraints in the Navy's situation. (10 minutes)

Source: Based on an article by George Dougherty, "Books Don't Float," *The Data Bus,* August 1987.

DESKTOP DOCTORS

By Ron Winslow

Burlington, Mass.—When Kelli Marcou took her 15-month-old son for a checkup at the Harvard Community Health Plan's clinic here earlier this year, Dr. Max Walten listened to the baby's heart with a stethoscope and checked his ears with an otoscope.

Then, facing Mrs. Marcou with a keyboard in his lap, he typed data about his young patient into his computer workstation and ordered a prescription.

In most businesses these days, such a scene would hardly raise an eyebrow. But in a doctor's office, it's as rare as an empty late-afternoon waiting room. While most physicians eagerly embrace the latest high-tech gadgetry for surgical and diagnostic procedures, they have been remarkably slow to log on to the desktop-computer revolution. Every time a patient visits a doctor, it generates seven to 10 pieces of paper; even in small practices, entire rooms are devoted to storing manila folders filled with medical data. Except for billing records, most doctors remain steadfastly low-tech.

Vying for Patients

At Harvard Community Health Plan, though, the goal is to create the near-paperless medical office. This is no pointy-headed quest for techno-nirvana. Managing clinical data more effectively is fundamental to the health maintenance organization's efforts to attract more patients in the competitive Boston market, as well as to maintain its reputation as an innovator in health care.

"We're trying to change the whole fabric of the business we're in," says Dr. John Ludden, medical director at the HMO, based in Cambridge, Mass.

The health plan's effort comes amid a growing movement to marshal electronic data processing power to fight two leading causes of soaring health costs: overutilization of services, and the enormous burden of processing claims and maintaining clinical information. At the same time, corporate America is beginning to steer employees to doctors and hospitals who can prove they provide cost-effective medical care.

"Employers are demanding that health-care organizations provide more information about what they're doing, where the money is going and what is the quality of care," says Dr. Albert Martin, president and chief executive of InterPractice Systems, which is developing the clinical-information system for Harvard Community Health. "It's impossible to provide that information when it's [stored] in thousands of paper documents."

That means HMOs and other health-care organizations that have computerized access to their clinical data will have a competitive advantage over those whose record of quality or effectiveness is buried in hundreds of file folders. Moreover, the Institute of Medicine, which is part of the National Academy of Sciences, issued a report last year urging that hospitals develop paperless medical records.

No Guarantees

But that hardly ensures that doctors and other medical organizations will be quick to adopt the idea. Hospitals, for instance, have been slow to acquire bedside computer terminals intended to help produce a paperless record, says Dr. David Nash, director of health policy and outcomes research at Thomas Jefferson Medical College in Philadelphia.

For one thing, many doctors don't like to type. Some experts think it will take advances in emerging technologies of voice and handwriting recognition to convert doctors to paperless records. For another, at most hospitals, doctors are independent contractors with different interests and loyalties than doctors who are salaried employees at group practices. "There's a physician culture that must be taken into account" when trying to develop a computerized chart, Dr. Nash says. "If paperless records are going to happen anywhere, they're going to start at group practices" such as Harvard Community Health.

The Harvard plan, which has more than 500,000 members in the Boston area and in Rhode Island, and which had revenue last year of $829 million, launched its prototype electronic medical-records project at its center here in Burlington about a year ago. Participants say the project began smoothly, thanks in part to several weeks of training and other support. But the HMO has been rocked by other controversy, including a recent physician uprising that led to the departure of Chief Executive Thomas Pyle. While the incident had no direct connection to the paperless-record project, insiders say it reflects the tensions that develop when an organization seeks to change the way it thinks about and delivers health care.

In any event, the plan expects to expand the project to its other 13 health centers around Boston. It's too early to show broad impact from the effort, but officials at the HMO believe it will prove a potent tool in the drive to both control costs and improve quality. InterPractice Systems—a joint venture of Harvard Community Health and General Motors Corp.'s Electronic Data Systems subsidiary—plans to market the system to other physician groups. Paper medical-record snafus are a major source of waste and customer complaints and could even expose a doctor or a health-care organization to liability. Studies show, for instance, that paper medical records are unavailable during 30% of visits; 11% of laboratory tests must be reordered because the results get lost enroute to the patient's file or aren't there when the doctor wants them.

And then there is the problem of doctors' handwriting. "My biggest nemesis is trying to figure out somebody else's handwriting on the chart," says Dr. Walten.

Reading Entries

With the automated system, Dr. Walten not only can read other entries in the record, he can order lab tests and find results entered in the chart when he calls up the record the next morning. He can, with a click or two of the computer's mouse, track a patient's medication record for, say, ear infections over several months, or make sure a child has been immunized according to the HMO's schedule. And he can order a prescription through the HMO's pharmacy, to be ready by the time his patient leaves his office.

Within a few months, doctors at the clinic will be able to call up suggested protocols for diagnosing symptoms or treating illnesses they may encounter only occasionally. "Some physicians may bumble through a workup and miss some important steps," Dr. Walten says. "This is a way of improving the quality of care."

It is expected to save money as well. Managing paper records alone costs at least an estimated $5 per patient visit—not including repeat visits and reordered tests required when the records aren't available. Dr. Martin, who was associate medical director at the plan before leaving to head InterPractice Systems, maintains that an electronic medical record will save as much as $10 a visit. Considering that the plan's 500,000 members visit a doctor on average nearly six times a year, total savings could approach $30 million—about 3.5% of the HMO's current annual revenue.

While both doctors and administrators of the plan worried that members would consider computers an impersonal imposition in their relationship with the doctor, patient complaints have been few. Indeed, when Dr. Walten typed in the wrong password and had to retype it to gain access to the system, Mrs. Marcou, who uses a computer in her family's jewelry business, felt it made the doctor seem "more human, like I'm more on his level." And after Dr. Walten (correctly) typed in the prescription for her son's ear infection, Mrs. Marcou picked up the medicine at the pharmacy on the way out. "It was ready before I got downstairs," she says.

A few days later, her son's ear infection flared up again. Because it was a weekend, she took him to a different Harvard plan clinic, but she forgot what medicine the child had taken. The other clinic wasn't equipped with the new technology, but its doctors have computer access to the records in Burlington; that enabled a doctor to determine what medicine the child had been taking and to prescribe a different one. "When I went back to see Dr. Walten" a few days later, Mrs. Marcou says, "he already knew what my son was taking. That was nice."

House Call

Meanwhile, in nearby Bedford, Mass., Mary Kyper and her family are participating in another part of the experiment. They have a computer terminal at home that is linked by telephone to a data base at the Burlington center. Mrs. Kyper has used it to seek help in treating a rash that broke out on her daughter's skin and for flu symptoms and other ailments for most of her family. "Most of the time, it eliminates a trip to the doctor's office," she says.

The plan has placed the terminals in homes of 150 members in an experiment to both promote health education and reduce unnecessary doctor visits. More than 30% of appointments are made for maladies that would cure themselves without doctor intervention, Dr. Martin says. When patients dial up the data base and type in symptoms, they get a series of questions that lead either to recommendations for home treatment or to make an appointment. If a member's answers indicate the possibility of serious illness, an alarm sounds at the clinic, alerting staff members to call the home.

Dr. Martin doubts whether it would make sense to provide a terminal for every member's home, but for people with young children or with chronic illnesses, it may prove a benefit. Mrs. Kyper is certainly satisfied, but now fears she may lose access to the system because her husband may take a job in another city.

"We're on the cutting edge of technology," she says. "If we have to go to another part of the country and have to go back to more routine things, I think we're going to be frustrated."

These and other experiences are winning converts on both sides of the doctor-patient relationship, but HMO officials believe the real benefits of the new system won't be apparent until it is up and running at all the plan's health centers. "For one of these systems to

Putting It on Paper

How much money would be saved if doctors' offices go paperless? Consider:

Percent of patients' visits during which a doctor can't get access to the patients' medical records	30%
Percent of hospital patients' paper records that are incomplete	70%
Percent of laboratory tests that have to be reordered because the results aren't in patients' records	11%
Percent of physicians' time spent writing up patients' charts	38%
Percent of nurses' time spent writing up patients' charts	50%
Weight of the average paper medical record (in pounds)	1.5
Percent of time a patient's age isn't included in a medical record	10%
Percent of time a diagnosis isn't recorded in a patient's record	40%
Number of paper medical records that a quality-assurance staff can review per hour	3
Number of automated medical records that a quality-assurance staff can review per hour	400
Percent of time that doctors, while taking a medical history, fail to note in the record the patient's chief complaint	27%
Number of people at a hospital who need access to a patient's medical record at a given time	22
Percent of total U.S. hospital expenditures spent on alcohol-related illness	20%
Percent of time a diagnosis of alcohol abuse is missing from a patient's medical record	90%

NOTE: Figures are based on various studies conducted between 1971 and 1990.

Sources: "The Computer-Based Patient Record," a publication of the Institute of Medicine; U.S. General Accounting Office; *Journal of the American Medical Association*

become a real powerhouse is going to take three to five years," says Dr. Ludden, "after the data pile up and it becomes a tool you can use to analyze what you're doing."

Once a few years worth of data have accumulated, for instance, plan managers can begin to evaluate the effectiveness of mammography-screening and prenatal-care programs, rates of birth by caesarean section, or approaches to treating coronary heart disease. "You need to look over time at what's happening to people to find out all the places where we can improve the work we do," Dr. Ludden adds. "You've got to have the data to know where those opportunities are."

CASE QUESTIONS

1. Doctors involved in the Harvard Community Health Plan say they are changing the entire fabric of their business. Describe the existing patient-doctor-treatment process and how it is changing from an operational standpoint.
2. The case reports a typical, and serious, problem of quality control for health-care and hospital environments. Describe in operational terms the quality problem, how it would affect health-care services and costs, and how process controls could be used to address the problem.
3. As this case illustrates, information technology is playing an important role in changing health-care organizations. Identify the types of information systems needed to address the problems of patient records and processing, physician care, and coordination among health agencies.

20

Entrepreneurship

OUTLINE

Entrepreneurship and Management
Historical Perspective
Entrepreneurship as a Process
The Entrepreneurial Spirit
Entrepreneurship as a Field of Study

Toward a Definition
How Entrepreneurs Are Perceived
Entrepreneurial Characteristics

Corporate Entrepreneurship
Intrapreneurship
Classifications of Corporate Entrepreneurship
New-Venture Units

New-Venture Creation
Stages of New-Venture Development
Crises in Development

Managing New Ventures
Planning
Organizing
Leading
Controlling

Managing Small Businesses
Defining Small Business
Common Types of Small Businesses
Perspective on Small Business

OBJECTIVES

- Explain the historic foundations of entrepreneurship in our free enterprise system.
- Discuss profiles of entrepreneurs and career implications for managers.
- Discuss the concept of corporate entrepreneurship, or intrapreneurship.
- Identify stages of development for new and growing firms.
- Explain planning, organizing, leading, and controlling in new ventures.
- Describe how entrepreneurship and small-business management differ.

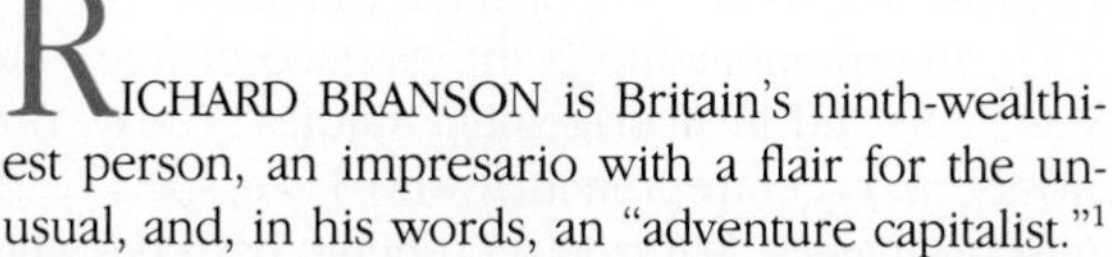

RICHARD BRANSON is Britain's ninth-wealthiest person, an impresario with a flair for the unusual, and, in his words, an "adventure capitalist."[1] He also owns one of the world's most unusual airlines, Virgin Atlantic Airways, which he inaugurated in 1984 with one tiny airplane. Today the airline earns more than a half-billion in annual revenues from routes throughout Europe and into New York and Florida. Branson is a compulsive entrepreneur who made Virgin Atlantic what it is through creative ideas and personal enthusiasm. He often shows up on flights, fills in as a flight attendant, jokes with passengers, and helps prepare the airline food. Branson has fun, and he makes sure passengers have fun too. Entrepreneurship, he explains, is the "business of pleasure."

He was born to upper-middle-class parents and sent to good private schools, which he promptly quit in 1968 at the age of 16. Never interested in academic studies, yet extremely well-read, Branson was a maverick who was told by his headmaster that he would eventually end up in prison or a millionaire. Today he is a billionaire. His first venture was a magazine called *The Student,* launched the year he quit school. It was a notable success. He sold issues through a mail-order system, one of the first attempts to market a slick magazine through the mail in Britain. This led to a mail-order recording business and eventually to his recording studio, where he sponsored rock stars like Phil Collins.

Branson sold the magazine and mail-order businesses, bought into nightclubs, and eventually sold the recording studio with its copyrights for more than $900 million. Then he leveraged his money into up-market retail outlets for youth fashions and sports contests such as hot-air ballooning. He once tried to set a transatlantic record himself in a balloon (and came close), but turned his attention to new challenges such as buying rights to unusual publications, movies, video games, and songs. His holding company, The Virgin Group, controls nearly 100 companies with $1.4 billion in annual sales, with Branson in control as owner-manager.

Typical of Branson's attitude toward his ventures is the way he describes Virgin Atlantic as an airline. "It is an entertainment business, meant to give pleasure, not simply a human freight express," he explains. Branson's genius lies in his determination to succeed by offering high value to customers. That, he says, is his only dogma for doing business.

Entrepreneurship is often associated with extraordinary successes—and failures—and entrepreneurs are thought to be creative individuals like Richard Branson who take huge risks in search of fame and fortune. These perspectives are sometimes true, but as we shall see in this chapter, entrepreneurship more often consists of long hours of hard work by ordinary people who have the tenacity to start and nurture their own businesses.

ENTREPRENEURSHIP AND MANAGEMENT

entrepreneurship
The process of creating wealth by bringing together resources in new ways to start a venture that benefits customers and rewards founders for their innovation.

Entrepreneurship is the process of creating wealth by bringing together resources in new ways to start a venture that benefits customers and rewards its founders for their innovation. We will expand this definition later, but initially it helps explain the connection between entrepreneurship and management. Successful entrepreneurs not only create new enterprises but also plan their ventures, organize their resources, furnish the inspiration and leadership necessary for the enterprise to succeed, and control the process of providing commercial benefits to customers. When they do all these things well, they acquire wealth and enjoy the personal satisfaction of providing something of value to society.

Entrepreneurship is the essence of free enterprise, yet until fairly recently, it was neglected in management studies. Today, however, there is a tremendous curiosity about entrepreneurs who have spearheaded industrial growth by creating new businesses. Many entrepreneurs have become folk heroes in the popular press; a number of them—like Richard Branson—are considered "characters," slightly out of step with the rest of the world.

Historical Perspective

Entrepreneurship is one of the four mainstream economic factors: land, labor, capital, and entrepreneurship. The word is derived from the seventeenth-century French word *entreprendre,* referring to individuals who were "undertakers" of the risk of new enterprise, "contractors" who bore the risks of profit or loss.[2] Many early entrepreneurs were soldiers of fortune, adventurers, builders, merchants, and, incidentally, funeral directors (how the term *undertaker* became associated with funerals is a mystery). There is a considerable body of literature on entrepreneurship. Fourteenth-century references to *entrepreneurs* concerned tax contractors, individuals who paid a fixed sum of money to a government for the license to collect taxes in their region. If these entrepreneurs collected more in taxes than the sum they paid for their licenses, they were allowed to keep the excess, and thus made a profit. But if they collected less, they suffered a loss. Entrepreneurship dominated economic writing in the eighteenth and nineteenth centuries in Europe and after the American Revolution, entrepreneurship became the driving force behind the new nation's economic development.

Economics and entrepreneurship. Richard Cantillon, a French economist of Irish descent, is credited with giving the concept of entrepreneurship a central role in economics. In his *Essai sur la nature du commerce en général,* published posthumously in 1755, Cantillon described an entrepreneur as a person who pays a certain price for a product to resell it at an uncertain price, thereby making decisions about obtaining and using resources and assuming the risk of enterprise.[3] A critical point in Cantillon's argument was that entrepreneurs *consciously make decisions* about resource allocations. Consequently, astute entrepreneurs would always seek the best opportunities for using resources for their highest commercial yields. Cantillon played out his theory in real life, becoming a wealthy arbitrageur who invested in

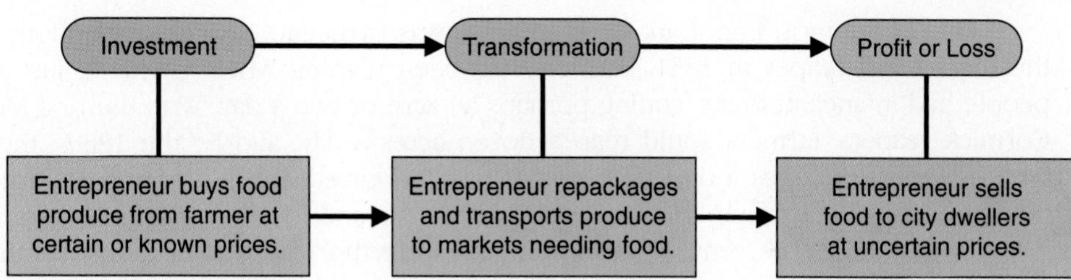

FIGURE 20-1 Cantillon's Early Vision of Entrepreneurial Behavior

European ventures, dealt in monetary exchange, and controlled farm commodities for auction in high-demand markets. His vision of entrepreneurship for farm produce is illustrated in Figure 20-1.

In 1776, Adam Smith wrote of the "enterpriser" in his *Wealth of Nations*[4] as an individual who undertook the formation of an organization for commercial purposes. He thereby ascribed to the entrepreneur the role of industrialist. But he also viewed the entrepreneur as a person with the foresight to recognize potential demand for goods and services. In Smith's view, entrepreneurs reacted to economic change, thereby becoming the economic agents who transformed demand into supply.

The French economist Jean Baptiste Say, in his 1803 *Traité d'économie politique* (translated into English in 1845 as *A Treatise on Political Economy*), described an entrepreneur as a person who possessed the arts and skills to create new economic enterprises, along with exceptional insight into society's needs and the ability to fulfill them. Say therefore combined Cantillon's "economic risk taker" with Smith's "industrial manager" to produce an unusual character who *influenced* society by creating new enterprises and at the same time was *influenced by* society to meet demand for innovative products through astute management of resources.[5]

In 1848, British economist John Stuart Mill elaborated on the necessity for entrepreneurship in private enterprise. The term *entrepreneur* subsequently became common as a description of business founders, and the "fourth factor" of economic endeavor was entrenched in economic literature as encompassing the ultimate ownership of a commercial enterprise.

In Austria, Carl Menger established the "subjectivist perspective of economics" in his 1871 *Principles of Economics*.[6] In Menger's view, economic change does not arise from circumstances but from an individual's awareness and understanding of those circumstances. The entrepreneur is the change agent who transforms resources into useful goods and services, often creating the circumstances that lead to industrial growth. Menger envisioned a causal chain of events whereby resources having no direct use in terms of fulfilling human needs were transformed into highly valued products that directly fulfilled human needs; this is the classic theory of production.

Although the European economists influenced our twentieth-century concept of entrepreneurship, most were concerned with models of macroeconomics, reducing their theories to precise mathematical formulas. Consequently, the human side of enterprise—the role of the adventurer or risk-taking entrepreneur—was ignored for several generations.

Antecedents in America. It is unlikely that the North American colonists paid attention to elaborate European economic theories on entrepreneurship. Instead they lived these theories out in their frontier adventures. Nearly every story of our early development, from the push west by French-Canadian fur trappers to the immigrant settlements on the Great Plains, is steeped in the folklore of individual initiative. During the 1800s, thousands of new products were developed that transformed North America. New plows, snowshoes, bridles, wagons, and mining tools were fashioned, and new hybrid crops were created. The telegraph became a commercial reality, and Samuel Colt introduced his six-shooter with replaceable parts (a significant innovation).

One of the most important developments was Cyrus McCormick's invention of the mechanical reaper in 1831. Farmers had been reaping wheat by hand, just as people had in ancient times, cutting perhaps an acre or two a day. With the first McCormick reapers, farmers could reap a dozen acres a day, and by the 1860s, they were reaping 100 acres a day.[7] The reaper revolutionized agriculture and inspired new industries in farm implements, grain processing, and food distribution.

In the nineteenth century, entrepreneurs were the "captains of industry," the risk takers, the decision makers, the individuals who aspired to wealth (and sometimes endured great losses) and who gathered and managed resources to create new enterprises. Menger's model of productive reallocation of resources flourished in the United States, and American adventurers created the chain that linked raw resources and useful products. Then the picture altered as huge, often embarrassing, fortunes were made. The connotation of entrepreneur changed from captain of industry to flimflam artist on the fringe of legitimate business who garnered profits at the expense of others. The term *entrepreneur* became associated with the "robber barons," yet it was exactly those individuals who drove the economy forward by launching steel mills, the oil industry, shipping, railroads, meat packing, and the automobile industry.

Entrepreneurship as a Process

Joseph Schumpeter, an Austrian economist, revived the honor of the entrepreneur when he joined Harvard University in 1934. Schumpeter wrote a series of economic treatises between 1911 and 1950 that addressed entrepreneurship, describing it as a force of "creative destruction" whereby established ways of doing things are destroyed by the creation of new and better ways to get things done. Entrepreneurship is often a subtle force, challenging the order of society through marginally small changes, but in Schumpeter's view, it can be an extraordinarily powerful force, such as McCormick's reaper or the processes that transformed crude oil into an energy resource. Schumpeter described entrepreneurship as a *process* and entrepreneurs as *innovators* who use the process to shatter the status quo through new combinations of resources and new methods of commerce.[8]

From time to time, proponents of entrepreneurship have surfaced to raise the banner of free enterprise. In 1964, Peter Drucker said, "Resources, to produce results, must be allocated to opportunities rather than to problems. . . maximization of opportunities is a meaningful, indeed a precise, definition of the entrepreneurial job. It implies that effectiveness rather than efficiency is essential in business."[9] Drucker returned to this theme in 1974: ". . . an entrepreneur. . . has to redirect resources from areas of low or diminishing results to areas of high or increasing results. He has to slough off yesterday and to render obsolete what already exists and is already known. He has to create tomorrow."[10]

There have been other proponents of entrepreneurship in recent years, but still the concept is elusive. Management literature has largely stayed away from the concept because of the popular myth that entrepreneurship and small business amount to the same thing, and small business has never been a popular subject in business schools. Other widely held myths about entrepreneurs depict them as gamblers or misfits who failed in corporate careers. (The latter point has merit because the strong individualism of many innovators has upset corporate management practices and led to unsolicited change.) Entrepreneurs are not necessarily small businesspersons, although many of them are, and most entrepreneurs do start small. Few are gamblers, but clearly they shoulder greater risk than most corporate managers, and they do create disequilibrium by championing new ideas.

The modern view of entrepreneurship accepts the reality that individuals play a critical role in introducing innovative change, that growth and development evolve from constructive change, and that stagnant bureaucracies need to be replaced by decentralized, adaptive, and creative forms of entrepreneurial organizations.[11] Management will continue to focus on systems development, leadership, and administrative efficiency, but entrepreneurs will continue to have important roles marked by ingenuity, individualism, and a zest for creative adventures.

The Entrepreneurial Spirit

Most growing, innovative companies exhibit an entrepreneurial spirit, corporations are urging managers to become entrepreneurially minded, universities are developing entrepreneurship programs, and individual entrepreneurs are making dramatic changes in our society. Small business is important to entrepreneurship because few firms begin large. Hewlett-Packard and Apple Computer Corporation were started by people with grand ideas tinkering with gadgets in garages; Ford, IBM, and Procter & Gamble were begun in the same way. The electric utility, telephone, and aerospace industries came out of similar humble surroundings, as did such major firms as J. C. Penney's, the Marriott Corporation, and McDonald's. The world of entrepreneurship is unlimited. Figure 20-2 is meant merely to stimulate your thinking; it would take an encyclopedic effort to relate how crucial entrepreneurs have been to industrial development. Most products and services we now take for granted emerged from the vision and determination of intrepid individuals.

We need to distinguish between professional managers—those working in established organizations—and entrepreneurs. Entrepreneurs *create* wealth and managers *administer* it. These are separate talents, equally worthy. Some creative geniuses are not able to manage their innovations; Alexander Graham Bell may have given us the telephone, but J. P. Morgan fashioned the organization to make it a

---

William E. Bindley, founder and CEO of Bindley Western Industries, perceived in 1968 that a revolution was occurring in the retail drug industry as giant chains were replacing small drugstores. So, at the age of twenty-eight, he decided to establish his own wholesale drug company to purchase drugs in volume and set up a highly effective warehouse operation so that Bindley would become the main supplier for the chains. After banks refused to back him, he mortgaged his house and began business in the basement of his father's small retail drug firm. Bindley had the managerial ability to realize his dream. In 1991, *Fortune* awarded the number-two spot on its list of most productive service companies to Bindley Western. Explains CEO Bindley, "We have a low-cost mentality."

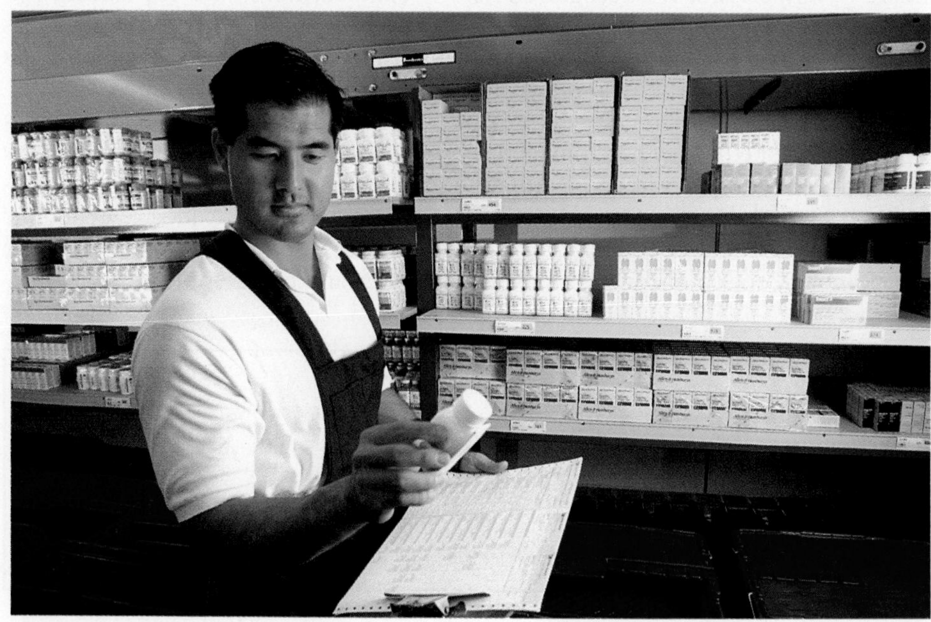

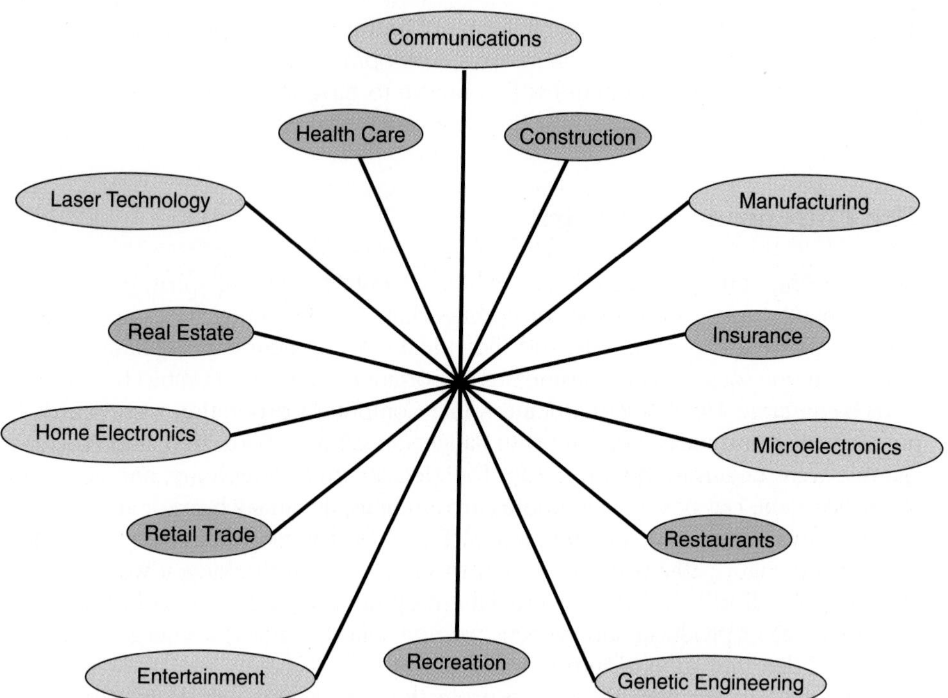

FIGURE 20-2 World of Entrepreneurs—Limited Only by Imagination

widespread reality. Similarly, Steven Jobs vaulted us into a new age of microcomputers, but John Sculley shaped Apple into a successful corporation capable of global marketing. Then there are a few people, such as Ted Turner and Ross Perot, who have the verve to both create and manage their ventures.

Entrepreneurship as a Field of Study

Entrepreneurship is an important field of study, not only because many students will become entrepreneurs, but also because many will manage new ventures created by others. Entrepreneurship is not a discipline in the same sense that marketing and accounting are; few people study the subject with a career in entrepreneurship in mind. Nevertheless, it is a recognized field of study in more than 400 leading colleges and universities. The resurgence of entrepreneurship in higher education has not come from the discipline of economics but from those who teach small-business management or have instituted new courses in entrepreneurship.[12]

Fortunately, entrepreneurs have ignored theoretical arguments and academe's opinion of the field. They have plunged ahead with tremendous energy to forge new enterprises in Europe, Asia, and North America. This phenomenon has been particularly strong in the United States through several generations of explosive economic activity. It is no accident that every *Fortune 500* enterprise that exists today was the creation of an entrepreneur who took a simple idea and persevered.

CHECKPOINT

- Compare the viewpoints of early economists with those of today's economists on entrepreneurship.
- Discuss Peter Drucker's description of entrepreneurship as a process for allocating resources to opportunities.

TOWARD A DEFINITION

We do not have one undisputed definition for *entrepreneurship* or *entrepreneur*. However, Schumpeter provided a framework for understanding both in terms of a process. The entrepreneur seeks, in Schumpeter's words,

> to reform or revolutionize the pattern of production by exploiting an invention or, more generally, an untried technological possibility for producing a new commodity or producing an old one in a new way, by opening up a new source of supply of materials or a new outlet for products. . . . Entrepreneurship, as defined, essentially consists in doing things that are not generally done in the ordinary course of business routine.[13]

Schumpeter did not equate entrepreneurs with inventors, suggesting instead that an inventor only creates a new product, while an entrepreneur gathers resources, organizes talent, and provides leadership to make that product a commercial success. Schumpeter's explanation has many interpretations, but for our purposes, we will use one interpretation recently put forward by Robert Ronstadt, which is:

> Entrepreneurship is the dynamic process of creating incremental wealth. This wealth is created by individuals who assume the major risks in terms of equity, time, and/or career commitment of providing value for some product or service. The product or service itself may or may not be new or unique but value must somehow be infused by the entrepreneur by securing and allocating the necessary skills and resources.[14]

Consequently, an **entrepreneur** is a person who starts a new business, taking the initiative and the risk associated with the new venture, and who does so by creating something new or by using resources in unusual ways to provide value for customers. The term is inappropriate for people who simply choose to run their own business rather than work for others, such as the typical gas station owner, small retail franchisee, or restaurateur. Most of these individuals, and many others in personal service businesses (e.g., barbers, beauticians, and independent insurance agents), have simply applied their money or skills to an enterprise instead of working for someone else as an employee. On the other hand, a gas station owner who plans a growing chain of stations, a retailer with a vision for a chain of unusual stores, and a restaurateur who creates a new approach to food service can properly be called entrepreneurs. The important distinctions are *vision* for growth, *determination* for constructive change, and *persistence* to turn an idea into a commercial success. As Figure 20-3 shows, these are the three most crucial aspects of success in new-venture management.

entrepreneur
A person who starts a new business, taking the initiative and the risk associated with the new venture, and who does so by creating something new or by using resources in unusual ways to provide value for customers.

The phrase *new-venture managment* used in the title of Figure 20-3 suggests that entrepreneurship is more than opening a new business. Vision by itself has little value; determination must be focused on an objective and persistence must be channeled in constructive ways. In opening a new business, these three qualities are needed to bring new ideas to life. In an existing organization, they are just as important to help a firm become innovative and to grow.

FIGURE 20-3 Crucial Aspects of New-Venture Management

Vision → Determination → Persistence

- Vision: Ideas for development
- Determination: Constructive use of resources
- Persistence: Commercial success

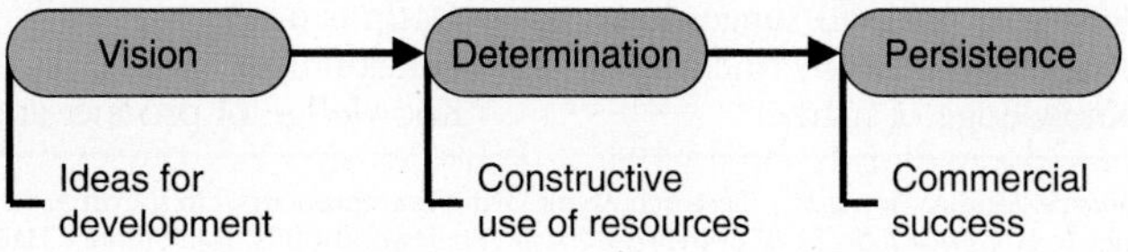

How Entrepreneurs Are Perceived

Even with a definition in mind, we still have trouble identifying entrepreneurs, finding them, or determining what they do. Does the local gas station owner have hidden aspirations to create a chain of self-service ministops? Are there entrepreneurs in corporations? In schools? In government? There are no short answers to these questions because there are no formal guidelines for classifying entrepreneurs. Who is characterized as an entrepreneur also may depend on who is doing the classifying.

Karl Vesper, in his research on entrepreneurship, found that the nature of entrepreneurship is often a matter of perception.[15] Economists—at least those who endorse free enterprise—subscribe to Schumpeter's view that entrepreneurs bring resources together in unusual combinations to generate profits. Psychologists tend to view entrepreneurs in behavioral terms as achievement-oriented individuals driven to seek challenges and new accomplishments. Marxist philosophers may see entrepreneurs as exploitative adventurers, representative of all that is negative in capitalism. Corporate managers too often view entrepreneurs as small businesspersons lacking the qualities needed in corporate managers. On a positive note, Vesper suggests that those of us who strongly favor a market economy view entrepreneurs as pillars of industrial strength—the movers and shakers who constructively disrupt the status quo.

Consequently, entrepreneurs are often identified by the way they behave and what they accomplish through their activities. This line of reasoning has prompted researchers to try to classify entrepreneurs according to behavioral characteristics. If a pattern could be identified, so the argument goes, then everyone would benefit by understanding why discordant behavior occurs in people like Richard Branson of Virgin Atlantic.

Entrepreneurial Characteristics

Research on entrepreneurial characteristics has focused on traits common to a majority of individuals who start and operate new ventures. John Hornaday of Babson College was among the first to use surveys and intensive interviews to develop a composite list of entrepreneurial traits.[16] These are summarized in Exhibit 20-1. Although this descriptive list is supported by impressive data, it has the restriction of relating only to highly successful entrepreneurs; there is no way of knowing how these traits relate to the majority of entrepreneurs. For example, some people may have the creative talent to generate new ideas but lack the ability to organize re-

EXHIBIT 20-1 Characteristics of Successful Entrepreneurs

Self-confidence	Perseverance, determination
Energy, diligence	Resourcefulness
Ability to take calculated risks	Need to achieve
Creativity	Initiative
Flexibility	Independence
Positive response to challenges	Foresight
Dynamism, leadership	Profit orientation
Ability to get along with people	Perceptiveness
Responsiveness to suggestions	Optimism
Responsiveness to criticism	Versatility
Knowledge of market	Knowledge of product and technology

Source: John A. Hornaday, "Research About Living Entrepreneurs," in Calvin A. Kent, Donald L. Sexton, and Karl H. Vesper (eds.), *Encyclopedia of Entrepreneurship* (Englewood Cliffs, N.J.: Prentice-Hall, Inc., 1982), p. 28. Adapted with permission.

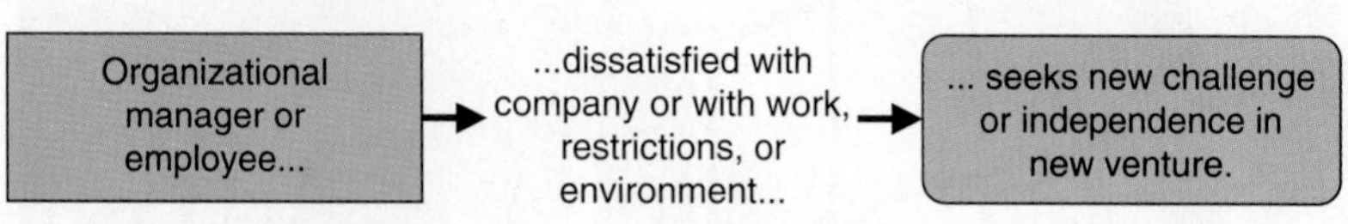

FIGURE 20-4 From Manager to Entrepreneur

sources, while others may have a compelling need to achieve but lack the resourcefulness to create a new venture. Many individuals with only a few entrepreneurial traits will start new businesses and succeed. Others with most of the traits may start new businesses and fail. Opponents of the trait approach also reverse Hornaday's logic and ask whether those among us who do not choose to be entrepreneurs have similar traits. Put another way, can a "nonentrepreneur" also be achievement oriented, persistent, and creative?

A. David Silver, a successful venture capitalist and author, described the entrepreneur as someone who is "energetic, single-minded, and has a mission and clear vision; he or she intends to create out of this vision a product or service in a field many have determined is important to improve the lives of millions."[17] Silver also suggests that entrepreneurs venture out on their own because of dissatisfaction with their organizations, although they are not necessarily unhappy with their career fields. This is illustrated by the proliferation of Silicon Valley firms started by engineers, inventors, scientists, and computer wizards who left established companies to pursue private enterprise, yet did so within the scope of their professions. For example, Robert Noyce was a successful research engineer with Fairchild Camera, Inc., when he walked out in 1968 to found Intel Corporation, now one of the top three international manufacturers of integrated circuits. Noyce has been called the "father of Silicon Valley" because so many young engineers and scientists began their careers at Intel, later leaving to start their own high-tech companies; Steven Jobs, cofounder of Apple Computer and founder and current CEO of NeXT Computers, is perhaps the most notable.[18] This route to entrepreneurship is illustrated in Figure 20-4.

Another way to explain entrepreneurship is from a sociocultural standpoint. Albert Shapero made comparative studies between nations, peoples, and ethnic groups, accumulated information about historical trends, and conducted many firsthand interviews with entrepreneurs. He concluded that individuals often become entrepreneurs by being thrown into situations that force them to fashion their own means of economic livelihood.[19] Immigrants fit this model well. A great many come to the United States to escape famine, war, or political oppression in their home countries. Many others flee desperate economic conditions. When they arrive here, most do not have the English language skills to secure well-paying jobs in American firms. Others find their employment opportunities hampered by stereotypes of their ethnic or religious group. These "displaced persons" have few options for success other than to establish independent ventures. Irving Berlin, profiled in the Management Application box, was one of many immigrants who overcame these barriers to succeed, and in so doing, enriched our culture.

The immigrant scenario is exemplified by well-known nineteenth-century adventurers such as Andrew Carnegie—the Scottish immigrant who founded the U.S. steel industry—but also by thousands of ordinary people who opened stores, brewed beer, started railroads, and turned barren prairies into lush farmlands. Most

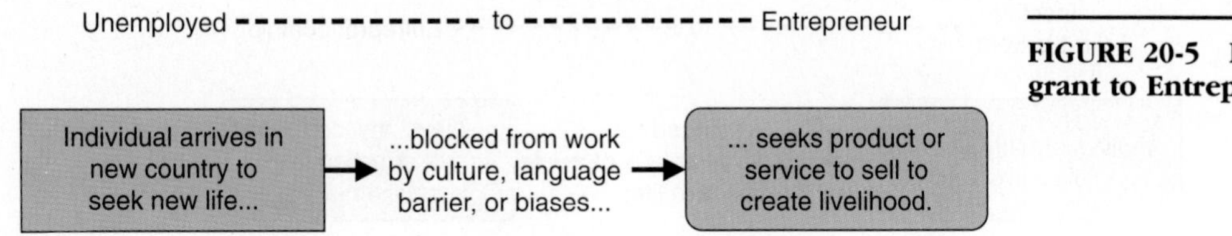

FIGURE 20-5 From Immigrant to Entrepreneur

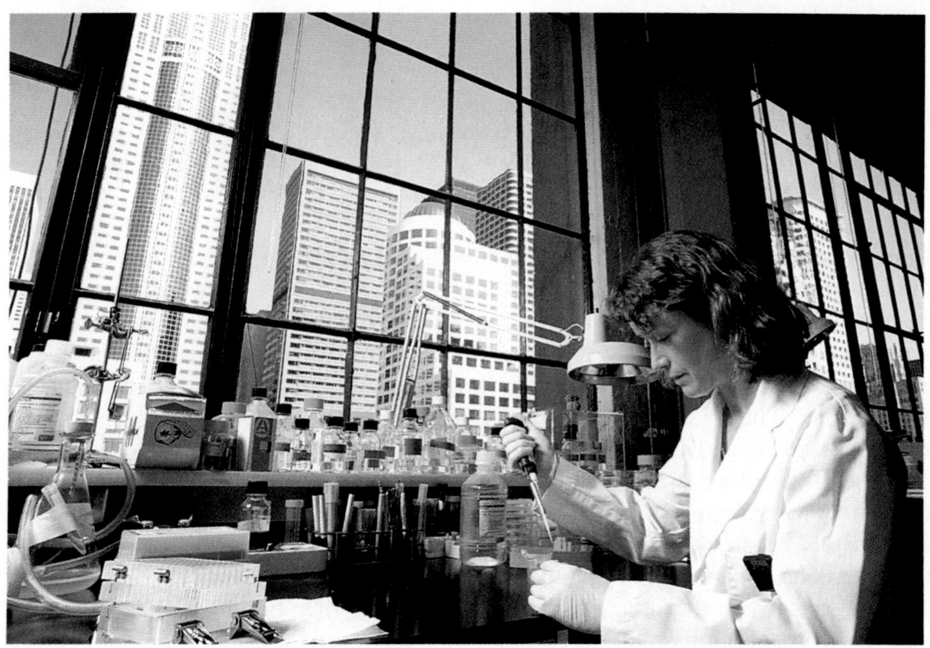

The recent surge of high-tech startups and spinoffs in the Pacific Northwest suggests that there is such a thing as an entrepreneurial environment. Like several of Seattle's biotech companies, Immunex is a spinoff of the Fred Hutchinson Cancer Center, a $92 million nonprofit research institution in the region. And the early success of such companies as Microsoft and Tektronix has caused hundreds of high-tech companies to spring up. Says Woody Howse of Cable & Howse Ventures, "When you see successful companies happen, you think, 'Gee, I know that guy. I could do that too.'"

of the early immigrants were from Europe, but Asians are more prevalent today. An Wang, for example, started Wang Laboratories as an out-of-work graduate engineer living in a low-rent apartment. Recent surveys show that roughly half of the one million Korean immigrants in the United States are self-employed. In New York—a microcosm of immigration—Koreans own 85 percent of the $500 million retail grocery business and 20 percent of all laundries, restaurants, and garment manufacturers.[20] Figure 20-5 on page 667 illustrates the immigrant route to entrepreneurship.

Shapero also found a high correlation between increases in new ventures and rising unemployment. Many "economically displaced" (unemployed) individuals become disillusioned with their faltering careers and find starting a new venture an exhilarating career change as well as a necessary survival tactic. In addition, individuals who retire, or are forced to retire early, frequently start new businesses. Colonel Harlan Sanders, for example, launched Kentucky Fried Chicken while on Social Security, Alexander Graham Bell helped found the National Geographic Society in his early retirement years, and Wilson Greatbatch invented the pacemaker after a long career in engineering. Figure 20-6 suggests how this route to entrepreneurship evolves.

The diversity of characteristics found among entrepreneurs and the variety of routes taken by individuals to become entrepreneurs present so many options that it

FIGURE 20-6 From Retirement to Entrepreneurship

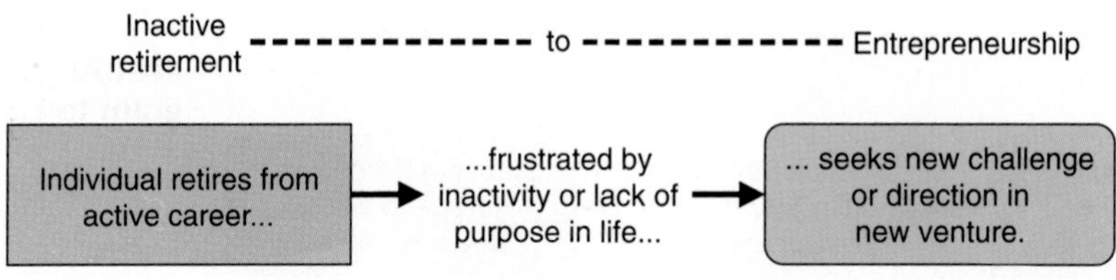

Inactive retirement
to
Entrepreneurship
Individual retires from active career...
...frustrated by inactivity or lack of purpose in life...
... seeks new challenge or direction in new venture.

MANAGEMENT APPLICATION

Irving Berlin

As a child, Irving Berlin sang for pennies on street corners in New York, but when he died in 1989, he left behind an unequaled legacy of music and theater innovations. Born in 1888, Israel Baline came to America as a Russian Jewish immigrant with his parents, and at the age of five, he was out on the streets of New York helping his family by earning food money with his singing. He published his first song in 1907 at the age of 19, and his first blockbuster hit came in 1911 with "Alexander's Ragtime Band." During his life, he composed more than a thousand songs, completed scores for nineteen Broadway shows, and wrote the music for a dozen movies.

Irving Berlin was also an astute businessman who started the Berlin Music Corporation, controlled his own copyrights, opened the Music Box, an innovative New York theater devoted to musical plays, and established foundations for creative artists and musicians. His musical innovations ranged from incorporating the syncopations of ragtime and jazz into popular music to composing "God Bless America"—a song many Americans regard as the unofficial national anthem. Berlin was one of the few composers who wrote both his own lyrics and music, and he even performed in several of his productions. However, he could only play the piano in the key of F sharp, and because so many scores had to be written in other keys, he had a special piano developed to transpose his compositions automatically to other keys.

Until a few months before his death, Berlin was still regularly calling into his office at Berlin Music Corporation, and he was an active supporter of the American Society of Composers, Authors & Publishers, an organization he founded to help artists protect their creations.

Source: "One of a Kind," *Sunday Morning Post* (Hong Kong), September 24, 1989, p. 1.

is hard to identify the "entrepreneurial individual." Yet there are individuals who are apparently more likely to become entrepreneurs and others who are more likely to flourish in structured environments.

CHECKPOINT

- Describe the critical elements in the definition of entrepreneurship.
- Identify the characteristics of entrepreneurs and discuss how they might differ from those of people not interested in new ventures.
- Discuss three different routes to entrepreneurship and what motivates people to take the entrepreneurial plunge.

CORPORATE ENTREPRENEURSHIP

Suggesting that entrepreneurship can take place in established, large bureaucratic organizations is controversial. Our definition would not exclude managers from being entrepreneurs, however, if they combined resources in unusual ways to create innovative new products or services. The concept also implies that entrepreneurs take risks, which generally means committing personal resources to a project. If successful, they will reap major rewards; if not, they will lose much or all they put at risk. Corporate managers do commit their time and energy to projects, and sometimes they risk their careers, but they seldom risk their personal capital or place themselves in a position to win or lose great wealth.

The greatest point of controversy is ownership. From an economic or legal viewpoint, entrepreneurs are narrowly defined as having an ownership interest in a clearly defined venture. This interpretation would exclude salaried managers or wage-earning employees. Nevertheless, entrepreneurship does occur in established organizations. As we shall see, it can happen through product innovations, "spin-off" new ventures underwritten by the mother company, development of subsidiaries, and in several other ways. Managers and employees who instigate these new corporate ventures behave similarly to founders of independent businesses.[21]

Corporate managers of entrepreneurial ventures are therefore expected to have vision, determination, and persistence. They are also given greater profit-and-loss responsibility, which can approach the autonomy enjoyed by independent business founders. The mother company provides the investment and is ultimately accountable for its success or failure; thus managers avoid the monetary risk of ownership. Still, more and more corporations are including managers in new-venture investments, and this further reduces the gap between "entrepreneurial managers" and "entrepreneurs." For example, Tektronix has encouraged new-venture management by creating special stock options for employees who become involved. General Electric has set up a new-venture fund to underwrite innovations, and gives employees who create operating units the opportunity to buy into their enterprises. One of GE's more successful spin-offs is GigaBite, a corporation engaged in research on superconductivity. Most often, the corporate approach is to reward an innovator through bonuses, put more resources at his or her disposal, and recognize the successful corporate entrepreneur through promotions. Art Fry, the 3M research engineer who developed the Post-it notepad, now enjoys easy access to resources, a higher position, greater latitude in his work, and substantial bonuses based on his innovations.[22]

Intrapreneurship

intrapreneurship
A term used in place of "corporate entrepreneurship," this label applies to managers who work within their existing organizations to create and commercialize new products or services for their organizations.

Corporate entrepreneurship has become known as **intrapreneurship,** a term meant to capture the notion of "intracorporate" venture activity. The implication is that formal entrepreneurship occurs within the established boundaries of existing organizations.[23] As we shall see, there are several models of intracorporate venture activity, but first it is important to understand that new products and services can be created through either *invention* or *innovation*.

Invention is the creation of something new. The resulting product of an inventor did not exist before. In contrast, innovation is a new way of using existing resources. Though both invention and innovation involve a tremendous amount of creativity, they are entirely different processes. Figure 20-7 illustrates this important

FIGURE 20-7 Invention versus Innovation

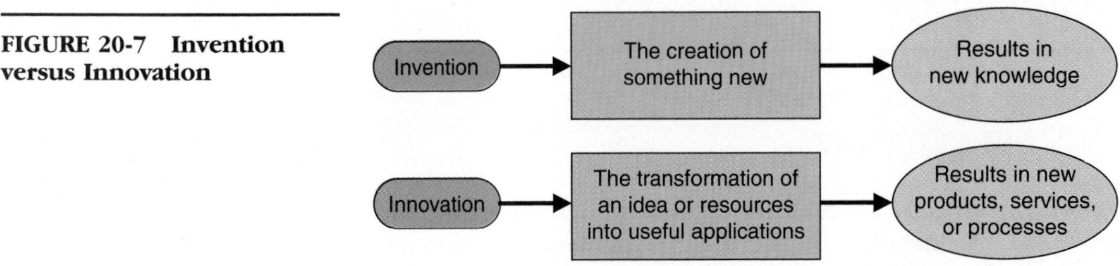

distinction. For example, an innovation may be a new combination of natural elements that results in a useful and commercially viable product. Gasoline is an innovation, a derivative of a natural resource. Fertilizers are often combinations of nitrates and other chemicals made through an innovative process. In contrast, the first bicycle was an invention, and the microcomputer resulted from a half dozen inventions, including a system of mathematical calculations and microelectronics. Combining these inventions innovatively culminated in a commercially viable microcomputer.

Neither inventors nor innovators are necessarily entrepreneurs; many creative people with unusual ideas never get beyond the stage of creativity. Entrepreneurs breathe commercial life into their ideas, and by that criterion, independent entrepreneurs and corporate intrapreneurs are very much alike.

Classifications of Corporate Entrepreneurship

The traditional approach for creating new products or processes within the corporate environment is research and development (R&D). R&D is the formal activity charged with specific design or engineering responsibilities; however, new ideas, product improvements, innovative services, and new technologies can surface from many sources besides the R&D laboratory. Hans Schollhammer, an educator with years of experience in entrepreneurship, has classified the various ways entrepreneurship can occur in organizations. He also suggests that corporate strategies formulated to specifically support each approach influence how a firm will position itself for growth. His five classifications follow.[24]

Administrative entrepreneurship. Traditional R&D management is closely approximated in the administrative mode. The firm simply moves a step beyond formal R&D projects to encourage greater innovation or new inventions. The distinction that makes R&D entrepreneurial may be a state of mind, a corporate philosophy of enthusiastically supporting researchers toward greater achievement. R&D personnel are only partial contributors to bringing a new product to market or implementing a new technology. Other corporate personnel and resources help commercialize R&D innovations.

For example, Boeing became the world's foremost commercial aircraft manufacturer through the Boeing 727 project. The key to the Boeing 727 was the fan-jet engine created in 1961 for greater thrust and high-speed cruising. Seven years later, 400 Boeing 727 aircraft rolled off company assembly lines, and by 1984, when the last 727 was produced, Boeing had produced nearly 2,000 of them. This remarkably successful plane required teams of designers, marketers, scientists, and production engineers.[25]

Opportunistic entrepreneurship. Formal structural ties are loosened as product champions seek out and take advantage of unique opportunities. The traditional R&D perspective is avoided in favor of encouraging individuals to pursue ideas inside and outside the organization.

At First American Bank & Trust, for example, managers are encouraged to take profit-and-loss responsibilities for investing branch funds in unusual high-risk opportunities. Branch managers can make independent capital acquisitions, such as creating subsidiary businesses in real estate, and a few of the bank's managers operate independently as investment consultants who are compensated according to their investment performance. Quad/Graphics, Inc., the company that prints *U.S. News & World Report, Newsweek,* and *INC.*, among other magazines, has taken opportunities a step further. When printing technology began to change rapidly with computers, Quad/Graphics designed state-of-the-art equipment through a subsidiary, called Quad/Tech, the company set up with its design engineers. Quad/Tech engi-

When Johnson & Johnson set up its Vistakon unit in 1987 to produce revolutionary disposable contact lenses, Bernard Walsh hesitated before deciding to accept the position of the unit's president. Recalls Walsh, "There was a perception of high risk." But *risk* is a word that flies at the corporation giant, whose decentralization has long encouraged managerial entrepreneurship. Vistakon is an example of how well that concept has worked for Johnson & Johnson. In 1983, after an employee heard about a new Danish technology to produce cheap disposable lenses, Johnson & Johnson bought the rights to it. After assembling a Vistakon management team and constructing a plant capable of mass-producing thousands of such lenses quickly, Johnson & Johnson began test-marketing them in 1987. Meanwhile, Vistakon established distribution routes, prepared consumer ads, and was ready to market the product in June 1988, an incredibly short time. Because the unit had so much autonomy, Walsh was able to run it as if it were a small startup, making decisions on every aspect of operations: development, production, advertising, and distribution.

neers were given full control and the autonomy to sell technology to anyone. The parent company, Quad/Graphics, funded the subsidiary and enjoys a majority of its profits, but the engineers—now executive managers—share in the profits and openly compete in the printing technology market.[26]

In sum, the opportunistic model suggests that managers accept some degree of isolation from corporate halls, alter their career paths, and work semiautonomously to exploit opportunities within reasonable boundaries. They also may share generously in rewards.

Acquisitive entrepreneurship. Even further removed from traditional R&D models, the acquisitive approach encourages corporate managers to look externally for innovations that can lead to rapid growth and profits. Instead of developing ideas internally, corporations actively seek other firms that have invented new products or processes. In recent years, this strategy has led to many mergers and acquisitions in virtually every sector of the economy. In the microcomputer industry, corporations have added thousands of new products to their assets by acquiring firms that hold patents or that have incubated unusual ideas.

Lotus Development Corporation, for instance, rapidly expanded beyond its initial computer spreadsheet product, Lotus 1-2-3, by acquiring Software Arts and the copyrighted products VisiCalc, TK!Solver, and Spotlight. In 1991, Lotus bought out Samna Corporation to acquire word processing software called Ami Pro. Meanwhile, Borland International, a competitor of Lotus, bought out sixth-ranked Ashton-Tate Corporation; and Novell, Inc., the third-ranked U.S. software company, purchased Digital Research. More than 200 acquisitions have occurred in the last ten years as computer software firms have jockeyed for market position and new products, yet Microsoft—the number-one company in the industry—relies primarily on internal team R&D efforts.[27]

Imitative entrepreneurship. Sometimes likened to corporate espionage, imitative entrepreneurship takes advantage of other firms' ideas and inventions. The Japanese have suffered this label for years, particularly when they study an American product and find a way to improve upon it or bring it to market at a lower cost. Imitation abounds in all cultures; it is a way of "shaking out" less efficient producers. Since many inventors suffer from poor underwriting or lack of resources, they are often forced to yield to more powerful and capable corporations. Other firms with talented people can often take a marginal product and create out of it something of high quality and value.

For example, the Korean electronics company Samsung assembled its first color television set in 1977. It was an amalgamation of parts and designs found in sets made by RCA, GE, and Hitachi. This was a prelude to Samsung's becoming the world's fifth-largest color TV manufacturer within eight years. By 1983, the company's engineers had created their own version of a color TV that was more reliable and less expensive than any other set on the market. The company penetrated the U.S. retail market, expanded into Europe, and now has the largest share of low-price discount sales worldwide.[28]

Incubative entrepreneurship. After acquiring new products or patents, corporations must allocate resources to commercialize the acquisitions. This activity begins with an intense focus on development. The corporate pattern has been to create semiautonomous venture development units that nurture the new product or technology. These units are high-impact implementation teams working in high-risk endeavors. Few projects will be successful—in fact, most will be scrapped early in the development stage—so this type of activity requires corporate managers not easily discouraged by failure. They have to have the temperament to discard a poor idea, yet enthusiastically pursue the next idea with the same vigor. Managers in traditional career positions who must rely on patterns of success for promotions can seldom risk these activities. Corporations therefore create venture units that can develop a style separate from corporate politics and lockstep performance.

Corporate use of out-of-channel venture teams to develop innovative new products has been increasing. We introduced the concept in Chapter 9 as an unusual, and unofficial, way to create project teams called *skunkworks*—small teams of employees asked to develop and champion innovations outside R&D and other formal departments and reporting relationships.[29] Today they have official charters and are called *new-venture units*.

New-Venture Units

A **new-venture unit (NVU)** is a separate team, division, or subsidiary created specifically to initiate new business ideas. By creating NVUs, companies de-bureaucratize the entrepreneurial process, giving a charter of autonomy for research and development to a volunteer team of employees. A small team can grow to division status, perhaps becoming incorporated as a subsidiary that pursues full commercialization of an innovation.[30]

new-venture unit (NVU) A team, division, or subsidiary created specifically to initiate new business ideas and bring them to fruition through commercial endeavors.

The small-team model is followed by 3M, where venture units have accounted for nearly 25 percent of the company's increased operating profits since 1983. As noted earlier, a 3M team developed the Post-it pad and planned its introduction as a commercial product. After the innovative notepads were integrated into 3M's main product line for manufacturing and sales, the original team regrouped on a voluntary basis for several other projects.[31] At IBM, the new-venture team that developed the personal computer was enlarged from a few individuals to fifty volunteers, who were given official status and encouraged to develop a full line of complementary computers. The PC team continued to expand until it was consolidated as IBM's Entry Systems Division.[32]

The corporate subsidiary model is less common than the small-team or division NVU, but has had many notable successes. For example, General Mills expanded away from its food line into toys several years ago by creating Kenner Toys. Kenner was financed through General Mills and given autonomy to establish a product line of toys. Some of Kenner's best products have been Star Wars toys, Care Bears, and Strawberry Shortcake dolls, all developed in the NVU. Creation of the Master Card—and the entire bank card industry—was the result of an unusual consortium of corporate investors who established Western States Bankcard Corporation to develop an interbank credit card clearinghouse system. Initial corporate investors included Wells Fargo, Crocker Bank, and United California Bank, and they were quickly followed by 200 others.[33]

New-venture units have proved to be more efficient than in-house R&D departments because they use fewer resources to bring product ideas to a commercial stage of development in about half the time. They have also had a higher percentage of successes, nearly two-to-one over R&D efforts. There are several reasons for these results. First, established R&D departments tend to follow a pattern of low-risk, systematic product development—designing, testing, and evaluating products methodically. Second, R&D departments are subject to formal reporting systems, annual budget reviews, and time-consuming performance reviews. Third, R&D staff are charged with working on a broad range of projects rather than with focusing on breakthrough, high-risk products. In contrast, new-venture teams do not have to follow an established research methodology, are relieved of complicated reporting systems, and are expected to focus on a narrow range of innovations.[34] Both have their uses in a corporation: the R&D department to meet existing design and engineering responsibilities, and the NVU to focus on the kind of breakthroughs that keep a firm competitive.

GLOBAL TRENDS

Mexican Entrepreneur Seeks to Solve Food Problem

Regina Garza, a successful young securities broker in Monterrey, Mexico, may revolutionize agriculture in her country. She has started a new venture to import a water-absorbing polymer product that can attract and hold up to 400 times its weight in water. The product looks like sugar crystals, and a teaspoon of it mixed into soil can retain enough moisture to keep a tomato plant healthy for several weeks. The polymer swells, slowing releasing water to a plant's roots. Because most rainwater runs off or quickly evaporates, the water-absorbing crystals solve an acute agricultural problem in Mexico—lack of water—and for a country where most produce is grown in semiarid fields, modern irrigation systems are rare.

Garza first saw the polymer in 1988 at a conference of the Association of Collegiate Entrepreneurs when an American college student sprinkled polymer crystals in several glasses of drinking water as a practical joke during a luncheon. The crystals quickly turned the drinking water to a clear gel, confusing luncheon guests. When the student explained how the product worked, Garza became excited about its possibilities for farmers in Monterrey.

On her return home, she located a British manufacturer that made the polymer and bought samples for testing. In February 1989, Garza started a small import company and convinced several commercial growers to use the polymer in field tests. The results were impressive: Polymer-treated fields increased crop yields by as much as 30 percent, and in several areas where water was too scarce for commercial agriculture, the polymer retained enough moisture to permit growing vegetables such as corn and beans.

The polymer is registered in Mexico as *Hydrogel* and sold through Garza's company Poliacrilamida Agricola de Mexico. The commercial possibilities are tremendous in Monterrey, where a population of four million relies on domestic food supplies grown predominately within a fifty-mile radius. There are approximately 280,000 acres planted in food products in this area, which gives Hydrogel a potential market of $30 million annually.

It is not the prospect for wealth that motivates Garza, however, but her vision of providing food for starving children and helping struggling farmers improve their livelihood. In fact, she has given away more Hydrogel than she has sold, enabling hundreds of families on the brink of starvation to plant backyard vegetable gardens in soil that otherwise could not hold enough water to be used.

CHECKPOINT

- Describe both sides in the controversy about whether entrepreneurship can take place in established organizations.
- Explain how administrative and opportunistic entrepreneurship differ.
- Discuss how imitative entrepreneurship occurs.
- Define a new-venture unit (NVU) and describe how small teams can encourage innovation.

NEW-VENTURE CREATION

Although corporate entrepreneurship has become popular, we still associate entrepreneurship with new, small businesses. A necessary distinction is that entrepreneurship is most often associated with those firms that are relatively new ventures *seeking rapid growth*. Specifically, new-venture creation aimed at high growth is the essence of entrepreneurship. New ventures do not blossom from bright ideas alone. They require the skill and daring of adventurers who choose to take risks. We have recently begun to establish business development methods to help budding entrepreneurs reduce their risks and learn how to manage their ventures.[35] One aspect of this business development process is understanding the various stages that a new venture goes between incubation and maturity, and another aspect is understanding the crises that entrepreneurs face during each of these stages.

Stages of New-Venture Development

Every new venture goes through four distinct stages of development before it matures as a successfully established enterprise. These stages are illustrated in Figure 20-8.[36]

Pre–start-up stage. During this initial phase, creative ideas evolve to the point of being consciously perceived as commercial endeavors. Entrepreneurs believe that their ideas are feasible, and they become fascinated by visions of their enterprises. Many entrepreneurs haphazardly plunge into business at this stage, following the popular adage that entrepreneurship is simply a manner of "finding a gap and filling it," but this lack of preparation often leads to early failure. Finding a gap and filling it is important, but seldom sufficient, for success.

More astute entrepreneurs ask questions about the actual potential of their products or services. They try to answer questions about production, operations, markets, competitors, costs, financing, and potential profits. And they try to resolve questions about their own abilities to start a business. Depending on the complexity of the proposed enterprise, the range of pre–start-up activities can be quite extensive, but the following four activities are common to all new ventures with a strong *planning* mandate.

The business concept is identified. Entrepreneurs must conscientiously plan the venture based on answering the question: What do I want to accomplish with this enterprise? For example, Steve Kirsch, who developed the concept for an electronic "mouse," a common accessory for computer systems today, was an MIT student working in a computer lab where three very expensive machines were all crippled because the mechanical mouse each machine used was broken. He said that it was a sad situation, "like having a Ferrari with only three wheels on it."[37] Kirsch soon

FIGURE 20-8 The Four-Stage Growth Model

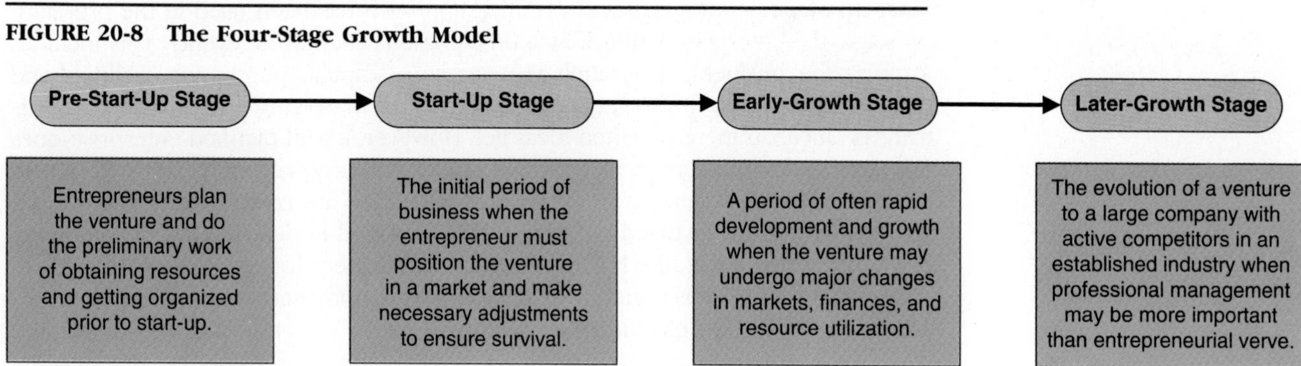
Pre-Start-Up Stage
Start-Up Stage
Early-Growth Stage
Later-Growth Stage
Entrepreneurs plan the venture and do the preliminary work of obtaining resources and getting organized prior to start-up.
The initial period of business when the entrepreneur must position the venture in a market and make necessary adjustments to ensure survival.
A period of often rapid development and growth when the venture may undergo major changes in markets, finances, and resource utilization.
The evolution of a venture to a large company with active competitors in an established industry when professional management may be more important than entrepreneurial verve.

designed a reliable electronic mouse, but the idea of a business evolved over a period of several months as he planned a way to have the mouse manufactured and marketed through his own company. He could have sold the idea to IBM or licensed it to Apple, but his business concept was to create a new venture for electronic computer accessories. Today his company, Mouse Systems, Inc., has clients that include most major manufacturers of microcomputers and scientific work stations.

A product-market study is completed. Pragmatic research is required to determine whether a product or service is feasible. This can involve complicated market research and product development, but it is essential to do before actually launching a new business. Too often entrepreneurs launch their ventures without taking the time and effort to accomplish this research. Steve Kirsch took the time to find out if potential competitors were developing similar electronic accessories, how much production might cost, whether the "mice" could be marketed successfully at a profitable price, and how he was going to protect his ideas through patents and copyrights. Consequently, he avoided jumping to early conclusions based on intuition that could have been in error.

A financial plan is defined. Although many new ventures are underwritten by personal savings and cookie-jar money, cash infusions are essential for any significant venture and for initial growth. Early cash flow is usually acquired through a combination of short-term loans, mortgages, and family investments. As the business evolves, a plan must be established for attracting sizable loans and large blocks of capital. Also, many ventures have a long pre–start-up development stage requiring so-called *seed money*. For example, Genentech, Inc., a biotechnology company that manufactures lab testing enzymes and experimental medicines, spent more than three years and $20 million before announcing it was "in business" with its first commercial product.[38] Having a financial plan before launching an enterprise is therefore crucial.

Pre–start-up activities are planned. If we define the pre–start-up stage as the period that precedes any attempt to generate sales, then it is a stage similar to that of an Olympic sprinter preparing for a race. The sprinter, like the entrepreneur, plans, trains, develops strategies, attracts sponsors, and gets physically and mentally prepared to run. Just before the race is to begin, the sprinter gets into the starting blocks to await the gun. Like the sprinter, an entrepreneur must commit to action and do certain things before the event: establish vendor relations with suppliers, obtain a business location, hire essential personnel, arrange for initial promotions, and set up administrative systems. These activities vary widely with the nature of the business, but they are all essential, and if the business is complicated like Genentech's, the company may have to acquire licenses from federal and state agencies, comply with federal regulations for testing and development activities, and accumulate substantial research equipment and assets.

Start-up stage. If a business planning approach has been used in the pre–start-up stage, the enterprise will follow a time-phased schedule of events. This includes forming the business, generating the necessary capital, purchasing facilities and equipment, building prototype products, and test marketing. The start-up stage is truly an "incubation" stage when ideas gel. However, a well-planned enterprise does not gear up for full-scale activity at this point; the entrepreneur is still engaged in product and market research. Only limited resources are committed to the project, and few people are involved outside of those engaged in determining the feasibility of the business. In fact, the business may be terminated during this stage if circumstances show the idea is untimely or infeasible. Initial investors then take their losses and look elsewhere. Unfortunately, entrepreneurs who did not plan well during the pre–start-up stage often fail to recognize potential difficulties and, operating more on impulse than plans, run headlong toward bankruptcy.

This is precisely what happened to Osborne Computers.[39] During its first year of operations, Osborne became the fastest-growing corporation in America. The company's founders had conceived of the first portable computer in 1980, several years ahead of Compaq and IBM, and estimated sales at less than a third of the $80 million in orders it actually achieved during its first few months in business. Because most sales were to distributors who had thirty-day credit terms, Osborne accumulated huge orders without getting any cash receipts. To meet manufacturing costs, the company acquired loans and shipped computers around the clock. Osborne seemed to be an enormous success, but it was hopelessly in debt. Creditors called in their loans, investors liquidated their positions, and the company disappeared as quickly as it had appeared. In contrast, Michael Dell started his PC Limited line of microcomputers modestly, stayed within a well-defined plan of operations during the early years, and by 1992, only six years after the venture started, topped a billion dollars in annual sales.[40]

Started in 1985 by college dropout Ted Waits, who borrowed $10,000 to set up business in a barn on the family farm, the mail-order computer company Gateway is in its early growth stage. Gateway's low prices have made it number one in the mail-order computer business. But the company's phenomenal growth is causing problems. Flooded by orders, Gateway recently has been delivering late and quality control has also declined. One customer, who ordered fifty Gateways, only to discover that three were defective when unpacked and fourteen monitors and ten more computers soon failed, says, "The company has grown so fast that its systems have not caught up." Gateway is trying to cope with the problems brought about by its phenomenal rise. For example, it has created the job of quality assurance manager and redesigned the main circuit board of one of its computers.

Early-growth stage. Once feasibility has been established, third-stage activity makes the firm fully operational. If the business is well planned, operations will be carefully monitored and activities will be maintained within the firm's resource capabilities. Managers and employees will be in a learning situation, testing their skills and products in real markets. A typical goal of operations in this stage is to reach a break-even point while fine-tuning growth strategies. If the firm has an unusual product or holds a lucrative patent, it may become a candidate for acquisitions by more powerful corporations when market performance brings it high visibility. Of course, market performance may be disappointing and the venture terminated. Many businesses, after experiencing early growth, find their enterprise has severe limitations. For example, the entrepreneurs may not have the marketing skills necessary to make the business a success. Then again, they may have the skills but lack access to a good distribution system. Either of these limitations could prompt the sale of the firm or influence the entrepreneur to license the product to an established firm, but if growth has been steady, the venture probably can attract capital for more rapid growth or diversification.

Karsten Solheim is a Norwegian immigrant who developed his first Ping putter as a hobby while working for GE. During the early stage of his business, he produced only putters, and for most of the 1970s, marketing was limited to select pro shops and distributors. Because his clubs became popular and his early growth record was respectable, Solheim was able to position Karsten Manufacturing Corporation to produce a full line of golf clubs during the early 1980s when demand for golf equipment was increasing exponentially with the rapid growth in new courses. Karsten's firm grew at nearly 200 percent annually, and by 1989, Ping putters were used by more than half of PGA touring pros. Today Ping produces 12,000 clubs a day, grossing $100 million annually without being able to meet demand for customer orders.[41]

Later-growth stage. If the enterprise proves successful in the early-growth stage and has momentum, it enters a mature stage when management must be structured, long-term financing must be established, and substantial facilities must be planned. Companies that reach this stage often "go public" with stock offerings. Family fortunes turn into corporate fortunes. Private investors convert their holdings to publicly traded investment instruments. Professional management teams replace individual entrepreneurial efforts, and the full range of planning, organizing, leading, and controlling becomes crucial for future growth. This is a critical transition stage for the entrepreneur. The firm may once again become a candidate for acquisition, and the entrepreneur may lose control of the enterprise through public financing.

Some entrepreneurs, like Steven Jobs at Apple, are ousted by their investor groups, but many entrepreneurs remain in control and build second- or third-generation family empires.

The DuPont family controlled its plastics manufacturing empire for three generations, and today the Mars family still owns and manages its global business in candy and convenience foods. Perhaps one of the most interesting companies is Mrs. Fields Cookies, a company started in 1978 by Debbi Fields at the age of twenty-two and now jointly operated by Debbi and Randy Fields. Their business has over 600 stores spanning five countries and grosses more than $100 million annually. The business is not franchised; all stores are owned by the company, which is managed by a staff of 120 people.[42] So growth does not necessarily mean emulating IBM or General Motors, but most ventures do outgrow their founders' abilities to manage them and are transformed through new infusions of capital and a professional organizational structure.

Crises in Development

Each stage of development brings new challenges and risks. Many of them can be foreseen by astute observers who have watched entrepreneurs stumble through often predictable crises in management as they nurture their enterprises toward success. During the pre–start-up stage, for example, entrepreneurs have a *planning crisis*. They must have the patience and skill to carefully develop plans before committing resources to a venture. If they plan well, the crisis is overcome, but if they move ahead with blinders on, they may hasten the next crisis of *cash flow*. During the start-up stage, cash is necessary to properly test products and markets. Capital needed is high-risk money known as seed capital. Investors are more likely to lose everything here than at any other stage of development.

Cash is also needed during the venture's growth, and this leads to a *capital crisis* as requirements for many enterprises become larger and more complex. During the early-growth stage, venture capital is often needed in several rounds of financing. Unlike seed capital, which usually comes from personal loans, venture money tends to come from knowledgeable investors. Small-business loans, partnership arrangements, and a wide array of government-sponsored programs offer special financing opportunities for first- and second-round venture capital underwriting. With continued growth, large infusions of capital are needed; this is often generated through public stock offerings.

Management crises may be far more important than capital crises. If a product is sound, there will be investors eager to put up development money. But if management is shaky, even a unique product may not be able to attract financing. The early-growth stage requires dynamic individual leadership. An *A* idea championed by a *D* entrepreneur is ripe for imitation by a tenacious competitor who has the managerial talent to commercialize it. As the firm grows, the entrepreneur must make a transition to professional management. It is at this stage that planning, organizing, leading, and controlling are emphasized. Perhaps the most severe crisis is that of delegation. Most entrepreneurs who have given birth to a new business and made it grow are reluctant to allow anyone else to be part of it. For some entrepreneurs, this may be an impossible transition.

Figure 20-9 shows the stages of new-venture development and the parallel crises stages. Each involves a certain amount of turmoil for entrepreneurs, yet most successful ones manage to translate the turmoil into challenges. The pre–start-up stage is full of exciting visions; the start-up period is exhilarating as the venture becomes reality; the early-growth stage tests an entrepreneur's determination; and the later-growth stage challenges his or her competitive endurance. Nothing will happen, however, without astute management skills tempered to the demands of the new venture.

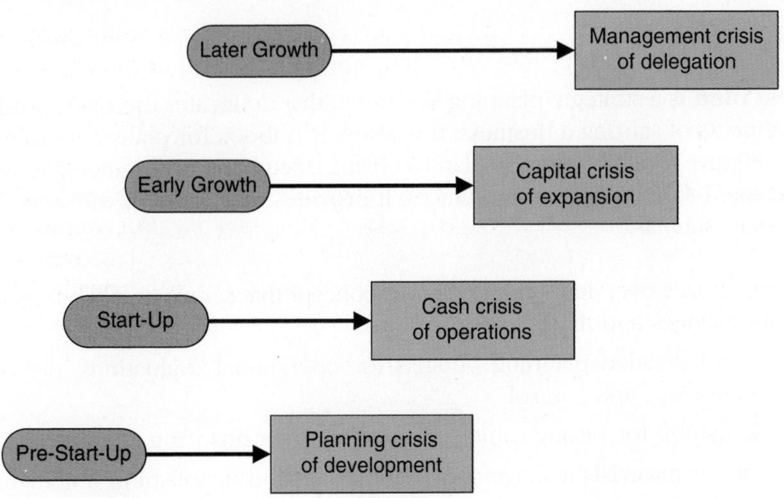

FIGURE 20-9 Crises Entrepreneurs Face in New-Venture Growth

CHECKPOINT

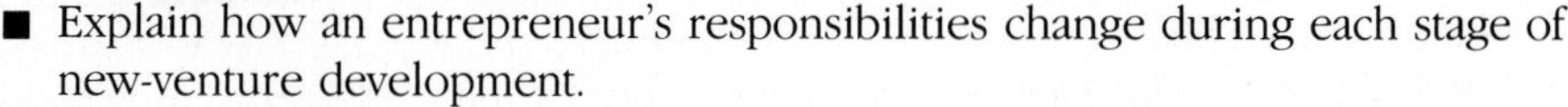

- Explain how an entrepreneur's responsibilities change during each stage of new-venture development.
- Describe the four crises entrepreneurs face as their venture matures.

MANAGING NEW VENTURES

We have alluded to a business plan, which is a concise summary of the best projections for detailed activities of a new venture or the expansion of an existing one.[43] Exhibit 20-2 provides an outline of the major components of a formal business plan.

EXHIBIT 20-2 Eight Common Elements in a Business Plan

Executive Summary	Defines venture, identifies products or services, summarizes market characteristics, introduces founders, and profiles financial structure.
Business Concept	Describes the purpose of the venture, the major objectives of its founders, and the distinct competency of the firm.
Product or Service	Describes the function and nature of products or services, proprietary interests, attributes, and technical profile.
Market Research & Analysis	Provides customer scenario, profiles markets, venture's niche, industry structure, and expected competition, and forecasts sales.
Market Plan	Outlines market strategy to compete, describes pricing, promotion, distribution, service and warranties, strategies, and indicates sales leadership.
Manufacturing or Operations	Describes facilities, location, inventory and materials needed, as well as human resources, operational processes, technology, security, insurance, and safety.
Entrepreneurial Team	Profiles founders, key personnel, investors, and management roles.
Financial Documentation	Contains financial statements for income and expenses, cash flow, assets and liabilities, break-even projections, and start-up underwriting needed.

Planning

business plan
A carefully prepared document that describes services and products, identifies customers, markets, and competition, evaluates capabilities, and provides supporting data for financing a new venture.

The **business plan** is a strategic planning document that delineates the often prodigious requirements of starting a business. It is also a handbook for plausibly managing the new venture. A viable business plan is a living document, updated at least annually and adapted to changing circumstances. It provides management with several valuable benefits, such as:[44]

1. A comprehensive overview of the business concept that serves as a benchmark for future changes and managerial decisions.
2. Forecasts and detailed planning budgets for operational evaluations, performance monitoring, and control.
3. A valuable exhibit for raising capital and seeking debt financing.
4. A guideline for materials management, purchasing, and establishing vendor relations.
5. An instrument of personnel management for planning, recruiting, and retaining human resources.
6. A marketing tool for targeting customers, products, and positioning the firm in its proper niche.

Like the strategic and tactical plans discussed earlier in the text, the business plan is an entrepreneurial exercise because it requires decisions about the fundamental concepts of the enterprise. New ventures are seldom well thought out; the business plan offers a process for bringing the entrepreneur down to earth. Not everything can be put on paper, but then, not everything should. The challenge of management is to plan and to make those plans work without becoming paralyzed by overanalysis.

Organizing

Managers of new ventures have two broad concerns. The first is how to legally institute the enterprise. The second is how to refine the structure to support the new company's planned strategies and obtain the necessary resources. Most of these issues are the same for large established firms and entrepreneurial start-ups, with obvious differences in magnitude. However, unlike managers in larger firms who work within an established legal form of enterprise, entrepreneurs must make a conscious choice about their legal status. If the new venture is a for-profit organization, there are several legal forms the firm may take. Exhibit 20-3 summarizes three of the most common legal forms of conducting business in the United States.[45]

EXHIBIT 20-3 Three Common Forms of Ownership

Sole Proprietorship	One owner solely responsible. Business earnings taxed as individual income. Owner personally liable for all business affairs.
General Partnership	Two or more owners with joint interests. Income taxed on prorated share of owner interest. Jointly and severally liable for business affairs.
Incorporation	Stock ownership defines separate legal entity. Corporate income taxed; stockholder dividends taxed. Stockholders have limited liability for business affairs.

Sole proprietorship. Individuals who conduct business as sole and unincorporated owners are known as **sole proprietors.** This form of business is quick and simple to start. Usually an owner must file forms with local authorities that identify the name and type of business. This process is controlled by municipal and state licensing laws. Practice varies widely, but a common filing form is the "DBA," which stands for "doing business as." The DBA identifies the legal owner and a business name. For example, Ajax Cleaners and Orchard Computer Store are possible DBAs; their owners are individuals who are solely and legally responsible for their enterprises. Sole proprietorships are not taxable entities, and owners include business profits or losses in their personal income. This practice can be beneficial if one's income is low and the lower personal income tax rate is applied to earnings, but it can be detrimental if the venture is extremely profitable and taxed at a much higher rate. In addition, since a sole proprietor cannot separate business liability from personal liability, a lawsuit or insurance claim can be brought against the entire personal holdings of the entrepreneur.

sole proprietor
A person who conducts business as an independent and unincorporated owner. Legally, a form of business that has no other investors beyond the independent owner.

Partnerships. The basic concept of a **partnership** is that two or more individuals have combined their efforts in a joint activity or created joint responsibility for the affairs of a business. Many types of partnerships exist, including a statutory form called a *limited partnership* (a subject for a business law course), but a *general partnership* can be created without formal agreement simply by having more than one person invest in an enterprise. Reason suggests, however, that the partners commit to writing their interests and responsibilities in any business venture. Because general partnerships are not legal entities, partners are taxed according to their percentage of ownership, with commensurate rights and liabilities. Partnerships are similar to sole proprietorships in that both have unlimited liability: Each partner can be held liable to the extent of his or her entire personal assets. Also, one partner can be held liable for the other's business obligations. The advantage of a partnership is that it normally brings together greater expertise and capital than a sole proprietorship could.

partnership
Two or more individuals with joint responsibility and investment in a business.

Incorporation. **Corporations** are legal taxable entities with lives of their own according to statutory law. Many laws and regulations, beyond the scope of this discussion, govern corporations, but it is worth noting that numerous small firms incorporate early to protect the owners' personal assets from the business's legal liabilities. Entrepreneurs incorporate to separate business from personal assets. Then if the venture fails, creditors can only satisfy claims against corporate assets. A major drawback to incorporation is tax treatment. All corporations pay taxes as legal entities, and then the income distributed as dividends is taxed again as ordinary income to owners.

corporation
A legal entity created by statute, subject to commercial laws; a form of ownership in which investors have limited liability through stock ownership.

Current Internal Revenue Code rules allow for small corporations with limited numbers of stockholders to file with "S-corporation status." This status relieves the double taxation problem by taxing net earned income as partnership distributions. Thus individual stockholders pay taxes on prorated shares but are exempt from corporate income tax.

The incorporation of new ventures has several other dimensions. First, the ability to raise venture capital may hinge on the legal form of the business. Individual investors in formal venture capital markets seldom risk capital on an unincorporated business. Sophisticated investors want stock, control of board functions, and legal leverage against owners. Sole proprietorships and most general partnerships do not provide the breadth of leverage needed to attract high-risk venture capital. Financial institutions prefer stock-based firms for debt underwriting. Yet certain forms of partnerships and trusts attract huge capital investments, particularly from investors seeking tax shelters and income benefits.[46]

Legal forms of business have other implications, concerning succession, dissolution problems, and rights under bankruptcy laws. State laws and methods of terminating a business are additional complicating factors. Although beyond the scope of our discussion, these topics are critical for new and growing ventures.

Leading

The reality is that more than half of America's workers are employed by firms with fewer than 100 employees, and nearly 90 percent of all registered business organizations have fewer than 20 employees.[47] Leadership in new ventures is therefore based less on hierarchical relationships and more on personal associations among a few individuals working in close proximity. The entrepreneur must wrestle with employees' personal problems, absenteeism, scheduling, stress, conflicts, discord, and a range of issues such as safety and employee theft without the assistance of professional personnel managers. He or she has to encourage quality workmanship, effective production, efficient materials management, and inventory control without the aid of professional production managers. Product and process design rest with the team, often without the benefit of professional engineering management. Marketing, customer research, advertising, and distribution decisions are the responsibility of one or two individuals who seldom have professional marketing experience.

Entrepreneurs wear many hats during the early stages of development. New ventures succeed or fail based on the adaptability and dynamic capabilities of one or a few key individuals. As the firm grows, these burdens should diminish because it will have the resources to hire expertise and install professional managers in key positions. Still, entrepreneurs often fail to make the leadership transition to an environment based on delegated management activity. In other words, lack of leadership becomes a primary limitation on growth at some stage in the growing venture. If the lead entrepreneur cannot adapt, the firm may become one more inelegant statistic on the list of failures.

Controlling

Preparation of the business plan is the heart of planning for most new ventures; it is also the critical control document in establishing benchmarks of activity and evaluation guidelines. Controlling a new venture is similar to controlling more complex corporations. However, the crises noted earlier during various growth stages suggest different degrees of emphasis. For new ventures, cash is the most crucial element to control. Managers can make marketing mistakes, experience production glitches, stumble through leadership, and still survive with a reasonable product. But no matter how extraordinary the product or service, when a business runs out of cash, the game is over. Unlike large corporations, entrepreneurial ventures usually lack alternatives for financing.

Controlling is a particularly painful problem for many entrepreneurs because ventures are usually created by individuals with technical or marketing expertise but without management training. Engineers, computer specialists, scientists, retailers, salespersons, doctors, lawyers, and many others bring to their ventures tremendous expertise. Few, however, have ever controlled costs in a formal environment. Few have had inventory management, contract purchasing, or quality assurance experience. As noted in the earlier chapters on control issues, effective management of any enterprise rests heavily on careful management of these functions.

Perhaps the key elements for entrepreneurs concern projected cost and expense items. A good business plan will carefully forecast them, but additional budget work will enhance the chance of winning in a new venture. Specifically, documented controls for cash flow, asset management, working capital, profit projections, and sales help new ventures survive. There is no substitute for an accurate and timely

ETHICS IN MANAGEMENT

Cultural Survival Enterprises Helps Solve Rain Forest Problems

Indigenous tribes of the Amazon are caught between two worlds—one of survival where their people need money today for life's necessities, and one where they live in traditional ways off their tribal forest lands. In order to obtain money for survival needs, they have been selling forest lands to miners and loggers, who denude the land that has traditionally supported the tribes. The result has been less land for cultivation and fewer forests to support wildlife, yet the money obtained is never sufficient to support the tribes' needs.

Entrepreneur and environmentalist Dr. Jason Clay, a Massachusetts anthropologist, may be reversing that trend. He started Cultural Survival Enterprises as a way of harvesting brazil and cashew nuts, selling them to retailers in the United States, and returning all profits to the Amazon tribes. Clay not only uses new methods of processing nuts, but has also found ways to use the husks and shells from nuts, improving profits. A small business with only a handful of employees and several volunteers, Cultural Survival Enterprises registered $1.2 million in sales in 1991 and expected $3 million in sales in 1992.

By helping the Amazon tribes profit by planting, harvesting, and processing native nuts, Cultural Survival Enterprises has created a self-sustaining rural agricultural base. Consequently, the tribes no longer need to sell their land rights, and several rain forests in the Western Amazon are beginning to recover from years of deforestation. The key to success was getting good prices for commercial nuts through a marketing system that would not exploit the tribes. It was Clay's plan to transform forest groups into self-supporting small businesses, each linked to a selling cooperative that ran as a commercial enterprise.

The company is now doing research on ways to use cashew juice for blended juices, and it is developing a process for producing concentrates from various fruits and nuts found in the rain forest. In addition, Clay and his associates are showing the Amazon tribal groups how to harvest sufficient products without doing environmental harm. After three years of effort, the company and its tribal associates have broken even and begun to build a profitable reserve. The next step is to use these profits for rebuilding the damaged Amazon environment.

Source: Udayan Gupta, "Some Firms Are Born to Alleviate the Ills of the World," *Wall Street Journal,* March 17, 1992, p. B2.

sales forecast that strips away illusions of grandiose markets at noncompetitive prices.

CHECKPOINT

- Describe how a business plan is used in the pre–start-up stage and at later stages of growth.
- Define and contrast sole proprietorships, general partnerships, and corporations as legal forms of business.
- Discuss how leadership responsibilities in a new venture differ from those in established organizations.

MANAGING SMALL BUSINESSES

Most business students probably want careers with major corporations, but employment statistics indicate they have a higher probability for careers in smaller firms. During the 1980s, small businesses created more than 6 million new jobs for Americans. Simultaneously, Fortune 500 firms cut employment by about 10 percent for more than a million net job losses. Today more than 16 million small businesses account for approximately 97 percent of all nonfarm businesses, and since 1980, 66 percent of all new jobs in the United States were created by firms with fewer than 1,000 employees and $10 million or less in annual sales.[48]

Although these statistics are impressive, the Small Business Administration and the annual U.S. Census of Business suggest that about 55 percent of new businesses fail each year. The popular idea is that owning or managing a small business is like riding a tiger—survival is not a probable outcome. This view is inaccurate for a number of reasons. In the official statistics, a firm that changes its name is listed as "out of business," and one that changes from a proprietorship to an incorporation may be listed as no longer in existence. Other firms that merge, take on new partners, or enfranchise also often inaccurately join the roll of failures. For these reasons, research really hasn't established the small-business failure rate. Recent inquiries suggest that perhaps fewer than one in ten actually dissolve or go bankrupt. Most new ventures and small firms simply go through many changes that disguise their existence.[49]

Defining Small Business

small business
Conceptually, an enterprise that does not dominate its industry, has few employees, and generates limited income. The SBA has defined a small business for qualifying loans as one with fewer than 1,000 employees and less than $10 million in annual sales.

According to the Small Business Administration, a **small business** does not dominate its industry, has less than $10 million in annual sales, and employs fewer than 1,000 people.[50] These are the criteria the SBA uses for qualifying borrowers. In reality, though, "small business" defies clear definition. For instance, in today's markets, firms with fewer than 100 workers but with high-speed production lines often generate $50 million or more in sales. Fast-food franchises such as McDonald's that generate millions in sales are staffed mainly with part-time employees. Conversely, companies with several hundred workers may have rather low sales volume. "Small" therefore is often in the eye of the beholder. The one part of the SBA's definition that is generally true is that small businesses do not dominate their industries.

Common Types of Small Businesses

Three types of businesses account for nearly all small-business enterprises: *family enterprises, personal service firms,* and *franchises.* These are summarized in Exhibit 20-4, and explained below. Do not confuse these types of businesses with legal forms of business; any of these enterprises can be proprietorships, partnerships, or corporations.

family enterprise
Legally defined as a company controlled by family members who hold a majority-owner interest through stock or other investments. Conceptually, an enterprise owned and operated by family members.

Family enterprises. A **family enterprise,** as defined by the U.S. Department of Commerce, is one in which a family has legal control over ownership. By this definition, nearly 90 percent of all business in the United States, including corporations, partnerships, and sole proprietorships, are family enterprises; in fact, 175 of the Fortune 500 companies are legally controlled by families.[51] These include Ford and Du Pont, whose names reflect the families with controlling stock, and Campbell Soup, where the John T. Dorrance family retains nearly 60 percent of corporate stock after three generations. Ownership of Estée Lauder is shared with the founder's son and daughter-in-law.

Locally owned family enterprises, such as those created by a husband and wife as a proprietorship, fit the small-business definition.[52] They include restaurants,

EXHIBIT 20-4 Types of Small Businesses: Advantages and Disadvantages

Type	Advantages	Disadvantages
Family enterprise	Offers economic independence; promotes family unity.	Family liability for the business; unsure succession.
Personal service firm	Offers personal freedom and opportunity for personal growth.	Personal liability for the business; lack of secure income; no succession.
Franchise	Franchisor provides financial, technical, and other assistance; offers relatively secure income.	Less freedom and adventure than other types; unsure succession.

small clothing stores, and the many types of franchises available to small-business owners. Their markets have a consistent clientele and a high turnover of inventory. Those selling merchandise rely on a family environment to perpetuate the business, and often sons, daughters, brothers, and sisters are brought into the business as it grows.

Service-based firms rely on the skills of individuals. The myth of small-business failure noted earlier is particularly irritating to family business owners who know that it is lack of successors that often limits the life of their firms to the working lives of their founders. For example, a florist may operate a successful business until retirement, but if there is no family member to succeed the owner, the business is sold or shut down. Many students reading this have parents who run service or retail businesses, yet few intend to follow in their footsteps. Succession is one of the most critical problems for small family-owned businesses. Entrepreneurs who have worked hard most of their lives to develop successful enterprises often must resign themselves to dissolving their firms or selling out at retirement. Still, a family enterprise can provide the tremendous personal benefits of an independent lifestyle and a respected position in the community.

Personal service firms. A common form of a small business is the **personal service firm** that succeeds or fails on the expertise of a few individuals. Many family-owned businesses are personal service firms engaged in skilled activities. Most crafts, such as plumbing, carpentry, and cosmetology, fall into this category. Specialized services that rely on the skill of one individual range from medical services to computer consulting and include interesting occupations such as golf professionals, interior designers, and freelance writers. Since the business *is* the person, family succession is unlikely unless a son or daughter develops comparable skills.

personal service firm
A form of small business that provides services to customers through the skilled activities of its owners or employees.

Franchises. A growing form of business ownership is the franchise. A **franchise** is created by contract whereby a buyer, the *franchisee,* contracts with the mother company, the *franchisor,* to open a complete business replicating the franchise enterprise. In exchange for a franchise fee and a percentage of sales from the franchisee, the franchisor provides the business concept and specific assistance for the new venture. A franchisor develops a network of income-producing enterprises that share a common name, use common materials, sell similar products, and benefit from national brand-name advertising. The franchisee may receive financial help, training, guaranteed supplies, a protected market, and technical assistance for site selection, purchasing, accounting, and operations management.

franchise
A form of business ownership created by contract whereby a company sells the rights to a business concept, providing products and services to the buyer in exchange for a royalty or share of profits.

We have grown accustomed to franchises such as Wendy's and McDonald's, but franchising extends to a great many industries other than fast foods. Most mall-type stores that sell clothing, books, toys, photographic supplies, records, shoes, and computers are franchises. Also, printers, furniture stores, auto rentals, convenience stores, and snack shops are frequently franchises. In contrast, most groceries, drugstores, hardware stores, and discount stores are locally managed outlets owned by major corporations. Most jewelers, music shops, sports stores, nurseries, auto dealers, contractors, and day-care centers are still independently owned, but franchising is making inroads in these businesses.

Today franchising extends to nearly every category of business, and in the ten years preceding 1988, more than 500,000 new franchise outlets were opened in the United States. The U.S. Department of Commerce has identified franchising as the fastest-growing business sector in the country, with the potential for $100 billion in sales by the end of the century.[53] Stunning changes have occurred in many industries where franchising has become common. For example, Red Carpet Realty began franchising in 1977, and now nearly a third of the home real estate market is under franchise management, with competitors that include Century 21, ERA, Better Homes, and Coldwell Banker. Barbers have a new image with the Hair Performers, The Hair Cuttery, UniSex, Image 21, and other franchises. Additional franchising examples are 1st Optometry, Franklin Mint, ACE Hardware, Omni Hotels, Budget Rent-a-Car, Merle Harmon's Fan Fair, Money Mart, Jiffy Lube, and Mail America. All together, more than 48 categories of franchise industries with nearly 1,500 business options operate in this country.[54]

Many franchisors are now subsidiaries of major corporations. For example, John Deere and ARCO changed to franchise formats, and PepsiCo bought into franchising with its purchases of Kentucky Fried Chicken, Taco Bell, and Pizza Hut. Similarly, Transamerica Corporation bought Budget Rent-a-Car. Still, most franchisors start with a simple idea by an entrepreneur, a small store or service, and then develop a business format that can be replicated successfully.

Perspective on Small Business

Franchising illustrates two viewpoints of entrepreneurship from a small-business perspective. First, for the local independent businessperson, a franchise offers collective help in a proven market niche to provide the owner with low-risk income substitution. Second, for more aggressive franchisees, there is a growth option. They can often buy into "master area" franchises, opening multiple store locations, or they can buy multiple sites, often owning businesses in several different franchise organizations. Most franchisees, however, are content with one location and a rewarding lifestyle in a business they can call their own.

Those that do expand often hold extensive chains of stores and, in effect, become corporate managers with an expanding layer of location managers. The next step up the line is becoming a franchisor who sells locations. The creators of Sir Speedy, Kwik-Kopy, Pier 1 Imports, and Mail America began as individual franchisees with competing companies, then grew to the point of opening their own franchise organization. Consequently, it is difficult to categorically label all franchises as "small" businesses or to conclude that all franchisees are locally operated by independent owners.

Family-owned businesses are equally difficult to categorize. Although most are local personal service enterprises focused on skills of individuals who would rather work for themselves than for larger companies, many of our major corporations grew out of these modest foundations. Macy's began as a small tailor shop, Kellogg's grew from a family grocery store, and Maytag emerged from a plumbing shop. Rags-to-riches stories are behind most successful companies, and although few individuals can aspire to great fortunes, many who are students today will create legends recounted in future textbooks.

CHECKPOINT

- Define small business and explain how it differs from entrepreneurship.
- Contrast large and small family enterprises and discuss why succession is a critical problem to resolve.
- Define franchising and describe what franchisees and franchisors receive through their contractual agreement.

LOOKING BACK to our opening comments on Richard Branson, it should be clear that he fits the stereotypical profile of an entrepreneur. Branson is a maverick who seems more concerned with the pleasure he gets out of creating new enterprises than with administering them once they are successful. His interest in money has always been secondary to his fascination with taking calculated risks, and although he can retreat to his own $10 million private island (where else but in the Virgin Islands?), he is more likely to be found in shirtsleeves conversing with customers or working alongside his employees. Branson's one compulsive trait is astute planning for all his ventures. None of his nearly 100 ventures was initiated without careful research and formal planning, and Branson hires the best managers he can find with a similar commitment. However, he does not allow planning to paralyze him, but enjoys being an "adventurer" always in search of opportunity-making activities.[55] ■

A SYNOPSIS FOR LEARNING

1. **Explain the historic foundations of entrepreneurship in our free enterprise system.**

   Entrepreneurship appeared in the economic literature of the sixteenth and seventeenth centuries as a description of merchants or craft workers who contracted their services. Entrepreneurship emerged as an explanation for free enterprise during the late eighteenth century, and then as the basis for industrial capitalism at the turn of the twentieth century. Only recently has it been recognized as a field of study in American business schools. We have now refined the definition of entrepreneurship to mean those people who create new ventures by bringing together resources in new ways to benefit society, undertaking the risk for profitable rewards.

2. **Discuss profiles of entrepreneurs and career implications for managers.**

   Entrepreneurs are motivated to achieve unusual results, persistent in their endeavors, and intensely focused, optimistic, self-reliant, and energetic. They also tend to persevere where others retreat, championing new ideas with determination. Although these characteristics may apply equally to many professionals and managers not involved in new ventures, entrepreneurs join to them a fierce independence and commitment to a new, often risky, idea. Managers can emulate this behavior, and many of the most successful corporate leaders have achieved success by behaving as entrepreneurs.

3. Discuss the concept of corporate entrepreneurship, or intrapreneurship.

   Corporate entrepreneurship, or intrapreneurship, is a label for corporate innovation that results in new products, new-venture units, and often new companies. Instead of starting companies from scratch, however, corporate entrepreneurs work within existing companies to launch new ideas. They are supported by company resources and encouraged to take risks beyond the normal scope of company operations.

4. Identify stages of development for new and growing firms.

   In the incubation, or pre–start-up stage of planning, entrepreneurs realize an idea is worth pursuing and set about to investigate how to bring it alive. In the second, or start-up, stage, entrepreneurs try to acquire seed financing to launch the enterprise, build product prototypes, and develop initial sales. In the third, or early-growth, stage, entrepreneurs recognize opportunities for rapid growth; they now need substantial capital, resources, and an organization capable of achieving growth objectives. In the fourth, or later-growth, stage, the entrepreneurial venture must make the transition to a professionally managed firm. Often companies "go public" at this stage to attract the investment needed for major operations.

5. Explain planning, organizing, leading, and controlling in new ventures.

   In planning new enterprises, entrepreneurs are without resources, market information, or experience with the new product or service. Planning is risky, and managers have little prior information on which to base future predictions of success. In organizing a new venture, entrepreneurs are concerned with acquiring resources, hiring employees, and making choices about how to structure the new enterprise. Leading new ventures can be a multirole responsibility because entrepreneurs can seldom afford to hire personnel to handle specialized tasks. In controlling a new venture, entrepreneurs are preoccupied with managing cash to keep the firm alive, but since they lack a cadre of supporting managers, they are often forced to personally control production, get involved in product design, lead field sales efforts, and do all the administrative work needed to keep the business going.

6. Describe how entrepreneurship and small-business management differ.

   Entrepreneurs seek to create growing business enterprises by commercializing new ideas and encouraging wealth formation through innovation. Small-business owners may also start new businesses that grow and create wealth, but frequently they seek autonomy of ownership by serving a local market with established products and services. According to the Small Business Administration, a small business does not dominate its industry, has less than $10 million in sales, and employs fewer than 1,000 people.

SKILL ANALYSIS

CASE 1 CareerTrack on a Roll

Entrepreneurs seldom march to the same cadence as others, and this out-of-step mindset often ends up costing them their jobs. Jimmy Calano experienced this in a corporate career that ended at age twenty-four. Together with Jeff Salzman, who left his job at age twenty-eight, the partners set up CareerTrack in 1982. Their corporate careers over, Calano and Salzman built an organization starting in Calano's bedroom that today has nearly $50 million in sales and is the leading business seminar company in the industry.

CareerTrack offers more than 3,000 seminars annually in nearly 400 cities on three continents, and the numbers are rising. The success of CareerTrack is based on astute marketing and a clear picture of the firm's customers. By pricing seminars as low as $45 rather than the more usual several hundred dollars per person, the company captured the market for women in emerging professional careers. "We gave more value at one-fourth the price," says Calano. "A lot of people price seminars according to their costs; we price our programs at what people can afford."

Among CareerTrack themes are "Image and Self-Projection," "Getting Things Done," and "How to Get Results with People." There are more than 500 seminar themes in the firm's portfolio, but when the business started, a determined effort was made to identify women in dynamic career positions. Once established, CareerTrack diversified to provide on-site seminars to large corporations, including IBM, AT&T, and General Motors. After reaching $25 million in sales in 1986, the entrepreneurs took aim at government agencies, including the I.R.S. and the C.I.A. New themes emerged for corporate and governmental clientele, such as productivity improvement, quality performance, creativity, and office systems development.

Calano recalls that the company began with a vision of success that had little similarity to what CareerTrack is today. "You have to understand that I was just out of college and still not entirely sure what my final grades were when Jeff and I decided to go," Calano explains. "Jeff had been through several jobs in sales, and I had been working for a guy who did the Saturday-morning-you-are-gonna-get-rich seminars. Every Saturday we'd collect a couple of hundred bucks from twenty or thirty people eager to hear how to get ahead in real estate or stocks or something. I realized very quickly that nearly anyone could put on a seminar with a sexy message, and Jeff and I decided to do it right."

CareerTrack's first seminar for working women on "assertiveness training" was held in a Colorado hotel conference room. Calano and Salzman worked for several months researching the topic and putting the seminar together. Then they decided on a $40 fee, placed several ads, and the company was born.

"The concept was to provide a valuable seminar worth $40," explains Calano, "and we felt good about what we were offering. The topic seemed obvious because no one seemed to be paying any attention to working women or their career problems. A half-day seminar on how to be more assertive in their jobs just seemed the ticket. But our so-called vision was just that—to offer one seminar to working women on assertiveness and hopefully make enough to buy tacos for a week or two. We had no idea of making lots of money, running courses for IBM, or hiring people like Tom Peters to lead seminars.

"Once we realized how many people wanted quality seminars," Calano notes, "opportunities seemed to be everywhere. If we had mapped out a business plan then, it would have looked like a spider web with market opportunities in every direction. College students needed—and still need—practical information on writing resumés and getting jobs. Women still need help negotiating for promotions and being assertive about their careers. Men need stress management. And we all need to improve our careers, our self-images, and our knowledge of the world around us. If we had not created CareerTrack, someone would have, and, in fact, a lot of companies are doing the same thing now. All we had to do in 1982 was pick a direction and go. We are still doing that."

Today Calano and Salzman spend their time on two distinct business activities. The first, and most consuming, is market research. The second is the actual development of CareerTrack training programs. Success, in their eyes, comes from first *understanding* the $4 billion seminar and training industry, then *planning* carefully to address a distinct customer within that industry. The firm's products evolve from a marketing base that today includes films, videos, audiotapes, books, and seminars ranging in topics from "How to Survive Your College Days" to "The Masters of Excellence" by Tom Peters.

Case Questions

1. Identify and discuss CareerTrack's window of opportunity. What social or economic changes occurred to create this window? Do you think the window is still open today? Explain.
2. Describe how the company's business concept changed to propel CareerTrack from a Saturday morning seminar to a global business.
3. Put yourself in Calano's shoes today. What opportunities exist now and in the immediate future for a similar business?

Source: Interview with Jimmy Calano and staff at CareerTrack. See also Jimmy Calano and Jeff Salzman, *CareerTracking* (New York: Simon & Schuster, 1988), pp. 32-34, 95-96.

VIDEO CASE Getting into a New Business: To Buy or to Start Up?

Many people dream of owning their own business. According to the outplacement firm Challenger, Gray, and Christmas, 50 percent of the people it counsels consider running their own business, and one out of five actually gives it a try. What makes running one's own business so attractive? The reasons that people pursue this dream include wanting the freedom to make their own decisions, wanting total control over their own situation, and wanting to enjoy the rewards of their own hard work.

Even before the work begins, would-be business owners need to make an important decision. Do they buy an existing business, or do they start their business from the ground up?

Consider those people who start a business from scratch. What challenges await these new-business owners? Choices about marketing, financing, operations, personnel, and other aspects of the business must be made. Some people rise to the occasion, their enthusiasm undimmed by the number and importance of these decisions.

Another significant demand in succeeding in starting up a business is the time that needs to be spent. New businesses often require long hours and offer start-up owners little leisure time for unwinding from the burden of their jobs. As an executive from an outplacement firm explains, "I think most people who start a business fail to realize how much time it takes. Seventy-, eighty-hour weeks are part of the norm. Doing a variety of tasks, in fact, from start to finish, are the norms."

Not every individual has the critical skills needed to start a new business. Even executives experienced at running large operations do not necessarily have these skills. Moreover, there is no financial history of income and expenses for a start-up business, so banks and other investors are often reluctant to lend money. This difficulty drives some people to fulfill their dream of business ownership by buying an existing business.

Buyers of a going concern usually have an easier time of getting outside capital because they can use the business as collateral or can arrange financing with the person selling the business. Also, many of the other struggles that owners of a start-up business face are already resolved in the existing business, as an executive at the National Federation of Independent Businessmen notes. "It usually has employees. It has suppliers. There's a whole bunch of problems that are already solved and all you've got to do is come in and manage them for a while." However, buyers of an existing business need to be aware that they may be buying someone else's problems. Nonetheless, Russ Miller, who purchased an existing golf car company, states, "I always feel that, if you can purchase a business and expand on it and improve upon it, I think your chances of success are greater." In fact, Miller, who bought his company after retiring from construction, says its earnings have nearly tripled in four years. Even individuals who purchase an existing business find that long hours are required and major lifestyle adjustments are often necessary. Hard work and few days off are normal for most entrepreneurs.

Yet most people who take the plunge into business ownership wouldn't trade what they do for anything. They want to be their own boss, and the only way to do that is to buy a business or start one. This is a dream that continues to lure entrepreneurs.

Case Questions

1. What are the benefits and drawbacks of starting a business from scratch?
2. What are the benefits and drawbacks of buying an existing business?
3. What factors should individuals who want to own their own business consider when deciding whether to buy or start a business?

Sources: Genevieve Soter Capowski, "Be Your Own Boss? Millions of Women Get Down to Business," *Management Review,* March 1992, p. 24ff; John Case and Anne Murphy, "Buy Now—Avoid the Rush: Why Smart People Aren't Starting Businesses—They're Buying Them," *Inc.,* February 1991, p. 36ff; Kerry M. Lavelle, "Legal and Financial Planning Considerations for Business Start-ups," *The Practical Accountant,* January 1991, p. 52ff; and Jay Finegan, "The Insider's Guide—Buying a Business," *Inc.,* October 1991, p. 26ff.

MIND-SCAPING: AN EXERCISE IN INNOVATIVE THOUGHT

SKILL PRACTICE

During a recent lecture to nursing students on entrepreneurship, the professor challenged students to think of careers, businesses, or new services that nurses could pursue besides working in hospitals. During a fifty-minute period, twenty-four nursing seniors mapped out seventy-one ideas for new opportunities. The process they used was simple brainstorming, but with a slight twist. The twist, to use the professor's terms, was "mind-scaping."

Mind-scaping is the process of starting with an obvious idea and branching out like a tree—each limb being a new idea stemming from the previous one. The following is a summary version of the nursing students' exercise.

The professor wrote one concept on the board to start the process: "health care." From that, students branched to these main topics: home health care, rehabilitation, meals on wheels, special nursing care, visitation, and counseling. Each branch created more ideas. For example, "rehabilitation" led to: cardiac rehabilitation, physical therapy, mental rehabilitation counseling, job retraining, accident recovery care, home dressing services, family aid, and kidney dialysis treatment. From home health care came: equipment sales, life-support systems calibration, pediatrics care, temporary nurse "on-call" services, and many others.

The same mind-scaping process can be applied to almost any category of technology or major interest area. Following are several major categories of topics to stimulate interest. They can be assigned or personally selected for in-class or written exercises. Begin by listing one category and circling it, perhaps in the center of the blackboard or in the center of a piece of paper. Then develop root ideas that are closely related to the main topic. Circle these and draw lines back to the original topic. Choose one category that seems most promising, like "rehabilitation" in the previous example, and build new branches. See how far you can extend the tree in a reasonable period of time.

microcomputers	laser technology	robotics
genetic engineering	mass transit	communications
home entertainment	student services	furniture
travel	training	sports

Next, choose one of the branched ideas to develop more thoroughly and brainstorm the possibilities by answering the following questions.

Suggested Exercises

1. With a prepared mind scape, define a business concept around one of the selected branch ideas. Include a definition of the product or service, the target customer, and other relevant information such as potential location, facility needs, and likely demand.
2. Explain the obstacles you might encounter trying to start this business.

FIGURE 20-A Mind-scaping for New Ideas

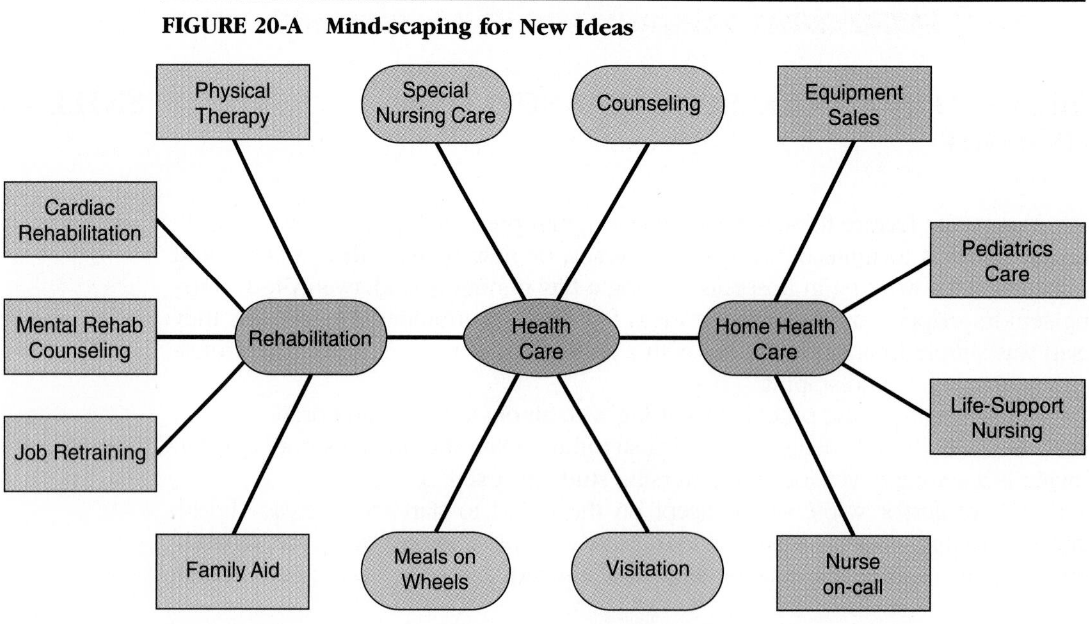

3. In general, what entrepreneurial skills would you need to ensure that this venture is successful? What finances?
4. What competition might exist in this venture's market? What might be the opportunities for growth? Would you be excited about running this venture? Explain.

21

Career Management

OUTLINE

Entering the Work Force and the Early Career
Finding the Right Job: The Employee's Perspective
Finding the Right Employee: The Organization's Perspective
The Psychological Contract

Life Stages and Career Development
Erikson's Eight-Stage Model
Levinson's Life Development Model

The Career Development Process
Making a Self-Assessment
Conducting an Environmental Analysis
Setting Objectives
Discovering a Range of Opportunities
Implementing an Action Plan
Evaluating Progress

Managing a Career
Creating a Success Pattern
Developing a Career Anchor
Resolving Personal Dilemmas

OBJECTIVES

- Explain how recruiting objectives are similar for individuals and organizations, and how both can improve career development during the early career stage.
- Identify potential crises in careers during the stages of life.
- Describe a career development plan and how it can be applied during the preparation stage.
- Describe how to create a pattern of success and why career anchors are helpful during the early career stage.

JACK KARSON, a 1983 graduate of the University of Alabama, has a second career following a fast-track in banking.[1] Armed with a degree in finance, Karson landed a job with the North Carolina National Bank, where he advanced rapidly during NCNB's expansion to a regional banking corporation. By 1990 he was vice president in charge of credit policy for NCNB in South Florida, but, with the banking industry in turmoil, his career seemed far from secure. Then, as bank mergers increased and NCNB combined with another bank system, C&S/Sovran, Karson began examining alternative career opportunities.

Research into openings in his own field of finance was disheartening. Downsizing in major industries meant fewer openings for experienced middle managers, particularly those in staff positions, where automated technology was replacing many functional occupations. A fresh, inexperienced graduate had a better chance of a job than did Karson even with his eight years of experience in banking and outstanding track record. Older managers fared even worse; they were either deadlocked in established career paths or "behind the curve" on new finance methods and computer applications.

But Karson had an advocation that eventually led him into a new career. A fishing enthusiast who enjoyed the environment of the southern Florida coast, he had been toying with investing in a coastal fishing business, when rumors of employment cutbacks first surfaced at NCNB. Knowing his limited options in financial banking, Karson bought into the Miami-based National Fisheries, Inc., a small private seafood wholesaler. He had only begun to learn how his new business operated, when the bank began eliminating jobs and consolidating many regional management positions. Although Karson did not lose his job, he realized his banking career had been sidetracked. In 1991, he gave up banking and became a full-time fishmonger, starting at the bottom at National Fisheries in order to learn the fundamentals.

The career move was exhilarating, and the challenge of actually "doing business rather than shuffling paperwork" an eye-opening experience. Explained Karson later, "I wanted to control my own destiny." By early 1992, Karson had learned the business enough to move into the company's executive offices, where his talents and financial skills, he believed, could be combined into an entrepreneurial career. In America, the social status of handling fish may be a step down from that of dealing with sophisticated loans, but for Karson, the career move not only made economic sense, but was personally gratifying.

In this final chapter, we explore what it means to have a career and then to successfully manage it. You may be reading this chapter early in the course rather than at the end; if so, some terms used in the management field may appear unfamiliar. Consequently, we keep the discussion on a general level of understanding and study careers from a "life perspective." Thus, we examine the life stages of career development, starting with student perceptions of what future careers can offer and ending with a brief introduction to career issues relevant to people of retirement age. In addition, we explore issues critical to young adults in the early stage of career development.

ENTERING THE WORK FORCE AND THE EARLY CAREER

career
The pattern of work-related experiences that span the course of a person's life.

One definition of a **career** is the pattern of work-related experiences that span the course of a person's life.[2] Work-related experiences are broadly construed in objective terms as the job positions, duties, activities, and expectations normally associated with a person's field of endeavor. A career also includes subjective criteria, such as individual values, feelings, needs, and perceived benefits a person derives from pursuing a particular field of work.

Recognizing that a career has objective and subjective elements is essential both for managing a career and considering career changes. Jack Karson, for example, changed the objective parameters for his career; he left the bank for ownership of a fishmonger business. But Karson did not feel as if he had abandoned his career interests in finance. To the contrary, his financial skills, he believed, were compatible with his entrepreneurial interests. What he left behind, in his view, was the lending process and the bank environment. What he added to his career profile was apparently greater satisfaction because of fulfilling his ambition to own his own business.

Entering the work force after graduation can be an exciting experience, but it can turn sour quickly if the job or the organization does not coincide with the person's occupational priorities. The experience can also be negative if the individual brings unrealistic expectations to the job or adapts poorly to the new work environment. The early-career period occurs during the following few years when the objective is to become established. This period can be exciting if the person progresses

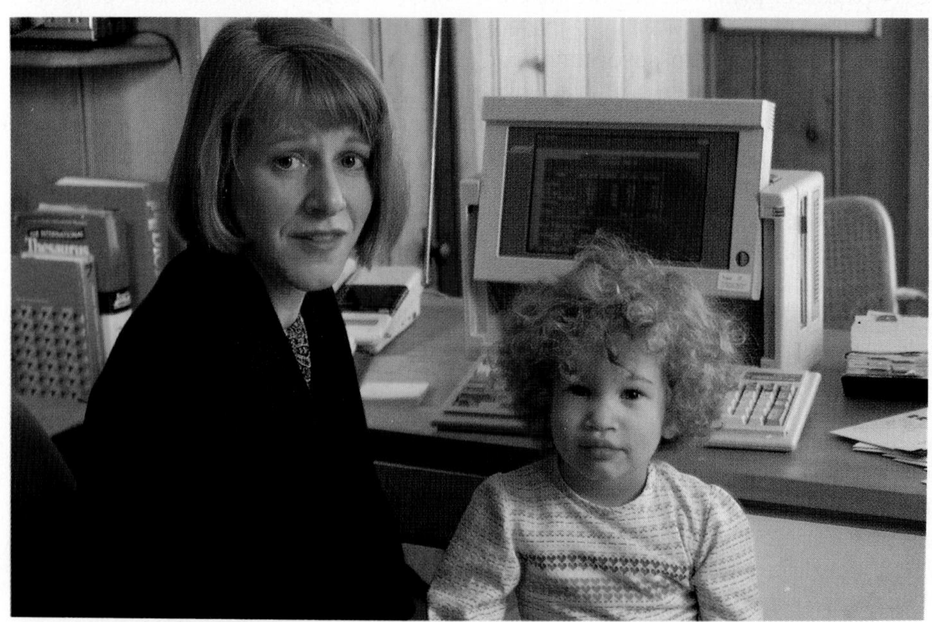

In 1988, after Debora Kane lost her $50,000 job as a computer systems specialist, she did not abandon her interests. Instead, she employed her skills as a freelancer, teaching computer newcomers how to use applications programs. The next step was starting her own business. In order to gain know-how, Kane worked part-time for companies offering computer training programs for corporations. In 1989, she was ready to create PC Basics. The new company's computer training targets: small businesses, nonprofit organizations, and hospitals. By 1992, PC Basics was doing so well that its founder and sole employee was thinking about hiring an assistant.

rapidly and feels a sense of achievement. Conversely, the early years of a career can be frustrating and punctuated by job changes, without achieving progress toward career objectives.

Successfully matching organizational needs with those of new employees during recruitment and the early career period benefits everyone. Yet researchers have found that nearly 75 percent of new employees are disappointed in their first jobs, and nearly a third leave within a year; as many as half are likely to leave within three years.[3] The reason for such high attrition is called the **reality shock syndrome,** the cumulative effect of newcomers being mentally unprepared for organizational work, being unable to adapt to new values or expected patterns of behavior, and failing to find the opportunities they expected in their occupations.[4]. Both employer and employee lose time and resources by negotiating a mismatch in employment that ends in turnover, and both are responsible for creating, during the recruiting process, such a situation.

reality shock syndrome
The disillusionment associated with a person's new job that results from differences between expectations and realities of organizational life.

Finding the Right Job: The Employee's Perspective

Unfortunately, most graduates accept job offers without a clear understanding of the organization they are poised to enter. This lack of clarity can occur for several reasons, but the most common explanation is that they are too anxious to find a job and therefore do not conduct a thorough job search. Those who do a formal job search generally employ a form of the *expectancy model* of motivation (see Chapter 13), in which alternative opportunities are compared and rated for how well they meet expectations.[5]

In expectancy theory terminology, a person rates the desirability of a job offer based on a variety of criteria, such as how interesting the work will be, what advancement opportunities exist, salary, location, potential to satisfy personal needs (e.g., travel or advanced training), and image of the company. These criteria—and any others seemingly relevant—are scored for each job offer. Then a probability is assigned to each item based on the applicant's judgment that the organization can satisfy the criteria. For example, a person may strongly desire to travel (rating the criteria high), and then assign a very high probability to a job offer by Club Med and a low probability to a job offer by Citicorp. If travel were the only criteria considered, Club Med would be the likely choice because the travel score given a high probability weight would result in a high total outcome score. Hypothetically, travel could be rated with a value of 10 on a 1-to-10 scale, and Club Med's offer would be assigned a probability for fulfilling that need of 0.9 when 1.00 is 100 percent. Consequently, travel-times-probability (10×0.9) equals an outcome score of 9.0. If Citicorp were assigned a probability of 0.3, the outcome score would be 3.0, and the applicant would obviously want to accept the Club Med offer. This procedure is repeated for all criteria, with outcome scores summed for all job offers. Then the applicant can make an informed choice.

Few students are likely to establish a formal expectancy model or to conduct the research required to compare organizations, but most will at least think implicitly in expectancy terms. They will wonder whether an organization can provide advancement opportunities, interesting work, or a satisfying environment, and they will mentally rate the importance of each criteria for making a job decision. Problems nevertheless occur when they focus too narrowly on one or two criteria, such as the starting salary or where the organization is located, without taking into consideration criteria that will have the greatest impact on job satisfaction. Such applicants are likely to jump at the offer with the highest starting salary or the one that sounds interesting, only to find the daily routine restrictive, their supervisors to be poor managers, the work environment unpleasant, or their position leading nowhere.[6]

Recent graduates without prior job experience, and particularly those from prestigious schools who have high expectations, are most likely to suffer from reality shock. There are several reasons for this response.[7] All students are accustomed to accomplishing activities in brief time cycles (one quarter or one semester) and to receiving frequent feedback through tests and grades. They complete blocks of activities, attain grades, and are "promoted" to the next level of study. These conditions seldom exist in organizations, where work is continuous, few employees enjoy "closure" on their efforts, and formal feedback from supervisors is infrequent. Graduates find themselves in positions where daily task expectations are unregulated by rules and procedures. Students can avoid unpleasant professors or choose not to take courses with uncomfortable task expectations; they are also relatively free to decide when and how hard they will study. None of these conditions exist in organizations. Instead, organizations have rigorous policies, rules, disciplinary codes, dress codes, and full-day schedules that employees cannot avoid or flaunt. Moreover, new employees will be expected to fit into groups with informal work norms and established patterns of associations, composed of co-workers from a wide variety of backgrounds and of equally varied ages, who keep newcomers at arms length until they prove themselves worthy of group membership. Thus, a new employee faces a tremendous number of changes that occur immediately at job entry.

Many of these problems can be minimized by systematically researching organizations under consideration for employment. This research can take the form of studying annual reports, news articles, recruiting materials, and employment guides published by government agencies. Research also usually includes enquiries to organizations such as the Better Business Bureau; often, the best source of information is a reliable employee with significant experience in a particular company. Finding an organization with a good match to your expectations can also be accomplished by job prospecting through personal networks rather than through college recruiting, or mailed resumes, or cold-call applications. Networks can include family members, friends, social acquaintances, professors, alumni, and friends or associates of these personal contacts. Jobs found through networks are almost always better suited to the individual and the organization than those attained through any other recruitment method. So, although network prospecting is more difficult and time consuming, it greatly reduces the likelihood of a mismatch.[8] Students can also reduce the effects of reality shock by gaining some work experience prior to graduating. Summer work, part-time work, internships, and volunteer work can provide experience without becoming disruptive events in the search for a career position. Having work experience will strengthen a person's qualifications, but more essentially, it will provide a student practical insights into daily routines, supervision, interviewing for work, and what an organization can offer to an employee in terms of psychological support.

Finding the Right Employee: The Organization's Perspective

While students are busy prospecting for jobs, organizations are busy recruiting to fill their labor pools with the best possible job candidates. An organization has the same mandate as a student to create an effective match of interests, but recruiters must first attract a sufficient number of qualified candidates. Because they are engaged in selling the benefits of their organizations, recruiters are unlikely to reveal anything unpleasant about the company or its operations. College recruiters are adept at representing their organizations in the best possible light; so students are unlikely to receive from them an unbiased picture on which to base a job decision.[9]

Although interviewing with recruiters will seldom result in sufficient information to reveal how a company really works, once a candidate is invited to the company for evaluation, interviews and assessment procedures tend to be extremely thorough. Company representatives want to discover how a candidate will fit into the organization. Therefore, information about work expectations and employment conditions are likely to surface.

GLOBAL TRENDS

Elizabeth McDougall: On a Fast Track in Asia

Owning a recreation consulting firm in Hong Kong was never remotely in Elizabeth McDougall's career plans, but eight years after graduating from an American university in Virginia, she is a Hong Kong entrepreneur advising Chinese business people how to stay healthy and improve their tennis game. Her work is not unusual, but how she got to the point of creating it, is.

McDougall came to the U.S. from her home in Canada under a tennis scholarship and graduated in 1984 with a management degree. Returning to Canada, she worked in a retail sporting goods store while trying to decide on a career. Following interviews with more than 60 companies, McDougall realized that a management graduate with no special qualifications and a modest GPA was not going to land a great job. She did have offers for sales positions, and finally decided to accept one in an insurance firm. But soon dissatisfied with this work, she took a different job with Namura Securities, a Japanese investment firm with offices in Canada. This job gave her a good salary. Meanwhile, her boss exerted tremendous pressure on McDougall to return to school to study finance and prepare herself for a proper career. Uncertain that she wanted a career in the investment field, she enrolled in a part-time MBA program, completing her initial courses with distinction.

Her academic achievement led to promotion and an offer to go to Seoul, Korea, where the company had a major office. Japanese companies often hire Canadians to work in foreign posts because Canadians are generally on good terms with other nationalities, whereas the Japanese themselves tend to be resented, particularly in Korea. So, McDougall found herself in Seoul, selling securities to Korean customers. She also continued her studies, and three years later earned her MBA. During this period, she established an excellent sales record, specializing in Asian mutual funds.

Then Namura announced expansion of their Hong Kong business and asked her to transfer there. McDougall accepted the transfer, moved to Hong Kong, and became a broker for Indonesian and Malaysian investment funds. Her income nearly tripled, enabling her to move into an apartment complex with a private recreation and tennis club. The club gave her the opportunity to renew her interests in tennis, which she had ignored for nearly four years. By 1991 she had become almost as well known for her tennis abilities as for her professional work. Meanwhile, McDougall was becoming disenchanted with Namura, which promoted men rapidly but seldom considered women for management positions. Feeling "topped out" at Namura, and also finding that tennis gave her tremendous pleasure, McDougall searched for a way to make a living in the tennis world. She began by giving private lessons on a spare-time basis, but this angered her boss, who demanded that she focus her energy on company business. McDougall refused, quit her job, and opened a tennis training business. By 1992, she expanded it to include recreation and fitness training, and had more clients than she could accommodate, many of them Japanese or British executives and their wives.

McDougall found her situation amazing. A Canadian with a U.S. degree in management and a Korean MBA, who had succeeded in a Japanese company selling Indonesian and Malaysian securities to Chinese clients, she had become a Hong Kong entrepreneur, involved in two activities she enjoyed most and did best—tennis and business management.

Source: "Making it in Asia—With a Few Twists," *The Montpilier* (A publication of James Madison University), Spring 1992, pp. 8–10. Also, personal interview by the author, March 1992.

Organizational interests are clearly best served by attracting suitable candidates. Recruiters must find employees who are likely to succeed in their organizations; those who make selection decisions often tend to be more concerned with personal characteristics than with a candidate's skills and qualifications. A method for accomplishing this objective is the **realistic job preview (RJP),** a formal process for evaluating skills, qualifications, expectations, and organizational compatibility of job candidates.[10] It constitutes a complex job selection process that can include aptitude testing, personality assessments, interviews with managers or employees, and in some instances a trial period of employment. (Chapter 12 addresses several methods of evaluation and job selection processes.)

realistic job preview (RJP)
A comprehensive evaluation of a candidate's skills, qualifications, aptitudes, expectations, and potential compatibility with the organization.

The Psychological Contract

When new employees have progressed well enough to understand what is expected of them, and when they have demonstrated to the organization their capabilities, a **psychological contract** evolves between them and the organization. This contract is a mutual understanding of what the organization and the employee will give to and receive from one another. It is unwritten, and is not legally binding on either party; yet it exists in terms of unarticulated expectations. The employee will work, meet job expectations, and behave appropriately in return for which the organization will provide compensation, job security, training, and meaningful career opportunities.[11]

psychological contract
A mutual understanding between the employee and his or her organization of expectations for what each will exchange in the employment relationship.

A psychological contract evolves during the early career period. The socialization process is crucial for both parties as a way of solidifying expectations and forming the contract. If the employee is slow in accommodating organizational values, or if the employee cannot adapt, the contract does not evolve. Therefore, the organization may not fulfill the employee's expectations (e.g., fail to recognize the employee for promotion, offer incentives, or make career opportunities available), and, subsequently, the employment relationship begins to deteriorate. In time, neither party will feel an obligation to the other, and the employee may leave or be terminated.

A successful psychological contract evolves when both parties grow closer in expectations and a positive exchange blossoms with new challenges, higher rewards, opportunities, and career growth. It is a win-win situation, which can continue to expand as both parties raise their expectations, meet those expectations, and are rewarded by the exchange. As noted at the beginning of this section, the relation between employer and employee is a matching one, and success for both begins with the initial exchange of a job offer and commitment by the candidate. If this match can be effected without unrealistic expectations by the candidate or inflated prospects by the company, then the psychological contract may be consummated quickly. Minimizing reality shock (perhaps through mentoring, training, or orientation) can help bring expectations into alignment or speedily identify a mismatch that should be terminated.

CHECKPOINT

- Explain "reality shock" and how it can be minimized by the new employee and the organization.
- How can students improve their prospects of a good match in their entry-level jobs?
- How does the psychological contract evolve to benefit the employee and the organization?

LIFE STAGES AND CAREER DEVELOPMENT

Each of us passes through several stages in life, which not only alter our personal priorities but also affect our careers. Early researchers developed models around life stages and suggested models for career management. The leading models and research are described in the following sections, but they are not generally applicable to everyone. Specifically, when the research was being conducted, little attention was given to gender differences in career development or to multicultural work environments. Consequently, the models do not address women's careers or minority career development. Later in the chapter, we will direct our attention to these points.

Erikson's Eight-Stage Model

Many career development models used today are based on the psychosocial profile of a human's life published in 1963 by psychiatrist Erik Erikson.[12] In Erikson's view, a person goes through eight stages. Four stages occur during childhood between birth and preadolescence, while the other four span the period from adolescence to maturity. Exhibit 21-1 illustrates the eight stages, the approximate age range in which they occur, and the individual's focal concern during these stages for life development.

Each of Erikson's stages describes a category of growth within a structure of social development. Although the childhood stages are very interesting, our concern is with the late adolescent and adult stages, when important career decisions are made. Most adolescents have some difficulty reconciling personal development objectives with their social objectives during their teenage years because, while society expects them to begin to fit into a "structured" environment of education and work, they are more concerned with "breaking away." Adolescents want to create some sense of individuality, to establish an "identity." With proper support and development the adolescent discovers this identity (frequently associated with educational or occupational goals) and enters young adulthood, when it becomes important to build friendships, marriages, and close social networks.

In general, the middle-adult stage appears when families and friendships are stabilized. In Erikson's model, this is the time when *generativity* occurs—Erikson's term for guiding the next generation through parenting or mentoring. In the middle-adult stage, people shift their focus away from "inwardly directed" priorities to "outwardly directed" support and social affiliations. Their behavior changes, and

EXHIBIT 21-1 Erickson's Eight Stages of Development

Life Stage	Age Range	Focus of Development
1 Infancy	Infancy to age 1	Basic trust, dependency
2 Early childhood	Ages 1 to 3	Autonomy within family
3 Childhood	Ages 4 to 5	Initiative
4 Late childhood	Ages 6 to 11	Personal industriousness
5 Adolescence	Puberty to late teens	Personal identity
6 Young adulthood	Early 20s to mid-30s	Intimate relationships
7 Middle adulthood	Late 30s to mid-50s	Generativity
8 Maturity	After mid-50s	Ego integrity

Source: Based on materials from Erik H. Erikson, *Childhood and Society,* 2nd ed. (New York: W.W. Norton, 1963), Chap. 1 and pp. 247–254; G.J. Craig, *Human Development* (Englewood Cliffs, N.J.: Prentice Hall, 1976), Chap. 3; and Jeffrey H. Greenhaus, *Career Management* (New York: Dryden Press, 1987), pp. 80–81.

their lifestyles tend to be characterized by the legacies they leave behind (i.e., successes in careers, at parenting, social and community involvement, and so on).

The final stage begins to unfold as children leave the home, careers level off, and there exists a stable order to the individual's lifestyle. People may still be strongly engaged in their careers and actually reach peak performance, but few contemplate major changes in behavior, other than to solidify their positions. It is a time for individuals to start planning for retirement while remaining personally and professionally active.

Levinson's Life Development Model

Although many researchers have built upon Erikson's model and published interesting work on career development, the most widely recognized life development model is Daniel J. Levinson's, based on efforts by a research team he headed that identified four stages in a human life cycle, as shown in Figure 21-1.[13] Levinson showed how in each stage there are transitional periods signifying critical periods of change. In addition, the model shows periods of stability lasting as long as six or seven years, which approximate the patterns of behavior suggested by Erikson. For our purposes, we can focus on the following adult stages in Levinson's model.

Early adult transition. This stage occurs between the ages of 17 and 22 when young adults strive for independence. It is the first incremental stage in the *early*

FIGURE 21-1 Levinson's Stages of Life

Source: Daniel J. Levinson, *The Seasons of a Man's Life.* Copyright © 1978 by Daniel J. Levinson. Reprinted by permission of Sterling Lord Literistic, Inc.

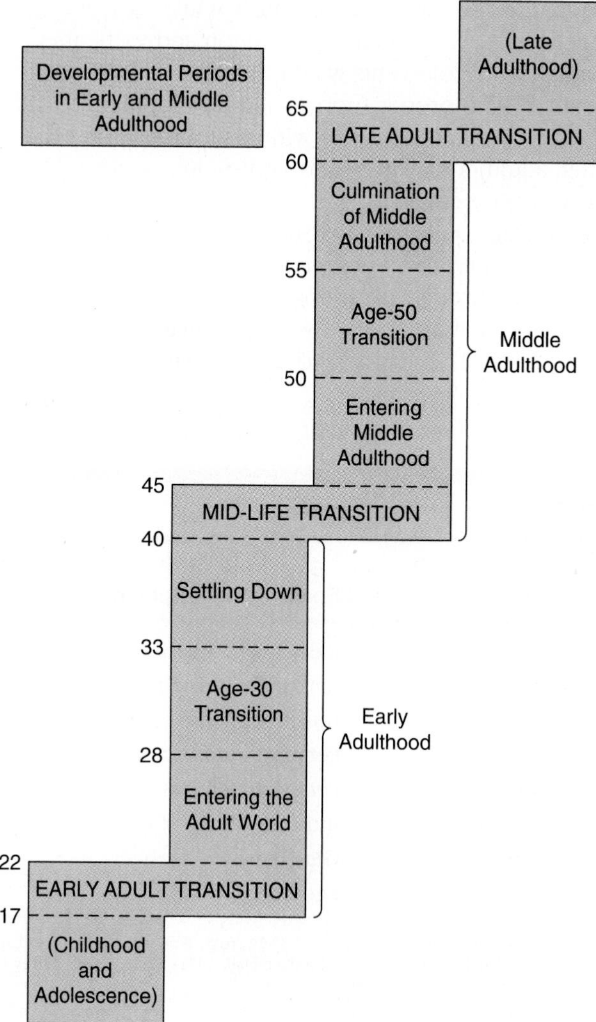

adulthood period, the period when most college-aged youth break away from family ties and begin to explore career opportunities. According to Levinson, young adults who fail to break strong family ties and, therefore, remain emotionally dependent on parental guidance, experience slower growth. He recommends a gradual transition to help build self-confidence and self-sufficiency.

Entering the adult world. Between the ages of 22 and 28, most young adults complete the transition away from their educational environment and into an organizational one. It is here that career tracks begin to clearly develop. Levinson notes that young adults who emerge from this period without having attained a clear picture of their careers often are frustrated over frequent job changes and ambiguous personal objectives.

Age-30 transition. Between the ages of 28 and 33, people either make a positive transition based on a sound track record and successful progress in their careers or are in turmoil, having "turned 30-something," still searching for a direction to their lives. A good track record obviously does not necessarily mean you are satisfied in a particular career field. Consider our opening description of Jack Karson, who succeeded in banking, yet made a significant change to become an independent business owner about 8 years after graduating from college. His timing is consistent with this age-30 transition stage when many people question their career paths.

Settling down. Having survived the age-30 transition period, people tend to make a genuine commitment to a career, which leads to a period of stability. This settling-down period can last for seven years or longer, as individuals focus their efforts on making a success of their chosen career—the one developed previously or a new one emerging during the transition. During the settling-down period, people create lasting personal friendships, often developing close relationships within their organizations. These relationships are frequently professional, with senior managers acting as mentors who guide (or actually sponsor) a person for career advancement. Many people may become too focused on career advancement, allowing work to dominate their time and energy at the expense of family and friends.

Mid-life transition. A critical transition occurs at "midlife," which tends to occur between the ages of 40 and 45. This incremental stage is the first in *middle adulthood,* and there are many similarities to the age-30 transition period. Now individuals seriously question their career progress. Because advancement opportunities begin to rapidly thin out at higher organizational levels, it is easy to become disheartened during the early 40s. This is particularly true if, after years of successful advancement, people feel as if their career has plateaued. In addition, many people go through physical and emotional changes called the "mid-life crises" during this period. Although these changes can also occur much later in life, when they appear, behavior can become erratic. A person who experiences a physical change in body functions, an emotional change in personal relationships with his or her spouse or close friends, and a feeling of frustration because career expectations have dimmed can make life- and career-wrecking decisions. Some adjust to these circumstances, working harder to get through the crisis years. Others, with strong support from spouses and friends, generally tolerate the turmoil without too much difficulty. Still others "cope" through maladaptive behavior, turning to alcohol or drugs or walking away from their jobs or marriages.

Entering middle adulthood. Having survived the mid-life transition, middle adulthood can be a fulfilling experience lasting from five to seven years. Levinson identifies the period as occurring mainly between the ages of 45 and 50 when a person's career is firmly established. Most people are in a comfortable position by this time in their lives. Some will have established a rewarding career launched from the ashes of a mid-life crisis. Others may experience a late mid-life crisis, but because they are nearing 50, often become reconciled to their existing career positions. In each situation, people tend to consolidate their positions and look forward to new challenges, building on hard work from prior years.

Age-50 transition. Turning 50 can be traumatic, as people realize that they are in the last full decade of career development. If they have not yet "made it" in a career of their choice, people between the ages of 50 and 55 can experience a sense of urgency to make a distinguished accomplishment while there is still time to make an effort. It can also be a period of frustration, reflecting languishing career opportunities and unfulfilled expectations. A gallant effort at this point may be a matter of too little, too late. Most people are unlikely to consider a career change during this transition period, and unless faced with a crisis (such as being laid off), will reconcile themselves to improving their current lifestyles.

Culmination of middle adulthood. Between the ages of 55 and 60, retirement plans begin to take priority over career advancements. Early dreams of wealth and success that most of us have, yet few of us attain, no longer cause anxiety; they are more often warm reflections of youthful expectations. It is a period of rejuvenation in which Levinson sees opportunities for harvesting wealth and reaching out for greater satisfaction through hobbies and avocations. For those who reached the upper echelons of their professions or have achieved their career dreams, this can be a period of peak performance. Executives may face their most difficult challenges during this time when they are called upon to guide strategic decisions or lead their organizations toward significant changes.

Late-adult transition. The last major stage occurs between the ages of 60 and 65 (or until retirement). Major decisions must be made during this time about retirement and how to live afterwards. The transition to retirement can be painful for those who have not found a constructive way to replace an active career. Many companies have developed pre-retirement programs to help employees make the transition from being active contributors to their organizations to entering a social environment without organizational responsibilities or career expectations.

Late adulthood. The final stage of late adulthood encompasses retirement activities, and although it is seldom considered important to career development, many senior citizens remain active in their career fields or constructively use their time in new endeavors. As life expectancy continues to rise, more older people are leading active lifestyles. Many retirees are opening franchise businesses (usually with younger family members), contracting as consultants, or seeking part-time or temporary employment in jobs where they feel they can contribute meaningfully.

THE CAREER DEVELOPMENT PROCESS

The models of Erikson and Levinson emphasize life phases in which certain critical personal decisions must be made. The career development process consists of making appropriate decisions during each of these life phases. Ideally, these decisions will be conscientious rather than haphazard responses to crises. Although a person cannot completely avoid making career decisions, it is relatively easy to drift along, allowing circumstances or other people to control those decisions. Being *proactive* to deliberately implement a career plan is obviously better.

Figure 21-2 illustrates a career-planning process that can be used at any stage in life. It is derived from the formal planning model presented in Chapter 6, and emphasizes activities required to manage career decisions. Students who want to solidify their interests and control their own decisions can follow the planning process as they prepare for a career.[14] We employ the model to describe how this can be accomplished within the framework of *preparing for a career*.

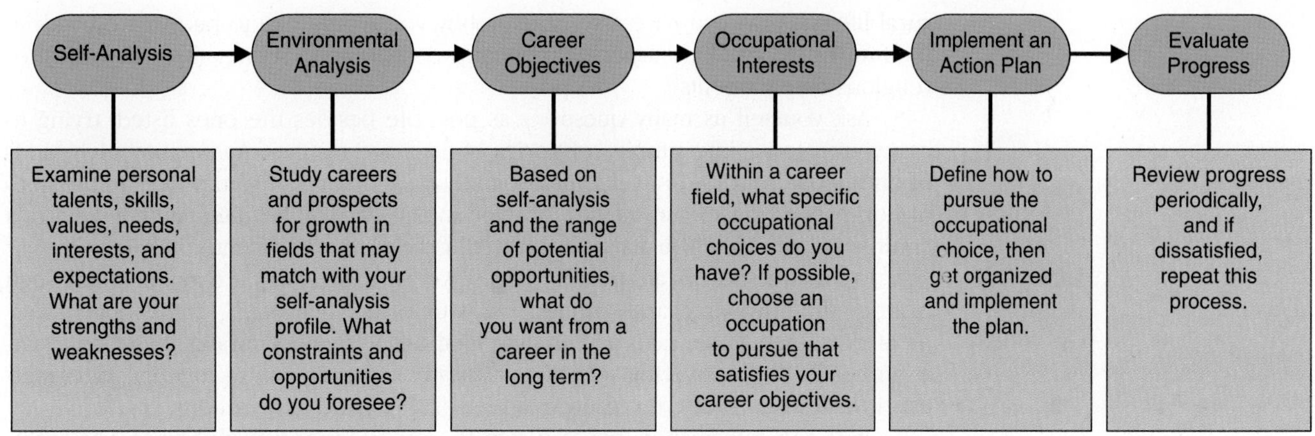
Self-Analysis
Environmental Analysis
Career Objectives
Occupational Interests
Implement an Action Plan
Evaluate Progress
Examine personal talents, skills, values, needs, interests, and expectations. What are your strengths and weaknesses?
Study careers and prospects for growth in fields that may match with your self-analysis profile. What constraints and opportunities do you foresee?
Based on self-analysis and the range of potential opportunities, what do you want from a career in the long term?
Within a career field, what specific occupational choices do you have? If possible, choose an occupation to pursue that satisfies your career objectives.
Define how to pursue the occupational choice, then get organized and implement the plan.
Review progress periodically, and if dissatisfied, repeat this process.

FIGURE 21-2 A Planned Approach to Career Preparation

Recall that the *preparation stage* described earlier is usually associated with young adulthood and involves planning for an occupation, initially choosing a career field, and gaining the required qualifications. **Career preparation** means being prepared for opportunities within an occupational discipline. People investigate occupations to discover which ones fit their interests, talents, and values. They next focus on a particularly promising field, gaining the capabilities necessary to seize potential opportunities. There are six steps in the career planning process.

career preparation
Being prepared for opportunities within a particular occupational field.

Making a Self-Assessment

The first step in planning a career consists of defining skills, values, needs, interests, and expectations about what might be a satisfying future lifestyle. This self-inventory results in a profile of characteristics and a definition of what seems to be important in a person's life. Such a profile is likely to change as individual priorities change, but periodic reassessment permits a person to make better career decisions. Most people engage in some form of self-analysis whenever they become aware of faltering progress, face a life crisis, or experience occupational dissatisfaction. Self-analysis may occur subconsciously, but the model suggests that people consciously assess their careers to ensure that they remain focused on desired objectives.

Professional counselors employ a variety of assessment methods to help people in their careers. Companies also commonly assess new employees by asking them to complete an aptitude test. Such methods form the basis for personality or psychological profiles revealing patterns of interests, values, and personal needs. Such profiles can be matched with occupations and career environments to assist in job counseling. In addition, they are frequently used to study patterns of behavior of candidates for jobs or promotions. *Acumen* software, packaged as a supplement to this textbook, is one of these assessment instruments. If you use *Acumen,* you will be asked to answer 135 predetermined questions; some assessment tools have hundreds of questions in dozens of categories.

You can conduct a self-assessment with little difficulty. Although this approach will not yield professional answers with statistical validation, it can help you identify issues to consider when making career decisions. For example, everyone has interests that tend to stand out as well as activities that we dislike. Apply this notion to education and construct a list of topics you enjoy and detest. Do you like or dislike math and quantitative modelling? Creative writing? Interactions with people? Foreign languages? Art? Working with machines? Agriculture or horticulture? Solving creative problems? Using a computer?

Develop a list of your personal activities that are pleasurable and unpleasurable. Do you like to travel or is it boring? Do you anticipate having a family and bringing up children, or is this a low priority in life? Are you drawn to a city or a rural lifestyle? Do you have a sport or hobby you would like to be involved with in the future? Do you have a personal need to contribute to society through ethical or religious commitments?

Ask yourself as many questions as possible besides the ones listed, trying to cast your queries into simple categories of likes and dislikes. Answers to such kinds of questions of course are seldom absolutely clear; many fall somewhere in the middle or depend on circumstances. For instance, you may be interested in having a family but only after you have established a career. As a student you might answer "no" to this question as an area of interest, yet in a few years it may become a high priority, thereby significantly influencing your career decisions. Professional assessment instruments use scales and scoring methods to more accurately describe evaluation results, but answering questions honestly will help you to identify your interests in education, work, recreation, lifestyle, values, and expectations.

With this information, you can start to outline long-term objectives. For example, you might discover that you enjoy travel and foreign languages, have strong interests in cultural studies and history, and enjoy working with other people who are creative. This profile might suggest several high-potential career fields, such as working in travel and tourism, following a career with the foreign service, or becoming a member of an organization that works with artists. These opportunities may be relatively unavailable. But hundreds of options for careers probably exist that fit your profile. Therefore, before career objectives can be established or an occupational choice made, a person must research the opportunities.

Conducting an Environmental Analysis

Conducting an environmental analysis in relation to choosing a career is a process of "external scanning" of opportunities, threats, constraints, and potential new occupational endeavors. For college students, this process can begin at career planning or university placement offices offering counseling help and published information about careers. For example, the U.S. Department of Labor publishes an annual *Occupational Outlook Handbook,* available in most placement offices and public libraries. Several other government publications also list hundreds of individual jobs. Figure 21-3 shows one of the many projections made by the Bureau of Labor Statistics.[15] In addition, many companies publish career opportunity brochures, pamphlets, and employment manuals, available through placement offices. Insights can also be gained from reading job ads, attending job fairs, visiting companies, participating in career seminars, writing to professional organizations for occupational information, and talking to professors, counselors, and family members.

For students who have not entered the job market, taking summer or part-time jobs can provide valuable hands-on experience in potential career fields. For example, if you are majoring in accounting, you may want to inquire about summer openings in an accounting firm, simply to gain access to a professional office and so be able to observe what accountants do on a daily basis. Although it would be ideal to obtain an intern position, with an opportunity to actually gain hands-on experience, even a janitorial job can get you inside the organization, and being inside is the first priority. People with work experience naturally will have a baseline of information for assessing opportunities, but if they are interested in new career opportunities, men or women in their 30s or 40s may also have to turn to paid job counselors or conduct their own searches through agencies, advertisements, job fairs, or professional organizations. Today almost anyone can access a data base with occupational listings. Many campuses have data base systems, while public systems like Prodigy or CompuServe cross-list more than 30,000 employers and occupational fields.[16]

Environmental analysis works well when combined with self-assessment. Each provides insight useful for the other, and by conducting both simultaneously, students can fine-tune their research while discovering latent interests. The cycling process of going back and forth between assessment and research on opportunities is,

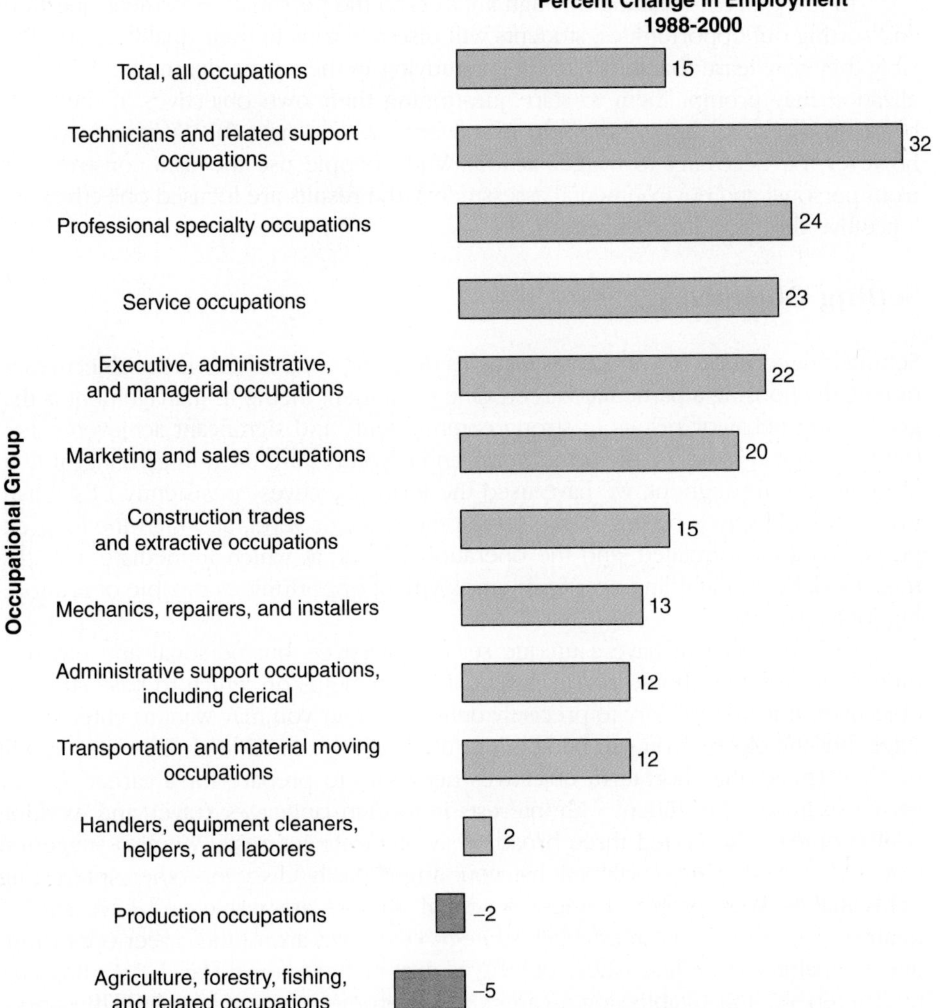

FIGURE 21-3 Employment Outlook for Broad Occupational Groups
Studies by government organizations provide broad-based forecasts as well as detailed reports. All jobs in each category here are considered, but the Bureau of Labor Statistics notes that managerial and mid-level skilled jobs are likely to be more pronounced in each area. For example, in the "service jobs" category, with a 23 percent increase expected through the year 2000, demand for skilled and managerial positions are expected to increase by about 32 percent, while similar positions in production are expected to decline by 11 percent.

Source: Bureau of Labor Statistics, "Tomorrow's Jobs" *Occupational Outlook Handbook* (Washington, D.C.: U.S. Department of Labor, 1991), p. 12.

in fact, a key dimension of the planning process. For example, an initial interest in foreign languages may lead you to research the travel industry, but during this process, you may discover that the World Bank is interested in business graduates to help develop new small businesses in Eastern Europe. For some students, this discovery might be tremendously exciting, and their minds will start racing about how to become qualified. They might then ask: What language skills will I need? Can I gain these language courses at my school? Will any business degree be acceptable, or will the World Bank need graduates with specific qualifications? What are those qualifications—knowledge of marketing? Small business development? International trade? How can I qualify, and do I really have an interest in this field? To determine whether a job at the World Bank can lead to a rewarding career, these questions, which require a reassessment of personal interests as well as more research into the opportunity, need to be answered.

After Eugene Stahnke lost his job as a corporation lawyer, he discovered the Career Renewal Center of Holy Cross Catholic Church. Not only did the Center provide Stahnke with an adviser on the legal-employment market, it also introduced him to a communications professor at a local university who now coaches Stahnke on how to conduct himself during job interviews.

In the process of sifting through answers to the personal assessment questions and sorting out opportunities, students will discover gaps in their qualifications. Possibly they may learn that they have been studying in the wrong degree field. This realization may prompt them to start questioning their own objectives. If they have been misdirecting their efforts, the discovery may be stressful. Such anxiety can, however, be necessary to trigger action. When people use the data constructively from personal and environmental assessments, the results are focused objectives and a positive direction for their efforts.

Setting Objectives

Setting long-term career objectives involves deciding what achievement objectives to pursue in choosing a particular career. One prominent theme in management is that goal-setting behavior results in strong commitments and significant achievements.[17] (See Chapters 13 and 14; the terms *goals* and *objectives* are used interchangeably in the field, but throughout, we have used the term objectives consistently.) Establishing career objectives occurs at two levels: the strategic level, at which life-long expectations are formulated, and the operational level, at which immediate activities must be defined, including near-term employment opportunities capable of reinforcing long-term plans.

Each person will have a unique set of objectives, but personal and environmental assessments should reveal potential career fields on which to base strategic objectives. It is unnecessary to precisely define a career you may want to enter at this stage, but the clearer you can be about a future occupational area, the easier it will be to articulate the short-term objectives necessary to prepare for a career. In our earlier example of a student with interests in foreign languages, travel, and working with people, we indicated three broad areas of career interests. We also suggested that, while researching occupations, you might easily discover other interesting fields that fit your profile. If these potential choices are viable and have similar qualifications, then you can establish strategic objectives any of the career opportunities is capable of fulfilling. These objectives may include global travel, pursuing cultural interests, and establishing a career in government (or perhaps just the opposite, becoming an entrepreneur and owning a travel or arts management agency).

Once you have articulated several long-term objectives, it is necessary to envision a path to achieve them. It may be impossible, for example, to attain a position with the World Bank without several years experience and specific language qualifications. Therefore, you might target entry-level occupations and immediate studies to achieve these prerequisites. Specifically, an entry-level position as an apprentice interpreter with the United Nations might be ideal experience; perhaps an economic research position with the Department of Commerce is a good alternative. If you discover a gap in your educational qualifications, then an immediate objective will be to fill it through course selections (or possibly a major curriculum change). There can be many permutations to this scenario, but without making an effort to identify realistic objectives, it is difficult to make effective decisions today that will pay dividends tomorrow.

Discovering a Range of Opportunities

If preliminary planning work has been satisfactory, the most interesting occupational fields will surface, and it may be, as previously noted, unnecessary to deliberately choose one. If the qualifications or career routes in these fields are similar, pursuing one option may open opportunities in the other fields. Nevertheless, this is the point at which most people stumble in the planning process. It may be possible to complete a thorough self-assessment and a detailed environmental analysis, and perhaps even to articulate clear objectives, yet have insufficient information or experience to feel comfortable about committing yourself to a specific occupation. Undergraduate marketing majors, for example, may feel confident that they want to work in the mar-

MANAGEMENT APPLICATION

Young Managers Eye Global Careers at GE and American Express

Nearly half of all Fortune 500 companies now have some form of global training exercises for young managers. Ten years ago no such programs existed. American Express and General Electric, two of the leading firms in global training and development, have set the pace, yet their efforts are distinctly different.

American Express instituted global training through its Travel Related Services unit during the late 1980s, offering exchange positions to foreign employees and domestically based young managers. Few employees initially took advantage of the opportunity to exchange positions, each exchange scheduled to last for two years. But, by 1990, 18 exchanges had been completed for 36 individuals who ended their two-year stints working in several United States or overseas posts. By 1992, there were nearly 500 applicants for similar posts, and American Express has sought to underwrite as many requests as feasible.

During their exchanges, U.S. employees are expected to learn to speak at least one other language fluently (preferably two languages), work in at least four functional posts, and demonstrate their skills through accountability controls for cross-cultural management skills. To qualify, employees must have two years experience with the company and be in junior-level management positions. The program is structured for managers with potential for advancement.

In contrast, GE's program was spearheaded through its Aircraft Engine division, which hired an educational consulting firm to develop a comprehensive program for repositioning younger managers and technicians in global careers. Unlike their counterparts in the American Express program, GE employees do not have to spend time overseas, although most would prefer to do so. The training is structured for domestic employees. Each candidate is expected to develop language skills in two foreign languages and to do business in two other countries. Nearly 500 employees were considered for the program in early 1992, and although a few of the selected will go overseas, most will take formal courses through structured seminars. All employees, however, must develop two projects in different functional areas such as marketing or product development with the ultimate aim to target their work toward customers in foreign markets.

As U.S. managers follow their new global career paths, companies envision more extensive training for spouses and family members. Procter & Gamble, for example, implemented a cross-cultural indoctrination experience in 1991 for wives of several managers headed for China. P&G decided to start a formal course in Beijing, where the wives spent two months in language training and cultural familiarization seminars, covering everything from local customs to shopping. The point of such orientation, according to P&G officials, is to reinforce their managers' career options by making foreign assignments family affairs.

Sources: Joann S. Lublin, "Younger Managers Learn Global Skills," *Wall Street Journal,* March 31, 1992, p. B1. See also Robin Pascoe, "Employers Ignore Expatriate Wives at Their Own Peril," *Wall Street Journal,* March 2, 1992, p. A12.

keting field but be skeptical about going into advertising, market research, or one of the many sales fields. An occupational choice, in other words, may constitute a rather broad commitment to prepare for a range of opportunities.

In North America, choosing an occupation has been a matter of free choice, without the pressure for an early or unchangeable decision. American students, therefore, are more likely to specify a general field of work—a career in foreign service or a marketing position in a major corporation. These selections may be general, but they are choices that can help students with their decisions. With a little refinement, such choices can be even more useful. For example, deciding to be "in marketing with a major corporation" might be better stated as: "to be in merchandising of personal care products with a major corporation." The first statement could be interpreted as working in any marketing discipline for almost any large company, but the second statement targets a discipline (merchandising), a product (personal care products), thus narrowing the field of companies to those such as Procter & Gamble, Lever Brothers, or Colgate-Palmolive.

Although marketing students have some latitude in their selections, many undergraduate programs require a specific commitment and early occupational choice. A nuclear engineering student, for example, must select the major early in order to complete prerequisite courses, and a pre-med student often must qualify for the program as an incoming freshman. Accounting majors will start their series of courses long before management or marketing students, who can often choose their fields as seniors. In most European countries, such a choice is expected before students enter college, and in many developing countries there is no choice; students prepare for jobs according to the dictates of society or their family status.[18]

Implementing an Action Plan

Implementation requires an action plan in order to be prepared for the occupational field of choice. More precisely, people will position themselves to take advantage of opportunities within career fields. For students, this means mapping out a program of studies and activities, so that when they graduate, they will be able to pursue entry-level jobs that reinforce their career objectives.

For example, a finance student who decided as a sophomore to pursue a career in securities brokerage followed a well-devised plan, and on graduation landed his first job as a stock analyst in Washington, D.C. Two years later, he was on a mutual fund management team, an occupational area of interest he had identified as a college junior. How did he do this? After identifying his area of interest, he had prepared for a career in it by becoming a finance major, then structuring his program to emphasize investment course electives (as opposed to banking courses or other electives). During summers he found work with brokerage firms, one year in a mail room and the next as a research assistant. As a mail room employee, the student not only had access to brokers, but studied how a securities firm operated. As a research assistant, he gained experience researching stock portfolios. As a student, he organized a small investment club with several other students, opened an investment account, and built a modest stock portfolio. And, during his first two years of employment, he maneuvered within his analyst position to work on mutual funds, thus positioning himself for advancement to a mutual fund team.

Evaluating Progress

The final step in the career-planning process involves periodically assessing how the plan is progressing and whether it is leading to your objectives. Students chart their degree programs to determine whether they are on track, and they assess coursework to determine whether their expectations are being fulfilled. They are often disappointed by their courses and modify their plans, changing majors or redirecting their efforts to achieve a better match between coursework and their interests. The finance major described previously, for example, could have discovered through his summer work that a career in securities brokerage was less engrossing than he originally envisioned, or through his coursework, he may have uncovered a keen interest in corporate finance. Or, during the early years in her first job, a client may have offered her a position that opened new opportunities in foreign exchange banking or estate planning.

As people gain more knowledge from coursework or as options surface during their work experience, the progress of reassessment occurs almost spontaneously. On the other hand, if plans are going as expected or no events provoke an assessment, they may have to deliberately question their progress. The critical point is that a person must be stimulated to make a career assessment. If nothing specific happens to awaken this interest, then it is necessary to instigate the process. In our opening scenario, Jack Karson had a comfortable banking position and was making sufficient progress not to be overly concerned about his future. Yet his misgivings about the stability of employment in the banking industry prompted him to examine alternatives. Fortunately, he began looking around long before he had to face a crisis, and although he was only "nibbling" at options, he found an entirely new direction to pursue.

Too often it takes a crisis to awaken individuals to a plateaued career or to the realization that they have pursued the wrong occupation.[19] It is not unusual for students to discover as seniors that they have mistakenly pursued the wrong degree, but rather than seek a more suitable field, they force themselves to finish a program and graduate on time. In the long term, this decision will probably produce frustration and extra effort will be required to redirect their career.

CHECKPOINT

- How does career planning help during the various life stages?
- Describe how to obtain help and what resources are available for conducting a self-assessment.
- What does an environmental analysis accomplish?
- Explain types of career objectives and occupational interests.

MANAGING A CAREER

Managing a career means making informed decisions about occupational activities to enhance future opportunities. The ability to make these informed decisions during the early stages of a career requires that people understand the nature of their occupations. It also means having sufficient experience with their organization to be able to envision how to achieve future progress. Active career management starts in earnest, then, when newcomers become reasonably well established. They can at this point begin to control their own decisions, sharpen their focus on career-directed activities, and build a record of achievement.

Creating a Success Pattern

Career success is usually associated with upward mobility within a field or advancement within an organization. This preoccupation with a linear focus on promotion is prevalent in Western societies; it is the gauge by which our success is measured, and by which we measure that of others. The linear concept of success is not as pronounced in other cultures. In most Buddhist, Hindu, and Islamic societies, for example, success is more often associated with values, such as loyalty and group harmony. Thus, in these cultures employee success is judged by the relationships a person develops within organizations. Promotions occur and carry tremendous esteem, fewer opportunities exist for advancement, and individuals are not expected to strive for higher organizational positions. We have mentioned similar differences in cultures and expectations throughout this text, and they are becoming more significant as younger managers work increasingly in a global business environment. Students directing their careers toward international endeavors may experience an even greater reality shock on the job on discovering that they are expected to set aside their interests in a linear career path, replacing it with organizational loyalty or the development of cohesive and harmonious relationships.

Differences in cultures illustrate that definitions of success will vary widely, but within a domestic organization, success will also be defined in many ways. Although linear advancement is important, promotions do not occur rapidly enough for it to be a sufficient gauge of success. Part of a newcomer's reality shock derives from understanding that, during his or her lifetime, there may be few opportunities for promotion. In the early-career stage, a newcomer may only experience a few mild transitions within a job category. Many people simply remain in their hired positions for years. Success must therefore encompass a pattern of achievements that reinforce a career profile. The following recommendations may help you to achieve success during your career.[20]

- *Demonstrate competence.* Do excellent, not merely acceptable, work. Organizations expect everyone to perform acceptably to remain employed, but advancement and recognition is reserved only for those few who excel.
- *Embrace responsibilities.* Actively seek new responsibilities that stretch your capabilities. A person does not grow by working "within oneself," but by challenging new tasks and developing new skills.
- *Make meaningful contributions.* Determine how best to help the organization, co-workers, and your immediate superior. Treat them as customers you want to satisfy with valuable services.
- *Learn to adapt.* Find a way to accommodate organizational expectations rather than resist them, and then adapt your behavior to become a member of the team. This suggestion is not meant to imply that you should abandon your ethical standards; instead, it suggests you reconcile your differences with the organization in order to strengthen the psychological contract.
- *Make a commitment.* Once you have accepted a job, make a commitment to give it your best effort. Do not go into a new position on the defensive or with the attitude of "wait and see"; such stances may keep you on the outside, retarding your ability to grow and contribute.
- *Continue to learn.* Although you may have graduated and have no intention of pursuing formal education further, career development is a life-long process of progressive learning. Successful people are recognized for their efforts to become better educated. Continuing education can occur formally, through seminars, development programs, evening courses, or other similar means, or informally, through membership in professional societies, participation in community activities, social networking, or self-development techniques.
- *Prioritize your loyalties.* Become known as a loyal employee, but not at the expense of your long-term career objectives. Ideally, a match between your objectives and those of the organization will allow you to be unreserved in your loyalty, but this ideal situation seldom exists. Showing loyalty should enhance your success profile but not prohibit you from pursuing your career objectives.

Developing a Career Anchor

Achieving success requires a focal reputation. Companies strive to create a *distinct competency* in their industry, and individuals strive to create the same distinction within their career profiles. This achievement is known as having a **career anchor,** a cluster of talents, motives, values, and abilities that form a nucleus of occupational characteristics. A career anchor is the foundation on which we base our career decisions and become recognized for our work efforts.[21]

career anchor
The cluster of talents, motives, values, and abilities that form a nucleus of occupational characteristics.

EXHIBIT 21-2 Schein's Career Anchors

Anchor	Characteristics
Technical/Functional Competence	Individual self-concepts associated with skills, specialized abilities, and technical expertise. A person relies on task-related results, while focusing on the functional requirements of occupations.
Managerial Competence	Individual aptitude for leadership, solving problems, making decisions, and possessing the desire to take charge emotionally to effect personal guidance of other people and resources in organizations.
Security	Individual priority of stability and occupational security, remaining in one location or career field. This can take the form of a strong commitment to an organization or a career path in order to protect valued lifestyle objectives.
Creativity	Individual concept of achievement, coinciding with starting something new or taking risks with new ventures or new ideas.
Autonomy	Individual preference for working independently and away from organizational relationships, often translating into occupations that rely on personal service or individual talents.

Source: Edgard H. Schein, *Career Dynamics: Matching Individual and Organizational Needs* (Reading, Mass.: Addison-Wesley, 1978), pp. 124-127.

Each person will develop an occupational self-concept around one of five career anchors described in Exhibit 21-2. These five anchors were identified by Edgar H. Schein, who found that people tend to lean toward one of these clusters of attributes very early in their careers. Most people come to rely on their anchor characteristics for deciding what to do in life as well as how to go about accomplishing specific objectives. However, because a person focuses on one category does not mean that he or she will exclude others; they may simply be relegated to a less important position in decisions. Also, a focal career anchor may change as a person becomes more experienced, changes careers, or enters a new life stage. A career anchor evolves, Schein suggests, through a process of individual adaptation. Thus, although people may be inclined to rely on their technical/functional competence during adolescence or young adulthood, through work experience and self-discovery, they may develop into outstanding managers, thereby shifting their focus to managerial competence.

Subsequent research into career anchors supports the model of adaptation, but also reveals many more anchoring categories than the five presented by Schein.[22] When asking what motivates a person to make a particular career decision, there can be many possible answers, each identified as a rationale, but the more significant point is that anchors do exist and that people are influenced by their self-perceived cluster of attributes. They will seek ways to succeed based on this self-perception of "distinct competency," as well as measure their accomplishments in terms of the clustered attributes.

Resolving Personal Dilemmas

Many of the most difficult problems to overcome in managing a career are personal, not occupational. Recall from the life-cycle models described earlier that young adults are preoccupied with developing personal relationships. Young adult patterns

EXHIBIT 21-3 Women at the Top Among the Fortune 500 Companies

Number of men and women directors and officers at Fortune 500 companies in the following industries, 1990.

	DIRECTORS			OFFICERS		
	Women	Men	% Women	Women	Men	% Women
AEROSPACE	8	213	3.6	7	272	2.5
APPAREL	6	84	6.7	10	89	10.1
CHEMICALS	17	609	2.7	14	629	2.2
COMPUTERS	12	221	5.2	15	461	3.2
ELECTRONICS	23	434	5	7	564	1.2
FOOD	26	522	4.7	12	698	1.7
INDUSTRIAL AND FARM EQUIP.	9	329	2.7	7	372	1.8
METALS	6	267	2.2	8	269	2.9
PHARMACEUTICALS	18	203	8.1	11	270	3.9
PUBLISHING AND PRINTING	18	235	7.1	13	244	5.1
SOAPS AND COSMETICS	17	84	16.8	8	185	4.1
TEXTILES	4	103	3.7	4	127	3.1
TRANSPORTATION EQUIP.	0	51	0	1	66	1.5
TOTAL*	254	5384	4.5%	175	6502	2.6%

*For all Fortune 500 companies

Source: Mary Ann Von Glinow, University of Southern California. Reproduced in Joann S. Lublin, "Rights Law to Spur Shifts in Promotions," *Wall Street Journal,* December 30, 1991, B1. Reprinted by permission of the Wall Street Journal,

of behavior are therefore quite different than patterns of behavior among middle-age adults, those in their late adult careers, or those about to retire. Yet obviously many managers and most executives are in these latter groups, while graduates in their first jobs are in the former group. The priorities, behavior, objectives, and values of these different age groups are seldom going to coincide with one another. Ample opportunity exists for conflict to arise over differences in personal perspectives. Chapters 12–15 deal with some of the potential conflicts over human resources, motivation, leadership, conflict, and stress management.

Several specific career issues are important to emphasize here. First, many young adults marry early in their careers and must reconcile career decisions for themselves and their spouses. Second, women now comprise nearly 40 percent of qualified applicants in business-related careers, and the percentage is rising rapidly.[23] Unfortunately, gender barriers still retard career advancement opportunities for many women. Even in companies that have made extraordinary efforts to support career aspirations for women, circumstantial obstacles still exist, such as few senior women executives for role models and ingrained myths about a woman's capabilities held by some employees. Exhibit 21-3 shows how few women executives there are in the Fortune 500 companies. Third, minorities in their early career periods are unlikely to have the same benefits as others in terms of support, mentors, role models, or socialization; consequently, their career hopes may dim.

Dual-career couples. Most people feel it is difficult enough to manage one career without being involved in decisions for another person at the same time. Almost invariably the career priorities of one person in a couple will clash with those of the other.[24] For example, if one person may be asked to relocate, the other will probably risk a career setback by changing jobs. Each may have different work schedules, with little remaining time to pursue their personal lives together. A woman may want to interrupt her career to start a family, while her husband prefers that they both work for several years. A husband and wife may have different ideas about when to start a family. Two people in separate organizations, or with separate career occupations, or both, are likely to develop divergent interests, different circles of friends, and different expectations for work, recreation, and social activities. Often their careers or interests may so diverge that they cannot share work insights or frustrations with one another. These obstacles can become almost insurmountable, forcing a choice between the relationship or the career.

The problems associated with dual-career couples are becoming widely recognized. Organizations have begun taking positive steps to minimize their affects. Scheduling problems are being addressed through flexible working hours, job-sharing systems, and various means of telecommuting (see Chapters 10 and 12). Many organizations have policies for maternity leave, protecting the job security of women who interrupt these careers to start families. Several programs help young mothers reenter an organization on a part-time or periodic work basis, while providing child-care or release time to accommodate the demands of motherhood. This practice has not extended to men so that even unmarried male parents may qualify for paternity leave.[25]

Relocation problems are especially acute because companies must fulfill their primary obligations—staff-expanding operations or promotion of their best people. Advancement frequently involves relocation, and the company must address how a move will affect an employee's personal life. Many companies now have relocation offices staffed with specialists and counselors who do everything they can to make the move a positive experience for the entire family. Their functions may include responsibility for the physical moving activities and housing arrangements, helping spouses find new employment opportunities, and assisting in adjustment to the new job environment. In a few companies, farsighted policies provide mentors for the employee and family members at the new location. And when the transfer involves an overseas assignment, relocation efforts can involve months of cross-cultural training, language classes, arrangements for child-care or schooling, and career counseling for the spouse who has interrupted his or her career.[26]

Gender barriers to career development. Beside the many difficulties of managing a career already mentioned, women must deal with discrimination, sex stereotyping, and life-stage priorities that create career obstacles. Discrimination persists as biased men in management positions control decisions affecting job assignments and promotions. Consequently, many qualified women plateau in their careers or find themselves shunted into assignments without advancement opportunities. Male co-workers can also create obstacles for women, preventing them from doing effective jobs or becoming socialized within the organization. Blatant discrimination is now being addressed through our legal system, but career barriers for women are often less obvious. These barriers comprise what is called the *glass ceiling*, a transparent but real barrier to advancement.[27]

The glass ceiling exists not only because of discrimination but also because until recently few women have been educated in disciplines—such as engineering or business—that lead to top management positions. Consequently, there are few experienced women positioned for top-echelon promotions. Some women also tend to seek a balance between family and work, focusing on different priorities than men do at different stages in their lives. This alters patterns of behavior, particularly for women who have children or are planning a family.[28]

In addition, many women have traditionally chosen careers in staff areas such as human resources and counseling, where fast-track line management experience necessary for general management promotions is lacking. These staff positions often provide rewarding careers for both men and women, but they are seldom "visible"

In 1990, Jill Barad broke the glass ceiling by becoming president of Mattel USA. Yet an April 1992 *Business Week* survey of 400 female managers shows that in these women's opinion the playing field is still not level. Thus, while 48 percent of the respondents agreed that American corporations were doing "somewhat better" in hiring and promoting women, 56 percent believed that there was a glass ceiling in their company.

in the sense of preparing an individual for rapid advancement. Sex stereotyping occurs to reinforce this trend, as many women are seen in gender-specific roles that isolate them from fast-track careers.[29] Whether women choose career areas with fewer advancement opportunities in general management or are guided into them is less important than the fact that many capable women find themselves in staff support areas. As noted, both men and women can find rewarding careers in staff positions, but recent studies show that men can easily move laterally to line positions or reposition themselves for advancement while women seldom enjoy lateral moves and are constrained in less mobile support roles. This has been called the *glass wall,* suggesting a gender-specific problem within organizations for equitable career development opportunities.[30]

To combat many of these problems, responsible organizations are taking steps to groom younger women for more rewarding careers and rapid advancement. For example, *mentoring* has proved useful. Successful, experienced women executives are encouraged to help younger women develop the organizational skills and job experience necessary to move into visible career corridors, and the mentor acts as an advisor and coach. This not only helps protect younger managers from potential stereotyping or threats of discrimination but also facilitates lateral transfers and career development opportunities when appropriate.[31] A somewhat controversial approach has been to suggest a "Mommy Track" for working mothers, whereby two separate career tracks could exist in one company.[32] The first track would be undifferentiated by gender, and women would compete with male counterparts for similar positions on similar criteria. The second track would be for mothers and women expecting children who would be given flexible working hours, responsibilities consistent with physical and schedule constraints, and the opportunity to interrupt a career with leave (or work in a part-time status) until they chose to resume full-time career responsibilities. Meanwhile, their positions and benefits would be protected.

Multicultural career issues. A persistent theme in this book has been that minority career problems are better addressed by enlightened managers, and most organizations are concerned with enhancing opportunities for minorities. Good intentions, however, do not automatically create systems of equality or the career opportunities needed in a multicultural environment. The term *multicultural* refers to the mix of many different ethnic groups: not only Caucasian men and women but also various minority groups including African Americans, Hispanics, Native American, Asians, and immigrant groups with various religious and geographic backgrounds. This topic was addressed in earlier chapters on group development and human resources, but in relation to careers, it is a particularly sensitive issue because of the underpinning problem of discrimination.

Research shows that career planning programs are needed to enhance opportunities for minorities, yet little has been accomplished to specifically address how that can and should occur. The prominent theme has been to rely on government mandates and guidelines for minority hiring, but advancement opportunities seem to rest more on resolving problems for ethnic minorities that are similar to those for women. Specifically, because so few minority executives exist, mentor-protege relationships rarely exist to enhance opportunities for younger minority candidates. Yet in some companies, such as Xerox and Corning Glass, minority executives are encouraged to become mentors, and programs have been formed to help younger minority managers develop.[33]

Sensitivity to race relations also prevents most white male managers from giving feedback—negative or positive—to members of minority groups. Many managers are uncomfortable with overseeing people of different racial characteristics. Consequently, minority employees receive less constructive help, even by well-intentioned managers, and they can become isolated. Discrimination aside, minority employees can find themselves outside mainstream career corridors. Legal mandates and affirmative action/equal opportunity efforts are aimed at correcting discrimination, but they cannot force improved communications or reduce sensitivity within the multicultural work environment.[34] One answer to this problem is to promote an organizational policy of lateral transfer and cross-training for potential managers. Another solution being studied is to periodically swap jobs among managers and employees (particularly in multiracial environments) to improve sensitivity to communication problems, thus enhancing a mutual understanding for career objectives and expectations among workers.[35]

As a concluding comment to this section and to the heart of this chapter, career problems for women and ethnic minorities have only begun to be addressed by research, and the barriers that exist are not well understood by most managers currently in responsible executive positions. Nevertheless, more young women and ethnic minorities are being educated in business-related fields, and promotions are occurring more rapidly. Consequently, more opportunities may evolve through mentoring and career development initiatives. In the meantime, individuals must take the initiative or seek out organizations with proactive programs of career development or companies where role models and mentors exist. Also, career opportunities can be enhanced by becoming positioned early in visible jobs with lateral and upward mobility.[37]

CHECKPOINT

- What problems do dual-career couples face, and how are companies trying to help resolve them?
- How does lateral immobility constrain careers for women?
- Explain how young members of minority groups can improve their opportunities for career advancement.

IN OUR OPENING PROFILE, Jack Karson made a major career change early in his life. Having graduated as a finance major and worked successfully in a major bank for nearly eight years, he became a partial owner and manager of a seafood wholesale company. This kind of change is not unusual, because many small business owners come from the ranks of young people with a few years experience who have realized that their career interests lie elsewhere than in the corporate world. Karson had a banking "job," but his career interests apparently were always in the small business world he eventually invested into. By coupling his personal desire for a lifestyle near the seacoast with his business interests, Karson made his transition successfully. ■

A SYNOPSIS FOR LEARNING

1. Explain the concept of a career from an individual and an organizational viewpoint.

   The concept of a career depends on perception. Each person has a vision of future occupational endeavors that shapes his or her career decisions about obtaining jobs, engaging in social activities, making friends, forming a lifestyle, and so forth. The combination of these occupational and personal interests and activities form the career path. Over the period of a lifetime, this path may change several times and be shaped more by circumstance than by decision. From an organizational viewpoint, a person's career interests concern what occurs within that organization—the employee's profile at work and whether he or she is loyal and contributes to the organization. This focus is naturally much narrower than the individual's.

2. Identify potential crises in careers during the stages of life.

Crises occur most often at transition points when major changes take place in a person's priorities. In late adolescence or young adulthood, there is an "early adult transition," when individuals leave school behind to enter the work force. During this stage young people tend to suffer from reality shock in their first jobs or discover that they have prepared incorrectly (or poorly) for their early careers. A second crisis may occur at the "age-30 transition," when a young adult shifts his or her interests away from being independent and adventurous toward establishing a family or close social affiliations and begins to settle down. During the early 40s, many people go through a "mid-life crisis," a result of emotional and physical changes. At this stage, some people become irrational, making major, unplanned changes in their lives and work. A mental change occurs during the "age-50 transition," when adults enter the late-adult stage and come to terms with their age and relative success (or failure) in their careers; it is a period of psychological reconciliation in order to solidify the efforts of a lifetime and prepare for retirement. The final crisis may occur at retirement, when a career is ended and retirement activities must be planned.

3. Describe a career development plan and how it can be applied during the preparation stage.

A career development plan is a conscious effort to make decisions enabling individuals to control their own destinies rather than allowing circumstances to dictate career events. Young adults may use the planning model to identify personal interests through "self-assessment" activities, which help them become better informed about their preferences, talents, skills, and values. With this information, they can improve their career preparations through education, work, or personal activities. An "environmental analysis" can identify occupational opportunities and potential career constraints. Along with results from self-assessment, it helps people determine realistic long-term career objectives. By forming career objectives, people can focus more clearly on short-term efforts needed to prepare for occupational fields most interesting to them. If the plan unfolds according to script, they will be positioned to take advantage of opportunities in areas that match well with their characteristics. At various times in the stages of their career, people will make occupational choices, and if these have planned well, choices will reinforce their career objectives. The planning process also emphasizes the need for a person to periodically review his or her progress, take stock of career advancement, and evaluate how well objectives are being met.

4. Explain how recruiting objectives are similar for individuals and organizations, and how both can improve career development during the early career stage.

Both individuals and organizations want satisfied employees able to grow and feel part of the organization. For management, recruiting those who can "fit in" is as critical as having qualified employees, while, for individuals, finding an organization with opportunities of reinforcing career objectives is crucial. Too frequently, however, the individual is preoccupied with immediate concerns over salary or job image and fails to prospect properly for a position that will reinforce career objectives. And because organizational recruiters, as indicated, tend to focus on filling labor pools, they inflate expectations about their organizations. Both parties are best served by careful research and reconciling realistic expectations so that a proper match can be made. During the early career stage, the culmination of work, activities, training, support systems, and organizational programs either help or hinder the completion of a psychological (unwritten) contract between the organization and the employee. The ultimate objective is to bring interests together through planned career development activities, with the individual and the organization sharing responsibilities to ensure the success of this process.

5. Describe how to create a pattern of success and why career anchors are helpful during the early career stage.

A pattern of success evolves through conscious efforts to do excellent work, demonstrate loyalty to an organization, adapt to organizational priorities, socialize rapidly into one's work group, continue to progress through active learning, and challenge personal limitations. Personal growth and achievement occur when individuals exceed their existing capabilities, stretching their abilities and using their talents in new and creative ways. A career anchor is a primary focus, or set of characteristics, on which to build a career path. Some people rely on technical/functional characteristics; others on leadership abilities or management talents; still others have unusual creative characteristics or other anchors. Anchors are derived from a person's self-concept and his or her profile of talents, values, interests, abilities, and personal perceptions.

SKILL ANALYSIS

CASE 1 Kodak Sacrifices Profits to Help Employees

Like many notable American companies, Kodak faced huge cutbacks in employment and operations during 1990 and 1991, but instead of downsizing en masse, the company sought ways to retain its employees. Explains the director of strategic staffing, "We have a psychological contract with each employee, and if we expect our people to be part of the organization, the organization must be concerned with their livelihoods."

Kodak has had a long-standing reputation for good employee relations and excellent management development procedures, but in 1991, the looming possibility of pink-slipping more than 6,700 workers due to realignment of its information services operations placed that reputation in jeopardy. Kodak made the hard decision to retrench its product lines for copiers, printers, microfilm, and graphic arts supplies, feeling it had overextended its position. Then the company established an early retirement program for most of its displaced workers. The first part of this program instituted a systematic pre-retirement planning process to ease employees into a retirement status without threatening their quality of life. Explains a human resource consultant, "The goal was to help employees make a transition, not from active work to inactive work, but from an active position at Kodak to an equally active lifestyle in an area of interest beyond the company. We wanted our people to reassess their life interests from a constructive viewpoint, and then help them achieve new career goals."

The program was successful, but costly, and it failed to alleviate the problem of shuffling several thousand more workers of non-retirement age. So a second program was begun, aimed at creating an "employee parking lot," which company managers could draw on when replacing workers or filling employment gaps. Most Kodak employees who were idled were retained on company rolls and given constructive tasks while waiting reassignment. Some of these tasks were public-service jobs; others involved retraining for potential promotion or new occupations. Although traumatic, the process saved or repositioned many career employees.

Its reputation intact, the company began its second year of repositioning its human resources in 1992, with a long-term commitment to pre-retirement retraining and internal job assessment. Most employees who wanted to remain were repositioned in jobs where they could use their existing skills, but rather than work on computer software, printers, or accessories, they did projects in the company's Imaging Division, a field where Kodak has retained its global prominence.

The company's actions were not lost on Wall Street, whose analysts backed the corporation's strategic moves with strong stock prices. Wall Street's support occurred despite Kodak's huge losses over the realignment period. The company's profits plunged to 7.3 percent in 1991, down from 12.8 percent for the previous year. Earnings were reported to plummet 40 percent in early 1992, yet sales actually increased. First-quarter 1992 imaging sales alone reached $1.42 billion, up from $1.36 billion a year earlier. Smith Barney investment analysts concluded that Kodak suffered productivity losses from its massive lateral moves and occupational realignment programs, yet they project that long-term benefits will far outweigh the short-term effects of regenerating a work force.

Case Questions

1. Explain what is meant by a psychological contract, and discuss the possible issues at stake for Kodak and its employees.
2. Describe how pre-retirement planning helps employees and what the career issues are for older adults in this transition period of life.
3. Using case and text materials, describe what might be crucial human resources issues for employees at various stages in their careers and how management can address those issues in a situation like the one Kodak faced.

Sources: Joan E. Rigdon, "Using Lateral Moves to Spur Employees," *Wall Street Journal,* May 26, 1992, pp. B1, B9. See also *Annual Report*, Eastman Kodak Company, Inc., 1991.

VIDEO CASE Executive Pay Ignites Controversy

During the spring of 1992, an intense controversy grew up around the issue of executive compensation. Just how much is a chief executive officer's job worth? How should that job be valued? Critics claimed that American CEOs earn way too much. Even Congress and the Securities and Exchange Commission are in on the debate.

What ignited this controversy were the astronomical compensation packages given to certain CEOs in recent years. Critics cited Stephen Wolf, chairman of UAL, the parent of United Airlines. He received $18 million during 1990, a year in which his company's profits dropped more than 71 percent. :The CEO of Reebok International, Paul Fireman, pulled down $74.3 million over the past five years, even though his company lost the number-one spot in the sneaker business to Nike and achieved only a minuscule 1 percent gain in profits for 1990. These are just a few of the examples that irate shareholders and other critics point to. An individual who serves on the boards of two public companies and eight mutual funds says, "I do think what we've done is let executive compensation get out of hand in this country."

For years, corporate shareholders tried to address the issue of executive pay levels at corporate annual meetings, but to no avail. Now, though, people are paying attention. Many experts on the subject believe that public and shareholder concern about executive compensation has escalated because of the recession. A spokesperson for Institutional Investors Service explains, "The recession has had a lot to do with focusing public attention and concern on the issue. It is not, by any means, unusual to see corporations paying top executives more than $1 million a year now, at the very time that workers are being laid off and plants are being closed." Many critics see this as a waste of scarce corporate resources.

The Securities and Exchange Commission chairman, Richard Breeden, has proposed a plan that would permit stockholders to vote on nonbinding resolutions concerning compensation for top corporate management. Says Breeden, "It was our judgment that, in light of the vast increase in public interest in this issue, that it had gone from being a matter of mundane, ordinary business of the compensation systems of the companies to being a matter of legitimate concern by the shareholders for the long-term future of their companies. . . ."

Critics point out that the current method used to establish executive compensation is absurd. The head of the United Shareholders Association states, "If you get through all the blood, guts, and feathers of this issue, these CEOs are setting their own pay, because the board of directors are totally beholden to them, and there's no accountability in the system." A corporate director counters, "One of the ways that salaries are set is outside consultants come in and give the board a range, which might be a range of reasonableness, and that tends to depend upon the size of the company, other companies in the industry, and what they pay their CEOs, the performance of the company, and that sort of thing. This is a very deliberate process these days."

The question of what is appropriate executive pay may not be answered for some time to come.

Case Questions

1. Explore the issue of executive compensation from the stockholders' and the CEOs' viewpoints.
2. As a new organizational recruit, should you be concerned about levels of executive compensation? Why or why not?
3. What are the good and bad aspects of what the video case describes as the methods of determining executive compansation?

Sources: Amanda Bennett, "A Little Pain and a Lot to Gain," *Wall Street Journal,* April 22, 1992, p. R1; Amanda Bennett, "Voices of Protest: In Today's Compensation Free-for-All, Everybody Has an Opinion About Changing CEO Pay," *Wall Street Journal,* April 22, 1992, p. R6; "Pressure to Perform," *U.S. News & World Report,* April 6, 1992, p. 49ff; John A. Byrne, "Executive Pay: Compensation Is Out of Control—Here's How to Reform It," *Business Week,* March 30, 1992, p. 52ff; and Carl Levin, "Executive Pay: Out of Control?" *Corporate Board,* January–February 1992, p. 1ff.

SKILL PRACTICE

A CLOSER LOOK AT CAREER PLANS

Although most students in this course will have much to do before they graduate, it is never too early to begin career planning. This exercise is designed to encourage the planning process with a brief look at where you are now in your plans, followed by an assignment to engage in self-assessment. The instructor may expand this exercise to include a research project encompassing the entire career planning process presented in the chapter. If so, these questions can help you get started.

Your Current Situation

List answers to the following questions on a separate sheet of paper. If you have no answer, make a note for future reference. If you have more than one answer, list each separately. (Time = 10 minutes)

1. What do I want to be?
2. Why am I in college?

3. Who am I trying to satisfy with my education?
4. Why have I selected the major I am now in?
5. What options do I see for these choices in the future?

Self-Assessment

This exercise constitutes only the beginning of a self-assessment. You should consult every available source of help in a complete assessment process, but for this exercise, answer each item below. (Time = 10 minutes)

1. What are my favorite activities?
2. What are my favorite educational topics?
3. What talents or special capabilities do I possess?
4. What particular skills do I have (or expect to acquire)?
5. What activities do I distinctly dislike?
6. What educational topics do I dislike or find very difficult?
7. What particular constraints do I have in terms of skills or capabilities?

Approximating Career Objectives

You may not be ready to firmly identify long-term career objectives, but if you can, list them. If you cannot, use information to approximate options that may be interesting to investigate further. (Time = 10 minutes)

Class Discussion

The instructor will ask students to answer each of the questions, selecting various students for a response (or several responses depending on class time constraints) in each category. You may take the opportunity to jot down ideas from these responses for further study.

The point of the discussion is not to discover whether students can answer the questions (there are no right or wrong answers), but to identify possibilities for careers and to prompt critical thinking about these initial career planning issues. If you have few answers and no objectives, it may be time to implement a solid career planning exercise.

Multinational Start-Up

by Hal Plotkin

With the rapid internationalization of the U.S. economy, more companies are looking overseas early in their development. Indeed, some new firms are predicating their success almost entirely on penetrating foreign markets for their goods and services.

Of course, there have always been companies—such as import/export operations, shipping firms, and consultants—that have done virtually all their business abroad. But the globalization of financial markets, along with new communication technologies—facsimile machines, in particular—has greatly expanded the opportunities for fledgling companies to start their business overseas.

Crucial to the success of this new breed of multinational start-up is the strong demand in many parts of the world for products uniquely American. Whether for cosmetics, fresh fruits, or television shows, this demand can create lucrative openings for entrepreneurial ventures.

Flexible Marketing

Beauty Products International, Inc. (BPI), a cosmetics-exporting firm founded in 1987 by three California businessmen, is a classic model of this new type of start-up. Rather than taking the usual route of building domestic sales and then hesitantly dipping a toe into foreign waters, company president James K. Yoder thought globally from the beginning. This focus paid off quickly.

Capitalized with only $25,000, by 1988, BPI had penetrated markets in Australia, Saipan, Malaysia, Indonesia, Singapore, South Korea, the Philippines, Malta, Kuwait, Nigeria, Greece, and Japan, with even larger deals pending in Mexico, France, and Taiwan. Since its creation, the company has shipped more than a million units of nail enamel and lipstick to wholesale customers around the world.

Central to BPI's success has been its capitalizing on the mystique of American women, particularly California women. By leveraging this asset with a finely developed network of distributors and a willingness to adjust products to meet local tastes, in less than two years BPI has racked up sales of nearly $1 million.

BPI's success came in a niche ignored by larger, more established companies. Yoder's partner, Maurice Rasgon, has a childhood friend, Mark Friedman, whose factory supplies cosmetics to discount stores such as K Mart, which sell them at two for a dollar. Though Friedman had frequently received inquiries from potential customers overseas, they had never piqued his interest.

"He would just throw the letters in the wastepaper basket," Rasgon recalls, "because he thought it was too big a bother. Many of the letters were in foreign languages, or they were from places he had never heard of."

But Rasgon and Yoder saw a better use for those letters. They took them to their friend Kenton Post and used them to convince him to put up the $25,000 they needed to get started. Seeking to take advantage of the fascination with California around the world, they repackaged their discount cosmetics for their export-only "California Colors" line.

But if the California concept piqued the interest of overseas merchandisers, BPI's success rests largely on its flexible approach to each market. "Jim listens closely to his customers, and he never argues," notes BPI's Japanese marketer, Yasunori Satomi. "Americans are always asking, 'Why do the Japanese do that?' But that is a question for scholars. The question businessmen should ask is, 'How do the Japanese do this or that?' And that is the question Jim is always asking me."

In Japan, Yoder's ability to listen and learn is reflected in BPI's willingness to place the brand name on the lipstick's base instead of on the removable cover and to change the packaging color scheme upon request. As a result, BPI's slightly altered product line is now being test-marketed at Daiei, Japan's popular 3,000-store retail chain. Yoder is quick to point out the power of Japan's mass market: Sales of just twelve pieces per day per store will add $6 million to BPI's annual sales volume.

Yoder carries this flexibility into other markets. In South Korea, for example, his customer wanted a lipstick that slid more smoothly from its sheath. "So it costs us two cents more per piece," Yoder explains, "but now it is a very elegant product. Basically, we just try to find out what they want, and then we sell it to them."

This willingness to customize may soon pay off in big sales in South Korea, believes Jason Shin, managing director of the Seoul-based Poong Jin Company. Last summer Poong Jin test-marketed $20,000 worth of BPI's lipstick, and plans to quadruple its purchases this year.

Building Relationships

Effective and flexible marketing is only one aspect of building a successful multinational start-up. Equally important, particularly in Asia, is the patient constructing of relationships with key business contacts. For example, Western Orient Trading Company founder and president Jeff Thompson cites his close ties with his largest Japanese customer, produce wholesaler Tomio Arimoto, as perhaps the key element in his success. In only four years, Thompson's Mission Viejo, California, which markets high-quality American fruits and vegetables in Asia, has seen its sales jump from $1.2 million to $14 million.

"The second time I visited Mr. Arimoto," recalls Thompson, who still addresses his most important customer formally, "he prepared a Matsutake mushroom feast." The fleshy fungi, which sell for about $100 each in Japan, were the centerpiece of a meal that Thompson will try to top the next time Arimoto visits him in California.

Arimoto, who spent thirty years as an employee of Nishimoto Trading Company, a distributor for fruit marketing giant Sunkist, beams when Thompson's name is mentioned. "Most Americans who want to sell products here, they have mouths, but no ears," he says. "But Mr. Thompson is different. I tell him what we need, what size, what color, and he finds the very best products for us."

Grabbing the Opportunity

Yet, more than anything else, it is classic entrepreneurial opportunism that characterizes the new breed of multinational start-ups. Take Lyric Hughes, founder and president of T.L.I. International Corporation, marketing services firm in Chicago.

When Hughes's favorite football team, the Chicago Bears, played in the 1986 Super Bowl, she made a bet with her friend, NFL representative Jim Bukata. The deal was that if her team won, she would get the exclusive rights to rebroadcast the game in China. The Bears won.

Paying the NFL a paltry $200 for the first-ever rights to broadcast a Super Bowl to China's potential megamillion-viewer TV audience, Hughes opened up a new market for American sports programming in that country. Offering entry advertising rates for 30-second spots on China Central TV (CCTV) for less than the equivalent time in any major U.S. metropolitan media market, Hughes netted some $75,000 worth of advertising from the Super Bowl rebroadcast.

For their part, Chinese television officials believe their audience—more than 300 million viewers watched the game in 1987—is only beginning to get interested in such events. "Refrigerator Perry was very popular," says Cen Chuanli, CCTV deputy director of sports programming. "A lot of people liked the Refrigerator, a man who could eat a lot of food."

Whether cosmetics or cantaloupe, the Refrigerator or the California Girl, the international appetite for American products seems insatiable. For the entrepreneur willing and able to exploit it, the time has never been better.

Case Questions

1. Using MNC classifications, discuss each firm's approach to business. In your answer, explain how each used licensing, exporting, contracting, and other forms of business internationally.
2. Explore how each entrepreneur used a knowledge of the culture of the countries he or she was doing business with to generate cooperation with clients. How might cultural awareness be important for each firm during the 1990s?
3. From an entrepreneur's perspective, choose a product or service that you think might be valuable to a foreign customer. Using the start-up planning criteria for a new venture and information from Chapter 20, International Management, describe your customers, markets, and critical success factors. Why might your product or service be a success, and what factors could spell doom?

Source: Hal Plotkin, "Multinational Start-Up," *Inc.'s Guide to Internationl Business,* Fall 1988, pp. 15–17. Adapted with permission.

Endnotes

CHAPTER 1

1. Thomas A. Stewart, "Brainpower," *Fortune,* June 3, 1991, pp. 44–46, 50, 54–56, 58–60.

2. Michael A. Hitt, Robert E. Hoskisson, and Jeffrey S. Harrison, "Strategic Competitiveness in the 1990s: Challenges and Opportunities for U.S. Executives," *Academy of Management Executive,* Vol. V, No. 2 (1991), pp. 7–22.

3. Timothy M. Collins and Thomas L. Doorley, *Teaming Up for the 90s* (Homewood, Ill.: Business One Irwin, 1991), pp. 65, 170–171, 292–301.

4. John Naisbitt, *Megatrends: Ten New Directions Transforming Our Lives* (New York: Warner Books, 1982), pp. 11–14.

5. L. D. Parker, "Control in Organizational Life: The Contribution of Mary Parker Follett," *Academy of Management Review,* Vol. 9, No. 4 (1984), pp. 736–745.

6. Evan Thomas, John Barry, Thomas M. DeFrank, and Douglas Waller, "The Reluctant Warrior," *Newsweek,* May 13, 1991, pp. 18–22.

7. Robert W. Rice, Dean B. McFarlin, Raymond G. Hunt, and Janet P. Near, "Organizational Work and the Perceived Quality of Life: Toward a Conceptual Model," *Academy of Management Review,* Vol. 10, No. 2 (1985), pp. 296–310.

8. Stuart Auerbach, "Westinghouse Leads Updating of Soviet Air Traffic Control," *Washington Post,* March 6, 1991, p. C12.

9. Michael H. Mescon, Michael Albert, and Franklin Khedouri, *Management: Individual and Organizational Effectiveness,* 2nd ed. (New York: Harper & Row, 1985), p. 10.

10. Peter F. Drucker, "We Have Become a Society of Organizations," *Wall Street Journal,* January 9, 1978, p. 12.

11. George A. Steiner, *Top Management Planning* (New York: Macmillan, 1969), p. 7.

12. Henry Mintzberg, "The Manager's Job: Folklore and Fact," *Harvard Business Review,* Vol. 53, No. 4 (1975), pp. 49–61.

13. Fred Luthans, "Successful vs. Effective Real Managers," *Academy of Management Executive,* Vol. II, No. 2 (1988), pp. 127–132.

14. "Can Chrysler Keep Its Comeback Rolling?" *Business Week,* February 14, 1983, pp. 132–136. See also "GM Moves into a New Era," *Business Week,* July 16, 1984, pp. 48–54.

15. Pradip N. Khandwalla, *The Design of Organizations* (New York: Harcourt Brace Jovanovich, 1977), pp. 2–4, 109, 515–516.

16. Michael W. Miller and Paul B. Carroll, "Vaulted IBM Culture Yields to New Values: Openness, Efficiency," *Wall Street Journal,* November 11, 1988, pp. A1, A9. See also Laurance Hooper, "IBM Plans Revamps, Hints at Price Cuts," *Wall Street Journal,* April 19, 1991, p. B1.

17. John Naisbitt and Patricia Aburdene, *Re-inventing the Corporation* (New York: Warner Books, 1985), pp. 12–13.

18. Robert H. Schappe, "The Production Foreman Today: His Needs and His Difficulties," *Personnel Journal,* July 1972, pp. 156–172.

19. Lester R. Bittel, *What Every Supervisor Should Know,* 4th ed. (New York: McGraw-Hill, 1980), pp. 7–8.

20. S. Prakash Sethi, Nobuaki Namiki, and Carl L. Swanson, *The False Promise of the Japanese Miracle* (Boston: Pitman, 1984), pp. 11–12.

21. Larry Reibstein and Laurdes Rosado, "Seeing Red at Big Blue," *Newsweek,* June 10, 1991, p. 40.

22. Peter F. Drucker, "The Coming of the New Organization," *Harvard Business Review,* Vol. 88, No. 1 (1988), pp. 45–53.

23. Robert L. Katz, "Skills of an Effective Administrator," *Harvard Business Review,* Vol. 52, No. 5 (1974), pp. 90–102.

24. Luthans, "Successful vs. Effective Real Managers," pp. 127–132.

25. *The State of Small Business: Report of the President 1987* (Washington, D.C.: U.S. Government Printing Office), p. xi, Appendix A.

26. Israel M. Kirzner, *Perception, Opportunity, and Profit: Studies in the Theory of Entrepreneurship* (Chicago: University of Chicago Press, 1979), p. 39.

27. Brett Kingstone, *The Dynamos: Who Are They, Anyway?* (New York: John Wiley, 1987), pp. 45–60. See also Eileen Davis, "'Small Caps' Tough It Out," *Venture,* April 1988, pp. 34–35, 37.

28. George M. Taoka and Don R. Beeman, *International Business: Environments, Institutions, and Operations* (New York: HarperCollins, 1991), pp. 21–23.

29. "Productivity Growth Lags Normal Pace," *Wall Street Journal,* July 15, 1985, p. 1. See also Joseph A. Maciariello, Jeffrey W. Burke, and Donald Tilley, "Improving American Competitiveness: A Management Systems Perspective," *Academy of Management Executive,* Vol. 3, No. 4 (1989), pp. 294–303.

30. Tim R. V. Davis, "Information Technology and White-Collar Productivity," *Academy of Management Executive,* Vol. 5, No. 1 (1991), pp. 55–67.

31. William H. Newman (ed.), *Managers for the Year 2000* (Englewood Cliffs, N.J.: Prentice Hall, 1978), pp. 32–33.

32. Joel Dreyfuss, "Victories in the Quality Crusade," *Fortune,* October 10, 1988, pp. 80–88.

33. Roy Rowan, "America's Most Wanted Managers," *Fortune,* February 3, 1986, pp. 18–25; Thomas A. Stewart, "GE Keeps Those Ideas Coming," *Fortune,* August 12, 1991, pp. 41–45, 48–49; and John Huey, "America's Most Successful Merchant," *Fortune,* September 23, 1991, pp. 46–48, 50, 54, 58–59.

CHAPTER 2

1. *General Motors Public Interest Report* (Detroit, Mich.: General Motors Corporation, 1991), pp. 1–2, 7–8; and James B. Treece, "The Board Revolt: Business As Usual Won't Cut It Anymore at a Humbled GM," *Business Week,* April 20, 1992, pp. 31–36.

2. Jacob M. Schlesinger and Paul Ingrassia, "GM Uses Employees by Listening to Them, Talking of Its Team," *Wall Street Journal,* January 12, 1989, pp. A2, A6.

3. "GM into the Nineties: Forging New Relationships," *Public Interest Report,* a GM reprint, May 15, 1991, pp. 2–12.

4. Harold Koontz, "The Management Theory Jungle Revisited," *Academy of Management Review,* Vol. 5, No. 2 (1980), p. 186.

5. Peter F. Drucker, *People and Performance:* (New York: Harper & Row, 1977), p. 19.

6. Adam Smith, *An Inquiry into the Nature and Causes of the Wealth of Nations,* 5th ed. (Edinburgh, Scotland: Adam & Charles Black, 1859), p. 3.

7. Edwin A. Locke, "The Ideas of Frederick W. Taylor: An Evaluation," *Academy of Management Review,* Vol. 7, No. 1 (1982), pp. 14–24.

8. Frederick Winslow Taylor, *Scientific Management* (New York: Harper & Row, 1947).

9. Daniel A. Wren, *The Evolution of Management Thought* (New York: Ronald Press, 1972), pp. 158–168.

10. Stephen P. Robbins, *The Administrative Process,* 2nd ed. (Englewood Cliffs, N.J.: Prentice Hall, 1980), pp. 194–195.

11. Warren G. Bennis, "The Coming Death of Bureaucracy," *Think,* Vol. 32 (November–December 1966), pp. 32–33. See also Lawrence Finley, *Entrepreneurial Strategies* (Boston: PWS-Kent, 1990), pp. 224–225.

12. Henri Fayol, *General and Industrial Management* (London: Sir Isaac Pitman & Sons, 1949).

13. Hugo Münsterberg, *Psychology and Industrial Efficiency* (Boston: Houghton Mifflin, 1913).

14. Chester I. Barnard, *The Functions of the Executive* (Cambridge, Mass.: Harvard University Press, 1938).

15. L. D. Parker, "Control in Organizational Life: The Contribution of Mary Parker Follett," *Academy of Management Review,* Vol. 9, No. 4 (1984), pp. 736–745. See also H. C. Metcalf and L. Urwick (eds.), *Dynamic Administration: The Collected Papers of Mary Parker Follett* (London: Sir Isaac Pitman & Sons, 1941).

16. Elton Mayo, *The Human Problems of an Industrial Civilization,* 2nd ed. (New York: Macmillan, 1946). See also F. J. Roethlisberger and William J. Dickson, *Management and the Worker* (Cambridge, Mass.: Harvard University Press, 1946).

17. Wren, *The Evolution of Management Thought,* p. 313.

18. Douglas McGregor, *The Human Side of Enterprise* (New York: McGraw-Hill, 1960).

19. Abraham H. Maslow, *Motivation and Personality,* 2nd ed. (New York: Harper & Row, 1970).

20. Victor H. Vroom and Arthur G. Jago, *The New Leadership: Managing Participation in Organizations* (Englewood Cliffs, N.J.: Prentice Hall, 1988), pp. 3–4.

21. William Ouchi, *Theory Z: How American Business Can Meet the Japanese Challenge* (Reading, Mass.: Addison-Wesley, 1981).

22. Philip B. Crosby, *Quality Is Free: The Art of Making Quality Certain* (New York: Mentor Books, 1979). See also Thomas J. Peters and Robert H. Waterman, Jr., *In Search of Excellence: Lessons from America's Best-Run Companies* (New York: Harper & Row, 1982).

23. Ludwig Von Bertalanffy, "General Systems Theory: A New Approach to the Unity of Science," *Human Biology,* Vol. 23 (1951), pp. 302–361. See also Fremon E. Kast and James E. Rosenzweig, "General Systems Theory: Applications for Organization and Management," *Academy of Management Journal,* Vol. 15, No. 4 (1972), pp. 447–465.

24. Fred E. Fiedler, "Predicting the Effects of Leadership Training and Experience from the Contingency Model: A Clarification," *Journal of Applied Psychology,* Vol. 57, No. 2 (1973), p. 110.

25. Fred Luthans, *Introduction to Management: A Contingency Approach* (New York: McGraw-Hill, 1975). See also Fred Luthans and Todd I. Stewart, "A General Contingency Theory of Management," *Academy of Management Review,* Vol. 2, No. 2 (1977), p. 181.

26. Richard B. Chase and Nicholas J. Aquilano, *Production and Operations Management: A Life Cycle Approach,* 4th ed. (Homewood, Ill.: Richard D. Irwin, 1985), pp. 4–8.

27. Starr Roxanne Hiltz and Kenneth Johnson, "User Satisfaction with Computer-Mediated Communication Systems," *Management Science,* Vol. 36, No. 6 (1990), pp. 739–764.

28. James C. Wetherbe, *Executive's Guide to Computer-Based Information Systems* (Englewood Cliffs, N.J.: Prentice Hall, 1984), pp. 7–8, 22.

CHAPTER 3

1. "AT&T Slowly Gets Its Global Wires Uncrossed," *Business Week,* February 11, 1991, pp. 82–83.

2. Benjamin Gomes-Casseres, "Joint Ventures in the Face of Global Competition," *Sloan Management Review,* Vol. 30, No. 2 (1989), pp. 17–26.

3. Henry A. Kissinger, "The New Russian Question," *Newsweek,* February 10, 1992, pp. 34–35. See also "Soviet Union: Staying On," *The Economist,* November 30, 1991, pp. 50–51.

4. Carroll Bogert, "The Battle Against Bottlenecks," *Newsweek,* January 27, 1992, p. 31; "End of an Empire," *Newsweek,* September 9, 1991, pp. 18–23; and Kenneth Auchincloss, "Falling Idols," *Newsweek,* September 2, 1991, pp. 26–29.

5. Ministry of Foreign Economic Relations and Trade, *Economic Record of Trade and Development,* January 1991, Tables 2 and 7, pp. 27–32. See also "Regional Affairs," *Far Eastern Economic Review,* August 5, 1991, pp. 13–14.

6. Neal E. Boudette, John S. McClenahen, and Joani Nelson-Horchler, "The East After the Fall," *Industry Week,* February 5, 1990, pp. 32–38; "Europe: Capitalism with a Worried Face," *The Economist,* November 27, 1990, pp. 59–63; and Andrew Nagorski, "Opening a New Frontier," *Newsweek,* January 27, 1992, p. 34.

7. Shawn Tully, "Doing Business in One Germany," *Fortune,* July 2, 1990, pp. 80–83; "Whoever Said Freedom Was Easy?" *The Economist,* March 17, 1990, pp. 42–43; and "Long Days, Low Pay, and a Moldy Cot," *Business Week,* January 27, 1992, pp. 44–45.

8. John Templeman, "A European Germany or a German Europe?" *Business Week,* December 9, 1991. See also "Germany's Immigrants: No Solution," *The Economist,* October 19, 1991, p. 58.

9. "Germany and the Soviet Union: A Friend in Need," *The Economist,* August 24, 1991, p. 22. See also John Templeman, Gail E. Schares, Stewart Toy, and William Glasgall, "Germany Takes Charge: It's Using Its Growing Power to Reshape Europe," *Business Week,* February 17, 1992, pp. 50–58.

10. Mark M. Nelson and Martin du Bois, "Pact Expands Europe's Common Market," *Wall Street Journal,* October 21, 1991, p. A10.

11. Heinz Weihrich, "Europe 1992: What the Future May Hold," *Academy of Management Executive,* Vol. IV, No. 2 (1990), pp. 7–18.

12. Kenichi Ohmae, *Triad Power: The Coming Shape of Global Competition* (New York: The Free Press, 1985), pp. 1–6, 28–30. See also Kenichi Ohmae, "The Global Logic of Strategic Alliances," *Harvard Business Review,* Vol. 89, No. 2 (March-April 1989), pp. 143–154.

13. Jordan E. Goodman, "Go for Global Profits with America's Best-Known Brands," *Money,* Vol. 20, No. 8 (August 1991), pp. 43–49.

14. Michael A. Hitt, Robert E. Hoskisson, and Jeffrey S. Harrison, "Strategic Competitiveness in the 1990s: Challenges and Opportunities for U.S. Executives," *Academy of Management Executive,* Vol. V, No. 2 (1991), pp. 7–21; Louis Kraar, "The Rising Power of the Pacific," *Fortune,* Special Issue, Fall 1990, pp. 8–12; and Louis Kraar, "Ten to Watch Outside Japan," *Fortune,* Special Issue, Fall 1990, pp. 25–27, 30–32, 34, 36.

15. Charles W. Joiner, "Harvesting American Technology—Lessons from the Japanese Garden," *Sloan Management Review,* Vol. 30, No. 4 (1989), pp. 61–70. See also Susan Bartlette Foote and Will Mitchell, "Selling American Medical Equipment in Japan," *California Management Review,* Vol. 31, No. 4 (1989), pp. 146–161.

16. "Money Trends," *Executive Wealth,* Vol. 14, No. 2, February 1992, p. 8.

17. "Making a Yanqui Boodle South of the Border," *Business Week,* February 10, 1992, pp. 40–41.

18. "We Have to Get Together: Mexico's President Makes the Case for Free Trade," *Newsweek,* February 3, 1992, p. 41.

19. Nancy J. Perry, "What's Powering Mexico's Success," *Fortune,* February 10, 1992, pp. 109–115.

20. Joseph Duffey, "U.S. Competitiveness: Looking Back and Looking Ahead," in Martin K. Starr (ed.), *Global Competitiveness: Getting the U.S. Back on Track* (New York: W. W. Norton, 1988), pp. 72–94.

21. "International Scoreboard of U.S. Corporations," *Business Week,* March 22, 1985, pp. 158–162. See also Timothy M. Collins and Thomas L. Doorley III, *Teaming Up for the 90s: A Guide to International Joint Ventures and Strategic Alliances* (Homewood, Ill.: Business One Irwin, 1991), pp. 8–9, 20–21, 143.

22. "Trade Across the Pacific," *Fortune,* Special Issue on the Pacific Rim, Fall 1990, pp. 92–93.

23. Richard N. Farmer, "International Management," in Joseph W. McGuire (ed.), *Contemporary Management: Issues and Viewpoints* (Englewood Cliffs, N.J.: Prentice Hall, 1974), pp. 300–301.

24. David P. Rutenberg, *Multinational Management* (Boston: Little, Brown, 1982), pp. xi, 3–5.

25. Collins and Doorley, *Teaming Up for the 90s,* pp. 266–269.

26. Simcha Ronen, *Comparative and Multinational Management* (New York: John Wiley, 1986), pp. 41–42, 134.

27. Collins and Doorley, *Teaming Up for the 90s,* pp. 142–144, 216–218.

28. Rutenberg, *Multinational Management,* pp. 374–377.

29. Richard T. Pascale, "Perspectives on Strategy: The Real Story Behind Honda's Success," *California Management Review,* Vol. 26, No. 3 (1984), pp. 47–72.

30. Masanori Moritani, "Japan's Next Export? Promoting and Managing Technology Transfer," *Speaking of Japan,* Vol. 8, No. 77 (1987), pp. 21–29.

31. Raymond Vernon and Louis T. Wells, Jr., *The Manager in the International Economy,* 6th ed. (Englewood Cliffs, N.J.: Prentice Hall, 1991), pp. 77–91.

32. Bernard A. Rausch, "Du Pont Transforms a Division's Culture," *Management Review,* March 1989, pp. 37–42.

33. Eric N. Berkowitz, Roger A. Kerin, and William Rudelius, *Marketing,* 2nd ed. (Homewood, Ill.: Richard D. Irwin, 1989), p. 587.

34. Alan C. Shapiro, *Multinational Financial Management,* 3rd ed. (Boston: Allyn & Bacon, 1989), pp. 9–10. See also U.S. Small Business Administration, *The World Is Your Market* (Washington, D.C.: SBA Office of International Trade, 1990), pp. 75–77.

35. Donald D. Boroian and Patrick J. Boroian, *The Franchising Advantage* (Schaumburg, Ill.: National Bestseller Corp., 1989), pp. 6–7.

36. "Regional Affairs," *Far Eastern Economic Review,* September 28, 1989, pp. 13–19. See also Robert Neff and Kimberly Blanton, "You Can't Get Sushi at the Local 7-Eleven—Yet," *Business Week,* November 12, 1990, p. 59.

37. Collins and Doorley, *Teaming Up for the 90s,* pp. 57–58.

38. Ibid., pp. 257–258.

39. David Warshaw, "Equal Partners: GE's Factory Automation Joint Venture with Fanuc of Japan Is a Key Link in a Global Chain," *Monogram,* Vol. 66, No. 2 (Spring 1988), pp. 3–7.

40. Shen Peng, "Across China: Promising Future for Guangdong–Hong Kong–Macao Trade," *International Business,* Vol. 9 (1988), pp. 14–17. See also "The Magnet of Growth in Mexico's North," *Business Week,* June 6, 1988, pp. 48–50.

41. U.S.-China Business Council, *U.S. Investment in China* (Washington, D.C.: The China Business Forum, 1990), pp. 7–13; "The Chill Is Gone, and U.S. Companies Are Moscow-Bound," *Business Week,* June 5, 1989, p. 64; and "Speedy Reversal of Soviet Coup Makes Some Westerners More Eager to Invest," *Wall Street Journal,* August 23, 1991, pp. B1–B2.

42. U.S. Department of Commerce, *A Basic Guide to Exporting* (Washington, D.C.: U.S. Government Printing Office, 1991), p. 82.

43. "Dickson's 10th Anniversary," *Dickson Group Report,* February 27, 1990, pp. 1–4.

44. Richard M. Hodgetts and Fred Luthans, *International Management* (New York: McGraw-Hill, 1991), pp. 507–510. See also Jeremy Main, "How to Go Global—and Why," *Fortune,* August 28, 1989, p. 70.

45. Maurice H. Bood, "France on the Move: Meeting the Challenges of the 90s," *Fortune,* January 18, 1988, p. 15–16.

46. Ronen, *Comparative and Multinational Management,* pp. 483–490.

47. G. A. Phillips and R. T. Maddock, *The Growth of the British Economy 1918–1968* (New York: Harper & Row, 1973), pp. 150–161.

48. Vernon and Wells, *The Manager in the International Economy,* pp. 103, 196.

49. "Collision Course: Can the U.S. Avert a Trade War with Japan?" *Business Week,* April 8, 1985, pp. 50–55, 58–59. See also Louis Kraar, "The New Powers of Asia," *Fortune,* March 28, 1988, pp. 126–132.

50. Rutenberg, *Multinational Management,* pp. 108–121.

51. Farmer, "International Management," pp. 296–297.

52. David Granick, *Managerial Comparisons in Four Developed Countries: France, Britain, United States, and Russia* (Cambridge, Mass.: M.I.T. Press, 1972). See also Mark E. Mendenhall and Gary Oddou, "The Overseas Assignment: A Practical Look," *Business Horizons,* September–October 1988, p. 13.

53. Granick, *Managerial Comparisons in Four Developed Countries,* pp. 356–358. See also Joseph J. Disefano and Henry W. Lane, *International Management Behavior,* 2nd ed. (Boston: PWS-Kent, 1992), pp. 17–28.

54. "Britain: In for the Kill," *The Economist,* November 17, 1990, pp. 73–75.

55. "Public Sector Enterprise," *The Economist,* December 30, 1988, p. 39.

56. Masami Atarashi, "Survival Strategy," *Speaking of Japan,* Vol. 9, No. 97 (January 1989), pp. 14–18.

57. Patricia G. Steinhoff and Kazuko Tanaka, "Women Managers in Japan," *International Studies of Management & Organization,* Fall–Winter 1986, pp. 121–123.

58. Hodgetts and Luthans, *International Management,* pp. 178–183.

59. "In Nigeria, Payoffs Are a Way of Life," *Wall Street Journal,* July 12, 1982, p. 16.

60. "AT&T Slowly Gets Its Global Wires Uncrossed," pp. 82–83.

CHAPTER 4

1. Stewart Toy, "The Defense Scandal," *Business Week,* July 1, 1988, pp. 28–30. See also *General Dynamics Standards of Business Conduct* (Los Angeles: General Dynamics Corp., 1989), pp. 1–2, 18.

2. Alvar O. Elbing, "On the Applicability of Environmental Models," in J. W. McGuire (ed.), *Contemporary Management* (Englewood Cliffs, N.J.: Prentice Hall, 1974), pp. 282–283.

3. Robert H. Pojasek, "Towards a New Pollution-Prevention Ethic," *National Underwriter,* August 6, 1990, pp. 10–11, 46. See also Laurie Hays and Gerald F. Seib, "Gorbachev Vows to Safeguard Human Rights," *Wall Street Journal,* September 11, 1991, pp. A3, A9.

4. Manuel G. Velasquez, *Business Ethics: Concepts and Cases,* 3rd ed. (Englewood Cliffs, N.J.: Prentice Hall, 1992), pp. 18–20.

5. John Hoerr, "Privacy," *Business Week,* March 28, 1988, pp. 61–66; W. Michael Hoffman, "The Cost of a Corporate Conscience," *Business & Society Review,* Vol. 69 (1989), pp. 46–54; and L. Gordon Crovitz, "Clarence Thomas Explains Natural Rights and Political Wrongs," *Wall Street Journal,* September 11, 1991, p. A17.

6. Barry Z. Posner and Warren H. Schmidt, "Ethics in American Companies: A Managerial Perspective," *Journal of Business Ethics,* March 1987, pp. 383–391.

7. Saul W. Gellerman, "Why 'Good' Managers Make Bad Ethical Choices," *Harvard Business Review,* Vol. 86, No. 4 (July–August 1986), pp. 85–90.

8. Robert B. Sweeney and Howard L. Siers, "Ethics in Corporate America," *Management Accounting,* Vol. 71 (June 1990), pp. 34–40.

9. "Ethical Context," *Personnel Journal,* Vol. 70 (1991), p. 75.

10. *America's Most Pressing Ethical Problems* (Washington, D.C.: The Ethics Resource Center, 1990), p. 1.

11. Milton R. Moskowitz, "Company Performance Roundup," *Business and Society Review,* Vol. 53 (Spring 1985), pp. 74–77. See also Howard L. Siers, "Enriching the Corporate Ethics Environment," *Management Accounting,* Vol. 71 (April 1990), pp. 49–52.

12. *Corporate Ethics: A Prime Asset* (New York: Business Roundtable, 1988), pp. 3–10.

13. *Business Conduct Guidelines,* Vol. 2 (Seattle, Wash.: The Boeing Co., 1990). See also *Corporate Ethics: A Prime Asset,* pp. 12–14.

14. Mark Methabane, "An Embargo That Backfires," *U.S. News & World Report,* July 2, 1990, p. 36.

15. R. Edward Freeman and Daniel R. Gilbert, Jr., *Corporate Strategy and the Search for Ethics* (Englewood Cliffs, N.J.: Prentice Hall, 1988), pp. 90–91.

16. Marcia Parmarlee Miceli and Janet P. Near, "The Relationship Among Beliefs, Organizational Positions, and Whistle-Blowing Status: A Discriminate Analysis," *Academy of Management Journal,* Vol. 27, No. 4 (1984), pp. 687–705. See also Gillian Sandford, "'Whistleblower' Protection Bill Cleared Easily by House," *Congressional Quarterly Weekly Report,* March 25, 1989, pp. 643–644.

17. Janet P. Near, "Whistle-Blowing: Encourage It!" *Business Horizons,* Vol. 32 (January–February 1989), pp. 2–6.

18. John Bussy, "Gerber Takes Risky Stand as Fears Spread About Glass in Baby Food," *Wall Street Journal,* March 6, 1986, p. 21. See also Felix Kessler, "Tremors from the Tylenol Scare Hit Food Companies," *Fortune,* March 31, 1986, pp. 59–62.

19. Archie B. Carroll, "A Three-Dimensional Conceptual Model of Corporate Performance," *Academy of Management Review,* Vol. 4, No. 3 (1979), pp. 497–505.

20. Marc J. Dollinger, "Environmental Boundary Spanning and Information Processing Effects on Organizational Performance," *Academy of Management Journal,* Vol. 27, No. 2 (1984), pp. 351–368.

21. William G. McGowan, "Telecommunications and Global Competitiveness," *Vital Speeches of the Day,* January 12, 1991, pp. 199–202.

22. Peter F. Drucker, "The Job as Property Right," *Wall Street Journal,* March 4, 1980, p. 8.

23. Ellen F. Jackofsky, John W. Slocum, Jr., and Sara J. McQuaid, "Cultural Values and the CEO: Alluring Companions?" *Academy of Management Executive,* Vol. II, No. 1 (1988), pp. 39–49.

24. John A. Pearce III and Richard B. Robinson, Jr., *Strategic Management: Strategy Formulation and Implementation,* 2nd ed. (Homewood, Ill.: Richard D. Irwin, 1985), pp. 625–643.

25. Kenneth M. York, "Defining Sexual Harassment in Workplaces: A Policy-Capturing Approach," *Academy of Management Journal,* Vol. 14, No. 4 (1989), pp. 830–850.

26. Tom L. Beauchamp and Norman E. Bowie (eds.), *Ethical Theory and Business,* 3rd ed. (Englewood Cliffs, N.J.: Prentice Hall, 1988), pp. 330–335. See also U.S. Equal Employment Opportunity Commission, *Affirmative Action*

and Equal Employment: A Guidebook for Employers (Washington, D.C.: Government Printing Office, 1990), Sect. D.

27. U.S. Department of Labor, Bureau of Labor Statistics, *Monthly Labor Review,* January 1991, summary trend data. See also *The 1991 Almanac* (Boston: Houghton Mifflin, 1991), pp. 54–59.

28. Colin Leinster, "Black Executives: How They're Doing," *Fortune,* January 18, 1988, pp. 109–114.

29. Carol Hymowitz, "One Firm's Bid to Keep Blacks, Women," *Wall Street Journal,* February 16, 1989, p. B1.

30. John Huey, "Wal-Mart: Will It Take Over the World?" *Fortune,* January 30, 1989, pp. 52–64.

31. Steven Kelman, "Regulation and Paternalism," in Beauchamp and Bowie (eds.), *Ethical Theory and Business,* pp. 151–157.

32. Michael E. Porter, *Competitive Strategy: Techniques for Analyzing Industries and Competitors* (New York: Free Press, 1980), Chap. 4. See also Michael E. Porter, *Competitive Advantage* (New York: Free Press, 1985), Chap. 2.

33. Thomas C. Richards and Ross L. Chan, "Microcomputer Software Piracy and the Law," *Security Audit & Control Review,* Vol. 7, No. 1 (1989), pp. 37–39. See also Richard H. Stein, "Micro Law: Appropriate and Inappropriate Legal Protection of User Interfaces and Screen Displays," *IEEE MICRO,* August 1989, pp. 7–10.

34. John W. Wilson, "Intel and Sequent Kiss and Make Up," *Business Week,* May 25, 1987, p. 120. See also George McKinney and Marie McKinney, "Forget the Corporate Umbrella—Entrepreneurs Shine in the Rain," *Sloan Management Review,* Vol. 30, No. 4 (1989), pp. 77–82.

35. James Ledvinka, *Federal Regulation of Personnel and Human Resource Management* (Boston: Kent, 1982), pp. 4–14. See also Keith Davis, "The Case For and Against Business Assumption of Social Responsibilities," *Academy of Management Journal,* Vol. 16, No. 2 (1973), pp. 312–322.

36. Jay A. Sigler and Joseph E. Murphy, "Should Government Regulators Try the Carrot Before the Stick?" *Business & Society Review,* Vol. 69 (Spring 1989), pp. 51–53.

37. Jerry B. Madkins, "Affirmative Action Is Necessary and Ethical," *Personnel Journal,* Vol. 68 (August 1989), pp. 29–30. See also Robert Wrubel, "Addicted to Fraud?" *Financial World,* June 27, 1989, pp. 58–61.

38. Sir Adrain Cadbury, "Ethical Managers Make Their Own Rules," *Harvard Business Review,* Vol. 65 (September–October 1987), pp. 69–73. See also Susan Dentzer and Leslie Mandel-Viney, "How to Avoid Another BCCI," *U.S. News & World Report,* August 12, 1991, p. 33.

39. Robert W. Crandall, "Environmental Ignorance Is Not Bliss," *Wall Street Journal,* April 22, 1985, p. 28.

40. W. Michael Hoffman, "The Cost of a Corporate Conscience," *Business & Society Review,* Vol. 69 (Spring 1989), pp. 46–48. See also Keith Stock, "Regulation May Kill My Bank," *Wall Street Journal,* September 5, 1991, p. A14.

41. Milton Friedman, *Capitalism and Freedom* (Chicago: University of Chicago Press, 1962). See also Henry Mintzberg, "The Case for Corporate Social Responsibility," *Journal of Business Strategy,* Fall 1983, pp. 5–6.

42. Rich Stranel, "A Systems Paradigm of Organizational Adaptations to the Social Environment," *Academy of Management Review,* Vol. 8, No. 1 (1983), pp. 90–96. See also Sigler and Murphy, "Should Government Regulators Try the Carrot Before the Stick?" pp. 51–52.

43. George C. Lodge and Jeffrey F. Rayport, "Knee-deep and Rising: America's Recycling Crisis," *Harvard Business Review,* Vol. 69, No. 5 (September–October 1991), pp. 128–139.

44. Melanie Menagh, "The Business of Going Green," *Omni,* June 1991, pp. 42–48.

45. Rogene A. Buchholz, *Business Environment and Public Policy: Implications for Management,* 4th ed. (Englewood Cliffs, N.J.: Prentice Hall, 1992), pp. 8–12, 524–525.

46. Susan J. Harrington, "What Corporate America Is Teaching About Ethics," *Academy of Management Executive,* Vol. 5, No. 1 (1991), pp. 21–30.

47. Karin Ireland, "The Ethics Game," *Personnel Journal,* Vol. 70 (March 1991), pp. 72–75.

48. Ken Wells and Charles McCoy, "How Unpreparedness Turned the Alaska Spill into Ecological Debacle," *Wall Street Journal,* April 3, 1989, p. 1. See also Charles McCoy, "Exxon Corp.'s Settlement Gets Court Approval," *Wall Street Journal,* October 9, 1991, pp. A3, A10.

CHAPTER 5

1. Norman MacRae, "World Banking in Trouble," *World Press Review,* January 1991, pp. 38–40.

2. "Trade Bill Highlights," *Wall Street Journal,* April 1, 1988, p. 12.

3. E. R. Archer, "How to Make a Business Decision: An Analysis of Theory and Practice," *Management Review,* Vol. 69, No. 2 (1980), pp. 30–37.

4. Herbert A. Simon, *The New Science of Management Decisions,* rev. ed. (Englewood Cliffs, N.J.: Prentice Hall, 1977), pp. 44–49.

5. Weston Agor, "The Logic of Intuition: How Top Executives Make Important Decisions," *Organizational Dynamics,* Winter 1986, pp. 5–18.

6. Nelson W. Aldrich, Jr., "Lines of Communication," *Inc.,* June 1986, pp. 140–144. See also "The Franchise 100," *Venture,* December 1988, pp. 35–47.

7. Henry Mintzberg, *The Nature of Managerial Work* (Englewood Cliffs, N.J.: Prentice Hall, 1980), pp. 54–94.

8. "Face-to-Face with '1-2-3' Creator Mitch Kapor," *Inc.,* January 1987, pp. 31–38.

9. Richard D. Robinson, *Union Carbide's Good Record* (Danbury, Conn.: Union Carbide Corp., 1991), p. 2.

10. Richard Sharwood Cates, "The Gordian Knot: A Parable for Decision Makers," *Management Review,* Vol. 79 (December 1990), pp. 47–48.

11. David H. Holt, *Entrepreneurship: New Venture Creation* (Englewood Cliffs, N.J.: Prentice Hall, 1992), p. 32.

12. Ellen Graham, "McDonald's Pickle: He Began Fast Food but Gets No Credit," *Wall Street Journal,* August 15, 1991, pp. A1, A5.

13. Thomas V. Busse and Richard S. Mansfield, "Theories of the Creative Process: A Review and a Perspective," *Journal of Creative Behavior,* Vol. 4, No. 2 (1980), pp. 91–103.

14. "The Mad Idea," in *Communicating and the Telephone,* a biographical monograph by American Telephone and Telegraph Company, July 1979, pp. 4–5.

15. *The Entrepreneurs: An American Adventure,* PBS Documentary, Vol. 1 (Boston: Enterprise Media, 1986).

16. Organisation for Economic Co-operation and Development, "Trends and Perspectives," *R&D, Invention, and Competitiveness* (Paris, France: OECD, 1990), pp. 50–57. See also Organisation for Economic Co-operation and Development, "Technology Indicators," *Innovation Policy* (Paris, France: OECD, 1988), pp. 48–57.

17. Gifford Pinchot III, *Intrapreneuring* (New York: Harper & Row, 1985), pp. 7–9.

18. Ibid., pp. 40–41.

19. Kenneth Labich, "The Innovators," *Fortune,* June 6, 1988, pp. 50–53, 56, 60. See also Ellen Schultz, "America's Most Admired Corporations," *Fortune,* January 18, 1988, pp. 32–39.

20. "The West Is Asking: Who's in Charge Here?" *Business Week,* September 9, 1991, pp. 32–33.

21. Ronald N. Taylor, *Behavioral Decision Making* (Glenview, Ill.: Scott, Foresman, 1984), pp. 1–6, 41–43.

22. A. F. Osborn, *Applied Imagination,* 3rd ed. (New York: Scribner's, 1963), pp. 154–163.

23. Don Hellriegel, John W. Slocum, Jr., and Richard Woodman, *Organizational Behavior* (St. Paul, Minn.: West, 1989), pp. 109–110.

24. Taylor, *Behavioral Decision Making,* pp. 44–45.

25. Marvin D. Dunnette, John P. Campbell, and K. Jaastad, "The Effect of Group Participation on Brainstorming Effectiveness for Two Industrial Samples," *Journal of Applied Psychology,* Vol. 47 (1963), pp. 30–37.

26. André L. Delbecq and Andrew H. Van de Ven, "A Group Process Model for Problem Identification and Program Planning," *Journal of Applied Behavioral Science,* Vol. 7, No. 4 (1971), pp. 466–492.

27. Taylor, *Behavioral Decision Making,* pp. 181–182.

28. Christopher Knowlton, "What America Makes Best," *Fortune,* March 28, 1988, pp. 44–54.

29. James S. Hirsch, "To One Xerox Man, Selling Photocopiers Is a Gambler's Game," *Wall Street Journal,* September 24, 1991, pp. A1, A12.

30. Laura Gardner, "Sludging Toward Profits," *Venture,* March 1985, pp. 85–86. See also

Dana Milbank, "Aluminum's Envious Rivals Turn Green, Rush to Show They, Too, Are Recyclable," *Wall Street Journal,* September 18, 1991, pp. B1, B7.

31. Mike Connelly, "Hospitals Try Franchising to Cut Costs, Add Services," *Wall Street Journal,* October 14, 1988, p. B1.

32. John Helyar and Bryan Burrough, "Buy-Out Bluff: How Underdog KKR Won RJR Nabisco Without Highest Bid," *Wall Street Journal,* December 2, 1988, p. A1.

33. "The Chairman Doesn't Blink," *Quality Progress,* March 1987, pp. 19–24; and follow-up interview by author, July 1991, with CGW director of quality.

34. Ralph Stayer, "How I Learned to Let My Workers Lead," *Harvard Business Review,* Vol. 68 (November–December 1990), pp. 66–75. See also "The Industry Cries Out for Help: Power to the People," *Lodging Hospitality,* Vol. 46 (September 4, 1990), pp. 52–54.

35. Robert I. Benjamin and Michael S. Scott Morton, "Information Technology, Integration, and Organizational Change," *Management in the 1990s,* reprint of the Sloan School of Management, Massachusetts Institute of Technology, April 1986.

36. Kevin Crowston and Thomas W. Malone, "Information Technology and Work Organization," *Management in the 1990s,* reprint by the Sloan School of Management, Massachusetts Institute of Technology, October 1987.

37. Robert A. Portnoy, *Leadership: What Every Leader Should Know About People* (Englewood Cliffs, N.J.: Prentice Hall, 1986), pp. 114–115.

38. Vilma Barr, "The Process of Innovation: Brainstorming and Storyboarding," *Mechanical Engineering,* November 1988, pp. 42–46.

CHAPTER 6

1. "IBM Europe Starts Swinging Back," *Business Week,* May 6, 1991, pp. 52–53.

2. Centre D'enseignement et de Recherche en Modelisation Informatique et Calcul Scientifique (CERMICS), *Strategic Alliances and Advances in Information Science* (Valbonne, France: CERMICS, 1991), pp. 22–24.

3. George A. Steiner, *Top Management Planning* (New York: Macmillan, 1969), p. 7.

4. Henry Mintzberg, "The Manager's Job: Folklore and Fact," in Arthur A. Thompson, Jr. and A. J. Strickland III (eds.), *Strategy Formulation and Implementation* (Plano, Tex.: Business Publications, 1980), pp. 35–36.

5. Fred Luthans, "Successful vs. Effective Real Managers," *The Academy of Management Executive,* Vol. II, No. 2 (1988), pp. 127–132.

6. Echo Montgomery Garrett, "My Catalog Is My Showroom," *Venture,* November 1988, pp. 32–33.

7. Arthur A. Thompson, Jr., and A. J. Strickland III, *Strategic Management: Concepts and Cases* (Plano, Tex.: Business Publications, 1987), pp. 6–7.

8. Joel Kotkin, "The Innovation Upstarts," *Inc.,* January 1989, pp. 70–76.

9. "Will Bush's Plan Work? Special Report," *Newsweek,* October 7, 1991, pp. 20–22, 24–26.

10. Henry Mintzberg, *Power in and Around Organizations* (Englewood Cliffs, N.J.: Prentice Hall, 1983), pp. 136–37.

11. Brenton R. Schlender, "Apple Unveils New Macintosh, Hints at Closer Unix Link," *Wall Street Journal,* January 19, 1989, p. B1; G. Pascal Zachary, "IBM, Apple Outline Plan, but Questions Remain on Products, Rivals' Response," *Wall Street Journal,* October 3, 1991, p. A3; and G. Pascal Zachary, "Apple and IBM Pact Came After Failure of Talks with Sun," *Wall Street Journal,* October 3, 1991, p. A4.

12. "Home-Computer Field Baffles Manufacturers and Many Buyers Too," *Wall Street Journal,* July 26, 1983, pp. 1, 18.

13. J. M. Juran, *Juran on Planning for Quality* (New York: The Free Press, 1988), pp. 35–36.

14. Kenneth R. Andrews, "Ethics in Policy and Practice at General Mills," in James Keogh (ed.), *Corporate Ethics: A Prime Business Asset* (New York: The Business Roundtable, 1988), pp. 41–52.

15. "World-Class Quality: The Challenge of the 1990s," *Fortune,* September 23, 1991, pp. 142, 173–174.

16. Ibid., p. 174.

17. Thompson and Strickland, *Strategic Management: Concepts and Cases,* p. 8.

18. Bernard Avishai, "A CEO's Common Sense of CIM: An Interview with J. Tracy O'Rourke," *Harvard Business Review,* Vol. 89, No. 1 (January–February 1989), pp. 110–117.

19. Steiner, *Top Management Planning,* p. 26.

20. Peter F. Drucker, *The Practice of Management* (New York: Harper & Row, 1954), pp. 128–129.

21. Stew Leonard, "Love That Customer," *Management Review,* October 1987, pp. 36–39.

22. Neil Barsky, "Does This Mean All the Fights Will Now Take Place on the Ice?" *Wall Street Journal,* January 27, 1989, p. B1.

23. Kathy Williams, "The Magic of Management Accounting Excellence," *Management Accounting,* February 1986, pp. 21–27.

24. Jim Jubak, "Think Like a Bee," *Venture,* January 1989, pp. 48–52.

25. Toyohiro Kono, "Japanese Management Philosophy: Can It Be Exported?" *Long Range Planning,* Vol. 15, No. 3 (1982), pp. 90–102. See also Mike Mansfield, "The Situation as I See It: Perspectives from a Decade as U.S. Ambassador to Japan," *Speaking of Japan,* Vol. 8, No. 84 (December 1987), pp. 1–3.

26. Dean M. Schroeder and Robert Hopley, "Product Development Strategies for High-Tech Industries," *The Journal of Business Strategy,* May–June 1988, pp. 38–43.

27. Robley D. Wood and Lawrence R. LaForge, "The Impact of Comprehensive Planning on Financial Performance," *Academy of Management Journal,* Vol. 22 (1979), pp. 516–526.

28. Richard M. Hodgetts, *Management: Theory and Practice* (Philadelphia: W. B. Saunders, 1979), p. 99. See also Thompson and Strickland, *Strategic Management: Concepts and Cases,* pp. 12–15.

29. Lester R. Bittel and Jackson E. Ramsey, "The Limited, Traditional World of Supervisors," *Harvard Business Review,* Vol. 82, No. 4 (July–August 1982), pp. 26–37.

30. Mintzberg, *Power in and Around Organizations,* pp. 137–139. See also Victor H. Vroom and Arthur G. Jago, *The New Leadership: Managing Participation in Organizations* (Englewood Cliffs, N.J.: Prentice Hall, 1988), pp. 11–12.

31. George A. Steiner, John B. Miner, and Edmund R. Gray, *Management Policy and Strategy: Text, Readings and Cases,* 2nd ed. (New York: Macmillan, 1982), pp. 182–183.

32. "The New Breed of Strategic Planner," *Business Week,* September 17, 1984, pp. 62–68.

33. Steiner, Miner, and Gray, *Management Policy and Strategy,* p. 186.

34. Paul B. Carroll, "IBM Is Seen Disbanding a Unit Set Up to Develop PC Software Applications," *Wall Street Journal,* October 9, 1991, p. B4; Paul B. Carroll, "IBM Net Tumbled 85% in 3rd Quarter, and the Outlook for 4th Period Worsens," *Wall Street Journal,* October 16, 1991, pp. A3, A10; and "IBM Europe Starts Swinging Back," *Business Week,* May 6, 1991, p. 53.

CHAPTER 7

1. Jack F. Reichert, "Brunswick's Dramatic Turnaround," *The Journal of Business Strategy,* January–February 1988, pp. 4–8.

2. Carol Kennedy, "How Marriott Corporation Grew Five-fold in Ten Years," *Long Range Planning,* Vol. 21, No. 2 (1988), pp. 10–14.

3. Carol Kennedy, "Planning Global Strategies for 3M," *Long Range Planning,* Vol. 21, No. 1 (1988), pp. 9–17.

4. James Brian Quinn, Henry Mintzberg, and Robert M. James, *The Strategy Process: Concepts, Contexts, and Cases* (Englewood Cliffs, N.J.: Prentice Hall, (1988), pp. 14–15. See also Charles E. Summer, *Strategic Behavior in Business and Government* (Boston: Little, Brown, 1980), p. 3.

5. Thomas J. Peters and Robert H. Waterman, Jr., *In Search of Excellence: Lessons from America's Best-Run Companies* (New York: Harper & Row, 1982), p. 31.

6. Ibid., p. 29.

7. Eric Rolfe Greenberg, "Downsizing and Worker Assistance: Latest AMA Survey Results," *Personnel,* November 1988, pp. 49–53.

8. John Naisbitt and Patricia Aburdene, *Reinventing the Corporation* (New York: Warner, 1985), pp. 12–16.

9. Tim R. V. Davis, "Information Technology and White-Collar Productivity," *Academy of Management Executive,* Vol. 5, No. 1 (1991), pp. 55–67.

10. Henry Mintzberg, "The Manager's Job: Folklore and Fact," *Harvard Business Review,* Vol. 53, No. 4 (July–August 1975), pp. 49–61.

11. Peters and Waterman, *In Search of Excellence,* p. 260.

12. Jacob M. Schlesinger and Joseph B. White, "The New-Model GM will Be More Compact but More Profitable: Over Next Five Years, Firm May Close Six Factories, Lay Off 100,000 Workers," *Wall Street Journal,* June 6, 1988, pp. 1, 6.

13. Amal Kumar Naj, "Clouds Gather Over the Biotech Industry," *Wall Street Journal,* January 30, 1989, p. B1; "The Ethics of Marketing Drugs," *The Economist, April 6, 1991, p. 72; and Thomas A. Stewart, "Brainpower," Fortune,* June 3, 1991, pp. 44–46, 50, 54, 56, 60.

14. Summer, *Strategic Behavior in Business and Government,* pp. 205–206.

15. Anthony V. Trowbridge, "'Titanic Planning' in an Uncertain Environment," *Long Range Planning,* Vol. 21, No. 3 (1988), pp. 9–17.

16. Ronald Henkoff, "Deals of the Year," *Fortune,* January 30, 1989, pp. 162–164.

17. Summer, *Strategic Behavior in Business and Government,* p. 203.

18. Peter F. Drucker, *Management: Tasks, Responsibilities, Practices* (New York: Harper & Row, 1974), p. 455.

19. John Huey, "America's Most Successful Merchant," *Fortune,* September 23, 1991, pp. 46–48, 50, 54; 58–59.

20. "Executive Summary," *The State of Small Business: A Report of the President* (Washington, D.C.: U.S. Government Printing Office, 1988), pp. xv–xvi.

21. William H. Newman, James P. Logan, and W. Harvey Hegarty, *Strategy: A Multi-level, Integrative Approach* (Cincinnati: South-Western, 1989), pp. 7–15.

22. James E. Ellis, "Sam Johnson Is 'Going Public to Stay Private,'" *Business Week,* December 5, 1988, pp. 58–60.

23. Leslie W. Rue and Phyllis G. Holland, *Strategic Management: Concepts and Experiences,* 2nd ed. (New York: McGraw-Hill, 1989), p. 57. See also Richard B. Robinson, Jr., and John A. Pearce II, "Planned Patterns of Strategic Behavior and Their Relationship to Business-Unit Performance," *Strategic Management Journal,* Vol. 9, No. 1 (1988), pp. 43–60.

24. Richard F. Vancil, *Decentralization: Managing Ambiquity by Design* (New York: Financial Executives Research Foundation, 1979), p. 5.

25. Ronald Henkoff, "How to Plan for 1995," *Fortune,* December 31, 1990, pp. 70–72, 75–76, 78.

26. Thompson and Strickland, *Strategic Management: Concepts and Cases,* p. 29.

27. Ibid., adapted from Chap. 1.

28. Control Data Corporation, *Annual Report of CDC, 1987.*

29. Hart, Schaffner & Marx, *Annual Report, 1986.*

30. Thompson and Strickland, *Strategic Management: Concepts and Cases,* pp. 8–9.

31. Robert O. Metzger, "Polish Your Crystal Ball," *Banker's Monthly,* Vol. 107 (August 1990), p. 70.

32. Thomson and Strickland, *Strategic Management: Concepts and Cases,* p. 61.

33. Eric N. Berkowitz, Roger A. Kerin, and William Rudelius, *Marketing,* 2nd. ed. (Homewood, Ill.: Richard D. Irwin, 1989), pp. 235, 298–299.

34. David B. Hilder and Roger Lowenstein, "Merger of 2 Banks in New York May Be the Start of a Wave," *Wall Street Journal,* July 16, 1991, pp. A1, A6.

35. Micheal E. Porter, *Competitive Strategy: Techniques for Analyzing Industries and Competitors* (New York: Free Press, 1980), Chap. 1. See also Michael E. Porter, *Competitive Advantage,* (New York: Free Press, 1985), Chap. 2.

36. Alecia Swasy, "P&G Gets Mixed Marks as It Promotes Green Image but Tries to Shield Brands," *Wall Street Journal,* August 26, 1991, pp. B1, B6.

37. Berkowitz, Kerin, and Rudelius, *Marketing,* p. 357.

38. Porter, *Competitive Strategy: Techniques for Analyzing Industries and Competitors,* pp. 27–28.

39. Thompson and Strickland, *Strategic Management: Concepts and Cases,* pp. 97–99.

40. Newman, Logan, and Hegarty, *Strategy: A Multi-level, Integrative Approach,* pp. 106–112. See also Thompson and Strickland, *Strategic Management: Concepts and Cases,* pp. 159–164.

41. Maria Shao, "The Next Step Up from Nintendo," *Business Week,* May 28, 1990, p. 107.

42. Sally Saville Hodge, "Chicago's Unabashed Centimillionaire," *Forbes,* May 30, 1988, pp. 252–260.

43. Anheuser-Busch Companies, Inc., *Annual Report to Stockholders, 1987.* See also Charles G. Burck, "While the Big Brewers Quaff, the Little Ones Thirst," *Fortune,* November, 1982, p. 107.

44. Statford P. Sherman, "Who's in Charge at Texaco Now?" *Fortune,* January 16, 1989, pp. 68–72.

45. Rue and Holland, *Strategic Management: Concepts and Experiences,* pp. 45–47.

46. Thompson and Strickland, *Strategic Management: Concepts and Cases,* pp. 167–170.

47. Maynard M. Gordon, *The Iacocca Management Technique* (New York: Ballantine, 1985), pp. 153–154, 172–177.

48. Victor Kiam, *Going for it! How to Succeed as an Entrepreneur* (New York: Morrow, 1986), pp. 207–226.

49. Pat Baldwin, "Smart Pricing Pays in Profits," *Dallas, Inc.,* March 21, 1988, p. 17.

50. R. Bruce McAfee and William Poffenberger, *Productivity Strategies: Enhancing Employee Job Performance* (Englewood Cliffs, N.J.: Prentice Hall, 1982), p. 2.

51. Reichert, "Brunswick's Dramatic Turnaround," pp. 4–8.

52. Robert M. Donnelly, "Exxon's 'Office of the Future' Fiasco," *Planning Review,* July–August 1987, pp. 12–15.

CHAPTER 8

1. Brian O'Reilly, "How to Manage for Recovery," *Fortune,* March 23, 1992, pp. 62–64. See also "Addressing Customer Needs," *Walker Manufacturing Company Report,* February 1992, p. 2.

2. "Sweet-Talking the Public," *Newsweek,* January 28, 1985, p. 57.

3. Alix M. Freedman, "New Sweeteners Head for the Sugar Bowl," *Wall Street Journal,* February, 6, 1989, p. B1.

4. Eric N. Berkowitz, Roger A. Kerin, and William Rudelius, *Marketing,* 2nd ed. (Homewood, Ill.: Richard D. Irwin, 1989), p. 171.

5. "Sneakers That Don't Specialize," *Business Week,* June 6, 1988, p. 146.

6. Berkowitz, Kerin, and Rudelius, *Marketing,* pp. 44–46.

7. "Marketing's New Look," *Business Week,* November 2, 1987, pp. 64–69.

8. "Taking It Personally: Special Report on Technology," *Wall Street Journal,* October 21, 1991, pp. R1, R15. See also Deidre A. Depke, "A Comeback at Compaq? Wait Till Next Year," *Business Week,* September 23, 1991, p. 38.

9. John B. Judis, "Innovation, a Casualty at IBM," *Wall Street Journal,* October 17, 1991, p. A23.

10. Al Ries and Jack Trout, *Marketing Warfare* (New York: McGraw-Hill, 1986), pp. 184–185.

11. Carl R. Anderson and Carl P. Zeithaml, "Stages of the Product Life Cycle, Business Strategy, and Business Performance," *The Academy of Management Journal,* Vol. 27, No. 1 (1984), pp. 5–24.

12. Philip Kotler and Gary Armstrong, *Principles of Marketing,* 5th ed. (Englewood Cliffs, N.J.: Prentice Hall, 1991), pp. 466–467.

13. Ann Hughey, "Sales of Home Movie Equipment Falling as Firms Abandon Market, Video Grows," *Wall Street Journal,* March 17, 1982, p. 25. See also "If You Put TV, CD, and VCR Together, They Spell 'Home Theater' to Marketers," *Wall Street Journal,* October 23, 1991, pp. B1, B5.

14. Kotler and Armstrong, *Principles of Marketing,* pp. 539–540.

15. John Huey, "America's Most Successful Merchant," *Fortune,* September 23, 1991, pp. 46–48, 50, 54, 58–59.

16. Walter Guzzardi, Jr., "The U.S. Business Hall of Fame," *Fortune,* March 14, 1988, pp. 142, 145.

17. Kotler and Armstrong, *Principles of Marketing,* pp. 587–593.

18. Thomas J. Peters and Robert H. Waterman, Jr., *In Search of Excellence: Lessons from America's Best-Run Companies* (New York: Harper & Row, 1982), pp. 115–116, 141.

19. Donald D. Boroian and Patrick J. Boroian, *The Franchise Advantage: Make it Work for You!* (Schaumburg, Ill.: National BestSeller Corporation, 1987), pp. 28–34.

20. Glenn A. Welsch, Ronald W. Hilton, and Paul N. Gordon, *Budgeting: Profit Planning and Control,* 5th ed. (Englewood Cliffs, N.J.: Prentice Hall, 1988), p. 210.

21. "Agricultural Lending and Cyclical Demand," *Dominion Bank Review* (Roanoke, Va.: Dominion Bank, 1991), p. 2.

22. D. M. Warner and J. Pranda, "A Mathematical Programming Model for Scheduling Nursing Personnel in a Hospital," *Management Science,* Vol. 19, No. 4 (1972), pp. 411–422.

23. J. M. Juran, *Juran on Planning for Quality* (New York: The Free Press, 1988), pp. 5–7, 283–284.

24. Ted Kumpe and Piet T. Bolwijn, "Manufacturing: The New Case for Vertical Integration," *Harvard Business Review,* Vol. 88, No. 2 (1988), pp. 75–81.

25. John W. Verity, "Rethinking the Computer," *Business Week,* November 26, 1990, pp. 116–119, 122, 124. See also Brenton R. Schlender, "The Future of the PC," *Fortune,* August 26, 1991, pp. 40–44, 46, 48.

26. Richard J. Schonberger, *Japanese Manufacturing Techniques: Nine Hidden Lessons in Simplicity* (New York, The Free Press: 1982), pp. 34–38.

27. William N. Cooke, "Factors Influencing the Effect of Joint Union-Management Programs on Employee-Supervisor Relations," *Industrial and Labor Relations Review,* Vol. 43, No. 5 (1990), pp. 587–603.

28. Donald F. Ephlin, "Revolution by Evolution: The Changing Relationship Between GM and the UAW," *Academy of Management Executive,* Vol. II, No. 1 (1988), pp. 63–66. See also Pat Choate, "Today's Worker in Tomorrow's Workplace," *Journal of Business Strategy,* Vol. 11 (July–August 1990), pp. 4–7.

29. Amar Bhide, "Why Not Leverage Your Company to the Hilt?" *Harvard Business Review,* Vol. 88, No. 3 (May–June 1988), pp. 92–98.

30. Paul Preston and Thomas W. Zimmerer, *Management for Supervisors,* 2nd ed. (Englewood Cliffs, N.J.: Prentice Hall, 1983), p. 311.

31. Sud Ingle, *In Search of Perfection: How to Create/Maintain/Improve Quality* (Englewood Cliffs, N.J.: Prentice Hall, 1986), pp. 1–14.

32. Kate Ludeman, "Instilling the Worth Ethic," *Training & Development Journal,* Vol. 44 (May 1990), pp. 53–59.

33. Preston and Zimmerer, *Management for Supervisors,* pp. 33–36.

34. Robert Landel, *Managing Productivity Through People: An Operations Perspective* (Englewood Cliffs, N.J.: Prentice Hall, 1986), p. 11. See also William Sandy, "Link Your Business Plan to a Performance Plan," *Journal of Business Strategy,* Vol. 11 (November–December 1990), pp. 4–8.

35. Brian O'Reilly, "How to Manage for Recovery," *Fortune,* March 23, 1992, pp. 62–64. See also "Addressing Customer Needs," *Walker Manufacturing Company Report,* (February 1992), p. 2.

36. "Alfa-Laval: Updating Its Know-how for the Biotechnology Era," *Business Week,* September 19, 1983, pp. 80, 84–85.

CHAPTER 9

1. Nancy Giges, "Saatchi's Global Shift," *Advertising Age,* Vol. 62, No. 32 (August 5, 1991), pp. 1–37.

2. Stephen P. Robbins, *Management,* 3rd ed. (Englewood Cliffs, N.J.: Prentice Hall, 1991), p. 7.

3. Ernest Dale, *Organization* (New York: American Management Associations, 1976), pp. 9–10. See also Howard M. Carlisle, *Management Concepts, Methods, and Applications,* 2nd ed. (Chicago, Ill: Science Research Associates, 1982), p. 478.

4. Adam Smith, *Wealth of Nations* (New York: Modern Library, 1937), pp. 3–4.

5. Henry Mintzberg, *Structure in Fives: Designing Effective Organizations* (Englewood Cliffs, N.J.: Prentice Hall, 1983), pp. 36–37.

6. Paul L. Blocklyn, "Making Magic: The Disney Approach to People Management," *Personnel,* December 1988, pp. 28–35.

7. Chris Argyris, *Personality and Organization* (New York: Harper & Row, 1957); Warren G. Bennis, "The Coming Death of Bureaucracy," *Think Magazine,* November–December 1966, pp. 30–35; Frederick Herzberg, Bernard Mausner, and Barbara Snyderman, *The Motivation to Work,* 2nd ed. (New York: John Wiley, 1959); Rensis Likert, *New Patterns of Management* (New York: McGraw-Hill, 1961); and Douglas McGregor, *The Human Side of Enterprise* (New York: McGraw-Hill, 1960).

8. Victor K. Kiam, "Growth Strategies at Remington," *Journal of Business Strategy,* January–February 1989, pp. 22–26.

9. Mintzberg, *Structure in Fives,* pp. 28–29. See also H. Thomas Johnson, "Managing Costs versus Managing Activities—Which Strategy Works?" *Financial Executive,* January–February 1990, pp. 32–36.

10. Mintzberg, *Structure in Fives,* pp. 28–29.

11. Dana Milbank, "Changes at Alcoa Point Up Challenges and Benefits of Decentralized Authority," *Wall Street Journal,* November 7, 1991, pp. B1, B2.

12. Mintzberg, *Structure in Fives,* p. 31.

13. Thomas J. Atchison, "The Employment Relationship: Un-tied or Re-tied?" *Academy of Management Executive,* Vol. 5, No. 4 (1991), pp. 52–62.

14. Max Weber, *The Theory of Social and Economic Organization,* trans. A. M. Henderson and H. T. Parsons (New York: The Free Press, 1974).

15. Mintzberg, *Structure in Fives,* pp. 35–36.

16. Paul D. Collins and Frank Hull, "Technology and Span of Control: Woodward Revisited," *Journal of Management Studies,* Vol. 23 (March 1983), pp. 143–164. See also John S. McClenahen, "Managing More People in the '90s," *Industry Week,* March 1989, pp. 30–38.

17. Bennis, "The Coming Death of Bureaucracy," pp. 32–33.

18. Tom Burns and George M. Stalker, *The Management of Innovation* (London: Tavistock, 1961).

19. Jim Bartimo, "Compaq Chief Maps Numerous Major Changes," *Wall Street Journal,* November 6, 1991, p. A3.

20. Mintzberg, *Structure in Fives,* pp. 37–38.

21. Ibid, pp. 121–149.

22. Ibid., p. 128.

23. Joan Woodward, *Industrial Organization: Theory and Practice* (London: Oxford University Press, 1965).

24. James Cook, "Where's the Niche?" *Forbes,* September 24, 1984, p. 54.

25. Mintzberg, *Structure in Fives,* p. 134.

26. John J. Keller, "AT&T's Bob Allen Is Pushing All the Right Buttons," *Business Week,* November 28, 1988, pp. 133, 136.

27. "Gillette Finds World-Brand Image Elusive," *Advertising Age,* June 25, 1984, p. 50.

28. Robert McGough, "Changing Course," *Financial World,* Vol. 160, No. 15 (July 23, 1991), pp. 42–45.

29. David E. Bowen, Gerald E. Ledford, Jr., and Barry R. Nathan, "Hiring for the Organization, Not the Job," *Academy of Management Executive,* Vol. V, No. 4 (November 1991), pp. 35–51.

30. Tom Peters, "The Best New Managers Will Listen, Motivate, Support," *Working Woman,* September 1990, pp. 142–143, 216–217.

31. John Paul Newport, Jr., "The Stalking of Gillette," *Fortune,* May 23, 1988, pp. 99–101.

32. Alfred A. Marcus, "Responses to Externally Induced Innovation: Their Effects on Organizational Performance," *Strategic Management Journal,* Vol. 9 (1988), pp. 387–402.

33. Mintzberg, *Structure in Fives,* p. 134.

34. "1-2-3 Creator Mitch Kapor: The Young Founder of One of the World's Leading Software Companies Gives Some Provocative Reasons for Walking Away from It All," *Inc.,* January 1987, pp. 31–38.

35. Thomas A. Stewart, "Brainpower," *Fortune,* June 3, 1991, pp. 44–46, 50, 54, 56, 60; Thomas A. Stewart, "GE Keeps Those Ideas Coming," *Fortune,* August 12, 1991, pp. 41–45, 48–49; and McGough, "Changing Course," pp. 42–45.

36. Patricia Galagan, "Work Teams That Work," *Training and Development Journal,* November 1986, p. 35. See also Ralph Stayer, "How I Learned to Let My Workers Lead," *Harvard Business Review,* Vol. 68 (November–December 1990), pp. 66–75.

37. Peter E. Mudrack, "Group Cohesiveness and Productivity: A Closer Look," *Human Relations,* Vol. 42 (1989), pp. 771–785.

38. *Handbook of Small Business Data* (Washington, D.C.: U.S. Small Business Administration, 1990), Chap. 2.

39. Larry E. Greiner, "Evolution and Revolution as Organizations Grow," *Harvard Business Review,* Vol. 50, No. 4 (July–August 1972), pp. 37–46.

40. Jack Cavanaugh, "When the Cheering Stops," *Venture,* February 1989, pp. 23–28.

41. "Publishing Magnate Pat McGovern," *Inc.,* August 1988, pp. 27–33.

42. James M. Higgins, "The Decline and Fall of W. T. Grant," in Melvin J. Stanford (ed.), *Management Policy,* 2nd ed. (Englewood Cliffs, N.J.: Prentice Hall, 1983).

43. Scott Donaton, "Murdoch's Package," *Advertising Age,* March 25, 1991, p. 50.

44. Victor H. Vroom and Arthur G. Jago, *The New Leadership: Managing Participation in Organizations* (Englewood Cliffs, N.J.: Prentice Hall, 1988), pp. 5–14.

45. James T. McKenna, "Pan Am Sets Up Asset Auction After Delta Rejects Takeover," *Aviation Week & Space Technology,* Vol. 135, No. 1 (1991), p. 31.

46. Max Messmer, "Strategic Staffing for the '90s," *Personnel Journal,* October 1990, pp. 92–97.

47. Laura L. Castro, "Managers Declare Independence to Run Businesses from Their Personal Utopias," *Wall Street Journal,* September 3, 1991, pp. B1, B4; Harlan R. Jessup,

"New Roles in Team Leadership," *Training & Development Journal,* Vol. 44 (November 1990), pp. 79–83; and Bowen, Ledford, and Nathan, "Hiring for the Organization, Not the Job," pp. 35–51.

48. John Naisbitt and Patricia Aburdene, *Reinventing the Corporation* (New York: Warner Books, 1985), pp. 9–43. See also "The Fortune Service 500: More Woes Than Winnings," *Fortune,* June 6, 1988, pp. D3–D7.

49. Walt Bogdanich and Michael Waldholz, "Hospitals That Need Patients Pay Bounties for Doctors' Referrals," *Wall Street Journal,* February 27, 1989, pp. A1, A4. See also Russell C. Swansburg, *Management and Leadership for Nurse Managers* (Boston: Jones and Bartlett, 1990), pp. 236–239.

50. James A. Fitzsimmons and Robert S. Sullivan, *Service Operations Management* (New York: McGraw-Hill, 1982), pp. 221–227; Ken G. Smith, Curtis M. Grimm, Martin J. Gannon, and Ming-Jer Chen, "Organizational Information Processing, Competitive Responses and Performance in the U.S. Domestic Airline Industry," *Academy of Management Journal,* Vol. 34, No. 1 (1991), pp. 60–85; and Daniel Pearl, "More Firms Pledge Guaranteed Service," *Wall Street Journal,* July 17, 1991, pp. B1, B4.

51. Susan Fraker, "High-Speed Management for the High-Tech Age," *Fortune,* March 5, 1984, pp. 62–68.

52. Ibid., p. 63.

CHAPTER 10

1. Kathleen Deveny, "Can Ms. Fashion Bounce Back?" *Business Week,* January 16, 1989, pp. 64–70. See also Jeffrey A. Trachtenberg and Teri Agins, "Can Liz Claiborne Continue to Thrive When She Is Gone?" *Wall Street Journal,* February 28, 1989, pp. A1, A11.

2. Pradip N. Khandwalla, *The Design of Organizations* (New York: Harcourt Brace Jovanovich, 1977), P. 489.

3. Erik W. Larson and David H. Gobeli, "Matrix Management: Contradictions and Insights," *California Management Review,* Vol. 29, No. 4 (Summer 1987), pp. 126–138.

4. Harvey F. Kolodny, "Evolution to a Matrix Organization," *The Academy of Management Review,* Vol. 4, No. 4 (1979), p. 548.

5. Ibid, pp. 549–550.

6. Paul R. Lawrence, Harvey F. Kolodny, and Stanley M. Davis, "The Human Side of the Matrix," *Organizational Dynamics,* Vol. 6, No. 1 (1977), pp. 43–61.

7. Ibid. pp. 46–48.

8. Kolodny, "Evolution to a Matrix Organization," p. 547.

9. Stanley M. Davis and Paul R. Lawrence, *Matrix* (Reading, Mass.: Addison-Wesley, 1977).

10. Rosabeth Moss Kanter, *The Change Masters* (New York: Simon & Schuster, 1983), See also Rosabeth Moss Kanter, "Quality Leadership and Change," *Quality Progress,* February 1987, p. 48.

11. "Allied Unit, Free of Red Tape, Seeks to Develop Orphan Technologies," *Wall Street Journal,* September 13, 1984, p. 31; "Keeping the Fires Lit Under the Innovators," *Fortune,* March 28, 1988, p. 45; and Andrall E. Pearson, "Tough-Minded Ways to Get Innovative," *Harvard Business Review,* Vol. 88, No. 3 (May–June 1988), pp. 99–106.

12. Stephen W. Quickel, "CEO of the Year: General Electric's Jack Welch," *Financial World,* April 3, 1990, p. 62.

13. Kenneth Labich, "The Innovators," *Fortune,* June 6, 1988, pp. 50–53, 56, 60. See also Brian Dumaine, "The New Turnaround Champs," *Fortune,* July 16, 1990, pp. 36–44.

14. Peter Nulty, "America's Toughest Bosses," *Fortune,* February 27, 1989, pp. 40–43.

15. Bro Uttal, "Behind the Fall of Steve Jobs," *Fortune,* August 5, 1985, pp. 20–24.

16. Ralph Stayer, "How I Learned to Let My Workers Lead," *Harvard Business Review,* Vol. 68 (November–December 1990), pp. 66–75.

17. Rosabeth Moss Kanter, "Power Failure in Management Circuits," in Robert W. Allen, and Lyman W. Porter (eds), *Organizational Influence Processes* (Glenview, Ill: Scott Foresman, 1983), pp. 87–104.

18. David A. Whetten and Kim S. Cameron, *Developing Management Skills,* 2nd ed. (New York: Harper Collins, 1991), pp. 397–400.

19. Mariann Jelinek, "Organization Structure: The Basic Conformations," in Mariann Jelinek, Joseph A. Litterer, and Raymond E. Miles (eds.), *Organizations by Design: Theory and Practice* (Plano, Tex: Business Publications, 1981), pp. 293–302.

20. Bernie Knill, "Quick Response: Technology Doesn't Stand Alone," *Material Handling Engineering,* Vol. 46, No. 7 (1991), pp. 52–54.

21. Otto Forchheimer, "Accountability for Functional Executives," *Advanced Management Journal,* April 1972, pp. 15–20.

22. William H. Newman, Kirby E. Warren, and Jerome E. Scnee, *The Process of Management: Strategy, Action, Results,* 5th ed. (Englewood Cliffs, N.J.: Prentice Hall, 1982), pp. 221–223.

23. French and Raven, "The Bases of Social Power," pp. 607–623. See also Dale McConkey, *No Nonsense Delegation* (New York: AMACOM Books, 1974).

24. Ramon J. Aldag and Arthur P. Brief, *Task Design and Employee Motivation* (Glenview, Ill: Scott Foresman, 1979), pp. 44–48.

25. Peter F. Drucker, *Management: Tasks, Responsibilities, Practices* (New York: Harper & Row, 1974), pp. 494–495. See also Gerald G. Fisch, "Toward More Effective Delegation," *CPA Journal,* Vol. 46, No. 7 (1976), pp. 66–67.

26. Noel M. Tichy and David O. Ulrich, "SMR Forum: The Leadership Challenge—A Call for the Transformational Leader," *Sloan Management Review,* Vol. 26, No. 1 (1984), pp. 59–68.

27. Robert Duncan, "What Is the Right Organization Structure?" in David A. Nadler, Michael L. Tushman, and Nina G. Hatveny (eds.), *Managing Organizations: Readings and Cases* (Boston: Little, Brown, 1982), pp. 302–318.

28. Labich, "The Innovators," pp. 50–58.

29. "The Chief's Personality Can Have a Big Impact—For Better or Worse," *Wall Street Journal,* September 11, 1984, pp. 1, 12; C. G. Burck, "A Group Profile of the Fortune 500 Chief Executives," *Fortune,* May 14, 1986, pp. 173–177, 311–312; and Nulty, "America's Toughest Bosses," pp. 40–43.

30. Robert D. Hof, "25 Executives to Watch: Carol Bartz," *The 1991 Business Week 1000,* August 1991, p. 52.

31. Maria Shao, "25 Executives to Watch: Sandra Kurtzig," *The 1991 Business Week 1000,* August 1991, p. 72. See also Sandra Kurtzig, "Meeting the Entrepreneurial Challenge," keynote address to the International Conference of the Association of Collegiate Entrepreneurs, March 12, 1989.

32. John Hillkirk, "Kodak Develops New Ways of Managing," *USA Today,* August 8, 1990, p. 4B.

33. Rosbeth Moss Kanter and Barry A. Stein, *Life in Organizations: Workplaces as People Experience Them* (New York: Basic Books, 1979), pp. 259–260. See also Bro Uttal, "The Corporate Culture Vultures," *Fortune,* October 17, 1983, p. 66.

34. Carol Davenport, "America's Most Admired Corporations," *Fortune,* January 30, 1989, pp. 68–69; Thomas A. Stewart, "Brainpower," *Fortune,* June 3, 1991, pp. 44–46, 50, 54, 56, 60; and Donald R. Sease and Craig Torres, "Industrials Tumble 41.15 Points; Gloom Spreads to Bonds, Dollar," *Wall Street Journal,* November 20, 1991, p. C1.

35. Paul B. Carroll, "How an IBM Attempt to Regain PC Lead Has Slid into Trouble," *Wall Street Journal,* December 2, 1991, pp. A1, A6; Brenton R. Schlender, "The Future of the PC," *Fortune,* August 26, 1991, pp. 40–44, 48; Joseph B. white, "GM Tries a New Tack: Build the Cars Right; But, Will It Work?" *Wall Street Journal,* November 21, 1991, pp. A1, A6; and "American Telephone & Telegraph: The Wrong Choice?" *The Economist,* April 27, 1991, p. 77.

36. John W. Slocum, Jr., and Sara J. McQuaid, "Cultural Values and the CEO: Alluring Companions?" *Academy of Management Executive,* Vol. II, No. 1 (1988), pp. 39–49.

37. Gene Bylinsky, "America's Best-Managed Factories," *Fortune,* May 28, 1984, pp. 16–24.

38. Ibid., p. 18.

39. William R. Torbert, "Pre-Bureaucratic and Post-Bureaucratic Stages of Organizational Development," *Interpersonal Development,* Vol. 5 (1975), pp. 1–25.

40. William N. Cooke, "Factors Influencing the Effect of Joint Union-Management Programs on Employee-Supervisor Relations," *Industrial and Labor Relations Review,* Vol. 43, No. 5 (1990), pp. 587–603.

41. Kanter, "Quality Leadership and Change," pp. 45–51.

42. Dana Milbank, "Changes at Alcoa Point Up Challenges and Benefits of Decentralized Authority," *Wall Street Journal,* November 7, 1991, pp. B1, B2.

43. "Akers Looks Ahead to IBM's Future Strategies, Principles," *Computer Reseller News,* April 3, 1989, pp. 44–46. See also Hollister B. Sykes, "Lessons from a New Venture Program," *Harvard Business Review,* Vol. 86, No. 3 (1986), pp. 69–74.

44. Christopher K. Bart, "New Venture Units: Use Them Wisely to Manage Innovation," *Sloan Management Review,* Vol. 29 (Summer

1988), pp. 35–43. See also David H. Holt, *Entrepreneurship: New Venture Creation* (Englewood Cliffs, N.J.: Prentice Hall, 1992), pp. 87–90.

45. John L. Cotton, David A. Vollrath, Kirk L. Froggatt, Mark L. Lengnick-Hall, and Kenneth R. Jennings, "Employee Participation: Diverse Forms and Different Outcomes," *Academy of Management Review,* Vol. 13, No. 1 (1988), pp. 8–22; Fraker, "High-Speed Management for the High-Tech Age," p. 63; and David J. Kautter, *Benefit Planning* (Washington, D.C.: Arthur Young & Co., 1984), pp. 11–12.

46. Timothy M. Collins and Thomas L. Doorley III. *Teaming Up for the 90s: A Guide to International Joint Ventures and Strategic Alliances* (Homewood, Ill: Business One Irwin, 1991), pp. 144–160. See also, "RDLPs and Consortiums: The New Wave in R&D," *Compressed Air Magazine,* March 1984, pp. 20–27.

47. D. Bruce Merrifield, "The Measurement of Productivity and the Use of R&D Limited Partnerships," U.S. Department of Commerce Publications, Office of Productivity, Technology, and Innovation, Summer 1984.

48. Collins and Doorley, *Teaming Up for the 90s,* pp. 77, 216.

49. Bruce Kogut, "Joint Ventures: Theoretical and Empirical Perspectives," *Strategic Management Journal,* Vol. 9 (1988), pp. 319–332; "Doctors Are Entering a Brave New World of Competition," *Business Week,* July 16, 1984, pp. 56–57, 59–61; and Carol Hurewitz, "TOM: Does Your Company Measure Up?" *Magazine of Service Management,* October 1991, pp. 19–20, 22, 24.

CHAPTER 11

1. Ellen Schultz, "America's Most Admired Corporations," *Fortune,* January 18, 1988, pp. 32–37. See also "Herman Miller's Secrets of Corporate Creativity," courtesy of Herman Miller, Inc., September 1991, pp. 1–6.

2. David Woodruff, "Herman Miller: How Green in My Factory," *Business Week,* September 16, 1991, pp. 54, 56.

3. D. Bruce Merrifield, *The Measurement of Productivity and the Use of R&D Limited Partnerships: A Productivity Update* (Washington, D.C.: Office of Productivity, Technology and Innovation, 1991), pp. 1–6.

4. Michael A. Cusumano and Chris F. Kemerer, "A Quantitative Analysis of U.S. and Japanese Practice and Performance in Software Development," *Management Science,* Vol. 36, No. 11 (1990), pp. 1384–1406.

5. Paul R. Erhlich, *The Population Bomb* (San Francisco: Sierra Club, 1969), pp. 16–18.

6. M. W. Thring, *Robots and Telechirs: Manipulators with Memory, Remote Manipulators, Machine Limbs for the Handicapped* (Chichester, U.K.: Ellis Horwood, 1983). See also Ronald Henkoff, "How to Plan for 1995," *Fortune,* December 31, 1990, pp. 70–76.

7. Wade Lambert, "Discrimination Afflicts People with HIV," *Wall Street Journal,* November 19, 1991, pp. B1, B6.

8. Joan S. Lublin, "Sexual Harassment Is Topping Agenda in Many Executive Education Programs," *Wall Street Journal,* December 2, 1991, pp. B1, B6.

9. Sue Shellenbarger, "More Job Seekers Put Family Needs First," *Wall Street Journal,* November 15, 1991, pp. B1, B12.

10. Joseph A. Raelin, "The '60s Kids in the Corporation: More Than Just 'Daydream Believers,'" *The Academy of Management Executive,* Vol. I, No. 1 (1987), pp. 21–30.

11. Albert Shapero and Lisa Sokol, "The Social Dimensions of Entrepreneurship," in Calvin A. Kent, Donald L. Sexton, and Karl H. Vesper (eds.), *Encyclopedia of Entrepreneurship* (Englewood Cliffs, N.J.: Prentice Hall, 1982), pp. 72–98.

12. Donald J. Campbell, "Task Complexity: A Review and Analysis," *Academy of Management Review,* Vol. 13, No. 1 (1988), pp. 40–52.

13. Robert Landel, *Managing Productivity Through People* (Englewood Cliffs, N.J.: Prentice Hall, 1986), pp. 90–95.

14. Richard J. Schonberger, *World Class Manufacturing Casebook: Implementing JIT and TQC* (New York: The Free Press, 1987), pp. xvi–xxi. See also Thomas A. Stewart, "GE Keeps Those Ideas Coming," *Fortune,* August 12, 1991, pp. 41–45, 48–49.

15. John F. Krafcik, "Triumph of the Lean Production System," *Sloan Management Review,* Vol. 30, No. 1 (Fall 1988), pp. 41–52.

16. David Kirkpatrick, "Smart New Ways to Use Temps," *Fortune,* February 15, 1988, p. 110.

17. Michael A. Verespej, "Part-Time Workers: No Temporary Phenomenon," *Industry Week,* April 3, 1989, pp. 13–18. See also Michael Selz, "Small Companies Thrive by Taking Over Some Specialized Tasks for Big Concerns," *Wall Street Journal,* September 11, 1991, pp. B1, B6.

18. Max Messmer, "Strategic Staffing for the '90s," *Personnel Journal,* October 1990, pp. 92–97.

19. Barbara Steinem, "Could Your Next Supervisor Be a Rent-a-Boss?" *Wall Street Journal,* December 2, 1991, p. A12.

20. Patricia Amend, "Workers Get a Share of the Action: Job Sharing Splits Hours," *USA Today,* April 27, 1989, p. 9B.

21. Ilan Salomon and Meira Salomon, "Telecommuting: The Employee's Perspective," *Technological Forecasting and Social Change,* Vol. 25, No. 1 (1984), pp. 15–28.

22. Sarah Glazer, "Setting Up an Office at Home," *Inc. Office Guide,* July 1988, pp. 28–32; Laura L. Castro, "Managers Declare Independence to Run Businesses from Their Personal Utopias," *Wall Street Journal,* September 3, 1991, pp. B1, B4; and Shellenbarger, "More Job Seekers Put Family Needs First," pp. B1, B12.

23. John R. Dorfman, "Stocks of Companies Announcing Layoffs Fire Up Investors, but Prices Often Wilt," *Wall Street Journal,* December 10, 1991, pp. C1, C2.

24. J. Richard Hackman and Greg R. Oldham, *Work Redesign* (Reading, Mass.: Addison-Wesley, 1980), pp. 135–142.

25. Aldag and Brief, *Task Design and Employee Motivation,* Chap. 4.

26. Joseph Luft, *Group Processes: An Introduction to Group Dynamics,* 3rd ed. (Palo Alto, Cal.: Mayfield, 1984), pp. 151–152.

27. Edgar H. Shein, *Organizational Psychology,* 3rd ed. (Englewood Cliffs, N.J.: Prentice Hall, 1980), pp. 146–153.

28. John P. Wanous, Arnon E. Reichers, and S. D. Malik, "Organizational Socialization and Group Development: Toward an Integrative Perspective," *Academy of Management Review,* Vol. 9, No. 4 (1984), pp. 678–683.

29. Luft, *Group Processes: An Introduction to Group Dynamics,* pp. 153, 155–156. See also Leonard R. Sayles, "Research in Industrial Relations," *Industrial Relations Research Association* (New York: Harper & Row, 1957), pp. 131–145.

30. Kenneth N. Wexley and Gary A. Yukl, *Organizational Behavior and Personnel Psychology* (Homewood, Ill.: Richard D. Irwin, 1977), pp. 126–128.

31. Harlan R. Jessup, "New Roles in Team Leadership," *Training and Development,* November 1990, pp. 79–83.

32. David O. Sears, Jonathan L. Freedman, and Letitia A. Peplau, *Social Psychology,* 5th ed. (Englewood Cliffs, N.J.: Prentice Hall, 1985), p. 368. See also Raef T. Hussein, "Informal Groups, Leadership and Productivity," *Leadership and Organizational Development Journal,* Vol. 10 (1989), pp. 9–16.

33. Jerry C. Wofford, *Organizational Behavior* (Boston: Kent, 1982), pp. 311–314. See also Victor H. Vroom and Arthur G. Jago, *The New Leadership: Managing Participation in Organizations* (Englewood Cliffs, N.J.: Prentice Hall, 1988), pp. 103–105.

34. Kate Ludeman, "Instilling the Work Ethic," *Training & Development Journal,* May 1990, pp. 53–59.

35. Davis C. Feldman, "The Development and Enforcement of Group Norms," *Academy of Management Review,* Vol. 9, No. 2 (1984), pp. 47–53.

36. Peter E. Mudrack, "Group Cohesiveness and Productivity: A Closer Look," *Human Relations,* Vol. 42 (September 1989), pp. 771–785.

37. Jessup, "New Roles in Team Leadership," pp. 79–83.

38. Warren G. Bennis and Herbert A. Shepard, "A Theory of Group Development," *Human Relations,* Summer 1963, pp. 415–457. See also W. Edwards Deming, "Improvement of Quality and Productivity Through Action by Management," *National Productivity Review,* Vol. 1 (Winter 1981–1982), pp. 12–22.

39. Edward E. Lawler III, "Let the Workers Make White-Knuckle Decisions," *Fortune,* March 26, 1990, pp. 49–50.

40. J. Stephen Heiner and Eugene Jacobson, "A Model of Task Group Development in Complex Organizations and a Strategy of Implementation," *Academy of Management Review,* Vol. 1, No. 4 (1976), pp. 98–111. See also John A. Wagner III and John R. Hollenbeck, *Management of Organizational Behavior* (Englewood Cliffs, N.J.: Prentice Hall, 1992), pp. 372–373.

41. Paul Hersey and Kenneth H. Blanchard, *Management of Organizational Behavior: Utilizing Human Resources,* 5th ed. (Englewood Cliffs, N.J.; Prentice Hall, 1988), pp. 333–336.

42. Richard W. Hallstein, "Team Un-Building," *Training & Development Journal,* June 1989, pp. 56–58. See also Jessup, "New Roles in Team Leadership," pp. 79–83.

43. Arthur K. Rice, *The Enterprise and Its Environment* (London: The Tavistock Institute, 1963).

44. Kichiro Hayaski, "The Internationalization of Japanese-Style Management," in *Japan Update* (Tokyo: Japan Institute for Social and Economic Affairs, Autumn 1987), pp. 20–23. See also Thomas F. O'Boyle, "Under Japanese Bosses, Americans Find Work Both Better and Worse," *Wall Street Journal,* November 27, 1991, pp. A1, A4.

45. Norman R. F. Maier, "Assets and Liabilities in Group Problem Solving," *Psychological Review,* Vol. 74 (1967), pp. 239–249.

46. Dorwin Cartwright, "Determinants of Scientific Progress: The Case of Research on the Risky Shift," *American Psychologist,* Vol. 28, No. 3 (March 1973), pp. 222–231.

47. Ibid., p. 337.

48. Irving L. Janis, "Groupthink," *Psychology Today,* November 1971, pp. 43–46.

49. Anne B. Fisher, "Morale Crisis," *Fortune,* November 18, 1991, pp. 70–72, 76, 80. See also "Even Uncle Sam Is Starting to See the Light," *Business Week,* October 25, 1991, pp. 132–134, 136–137.

50. Edgar H. Schein, *Organizational Culture and Leadership* (San Francisco: Jossey-Bass, 1985), pp. 223–242. See also Jessup, "New Roles in Team Leadership," pp. 79–83.

51. Woodruff, "Herman Miller: How Green in My Factory," pp. 54, 56. See also "Herman Miller's Secrets of Corporate Creativity," p. 2.

CHAPTER 12

1. Information about the Blackfeet Indian Writing Company was provided by Bill Oswald, Vice President of Marketing for the company, on April 14, 1992

2. Gary Dessler, *Personnel Management,* 4th ed. (Englewood Cliffs, N.J.: Prentice Hall, 1988), pp. 2–6.

3. Andrew F. Sikula, *Personnel Administration and Human Resources Management* (New York: John Wiley and Sons, 1976), pp. 7–8. See also Jack English, "The Road Ahead for the Human Resources Function," *Personnel,* Vol. 57 (March–April 1980), pp. 35–39.

4. James Morris, "Those Burgeoning Worker Benefits," *Nation's Business,* February 1987, pp. 53–54. See also Kenneth A. Kovach and John A. Pearce II, "HR Strategic Mandates for the 1990s," *Personnel,* Vol. 67 (April 1990), pp. 50–55.

5. William F. Glueck, *Personnel: A Diagnostic Approach,* 3rd ed. (Plano, Tex.: Business Publications, 1983) p. 89.

6. "Opportunities in Field Engineering," *Careers with Exxon,* a career guide for college recruitment from Exxon Corporation USA (Fall 1991), pp. 3, 7–8.

7. Thierry Wils, Christiane Labelle, and Jean-Yves Le Louarn, "Human Resource Planning at Quebec-Telephone," *Human Resource Planning,* Vol. 11, No. 4 (1988), pp. 255–269.

8. George T. Milkovich and John W. Boudreau, *Human Resource Management,* 6th ed. (Homewood, Ill.: Richard D. Irwin, 1991), pp. 130–133.

9. Max Bader, "Attitudes Harden Before Arteries When Hiring the Elderly," *Wall Street Journal,* June 6, 1988, p. 20.

10. Alan Murray and David Wessel, "Torrent of Layoffs Show Human Toll of Recession Goes On," *Wall Street Journal,* December 12, 1991, pp. A1, A8.

11. Suzanne Alexander, "Firms Get Plenty of Practice at Layoffs, but They Often Bungle the Firing Process," *Wall Street Journal,* October 14, 1991, pp. B1, B4.

12. "Management Summary," *Fourth Quarter Report of Earnings and Operations,* Xerox Corporation, January 1992, p. 2.

13. Brian D. Steffy and Steven D. Maurer, "Conceptualizing and Measuring the Economic Effectiveness of Human Resource Activities," *Academy of Management Review,* Vol. 13, No. 2 (1988), pp. 271–296. See also Richard B. Frantzreb, "Human Resource Planning: Forecasting Manpower Needs," *Personnel Journal,* Vol. 60, No. 11 (1981), pp. 850–857.

14. Roger Ricklefs, "Victims of AIDS-Related Discrimination Are Fighting Back—and Getting Results," *Wall Street Journal,* July 15, 1988, p. 17; David Ritter and Ronald Turner, "AIDS: Employer Concerns and Options," *Labor Law Journal,* Vol. 38, No. 2 (1987), pp. 67–83; and Judy D. Olian, "AIDS Testing for Employment Purposes? Facts and Controversies," *Journal of Business and Psychology,* Vol. 3, No. 2 (1988), pp. 135–153.

15. Harvey Mackay, *Swim With the Sharks Without Being Eaten Alive,* rev. ed. (New York: Ballantine Books, 1990), pp. 207–212.

16. Amy Dunkin (ed.), "Laying Off the Layoffs in Lean Times," *Business Week,* January 20, 1991, pp. 100–101.

17. Richard Neidig and Manela Neidig, "Multiple Assessment Center Exercises and Job Relatedness," *Journal of Applied Psychology,* Vol. 69, No. 1 (1984), pp. 182–186. See also Craig Russell, "Individual Decision Processes in an Assessment Center," *Journal of Applied Psychology,* Vol. 70, No. 4 (1985), pp. 737–746.

18. Milkovich and Boudreau, *Human Resource Management,* pp. 386–387.

19. William J. Hampton, "How Does Japan, Inc., Pick Its American Workers?" *Business Week,* October 3, 1988, pp. 84–85.

20. Meryl Reis Lous, "Surprise and Sense Making: What Newcomers Experience in Entering Unfamiliar Organizational Settings," *Administrative Science Quarterly,* June 1980, pp. 226–251. See also Joan P. Klubnik, "Orienting New Employees," *Training and Development Journal,* April 1987, pp. 46–49.

21. Milkovich and Boudreau, *Human Resource Management,* p. 407.

22. Ibid., pp. 417–419.

23. Lois Therrien, "Motorola Sends Its Work Force Back to School," *Business Week,* June 6, 1988, pp. 80–81.

24. Walter Kiechel III, "The Organization That Learns," *Fortune,* March 12, 1990, pp. 133–136.

25. Susan B. Garland, "909 Days to Learn to Scrub? Sure, if Uncle Sam's Paying," *Business Week,* January 20, 1992, pp. 70–71.

26. Patricia A. Galagan, "IBM Gets Its Arms Around Education," *Training & Development Journal,* January 1989, pp. 35–41.

27. Dessler, *Personnel Management,* pp. 272–280.

28. Milkovich and Boudreau, *Human Resource Management,* pp. 452–458.

29. "Financial Freedom: Do Workers Need More Help Managing Pension Assets?" *Wall Street Journal,* September 10, 1991, p. A1.

30. Sue Shellenbarger, "Companies Team Up to Improve Quality of Their Employees' Child-Care Choices," *Wall Street Journal,* October 17, 1991, pp. B1, B11.

31. David Wessel, "The 1993 Budget: Bush's Antidote to Recession, Proposal Indicates Bush Is Willing to Bend on the Issue of the Deficit," *Wall Street Journal,* January 30, 1992, p. A6.

32. Hilary Stout, "Paying Workers for Good Health Habits Catches On as a Way to Cut Medical Costs," *Wall Street Journal,* November 26, 1991, pp. B1, B7.

33. Milkovich and Boudreau, *Human Resource Management,* pp. 568, 605.

34. John P. Bucalo, "Successful Employee Relations," *Personnel Administrator,* April 1986, pp. 63–84.

35. Joann S. Lublin, "Companies Try a Variety of Approaches to Halt Sexual Harassment on the Job," *Wall Street Journal*, October 11, 1991, pp. B1, B7; "Harassment: Views in the Workplace," *Wall Street Journal*, October 10, 1991, p. B1; and Cynthia Croseen, "Are You from Another Planet, or What?" *Wall Street Journal*, October 18, 1991, p. B1.

36. Craig Mellon, "The Dope on Drug Testing," *Human Resource Executive*, Vol. 2, No. 4 (1988) pp. 34–37.

37. "Privacy," *Business Week*, March 28, 1988, pp. 61–68.

38. Milkovich and Boudreau, *Human Resource Management,* pp. 605–608.

39. Bureau of Labor Statistics, *Digest of Employment and Earnings,* series summaries, January 1990 and January 1991.

40. Jeffrey S. Zax, "Employment and Local Public Sector Unions," *Industrial Relations,* Winter 1989, pp. 21–31.

41. Jeanne M. Brett, "Why Employees Want Unions," *Organizational Dynamics,* Spring 1980, pp. 316–332. See also John A. Fossum, "Labor Relations: Reserach and Practice in Transition," *Journal of Management,* Summer 1987, pp. 281–300.

42. Fossum, "Labor Relations: Research and Practice in Transition," pp. 281–300. See also George Strauss, "Industrial Relations: Time of Change," *Industrial Relations,* Vol. 23, No. 1 (1984), pp. 1–15.

43. Jai Ghorpade, *Job Analysis: A Handbook for the Human Resource Director* (Englewood Cliffs, N.J.: Prentice Hall, 1988), pp. 6, 96, 141. See also Allan M. Mohrman, Jr., Susan M. Resnick-West, and Edward E. Lawler III,

Designing Performance Appraisal Systems (San Francisco: Jossey-Bass, 1989), pp. 5–22.

44. "Firms Debate Hard Lines on Alcoholics: Oil Spill Spurs Exxon to Shift Job Guarantees," *Wall Street Journal,* April 13, 1989, p. B1.

45. Jeffrey Rothfeder, Michael Galen, and Lisa Driscoll, "Is Your Boss Spying on You?" *Business Week,* January 15, 1990, pp. 74–75.

46. Brian Dumaine, "Those Highflying PepsiCo Managers," *Fortune,* April 10, 1989, pp. 78–79, 84.

47. Mohrman, Resnick-West, and Lawler, *Designing Performance Appraisal Systems,* Chap. 1.

48. Jerry W. Hedge and Michael J. Kavanagh, "Improving the Accuracy of Performance Evaluations: Comparison of Three Methods of Performance Appraisal Training," *Journal of Applied Psychology,* February 1988, pp. 68–73.

49. Donald P. Schwab and Herbert G. Heneman III, "Behaviorally Anchored Rating Scales," in Herbert G. Heneman III and Donald P. Schwab (eds.), *Perspectives on Personnel/Human Resource Management* (Homewood, Ill.: Richard D. Irwin, 1978), pp. 65–66.

50. Uco Wiersma and Gary P. Latham, "The Practicality of Behavioral Observation Scales, Behavioral Expectations Scales, and Trait Scales," *Personnel Psychology,* Vol. 39, No. 3 (Autumn 1986), pp. 619–628. See also Milkovich and Boudreau, *Human Resource Management,* pp. 101–103.

51. Joane Pearce and Lyman Porter, "Employee Response to Formal Performance Appraisal Feedback," *Journal of Applied Psychology,* Vol. 71, No. 2 (1986), pp. 211–218.

52. Patrick J. Montana, *Retirement Programs* (Englewood Cliffs, N.J.: Prentice Hall, 1985), pp. 3–5.

53. E. Thomas Garman and Raymond E. Forgue, *Personal Finance,* 3rd ed. (Boston: Houghton Mifflin, 1991), p. 486.

54. F. Lee Van Horn, international consultant, quoted in *Vista,* July–August 1989, p. 58.

55. "OSHA Training Guidelines (Part II): Developing Learning Activities," *Personnel Manager's Legal Report,* February 1984, pp. 7–8.

CHAPTER 13

1. Howard Banks, "Is Delta Too Nice for Its Own Good?" *Forbes,* November 28, 1988, pp. 91–94.

2. "Dogfight! United and American Battle for Global Supremacy," *Business Week,* January 21, 1991, pp. 56–62; James Ott, "Delta Faces Fight to Regain Lost Shuttle Passengers," *Aviation Week & Space Technology,* September 9, 1991, pp. 35–37; and Michael Mecham, "Lufthansa Protests Delta Takeover of Pan Am's European Routes," *Aviation Week & Space Technology,* September 9, 1991, p. 37.

3. Craig C. Pinder, *Work Motivation* (Glenview, Ill: Scott Foresman, 1984), p. 8.

4. Edward E. Lawler III, *High Involvement Management: Participative Strategies for Improving Organizational Performance* (San Francisco: Jossey-Bass, 1986), pp. 5–8.

5. Thomas A. Stewart, "GE Keeps Those Ideas Coming," *Fortune,* August 12, 1991, pp. 41–45, 48–49.

6. Aaron Bernstein and Ronald Grover, "Union Workers Will Get Some Breaks in '92," *Business Week,* February 3, 1992, p. 50; "The Push to 'Buy American,'" *Newsweek,* February 3, 1992, pp. 32–35; and Bob David and Dana Milbank, "If the U.S. Work Ethic Is Fading, Alienation May Be the Main Reason," *Wall Street Journal,* February 7, 1992, pp. A1, A4.

7. Joseph Weber, "A Big Company That Works," *Business Week,* May 4, 1992, pp. 124–127, 130, 132.

8. Jeremiah J. Sullivan, "Three Roles of Language in Motivation Theory," *Academy of Management Review,* Vol. 13, No. 1 (1988), pp. 104–115. See also Edward E. Lawler III, "Job Design and Employee Motivation," *Personnel Psychology,* Vol. 22 (1969), pp. 426–435.

9. Douglas M. McGregor, "The Human Side of Enterprise," in Louis E. Boone and Donald D. Bowen (eds.), *The Great Writings in Management and Organizational Behavior* (New York: Random House, 1987), pp, 126–138.

10. Victor H. Vroom and Arthur G. Jago, *The New Leadership: Managing Participation in Organizations* (Englewood Cliffs, N.J.: Prentice Hall, 1988), pp. 7–14.

11. Thomas L. Daniel and James K. Esser, "Intrinsic Motivation as Influenced by Rewards, Task Interest, and Task Structure," *Journal of Applied Psychology,* Vol. 65, No. 5 (1980), pp. 566–573.

12. Abraham H. Maslow, *Motivation and Personality,* 2nd ed. (New York: Harper & Row, 1970).

13. Howard S. Schwartz, "Maslow and the Hierarchical Enactment of Organizational Reality," *Human Relations,* Vol. 36, No. 10 (1983), pp. 933–956. See also Gary Johns, *Organizational Behavior: Understanding Life at Work,* 3rd ed. (New York: Harper Collins, 1992), pp. 175–176.

14. Clayton P. Alderfer, "An Empirical Test of a New Theory of Human Needs," *Organization Behavior and Human Performance,* Vol. 4 (1969), pp. 142–175. See also Clayton P. Alderfer, *Existence, Relatedness and Growth: Human Needs in Organizational Settings* (New York: Free Press, 1972), pp. 26–28.

15. John P. Wanous and A. Zwany, "A Cross-Sectional Test of Need Hierarchy Theory," *Organizational Behavior and Human Performance,* Vol. 18 (1977), pp. 78–97.

16. Frederick Herzberg, "One More Time: How Do You Motivate Employees?" *Harvard Business Review,* Vol. 87, No. 5 (September–October 1987), pp. 109–117.

17. Frederick Herzberg, Bernard Mausner, and Barbara Snyderman, *The Motivation to Work* (New York: John Wiley, 1959), Chaps. 2 and 3 in particular.

18. "The Best of America—Making a Difference," *U.S. News & World Report,* August 26–September 2, 1991, p. 91.

19. John W. Atkinson, *An Introduction to Motivation* (New York: Van Nostrand, 1961).

20. David C. McClelland, *The Achieving Society* (Princeton, N.J.: Van Nostrand, 1961). See also David C. McClelland, *Power: The Inner Experience* (New York: Irvington, 1975).

21. Robert H. Brockhaus, Sr., and Pamela S. Horwitz, "The Psychology of the Entrepreneur," in Donald L. Sexton and Raymond W. Smilor (eds.), *The Art and Science of Entrepreneurship* (Cambridge, Mass.: Ballinger, 1986), pp. 25–48.

22. Brian Dumaine, "Who Needs a Boss?" *Fortune,* May 7, 1990, pp. 52–55, 58–60.

23. David C. McClelland, "Toward a Theory of Motive Acquisition," *American Psychologist,* Vol. 20, No. 5 (1965), pp. 321–333.

24. David C. McClelland, "That Urge to Achieve," in Boone and Bowen, *The Great Writings in Management and Organizational Behavior,* pp. 384–393.

25. Victor H. Vroom, *Work and Motivation* (New York: John Wiley and Sons, 1964). See also Vroom and Jago, *The New Leadership: Managing Participation in Organizations,* pp. 121–127.

26. David A. Nadler and Edward E. Lawler III, "Motivation: A Diagnostic Approach," in Barry M. Staw (ed.), *Psychological Foundations of Organizational Behavior,* 2nd ed. (Glenview, Ill.: Scott Foresman, 1983), pp. 36–45.

27. A. Bandura, "Self-Efficacy Mechanism in Human Behavior," *American Psychologist,* Vol. 37 (1982), pp. 122–147.

28. A. Bernstein, "How to Work the Line and Influence People," *Business Week,* May 7, 1990, pp. 140–141.

29. Barbara Dutton, "Quality in the Glen," *Manufacturing Systems,* March 1992, pp. 20–26; "Processing Monitoring with Vision," *Quality,* April 1992, pp. 39–41; and Larry Armstrong and William C. Symonds, "Beyond 'May I Help You?'" *Business Week/Quality,* October 25, 1991, pp. 100–103.

30. J. Stacy Adams, "Toward an Understanding of Inequity," *Journal of Abnormal and Social Psychology,* Vol. 67, No. 5 (1963), pp. 422–436. See also Steven Kerr, "On the Folly of Rewarding A While Hoping for B," *Academy of Management Journal,* Vol. 18, No. 4 (1975), pp. 769–783.

31. Steven E. Markham and Michael J. Vest, "Merit Pay: Just or Unjust Deserts?" *Personnel Administrator,* September 1987, pp. 53–59.

32. Edwin A. Locke, "Toward a Theory of Task Motivation and Incentives," *Organizational Behavior and Human Performance,* Vol. 3 (1968), 157–189.

33. Gary P. Latham and Edwin A. Locke, "Goal Setting—A Motivational Technique That Works," *Organizational Dynamics,* Vol. 8, No. 2 (1979), pp. 68–80. See also Miriam Erez, P. Christopher Earley, and Charles L. Hulin, "The Impact of Participation on Goal Acceptance and Performance: A Two-Step Model," *Academy of Management Journal,* Vol. 28, No. 2 (1985), pp. 50–66.

34. W. E. Craighead, A. E. Kazdin, and M. J. Mahoney, *Behavior Modification* (Boston: Houghton Mifflin, 1976), pp. 134–148. See also Fred Luthans and Robert Kreitner, *Organizational Behavior Modification and Beyond: An Operant and Social Learning Approach* (Glenview, Ill.: Scott Foresman, 1985), Chap. 1.

35. B. F. Skinner, *Science and Human Behavior* (New York: Macmillan, 1953). See also B. F. Skinner, *Beyond Freedom and Dignity* (New York: Alfred Knopf, 1971).

36. E. L. Thorndike, *Animal Intelligence* (New York: Macmillan, 1911). See also Pinder, *Work Motivation,* pp. 187–208.

37. W. F. Dowling, "At Emery Air Freight: Positive Reinforcement Boosts Performance," *Organizational Dynamics,* Vol. 2, No. 1 (1973), pp. 41–50.

38. W. Clay Hamner, "Using Reinforcement Theory in Organizational Settings," in Henry L. Tosi and W. Clay Hamner (eds.), *Organizational Behavior and Management: A Contingency Approach* (Chicago: St. Clair Press, 1977), pp. 388–395.

39. Andrea Rothman, "Can Wayne Calloway Handle the Pepsi Challenge?" *Business Week*, January 27, 1992, pp. 90–92, 94–95, 98.

40. Fred Luthans and Robert Kreitner, "The Management of Behavioral Contingencies," *Personnel,* Vol. 51, No. 4 (1974), pp. 7–16.

41. Pinder, *Work Motivation,* pp. 229–232.

CHAPTER 14

1. Toni Mack,"Eager Lions and Reluctant Lions," *Forbes*, February 17, 1992, pp. 98–101.

2. John B. Goodman and Gary W. Loveman, "Does Privatization Serve the Public Interest?" *Harvard Business Review,* Vol. 69 (November–December 1991), pp. 26–38.

3. Robert R. Blake and Jane S. Mouton, *The Versatile Manager: A Grid Profile* (Homewood, Ill.: Richard D. Irwin, 1981), p. vi.

4. Ralph M. Stogdill, *Handbook of Leadership* (New York: The Free Press, 1981), pp. 6–8, 14–17. See also Karl W. Kuhnert and Philip Lewis, "Transactional and Transformational Leadership: A Constructive/Development Analysis," *Academy of Management Review,* Vol. 12, No. 4 (1987), pp. 648–657.

5. John R. P. French and Bertram Raven, "The Bases of Social Power," in Dorwin Cartwright (ed.), *Studies in Social Power* (Ann Arbor: University of Michigan Press, 1959), pp. 150–167. See also Jay A. Conger and Rabindra N. Kanungo, "The Empowerment Process: Integrating Theory and Practice," *Academy of Management Review,* Vol. 13, No. 3 (1988), pp. 471–482.

6. Chester I. Barnard, *The Functions of the Executive,* 30th Anniversary Edition (Cambridge, Mass.: Harvard University Press, 1968), pp. 164–167.

7. Zachary Schiller, "No More Mr. Nice Guy at P&G—Not by a Long Shot," *Business Week,* February 3, 1992, pp. 54–56.

8. Gary A. Yukl, *Leadership in Organizations,* 2nd ed. (Englewood Cliffs, N.J.: Prentice Hall, 1989), p. 13. See also Robert P. Vecchio and Mario Sussmann, "Choice of Influence Tactics: Individual and Organizational Determinants," *Journal of Organizational Behavior,* March 1991, pp. 73–80.

9. Tom Callahan, "I Consider Chipmunks Therapy," *U.S. News & World Report,* August 26–Septembher 2, 1991, pp. 86–87.

10. Ralph M. Stogdill, "Personal Factors Associated with Leadership: A Survey of the Literature," *Journal of Psychology,* Vol. 25, No. 1 (1948), pp. 35–71.

11. Robert A. Portnoy, *Leadership! What Every Leader Should Know About People* (Englewood Cliffs, N.J.: Prentice Hall, 1986), pp. 12–20. See also Paul Hersey, *The Situational Leader* (Escondido, Cal.: Center for Leadership Studies, 1984), pp. 13–14.

12. Cynthia Epstein, "Ways Men and Women Lead," *Harvard Business Review,* Vol. 69, No. 6 (November–December 1991), pp. 150–160.

13. Ralph M. Stogdill and Alvin E. Coons (eds.), *Leader Behavior: Its Description and Measurement,* Research Monograph No. 88 (Columbus: Bureau of Business Research, Ohio State University, 1957). See also Chester C. Schriesheim and Steven Kerr, "Theories and Measures of Leadership: A Critical Appraisal of Current and Future Directions," in James G. Hunt and Lars Larson (eds.), *Leadership: The Cutting Edge* (Carbondale, Ill.: SIU Press, 1977), pp. 9–21, 51–56.

14. Rensis Likert, *New Patterns of Management* (New York: McGraw-Hill, 1961). See also Rensis Likert, "An Integrating Principle and an Overview," in Louis E. Boone and Donald D. Bowen (eds.), *The Great Writings in Management and Organizational Behavior* (New York: Random House, 1987), pp. 216–238.

15. Peter Coy, "Twin Engines: Can Bob Allen Blend Computers and Telecommunications at AT&T?" *Business Week,* January 20, 1992, pp. 56–59, 62–63.

16. Rensis Likert, *Past and Future Perspectives on System 4 and Appendices A and B* (Ann Arbor, Mich.: Rensis Likert Associates, 1977), pp. 3–5, 9.

17. Blake and Mouton, *The Versatile Manager: A Grid Profile,* pp. 239–261.

18. Dean M. Ruwe and Wickham Skinner, "Reviving a Rust Belt Factory," *Harvard Business Review,* Vol. 87, No. 3 (May–June 1987), pp. 70–76.

19. Alex Taylor III, "A U.S.-Style Shakeup at Honda," *Fortune,* December 30, 1991, pp. 115–120. See also Brenton R. Schlenor, "How Sony Keeps the Magic Going," *Fortune,* February 24, 1992, pp. 76–82.

20. Robert Tannenbaum and Warren H. Schmidt, "How to Choose a Leadership Pattern," *Harvard Business Review,* Vol. 36, No. 2 (March–April) 1958, pp. 95–101. See also Jeffrey Pfeffer and Gerald R. Salancik, "Determinants of Supervisory Behavior: A Role Set Analysis," *Human Relations*, Vol. 28 (1975), pp. 139–153.

21. Louis S. Richman, "America's Tough New Job Market," *Fortune,* February 24, 1991, pp. 52–54, 58, 61.

22. Blake and Mouton, *The Versatile Manager: A Grid Profile,* pp. 10–26.

23. Stratford P. Sherman, "The Mind of Jack Welch," *Fortune,* March 17, 1989, pp. 39–50.

24. Blake and Mouton, *The Versatile Manager: A Grid Profile,* p. 5.

25. Fred E. Fiedler, "Engineer the Job to Fit the Manager," *Harvard Business Review,* Vol. 43, No. 5 (September–October 1965), pp. 115–122. See also Fred E. Fiedler, *A Theory of Leadership Effectiveness* (New York: McGraw-Hill, 1967).

26. Blake and Mouton, *The Versatile Manager: A Grid Profile,* pp. 252–258.

27. Robert J. House, "A Path Goal Theory of Leader Effectiveness," *Administrative Science Quarterly,* Vol. 16, No. 5 (1971), pp. 321–328.

28. Michelle Neely Marinez, "The High Potential Woman," *HR Magazine,* June 1991, pp. 46–51.

29. Ibid, p. 324.

30. Robert J. House and Terence R. Mitchell, "Path-Goal Theory of Leadership," in Boone and Bowen, *The Great Writings in Management and Organizational Behavior,* pp. 341–353.

31. Yukl, *Leadership in Organizations,* pp. 99–104. See also Blake and Mouton, *The Versatile Manager: A Grid Profile,* p. 153; Robert J. House, "Retrospective Comment," in Boone and Bowen, *The Great Writings in Management and Organizational Behavior,* pp. 354–364.

32. Victor H. Vroom and Phillip Yetton, *Leadership and Decision Making* (Pittsburgh: University of Pittsburgh Press, 1973). See also Victor H. Vroom and Arthur G. Jago, *The New Leadership: Managing Participation in Organizations* (Englewood Cliffs, N.J.: Prentice Hall, 1988), pp. 49–77.

33. Paul Hersey and Kenneth H. Blanchard, *Management of Organizational Behavior: Utilizing Human Resources,* 5th ed. (Englewood Cliffs, N.J.: Prentice Hall, 1988), pp 169–201.

34. Yukl, *Leadership in Organizations,* pp. 107–108. See also Vroom and Jago, *The New Leadership: Managing Participation in Organizations,* pp. 53–54.

35. Richard E. Boyatzis and Florence R. Skelly, "The Impact of Changing Values on Organizational Life," in David A. Kolb, Irwin M. Rubin, and Joyce S. Osland (eds), *The Organizational Behavior Reader,* 5th ed. (Englewood Cliffs, N.J.: Prentice Hall, 1991), pp. 1–3, 13.

36. Anne Wilson-Schaef, "The Female System and the White Male System: New Ways of Looking at Our Culture," in Peter J. Frost, Vance Mitchell, and Walter R. Nord (eds.), *Organizational Reality: Reports from the Firing Line,* 4th ed. (New York: HarperCollins, 1992), pp. 132–143.

37. Julie Amparano Lopez, "Study Says Women Face Glass Walls as Well as Ceilings," *Wall Street Journal,* March 3, 1992, pp. B1, B2.

38. Gary N. Powell, "One More Time: Do Female and Male Managers Differ?" *Academy of Management Executive,* Vol. 4, No. 3 (1990), pp. 68–75. See also Epstein, "Ways Men and Women Lead," pp. 150–160.

39. Dorothy J. Gaiter, "Short-term Despair, Long-term Promise," *Wall Street Journal,* April 3, 1992, pp. R1, R4.

40. Brent Bowers, "Black Boss, White Business," *Wall Street Journal,* April 3, 1992, p. R7. See also David A. Thomas, "The Impact of Race on Managers' Experiences of Developmental Relationships (Mentoring and Sponsorship): An Intra-Organizational Study," *Journal of Organizational Behavior,* November 1990, pp. 479–492.

41. Richard Lacayo, "When the Boss Is Black," in Frost, Mitchell, and Nord, *Organizational Reality: Reports from the Firing Line,* pp. 152–153.

42 Boyatzis and Skelly, "The Impact of Changing Values on Organizational Life," pp. 1–16.

43. "Older Workers Chafe Under Young Managers," *Wall Street Journal,* February 26, 1990, p. B1.

44. Charles C. Manz and Henry P. Sims, Jr., "Leading Workers to Lead Themselves: The External Leadership of Self-Managing Work Teams," *Administrative Science Quarterly,* Vol. 32 (1987), pp. 106–122.

45. Joseph Seltzer and Bernard M. Bass, "Transformational Leadership: Beyond Initiation and Consideration," *Journal of Management,* Vol. 16 (December 1990), pp. 24–33.

46. Bernard M. Bass, "From Transactional to Transformational Leadership: Learning to Share the Vision," *Organizational Dynamics* Winter 1990, pp. 19–31.

47. Bulent Kobu and Frank Greenwood, "Continuous Improvement in a Competitive Global Economy," *Production and Inventory Management Journal,* Vol. 32, No. 4 (1991), pp. 58–63; Michael J. Stickler, "Manager or Leader, Which Are You?" *Production & Inventory Management,* January 1992, pp. 14–15; and Susan Caminiti, "The Payoff from a Good Reputation," *Fortune,* February 10, 1992, pp. 74–77.

48. Noel M. Tichy and David O. Ulrich, "The Leadership Challenge—A Call for the Transformational Leader," in Kolb, Rubin, and Osland, *The Organizational Behavior Reader,* pp. 430–441.

49. Bass, "From Transactional to Transformational Leadership: Learning to Share the Vision," pp. 19–31.

50. Gary Johns, *Organizational Behavior: Understanding Life at Work,* 3rd ed. (New York: HarperCollins, 1992), pp. 362–364.

51. Mack, "Eager Lions and Reluctant Lions," pp. 98–101.

CHAPTER 15

1. Joann S. Lublin, "Trying to Increase Worker Productivity, More Employers Alter Management Style," *Wall Street Journal,* February 13, 1991, pp. B1, B3.

2. Larry E. Greiner, "Patterns of Organizational Change," *Harvard Business Review,* Vol. 67, No. 3 (May–June, 1967), pp. 119–128.

3. Michael Beer, *Organization Change and Development: A Systems View* (Santa Monica, Cal.: Goodyear, 1980), p. 47.

4. Jeremy Main, "The Recovery Skips Middle Managers," *Fortune,* Feburary 6, 1984, pp. 112–120.

5. Paul R. Lawrence, "How to Deal with Resistance to Change," in G. W. Dalton, P. R. Lawrence, and L. E. Greiner (eds.), *Organization Change and Development* (Homewood, Ill.: Richard D. Irwin, 1970), p. 183.

6. Larry Armstrong, "How Packard Bell Broke Out of the Pack," *Business Week,* January 27, 1992, p. 88.

7. Bob David and Dana Milbank, "If the U.S. Work Ethic Is Fading, Alienation May Be the Main Reason," *Wall Street Journal,* February 7, 1992, pp. A1, A4.

8. Tracy E. Benson, "Caterpillar Wakes Up," *Industry Week,* May 20, 1991, pp. 33–37. See also "Industry Notes," *Forbes,* January 6, 1992, p. 72; and Jonathan P. Hicks, "Progress Is Slight in Contract Talks," *New York Times,* April 14, 1992, p. A21.

9. Susan Caminiti, "The Payoff from a Good Reputation," *Fortune,* February 10, 1992, pp. 74–77.

10. Edgar H. Schein, *Organizational Psychology,* 3rd Ed. (Englewood Cliffs, N.J.: Prentice Hall, 1980), pp. 243–244.

11. Kurt Lewin, "Group Decision and Social Change," in G. E. Swanson, T. M. Newcomb, and E. L. Hartley (eds.), *Readings in Social Psychology* (New York: Holt, Rinehart & Winston, 1952), pp. 459–473.

12. Schein, *Organizational Psychology,* p. 244.

13. Ibid., pp. 245–246.

14. Donald F. Harvey and Donald R. Brown, *An Experiential Approach to Organizational Development,* 4th ed. (Englewood Cliffs, N.J.: Prentice Hall, 1992), pp. 199–200.

15. Richard Beckhard, "Planned Change and Organization Development," in D. A. Kolb, I. M. Rubin, and J. M. McIntyre (eds.), *Organizational Psychology: A Book of Readings,* 3rd ed. (Englewood Cliffs, N.J.: Prentice Hall, 1979), pp. 461–472.

16. Louis P. White, and Kevin C. Wooten, "Ethical Dilemmas in Various Stages of Organizational Development," *Academy of Management Review,* Vol. 8, No. 4 (1983), pp. 690–697.

17. Schein, *Organizational Psychology,* p. 243.

18. David A. Nadler and Michael L. Tushman, "Organizational Frame Bending: Principles for Managing Reorientation," *Academy of Management Executive,* Vol. III, No. 3 (1989), pp. 194–204.

19. Henry A. Kissinger, "The New Russian Question," *Newsweek,* February 10, 1992, pp. 34–35. See also "A Vision Thing," *Newsweek,* February 10, 1992, pp. 54–57.

20. Nadler and Tushman, "Organizational Frame Bending: Principles for Managing Reorientation," pp. 194–204.

21. Patricia Sellers, "Pepsi Keeps Going After No. 1," *Fortune,* March 11, 1991, pp. 62–70.

22. Nadler and Tushman, "Organizational Frame Bending: Principles for Managing Reorientation," pp. 194–204.

23. Howard Banks, "Preparing for Even More Draconian Cuts in Defense Spending, Suppliers Are Cutting Jobs and Costs," *Forbes,* January 6, 1992, pp. 96–97.

24. Beer, *Organizational Change and Development: A Systems View,* p. 52.

25. Jeffrey R. Williams, Betty Lynn Paez, and Leonard Sanders, "Conglomerates Revisited," *Strategic Management Journal,* Vol. 9, No. 5, (October 1988), pp. 403–414.

26. Christopher Knowlton, "What America Makes Best," *Fortune,* March 28, 1988, pp. 40–45.

27. Edward E. Lawler III, "Choosing an Involvement Strategy," *The Academy of Management Executive,* Vol. II, No. 3 (August 1988), pp. 197–204.

28. Harvey and Brown, *An Experiential Approach to Organizational Development,* pp. 199–200.

29. Lublin, "Trying to Increase Worker Productivity, More Employers Alter Management Style," pp. B1, B3.

30. Ibid., p. B1.

31. John P. Kotter and Leonard A. Schesinger, "Choosing Strategies for Change," *Harvard Business Review,* Vol. 57, No. 2 (March–April 1979), pp. 106–114. See also Gregory Moorhead and Ricky W. Griffin, *Organizational Behavior: Managing People and Organizations,* 3rd ed. (Boston: Houghton Mifflin, 1992), pp. 667–668.

32. Wendell L. French and Cecil H. Bell, Jr., *Organizational Development,* 4th ed. (Englewood Cliffs, N.J.: Prentice Hall, 1990), pp. 21–22.

33. Larry E. Greiner, "Red Flags in Organization Development," in J. R. Hackman, E. E. Lawler III, and L. W. Porter (eds.), *Perspectives on Behavior in Organizations* (New York: McGraw-Hill, 1983), pp. 536–542.

34. Terrence E. Deal and Allan A. Kennedy, "Culture: A New Look Through Old Lenses," *The Journal of Applied Behavioral Science,* Vol. 19, No. 4 (1983), pp. 107–108.

35. French and Bell, *Organizational Development,* p. 141.

36. Ibid., pp. 192–193. See also Richard Woodman, "Organization Change and Development," *Journal of Management,* June 1989, pp. 205–228.

37. Michael Beer, Russell A. Eisenstat, and Bert Spector, "Why Change Programs Don't Produce Change," *Harvard Business Review,* Vol. 68, No. 6 (November–December 1990), pp. 158–166.

38. French and Bell, *Organizational Development,* pp. 116–119. See also Gary Johns, *Organizational Behavior: Understanding Life at Work,* 3rd ed. (New York: HarperCollins, 1992), pp. 629–638.

39. Robert R. Blake and Jane S. Mouton, *The Versatile Manager: A Grid Profile,* (Homewood, Ill: Richard D. Irwin, 1981), Chap. 3 and pp. 239–261. See also Robert R. Blake and Anne Adams McCanse, *Leadership Dilemmas—Grid Solutions* (Houston, Tex.: Gulf, 1991), pp. 29–30, 38–40.

40. Stephen P. Robbins, *Organizational Behavior: Concepts, Controversies, and Applications,* 5th ed., (Englewood Cliffs, N.J.: Prentice Hall, 1992), pp. 428–430.

41. Yoshio Maruta, "Tetsuri: Advocated by Prince Shotoku as the Guideline of Management and R&D," unpublished invited paper, Second Annual Japan-U.S. Business Conference, Tokyo, April 1983.

42. Robbins, *Organizational Behavior: Concept, Controversies, and Applications,* p. 428.

43. Alfie Kohn, *No Contest: The Case Against Competition* (Boston: Houghton Mifflin, 1986), pp. 11–24. See also Richard Tanner Pascale, "The Renewal Factor: Constructive Contention," *Planning Review,* Vol. 18 (July–August 1990), pp. 4–13, 47–48.

44. Arthur G. Bedeian, Beverly G. Burke, and Richard G. Moffett, "Outcomes of Work-Family Conflict Among Married Male and Female

Professionals," *Journal of Management,* September 1988, pp. 475–485. See also Robert L. Kahn, "Role Conflict and Ambiguity in Organizations," *The Personnel Administrator,* Vol. 9 (1964), pp. 8–13.

45. Carl Kotchian, "Case Study—Lockheed Aircraft Corporation," in T. Donaldson and P. H. Werhane (eds.), *Ethical Issues in Business: A Philosophical Approach,* 2nd ed. (Englewood Cliffs, N.J.: Prentice Hall, 1983), pp. 25–43. See also Kenneth D. Alpherm, "Moral Dimensions of the Foreign Corrupt Practices Act: Comments on Pastin and Hooker," in Donaldson and Werhane, *Ethical Issues in Business: A Philosophical Approach,* pp. 52–57.

46. Jeffrey Pfeffer, *Power in Organizations* (Marshfield, Mass.: Pitman, 1981), p. 32.

47. Melville Dalton, "Conflicts Between Staff and Line Managerial Officers," *American Sociological Review,* Vol. 15 (1950), pp. 342–351.

48. Roger J. Volkema and Thomas J. Bergmann, "Interpersonal Conflict at Work: An Analysis of Behavioral Responses," *Human Relations,* Vol. 42 (September 1989), pp. 757–770. See also Robbins, *Organizational Behavior: Concepts, Controversies, and Applications,* pp. 434–436.

49. Stephen P. Robbins, *Managing Organizational Conflict: A Nontraditional Approach* (Englewood Cliffs, N.J.: Prentice Hall, 1974), p. 23.

50. Johns, *Organizational Behavior: Understanding Life at Work,* pp. 486–487.

51. Hans Selye, *Stress Without Distress* (New York: Signet Books, 1974), pp. 24–27. See also Hans Selye, "On the Real Benefits of Eustress," *Psychology Today,* March 1978, pp. 60–70.

52. James C. Quick and Jonathan D. Quick, *Organizational Stress and Preventive Management* (New York: McGraw-Hill, 1984), Chap. 2, pp. 18–42.

53. Ibid., pp. 59–63.

54. Ibid., pp. 294–295. See also Donald M. Vickery and James F. Fries, *Take Care of Yourself: A Consumer's Guide to Medical Care* (Reading, Mass.: Addison-Wesley and Xerox Corporation, 1979).

55. Selye, *Stress Without Distress,* pp. 27, 62–68. See also Quick and Quick, *Organizational Stress and Preventive Management,* Chap. 3.

56. Lublin, "Trying to Increase Worker Productivity, More Employers Alter Management Style," pp. B1, B3.

CHAPTER 16

1. Morey Stettner, "Salespeople Who Listen (and What They Find Out)," *Management Review,* June 1988, pp. 44–45.

2. Paul R. Timm, *Managerial Communication: A Finger on the Pulse* (Englewood Cliffs, N.J.: Prentice Hall, 1980), p. 4.

3. Linda M. Micheli, Frank V. Cespedes, Donald Byker, and Thomas J. C. Raymond, *Managerial Communications* (Glenview, Ill.: Scott Foresman, 1984), pp. 186–188.

4. Patricia L. Fry, "More Power to 'Em," *Entrepreneurial Woman,* January–February 1992, pp. 12–15.

5. Leslie Lamkin and Emily W. Carmain, "Crisis Communication at Georgia Power," *Personnel Journal,* Vol. 70 (January 1991), pp. 35–37.

6. Donald Jay Korn, "Dos and Don'ts in Managing Your Pension Plan: How to Assure Compliance with ERISA and the IRS," *Your Company,* Winter 1992, pp. 14–15.

7. Harold J. Leavitt and Ronald A. H. Mueller, "Some Effects of Feedback on Communicating," *Human Relations,* Vol. 4, No. 4 (1951), pp. 401–410.

8. Peter F. Drucker, *Management: Tasks, Responsibilities, Practices* (New York: Harper & Row, 1974), p. 483.

9. Fred Luthans and Janet K. Larsen, "How Managers Really Communicate," *Human Relations,* Vol. 39 (February 1986), pp. 161–178.

10. Christopher Knowlton, "How Disney Keeps the Magic Going," *Fortune,* December 4, 1989, pp. 111–132.

11. Michael J. Glauser, "Upward Information Flow in Organizations: Review and Conceptual Analysis," *Human Relations,* Vol. 37, No. 4 (1984), pp. 613–643.

12. Jonathan H. Amsbary and Patricia J. Staples, "Improving Administrator/Nurse Communication: A Case Study of 'Management by Wandering Around,'" *Journal of Business Communications,* Vol. 28, No. 2 (1991), pp. 101–111.

13. David Kirkpatrick, "Here Comes the Payoff from PCs," *Fortune,* March 23, 1992, pp. 93–97, 100, 102.

14. Patricia Galagan, "Donald E. Peterson, Chairman of Ford and Champion of Its People," *Training & Development Journal,* August 1988, pp. 20–24.

15. Keith Davis, "Management Communication and the Grapevine," *Harvard Business Review,* Vol. 31 (September–October 1953), pp. 43–49. See also Keith Davis, "Grapevine Communication Among Lower and Middle Managers," *Personnel Journal,* Vol. 48 (April 1969), pp. 269–271.

16. Hugh B. Vickery, "Tapping into the Employee Grapevine," *Association Management,* Vol. 36 (January 1984), pp. 59–60.

17. Roy Rowan, "Where Did That Rumor Come From?" *Fortune,* August 13, 1979, pp. 130–137. See also Janet Barnard, "The Information Environments of New Managers," *Journal of Business Communications,* Vol. 28, No. 4 (Fall 1991), pp. 312–324.

18. Kathleen J. Krone, "A Comparison of Organizational, Structural, and Relationship Effects on Subordinates' Upward Influence Choices," *Communication Quarterly,* Vol. 40, No. 1 (Winter 1992), pp. 1–15.

19. Walter Kiechel III, "The Art of the Corporate Task Force," *Fortune,* January 28, 1991, pp. 104–105.

20. Samuel A. Culbert and John J. McDonough, "The Invisible War: Pursuing Self-Interest at Work," in Peter J. Frost, Vance Mitchell, and Walter R. Nord (eds.), *Organizational Reality: Reports from the Firing Line,* 4th ed. (New York: HarperCollins, 1992), pp. 386–394.

21. Suellyn McMillan, "Squelching the Rumor Mill," *Personnel Journal,* Vol. 70 (October 1991), pp. 95–100.

22. Lyman W. Porter and Karlene H. Roberts, "Communication in Organizations," in Marvin D. Dunnette (ed.), *Handbook of Industrial and Occupational Psychology,* 2nd ed. (New York: John Wiley & Sons, 1983), pp. 1553–1589.

23. Robert H. Lengel and Richard L. Daft, "The Selection of Communication Media as an Executive Skill," *Academy of Management Executive,* Vol. 2 (August 1988), pp. 225–232.

24. Karin Ireland, "The Ethics Game," *Personnel Journal,* Vol. 70 (March 1991), pp. 72–75.

25. William G. Scott and Terence R. Mitchell, *Organizational Theory: A Structural and Behavioral Analysis* (Homewood, Ill.: Richard D. Irwin, 1972), p. 43.

26. James C. McCroskey and V. P. Richmond, "Willingness to Communicate: Differing Cultural Perspectives," *Southern Communication Journal,* Vol. 56 (1990), pp. 72–77.

27. James C. McCroskey, "Reliability and Validity of the Willingness to Communicate Scale," *Communication Quarterly,* Vol. 40, No. 1 (1992), pp. 16–25.

28. Gary Johns, *Organizational Behavior: Understanding Life at Work,* 3rd ed. (New York: HarperCollins, 1992), pp. 273–274, 384–385.

29. Henry W. Lane and Joseph J. DiStefano, *International Management Behavior,* 2nd ed. (Boston: PWS-Kent, 1992), p. 18.

30. Timothy M. Collins and Thomas L. Doorley, *Teaming Up for the 90s: A Guide to International Joint Ventures and Strategic Alliances* (Homewood, Ill.: Business One Irwin, 1991), pp. 315–320.

31. R. S. Teitelbaum, "Language: One Way to Think Globally," *Fortune,* December 4, 1989, pp. 11, 14.

32. Joann S. Lublin, "Young Managers Learn Global Skills," *Wall Street Journal,* March 31, 1992, p. B1.

33. Nancy J. Adler, *International Dimensions of Organizational Behavior* (Boston: PWS-Kent, 1986), pp. 52–54.

34. Lane and DiStefano, *International Management Behavior,* p. 19.

35. Richard E. Porter and Larry A. Samovar, "Approaching Intercultural Communication," *Intercultural Communications,* 5th ed. (Belmont, Calif.: Wadsworth, 1988), pp. 15–30. See also Patricia A. Galagan, "Executive Development in a Changing World," *Training and Development Journal,* June 1990, pp. 23–41.

36. Johns, *Organizational Behavior: Understanding Life at Work,* pp. 395–396.

37. André Laurent, "The Cross-Cultural Puzzle of International Human Resource Management," *Human Resource Management,* Vol. 25, No. 1 (1986), pp. 91–102. See also Albert H. Yee, *A People Misruled: Hong Kong and the Chinese Stepping Stone Syndrome* (Hong Kong: API Press, 1989), pp. 164–165.

38. A. Furnham and S. Bocher, *Culture Shock: Psychological Reactions to Unfamiliar Environments* (London: Methuen, 1986), pp. 207–208. See also Koh Sera, "Corporate Globalization: A New Trend," *Academy of Management Executive,* Vol. 6, No. 1 (1992), pp. 89–96.

39. "MBA's Learn a Human Touch," *Newsweek,* June 16, 1986, pp. 48–50; Johns, *Organizational Behavior: Understanding Life at*

Work, pp. 397–398; and T. S. Li, "Cultural Accommodation Can Open Doors," *China Progress,* March 9, 1992, p. 31.

40. Kim Griffin and Bobby R. Patton, *Fundamentals of Interpersonal Communication* (New York: Harper & Row, 1971), p. 111.

41. Kerry Rottenberger, "The Next Voice You Hear . . . ", *Sales & Marketing Management,* July 1991, pp. 50–54.

42. Stephen C. Rafe, "Credibility—Key to Communications Success," *Public Relations Journal,* Vol. 18 (1972), pp. 14–15.

43. Joan P. Klubnik, "Orienting New Employees," *Training and Development Journal,* April 1987, pp. 46–49.

44. Judi Brownell, "Perceptions of Effective Listeners: A Management Study," *Journal of Business Communications,* Vol. 27 (Fall 1990), pp. 401–415.

45. Selma Friedman, "Where Employees Go for Information," *Administrative Management,* Vol. 42 (1981), pp. 72–73. See also Cynthia Hamilton and Brian H. Kleiner, "Steps to Better Listening," *Personnel Journal,* Vol. 66 (February 1987), pp. 20–21.

46. A. Nicholas Komanecky, "Developing New Mangers at GE," *Training and Development Journal,* June 1988, pp. 62–64.

47. Ernest G. Bormann, William S. Howell, Ralph G. Nichols, and George L. Shapiro, *Interpersonal Communications in Modern Organizations* (Englewood Cliffs, N.J.: Prentice Hall, 1969), pp. 148–149.

48. William V. Haney, *Communication and Organizational Behavior* (Homewood, Ill.: Richard D. Irwin, 1973), pp. 379–381.

49. Ibid., p. 522.

50. Jay A. Conger, "Inspiring Others: The Language of Leadership," *Academy of Management Executive,* Vol. 5, No. 1 (1991), pp. 31–45; J. P. Kahn, "Steven Jobs of Apple Computer: The Missionary of Micros," *Inc.,* April 1984, p. 83; Brian O'Reilly, "Growing Apple Anew for the Business Market," *Fortune,* January 4, 1988, pp. 36–37; Brenton R. Schlender, "The Future of the PC," *Fortune,* August 26, 1991, pp. 40–44, 48; and "Jobs and Gates Together," *Fortune,* August 26, 1991, pp. 50, 54.

51. Jaclyn Fierman, "Why Women Still Don't Hit the Top," *Fortune,* July 30, 1990, pp. 40–44. See also Joann S. Lublin, "Rights Law to Spur Shifts in Promotions," *Wall Street Journal,* December 30, 1991.

52. Anne Wilson-Schaef, "The Female System and the White Male System: New Ways of Looking at Our Culture," in Frost, Mitchell, and Nord (eds.), *Organizational Reality: Reports from the Firing Line,* pp. 132–143.

53. Fierman, "Why Women Still Don't Hit the Top," p. 41. See also Wilson-Schaef, "The Female System and the White Male System: New Ways of Looking at Our Culture," pp. 134–135.

54. Leland Brown, *Communicating Facts and Ideas in Business,* 3rd ed. (Englewood Cliffs, N.J.: Prentice Hall, 1982), pp. 14–15. See also Carl R. Rogers and F. J. Roethlisberger, "Barriers and Gateways to Communication," *Harvard Business Review,* Vol. 69 (November–December 1991), pp. 105–111.

55. Johns, *Organizational Behavior: Understanding Life at Work,* pp. 400–403; Brian Dumaine, "Creating a New Company Culture," *Fortune,* January 15, 1990, p. 130; Peggy Yuhas Byers and James R. Wilcox, "Focus Groups: A Qualitative Opportunity for Researchers," *Journal of Business Communications,* Vol. 28, No. 1 (1991), pp. 63–77; and William H. Peace, "The Hard Work of Being a Soft Manager," *Harvard Business Review,* Vol. 69 (November–December 1991), pp. 40–42, 46–47.

56. Stettner, "Salespeople Who Listen (and What They Find Out)," pp. 44.

CHAPTER 17

1. Hal Lancaster and Michael Allen, "Dell Computer Battles Its Rivals with a Lean Machine," *Wall Street Journal,* March 30, 1992, p. B4.

2. Peter F. Drucker, *People and Performance: The Best of Peter Drucker on Management* (New York: Harper & Row, 1977), p. 343.

3. Helmut A. Welke and John Overbeeke, "Cellular Manufacturing: A Good Technique for Implementing Just-in-Time and Total Quality Control," *Industrial Engineering,* (November 1988), pp. 36–41.

4. William P. Barrett, "Annual Report on American Industry: Energy," *Forbes,* January 6, 1992, pp. 134–137.

5. Joel Dreyfus, "Victories in the Quality Crusade," *Fortune,* October 10, 1988, pp. 84–85.

6. Jeremy Main, "Is the Baldrige Overblown?" *Fortune,* July 1, 1991, pp. 62–65.

7. J. M. Juran, *Juran on Planning for Quality* (New York: The Free Press, 1988), pp. 71–73.

8. Michael A. Cusumano, *The Japanese Automobile Industry: Technology and Management at Nissan and Toyota* (Cambridge, Mass.: Harvard University Press, 1985), p. 351. See also Richard J. Schonberger, *Japanese Manufacturing Techniques: Nine Hidden Lessons in Simplicity* (New York: The Free Press, 1982), pp. 53–55.

9. James B. Teece and David Woodruff, "Crunch Time Again for Chrysler," *Business Week,* March 25, 1991, pp. 92–94.

10. Lois Therrien, "Motorola and NEC: Going for the Glory," *Business Week: Quality,* Special Issue, October 25, 1991, pp. 60–61.

11. David H. Holt, personal communication and consulting with Falconer Glass Industries, Inc., Jamestown, New York.

12. Peter F. Drucker, *Management: Tasks, Responsibilities, Practices* (New York: Harper & Row, 1974), p. 494.

13. William H. Newman, *Constructive Control* (Englewood Cliffs, N.J.: Prentice Hall, 1975), pp. 5–9. See also Robert H. Hayes, Steven C. Wheelwright, and Kim B. Clark, *Dynamic Manufacturing* (New York: The Free Press, 1988), pp. 219–228.

14. Schonberger, *Japanese Manufacturing Techniques: Nine Hidden Lessons in Simplicity,* pp. 89–90. See also Eric N. Berkowitz, Roger A. Kerin, Steven W. Hartley, and William Rudelius, *Marketing,* 3rd ed. (Homewood, Ill.: Irwin, 1992), pp. 231, 504.

15. Welke and Overbeeke, "Cellular Manufacturing: A Good Technique for Implementing Just-in-Time and Total Quality Control," pp. 37–38.

16. Joseph M. Juran and Frank M. Gryna, Jr., *Quality Planning and Analysis,* 2nd ed. (New York: McGraw-Hill, 1980), pp. 275–276.

17. Elwood S. Buffa and Jeffrey G. Miller, *Production-Inventory Systems: Planning and Control,* 3rd ed. (Homewood, Ill.: Irwin, 1979) p. 161.

18. Juran, *Juran on Planning for Quality,* pp. 297–300.

19. John H. Sheridan, "Racing Against Time," *Industry Week,* June 17, 1991, pp. 23–26.

20. Larry Armstrong and William C. Symonds, "Beyond 'May I Help You?'" *Business Week/Quality,* October 25, 1991, pp. 100–103.

21. Ross H. Johnson and Richard T. Weber, *Buying Quality* (New York: Franklin Watts, 1985), pp. 19–23. See also Robert L. Frigo, "How to Improve Productivity," *Financial Executive,* Vol. 7 (March–April 1991), pp. 14–16.

22. Glenn A. Welsch, Ronald W. Hilton, and Paul N. Gordon, *Budgeting: Profit Planning and Control,* 5th ed. (Englewood Cliffs, N.J.: Prentice Hall, 1988), pp. 49–51, 631–639.

23. W. Edwards Deming, *Out of the Crisis* (Cambridge, Mass.: MIT Center for Advanced Engineering Study, 1986), p. 3.

24. Robert C. Camp, *Benchmarking: The Search for Industry's Best Practices That Lead to Superior Performance* (Milwaukee, Wis.: ASQC Quality Press, 1989), p. 1.

25. David Altany, "Copycats," *Industry Week,* November 5, 1990, pp. 11–18.

26. A. Steven Walleck, "A Backstage View of World-Class Performers," *Wall Street Journal,* August 26, 1991, p. A10.

27. Charles G. Mertens, "APICS Initiates New Program Format," *Production & Inventory Management Review,* April 1988, p. 11.

28. *Annual Survey of Manufacturers, 1989–90* (Washington, D.C.: U.S. Department of Commerce, 1990), p. 2. See also Charles G. Andrew and George A. Johnson, "The Crucial Importance of Production and Operations Management," *The Academy of Management Review,* Vol. 7, No. 1 (1982), pp. 143–147.

29. Alan Radding, "Super Servers: Waiting in the Wings," *Infoworld,* April 6, 1992, pp. 46–50.

30. Richard J. Schonberger, *World Class Manufacturing Casebook: Implementing JiT and TQC* (New York: The Free Press, 1987), pp. 13–14.

31. Ned Snell, "Bar Codes Break Out," *Datamation,* April 1, 1992, pp. 71–73.

32. Richard J. Schonberger, *Building a Chain of Customers: Linking Business Functions to Create the World-Class Company* (New York: The Free Press, 1990), pp. 154–160. See also Robert G. Eccles, "The Performance Measurement Manifesto," *Harvard Business Review,* Vol. 69 (January–February 1991), pp. 131–137.

33. Mark Schlack, "IS Has a New Job in Manufacturing," *Datamation,* January 15, 1992, pp. 38–40.

34. Paul L. Blocklyn, "Making Magic: The Disney Approach to People Management," *Personnel,* December 1988, pp. 28–35.

35. Brad Stratton, "How Disneyland Works," *Quality Progress,* July 1991, pp. 17–30. See also Rick Johnson, "A Strategy for Service—Disney Style," *The Journal of Business Strategy,* Vol. 12 (September–October 1991), pp. 38–43.

36. Thomas Moore, "Goodbye, Corporate Staff," *Fortune,* December 21, 1987, pp. 65–76.

37. Bridget O'Brian, "American to Simplify Fares, Shrink Price Range," *Wall Street Journal,* April 9, 1992, pp. B1, B6.

38. Berkowitz, Kerin, Hartley, and Rudelius, *Marketing,* pp. 382–384, 446.

39. J. Fred Weston and Eugene F. Brigham, *Essentials of Managerial Finance,* 8th ed. (New York: The Dryden Press, 1987), pp. 240–248.

40. Mark Taber, "Systems Management Beyond the Glass House," *Datamation,* March 15, 1992, pp. 63–67.

41. Jack L. Smith, Robert M. Keith, and William L. Stephens, *Accounting Principles,* 3rd ed. (New York: McGraw-Hill, 1989), p. 10.

42. Ibid., pp. 1012–26.

43. Thomas E. Gorley, Jr., and Paul D. Applegate, "Managing Investment in Technology Assets," *Public Utilities Fortnightly,* January 1992, pp. 39–40.

44. Welsch, Hilton, and Gordon, *Budgeting: Profit Planning and Control,* pp. 41–42, 596–598.

45. Linda J. Shinn and M. Sue Sturgeon, *"Budgeting from Ground Zero," Association Management,* Vol. 42 (1990), pp. 45–48.

46. Mark W. Dirsmith and Stephen F. Jablonsky, "Zero-Base Budgeting as a Management Technique and Political Strategy," *Academy of Management Review,* Vol. 4, No. 4 (1978), pp. 215–225.

47. "Hospitals Dismantle Elaborate Corporate Restructurings," *Hospitals,* Vol. 65 (July 1991), pp. 41–48. See also John B. Goodman and Gary W. Loveman, "Does Privatization Serve the Public Interest?" *Harvard Business Review,* Vol. 69 (November–December 1991), pp. 26–38.

48. D. R. Carmichael, Wayne G. Bremser, Lawrence J. Gramling, and Philip E. Lint, "Auditing," *The CPA Journal,* (May 1988), pp. 75–78.

49. Keith Davis and Robert L. Blomstrom, *"Implementing the Social Audit in an Organization," Business and Society Review,* Vol. 16 (1975), pp. 13–18.

50. Maynard M. Gordon, *The Iacocca Management Technique* (New York: Ballantine Books, 1985), pp. 61, 131. See also James T. MaKenna, "Delta Weighs Aid to Pan Am After Talks with United Fail," *Aviation Week & Space Technology,* Vol. 135 (1991), pp. 18–19.

51. William H. Newman, *Constructive Control: Design and Use of Control Systems* (Englewood Cliffs, N.J.: Prentice Hall, 1975), pp. 80–81. See also Terry Newell, "Applying a Consulting Model to Managerial Behavior," in J. William Pfeiffer (ed.), *The Annual 1988: Developing Human Resources* (San Diego, Cal.: University Associates, 1988), pp. 229–243.

52. Lancaster and Allen, "Dell Computer Battles Its Rivals with a Lean Machine," p. B4.

CHAPTER 18

1. Barbara Dutton, "Quality in the Glen," *Manufacturing Systems,* March 1992, pp. 20–26.

2. Glenn A. Welsch, Ronald W. Hilton, and Paul N. Gordon, *Budgeting: Profit Planning and Control,* 5th ed. (Englewood Cliffs, N.J.: Prentice Hall, 1988), pp. 639–640.

3. Peter F. Drucker, *People and Performance: The Best of Peter Drucker on Management* (New York: Harper & Row, 1977), p. 97.

4. David A. Garvin, "Competing on the Eight Dimensions of Quality," *Harvard Business Review,* Vol. 87, No. 6 (November–December 1987), pp. 101–109.

5. Robert E. Cole, "The Quality Revolution," *Production and Operations Management,* Vol. 1, No. 1 (Winter 1992), pp. 118–120.

6. Armand V. Feigenbaum, *Total Quality Control,* 3rd ed. (New York: McGraw-Hill, 1983), pp. 823–829.

7. Steve D. Doherty, "Roadblocks to Total Quality Management," *Quality,* April 1992, pp. 62–66.

8. John A. Byrne, "The Prophet of Quality," *Business Week,* January 28, 1991, p. 14. See also W. Edwards Deming, *Out of the Crisis* (Cambridge, Mass.: MIT Center for Advanced Engineering Study, 1986), pp. 1–12.

9. Kate Ballen, "America's Most Admired Corporations," *Fortune,* February 10, 1992, pp. 40–43, 46; "How Companies Rank in 32 Industries," *Fortune,* February 10, 1992, pp. 52–53, 57–59, 76; and Steve Kichen, "Annual Report on American Industry," *Forbes,* January 6, 1992, pp. 94–95.

10. Feigenbaum, *Total Quality Control*, pp. 339–340.

11. J. M. Duran and Frank M. Gryna, Jr., *Quality Planning and Analysis,* 2nd ed. (New York: McGraw-Hill, 1980), p. 14.

12. Ross H. Johnson and Richard T. Weber, *Buying Quality* (Milwaukee, Wis.: Quality Press, 1988), pp. 12–15.

13. Jeremy Rifkin, *Entropy* (New York: Bantam Books, 1980), p. 3.

14. "The Quality Imperative," *Business Week/ Quality 1991,* Special Issue, August 1991, pp. 7–11.

15. Philip B. Crosby, *Quality Without Tears* (New York: New American Library, 1984), pp. 3–5.

16. Juran and Gryna, *Quality Planning and Analysis,* pp. 408–409.

17. J. M. Juran, *Juran on Planning for Quality* (New York: The Free Press, 1988), p. 1. See also Tracy E. Benson, "International Quality Study: Challenging Global Myths," *Industry Week,* October 7, 1991, pp. 13–25.

18. Personal communication with David B. Landry, vice president, Dental Research Corporation, manufacturer of Interplak, April 1990. See also Erik Calonius, "Smart Moves by Quality Champs," *Fortune,* Special Issue, Fall 1991, pp. 24–28.

19. Juran and Gryna, *Quality Planning and Analysis,* pp. 464–470.

20. Ibid., p. 467; Suein L. Hwang, "Its Big Brands Long Taunted as Fatty, CPC Tries a More 'Wholesome' Approach," *Wall Street Journal.* April 20, 1992, pp. B1, B8; and Bruce Ingersoll, "Label Rules to Foster Healthful Foods," *Wall Street Journal,* December 26, 1991, pp. B1, B4.

21. Richard A. Bettis, Stephen P. Bradley, and Gary Hamel, "Outsourcing and Industrial Decline," *Academy of Management Executive,* Vol. 6, No. 1 (1992), pp. 7–22.

22. Otis Port and John Carey, "Questing for the Best," *Business Week/Quality,* October 25, 1991, pp. 8–11, 14–16.

23. Elwood S. Buffa and Jeffrey G. Miller, *Production-Inventory Systems: Planning and Control,* 3rd ed. (Homewood, Ill.: Irwin, 1979), pp. 609–610.

24. "Problem Identification and Progress Planning in Systems Development," *Field Protocols* (Denver: Price Waterhouse, 1992), pp. 45–58.

25. Bulent Kobu and Frank Greenwood, "Continuous Improvement in a Competitive Global Economy," *Production and Inventory Management Journal,* Vol. 32, No. 4 (1991), pp. 58–63.

26. Robert E. Stein, "Beyond Statistical Process Control," *Production and Inventory Management Journal,* Vol. 32, No. 1 (1991), pp. 7–10.

27. "On-line Monitor," *Quality,* April 1992, p. 55.

28. John A. Buzacott and J. George Shanthikumar, "A General Approach for Coordinating Production in Multiple-Cell Manufacturing Systems," *Production and Operations Management,* Vol. 1, No. 1 (1992), pp. 34–52.

29. Lee Kneppelt, "The 'Real' Real-Time Manufacturing Systems," *APICS—The Performance Advantage,* October 1991, pp. 24–26.

30. Tom Inglesby, "Time Waits for No Man(ufacturer)," *HP/Manufacturing Systems,* June 1991, pp. 4–20; Kalyan Singhal, "Introduction: Shaping the Future of Manufacturing and Service Operations," *Production and Operations Management,* Vol. 1, No. 1 (1992), pp. 1–4; and Dutton, "Quality in the Glen," pp. 20–26.

31. Tom Baker and Gerry Cleaves, "World-Class Performance," *APICS—The Performance Advantage,* October 1991, pp. 28–31.

32. Eberhard E. Scheuing, *Purchasing Management* (Englewood Cliffs, N.J.: Prentice Hall, 1989), p. 4.

33. John C. Malley and Ruthann Ray, "Informational and Organizational Impacts of Implementing a JIT System," *Production and Inventory Management Journal,* Vol. 29, No. 2 (1988), pp. 66–70.

34. "Getting to World Class: What Carriers Do," *Purchasing,* August 15, 1991, p. 81.

35. John R. Emshwiller, "Suppliers Struggle to Improve Quality as Big Firms Slash Their Vendor Rolls," *Wall Street Journal,* August 16, 1991, pp. B1, B2.

36. Robert W. Hall, *Zero Inventories* (Homewood, Ill.: Irwin, 1983), pp. 109–111, 166. See also Johnson and Weber, *Buying Quality,* p. 2.

37. Joseph Sarkis, "Production and Inventory Control Issues in Advanced Manufacturing Systems," *Production and Inventory Management Journal,* Vol. 32, No. 1 (1991), pp. 76–82.

38. Ibid., p. 77.

39. Susan Connor, "Integrating Quality Efforts in Process Production," *Manufacturing Systems,* March 1992, pp. 35–36, 38, 40.

40. Stephen H. Replogle, "The Strategic Use of Smaller Lot Sizes Through a New EOQ Model," *Production and Inventory Management Journal,* Vol. 29, No. 3 (1988), pp. 41–44. See also T. C. E. Cheng, "An EOQ Model with Learning Effects on Setups," *Production and Inventory Management Journal,* Vol. 32, No. 1 (1991), pp. 83–84.

41. Stuart F. Heinritz and Paul V. Farrell, *Purchasing: Principles and Applications,* 6th ed. (Englewood Cliffs, N.J.: Prentice Hall, 1981), p. 154.

42. Marcia Migliorelli and Robert J. Swan, "MRP and Aggregate Planning—A Problem Solution," *Production and Inventory Management Journal,* Vol. 29, No. 2 (1988), pp. 42–44.

43. Buzacott and Shanthikumar, "A General Approach for Coordinating Production in Multiple-Cell Manufacturing Systems," pp. 34–52. See also Richard J. Schonberger, *World Class Manufacturing Casebook: Implementing JIT and TQC* (New York: The Free Press, 1987), pp. xi–xxii.

44. Ed Shankle, "How About JIT and MRP II?" *Production and Inventory Management,* January 1992, p. 12–13.

45. Richard J. Schonberger, *Japanese Manufacturing Techniques: Nine Hidden Lessons in Simplicity* (New York: The Free Press, 1982), p. 158.

46. Ibid., p. 220. See also Alex Taylor, "Why Toyota Keeps Getting Better and Better and Better," *Fortune,* November 19, 1990, pp. 66–68, 78–79.

47. Schonberger, *Japanese Manufacturing Techniques: Nine Hidden Lessons in Simplicity,* pp. 15–16.

48. M. T. Midas, "The Productivity/Quality Connection," in Y. K. Shetty and V. M. Buehler (eds.), *Quality and Productivity Improvements: U.S. & Foreign Company Experiences* (Chicago: Manufacturing Productivity Center, 1983), pp. 27–40.

49. David A. Garvin, "Quality on the Line," *Harvard Business Review,* Vol. 83, No. 5 (September–October, 1983), pp. 65–75.

50. Schonberger, *Japanese Manufacturing Techniques: Nine Hidden Lessons in Simplicity,* p. 16.

51. Don Sheldon, Jr., "MRP II—What It Really Is," *Production and Inventory Management Journal,* Vol. 32, No. 3 (1991), p. 12–15.

52. Terence R. Lautenbach, "MIS at IBM: Improving the Business Through Better Communications," *Academy of Management Executive,* Vol. III, No. 1 (1989), pp. 26–28.

53. Jack B. ReVelle and Hugh Jordan Harrington, "Use of Statistical Process/Quality Control in the Defense Industries," |*IE*|, February 1988, pp. 36–40.

54. Alan Luber, "Living in the Real World of Computer Interfaced Manufacturing," *Production & Inventory Management,* September 1991, pp. 10–11.

55. Shankle, "How About JIT and MRP II?", pp. 12–13.

56. W. Calvin Wasco, Robert E. Stonehocker, and Larry H. Feldman, "Success with JIT and MRP II in a Service Organization," *Production and Inventory Management Journal,* Vol. 32, No. 4 (1991), pp. 15–21.

57. Shankle, "How About JIT and MRP II?", pp. 12–13.

58. Dutton, "Quality in the Glen," pp. 20–26.

CHAPTER 19

1. Mark Taber, "Systems Management Beyond the Glass House," *Datamation,* March 15, 1992, pp. 63–67.

2. Torsten Busse, "Enterprise Computing: Say Goodbye to Sneakernet," *Infoworld,* March 2, 1992, pp. 49–57.

3. Larry Long, *Management Information Systems* (Englewood Cliffs, N.J.: Prentice Hall, 1989), pp. 10–11.

4. Houston H. Carr, *Managing End User Computing* (Englewood Cliffs, N.J.: Prentice Hall, 1988), p. 3.

5. Ken Yamada, "Almost Like Being There," *Wall Street Journal,* April 6, 1992, p. R10.

6. Mike Ricciuti, "Software Manufacturing: Connect Manufacturing to the Enterprise," *Datamation,* January 15, 1992, pp. 42–44.

7. "Process Monitoring with Vision," *Quality,* April 1992, pp. 39–41.

8. Mark Schlack, "IS Has a New Job in Manufacturing," *Datamation,* January 15, 1992, pp. 38–40. See also Cheryl Currid, "IS Departments Haven't Dispelled Their Images as Villains," *Infoworld,* February 17, 1992, p. 53.

9. Long, *Management Information Systems,* pp. 16–18, 26.

10. David Coursey, "CIO Shares Advice on Avoiding Pitfalls," *Management Information Systems Week,* April 3, 1989, p. 38.

11. Steven L. Mandell, *Computers and Data Processing: Concepts and Applications with BASIC,* 2nd. ed. (New York: West Publishing Company, 1982), p. 378.

12. Alice LaPlante, "Help from End-users Strengthens I.S. Department's Efficiency," *Infoworld,* February 3, 1992, p. 51.

13. Mandell, *Computers and Data Processing,* pp. 379–380.

14. Douglas W. Richardson, "A Call for Action: Integrating CIM and MRP II," *Production and Inventory Management Journal,* Second Quarter 1988, pp. 32–35.

15. Olin Thompson, "Computer-Integrated Manufacturing in the Process Industry," *P&IM Review,* February 1991, pp. 38–39.

16. Kalyan Ginghal, "Introduction: Shaping the Future of Manufacturing and Service Operations," *Production and Operations Management,* Vol. 1, No. 1 (1992), pp. 1–4; Alice LaPlante, "Retraining Staff Is Crucial to a Shift to Information Management," *Infoworld,* February 17, 1992, p. 52; and Ricciuti, "Software Manufacturing: Connect Manufacturing to the Enterprise," pp. 42–44.

17. Alice LaPlante, "Decentralizing Systems Is Not the Best Solution for Everyone," *Infoworld,* March 9, 1992, p. 57.

18. "Office Automation: Making It Pay Off," *Business Week,* October 12, 1987, pp. 134–146.

19. Michael Fitzgerald, "System Odyssey Leads to Outsourcing," *Computerworld,* February 17, 1992, pp. 75–76.

20. Matt Kramer, "Keep an Ear Out for New Voice Technology," *PC Week,* April 10, 1989, p. 63.

21. Carr, *Managing End User Computing,* pp. 130–131.

22. Mike Feuche, "MIS Managers Aided Now by PC Programs," *Management Information Systems Weekly,* April 10, 1989, p. 44.

23. Charles S. Parker, *Management Information Systems: Strategy and Action* (New York: McGraw-Hill, 1989), pp. 368–369.

24. Long, *Management Information Systems,* pp. 234–235.

25. Richard Chen, "Distributed Data Processing Considerations," *Journal of Systems Management,* June 1986, pp. 10–13.

26. Taber, "Systems Management Beyond the Glass House," pp. 63–67. See also Alan Radding, "Enterprise Computing: Super Servers Waiting in the Wings," *Infoworld,* April 6, 1992, pp. 46–50.

27. Ibid., p. 50.

28. Dorothy Leonard-Barton and John J. Sviokla, "Putting Expert Systems to Work," *Harvard Business Review,* Vol. 88, No. 2 (March–April 1988), pp. 91–98.

29. John P. Gallagher, *Knowledge Systems for Business: Integrating Expert Systems & MIS* (Englewood Cliffs, N.J.: Prentice Hall, 1988), p. 23.

30. Robert Haavind, "Playing to Win a New Generation," *High Technology,* August 1985, pp. 63–65. See also Marilyn M. Parker and Robert J. Benson with H. E. Trainor, *Information Economics: Linking Business Performance to Information Technology* (Englewood Cliffs, N.J.: Prentice Hall, 1988), pp. 21–22.

31. Gallagher, *Knowledge Systems for Business: Integrating Expert Systems & MIS,* pp. 24–25.

32. M. W. Thring, *Robots and Telechirs: Manipulators with Memory; Remote Manipulators; Machine Limbs for the Handicapped* (New York: Wiley, 1983), pp. 33–39. See also Kenneth Fordyce, Peter Norden, and Gerald Sullivan, "Review of Expert Systems for Management Science Practitioner," *Interfaces,* Vol. 17, No. 2 (1987), pp. 64–77.

33. *Commercial Biotechnology: An International Analysis* (Washington, D.C.: U.S. Government Printing Office, 1984), pp. 2–4. See also Jay Liebowitz, *Introduction to Expert Systems* (Santa Cruz, Cal.: Mitchell, 1988), pp. 17–19.

34. Tim R. V. Davis, "Information Technology and White-Collar Productivity," *Academy of Management Executive,* Vol. 5, No. 1 (1991), pp. 55–67.

35. Charles E. Catlett, "The NFSNET: Beginnings of a National Research Internet," *Academic Computing,* January 1989, pp. 18–21, 59–64. See also Richard A. Danca, "EPA Reorganizes Data Division, Focuses on Network Computing," *Federal Computer Week,* February 3, 1992, p. 8.

36. David Kirkpatrick, "Here Comes the Payoff from PCs," *Fortune,* March 23, 1992, pp. 93–97, 100, 102.

37. "Information Power: How Companies Are Using New Technologies to Gain a Competitive Edge," *Business Week,* October 14, 1985, pp. 108–116. See also William M. Bulkeley, "Special Systems Make Computing Less Traumatic for Top Executives," *Wall Street Journal,* June 20, 1988, p. 17.

38. Karyl Scott, "LAN Interconnection Demands on the Rise," *Infoworld,* February 3, 1992, p. 43. See also Susan Kerr, "Wireless Works, Within Limits," *Datamation,* February 1, 1992, pp. 38–40.

39. Lynda M. Applegate, James I. Cash, Jr., and D. Quinn Mills, "Information Technology and Tomorrow's Manager," *Havard Business Review,* Vol. 88, No. 6 (November–December 1988), pp. 128–136.

40. Tom McCusker, "HP Opens Up Network Management," *Datamation,* February 15, 1992, pp. 22–26; Kim Spitznagel, "Micro or Workstation? NeXT Computer's View," *Manufacturing Systems,* March 1992, p. 14–MM; and Mark Taber, "Can OfficeVision Take Off with Notes?" *Datamation,* February 15, 1992, pp. 65–68.

41. David Owen, "Expect the Worst" *Information Strategy: The Executive's Journal,* Vol. 6 (1990), pp. 46–48. See also Ed Foster, "It Makes Me Very Insecure When People Say That Even Unix Isn't Safe," *Infoworld,* February 3, 1992, p. 52.

42. Helena Stalson, "Intellectual Property Rights and U.S. Competitiveness," *Economic Impact,* Vol. 64, No. 3 (1988), pp. 6–11. See also U.S. Office of Technology Assessment, "Disseminating Information: Evolution of a Concept," *Economic Impact,* Vol. 64, No. 3 (1988), pp. 18–23.

43. Kenneth P. Weiss, "Controlling the Threat to Computer Security," *Management Review,* Vol. 79 (June 1990), pp. 54–57. See also John Schwartz, "The Hacker Dragnet," *Newsweek,* April 30, 1990, p. 50.

44. Long, *Management Information Systems,* pp. 448–449.

45. Rita P. Hull and Louis E. Serio, Jr., "What Managers Should Know About Computer Security," *Business,* Vol. 37 (October–December 1987), pp. 3–8.

CHAPTER 20

1. Ken Wells, "Adventure Capitalist Is Nipping at the Tail of Big British Airways," *Wall Street Journal,* May 22, 1992, pp. A1, A6.

2. David H. Holt, *Entrepreneurship: New Venture Creation* (Englewood Cliffs, N.J.: 1992), pp. 3–4.

3. Richard Cantillon, *Essai sur la nature du commerce en général,* trans. H. Higgs (London: Macmillan, 1931), pp. 47–49, 151–153.

4. Adam Smith, *Inquiry into the Nature and Causes of the Wealth of Nations,* originally printed in Glasgow, Scotland, 1776; reprinted as *The Wealth of Nations* (New York: Random House, 1937), pp. 48–49, 86, 114.

5. Jean Baptiste Say, *A Treatise on Political Economy,* 4th ed., trans. C. R. Prinsep (Philadelphia: Grigg & Elliot, 1845), pp. 99–100, 330–332.

6. Carl Menger, *Principles of Economics,* trans. J. Dingwall and D. F. Hoselitz (Glencoe, Ill.: The Free Press, 1950), pp. 8–14, 56–57.

7. *The Entrepreneurs: An American Adventure,* Film Series Vol. 2 and Academic Supplement (Boston: Enterprise Media, 1987), pp. 4–6.

8. Joseph A. Schumpeter, *The Theory of Economic Development,* trans. R. Opie (Cambridge, Mass.: Harvard University Press, 1934), pp. 42–46, 78–79. See also Joseph A. Schumpeter, "Economic Theory and Entrepreneurial History," in Hugh G. J. Aitken (ed.), *Explorations in Enterprise* (Cambridge, Mass.: Harvard University Press, 1965), pp. 45–64.

9. Peter F. Drucker, *Managing for Results* (New York: Harper & Row, 1964), p. 5.

10. Peter F. Drucker, *Management, Tasks, Responsibilities, Practices* (New York: Harper & Row, 1974), p. 45.

11. Arnold C. Cooper, Carolyn Y. Woo, and William C. Dunkelberg, "Entrepreneurs' Perceived Chances for Success," *Journal of Business Venturing,* Vol. 3, No. 2 (Spring 1988), pp. 97–108.

12. Robert D. Hisrich, "Entrepreneurship: Past, Present, and Future," *Journal of Small Business Management,* Vol. 26, No. 4 (1988), pp. 1–4. See also Karl H. Vesper, *Entrepreneurship Education* (Wellesley, Mass.: Center for Entrepreneurial Studies, Babson College, 1991).

13. Schumpeter, *Theory of Economic Development,* p. 74.

14. Robert C. Ronstadt, *Entrepreneurship: Text, Cases and Notes* (Dover, Mass.: Lord, 1984), p. 28.

15. Karl H. Vesper, *New Venture Strategies* (Englewood Cliffs, N.J.: Prentice Hall, 1980), p. 2.

16. John A. Hornaday, "Research About Living Entrepreneurs," in Calvin A. Kent, Donald L. Sexton, and Karl H. Vesper (eds.), *Encyclopedia of Entrepreneurship* (Englewood Cliffs, N.J.: Prentice Hall, 1982), pp. 20–34.

17. A. David Silver, *The Entrepreneurial Life* (New York: Wiley, 1983), p. 26.

18. John W. Wilson, *The New Venturers: Inside the High-Stakes World of Venture Capital* (Reading, Mass.: Addison-Wesley, 1985), pp. 38–39.

19. Albert Shapero and Lisa Sokol, "The Social Dimensions of Entrepreneurship," in Kent, Sexton, and Vesper, *Encyclopedia of Entrepreneurship,* pp. 72–88. See also Jeanne Saddler, "Start-ups Bloom Amid Economic Gloom," *Wall Street Journal,* March 30, 1992, p. B1.

20. Matthew Schifrin, "Horatio Alger Kim," *Forbes,* October 17, 1988, pp. 92–96.

21. Eric Flamholtz, *How to Make the Transition from an Entrepreneurship to a Professionally Managed Firm* (San Francisco: Jossey-Bass, 1986), pp. 3–16.

22. Gifford Pinchot III, *Intrapreneuring* (New York: Harper & Row, 1985), pp. 282–284.

23. Hans Schollhammer, "Internal Corporate Entrepreneurship," in Kent, Sexton, & Vesper, *Encyclopedia of Entrepreneurship,* pp. 209–223.

24. Ibid., pp. 211–219. See also Terry E. Winters and Donald L. Murfin, "Venture Capital Investing for Corporate Development Objectives," *Journal of Business Venturing,* Vol. 3, No. 3 (1988), pp. 207–222.

25. Watts S. Humphrey, *Managing for Innovation: Leading Technical People* (Englewood Cliffs, N.J.: Prentice Hall, 1987), pp. 92–93.

26. M. C. Sherman, "The Small Bank That Thinks Big," *Bankers Monthly,* January 1988, pp. 60–62. See also "They Sell Their Secrets," *Intrapreneurial Excellence,* March 1987, p. 5.

27. John J. Kao, *Entrepreneurship, Creativity, & Organization* (Englewood Cliffs, N.J.: Prentice Hall, 1989), pp. 236–237; William M. Buckeley, "Software Industry Loses Start-up Zest as Big Firms Increase Their Dominance," *Wall Street Journal,* August 27, 1991, pp. B1, B5; and Julie Pitta, "Lean, Mean & Smart: Computers & Communications," *Forbes,* January 6, 1992, pp. 112–114.

28. Ira C. Magaziner and Mark Patinkin, "Fast Heat: How Korea Won the Microwave War," *Harvard Business Review,* Vol. 89, No. 1 (January–February 1989), pp. 83–92.

29. Dennis P. Slevin and Jeffrey G. Covin, "Juggling Entrepreneurial Style and Organizational Structure: How to Get Your Act Together," *Sloan Management Review,* Vol. 30, No. 1 (1990), pp. 43–53.

30. Christopher K. Bart, "New Venture Units: Use Them Wisely to Manage Innovation," *Sloan Management Review,* Vol. 28, No. 3 (1988), pp. 35–43.

31. Hollister B. Sykes, "Lessons from a New Ventures Program," *Harvard Business Review,* Vol. 86, No. 3 (May–June 1986), pp. 69–74.

32. Pinchot, *Intrapreneuring,* pp. 205–206.

33. Ibid., pp. 60–61, 280–281.

34. Bart, "New Venture Units: Use Them Wisely to Manage Innovation," pp. 36–37.

35. Holt, *Entrepreneurship: New Venture Creation,* pp. 101–132. See also Robert Ronstadt, "Ex-Entrepreneurs and the Decision to Start an Entrepreneurial Career," in John A. Hornaday, Fred Tarpley, Jr., Jeffry A. Timmons, and Karl H. Vesper (eds.), *Frontiers of Entrepreneurship Research* (Wellesley, Mass.: Center for Entrepreneurial Studies, Babson College, 1984), pp. 437–460.

36. Arnold C. Cooper, "The Entrepreneurship–Small Business Interface," in Kent, Sexton, and Vesper, *Encyclopedia of Entrepreneurship,* pp. 193–205.

37. Brett Kingstone, *The Dynamos: Who Are They Anyway?* (New York: Wiley, 1987), pp. 78–79.

38. Amal Kumar Naj, "Clouds Gather over the Biotech Industry," *Wall Street Journal,* January 30, 1989, p. B1. See also "Biotech: Where to Invest Now," *Changing Times,* August 1990, pp. 69–75.

39. Kathleen K. Wiegner, "The Anatomy of a Failure," *Forbes,* November 5, 1984, p. 42.

40. Patrick Oster and Igor Reichlin, "Dell: Mail Order Was Supposed to Fail," *Business Week,* January 20, 1992, p. 89.

41. Wendy Cole, "Tee Time for Baby Boomers," *Venture,* June–July 1989, pp. 69–73.

42. Tom Richman, "Mrs. Fields' Secret Ingredient," *Inc.,* October 1987, pp. 65–72; Craig J. Cantoni, "Quality Control from Mars" *Wall Street Journal,* January 27, 1992, p. A12; and Joel Glenn Brenner, "Planet of the M&M's," *The Washington Post Magazine,* April 12, 1992, pp. 10–19, 24–32.

43. John A. Welsh and Jerry F. White, *The Entrepreneur's Master Planning Guide* (Englewood Cliffs, N.J.: Prentice Hall, 1983), p. 1.

44. Ibid., p. 2.

45. E. Thomas Garman and Raymond E. Forgue, *Personal Finance,* 3rd ed. (Boston: Houghton Mifflin, 1991), pp. 569–571.

46. Arthur Lipper III, *Guide to Investing in Private Companies* (Homewood, Ill.: Dow Jones-Irwin, 1984), pp. 57–65.

47. U.S. Small Business Administration, "Business Development Activity," *SBA Update* (Washington, D.C.: U.S. Small Business Administration, 1992), pp. 2, 6–7.

48. *The State of Small Business: A Report of the President* (Washington, D.C.: U.S. Small Business Administration, 1991), pp. ii, 1–3. See also Bruce A. Kirchhoff and Bruce D. Phillips, "Research Applications of the Small Business Data Base of the U.S. Small Business Administration," in Donald L. Sexton and John D. Kasarda (eds.), *The State of the Art of Entrepreneurship* (Boston: PWS-Kent, 1992), pp. 243–267.

49. David B. Greenberger and Donald L. Sexton, "An Interactive Model of New Venture Initiation," *Journal of Small Business Management,* Vol. 26, No. 3 (1988), pp. 1–7. See also Arnold C. Cooper and William C. Dunkelberg, "Entrepreneurial Research: Old Questions, New Answers and Methodological Issues," *American Journal of Small Business,* Vol. 11, No. 3 (1987), pp. 11–23.

50. Charles L. Martin, *Starting Your New Business: A Guide for Entrepreneurs* (Los Altos, Cal.: Crisp, 1988), pp. 1–2.

51. Ronald E. Berenbeim, "Family Business Is Big Business," *Across the Board,* December 1987, pp. 20–30.

52. Jeffrey A. Barach, Joseph Gantisky, James A. Carson, and Benjamin A. Doochin, "Entry of the Next Generation: Strategic Challenge for Family Business," *Journal of Small Business Management,* Vol. 26, No. 2 (1988), pp. 49–56.

53. U.S. Department of Commerce, International Trade Association, *Franchising in the Economy,* January 1988, p. 1. See also Erika Kotite, "Recession or Not, Franchising's Hot: Way to Grow!" *Entrepreneur,* April 1992, pp. 108, 110.

54. Donald D. Boroian and Patrick J. Boroian, *The Franchise Advantage* (Schaumburg, Ill.: National BestSeller, 1988), pp. 16–20, 68–77. See also "Entrepreneur's 5th Annual Survey of New Franchises," *Entrepreneur,* April 1992, pp. 113–127.

55. Wells, "Adventure Capitalist Is Nipping at the Tail of Big British Airways," pp. A1, A6.

CHAPTER 21

1. Bruce Nussbaum, Ann Therese Palmer, Alice Z. Cuneo, and Barbara Carlson, "Downward Mobility," *Business Week,* March 23, 1992, pp. 56–63.

2. Jeffrey H. Greenhaus, *Career Management* (New York: Dryden Press, 1987), pp. 6–7.

3. Edgar H. Schein, "The First Job Dilemma," *Psychology Today,* March 1968, pp. 22–37.

4. Jeffrey H. Greenhaus, C. Seidel, and M. Marinis, "The Impact of Expectations and Values on Job Attitudes," *Organizational Behavior and Human Performance,* Vol. 31 (1983), pp. 394–417. See also Hall, *Careers in Organizations,* Chap. 3.

5. Victor H. Vroom and Arthur G. Jago, *The New Leadership: Managing Participation in Organizations* (Englewood Cliffs, N.J.: Prentice Hall, 1988), pp. 54–69.

6. Lee, "What Kind of Job Are You Likely to Find?" pp. 5–6.

7. Lyman W. Porter, Edward E. Lawler III, and J. Richard Hackman, *Behavior in Organizations* (New York: McGraw-Hill, 1975), pp. 131–135.

8. Clawson, Kotter, Faux, and McArthur, *Self-Assessment and Career Development,* pp. 144–150, 188–197. See also Jack Falvey, "A New Set of Rules for the 'Real World'," *Wall Street Journal, National Business Employment Weekly,* Fall 1991, p. 90.

9. John P. Wanous, *Organizational Entry: Recruitment, Selection and Socialization of Newcomers* (Reading, Mass.: Addison-Wesley, 1980). See also Brooks Mitchell, "Interviewing Face-to-Interface," *Personnel,* January 1990, pp. 23–25.

10. Richard E. Boyatzis and Florence R. Skelly, "The Impact of Changing Values on Organizational Life," in David A. Kolb, Irwin M. Rubin, and Joyce S. Osland (eds.), *The Organizational Behavior Reader* (Englewood Cliffs, N.J.: Prentice Hall, 1991), pp. 1–16; Greenhaus, *Career Management,* pp. 130–132; and David E. Berlew and Douglas T. Hall, "The Socialization of Managers: Effects of Expectations on Performance," *Administrative Science Quarterly,* Vol. 11, No. 2 (1966), pp. 207–223.

11. John P. Kotter, "The Psychological Contract: Managing the Joining-Up Process," *California Management Review,* Vol. 15, No. 3 (1973), pp. 91–99.

12. Erik H. Erikson, *Childhood and Society,* 2nd ed. (New York: W. W. Norton, 1963), pp. 247–274.

13. Daniel J. Levinson, Charlotte N. Darrow, Edward B. Kein, Marie H. Levinson, and Braxton McKee, *The Seasons of a Man's Life* (New York: Alfred A. Knopf, 1978).

14. William L. Mihal, Patricia A. Sorce, and Thomas E. Comte, "A Process Model of Individual Career Decision Making," *Academy of Management Review,* Vol. 9, No. 1 (1984), pp. 95–103.

15. Michael J. Driver, "Careers: A Review of Personal and Organizational Research," in C. L. Cooper and I. Robertson (eds.), *International Review of Industrial Psychology* (London: John Wiley, 1988), pp. 245–277.

16. Erik Page Bucy, "Scrolling for Jobs," *Wall Street Journal, National Business Employment Weekly,* Fall 1991, pp. 42–43.

17. John A. Wagner III and John R. Hollenbeck, *Management of Organizational Behavior* (Englewood Cliffs, N.J.: Prentice Hall, 1992), pp. 219–222.

18. Tom Baum, "The U.S. and U.K.: Comparing Expectations of Management Trainees," *Cornell Hotel and Restaurant Administration Quarterly,* Vol. 32 (1991), pp. 79–84.

19. James G. Clawson, John P. Kotter, Victor A. Faux, and Charles C. McArthur, *Self-Assessment and Career Development,* 2nd ed. (Englewood Cliffs, N.J.: Prentice Hall, 1985), pp. 277–279.

20. Schein, "Culture as an Environmental Context for Careers," pp. 71–81. See also Greenhaus, *Career Management,* pp. 134–135.

21. Edgar H. Schein, "How 'Career Anchors' Hold Executives to Their Career Paths," *Personnel,* Vol. 52, No. 3 (1975), pp. 11–24.

22. Michael J. Driver, "Career Concepts—A New Approach to Career Research," in Ralph Katz (ed.), *Career Issues in Human Resource Management* (Englewood Cliffs, N.J.: Prentice Hall, 1982), pp. 23–32.

23. Elizabeth Dole and Janet L. Norwood, "Tomorrow's Jobs," *Occupational Outlook Handbook, Bulletin 2330,* April 1990, pp. 8–12.

24. Calvin Reynolds and Rita Bennett, "The Career Couple Challenge," *Personnel Journal,* Vol. 7, No. 3 (1991), pp. 46–48.

25. Chris Lee, "Balancing Work and Family," *Training,* September 1991, pp. 23–28. See also Douglas Bell, "Three Men and Their Babies," *CA Magazine,* February 1991, pp. 27–33.

26. Robin Pascoe, "Employers Ignore Expatriate Wives at Their Own Peril," *Wall Street Journal,* March 2, 1992, p. A12. See also Michael Selz, "Hiring the Right Manager Overseas," *Wall Street Journal,* February 27, 1992, p. B2.

27. Jaclyn Fierman, "Why Women Still Don't Hit the Top," *Fortune,* July 30, 1990, pp. 40–42.

28. K. R. Yount, "A Theory of Productive Activity: The Relationship Among Self-Concept, Gender, Sex Role Stereotypes, and Work-Emergent Traits," *Psychology of Women Quarterly,* Vol. 10 (1986), pp. 63–88.

29. Julie Amparano Lopez, "Study Says Women Face Glass Walls as Well as Ceilings," *Wall Street Journal,* March 3, 1992, pp. B1, B2.

30. Michelle Neely Martinez, " The High-Potential Woman," *HR Magazine,* June 1991, pp. 46–51.

31. Kathy E. Kram and Lynn A. Isabella, "Mentoring Alternatives: The Role of Peer Relationships in Career Development," *Academy of Management Journal,* Vol. 28, No. 1 (1985), pp. 110–132.

32. Felice N. Schwartz, "Management Women and the New Facts of Life," *Harvard Business Review,* January–February 1989, pp. 65–76.

33. Wagner and Hollenbeck, *Management of Organizational Behavior,* pp. 317–318.

34. Lise M. Saari, Terry R. Johnson, Steven D. McLaughlin, and Denise M. Zimmerle, "A Survey of Management Training and Educational Practices in U.S. Companies," *Personnel Psychology* (Winter 1988), pp. 731–743.

35. Philip R. Harris and Robert T. Moran, *Managing Cultural Differences* (Houston, Tex. Gulf Publishers, 1987), p. 201.

36. Ruth B. Ekstrom, "Women in Management: Factors Affecting Career Entrance and Advancement," *Selection,* Vol. 2, No. 1 (1985), pp. 29–32.

37. Kenneth Labich, "Take Control of Your Career," *Fortune,* November 18, 1991, pp. 87–88, 96–98.

Glossary

A items Materials and parts imperative to operations that seldom have substitutes and therefore require extremely close control.

ABC inventory system A formal method for rank-ordering inventory and matching cost-effective controls to items with relatively different values.

accuracy of information The degree to which information is error-free.

acquired-needs theory A theory developed by David C. McClelland that proposes people develop a profile of needs through life experiences.

activity budget Usually expressed in nonmonetary terms, an activity budget is used to plan and control operational tasks.

adaptability The ability to adjust to new or changed circumstances; a reaction to internal and external conditions requiring managers to adapt decisions.

aggregate capacity plan This establishes the maximum feasible output that can be manufactured and delivered during a strategic planning period.

algorithms Mathematical rules for finding unique solutions to well-established problems.

alternatives Viable options from which managers can select a course of action to resolve a problem or take advantage of an opportunity.

artificial intelligence (AI) Fifth-generation computer technology that enables computers to emulate human brain processes for problem solving.

assessment center A method of evaluating employees—usually managers—by conducting exercises, simulated work situations, tests, interviews, and psychological testing to determine skills and managerial potential.

attitude A predisposition to respond favorably or unfavorably to objects, persons, and concepts.

authority The right to make decisions within predetermined boundaries sanctioned by an organization, often taking the form of legal or institutionalized responsibility.

autocratic leadership A directive style of leadership with power centered in one or a few key individuals; autocratic leaders typically focus on tasks, centralize personal power, and have a low concern for people.

B items Materials and parts that are important and require close control, but can be replaced even though costly.

behavioral approach An approach that explains how managers influence others to achieve organizational objectives through human relations and motivation.

benefits management The management of pensions, insurance, workers' compensation, dental plans, educational benefits, vacations, health care, and other "fringes" important to employees.

bottom-up change An open environment for change where employees are encouraged to take independent action, initiating or recommending organizational adaptations.

bottom-up planning An approach to planning in which authority to establish objectives and planning responsibilities is delegated to lower-level managers, who are expected to initiate planning activities.

boundary-spanning role A managerial responsibility created by proximity to external constituents to link those constituents' interests to the company's interests through effective communications.

brainstorming Associated with group decision making and creativity, it is a technique for generating many diverse ideas in an atmosphere free from criticism and explicit boundaries.

budget A plan transformed into quantitative terms (such as money or units) to allocate resources, articulate performance expectations in measurable terms, and provide control documents for monitoring progress.

budget variance The difference between budgeted results and actual results used to analyze unacceptable variations, causes, and potential consequences.

budgets Plans expressed in commonly understood numerical terms such as dollars or units that serve the reciprocal purpose of providing measurable standards for controlling operations, expenses, and performance.

bureaucracy A model of organization based on defined positions, formal authority, and a regulated environment that includes well-documented rules, policies, and procedures.

business ethics The concept of moral right and wrong as applied to business enterprises, executive policies, and behavior.

business plan A carefully prepared document that describes services and products, identifies customers, markets, and competition, evaluates capabilities, and provides supporting data for financing a new venture.

business-level strategies Managers focus on well-defined business lines or divisions of services to determine how to compete in their respective industries.

C items Materials and parts that have many substitutes and are usually inexpensive to purchase and store; C items are not closely controlled.

capital expenditure budget A budget document used to make strategic decisions about facilities, equipment, technological processes, and other assets that represent long-term investments.

career The pattern of work-related experiences that span the course of a person's life.

career anchor The cluster of talents, motives, values, and abilities that form a nucleus of occupational characteristics.

career preparation Being prepared for opportunities within a particular occupational field.

cash budget A summary budget that shows actual receipts and disbursements from all sources to identify cash required to remain solvent.

centralization The concentration of decision-making authority at top levels of management with little delegation to others.

certainty The condition of knowing the outcomes under each set of alternatives.

chain of command A vertical line of authority between successively higher levels of management, unbroken and direct, linking each stratum in the hierarchy of management.

channel A medium of communication between sender and receiver; the method of delivering a message.

channels The reporting relationships determined by the structure of management through which prescribed messages are sent.

clarity Managers must be explicit about how they expect subordinates to make decisions and the extent to which subordinates have authority to make decisions.

client/server systems (C/SS) A network that allows distributed computing among network users, yet retains full access to a central mainframe file server.

closed system A control system that can be substantially operated without management intervention once standards are set; monitoring and corrective actions are performed by the system technology.

cluster organization A organizational structure based on work groups that work together to solve problems, manufacture products, or serve clients.

coercive power The capability to punish, rather than reward, or to withhold rewards to influence preferred behavior; power based on fear and force.

command group A permanent group with jobs clustered within a formal structure that reports through the chain of command.

communication The interpersonal process of sending and receiving messages through symbols or gestures.

compensation management The management of wages and salaries, including raises, bonuses, and monetary incentives.

competition A systematic approach to evaluating a company's competitive position relative to its industry and economic power in society.

completeness of information The degree to which information is sufficient to support decisions, addressing issues without omissions.

comprehensive planning The total involvement of an organization in systematic planning at all levels to integrate objectives and coordinate formal planning processes.

computer-integrated manufacturing (CIM) A process using information resources to integrate activities required for a complete manufacturing system.

concentration strategy A strategy of trading on a distinctive competency to prevail in one product, market, or technology.

concentric diversification A growth strategy achieved by developing new products or services that complement the company's existing line of business.

conflict An effort by one party to purposely interfere with another's ability to perform or attain objectives, thereby creating tension and discord.

conglomerate diversification A conscious effort to develop or acquire unrelated products, services, or technologies, thereby reducing the risk of being in one business subject to economic cycles or industry competition.

content theory The management theory usually associated with motivation that focuses on helping individuals fulfill their needs and improve their performance through behavioral techniques and enhanced job satisfaction.

contingency leadership An approach to leadership that suggests the most effective management behavior depends on circumstances.

contingency management An approach to management that suggests leadership behavior should be adapted to accommodate different situations, or, alternatively, leaders should be assigned to situations that best fit their leadership styles.

contingency plan An alternative plan to replace the preferred plan if conditions change.

control points Designated places or times during operational activities to measure progress, sample results, or test products.

controlling The management function of monitoring performance and adapting work variables to improve results.

corporate responsiveness Public perception of how a company reacts to protect the public interest or how it resolves questionable practices, not what the company does in absolute terms.

corporate-level strategy Also called the portfolio-level strategy, it concerns board-level decisions for acquisitions, mergers, major expansions, and divestitures that add to or reduce product lines.

corporation A legal entity created by statute, subject to commercial laws; a form of ownership in which investors have limited liability through stock ownership.

cost center A work unit where managers are responsible for controllable expenses, but not revenues, profits, or investments.

creativity The ability to bring something new into existence.

critical path method (CPM) A network scheduling technique for planning and controlling operations (usually projects) based on critical time increments to complete defined tasks.

cross-cultural communication The process of communicating with people of different cultures who have substantial differences in assumptions and behavior that influence language usage, perception, and attribution of meaning.

culture A shared set of values and beliefs that determine patterns of behavior common to groups of people; corporate culture refers to patterns of behavior based on shared values and beliefs within a particular firm.

customer pattern An approach to departmentalization based on well-defined customer groups whereby employees and activities are focused on unique needs of clientele.

customer scenario A customer scenario describes a group of prospective buyers with common needs who are expected to respond similarly to a marketing program.

data Raw information and facts, figures, and results that become source inputs for analyzing activities, events, and circumstances.

data base A pool of raw data stored in such a way that parts of it can be selected, changed, used in calculations, and transformed into useful information for end users.

decentralization Dispersal of authority through delegation that gives successively lower-level managers greater decision-making responsibility.

decision support systems (DSS) Systems based on standalone microcomputers or work stations that allow independent application or access to central data bases to support management decisions. Also called *executive support systems (ESS).*

decoding A message is decoded by a receiver, who interprets symbols, words, pictures, or gestures to give them meaning.

deficit principle A crucial aspect of Maslow's theory of motivation based on human needs that suggests an unsatisfied need becomes a focal motivator, while a satisfied need no longer influences an individual's behavior.

delegation The process of partially distributing authority to subordinates for making decisions or performing tasks.

Delphi technique Used in forecasting, problem solving, and creative processes, the Delphi technique surveys experts through several rounds of investigation to develop a profile of information, ideas, or solutions.

democratic leadership An approach to leadership that involves employees in decisions through group efforts and team-building techniques.

departmentalization Logical grouping of work activities based on expertise, products, markets, customers, or projects to enhance planning, leading, and controlling.

development Programs focused on leadership, productivity, and organizational issues, often associated with management.

distress The destructive dimension of stress, which exceeds the normal tension associated with healthful living and threatens an individual physically or psychologically.

distributed computing Also called *distributed processing,* it is the decentralization of information processing from a central computer to multiple work stations.

diversification Expanding into new products, markets, or technologies to deploy a company's assets more effectively.

divestiture The process of selling off divisions or subsidiaries that are either poor performers or do not fit well with the company's long-term strategic objectives.

downward communication Messages and information initiated by superiors to subordinates, usually in the form of directives.

economic order quantity (EOQ) A mathematical model for determining the optimal quantity of materials or inventory to purchase based on inventory usage, carrying costs, and purchasing costs.

effectiveness The result of making decisions that lead to doing the right things, which helps to fulfill the mission of an enterprise.

efficiency The result of making decisions that lead to doing things right, which helps to achieve objectives with fewer resources and at lower costs.

electronic data interchange (EDI) A process that allows information with predetermined formats to be exchanged electronically between end users.

empathy The conscious effort to understand another person's viewpoint or to psychologically adapt to the other's frame of reference.

employee orientation A style of management that emphasizes motivation, social cohesion, participative decision making, and a concern for employees.

employee relations A field of activities to help employees resolve personal problems and to improve their performance.

Employee Stock Ownership Plan (ESOP) A program designed to transfer stock ownership to employees through a formula that shares profit increases with employees.

encoding A message is encoded by a sender, who uses symbols, words, pictures, or gestures to formulate the message content.

entrepreneur An individual who assumes the risk of starting a new business, creating a new commercial product or service, and consequently seeking profitable rewards within a free enterprise system.

entrepreneurship The process of creating wealth by bringing together resources in new ways to start a venture that benefits customers and rewards founders for their innovation.

equity theory A theory of motivation that suggests individuals modify their behavior based on perceptions of fair treatment and equitable rewards.

ethnocentric management An approach to managing a global company whereby the home-office executives impose standards, ethics, and values on those who manage overseas operations.

ethnocentrism The fundamental belief in the superiority of one notion (race, creed, or culture) over another.

eustress The constructive dimension of stress, which is essential for a healthy mind-body response to life.

expectancy theory A theory concerned with motivation that suggests people make conscious decisions about their behavior based on expectations of outcomes.

expense budget A budget that identifies specific operational costs to evaluate how efficiently a firm's resources are being deployed.

expert power The ability to lead others and influence behavior based on perceived expertise or special knowledge.

expert systems (ES) Software programs that are capable of mimicking the human thought process by using extensive human knowledge stored in complex data bases.

exporting A strategy of selling domestic goods or services overseas, usually through international brokers or distribution centers.

feedback Reports, performance information, results from operations, and other data routed back to planners and decision makers to enhance future decisions or correct deviations in performance. In communications, a response or acknowledgment that a message has been received and understood.

feedback control The use of information from recently completed operations to learn how to improve performance or to avoid repeating mistakes.

feedforward control The use of information to project what might occur in the future, thus allowing managers to take preventive measures.

financial ratios Computations of selected data used to analyze performance, track company results over time, and compare companies to one another.

financing budget A budget derived from cash flow projections and capital expenditure plans to identify how assets can be financed.

five forces model of competition A systematic approach to evaluating a company's competitive position relative to its industry and economic power in society.

foreign subsidiary A company organized under a foreign legal code with separate liability and accountability, although wholly owned by a parent corporation.

formal communication channels The reporting relationships determined by the structure of management through which prescribed messages are sent.

formal group Created through formal authority, a formal group has defined purposes and reporting relationships.

formal organization Two or more people involved in a mutual effort with formal authority for creating tangible benefits.

formal planning The process of using systematic criteria and rigorous investigation to establish objectives, decide on activities, and formally document organizational expectations.

formulating strategies Strategies formulated by managers through their planning efforts to explain how the company will achieve its objectives.

franchising A special form of licensing based on a contract that grants to a franchisee the right to offer, sell, or distribute goods or services through a business system created by the franchisor.

friendship group Developed spontaneously by employees with similar characteristics or needs to affiliate socially.

frozen evaluation Assumption of "no change," in which a person shuts out information, thereby protecting the status quo and avoiding the threat of having to alter values or beliefs in a changing world.

functional management A definition of management authority based on expertise and specialization.

functional pattern An approach to departmentalization based on grouping people according to their skills and expertise, giving them authority within their areas of expertise.

functional perspective An approach that explains managers' responsibilities and activities according to general principles of management for planning, organizing, leading, and controlling.

functional-level strategies Carried out by executives in functional areas, these strategies support business-level decisions to introduce new technologies, develop new products, open new markets, or implement functional action plans to help the firm compete effectively.

gainsharing A method of bonus compensation based on a formula that shares profits or productivity gains among investors and employees.

Gantt Chart A graphic illustration (usually a bar graph or diagram) that indicates time allocations for sequential operations and traces progress, routing, scheduling, and tasks in time intervals.

general adaptation syndrome (GAS) The psychophysiological (mind-body) reaction that is a natural mobilization and recovery process to stress stimuli.

general manager A person who oversees collective operations and supervises multifunctional subordinate activities.

geocentric multinational A company that has diversified global operations but is controlled through decisions made by a centralized cadre of executives at the home office.

geographic pattern An approach to departmentalization based on territorial control and localized decision making, with functional activities subordinated to geographic divisions.

go/no-go controls Another term for "yes/no controls," go/no-go controls have fail-safe standards dictating absolute corrective action or no action.

group Two or more individuals regularly interacting with one another in pursuit of one or more common goals.

group cohesiveness The extent to which employees are attracted to their group and feel compelled to stay in it.

group norms Informal rules of conduct and patterns of behavior that all group members are expected to follow.

group objectives Objectives developed by group members that relate to task achievements and maintenance of the group; they can be purposely created or they can evolve through group behavior.

group technology The combination of several jobs into one that integrates job activities through new technology or redefined work processes.

growth A growth strategy is the expansion of sales achieved either through marketing existing products more aggressively or through pursuing new products or new markets.

halo effect (halo error) Positively or negatively skewing an individual's evaluation on the basis of a limited number of traits.

hardware The physical equipment employed to input, store, retrieve, and output data.

Hawthorne Studies Social and psychological experiments conducted at Western Electric Company during the 1920s that revealed how human relations affected productivity.

heuristics A process of "learning" through which decision makers analyze ideas and "progress" toward a solution as ideas unfold.

hierarchy of needs The progressive categories of needs set forth by Maslow that he suggested motivate human behavior when they are deemed unfulfilled.

horizontal communication The process of exchanging information between peers at any organizational level, usually to coordinate activities.

horizontal integration A strategy to acquire similar products or services in order to reduce competition or to improve the firm's product mix or market coverage.

horizontal job specialization The result of dividing complicated tasks into simpler jobs or operations, reducing the scope of tasks.

human resource forecasting The process of estimating future demand for employees, based partially on estimated demand for products and services, and partially on productivity, technological changes, and social changes.

human resource management The sum of activities required to attract, develop, and retain people with the knowledge and skills needed to achieve an organization's objectives.

human resource planning Planning for future personnel needs, skills, labor changes, and related issues (such as compensation and retirement).

hygiene factors In Herzberg's two-factor theory, those potential dissatisfiers that can be troublesome if not properly managed, yet are factors having little motivation potential.

incremental change An adjustment that can be implemented within the existing framework of operations.

informal channel of communication The unsanctioned personal network of information among employees fostered by social relationships and friendships.

informal group Created by their members without formal authority for the purpose of pursuing mutual interests or satisfying social needs.

informal organization Two or more people involved in a mutual effort without deliberate structures of authority or the necessity of common objectives.

informal planning A process of intuitively deciding on objectives and the activities needed to achieve them without rigorous and systematic investigation.

informal structure A shadow structure that exists apart from the formal organization, resulting from personal interactions, sentiments, and social activities.

innovation Finding new ways to use or combine resources to create new products, services, processes, or technologies.

integration strategies Companies integrate either backward or forward to stabilize supply and distribution lines, often reducing costs or securing raw materials or markets related to the firm's products.

integrationist A theorist who integrates concepts of several schools of management thought to suggest improved management practices.

interest group An informal group that comes together to pursue specific objectives of interest to its members.

interpersonal communication The personal interaction between individuals that involves their perceptions during a dialogue in which specific meanings are attached to messages.

intrapreneurship A term applied to corporate entrepreneurship (literally "intracorporate entrepreneurship"), suggesting innovation and new-venture creation from within established organizational boundaries.

inventory control The management of incoming materials and supplies, work-in-process inventory, and finished products.

investment center An organization unit whose managers are held responsible for capital expenditures and the structure of investments.

IS management The concept of responsibility by all managers for the management of integrated information systems.

job analysis A formal method of identifying tasks, skills, physical requirements, and duties specific to an individual job.

job characteristics model A conceptual framework for identifying activities, relationships, and responsibilities using core job dimensions that influence job design and redesign decisions.

job depth The relative responsibility employees have for decisions about their task activities and jobs.

job description A written statement of expectations and duties related to a specific job. It may also include the particular responsibilities and personal characteristics needed to fulfill job assignments.

job design The process of combining tasks into a well-defined job to be performed by each employee.

job enlargement An organizational development technique for combining two or more tasks into one, usually at one level of skill, to add variety, reduce boredom, or improve efficiency in work.

job enrichment The vertical combination of tasks that increases one's duties and responsibilities; job depth is enhanced to improve job satisfaction.

job inventory A descriptive list of task activities and attributes for a job derived from a thorough job analysis.

job range The horizontal scope of activities expected within a specific job.

job rotation Periodic temporary assignment to jobs with complementary skills.

joint venture A contractual alliance between two or more independent companies, often including foreign government interests, to jointly invest in and pursue a new commercial enterprise.

just in time (JIT) A comprehensive system that seeks to eliminate inventory by purchasing materials just in time for use in production, producing just in time for shipment, and shipping just in time to meet customer orders without errors or quality defects.

kanban An inventory system based on scheduling cards prepared for each order and used in production to track progress and alert management to problems.

labor relations Activities concerned with relationships between an organization's management and legally recognized unions and associations.

leadership The process of influencing others to behave in preferred ways to accomplish organizational objectives.

legitimate power Also called *formal authority,* it is the right to manage derived from delegation based on ownership or property rights.

licensing In international business, the process of contracting with foreign companies, granting them the rights to use proprietary technology, patents, copyrights, or trademarks or to market products and services.

life cycle model An approach to leadership in which managers adopt behavior to coincide with the maturity of subordinates; the four behavior modes are delegating, participating, selling, and telling.

line manager A person who has direct control over primary operations of an organization such as production.

liquidation The "final" option, liquidation is the decision to terminate a business in a systematic way through bankruptcy or a complete sale of the company.

local area network (LAN) A system of interconnected hardware, software, and communication devices, linking various work centers together within an organization so that information can be shared.

management The art of getting things done through people.

management audit A method of appraising leadership behavior through surveys, interviews, and observations of managers, often employing evaluation teams of peer managers, consultants, and employees.

management by objectives (MBO) A technique used in planning and controlling in which subordinates determine their objectives jointly with superiors and evaluation follows periodic monitoring and performance reviews.

management information system (MIS) A service that uses total information resources in a way that enhances managerial decisions, monitors activities, and ensures accurate and timely performance feedback.

management science An approach to management that relies on models and mathematical analysis to improve decision making; alternatively called *the quantitative school* or *operations research*.

manager-assisted objectives Derived from the purpose of the group, these objectives may be expressed by management or jointly developed with employees.

Managerial Grid An organizational development model created by Robert Blake and Jane Mouton that is based on a matrix of values between 1 and 9 for two primary variables explaining a manager's orientation: concern for production and concern for people.

manufacturing cell An integrated process of related activities based on group technology that includes individuals or autonomous work teams responsible for a set of operations, equipment utilization, and product quality.

manufacture resource planning (MRP II) A comprehensive planning system that encompasses production resources and activities of MRP plus financial, capital, and marketing resources and activities.

market diversification A method of growing by positioning existing products or services in new markets or for sale to new customers.

marketing plan Managers develop marketing plans to support strategic objectives using customer scenarios to position products or services in markets according to well-documented sales forecasts.

marketing program A marketing program addresses specific product characteristics, pricing decisions, promotional activities, and distribution channels.

master strategies Also called grand strategies, these define in broad terms the long-term direction of an organization.

materials requirements planning (MRP) A computer-integrated process of coordinating master production schedules, purchasing, inventory control, and resource allocation based on projected orders.

matrix organization An approach to organizing work based on forming temporary teams from the ranks of existing employees that are responsible for completing well-defined projects.

media richness The capability of a given form of communication to convey information.

mentor An experienced employee assigned to help a newcomer by fulfilling the roles of counselor, coach, role model and sponsor.

motion study The study of physical actions required to perform a task in the most efficient way possible.

motivation The concept of behavioral change as a result of an influence that alters an individual's performance.

multicultural environment Refers to an organization that has employees from diverse cultural backgrounds or that has relationships with customers and other external constituents who represent diverse sociocultural interests.

multinational corporation (MNC) A corporation that operates on a global scale with branches, outlets, distribution centers, facilities, or sales in foreign countries.

needs assessment review A process of matching projected activities with projected employment requirements.

new-venture unit (NVU) A team, division, or subsidiary created specifically to initiate new business ideas and bring them to fruition through commercial endeavors.

nominal group A panel established to develop ideas independently for resolving a particular problem that then, through an exchange of ideas, refines those ideas until a group consensus emerges.

nominal group technique (NGT) A group decision-making process in which members independently identify solutions to a problem or alternative opportunities. Then, after options are fully articulated and discussed, members vote confidentially for preferences.

nonprogrammed decisions Decisions derived from unstructured analysis or generated from individual evaluation of nonroutine situations; decisions that lack clear analytical parameters or substantial precedent.

obfuscate Literally, "to cloud an issue," obfuscate implies a purposeful attempt by one person to confuse another through the use of perplexing language.

office automation system (OAS) Designed to improve productivity, an OAS is meant to reduce clerical work and increase the efficiency and effectiveness of office administration.

open system A control system in which managers intervene to set standards, monitor performance, decide whether results meet expectations, and take corrective actions.

operant conditioning The process of reinforcing behavior through positive or negative consequences to condition future behavior.

operational objectives Immediate short-term performance targets for daily, weekly, and monthly activities that, when attained, will reinforce tactical planning objectives.

operational planning Operational planning occurs at the lowest management levels and focuses on specific performance objectives for immediate results.

operations management The application of quantitative techniques in production and operations control using analytical models to improve organization activities.

organization The structure of relationships that exists when two or more people mutually cooperate to pursue common objectives.

organizational behavior modification (OB Mod) The process of changing human behavior by influencing individuals through such methods as operant conditioning.

organizational development (OD) The process of changing organizations through behavioral science techniques such as consulting, intervention to improve performance, leadership, and decision-making systems.

organizational objectives Performance targets or the end results that managers seek to attain through organizational efforts.

organizational socialization The process of accommodating to the values, behavior, and role expectations required to be accepted as an organizational member.

organizing The function of gathering resources, allocating resources, and structuring tasks within an organization.

orientation A formal indoctrination program that introduces new employees to their job responsibilities, co-workers, and work environment.

overseas branch An extension of domestic operations located overseas that is wholly owned and managed by the parent company.

parity The condition of being equal in power, value, wealth, and status.

participative change A strategy of implementing change through cooperative efforts, team decision making, and group initiatives.

partnership Two or more individuals with joint responsibility and investment in a business.

path-goal theory A contingency approach to leadership that holds managers responsible for influencing employees to work for rewards linked to specific tasks.

perceptual noise A distortion of meanings and selective filtering of messages created by a receiver's personal frame of reference and attitude.

performance evaluation The process of appraising subordinates' behavior and providing feedback to help them improve their performance.

personal staff Expert advisers who provide special services or advice related to particular responsibilities such as legal affairs, economic consulting, or affirmative action.

piece rate An approach to compensation whereby employees are paid for each unit of work completed.

planning One of the four major functions of management. It is the process of defining organizational objectives and then articulating strategies, tactics, and operations necessary to achieve those objectives.

planning premises Those considerations taken into account by managers that will likely affect plans or activities.

polarization A jaundiced viewpoint in which a person interprets information in extreme—black and white—contexts.

policy A standing-use plan that provides a general framework for decision making.

polycentric multinational A company with diversified global operations in which authority is decentralized, giving overseas managers broad-based authority for making decisions.

positioning Positioning is the act of targeting specific products or services to specific markets.

postaction controls Systems that periodically monitor results "after the fact," comparing actual performance with standards to prompt corrections and thus avoid repeating mistakes in the future.

power The ability to influence others' behavior to accomplish preferred results.

proactive response A self-initiated action by a company to resolve, or protect against, unethical behavior.

procedure An explicit set of actions, often sequential in nature, required to achieve a well-defined result.

process theory The motivation theory that focuses on individual attitudes, thoughts, and preferences to understand and influence personal performance.

product control Product control is concerned with reducing costs associated with poor quality and unreliable products.

product diversification A specific choice of growing by adding new products, either through internal development or acquisitions.

product life cycle A product life cycle describes the stages a product goes through in the marketplace from introduction to decline.

product pattern An approach to departmentalization based on grouping people according to an organization's products or services, with functional activities relocated under product or service divisions.

production control Production control is concerned with controlling the manufacturing process.

production plan A formal production plan specifies the planned volume of each product to be manufactured consistent with marketing plans for projected sales during a planning period.

production planning Managers in production planning are concerned with manufacturing quality products in the right quantities for delivery to customers at the right time.

productivity The relationship of combined inputs such as labor, materials, capital, and managerial verve to outputs such as products or services. It is the summation of quality performance that results in more efficient utilization of organizational resources.

productivity planning The conscious attention to quality, costs, and work processes to improve resource allocation while achieving higher total company performance.

profit budget A budget that consolidates revenue and expense information to identify planned net income and to record actual results.

profit center An organization unit that is held responsible for both costs and revenues; performance is evaluated in terms of the resulting net income.

program A single-use plan with multiple activities that can be orchestrated to achieve one important objective.

program budget A method of separating budget criteria so that allocations are tied directly to programs or projects rather than to functional departments or operating units.

program evaluation and review technique (PERT) A network model that identifies sequential events necessary to complete a project while defining activities that individually lead to the next event.

programmed decisions Decisions that have been made so often under similar circumstances that past experience provides clear guidelines for managers.

progression principle Abraham Maslow's concept that successively higher-order needs in his hierarchy of needs are not active motivators until lower-order needs are fulfilled.

project A single-use plan with a specific short-term objective that is seldom repeated.

psychological contract A mutual understanding between the employee and his or her organization of expectations for what each will exchange in the employment relationship.

purchasing The acquisition of needed goods and services at optimal costs from competent, reliable sources.

purpose The reason a company exists; it is the fundamental rationale for being in business.

quality The concept of doing things better, not just more efficiently.

quality of work life (QWL) The concept of making work meaningful for employees in an environment where they are motivated to perform and satisfied with their work.

quantitative management An approach to management based on decision theory, use of statistical techniques for problem solving, and application of mathematical models to organizational processes.

rational decision making A process of systematically analyzing a problem to find an optimal solution.

reactive response A forced action by a company to resolve problems or unethical behavior that is brought about by external pressure groups or government intervention.

realistic job preview (RJP) A comprehensive evaluation of a candidate's skills, qualifications, aptitudes, expectations, and potential compatibility with the organization.

reality shock syndrome The disillusionment associated with a person's new job that results from differences between expectations and realities of organizational life.

recruitment The process of attracting qualified applicants to an organization through activities such as advertising and campus visitations.

referent power The ability to generate in others a sense of admiration and devotion; often associated with charisma.

reinforcement theory A theory of motivation that explains behavior in terms of consequences learned from past experiences that teach individuals what to do to avoid pain and to gain pleasure.

relevancy of information Appropriate information that helps managers make decisions without creating an overload.

research and development limited partnership (RDLP) A legal partnership of limited life that allows public and private organizations to contribute resources to a separate organization that operates independently for a specific purpose.

resource allocation The planned used of facilities, equipment, material, energy, cash, and supplies during a company's budgeting period.

responsibility center A work group, department, or division of a company with budgetary controls focused on relevant and controllable activities.

retrenchment A strategy of "regrouping," usually through consolidation, to retreat from an overexpanded position.

revenue budget A budget derived from sales data and used to evaluate the effectiveness of marketing efforts.

revenue center An organization unit that is evaluated on its ability to generate operating income, but not income from investments or costs or profits from operations.

reward power The ability to influence behavior by controlling rewards in a positive, motivating way.

risk The condition of not being certain about the outcome of a decision while also having enough information to sense probabilities.

risk averse Having an aversion to taking perceived risks, preferring instead to make decisions with a high degree of clarity.

risk takers Those who have a propensity to pursue risks to resolve problems with uncertain outcomes.

rule A statement that tends to restrict actions or prescribe specific activities with no discretion.

sales forecast A sales forecast is an estimate of expected sales for a specific time period related to target markets.

satisfice A decision-making behavior in which an individual chooses a satisfactory alternative, one thought to be adequate, though not necessarily the best.

satisfier factors Motivating factors associated with job content, achievement, recognition, and intrinsic rewards, including promotion.

scalar chain The concept of a clear, unbroken line of authority derived from unambiguous delegation throughout the management hierarchy.

schedule A time-phased series of activities to be performed to achieve specific and measurable objectives.

scientific management A major approach to management advocated by Frederick W. Taylor that focuses on standardized work methods and rational selection of employees coupled with training and job development.

screening A subconscious blocking of information to avoid unpleasant facts; also, a conscious and deliberate filtering of messages to manipulate information to one's benefit.

selection The process of choosing and hiring employees from among those candidates recruited for the organization.

semantics The nature and meaning of words and phrases and how they are used in the context of messages.

single-use plans These plans are developed for unique activities and are seldom repeated exactly; they include programs, projects, and budgets.

situation analysis An examination of industry structure, economics, competitive forces, and other external factors and internal conditions essential for strategic planning.

skills inventory A data base detailing each employee's qualifications, education, interests, and career aspirations.

small business Conceptually, an enterprise that does not dominate its industry, has few employees, and generates limited income. The SBA has defined a small business for qualifying loans as one with fewer than 1,000 employees and less than $10 million in annual sales.

social audit Evaluation of organizational activities that have a significant influence on social responsibility and external relationships.

social responsibility Refers to an organization's obligation to conduct business in such a way as to safeguard the welfare of society while pursuing its own interests.

software The means for driving hardware and controlling an information system.

sole proprietor A person who conducts business as an independent and unincorporated owner. Legally, a form of business that has no other investors beyond the independent owner.

span of control Also called the *span of management,* it is the number of subordinates who can be effectively supervised given the type of task, technology, and environment of work.

specialization Defining tasks that relate to expertise and then horizontally separating jobs for formal activities.

staff assistants Assistants and advisers to line managers who directly support operational activities but do not become involved in those decisions.

staff managers Staff managers concern themselves with the support and advising activities that reinforce line operations, but do not have direct authority for operational results.

stakeholders Those individuals and groups that have interests in, or are affected by, an organization's performance.

standardization Making work uniform throughout repeated use of similar methods, machines, and materials to achieve similar and predictable results over time.

standing-use plans These are plans used on a continuous basis to achieve consistency in organizational activities; they include policies, procedures, and rules that can be repeated.

statistical process control (SPC) A method of collecting information and analyzing results during operations to improve quality and in-process performance.

statistical quality control (SQC) A method of analyzing deviations in manufactured materials, parts, and products.

steering controls Controls used to adjust behavior or operations, such as correcting the speed and direction of a car.

stereotyping The belief that certain people have attributes based on group characteristics such as sex, race, and ethnic origin that make them superior or inferior.

strategic business unit (SBU) A major subunit or group at the strategic level of a large, complex firm. SBUs provide a focus on related services, products, markets, customers, or technologies to improve management and decision making.

strategic change A major effort that redefines an organization, its objectives, or its methods of doing business.

strategic implementation The deliberate execution of strategies that achieve objectives through incremental activities defined in policies, programs, projects, budgets, procedures, and rules.

strategic management The senior management responsibility for defining the firm's mission, formulating strategies, and guiding long-term organizational activities consistent with internal and external conditions.

stress Associated with tension and anxiety, stress can be destructive both physically and psychologically, but it is also essential for life.

sufficiency Subordinates can only be held accountable if they have sufficient authority to make decisions relating to activities for which they are responsible.

supportive leadership A style of leadership that encourages employees through motivation techniques and acceptance.

SWOT A situation analysis that examines external factors and internal conditions of an organization to identify strengths, weaknesses, opportunities, and threats.

system A system that includes plans and controls linking together all organizational activities to ensure quality performance.

System 4 Management Developed by Rensis Likert, it is a description of four approaches to leadership taken by managers, ranging from autocratic to participative. Likert believes the one best way to lead is through "System 4 participation."

tactical objectives Medium-term performance targets for achieving limited results, such as annual sales, quarterly profits, or incremental changes in products or services.

tactical planning The transformation of strategies into medium-term objectives and activities usually implemented by middle managers in functional roles.

task group A formal group with selected members who work together on focused tasks; a task group is seldom permanent and rarely reports through a chain of command.

task orientation Management style emphasizing control of, rather than encouragement of, employees' work, focusing on work results, task responsibilities, and work standards.

team planning A participative approach to planning whereby planning teams comprising managers and staff specialists initiate plans and formulate organizational objectives.

technological imperative The concept that an organization's structure and relationships among its members are often dictated by the technology employed.

technology The total accumulation of tools, systems, and work methods used collectively to transform inputs into outputs.

telecommuting The practice of allowing employees to work at home or in other locations away from the organization; usually associated with job tasks that can be accomplished with computers and telecommunications.

termination Employees are terminated when they are formally severed from the organization through retirement, death, resignation, or dismissal.

Theory X A set of assumptions that employees are lazy, unambitious, and must be coerced to work; hence, a managerial approach based on fear tactics.

Theory Y A set of assumptions that employees are generally responsible, want to do meaningful work, and are capable of self-direction; hence, a managerial approach based on conciliatory behavior.

Theory Z A reference to Japanese management practices of consensus decision making, quality circles, and employee participation to enhance productivity.

timeliness of information The concept of not only having accurate and complete information, but also having it at the right time.

top-down change The traditional approach to change that emphasizes unilateral decisions by superiors who direct how organizational change is to occur.

total quality management (TQM) The comprehensive approach to quality by everyone in an organization to provide customers with reliable products and services.

training Instruction for specific job skills, usually associated with nonmanagement employees.

transaction processing system (TPS) Also called *electronic data processing (EDP),* a TPS is configured to handle repetitive data and programmed calculations for efficient transactions and report summaries, not to handle decision-making support information.

transfer A transfer is a formal change in an employee's job or position to satisfy employee preferences or to accommodate organizational shifts in resources.

transformational leadership The ability of leaders to make profound changes, introduce new visions for their organizations, and inspire people to work toward achieving those visions.

transnational services Professional and commercial services that are offered through contracts or provided to foreign customers through overseas branches and subsidiaries.

two-factor theory A motivation theory developed by Frederick Herzberg that defines hygiene factors generally associated with dissatisfaction and motivation factors generally associated with satisfaction.

uncertainty The condition of not knowing, and of having insufficient information to assign probabilities, in a decision situation.

unity of command The concept that a subordinate should report to only one superior or receive only one set of directions from one superior at one time.

upward communication Messages and information initiated by subordinates for their superiors, usually in the form of reports.

verifiability The extent to which information can be traced to its source and its accuracy determined.

vertical integration A strategy to gain control of resources, supplies, or distribution systems that relate to a company's business.

vertical job specialization The result of delegating responsibilities for tasks and decisions to subordinates, thereby compressing the depth of tasks.

Vroom-Yetton model A theory of leadership that suggests conditions that influence subordinates to participate in various ways in decision making.

wage and benefit management Usually the responsibility of specialists in the field, wage and benefit management in planning terms is the professional planning and control of compensation and employee benefits.

whistleblowers Employees who in an act of conscience go against their employers to publicly reveal unethical behavior.

work design The process of structuring individual jobs, integrating them within work groups, and making work efficient and interesting.

work groups Small formal teams of co-workers who, together with their managers, share tasks and responsibilities for well-defined segments of work activities.

yes/no control A screening technique that yields a "yes" or "no" (go or no-go) decision at selected checkpoints in an operation.

zero-based budgeting (ZBB) A process that requires budgeting to start from scratch rather than build on previous budget allocations.

zone of indifference A concept articulated by Chester Barnard that implies a range of acceptance by subordinates to orders with few objections. Beyond the zone, subordinates are no longer indifferent and object to orders.

Photo Credits

CHAPTER 1

page 1—SABA/Merrill Lynch; page 4—(left) J. L. Atlan/Sygma, (right) J. Langevin/Sygma; page 9—Wide World Photos; page 17—Will McIntyre; page 19—Mike Clemmer; page 26—SABA/Merrill Lynch.

CHAPTER 2

page 35—Peter Yates/SABA; page 39—The Bettmann Archive; page 44—Courtesy Western Electric; page 45—John S. Abbott; page 46—Gordon Reflex/Picture Group; page 52—Tom Tracy/The Stock Market; page 54—Blake Little; page 55—Peter Yates/SABA.

CHAPTER 3

page 63—Andrew Popper/Picture Group; page 64—Shone/Gamma-Liaison; page 70—Kaku Kurita/Gamma Liaison; page 78—R. Ian Lloyd, Singapore; page 79—Sergio Dorantes/Sygma; page 88—Andrew Popper/Picture Group.

CHAPTER 4

page 95—Courtesy General Dynamics/Electric Boat Division; page 98—Kevin Harvey/SIPA; page 102—Courtesy the Hewlett-Packard Company; page 109—Courtesy Xerox Corporation; page 110—Courtesy of Larry Taylor, president, Taylor Corporation; page 116 (top of page)—The Granger Collection; page 116 (bottom of page)—Ron Haviv/SABA; page 120—Courtesy General Dynamics/Electric Boat Division; page 122—*Anchorage Daily News*/Gamma-Liaison.

CHAPTER 5

page 129—Copyright © The Walt Disney Co.; page 135—The Bettmann Archive; page 136—Michael Abramson; page 139—Katherine Lambert; page 152—Courtesy Cadbury Schweppes; page 153—Courtesy Cadbury Schweppes; page 154—Copyright © The Walt Disney Co.

CHAPTER 6

page 163—Christophee Ena/REA/SABA; page 165—John Madere; page 169 (top)—Andy Freeberg, (bottom)—Mark Hanauer/Onyx; page 174—Courtesy Corning Glass Works; page 178—Courtesy Stew Leonard; page 181—Hans Neleman; page 188—Christophee Ena/REA/SABA.

CHAPTER 7

page 195—Courtesy Brunswick Bowling; page 198—Courtesy Marriott Corporation; page 201—Walker/Gamma-Liaison; page 209—Robert Holmgren; page 214—T. Simon/Gamma-Liaison; page 221—Courtesy Brunswick Bowling.

CHAPTER 8

page 227—Courtesy Tenneco Automotive; page 229—Bob Nelson/Picture Group; page 232—Teri Stratford; page 335—Barbara Alper/Stock, Boston; page 238—Peter Niland; page 241—Courtesy Spokes Bicycles; page 246—Mike Clemmer/Picture Group; page 253—Tenneco Automotive.

CHAPTER 9

page 263—Teri Stratford; pages 274–275—Courtesy Benetton Services Corp.; page 276—Bob Sacha; page 284—Robb Kendrick/Contact Press; page 288—Courtesy Ben & Jerry's Ice Cream/photo by Lee Holden; page 290—Wide World Photos; page 291—Teri Stratford.

CHAPTER 10

page 297—Louis Psihoyos/Matrix; page 305—Courtesy Johnson Space Center/NASA; page 312—P. Robert/Sygma; page 319—Tim Wright; page 321—Courtesy ASK Computer Systems; page 323—(left) Courtesy Hyatt Hotels Corporation, (right) Will & Deni McIntyre; page 330—Louis Psihoyos/Matrix.

CHAPTER 11

page 337—Courtesy Herman Miller, Inc.; page 341—Alain Kelert/Odyssey, Matrix; page 347—John S. Abbott; page 357—Michael L. Abramson; page 360—Comstock; page 363—Courtesy Herman Miller, Inc.

CHAPTER 12

page 369—Courtesy the Blackfeet Indian Writing Company, Inc.; page 381—Rex Rystedt; page 385—Doug Menuez; page 392—Roger Mastroianni; page 398—Steven Pumphrey; page 399—Courtesy the Blackfeet Indian Writing Company, Inc.

CHAPTER 13

page 409—Roy Morsch/The Stock Market; page 418—Jim Knowles/Picture Group; page 420—Rhoda Baer; page 424—Peter Sibbald; page 430—Bill Luster; page 432—Roy Morsch/The Stock Market.

CHAPTER 14

page 439—Courtesy British Petroleum Co. Ltd.; page 445—John S. Abbott; page 449—Andy Freeberg; page 453—Ed Kashi; page 456—Courtesy Lincoln Electric Co.; page 465—Courtesy British Petroleum Co. Ltd.

CHAPTER 15

page 473—Shawn Henry/SABA; page 480—Katherine Lambert; page 483—Michael L. Abramson; page 489—Michael Greenlar; page 495—Eobert Hower/Quadrant; page 502—Shawn Henry/SABA.

CHAPTER 16

page 509—Wally McNamee/Woodfin Camp; page 516—Courtesy Hewlett Packard; page 522—Dan Lamont/Matrix; page 527—R. Ian Lloyd; page 533—Michael L. Abramson; page 538—Wally McNamee/Woodfin Camp.

CHAPTER 17

page 547—Courtesy Dell Computer Company; page 550—Jamie Tanaka; page 553—Steve Winter/Black Star; page 558—Chris Usher; page 571—Mark Richards; page 582—Courtesy Dell Computer Company.

CHAPTER 18

page 589—Reprinted with permission of Compaq Computer Corporation—all rights reserved; page 593—Jeff Topping; page 594—Blake Little; page 596—Courtesy ICI Americas, Inc.; page 618—Michael L. Abramson; page 621—Reprinted with permission of Compaq Computer Corporation.

CHAPTER 19

page 627—Courtesy The Travelers Corporation; page 630—Andy Freeberg; page 632—Reinhold Spiegler; page 638—Andy Freeberg; page 646—Phil Schofield; page 650—Courtesy The Travelers Corporation.

CHAPTER 20

page 659—Mark Greenberg/Visions; page 663—Mark Richards; page 668—Robbie McClaran; page 671—Courtesy Vistakon; page 677—Layne Kennedy; page 687—Mark Greenberg/Visions.

CHAPTER 21

page 695—Brian Smith; page 696—Alen MacWeeney; page 708—Alice Q. Hargrave; page 715—Alan Levenson; page 717—Brian Smith.

Company Index

Name Index

Subject Index

BEAUFORT SEA
ALASKA (U.S.A.)
Brooks Range
Alaska Range
Gulf of Alaska
Alaska Peninsula
Bering Strait
BERING SEA
RUSSIA
YUKON
NORTHWEST TERRITORIES
District of Mackenzie
District of Keewatin
District of Franklin
Queen Elizabeth Islands
Parry Islands
Victoria Island
Banks Island
Baffin Island
BAFFIN BAY
Davis Strait
HUDSON BAY
Kalaallit Nunaat
Greenland (DENMARK)
Denmark Strait
ICELAND
LABRADOR SEA
CANADA
BRITISH COLUMBIA
ALBERTA
SASKATCHEWAN
MANITOBA
ONTARIO
QUÉBEC
NEWFOUNDLAND
NOVA SCOTIA
NEW BRUNSWICK
UNITED STATES
Rocky Mountains
Appalachian Mountains
Great Basin
Colorado Plateau
Gulf of Mexico
Gulf of California
MEXICO
BAHAMAS
CUBA
HAITI
DOMINICAN REP.
JAMAICA
BELIZE
GUATEMALA
HONDURAS
EL SALVADOR
NICARAGUA
COSTA RICA
PANAMA
Caribbean Sea
ATLANTIC OCEAN
PACIFIC OCEAN
COLOMBIA
VENEZUELA
GUYANA
SURINAM
FR. GUIANA
ECUADOR
PERU
BRAZIL
BOLIVIA
PARAGUAY
URUGUAY
ARGENTINA
CHILE
Mato Grosso
Falkland Islands (U.K.)
Tierra del Fuego
Cape Horn
South Georgia (U.K.)
South Sandwich Is. (U.K.)
South Orkney Islands
South Shetland Islands (U.K.)
Antarctic Peninsula
WEDDEL SEA
BELLINGHAUSEN SEA
UNITED KINGDOM
IRELAND
PORTUGAL
MOROCCO
WESTERN SAHARA
MAURITANIA
SENEGAL
THE GAMBIA
GUINEA-BISSAU
GUINEA
SIERRA LEONE
LIBERIA
CAPE VERDE ISLANDS
Azores (PORT.)
Canary Islands (SPAIN)
Bermuda Islands (U.K.)
Hawaiian Islands (U.S.A.)
Marquesas Islands (FRANCE)
Tuamotu Archipelago (FRANCE)
Society Islands (FRANCE)
Tubuai Islands (FRANCE)
Galapagos Islands (ECUADOR)
Isla de Pascua (Easter Island) (CHILE)
Juan Fernandez Islands (CHILE)
EQUATORIAL SCALE 1:60 000 000
VAN DER GRINTEN PROJECTION
• Reykjavik ■ Oslo ■ London NATIONAL CAPITALS
● Hamburg TOWNS OVER 1 000 000 INHABITANTS
○ Örebro • Riga OTHER TOWNS
IMPORTANT RAILWAYS
World Map © 1992 by GLA Kartor AB, Stockholm, Sweden
Distributed by Interarts, Ltd., Cambridge, Massachusetts, USA
International marketing MAPS INTERNATIONAL, Stockholm
Printed on DuPont TYVEK® in the United States
Product Number 100-11T
ISBN # 1-879856-14-1